THE WHIRLWIND OF WAR

Voices of the Storm,
1861–1865

BOOKS BY STEPHEN B. OATES

·

*The Whirlwind of War: Voices of the Storm,
1861–1865* (1998)

*The Approaching Fury: Voices of the Storm,
1820–1861* (1997)

A Woman of Valor: Clara Barton and the Civil War (1994)

Portrait of America (2 vols., 6th edition, 1994)

Biography as History (1991)

*William Faulkner, The Man and the Artist:
A Biography* (1987)

*Biography as High Adventure: Life-Writers
Speak on Their Art* (1986)

Abraham Lincoln: The Man Behind the Myths (1984)

*Let the Trumpet Sound:
A Life of Martin Luther King, Jr.* (1982)

*Our Fiery Trial: Abraham Lincoln,
John Brown, and the Civil War Era* (1979)

*With Malice Toward None:
A Life of Abraham Lincoln* (1977)

The Fires of Jubilee: Nat Turner's Fierce Rebellion (1975)

*To Purge This Land with Blood:
A Biography of John Brown* (1970)

Visions of Glory (1970)

The Republic of Texas (1968)

Rip Ford's Texas (1963)

Confederate Cavalry West of the River (1961)

THE WHIRLWIND OF WAR

VOICES OF THE STORM, 1861–1865

STEPHEN B. OATES

HarperCollins*Publishers*

HarperCollins books may be purchased for educational, business, or sales promotional use. For information please write: Special Markets Department, Harper-Collins Publishers, Inc., 10 East 53rd Street, New York, NY 10022.

FIRST EDITION

Designed by Interrobang Design Studio

Library of Congress Cataloging-in-Publication Data
Oates, Stephen B.
    The whirlwind of war : voices of the storm, 1861–1865 / Stephen B.
Oates. — 1st ed.
        p.   cm.
    Includes index.
    ISBN 0-06-017580-X
    1. United States—History—Civil War—1861–1865. 2. United States—
History—Civil War, 1861–1865—Biography. I. Title.
E462.O27   1998
973.7—dc21   97-51171

98 99 00 01 02 ❖ 10 9 8 7 6 5 4 3 2 1

Dedicated in loving memory to Mr. Key

Events by themselves are unimportant; it is the perception of events that is crucial.

—JOHN FERLING

I think that no one individual can look at truth. It blinds you. You look at it and you see one phase of it. Someone else looks at it and sees a slightly awry phase of it. But taken all together, the truth is in what they saw though nobody saw the truth intact.

—WILLIAM FAULKNER

CONTENTS

THE SPEAKERS

ABRAHAM LINCOLN

R. E. LEE

MARY LIVERMORE

JEFFERSON DAVIS

WILLIAM TECUMSEH SHERMAN

MARY BOYKIN CHESNUT

ULYSSES S. GRANT

FREDERICK DOUGLASS

CORNELIA HANCOCK

JOHN WILKES BOOTH

CODA: WALT WHITMAN

PREFACE

This is the story of the American Civil War. It is a sequel to *The Approaching Fury*, which covers the forty tumultuous years that led to America's Armageddon. Like that book, *The Whirlwind of War* is told from the viewpoints of several principal players in the drama: the rival presidents, Abraham Lincoln and Jefferson Davis; the rival generals, Robert E. Lee, Ulysses S. Grant, and William Tecumseh Sherman; the great black abolitionist, editor, and orator, Frederick Douglass; the young Union battlefield nurse, Cornelia Hancock; the brilliant head of the Chicago Sanitary Commission and cocreator of the northern Sanitary Fair, Mary Livermore; the Confederate socialite and political insider, Mary Boykin Chesnut; the assassin, John Wilkes Booth; and the greatest poet of the era, Walt Whitman, who speaks in the coda about the meaning of the war and Lincoln's death.

The fiction of William Faulkner inspired me to tell the story of the Civil War from multiple points of view. This technique illustrates the profound truth that the people of the past responded to events and to one another according to their perception of reality, and that their responses shaped the course of succeeding events. Like all people, Civil War Americans acted according to what they *thought* was true. Their perception of events, therefore, played a crucial role in how they shaped and fought the war, and what they did to win or lose it.

This book employs the same technique I used in *The Approaching Fury*. It is told in the first-person voices of the principal players, in the form of interconnecting dramatic monologues. This technique gives the story a passion and a sense of immediacy and freshness it could not possibly possess had it been told in the third-person voice. It fascinates me that the protagonist in one monologue becomes the antagonist in another.

Each speaker takes his or her turn on stage, serving as narrator for critical events in which he or she was the major instigator and participant or eyewitness. In adopting this technique, I was strongly influenced by Robert Altman's films *Nashville* and *Short Cuts,* and John Sayles's film *City of Hope,* which employ multiple viewpoints and segue ingeniously from one character to another. My narrative likewise segues back and forth from one historical figure to another, showing how their lives intersected—how they perceived and argued with one another, influenced one another's actions, and shaped the events and direction of the Civil War. I also drew inspiration from Hal Holbrook's one-man portrayal of Mark Twain, *Mark Twain Tonight!*, and Julie Harris's staged impersonation of Emily Dickinson, *The Belle of Amherst*, both of which showed me the power and the possibilities of the dramatic monologue.

The Whirlwind of War is my impersonation of eleven central figures of the Civil War. The metaphor in the title comes from them: one after another, they described the war in terms of a violent storm, a whirlwind, or a tornado. By necessity, my cast is dominated by white men, for they controlled the Union and the Confederacy and were mainly responsible for how the war turned out. To write the monologues, I steeped myself in the words of my speakers—their letters, speeches, interviews, reminiscences, and other recorded utterances—and then simulated how, if they were reminiscing aloud, they would describe historical events in which they were the principal players or eyewitnesses. In each case, I found that I had to get into character, much as an actor gets into a role. As much as possible, I used the actual words of my characters—their phrases, even whole sentences. When that was not possible, I simulated their language and rhythms of speech in order to recount developments in which they participated. As my references indicate, the events and themes in the monologues adhere to the actual historical record.

There are many dramatic scenes in my story. These are a matter of the record and are fully documented in my notes. There is also a fair amount of dialogue. Much of it comes from authentic sources—letters, memoirs, personal histories—though I took the liberty to rewrite such dialogue that seemed too formal for the spoken word. On other occasions, I created dialogue from factual descriptions in letters, reports, testimony, and similar sources. An example is the scene in 1861 when Senators Charles Sumner, Benjamin Franklin Wade, and Zacharia Chandler importune Lincoln to issue an emancipation proclamation. Their arguments are fully recorded in the third person and past tense in various sources. I simply cast the information in dialogue form, in the first person and the present tense.

In short, in this and similar instances, I simulated how my figures spoke by using facts imaginatively. The technique is not new with me. Allan Nevins, one of the greatest American historians of all time, wove historical data into graphic scenes and simulated dialogue in his widely acclaimed work of nonfiction, *The Emergence of Lincoln*.[1] Like Nevins, I believe that a little fact-based creativity of this sort enhances our appreciation and understanding of the people of history.

A word about my telling of Booth and the assassination of Lincoln. The modern, authoritative treatments of the story by William A. Tidwell, James O. Hall, David Winfred Gaddy, William Hanchett, and Betty J. Ownsbey convince me that Booth had ties to the Confederate secret service, that his abduction and assassination plots were part of several schemes of retribution to be executed by rebel agents, and that Booth had the approval and support of the highest authorities in Richmond, possibly Jefferson Davis himself. In their view, the North's ruthless military policies, especially against civilians, justified covert retaliation against Lincoln and his colleagues in Washington. My reference notes, I believe, provide convincing documentation for the revisionist version of the story. For a discussion of that version, see Barbara Hughett, "William Hanchett on 'Lincoln's Assassination After 130 Years,'" *The Civil War Round Table* (Chicago, Ill., Apr. 1995), 1.

My portrait of Sherman also requires an explanation. The red-headed warrior was a profane man. Those who knew him spoke of his profanity in their letters, reminiscences, and histories of the war; however, they seldom quoted him beyond a *damn* or a *hell*. The truth is, Sherman was a good deal more profane than that. In re-creating his voice, I honored his character and let him curse with fervor. I don't think this technique violates the truth of history. On the contrary, it gets closer to what the historical Sherman was like than does a rigid adherence to his recorded utterances—his letters and memoirs, for instance—which were highly sanitized.

Lincoln also swore on occasion, and some of his jokes would have made the prudish squirm. You will find one such joke early on in my story. Humor, of course, was Lincoln's antidote for depression, which plagued him all his life. In his day, the popular term for melancholia was "hypochondria" or the "hypo." The latter was Lincoln's favorite word for it; and in his monologues he uses it frequently to describe how inept generals, military reversals, and other bad news affected him.

[1]See Nevins, *The Emergence of Lincoln* (2 vols., New York: Charles Scribner's Sons, 1947), 1:151, 261–62, 2:11–20.

There are many legitimate ways to write history. Indeed, the great strength of the field is its Renaissance breadth and diversity. By composing this book in the first person, from multiple viewpoints, I hope to suggest a bona fide alternative to the more traditional third-person approaches. This alternative allows us to walk in the footsteps of the people of history, to think their thoughts and feel their feelings, to experience them in all their flawed and glorious humanity. For me, assuming the roles of eleven other human beings—which required that I show them all an equal degree of empathy—was a creative adventure of the highest order. I hope that the first-person approach enables readers to relate directly to my speakers, to empathize with them, understand them, be touched and enlightened by them, without the intrusion of an omniscient, third-person narrator.

THE WINDS OF 'SIXTY-ONE

The Union forever, hurrah! boys, hurrah!
Down with the traitor, up with the star,
While we rally round the flag, boys,
Rally once again,
Shouting the battle cry of freedom.

We are a band of brothers, and native to the soil,
Fighting for the property we gained by honest
        toil;
And when our rights were threatened, the cry rose
        near and far,
Hurrah for the Bonnie Blue Flag that bears
        a single star!

1. ABRAHAM LINCOLN

The Sunday morning headlines screamed with the latest news from Charleston harbor: Fort Sumter had fallen after a two-day bombardment by rebel shore batteries. The only good news was that the defenders hadn't suffered any casualties and the rebels had allowed our navy to evacuate the garrison. I guess they expected us to thank 'em for their charity. The fall of Sumter was the climax of almost six weeks of maneuvering in which I'd elected to send down a provisioning flotilla and leave it up to Jeff Davis and his pretended government, the Confederate States of America, so-called, whether to open fire on the fort and start a civil war. The blast of their guns at our flag gave me my answer.

Tossing the papers aside, I called the Cabinet together in my second-floor office and told them that the insurgents, by firing the first shot, had forced on us the decision of immediate dissolution or blood. We all realized that it would be a gigantic contest and that the small regular army—about sixteen thousand men all told—was wholly inadequate for the job; it was scattered across the country, mostly on the frontier, and southern resignations had badly depleted it. To maintain the government, we would have to rely on state militia. How many would we need? Some of the secretaries thought at least fifty thousand; but Secretary of State Seward croaked that it ought to be a hundred thousand. We settled on seventy-five thousand.

The next day, April fifteenth, I issued a proclamation calling up seventy-five thousand militia from the several states to suppress the rebellion, and I summoned Congress to convene in special session on Independence Day. "I appeal," I said, "to all loyal citizens to favor, facilitate and aid this effort to maintain the honor, the integrity, and the existence of our National Union, and the perpetuity of popular government."

Just two days later—two days!—the Virginia convention, which had been in continual session, waiting to see what I would do, adopted a secession ordinance, which Virginia voters would later ratify in a special election. Virginia Unionists went over to the rebellion, they claimed, because they could not tolerate the specter of Federal troops marching across their soil to suppress the insurrection in the seven cotton states, which had formed the so-called Confederacy in Montgomery before I'd even been inaugurated.

"Those traitors," I said bitterly in the privacy of my office. "How many times have I heard Virginia Unionists, right here in this room, proclaim their loyalty to the flag? I was sure on that basis that Virginia would remain loyal. But when I choose to defend the flag against treason, these professed Union men almost instantly embrace the rebellion and become traitors themselves. The sons-of-bitches! With Virginia on its way out, we may lose the entire upper South. Damn, damn, *damn*. Well, Virginia will be exceedingly sorry for this. I have no choice but to deal with the rebellion where I find it."

I tell you, it was chaos in Washington that day. We had no plan of operations and no idea how we were going to equip and supply seventy-five thousand men for the ninety days I'd called them to serve. It would be the largest force ever assembled in the country—more than seven times the size of the expeditionary force old Winfield Scott had led into Mexico in 'forty-seven. Our most pressing problem was the want of a capable officer to command the troops in the field. I greatly admired Scott, the general-in-chief of the army. He was a hero of two wars and though a Virginian was an unqualified patriot and a friend of the Administration. But it was plain to everybody that at seventy-five he was too old and sickly to command in the field. He was exceedingly stout and suffered from gout, vertigo, dropsy, and I don't know what else. It hurt him so much to walk that he had to pause every few steps to gather his strength. He couldn't ride a horse or climb the steps of the Capitol without help.

In the afternoon, Seward and I paid a visit to the old general, setting out on a tree-shaded brick walkway that led to the War Department and army headquarters on Seventeenth Street. It was a warm spring day and the lilacs were blooming along the way. Seward chewed on a cigar and talked nonstop about the crisis, using "damn" and "hell" liberally. A jocular little New Yorker with white hair, a beaked nose, and a scraggly neck, he tipped his hat at everybody we passed and said "How-de-do?" He seemed to think they all knew him. Some fellows, I noticed, openly sported secessionist buttons. The damn traitors probably worked for the government, too. I tell you, it gave me the hypo.

We passed the little War Department building and crossed the street to the five-story Winder Building, where army headquarters were located. Going upstairs to Scott's office, I noticed how many of his staff officers were old codgers who sat in little rooms off the hallway, writing memos or staring out the window. We found General Scott seated at his desk, which was cluttered with maps and papers.

An enormous fellow with bushy gray brows and side whiskers, he was dressed in full uniform with a yellow sash and expansive epaulettes.

Seward got down to business. "We're gathering a large army," he said around his cigar. "What we don't foresee is how it's to be led. What will we do for generals?"

"Mr. Secretary," Scott said, his face trembling, "I've thought a great deal about that. If I could only mount a horse—" He paused, shaking his head sadly. "But I'm past that. I can only serve my country here, in my chair." Who, then, would command the army in battle? Only one other general, John Wool, had ever led an army in the field. But Wool was two years older than Scott and equally unfit for field command. Wool's hands shook, he constantly repeated himself, and couldn't remember whatever subject was being discussed.

"Few of our officers have commanded even a brigade in the field," Scott conceded. "There are good officers, but unfortunately for us, the South has taken most of those holding the higher grades. We have captains and lieutenants that, with time and experience, will develop and give good service." He named McClellan, Hooker, Hancock, Sherman, Halleck, and others.

"There is one officer who would make an excellent general right now," Scott went on, "but I don't know if he's with us or not. He's a Virginian and lives just across the river: Colonel Robert E. Lee of the Second Cavalry. He's by far the best soldier I've ever seen in the field. His bold reconnaissance in the Mexico City campaign, back in 'forty-seven, enabled us to defeat the Mexican Army and capture the capital. I think he's a military genius."

Lee had my vote on Scott's praise alone. "I tell you what," I said. "Why don't I get Frank Blair, Sr., to talk to him. Blair is the best elder statesman we have. And he's mighty persuasive."

Scott thought it a good idea. He would also send for Lee, he said, and have a talk with him after he saw Blair.

I went at once to see Old Man Blair. When he visited Washington City, he stayed in a big house across Pennsylvania Avenue from the Executive Mansion. Seventy years old now, he was a fixture in Washington politics, an old-time Jacksonian, long-time editor of the *Congressional Globe*, and later one of the founders of the Republican Party. His shoulders were stooped and his wrinkled face reminded me of a walnut shell. But his blue eyes were clear and lively, and he enjoyed talking and laughing and spinning stories as much as I did. Friends begged him and his wife, Violet, not to come to the city alone, for fear that rebel sympathizers would bushwhack 'em. But day after day, the two Blairs would ride boldly in from their Maryland estate, Violet to see her daughters-in-law and Frank to advise me and other Republicans. He liked to say, "Van Buren was right, times are out of joint for us old Jacksonians." The idea of civil war, he said, held nothing but horror for him, as it did for all of us. "The young men of the land marching off to slaughter one another—how in hell did we get into this mess?"

"I'm hoping it won't last long," I said. "If we get the right man to command the army, one great battle ought to do it. That's why I'm here." I told him what Scott had said about Lee. "I wonder if you would talk with him and find out his intentions and feelings. If he's with us, offer him field command of the army we're raising. A promotion to general goes with it, of course. You can tell him the offer comes on the authority of the president of the United States."

Blair said, "I'll send word through his cousin John Lee that I'd like to see him tomorrow morning."

"Let me know right away what he says."

2. R. E. Lee

I had an idea what they wanted to see me about in Washington. Six weeks ago, with several southern states already out of the Union, General Scott had called me back from Texas, where I had been serving with the Second Cavalry. With the nation threatened, he desired me to be second in command of the army. I thanked him for his confidence in me, but said that I could never fight with an army of northern men against the South.

"I don't want you to do that," General Scott said. "I want you to command a Union force strong enough to keep peace and prevent civil war, which I deplore as much as you." I looked at him without replying. "Colonel," he said, "you know my esteem for you. You are the best soldier in Christendom. I want you to think over what I've said." I assured him I could think of little else. Civil war, after all, was a terrible, unthinkable alternative.

Now that alternative was upon us: the Confederate forces had seized Federal forts and posts within their borders—"Has it come so soon as this?" I asked—and the Republicans had called up a huge force of northern militia to subjugate the South. When I received the summons to see Mr. Blair and General Scott, I did not yet know the verdict of Virginia's secession convention after Lincoln's call for troops. I had long since decided that my loyalty to Virginia took precedence over what was due the Federal government. I had therefore resolved that if Virginia stood by the old Union, so would I. But if she seceded, though I did not believe in secession as a constitutional right, I would still follow my native state with my sword, and if need be with my life.

The next morning, April eighteenth, I rose early, as was my habit, and rode about Mr. Custis's estate. Mary, my wife, called it the Custis-Lee plantation, but out of respect for Mr. Custis, who was like a father to me, I still referred to it as his place. He was the grandson of Martha Washington, and had built the mansion partly as a shrine to the first president and kept many of his precious relics on display. Mr. Custis had passed on four years ago and had named me as executor of his estate, which included the Arlington, White House, and Romancock plantations and their 196 slaves. Mr. Custis's will gave Mary life estate at Arlington and our son Custis the rights and title. The other two plantations went to our other sons, Rooney and Rob, respectively. Mr. Custis's will stipulated that, after legacies were paid to our daughters, the 196 slaves were to be set free, no later than five years after his death. I vowed to fulfill that stipulation to the letter, even though it would work a great hardship on us.

I had much to do as manager of Arlington. The two-story mansion and outbuildings were in a state of disrepair, the fields were badly neglected, the slaves were poorly disciplined and indifferent to work; and I had little money and considerable debts to pay off. Nevertheless, granted an extended leave from the army, I set upon my duties as manager with a singular resolve to restore Arlington to her former majesty. I had the buildings renovated and struggled to make the fields productive again. I would be less than truthful if I didn't say it was a dreary, unhappy period for me, trying to turn a run-down plantation into a self-sufficient farm again. I even found myself missing the army.

Since I had more slaves than I could use given my land and capital, I hired several out for a year to supplement my income. Two of the Negroes, a male and a young female, became rebellious and tried to escape to Pennsylvania. They were captured, however, and returned to me. I sent them to lower Virginia, where it would be harder to escape to the North. This episode inspired an outrageous accusation in the abolitionist *New York Tribune*, that not only had I ordered the man brutally whipped by my overseer, but that I had personally laid thirty-nine lashes on the female when my overseer had refused to do so. It was all a lie; I never whipped any of Mr. Custis's servants, or any of my own family's either.

Though Mr. Custis had left me an unpleasant legacy in his slaves, I had great affection for Arlington and the magnificent old mansion on the hilltop, with its commanding view and what my dear daughter Agnes called "the soft wild luxuriance of its woods." It was the only real home I had ever known; it was where our children had been born, and where Mary and I had hoped to pass our final years.

Poor Mary feared that her time was already near, and I admit she suffered from crippling pain. When I first returned from Texas, after Mr. Custis's death, I was shocked to find dear Mary in bed, her feet and ankles terribly swollen, her right arm and hand entirely useless. She thought she had "a tumor," but the physicians said her trouble stemmed from "child-bed fever," suffered in bearing seven children in fifteen years; the fever had spread to her hips and pelvis, causing the swelling and pain. When I returned from Texas in 'sixty-one, she was confined to a wheel-chair and looked as if she had aged twenty years. Always small of frame, she appeared bent and shrunken, and her dark eyes, once so bright and cheerful, were dulled from pain.

Poor Mim, I remember what a difficult time she'd had bearing our second child, our little Mee. It left Mim so distracted that she suddenly seized a pair of scissors and cut off all her hair. Our physician treated her with leeching and fomentation. But she only grew sicker and weaker with every subsequent childbirth, with Rooney, Annie, Agnes, Rob, and Milly. Ah, what a toll it took on you, dear Mary. And yet with seven beautiful children, surely we were blessed. "They are so entwined around my heart," I said, "that I feel them at every pulsation." On winter evenings at Arlington, I liked nothing better than to sit before a fire, remove my slippers, and tell them a story while they tickled my hands and feet. But if they became so absorbed in the story that they forgot to tickle, I would tell them, "No tickling, no story!"

Custis, our oldest, was always Mary's favorite child, and he was a sweet boy, but rambunctious, hard to manage. As a child, little Mee was the brightest flower that ever bloomed. Oh she was a rare one. But so were gentle Annie, my little Agnes, and Milly, my Precious Light. It doesn't trouble me that my daughters chose not to marry when they were grown. To me they will always be the most beautiful blossoms in the world. Precious Light merely said, "All other men are small in comparison to you, father." I thank merciful Providence that my daughters remained free to care for poor Mim when she could no longer get about.

When I finished my rounds this April morning, I made certain that Mim was comfortable in the parlor, then rode down the winding path and across the Long Bridge into Washington. I could not stop thinking of the crisis and asking, *how, how has it come to this?* It had seemed to me, for some time, that the systematic and progressive efforts of the abolitionists and Black Republicans of the North, to interfere with and change the domestic institutions of the South, were chiefly to blame for the hostilities between the two sections. The object of those people, the freeing of our slaves, was both unlawful and irresponsible, and could only be accomplished through the agency of civil and servile war. That had been the object of the abolitionist attack at Harpers Ferry, servile war, and the result proved that the leader, John Brown, was a fanatic or a madman, and so were all those who thought like him. When I reflected on recent events, I not only felt *aggrieved* by the aggressions of the North against us; I also resented their *denial* of the South's equal rights to the common territories, including the right to take slaves there.

Do not misunderstand me: I was no defender of slavery. How could I have been? I believed that, in this enlightened age, few would deny that slavery as an institution was a moral and political evil in any country. I thought it a greater evil, however, to the white than to the black race, and my sympathies were with my own race. The blacks, I maintained, were immeasurably better off here than in Africa, morally, socially, and physically. The painful discipline they were undergoing, as slaves, was necessary for their instruction as a race, and I hoped it would prepare and lead them to better things. Their emancipation would sooner result from the mild and melting influence of Christianity, however, than from the storms and tempests of fiery controversy. How long their subjugation might be necessary was known and ordered by a wise and merciful Providence. As I told Mary, we must leave the final abolition of human slavery to Him who sees the end, who chooses to work by slow influences and for whom two thousand years are but a single day. The abolitionists must know this, but I feared they would persevere in their evil course. And I wondered: Was it not strange that the descendants of the pilgrims who crossed the Atlantic to preserve their own freedom of opinion were now proving themselves intolerant of the spiritual liberty of others?

Still, though I deplored northern aggressions against us, I was not a disunionist and was not pleased with the course or the selfish, dictatorial bearing of the cotton states following Lincoln's election. As an American citizen, I took great pride in my country, her prosperity and institutions, and I could anticipate no greater calamity for the nation than the dissolution of the Union. I agreed with what President Buchanan said in his last congressional message: *secession was nothing but revolution.* The framers of the Constitution, which created the old Union, would never have exhausted so much labor, wisdom, and forbearance in its formation and surrounded it with so many guards and securities, if they had intended for it to be broken by every member of the confederacy at will. I remembered that when the New England states resisted Mr. Jefferson's embargo law and the Hartford Convention assembled, a Virginia statesman had deemed secession to be treason. What could it be now?

Still, like Mr. Buchanan, I did not favor the use of force to maintain national integrity. "If the bond of the Union," I said, "can only be maintained by the sword and bayonet, instead of brotherly love and friendship, and if strife and civil war are to take the place of mutual aid and commerce, its existence loses all interest with me. I can however do nothing but trust in the overruling providence of a merciful God. I am particularly anxious that Virginia should keep right, as she was chiefly instrumental in the formation and inauguration of the Constitution, and I wish that she might be able to save the Union." But as the secession crisis deepened, I grieved for the condition of our country. "God alone can save us from our folly, selfishness & short sightedness," I wrote Markie Williams, Mary's young cousin. "I only see that a fearful calamity is upon us, and fear that the country will have to pass through a fiery ordeal for its sins."

I rode down Pennsylvania Avenue and reined up at Mr. Blair's house. A stooped, emaciated gentleman with a deeply wrinkled face, he received me with great fanfare in the parlor.

"I speak on the authority of President Lincoln," he said. "He wants to know if he can induce you to take command of the army that will be put into the field. I've spoken to the secretary of war, too, and he agrees that you are the man for the job."

Considering my record, I thought the offer painfully ironic. Although I had graduated second in my class at the Academy, I had been terribly frustrated with the peace-time army, with the low pay, slow advancement, and constant reassignment from one post to another. At times I feared I was inadequate, even a complete failure. I made many resolutions and attempts to do better but always failed. I told young Markie: "You who know my weaknesses will I fear have little confidence in my success." After thirty-two years in the army, with service in the Mexican War and a stint as superintendent of the Academy, I had only risen to the rank of colonel. Now the Black Republicans were offering me what I had never thought would be mine: the rank of general and the command of an army. And I had to say no.

"Please tell your president," I said, "that while I oppose secession and deprecate war, I can take no part in an invasion of the southern states. I must therefore decline his offer."

"I'll tell him," Mr. Blair said, frowning.

I then went to see General Scott and told him what Blair had offered and that I had turned him down.

The general looked pained. "Lee," he said, "you have made the greatest mistake of your life. But I feared it would be so." I saluted and turned to go. "One more thing," he said. "Every officer in the army should decide what course he will pursue and announce it. No one should continue in the employ of the government unless he intends to defend it. If you propose to resign, Colonel, it is proper that you do so at once, since your attitude is unequivocal."

I rode back to Arlington with a heavy heart. General Scott had been a kind friend and mentor to me, ever since we had served together in the Mexican War, and I felt that I had let him down. But what choice did I have? I thought I ought to resign my commission, as Scott said, but I felt such a strong sense of honor and duty to the United States that I could not bring myself to do it.

The next day, in town on business, I bought a newspaper and read that Virginia had in fact seceded *two days before*. This was terrible. It was the beginning of sorrows—the start of what I was certain would be a horrible and protracted war that would ruin the country. In Leadbeater's Apothecary, the proprietor asked what I thought of the news from Richmond.

"I am one of those dull creatures that cannot see the good of secession," I said.

I slept little that night. *We are now in a state of revolution*, I thought, *and Virginia has been brought into it. I do not recognize the necessity for this state of things and would have forborne and pleaded to the end for a redress of grievances, real or supposed; yet with all my devotion to the Union and the feeling of loyalty and duty I have as an American citizen, I cannot raise my hand against my native state, my relatives, my children, my home. I have no choice, therefore, but to resign from the army.*

Early the next morning, I wrote my letter of resignation and appended a personal note to General Scott. "Save in defense of my native State," I told him, "I never desire again to draw my sword."

Then I walked into the parlor. "Well, Mary," I said, "the question is settled."

The next day I took the train to Richmond and offered my services to Governor Letcher, who appointed me major general in command of the Virginia state forces, which were to be put into the field to repel the northern invasion. I thought: *I have done only what my duty demanded. I can take no other course without dishonor.* I felt that the question was now out of the power of man and in the hands of God alone. I could only trust that a merciful Providence would not dash us from the height to which his smiles had raised us.

3 . LINCOLN

When I heard that Lee had taken command of Virginia's insurgent army, it gave me the hypo. I'd understood from Scott and Blair that the colonel was not going to take sides, that he was going to sit the war out because he could not "raise his hand" against his home. But this latest news was vexing. I hadn't figured Lee for a traitor. Well, I was learning every day to expect the worst, as many other supposedly loyal southern officers also violated their oaths of allegiance and went over to the rebellion. Captain John Bankhead Magruder of the artillery, a theatrical Virginian with a sweeping mustache, actually came to see me, stood right here in this room, and repeated over and over his "undying devotion to the Union." Three days later he resigned his commission and joined the insurgents. No southern resignation pained me more. I didn't know who to trust anymore.

With Virginia gone and Maryland also threatening to secede, Washington City was in great danger. On the very day that Scott and Blair talked to Lee, rumors flew that rebel ships were sailing up the Potomac to bombard us, that Virginia troops were on the march from Richmond, that forty thousand of 'em were already approaching the Long Bridge! As rumor followed rumor, Washington residents armed themselves and barricaded their doors, and government clerks, the loyal ones, were issued muskets. James H. Lane of Kansas, "a gaunt, tattered, uncombed and unshorn figure," as one of my young secretaries described him, organized loyal hotel guests into a company and had them patrol the streets. While telegraphic dispatches indicated that the Seventh New York and Sixth Massachusetts militia were on their way to save the capital, we feared they would never get here in time.

4 . MARY LIVERMORE

When Mr. Lincoln called for troops, Boston was transported with excitement. The next day the militia arrived in clanging trains and marched through the crowded, cheering streets and women opened their windows and waved flags and handkerchiefs as the swaying lines of troops passed below. I had never seen anything like this before, had never dreamed that New England, slow to wrath, could be fired with such a warlike spirit. My father insisted that I help him out to his carriage to see the spectacle, and we followed the columns of troops and surging crowd to Faneuil Hall, where Old Glory went racing up the flagpole on the roof to resounding hurrahs. Never before had the national flag signified anything to me. But as I saw it now, kissing the skies, all that it symbolized as representative of government and emblematic of national majesty became clear to me. It was *this* holy flag that had been insulted—it was our people's government, the grandest on earth, with all its faults, that the South was determined to slay. And I thought, *if it be a question of the supremacy of freedom or slavery, then I pray to God it may be settled now, by us, and not by our children. Oh that I may be a hand, a foot, an eye, a voice, an influence, on the side of freedom and my country!*

On the afternoon of April seventeenth, the Sixth Massachusetts, a full regiment one thousand strong, started from Boston by rail. And the women left behind—the mothers, wives, sisters, and daughters—watched the train depart with flags in their hands and tears in their eyes. For women to send their men to the fearful chances of the battlefield, knowing well the risks they run—this involves exquisite suffering, and calls for another kind of heroism.

I had come from Chicago to nurse my father through an illness, but his condition had so improved that there was no longer any need of my remaining in Boston. My husband's letters from Chicago were full of the war excitement in the West. The doubtful position of slaveholding Missouri, and the fact that the lower counties of Illinois and Indiana were allied to the South by kinship, trade, and political sympathy, caused great distress, and I was anxious to return home.

Before leaving Boston, though, I went to see William Lloyd Garrison, the great abolitionist editor of the *Liberator*. My husband and I had met him years ago when we were living in Auburn, Massachusetts—we invited him to our house and took tea with him. I remember being struck by his appearance: he had a balding head and wore spectacles and seemed as calm and serene as a summer day. I could not believe that this harmless-looking man was the northern agitator so feared and despised in the South. My husband and I were already abolitionists, had long been readers of the *Liberator*, and I for one could attest to the accuracy of its descriptions of the southern slave system. For three years, I had been a tutor on a Virginia plantation and had witnessed with my own eyes the evils of slavery, saw the abject and hopeless condition of the poor Negroes, saw their families broken up and sold apart, saw one poor man whipped with his wrists roped to a beam from the roof of the cooper's shed. I can still hear the swish of the whip, the cries for mercy, the shrieks of anguish.

When I called on Garrison in his Boston office, I found him with composing-stick in hand, setting up print for the next issue of the *Liberator*.

I asked him, "Mr. Garrison, what is your opinion of this southern rebellion? Will it be a 'sixty-day flurry' as people say, or are we to have a war?"

"We are to have a war—a bloody, merciless war—a civil war, always more dreadful than one with a foreign nation. The North underestimates the power, purpose, and ability of the South. It will be a desperate struggle."

"How will it end?"

"You mean who will win? No one can answer that question. But I'm certain of one thing: the war will result in the death of slavery."

The next day, determined to do something for my country, to serve the flag somehow, I left for Chicago by train. All along the route were excited groups of people, eager for news from Washington. At Albany, where we stopped for dinner, we learned that something terrible had happened to the Sixth Massachusetts—that war had already begun.

5 . LINCOLN

It happened on Friday, April nineteenth, the anniversary of the battle of Lexington that had helped touch off the American Revolution. The Sixth Massachusetts, on its way through Baltimore, was attacked by a mob of pro-secession plug-uglies—like the bunch that had laid in wait for me earlier in the year—and several militiamen and civilians had been killed. The news upset my wife, Mary. She was afraid that another attempt would be made to assassinate me. Young Hay, my personal secretary, said he had to do some "dexterous lying" to calm her down. Ironic, I thought, that on this historic date the first blood of the Civil War should be spilled. Only God knew where it would all end.

The survivors of the Sixth regiment finally got away to Washington City by train. Many of them were bandaged and on crutches—they made quite a stir as they walked up to the Capitol, where they took up quarters. We had no place else to put them. I told Colonel Ed Jones, who commanded the regiment, that if they hadn't arrived that day, we'd have been in the hands of the rebels before morning. By then, dire warnings had come from Governor Hicks of Maryland and Mayor Brown of Baltimore that no more troops could pass through that city unless they were prepared to fight their way through.

By nightfall, malignant rumors swept Washington that the Baltimore mob was now on its way to burn us out. John Nicolay, my official private secretary, reported that "a vigilant watch is out at all the possible directions of approach," but to our relief no mob appeared that night. Early the next morning, a delegation from Baltimore intercepted me as I hurried down the stairs of the Executive Mansion, on my way to see General Scott, who sat in his carriage by the door. Grim-faced, they importuned me not to bring any more troops through their city.

That made me bristle. "If I grant you this concession," I said, "you'll be back here tomorrow, demanding that I can't march soldiers around it either." Scott at once proposed a compromise. "Why not send the troops around Baltimore?" I agreed to this if from a military viewpoint it was practicable, and I gave the committee a note to that effect, in order to avoid further bloodshed. I agreed to this contrary to the advice of several prominent friends of the Administration. I vowed that this was the last time I was going to interfere in strictly military matters, that from now on I would leave them entirely to military men.

Still, I appreciated the dilemma of Governor Hicks and Mayor Brown, and I called 'em to Washington for a conference with General Scott and me. Hicks struck me as a reasonable man, a loyal man, and I wanted to assure him of our goodwill toward the loyal people of Maryland; our beef was with the secessionists. Round about midnight a dispatch came from the mayor. "Governor Hicks has gone to Annapolis," it said. "Should I come alone?"

"Come," I said.

I was right about making concessions. Next day Mayor Brown showed up with a second and larger Baltimore delegation. They informed me that Union troops must not be permitted to "pollute" Maryland soil anywhere. Not only that, they urged me to make peace with the rebels "on any terms."

What a supplicating lot! "You, gentlemen, come here to me and ask for peace on any terms," I said, "and yet have no word of condemnation for those who are making war on us. You express great horror of bloodshed, and yet would not lay a straw in the way of those who're organizing in Virginia and elsewhere to capture this city. The rebels attack Fort Sumter, and your citizens attack troops sent to defend this government, and yet you would have me break my oath and surrender it without a blow. There is no Washington in that—no Jackson in that—no manhood nor honor in that.

"Gentlemen, I must defend the capital. And the only way I can do it is by marching men *over the soil of Maryland*. Our men are not moles—they can't dig under the earth. They're not birds—they can't fly through the air. There is no way but to march across, and that they will do."

By Sunday, April twenty-first, there were confirmed reports that secessionists had burned the wooden railroad bridges north and west of Baltimore. Virginia forces had seized Harpers Ferry and cut the Baltimore & Ohio, the east-west railroad connecting Washington to the northwestern states. All rail and telegraph connections between Washington and the North were now cut. The capital was isolated, trapped between secessionist Virginia and hostile Maryland. So far only the Sixth Massachusetts and a few hundred "unlicked patriots from Pennsylvania" (as young Hay put it) had come to the defense of the government. Where were all the other troops? I climbed to the roof of the Executive Mansion and scanned the Potomac through a telescope, looking for a sign of military transports. Then I focused on Alexandria, where rebel troops were reported to be massing. I could see a rebel flag floating over a hotel there, and smoke rising from what appeared to be rebel campfires on the wooded hillsides. Any day now, I expected an insurgent army to storm over the Long Bridge and burn and pillage the entire capital. The Executive Mansion would be a prime target for their torches. I didn't like to think of what might happen to Mary and our two little boys, Willie and Tad.

That same Sunday I called an emergency meeting of the Cabinet and Attorney General Bates in the Navy Department. As we took seats around a table, I thought how much I was going to need this bunch in the stormy days we faced. There was Seward with his perpetual cigar and endless flow of anecdotes and advice. There was Simon Cameron, the secretary of war, a tall man with a thin mouth and thick gray hair, who had a remarkable memory for faces and names and who had the responsibility of managing the war effort. There was Secretary of the Navy Gideon Welles, an ill-tempered fellow with a flowing white beard, who frowned when I kiddingly called him Neptune. Next to Welles sat Postmaster General Monty Blair, one of Old Man Blair's sons; he was tall and lean, with a high forehead and small, deep-set eyes. Then came Interior Secretary Caleb Smith, a prosaic Indianan with a slight speech defect, and Attorney General Ed Bates, a stout, barrel-chested Missourian with a thick white beard. Rounding out the group was portly Salmon Chase, the Treasury secretary. He also spoke with a slight lisp and had a huge, balding head and a soft, smooth-shaven face. He had no sense of humor and struck others as a tad arrogant. "Chase is a good man," Ben Wade of the Senate liked to say, "but his theology is unsound. He thinks there is a fourth person in the Trinity." A widower, he had buried three wives and several children, but his sorrows had not dulled his political ambitions: he wanted pretty desperately to be president and would bear some watching if we made it till 'sixty-four.

"Gentlemen," I said, "we face the worst crisis in the history of our young Republic. The government is rife with traitors. There is no effective and adequate organization for the public defense and no time to call Congress into session so that it can enact what we need. As I see it, we have only two options. We can work within the limited means Congress has provided, and let the government fall. Or we can assume broad emergency powers and try to save it. I vote for the last option." No argument there. They all nodded in solemn agreement. Accordingly, I named several private citizens, all known for their ability, loyalty, and patriotism, who would be authorized to spend public money without security or compensation. I instructed Chase to advance $2 million to three loyal New Yorkers for the purpose of buying arms and making military preparations; directed Welles to appoint several Unionists, including his brother-in-law, to forward troops and supplies to the imperiled capital; and allowed Cameron to authorize his Pennsylvania crony Alexander Cummings and the governor of New York to buy supplies and transport troops for the public defense. Maybe these emergency actions were without authority of law, but I believed them absolutely necessary to save our people's government from this clear, flagrant, and gigantic case of rebellion. I trusted that Congress, when it convened on July fourth, would approve my actions retroactively. Without them, I argued, the world's last best hope—our democratic experiment— would collapse. Despotism, with class and caste, would triumph in the world, and the monarchists would gloat that popular government was dead forever.

When two days passed and still no troops had arrived, I feared even our emergency actions were too late. Alone, I paced back and forth in my office, pausing now and then to peer out a window. "Why don't the troops come?" I asked aloud. "The governors of Indiana, Pennsylvania, Ohio, Illinois, New York, and Rhode Island have all promised to send thousands of men. Where are they?" The next day, in a climate of doubt and gloom, the wounded men of the Sixth Massachusetts called at the Executive Mansion. "I don't believe there is any North," I told them. "*You* are the only northern realities."

The next day, April twenty-fifth, young John Hay hurried off to the depot to see if there was any news. He was a witty, boy-faced dandy who had accompanied us from Illinois to help out Nicolay. Presently, Hay came dashing up the stairs of the Executive Mansion. "The Seventh New York is here!" he cried. "The capital is saved!" I tell you, that news gladdened my heart. The regiment marched slickly up Pennsylvania Avenue to the White House, with banners snapping overhead and bands playing patriotic and martial airs. Next day the Eighth Massachusetts and the First Rhode Island regiments reached Washington City, and cannon crashed and boomed, rattling windows in the Executive Mansion. Soon thousands of other soldiers arrived in the city, filing off trains and steamers from all over the North. They camped in the Navy Yard, in the Treasury Department, in the Capitol, in the Center Market, behind City Hall, on Market Square, and on the nearby hills. Washington was transformed into an armed city. From the open windows in the Executive Mansion, we could see soldiers everywhere on the avenue. We could smell the smoke of army campfires and hear the rumble of caissons, the roll of drums, the tramp of drilling men, the bark of officers, and the cry of bugles on the wind. Washington had indeed been saved.

To defeat the rebellion, however, we had much work to do. Resorting to more emergency measures, I declared a blockade of the rebel coast, ordered the national armories into full production, added twenty-two thousand men to the regular army and eighteen thousand to the navy, and called for forty-two thousand three-year volunteers, again trusting to Congress to ratify what I'd done after it met. On paper, we would have a total of almost 157,000 soldiers to put into the field. Everybody in Washington hoped that such a formidable army would end the rebellion within ninety days.

We still hadn't found a field commander. But we were working on a plan of operations. I'll be the first to admit that I lacked military experience, unless you count the time I led a company of raw volunteers in the Black Hawk Indian War. We never did any fighting, though. The only enemy we bloodied were the mosquitoes. Even so, I had a plan to suppress the insurrection, and I shared it with Caleb Smith and young Hay. "I intend to fill Fort Monroe, down on the tip of the Virginia Peninsula, with men and stores, tighten the blockade, provide for the entire safety of Washington, and then go down to Charleston and pay her the little debt we owe her for the fall of Fort Sumter."

I admit the plan was pretty naive, since it assumed the war could be won in the East and entirely overlooked the Mississippi Valley. I deferred of course to General Scott, leaving it up to him to devise a winning strategy. In early May, he submitted a "plan of campaign" that called for an effective blockade of the enemy coast and military operations on the Mississippi River. As Scott conceived it, an army, led by young George B. McClellan, with some "rough-vigor fellows" as his assistants, would seize the river from Cairo to the Gulf of Mexico, thereby cutting the Confederacy in two. Once the blockade was in place, we would have 'em surrounded.

What about the huge army we were assembling at Washington? I asked. Scott said he wanted to use it entirely for defensive purposes. "We don't want to invade the South with that army," he said. "It would only alienate southern Unionists. Once we capture the Mississippi, we should halt operations and wait. Wait for the Unionists to assert themselves and end the rebellion. If we're patient, we can win the war that way."

Instinctively, I distrusted that advice. How could you put down a rebellion without offensive operations? I appreciated Scott's emphasis on the importance of seizing the Mississippi. But I had little hope that southern Unionism could end the rebellion. Last winter, it had done damn little to halt the spread of secession in the Deep South, had in fact been all but nonexistent. Nope, that was too thin a reed to hang our hopes on. If we wanted to win this thing, we had to *invade* the South, had to *defeat* rebel forces on the field of battle.

May sixth brought more bad news from the slave states. The legislatures of Arkansas and Tennessee voted to secede, and the Confederate government, so-called, announced that a state of war existed with the United States. A couple of weeks later a convention in North Carolina unanimously approved a secession ordinance, making a total of eleven slave states seized by the insurgents. Only the border slave states—Missouri, Kentucky, Maryland, and Delaware—were still in the Union with us, but the first three, the crucial ones, all had powerful secessionist elements. We had to do everything possible to neutralize those elements and keep the border states loyal. If we lost 'em, it would cost us the whole game. A rebel Maryland would leave Washington City trapped in the center of an insurrectionary state— an unimaginable calamity. A rebel Missouri would make it difficult for us to hold the upper Mississippi; it would cut off Kansas and leave Illinois and Iowa vulnerable to attack. The loss of Kentucky would be even worse. It would give the insurgents a base from which to attack Illinois, Indiana, and Ohio. We would not be able to control the strategic Ohio River, or hold Missouri, which meant the Mississippi would probably be lost to us. I hoped to have God on our side, I said, but I *had* to have Kentucky.

As it turned out, the governor of Kentucky, a secesh named Beriah Magoffin, rejected my call for troops and proclaimed the state "neutral" in the conflict, forbidding "any movement upon Kentucky soil." I tell you, Magoffin tried my patience. Still, I decided to use diplomacy to keep Kentucky loyal; I ignored Magoffin and dealt directly with the pro-Union legislature. I promised that we would not use force against Kentucky, would not invade her territory, burn her cities, make war on her people, or free her slaves. But I did send out loyal officers to recruit volunteers, and chose friends of the Union out there to distribute guns to loyal regiments.

Swift and decisive military action saved the other two critical border states. In Missouri, General Nathaniel Lyon broke up the pro-secessionist state militia, chased off the pro-Confederate governor and legislature, and then turned the "vacant" government over to Missouri Unionists, who cooperated fully with us. Their leader was Frank Blair, Jr., Old Man Blair's son and a loyal Administration man.

Something like that happened in Maryland, too. General Benjamin F. Butler, commanding a militia force at Annapolis, begged me to let him "bag the whole nest of traitors" in Maryland and herd 'em down to Washington City like so much captured cattle. I refused his request because I wanted to use diplomacy in dealing with Maryland. But Butler, always an impetuous sort, ignored my orders and occupied Baltimore during a violent thunderstorm. Then he jailed the leading secessionists and confiscated more than two thousand muskets sent up from rebel Virginia. It was bad enough that Virginia had resorted to treason—now that damned state was trying to export it to Maryland.

Anyhow, Union troops could now march unimpeded through troublesome Baltimore, and northern newspapers hailed Butler as our first war hero. It was a beguiling irony, since Butler, a successful Massachusetts lawyer and Democratic politician, had favored Jeff Davis for president in the last canvass. I forgave our hero for acting without orders and promoted him to major general of volunteers, the first "political general" to attain that rank. I would make generals out of other politicians, too. It was a good way to keep political rivals from attacking Administration policies. Oh, yes, a good many Marylanders howled about Butler's "invasion," but the state soon quieted down. Thanks to the efforts of Governor Hicks, Maryland even sent a thousand volunteers to Washington.

Later, we uncovered tangible and unmistakable evidence that Mayor Brown of Baltimore and the secessionist members of the legislature were actively plotting treason. With Seward, I set out by carriage to confer with General John A. Dix, commander of eastern Maryland. We raced over rutted roads and swept into the village of Rockville in a swirl of dust, reining up at a tavern which doubled as Dix's headquarters. A New York Democrat who refused to coddle treason, the general escorted us to a grove of trees with thick bushes, where we could talk in private, beyond the hearing of subordinates whose loyalty was suspect. The Maryland legislature was soon to convene in Frederick City, and we had sound intelligence that the disunionists, who held the majority, would adopt a secession ordinance. The Unionist minority was deeply divided over what to do, and Governor Hicks, though a loyal Union man, was unable to control the secessionists. We knew who they were and agreed that we had to take a bold step to prevent them from handing Maryland— and the national capital with it—over to the rebels. I therefore authorized the army to keep the legislators under surveillance, permitting only the Union men to go to Frederick City. "You won't have any trouble separating the sheep from the goats," I told Dix. When the legislature convened, no goats were present. They had been arrested and thrown in prison. So had Mayor Brown. The pro-secession elements in the state, especially the Baltimore press, put up a terrible clamor, damning the arrests as "high-handed usurpation." Maybe it was, but I'll tell you this: it redeemed Maryland. The truth is, I was willing to do whatever was necessary to keep the border states in the Union. Necessity, after all, knows no law.

I took the same line in dealing with the enemy in the rear, a most efficient corps of spies, informers, suppliers, and aiders and abettors of the rebellion who, under the guise of liberty of speech, liberty of the press, and habeas corpus, did everything they could to obstruct our efforts to save the country. I suspended the writ of habeas corpus and declared martial law in vast areas behind the lines. This replaced civil courts with military tribunals, which had the power to try civilians suspected of disloyal activities. My actions may have been a violation of civil liberties, but I thought they were unavoidable if the laws of the Union, and liberty itself, were to survive the storm.

My suspension of the writ angered the chief justice of the U.S. Supreme Court, old Roger Taney of Maryland. He'd written the majority decision in the infamous Dred Scott case of 'fifty-seven, which in net effect had legalized slavery in all the national territories. A former slaveowner and a dedicated defender of that mischievous class, Taney was well over eighty now, stooped and white-haired, with an emaciated, withered face and loose-hanging jowls. From his office in the Capitol, he accused me of usurping power and argued that Congress alone had the constitutional right to suspend the writ.

"I admonish you," he said, "not to violate the very laws you have sworn to defend."

I answered the chief justice: "Are all the laws, *but one*, to go unexecuted, and the government itself go to pieces, lest that one be violated?" I went on to say I didn't believe any law had been violated. The Constitution states that the writ of habeas corpus can be suspended when, in cases of rebellion or invasion, the public safety requires it. But the Constitution is silent as to which branch, Congress or the Executive, is to exercise the power; and as the provision was plainly made for a dangerous emergency, I could not believe that the framers of the Constitution intended the danger to run its course until Congress could be called together, by which time the country might be destroyed. No sir, they intended that the Executive, too, should exercise the power. Accordingly, I suspended the writ and authorized the military to imprison people who were known disloyalists, who discouraged volunteering and otherwise aided and abetted treason.

Ah! you say. Lincoln made himself a dictator! He doesn't care one whit about the people!

That is *not so*. I've done what I've done to save the nation and its experiment in popular government, the noblest form of government the world ever saw. Whatever is *necessary* to save it, I'll do. You've got to remember, the war is an utter novelty. Nothing like it has ever occurred before in this country. We have no precedents, no guidelines, for dealing with internal dissent and security in the midst of a gigantic and confusing domestic insurrection that threatens the very life of the nation. From the outset, we had to feel our way in a fog of uncertainty, knowing that we were in uncharted waters where no previous administration had ever been. Maybe that's why I keep having this recurring dream in which I seem to be on the prow of a ship, moving through the mist toward a dark, indefinite shore.

I tell you, things were a colossal mess in those first months of the war, and it gave me fits of the hypo. Every agency from the White House to the army operated in a state of confusion. There was such a surge of patriotism and flood of volunteering across the North that the understaffed War Department completely lost track of all the regiments pouring into Washington. The job was already proving too much for War Secretary Cameron. Overwhelmed by his responsibilities, he used bad judgment in signing contracts for defective military equipment and often refused to accept state regiments, which caused officers and governors to come banging on my door. In addition to my other worries, I found myself having to send a steady stream of memos to Cameron, advising him to take the latest outfits from Indiana, from Michigan and Minnesota, from Ohio and Pennsylvania. When rival recruiters complained to me about whose regiments should be inducted, I ordered the War Department to take 'em all.

We soon had more than thirty thousand men encamped in and about the city, but the understaffed Commissary, Quartermaster, and Ordnance departments lacked the means to feed, clothe, or equip a force of that size. Hundreds of men came down sick, yet the Medical Department did not have the staff or the facilities to care for them. There were few army surgeons and nurses—the nurses were soldiers detailed from the line—and not a single military hospital in Washington. The responsibility for medical care fell back on the individual regiments, but they too were hopelessly short of doctors and medical stores. I read where one poor fellow had fallen sick and starved to death in his tent for lack of care.

When Dorothea Dix came to me with a plea to let her raise a corps of lady nurses, I told her to have at it. She had marched up and down the War Department, she said, but the "old men" in charge were horrified at the idea of enlisting women in government service to serve as nurses. Officially military nursing was a *man's* domain, they told her, and had been as long as they could remember. But Miss Dix, though sixty years old and thin as a fence rail, was one determined lady. I tell you, with her willpower and stiff back, she would have made a good general. We gave her a commission and authorized her to raise a corps of female nurses to help relieve our suffering soldiers.

We owe a lot to the women of the North. They did a great deal more for us than work in improvised army hospitals. Without 'em, we would never have been able to feed and clothe the huge army assembling in Washington, not to mention the forces organizing in Chicago, Cairo, and other strategic points in the West.

6. LIVERMORE

When I reached Chicago, there was more stir and excitement than I had seen anywhere on my journey back from Boston. The war spirit, war news, and war preparations engrossed everybody. Within eight days after the president's call, hundreds of troops were in Chicago, preparing to leave for the muddy little town of Cairo, situated at the confluence of the Ohio and Mississippi rivers and thus of vital military importance. When the troops set out through the unpaved streets, heading for the railroad station, people thronged the plank sidewalks and waved flags and cheered, and the prairie breeze not only kept the dust in perpetual motion, but caught up the litter and debris strewn about the streets, and sent that whirling through the air in clouds that blinded the eyes and choked the throats and nostrils. At the depot, the troops boarded a flag-draped train—it required twenty-six cars to hold them all—and it steamed out and headed south with a shrill blast of its whistle. Once again, I was struck by the heroism of the women who waved good-bye to them—who gave up their husbands, sons, and brothers, perhaps to a violent fate.

The great uprising among men, however, was paralleled by a similar uprising among the women. Across the North they formed thousands of Soldiers' Aid Societies and set about preparing boxes of food, stockings, medical stores, sheets, and blankets, and forwarding them to the military camps. In short order, there were a dozen or more such societies at work in Chicago alone, busily gathering supplies for our men at Cairo.

I presided over a Chicago Soldiers' Aid Society and saw right away that relief work was how I was meant to raise my voice and influence on the side of freedom and my country. In this, I was fully supported by my husband, Daniel, my lover, friend, housemate, and efficient helpmate. He was then pastor of the Second Universalist Church and editor of a Universalist monthly, the *New Covenant*. Before the war, he had encouraged me to write and sell poems and religious stories and had made me associate editor of his paper. When he was away on church matters, I wrote for every department except the theological and took charge of the business operations. I thanked God that I was endowed with an almost phenomenal capacity for work: in addition to my responsibilities at the *Covenant*, I worked with the Chicago Home for the Friendless and other charities and I conducted my own Sunday school class, consisting of sixteen young men, all of whom would later enter the army. All the while I was my own housekeeper, I directed my servants, gave personal supervision to the education and training of my two daughters, Marcia and Etta, and provided hospitality for my husband's many patrons and friends. Daniel said I was strong and forceful—"it shows in those clear, confident eyes," he said. My dear Daniel: I can still see him at our wedding—a handsome, clean-shaven man, dressed in a black suit with a white cravat, holding a Bible in one hand, with his other arm around my shoulder.

In managing a Soldiers' Aid Society, I enjoyed the assistance of Jane Hoge—pronounced "Hodge"—an ample, forceful, practical woman, fifty years old when the war began (I was forty). Our war work developed in both of us executive capabilities we did not know we possessed, and we surprised others, as we surprised ourselves, by the exercise of hitherto unsuspected gifts. We established a network of Chicago's most talented women—the wives and daughters of the city's most prominent and successful business and professional men—to assist in our war work. When additional regiments poured into the city and set up camps of instruction, we kept them supplied with food and drink and assorted indigestible dainties, which is why they called us "the cake and pie brigade."

When our "brigade" visited the Nineteenth Illinois, a captain pointed at one soldier and asked me if I noticed anything peculiar about him. I saw at a glance that it was a young woman masquerading as a man, and I said so. "That's the rumor," the captain said, "and my suspicion." He confronted the young woman, and she clutched his arm and begged him not to expose her, but to allow her to keep her disguise. Her husband had enlisted in this company, she said, and it would kill her if he marched without her. "Sir, let me go with you," she begged the captain. But she was quietly conducted outside the camp. I overtook her in my carriage and offered to take her to my home, but she leaped from the carriage and disappeared in the crowd. That night she jumped into the Chicago River, but a policeman rescued her and took her to the Home of the Friendless. Here I found her a few days later. She was extremely dejected. "I have only my husband in all the world," she said. "When he enlisted he promised that I could go with him; and that was why I put on his clothes, cut my hair, and joined the same regiment. And I *intend* to go with him, in spite of everybody." Her husband's regiment was ordered to Cairo, and she disappeared from the Home that same night. None of us doubted but that she had left to carry out her purpose.

Hers was not an isolated case. Hundreds of women joined the army masquerading as men and marched off to war with their regiments. Some did so for the same reason as the poor girl I just described—they wanted to be with their husbands or sweethearts. But many others enlisted disguised as men in order to defend the country—to *fight*. And the sad thing is, few records exist to document their contributions and their fate.

I was moved to admiration by the regeneration of women in our land and said so in an article in the *Covenant*. "Before Sumter," I wrote, "so many of our young women aspired to be fashion setters, their highest happiness being found in shopping, polkaing, and the schottische. They were pretty, petted, useless, expensive butterflies. But after Sumter, we find them lopping off superfluities, retrenching expenditures, deaf to the calls of pleasure or the mandates of fashion, swept by the incoming patriotism of the time to the loftiest height of womanhood, willing to do, to bear, or to suffer for the beloved country."

Oh there was an *uprising* of women, all right. The Women's Central Association of Relief, based in New York City, was instrumental in the formation of the United States Sanitary Commission, which became the Union's official civilian relief agency, with its main offices in Washington City and ten branch or regional offices in such major cities as Boston, New York, Philadelphia, Cincinnati, and Chicago. While men held the top executive offices in Washington, women served in managerial posts in the branch offices and made up the Commission's rank and file. The numerous Soldiers' Aid Societies—ten thousand of them ultimately—became affiliated with the Sanitary Commission and sent supplies to the central office or one of the regional offices for distribution to the troops. Thus it was that the Sanitary Commission harnessed the energy of women across the entire North on behalf of the great cause of our country.

Jane Hoge and I became associated with the Chicago branch—it was first called the Chicago Sanitary Commission, and later the Northwestern Sanitary Commission. Eliza Chappell Porter was the first office manager, and women made up the workforce. To our office on Wabash Avenue, in the heart of the business district, came a steady flow of blankets, shirts, pillows, comforters, drawers, sheets, pillowcases, towels, gowns, socks, Bibles, and assorted foods and drink, all neatly boxed, from our affiliated Soldiers' Aid Societies. Our office then distributed the boxes to the principal military camps of instruction in and about Chicago and elsewhere in the state. Dr. Charles H. Ray, a friend of President Lincoln's and the main editor of the *Chicago Press & Tribune*, issued an eloquent and stirring appeal for the entire Northwest to support our office, and we were soon receiving relief boxes from Soldiers' Aid Societies from as far away as Allen's Grove, Wisconsin.

At first, the women of a local affiliate marked their boxes for specific regiments from their own districts and even for their own brothers, husbands, or sons. But the requirements of the enormous armies Mr. Lincoln was assembling proved so great that we started shipping boxes to wherever they were needed. We did so in the spirit of Mrs. E. P. Teale, secretary of the Allen's Grove Soldiers' Aid Society. "In the light of war," she said, "*I view every loyal soldier as my brother.*"

7. LINCOLN

The Soldiers' Aid Societies did a great service that spring in providing our forces with rations and stores. But so many regiments were mustering in every day that the army remained short of everything in the fighting department. Our biggest headache was a want of adequate weapons. I was a big advocate of the modern repeating rifle, by far the best weapon for infantry because of its accuracy and rapid rate of fire. But the chief of army ordnance, James Wolfe Ripley, a white-haired, ruddy-faced old soldier with a bad temper and a constitutional aversion to change, insisted on arming our men with old smoothbore muskets, which were inaccurate beyond fifty yards. Mule-headed as they come, Ripley dismissed gun manufacturers and inventors with a curt, "han't got time." So they all came to me. I was interested in guns, especially the newfangled ones, and made it a policy to hear the inventors out. Most of 'em were men of character, though some were amusingly eccentric and others hare-brained crackpots. My personal secretaries joked about the "specimens of new rifles and cannon" that came to me by the score. Soon so many new guns leaned against the wall of my office that it looked like an ordnance bureau.

Six weeks after the fall of Fort Sumter, the Grand Army of the United States finally launched its first offensive movement. During the night of May twenty-fourth, under a full moon, several regiments charged across the Long Bridge, occupied Lee's plantation on Arlington Heights, and converted it into army field headquarters. Our men also seized Alexandria and ripped down that offensive rebel flag floating over the hotel.

With the attacking force was a close personal friend of my family, Colonel Elmer Ephraim Ellsworth. He was a cheerful, honest, fine-looking fellow—had accompanied us from Springfield, where he'd once worked in my law office. Mary said he was "an exemplary young man," and our little boys practically worshipped him. I think he was more of a big brother to them than our oldest son, Robert, and we came to regard him as part of our family. I felt a fatherly pride that he had participated in our first offensive thrust.

I was in the library when a captain came in, apologized for the interruption, and said he had some bad news. It was about Colonel Ellsworth. He'd been killed in Alexandria that morning. It was Ellsworth who had taken the rebel flag down from the roof of the hotel, the captain said. As he was doing it, a secessionist had blasted him to eternity with a double-barrel shotgun. The captain said he was sorry and made his leave. I stood at an open window for a long time, unable to believe what had happened to poor Ellsworth. The last time I saw him, he was dressed in his colorful Zouave uniform of red cap, red shirt, gray breeches, and gray jacket, and was armed with a sword, a heavy revolver, and a huge Bowie knife that was a full foot in length. We'd laughed and laughed together, he was such an amusing sight. How could such a fine young man be dead?

I heard someone come into the room and turned to see Senator Henry Wilson and a reporter advancing toward me.

"I can't talk," I said with tears in my eyes. "Ellsworth is dead and it's unnerved me."

I left to tell Mary and the boys the terrible news. I held them tight as they cried and cried. Later Mary and I went down to the Navy Yard near the river to see Ellsworth's body. We passed through the stone gate, where two sentries in dark blue tunics were on duty, and found Captain Dahlgren, the yard's chief ordnance officer. A spare, lean man with piercing eyes, he was the inventor of the famous Dahlgren gun, an eleven-inch howitzer, and was a trusted friend who served as my chief adviser on war ordnance. He showed us young Ellsworth's body where it lay amid trophies of guns from the Revolution and the Mexican War. "We can't leave him here," I said and had him brought up to the Executive Mansion, where he lay in state and received a full military funeral. Somebody brought us the blood-smeared flag he'd torn down from the hotel in Alexandria, but we couldn't bear to look at it, and Mary put it away. And so young Ellsworth was gone, killed in the first winds of war, and it left a wound in our hearts that would never quite heal. I worried about how many other young men would die before the whirlwind was over.

8. LEE

Our beloved Arlington was *lost*. I could not believe it. The news sent an arrow of pain through my heart. I was standing at a window of my office on the top floor of the Mechanics Institute in Richmond, shaking my head at our misfortune. Our old home, if not destroyed by our enemies, was so desecrated that I could not bear to think of it. I would rather that the mansion had been wiped from the earth than for it to be degraded by the presence of enemy soldiers who reveled in the evil they did. I could only thank merciful God that my wife and daughters had managed to flee to the safety of friends in Fauquier County.

Mary wrote me how anxious and uneasy she felt about Arlington. "Dearest Mary," I replied, "I sympathize deeply with your feelings at losing your dear home. I have experienced them myself and they are constantly revived. I fear we have not been grateful enough for the happiness at Arlington within our reach, and our Heavenly Father has found it necessary to deprive us of what He gave us. I acknowledge my ingratitude, my transgressions and my unworthiness, and submit with resignation to what He thinks proper to inflict upon me."

Trying to put Arlington out of my thoughts, I immersed myself in my military duties. Two weeks earlier, I had accepted a commission as brigadier general in the Confederate Army, then its highest rank. I gave my allegiance to the Confederacy because I deemed its cause sacred and worthy and felt it my duty to serve. My sons also enlisted in the Confederate Army: Custis became an officer of engineers, Rooney a cavalry captain, and Rob a captain in a student company at the University of Virginia.

I worried about them, though. I had especially wanted Rob to remain in school: I feared that this war could last ten years, and that later there would be no young men left to fight for us if we took them all into the army now. I loved my sons as I loved my daughters, yet I feared that I had failed them as a father. The army had taken me away from them for so many years; all I could do, from afar, was write them long letters of advice: hold yourself above every mean action. Be strictly honorable in every act, and be not ashamed to *do right*. I agonized when they did not do right, when they succumbed to evil ways, which I now know was God's way of punishing me for my own weakness and failures. I was especially worried about our second son, Rooney. His application to West Point, to my great sorrow, had been rejected, and he had gone to Harvard instead. Yet all he seemed to care about was running around and amusing himself. The boy thought entirely of his pleasures and not of what was proper to be done. Stationed in distant Texas, I could not sleep at night worrying about him, worrying that I had raised him and the other children badly. Somehow the boy had to learn self-control, as I had learned it from my dear departed mother; otherwise he was just throwing himself away.

As I feared, he left Harvard without completing his studies, and it grieved me that he might be good for nothing. Then General Scott, interceding in my behalf, arranged for Rooney to enter the old army with a commission in the infantry. Rooney, however, announced that he wanted to be a farmer, not a soldier, complaining to Mim that I had always discouraged him. I was furious. What did he want—that I should *praise* him for his mistakes? This farming idea was nonsense. "If at twenty he was unable to be his own guardian," I told Mim, "how does he expect to be so at twenty-one?" But now that civil war had taken control of our lives, I hoped that Rooney would learn self-discipline and would make a reliable officer in the Confederate Army. I must say, he did look manly in his gray uniform and his full black beard.

Though others deserved the honor, President Davis gave me command of all the Confederate forces being put into the field in Virginia. As regiments arrived in Richmond, I dispatched them to the state's crucial points, especially Harpers Ferry and Manassas Junction in northern Virginia, with orders to contest the enemy step by step once he began advancing into the interior. I will be frank, however: I chafed at being confined to a desk in Richmond. I wished to take the field. I was a soldier, not an administrator. My place was the battlefront, not an office. I let the president know that I would go at a moment's notice, and to any point where I might best defend the cause.

9. JEFFERSON DAVIS

My presidential office in Montgomery was situated in a large brick building with a Confederate flag flying overhead. Here I studied the dispatches from the North and congratulated us for our wisdom in separating from the diabolical Yankees. They had allowed the ignorant usurper who passed for their president to trample upon all the prerogatives of citizenship—to suspend the writ of habeas corpus and throw innocent civilians into his dungeons—and then to ignore the admonishing of their brave chief justice, the venerable Mr. Taney. The usurper justified his acts of despotism with the same plea that tyranny has ever employed against liberty and justice—the time-worn excuse of usurpers—*necessity*. We Confederates could rejoice that we had forever severed our connection with a government that thus trampled on individual rights. The Yankees, I said, were unfit to possess a free government. Upon us, not those swine, devolved the high and holy responsibility of preserving the constitutional liberty of a free government.

The enemy's sudden thrust against Arlington and Alexandria, however, gave all of us in Montgomery great alarm. Convinced that it was the first step in an all-out invasion of Virginia, we Confederate authorities made haste to transfer the Confederate government to Richmond so that we could expedite the mobilization of the country. We had agreed to move the seat of government because Richmond was a larger city with better accommodations and because we wanted to demonstrate the Confederacy's commitment to Virginia, the South's richest, most populous, and most important state.

I was in exceedingly poor health—my face burned with pain, on account of neuralgia, and I suffered excruciating headaches. "From anxiety and unremitting labor," said Varina, my wife of sixteen years. Presiding over the birth of the new southern nation was by far the most demanding and difficult task I had ever undertaken, yet few people appreciated my efforts. When, by authority of Congress, I created a national army under my exclusive control and began raising troops directly, without going through the state governors, Joe Brown of Georgia cried *usurpation* and threatened to disarm Georgia volunteers who attempted to leave the state. It was the start of a running feud I would have with that implacable scoundrel. There were also endless complaints from local politicians that, in disseminating public offices, I had overlooked them and their constituents.

The mails even brought threats to assassinate me. Just before I departed for Richmond, I saw a potential assassin, an armed man staring inside, through the window of my sleeping chambers; I ran outside after him, but the man leaped over a fence and escaped.

On May twenty-seventh, I left Montgomery in secret on an eastbound train. Varina and our children would follow a few days later. My traveling party included Louis Wigfall and his wife, Charlotte. A hot-tempered Texan with a square jaw and an unkempt beard, Wigfall was at this time one of my aides. I was now so ill that I was obliged to keep to my bed under the care of my body slave. But the news that the president of the Confederacy was on the train leaked out, and everywhere we stopped crowds clamored for me to speak. I tried to give them all a few encouraging words, but my voice was frail and hoarse.

The whole country we passed through resembled a military camp. The cars were crowded with troops dressed in butternut trousers and gray homespun coats and armed with every conceivable weapon from squirrel rifles to shotguns. "They are all as jubilant," said Charlotte Wigfall, "as if they are going to a frolic, not a fight." I kept warning our people that it was going to be a protracted and bloody war, the likes of which mankind had never seen before. But few listened. There was a prevailing notion that the Yankees were too cowardly to fight. Others claimed that it did not matter if they outnumbered us almost four to one, since one southern man was equal to seven of them. I knew the Yankees to be a cruel and vicious race of men. To beat them would require complete unity, all our strength and perseverance, and unimaginable sacrifice.

When at last the train steamed into the depot at Richmond, cannon boomed a fifteen-gun salute and an escort took us to the flag-draped Spotsylvania Hotel, where many luminaries and a large crowd welcomed me to Virginia. "Thank God!" cried L. Q. C. Lamar, my fellow Mississippian. "We have a country at last, to live for, to pray for, and, if necessary, to die for."

Two days later, Varina and the children arrived in Richmond, and we moved into temporary quarters in the Spotsylvania Hotel until an appropriate Executive Mansion could be found for us. From the hotel balcony, I told a crowd of serenaders that it was up to us to preserve the institutions of our fathers. "We have now reached the point," I said, "where arguments being exhausted, it only remains for us to stand by our arms, and we will make a history for ourselves."

The influx of troops and government employees transformed this city of thirty-eight thousand into a sprawling military camp. A steady traffic of wagons, horses, and horse-drawn artillery stirred up so much dust that it drifted across the city like a brown mist. Swarms of office seekers, gun merchants, concessionaires, camp followers, and hangers-on added to the mayhem. The soldiers camped beyond the city limits and began drilling for the coming battle, though many people still doubted that the Yankees would dare to attack the manhood of Dixie. Despite my dire warnings, a frivolous air prevailed, with a plethora of parties and parades.

The executive offices of the Confederacy were located on the third floor of the Treasury Building, which stood on Main Street, facing the grassy slopes and winding walkways of Capitol Square. Anxious to get to work, I called on General Robert E. Lee in his office on the top floor of the Mechanics Institute. I thought to myself, what a fine specimen of a man he is. In his mid-fifties, he stood almost six feet tall, with broad shoulders, a powerful torso, and narrow hips. I could not help but notice how small his feet were. His dark hair was streaked with gray, and he wore a short black mustache. In his gray uniform and polished black boots, he was the very picture of a soldier.

He said, "Welcome to Richmond, Your Excellency. Allow me to brief you on what we've done so far to secure the state." Pointing to a map of Virginia, he said that he had sent some thirty thousand men into the field, including those I had dispatched from the cotton states. General Joseph E. Johnston commanded our troops at Harpers Ferry at the convergence of the Potomac and Shenandoah Rivers. General Pierre G. T. Beauregard, the hero of Fort Sumter, commanded our forces in northern Virginia. His headquarters and most of his troops were at Manassas, a critical railroad junction about twenty-two miles southwest of Washington.

"We must strengthen Manassas at once," Lee said, "because that is where the enemy is most likely to attack." As we talked, he referred to the Yankees as "our cruel enemy" and spoke of "the evil designs of the North." I am certain that the seizure of his Arlington plantation had much to do with the anger flashing in his eyes. "Sir," he said, "I can tell you this. You can count on my voice and counsel as long as I have one arm that can wield a sword. I prefer annihilation to submission." In speaking thus, he sounded like me. Plainly he had been studying my speeches to the country.

"Arlington Heights and Alexandria," I assured him, "will be retaken."

I repeated what I had told our other generals, that I hoped to change from the defensive to an offensive attitude. Our objective must be to drive the invader from Virginia and teach our insolent foe some lessons that would incline him to seek a speedy peace. With confidence in my military abilities, I assumed direct control of our forces in northern Virginia and gave Lee the responsibility of defending eastern Virginia, which included Richmond. He put gangs of impressed slaves to work constructing elaborate earthworks around the capital while I dealt with Beauregard. Already he was demanding immediate reinforcements of ten thousand men. As if I were a genie who could conjure troops from a bottle! I was sending him every man and weapon we could spare.

To Johnston I stressed the importance of holding Harpers Ferry, which commands the northern gateway to the Shenandoah Valley, the rich farming region the Confederacy relied on as its "breadbasket." On June fifteenth we were shocked to learn that Johnston had evacuated Harpers Ferry and retreated southward through the Shenandoah to Bunker Hill, near Winchester. I was furious. I demanded an explanation.

He had fallen back, he said, because he feared that Federal troops were closing in on him. It was the first of a great many disastrous retreats for this irritable and irritating officer. I recalled that he had served with distinction in the Mexican War—had been wounded at Cerro Gordo and again at Chapultepec. "Johnston is a good soldier," General Scott once said, "but he has an unfortunate knack of getting himself shot in nearly every engagement." Short and slight, with a Vandyke beard and a balding head, he affected an exaggerated swagger, probably to cover up his natural indecisiveness. He was so sensitive about his baldness that he even wore his hat at table.

Our biggest concern now was the huge Federal buildup in Arlington and Alexandria. Our intelligence estimated the force at 45,000 men and warned that an attack against our lines at Manassas Junction could come at any time. Against the Yankee hordes Beauregard had only about 16,500 men to put into battle, with an additional 1,500 held back as camp guards, pickets, and garrison troops. Beauregard advised us that if he had to do so, he would retreat before overwhelming numbers. "I wish it distinctly understood, however, that if the enemy should offer battle I shall accept it for my command against whatever odds he may array in my front on the line of Bull Run." I replied that retreat would expose Virginia to temporary, if not permanent, disintegration and was only to be contemplated as a necessity; that I daily sought arrangements for a more steady and rapid advance of troops to Manassas; and that I was sorely tempted to leave Richmond to share the fortunes of the army in the field. I was a West Point graduate and a Mexican War hero, and I thought myself better adapted to command an army in battle than to the presidency.

10. LINCOLN

Beyond the windows of the Executive Mansion, Washington thronged with politicians assembling for the special session of Congress, to commence on July fourth, and red, white, and blue flags fluttered all along Pennsylvania Avenue. Congressmen and senators alike hurried across the Potomac to inspect the Grand Army and talk with General Irvin McDowell, in his headquarters in the Lee manor on Arlington Heights. We had finally chosen McDowell to command the army in the field, and he was working up plans for the coming campaign. In pairs and groups, the legislators also came to me and demanded: "When will the army fight? It's been more than two months since you issued your proclamation. What, sir, is the army waiting for?" They insisted that I send the army forward at once, that it smash the rebels at Manassas, march to Richmond, and end the rebellion in a stroke. With the cry of "On to Richmond" ringing across the land, I felt I had to do something or face charges of incompetence and cowardice, maybe even impeachment.

I called McDowell and Scott to the Executive Mansion, to discuss a summer offensive with McDowell in command. A stout fellow with thick, dark hair, blue eyes, and a tuft of iron gray whiskers on his chin, McDowell was about forty years old and an unproven officer. As we sat around the big oak table used for Cabinet meetings, he spoke fervently of the difficulties he faced in trying to forge an army out of a mob of raw volunteers. He was too apologetic about his own shortcomings to suit me.

I directed his attention to a map of Virginia on the wall and said I wanted him to attack the rebel army at Manassas railroad junction, just across Bull Run about twenty-two miles southwest of Washington.

"Mr. President," General Scott said, "that's not wise, not wise. The Grand Army is not prepared for an offensive. Won't be until October. With due respect, sir, the best plan is the one I submitted last May. We should seal off the Confederacy by seizing the Mississippi and tightening the blockade, and then wait for southern Unionism to end the rebellion."

I shook my head. We had been through all this before. "General," I said, "with all the public clamor for battle, we can't postpone an offensive until the autumn. The public will not tolerate any more delay." I turned back to the map. The rebel forces in northern Virginia were split, with the main force of some twenty thousand at Manassas under Beauregard and the rest in the Shenandoah Valley. "Here is what I propose: General Patterson has a force in the valley that is larger than the enemy force there. While Patterson neutralizes the enemy in the valley, McDowell can whip Beauregard, seize Richmond, and end the rebellion."

"Mr. President," McDowell said. "General Scott is right, the army is not ready for battle. I need more time to organize and discipline it. The troops are too green to fight. I can't train them and take them into battle at the same time."

"You're green, it's true," I said; "but they're also green; you're green alike. Yes, giving battle is a risk, but we believe it's a risk worth taking. Unless the Grand Army fights now, public morale will likely collapse. We can't afford to wait." I rose. "Go now," I said, "and prepare for offensive operations."

The generals left, grumbling to themselves, and I returned to work on my message to Congress. I wrote at a table between two high windows, sitting in a large armchair with my legs crossed. In the message, I was trying to explain our cause to the world and for posterity. As I told young Hay, "The central idea of this struggle is the necessity that is upon us, of proving that popular government is not an absurdity. We must settle this question now, whether in a free government the minority have the right to break up the government whenever they choose. If we fail it will go far to prove the incapability of the people to govern themselves."

I elaborated on that point in my message. "This issue embraces more than the fate of these United States," I wrote. "It presents to the whole family of man, the question, whether a constitutional republic, or a democracy—a government of the people, by the same people—can, or cannot, maintain its territorial integrity against its own domestic foes. It presents the question, whether discontented individuals can always, upon the pretenses made in this case, or on any other pretenses, or arbitrarily, without any pretense, break up their government, and thus practically put an end to free government upon the earth."

In Europe, the monarchists maintained that secession movements, anarchy, and civil war were inherent weaknesses of popular government, and that a constitutional monarchy was the most stable form of government. British monarchists, in fact, cheered "the trial of Democracy and its failure" in America and declared it good "riddance to a nightmare." Good riddance to a nightmare! The beacon of liberty for oppressed people the world over is a nightmare? These monarchists give me the hypo. You know there are monarchists right here in this country, in the South, even in the North, who argue that our troubles come from too much democracy, too many elections and warring political agendas, all of which make for an unstable system. I tell you, these monarchists are our ideological enemies. Let them prevail, and back will come everything we're fighting against. Back will come class, caste, and despotism. The equality doctrine of the Declaration will be expunged, all the gains made since the Enlightenment will be lost, and mankind will spin backward into the Dark Ages.

As I labored on my message, I kept thinking that in this great crisis, popular government—the political offspring of the Enlightenment—was on trial for its very existence. To preserve democracy for this and all future generations, I wrote, the government must meet force with force. It must teach southern insurgents the folly of being the beginners of war. It must show the world that those who can fairly carry an election, can also suppress a rebellion. It must show the world that popular government *is* a viable system, that the people *can* rule themselves. "This is essentially a people's contest," I wrote. "On the side of the Union, it is a struggle for maintaining in the world, that form, and substance of government, whose leading object is, to elevate the condition of men—to lift artificial weights from all shoulders—to clear the paths of laudable pursuit for all—to afford all, an unfettered start, and a fair chance, in the race of life."

I also denied the right of secession, which was based on the ingenious sophism that any state of the Union may, *consistently* with the national Constitution, and therefore *lawfully* and *peacefully*, withdraw from the Union, without the consent of the Union, or any other state. "With rebellion thus sugar-coated," I wrote, "southern secessionists have been drugging the public mind of their section for more than thirty years. The sophism derives the whole of its currency from the assumption that there is some omnipotent and sacred supremacy, pertaining to a state—to each state of our Federal Union. This principle, however, is not guaranteed by the Constitution. The principle itself is one of disintegration, and upon which no government can possibly endure."

I reviewed the events and decisions relating to Fort Sumter, pointing out that I had sent a provisioning flotilla to relieve the fort and that the insurgents, by firing the first shot, had begun the conflict of arms. They had forced on the country the distinct issue: "Immediate dissolution, or blood." To save the nation and its people's government, I wrote, the Executive had been forced to employ the war power: he had called up seventy-five thousand militia and adopted other emergency measures such as the suspension of the writ of habeas corpus. The Executive had to perform this duty or surrender the existence of the government. "It is now recommended that you give the legal means for making this contest a short, and a decisive one," I told Congress; "that you place at the control of the government, for the work, at least four hundred thousand men, and four hundred millions of dollars." With such means, we would teach the enemies of the government the folly of starting the war. "Having thus chosen our course," I said in conclusion, "without guile, and with pure purpose, let us renew our trust in God, and go forward without fear, and with manly hearts."

On July fourth, I sent the message to Capitol Hill, and it was read the next day while I reviewed troops from Pennsylvania. As I'd hoped, Congress went on to ratify the Administration's emergency measures and to enact a confiscation bill, which I signed, authorizing the army to seize enemy property, including property in slaves, used for insurrectionary purposes. Those slaves employed by the rebels to make war would henceforth be free.

At this juncture, that was as far as I would go in molesting slavery in the rebel states. My official stance was that we were trying to save the old Union with slavery as an *institution of the states* left intact. The Republican Party had always taken the stand that slavery as an institution, in the states where it already existed, must be left alone; our goal was to hem it into the narrowest possible limits, preventing it from expanding into the territories. Thus restricted, it would be placed on the course of ultimate extinction—would die a natural death someday. I did not think that we could throw that policy aside and emancipate all the slaves at once. And who would do the emancipating? Certainly not Congress. It has no constitutional authority to destroy a state institution like slavery by ordinary statute. A constitutional amendment to be ratified by the states, yes, but not by ordinary law. I also doubted the legality of emancipation by presidential fiat. I feared it would destroy our efforts to organize a bipartisan war effort, would alienate the loyal Democrats, and cause an insurrection in the rear. Worse, I was sure it would cost us the border slave states, without which we would lose the war for certain.

I've got to admit, there were Radical Republicans who challenged that policy from the start. Three in particular—Senators Charles Sumner of Massachusetts, Zacharia Chandler of Michigan, and Benjamin Franklin Wade of Ohio—came regularly to the Executive Mansion and argued long and loudly for a presidential proclamation of emancipation. They're an intimidating group, those three. Rawboned, smooth-shaven Chandler is a prominent Detroit businessman who wears an eternally grim expression and is known for "a bold and somewhat reckless audacity," as a friend of mine put it. Wade, who got his nickname, "Bluff Ben," from his readiness to duel southerners, is short and stout, with iron gray hair, brilliant eyes, a firm jaw, and the tenacity of a bulldog. He sometimes gets so riled at my perceived sluggishness that it throws him into a tirade.

I felt closest to my friend Sumner, the conscience of the Republican Party. Even in those early days of the war, he often accompanied me on my afternoon carriage rides and became a confidant of my wife, Mary, and called on her regularly. A tall, scholarly Bostonian with a somewhat dictatorial bearing, he speaks with polished elegance compared to me. He was educated at Harvard, while the aggregate of all my schooling did not amount to one year. My real schooling was in the University of Hard Knocks. Sumner's an Anglophile and likes to wear tailored coats, checkered trousers, and shoes with English gaiters. A lot of men think he's a strange buzzard. "I'm so conscious of manners," he likes to say, "that I never allow myself, even in the privacy of my own chamber, to fall into a position which I would not take in my chair in the Senate. Habit, after all, is everything." Once, trying to inject a little levity into our discussions, I dared him to stand up with me, back to back, to see who was the taller man. Chuckling, I made a fine speech about this being the time for uniting our *fronts* against the enemy and not our backs. With a pompous grunt, Sumner declined to measure—I think he was afraid of losing. Still, he's a good piece of a man. I've never had much to do with bishops where I live, but, you know, Sumner is my idea of a bishop.

I was not, however, his idea of a president, not when it came to the vexing slavery question. "Mr. President," he said, "this is not the time to be lenient with traitors. They have thrown off the Constitution and cannot now invoke that same Constitution to protect slavery."

That was exactly what General Butler had said when he took command at Fort Monroe in May. That's our great bastion on the tip of the Virginia Peninsula. Slaves who made it to his lines he deemed "contraband of war" and refused to return them to their rebel masters. After some discussion with the Cabinet, I approved Butler's action. I tell you, once that got out to the black population in the insurgent districts, the slaves turned up at our lines in ever-increasing numbers, saying: "I's contraband." "So's I." "So's me and all my young-uns."

The contrabands, however, raised another problem. Were they free? Still slaves? The confiscation act of 'sixty-one freed the ones employed in the rebel war effort. But what about the others? For now, we tended to let army commanders solve the contraband problem in their own way. Some sent runaways back to the Confederacy, others turned them over to refugee camps administered by benevolent organizations.

"Like you," Wade was saying, "we fully endorsed the Republican Party position before the war—that slavery ought to be let alone where it already exists. But the rebels sacrificed all constitutional guarantees when they fired on the flag. The first blast of civil war was the death warrant for their institution. Sir, we're faced with *national annihilation.* We have to take every necessary step to save the country. What better step is there than to destroy the cornerstone of the Confederacy? That's what Alex Stephens, the traitors' vice president, said slavery was, the cornerstone of the rebellion, its indispensable labor force. We feel that either the president or Congress can abolish slavery by the war power, and we think you ought to do it in your capacity as commander in chief. If you free the slaves by proclamation, it will cripple the enemy's ability to fight and bring a speedy end to the insurrection."

He paused. "Now, don't misunderstand me. I'm no nigger-lover. Personally can't stand 'em. They've got an offensive odor and shouldn't be allowed to cook for us. Too Goddamned many nigger cooks in this city alone. I've eaten food cooked by niggers till I can smell and taste the nigger in everything I eat. The country will never be right until we ship the lot of 'em back to Africa."

"You're talking about removing more than four million people," I said. "Wouldn't that be a tad expensive? Where would we get the money? All the necessary ships?" Actually, I favored colonization myself as the ultimate solution but liked raising the opposing viewpoint. It's long been my habit to study the opposite side of every disputed question.

Chandler jumped in with another argument for emancipation. "Mr. President, slavery is the *cause* of the rebellion, you've said so yourself. To protect it was the fundamental reason the rebels seceded. Is it not *absurd* to fight a war without removing the Goddamned thing that caused it? If we follow your policy and save the old Union with slavery, it will only cause another war down the road, whenever the southern master class thinks its property in slaves is threatened again. We'll be fighting civil wars over slavery ad nauseam, until the Goddamned curse is expunged once and for all. If you really want to save the Union and its experiment in popular government, you've got to abolish slavery."

"Slavery and the rebellion," Sumner chimed in, "are wedded and will stand or fall together."

Sumner went on: "There are foreign policy considerations, too. As you know, Mr. President, I have a great many powerful British friends. I can tell you frankly, it is altogether probable that the British Cabinet will soon recognize the Confederacy as a nation." Which, of course, would be a calamity. Being admitted into the family of nations, the so-called Confederacy would be able to form alliances with the European powers, to seek mediation and even armed intervention by them. "But if you make emancipation a war aim," Sumner went on, "I think the British will refrain from recognizing or helping the Confederacy because of their strong antislavery heritage."

Sumner added: "I would remind you, sir, that emancipation is also the *morally right thing to do*. You've said yourself, slavery is a monstrous moral evil. Well, here is your chance to remove that evil and free several million oppressed human beings."

I had great respect for the senators and wanted to maintain a close association with them and their Radical associates in Congress—after all, they controlled most of the important committees. To win the war, we had to work together. I was also sympathetic to all their arguments for emancipation, many of which had already occurred to me.

"I've always hated slavery," I said, "as much, I think, as any abolitionist. But I tell you frankly, emancipation by presidential proclamation is too big a lick. It would upset our applecart altogether. We didn't go into the war to put down slavery, but to put the flag back; and to act differently at this time would not only weaken our cause but smack of bad faith. Gentlemen, this thunderbolt will keep."

They grumbled a good deal but indicated that for the sake of party harmony they would go along with me for now. In private, Sumner said he still regarded me as "a deeply convinced and faithful antislavery man" and argued that the sheer force of the war would drive me to abolish slavery, "willy nilly."

I led him to the door by the elbow. "Sumner," I said, "I would appreciate your advice on foreign policy matters. Seward, of course, handles that field and does it well. But I don't know anything about it and can use your know-how, especially in dealing with Great Britain. Come by and talk any time."

11. DAVIS

The Independence Day message of the crude usurper in Washington made my face twitch with anger. A special place in hell was reserved for that lying blackguard. *We* were fighting to preserve free government and constitutional liberty, not that despicable tyrant and his servile constituents; it was he who authorized justice and law to be trampled under by the armed heel of military authority, he who sought to coerce sovereign states back into a union they had every constitutional right to leave. That this pettifogging backwoods lawyer should lecture *us* on constitutional law made me gag. Worse still, he blamed *us* for starting the war, when in fact it was *he* who sent the hostile fleet to Charleston harbor, forcing us to open fire in self-defense. Then he abandoned all further disguise and proposed to make the contest "a short and decisive one" by calling out 400,000 men and asking for $400 million in revenue. These enormous preparations in men and money, for the conduct of a war on a scale more gigantic than any which the new world had ever witnessed, was a distinct avowal, in the eyes of civilized man, that the United States were at last compelled to abandon the pretense of being engaged in dispersing rioters and suppressing insurrections. They meant to wage an indiscriminate war upon everyone in the Confederacy, with a savage ferocity unknown to modern civilization. In this war, rapine was to be the rule; private residences, in peaceful rural retreats, were to be bombarded and burnt; grain crops in the fields were to be consumed by the torch. The blockade declared around our shores demonstrated what sort of war the North intended to wage. By this cool and deliberate malignity, they had struck at the sick and the infirm, including women and children, by cutting off our medical supplies.

They also meant to invade the Confederate States, seize all property as plunder, and let the Negroes go free. Our posterity, reading that history, will blush that such facts are on record. Before the war, Sumner told the U.S. Senate: "I take occasion to declare most explicitly that I do not think that Congress has any right to interfere with slavery in a state." I know he said that because I was there. Yet with its barbarous first confiscation act, the Congress of the United States decided that it *did* have the power to interfere with slavery in a state and resorted to a despotic measure that violated all the principles of the law of nations, without a shadow of authority for it under the Constitution of the United States. If Congress had the power now to do what it had not before, whence was it derived? The answer, again, was *necessity*, the hackneyed excuse of all usurpers. The Federal Congress declared that our institution of slavery was the cause of all the troubles of the country, and therefore the whole power of the government must be so directed as to remove it.

On the battlefront, the usurpers committed their first act of aggression against us in western Virginia. In mid-July a Federal force of eight thousand men under George McClellan routed our undermanned columns at Rich Mountain and Corrick's Ford, forcing them to retreat toward the east. This gave the invader control of the mountainous region west of the Shenandoah, enabling him to protect his railroads running east and west. It was, I feared, a harbinger of evil to come.

On July seventeenth an urgent telegram came from Beauregard: "Enemy is advancing on Fairfax CH." The long-awaited main attack had begun, and the news threw all Richmond into a state of alarm. People thronged the streets wanting to know if the city would be overrun. From Beauregard came frantic appeals for reinforcements lest he be overwhelmed by an enemy that outnumbered him two to one. According to a plan devised by me and General Lee, the War

Department ordered General Johnston to move nine thousand of his twelve thousand troops from the Shenandoah to Manassas if practicable. It proved practicable indeed when the Federal commander in the valley stupidly pulled his force back from Winchester, relieving the pressure on Johnston and allowing him to disengage from his front. As I read the dispatches, I longed to join Johnston and Beauregard in the field. But it was impossible, impossible, what with the Congress soon to convene, and my accursed obligations to address it on the "state of the nation."

The next day came another dispatch from Beauregard: "The enemy advanced in great force by at least three approaches and encamped last night at Centreville ready to envelope it this morning. I shall fight on line of Bull Run." I wired Beauregard that Johnston would reinforce him and that I had also ordered to Manassas three thousand men under General Theophilus Holmes. "God be praised for your successful beginning," I said. "I have tried to join you, but remain to serve you here."

Johnston meanwhile was moving his troops by foot and rail, and we assumed that everything was going smoothly. On the twentieth, however, Johnston sent us a wire asking what his rank and status were in relation to General Beauregard, whom he had outranked in the old army. Johnston wanted to know who would command the combined Confederate armies at Manassas, him or Beauregard. He asked this, he said, to avoid any misunderstanding. "With the Federals on the attack, he wants to know about his *rank?*" I said. This was unimaginable. It filled me with anxiety, lest there should be some unfortunate complication, or misunderstanding, between my two field commanders. I wired him back that he was a general in the Confederate Army, with all the power attaching to that rank, and that I wanted him to cooperate in harmonious action with *Brigadier General* Beauregard in the provisional service. The reference to Beauregard's lower rank made it clear that Johnston was the senior officer.

Congress assembled that day amid intense excitement about the "big battle" impending in the north. In my address, read before the two houses, I elaborated on the theme of the Yankees as our hated enemy. Mankind, I said, would shudder to hear the tales of outrages committed on defenseless females by soldiers of the United States now invading our homes. These outrages were prompted by inflamed passions and the madness of intoxication. The people of the Confederacy, however, were not afraid, for they were united and determined. To speak of subjugating such a people, I said, was to speak a language incomprehensible to them. Whether this war should last one, or three, or five years, was a problem they left to be solved by the enemy alone; it would last till the enemy withdrew from their borders—till their political rights, their altars, and their homes were free from invasion. Then, and then only, would they rest from this struggle to enjoy in peace the blessings which with the favor of Providence they have secured by the aid of their own strong hearts and sturdy arms.

Reports on the twenty-first indicated that a great battle had at last broken out at Manassas. Unable to remain in Richmond, I left for the battlefield on a single-coach train with my nephew and an aide. I'm sure that General Lee wanted to come with us, but we needed him in Richmond, in case the fortunes of war should turn against us. When we reached Manassas, we detached the locomotive and set out in it for army field headquarters, the engine roaring at top speed, the hot wind whipping at my face as I leaned out the window of the locomotive. As we approached headquarters at more than thirty miles an hour, we could hear the rattle of musketry and boom of artillery in the direction of Bull Run.

12. WILLIAM TECUMSEH SHERMAN

I commanded a brigade in McDowell's rabble army and had no delusions that the battle we were about to fight at Bull Run would end the war. I thought the contest was going to be long and bloody and had said so from the beginning, when I was superintendent of the Louisiana State Seminary of Learning and Military Academy, located near Alexandria. I was a Goddamned fish out of water there, being an Ohio man, a West Point graduate who took his oath of allegiance to heart, and a defender of the general government, the most mild and paternal government ever designed for ungrateful man. Don't get me wrong, I'm no nigger-lover and had no stomach for abolition. Niggers in the great numbers that existed in the South had to be slaves out of necessity. All the Congresses on earth could not make the nigger anything else than what he was, an inferior brute. He had to be subject to the white man, or be destroyed; two such races could not live in harmony save as master and slave. I objected to abolition because it would lead to universal anarchy on this continent. I hated secession for the same reason: it was nothing but revolution—the beginning of the end. It meant chaos, the destruction of all order and stability, and I blamed the whole cockeyed idea on the Goddamned politicians and on too much democracy—hyper-democracy—and a suicidal tendency toward anarchy. I had seen that tendency all over America, from the lynch mobs of gold-rush California to the rabble-rousing secessionists of Dixie and their modern anarchist doctrine. What we needed in this country was a Goddamned *monarch*, to halt the drift toward unadulterated democracy and demagogism. And if Congress refused to provide one, the army ought to. If we'd had a monarch in power in 'sixty, he would have stopped secession at the beginning by sending in the army and *shooting* every Goddamned disunionist in sight.

When the cotton states started to secede, I told a Louisiana professor at the seminary what I thought about their fateful course. I paced the floor, back and forth, gesticulating with both hands. "You people of the South believe there can be such a thing as peaceable secession," I said. "You don't know what you're doing. I know there can be no such thing. Secession means war, and this country will be drenched in blood. God only knows how it will end." I threw up my hands. "It's all folly, madness, a crime against civilization. You people speak lightly of war. You don't know what you're talking about. War is terrible. You mistake the people of the North if you think they won't fight you. You're rushing into war with one of the most powerful, ingeniously mechanical and determined people on earth. You're bound to fail."

When Louisiana's secessionists seized the Federal arsenal in Baton Rouge, in what amounted to a declaration of war, I resigned my post, made my arrangements at the academy, and returned to the North. As I told my southern friends: "You're driving me and hundreds of others out of the South who've cast our fortunes here and love your people, and want to stay. Yet I must give it all up and go away; and once war comes, as it surely will, I must fight you."

Now, six months later, I was on my way to fight them, as the colonel of a predatory mob that called itself a brigade. Since taking command, I'd been able to drill them exactly six times. It was early in the morning of July twenty-first, and we were leading our division, under General Daniel Tyler, down a dirt road toward the rebel army at Bull Run. General David Hunter's division of some ten thousand men was moving around by the right in order to fall upon the enemy flank. General Samuel Heintzelman's division of similar strength was marching in support of Hunter. Our division was supposed to threaten the rebels while Hunter and Heintzelman made their circuit and launched the attack.

It was already hot and sultry, and the mosquitoes were out in force. "Come on, close up," I kept shouting at my men. "Keep in ranks. You can't chase pigs and chickens, Goddamn you!" I cried. It struck me that there was nothing worse than an invasion by a volunteer army. Since leaving Washington, they had looted every homestead we passed, like a bunch of Vandals and Goths.

We halted near the Stone Bridge across Bull Run, and deployed in line along a skirt of timber to the right of the road. Schenck's brigade deployed to the left of the road, and Keyes's stayed behind, in reserve. I rode down to the Stone Bridge to reconnoiter and saw rebel soldiers on the other side of the Run, moving around in the gray light of morning. I saw plenty of trees cut down, some bush huts such as soldiers used on picket guard, but no evidence of strong field fortifications, which was a good sign. Since our business was to threaten the enemy, I returned with some skirmishers and noticed two men riding horseback along a hill; they descended, crossed the Run, and headed toward us. One had a gun and was waving it overhead. "You Goddamned black abolitionists," he yelled, "come on!" My men opened fire, driving him off.

About ten in the morning we saw a great mass of rebels leave their cover in our front and proceed at double quick time down the road toward Sudley. Hunter and Heintzelman were supposed to be approaching by that road—in fact, we could see a cloud of dust in their direction. The rebels were going on the attack! I directed my batteries to commence firing, but our smoothbores couldn't reach 'em. I'll never forget the sight of a poor nigger caught between our lines. Frozen with fear, he hunkered down with our shells shrieking over him. Soon we heard the roar of cannon and musketry in the direction of the cloud of dust. The rebels had engaged the head of Hunter's column! The brisk firing, growing louder, convinced us that the rebels were falling back this way. About noon, however, the noise of battle stabilized, indicating that the rebels were making a stand against our infantry and artillery forces on the other side of Bull Run.

An order came from our commanding general to go to Hunter's assistance, and I led my entire brigade across Bull Run. I was afraid we might be mistaken for secessionists and fired on by our own men, since one of my regiments wore gray uniforms like the uniforms of the Virginia troops. When we came on a group of rebels retreating through a cluster of pines, Lieutenant Colonel Haggerty of the Sixty-Ninth New York foolishly rode forward to intercept them, only to be shot dead from his horse. His body lay quivering in a spreading pool of blood. My men opened fire on the rebels, but I ordered them to stop and we moved on to join Hunter's division on a high field with a house. Hunter himself was wounded, and the ground was strewn with dead men and dead horses, all covered by flies.

At this point, the rebels appeared to be retreating to nearby Henry House Hill, and our men were cheering lustily. My brigade moved on to support Heintzelman's division, which was pursuing the rebels. We crossed a small stream and ascended Henry House Hill, at the summit of which a furious battle was raging. The ground was swept by the most severe fire of artillery and musketry I'd ever seen, and confusion reigned. When we reached the crest of the hill, I put in each of my regiments, but they were beaten back by a hail of canister, fired by an enemy battery from a nearby hill. The canister struck our ranks with a terrific shuttering noise, literally blowing men apart. Pieces of bodies were flying all over the place.

It was impossible to get a good view of the Goddamned ground. At one point, I tried to make an observation without a field glass, when a civilian materialized at my side and offered to loan me his. I whipped around and demanded: "Who the hell are you?"

"Owen Lovejoy," he said. "I'm a member of Congress."

"What in the Goddamned hell are you doing here?" I said. "Get out of my lines!" He didn't seem to comprehend. "*Out*, Goddamnit!" He got out.

I kept to my horse at the head of my brigade and moved slowly across the ridge under constant fire. My horse was shot from under me; musket balls grazed my shoulder and knee. I found another mount, but soon my men started to fall back in confusion. Other regiments also fell into disorder with an incessant clamor of tongues, some saying they were not properly supported, others that they could not tell friend from foe. I did all I could to get them to make a stand. At one point, I could see the entire carnage of battle, men lying in every conceivable shape and mangled in horrible ways—faces blown off, heads and limbs shorn away, and intestines hanging out. Horses were running about, riderless, with blood streaming from their nostrils. Other animals lay on the ground hitched to cannon, gnawing their sides in death. But I was so numb that none of it made a particle of impression on me.

At this juncture, I had no idea we were beaten; I reformed my regiments in line and saw to my horror that we were alone except for a body of regulars, who had formed a square against enemy cavalry. I realized now that the whole army was in retreat. Retreat hell: it was a Goddamned stampede! My own men ran, too, across the Stone Bridge and down the road to Centreville. The soldiers fell back on the army's commissary wagons, whose civilian drivers had moved closer to the front when told that victory was imminent. Now they whipped their mules around and fled hysterically northward. This in turn stampeded crowds of politicians and their wives, who'd followed the army in carriages, with picnic baskets and opera glasses through which to view the show. Well, they saw the Goddamned show all right: a screaming melee of soldiers, wagon drivers, and sightseers streaming back toward Centreville.

I found General McDowell at Centreville and understood that several of his divisions had not been engaged at all, and that he would reorganize the army and make a stand against the enemy. I got my four regiments into parallel lines in a field, but to no avail. The next day the entire army slunk back to Washington, a defeated rabble. All order seemed at an end. It was as disgraceful an exhibition as words can portray—the inevitable consequence of taking an armed mob of volunteers into battle. The lesson was plain as hell. We needed to fight this Goddamned war with *regulars*.

Back at Fort Corcoran, our base camp, my staff and I did our best to stop the flying masses, and partially succeeded, forming broken units into a makeshift front to fight the rebel columns when they came charging after us. I was sure they would stampede us again and drive right into Washington, capturing the president and the Congress and planting the rebel flag on the Capitol.

13 . LINCOLN

I spent most of that Sunday at the telegraph office, located at the head of the first stairway of the little brick building on Seventeenth Street that housed the War Department. A small group of cipher-operators kept track of McDowell's movements and rebel positions on field maps spread before them. General Scott assured us it was going to be a great Union victory that would end the war, but I was filled with apprehension. Though not a regular churchgoing man, I went to church that morning. At first, the telegrams from Bull Run were encouraging. A considerable part of our army was engaged and seemed to be driving the rebels back. Then abruptly the dispatches stopped, throwing the little room into great suspense.

In the afternoon, the operator at Fairfax Station reported that he could hear "the fluctuations of the firing" in the direction of Bull Run. I became uneasy again when the fluctuations seemed to indicate that our army was retreating. After dinner, I called on General Scott in his office at the Winder Building and found him asleep at his desk. I woke him up and told him about the dispatches from Fairfax Station, saying I feared we might be beaten.

"These reports are worthless," he said. "The changes in the currents of wind, the echoes and so forth, make it impossible for a distant listener to determine the course of a battle." He repeated that he was confident of "a successful result" and went back to sleep.

About six I went for a carriage ride, leaving my personal secretaries, Nicolay and Hay, sitting by the window in the president's room. When I returned, I met them as they bolted down the stairs in great excitement. "Seward was just here," they blurted out, giving me the news separately and together. "He says the battle is lost. The telegraph reports McDowell is in full retreat, and calling on General Scott to save the capital. Seward said to find you and tell you to come immediately to General Scott's."

I left at once. Hurrying along the walkway to the Winder Building, I could hear the sound of heavy artillery fire south of the Potomac. At army headquarters, Scott and his staff confirmed the news. The Grand Army was in full retreat. All was lost, *lost*. But how did it happen? I demanded. Who was to blame? Nobody seemed to know. Scott appeared to be in a daze.

I returned to the Executive Mansion and lay down on a sofa in my office. Within the next few hours, I feared, the victorious rebel army would be upon us. I told myself, *I'll have to get Mary and the boys out of Washington. But no need to upset them right now. Time enough to get them away when we know for certain the rebel army is coming.* As night fell, I could see, through the windows, heavy clouds swirling across the moon in fantastic formations. It started to rain. Around midnight Chandler called. He was dripping wet and furious. He and Wade had gone out to Bull Run in a carriage to watch the battle, only to be engulfed by fleeing Union soldiers. "We pulled our carriage across the road," Chandler said, "and pointed our revolvers at 'em, crying, 'Stop, you Goddamned cowards! Go back and fight!' But it was no use. The bastards didn't stop running until they reached the Potomac."

What had caused this? I asked. Raw volunteers? A premature advance? "It was stupid Goddamned generalship," Chandler said flatly. "But there's no time to grieve. You must show the country and the rebels that this government is not discouraged one whit, but is just beginning to get mad."

I agreed. The next day I signed a bill calling up 500,000 volunteers to serve for three years. Three days later we called up 500,000 more. I also relieved McDowell of command and summoned young George McClellan out of western Virginia to take charge of the remnants of the army.

14. DAVIS

When we reached army field headquarters near the battlefield, Beauregard's adjutant general stated his opinion that it was dangerous and improper for me, the president, to go into battle. What impertinence! Who did that man think he was? But I had no time to lecture him about his attitude. I located a horse and rode on to Henry House Hill, where I found General Johnston seated on his mount in the smoke of battle.

"Mr. President," he said, taken aback to see me on the battlefield. "We've won a great victory. The enemy is in full retreat."

Riding farther west with Johnston and his aides, we heard ominous warnings that the Federals were not retreating after all. They were reported to be attacking and on the verge of winning the battle! But our men cheered and cheered when they recognized me. My presence seemed to instill new fight in them. They rallied and charged forward, and the next we heard they had routed the enemy, capturing several field batteries and regimental standards and one U.S. flag. I raised my hat in jubilation as we rode past our victorious columns. There were signs of utter rout on the part of the Yankee army: discarded muskets, cartridge boxes, canteens, haversacks, and overcoats littered their line of retreat. The ground was strewn for miles with the dead and dying. The corpses were already emitting a sickening stench. The farmhouses and surrounding grounds were filled with wounded, and physicians were performing amputations and throwing the severed limbs into piles.

Back at army headquarters that night, I wired Richmond that we had won a glorious but dear-bought victory, that the enemy had been routed and had fled precipitately. That same night, in a conference with Johnston and Beauregard at Moss Mansion, it became clear that Johnston's timely arrival from the Shenandoah had saved Beauregard from destruction. I was pleased that the plan devised by me and General Lee had worked so well. Aiding matters was a brave stand by Thomas J. Jackson near a stone wall that earned him a new nickname.

As we talked in the Moss Mansion, I studied Beauregard, gazing upon a lean man with a bronze complexion, high cheekbones, and a thick black mustache. His large melancholy eyes, I thought, gave him the look of a bloodhound. He spoke with a slight French accent and was vain to the point of arrogance. He kept calling Manassas "his victory." *His* victory! It was the *president* who, coming upon the field, had rallied the troops and saved the day! Even so, I thanked Beauregard for his skill as a commander, gallantry as a soldier, and zeal as a patriot.

I wanted Beauregard and Johnston to pursue the beaten Yankees to the Potomac. But Johnston, his restless black eyes fixed on mine, insisted that such an advance was quite impossible. "We are more disorganized by victory," he said, "than the Yankees are by defeat." Beauregard agreed, saying it would take them weeks to regroup and reorganize.

"Whatever you do," I said, eyeing Johnston, "don't retreat from Manassas. This line *must* be held. *At all costs.*"

With that, I took the train back to Richmond, where a boisterous, flag-waving crowd greeted me at the depot. Tired and hoarse, I addressed them from a buggy. "Your little army—derided for its want of arms—derided for its lack of all the essential materiel of war—has met the grand army of the enemy, routed it at every point, and it now flies, in inglorious retreat, before our victorious columns. We have taught them a lesson in their invasion of the sacred soil of Virginia. We have taught them that the grand old mother of Washington still nurses a band of heroes; and a yet bloodier and far more fatal lesson awaits them, unless they speedily acknowledge that freedom to which you were born."

Back in my office in the Treasury Building, I set to work on the enormous stacks of paper on my desk, carefully reading every report, every letter, and every request for a transfer, pass, or promotion and duly forwarding each document, with notations if necessary, to the appropriate office. The day-to-day demands of the presidency required an incredible amount of my energy and time, but I did not complain like some of my subordinates and a general or two I could name. In fact, I enjoyed attending to the details, whether small or large, of an ever-growing bureaucracy. Varina says that when I took my papers home, she could hear me singing as I tended to them.

The post-Manassas reports from our spies alarmed me, for they indicated that the Black Republican Administration was making every effort to organize an even more powerful army than the one we had routed. We knew that McClellan, who had driven us from western Virginia, was on his way to Washington to assume command of the forces being assembled for our annihilation. We had reports, too, of extensive mobilization of enemy forces in Kentucky, southern Illinois, and Missouri. I resolved to employ all the power of my office to increase the strength of our army so that we could defend the entire breadth of the Confederacy, from the Northern Neck of Virginia, out to the northern and western borders of Arkansas, and down to the Big Bend of Texas—a seventeen-hundred-mile front.

To successfully guard our far-flung borders, I realized, the national government would have to assume control of the telegraphs, complete the building of new railroads to connect key points, enjoy exclusive control of all the forts, navy yards, armories, weapons, and ammunition within the states, and establish more manufactures to produce weapons. At this juncture, Richmond's Tredegar Iron Works was the only factory in all the Confederacy that could produce heavy ordnance. Until the government could build more arms manufactures, we must buy from Europe what we needed beyond what the states could provide, relying on blockade runners and the trade route from Mexico through Texas to bring us war materiel. In order to survive as an independent nation, I believed, the Confederacy had to achieve industrial self-sufficiency, by stimulating manufacturing and developing our natural resources.

Alas, the strong national government I desired put me at odds with certain state-rights men, who accused me of trying to build a monster government in Richmond like the one in Washington we had thrown off. They were wrong. It's true that, before secession, I had been an uncompromising foe of a consolidated Federal government. But that was because I feared it would be taken over by rabid abolitionists, as in fact it was. We had no such fear in the Confederacy.

We could afford to put aside our state-rights doctrines. We had to have a strong national government with the power to mobilize our resources and our people; otherwise, as the *Charleston Mercury* said, we would never "rid ourselves of Yankee domination, commercially, socially, and politically."

When it came to proper military strategy, I preferred the offensive-defensive to the purely defensive. This meant that wherever the enemy invaded our soil, we would destroy him with offensive counterstrokes and thereby break the Union will to fight. I even pledged to carry the war into the *enemy's* country if he would not let us go in peace.

The offensive-defensive mode dictated that we organize the Confederacy into largely autonomous and self-sufficient military departments, each under an army commander whose objective was to meet and repel Yankee threats against his realm. We hoped that this cordon of military departments would make the Confederacy invulnerable. The president, aided by the War Department, would direct all the regional departments, shifting troops from one point to another—even one state to another—as events dictated. Our safety—our very existence—depended on the complete blending of the military strength of all the states into one united body under my control, to be used anywhere and everywhere as the exigencies of the contest might require or for the good of the whole. The idea of each state retaining its own troops, which certain of our governors advocated, was a profoundly fatal error.

To implement the offensive-defensive strategy, I took great pains to put the best generals in command of the various military departments. By virtue of his seniority in rank, General Joseph E. Johnston headed our forces in northern Virginia, with Beauregard now reduced to corps command. To run the Department of distant Texas, with its important trade route through Brownsville and Matamoras, Mexico, I chose General Earl Van Dorn, an elegant little gentleman, a fellow West Pointer, and a fellow hero of the Mexican War. General David Twiggs, a veteran warrior from the old army, would command Department Number 1, which embraced the Gulf Coast of Alabama, Mississippi, and Louisiana. To command Department Number 2, which encompassed the vital Mississippi Valley, from the southwestern border of Mississippi north to the state lines of Kentucky and Missouri, I chose an old friend and West Point classmate, Leonidas Polk, who had resigned his commission in the old Federal army and become an Episcopalian bishop. He may have lacked military experience, as my critics were quick to point out, but he was an extremely capable man and utterly loyal to the Administration.

When he came to Richmond at my summons, I spoke with him at length, as did General Lee and Secretary of War Walker. Tall and erect, with broad shoulders and a red face framed by prodigious white side whiskers, Polk spoke in a clear, distinct voice and carried himself with great dignity. Frankly, I congratulated myself for my sagacity in naming him to command in the West.

In our discussions, I explained how crucial it was for us to hold Tennessee and honor Kentucky's "neutrality." Stretching from the Mississippi to the Appalachians, a neutral Kentucky would serve as an impenetrable buffer, shielding the Confederate heartland from Yankee aggressions. After Polk left for the West, I wrote the governor of Kentucky, assuring him that we would not violate his state's neutrality. I added, however, that I had heard that Kentucky authorities were allowing Union regiments to form, drill, and receive arms from the North. "Neutrality to be respected," I said, "must be strictly observed."

In the East, my most immediate concern was the Yankee presence in the mountains of northwestern Virginia. I needed a competent commander out there to coordinate the separate forces of John B. Floyd and Henry A. Wise, both former governors of Virginia. On July twenty-eighth I assigned General Lee to serve there as military "coordinator" over Floyd and Wise. His objective was to concentrate their forces and drive the Yankee invaders out. If anybody could bring success to our arms in that region, it was General Lee.

"Your Excellency," he said, "I fear such a campaign is hopeless. But I shall do as you command." That is why I had such high regard for Lee: he obeyed orders. That same day, he started west with two of his slaves—a cook and a body servant. When he reached western Virginia, however, he reported that our troops were ill-clad and ill-fed and appallingly demoralized. Worse still, Floyd and Wise hated each other and, despite Lee's efforts, quarreled constantly. I finally removed Wise, whose behavior was scandalous, but it made little difference. The reports from out there remained disconcertingly pessimistic.

At the same time, there were endless complaints from the army at Manassas: food was in short supply, the sick suffered from a want of care, good weapons were scarce, desertions were on the rise. We did everything within our power to provide for the army, but shortages of everything were a grim fact of life in the Confederacy. Then General Johnston, vaguely proposing an attack on Washington, demanded that I send him ten thousand of the twenty thousand soldiers he assumed I was withholding from him to defend Richmond. I informed him that he was deceived. We had never had anything near twenty thousand men in the defenses of Richmond, more like one-fourth that number. As for an attack on Washington, I said, we could not afford an offensive movement without a reasonable assurance of victory, or necessity so pressing as to overrule our present general policy, which was to hold what we now possessed. We had no second line of defense. The cause of the Confederacy was staked upon the army at Manassas, and it could not be squandered in a reckless foray. Had I the requisite arms, however, the argument would soon be changed.

Meanwhile my family and I had moved to new quarters, a three-story stucco mansion known as the Old Brockenbrough House, which the city of Richmond had bought and leased to the Confederate government. This "Confederate White House," as it was popularly known, stood on the brow of a high, steep hill, overlooking a plain through which ran the railway to Danville. A garden, sloping down the hill in steep terraces, featured cherry, pear, and apple trees. Among the outbuildings were a stable and carriage house, a brick kitchen, and quarters for our slaves.

The mansion itself was lighted by gas lamps and boasted wide windows, high ceilings, and a bathroom with every modern convenience. The first floor consisted of a drawing room, parlor, reception room, dining room, and library. Staircases wound upward toward the "airy rooms" above. My private office was on the second floor, along with the master bedroom, a dressing room, and a nursery for our children. From an upper window, we could see Richmond's tree-shaded suburbs and, off to the southeast, the James River winding through a hazy, timbered landscape to Drewry's Bluff.

Once we were comfortably settled, we began entertaining a few friends. Our favorites were the Chesnuts of Camden, South Carolina. James Chesnut, my protégé before the war, had served on Beauregard's staff at Manassas and now hoped to win a seat in the Confederate Senate. His wife, Mary, a small woman with high cheekbones and dark, radiant, deep-set eyes, is an altogether charming woman with a wonderful gift for conversation. I always had her sit across from me when the Chesnuts dined with us.

15. MARY CHESNUT

The president said he liked my style of chat. But really I must have been quite *morbid* with all the military funerals taking place in Richmond. Our glorious victory at Manassas had been purchased with the lives of so many of our young men. I dream even now of the everlasting Dead March in the streets of wartime Richmond—the muffled drum and empty saddle and the lead warhorse. To me the Dead March was the saddest of all human pageants, and it was a happy day when an hour's interval came between acts of it.

My husband had fought at Manassas, and I shall never forget how relieved I was when he came back, safe, striding into our hotel room in his dusty uniform. Was I glad to see him! He had brought up regiments all that day, he said, and carried orders with shot whizzing around him. "What a rout it was," he said.

The next day I called on Mrs. Davis in her drawing room and we sat together while the president, an old warhorse, addressed a crowd of thousands outside. He took all the credit to himself for the victory, said our men rallied at the sight of him and rushed on and routed the enemy. The truth was, Jeff Davis was not two miles from the battlefield—so James said. The president was just greedy for military fame. Mr. Chesnut was then called for and delivered a capital speech, giving the glory of victory entirely to Beauregard. Afterward James told me that if the president had not bragged so much about himself, he would have praised him.

My gallant and honorable husband! If only he had had more *ambition*. His cherished code of honor precluded self-promotion, and he was content merely to accept a seat in the Senate, if the South Carolina legislature was disposed to elect him next November. President Davis had offered him a choice of positions in the army—"anything you want," he said. But James could not make up his mind about a military commission. So typical of him! I had far greater plans for my laconic husband than some insignificant position in the army: I wanted him to be the Confederate minister to London or Paris. Actually, I wished the president would send *me* to Paris as his ambassador—then I should not care a whit about the South Carolina legislature. Wouldn't that just be the life, courting fame and honor in one of the world's most charming cities, far removed from the funerals of Richmond and the privations of civil war?

I spoke harshly of the president. The truth is, I felt sorry for him. He was such a sickly man, stooped and thin as a rail, with only one good eye, the other blind and covered with a film—the result of excruciating sieges of neuralgia. He had high cheekbones, a tuft of whiskers on his chin, and very wide nostrils, which flared when he was angry. He often wore a black silk handkerchief about his neck, and the expression on his careworn face was almost always anxious and pained.

Now that Congress was in session, the president was under attack by a growing circle of malcontents. Charlotte Wigfall told me that Robert Toombs and Howell Cobb of Georgia headed the opposition; with them were Hammond, Keitt, Boyce, and Banks. Mrs. Wigfall doubted that the president had a personal friend in Congress unless it be Clement Clay of Alabama. Her own husband, once Davis's friend, was now his worst enemy. That was Louis T. Wigfall, the "stormy petrel" of Texas, who had a scraggly black beard and ferocious eyes and wore those huge spurs.

Wigfall's conversion to the opposition complicated my affairs no little, since Mrs. Wigfall and Mrs. Davis were both my friends. Forced to make a choice, however, I sided with the Davises. "Right or wrong," I wrote in my diary, "we must stand by our president and our generals, and stop all this fault-finding. Mr. Davis's hands ought to be strengthened. He ought to be upheld."

Mrs. Davis heard about the carping to which her husband was daily subjected. "There must be an opposition in a free country," she said, "but it is very uncomfortable. United we stand, divided we fall." I adored her for speaking her mind. She was a tall, handsome woman with full lips and dark eyes.

In mid-August, I sat all evening with Mr. Barnwell and learned that the opposition to Davis in South Carolina was stronger than I had expected: Orr, Marshall, McGowan, Hammond, Keitt, Boyce, the Rhetts and their influential newspaper, the *Charleston Mercury*— all were against the president. Which meant that they were also against James Chesnut, the president's friend. "So he will be left out of the next Senate," Barnwell said. "Nobody can win an election in South Carolina against that kind of opposition." This intelligence gave me a terrible headache. It left me looking right in the face of defeat of my personal ambition. It meant in all probability that we would return to Mulberry, the family plantation in South Carolina, to live with James's elderly parents. How would I *survive* so dark a fate—having to cope with people who had always treated me badly, without outside friendship, without intercourse with those who were close to me? But if that was to be my fate, I said, God's will be done. I would bear it as best I could. After all, so many other people were more miserable.

My only real hope was that James would accept a colonel's commission in the army. If only I had been a man! I would have taken the colonelcy without a moment's thought. Just as I feared, though, Mr. Chesnut announced that he would not accept it, would not be joining the army. I felt deeply mortified, what with everybody saying he could get whatever he wanted. Then James Mason and John Slidell were chosen as commissioners to Great Britain and France respectively, and all my pretty chickens were destroyed at one fell swoop. The purgatory of Camden now awaited me. I was bitter—I admit it. James would have been a better diplomat than either of those men. How could the president send to England a man who had shot and wounded his wife's uncle in a political row? What the country needed was someone who could carry on a civilized conversation with the Europeans. I could have done that better than Mr. Mason, Mr. Slidell, *or* Mr. Chesnut. "I think these times make all women feel their humiliation in the affairs of the world," I confided in my diary. "With *men* it is on to the field—'glory, honor, praise, power.' Women can only stay at home—yet every paper reminds us that women are to be violated by the Yankees—ravished and humiliated."

Still, I did what I could—I took biscuits to the makeshift hospitals in Richmond. Entering the one at Gilland's factory, I saw men sick with measles and typhus fever, and others eating at a dinner table, all in the same room. Dreadful, dreadful. I distributed biscuits to our Carolinians, one of whom was dying, the poor boy. The others seemed so pleased, telling me to come often. Then I called at the hospital in the St. Charles Hotel—what horrors I saw there, dirt and discomfort and bad smells enough for the stoutest man. Another Carolinian was dying in this woeful place—one had died in that very room the day before. "God help us," I said.

Later, in our rooms at the Arlington House, I came down with a fever, probably contracted at the hospitals, and took opium, which put me into the dreamy state I so enjoyed. A few days later, feeling improved, I called at the Davis mansion on top of the hill and found that the president himself was ill, so much so that Varina couldn't talk. I then called on Mrs. Robert Toombs, whose husband was now in the army. She ridiculed Varina and pronounced the president's illness "all humbug." Mrs. Toombs also said that Mrs. Reagan, wife of the postmaster general, was the lowest woman she ever saw. "She lets her children and little Negroes *sleep* together," Mrs. Toombs said.

James and I were scheduled to depart for South Carolina on September second, but before we left we called again at the Executive Mansion, to see if there was something we could do for poor Mr. Davis. The president was shut in his bedroom, so weak that even talking made him flushed and feverish. In a weak voice, his face drained of all color, he asked James to look around at South Carolina's defenses and assured him again that he could have any office or position he desired, which gave me a fleeting hope that my exile in South Carolina might be short. It all depended on my vacillating husband.

Later, we learned that the president had taken a turn for the worse. Some feared he might die. The Yankee papers, in fact, reported that he *had* died, attributing the cause to "congestive fever." One could only imagine how the news must have cheered his counterpart at the north, the ugly and uncouth man who was plotting our destruction.

16. LINCOLN

The report turned out to be wrong, and anyway I had more important things on my mind than the health of Jeff Davis. Everybody was pointing fingers over the Bull Run fiasco. The Republicans and the Democrats blamed each other, the *New York Herald* blamed the abolitionists, the younger officers blamed "senile" General Scott, the regular army blamed the volunteers, Chandler still blamed stupid generals, and just about everybody blamed the tall fellow at the White House window. That fellow deserved to be criticized—for naively believing that this gigantic insurrection could be put down in a single battle.

When I discussed the disaster with General Scott, he fumed and fussed. "I'm the greatest coward in history," he said, "and ought to be relieved of command. I should've stood up to you and resisted fighting a battle when the army was not ready."

"You seem to imply that *I* forced you to fight this battle," I said. He backed off from that insinuation, but others complained that I hadn't been anywhere near aggressive enough. Lyman Trumbull, senator from Illinois, told me to my face that I'd been "weak" and "irresolute."

"You're probably right," I said.

Trying to be resolute, I went across the river to shore up the morale of the army. The troops were disorganized and badly demoralized, but a regiment stationed at Fort Corcoran gave me the first bright moment since the defeat. It was the Sixty-Ninth New York of Colonel Sherman's brigade, one of the last brigades, I'd heard, to leave the field at Bull Run. Compared to the other camps along the Potomac, the Sixty-Ninth's was a model of discipline. When Seward and I drove up in our carriage, the regiment sprang into line, presented arms, and stood at "parade rest."

Rising in the carriage, I told 'em: "The days are sad, but brighter ones will come. The rain is falling, but the sky will be clear again. Don't be discouraged—think of tomorrow. Have faith in the nation and in our final success, which will come as sure as there is a God in Heaven."

Colonel Sherman was present, and when I finished, he grabbed my hand. "That speech reached every heart, nerved every arm," he said, and went on talking in that vein without letup, gesticulating with a long black cigar. I'd never heard anybody talk so fast—words spewed out of his mouth like water out of a pipe. He struck me as an unforgettable specimen—tall, gaunt, and ramrod straight, with a shock of sandy red hair, a rusty, grizzled beard, and sharp, piercing eyes. He wore a black felt hat slouched low over his eyes and a ragged blue coat whose sleeves were too short, exposing a pair of bony wrists. As he talked, his face twitched and his hands were constantly on the go, rubbing his red hair, flicking his cigar, twisting this way and that.

When there was finally a break in his monologue, a captain stepped forward. "Mr. President, I have a grievance," he said. "This morning I went to speak to Colonel Sherman, and he threatened to shoot me."

"He threatened to *shoot* you?"

"Yes sir, he threatened to shoot me." I looked at Sherman, then back at the captain. Stooping toward him, I said in a loud stage whisper: "Well, if I were you, and he threatened to shoot me, I wouldn't trust him—I think he'd do it."

The other soldiers broke out laughing, and the captain's face visibly reddened. Didn't hear another peep out of him. Later, riding on with us, Sherman explained that the captain had tried to leave camp without authorization, on account of his ninety days of service being up. "A good many soldiers of the Sixty-Ninth had gathered around us," Sherman said. "If the captain could defy me, so would they, so I turned on the officer sharply and told him, 'If you try to leave without orders, it will be mutiny, and I'll shoot you like a dog!'"

I told Sherman: "I figured you knew your own business best." What impressed me most about Sherman was the expression in his eyes: it hinted of a ruthlessness, a killer instinct, that convinced me he would make a successful general, and I had him duly promoted to brigadier.

To all of us, the Bull Run disaster showed that the war was going to last a lot longer than any ninety days. If we were going to win it, we needed a coherent plan of operations embracing both the eastern and western theaters. Toward that end, trying to hold the big picture in mind, I proposed three coordinated movements. The Grand Army would attack the rebels at Manassas. At the same time, a second force would drive down the Mississippi and seize the vital river port of Memphis. A third force, acting in concert with the Mississippi expedition, would move down from Cincinnati and liberate East Tennessee, a mountainous region full of loyal Unionists. To fill up the ranks, we would bring up hundreds of thousands of three-year volunteers. At the same time, we would tighten the blockade, as General Scott advised.

Formulating the plan was easy enough. The hard part was finding the right commanders to execute it. The details of the East Tennessee operation still had to be developed. The Mississippi River expedition, however, would be carried out by General John Charles Frémont, commander of the Western Department with headquarters in St. Louis. He was a political general—the same Frémont who'd first carried the Republican presidential banner, back in 'fifty-six. In his late forties now, he was a colorful figure—tempestuous, magisterial, and wholly untested as an army commander. I assured the general, however, that I had full faith in him and extended him carte blanche in the administration of his department. As to getting up the Mississippi expedition, I told him to use his best judgment and do the best he could, but not to delay too long.

George McClellan, the new commander of what was soon called the Army of the Potomac, would carry out the second offensive against the rebel army at Manassas. The day after he reached Washington, I called him to the Executive Mansion to have a look at him. He was a stocky little fellow, in his mid-thirties, with red hair and a red mustache. He chewed tobacco and was a pretty fair shot at a spittoon. When he talked, he puffed up, stuck one hand in his coat, and swept the air with the other. No wonder they called him the Little Napoleon. He had impeccable military credentials: had graduated second in his class at West Point, fought in the Mexican war as an engineer on Scott's staff, observed the war in the Crimea, written a manual on warfare. Scott said he had no equal in America when it came to the theory of war. But he'd grown tired of the army and resigned his commission to enter the railroad business, winding up as vice president of the Illinois Central. I'd often represented that same railroad in court.

McClellan was a Democrat and a crony of Judge Douglas, and it got around that the vice president of the Illinois Central thought of yours truly as a frivolous feller who told too many stories. Well, he's probably right. "That reminds me of a story" is my favorite line. Did you hear the one about the short-legged man in a big overcoat? Its tail was so long it wiped out his footprints in the snow. Then there's the one about the traveler passing a farmhouse in his carriage. A drunk man stuck his head out of the upstairs window and shouted, "Hullo! Hullo!" The traveler stopped and asked what the drunk man wanted. "Nothing of you," he said. "Why in hell are you shouting hullo for when people are passing?" the traveler asked angrily. "Why in hell are you passing for when people are shouting hello?" replied the drunk man. I've got a better one. Do you know what the Irishman called soda water? "It's a tumbler of piss with a fart in it."

I tell you the truth when I say a funny story has the same effect on me that a square drink of whiskey has on an old toper; it puts new life into me.

I'll be frank, though: I worried about young McClellan. I didn't mind his self-confidence—nothing wrong with that. There was something else about him—a nervous streak, a penchant for exaggeration—that bothered me.

"General," I told him as we parted, "it's up to you to save the country."

"Sir," he said, "it *is* an immense task I have on my hands, but I assure you *I* can accomplish it."

From a White House window, I watched him ride off toward the army camps with a retinue of aides trotting after him. Sitting high in the saddle, he was a superb horseman, and people stopped to stare at him as he rode by.

I tried to convince myself that I'd made sound military decisions, that McClellan in the East and Frémont in the West would lead their armies forward to victories. But I tell you, my job was wearing me out. It was the damned trivia that drained me the most: while trying to formulate a grand military strategy that would win the war for us, I had to dispense the accursed patronage, fretting over who would be the consul at Jerusalem, or who would be the Indian agent for the Choctaws. At ten every morning, I had to throw my office door open and let in a blast of raucous humanity—office seekers, politicians, interviewers, businessmen, weeping mothers who wanted their sons released from the army, and coquettish young wives who urged me to promote their military husbands. I'd be a liar if I denied the pleasure I felt in listening to the young wives. But I tried to be attentive to the others too—the jobless and the infirm, even the parvenus. I would tell the caller, "What can I do for you?" Then I would listen, stroking my beard, and promise to do what I could if the request was reasonable. If I needed to get rid of somebody, I would tell him a story, and while both of us laughed I would ease him to the door.

These public opinion baths are important. It's the best way I have of finding out what people are thinking. But I tell you frankly, I sometimes get tired of the numerous grist that grinds through here daily; I'll lose my temper, call somebody a damned rascal, tell a persistent pest: "Now go away! I can't attend to all these details. I could as easily bail out the Potomac with a teaspoon." Every caller, from some senator wanting a war with France to a poor woman after a Treasury job, takes away a special piece of my vitality. When I get through with such a day's work, there's only one word to describe my condition, and that is *flabbiness*.

During this first summer of the war, I gathered Mary and the boys and retreated to the Soldiers' Home, located in the woods on higher ground, just beyond the city limits. The cool breezes there offer wonderful relief from the sweltering heat and aggressive mosquitoes of Washington.

"It's beautiful!" Mary exclaimed when she first saw the immaculate grounds. "We can be as *secluded* here as we please." Only five feet two, with round cheeks and an upturned nose, she was admiring the commodious main building, which serves as a home for aged and disabled soldiers of the regular army. A tower affords a fine view of Washington, with its spires and busy thoroughfares, and the farms and countryside for miles around.

There was a cottage on the grounds, which we converted into a summer White House. I hoped Mary would find some peace here. The stuck-ups of Washington society had been pretty rough on her, calling her a country hussy who smelled of the barnyard. Nothing was farther from the truth: she's the educated daughter of a prominent Kentucky lawyer. But that's what they called her—a country hussy.

Since several of her relatives had sided with the Confederacy, ugly rumors spread around that she was a spy who passed state secrets to rebel agents. Can you imagine anybody believing that? I tell you, Mary loved the government and the Union as much as I did, and the accusation of disloyalty hurt.

They undoubtedly aggravated her headaches. She had suffered from them ever since I'd known her. When the pain was on her, she said, it felt like somebody was pulling wires out of her eyes, and she would scream at me and everybody else who crossed her path. I overheard my personal secretaries calling her "the hellcat" and complaining that she was getting "more hellcattical" every day. Chalk that up to youthful intolerance. I was glad to get her away into the country, to spare her that kind of carping at least for the summer.

In the morning I would ride alone into Washington and return at night to cool seclusion with Mary and the boys. In the cottage, while they slept, I would do some late-night work by lamplight. Later, waiting for sleep to come, I liked to read my worn copy of Shakespeare's tragedies—my favorites are *Hamlet* and *Macbeth*—or a volume of poetry—say, Burns, Whittier, or Holmes. Lying in the darkness, I often recited a stanza from Holmes I knew by heart: "Green be the graves where her martyrs are lying! Shroudless and tombless they sunk to their rest. . . ." Then at last, I would fall into a brief and fitful sleep, filled with dreams of clashing armies and a phantom ship moving in the mist.

I tell you the truth, I was feeling pretty low this summer. Word came from Chicago that my longtime political rival, Stephen A. Douglas, was dead at the age of forty-eight. He'd declared his unwavering support for the cause and had gone home to rally loyal Democrats, and his death was a great loss. The doctors said he'd died of something called "acute rheumatism," but friends said it was bad whiskey that got him. "He killed himself with it while stumping for the Union, all over the country, in eighteen and sixty." That's what they said. I had the Executive Mansion draped in black to commemorate his passing. The drapes didn't help my mood none.

Governor Yates appointed Orville Browning to fill out Douglas's Senate seat. One evening, Browning came to the Executive Mansion for dinner, and we had a long private talk in my office. I'd known Browning for years and confided to him that I had the hypo pretty bad and was not at all hopeful about my future. Many important people insisted that I was unfit for the presidency, that the war and the other demands of the office were too much for me. "You are not considered a great man," wrote Horace Greeley, editor of the powerful *New York Tribune*, and he demanded that I sign an armistice with the insurgents on their own terms. Later he changed his mind and urged the government to fight on, but his vacillations mirrored the confusion of many other loyal men, who struck out at me in frustration.

"It makes me depressed," I told Browning. "If to be the head of hell is as hard as what I have to undergo here, then I pity Satan himself."

"You do yourself a great injustice in feeling that way," Browning said. "You have control of your fortune and the power to make yours one of the most memorable names in the history of the human race. You must hold the reins of government with a steady hand—must be firm, earnest, and, if need be, even inexorable."

Depressed or no, I called frequently at the camps across the river, and I'll confess I was impressed with the sensational energy McClellan displayed in reorganizing the army. When he took command, it was "merely a collection of broken regiments cowering on the bank of the Potomac," as he put it. Now he was pulling those broken regiments into a real army. He had them drilling and practicing war with a zeal that even rubbed off on me.

Because the army still suffered from a want of weapons, I dispatched Colonel George S. Schuyler to Europe to buy two million dollars' worth. Secretary of War Cameron also bought guns from foreign arsenals. Many of 'em proved to be useless—"Goddamned *swindles*," was how Seward described them. But we also acquired thousands of excellent British Enfields—.577 caliber, muzzle-loading rifled muskets.

The big debate, of course, was which was the better rifle for infantry—the muzzleloader or the breechloading repeater? Old General Ripley, chief of army ordnance, dismissed the breechloader as "a newfangled gimcrack" and threw his support behind the muzzleloader, but I was more than ever convinced that the breechloading repeater was the better weapon.

One day I tested one of these remarkable rifles—I believe it was a Henry—at the firing range in Treasury Park. Young William Stoddard, one of my private secretaries, was with me, and he tested a single-shot Marsh breechloader. As we blasted away at a wooden target, I found that the metallic cartridges used in the repeater were far superior to the paper cartridges required in muzzleloaders, and the breechloader was a good deal more accurate. Now, it was against the law to fire a weapon in the capital, and our gunshots brought a detail of soldiers on the run. "Stop that firing!" they yelled. "Stop that firing!" When they recognized who I was—my stovepipe hat gave me away, I suspect—they wheeled around and ran off.

"Well," I told Stoddard, "they might've stayed and seen the shooting."

Another big advocate of the breechloader was Colonel Hiram Berdan, who was getting up a unit of sharpshooters. An aggressive New Yorker with a drooping mustache, he wanted to arm his men with single-shot breechloaders. To demonstrate the effectiveness of that weapon he invited a crowd of luminaries, including General McClellan, me, three Cabinet members, and a retinue of other officers, to observe some of his men at target practice with the coveted weapons. When we came up, they were firing at lifelike targets more than six hundred yards off. I borrowed a rifle and banged off three rounds, which found their mark well enough. Then Berdan took aim with a breechloader, only to pause when he saw the name JEFF DAVIS scrawled at the bottom of his target.

"Is that proper?" Berdan asked.

"Colonel," I said, "if you make a good shot it will serve him right."

Goaded by an assistant secretary of war to fire at the eyes, Berdan blasted away. When a soldier brought the target in, the pupil of Jeff Davis's right eye was blown off.

"Colonel," I said, "come down tomorrow, and I'll give you the order for the breechloaders."

Ripley, however, refused to buy the newfangled gimcracks until I sent him an executive order to do it. By year's end, under constant pressure from me, he'd ordered about thirty-seven thousand single-shot and repeating breechloaders. But the army remained an adamant foe of change, and the muzzleloader—the British Enfield and the .58 caliber American Springfield—remained the standard weapon for our infantry.

I said I liked the company of inventors hawking military gadgetry. Let me tell you about one fellow in particular, Professor Thaddeus Sobieski Constantine Lowe. This ingenious young man had flown a balloon from Cincinnati to South Carolina, landing on enemy soil several days after Fort Sumter. He claimed to be "the first prisoner of the Civil War." When the rebels let him go, he came to Washington and sold me on the possibilities of using balloons for "telegraphic air-ground communication." What a boon this would be for army reconnaissance! Delighted with the prospect, I had the War Department advance the professor funds to do some testing. A week later, he went aloft in a balloon named *Enterprise*, which hovered over the armory between Sixth and Seventh Streets. He sent a communication down to me: "This point of observation commands an area near fifty miles in diameter. I have the pleasure in sending you this first dispatch ever telegraphed from an aerial station." The next day he went up again in his aerial station, this time floating over the Executive Mansion. A bugler ascended a rope connected to the balloon, and as he rose the strains of his horn sounded across the city.

Convinced that Lowe was right, that the army could use a corps of balloons like *Enterprise*, I gave him a letter of introduction to show General Scott. Back he came, disappointment etched on his face. "The general in chief," he said, "was very firm and pompous with me, and it was hard to get his attention. He was preoccupied with the makeup of the army as he's always known it, and he had no interest in innovations like a balloon corps."

"Come on," I said, donned my stovepipe hat, and accompanied the professor to Scott's office, where I insisted that the general give the young man a hearing. Scott subsequently admitted him into the service, and soon several of his balloons were moored to a warship on the Potomac, ready for reconnaissance service once the army moved forward.

But the Potomac Army did not move forward, not this summer. General McClellan announced that it was not ready for battle—that it would require thousands of reinforcements and a great deal more drilling before he could advance against the insurgent army at Bull Run.

So much for my plan for the armies in the East and West to act in concert. The Western Department, in fact, was in utter chaos. From St. Louis, Frémont bombarded us with volleys of complaints: *I can't attack Memphis, I can't even hold Missouri if you don't send reinforcements at once. My army is undermanned, the people here are divided in their loyalties, a large rebel force has invaded the state, I'm about to be overwhelmed, why do you not send reinforce-*

ments? To make matters worse, Frémont and Frank Blair, Jr., were locked in a destructive feud. Blair sent me a stream of letters—passed on by his brother Monty—filled with complaints about Frémont. He was hysterical, he'd lost control of his troops, he'd shown favoritism to his California cronies (Blair called 'em "vampires"), his entire department was shot through with corruption.

Late August brought more alarming dispatches from Missouri. The rebels had defeated a Union force in southeast Missouri—that was the battle of Wilson's Creek, where General Lyon was killed—and the insurgents were now advancing toward St. Louis. On August thirtieth, Frémont issued a proclamation to meet the crisis. The proclamation put Missouri under martial law and announced that the slaves of rebels there were to be seized and "declared freemen."

I was stunned. I hadn't authorized Frémont to issue that decree. It went far beyond the first confiscation act, which held that only slaves employed *in the enemy war effort* were to be seized and set free. Slavery was a political matter; decisions about it had to be made by the president and Congress, not by commanders in the field. Frémont's proclamation was a *political* act which failed to come within the range of military law or necessity.

Just as I feared, slaveowners in the loyal border put up a howl. Was this now the Administration's policy? they wanted to know. My friends James and Joshua Speed wrote from Kentucky that Frémont's "foolish" edict would destroy the Union party there and incite a slave revolt. A telegram from Robert Anderson, the defender of Fort Sumter, reported that the proclamation had caused an entire company of Kentucky volunteers to throw down their arms and quit the Federal service. Unless I revoked that "pernicious decree," others warned, "Kentucky is gone over the mill dam."

On the other side, abolitionists and Radical Republicans called Frémont a hero and fell all over themselves in praising the proclamation as a major step toward universal emancipation. Fred Douglass, in his Negro newspaper, called the proclamation "the most important and salutary measure" to come "from any general during the whole tedious progress of the war."

I cared about what he and the Radicals thought, don't get me wrong, but I was desperate about Kentucky. If she "went over the mill dam" the Union cause was lost. On September second, therefore, I sent Frémont a confidential letter warning that his proclamation would "alarm our Southern Union friends, and turn them against us—perhaps ruin our rather fair prospect for Kentucky."

Accordingly, "in a spirit of caution and not of censure," I asked him to modify his proclamation so that it conformed to the confiscation act, a copy of which I enclosed.

The general sent his wife, Jessie, to Washington with his response. I showed her into the Red Parlor, but she seemed so hostile that I didn't even bother to offer her a seat. "Well?" I said. A hard woman with frowning eyes and a turned-down mouth, she handed me the letter from her husband as if it were an ultimatum, and I read it under the chandelier. The general announced that his proclamation was "equal to a victory in the field" and that he would not "change or shade" anything in it. If I desired to amend the section on emancipation, I must "openly direct him to make the correction."

I folded the letter and faced Mrs. Frémont. "I have written to the general and he knows what I want done."

"Yes," she replied, "but we think it best that I present his views, since our enemies enjoy your personal confidence."

"Enemies? What enemies? What do you mean?"

"I think you know what we mean," she said. She went on: "My husband understands the English feeling for emancipation, and both of us think his proclamation will win us friends abroad."

"You're quite a female politician," I said. She stared hard at me, then sneered. "This is a war," I said, "for a great national idea, the Union, and General Frémont should not have dragged the Negro into it. He wouldn't have, if he'd listened to Frank Blair."

She flung back a warning. "It will be hard on you if you oppose my husband. If you do, he will set up for himself."

What a woman! She taxed me so violently that I had to exercise all the awkward tact I had to avoid further quarreling with her. After she left, I wrote a terse reply to her husband. Assuming, I said, that he, being upon the ground, could better judge of the necessities of his position than I could, I did not object to that part of his proclamation placing Missouri under martial law. I did, however, object to the part dealing with the liberation of slaves. Therefore, as he requested, I "very cheerfully" directed him to revise the slave provision so that it conformed to the confiscation act, and I released a copy of the order to the newspapers.

The order, I'm happy to say, quieted down the loyal border. But it enraged the Radical Republicans. Sumner groaned that "Lincoln is now a dictator," and Ben Wade announced that Lincoln's views on slavery "could only come of one, born of 'poor white trash' and educated in a slave State." The abolitionists were even madder. Fred

Douglass demanded to know when I would stop my "abominable truckling to the cause of all our calamities." Another abolitionist damned me for my "pigheaded stupidity," and Garrison's American Anti-Slavery Society, which had suspended operations and urged its members to support the Administration, declared that its "truce" with Lincoln was over.

It was a dismal time for our cause. The Treasury was empty, the War Department in chaos. Secretary of War Cameron was utterly ignorant and—regardless of the course of things—was incapable of organizing details or conceiving and advising general plans. On top of which he was openly discourteous to me. And then there was the military situation. The rebels had virtually seized Missouri. They had also invaded Kentucky, capturing the strategic river port of Columbia on the Mississippi. Everything in the West was in hopeless confusion. Only the timely move of a man named Grant kept Paducah, Kentucky, a vital point at the mouth of the Tennessee River, from falling into enemy hands.

17. ULYSSES S. GRANT

When the enemy seized Columbus, I'd just taken command of the military district of southeast Missouri and southern Illinois and established my headquarters in Cairo—that's at the tip of Illinois, where the Ohio joins the Mississippi. A spy told me that four thousand rebel troops were now on their way to capture Paducah on the Ohio, near the mouth of the Tennessee. Meant I had to move without delay, or the enemy would cut us off on the Ohio and gain control of the whole of Kentucky. I wired departmental headquarters in St. Louis that I aimed to beat the rebels to Paducah unless otherwise instructed. Not being otherwise instructed, I loaded two regiments and a battery of artillery on three river steamers and started up the Ohio escorted by a couple of gunboats.

Next morning, September sixth, my troops occupied the city without a fight and ran up the national colors. Pro-secession citizens, who were expecting the rebel army, milled about the streets in a daze, unable to believe that Federal troops occupied their city and Federal warships guarded their riverfront. A soldier reported that some women gave hurrahs for Jefferson Davis, but the town as a whole was stunned. I never saw such consternation. To assure the citizenry of our peaceful intentions, I issued a proclamation:

> *An enemy, in rebellion against our common government, has taken possession of the soil of Kentucky and fired upon our flag. He is moving upon your city. I am here to defend you against this enemy and to assert and maintain the authority and sovereignty of your government and mine.*

Also sent a column to occupy nearby Smithland, at the head of the Cumberland. Now we controlled the entrances to two great waterways—the Tennessee and the Cumberland—that ran deep into enemy territory. The secessionist governor condemned my "invasion" of Paducah and the rebel attack on Columbus as wanton violations of Kentucky's neutrality. But the pro-Union legislature ordered all rebel forces out of the state and invited Union troops to come and drive 'em out. With that, Kentucky entered the war on our side.

I returned to Cairo and wrote Julia, my wife, that my move against Paducah was of much greater importance than was probably generally known, and that my new command was an extensive one—third in importance in the country. I'd invited John Rawlins, of Galena, Illinois, to act as my adjutant, but he hadn't arrived yet, on account of his wife was dying and he was with her and their children. Without Rawlins, I had to do the staff work myself in my small office in the bank building. It was a rare thing when I got to bed before two or three in the morning. Just as well, 'cause there was nothing to do in that miserable river town except work. The place was crawling with rats and infested with mosquitoes, and the stinking carcasses of dead horses and mules floated in the river along the waterfront. The St. Charles hotel was a haven for the human flotsam of war—army contractors, reporters, speculators, river men, and spies, who drank whiskey and played poker and quarreled, cussed, and caroused in its dancing saloon. I prohibited my officers and soldiers from frequenting it or any place like it.

It was good that my duties demanded all my time. If I'd had time to myself, I would've started missing Julia and feeling sorry for myself, and that would've led to trouble. I mean the kind of trouble I got into before the war, out in California. That trouble was what they served in the St. Charles. Why I stayed away from there.

In mid-September, Rawlins arrived in Cairo and took over the operations of my staff. His wife had passed on and I was sorry for him and said so, but he bore it manfully. We had one similarity—we were both from Galena, Illinois. In all other respects he was my opposite—talked constantly and with passion, dark eyes flashing, black hair askew, pale face twisted with impatience. Most profane man I've ever known, Rawlins. Cussed a blue streak when things didn't suit him, or somebody did something wrong. Had no patience for laggards or what he called "roistering, hard-drinking sons-of-bitches" who tried to latch on to me. Had no qualms about lighting into me, his commanding officer and nine years his senior—he was thirty at the time, I was thirty-nine—if he thought I was slipping. He kept telling me I was "a man of destiny." He conceived it his job to keep me out of trouble—"to save you from yourself," as he put it. He made me promise on my word of honor not to touch a drop of anything stronger than water.

Rawlins was the man who convinced me to return to the service and defend the flag. It was the day after Lincoln's call for troops, and Galena's stores were closed and a great patriotic meeting was under way. Several prominent men spoke, then there were cries of "Rawlins—Rawlins!" He was the city attorney and had a private law practice—he handled the legal affairs of my father's leather store, which I operated with my brother Orvil. Nominally I was just a clerk and lucky to be that, given my record. I'd managed to graduate from West Point and acquired a way with horses, but beyond that I was good for nothing. Got in that trouble in California and had to quit the army. Failed at everything else I tried—farming, selling real estate—until the war gave me another chance.

Only thing I hadn't failed at was my marriage to Julia. Best day of my life when she said yes. Happened on a buggy ride, when we came to a bridge across a swollen stream—the water was surging right up across it. "If anything happens," Julia cried, "I'll cling to you." When we were safely across, I mumbled, "How would you like to cling to me for life?" Fact was, *I* was the one who clung to her. Couldn't have survived without Julia and the children, Fred and Buck, Jess and Nellie. Other men might not think so, but to me Julia's always been the most beautiful woman in the world.

Anyway, Rawlins stood before the mass meeting in Galena and cried: "I've been a Democrat all my life; but this is no longer a question of politics. It's a question of Union or disunion, country or no country. I've favored every compromise, but the time for compromise has passed. Only one course is left for us. We will stand by the flag and appeal to the God of battles!"

I thought over what he said. Seemed to me no impartial man could deny that in all our troubles the South had been the aggressor and that the integrity of the glorious old Stars and Stripes, the Constitution and the Union, had to be defended. The government had a right to expect me to support it, since it had educated me, at its expense, for such an emergency.

"I think I ought to go into the service," I told Orvil, and he said he would mind the store. I told my father there were but two parties now, Traitors and Patriots.

My first command was as colonel of the Twenty-First Illinois. We fought our first battle in Missouri, near the settlement of Florida. As we approached the top of a hill from which we expected to see the camp of the enemy, commanded by a man named Tom Harris, I was afraid he might have formed his men to meet us. My heart pounded harder and harder till it felt like it was in my throat. I would have given anything to have been back in Illinois, but I didn't have the moral courage to halt and consider what to do, so I kept on. At the crest of the hill, I halted my men and studied the enemy camp in the valley below. To my amazement, the camp was empty. *The rebels had fled.* It occurred to me at once that Harris had been as much afraid of me as I'd been of him. This was a view of the question I'd never taken before; but it was one I never forgot. From then on, I was never afraid to confront an enemy. I never forgot that he had as much reason to fear my forces as I had his.

In August I read in the St. Louis paper that I'd been promoted to brigadier general. A chaplain called the story to my attention. "It never came from any request of mine," I told him about that promotion. "That's some of Washburne's work," Washburne being the congressman from my district. "I knew Washburne in Galena," I said. "He was a strong Republican and I was a Democrat, and I thought because of that he never liked me very well, and we never had more than a business or street acquaintance. But when the war broke out I found that he'd had something to do in having me commissioned colonel of the Twenty-First Regiment, and I suppose this is more of his work."

So now I was General Grant, in command of all Federal forces from Cairo to Ironton in southeastern Missouri. Didn't seem possible, given my peacetime record. When I thought about what a general ought to do, I thought he ought to take the offensive. Invade the Confederacy. Remember sitting under a tree one day, studying a map of southeastern Missouri, southern Illinois, and western Kentucky. I ran a finger down the Mississippi, muttering to myself that we had to clean all the rebels out of the valley there. With a red pencil I traced a line down the Mississippi and made another line south by the Cumberland and the Tennessee. A civilian by the name of Emerson, who'd given me the map, saw my red pencil markings and said I must be up to serious business.

"Possibilities," I said, "just possibilities."

But once we had control of Paducah and Smithfield, along with our strong river base at Cairo, a campaign into the heart of the Confederacy was more than a possibility. Of course in the fall of 'sixty-one I didn't have enough men or boats to carry it off. I was working on that. And impatient to get going, believe me. I was glad when Foote—Commodore Andrew Hull Foote—arrived in Cairo because he thought like I did about offensive warfare. He was commander of the "Western flotilla," which at that time amounted to three wooden gunboats armed with thirty-two-pounders and eight-inch shell guns. More modern boats would be built for us, but for now that was all we had. We made a good team, Foote and me, and probably looked a sight as we strolled through town together: the short, skinny, blue-eyed general with his scruffy beard, and the tough old sailor with his disheveled hair and full gray beard. A God-fearing man, Foote. Liked to preach sermons to his sailors and was always damnin' slavery, said he hated that infernal institution like Hades itself. I didn't care for slavery either, even though Julia came from a slaveowning family over in Missouri and owned some house servants herself. I owned a man once, when we were living in St. Louis. But I freed him. Had to go to court to do it.

It was quiet in the Cairo sector, but I thought it was the quiet before a storm. The rebels were fortifying the river bluffs at Columbus and reinforcing the garrison, no doubt to attack Paducah. I wanted to attack before they did, seize Columbus, and strike southward. "What I want is to *advance*," I wrote Julia. But because of the enemy threat in Missouri, St. Louis kept my force too much reduced to permit offensive operations. Frustrated me. Felt like my fists were chained to the wall.

I was right about a coming storm. It broke in mid-September, when a large rebel army under Albert Sidney Johnston invaded Kentucky. Sidney Johnston was a good soldier, tough, wouldn't stop till he controlled the state. This was a disaster in the making, yet there was nothing I could do about it.

18. DAVIS

Albert Sidney Johnston was by far the best general in our army and the great pillar of the southern Confederacy. Back in the spring, the powers in Washington had offered him field command of the Federal army after Lee had told them no, but Sidney had also turned them down and resigned his commission in the old regular army to throw in with us. Quitting his post in California, he undertook an arduous trip overland to Richmond and arrived the day after our forces seized Columbus, Kentucky, in early September. When he called at the Executive Mansion, he was told that I was ill and confined to my chamber, and he started to leave. But hearing his voice, I leaped out of bed and hurried downstairs to shake his hand. I was delighted to see my old friend—we had known each other since West Point—and to welcome him into our army. He was a magnificent-looking soldier, bronzed by the sun, tall, straight, and strong, with an imposing mustache and calm, steady eyes. I felt strengthened, knowing a mighty support had been added to our cause. I told some friends that if I had the power, I would resign and transfer to Sidney Johnston the presidency of the Confederacy.

So great was my admiration for my old friend that I appointed him overall commander of the entire western Confederacy. I was completely confident that with his capacity for organization and administration, he would make the undeveloped power of the West sufficient not only for its own protection, but for the support of the more seriously threatened eastern Confederacy.

In my discussions with Sidney, I expressed my unhappiness over General Polk's unauthorized seizure of Columbus. Despite my warning that Kentucky's neutrality must be honored (I had promised the governor that it would be), Polk had sent troops under Gideon Pillow to take the city without consulting with me or the War Department. It made me furious and sicker than ever. Polk was a personal friend in whom I had put my complete trust and confidence, and his rash act unquestionably damaged the secessionist cause in Kentucky. At my direction, Secretary of War Walker ordered Polk to withdraw his forces, and demanded an explanation. Polk replied that he had acted out of military necessity: had he not seized the city, an important point on the Mississippi, Federal forces would have captured it, as they subsequently captured Paducah. Once I was fully apprised of the military situation, I accepted his explanation; and since the act was done, a fait accompli, I allowed Polk to keep his troops in Columbus and reinforce the garrison. Despite the pernicious caviling of my enemies, I also kept Polk in command at Columbus because I still believed him, on the whole, a highly capable soldier.

Now I had Sidney Johnston to command the West and coordinate its military efforts. He had indeed a vast domain to defend, stretching from the Blue Ridge to the Great Plains and encompassing the Confederate states of Tennessee, Arkansas, and western Mississippi, the border states of Kentucky, Missouri, and Kansas, and the Indian Territory. I saw Sidney off with soaring hopes that with a man such as him in charge, our western forces would win us great victories.

But from his headquarters in Memphis, Johnston complained that he had fewer than forty thousand men to defend the vast border, and many of them were armed with obsolete flintlock smoothbores or had no weapons at all. He insisted that he had reliable intelligence that the enemy in his front had in excess of ninety thousand troops, who were well armed and were being reinforced. I told him the same thing I told Joseph Johnston and Beauregard: we were doing everything within our power to buy or produce more and better weapons. In the meantime, I was certain that Sidney had the ability to solve most of his problems by drawing on his own resources.

With my approval, since Kentucky neutrality was no longer an issue, Johnston threw an army under Simon Bolivar Buckner into the state, and Buckner occupied and fortified strategic Bowling Green. Next day Johnston sent another force to seize Barboursville. These two actions secured the western end of Johnston's defensive line on the eastern side of the Mississippi, which extended eastward from Columbus through Bowling Green to the Cumberland Gap. Johnston's bold and decisive move vindicated my choice of him as western commander.

Buckner, of course, complained that his minuscule army of six thousand could not possibly contend against the opposing Federal army in Kentucky, which Buckner claimed numbered fifteen thousand men and was being augmented. Johnson, however, had Buckner move his men around, marching and feinting, so as to deceive the Federals into believing they faced overwhelming numbers. Buckner even sent an advanced guard to threaten Louisville on the Ohio River.

19. SHERMAN

The approach of Buckner's columns, said to be in division strength, scared the Goddamned hell out of us. At army headquarters in Louisville, we followed his course of march on a large map. The latest intelligence put him at the Rolling Fork of Salt Creek, just thirty miles from Louisville. Consternation reigned in the city—disorder in the streets—civilians fleeing by horse and wagon. We were totally unprepared to meet the crisis—were short of everything—troops, muskets, artillery, provisions, uniforms, horses, you name it, we lacked it. All we had for troops were Rousseau's Legion and a few Home Guards—a Goddamned rabble was all we were, facing an entire division of Sidney Johnston's rebel army. I kept thinking, how the hell did I get into this nightmare?

I could thank the president for that. He'd put Bob Anderson of Kentucky in command of the Department of the Cumberland, which embraced Kentucky and Tennessee, and authorized him to take three newly commissioned brigadier generals with him. Anderson picked me as his senior brigadier, I being newly commissioned, again thanks to Mr. Lincoln. When I conferred with Anderson at Willard's Hotel in Washington, he said our main objective was to hold Kentucky, but we were dangerously short of troops. Hence my first assignment. I rode the cars across the northwestern states, urging the governors to raise regiments for us and to do it in a hurry because time was of the essence; otherwise the rebels would have Kentucky and their northern line would be planted on the Ohio, with invasions of the Northwest sure to follow.

The governors of Indiana and Illinois, I found, were recruiting regiments with gusto, but as soon as they were mustered into Federal service they were sent to Frémont in Missouri or to McClellan in the East. Still, I had every hope that the Administration would see the importance of Kentucky as the center of the vast battlefield of America and would order from the East and elsewhere an army strong enough to hold that vital center.

When I joined Anderson in Louisville, I kept thinking of the war as a Goddamned *monster*, demanding more and more victims to eat up as it stomped across the land, frothing and bellowing and breathing fire. And now to our horror the monster was at Rolling Fork, on its way here. We didn't want it coming into Louisville—better to gather up what troops we had and go out there and face the grim brute. So I took maybe a thousand men of Rouseau's Legion by train to Rolling Fork and found the bridge there burned down, but no sign of the rebels. Wherever they had gone, they were sure to come back to seize or destroy the railroad. So I took up a defensive position across the road at Muldraugh's Hill, in a range of hills between the Green River and Salt Creek. Anderson forwarded troops to me as they arrived in Louisville, until I had between four and five thousand men. But we were no match for Buckner's force, said to be fifteen thousand strong, with thousands more pouring into the state. Here, I believed, in the great center, was where the enemy was concentrating all his forces not employed elsewhere.

I was certain my command was crawling with spies and took precautions to maintain security. One day, a New York reporter came to me and demanded to know the strength and position of my forces in the most insolent tone and manner.

"Friend," I said, "I give you exactly fifteen minutes to get the hell out of my camp or I'll hang you as a spy."

"But, General!" he complained. "The people are anxious to know. I'm only after the truth."

"We don't want the truth told about things here—that's what we *don't* want. The enemy can read the papers, too. We don't want him any better informed than he is."

The reporter left under protest. My mistake was in not hanging the insolent bastard.

In early October I went back to Louisville to see Anderson and found him a nervous wreck, his hands were shaking, a haunted look in his eyes. He said he could no longer stand the mental torture of his job—had to leave it or it would kill him. He therefore relinquished the command of the Department of the Cumberland. Handed it right to me, is what he did, because I was now the senior officer. I didn't want the Goddamned thing, but there was nobody else to do the job—either I took it or everything would go to hell. So against all my desires I became commander of the Department of the Cumberland, and I hated it. I kept telling Washington that our men and arms were insufficient to hold this crucial line. I even sent a list of complaints directly to the president, signing off with one desperate word: "Answer!" Washington replied: "We are moving heaven and earth to get arms, clothing, and money necessary in Kentucky, but McClellan and St. Louis have made such heavy drafts that the supply is scant." Moving heaven and earth, my ass! With all the vast resources available in the North, how was it that the supply was *scant*? It wasn't scant, that's what I'm telling you. They had plenty of men and guns and money, but they gave everything to Frémont and McClellan, and left me to hold the great center with the puniest force of all. We were so Goddamned weak that Sidney Johnston could have walked into Louisville. But Washington didn't give a shit. Washington seemed to think we could win the war in Kentucky with words and hot air. The president even wanted me to take the *offensive*—can you believe that?—and liberate the Unionists in the mountains of East Tennessee.

It was fucked up. It drove me crazy. In my rooms on the ground floor of the Galt House, I studied maps, read troop reports, scratched off dire warnings to Washington. I had no patience for incompetence and yelled at dilatory subordinates, giving them an order and shoving them out the door. Every night I hurried to the Associated Press telegraph office to fire off my complaints, examine the latest reports, and talk with the only two reporters I ever trusted, Shanks and Villard. Shanks said I was "a bundle of nerves all strung to their greatest tension," and he was right. Haranguing Washington for its neglect, I paced up and down the telegraph room with my head tilted forward, puffing on a cigar, flicking the ashes away with a finger, running my hands through my hair. I sat down, got back up to pace, sat down again, drumming a tattoo on the table. To make a point, I would snatch the cigar from my mouth and gesticulate furiously with it. I was tied up in knots, a Goddamned time bomb ready to explode—hell, Lincoln himself would've been the same way in my place. When my cigar was burned down to near the end, I would stub it out on the agent's table and light up a fresh cigar. Eight or ten stubs would accumulate in a single evening. The porter called them "Sherman's old soldiers." Shit, I wish I'd *had* a soldier for every cigar I smoked in that telegraph office. It would've been a hell of a big force.

Back in my rooms, I would be up all night, unable to sleep, my head aching from too many cigars. I wrote my wife, Ellen, back in Ohio, that I felt a powerful desire to hide myself in an obscure place to avoid the monster that threatened us. "We could be surprised and overwhelmed any night," I told her. "This thought alone disturbs my sleep, and I cannot rest. I find myself riding a whirlwind unable to guide the storm. The idea of my name going down in history as the commander who lost Kentucky, and therefore cost us the war, nearly makes me mad. Sometimes I think I *am* mad."

I was Goddamn *mad* all right—at the blockheads in Washington.

Somehow I had to make them understand what was at stake out here, make them see what I saw. I got the chance when Secretary of War Cameron and Adjutant General Lorenzo Thomas stopped off on their way back from St. Louis and an investigation of Frémont's department. Six or seven men were with them—one turned out to be a slimy reporter, Samuel Wilkeson of the *New York Tribune*, but I didn't know it at the time. We had a conference at the Galt House, and though Cameron was feeling poorly and lay down in bed, he joined freely in the discussion.

"Now, General Sherman," he said, "tell us your troubles."

"I prefer not to discuss military matters with so many strangers present," I said.

"They're all friends, all members of my family. You can speak freely."

I'm sure I stepped to the door and locked it, to guard against intruders. Then I fully and fairly represented the state of affairs in Kentucky. I reminded Cameron that he'd promised General Anderson forty thousand of the best Springfield muskets. But all we'd received were about twelve thousand rejects—Belgian muskets turned down by the governor of Pennsylvania as worthless. But our worst problem was the shortage of troops. "The new levies of Ohio and Indiana," I said, "are diverted East and West, and we get little. Sidney Johnston, if he chooses, can seize Louisville any day. He has *five times* my forces and is preparing for an onslaught."

"You astonish me!" Cameron said, rising on one arm. His mop of gray hair was mussed up in back where he'd laid on it. "The Kentucky senators and congressmen all claim there are plenty of men here ready to fight for our cause," he said. "Why not recruit them?"

"Not true," I said. "The young men of Kentucky are arming themselves and going off in broad daylight to enlist in the rebel army."

That seemed to disturb him. He turned to Adjutant General Thomas and asked him if he knew of any northern troops that might be sent to me. A nondescript army bureaucrat with full side whiskers and a talent for obfuscation, Thomas babbled to himself, hemmed and hawed, and finally came up with one brigade at Pittsburgh and a couple of other regiments on their way to St. Louis, and Cameron promised they would be diverted to me.

"I'll be frank, Mr. Secretary," I said. "We need a hell of a lot more men than that to hold the great center. Here, let me show you." I produced a large map of the United States and laid it on my table. "You can see that McClellan, in the East, has a front of less than a hundred miles and a force of a hundred thousand men to cover it. Frémont, in St. Louis, has about a hundred miles to cover in the Western Department and has sixty thousand men. By contrast, I'm holding a line *three hundred miles long,* from Paducah to the Big Sandy, with only eighteen thousand men, not counting the driblets you'll send me. It's ridiculous. Can't be done. I need at least sixty thousand men just to *hold* the line against the overwhelming numbers I face. But, gentlemen, the rebellion can never be put down by maintaining the defensive. We have to take the *offensive.* And to do that, to clean the rebels out of Kentucky and carry the war into the Confederacy, clear to the Gulf of Mexico, which is what it will take to end the rebellion, I'll need a force of two hundred thousand. Not a man less."

"Great God!" Cameron said. "Where are they to come from?"

I told him that there were plenty of men in the North ready and willing to come, if he would accept their services. It was notorious that the War Department had refused to accept a great many regiments from the Northwest, on the grounds that they were not needed. When I finished, Cameron turned to Thomas and told him to write a memorandum of our conversation so that he could attend to my requests when they got back to Washington. We'd discussed my concerns in the most friendly spirit, and I thought I'd made Cameron realize that a great war was upon us, so I was in better spirits when they left.

At about this time the *New York Tribune* published a dispatch from its Louisville correspondent, saying that I had at least twenty thousand men in various camps between that city and Green River. It was all there for the rebels to see! I was so Goddamned mad I banned all reporters from my lines. Goddamned press was our worst enemy. I told 'em what I thought: told 'em that if we were going to win this war, every newspaper in the country had to be suppressed. That got the whole stinking tribe of journalists after me, but I didn't give a rat's ass. Once you establish the principle that the press had the right to keep paid agents in our camps, independent of army commanders, the army would be destroyed.

But back to Cameron. I was wrong in thinking I'd made him face reality. As I learned later, he told Wilkeson, the reporter who was with him, that Sherman was "unbalanced by exaggerated fears as to rebel strength, and that it would not do to leave him in command." He said *that* to a fucking reporter! Cameron himself later admitted to me that General Thomas's memo made reference to my *insane* request for two hundred thousand men. That's how it got started, the public charge that I was gone in the head, loony as a God-damned hyena. Cameron's report, based on Thomas's memo, was published in the newspapers—whether released by the secretary or General Thomas, I never found out—and there it was, in print, for all the country to see, that I was "insane, crazy, mad" because I said it would take two hundred thousand men to win the war.

I'll tell you this: if at the start Mr. Lincoln had accepted the fact of a long and costly war and raised an army, as I advised, of a million men, the South would have seen they had aroused a lion in the North and might have given up. But no, Washington resorted to expedients, first calling up seventy-five thousand militia, then ten new regiments, then half a million volunteers, then another half million—again and again finding it necessary to increase the call. At some point, I said, Washington would have to realize that if the North was to defeat the South, we had to begin in Kentucky and *reconquer every inch of enemy territory.* It was this conviction that made men think I was crazy.

Fuck 'em. I'd had it. In early November I asked to be relieved of departmental command, and Washington named Don Carlos Buell to replace me. I was in rough shape, nerves shot. One of my staff summoned my wife, Ellen, by telegram, and she hurried out by train and stayed a week with me at the Galt House.

I was damned glad to see her. She was my best friend—her family, the Ewings of Lancaster, Ohio, had taken me in after my father died, and gave me a Christian name, William, to go with Tecumseh, the name my father had given me out of admiration for the great Indian chief. I'd vowed I'd never marry, went off to West Point—graduated sixth in the class of 'forty-three—fought the Seminoles in Florida. But when I returned home on furlough and saw how pretty Ellen was, all grown up now, with long dark hair and a wide and pretty mouth, that was the beginning of the end of my bachelor days. We began courting, mostly by mail, got married, and went on to have six wonderful kids—two sons and four daughters, all but one born before the war broke out. Ellen and I struck certain people as an odd pair—I was a redheaded, hot-tempered agnostic—I believed in good works rather than faith—while she was as pious as they come, one hundred percent Roman Catholic, and positively obsessed with getting me into the church and ensuring my tortured soul a place in the hereafter. We'd spent most of our marriage apart, thanks to the peregrinations of my career, but Ellen knew my moods better than anyone, and she was alarmed at the "state of morbid anxiety" she found me in at the Galt House.

"Cump," she said, "you look *terrible*."

I'd eaten and slept little for some time, and she did her best to get me to eat and rest, but I just paced, back and forth, saying that the whole country was irrevocably gone and that ruin and desolation were at hand.

20. LINCOLN

Ball's Bluff was another disaster for our arms. It hurts to talk about it because of what happened to Edward Baker. He was an old friend of mine from Whig days in Illinois, and Mary and I had named our first child after him—Eddie, who passed on in eighteen and 'fifty. The day before the affair at Ball's Bluff, October twentieth it was, Baker called at the Mansion to pay his respects, and we went out to the front lawn where my boy Willie was playing in some fallen leaves. It was a golden fall day and the foliage and leaves blazed with colors. I leaned against a tree and Baker stretched out on the grass, and we talked about the war. It was now in its seventh month, and we had not won a single victory anywhere. General McClellan had drilled the Army of the Potomac, now seventy-five thousand strong, into a potentially lethal instrument of destruction, and the pressure from the country was unrelenting for him to attack the rebels across the river.

"You know what he told me?" I asked Baker. "'Don't let them hurry me, is all I ask.' I said to him, 'You'll have your way, General.'"

Baker laughed; he was colonel of one of McClellan's regiments, and he knew what a stickler the general was about discipline and fitness. McClellan seemed bent on creating the perfect army before he took it into battle.

"He don't get it yet," Baker said. "Only way we're going to win this war is by bold and determined offensive action."

"What I've been saying all along. Well, at least there's going to be some action tomorrow."

McClellan had ordered a reconnaissance in force against the rebels at Leesburg, forty miles upriver. Baker's regiment was to be in on it, and he hoped there would be a fight. "Maybe I'll become a martyr," he said. I stared hard at him, but he just grinned and said he was kidding. "Don't worry. I don't even have my will made out." He was fifty years old and looked right soldierly in his uniform. He wore thick side whiskers, and had a fine face and steady eyes.

After a while we got to talking about the old days, about Whig politics and Sangamon County and the high times we'd had in the state legislature. I reminded him that early on he'd shown a peculiar aptitude for the champagne glass and the gambling table, and he goaded me for being a teetotaler. Then, all too soon, Baker said he had to go. Willie ran over and Baker lifted the boy up and kissed him on the cheek. Mary came out and gave Baker some flowers, and we all stood around talking on the lawn. Then Baker mounted and rode out of the gates, and I watched until he disappeared from view.

The next day, around sunset, I went to McClellan's headquarters and asked if there was any news about the Leesburg operation. A lieutenant took me into the inner office, where the telegraphs were ticking, and told me what had happened. There had been a fierce skirmish at Ball's Bluff near Leesburg. Baker had led an impetuous attack against the rebel works there, and enemy guns had cut him down. Colonel Baker, the lieutenant said, was dead.

I was stunned. *Not Baker—not Baker, too.* I vaguely remember leaving the telegraph room with my hands pressed against my heart, and stumbling when I stepped into the street. On my way back to the Executive Mansion, I kept my head bowed—didn't speak to a soul. I told Mary and the boys what had happened, and then went into seclusion in my office. I was still there that night, pacing the floor, dimly aware of the rain beating against the windows. Ellsworth's death had hurt, but Baker was an old, old friend, and the loss of a man like him smote like a whirlwind.

There was more finger-pointing over Ball's Bluff, cries of outrage over the senseless loss of a patriot like Baker, and accusations of bungling and ineptitude that stretched from the Executive Department to the army. A day or so after Ball's Bluff I looked out the White House window and saw Senators Wade, Chandler, and Trumbull hurrying up the steps. "The Jacobin club," young Hay called 'em. They filed grimly into my office. Wade, of course, was furious.

"The people want a battle and a victory," he said. "They won't tolerate any more debacles and delays."

"McClellan's been drilling and organizing the army for more than two months," Chandler said. "Why don't he attack the enemy at Manassas? I think he's a Goddamned coward."

"No," said Trumbull, "it's because he's a Democrat who sympathizes with the South and supports slavery. That's why he won't fight."

"He's just deliberate," I said. But the senators had no stomach for my excuses. I'd heard that they had their doubts about me, too. Called me "weak" and "inefficient" or words to that effect.

After they'd gone, Hay came in, shaking his head. "So," he said, "the wild howl of the summer is to be renewed. Onward to Richmond."

"I'd better go see McClellan," I said, reached for my stovepipe hat, and strode off to headquarters. First, I told the general about a wonderful new rifled cannon, a repeater that fired fifty balls a minute, and said I had ordered ten and asked the general to go down to army ordnance and see it. Then we talked about the three senators.

"I don't like this popular impatience," I told McClellan, "but it's a reality and has to be taken into account."

He became extremely agitated. "I'm preparing the army for a mighty conquest," he said, "but it's not ready for battle yet. It needs more training and more men. The enemy has more than 130,000 troops behind the earthworks at Bull Run—our intelligence confirms it. Before I advance, I must have 273,000 men. *Then* I'll show you a campaign *en grand*. I'll attack Manassas, march on Richmond, and end the war."

He went on in a shrill voice: "I resent meddling politicians who know nothing about warfare—nothing about strategy and logistics, assault and supply. Men like Wade prefer a defeat to a delay. If you let them hurry me into a premature offensive, there will be another rout—another Bull Run. Is that what you want?"

"Well," I said, "you must not fight until you're ready."

"I have everything at stake in this—my reputation, the fate of the country."

"When you *are* ready," I said, "I have a notion to go out with you and stand or fall with the battle."

21. GRANT

Gloom filled the country after Ball's Bluff. The North was desperate for a victory and I was anxious to give 'em one. Hated being cooped up in Cairo. Had a bunch of raw volunteers who needed a battle—needed to see the elephant—to make 'em soldiers. I still wasn't strong enough to attack the fortifications on the river bluffs of Columbus, but I was strong enough to attack a smaller enemy force of some three thousand encamped at Belmont, Missouri, across the Mississippi from Columbus and about eighteen miles south of Cairo. The rebels, I figured, had occupied Belmont for a reason: so they could funnel reinforcements through to their General Price, who was operating in central Missouri. I aimed to destroy the enemy camp at Belmont, then get away before reinforcements could be thrown across the river from Kentucky. I aimed to give the North and my raw recruits a victory that'd make 'em proud.

Trouble was, I had vague and contradictory orders from St. Louis. They were in turmoil up there—height of the Frémont scandals, investigators out from Washington, Rebel General Price loose in the state, everything in confusion. First they tell me to "make demonstrations" down both sides of the Mississippi, but not to attack the enemy. Then they tell me to go after a small rebel force now operating in southeastern Missouri and help "drive" it back into Arkansas. Forget that, I told myself. I sent Dick Oglesby and three thousand men downriver with orders to *destroy* the rebel force. That gave me the opportunity to attack Belmont, so as to prevent the enemy from cutting off Oglesby or from reinforcing Price. I admit I had no orders to attack but didn't let that stop me. I saw a chance to hit the enemy and took it.

Night of November sixth, I headed down the Mississippi with more than three thousand men and two batteries of light artillery loaded on five transports. Two of Foote's wooden gunboats went along as escorts. We landed next morning in a cornfield above the rebel camp and prepared to attack. I posted a guard on the road to cover the transports, then rode out front with my skirmish line and led my men southward at double quick. Before long, we ran up against enemy skirmishers and drove 'em back across the fields and sloughs toward their encampment on the riverbank.

All of a sudden we ran into a wave of attacking rebels screaming their ungodly yell. Their musketry and canister ripped into our ranks and their shells fell on us fast and thick. My horse was shot from under me, but I borrowed another from an aide and rode ahead through the smoke. My men, I'm proud to say, broke the Johnnies' charge and drove 'em back through the woods, foot by foot and from tree to tree, and then overran their encampment in a wild melee. Most of the rebels got away and hid under the riverbank, but we had their camp, making the victory complete. My men, though, lost all discipline, threw down their arms, and started plundering the enemy tents while a regimental band played "Yankee Doodle."

"Sir! Look!" It was an aide, pointing at two large, triple-deck transports, steaming across from the Kentucky side of the river. They flew the enemy flag and were loaded with troops—reinforcements from Columbus! At the same time, enemy artillery on the opposite bluffs opened fire on us, but their aim was too high and the shells roared over the camp and exploded in the woods beyond.

We had to get back to our transports, not a minute to lose. Had my officers burn the camp. Torched everything—smoke and flame billowing up. Tell you one thing, it put an end to the looting. We spiked the enemy cannon, regrouped the men, and set out for our transports upriver. On the way we met a frightened staff officer, who told us that the reinforcements from Columbus had landed upriver and had gotten between us and our transports. At the same time, the rebels hiding under the riverbank had reformed and were closing in on our rear troops, including a detachment I'd detailed to carry our wounded.

"We're surrounded!" another aide cried.

"Well," I said, "if that's so, we'll cut our way out as we cut our way in."

I formed the men into line of battle and moved 'em out. Finding the rebels drawn across the road, I ordered an attack, and my men gave a *Yankee* yell and cut right through 'em in a rout. Then we marched unimpeded to our transports. As the men were filing on board, I rode back down the road to check on the rear guard I'd posted to protect the transports, but the guard was nowhere in sight. I was furious. The officer in charge, without orders, had withdrawn his troops to the transports, leaving our rear completely exposed. There was nothing to stop the enemy from advancing to the shore and firing on the main body of my troops as they were boarding the transports.

I was afraid the rebels were already approaching unseen, so I rode out across the cornfield to reconnoiter. The corn stalks were so high and thick that I couldn't see clearly, but neither could the enemy. Then I saw a column of Johnnies marching by me not fifty yards away. Trying to make as little noise as possible, I turned my horse slowly around and rode at a walk back toward the river, where our transports were now under enemy fire, our gunboats thundering in reply. As I rode along, I saw that the last of our men had made it on board and the boats were pushing away. At that moment, I was the only man of the national army between the rebels and our transports, and I was in danger of being left. I put the spur to my mount and rode like thunder, waving my hat. At last I saw a gangplank being run out from one of the transports—they had seen me. When I got to the river, my horse slid down the steep bank and trotted across the plank onto the deck of the steamer, with rebel bullets smacking into the smokestack. A little unsteady from my narrow escape, I made my way up to the captain's room on the upper deck and lay down on a sofa. But in a minute I got up to see what was happening. When I did, a stray bullet struck the head of the sofa, passed through it, and lodged in my foot.

We made it safely back to Cairo, and I wired St. Louis that we'd achieved a complete victory in terms of the objective of the expedition: we'd wiped out the enemy camp, inflicted heavy casualties (three to our one), taken 130 prisoners, and no doubt defeated a move by the enemy to reinforce Price, all at a cost of some 600 killed, wounded, and missing on our side. Our worst wounded, I'm sorry to say, fell into the hands of the enemy.

Later, under a flag of truce, I returned to Belmont and arranged for the burial of our dead. I talked with a friend from West Point days who was now in the rebel army, and mentioned my predicament in the cornfield near the advancing rebel line.

"Was that you?" he asked. "We saw you, and General Polk called to some of our troops: 'There, men, is a Yankee, if you want to try your aim.' But they were more interested in firing on the transports than on you. Grant's luck, hey?"

Grant's luck saved him from the rebels, but not from his detractors in the northern press, who seemed to think that we'd been whipped and driven from the field at Belmont, which was what the rebels claimed. Since the enemy reestablished his camp at Belmont, my detractors declared it a pointless battle, a useless waste of lives. But that's wrong. We'd won a victory when the North needed one, twice routing an enemy that, all told, had outnumbered us more than two to one. As I reported to St. Louis, Belmont afforded my officers and men invaluable battle experience, in which they saw the elephant for the first time. It gave me a confidence in them that would enable me to lead them in future campaigns without fear of the result.

22. LINCOLN

I tell you, I liked that man Grant. No delays and excuses from him. He saw the enemy at Belmont and went down there and bloodied his nose. Oh, I read the stories in the newspapers about Grant and heard the rumors, you know, that he was drunk a good deal at Cairo, but Washburne said it wasn't true: he had assurances from Grant's adjutant, man named Rawlins, that we need have no fear that General Grant, "by bad habits or conduct," would ever disgrace himself or the cause.

He was the only good thing about the Western Department. I had my hands full with that unholy mess. On November second I finally relieved Frémont of command; it was either that or risk a public scandal. I still don't think he was personally dishonest. His cardinal mistake was that he isolated himself and didn't know about the waste and corruption in his department. To placate the Radicals, I named Major General David Hunter, an abolitionist, as temporary commander.

In the East, meantime, we'd prepared a surprise for the rebels at Port Royal, on the South Carolina coast: an armada of two warships and fourteen transports carrying some ten thousand soldiers left Hampton Roads, swooped down the coast, and seized Hilton Head on the same day that Grant attacked Belmont. By nighttime, we had control of Port Royal and all the sea islands, which became the base of our South Atlantic Blockading Squadron and a staging area for operations against Charleston, a major blockade-running port and the place where treason began.

More good news came a few days later: Captain John Wilkes of the navy had captured Mason and Slidell, the enemy commissioners to England and France, on the high seas and hauled 'em off to jail. I reported the news to Edward Everett, the Boston statesman and orator, with an exclamation mark.

On the Virginia front, I wanted McClellan to show some of Grant's spunk and bloody the enemy's nose at Manassas, but I kept my promise about not hurrying him into battle. In fact, to show my faith in McClellan, I promoted him to general in chief of all the armies. General Scott had finally resigned, pleading the infirmity of old age. I was reluctant to let him go—on account of his long and distinguished service to the country—but the Cabinet insisted that he could no longer command, and so I accepted his resignation and on November first named McClellan to replace him, but without giving him Scott's rank as lieutenant general. Just going on thirty-five, McClellan was young for the supreme command, but I didn't have anybody else to choose.

I called on the general that night and told him: "I hope this vast increase of responsibility won't embarrass you."

"It's a great relief, sir. I feel as if several tons have been taken off my shoulders today." He meant, of course, that he no longer had Scott on his back. The two generals had clashed from day one; Scott thought McClellan an arrogant young upstart, which he was, and scolded him for grossly exaggerating enemy strength at Manassas, which he probably did. Scott told me flatly that *McClellan* had the superior force, not the other way around, as McClellan shrilly insisted. McClellan, on the other hand, told me that Scott was his "most dangerous antagonist"—even worse than the Radical Republicans—and that their ideas were so far apart that they could never work together. No wonder McClellan felt relieved when Scott was gone.

I told the young general: "Draw on me for all the sense I have, and all the information. In addition to your command of the Army of the Potomac, the supreme command of all our armies will be a vast labor on you."

"I can do it all," he replied.

All we could do was hope. But I tell you, McClellan's penchant for secrecy troubled me. Seward and I often called at army headquarters or McClellan's house to divine the general's plans for the coming campaign, but he put us off, even seemed insulted by our inquiries. I'd heard he thought me an odd duck and Seward and the other secretaries a bunch of geese, and told Democratic politicians that he deeply resented our meddling. That I was commander in chief didn't impress him one whit—to him, I was an interloper in the military domain. I confess to being an ignoramus in military matters and was trying to correct that by boning up late at night, reading every volume on warfare my secretaries could find in the Library of Congress. To escape me and Seward and his other "enemies," McClellan took to hiding out over at Ed Stanton's house. Stanton was a Pennsylvania lawyer and a fellow Democrat, and I could imagine what they talked about, since Stanton had once derided me for my shortage in the intelligence department and called me "a giraffe." At six feet four, almost, with a long neck and a big Adam's apple, I probably do resemble a giraffe.

Anyhow, one night in mid-November I called on McClellan at his house—Seward and young Hay were with me. The porter said that McClellan was attending a wedding but should be back soon, so we decided to wait for him in the parlor. He returned an hour or so later but ignored the porter when he announced that the president and secretary of state were waiting to see him, and went upstairs. Walked right by the doorway to the room where we were seated. When a half hour passed and he didn't come down, we asked the porter to remind General McClellan that we were here. The porter did so and returned to the parlor.

"The general," he said, "wishes me to tell you he's gone to bed."

On the way back to the Executive Mansion, Hay was furious about McClellan's conduct—called it "an act of unparalleled insolence" and "a portent of evil to come." But I told him it was better at this time not to worry about etiquette and personal dignity.

Still, McClellan's behavior rankled me. With everybody from Radical Republicans to Democrats calling me a failure, I thought I'd better start acting like a commander in chief. After that affair, I didn't call on McClellan anymore. I made him come to see me at the Executive Mansion. "It's about *time*," said Hay and Nicolay. McClellan didn't like it, but I was involved in his reorganization of the entire Western theater. The Department of the Cumberland, Sherman's former command, now became the Department of the Ohio. By the way, I was sorry when I learned of Sherman's breakdown and request to be relieved—he'd struck me as a fighter. Not like him to go "crazy." Buell, who now replaced him, was supposed to be a good man. At least he didn't think we needed 200,000 troops to wage offensive warfare in Kentucky, and it was a damn good thing because we didn't have that number to spare.

As for the rest of the reorganization, the Western Department now became the Department of the Missouri, with General Henry W. Halleck, a West Pointer and the author of a textbook on military arts and science, in command. Grant, still at Cairo, was Halleck's subordinate, and McClellan sent him "Crazy Bill" Sherman, too. Major General Hunter, incidentally, was put in command of the Department of Kansas, but he thought it an insignificant outpost and wrote me an ugly letter saying he was "mortified," "humiliated," and "disgraced." He accused me of "banishing" him, a major general, to an outpost with only three thousand effectives, while Buell, a mere *brigadier*, had command of a major department with many times that number of men. I wrote Hunter that it had never occurred to me that he was being "humiliated, insulted, and disgraced," told him that Kansas was important to us and that I remained his friend. As such, I quoted him a piece of wisdom, "Act well your part, there all the honor lies," and reminded him that he who does *something* at the head of one regiment will eclipse him who does *nothing* at the head of a hundred. That of course was a reference to a certain stationary general in chief.

McClellan and I, meantime, had agreed on a strategy that called for coordinated offensive movements of our three major armies. Halleck's was to push down the Mississippi, as Scott had long proposed, while Buell's was to drive into east Tennessee and liberate the Unionists there. He would then be in a position to cooperate with McClellan, once he got around to campaigning in Virginia. But, as would always be the case, our forces encountered seemingly insurmountable *impedimenta*. Buell showed a McClellan-like propensity for meticulous preparation that consumed valuable time. Then he announced that he could not possibly invade east Tennessee, on account of poor railroads and impossible logistical problems. This meant that Buell could not cooperate with McClellan in Virginia, which, in turn, left McClellan to deal with the rebel hordes he saw at Manassas with only the 100,000 men of the Army of the Potomac. And *that*, in turn, gave the general of all our armies an excuse to postpone his own offensive, and he announced, yet again, that the Potomac Army was not prepared to advance.

What had I got myself into with him? I kept rationalizing McClellan's behavior, reminding myself that he was a professional soldier and must know what he was doing. But, in an effort to light a fire under him, I sent him a blunt memo, dated December first: "If it were determined to make a forward movement of the Army of the Potomac, without awaiting further increase of numbers, or better drill & discipline, how long would it require to actually get in motion?"

He replied: "I have now my mind actively turned towards another plan of campaign that I do not think at all anticipated by the enemy nor by many of our own people." Of course, he didn't bother to reveal what that other campaign entailed or when he would put it into motion. Meanwhile our most powerful army went on drilling. And drilling. And drilling.

23. DAVIS

A succession of glorious victories at Manassas, Springfield, Lexington, Ball's Bluff, and Belmont had checked the wicked Yankee invasion which greed of gain and the unhallowed lust of power had brought upon our soil. After more than seven months of war, the enemy had not only failed to extend their occupancy of our territory, but new states with provisional governments—Kentucky and Missouri—had been added to our Confederate nation. Our people now looked with contemptuous astonishment on those with whom they had been so recently associated. They shrank with aversion from the bare idea of renewing such a connection. They knew that with such a people, ruled as they were by an ignorant despot, the separation was final, and for the independence we had asserted we would accept no alternative.

The nature of the hostilities the enemy waged against us must be characterized as barbarous. They bombarded undefended villages without giving notice to women and children to enable them to escape. Arson and rapine, the destruction of private homes and property, and injuries of the most wanton character, even on noncombatants, marked their forays along our borders and upon our territory. By converting their soldiers into robbers and criminal incendiaries and by waging a species of war which claimed innocent civilians as its victims, they could expect to be treated as outlaws and enemies of mankind. As I told Congress, he who refused to regard the rights of humanity forfeited his claims, if captured, to be considered as a military prisoner of war, and must expect to be dealt with as an offender against all law human and divine.

The tyrant who ruled the enemy had even carried his violations into international jurisdictions when he declared an unenforceable "blockade" of our coastal borders, which was a blatant violation of international law, and which we thought the neutral nations of the earth would surely condemn. We had of course justly asked for admittance into the family of nations and achieved the first step toward that

objective when Great Britain recognized the Confederacy as a belligerent power. We now had every reason to believe that Britain, France,
and the other great powers would now recognize us as a nation,
because we possessed one commodity, cotton, that Great Britain and
France could not do without. King cotton, we believed, ruled the commerce of the world and would dictate our admission into the family of
nations.

It was my hope, this autumn of 'sixty-one, that the army at Manassas might *attack* our barbarous enemy to the north, as Johnston
had earlier proposed to do. Toward that end, sick though I still was,
I visited the camps in northern Virginia but found that many of the
men were prostrate with disease and many others had died. Desertions further depleted our ranks. Generals Johnston and Beauregard,
supported by General Woodson Smith, wanted to launch an offensive against McClellan's army, but they admitted that it would
require sixty thousand men, twice the number they had at present,
even counting the sick and infirm. An advance, I concluded, was still
out of the question, since the want of arms restricted our ability to
reinforce the army.

At the end of October, General Lee, wearing a cap and a tattered
uniform, returned to Richmond and reported that he had failed to
dislodge the enemy from the mountains of western Virginia. Despite
feuding officers and the demoralized condition of his troops, he had
pushed an expedition against the enemy works at Cheat Mountain,
hoping to catch the Yankees by surprise, but bad weather and poor
coordination between the two attacking columns had doomed the
effort. A second campaign in the Kanawha Valley had met a similar
fate.

"Your Excellency, I cannot tell you my regret and mortification," Lee said.

I assured him that he had done all that could be done. The enemies of the Administration, however, dubbed him "Granny Lee," in
reference to the "lethargic" campaign he had supposedly waged, and
hostile stories about him appeared in the newspapers. He bore the
criticism stoically, and waited with patience for me to give him a
new command.

That opportunity came when the enemy, in another display of
his cruel and relentless spirit, fitted out a large naval expedition with
which to attack Port Royal, for the confessed purpose not only of
plunder, but to incite a slave insurrection in our midst. To meet this
contingency, I organized our southern coast from Georgetown to

Savannah and the Saint John's River, a stretch of three hundred miles, into a single department and sent General Lee to command it. But there was such opposition in South Carolina to the appointment of "Granny" Lee that I had to assure the governor, by letter, that General Lee was the best soldier for the assignment.

24. LEE

My detachment to South Carolina was another forlorn hope expedition, worse than the western Virginia campaign, and I could only trust that a generous Providence would save me from still another failure. Yet the very day I arrived in Charleston, Hilton Head and Port Royal fell to the enemy. Now the coasts of Georgia and South Carolina, including Charleston, were vulnerable to enemy thrusts. To my dismay, I discovered that I had fewer than thirteen thousand troops to defend my vast seacoast command, and the prospects were worse than dim. Nevertheless, I set about trying to establish an effective system of defense and to bring out the military strength of South Carolina. I reminded state officials that the Confederacy had but one great object in view: the successful issue of their war of independence. By a combination of pressure and cajolery, I managed to increase my forces to twenty thousand men and to strengthen the forts ringing Charleston harbor. But it would require a larger force than that to contend effectively with the formidable enemy presence on the sea islands, whose objective, as President Davis said, was to stir up a servile revolt on the mainland.

A month after I took command, the Federals tried to block the entrance to Charleston harbor by sinking between thirteen and seventeen ships, loaded with stone, in the main ship channel. This achievement, so unworthy of any nation, was the abortive expression of the malice and revenge of a hateful people. It was also indicative of their despair of ever capturing a city they hoped to ruin. If I had had the strength to *attack* those people, I would have driven them from Hilton Head and the other islands and sent them fleeing back to their origins.

It was an utterly thankless post, this seacoast command. I found myself trapped on a treadmill of paperwork relating to ordnance and supply and troop organization and recruitment. I was *not* a desk general and felt consigned to purgatory in damp, mosquito-ridden Charleston. In my office, I could only read reports about how safe the enemy was with his big boats and how—where he could venture with impunity—he pillaged, burned, and robbed, and alarmed women and children. Every day I received reports of some landing in force, marching and so on, which always turned out to be some marauding party bent on burning out plantations and stealing slaves.

I tried my best to remain in contact with Mim and the children. I wrote dear Mildred, my Precious Light, who was then at school in Winchester, that she must labor at her books and gain knowledge and wisdom, and pay no attention to what Rob said. I shared with her what family news I had: Mim and Fitzhugh's wife, Charlotte, were at Shirley, and Charlotte had written me of the death of cousin Annie Leigh's little baby, which had just occurred there. Happy little creature to be spared the evil of this world. I added one personal piece of news: "I have a beautiful white beard. It is much admired. At least, much remarked on."

Along with the forlorn hope of my command, I was mortified to hear people in Charleston talk so much about help from abroad. We of the South had to make up our minds to fight our own battles and win our independence alone. We required no outside aid, if we were true to ourselves—if we were prudent, just, fair, and bold. Yes, I was dreadfully disappointed at the spirit shown in Charleston. The people there, with their fine carriages and iron-grilled palatial homes, had all of a sudden realized the asperities of war, in what they must encounter, and did not seem to be prepared for it. They were content to nurse themselves and their dimes and leave the protection of their country to others. This was not the way to accomplish our independence. I wrote Annie that I was doing all I could, with our small means and slow workmen, to defend the cities and coast. Against ordinary numbers we were pretty strong, but against the hosts our enemies seemed able to bring everywhere, there was no calculation. If I'd had some *veteran* troops in my command, they would have rallied against our deadly enemy and been inspired with the great principle for which we were fighting. I could only trust that a merciful God would arouse us to a sense of our danger, bless our honest efforts, and drive back our enemies to their own territory.

2 5 . DAVIS

I appreciated General Lee all the more because he seldom complained to us about the shortages of men and weapons and supplies that plagued his department. Despite the immense difficulties he encountered, he established excellent defensive fortifications in Charleston harbor that would withstand the enemy's most determined efforts to seize the city.

If only generals Johnston and Beauregard had been more like Lee. With those two, however, I had nothing but a vortex of difficulties. By authority of Congress, I had made Samuel Cooper, the adjutant general, and Sidney Johnston, Lee, Joseph Johnston, and Beauregard full generals in that order. Their ranking was determined by their former rank in the old Federal army. No sooner had Congress confirmed the promotions than Joseph E. Johnston, ever petulant about his rank, sent off a furious letter to me expressing his "surprise and mortification" that, by my act, Cooper, Sidney Johnston, and Lee outranked him. How could this be, he demanded, when he had been quartermaster general in the old army, with the staff rank of brigadier general, whereas Sidney Johnston and Lee had only been colonels and Samuel Cooper only a captain? "I ought to hold the rank of first general," he complained. "By denying me that rank, you tarnish my fair name as a soldier and as a man."

Johnston's argument about rank was wrong on the face of it. There was a great difference in the old army between a staff rank and a line rank, and Joe Johnston's line rank had been lieutenant colonel; hence the reason for ranking him behind Sidney Johnston and Lee in the Confederate Army. As for Samuel Cooper, he was our adjutant and inspector general—the same position he had held in the old Federal army—and an unswervingly loyal assistant to me. He had helped me build our military system from nothing and now assisted me in controlling our far-flung armies. Hence the reason he became our ranking general.

Johnston's letter of protest was unforgivable insubordination, written in a fit of jealousy against men who were vastly his superior in every respect, and I dispatched an indignant reply. The arguments and statements in his letter, I informed him, were utterly one-sided, and its insinuations as unfounded as they were unbecoming. Instead of putting Johnston in his place, however, my letter appeared to have the opposite effect. He declared himself "offended" and remained so forever after. All my subsequent troubles with him commenced with this notorious affair.

My difficulties with Beauregard began when he submitted his official report of the battle of Manassas and released a synopsis of it to the press. In the report, Beauregard claimed that after the battle he had proposed to advance north, capture Washington, seize Baltimore, and liberate Maryland, but that *I* had overruled him. It was a shocking piece of slander, all the worse because it aired in our newspapers, and I called Beauregard to account for it. I wrote him that his report "surprised" me because even if we had differed about a contemplated campaign, it had no place appearing in his battle report; and further because it seemed to be an attempt to exalt himself at my expense; and especially because no such plan as that described was ever submitted to me.

I called on General Johnston to vindicate me. He was a party to all our conferences. I asked him: had I ever obstructed the pursuit of the enemy after the victory at Manassas? Had I ever objected to an advance or other active operation if it was feasible for the army to undertake it? That peevish officer would only repeat what he had said in his own report, that fresh enemy troops had checked our pursuit at Centreville, and that a want of ammunition, provisions, and transportation had made an advance against Washington impracticable. That was all the vindication I would get from him.

I then asked Beauregard to delete the "extraneous" part of his report, containing that mendacious claim about me, but he refused to modify any portion of the document and declared that nowhere in it had he sought to "exalt" himself at my expense. He had the temerity to suggest that I *reread* the report, so as to rid my mind of "all suspicion" that he had tried to enhance his reputation to my detriment. *Gross* insubordination, that is what this was! Before the controversy subsided, James Chesnut, Beauregard's aide at Manassas, got drawn into it. "I am sure that a full and dispassionate investigation and consideration of this subject," he wrote me from South Carolina, "will leave little ground for reasonable dissatisfaction. The success of our cause depends not merely on the ability and fidelity—but on the harmony and hearty cooperation—of those who are chief and chosen instruments in the direction of our affairs." Perhaps so, but Beauregard's behavior was intolerable. In the end, Congress took the side of the president and directed that the published version of Beauregard's report omit the portion to which I objected. Just as I expected, the deleted portion found its way into the newspapers, which accused me of trying to destroy the reputation of a popular general.

I must say that in all my difficulty with Johnston and Beauregard, I enjoyed the complete support of Adjutant General Cooper and Secretary of War Judah P. Benjamin, who had replaced Walker in September. This short, stout, intelligent Jew, with his olive complexion and bright black eyes, became my closest adviser in the Cabinet and ran the War Office with the same unswerving devotion to duty that Samuel Cooper displayed in overseeing the adjutant and inspector general's office.

The Confederate electorate, meanwhile, had expressed their support of my policies by electing me on November sixth to a single six-year term as president of the permanent Confederate government. Up to now, I had served as provisional president, having been chosen by the Montgomery convention that had established the Confederacy and written its Constitution. That same November sixth, the voters also elected members to the first regular Congress.

Two days later our hated enemy committed yet another crime in the international sphere when one of their ships of war interdicted a British steamer, the *Trent*, in the neutral Spanish port of Havana, Cuba, and seized our two commissioners, Mason and Slidell, who were on board, on their way to England and France, respectively, as permanent envoys. The enemy captain then took our commissioners to Boston as contraband of war. The British were outraged. So were we. By this sordid act, the United States illegally claimed general jurisdiction over the high seas. Entering a British ship sailing under its country's flag and seizing our ministers while under the protection of a neutral nation, violated the rights of embassy, held sacred even amongst barbarians. It would be the act of a merciful God, I thought, if Great Britain should now enter the war on our side.

26. LINCOLN

I'll tell you this about the capture of Mason and Slidell: Captain Wilkes acted without instructions and without the knowledge of this government. I was an ignoramus when it came to international law, but at the outset of the *Trent* affair I thought the two traitors would prove to be white elephants: if Great Britain demanded their release, we would have to give them up. Still, I was not displeased. The British had long practiced a policy of search and seizure on the high seas, especially against American ships. That had been a major cause of our second war with them. If the British protested, and we did give the traitors up, it would forever bind Britain to keeping the peace in relation to neutrals and so acknowledge that she had been wrong for sixty years. I chuckled at the irony.

Trouble was, the country needed a hero, and Captain Wilkes fit the bill. The papers ballyhooed his action, and Congress voted him a gold medal. There was a lot of proud and belligerent talk about how the United States had given the haughty British a dose of their own medicine. I saw that giving up Mason and Slidell might not be so easy as I'd thought.

Then came the British reaction. On December nineteenth, Lord Lyons, the British minister in Washington, handed Seward an official demand from the British Cabinet. The United States, it said, must not only release the prisoners within eleven days of receipt of this communication, but also apologize for violating British neutrality. There were rumors that if we refused, Lyons could sever diplomatic relations, close the British embassy, and return to London with his entire legation. This of course was the first step toward war.

I tell you, the British reaction caused great consternation in Washington. Sumner showed me disturbing correspondence from his liberal friends in England, Cobden and Bright. America, they said, must release the envoys; no other solution was acceptable. "I need not tell you," Bright warned, "that nations drift into wars often through the want of a resolute hand at some moment early in the quarrel. So now, a courageous stroke, not of arms but of moral action, may save you and us."

"What do you think?" I asked Sumner.

"Mr. President, war with Britain would be an absolute catastrophe for the United States. Britain has the most powerful navy in the world. It would crush our navy and blockade our ports. France, Britain's ally, would join her in recognizing the Confederacy as a nation, and all three would form an alliance against us. A super added war against Britain would ensure our defeat and Confederate independence. "

"There will be no such war," I said gloomily, "unless England is bent on having one."

Seward, meanwhile, spoke with McClellan about the *Trent* affair, and the general of all our armies for once agreed with Sumner. McClellan warned flatly that the Union could not fight Great Britain and the Confederacy at the same time. "If the matter takes that turn," Seward said, "the commissioners will have to be released."

I was caught in the worst imaginable dilemma. I'd already been accused of spineless incompetence and a hell of a lot worse. If I backed down, I would be charged with crumbling under British pressure and sacrificing the national honor. It would create an uproar in Congress, the press would howl, the morale of the army would suffer, people would demand my impeachment. Still, McClellan was right: we could fight only one war at a time. Somehow I had to convince the British that I wanted to avoid a violent showdown.

I sent for Sumner. "Let's cut through all this diplomatic protocol," I said. "You bring Lord Lyons here for a personal talk with me. I want him to hear from my lips how much I want peace."

But Sumner argued that this would be improper. The best solution, he said, would be to submit the entire question to arbitration, say with the sovereign of Prussia.

"Good idea," I said. "I'll have Seward work up a draft." I added: "Don't worry, I'll go over the proposal word for word, to make sure it won't contain anything that would create more bad blood."

As it turned out, arbitration wasn't necessary because the British were as anxious as we were to settle the dispute without a war. Accordingly, they dropped the demand for an apology, as long as we assured them that Wilkes had acted without authority. As I'd figured, though, they still insisted that we release the prisoners.

On Christmas day, Sumner and I met with the full Cabinet to decide what to do. Seward had studied up all the works ever written on international law and came to the meeting loaded to the muzzle with the subject. Twirling his watch, he argued that Wilkes had simply been in the wrong. By international law, he had the right to search the *Trent* and confiscate enemy war materiel, but not to impress men from the decks of a neutral ship. Therefore Seward voted to surrender the prisoners. Sumner backed him up and read the letters from Cobden and Bright. Some of the other secretaries, however, hated to knuckle under to British pressure, and there was a good deal of debate pro and con. In the end, however, we all agreed that Sumner was right, that the United States could not win "in a super added war with England." So we yielded to necessity and decided to give the prisoners up. It was a pretty bitter pill to swallow, "all gall and wormwood," as Chase described it, but I contented myself with believing that England's triumph in the matter would be short-lived, and that after we won the war, we would be so powerful that we could call her to account for all the embarrassments she'd inflicted on us.

So the *Trent* affair ended peacefully. In Congress, Vallandigham of Ohio damned Lincoln's "unmanly capitulation" and vowed that the president would pay for humiliating the nation, and there were similar rumblings in the Senate. But Sumner defended the Administration there with what the experts said was a masterful discourse on international law. Seward, meantime, drafted a crafty reply to Lord Lyons and read it to me with a cigar in his mouth and one leg over the arm of his chair. Wilkes, he said, had indeed acted without authorization—hence there was no need for an apology. His biggest mistake was that he'd followed the British example of the Napoleonic wars, when they had boarded American ships and impressed men to serve in their navy. Now, in demanding that neutral rights be honored on the high seas, Britain was endorsing "an old, honored, and cherished" American principle. Therefore the United States would "cheerfully" release the prisoners and send them on their way.

Reflecting on the *Trent* affair, I saw that Britain had passed up a great opportunity to enter the war and make the Confederacy an independent nation. For that, every patriot in the country could give thanks.

27. FREDERICK DOUGLASS

When the war commenced, I stood in front of my house in Rochester and cried to the heavens, "God be praised! It has come at last!" In the first blast of rebel gunpowder I could hear the roar of a just God. The country was now to weep and howl in compensation for the sins of two centuries against millions of slaves on both sides of eternity. Could I write as with lightning, and speak as with the voice of thunder, I would write and cry to the nation: "Repent, put an end forever to slavery, the primal cause of the rebellion. Break every slave's yoke, let the oppressed go free for herein alone is deliverance and safety! It is not too late. The moment is propitious, and we may yet escape the complete vengenace of God's wrath and fury, whose balls of fire are already dropping to consume us."

The white abolitionists agreed. "The hour has struck!" Wendell Phillips, the great orator, told the North. "Seize the thunderbolt God has forged for you, and annihilate the system which has troubled your peace for seventy years!" Mr. *William Lloyd Garrison*, however, from his *high* station as editor of the *Liberator* and leader of the Massachusetts Anti-Slavery Society, called on all abolitionists to rally behind the Administration regardless of what it did. "This is no time for minute criticism of Lincoln, Republicanism, or even the other parties, now that they are fusing for a death-grapple with the Southern slave oligarchy." Toeing his line, the executive committee of the American Anti-Slavery Society even voted to suspend its meetings and operations.

But when Mr. Lincoln announced his slavery policy, many of us were numb with disbelief. He would not free the slaves. It would "weaken our cause." It would "smack of bad faith." It would alienate the "loyal" border. Nor would he let free colored men fight in his armies. In a burst of patriotism—this is our country too!—black men of the North rushed to enlist, only to be told by Lincoln's War Department that this was "a white man's war," that there would be no colored soldiers. That was the policy Lincoln announced in this year of 'sixty-one. The Negro could play no part in the Federal cause, not as a free man and not as a slave. What would happen if the Negro tried? Down in traitorous Florida, a brave group of slaves attempted to help defend Fort Pickens against the rebels, but the Federal defenders seized them, put them in irons, and returned them to their masters to be whipped to death. At Fort Monroe, it is true, General Butler received fugitive slaves as "contraband of war" and put them to work on his defenses. But with Lincoln's consent, other Federal commanders cruelly announced that their departments would not become "harbors for escaping slaves" and handed them back to southern masters who claimed to own them.

The president had not yet seen the hand of God in the blood red clouds of battle, had not yet heard His voice in the whipping winds. Well, I would help him open his eyes and ears. I vowed to *agitate, agitate,* until I had converted him to an emancipation policy that would remove the curse of centuries. On the platform and in the columns of my paper, *Frederick Douglass's Monthly*, which I sent regularly to Washington, I aimed a steady volley of words at the Man in the White House, playing on his own oft-stated personal hatred of slavery.

"What is the mission of the war?" I asked him. "It is the *liberation* of the slave as well as the *salvation* of the Union. We cannot afford to be lenient toward the rebel traitors. A lenient war is a lengthy war, and therefore the worst kind of war. Let us stop it, and stop it effectually—stop it on the soil upon which it originated, among the traitors and rebels who started it. This can be done at once, by 'carrying the war into Africa.'"

What would we tell the president if we hazarded a trip through slaveowning Maryland and called on him in person? "We would tell him," I said, "that this is no time to fight with one hand when both are needed; that this is no time to fight with your soft white hand, and allow your black iron hand to be chained and tied. Let the slaves and free colored people be called into service, and formed into a liberating army, to march into the South and raise the banner of emancipation among the slaves. The slaveowners have brought revolution and war upon the country, and having elected and consented to play at that fearful game, they have no right to complain if calamity shall result from their own acts and deeds."

"The Negro," we would tell him, "is the key of the situation—the pivot upon which the whole rebellion turns. Teach the rebels and traitors that the price they are to pay for the attempt to abolish this government must be the abolition of slavery. Henceforth let the war cry be down with treason, and down with slavery, the cause of treason."

We would tell him how useless it was to appease the border slave states. "The ties that bind slaveholders together are stronger than all other ties, and in every state where they hold the reins of government, they will take sides openly or secretly with the slaveholding rebels. Conciliation is out of the question. They know no law, and will respect no law but the law of force. The safety of the government can be attained only in one way, and that is, by rendering the slaveholders powerless by stripping them of the cornerstone of their power."

We would tell him: "You are the statesman of the hour. For you to permit any settlement of the present war between slavery and freedom, which would leave untouched and undestroyed the relation of master and slave, would not only be a great crime, but a great mistake, the bitter fruits of which would poison the life blood of unborn generations. It is the critical moment for us. The destiny of the mightiest Republic in the modern world hangs upon the decision of this hour. If our government shall have the wisdom to see, and the nerve to act, we are safe. If it fails, we perish, and go to our own place with those nations of antiquity long blotted from the maps of the world."

We would tell him: "All signs portend that we are to have a long, revengeful and desolating war, in which both parties will be driven to extremities not dreamed of at the beginning. We are not fighting a servile people, but our masters, the men who have ruled us during a half a century. They are proud, brave, willful, determined, skillful, unscrupulous, and cruel; and to their savage villainy, more than to the moral virtue and humanity of the North, do we look for that iron necessity, which shall compel our government to aim a deathblow at slavery, the life-support of the rebellion."

But at this time only one Federal commander, John Charles Frémont, saw as I saw and heard as I heard, and he hurled at slavery in his department an iron-fisted proclamation of freedom. But Lincoln, as a sop to the accursed border, overruled and ousted Frémont in what I publicly called a pusillanimous and pro-slavery interference with a noble act. Then Lincoln turned about and *promoted* a man who defended slavery and sympathized with southerners, George B. McClellan. I asked Lincoln: was it not the height of imbecility to displace a general who was a *terror* to the rebels, who had the foresight to strike at the very *stomach* of treason, while at the same time promoting a lusterless general who excited no alarm whatever?

The Frémont affair upset my white brothers—Garrison, Phillips, and their followers—so much that they broke their seven-month truce with the Administration and joined me in putting pressure on Lincoln and the northern public to convert this into an emancipation war. They thundered in their press and their pulpits, circulated petitions, sponsored lectures—one antislavery group in Washington even launched a lecture series in the Smithsonian, near the Executive Mansion, to attract Lincoln's attention and that of Congress. From a hundred platforms, my white brothers rehearsed the very arguments I had been making: Lincoln must not put the old Union back together; he must use the war power to "abolish slavery throughout the land" and with it the traitorous master class that had fomented the rebellion. The "only feasible method" of *winning* the war was by removing the *cause* of it.

I called on my abolitionist brothers to put aside all our prewar differences and form a common league against slavery. Every one who was ready to work for the overthrow of slavery, whether a voter or nonvoter, a Gerrit Smith man or a Garrisonian, black or white, was both clansman and kinsman of ours. Even though Garrison and I had become bitterly estranged before the war, I was willing to put aside our ideological and personal differences to achieve a common goal. At Syracuse, I even shared the platform with him for the first time in many years.

Did Lincoln have ears to hear? Even with our message resounding in the Smithsonian itself, could Lincoln hear us? *Emancipate, Mr. President! Enlist colored troops! Strike treason with your iron black hand.*

28. LINCOLN

I still argued that Federal emancipation—emancipation by executive fiat and enforced by the army—was too big a lick. Still believed it would alienate northern Democrats and cost us the loyal slave states. Without them we would lose the war, the nation, popular government—everything worth living for. Even so, I attended some of the antislavery lectures at the Smithsonian and listened carefully to what the speakers said. One lecturer, I remember, was Horace Greeley of the *New York Tribune*, an odd-looking fellow with a balding head, white throat whiskers, and a round, pink-skinned face. I told Congressman Julian that Greeley's sermon on emancipation was full of good talk and I would like to take his manuscript home with me and study it some Sunday.

The abolitionist argument echoed what Sumner, Wade, Chandler, and other Radicals told me almost every day right here in my office. The cause-of-the-war argument, the cripple-the-cornerstone-of-the-Confederacy argument, the slavery-as-a-moral-wrong-and-national-disgrace argument—all were persuasive and vigorously presented. I conceded that. But the arguments *against* emancipation were equally compelling. I felt damned if I did and damned if I didn't, and it gave me the hypo.

Still, as I mulled the matter over at the window of my office, I thought there might be a way out, a way to remove slavery without losing the loyal border and alienating the Democrats and without violating everything the Republicans had always said about the sanctity of slavery as a state institution. Why not try gradual, compensated emancipation, *paid for* by the general government, but *carried out* by the states? Jefferson and Clay had both advocated gradual, compensated emancipation, and I'd championed it, too, before the war. As I thought about the possibilities now, I got excited. This just might work. We could begin in Delaware, an innocuous border state with a relatively small slave population, and go from there.

I went to my desk and drafted a model plan to be tested in the Delaware legislature; it called for the state to gradually free its slaves over the next thirty years and for the Federal government to compensate Delaware slaveowners for their loss, at the rate of five hundred dollars for every slave held there in 1860. I figured that a similar plan for the other border slave states would cost the Federal government about one-third of what it had expended on the war so far.

I told my Illinois friend Senator Orville Browning about my plan, and he said he liked it but wanted to know what we would do with "the liberated niggers."

"Colonize 'em," I said. "Either in new territory to be acquired or outside the country." A fellow named Redpath already had a private project under way to colonize free coloreds in Haiti on a voluntary basis. Maybe we could do something like that. Without some kind of colonization project on the drawing boards, I knew, the vast majority of northern white folk would never accept emancipation, even if it was done by the states, for fear that all the blacks would come north.

I thought my border-state plan was the best way out of an impossible situation. The leaders of the rebellion placed great hope in the border slave states joining the Confederacy. To deprive them of that hope would help bring the rebellion to an end, and state-initiated emancipation would indeed destroy that hope. By removing slavery themselves, the loyal border states would send a message to the insurgents that at no event would the border ever join their cause. State action meant that Federal action and all the dangers attached to it could be avoided. Once we won the war, and I kept telling myself we would win, we could urge the conquered states to adopt gradual, compensated emancipation as well and colonize their liberated Negroes like those of the border. By this slow, salutary process, the cause of the war would be removed and the Union and its experiment in popular government saved for this and all future generations.

Yes, popular government, as I kept telling everybody, was what we were fundamentally fighting for—and, conversely, what the enemy was fighting against. We found conclusive evidence of this in the public documents and general tone of the insurgents. They took pride in the existence of only one party, the Democrats, which hampered the expression of the people's will. In the recent elections down there, Davis had run without an opponent. The voters could not have chosen anybody else. That's not democracy, not in my book. We also found evidence of the abridgement of the right of suffrage—South Carolina, for example, did not permit a popular vote in presidential elections. In fact, there was a movement within the ruling slaveholder class to restrict the suffrage, even to deny the people any right to participate in the selection of public officers, with labored arguments to prove that large control of the people in government is the source of all political evil. Monarchy itself was sometimes hinted at as a possible refuge from the power of the people.

I pointed this out in my December message to Congress. I felt it my duty, I said, to raise my voice against this approach of returning despotism. I reminded Congress, and the nation beyond, that we of the North were trying to preserve a just, generous, and prosperous system, which opens the way to all—gives hope to all, and consequent energy, and progress, and improvement of condition to all. The struggle *of* today, however, was not altogether *for* today. It was for a vast future also, a future when this would be a nation of 250 million, and the door of advancement would be open to them, as it had been to us.

In that same message, I also asked that Federal funds be appropriated for the colonization of all slaves freed by the states or by the first confiscation act, which provided for the seizure of all slaves used in the enemy war effort. But I made it clear that I did not want the war to degenerate into a violent and remorseless revolutionary struggle. That was my way of saying I would not issue an emancipation proclamation. In every case, I said, I'd thought it proper to keep the integrity of the Union as the primary object of the contest. "The Union must be preserved, and all indispensable means must be employed to preserve it. Yet we must not be in haste to determine that radical and extreme measures, which may reach the loyal as well as the disloyal, are indispensable."

By "radical and extreme measures," I also meant the use of colored troops. Sumner, Secretary of War Cameron, and abolitionists like Fred Douglass were exhorting me to enlist colored men in the army and hit the rebellion with my "iron black hand." Now I had no objection to employing Negroes as military foragers and laborers, no objection to enlisting them in the navy to serve on warships and coastal installations—we were already doing that. But I said *no* to colored soldiers, and for a good reason: the army, unlike the navy, was a *physical presence* in the border states, and the loyal slaveowners there would throw in with the Confederacy if we sent black troops to serve on their soil. Put the colored man in a blue uniform and give him a rifle and send him to fight in slave territory, and the war would indeed become a remorseless revolutionary struggle.

I made it clear to the Cabinet that this was Administration policy, yet War Secretary Cameron brazenly disregarded it. In his annual report, to be circulated by postmasters and released to the press simultaneous with my congressional message, the secretary of war advocated both emancipation *and* the enlistment of Negro troops, on the grounds that this would be just punishment of "rebellious traitors." When I saw an advance copy of his report, I was appalled. Cameron had written the offending section without once consulting me. I immediately ordered Postmaster Blair to seize all the advance copies of the report, and instructed Cameron to delete the unauthorized remarks about emancipation and colored troops. But wouldn't you know, both versions found their way into the public prints—some papers published them side by side—and it made the Administration look more inept and confused than ever. This insidious affair put a severe strain on my relationship with Mr. Cameron. With all the reports I was getting of graft and corruption in his department, it was but a matter of time, I knew, before I would have to let him go.

My stand against emancipation, of course, infuriated the Radical Republicans and brought the leaders of that crowd, Sumner, Wade, and Chandler, on the run. Sumner now made it his personal crusade to convert me to an emancipation policy. It seemed to be his raison d'être to torture me on the subject. He even did it in his eulogy in the Senate to Edward Baker, who had once served there. I was sitting in the galleries that day and became uneasy when Sumner got off on slavery. I feared what was coming. The Administration, he thundered, was to be *condemned* for protecting this evil thing that caused all our woes. Gesturing dramatically, he told how Baker was killed at Ball's Bluff and then—looking straight at me—Sumner shouted that slavery was "the murderer of our dead senator." I tell you, I started violently. It felt like I'd been stabbed.

One day that December, Sumner rushed into my office even more excited than usual. I figured it had something to do with the Radicals' legislative offensive against slavery: they had introduced petitions and bills attacking it from various directions. One proposed measure went further than the confiscation act; it would free the slaves of everyone who supported the rebellion. Sumner in the course of things would pitch a determined argument for these proposals. But right now they were not what he wanted to see me about.

"Mr. President," he said, "I hear that you are maturing a plan of gradual and compensated emancipation. If that is true, I beseech you to introduce it. I want you to make it a New Year's present to Congress."

I would have, except for two problems. All my Kentucky friends warned me that it was a bad idea—that Kentucky would never go for it. Nobody in Delaware liked it either. I was promoting it there myself, but it made no difference. No bill incorporating my plan would ever come out of the Delaware legislature. I had a long and candid conversation with Sumner about all this, and I assured him that I hated slavery as much as he did, and that on the subject of emancipation I really wasn't very far behind him. About a month to six weeks, is what I told him.

"Mr. President, if that is the only difference between us, I will not say another word to you about it till the longest time you name has passed."

29. DOUGLASS

Lincoln's message to Congress was an affront and an outrage to all true antislavery men. We *wanted* radical and extreme measures, *wanted* a remorseless revolutionary struggle. The message, as Gerrit Smith said, was all "twattle and trash" and showed that Lincoln was "bound hand and foot by that proslavery regard for the Constitution in which he was educated." We still hoped that slavery would receive its death wound from the rebellion, yet we saw nothing in the temper or disposition of our rulers in Washington to justify our hope. On the contrary, antislavery men felt betrayed on the vital and all-commanding question of the age. Our government was not what it was elected to be, and Lincoln showed himself to be as destitute of antislavery principle or feeling as did James Buchanan.

"In this state of facts," I wrote in my paper, "we find our hopes of the speedy abolition of slavery by the war power greatly diminished, and the possibility of slavery coming out of the present struggle stronger than when it began. This is the aspect of the case at the beginning of the year of our Lord one thousand eight hundred and sixty-two. But a single day, but a single event may change the whole prospect. Let us, therefore, hope for that day and continue to labor for that event. God grant that that day may not be long delayed!"

30. DAVIS

William Preston, of Bowling Green, Kentucky, a pro-Confederate who had once served in the Federal Congress and as minister to Spain, divined the true intentions of the Black Republicans in Washington. "Recent events in the Federal Congress," he wrote me at year's end, "show that the extreme Republicans will force the Administration to confiscate or enfranchise the slaves, and that New England will compel the government to adopt her policy or abandon the war. Since the report of Mr. Cameron and the message of Mr. Lincoln, great discontent has manifested itself among the Union men in Kentucky. Universal dissatisfaction prevails, and information from various sources proves that the Kentucky troops in the Federal service are discontented and distrusted. Many officers have announced their intention to resign if the antislavery measures before Congress should pass. The people of Kentucky have been deceived by the promises that the war is not to be conducted in a spirit of hostility to the institution of slavery. The mask is now laid aside and the true character of the contest is revealed."

THE WINDS OF 'SIXTY-TWO

Where are you going, soldiers,
With banner, gun and sword?
We're marching south to Canaan
To battle for the Lord.

Your country every strong arm calling,
To meet the hireling Northern band
That comes to desolate the land
With fire and blood and scenes appalling,
To arms, to arms, ye brave;
The avenging sword unsheathe!
March on! March on! All hearts resolved
on victory or death.

1. LINCOLN

With snow falling outside my office windows, I studied a House committee report on the charges of corruption in Cameron's War Department. It made me cringe. According to the committee's investigations, Cameron and his agents had ignored competitive bidding and bought war materiel from favorite suppliers, many of them as dishonest as they were unscrupulous. They'd sold the War Department—all at exorbitant prices—huge quantities of tainted meat and rotten blankets, uniforms, shoes, and knapsacks that fell apart, and hundreds of diseased and dying horses. One agent spent $21,000 for straw hats and linen pants and contracted for seventy-five thousand pairs of overpriced shoes from a firm that sometimes loaned him money. In one scandalous episode, the War Department sold a lot of condemned carbines for a few dollars apiece, bought 'em back at $15 apiece, sold 'em again at $3.50 apiece, and bought 'em back again at $22 apiece. Cameron hadn't enriched himself in the scandals—no evidence of that—but his department, in the words of the report, had treated congressional law as "almost a dead letter," awarded contracts "universally injurious to the government," and promoted favoritism and "colossal graft."

It all reflected on me. As my critics pointed out, I'd shown poor judgment in appointing Cameron in the first place, and compounded the error by leaving him in office too long. In January I asked for his resignation—he'd said he would step down without making a fuss—and dispatched him to Moscow as our minister to Russia. That inspired a wisecrack from Congressman Thad Stevens: "Send word to the czar to bring in his things at night."

The House went on to censure Cameron, and that troubled me. The president and all the other departmental heads were equally responsible for whatever error, wrong, or fault had been committed, and I told Congress so in a subsequent message. I described the Cabinet meeting of April twenty-first of 'sixty-one, when the capital was in danger of attack and we'd decided to take emergency action to save the government. We'd given public funds to private individuals to buy supplies and forward them to Washington. I admitted the terrible misdeeds that had followed, but said I wasn't willing for Cameron to bear the burden of censureship alone.

Who to replace him with? If we were ever going to win this war, I needed a hard disciplinarian in the War Office with the administrative skill to manage our huge armies. The man I chose, to the shock of many Republicans, was Edwin McMasters Stanton, the War Department's chief legal adviser, a Democrat, and a friend of the inert general of all our armies. I consulted with nobody except Seward, and some of the Cabinet members were horrified. How could I name a man who'd once called me a giraffe and an imbecile and made no secret of his extreme hostility toward me? Easy, I said. He was the best man for the job.

I told him so. "I expect a lot from you, Stanton. The War Office is a rat's nest. Needs to be cleaned up from top to bottom. The waste and corruption has to stop. We need an efficient central agency to manage the war effort and keep generals in line with Administration policies."

"I can do the job, Mr. President."

Sizing him up this day, I liked what I saw. Behind his small round spectacles, he peers at you with stern, irritable little eyes that mean business. He wears a long, heavy beard to protect his chest from asthma attacks. With his huge torso and short thick legs, he looks like a gnome. It makes me chuckle to see him hurrying along on those stout little legs.

On his first day on the job, he started sweeping the rats out of the War Department with a vengeance. Talk about a workhorse! He audited government contracts and saved $17 million in adjustments. He reorganized the entire supply system, kept meticulous track of all new army units, and displayed a mastery of technical military data I found indispensable. Under my orders, he took charge of security matters and created a corps of civilian provost marshals to handle them. Before long, he'd transformed a corrupt, inept little department into a smoothly operating agency, with three chief assistants and a couple dozen secretaries.

Stanton's a harsh, irascible administrator. Army contractors are scared to death of him, which I like. No way they can pull anything on him. He pounds his desk, cusses foul-ups with gusto, screams at his aides, and drives 'em as hard as he drives himself. One staff member complained that Stanton "is exceedingly violent, reckless of the rights and feelings of others" and "often acts like a wild man, throwing his arms around." More than once, though, I've gone over there after he's had a hectic day, and found him alone, sobbing, with his head on his desk.

I'll tell you this, Stanton became a loyal friend and is as honest as they come. I can depend on him to tell me the truth. He knows he can protest a decision of mine—disagreement don't bother me, I like to get all the viewpoints I can. Now I'll admit it, I'm slow. My mind's like a piece of steel, hard to scratch anything on it and impossible after you get it there to rub it off. When my mind's made up, Stanton knows it and does what he's told. He's never failed to carry out an order. Yes, he's made a lot of dedicated enemies. Folks come up here and tell me there are a great many men who have all of Stanton's excellent qualities without his defects. All I can say is, "I haven't met 'em yet." Since he took charge of the War Department, I've probably spent more time with him than with any other Cabinet secretary. I go over to the War Department several times a day, to talk with Stanton about the army and military problems, and get the latest telegrams. Next to Seward, who amuses me with his stories, Stanton is my most frequent companion on my late afternoon carriage rides.

I said that Stanton was McClellan's friend. That may have been so, but it didn't blind Stanton to McClellan's tendency toward inertia. Four days after taking office, Stanton told me that McClellan *had* to fight. The Joint Committee on the Conduct of the War, established in December of 'sixty-one to investigate Ball's Bluff, weed out traitors, and put pressure on balking generals and dilatory presidents, had been telling me the same thing. Repeatedly. Ben Wade, the chairman, and Chandler, one of the members, accused me of "murdering" the country with inept commanders and a "want of a distinct policy" about slavery. The other members—three Republicans and two Democrats—backed 'em up on the murdering-the-country part.

One of the original Democrats was Andy Johnson, a Union man from Tennessee. He's strong and hot-tempered, with black hair and deep-set black eyes. Nobody hates slaveholding aristocrats and secesh more—they say he once held off a crowd of 'em with a pistol while he damned secession. Andy Johnson is a capable man, nowhere near the buffoon his enemies make him out to be. But I tell you what, he can match Seward in the cussing department. McClellan inspired Johnson to some pretty creative outbursts. "For five blah blah months," Johnson thundered, "McClellan ain't done a blah blah thing except drill his blah blah army. What a blah blah waste! What that blah blah blah needs is a blah blah kick in his test-ee-cles to get him off his blah blah ass."

The general had been prostrated with typhoid since late December. His aides wouldn't let me see him when I called at his house to find out what his plans were. He refused to send any word about them to me or the Cabinet, and nobody in Washington had any idea what he intended to do. When the Committee came to complain in early January, Wade was in a tirade. Never saw him so mad.

"What do you know about McClellan's plans?" he demanded.

I confessed I didn't know anything.

"That business about typhoid is a Goddamned excuse not to fight," Wade said. "It's a fact that the Army of the Potomac outnumbers the rebels at Manassas, but McClellan will do anything to keep from fighting because he's a Goddamned southern *sympathizer*. We've heard reports that he's scheming to become a dictator once the old Union with slavery is put back. I'm telling you, you've got to get rid of that Goddamned scoundrel."

"If I remove McClellan," I said, "who'll I put in command?"

"Anybody!" Wade stormed.

"Wade, *anybody* will do for you, but not for me. I have to have *somebody*." I added: "I have to use the tool I have."

Attorney General Bates said I ought to *order* McClellan forward. "Command the commanders" was the way he put it. Well, I couldn't very well order a sick man forward. But I did urge Buell in Louisville and Halleck in St. Louis to mount a concerted operation to liberate east Tennessee, where our friends were being hanged and driven to despair. "Delay is ruining us," I said. "It's indispensable for me to have something definite." I asked them to name as early a day as possible when they could move in concert. But it was the same old "can't-do" out there. Buell replied that he couldn't name the day he would be ready to advance. And Halleck insisted that he lacked the resources to take the offensive—it was all he could do to hold Missouri, he said. "It is exceedingly discouraging," I wrote on the back of Halleck's letter. "As everywhere else, nothing can be done."

In great distress, I went to see Quartermaster General Montgomery Meigs and sat down before a fire in his office. "General, what should I do? The people are impatient. Chase has no money and tells me he can't raise any more. The general in chief has typhoid fever. The bottom is out of the tub. What should I do?"

"Maybe you ought to confer with McClellan's division commanders," he said.

I took his advice. On the night of January tenth I summoned Generals McDowell and Franklin and several Cabinet members to a war council in my office. Told 'em I was greatly disturbed about the state of affairs and said I'd been to McClellan's house, but McClellan wouldn't see me. I had to talk to somebody, and that was why I'd called this meeting. If McClellan didn't intend to use the army, I said, I wanted to borrow it. What did the generals think about starting active operations?

Franklin, a friend of McClellan's, suggested a move against Richmond by the rivers to the east of the enemy capital. McDowell, however, favored an early advance against Manassas, and I agreed. A few days later I told Browning I was thinking of taking the field myself.

On January thirteenth, in the midst of my many cares (an empty treasury, the War Department scandals), I sent a joint communiqué to Halleck and Buell in which I set forth my general idea of the war and how it ought to be fought. I drew on the strategical studies from the congressional library I'd been reading and amplified what I'd been saying about concerted action since Bull Run. "We have the *greater* numbers," I said, "and the enemy has the *greater* facility of concentrating forces upon points of collision. We must fail, unless we can find some way of making our advantage an overmatch for *his*. This can only be done by menacing him with superior forces at *different* points, at the *same* time; so that we can safely attack one or both, if he makes no change; and if he *weakens* one to *strengthen* the other, forbear to attack the strengthened one, but seize and hold the weakened one, gaining so much." Applying the principle to the West, I said that Halleck should menace Columbus and downriver generally, while Buell menaced Bowling Green and east Tennessee. If the enemy concentrated at Bowling Green, it would leave Columbus exposed to Halleck and east Tennessee exposed to Buell, and one or both could be seized.

That same day—the very day, in fact, that I called Stanton to the War Office—I summoned several generals to the Executive Mansion for another talk. This time the general of all our armies himself showed up, like a sickly apparition. He said he'd been told about the previous meeting and believed there was a conspiracy afoot among his subordinates to remove him from command and give the army back to McDowell. He was furious. When McDowell proposed an advance against Manassas, McClellan rudely rejected it. There were whispers, an embarrassing silence. Then Chase and I both asked McClellan what he planned to do.

"I know what I'm doing," he said, looking at me. "If you have confidence in me, it's not necessary that I entrust my designs to the judgment of others. If, however, your confidence is so slight that you require the approval of others, then I suggest you replace me with someone who has your full confidence. No general in command of an army would willingly submit his plans to the judgment of an assembly like this. Some people in this room are incompetent to form a valuable opinion. Others can't keep a secret"—he looked straight at me when he said that. "So that anything made known to them would soon spread over Washington and become known to the enemy. I decline to give further information to this meeting, unless the president gives me the order in writing and assumes the responsibility of the result."

I tell you, that arrogant little rooster tried my patience. He did allow that operations in Kentucky took precedence over those in the East, yet typically refused to elaborate. That was enough for Seward. He stood, put on his coat, and said with a laugh, "Well, Mr. President, I think the meeting had better break up. I don't see that we're likely to get much out of General McClellan." Still, I was encouraged by his hint of action in Kentucky and assured the general that he still had my confidence.

Two days later, McClellan went before the Joint Committee, and Wade and Chandler accused him of "infernal, unmitigated cowardice." By then, Stanton had added his voice to the clamor for McClellan to move. But the only sign of movement in the eastern theater was an army-navy expedition under Brigadier General Ambrose E. Burnside, a tall, easygoing Rhode Islander who owns the bushiest set of side-whiskers of anybody in the army. With McClellan's approval, Burnside had assembled an amphibious division of twelve thousand men at Annapolis and in January had set off with a mighty armada of eighty ships, bound for the North Carolina coast. But the last we heard, in late January, was that high winds had stalled the fleet somewhere off Pamlico Sound.

By the end of the month, with all our major armies still inert, I lost all patience with my three principal generals and decided to "command the commanders." On my own hook, without consulting anybody, I issued General War Order No. 1, directing the Army of the Potomac, the army at and about Fort Monroe, the army in western Virginia, the army in Kentucky, the army and flotilla at Cairo, and the naval force in the Gulf of Mexico, to begin simultaneous operations against the insurgents, all movements to commence on or before February twenty-second, which was Washington's birthday. In Special War Order No. 1, issued February third, I specifically instructed McClellan to seize and occupy the railroad at Manassas Junction.

That broke the seal on his mouth. He marched in here and said, with "all due respect," that he preferred his own plan to mine. And what might that plan be? I asked. With a sigh, the general of all our armies at last revealed his plan of operations. "A frontal attack against the rebels at Manassas, as you propose, is not feasible. The enemy is too strongly fortified there with superior numbers. What I propose to do is this," he said, and pointed at the large map on the wall of my office. "Take the army down the Potomac to the Chesapeake, then up the Rappahannock to Urbana, land it there, and march on Richmond by the shortest possible land route. The enemy will be forced to fall back from Manassas to defend Richmond, but the Army of the Potomac will get there first. Once I've seized the enemy capital, all Virginia will fall. The enemy will be forced to abandon Tennessee and North Carolina. Then we can launch concerted operations in all theaters, crush out the Deep South, and end the rebellion."

I thought it was crazy. While the army was off on a wild goose chase on the Chesapeake and Rappahannock, the rebel army in Manassas could jump on Washington City. "I can't endorse that plan," I said and pointed in the direction of Manassas. "There, General, is your enemy. And there you will attack him. I order you to do it, no later than February twenty-second."

McClellan was clearly taken aback. "Is this order final? Or can I submit my objections to that plan in writing, and explain why I prefer my plan?" I told him to submit away. Later that same day I sent him a memorandum saying if he could give satisfactory answers to the following questions I would gladly yield my plan to his. First, did his plan not involve a greatly larger expenditure of *time* and *money* than mine? Second, wherein was a victory *more certain* by his plan than mine? Third, wherein was a victory *more valuable* by his plan than mine? Fourth, wouldn't it in fact be *less* valuable, in this, that it would break no great line of the enemy's communications, while mine would? Finally, in case of disaster, wouldn't a safe retreat be more difficult by his plan than mine?

Back came a twenty-one-page letter addressed to Stanton. In it, the general in chief contended once again that "the great advantage possessed by the enemy in the strong central position" he occupied at Manassas rendered an attack there impossible. Then, taking Stanton and me into his full confidence for the first time, he gave a lengthy technical defense of his Urbana plan. I thanked him for being frank with us and yielded my plan to his. Yes, I still had strong reservations about the practicality of that operation, but what did I know? I was an amateur, McClellan was a professional soldier, and so with reluctance I told the general of all our armies to go ahead with his preparations.

A few days later, encouraging news came from Burnside's North Carolina expedition. The flotilla had finally got across Hatteras Inlet and headed for Roanoke Island with all flags flying. On February seventh, sixteen Union warships destroyed a ragged rebel fleet and shelled enemy shore batteries into submission. Then 7,500 assault troops seized the rebel garrison in a stirring bayonet charge, taking some 2,500 prisoners and thirty pieces of artillery. The capture of Roanoke Island made a war hero out of Burnside and set church bells to ringing in triumph in Washington City and throughout the land.

2. DAVIS

The disastrous loss of Roanoke Island gave the invaders a strategic base from which to strike mainland North Carolina and even send an army against Richmond from the South. We were threatened by such a sea of difficulties that I despaired of the success of our cause. Our armies everywhere suffered from a want of men and arms. In January, the governors of South Carolina, Georgia, Florida, and North Carolina had all demanded that I return to them all their state-owned weapons. If such was to be the course of the states, I moaned, then we had better make terms with the Yankees as soon as we could.

One day an officer on Sidney Johnston's staff arrived in Richmond with a long list of complaints from his commander. The Yankees were amassing colossal forces in Kentucky and southern Illinois for offensive operations. Against them Johnston could muster only forty-three thousand men, he said, and they were stretched dangerously thin, holding a four-hundred-mile defensive line from Columbus on the Mississippi eastward across Kentucky to the Cumberland Gap in the Appalachians. Just south of the Kentucky-Tennessee border, Johnston had two stout earthworks, Fort Henry and Fort Donelson, standing guard on the Tennessee and Cumberland rivers respectively, to prevent Yankee invasions along those water routes deep into our heartland. But the forts were short of heavy guns, Johnston's aide said, and indeed his army remained disastrously short of proper weapons of all kinds, and Sidney had sent his aide to apprise me of that.

"My God!" I told the staff officer. "Doesn't General Johnston know that I have neither arms nor reinforcements to send him? He has plenty of men in Tennessee, and they must have arms of some kind—shotguns, rifles, even pikes could be used. He expects the impossible of me. Where am I to get more arms or men for him?" Johnston's aide had the temerity to point out that troops could be shifted from "less important places" such as Charleston, Pensacola, Savannah, or New Orleans. But I cut him off. "Tell my friend General Johnston that I can do nothing for him, that he must rely on his own resources."

Affairs in the West grew worse when a Federal force under George Thomas, a Virginian and a traitor to the South, routed a small Confederate garrison in the battle of Mill Springs in eastern Kentucky. This punctured a hole in Johnston's eastern defensive line, opening a path for the Yankees into eastern Tennessee. If they broke Johnston's western line in Kentucky, all Tennessee would lay exposed, and we would be facing a disaster of catastrophic proportions. I could spare no troops to shore up Johnston's defenses, but I did send him Pierre Beauregard to command his line in western Kentucky. I hoped that this petulant general could better serve our cause in the West. He stopped in Richmond on his way to Kentucky, and I found it curious that his raven hair had turned almost completely white, reportedly because the blockade had cut off the hair dyes he had imported from Europe. I had heard how he had lavishly indulged himself at Centreville, sipping cognac juleps and dining on roast duck with visiting dignitaries such as Prince Jerome Bonaparte of France and the three Cary sisters of Baltimore. He had continued to make a nuisance of himself, too, by sending letters to my congressional enemies proposing grandiose and outrageous strategic plans. Frankly, I was glad to send him out to Kentucky, far away from the ears of my enemies in Richmond.

I was mistaken, however, in thinking that Beauregard could help stave off disaster in the West. Just two days after he reached Bowling Green, we received the news that Fort Henry had fallen.

3 . GRANT

In late January, I'd gone up to St. Louis and asked Halleck for permission to move against Fort Henry on the Tennessee River. "I'll take and hold the fort," I told the general, who stared at me with watery, bulging eyes. Forts Henry and Donelson on the nearby Cumberland held the center of the rebel line in Kentucky, I pointed out. Capture Henry, and Union gunboats could penetrate clear to Muscle Shoals, Alabama. I started to elaborate further, but Halleck cut me short as if my plan was preposterous.

"And in any case, General Grant, all of this relates to the business of the general commanding the department," meaning Halleck. "When he wishes to consult *you* on the subject of an offensive movement, he will notify you."

Went back to Cairo feeling like I'd been kicked. But I wasn't going to give up. Had the full support of Commodore Foote, who wired Halleck that "Grant and myself are of opinion that Fort Henry on the Tennessee can be carried with four ironclad gunboats and troops. Have we your authority to move for that purpose?" A few days later I wired Halleck myself, thinking he couldn't cut off an argument by telegraph: "In view of the large force now concentrating in this district and the feasibility of the plan I would respectfully suggest the propriety of subduing Fort Henry and holding the position. If this is not done soon there is but little doubt that the defenses on both the Tennessee and Cumberland rivers will be materially strengthened. From Fort Henry it will be easy to operate either on the Cumberland, only twelve miles distant, Memphis, or Columbus."

Halleck finally gave his approval, not because of my telegraph, but because the president had ordered him and all the other Federal forces to move in concert, and because of a report that Beauregard was on his way to Kentucky with fifteen regiments of reinforcements. It was snowing in Cairo when Halleck's order to "take & hold Fort Henry" arrived, and it threw my headquarters into pandemonium. Staff officers tossed their hats into the air and kicked 'em when they came down. Rawlins, my adjutant general, was so excited he uttered some choice expletives and pounded the wall with his fist. I told 'em they'd better quiet down or they'd alert the rebels at Columbus that something was up.

February second, I took a convoy of twelve thousand troops up the Ohio to Paducah, where we picked up three thousand more. Foote commanded the escorting naval force—three wooden gunboats and four new ironclads that looked like giant turtles. That was their nickname, Turtles. They were long and wide, with sloping flat sides plated with iron two and a half inches thick. Each of them monsters carried twelve to fourteen heavy cannon—nine- and ten-inch guns, twelve-, thirty-two-, and forty-two–pounders. Looked to me like they could pulverize all of Chicago.

From Paducah, we steamed southward on the Tennessee to the Kentucky-Tennessee border. As we neared Fort Henry, which stood on the east bank of the river, just inside the Tennessee line, I went ahead on the ironclad *Essex* to look for a good landing spot and draw enemy fire to test the range of their guns. With a sweep of my glass, I saw that the fort occupied a bend in the river, which gave the guns in the water batteries a direct fire downstream, in our direction. The camp outside the fort was entrenched, with rifle pits and outworks. According to our intelligence, the fort had seventeen heavy guns, eleven on the river side, and a garrison of about 2,800 men.

Suddenly, the fort opened fire with solid shot, which fell short of the *Essex*, kicking up spouts of water. Then the enemy fired a rifled cannon—we could tell because its shell made a wild shrieking sound as it hurtled through the air. One shell hit the *Essex*, ripping through the deck close to where I was standing with Captain William D. "Dirty Bill" Porter. It was another close call for Grant. The *Essex* pulled back, out of range of that deadly gun. When the flotilla came up, I had the army disembark at a point three miles north of Henry and encamp for the night. I wrote Julia that the sight of our campfires on the riverbank was beautiful but tomorrow would come the tug of war.

On the flagship, *Cincinnati*, Foote and I went over our plan of battle. While the gunboats shelled Henry's water batteries, my troops would invest the fort on the landward side. McClernand's division—Brigadier General John McClernand, a horse-faced politician from Illinois—would complete the investment by marching around behind the fort and cutting off the garrison's route of escape.

A hard rain was falling, which meant miserable marching conditions for my infantry. Foote took note of it. "General," he said, "I'll have the fort in my possession before you get your troops into position."

It rained all night, but by late morning of the sixth the weather had cleared and McClernand set off on what we calculated would be an eight-mile march to get in the rear of the fort. Meanwhile Foote's gunboats attacked Henry with the ironclads in front, four abreast, belching smoke and fire from the guns in their bows. The enemy's water batteries answered with their eleven heavy guns, until the entire front was ablaze with flame. Shells and solid shot rained down on the gunboats with a roar like continuous thunder, the heavy shot shattering the plating on the ironclads "as if it were putty," as one sailor said. The *Essex* was the worst hit. A solid shot, weighing 128 pounds, pierced its casemate and slammed into the middle boiler, which exploded in a blast of scalding water and steam that struck one man in the face, killing him instantly, and scalded the pilot and twenty-seven other sailors to death.

The gunboats, however, gave better than they got, knocking out four enemy cannon and hurling projectiles right through the earth embankments. The enemy commander, finding himself with only a few guns that could fight, was forced to surrender the fort, but not before the bulk of the garrison escaped to Fort Donelson on the Cumberland, twelve miles to the east. They got away because McClerand's columns, slowed by swollen streams and virtually impassable roads, failed to complete the investment in time to cut off their escape. Even so, the navy had won a decisive victory, and I rode down to the river to congratulate Foote.

I wired Halleck: "Fort Henry is ours. The gunboats have proven themselves well able to resist a severe cannonading." Annoyed that the garrison had got away, I added a boast: "I shall take and destroy Fort Donelson on the eighth and return to Fort Henry." Then a quick note to Julia about our victory. "I am not hurt," I assured her. "This is news enough for tonight. I have been writing until my fingers are tired and therefore you must excuse haste and a bad pen. I have written to you every day so far. Kiss the children for me. Kisses for yourself. Ulys."

Donelson was an even bigger prize than Henry: it was the gateway to Nashville, the Tennessee capital and a key rebel military center on the banks of the Cumberland. I was confident I could take the fort and was raring to attack, but heavy downpours flooded the country, rendering the roads utterly impassable for wagons and artillery. On top of that, Foote had to take three of the ironclads back to Cairo for repairs. The wooden gunboats, meantime, went on a raid up the Tennessee: burned the Memphis & Ohio Railroad bridge, destroyed three rebel steamers, and spread terror clear into

Alabama. Locked in by high water and weakened by the absent gunboats, my army wasn't able to seize Donelson on the eighth.

Next day, with my staff and a regiment of cavalry, I reconnoitered Donelson, which was located on high ground above the western side of the Cumberland and surrounded by an entrenched camp. My glass revealed batteries in place in the side of the river bluff and the outer entrenchments. Enemy strength, we believed, was sixty-five guns and twenty-one thousand men, which made it one of the strongest forts in the country. According to our intelligence, Gideon Pillow was the commander. I remembered him from Mexico and thought him unaggressive. "General Pillow," I told my staff, "will not come out of his works to fight."

It was imperative that we attack Donelson before Pillow was reinforced. But I couldn't move until the gunboats rejoined us, and I chafed with impatience. The wooden gunboats returned late on the tenth. When word came, on the twelfth, that Foote was on the way with the ironclads and reinforcements for my army, I gave the order to advance at once. Some fifteen thousand infantry marched in double columns across the broken, hilly countryside to Fort Donelson, drove in the rebel pickets, and took positions on the heights commanding the fort on the land or western side. By the end of the following day, we had the fort completely invested on the landward side, with all our artillery in place. Our reconnaissance, however, reported that the enemy had been heavily reinforced during the previous night, putting his total strength at not less than thirty thousand men. My brave little army, with a longer line of communication, now besieged a garrison twice its size. Frankly, I didn't give a hoot that the Johnnies outnumbered us, or who was now in command of the fort. Once the gunboats came up, I meant to attack.

Foote arrived during the night of the thirteenth and next morning I rode down to see him with my staff. We found the squat, menacing ironclads and two wooden gunboats tied up two miles downriver from the fort. I was confident of an easy victory, certain that the gunboats would pound Donelson into submission, as they had Fort Henry. It occurred to me that today was Valentine's Day and it made me miss my Julia.

That afternoon, as my staff and I watched from a point close to the river, the four ironclads and two wooden gunboats bore down on the fort with flags flying. But when they closed the range and opened fire with their forward guns, they were no match for the enemy's powerful cannons, which blasted 'em with heavy shells and solid shot. The heavy iron shot produced a peculiar ringing sound when it struck the gunboats' metal armor. To our horror, Foote's flagship, the *St. Louis*, was hit repeatedly—fifty-nine times, we learned later—and was knocked out of action. The *Louisville*, too, was so badly shot up that she drifted aimlessly downriver. The remaining two ironclads also suffered heavy damage and withdrew. The attack had failed. I couldn't believe it. So much for the idea that ironclads could reduce a well-armed fort.

During the night, Foote sent a message that he wanted to see me, and I set out on horseback for the landing downriver where his boats were anchored. It was about four in the morning, and the air was extremely cold, the ground frozen solid, patches of snow in the woods. I felt badly for my men, knew they were suffering in their meager blankets, and it made me more impatient than ever to get on with the job. As I rode along, I heard a muffled *thump, thump* behind me, heard it again. Was that cannon fire? Maybe a skirmish developing. When I reached the landing, I took a small boat out to the *St. Louis*, where Foote, who was wounded in the arm and ankle, gave me the bad news.

"Have to take all four ironclads back to Cairo for repairs," he said. "Hope to be back in ten days with mortar boats and the *Thomas Hart Benton*, the most powerful boat in my command. I suggest you have your men entrench till then."

Frustrated me. He was proposing *a siege*. "Foote," I said, "I want to take that fort. With the reinforcements, I've got more than twenty-five thousand men on the heights up there, just itching to attack. Can't the gunboats stay long enough to support us?"

He thought it over and finally agreed to leave me the wooden gunboats and the least-damaged ironclad, the *Carondelet*. But the other ironclads, he insisted, had to be repaired before they could fight again. One ironclad and three obsolete wooden gunboats wouldn't do us much good, but how could I argue? The *St. Louis* was a wreck, so were the two other ironclads. Wounded sailors, some badly mangled, lay groaning on the *St. Louis*'s decks. I headed back to shore all upset. It looked like we were in for a siege.

At the landing, Captain Hillyer of my staff was waiting for me with terrible news. The enemy, he said, had attacked McClernand's division, which held our right, and his men were in full retreat. "Let's go," I said, and we set out at full gallop. *Should've anticipated this*, I thought. *So dang busy thinking about attacking the Johnnies, didn't think about them attacking me. Bet it's a breakout attempt, bet they're trying to fight their way to the Dover Road, so they can escape to Nashville. Not if I can help it.* We spurred our horses faster over the frozen road.

When we got to the left end of our line, I located General Charles F. Smith, commanding this sector, and told him to prepare his division for an attack. Then we rode in the direction of the gunfire and that unmistakable wildcat screech of the rebel yell. We trotted by remnants of McClernand's division and found him and General Lew Wallace standing in a clearing, with gunsmoke swirling over the trees in their front. Wallace's division held the center of our line.

"What happened?" I asked McClernand.

"Enemy attacked in overwhelming force, broke through my line. At least fifteen hundred casualties. Some of my men are trying to rally behind Wallace's division, but the escape route to the south's wide open." *So is the road to our rear,* I thought. *If the rebels aim to stay here and fight us, it could be a disaster.* I had some papers in my hand and twisted them violently.

"Gentlemen," I said, "the position on the right must be retaken."

We rode across the battleground and the situation was not so bad as I feared. The rebels had driven McClernand's troops back into Wallace's line and had almost turned our right; but Wallace had actually checked the rebel advance. I had no doubt the enemy was reforming to renew the attack.

Many of McClernand's men had run out of ammunition and had withdrawn out of rifle range. I rode over and talked to them. They described the enemy charge and said the rebels had haversacks and knapsacks, too, as if they meant to stay out and fight.

"Are the haversacks filled?"

There were prisoners nearby. An examination of their haversacks showed they had rations for three days.

Just as I'd thought. "They mean to cut their way out," I said. "They don't have enough rations to stay here and fight us. Whichever side attacks now will win the battle. The rebels will have to be quick to beat me. We're going to counterattack. With everything we have."

Seize the initiative. That wins battles every time. I was sure the enemy had weakened his right in order to concentrate his forces for the attack on his left. Therefore we would attack his right before he could redeploy. *Glad I had Smith prepare his division for just such a move.* Headed back to find McClernand and Wallace with one of McClernand's colonels. As we passed knots of soldiers, the colonel called out my instructions: "Fill your cartridge-boxes quick and get into line. The enemy's trying to escape and must be stopped." They did as they were told. All they wanted was for somebody to give 'em a command.

I found Wallace and told him we would counterattack. "Hit the enemy in the front with all the men you can get into line. Reform McClernand's broken units and throw 'em in as well."

Then I galloped back around to Smith's headquarters. "General Smith," I said, "all has failed on our right. You must attack and take Fort Donelson."

"General, I'll do it," he said.

A tall, straight, broad-shouldered man with a ruddy face and a swooping, snow white mustache, Smith rode out ahead of his division and waving his saber overhead led 'em forward with bayonets fixed. It was a sight. They caught the rebels completely by surprise and broke right through their works without firing a shot. By nightfall of the fifteenth, Smith's division was camped inside the rebel lines. Meanwhile Wallace had mounted a successful attack of his own, sweeping the startled rebels in his front clear back to their trench lines.

That night I rode with an aide back across the battleground on our right. A full moon was out, and it cast an eerie glow on dead soldiers of both sides, lying all around. We came to a farmhouse hospital, where corpses were lined up in rows. "Let's get away from this dreadful place," I said. "I guess this work is part of the devil in us all." We rode past wounded men who were limping, crawling, or hobbling on makeshift crutches toward the rear. "Man's inhumanity to man," I muttered, "makes countless thousands mourn." I spent that night in a log house, sleeping on a mattress on the kitchen floor.

Before daylight, General Smith brought me a note from General Simon Boliver Buckner, now in command of Fort Donelson: "I propose the appointment of commissioners to agree upon terms of capitulation of the forces and fort under my command."

I handed the note to Smith. "What should I say to this, General?"

"No terms to the damned rebels!"

I laughed and wrote a brief reply: "No terms except an unconditional and immediate surrender can be accepted. I propose to move immediately upon your works." I signed it "U. S. Grant" and gave it to Smith to pass on to the enemy messenger.

Just as my army was preparing to attack all along the line, a second note came from Buckner. "Sir: The distribution of the forces under my command, incident to an unexpected change of commanders, and the overwhelming force under your command, compel me, notwithstanding the brilliant success of the Confederate arms yesterday, to accept the ungenerous and unchivalrous terms which you propose."

I accepted Buckner's surrender and had breakfast with him inside the fort. We'd been friends before the war, had attended West Point together; he'd loaned me money when I was poor and down on my luck, after the trouble in California. He wore a coat with a long cape and gold lace on the sleeves, and looked stouter than I remembered him, with graying hair and whiskers.

"We intended to fight our way out yesterday," he said, "but your attack foiled us. After I offered to surrender, Generals Floyd and Pillow escaped upriver on transports, taking part of the garrison with them. Nathan Forrest also escaped with another thousand men, across the flooded backwater south of the fort." I asked him how many men he was surrendering. "Don't know for sure. Not fewer than twelve thousand, nor I think more than fifteen thousand." He also gave up about twenty thousand stands of arms, forty-eight pieces of artillery, seventeen heavy guns, two to four thousand horses, and large quantities of commissary stores. Our total casualties came to just over 2,000, theirs about 2,500.

I telegraphed Halleck: "We have taken Ft. Donelson." Next day it was on the front page of the papers. Halleck wired me that I had a new command: the District of West Tennessee, limits not defined. Bill Sherman took my old command at Cairo. I wrote my Julia: "There is but little doubt that Fort Donelson was the hardest fought battle on the continent. I was extremely lucky to be the commanding officer. From the accounts received here it must have created a perfect furor through the North."

4 · LIVERMORE

In Chicago the news was on everyone's lips. "Fort Donelson is taken! Our boys are victorious!" Cannon boomed, church bells rang, flags flew, people danced in the streets. But behind all this delirium a civilian corps of men and women were quietly and efficiently addressing the ugly aftermath of battle: the plight of the wounded at Donelson. The surgeons of the government were few in number, and its medical supplies utterly inadequate to the occasion, and it had to turn to the heroes and heroines of the home front to make up the shortages. The Chicago Board of Trade immediately raised $3,000 for the purchase of blankets, winter clothing, and medical stores, and a committee of citizens started for the scene of suffering. Seven volunteer physicians rode down on the first train that left Chicago after the fall of Donelson was known. Our Chicago Sanitary Commission had been sending supplies to its depot in Cairo for weeks, at the rate of a thousand dollars' worth daily, and it continued to do this for weeks afterward.

To evacuate the wounded, the Chicago and St. Louis sanitary offices fitted up floating hospitals, or "hospital steamers," loaded them with stores, and sent them on their errands of mercy. On board were volunteer nurses in the form of ministers, merchants, lawyers, and women, who were bent on challenging the proscription of women from the battlefield. Their motto was: "It is better to *heal* a wound than to make one." The first relief boat to reach Fort Donelson was *The City of Memphis*, but the *Allen Collier*, dispatched by the Cincinnati branch, soon joined her.

Jane Hoge and I remained at our Chicago headquarters, forwarding stores and supplies to the valiant hospital crews at the front. Thus we did not witness the horrors of the Donelson battlefield. But Dr. Newberry did. The secretary of the Sanitary Commission's Western Department, he reported what the public never saw and what the newspaper stories almost always left out. "We found ourselves surrounded by all the realities and many of the horrors of war," he wrote. "The batteries, the entrenchments, the white tents of our victorious army which covered the hills for miles around, the battlefield with its unburied dead, strewn with arms, clothing and accouterments, everywhere showing traces of the death storm by which it had been swept. The wounded who were being brought in on litters or in ambulances demanded and received our first thought and attention." Soon, he said, each hospital boat overflowed with some 250 wounded, many with grotesque wounds. They lay side by side on the hard decks and floors, shivering in the February cold.

They tell a story about one woman who turned up at Donelson, bearing stores from the Soldiers' Aid Society of Galesburg, Illinois. "It was after the battle that an officer, on looking out of his tent, near midnight, noticed a light flitting singularly about the hillside; like a will-o'-the-wisp, now moving, now standing still—moving again, and again stationary. He sent a servant to see what it meant. It proved to be Mrs. Bickerdyke, groping among the sad, still forms, that were left on the field for dead. She had a lantern in her hand, which she used for a narrower examination of the dead faces, as she stooped down, and turned them toward her. She was uneasy with the thought that some of them might be yet alive." Mary Ann Bickerdyke would become a legend in the western war as a Sanitary Commission nurse and relief worker.

The hospital boats evacuated the wounded to general military hospitals in St. Louis, Cairo, and Mound City. Mrs. Hoge and I saw these asylums of suffering when the Sanitary Commission sent us on an inspection tour, to find out how the general hospitals might be better supplied and prepared for the next battle. We would never forget what our eyes registered. In the first hospital we visited, that in St. Louis, a long ward stretched before us, containing more than eighty of the most fearfully wounded men, some with bloody stumps where limbs had been. The sickening odor of blood and healing wounds almost overpowered us. In the nearest bed lay a young man whose entire lower jaw had been shot away, and his tongue with it. The surgeon came to dress his wounds, and asked me to assist him. The process of healing had drawn down the upper part of the face, so that when the ghastly wound was concealed by plasters and bandages, the exposed portion of the face was badly distorted. But when the surgeon removed the bandages to examine the wound, its horrible nature became apparent, and I felt so sick that I had to leave the room.

Three times I returned, and each time saw some new horror, smelled some more nauseating odor, and I had to leave again.

"A great many people can't stay in hospitals, or render any service in them, they are so affected by the sights and smells," said the surgeon. "I wouldn't try to do anything here if I were in your place."

Perhaps that was a polite way of saying this was no place for a lady. Well, I vowed I was not going to shrink from the sight of misery. Holding myself in iron control, I forced myself to remain in the ward without getting sick. In the second bed, a rebel prisoner, a mere boy, lay dying. Both legs had been amputated above the knees, inflammation and fever had set in, and he was wild with delirium—singing, gesticulating, babbling. There was nothing I could do for him.

Another poor fellow had the unmistakable look of death settling in. He struggled painfully for breath, and large drops of sweat stood out on his forehead.

"You're suffering a great deal," I said.

"Yes! Yes!" he gasped. "I am, I am! but not in body. I can bear that. I don't mind pain—but I can't die. *I can't die!*"

"Maybe you won't die. While there is life there is hope."

"Oh, no, I can't live—I know it—there's no chance for me. I'm going to *die* and I'm *afraid*," he gasped, "*afraid to die.*"

I went to the surgeon, who was still in the ward, and asked about the poor fellow's chances. "None," the surgeon said. "He was horribly cut up when he got here. One leg had been amputated, the other had had two amputations, the last one was taken off between the knee and hip. The right arm had been broken, a caisson had crushed the lower left arm, and he'd been shot twice through the abdomen. Wounds in the abdomen are almost always mortal. He seemed an utterly hopeless case. But he's pulled along from day to day, staying alive somehow. But now gangrene has set in—smell that sweet sickening odor? That's gangrene. It defies treatment. He'll be dead in a few hours. All you can do is help him die easily."

I went back to his bedside. "I ain't fit to die," he rasped. "I've lived an awful life—that's why I'm afraid to die. I'll go to hell." I pulled up a campstool, sat down, and put my hand on his shoulders. "Stop screaming. Be quiet. This excitement is cutting your life short. If you must die, die like a man, not like a coward. Be still and listen to me." To combat his fear of death and sense of guilt, I assured him that however great his sins, God would forgive them, since he was penitent. When that seemed not to register, an attendant fetched the hospital steward, who was a Methodist minister, and the steward prayed with the dying boy and sang hymns with him, *Come, sing to me of Heaven, For I'm about to die.* I started to leave, but the dying man whispered: "Don't go. Stay. Please." I stayed with him to the end, then watched as his lifeless and mutilated body was carried to the dead house.

Mrs. Hoge and I moved on to Cairo, where a half dozen regimental hospitals had been improvised in sheds, homes, and carriage houses. Compressed within their narrow limits was more filth and discomfort, neglect and suffering, than would have sufficed to defile and demoralize ten times as much space. The fetid odor of healing wounds, typhoid fever, erysipelas, dysentery, and measles was rendered more nauseating by unclean beds and unwashed bodies; while from the kitchen, which opened into the hospital wards, came the smell of boiling meat and coffee, befouling still more the air of the unventilated apartments.

I doubted that I would ever become entirely habituated to the shocking sights that result from the wicked business men call war.

5 · LINCOLN

Grant's victories made him a bigger war hero than Burnside and Wilkes put together. People who read about Grant in the newspapers decided that his initials, U.S., must stand for Unconditional Surrender. What did "Unconditional Surrender" Grant accomplish? Just this: the capture of the two forts cracked the center of the enemy line in Kentucky—exposed both his flanks and opened the Cumberland and Tennessee rivers to Federal thrusts deep into the heart of the so-called Confederacy. The rebels were forced to abandon their entire Kentucky line and fall back into Tennessee. Everywhere Union men were cheering: "Columbus, the Gibraltar of the West, is ours, and Kentucky is free."

Trouble was, Halleck from his desk in St. Louis tried to discredit Grant. It's pretty clear now that Halleck had it in for "Unconditional Surrender," probably out of jealousy. Don't get me wrong: I admired Halleck—scholarly soldier, taught at the Academy, wrote a couple military treatises, translated Jomini's *Political and Military Life of Napoleon* from the French, all of which earned him the sobriquet "Old Brains." But his treatment of Grant cost me more than one night's sleep. The trouble started after Grant took Fort Henry. Old Brains tried to get McClellan to remove U.S. from command and give the river expedition to Buell, the same Buell who had the "can't-do" when it came to liberating east Tennessee. After Donelson fell, Halleck begged McClellan to put him, Old Brains, in overall command of the entire western theater, saying, "I ask this for Forts Henry and Donelson." Meaning, I suppose, that the campaign was *his* accomplishment. I tell you, Halleck knew no shame. A subsequent telegram from him gave Smith all the credit for the capture of the second fort. "Brig. Gen. Charles F. Smith, by his coolness and bravery at Fort Donelson when the battle was against us, turned the tide and carried the enemy's outworks. Make him a major-general. You can't get a better one."

Stanton and I disagreed with Halleck, and we first promoted

Grant to major general, then we promoted Smith and the other divisional brigadiers in Grant's command. This ensured that Grant would remain the senior officer in his army. February nineteenth, Congressman Washburne telegraphed the news to Grant: "You are appointed major general."

The next day a cloud passed over the Executive Mansion, dimming the luster of Grant's triumph for those of us who lived there. While Grant was pounding the river garrisons, both of our boys, Willie and Tad, had come down sick. The physician said not to worry. It was just a fever. Both ought to recover soon enough. But Willie's fever grew worse. Mary and I were both anxious and upset. She'd planned an extravagant dinner, complete with martial music from the marine band, in the main to show off her remodeling of the Executive Mansion. When we first moved in, she'd declared it a national disgrace—walls were dirty, furniture all broken down, carpets stained with tobacco juice. Over the winter she'd redecorated the place with imported drapes, custom-made carpets, and ornately carved furniture, installed by a small army of workmen. Under her watchful eye, servants painted the walls, installed new gaslights in the rooms, and scrubbed the windows until they were spotless. She was proud of her work. Now, she said, the mansion was a fit place for the president of the United States.

Congress had awarded her twenty thousand dollars to cover the renovations, but she wound up overspending that sum by almost seven thousand. I was furious and refused to pay the excess bills with government funds. "I'll pay it out of my pocket first. It would stink in the nostrils of the American people to have it said that the president of the United States had approved a bill overruning an appropriation of twenty thousand dollars for *flub dubs* for this damned old house, when the soldiers can't have blankets."

Congress solved the problem by burying an extra appropriation in the White House budget for 'sixty-two. But poor Mary. The people she wanted to impress—the high-nosed socialites who'd called her a country hussy—now gossiped about how extravagant she was. Well, she certainly loved to entertain and on a big scale—that was what the first lady was supposed to do, she said—which was why she'd scheduled the huge dinner party I was talking about. With Willie so sick, we wanted to cancel, but it was too late: the invitations had already gone out. The doctor told us not to worry. Go on, he said, enjoy yourselves. You can send for me if Willie gets any worse. So we went ahead with it.

When Mary swept out of her dressing room wearing a white satin dress trimmed in black lace with long tails, I was standing with my back to the fire, my hands folded behind my back. "Whew!" I said, "our cat has a long tail tonight." I nodded in the direction of her bare neck, exposed bosom, and naked arms. "Mother, it's my opinion, if some of that tail was nearer the head, it would be in better style." She made a face at me. Then we went downstairs to our guests. But throughout the evening either she or I would slip away to check on Willie.

By the next morning he was really bad, burning up with fever, eyes had a vacant look, face wet with sweat. More physicians came, but said it was no use; the boy was dying. All Mary and I could do was bathe his face with a wet cloth and whisper something comforting to him. It hurt to look at him, knowing there was nothing I could do. He was just twelve years old, smart beyond his years, liked nothing better than to curl up in a chair in Mary's room and read a book of poetry, or write verse on a writing pad, like I used to do when I was a boy in Indiana. He had a good sense of history, too—kept a scrapbook of important events, pasting in news clippings about my inauguration, the war, and the deaths of important people like Colonel Baker. He was such a gentle, affectionate boy, our Willie. Mary said she depended on him—"he'll be the hope and stay of my old age," she said. But in his room now, wiping his face with the cloth, I knew his time was near. Mary and I stayed by his bedside all day and all that night, one of us leaving only to give little Tad his medicine.

Finally, on February twentieth, at five o'clock in the afternoon, with Mary and me at his bedside, Willie died. Mary collapsed in a convulsion of hysterical weeping, and Lizzie Keckley, her black seamstress, led her away. I looked down at the little body that had been my son. "My poor boy," I whispered, "he was too good for this earth . . . but then we loved him so." Numb with grief, I found myself going down the corridor to Nicolay's office. "Well, Nicolay, my boy's gone—he's actually gone." Then I started crying and headed to Tad's room. I lay down with him and tried to explain that Willie was dead and would no longer play with him.

"Speak to me either?"

"Or speak to you either." Then he also started to cry.

The Brownings came at once and made all the funeral arrangements. Miss Dix, head of the government nurses, also called and asked if she could help. The doctor said we needed a real nurse for

Tad, and I asked Miss Dix if she could recommend one. She said without hesitation that there was one in her nursing corps who would give us "perfect satisfaction." She named Rebecca Pomroy.

"Oh yes, I've heard of her," I said. "Will you get her for me?"

When Mrs. Pomroy arrived, I showed her to Tad's room. Later, when the two of us were alone, I asked about her own family. "I have a husband and two children in the other world, and a son on the battlefield. One of my departed children was also named Willie."

I asked her, "Did you always feel that you could say, 'Thy will be done'?"

"No, not till the Lord found me at a camp meeting. Then I could say it."

"This is the hardest trial of my life," I said.

"Thousands of people are praying for you every day."

"I'm thankful for that."

But alone, I kept asking, "Why, God? Why Willie?" And all I could think of was the poem "Mortality," and its theme that all people in this world are destined to die, even my gentle Willie.

We buried him in a cemetery in Georgetown. Poor Mary was too distraught to attend the funeral and remained locked in her room for three months. You could hear her sobbing and crying out for Willie all over the Mansion. I did what I could to soothe her; so did Mrs. Pomroy and Lizzie Keckley, but Mary was inconsolable. I feared for her sanity—warned her she had to control her grief or it would drive her mad. Gradually she improved a little. But the mere mention of Willie's name would set her to crying again. She couldn't bear any memory of him and gave away all his toys and clothes and his scrapbook and everything else he'd owned and everything that reminded her of him and she never again went into the guest room where he'd died or the Green Room where he'd laid in state in his little metal coffin. She dropped all but the most vital social functions and lived in near seclusion in her room, finding a little solace in writing her friends back home about our "furnace of affliction." "But sometimes," she told me, "when I'm all alone, I realize again that *he isn't with us*, and the anguish of the thought overcomes me for days."

That same realization hurt me, too, once so badly I shut myself up in my office, wouldn't see anyone, and gave way to the hurt. Finally, I found what comfort I could in the doctrine of fatalism in which my long-dead mother had gloried. "Nothing can hinder the execution of the designs of Providence. What is to be will be and we can do nothing about it." That's the creed. I reckon I've believed it all my life. Hamlet had it right: "There is a divinity that shapes our ends"—mine, dear Willie's, everybody's. I know I'm an instrument of Providence. I'm conscious every minute that all I am and all I have is subject to the control of a Higher Power. We are put here for a purpose and taken away for a purpose. Nothing we can do about it.

I also found escape in work. Even the administrative tedium I despised helped dull the pain for a while. And of course there was always the war, the cruel war, demanding almost all my energy and time. I conferred with Stanton about the situation in the West, and on my instruction, Stanton wired Halleck that I still expected him and Buell "to cooperate fully and zealously with each other." They didn't cooperate, of course, but Buell, prodded into action by my General War Order No. 1, did move against Nashville in late February, forcing the enemy to evacuate the Tennessee capital. Now we controlled a major city on the Cumberland River from which to strike east, west, or south.

6. DAVIS

The fall of Forts Henry and Donelson shocked and sickened me. Reading the reports of the Donelson fiasco, I was unable to believe that a large army of our people had surrendered without a desperate effort to cut their way through the investing forces. The explanations offered up by Floyd and Pillow I deemed "unsatisfactory" and I relieved both generals from command. The loss of the Henry and Donelson caused Sidney Johnston's entire defensive line in Kentucky to collapse and led to a string of evacuations and retreats that made me ill. When the approach of two hostile armies, Buell's and Grant's, forced Sidney Johnston to abandon Nashville—it was either that or sacrifice his army—we lost to the enemy an invaluable military, industrial, and railroad center, a gunpowder plant, and enormous quantities of supplies we could not replace.

The day I learned of Donelson, February twenty-second, I was inaugurated as president of the permanent government of the Confederacy and gave my Inaugural Address outside the Capitol, before George Washington's statue, during a cold, hard rain. Though quite ill, I had resolved to go through with the ceremony because the people needed me to be strong in the wake of our misfortunes. Gazing out over a crowd of umbrellas, I spoke of how a million men were now standing in hostile array against us, waging war along a frontier of a thousand miles. Yes, we had recently met with serious disasters and the tide for the moment was against us, but the picture had its lights as well as its shadows. This great strife had awakened in our people the highest emotions and qualities of the human soul. It was, perhaps, in the ordination of Providence that we were to be taught the value of our liberties by the price we paid for them. Saying that, I raised my hands and eyes toward the weeping heavens.

At the mansion afterward, Varina complained: "As you stood pale and emaciated, dedicating yourself to the service of the Confederacy, you seemed to be a willing victim going to his own funeral. The idea so affected me, Banny, that I made an excuse, called for my carriage, and came home."

"There are many who would like to see me fail," I said. "My enemies in Congress—Wigfall, Foote, and Toombs especially. Vice President Stephens. Governor Brown of Georgia. John Daniel of the *Richmond Examiner*. Beauregard and Joe Johnston." Indeed, the clamor of abuse and vituperation against the Administration was all but unendurable. The evacuation of Nashville, and the evident intention of Sidney Johnston to retreat still farther, created a panic in the public mind. The press exploded with abusive tirades against the general and me. There were accusations of imbecility, cowardice, and treason. The national House of Representatives created a special committee "to inquire into the military disasters at Fort Henry and Fort Donelson, and the surrender of Nashville to the enemy." The Tennessee congressional delegation grimly waited on me in my office in the Treasury Building, and Senator G. A. Henry, speaking in their behalf and that of the state of Tennessee, requested that Johnston be removed and his department turned over to a competent general.

This exhibition of distrust toward an officer who had no equal pained me deeply. I was wounded by the injustice done to one I had known intimately in peace and in war and believed to be one of the *noblest* men I had ever been associated with. I paused under conflicting emotions, and then merely answered: "If Sidney Johnston is not a general, the Confederacy has none to give you."

From W. M. Brooks of Alabama, who had presided over the state's secession convention, came an abusive letter attacking me for adopting a purely defensive strategy and for having few friends and no defenders in Congress and the army. In the midst of all my vexations and responsibilities, I took the time to sit down at my desk and write Mr. W. M. Brooks a long reply. I acknowledged the error of my attempt to defend the entire Confederacy. As I'd said elsewhere, the government had attempted more than it had the power to achieve. In the effort to protect by our arms the whole of the territory of the Confederate states, seaboard and inland, we had been too exposed to the thrusts of our more numerous foe. But I informed Mr. Brooks that this was less my fault than that of the states. Had the states sent the government enough arms and ammunition in the first place, the attempt to defend the whole of the Confederacy would have been successful, and the battlefield would now be on the *enemy's soil.*

As for my strategy, I said: "You seem to have fallen into the not uncommon mistake of supposing that I have chosen to carry on the war upon a 'purely defensive' system. This is not so. Without military stores, without the workshops to create them, without the power to import them, *necessity* not *choice* has compelled us to occupy strong positions and everywhere to confront the enemy without reserves. The country has supposed our armies more numerous than they are, and our munitions of war more extensive than they have been. I have borne reproach in silence, because to report by an exact statement of facts I would have exposed our weakness to the enemy.

"If, as you inform me, it is 'credibly said' that 'I have scarcely a friend and not a defender in Congress or in the Army,' yet for the sake of our country and its cause I must hope it is falsely so said, as otherwise our fate must be confided to a multitude of hypocrites. When everything is at stake and the united power of the South alone can save us, it is sad to know that men can deal in such paltry complaint and tax their ingenuity to slander."

I had so many responsibilities—military, financial, diplomatic, administrative—that I needed a capable military man at my side, to help me run the War Department and manage and coordinate our defenses. I needed General Lee. Accordingly, on March second, I recalled him from Charleston, and he reported for duty four days later

"Your Excellency," he said.

"Welcome to Richmond, General Lee."

He now wore a white beard, which made him look even more distinguished. Directing him to sit down, I explained what his new duties entailed. "Under my direction, you are to conduct the military operations of our armies. You will function, unofficially, as a sort of military secretary of war. Brigadier-General George Randolph of Virginia will be the new secretary of war, and Judah Benjamin will move to state. You, Randolph, and General Cooper will assist me in devising a defensive strategy, especially for Tennessee and Virginia. We cannot afford further disasters."

The next day, however, brought news of further disaster, this time in the Trans-Mississippi theater. Our forces had already retreated out of Missouri, pursued by a more powerful Federal army. General Earl Van Dorn, now commander of the Trans-Mississippi Department, had tried to check their advance in the battle of Elkhorn Tavern in northwestern Arkansas, near the Missouri border. But he had gone down to defeat and was now falling back southward toward the Arkansas River. I feared that Missouri as well as northern Arkansas were now completely lost to us.

Meanwhile, threatened by overwhelming forces, deficient in arms, wanting in discipline, and inferior in numbers, Sidney Johnston's ragged army had fallen back to Murfreesboro in central Tennessee and was now on its way to Corinth, a vital railroad junction in northwestern Mississippi, which was threatened by the Federal presence on the Tennessee River. I did everything in my power to strengthen Johnston and retrieve our waning forces in the West: I sent him General Braxton Bragg with ten thousand disciplined men from Mobile and Pensacola, informing Sidney that he would find in my friend Bragg a man of the highest administrative capacity. "My confidence in you has never wavered," I told Johnston, "and I hope the public will soon give me credit for judgment rather than to continue to arraign me for obstinacy." My concern for Johnston was so great that I very nearly went out there and took the field with him.

7 . LINCOLN

All our triumphs in the West we owed to Grant. So you can imagine how shocked I was when, on March fourth, Halleck relieved Grant of his command, gave it to Smith, and restricted Unconditional Surrender to Fort Henry—in effect, putting him under arrest—on the grounds that he had disobeyed orders to report the position and strength of his troops. I thought Halleck's action was pretty damned petty. In a series of dispatches to McClellan, which Stanton and I saw, Halleck added more charges—claimed that Grant's army was as "demoralized" after Donelson as McDowell's had been after Bull Run; that he, Halleck, got no reports, returns, or information "of any kind" from Grant; that he sat at Fort Henry smugly satisfied with himself; that he'd left his troops and gone down to Nashville without authority; that he ought to be censured ("he richly deserves it"); and that Smith was "almost the only officer equal to the emergency." Halleck even threw in the "rumor" that Grant had "resumed his former bad habits," meaning he was drinking again.

McClellan fully supported Halleck's action against Grant. "The future success of our cause," he wired St. Louis, "demands that proceedings such as Grant's should at once be checked. Generals must observe discipline as well as private soldiers." Now I tried not to interfere in purely military matters—had no facts to dispute Halleck's claims anyway—but relieving a man like Grant of his army troubled me. It was not the way to win the war.

8 . GRANT

Halleck's telegram fell on me like a bombshell. I was stunned. It didn't make sense. First I'm ordered to command an important expedition, then I'm made major general, and now an order comes directing one of my juniors to take the command while I'm left behind with a small garrison. I was virtually under arrest. Couldn't believe it. Felt disgraced. Miserable. Had tears in my eyes when I showed the telegram to Rawlins, who cussed Halleck to hell and back.

We were on the steamer *Tigress*, anchored in the river by Fort Henry. Despite a severe cold, I'd been planning a major expedition up the Tennessee River to wreck the railroad bridge at Eastport, Mississippi, which would cut rebel connections with the strategic rail center of Corinth. Now Halleck's telegram had taken the expedition away from me and given it to Smith. Only reason Halleck gave for relieving me was: "Why do you not obey my orders to report strength & positions of your command?" What orders? I'd never gotten any such orders. Didn't know what he was talking about.

Halleck elaborated in a second bombshell: "Genl McClellan directs that you report to me daily the numbers and positions of forces under your command. Your neglect of repeated orders to report the strength of your command has created great dissatisfaction, & seriously interfered with military plans. Your going to Nashville without authority & when your presence with your troops was of the utmost importance, was a matter of very serious complaint at Washington, so much so that I was advised to arrest you on your return."

I didn't know who'd complained about me to Washington, but this letter from Halleck hurt to the quick. Couldn't figure out why he had such disposition to find fault with me. He even sent a copy of an anonymous complaint against me—from "a man of integrity and perfectly reliable," Halleck said—that was apparently the basis for the general's severe censure of me.

I wrote Halleck from the *Tigress*: "I have done my very best to obey orders and to carry out the interests of the service. If my course is not satisfactory remove me at once. I do not wish to impede in any way the success of our arms. I have averaged writing more than once a day, since leaving Cairo, to keep you informed of my position; and it is no fault of mine, if you have not received my letters."

Halleck's reply: "There is no letter of yours stating the number & position of your command since the capture of Fort Donelson. Genl McClellan has asked for it repeatedly, but I could not give him the information. He is out of all patience waiting for it."

That made me mad and I let Halleck know it. "You had a better chance of knowing my strength while my command was surrounding Ft. Donelson than I had. Troops were reporting daily by your order. I renew my application to be relieved from further duty in the department." In short, I was inviting a court of inquiry where I would have a chance to defend myself.

At that Halleck totally reversed himself. "You cannot be relieved from your command. There is no good reason for it. I am certain that all which the authorities at Washington ask, is, that you enforce discipline & punish the disorderly. Instead of relieving you, I wish you, as soon as your new army is in the field, to assume the immediate command & lead it on to new victories."

I was stunned again. Apparently all was forgiven. Not only did I have my army back, but I was to be reinforced. Hard to believe. I wrote Halleck: "After your telegram enclosing copy of an anonymous letter upon which severe censure was based I felt as though it would be impossible for me to serve longer without a court of inquiry. Your telegram of yesterday however places such a different light upon my position that I will again assume command and give every effort to the success of our cause."

Halleck also sent me a copy of a report he'd sent to Washington exonerating me of the Nashville charge. "Grant did go to Nashville without my permission. I am satisfied, however, from investigation that Genl Grant did this from good intentions and not from a desire to subvert the public interest."

I was grateful that he'd set things right for me with the government, and I told him so. "I most fully appreciate your justness, General, in the part you have taken." Still couldn't figure Halleck—still had a lot of anger toward him—but at least I was off the steamer and back in charge of the Corinth expedition. I wrote Julia: "I want to whip these rebels once more in a big fight and see what will then be said. I suppose such a result would make me a host of enemies."

I moved my field headquarters down to Savannah, a river port on the Tennessee, and began concentrating my army, now called the Army of the Tennessee, at Pittsburg Landing. My objective was the railroad center of Corinth in northeastern Mississippi.

9. LINCOLN

Reckon I had something to do with Halleck's exoneration of Grant. At the least, I thought Grant deserved a fair hearing of the charges against him, and so I had a set of interrogatories wired to Halleck. "By direction of the president, the secretary of war desires you to ascertain and report—Whether General Grant left his command at any time without proper authority, and if so, for how long? Whether he made to you proper reports and returns of his force? Whether he has committed any acts which were unauthorized?" In short, I was telling Halleck to put up or shut up, press formal charges against Grant or drop the whole matter. Next we heard, Grant was back in command of his army and getting up a new campaign, and Halleck was urging him on to new victories.

I was sure Grant would not disappoint. It was McClellan I was worried about. By early March, McClellan still hadn't budged. He put forth the same old excuses: the army wasn't ready for battle yet, his lines of retreat weren't secure yet. Which gave fits to Wade and his Committee on the Conduct of the War. "That son-of-a-bitch is a

Goddamned coward *and* a traitor," was Wade's delicate way of putting it. One day I warned McClellan that there were men who questioned his loyalty, and he became extremely upset, tears welling up in his eyes. "Your Excellency, I resent the imputations upon my loyalty." I assured him that *I* didn't doubt his loyalty. I didn't think he was a coward either. But I agreed with Wade and his Committee that *hard* fighting, and *only* hard fighting, would ever win this war.

Sumner told me I was crazy to entrust the army and the fate of the country to the likes of McClellan. It wasn't just his inertia Sumner despised. He and the general had exchanged heated words about Sumner's favorite topic: emancipation. McClellan declared himself categorically opposed to emancipation in any shape or form and to any other encroachment on southern property rights. The general pained me with his outbursts on the subject. I wished he would confine himself to fighting the enemy and leave political policy to me.

On the other hand, Sumner and many other Republicans saw the army as a powerful weapon to root out slavery, and Sumner reminded me of that when he again raised the issue of emancipation. "I promised, Mr. President, not to criticize your slavery policy because you assured me you were only a month to six weeks behind me on that subject. But it's more than two months since I made my promise, and you've done nothing."

"It's been on my mind constantly," I said. "And I'll tell you this, Sumner. The war goes on with no end in sight, and it goes on for a reason. I'm convinced it's a great movement of God to end slavery and the man would be a fool who would stand in the way."

Now, I still opposed Federal emancipation as too radical and dangerous. That was why I'd come up with my gradual, state-guided plan for Delaware—to avoid the extremity of Federal abolishment. I'll put it another way. Generally you try to save life and limb. Sometimes, though, a limb must be amputated to save a life. But a life must never be given to save a limb. In this case, I was trying to amputate the limb with as little pain as possible.

My plan, however, hadn't had any luck in Delaware, and it made me rethink my approach. Last December, Sumner had begged me to make my plan a New Year's gift to Congress. Maybe he was right: maybe it was better to introduce my plan on the national level first and then work back to the states. That was the approach I took in a message to Congress in early March. When I had it written, I called Sumner to my office. "I want to read you my message to Congress. I want to know how you like it. I'm going to send it in today." I read the message aloud, and if I haven't said this before, I'll say it now. My voice is peculiarly high-pitched, some say it's shrill, and betrays my Kentucky and southern Indiana origins. The way I say *inageration, thar, git, kin do it, one of 'em,* and *the army turned tail and ran* makes Sumner grimace and moan and cover his face with his hands. Fortunately for me, not many of those words were in the document at hand.

"Fellow-citizens of the Senate and House of Representatives," I read, "I recommend the adoption of a Joint Resolution that the United States ought to co-operate with any state which may adopt gradual abolishment of slavery, giving to such state pecuniary aid, to be used by such state in its discretion, to compensate for the inconveniences public and private, produced by such change of system. The Federal government would find its highest interest in such a measure, as one of the most efficient means of self-preservation. The leaders of the existing insurrection entertain the hope that this government will ultimately be forced to acknowledge the independence of the rebellious states, and that all the loyal slave states will then choose to go with the southern section. To deprive them of this hope, substantially ends the rebellion; and the initiation of emancipation completely deprives them of that hope. I do not expect that all the slave states will very soon, if at all, initiate emancipation. What I expect is that the loyal border states, by such initiation, will make it certain to the insurgent states that at no event would they ever join them in their proposed Confederacy. I say 'initiation' because, in my judgment, gradual and not sudden emancipation is better for all. Should the people of the insurgent districts now reject the councils of treason, revive loyal state governments, and again send senators and representatives to Congress, they would at once find themselves at peace, with no institution changed, and with just influence in the councils of the nation fully re-established."

Then I gave the insurgents a warning. "In my annual message last December, I thought fit to say, 'The Union must be preserved; and hence all indispensable means must be employed.' A practical re-acknowledgment of the national authority would render the war unnecessary, and it would at once cease. If, however, resistance continues, the war must also continue; and it is impossible to foresee all the incidents, which may attend and all the ruin which may follow it. Such as may seem indispensable, or may obviously promise great efficiency towards ending the struggle, must and will come."

Sumner asked to see the manuscript and read it over many times.

He had some reservation about its language. "Your style is so clearly aboriginal, autochthonous, that it will not admit of emendation. As for content, I object most strenuously to the sentence offering to let the insurgents back into the Union with no institution changed, if they would but lay down their weapons. That invites the *preservation* of slavery, when you admit that the war is God's movement to end it." I was in a hurry to get the message printed and agreed to delete the offending line. "The rest of the message," Sumner went on in his clipped Boston accent, "is superb. You do realize, don't you, that it's the first time in the history of the Republic that a president has submitted an emancipation program to Congress? I wholeheartedly approve. So, I think, will most of the party."

He was right: most Republicans embraced it enthusiastically as a step in the right direction. Nicolay read me what Horace Greeley said in the *New York Tribune*: "This Message constitutes of itself an epoch in the history of our country. It is the day-star of a new national dawn. Even if it were no more than a barren avowal by the Chief Magistrate of the Nation that IT IS HIGHLY DESIRABLE THAT THE UNION BE PURGED OF SLAVERY, it would be a great fact, of far weightier import than many battles."

Congressman William Wadsworth of Kentucky, on the other hand, was up in arms. "I utterly spit at it and despise it," he said of the message. "Emancipation in the cotton states is an absurdity. There is not enough power in the world to compel it to be done."

Maybe so, but I tried to compel it. On March tenth, I called the border-state delegations to the White House and told 'em: "I won't pretend to hide my antislavery feeling. I think slavery is wrong and ought never to have existed. But that's not the question we have to deal with now. Slavery exists, and I've no desire to do injury to the interests and sensibilities of the slave states. But we're engaged in a terrible, wasting, and tedious war. Immense armies are in the field and out of necessity come into contact with slaves in the states you represent and in the insurgent states as the armies advance into them. The slaves come to our camps and cause continual irritation. I'm constantly annoyed by conflicting and antagonistic complaints. One side complains if the army does not protect the slave. The other side—the slaveholders—complains that their rights are being interfered with, their slaves are induced to run away and find protection within our lines. These complaints are numerous, loud, and deep. They cause hostility to the government in the states you represent. And they strengthen the hope of the Confederates that some day the border states will unite with them, and that hope prolongs the war. If the joint resolution I've recommended is adopted by Congress and accepted by your states, it will remove the cause of these complaints and the hopes of the rebels. It will do more to shorten the war than the greatest victory of our arms. I assure you that emancipation is the exclusive right of the states. I'm not trying to coerce you. This government has no power to coerce you. I know you can't give me an answer now, but I hope you will take the subject into serious consideration, confer with each other and with your constituents."

They were "full of doubt, of qualified protest, and of apprehensive inquiry," as Nicolay put it, and when they left, grumbling and shaking their heads, I feared the worst. Sure enough, when Congress approved my plan, offering Federal funds to any state adopting a gradual emancipation program, not a single border-state representative voted for the resolution. They did not heed my warning, did not see the signs of where this war—God's war—was carrying us.

The signs were right there before them, in the steady parade of antislavery legislation pushed through by the Republican majority and sent to me for my signature. One measure, an additional article of war, prohibited the military from returning fugitive slaves, and I signed it. "The slave of every rebel master who seeks the protection of our flag," I said, "shall have it and be free." Another bill outlawed slavery in the territories, thereby reversing the hated Dred Scott decision, and I signed it, too. A third measure abolished slavery in the District of Columbia, compensated the owners, and appropriated funds for the voluntary colonization of liberated blacks in Haiti and Liberia, and I signed it into law, despite the wails of Democrats that "niggers" would now crowd white ladies out of congressional galleries and that the law was "the entering wedge of an abolition program." Sumner thought that was exactly what it was. "It is the first installment of the great debt which we all owe to an enslaved race," he said, "and will be recognized as one of the victories of humanity."

10. DOUGLASS

I thanked all the powers of earth and sky that I was permitted to witness the event of the president's message to Congress. That the vile system of slavery must eventually go down I had never doubted, even in the darkest days of my life in slavery. But that I should live to see the president of the United States deliberately advocating emancipation was more than I ever ventured to hope for. Yet there it was, right before me, an emancipation proposal. Yes, there were qualifications in Lincoln's message, but a blind man could see where his heart was. I read the spaces as well as the lines of that document and I saw in them a brave man trying against great odds to do right—an honest patriot endeavoring to save his country in its day of peril. Time and practice, I believed, would improve the president as they improved other men. He was tall and strong but he was not done growing. He grew as the nation grew, as the war and God *forced* them both to grow.

When Congress went on to abolish slavery in the District of Columbia, I wrote Sumner: "I trust I am not dreaming but the events taking place seem like a dream." Let high swelling anthems now roll along the earth and sky! I cried. This was the first great step toward a redeemed and regenerated nation. But, alas, this measure, so noble in its other respect, also appropriated $500,000 for that old bugbear, colonization. When would they ever learn? This was *our* country, too, and we would *never* participate in a voluntary expatriation program. We told the government: if you want to colonize people, colonize slaveowners.

11. DAVIS

Thus did the ignorant usurper and his Black Republican acolytes initiate a series of unconstitutional encroachments against the guaranteed right to property in slaves. The emancipation of slavery in the District of Columbia seized slave property without due process. The prohibition of slavery in the territories violated the spirit of the Constitution that slaveholders had equal rights in the national lands. The prohibitions against the return of fugitive slaves committed an even more flagrant outrage upon the constitutional obligation. The Federal Constitution *required* the return of fugitives from service or labor, but the Black Republicans ground that article to dust by the iron heel of despotism. At the same time, the ignorant usurper himself demanded that the national government, by an offer of funds, put pressure upon the states to surrender their slave property. Thus the Federal government was, step by step, "educating the people" up to a proclamation of emancipation, so as to make entire abolition one of the positive and declared issues of the contest.

You may argue, as an objection, that the Confederate States were out of the Union and beyond the protection of the provisions of the Federal Constitution. This objection, however, cannot excuse the crimes of the Congress and the Executive of the United States. Thus far, there was no act of Congress, no proclamation of the Federal president, showing that either of them regarded the Confederate States in any other position than as states within the Union, whose citizens were subject to all the penalties contained in the Constitution, and therefore entitled to the *benefit* of all its provisions for their protection. All the conduct of the Confederate States in the war consisted in justifiable efforts to preserve to themselves and their posterity rights and protection guaranteed to them in the U.S. Constitution. But the Federal government, under the Black Republicans, made every effort to subvert those rights, destroy those protections, and subjugate us to compliance with its arbitrary will. Its acts subverted the Constitution and destroyed the fundamental principles of liberty. I ask you, *who* in this case is the criminal? Posterity will answer that.

12. LINCOLN

Wade was back, accusing McClellan of being guilty of criminal negligence. "You don't think so?" he cried. "Then why the Goddamned hell don't he attack the traitor army at Manassas? It's been more than six months since he took command, and his army sits exactly where it was when he took it over."

I wanted McClellan to attack Manassas, too, not go chasing off down the Chesapeake and up the Rappahannock, far away from Washington, as his Urbana scheme called for. Yet McClellan still adamantly rejected a straight-ahead attack at Manassas. He now had reliable intelligence, he claimed, that more than 220,000 rebels were entrenched there. He said they had heavy guns too—said Union patrols had seen them. He was so obstinate on this point that I gave up pressing an attack on Manassas and told him, once more, to get on with the Urbana operation—as long as he left Washington City adequately protected.

The next day, Sunday, March ninth, an ominous telegram arrived from our station on Cherrystone Point, on the Virginia shore across from Fort Monroe. The day before, a mammoth rebel iron-clad ram, the *Virginia*, had steamed out of the Elizabeth River and attacked our wooden warships blockading the Virginia coast off Hampton Roads. The clanking monster had sunk the *Cumberland*, burned the *Congress*, and run the *Minnesota* aground, and was now reported to be heading up the Potomac to shell Washington and destroy McClellan's huge armada of wooden troop transports.

I called an emergency Cabinet meeting, and the army and navy prepared to block the Potomac with obstructions to keep the monster at bay. But a second dispatch from Fort Monroe, dated the day before but delayed because of a cable break, reported that our own experimental ironclad, the *Monitor*, with two eleven-inch Dahlgren guns mounted in a revolving turret, was on its way to Hampton Roads under Lieutenant John Worden. We hurried over to the telegraph office and waited for news in a state of high tension.

In late afternoon another telegram came ticking in from Fort Monroe: an unprecedented naval battle between two seagoing iron-clads had occurred that Sunday morning and the little *Monitor* had dueled the *Virginia* to a draw. After the two ships had bounced shells off each other for two hours, the rebel Goliath had steamed back to Norfolk. The crowd in the telegraph office broke out in cheers. The *Virginia* was neutralized, the blockade was saved. McClellan could proceed with his Urbana operation.

But that night brought more astounding intelligence, this time from contrabands. The rebel army had abandoned Manassas and fallen back to a new defensive position behind the Rappahannock. That galvanized McClellan into action. He promptly advanced (quote unquote) his giant army into the abandoned enemy camps. What he found there made us "the scorn of the world," as Senator Fessenden put it. Those menacing cannon that had deterred the general of all our armies turned out to be fake—made out of wood. "Quaker guns," they were called. Not only that. Camp remains indicated that the rebel army was far smaller than the massive hordes McClellan believed had been entrenched there. I tell you, his penchant for exaggeration was the best weapon the rebels had. If he'd only adopted my plan and attacked Manassas with the 120,000 men of his army, McClellan might have won a decisive victory.

Instead, he was in disgrace, I was in despair, Wade and the Joint Committee were beside themselves, and Congress and the country were in an uproar. Vice President Hamlin, dark and grim, told me plainly that McClellan had to go. Deeply pained, I called a Cabinet meeting to talk about "the McClellan problem." Stanton, Seward, Chase—all condemned McClellan's "imbecilic" behavior. Bates fumed, "McClellan has no plans, but is fumbling and plunging in confusion and darkness. Mr. President, you *must* command the commanders."

That I resolved to do. On March eleventh, in the President's War Order No. 3, I reorganized the entire command system. McClellan was forthwith relieved as general in chief. It was a painful decision, but it had to be done. However, I left him in command of the Potomac Army as a service, giving him the opportunity to retrieve his errors. In the West, I consolidated the departments of Kansas and Missouri and the western part of the Department of the Ohio into the Department of the Mississippi and put Halleck, the ranking general out there, in command. He'd been pushing for a consolidated western department and it made sense: now he commanded Buell as well as Grant and could coordinate their operations in the impending campaign against Corinth. I called Frémont out of obscurity and put him in charge of the new Mountain Department embracing the Shenandoah Valley and western Virginia. From now on, I would function as overall commander, watching all points on the big picture and coordinating campaigns east and west. All departmental commanders, including McClellan as head of the Potomac Department, would report directly to the secretary of war.

I'll say this for McClellan: he accepted his demotion manfully. I think he was embarrassed at how the rebels had fooled him with their Quaker guns and was anxious to redeem himself. The trouble was, by falling back to the Rappahannock, between Urbana and Richmond, the rebel army had also wrecked his plan of operations. No matter. He came up with another one. He thought it better than Urbana, claimed it would win the war in a masterstroke. He would take the Potomac Army down the Chesapeake, land at the sandy peninsula between the York and James rivers, and, with Fort Monroe as his base, dash upland into Richmond before the rebel army on the Rappahannock could fall back to defend it. He proposed to win the war, not by fighting the enemy army, but by outmaneuvering it.

I studied McClellan's plan carefully, noting that all his corps commanders had approved the "peninsula" campaign so long as McClellan left forty thousand men to secure Washington. That part of the plan I liked. The other part—taking the magnificent Potomac Army far off on the other side of Richmond—gave me the hypo. This whole business of winning the war by maneuver was crackbrained. Only *hard fighting* would win the war. When would our generals ever learn that? Stanton didn't like McClellan's new plan any more than I did. Still, how could a couple of civilians go against the entire leadership of the Potomac Army? With great reluctance, against my better judgment, I approved the new plan of operations in an order issued through Stanton. The order directed McClellan to secure Washington and Manassas from attack—by that, I meant leaving forty thousand men around the capital. Then he was to move his army down to Fort Monroe, or land it anywhere between Washington and there. "At all events," I said, "move the army at once in pursuit of the enemy by some route."

March seventeenth the Potomac Army began embarking at Alexandria for the Virginia Peninsula. Before McClellan left, I called on him at this old brick town, now transformed into a vast staging area for the general's expeditionary force of 120,000 men. A great fleet stretched up and down the river: warships bristling with cannon, triple-deck steam-powered transports, brigs and schooners with stalls for horses on their decks. Whistling tugboats moved among the anchored vessels and from pier to pier. Columns of troops were filing onto the transports to the accompaniment of regimental bands, and Negro laborers were busily loading the ships with huge quantities of supplies, heavy artillery, pontoons, horses, telegraphic materials, and other accouterments of war, including Professor Lowe's observation balloons. The *power* radiated by this immense force filled me with awe.

When I located McClellan, he was curt, in a hurry, too busy to talk to a meddling politician, except to say vaguely that, yes, yes, he was leaving Washington secure. On April first he sailed for Virginia, obviously glad to get away from me and the Joint Committee and the whole pack of politicians in Washington.

Back at the Executive Mansion, in conversation with Orville Browning, I said that I'd studied McClellan and taken his measure as best as I could: I was not at all satisfied with his conduct of the war—he was not energetic and aggressive enough. He had the capacity to make proper arrangements for a great conflict, but as the hour for action approached he became nervous and oppressed and hesitated to meet the crisis. That was why I'd given him peremptory orders to move.

On April second, Stanton came to me with an astounding discovery. He'd investigated Washington's defenses to see if McClellan had left forty thousand men in the fortifications around the city. He had not. Only nineteen thousand troops manned the capital's forts and redoubts—wholly inadequate to guard the city, especially with reports that the rebels were back in the Shenandoah in force. I tell you, this was an outrage. McClellan had *deliberately* and *arrogantly* disobeyed my order to secure Washington. Therefore I detached McDowell's corps of twenty thousand men from the Army of the Potomac and assigned it to defend Washington City. I explained all this in a dispatch to McClellan, who had now landed at Fort Monroe and was facing a rebel defensive line from Yorktown to the Warwick River. Back came a shrill protest: "I beg that you will reconsider the order detaching the first corps from my command. I am now of the opinion that I shall have to fight all of the available force of the rebels, not far from here. Do not force me to do so with diminished numbers."

In those words I spotted McClellan's propensity to get nervous and depressed when the hour of battle approached. I wired him that he had more than 100,000 troops (far more, let me add, than the rebels could possibly have had in his front) and urged him to break the enemy line at Yorktown at once and move on Richmond. The whole campaign, after all, hinged on speed—on McClellan's seizing the rebel capital before the main rebel army on the Rappahannock realized what was happening.

But this is McClellan we're talking about. He complained that my detachment of McDowell's corps left him with only *eighty-five thousand* men, not one hundred thousand, and that his diminished numbers made it impossible for him to attack at once. So, instead of knocking aside the little squad of insurgents at Yorktown, General McClellan called up his heavy guns and put the city under a month-long siege. Two words describe that unhappy action: "indefinite procrastination."

13. DAVIS

"No one but McClellan would have hesitated to attack." So said Joseph Johnston of McClellan's decision to lay siege to Yorktown. General Magruder had only twelve thousand men to defend the Yorktown line and would have been overrun had McClellan attacked with his huge, well-armed and well-supplied army. But by noisily marching and shifting his men around, Magruder invited McClellan to believe his own worst fear—that he faced superior numbers. By undertaking a lengthy siege, McClellan gave us time to bring General Johnston's army down from the Rappahannock to reinforce Magruder and avoid an even worse calamity than the disasters our arms had already suffered in the West. My fear now was that Johnston, the "retreating general," would abandon the Peninsula and along with it the indispensable navy yard at Norfolk.

In fact, in conference with me, General Lee, and Secretary of War Randolph in Richmond, Johnston announced that he did indeed plan to withdraw his forces from the Peninsula, on the grounds that Magruder's line was indefensible. Randolph objected at once, because the navy yard at Norfolk offered our best if not our only opportunity to construct gunboats for coastal and harbor defense. General Lee, always bold in his views and unusually sagacious in penetrating the designs of the enemy, insisted that the Peninsula offered great advantages to a smaller force in resisting a numerically superior assailant. I agreed with Lee and Randolph and resolved to resist the enemy on the Peninsula—to hold Norfolk and keep command of the James as long as possible.

Meanwhile I was making every effort to assemble a sufficient force to defeat the Yankees in Tennessee. I stripped Florida of its entire coastal defenses, save one garrison, and sent them to Sidney Johnston at Corinth. By early April he had at least forty thousand men there organized into "three grand divisions" under Beauregard, Polk, and Bragg. As far as we were concerned, Corinth had to be held at all cost. Two of the Confederacy's greatest railroads intersected there: the Mobile & Ohio, which was the principal north-south railroad, and the Memphis & Charleston, which was the only east-west railroad in the entire Confederacy. The Memphis & Charleston was "the vertebrae of the Confederacy," whose severance would threaten the very life of the nation.

Our intelligence placed Grant's army of forty thousand at Savannah and Pittsburg Landing on the Tennessee, and Buell's army of forty thousand at Columbia on the Mississippi. On April third Sidney Johnston reported that Buell was moving rapidly on Savannah with thirty thousand men, another force of ten thousand following. The enemy was plainly concentrating at Savannah for an attack on Corinth. "Have ordered my army of forty thousand forward to offer battle near Pittsburg," Sidney said. I saw in an instant that he intended to defeat the enemy forces in detail, destroying Grant before Buell could join him, then routing Buell. I offered a prayer of thanks for such a man as Albert Sidney Johnston! This bold and aggressive move justified all my faith in my old friend.

"I hope you will be able to close with the enemy before his two columns unite," I wired him. "I anticipate victory."

14. GRANT

Our best intelligence indicated that Sidney Johnston had around forty thousand armed effectives at Corinth, and I chafed at my orders from Halleck. Stay put at Pittsburg Landing, he said, till Buell's Army of the Ohio, forty thousand strong, can join you from Nashville. *Don't* move against Corinth, he said, and *don't* bring on a general engagement till Buell reaches you. Didn't like it one whit. Wasted valuable time. Gave the enemy a chance to reinforce. Wanted to hit 'em *now*, destroy 'em *now*. That was the way to capture Corinth.

By early April, I had five divisions, totaling 37,000 men, at Pittsburg Landing and another division of 7,500—Lew Wallace's—at Crump's Landing five miles north of there. Also had two wooden gunboats, the *Tyler* and the *Lexington*. Most of my infantry were armed with Springfields and Enfields—good rifles for infantry—but many had worthless Australian and Belgium rifled muskets. Of my six divisions, only McLernand's, Lew Wallace's, and Smith's had seen combat. Smith had cut his leg badly in an accident and was confined to his bed with a fever, and William H. L. Wallace was acting commander of his troops. The other three divisions were full of green, hastily recruited volunteers. Stephen A. Hurlbut, a friend of the president, commanded one of these raw divisions, and Benjamin Prentiss another. The third was under Bill Sherman—Halleck had assigned him to me, and I was glad to have him. Never once believed the rumors he'd gone "crazy." Not a false line in Sherman's character—a fighter.

Had my headquarters in the one-street river port of Savannah, in an old mansion overlooking the Tennessee. I was waiting there for Buell. But every day I took the *Tigress* to Pittsburg Landing, nine miles to the south, to check on my army. Huge quantities of supplies and equipment were piled up on the bluff overlooking the Landing, and a vast sea of white tents spread out on the high ground across the main road to Corinth, between the river and Owl Creek to the west. The smoke of thousands of campfires drifted overhead, filling the air with the scent of burning timber. A third of the army was hardly fit for duty, on account of dysentery and diarrhea. The men called it "the Tennessee quickstep." Had a bout of it myself, chills and fever. Rawlins had it, too, said it kept him "dancing" day and night near a week.

Sherman had field command of the five divisions at the Landing. He was camped just beyond a log church, Shiloh Meeting House, and held the center of our lines, in advance of the other divisions. McClernand's division, veterans of Henry and Donelson, was off to the right and somewhat to the rear of Sherman, with Wallace in reserve behind him. Prentice's brand-new division, the rawest of the lot, was farther back to Sherman's left, with Hurlbut in reserve behind them.

On the fifth, alarmed by reports of an enemy cavalry force in Sherman's front, I took the *Tigress* down to the landing to confer with him. I was on crutches with a sprained ankle—swollen so bad couldn't get my boot on. Happened the night before: it had rained and my horse stumbled on the muddy ground and fell on his side with my leg under him. When I got back to headquarters, ankle was so swollen up my aides had to cut the boot off.

When I reached the Landing on the fifth, Sherman reported that enemy cavalry had attacked his outposts, but everything was quiet now. We decided that the rebels designed nothing more than a strong demonstration. To be safe, I had already ordered Sherman to be on alert. But since I aimed to take the offensive as soon as Buell arrived, my army wasn't fortified and lacked a continuous defensive line. Frankly, I didn't think the rebels would leave their strong entrenchments at Corinth and attack us. Sherman swore up and down they wouldn't do it. Even if they did, I thought they wouldn't try it before the seventh or eighth. I hoped Buell would be up before then, so we could attack first. Other words, had my mind on what I was going to do to *them*, not what they were going to do to me.

Sherman said he was concerned about his "undisciplined mob"—said they had "as much idea of war as children." I liked the way he talked, quick, decided, loud, like Rawlins. Cussed like Rawlins, too. One of my aides described Sherman right, said he was "spare and angular, as if his superabundant energy had consumed his flesh." Said Sherman's "gray eyes flashed fire as fast as lightning on a summer's night."

Back at Savannah late that night, I told my staff we would move headquarters to Pittsburg tomorrow. Then hobbled upstairs to my room for a little sleep. Next morning, April sixth, a Sunday, we were all up at dawn. The horses were saddled and the boats were getting up steam for the trip south. I sat down to breakfast with my staff, but before we were half through we heard a faint rumbling.

"That's firing," Webster said.

"Sounds like it," I said.

My orderly, a sad-faced Frenchman called Napoleon, burst in. "General, there's terrific firing up the river." We rushed outside and heard the telltale roar of artillery off to the south.

"Where is it, at Crump's or Pittsburg Landing?" Webster asked.

"I think it's at Pittsburg," I said and buckled on my sword. "Orderly, get those horses on the boat and tell the captain we're leaving at once. Gentlemen, the ball is in motion. Let's be off."

On board ship, I dashed off a quick note to Buell that cannonading upriver indicated a battle had broken out and that I couldn't wait for him at Savannah. His lead division, under Nelson, was not far away on the east side of the river, and I sent Hillyer with an order for him to march to Pittsburg at once. "Tell him to hurry," I said. "Maybe Walker here can find him guides." Walker said he could do it. "Good," I said, then back to Hillyer: "Take two guides to Nelson, and then ride to Buell and get him to march up the rest of his army as fast as possible."

We steamed south to Crump's Landing and found Lew Wallace standing at the guardrail of his headquarters steamer. "General," I yelled from the *Tigress*, "have your men ready to march at a moment's notice."

"They're already under arms," Wallace yelled back

As we steamed south to Pittsburg Landing, the roar and tumult of battle grew louder. We could see columns of smoke rising up over the trees.

15. SHERMAN

When my skirmishers were driven in that morning, I had a suspicion that something was up. I had my entire division under arms and was mounted on a beautiful sorrel horse, sweeping the field with my glass, when I saw the glistening bayonets of heavy masses of infantry, which satisfied me that the rebels were attacking our entire army in great force. Since my camp was in advance, we caught bloody thunder—wave after wave of Johnnies coming at us with muskets blazing and screaming their crazy yell. They overran the first line of tents and put the torch to 'em. My sorrel was shot dead under me and I took the horse of my aide, McCoy, till it was shot, when I took my doctor's horse and that was shot. It was a blazing furnace of gunfire—sheets of flame—hotter than anything I'd seen at Bull Run. The very ground shook from the thunderous volley fire of their guns. Solid shot shattered thick oaks and struck horses and riders to the ground. Minnie balls filled the air with an incessant hum like thousands of malignant bees. Grapeshot and canister slammed into men with a whirling shudder, spraying the soldiers behind them with blood, intestines, eyeballs, and brains.

I was shot in my right hand and an orderly close by my side was killed, a handsome, faithful young soldier who carried his carbine ever ready to defend me, and the shot that killed him was meant for me. I saw hundreds of my raw volunteers throw down their rifles and run back toward the river, the Goddamned cowards. Others put up a fight, though, mixing it up with the rebels, and wounded men, charred and blackened by the burning tents and underbrush, were crawling about, begging for somebody to end their misery.

My line was crumbling, virtually all order gone. It looked like the shrieking rebel army would overrun us entirely and turn our flank. We were that close to a total disaster. Even so, I felt *exhilarated,* never more so—kept thanking General Halleck for giving me this chance, for believing in me and supporting me when I was disgraced by the insanity charge, when I was morbid, nerves gone—wild-eyed Ellen said—a failure, the terrible judgment of Providence on me. I'd written Ellen *I have given you pain when it should have been pride, honor and pleasure, ought to get on my knees and beg your pardon for the anxiety and shame I have caused you.* But Halleck gave me a leave of absence to go home, and wrote me soothing letters, and when I came back, feeling better, he showed his faith in

Bill Sherman—gave me command of an instruction camp and then promoted me to district command in Cairo and then assigned me to Grant's army. Grant's the best damned field general in this man's army. And now here I was in the thick of the greatest battle ever fought on this continent, to date, and feeling in total control, nerveless, in my element, and I rode back and forth across that flaming field, reforming broken units and stabilizing my line. Then I had my division fall back slowly, step by step, in good order, and in that way prevented a breakthrough. By ten that morning, we had checked the headlong assault of the enemy and were holding our own. Then, when the battle was raging fiercest, I saw Grant riding up in the pall of smoke with a cigar in his mouth and one boot off.

16. GRANT

Sherman was chewing a cigar, face and beard black with gunpowder and smeared with blood, bullet holes in his uniform, a bloody handkerchief wrapped around his hand. Showed no sign of panic: with bullets whizzing and shells exploding all around that deadly field, he was completely cool and confident as he explained to me what had happened on his front.

"General," I said, "you've made a gallant stand. Need you to hold your line. Can I count on you?"

"You can indeed," he said. Figured I could and set out on a jingling trot to check on McClernand. Far as I could tell, it was an attack all along our line. They had routed Prentiss and driven him back toward the Landing. Mess back there, mass of broken units, hundreds of men cowering behind the bluff. I'd brought up Hurlbut to reinforce what was left of Prentiss's division and keep 'em from turning our left. Moved William Wallace up to bolster our center. Lew Wallace was on his way from Crump's Landing—had sent Captain Baxter to get him. Lead division of Buell's army was coming up, too. Just had to hold till all of 'em got here.

We found McClernand's division in a desperate fight along the Purdy Road. I ordered up two reserve Iowa regiments to reinforce him and then headed back to our left, where the situation was critical. There Hurlbut's and Wallace's divisions and the remnants of Prentiss's had formed a ragged battle line from the Corinth Road back across a cotton field and a peach orchard to a point near the Tennessee River, but they were barely holding on. The ferocity of the enemy assaults in this sector, especially at a place called "the hornet's nest," convinced me that Sidney Johnston greatly outnumbered us and that he intended to turn my left flank, cut the army off from the Landing, and destroy it piecemeal in the swamps around Snake and Owl creeks. I told the three generals they had to hold on at all hazards, and with my staff raced back toward the Landing to bring up Lew Wallace's division, which should have arrived by now. Suddenly enemy artillery opened up on us and shells and balls whistled about our ears as we dashed for cover. I discovered that a ball had struck the metal scabbard of my sword, just below the hilt, and broken it nearly off.

When we reached the bluff above the Landing, Lew Wallace was nowhere to be seen. Where the devil was he? Needed his division, the battle was going against us. We'd just learned that Sherman and McClernand had both fallen back from repeated rebel assaults. But Sherman rallied his troops, reformed McClernand's broken units, and again stabilized his line. Heck of a job of soldiering. Could depend on Sherman all right. I sent Lieutenant Rowley to find Wallace, then rode to the edge of the bluff and swept the far shore with my glass, looking for a sign of Nelson. Below me, cowering behind the river bluff, was a panic-stricken mob, maybe four to five thousand men. What happened when you had to fight with raw troops.

Went down to the *Tigress*. Bad ankle was killing me. Tried to keep calm, not show how agitated I felt. I was standing in the doorway of the ladies' room when General Buell came aboard. Was I glad to see him. He said that Nelson ought to be here in a couple hours and asked for steamers to bring up Crittenden's division. "You got 'em," I said. As we stepped off the boat, Buell yelled at the cowards huddled behind the bluff, telling 'em to go back to their units or he would have the gunboats blast 'em to hell. But nobody moved. "Useless," I mumbled, "useless."

At the Landing, Buell turned to me and asked, "What preparations have you made for retreating, General?"

"Haven't despaired of whipping 'em yet."

Staff and I hurried back to the front—rode on every part of the field—reformed broken regiments and beaten troops and sent 'em back into line. Rawlins got on me for repeatedly exposing myself to enemy fire, but I had to see what was going on. At two o'clock the enemy mounted massive assaults against our left, at the peach orchard, where bullets and canister flew so thick it mowed down leaves and blossoms. All down our line, men tore paper cartridges, rammed 'em down musket barrels, capped the guns, and fired, repeating the process frantically, the best getting off three shots a minute. Sometimes they forgot to remove the ramrods and fired 'em like arrows. The attacking rebels fell in heaps, some without heads, others disemboweled or cut in half. The crash of exploding shells and shrieks of death made a hellish racket as white clouds of gunsmoke drifted through the trees, getting into the eyes and mouth.

We had to have reinforcements or the enemy was going to break through this sector. Where was Lew Wallace? Ought to have been here long ago. I sent two more aides to try to find him. But they reported back that Wallace was marching *west*, away from the river, and was further away from the Landing now than when he'd started. *Useless, Useless*. I galloped back to Sherman's side of the line and found that he and McClernand had been forced to fall back behind the river road, where they made another stand, with the Tennessee behind them. This wasn't good, wasn't good at all.

It was even worse at the peach orchard sector. About four-thirty the rebels opened a terrific artillery bombardment there—most deafening roar of artillery and musketry I'd ever heard. Sounded like seventy or eighty guns were in action, hurling solid shot, explosive shells, grape and canister at our line. Then came that infernal infantry again, screaming insanely. Wallace's division disintegrated and Wallace himself was mortally wounded while trying to get away. Hurlbut's division gave way, too, and fell back toward the Landing. Prentiss, however, refused to retreat even though both his flanks were exposed. Cut off and surrounded, he had to surrender his command of more than two thousand men.

With the collapse of our left, disaster was at hand. Panicked soldiers rushed past us in headlong flight to the shelter of the river. Double-decked ambulances careened wildly by—the drivers in the front seats were yelling at the horses and spurring them with bayonets while the load of wounded men inside screamed in agony. Shells shrieked and hissed through the air and exploded in clouds of flame and dust. In all the pandemonium, my staff and I managed to establish a new defensive line around the Landing, under the cover of our two gunboats, consisting of the remnants of Sherman's, McClernand's, and Hurlbut's divisions. I figured the rebels would attack our left again with everything they had, so I put all the available field and siege guns, including five twenty-four–pounders and several thirty-pounder Parrotts, on the high ground on our left, overlooking a steep ravine. The Tennessee River was now at our backs. Some of my officers feared all was lost, but I didn't think so.

"I think we'll stop 'em here," I said.

I went down to the crowd of laggards clinging to the side of the bluff and yelled at them, "We need you! Get back into line, redeem yourselves!" When nobody moved, I sent a squadron of cavalry down there to drive 'em back at sword point, but the cowards crawled up the bank and hung on to exposed roots of trees, beyond the reach of the horsemen as they swept by with whirling sabers.

Useless, useless.

The rebel artillery fire was intensifying when steamboats started across from the opposite shore with blasts of their whistles. It was Nelson's division at last; the rest of Buell's force could not be far away; and cheer after cheer rolled across my army. When Bull Nelson, a three-hundred-pounder, saw the mob hiding under the bluff, he mounted his horse, leaped over the gunwale, and cried at them: "Damn your souls, if you won't fight get out of the way and let men through who will!" Yelling "Buell! Buell!" Nelson's troops followed him to the top of the bluff and formed a line to the left of our guns. As they filed past, a cannonball barely missed me and decapitated a captain on my staff, spattering his brains against another man's back, and cut off both legs of a soldier in Nelson's ranks.

At about five-thirty that afternoon, the rebel infantry launched a final all-out attack against my left flank, as I figured they would. I rode down the line shouting, "They're coming! Army of the Tennessee, stand firm!" Down the ravine and up this side they came, but as they reached the crest of the ridge our artillery and gunboats cut 'em to pieces. The concussions of the big siege guns shook the ground and knocked the hats off our soldiers standing nearby. The murderous fire of artillery and musketry broke the assault and forced the rebels to withdraw, ending the fighting that day. I sensed that the rebel army had spent itself and resolved to seize the initiative like I'd done at Donelson. Told my officers to prepare their commands to take the offensive. We would counterattack at dawn.

That night, twenty thousand men of Buell's army came up and regiment after regiment filed into line and prepared for the attack. To keep the rebels off guard, our gunboats took turns shelling their lines at ten-minute intervals, and the huge eight-inch shells shrieked over our heads and exploded in the night. At midnight a fierce storm struck, with drenching rain and thunderclaps that mocked the boom of the gunboats. Bolts of lighting lit up an eerie landscape of twisted corpses, wrecked equipment, and dead horses.

I took shelter under a tree with my hat pulled down on my head and my collar up around my ears. Bad ankle was throbbing to beat all, so I sat down and lit a cigar. In a little while Sherman came up.

"Well, Grant, we've had the devil's own day, haven't we?"

"Yep. Lick 'em tomorrow, though."

We moved out at dawn, fifty thousand strong, and fell on the rebel army as it lay in our former camps around Shiloh church. The rebels fought with desperate tenacity—fine infantry, give 'em that—and the two armies reeled back and forth in what Sherman said was "the severest musketry-fire" he'd ever heard. At the height of the fighting, I formed some Ohio troops into an attacking column, rode out in front, and led 'em against a key rebel position on the road to Corinth. "Charge!" I cried, and those boys did me proud. Ran forward yelling and brandishing bayonets, and the rebels turned and fled. That charge broke the enemy resistance. By nightfall the rebel army was in headlong retreat down the muddy roads to Corinth. I wanted to pursue, but the roads were too bad and my men too exhausted to mount an effective pursuit. Even so, I took satisfaction in wiring Halleck that we'd won a tremendous victory. Halleck wired back that he was coming with reinforcements to assume field command. I guessed he was mad because I went into battle without Buell—technically a violation of Halleck's orders.

Day after the battle I rode out to examine the field and came to the peach orchard sector where the hardest fighting had taken place. Not a single peach blossom was left on the shattered trees. The ground was so covered with swollen corpses that it would have been possible to walk across the clearing in any direction, stepping on dead bodies, without a foot touching the ground. Hundreds of dead horses, wrecked wagons, caissons, guns, and all manner of equipment littered the battleground. I figured more than 110,000 men had fought here. Our total casualties came to 13,000 in killed, wounded, and missing. Enemy casualties were worse. Learned that Sidney Johnston himself was killed.

In my official report, I singled out Sherman for special praise. In both days of fighting, he'd displayed great judgment and skill in the management of his men. Though severely wounded in the hand on the first day, he'd kept his division in place when it counted and aided materially in keeping the divisions to his right and left in place. "In General Sherman," I wrote Julia, "the country has an able and gallant defender, and your husband a true friend."

17. SHERMAN

The sights of that battlefield ought to cure anybody of war. Wagons hauled in dead men and dumped 'em on the ground, like cords of wood, for mass burial in long trenches, like sardines in a box. Wounded men with mangled legs and arms and heads half shot off lay on the ground, and still more of the injured were crying for water and help in any form. The worst wounded were left at the little log house on top of the bluff, now an emergency field hospital, where surgeons sawed off legs and arms on outdoor tables and flung them into careless heaps. The other wounded, thousands of 'em, were taken down to the hospital boats for evacuation, and the ones who didn't make it, who died on those bloody decks, were left in a grim line on the shore. You know what they called that battle? Shiloh, after the little church on the bluff. In the Bible, the chaplain said, Shiloh meant "A Place of Peace." It was a Goddamned place of *peace* all right—for the four thousand blue and gray soldiers who were buried there.

I wrote Ellen I still felt the terrible nature of this war, and the piles of dead and wounded and maimed made me more anxious than ever for an end to it. But I knew such a thing could not be for a long, long time, and I had a feeling I'd never survive it. At the same time I felt *elated. Reborn.* I'd seen the Goddamned monster again, and I'd triumphed over the worst that son-of-a-bitch could do to me. Shiloh had given me the chance to redeem my good name. General Halleck, when he arrived and assumed command of the army, said I'd "saved the fortune of the day on the sixth" and he'd told Washington so. He even recommended me for promotion to major general, and I was duly promoted. Grant, too, kept praising me to the skies, said I'd displayed "great judgment and skill," said I was his "standby." I'd never felt so good. Never.

But the Goddamned newspapers! Their tribe of scribblers swarmed over the battlefield afterward, talked to the cowardly bastards who'd hidden under the bluff, and leaped to conclusions about what had happened. They reported that Grant had made no preparations, that our army was taken completely by surprise, that the rebels caught us in our tents and bayoneted the men in their beds, that divisional leadership was terrible, that Sherman and McClernand been routed, and that Buell's opportune arrival saved the Army of the Tennessee from annihilation. One paper even raised the old charge against me. Question: "Is Sherman Insane?" Answer: "The general impression here is, he's demented." But poor Grant got the worst of the slander. They accused him of being drunk, careless, criminal, a tyrant—you name it—when in reality he was a good and brave soldier and *victorious*. He'd won a Goddamned *victory*. Yet, just as they'd done with me, the papers tried to pull him down, destroy him.

Now you understand why I hate journalists. Nothing but Goddamned mongrels. Toadies and croakers. Fawning sycophants. And spies. Whole lot of 'em ought to be hanged. The more I thought about the fucking bastards, the more I was convinced that the howling tribe of 'em, North and South, had whipped up public passions into a frenzy and *brought on this infernal war*. You Goddamned right, I blamed the *journalists* for causing it.

I wrote my brother John: "I would rather be ruled by Jefferson Davis than be abused by a set of dirty newspaper scribblers who have the impudence of Satan. They come into camp, poke about among the lazy shirkers and pick up their camp rumors and publish them as facts, and the avidity with which these rumors are swallowed by the public makes even some of our officers bow to them. I will not." And I did not. I wrote John what really happened on the first day of Shiloh. He was a U.S. Senator of great influence in Washington and could show my letters to the president and anybody else who doubted us. I told John that the hue and cry against Grant was all wrong. Not a man was bayoneted in or near his tent. As to surprise, we'd had constant skirmishes with the enemy cavalry the week before, and I had strong guards out in front of each brigade. Yes, the guards were driven in on the morning of the battle, but before the enemy came within cannon range of my position every regiment was under arms at the post I'd assigned them. "I am out of all patience," I told John, "that our people should prefer to believe the horrid stories of butchery, ridiculous in themselves, gotten up by cowards to cover their shame, than the plain natural reports of the officers who were responsible and who saw what they described."

I sent a note to Grant: "Military men are chained to a rock, while the vultures are turned loose. We must be silent, while our defamers are allowed the widest liberty and license. Reputations are not made by honest soldiers who stand by their colors, but by the crowd that flies back to their homes and employs the press. I'm not dependent on the press in any manner, never having sought popularity. In fact, I *despise* popularity obtained by the usual process of flattery and pusillanimity." As for the croaking bastards who called themselves newsmen, I declared unrelenting *warfare* on the whole stinking lot.

Grant bore the newspaper tirades in silence. But I knew they hurt him. So did Halleck when he arrived and personally took charge of the army, thus stripping Grant of active command. Halleck proceeded to reorganize the army into three corps under Buell, Pope, and Thomas, with McClernand in command of the reserve. True, Halleck named Grant second in command, nominally in charge of the right wing and the center, but in reality he was substantially left out, since Halleck ignored him and issued orders directly to the corps commanders. Halleck, it seems, believed the newspaper carping about Grant's alleged lack of preparedness at Shiloh and was punishing him for it.

Don't get me wrong. I held Halleck in high esteem, had known him for twenty-five years and had always thought him a man of great capacity. As a grand strategist and theorist, he was one of the best we had—naturally of good strong mind, a head as strongly marked as Webster's. We'd served together in California, and on our voyage there around the South American cape, while others were struggling to kill time, he'd used it in hard study. When the sea was high and the ship was rolling, and the sky so dark that daylight did not reach his stateroom, he stood on a stool, with his book and candle on the upper berth and a bedstrap around his middle secured to the frame to support him in the wild tossing of the ship, and in that manner he studied military theory. In such a man the country in its time of trial had to have confidence.

Halleck concentrated a force of a hundred thousand men and two hundred guns from all corners of his vast department, the biggest army yet assembled in the West, and made his preparations for the campaign against Corinth. Yes, I still thought the hardest fighting lay ahead of us, but I had absolute faith that Halleck and Grant could whip Beauregard or any other general Jeff Davis sent against us.

18. DAVIS

I was at home that Sunday, April sixth, anxiously awaiting news about Sidney Johnston's attack on Pittsburg Landing. Initial dispatches were fragmentary and I knew nothing for certain until a courier brought me a telegram from Beauregard.

> *We this morning attacked the enemy in strong position in front of Pittsburg & after a severe battle of ten hours, thanks to the Almighty, gained a complete victory driving the enemy from every position. Loss on both sides heavy including our Commander in Chief, Genl A.S. Johnston who fell gallantly leading his troops into the thickest of the fight.*

I stared at the words in disbelief, then in despair. Then I broke down and wept. Sidney was my good, true, and tried friend. The only man I felt able to lean upon with entire confidence. There was no purer spirit, no more heroic soul, than his. Later I learned that his death could easily have been avoided. A bullet had cut the artery running down his thigh. It was fatal only because the flow of blood was not stopped by a tourniquet. How in God's name such a thing had been allowed to happen, I could not fathom. It made me all the more distressed.

In my message to Congress that same April sixth, I announced that we had won a glorious and decisive victory over the invaders at Pittsburg Landing and that the Federal army had abandoned the field. Then I reported Sidney Johnston's death. "My long and close friendship with this departed chieftain and patriot," I said, "forbids me to trust myself in giving vent to the feelings which this intelligence evokes. Without doing injustice to the living, it may be safely said our loss is irreparable."

The next dispatches from Beauregard filled me with woe. He had retreated to Corinth, leaving the *invaders* in command of the battlefield. We had somehow lost a battle I had announced to the world we had won! How could this be? When the official reports came in from Beauregard, Bragg, and the other officers, I had the answer to that question. Those reports showed clearly where the failure lay: with Beauregard. They proved that, when Sidney Johnston fell, the Confederate Army was so fully victorious that, had the attack been vigorously pressed, Grant and his army would before the setting of the sun have been fugitives or prisoners. But Beauregard, upon assuming command, had failed to press the attack, offering the pitiful excuse that darkness was near, that his troops were exhausted, etcetera. In calling off the attack, he had given Buell time to save Grant. Beauregard had withdrawn the army at the moment of victory, and thus had sacrificed all which the skill and heroism of Johnston had achieved.

All this pained and sickened me. In Johnston's fall the great pillar of the southern Confederacy was crushed, and beneath its fragment the best hope of the Southwest lay buried. I believed that in the history of this war the fate of an army depended on one man; more, that the fortunes of a country hung by the single thread of that one life that was yielded on the field of Shiloh.

Certain that the combined forces of Grant and Buell would attack Corinth, I took great pains to reinforce Beauregard, sending him twenty thousand men under Van Dorn from the Trans-Mississippi and transferring other troops from Charleston. I wrote the governors of five southwestern states that Beauregard must have more men to meet the vast accumulation of the enemy before him, and I beseeched them to forward to Corinth all the armed men they could furnish. I asked them for weapons, too, telling them that if rifles or muskets were not available, pikes and knives would be acceptable. But the governors had few men and weapons to send.

We had reached a critical hour. On every front, our armies suffered from severe shortages of men. On the peninsula, Joseph Johnston had only 58,000 troops to contend against McClellan's army of 100,000 besieging Yorktown. At Corinth, Beauregard, even with the reinforcements I sent him, was no match for the huge army the enemy was now assembling at Pittsburg Landing. To make matters worse, most of the 148 regiments of twelve-month volunteers were approaching the end of their service. The harried secretary of war had done all he could to stimulate reenlistment and volunteering, but with little success.

Faced with catastrophe East and West, I took a drastic step and asked Congress for a conscription law to produce the needed manpower. Congress responded with a measure, which I signed into law on April sixteenth, authorizing the states to conscript every white man between the ages of eighteen and thirty-five for three years in the national service. The law allowed conscripted men to hire substitutes. A few days later, Congress exempted, among other classes, railroad workers, river pilots, telegraph operators, foundrymen, superinten-dents and workers in cotton and wool factories, and officers in the state and Confederate governments. Execution of the law depended on state authorities. I expected them to enroll the conscripts within the limits of their respective states; Confederate officers would then receive the conscripts in camps of instruction and forward them to the requisite destinations.

Governor Brown of Georgia, however, protested bitterly against conscription, writing me in one hateful letter after another that the measure was an unconstitutional violation of state sovereignty—that it consolidated "almost the entire military power of the states" with the Confederate president—and forbidding state militia officers to be enrolled. He was utterly and completely wrong on all points, and I told him so in a series of dispatches—one of them more than forty pages in length. I pointed out that the constitutionality of the con-scription act derived from the power of the government to raise troops, and that the measure was not only necessary but absolutely indispensable because of the twelve-month regiments that were soon to be disbanded.

Meanwhile, even with this essential measure in place, our mili-tary situation continued to deteriorate. A powerful enemy fleet of wooden warships, mortar boats, and troop transports appeared at the mouth of the Mississippi, seventy-five miles below New Orleans. Only three thousand men under General Mansfield Lovell guarded that city, and the mayor sent frantic pleas for help, but I telegraphed him that I had none to give. I was confident, however, that Forts St. Philip and Jackson, situated at the mouth of the river, could stop the enemy's wooden fleet.

We were wholly unprepared for what happened next. Somehow seventeen Federal warships ran past the forts under cover of dark-ness with the loss of only three smaller vessels. I was shocked. Why was the channel not lit up by bonfires? Why was there no obstruc-tion to detain the enemy fleet under the fire of the forts? The enemy warships then steamed up the Mississippi and seized New Orleans after General Mansfield had abandoned the city and fled upriver to Vicksburg. Three days later Forts St. Philip and Jackson also surren-dered.

The fall of New Orleans, our chief commercial city, was an irre-versible catastrophe. Federal troops under that miserable cur, Ben-jamin Butler, then occupied the city and hanged an innocent civilian. Then Butler inaugurated a reign of terror, pillage, and a long train of infamies too disgraceful to be described without a sense of shame by anyone who is proud of the name American. The soldiers of the invading force were incited and encouraged by general orders to insult and outrage the wives and mothers and sisters of the citizens; helpless women were torn from their homes and subjected to solitary confinement, some in fortresses and prisons. Repeated pretexts were sought or invented for plundering the inhabitants of the captured city, by fines levied and collected under threat of imprisonment at hard labor with ball and chain. The entire population was forced to choose between starvation by the confiscation of all their property and taking an oath against their conscience to bear allegiance to the invader.

At about the time New Orleans was lost, General Lee came to me with a plan for countering the enemy's overwhelming superiority in numbers in Virginia. He proposed offensive warfare in the Shenandoah Valley with General Jackson and General Ewell, who had seventeen thousand men between them. The Federals had two forces in the Shenandoah, one under Banks, the other under Frémont, with McDowell's corps of McClellan's army guarding Washington. It was Lee's belief—and I agreed with him—that Frémont and Banks planned to attack our valley forces while McDowell's corps marched on Richmond by way of the Rappahannock and connected with McClellan to put Richmond under siege. Instead of waiting for the enemy to make his move, Lee proposed that Jackson and Ewell seize the initiative and attack Frémont and Banks, thereby throwing such a scare into the Federals that they would hold McDowell to defend Washington. I thought this a brilliant application of the offensive-defensive and told Lee himself to direct the operation.

On May first we received more shocking news, this time from the peninsula. It was a dispatch from Johnston announcing his intention to withdraw the following night. I wired him that this took us by surprise and must involve enormous losses, including the unfinished gunboats at Norfolk. I was filled with woe. Above all, I did not want Johnston to fall back upon Richmond and leave the capital vulnerable to a siege. To my dismay, however, Johnston abandoned the Yorktown line and began a long, dreary retreat up the peninsula, with McClellan in cautious pursuit. This, in turn, compelled the abandonment of Norfolk and the navy yard, which necessitated the scuttling of our great ironclad, the *Virginia*, and left the James River and southern Virginia and northern North Carolina vulnerable to enemy thrusts.

General Lee, if anything, was more upset than I was about John-ston's retreat. His crippled wife was at White House on the Pamunkey, and with the enemy advance she found herself behind the Yankee lines. McClellan, in an unusual display of magnanimity, allowed her to pass through his lines with an escort of two Federal officers. Then McClellan converted White House, George Washington's home in his early years, into a military hospital and made the grounds and landing his base of supplies.

Meanwhile another ominous dispatch came from Beauregard: an immense army of 100,000 to 120,000 men under Halleck was advancing toward Corinth. Against this force Beauregard only had 45,000. There seemed no end to the parade of disquieting dis-patches. But alarmed though I was about the fate of Corinth, it was the approach of the Federal army on Richmond that caused me the greatest anxiety. My first concern was the safety of Varina and the children, Maggie, Jeff, Joe, and Billy. I knew I ought to send them away, but I couldn't bear the thought and neither could Varina. She wept when I raised the possibility. But there really was no choice, and on the ninth of May we agreed they should start in three days for Raleigh, North Carolina.

That night, during a reception, a courier brought me dispatches. Passing Varina on my return to the drawing room, I whispered, "The enemy's gunboats are ascending the James." As soon as the guests departed, I told Varina that if the enemy gunboats got past our fortifications at Drewry's Bluff, they would shell Richmond. She and the children, therefore, must leave the city at once.

"Please, Banny, grant me a few days, you know how I dislike run-ning away." But I insisted, and the next morning they boarded the train and were gone. Two days later I wrote her: "My dear wife, I am quite desolate and at every look see something of yours or the chil-dren to remind me that I am alone. I have but a moment to send you my love and prayers. May God have you all in his holy keeping. Kiss my dear children and let each one give you a kiss from me. Love to all."

By May fourteenth, Johnston was within four miles of Rich-mond, on the north side of the Chickahominy, and my anxieties were so great that I rode out with General Lee to divine Johnston's plans. We talked late into the night, but Johnston was guarded and vague as always, a trait that infuriated me. Try as we might, we were unable to draw from Johnston any more definite purpose than that of improving his position as far as practicable and waiting for the enemy to leave the protection of his gunboats on the rivers, when an opportunity might present itself to give him battle.

The next day five enemy gunboats attacked our fortifications at Drewry's Bluff, seven miles south of Richmond. The booming of the guns could be heard in the city and it threw the population into a panic. I rode down to Drewry's Bluff to watch the battle, but arrived too late: our batteries had already repulsed the enemy vessels and our gunners were elated and prompt to tell me that "the gunboats were clear gone." I returned to Richmond in rain and mud and found that the panic had subsided. The talkers were boasting that they would rather see the city destroyed than surrendered. I thought: "They lightly talk of scars who never felt a wound." *Romeo and Juliet*, act two, scene two. The talkers had little idea of what scenes would follow if the enemy's guns bombarded rows of brick houses in Richmond. I told them that the enemy might be beaten before Richmond or on either flank and we would try to do that, but I could not allow the army to be penned up in the city.

I was therefore surprised and dismayed when Johnston brought the army across the Chickahominy to the immediate vicinity of Richmond. He attempted to justify this unexpected movement to me, arguing that it was to his advantage to have the river in his front rather than his rear. I made it plain to him that Richmond must *not fall* and that its defense must be made *outside the city*, but when in my anxiety I rode out to confer with the general, I found no visible preparations for defense and my brief conversations with him afforded no satisfactory information as to his plans and purposes.

By May twenty-fifth, McClellan's huge army was at the very gates of Richmond, with two of his corps across the Chickahominy—probably to connect with McDowell, when he came down from the north. From the top of the Executive Mansion, we could hear the rumble of artillery and see McClellan's two observation balloons hovering menacingly over the lines. Johnston had made no effort to contest the invaders' crossing of the Chickahominy, and I was indignant. Did "the great retreater," as Mary Chesnut referred to him, mean to retreat into the city? Even give it up? Why else would he make no preparation to keep the enemy at a distance? General Lee and I both agreed that Johnston had to stand and fight.

As we conferred about Johnston, electrifying dispatches came in from the Shenandoah Valley. General Jackson was executing Lee's offensive-defensive perfectly.

19. LINCOLN

We'd sent McClellan every spare man we had. Result was, we thinned the line on the upper Potomac too much and the rebels broke it and put Banks in great peril. Here's how that developed. McClellan, almost in spite of himself, had inched his way to the outskirts of Richmond but was crying for reinforcements—claimed he could only bring about eighty thousand men into battle while the enemy had "perhaps double" that number. He was sure he faced total annihilation unless we sent him by the water routes McDowell's corps and all the other disposable troops in the Washington area.

Stanton and I worked out a new plan to help McClellan and at the same time keep Washington secure: McDowell's corps, now encamped at Falmouth on the Rappahannock, would cooperate with McClellan by advancing on Richmond by land. That way McDowell would be in position to protect Washington in case of an enemy attack from the Shenandoah. Once he reached Richmond, he could harass it from one direction while McClellan harassed it from another. The rebel capital would be trapped between them while Washington remained secure.

But that plan got McClellan's hackles up. Back came a ten-page telegram informing us that McDowell should join him, McClellan, by water and come under his command. It was the only way. A separate command for McDowell would only cause confusion. "I believe that there is a great struggle before this army," McClellan informed us, "but I am neither dismayed or discouraged. I trust that the result may either obtain for me the permanent confidence of my government or that it may close my career."

But we thought our plan was sound and stuck to it. On May twenty-third I went down to Aquia Creek to talk to McDowell as he prepared for the overland march against Richmond. Got back to Washington at five the next morning and went directly to the War Department, where Stanton handed me a batch of dispatches from Banks in the Shenandoah. A rebel army under Jackson was on a rampage down there, had routed a small Federal garrison at Front Royal, which put Jackson in position to cut off Banks's army at Winchester.

Secretary Chase joined us for a conference at the War Department. Was this a diversion or the beginning of an attack on Washington by way of Harpers Ferry? Either way we saw a chance to trap Jackson. If Frémont, in western Virginia, made a forced march to the Shenandoah from the west and McDowell did the same from the east, they could cut off Jackson's escape. We sent out the orders at once. McDowell was to cancel the Richmond operation and dispatch twenty thousand men immediately to cooperate with Frémont. *Hurry*, we told both generals. *Move with utmost speed.* I then explained to McClellan that Banks's critical position in the valley had forced us to withhold McDowell a second time.

All the next day we were bombarded with distressing news about Banks. Jackson had routed his army at Winchester and was now pursuing him toward Harpers Ferry and the Potomac. This convinced us that Jackson's was a general and concerted movement on Washington and we wired McClellan so. "I think the time is near," I said, "when you must either attack Richmond or give up the job and come to the defense of Washington."

Back came his reply: "The time is very near when I shall attack Richmond. The object of the enemy's movements is probably to prevent reinforcements being sent to me. All the information obtained from balloon, deserters, prisoners, and contrabands agrees in the statement that the mass of rebel troops are still in immediate vicinity of Richmond, ready to defend it."

McClellan, it turned out, was right. The next thing we heard from the valley, Jackson was retreating rapidly southward. "*Damn*," I said. "It was a diversion all along, to draw us off from Richmond. Well, we've got some tricks, too. We can bag Jackson before he leaves the valley." I ordered Frémont, McDowell, and Banks to march at once and cut Jackson off before he got away. From the map in Stanton's office, I did not see how they could fail if they only moved. "Hurry," I telegraphed them. "I have arranged this trap and am very unwilling to have it deranged." But they seemed unable to move with the speed that Jackson did. Frémont complained that marching over mountainous terrain slowed him down, and all three pleaded insurmountable logistical problems.

"I see you are at Moorefield," I stormed at Frémont. "You were expressly ordered to march to Harrisburg. What does this mean?" I prodded and begged and threatened the three generals. "Do not let the enemy escape you," I wired them. But Jackson did escape, whipping Frémont and McDowell's advance units as he went. Jackson fought so ferociously that Frémont swore he had from thirty to sixty thousand men. Turned out to be more like fifteen to sixteen thousand.

Frankly, I was disgusted with my three generals, and disgusted with myself for falling for Jackson's ruse in the first place and detaining McDowell. Now his corps was too beat up to cooperate with McClellan, and that unhappy general was screaming louder than ever for reinforcements. The rebels, he said, were massing "everything" against him. The government must send help at once by water or be guilty of "irreparable fault." I wired him back: "That the whole force of the enemy is concentrating in Richmond, I think can not be certainly known to you or me. I shall aid you all I can consistently with my view of due regard to all points."

It was the same complaint on all fronts. Each of our commanders along a line from Richmond in the East to Pittsburg Landing in the West supposed himself to be confronted by numbers superior to his own and cried for reinforcements. When Halleck raised the cry, I told him what I told McClellan: we did the best we could. Besides, Halleck had an army of more than 100,000 men. Surely the rebels at Corinth could not outnumber him. How could they outnumber Halleck *and* McClellan? Didn't seem possible.

Let me add right here why I liked that man Grant. Never once called for reinforcements. Simply asked, where's the enemy? and went after him. You know, they said he was drunk at Shiloh; said that was why the rebels surprised him. One fellow came here and demanded that I dismiss Grant. "I can't spare this man," I said, "he fights." I wished McClellan, Frémont, and Halleck would show some of Grant's spunk. I was glad, at least, when Halleck finally began his movement on Corinth with the huge force he had.

20. GRANT

Slowest campaign I ever saw. Gave me fits. Halleck was so afraid of being attacked that the army crawled along at a snail's pace, fortifying as it went. Why they called it "the pick and shovel campaign." Even commanders of reconnaissance patrols were cautioned not to bring on an engagement and informed in so many words that it would be better to retreat than to fight. At the time, I refrained from criticizing the commanding general, even wrote Julia he was one of the greatest men of the age. Same time, I thought he was too cautious.

Had a great army, thought he could've taken Corinth and destroyed the enemy force if he moved fast.

I regarded the campaign as the last great battle to be fought in the valley of the Mississippi. Was itching to take an active part. Instead, I was little more than an observer, and it got the best of me. Protested to Halleck in writing: "As I believe it is generally understood through this army that my position differs but little from that of one in arrest, and as this opinion may be much strengthened from the fact that orders to the Right Wing and the Reserve, both nominally under my command, are transmitted direct from General Headquarters, without going through me, I deem it due myself to ask either full restoration to duty, according to my rank, or to be relieved entirely from further duty."

Halleck replied: "I am very much surprised, General, that you should find any cause of complaint in the recent assignment of commands. *You have precisely the position to which your rank entitles you.*" Why I was under a dark cloud with Halleck I didn't know— maybe the newspaper accounts of Shiloh, like Sherman said. Whatever, I kept my mouth shut and stayed out of Halleck's way, crawling along as the army crawled along.

Took us one month to cover the eighteen or twenty miles to Corinth. When we got there, Halleck refused to attack and put the city under siege. That caused me to make my only recommendation of the campaign. Went to headquarters and told Halleck that the rebel works on the extreme right of our line, on Sherman's front, were defective, and that we ought to attack with Sherman's and Pope's columns, turn the rebel flank, and sweep the entire field. Halleck, an overweight man with a suspicious disposition, trained his bulging eyes on me, scratched his elbows indignantly, and told me in so many words: "When I want *your* opinion, I'll ask for it." I went back to my tent resolved to say no more.

When our troops near the railroad reported that trains could be heard steaming in and out of Corinth, many of us were sure the enemy was evacuating the city. General Logan thought it could be taken with a single brigade. *Nope,* says Halleck. *Trains are bringing in reinforcements. Enemy's going to attack. Certain of it.* Then he orders the entire army into a defensive line of battle. The attack never came. Instead the enemy batteries fell silent. A scout reported that his works were empty. The biggest army in the West then marched into town to find no enemy troops anywhere. Beauregard had made good his escape.

I rode over to inspect the rebel left. Just as I expected, it proved to be the weakest segment of the enemy line. Satisfied me that if Halleck had followed my advice and ordered an assault there, a good general could have demolished the rebel army and delivered a fatal blow to the Confederate cause.

Disgusted with everything, I asked Halleck for a thirty-day leave of absence and made plans to go home to Julia.

21. SHERMAN

When I was at headquarters, Halleck casually mentioned that Grant was leaving the army the next morning—said he'd asked for a leave and Halleck had granted it. Why? I asked. Halleck said he didn't know. Hell, he didn't. We all knew Grant was chafing under the slights of his anomalous position. On the way back from headquarters, I stopped at Grant's camp in the woods just off the road. His office and camp chests were all packed and ready for departure. Grant was in his tent, sitting on a campstool, tying up bundles of his papers at his rude table.

"Is it true?" I asked. "You leaving?"

"Yep."

"But why?"

"You know, Sherman. I'm in the way here. Stood it as long as I can."

"Where you going?"

"St. Louis."

"Business there?"

"Nope."

I begged him not to leave and compared his situation to mine before Shiloh. "Grant, before Shiloh I was cast down by a newspaper assertion that I was crazy. But that one battle gave me new life, and now I'm in high feather. If you go away, the war will go on, and you'll be left out. But if you stay, some happy accident may well restore you to favor and your true place at the head of an army."

He didn't respond. "Well," I said finally, "if that's your decision, I wonder if I might have your cavalry escort, if you're not going to need it."

A day or so later Grant sent me a note that he was staying. I'd heard that Halleck had also asked him not to go. I wrote Grant: "Just received your note and am rejoiced at your conclusion to remain. For yourself, you could not be quiet at home for a week, when armies were moving, and rest could not relieve your mind of the gnawing sensation that injustice has been done you. There is a power in our land, irresponsible, corrupt and malicious, the press, which has created the intense feelings of hostility that have arrayed the two parts of our country against each other, which must be curbed, and brought within the just limits of reason and law, before we can have peace in America. War cannot cease as long as any flippant fool of an editor may stir up the passions of the multitude, arraign with impunity the motives of the most honorable, and howl on their gang of bloody hounds to hunt down any man who despises their order. We can deal with armies who have a visible and tangible existence, but it will require tact and skill and courage to clip the wings of this public enemy, and I hope you have sufficiently felt the force of what I say to join in their just punishment before we resign our power and pass into the humble rank of citizens. The moment you obtained a just celebrity at Donelson, by a stroke of war more rich in consequences than was the battle of Saratoga, envious rivals and malicious men set their pack of hounds at you, to pull you from the pinnacle which you had richly attained. By patience and silence we can quiet their noise, and in due time make them feel that in defaming others, they have destroyed themselves. Already is their power of mischief on the wane, and as soon as a few I could name drop the dirty minions of a corrupt press, they will drop back into the abyss of infamy they deserve. Of course I only asked for your escort, when I believed you had resolved to leave us, and assure you that I rejoice to learn of your change of purpose."

22. DAVIS

I was furious and disgusted when Beauregard abandoned Corinth and fell back to Tupelo, fifty miles to the south. He had vowed to hold Corinth "to the last extremity," but had retreated long before that extremity had arrived. The fall of Corinth cut off our remaining northern outposts on the Mississippi—first Fort Pillow and then Memphis fell to the barbarous invader. Beauregard meantime claimed to have made "a brilliant and successful retreat" but I demanded an explanation. He pleaded his constant occupation as the cause of his delay to make a reply. Constant occupation! With what? Certainly not with fighting. I wrote Varina: "There are those who can only walk a log when it is near the ground, and I fear Beauregard has been placed too high for his mental strength."

My judgment as to his mental strength was confirmed when a wire came from Bragg that Beauregard had announced that his health did not permit him to remain in command; he had thereupon turned his command over to Bragg and departed for Bladen Springs. What brash impertinence! He did not even notify his government, still less ask permission to retire. I immediately appointed Bragg as permanent commander of the Western Department. At the same time, I named Van Dorn commander of the Department of Southern Mississippi and East Louisiana, and he made preparations for a desperate defense of Vicksburg, our great garrison on the Mississippi.

In Bragg and Van Dorn I believed I had competent departmental commanders. But I could not say the same for General Johnston. Seeing no preparation for keeping McClellan at a distance, and being kept in ignorance of any plan for such a purpose, I went to see General Lee and told him I was highly dissatisfied with the condition of affairs in front of Richmond.

"What do you think ought to be done?" he asked.

"I think McClellan should be attacked on the other side of the Chickahominy before he can mature plans to besiege Richmond."

"Let me go and see General Johnston. Defer a decision until I return."

When Lee came back, he told me that Johnston proposed to attack the enemy on May twenty-ninth and that he, Lee, expected excellent results from this offensive-defensive program. As the hour of battle approached, I felt a peculiar exhilaration: I felt like mustering claws were in me and that cramping fetters had fallen from my limbs. *Richmond would not fall, not if I could help it.* On the twenty-ninth, I rode out to Meadow Bridge to observe the battle. I grew anxious, however, when I saw General Smith's division halted in the road. Riding on, I found General Longstreet, a tall, thickset soldier with a full beard and steel blue eyes, walking to and fro in a fretful manner. He said his division had been under arms all day waiting for orders to advance. But the day was now so far spent an advance was not possible. He said he did not know what was the matter. I knew where the trouble lay: Joe Johnston. He seemed congenitally incapable of launching an attack, and I had lost all patience with him. I sent him a warning: "If you will not give battle, I will appoint someone to command who will."

While awaiting his attack back in Richmond, I was stunned to read on the front page of the *Richmond Examiner* the following article about the plundering of our plantation at Davis Bend on the Mississippi: "We learn that the vandals have come off their boats and battered down and utterly destroyed the residence of Jefferson Davis, and also that of Joseph Davis. Their acts of destruction and vandalism in that neighborhood were complete, leaving nothing but a bleak and desolated track behind." I was filled with anger and sorrow. Our manor sacked, our fine library destroyed, our blooded stock lost, our Negroes forcibly deported. I wrote Varina: "You will have seen a notice of the destruction of our home. If our cause succeeds we shall not mourn over any personal deprivation; if it should not, why, 'the deluge.'"

On May thirty-first, we heard the boom of artillery in the direction of Nine Mile Road. Was Johnston finally attacking? Typically of him, he had said nothing to me or General Lee about any plan of battle that day. General Lee rode to the front at once. I put on a high silk hat and followed with Reagan and two aides, heading out New Bridge Road in the direction of the firing, which seemed to be coming from Seven Pines. We found General Lee at Johnston's headquarters, located in a house.

"It's not a battle," Lee said in answer to my question. "I spoke with General Johnston before he went to the front and he assured me it could be nothing more than an artillery duel."

We walked to the rear of the house and listened: that was musketry. It sounded like hail striking the ground. Satisfied that an action, or at least a severe skirmish, must be going on, we rode to the field of battle, which extended along the Nine Mile Road across York River Railroad and the Williamsburg stage road, where the Federals had constructed redoubts with long lines of rifle pits covered by abatis— sharpened branches of trees aimed at the enemy. When we reached the left side of our line, we found Whiting's troops hotly engaged. They had attacked the enemy and driven him from his advanced encampment back across an open field to the bank of the Chickahominy, a deep, sluggish, narrow river bordered by marshes and covered with tangled wood and swollen now from heavy rains during the night. Sitting motionless on my horse, I watched the enemy intently, impervious to the bullets flying around me. Reagan protested that I was unnecessarily exposing myself, but I kept my eye on the battle, known as the Battle of Seven Pines.

What was happening now? Whiting's men appeared to be falling back in confusion. I dispatched three separate couriers to General Magruder, directing him to send reinforcements by the wooded path, just under the bluff, to attack the enemy in flank and reverse. But the fighting in front ceased; now it was too late for reinforcements to effect anything. It was clear to me that improper preparations and unaccountable delays in bringing some of our troops into action prevented us from gaining a decisive victory.

General Johnston meanwhile had been carried back severely wounded. I must say, the poor fellow bore his suffering most heroically. When he was about to be put in the ambulance to be removed from the field, I dismounted to speak with him. He opened his eyes, smiled, gave me his hand, and said he did not know how seriously he was hurt, but feared a fragment of a shell had injured his spine.

As darkness fell, Lee and I rode back to Richmond. "General Lee," I said, "I am assigning you to the command of the army."

23. LINCOLN

I was at the War Department telegraph office on the afternoon of June first when a dispatch came ticking in from McClellan. I grabbed it as soon as it was complete. "We have had a desperate battle in which the corps of Sumner, Heintzelman & Keyes have been engaged against greatly superior numbers. Yesterday at one the enemy taking advantage of a terrible storm which had flooded the valley of the Chickahominy attacked our troops on the right bank of that river. But Heintzelman & Kearny most gallantly brought up their troops, which checked the enemy. This morning the enemy attempted to renew the conflict but was every where repulsed. Our loss is heavy, but that of the enemy must be enormous."

This was good news. But what did McClellan intend to do? Could we dare hope for a counterattack? Next day came another dispatch: "Our left is now within four (4) miles of Richmond. I only wait for the river to fall to cross with the rest of the force & make a general attack. Should I find them holding firm in a very strong position I may wait for what troops I can bring up from Fort Monroe—but the morale of my troops is now such that I can venture much & do not care for odds against me."

This was almost too good to be true. Had the taste of battle stiffened McClellan's spine? Stanton and I expected to hear of an attack at any hour. But of course it didn't happen. On June fourth McClellan wired his excuse for inaction directly to me: "Terrible rain storm during the night & morning—not yet cleared off. Chickahominy flooded, bridges in bad condition—are still hard at work at them. I have taken every possible step to insure the security of the Corps on the right bank, but I cannot reinforce them from here until my brigades are all safe as my force is too small to insure my right & rear should the enemy attack in that direction, as they may probably attempt. I have to be very cautious now." There it was—McClellan's favorite word again. Not a good sign. "Our loss in the late battle will probably exceed 5,000," the dispatch continued. "On account of the effect it might have on our own men & the enemy I request that you will regard this information as confidential for a few days. I am satisfied that the loss of the enemy was very considerably greater— they were terribly punished." If so, then I wondered why he hadn't pitched into 'em with everything he had. Might have won a decisive victory. I also worried about the Chickahominy being so close to his rear, and crossing his line of communication, and urged him to look well to it. He answered: "Your Excellency may rest assured that it has not been overlooked."

He also reported that Lee had taken command of the rebel army, which he said he liked, because Lee was "too cautious and weak." This of course was a case of the skillet calling the kettle black. Even so, Stanton and I expected him to counterattack. But wouldn't you know? He dug his heels in and cried for reinforcements—even suggested we transfer 'em from Halleck in the West. When we sent McClellan one of McDowell's divisions, he found another excuse for inaction: heavy rains, McClellan said, had made the roads impassable. His artillery and wagon trains were bogged down in the mud. Before he could move against Richmond, he had to build footbridges and corduroy the roads.

Pacing back and forth in the telegraph office, I pointed out that the rebels had attacked in bad weather. Why couldn't McClellan? He seemed to think heaven sent rain only on the Just. "I should never have let him go down there," I told Browning. "Manassas is where we should have fought the rebels, when their supply line was stretched. Now they're entrenched in front of Richmond in greater force. I don't think McClellan will ever attack now."

On June twenty-fifth I took the train up to West Point to confer with General Scott. This generated speculation in the public prints that I intended to restore Scott to command. Scott issued a denial, but I didn't say a thing—maybe McClellan would be galvanized into action if he thought he was about to be replaced. When I got back to Washington, a dispatch from McClellan was waiting for me at the telegraph office. "Several contrabands just in give information confirming supposition that Jackson's advance is at or near Hanover CH & that Beauregard arrived with strong reinforcements in Richmond yesterday. I incline to think that Jackson will attack my right & rear. The rebel force is stated at 200,000 including Jackson & Beauregard. I shall have to contend against vastly superior odds if these reports be true. I regret my great inferiority in numbers but feel that I am in no way responsible for it as I have not failed to present repeatedly the necessity of reinforcements, that this was the decisive point, & that all the available means of the government should be concentrated here. I will do all that a General can do with the splendid army I have the honor to command & if it is destroyed by overwhelming numbers can at least die with it & share its fate. But if the result of the action which will probably occur tomorrow or within a short time is a disaster, the responsibility cannot be thrown on my shoulders—it must rest where it belongs."

That arrogant little rooster! This was close to insubordination. I looked at Stanton. He shook his head, his narrow little eyes flashing with irritation. "He doesn't even mention that we sent him a division by water," Stanton growled.

"You send him one division, he demands two," I said. "Send him two and he demands four. Sending men to that army is like shoveling fleas across a barnyard. Half never get there."

I wired McClellan back: "Your dispatch pains me very much. I give you all I can, and act on the presumption that you will do the best you can with what you have, while you continue, ungenerously I think, to assume that I could give you more if I would. I have omitted and shall omit no opportunity to send you reinforcements whenever I possibly can."

That same day, June twenty-sixth, I did something I should've done earlier: I brought the forces of Frémont, Banks, and McDowell together in a single army, the Army of Virginia, and appointed John

Pope to command it. Pope had been with Halleck in the West, had captured Island No. 10 in the Mississippi, and impressed us with his no-nonsense approach to fighting. He's a big, striking man, with burning eyes and a bewhiskered chin. His daddy was a district judge back home—I'd practiced in his court.

When Pope reached Washington, he impressed everybody with his blustering talk. Said we had to fight an *offensive* war, had to attack and destroy the enemy *now*. That kind of zeal excited Wade and Chandler no end. "If Pope was in command of the Army of the Potomac," they said, "he'd seize Richmond at once and drive clear to the Gulf of Mexico." I told Pope that his army, while protecting western Virginia and Washington City from danger or insult, should in the speediest manner attack and overcome the rebel forces under Jackson and Ewell, threaten the enemy in the direction of Charlottesville, and render the most effective aid to relieve McClellan and capture Richmond.

That evening another telegram came from McClellan. The enemy had attacked him in "superior numbers" just below a place called Mechanicsville near the Chickahominy. "My men are behaving superbly. But you must not expect them to contest too long against great odds."

24. LEE

We faced long odds. General McClellan's army, I believed, outnumbered mine 150,000 to 85,000 and was entrenched in field works vast in extent and formidable in character within sight of Richmond. Yet he had left himself vulnerable by dividing his army: the bulk of his troops were on the south side of the Chickahominy and the rest, a corps of about 35,000, were on the north side with their right flank in the air. This I learned from Jeb Stuart after he made his celebrated ride around McClellan's army with 1,200 handpicked cavalry.

When Stuart reported the enemy dispositions, I proposed to President Davis that we take the offensive. While Magruder, with 27,000 men, remained south of the Chickahominy to hold the huge enemy left in check, I planned to move the rest of my army—which I now called the Army of Northern Virginia—across to the north side of the Chickahominy and fall on the exposed enemy corps. Jackson's four divisions—which included my youngest son, Rob, who served as a private in one of Jackson's batteries—would launch the attack, striking the enemy's right flank and rear. A. P. Hill's division, followed by D. H. Hill and Longstreet, would cross the river and advance against the enemy front at Mechanicsville. Then, linking up with Jackson, they would advance en echelon from left to right, and the army would sweep McClellan's entire force from the field. Then we could march unimpeded on McClellan's supply line, cutting him off from his base at White House on the Pamunkey River.

The president looked grave and careworn. "A bold plan, General Lee. Audacious."

"Your Excellency, we have to be audacious if we are going to win this war against the odds we face."

"I have one reservation," he said. "Won't McClellan move immediately on Richmond as soon as he finds that most of your army is on the north side of the river? How can Magruder's twenty-seven thousand hold off more than a hundred thousand men? On the other hand, if McClellan behaves like an engineering officer and deems it his first duty to protect his line of communication, I think the plan will be a success."

"I don't know if engineering officers are more likely than others to make such a mistake," I said—I had been an engineer myself in the old army. But I added: "General McClellan is cautious. If Magruder can hold the enemy's left wing at his entrenchment as long as he can, and then falls back on the detached works around the city, I will be on McClellan's heels before he gets there." As I said that, I slapped the palm of one hand with the fist of my other hand. My blood was up—I could sense a weakness in McClellan— did not think he would attack Magruder or cross the Chickahominy with the rest of his army—and all my instincts said *attack.*

On the day of battle, June twenty-sixth, I waited with growing impatience for General Jackson to begin the attack on the Federal right. When three o'clock came without any word from Jackson, I thought I would have to call off the battle. But then the rattle of musketry and roar of artillery sounded from Powell Hill's front, which meant that Hill was crossing the river and going into action. But what about Jackson? Followed by my staff, I set out through the swampy woodlands hoping that Hill was now fighting his way into Mechanicsville and clearing the turnpike. Then he could go forward and support Jackson, if Jackson was where he was supposed to be.

When I reached Mechanicsville, I saw that nothing was going according to plan. Hill hadn't waited for Jackson, but had attacked on his own initiative—had driven the enemy from his entrenchments and forced him to take refuge in new works on the left bank of Beaver Dam Creek, about a mile from Mechanicsville and some six miles northeast of Richmond. Hill had attempted to carry the new position by assault, but had been repulsed. Jackson was expected to pass Beaver Dam above and turn the enemy's right, but nobody knew where Jackson was, so I sent an aide to find out.

Shells were exploding all around the plain, knocking riders and horses down. As I sat Traveller, I noticed President Davis with a group of excited politicians, all on horseback. What in God's name was he doing here? A single Yankee shell burst could obliterate the chief of state.

I rode over and saluted. "Mr. President"—I gestured at the group with him—"who are these men and what are they doing here?"

"They are with me, General."

"Your Excellency, this is no place for you or them." Davis blanched at that, but then lifted his top hat and rode toward the rear. Later I learned that a shell had exploded close to Davis, killing a young man.

As soon as the Mechanicsville Bridge was repaired, Longstreet's and D. H. Hill's divisions crossed the creek, but it was late when they reached the north bank of the Chickahominy. The firing continued sporadically until nine that evening, when the engagement ceased. By any reckoning, the battle of Mechanicsville had not been a success. We had had 56,000 men north of the Chickahominy, yet only 14,000 had gone into action and 1,400 of those had fallen. I learned from General Jackson that in consequence of unavoidable delays, he had arrived at his position too late to begin his movement against the enemy right, as planned.

25 · LINCOLN

That night McClellan sent us an ecstatic telegram: "Victory of today complete & against great odds. I almost begin to think we are invincible." A *complete victory*! Stanton and I were so excited we practically danced around the crowded telegraph room. If this report was true, McClellan must have destroyed Lee's army and would march into Richmond tomorrow. This was an astounding development. I was ready to take back every harsh word I'd ever said about McClellan and his peninsula campaign.

As it turned out, McClellan's idea of a "complete" victory was not the destruction of the enemy army, but merely repulsing it, which led him into hysterical exaggeration of what he'd accomplished. The next day, he reported to Stanton that he was once again under heavy attack by "superior numbers" and that the "most severe struggle" was yet to come. "If I am forced to concentrate between the Chickahominy & James," he said, "I will at once endeavor to open communications with you. All reinforcements should for the present go to Fort Monroe. It is absolutely certain that Jackson, Ewell, and Whiting are here. As this may be the last dispatch I send you for some time I will beg that you put some one General in command of the Shenandoah & of all the troops in front of Washington. For the sake of the country secure unity of action & bring the best men forward. Good bye & present my respects to the President."

I appreciated that last line, but the rest of this telegram had me worried. Was McClellan contemplating a retreat? Dear God, I hoped not. What would the country say? In the absence of detailed reports, Washington was "almost wild with rumors and suspense," to quote young Nicolay, and crowds gathered at Willard's Hotel in anticipation of the latest bulletins. I camped out in Stanton's office, lying on a sofa while General Pope exhorted me not to let McClellan retreat.

26. LEE

On June twenty-seventh, our reconnaissance discovered that the enemy corps on the north side of the Chickahominy had evacuated their fortifications at Beaver Dam Creek—the conflagration of wagons and stores marked the way of their retreat toward Cold Harbor and Gaines Mill. "We must pursue quickly and press the attack," I told my aides and sent them down our lines to give the order. A courier brought word that Jackson was on the ground on our left, and I trotted off to confer with him.

When I found him, I thought, again, what a strange man he was, eating fruit and quoting Scripture so often that his men called him Old Blue Light. He walked in an awkward, ungainly manner, as if he could not quite coordinate the movement of his legs with the rest of his body. He wore knee-length cavalry boots over the biggest feet I have ever seen on a man, in addition to a red coat and a faded old cadet cap pulled so low over his forehead that he had to tilt his head up to see under it. When it came to fighting, though, I had no better soldier in the army.

I dismounted and sat with Jackson on a tree stump near a way-side church. He spoke slowly and did not look in such good shape, owing to his forced march from the Valley. He offered no excuses for his tardiness yesterday, and I asked for none, merely telling him to move on Cold Harbor without delay. Then I rode to Hill's division, which led the advance of the army, and told him to find the enemy and attack him.

Hot and humid though it was in the fierce glare of the sun, I wore my full uniform—regulation gray woolen coat, pants tucked into high boots, and a handsome hat surmounting my gray head (the latter was not prescribed in the regulations) and shielding my face, which was masked by a white beard as stiff and wiry as the teeth of a card. The mosquitoes assailed us dreadfully as we bore down on the enemy, yet there was no protection against those tenacious insects.

We found the enemy fortified on the high ground behind Boat-swain's Swamp, near Gaines Mill. I devised a plan of battle forth-with and sent instructions by couriers to my divisional commanders: Jackson was to attack the enemy right while A. P. Hill assaulted his center and Longstreet demonstrated against his left. If the enemy moved troops to meet Jackson's thrusts, Longstreet would shift to the attack, and the entire army would go forward in concert and drive the enemy from the field. Then we would get behind McClellan's army and upon his supply line, and his destruction would be at hand.

But once again Jackson was late in coming up. Powell Hill's lone division of fewer than sixteen thousand, leading our advance, rushed to the attack with the impetuous courage for which that officer and his troops were distinguished, but the smoke of battle was so heavy that I could make out little of the action through my glass. I had to judge the progress of the fighting mostly by the sound of the gunfire. Soon word came that Hill had been repulsed and that many of his men had fallen back in panic and disorder into the woods along the Cold Harbor Road.

By the sound of the firing, the Federals appeared to have gone on the offensive. This was critical. Where was Jackson? I sent one courier after another to hurry him forward. Since the enemy plainly had not shifted troops to meet any threat on his left, I dropped my previous plan of battle and ordered an attack all along the line once the army was in position. Meanwhile, to relieve the pressure on Hill, I instructed Longstreet to make a diversion against the enemy's right. But Old Pete sent word that the enemy was too strong in his front for a demonstration to do any good. To help Hill, he would have to mount an all-out assault against the heights, and that he was preparing to do.

That was the situation when down the road from Old Cold Harbor came General Jackson, riding a homely little horse and sucking on a lemon. "Ah, General," I said, "I am very glad to see you. I had hoped to be with you before now." That was a mild reprimand for his delay. He mumbled something I couldn't make out, due to the roar of battle sounding from the south. "That fire is very heavy," I said. "Do you think your men can stand it?"

He listened for a moment, then said matter-of-factly, "They can stand almost anything. They can stand that. Already gave them orders to sweep the field with the bayonet." With that he rode away to join them.

At last the entire army was up. I saw Jackson's right division, that of Whiting, going into position to the left of Longstreet. At the head of Whiting's column was Brigadier General John Bell Hood's Texas brigade. I rode up to Hood, a tall, rangy, rawboned soldier with sad eyes, and told him that gallant troops on the front had tried but failed to dislodge the enemy.

"This must be done," I said. "Can you break his line?"

"I'll try," he said.

I was anxious for the attack to commence from right to left. Twilight was settling, the day still could be lost. Then I heard that shrill cry, which always thrilled me: the rebel yell. On the right Whiting's troops moved forward steadily, unchecked by the terrible fire from triple lines of enemy infantry on the hill and enemy cannon on both sides of the river, which burst upon them as they emerged upon the plain. Shells exploded among them and canister and solid shot slammed into their ranks, yet on they went, advancing over ground strewn with the dead and wounded, the brave Texans and their commander out in front, leading the attack. The charge of those Texans won them a special place in my heart. Braving that storm of musketry and canister, without once breaking alignment, they routed the enemy from his first line of works, drove him up the hill to the entrenchments on the crest, and broke through those as well, which cracked the enemy line. From the crest Hood could be seen holding up a triumphant sword that reflected the red sun sinking on the wooded horizon.

Now came the rest of the army, widening the breach made by the Texans, driving the enemy back into the field beyond the hill and capturing fourteen guns. Fresh troops came to the enemy's support and he endeavored repeatedly to rally, but in vain. Our columns drove their broken forces back with great slaughter, and they fled to the banks of the Chickahominy, or wandered through the woods, until night put an end to the pursuit. Our troops had full possession of the field, which was covered with the Federal dead and wounded and, alas, with our own fallen, perhaps eight thousand of them. I sent a message to the president that I was profoundly grateful to Almighty God that He had blessed us with a victory.

I could have thanked God for General McClellan, too. In both battles, Mechanicsville and Gaines Mill, he had kept the principal part of his army south of the Chickahominy and out of the action on the north side. Much of this was due to General Magruder's theatrics—his artillery fired repeated salvoes and his men moved around noisily, apparently convincing McClellan that he was outnumbered on both sides of the river.

27 . LINCOLN

This came in from McClellan in the early morning of June twenty-eighth: "On this side of the river—the left bank—we repulsed several very strong attacks. On the right bank our men did all that men could do, all that soldiers could accomplish—but they were overwhelmed by vastly superior numbers even after I brought my last reserves into action. The loss on both sides is terrible—I believe it will prove to be the most desperate battle of the war.

"If we have lost the day we have yet preserved our honor & no one need blush for the Army of the Potomac. I have lost this battle because my force was too small. I again repeat that I am not responsible for this & I say it with the earnestness of a General who feels in his heart the loss of every brave man who has been needlessly sacrificed today. I still hope to retrieve our fortunes, but to do this the Govt must view the matter in the same earnest light that I do—you must send me very large reinforcements, & send them at once. I shall draw back to this side of the Chickahominy & think I can withdraw all our materiel.

"In addition to what I have already said I only wish to say to the President that I think he is wrong, in regarding me as ungenerous when I said that my force was too weak. I merely reiterated a truth which today has been too plainly proved. I know that a few thousand men more would have changed this battle from a defeat to a victory—as it is the Govt must not & cannot hold me responsible for the result.

"I feel too earnestly tonight—I have seen too many dead & wounded comrades to feel otherwise than that the Govt has not sustained this Army. If you do not do so now the game is lost."

I tell you, that telegram made me mad and depressed at the same time. I wired McClellan back: "Save your Army at all events. Will send reinforcements as fast as we can. Of course they can not reach you today, tomorrow, or next day. I have not said you were ungenerous for saying you needed reinforcements. I thought you were ungenerous in assuming that I did not send them as fast as I could. I feel any misfortune to you and your Army quite as keenly as you feel it yourself."

The truth was, Stanton and I were doing all in our power to send McClellan reinforcements. We ordered Burnside to bring ten thousand men from the North Carolina coast and asked Halleck to transfer twenty-five thousand of his troops to Richmond by the nearest and quickest route. But Halleck was getting up an important expedition against Chattanooga and couldn't spare twenty-five thousand men. So we had no choice but to appeal to the governors for more volunteers, no matter how unpopular that might be. Already the papers were fulminating about McClellan's failure to seize Richmond and there were bitter blasts against me and the Cabinet for letting him go down there. In an open letter to Seward, which the secretary of state took to a conference of governors in New York, I explained that the enemy had concentrated too great a force in Richmond for McClellan to successfully attack. But if we sent all the forces in Washington to McClellan, the enemy would send a force from Richmond and take Washington. Or, if a large part of the western army be brought here to McClellan, they would let us have Richmond and retake Tennessee, Kentucky, and Missouri. What ought to be done was to hold what we had in the West and defend Washington in every event. Then let the country give us 100,000 new troops in the shortest possible time, which when added to McClellan, directly or indirectly, would enable him to take Richmond without endangering any other place we now held—and would substantially end the war. "I expect," I said, "to maintain this contest until successful, or till I die, or am conquered, or my term expires, or Congress or the country forsakes me."

Thanks to Seward's persuasive powers, eighteen governors offered me a levy of all the men I needed. I asked them for 300,000 volunteers and wired McClellan that help would be on the way as soon as possible. "We still have strength enough in the country and will bring it out."

28. LEE

On the morning of the twenty-eighth, we discovered that none of the enemy remained on the north side of the Chickahominy. What was McClellan up to now? Great fires could be seen blazing and smoking within Federal lines south of the river. In the afternoon, columns of dust indicated that the entire Federal army was in motion, but to where? Was McClellan retreating down the Peninsula or changing his base from the Pamunkey to the James River? By nightfall, there were no indications that the Federals were approaching the lower bridges of the Chickahominy, so as to retire down the Peninsula. This meant that McClellan was retreating to the James and the cover of his gunboats.

I put my army into motion early on the twenty-ninth, intending to smash the retreating Federals by attacking their flank and rear. Magruder and Huger led the pursuit and found the whole line of McClellan's works deserted and large quantities of military stores of every description abandoned or destroyed; the fields were littered with discarded weapons and equipment, indicating the haste and panic with which the enemy had withdrawn. My advance columns came upon his rear guard at Savage Station, and I ordered Jackson to attack the flank and rear of this position from the north while Magruder struck from the west. Jackson, however, was delayed by the necessity of reconstructing the Grapevine Bridge, and in late afternoon Magruder finally attacked the enemy with one of his divisions in a severe action that ended with nightfall. I was disappointed that a decisive blow had not been delivered, and frustrated that the enemy was able to continue his retreat under cover of darkness. At Savage Station we found about 2,500 Federals in a hospital, but stores of much value, including hospital supplies for the sick and wounded, had been put to the torch.

I was determined to overtake McClellan the next day, the thirtieth, and destroy his army. Jackson reached Savage Station early in the morning, and I was concerned about him: he was covered with dust and his eyes had a vacant look, a sure sign of exhaustion. Nevertheless, I ordered him to pursue the enemy on the road he had taken, and then I joined Longstreet's division as it followed the enemy by the Darbytown Road. About mid-afternoon artillery fire sounded from the direction of Huger's advance, and I rode ahead to find out what it meant. I found Longstreet standing with President Davis in a clearing of small pine trees, within range of an enemy battery. It was a hot, cloudless day, and the sun bore down oppressively as I dismounted and saluted Davis.

"General," he said, "what are you doing here? You're in too dangerous a position for the commander of the army."

"I'm trying to find out something about the movements and plans of those people," I said. "But you must excuse me, Mr. President, for asking what *you* are doing here and for suggesting that this is no place for the commander in chief of all our armies."

"I'm here for the same reason you are."

As we spoke, red-bearded little Powell Hill rushed up. "Gentlemen, this is no place for either of you. I beg you to go to the rear. In fact, as commander of this part of the army, I *order* you to the rear."

We moved off a ways and then halted. But we were still in range of the enemy guns, and shells were exploding nearby. Hill galloped over. "Did I not order you to the rear? Did you not promise to obey me? A single shot from that battery over yonder could deprive the Confederacy of its president and the Army of Northern Virginia of its commander." This time we moved beyond the range of the enemy guns.

A courier from our cavalry brought discouraging news: the Federals were moving across Malvern Hill, which put them close to the

James. Could this be true? I rode forward and found that the report was correct: the Federals could be seen on top of Malvern Hill, which had been one of my maternal grandfather's large estates. I had no idea where Jackson or Huger were (Jackson, I learned later, was unable to force the passage of White Oak Swamp). Only Longstreet's and Powell Hill's divisions were in position to attack an enemy of unknown strength. I ordered them to proceed without delay.

Further reconnaissance placed the enemy's defensive line, unfortified, across the Charles City road near the settlement of Glendale, in a neighborhood of small farmhouses, impenetrable woods, bogs, and thick underbrush. At five in the afternoon, Longstreet and Hill sent their brigades forward across this difficult terrain. The battle raged furiously until nine that night, by which time the enemy had been driven with great slaughter from every position but one, which he held until he was able to withdraw under cover of darkness. Though we possessed the entire field, I was frustrated and angry. Had the other commands cooperated in the attack of Longstreet and Hill, the result might well have been the total destruction of McClellan's army.

The next day, July first, the Army of Northern Virginia was again united and ready for a pursuit that many now thought was hopeless. I could not conceal my bitterness. When Jubal Early said he feared that McClellan would escape, I exploded: "Yes, he will get away because I cannot have my orders carried out!" I admit I have naturally a terrible temper which requires great force to keep it in control. But in particularly vexing moments, like this one, I lost control, and the tone of my voice and the look in my eyes were of such force that it silenced everyone in my presence.

I went forward to reconnoiter and found that the enemy had established a new defensive line on top of Malvern Hill, three miles south of Glendale. Flanked by deep ravines, Malvern Hill was a position of great natural strength. Through my glass, I saw that McClellan had concentrated his powerful artillery up there—maybe one hundred guns—and these were supported by masses of infantry, partially protected by earthworks. The only way we could carry the position was by frontal assault, uphill, across open ground completely swept by the fire of McClellan's infantry and artillery. At first glance, it looked hopeless. But I sensed panic in McClellan's retreat— the discarded equipment suggested that—and thought his army was demoralized. A frontal attack was a risk, but one worth taking if it resulted in the annihilation of McClellan's army.

"D. H. Hill don't like it," Longstreet said. "Says if McClellan is on the hill in force we had better let him alone. 'Don't get scared now that we have got him whipped,' I told him." Longstreet said that he had found an advantageous position for our artillery, a hill on our right. If our guns were deployed there and in the field, they could lay down a converging fire on the Federals that would demoralize them further and clear the way for our infantry. I gave the order for the guns to be so deployed. Once they had done their work, the infantry of Jackson and Magruder were to attack at the same time, with Longstreet and Powell Hill in reserve.

Things went wrong from the start. The woods and swamps made it impossible to bring up sufficient artillery to contest the enemy's extraordinary force of guns. As fast as we could get batteries into the field, the enemy artillery knocked them out with thunderous cannonades. Owing to ignorance of the country, to the dense forests impeding necessary communication, and to the extreme difficulty of the ground, the whole line of attack was not formed until a late hour in the afternoon. The same obstacles prevented my field commanders from acting in concert, and the attack, when it came, was badly coordinated. D. H. Hill advanced up that deadly slope into the very muzzles of the Union guns, but not being supported by a simultaneous advance of the other troops, Hill was unable to keep the ground he had gained. Jackson sent his old division and part of Ewell's in to support Hill, but they arrived too late to help. On our right, Magruder and Huger led their troops forward and made several determined efforts to storm the hill at Crew's house. The brigades advanced bravely across the open field, raked by the fire of a hundred cannon and the musketry of large bodies of infantry. From where I was, watching through my glass, I could see our bullet-torn battle flags rising and falling in the thick pall of smoke. Some of our units broke and gave way, but others approached close to the flaming guns and drove the enemy infantry back, compelling his advance batteries to retire or risk capture. Here and there in the drifting smoke I could see our men battling the enemy at close quarters, mingling our dead with theirs. But for want of concert among the attacking columns, the assaults were too weak to break the enemy lines, and after struggling gallantly, our columns were forced to retire, leaving 5,500 of our dead and wounded on the field.

Many of my officers thought the battle had been a mistake. D. H. Hill complained bitterly, "It was not war—it was murder."

"Rivers of good blood flowed that evening," said young Porter Alexander of the artillery, "all in vain."

The next morning, we discovered that the enemy had withdrawn during the night, leaving the ground covered with his dead and wounded, and his route exhibited abundant evidence of a precipitate retreat. I ordered our cavalry to pursue him, but a torrential downpour greatly impeded my efforts to organize a full-scale pursuit. I was in the dining room of a plantation house, reading reports from my subordinates, when Pete Longstreet came in, dripping wet and downcast. Old Pete, I thought, my dependable old warhorse. He's over six feet tall, strong and stout, with a thick beard and dark, steady eyes. Last winter, he and his wife, Louise, had lost three of their four surviving children to scarlet fever. He had not talked about it—he is a stolid man of few words—but it was clear how much it hurt him.

"Have you ridden over the battlefield?" I asked.

"Pretty much all of it."

"What are your impressions?"

"Terrible sights. Slaughtered horses. Wrecked equipment. Mangled corpses everywhere. Heads without bodies. Torsos without limbs. Ambulance details picking up the wounded." He paused. "I think you hurt them about as much as they hurt you."

"I'm glad we punished them well, at any rate."

President Davis came in. I was so astonished to see him that I blurted "President" instead of "Mr. President" and said I was glad to see him. As we sat at the table, reviewing our situation, the rain beat at the windows and lightning rent the sky with ear-splitting thunderclaps. We agreed that the violent storm and the poor condition of the army made pursuit that day impracticable.

The next day we found that McClellan had made good his escape and was on the banks of the James, under the protection of his gunboats. His position was too strong to risk an attack—I did not want to expose my men to the destructive missiles of the Federal gunboats.

I was exceedingly disappointed. Throughout the Seven Days campaign, we had been impeded by poorly coordinated troop movements and assaults and by ignorance of the country roads and dense woods and swamps through which we had chased the retreating foe. We had lost twenty thousand men, almost one-quarter of the army. While inflicting heavy loss on the enemy, we had failed to destroy his army, and so our success was not so great or complete as I had desired. Yet we had raised the siege of Richmond and had driven a once confident and threatening host to the James, thirty miles from the capital. And for that I gave thanks to the Sovereign Ruler of the Universe, the Giver of all victory.

29. DAVIS

I issued a public letter of thanks to the brave soldiers of our army for their series of brilliant victories. Yes, it came at terrible cost in human life, attested to by the constant death marches through the Richmond streets and the newly dug graves multiplying on the city's hillsides. There were so many dead that the gravediggers could not work rapidly enough, and many of the corpses, lying above ground in their coffins, swelled up and burst them. Yet if our gallant dead helped secure our independence, perhaps their families would think the sacrifice worth the cost.

Lee had more than vindicated my decision to give him command of our greatest army. With the skill he showed in driving McClellan away, I began to believe that we might yet win the war. I wrote Varina that we had reason to think that the Yankees had gained from England and France an extension of one month and that I expected foreign intervention if we could hold the enemy at bay until the first of August. With Lee reorganizing his army and talking about ultimately carrying the war to the North, I was certain that we would more than hold our own against our hated foe. I do not exaggerate when I say that I pined for the day when our soil would be free from invasion and our banners would float over the fields of the enemy.

The Richmond newspapers, which had once disparaged the general as "Granny Lee," now extolled him in the highest terms. "The operations of General Lee," said the *Dispatch*, "were certainly those of a master." "He amazed and confounded his detractors by the brilliancy of his genius," said the *Whig*. Before the Seven Days, his own men, put to work digging trenches, had called him "the King of Spades." Well, no longer. Lee was now "the savior of Richmond" and "the first captain of the Confederacy."

As for McClellan, he certainly showed capacity in his retreat, but there was little cause to laud a general who was driven out of his entrenchments by a smaller and worse-armed force than his own, and compelled to abandoned a campaign in the preparation of which he had spent many months and many millions of dollars and seek safety by flying to the James for cover, burning his depots of provisions and marking his route by scattered arms, ammunition, and wagons.

30. LINCOLN

McClellan bragged about his retreat to Harrison's Landing on the James. "I have not yielded an inch of ground unnecessarily," he informed us, "but have retired to prevent the superior force of the enemy from cutting me off and to take a different base of operations." He added in another telegram: "When the circumstances of the case are known it will be acknowledged by all competent judges that the movement just completed by this army is unparalleled in the annals of war." He had saved not only the army, but his guns and trains "and, above all, our honor." The troops were now in review, "bands playing, salutes being fired, and all things looking bright." Now, he added, if Washington would send him 100,000 reinforcements, he could renew the offensive in a month or six weeks, take Richmond, and win the war.

One hundred thousand new men! For God's sake, I said, didn't McClellan understand what I'd been telling him? I offered him a thousand thanks for saving the army, and I did squeeze twenty-five thousand more men for him from Washington and the South Carolina sea islands. I also reminded him that Burnside was on the way from North Carolina with another ten thousand men and should be arriving soon. But I couldn't possibly raise enough volunteers for McClellan to mount an offensive in a month or even six weeks. "Under these circumstances, the defensive must be your only care," I wired McClellan. "Save the Army—first, where you are, if you *can*; and secondly, by removal, if you must."

I thought I'd better have a man-to-man talk with McClellan. The public outcry over his fiasco on the peninsula was shrill and threatening, and I was as nearly inconsolable as I could be and still live. The hostile *New York Herald* blamed me for McClellan's debacle— me and "the imbeciles" in the War and Navy Departments. Leading Republicans, moderate and Radical, demanded McClellan's head

and warned that if we didn't win a victory in the critical Eastern theater, the party would suffer terrible losses in the upcoming off-year
elections.

And the casualties! From Yorktown to Malvern Hill, we'd lost
more than twenty-three thousand men killed, wounded, and missing.
Every day now hospital steamers packed with the wounded arrived
from the James River, and crowds gathered at the wharves to watch
them being unloaded and transported to the scores of hospitals in
Washington City. The sight of those broken and blasted men left us
all in despair.

There was no end to our difficulties. On every front we suffered
critical shortages of troops. There was grave danger that Great
Britain and France, focusing their attention on the Eastern theater,
might conclude that the so-called Confederacy was invincible and
not only recognize her as an independent nation, but form alliances
with her.

All this was weighing down on me when I set off for Harrison's
Landing on board the steamer *Ariel*. Down the storied Potomac we
steamed, past army camps and fortifications bristling with guns; past
our teeming military camp at Aquia Creek; on down the Chesapeake,
round formidable Fort Monroe, and up the wide and wandering
James River to McClellan's fortified camp at Harrison's Landing. It
was late afternoon of a hot and hazy July day when we docked and
went forward to meet McClellan, who struck me as a little more grim-
faced and stiffly erect than usual. He spat tobacco and tugged at his
mustache a good deal as we talked. At sundown we reviewed troops,
line after line of 'em, with drums beating and banners and flags flying,
and as I rode past, tipping my stovepipe hat, I was surprised and
impressed that they appeared to be in such good condition.

Next day, in a candid talk with McClellan on the *Ariel*, I asked
if the army could be safely removed from here, and he seemed taken
aback, insulted even, and replied that it would be "a delicate and
very difficult matter." In other words, he wanted to stay put. I put
the same question to his five corps commanders—white-haired General Sumner, Heintzelman, Keyes, Porter, and Franklin—and three
of them also wanted to stay. Well, considering the high spirit of the
army, maybe they were right, maybe the army was safe enough
here.

Before I left, McClellan handed me a confidential letter that troubled me as I read it. The general said not a word about future operations of his army. Instead he gave his "general views"—"convictions"

from his heart—on "the existing state of the rebellion." The gist of it went like this:

> *Our cause must never be abandoned. This rebellion has assumed the character of a war, and it should be conducted upon the highest principles known to Christian civilization. It should not be a war looking to the subjugation of a people, but a war against armed forces and political organizations exclusively. Neither confiscation of property, political executions of persons, territorial organization of states or forcible abolition of slavery should be contemplated for a moment. Pillage should be punished as a high crime, military arrests should never be tolerated, military power should not be used to interfere with the relations of servitude, either by supporting or impairing the authority of the master. In carrying out a conservative and constitutional policy, you will require a Commander in Chief of the Army who possesses your confidence, understands your views. I do not ask that place for myself. . . .*

I thanked McClellan for the letter and left for Washington without responding to it. I wasn't offended that he'd written me confidentially on public policy, which of course was the province of the president and Congress, not commanders in the field. What disturbed me was that there were great differences between McClellan and me on how the war ought to be fought, especially in the matter of subjugation and slavery. Before I get into that, though, let me say that I agreed with McClellan on one point—the office of general in chief ought to be restored—and when I got back to Washington, I named Henry Halleck to that post and called him to Washington. I did so out of respect for the job he'd done in managing the Western Department. Grant, whose fighting pluck I liked so much, was given command of the District of West Tennessee with his headquarters in Memphis.

As for the other points in McClellan's letter, I was coming around to Stanton's view that we could no longer wage the kind of restrictive war McClellan called for, not with the war growing more and more violent with no end in sight. Like Wade, Chandler, Sumner, and many other Radicals, War Secretary Stanton advocated an all-our war of subjugation, using any and all means to win it, no matter how drastic they were. And two of those means were truly drastic: the abolishment of slavery and the use of colored troops.

Throughout the peninsula campaign, I'd brooded on the emancipation question, with pressures to strike at slavery thrust at me from various quarters, until it occupied my thoughts day and night. The abolitionists and Radical Republicans kept up relentless pressure on me to strike slavery a fatal blow, thus depriving the rebels of their labor force and removing the cause of the war. In Congress, Republicans and conservative Democrats conducted a rowdy debate over the new confiscation bill and its slave liberation provision. Because Trumbull had added a colonization clause, the new bill now had the support of moderate and Radical Republicans and was almost certain to pass. They were sending me a clear message that the majority of Republicans in Congress now favored emancipation by the Federal government.

Sumner was in here constantly, pleading and arguing that point with me and demanding that I issue an executive proclamation of emancipation. "Mr. President, Great Britain is close to recognition of the Confederacy and quite probably intervention. If you force the slavery issue into the open, making it clear that we are fighting to abolish slavery while the rebels are fighting to preserve it, Great Britain will neither recognize nor side with the Confederacy."

"You mean issue an emancipation proclamation," I said.

"Exactly. You've said yourself that we suffer shortages of troops along our entire line. You need more men, not only at the North, but at the South, in the rear of the rebels: you need the slaves. You can get them by issuing a proclamation of freedom."

"Sumner, I don't see any merit in issuing a decree I can't enforce. And if I did issue a proclamation as you want, Browning insists that half the officers would throw down their arms and three more states would join the rebellion."

"You are plainly mistaken, Mr. President."

"I've mulled over this great trouble, turning it over and over in my mind, looking at it from every conceivable direction. And I admit, I don't fully understand it. But I'm placed here, I'm obliged to do the best I can. And I can only go as fast as I can see how to go."

What I did see was this: things were near the end of the rope on the slavery question. We had to change our tactics or lose the whole game. Still, I wanted to give my gradual, compensated, state-guided plan one more try. I wanted to make the border-state senators and representatives understand that my plan was the only alternative to emancipation by the Federal government and the army.

Two days after I got back from seeing McClellan, I called the twenty-eight border-state men to the Executive Mansion, put on my spectacles, and read them a statement.

Gentlemen. After the adjournment of Congress, now very near, I shall have no opportunity of seeing you for several months. I feel it a duty which I cannot justifiably waive, to make this appeal to you. If you all had voted for the resolution in the gradual emancipation message of last March, the war would now be substantially ended. And the plan therein proposed is yet one of the most potent and swift means of ending it. Let the states which are in rebellion see, definitely and certainly, that in no event will the states you represent ever join their proposed Confederacy, and they cannot much longer maintain the contest.

Discarding punctilio and maxims adapted to more manageable times, and looking only to the unprecedentedly stern facts of our case, can you do better in any possible event than my plan? You prefer that the constitutional relation of the states to the nation shall be practically restored, without disturbance of the institution of slavery; and if this were done, my whole duty under the Constitution would be performed. But it is not done, and we are trying to accomplish it by war. If the war continues long, as it must, the institution in your states will be extinguished by mere friction and abrasion—by the mere incidents of the war. It will be gone, and you will have nothing valuable in lieu of it. Much of its value is gone already. How much better for you, and for your people, to take the step which at once shortens the war and secures substantial compensation for that which is sure to be wholly lost in any event.

I do not speak of emancipation at once, but of a decision at once to emancipate gradually. Room in South America for colonization can be obtained cheaply and in abundance; and when numbers shall be large enough to be company and encouragement for one another, the freed people will not be so reluctant to go.

The pressure on me to issue a proclamation of emancipation is increasing. By conceding what I now ask, you can relieve me, and much more, can relieve the country, in this important point. Before leaving the capital, consider and discuss my message of March last; and, at the least, commend

its proposition to the consideration of your states and peo-
ple. As you would perpetuate popular government for the
best people in the world, I beseech you that you not omit
this. Our common country is in great peril, demanding the
loftiest views and boldest action to bring it speedy relief.
Once relieved, its form of government is saved to the world;
its beloved history and cherished memories are vindicated;
and its happy future fully assured and rendered inconceiv-
ably grand. To you, more than to any others, the privilege is
given to assure that happiness and swell that grandeur, and
to link your own names therewith forever.

Most of the border men looked unhappy and hesitant, and when
they left I knew they would turn me down. In fact, twenty of them
rejected my appeal, on the grounds that my plan would cost too
much, would make the rebellion worse, would sow discord and discontent in their own states. They thought it unjust that their states,
which were loyal to the government, were asked to give up their
slaves, while those in flagrant rebellion kept theirs. In short, they
would do nothing.

Their intransigence taught me a lesson, I can tell you that. Slaveowners—even loyal ones like them—were too caught up in the institution to eradicate it themselves. They would never do it voluntarily.
That meant it was back in my lap. Turn which way I would, this disturbing element which caused the war rose against me. I saw that *I*
had to throw off the punctilio and maxims of a quieter time and
strike at slavery myself.

Next day, on a carriage ride with Seward and Welles, my navy
secretary, I said I'd about concluded that if the rebellion persisted, it
would be a necessity and a duty on our part to free the slaves. "I'm
convinced that we can't win the war by a temporizing and forbear-
ing policy toward the insurgents. The time has come for bolder and
more decisive action. The Administration must set an example, and
strike at the heart of the rebellion, by using the army to set the slaves
free. I think the country is ready for it. The army will be with us.
Maybe the government has no constitutional authority to emancipate the slaves. But there's no constitutional authority, specified or
reserved, for the slaveholders to resist the government or secede
from it. They can't throw off the Constitution and at the same time
invoke it to protect slavery. They started the war and have to face its
consequences."

The two secretaries were staring at me. "I know," I said. "You've not heard me say this before."

"Until now, you've always been prompt and emphatic in opposing any administrative interference with slavery," Welles said.

"Yes, I've tried various expedients to avoid having to issue an executive order of emancipation. But I can't avoid it any longer. Believe me, I've thought about this day and night, and I've concluded that emancipation by the Federal government and the army is a military necessity, absolutely essential to save our Union and our system of government. We must free the slaves or ourselves be subdued. Can't deny that the slaves are an element of strength to the rebels—we have to decide whether that element is for us or against us. We must invite 'em to desert and come to us, and uniting with us they must be made free from rebel authorities and rebel masters. My interview yesterday with the border men forced me to this conclusion. This is the first chance I've had to tell anybody what I've decided has to be our course. I'd like you both to think on this and then give me your frank opinion."

"Mr. President," Seward said, "the consequences of what you propose are so vast, so momentous, that I'll need mature reflection before giving you a decisive answer. But my immediate reaction is that the measure you propose is justifiable, you might say expedient and necessary."

"I agree," Welles said.

Next day, Orville Browning brought me a copy of the second confiscation bill, which Congress had adopted on the day I'd spoken to the border-state men. Browning begged me to veto the measure. He and other conservative Republicans had broken with the party and sided with the Democrats against full-scale confiscation of slaves and other property in the rebel South.

"This thing violates the laws of civilized warfare and I think it's patently unconstitutional," Browning said. "Lincoln, you've reached the culminating point in your Administration. What you do with this bill will determine whether you are to control the abolitionists and the Radicals or whether they will control you. If you veto this bill, it will bring you strong and enthusiastic support from the loyal border states. It will be worth a hundred thousand muskets to our cause. But if you approve this bill, it'll cause dangerous and fatal dissatisfaction in our army and cost us the loyalty of the border states."

I revealed nothing about my own emancipation plan—that thunderbolt would keep until I'd had a chance to go over the details with the entire Cabinet. After Browning left, I read the second confiscation bill and liked most of the things in it. If the rebellion did not end in sixty days, the bill authorized the executive to seize the property of all people who incited, supported, aided, gave comfort to, or participated in the rebellion. Federal courts would rule on which southerners were guilty and which had remained loyal to the Union. The latter would be permitted to keep their slaves and other property. Those convicted, among other penalties, would forfeit their estates and their slaves to the Federal government, and the slaves would be freed. Section nine specified that the slaves of rebels who'd escaped to our lines, who were captured by Federal forces, or who were abandoned by their owners, "shall be deemed captives of war, and shall be forever free." Section eleven authorized the president to "employ as many persons of African descent as he may deem necessary and proper for the suppression of this rebellion"—which meant, in plain language, that I could enlist colored men as soldiers. Another section, aimed at easing the fears of the white North, provided for the voluntary resettlement of liberated blacks "in some tropical country."

I fully agreed with the spirit of the bill: the traitor against the general government, if found guilty in a regular trial in a duly constituted court, ought to forfeit his slaves and other property as just punishment for treason. But the wording about the loss of his slaves was too vague to suit me. It was startling to say, as this bill did, that Congress could free a slave *within a state*, which implied that it could eradicate slavery *as the institution of a state*. That was an unfortunate form of expression, since Congress had no constitutional authority to do that by regular legislation. It would be better to state that the ownership of the slaves had first been transferred to the nation, and that Congress had then liberated them. More precise wording, I thought, could easily clear the vagueness up. In any case, I had no substantial objection to the sections on slave liberation.

But I did object to sections that divested the title of property forever, beyond the lives of the guilty parties. The Constitution states, "no attainder of treason shall work corruption of blood, or forfeiture, except during the life of the person attained." This feature of the bill was therefore unconstitutional, and I drafted a message setting forth my complaints and hinting that I would veto the bill as it was currently worded. Before I sent the message, Congress adopted a joint resolution removing most of my objections, particularly the one on forfeiture forever, and so I signed the bill into law, sent my message anyway with an appended explanation, and commanded the army to start enforcing the act.

As for the slaves who reached our lines, Stanton explained the new policy succinctly. "The president is of the opinion that, under the law of Congress, the slaves cannot be sent back to their masters; that in common humanity they must not be permitted to suffer for want of food, shelter, or other necessities of life; that to this end, they should be provided by the Quartermaster and Commissary departments; and that those who are capable of labor should be set to work and paid reasonable wages."

Sumner and Stanton were "delighted" that I'd sided with those who wanted to wage a hard war against southern traitors. But some Radicals were angry about my threatened veto and my "legalistic quibbling" when the nation was struggling for its existence against a mutinous aristocracy founded on slavery. When Congress adjourned, George W. Julian of Indiana, who's on the Joint Committee and wears a Quaker beard, stormed into the Executive Mansion and declared my behavior "inexpressibly provoking." He demanded that I tell him once and for all where I stood on emancipation and all-out war against the insurgents.

"When I get home," he said, "I'd like to assure my constituents that you'll cooperate with Congress. That you'll vigorously carry out the measures we've adopted to crush the rebellion. That you'll deal the quickest and hardest blows and among them will be a decisive blow against slavery."

"You Radicals criticize me unfairly, Julian. I've no objections at all to what you want to tell your constituents."

Without consulting anybody, I drafted a preliminary emancipation proclamation and read it to my Cabinet and Attorney General Bates. "I'm not seeking your advice," I told them. "I've already made up my mind to issue the proclamation. But I welcome suggestions on details." The proclamation announced that on January first of 'sixty-three, in my capacity as commander in chief of the army and navy, I would liberate all the slaves in the rebellious states—meaning those of secessionists and loyalists alike. The loyalists, however, would be compensated for their loss. The decree also commanded the army and navy to enforce the new confiscation act and quoted the sections dealing with slave liberation. I deemed the proclamation "a fit and necessary military measure" to save the Union and its system of popular government.

The proclamation went beyond the second confiscation act because it freed all the slaves within an insurgent state. If Congress lacks the authority to do that by regular statute, I thought the president might do it by the war power, which grants him broad "discretionary power" to save the government in a national emergency. The Constitution, of course, does not specifically state this, but implies it by charging the president, as commander in chief of the army and navy, to "preserve, protect, and defend" the Constitution and the country. At least that was my rationale for what I knew was a provocative and potentially explosive step.

Only Seward and Welles knew about my intentions beforehand. The other secretaries were astounded. "The measure goes beyond anything I've recommended," Stanton said. "But I urge you to issue it at once." Bates agreed. Postmaster Blair, however, warned that the country was not ready for an emancipation edict and that it would damage the Republican Party in the fall elections. Chase said he was "surprised." Oh, he was all for using colored troops and arming the slaves, but he feared that emancipation by presidential fiat was dangerous and would hurt the government's fiscal position. "Emancipation can be much better and more quietly accomplished by allowing generals to organize and arm the slaves," he argued.

The secretaries offered nothing that I hadn't already anticipated and settled in my own mind until Seward spoke. "Mr. President, I approve of the proclamation, but I question whether it's expedient to issue it at this time. We've won no military victories in the great eastern theater, and the public mind is greatly depressed. The proclamation might be viewed as the last measure of an exhausted government, a cry to the slaves for help. It might be considered as our last *shriek* on the retreat. Sir, I suggest that you postpone issuing it until it can be supported by military success, instead of issuing it now, in the wake of our disasters in Virginia."

I tell you, Seward's wisdom struck me with great force. It was an aspect of the case I'd entirely overlooked. That night, after mulling the matter over, I put the proclamation away in my desk. Seward was right: it would have to wait until we'd won a decisive victory in the East. But how long would that take? How long before McClellan attacked and whipped Lee? The idea that the proclamation depended on McClellan's winning a victory gave me the hypo.

At least General in Chief Halleck was acting aggressively, telling our field commanders that it was time to make the rebels feel the hard hand of war. "If necessary," Halleck wired Grant, "take up all active sympathizers and either hold them as prisoners or put them beyond our lines. Handle that class without gloves and take their property for public use. It is time that they should begin to feel the presence of war. The policy is to be terrible on the enemy." Stanton and I fully agreed with that policy. General Pope, whose Army of Virginia, forty thousand strong, was now south of the Rappahannock, to help relieve the pressure on McClellan, applied the new policy with a vengeance. He also declared himself a fighter. "I've come to you from the West," he told his army, "where we've always seen the backs of our enemies." If only we could say the same in the East.

I was so sure that McClellan would never fight that I authorized Halleck to remove him from command. He didn't go that far, but at my direction he did order McClellan to bring his army of ninety thousand back to northern Virginia, so that he could join Pope. If Lee had two hundred thousand men, as McClellan claimed, then this was the best move to save both the Potomac Army and the Army of Virginia for offensive operations that might win us a victory. McClellan complained bitterly, but I saw that the order stuck.

31. DAVIS

By a series of sweeping usurpations, the Yankees changed the character of the war into a campaign of indiscriminate robbery and murder. The second confiscation act, to begin with, violated all the principles of the law of nations, without a shadow of authority for it under the U.S. Constitution. The armies of the Union were literally empowered to invade the Confederate States, seize all property as plunder, and let the Negroes go free. Our posterity, reading that history, will be horrified that such facts are on record. It was estimated in the enemy House of Representatives that this new act would deprive upward of six million people of property valued at nearly five thousand million dollars. The Yankee Congress treated us as holding the twofold relations of enemies and traitors and used against us all the instruments of war, and all the penalties of municipal law, which made death the punishment for treason. The practical operation of the second confiscation act was that the U.S. government proceeded, without indictment, without trial by jury, and without the proof of two witnesses, to adjudge our six million people guilty of treason in levying war, and sought to deprive us of all our estate, real and personal, for life.

I read Lincoln's message in which he stated his objections to the new confiscation act and then signed it anyway. "It is startling," Lincoln said, "to say that Congress can free a slave within a state, and yet, if it were said that the ownership of the slave had first been transferred to the nation and that Congress had then liberated him, the difficulty would at once vanish." It is *amazing* to see the utter forgetfulness of all constitutional obligations and the entire disregard of the conditions of the laws of nations manifested in these words of the president of the United States, *so-called*.

Equally despotic and murderous were the acts of Lincoln's commanders in the field. By his authority, General Pope of the so-called Army of Virginia issued a series of orders in July 1862 that inaugurated a policy of pillage and outrage upon unarmed, peaceable civilians. First, he declared that his troops would "subsist upon the country," which meant that they would plunder the homesteads of our people who fell within his jurisdiction in Virginia. Second, he announced that he would hold them responsible for any damage done to the Union's military railroad or "for any attacks upon the trains or straggling soldiers by bands of guerrillas." He said, further, that "if a soldier or legitimate follower of the army be fired upon from any house, the house shall be razed to the ground and the inhabitants sent as prisoners to the headquarters of this army. If such an outrage occurs at any place distant from settlements, the people within five miles around shall be held accountable, and made to pay an indemnity sufficient for the case; and any person detected in such outrages will be shot." Furthermore, he decreed that all "disloyal male citizens" within his lines were to be arrested and given two choices: they could take an oath of allegiance to the U.S. and remain in their homes and at their work; or be conducted beyond the extreme pickets of his army and warned that they would be hanged as spies if they were caught within his lines or "at any point in the rear."

One of Pope's brigadier generals, a German named Steinwehr, used these orders to seize innocent and peaceful inhabitants, to be held as hostages and murdered in cold blood if any of his soldiers were killed by unknown persons whom he designated as "bushwhackers." By that he must have meant our citizens who had taken up arms to defend their homes and families.

I was empurpled with rage. Rapine and wanton destruction of private property, war upon noncombatants, murder of captives, bloody threats to avenge the death of an invading soldiery by the slaughter of unarmed citizens, confiscation acts of a character so atrocious as to insure the utter ruin of the population of our young nation—this was how our hated enemy now waged war.

How to retaliate against such ruthless insults to the defenseless? It so happened that representatives of the U.S. and the Confederacy had recently negotiated a cartel, which stipulated that all prisoners of war hereafter taken would be discharged on parole until they could be exchanged. We retaliated against Pope by issuing our own General Orders: the terms of that cartel would not apply to him, Steinwehr, and all their officers if they were captured; they would not be paroled until the offensive Federal orders were withdrawn. Moreover, for every citizen murdered under Pope's or Steinwehr's orders, we would hang a captured Yankee officer.

I sent Lee a copy of our retaliatory orders and pointed out in an accompanying letter that we found ourselves driven by our enemies toward a practice which we abhorred and which we were vainly struggling to avoid. But some of the Yankee military authorities seemed to suppose that better success would attend a savage war in which no quarter was to be given and no sex to be spared. I asked Lee to send a copy of our retaliatory orders to the commander in chief of the U.S. armies, along with a warning from me that if these savage practices were continued, we would be forced to the last resort of accepting the war on the terms chosen by our foes, until the outraged voice of a common humanity forced a respect for the recognized rules of war. Lee did as I asked, but the Federal general in chief, Halleck, refused to accept the dispatches because they were "couched in language exceedingly insulting to the government of the United States."

Lee was also furious at Pope, called him a murderer and a robber, and said he wanted that general "suppressed." Lee dispatched Jackson with one wing of the army to accomplish that feat while Lee remained in McClellan's front with the remainder of the army. Jackson found that Pope had advanced south of Culpeper in the direction of Orange Court House, and set off to give him battle. The Federals, however, struck Jackson first, attacking two of his divisions at Cedar Run, but Jackson brought up his third division and won a triumph for our arms, checking Pope's invasion for the moment.

Meanwhile we learned that Burnside was on his way to Fredericksburg with a large force and that McClellan's army was embarking on troop transports. It seemed clear that both Burnside and McClellan were on their way to reinforce Pope for a major offensive on the line of the Rapidan northwest of Richmond. Which meant that Jackson was in peril. On August thirteenth Lee set out to join Jackson with the rest of the army and to destroy Pope before Burnside and McClellan could reach him.

32. LEE

On our way to Gordonsville to join Jackson, I felt mortified that McClellan's army had escaped us. Though the material damage dealt him in the battles of the Chickahominy was not so great as I could have wished, he must have been so morally shattered that he decided retreat was necessary to save his army. I was relieved that Richmond was no longer threatened, but McClellan ought not to have gotten off so easily. Where was he heading? I thought he would either ascend the Rappahannock, occupy Fredericksburg, and threaten Richmond from the north, or he would unite with Pope.

"We must lose no time in preparing to meet him wherever he may appear," I wrote the president. But first, we had to suppress that miscreant, Pope. Then we would deal with Mr. McClellan.

Because I had left twenty thousand men to guard Richmond, the army, when it was united at Gordonsville, numbered only fifty-five thousand men. It was a far more efficient force now, thanks to the reorganization I had imposed after the difficulties of the Chickahominy campaign: I had grouped the divisions into two wings, with Jackson in command of one wing of twenty-three thousand men and Longstreet, the most effective field commander in the last campaign, in command of the other, larger wing. This would give me greater flexibility in battle, making it easier to shift divisions from flank to flank or to the center to close gaps in our line.

In a war council with my two wing commanders, I laid down a plan of battle for disposing of Mr. Pope, whose army lay to the north, between the Rapidan and the Rappahannock. Our cavalry would destroy the bridges across the Rappahannock, thus removing Pope's means of retreat. Our infantry would then attack his front and destroy him.

But before we could lay the trap, the Federals retreated to the north side of the Rappahannock. I was flustered that Pope had eluded our grasp. I had not thought that he would turn his back on us this early in the campaign. I moved my army north across the Rapidan, and on the rainy night of August twenty-second, at his request, I sent Major General Stuart on a raid behind enemy lines with 1,500 horsemen. His object was to destroy the railroad bridge over Cedar Run, thus cutting Pope's supply line and forcing him to retreat. Stuart also intended to avenge a raid of enemy horsemen several days before. They had slipped through our lines and surprised him while he was taking a nap at a farmhouse; he got away but lost his plumed hat. Now, he said with a merry smile, he meant to get it back.

James Ewell Brown Stuart, nicknamed "Beauty" at West Point and known as "Jeb" after his famous ride around McClellan, was a flamboyant and garrulous young fellow, with a huge mustache, flowing beard, blue-gray eyes, and reddish brown hair combed straight back. He wore a gray coat buttoned to his chin and cavalry boots above the knees, and carried a light French sword and a pistol at his waist. He loved to kiss the young ladies—"my sweethearts," he called them—and to sing and dance to the banjo. Like Hood and his Texans, Jeb Stuart would always have a special place in my heart.

When he returned from the raid a few days later, he did not have his plumed hat, but he had something far more valuable: Pope's letter-book and papers and his best uniform and cloak, not to mention money chests with $500,000 in Union greenbacks and $20,000 in gold. Stuart reported that he had ridden around behind the Federal Army and had descended on Pope's railroad headquarters and supply base at Catlett's Station during a violent thunderstorm. His men had found the booty in Pope's tent. Too bad Pope wasn't at home or Stuart would have made off with him, too. Stuart had burned valuable quantities of supplies, but owing to the driving rain, he had failed to destroy the railroad bridge over Cedar Run.

Even so, I was delighted with the invaluable information contained in the confiscated papers. These indicated that Pope had forty-five thousand men, plus reinforcements from Burnside, and that he intended to hold his position on the Rappahannock until Porter's corps—the advance of McClellan's army—arrived from Fredericksburg. Then he meant to take the offensive. I had speculated that this might be the case; now I knew it for a fact. We had to act quickly if we were to reach Pope before McClellan did. In order to fight Pope, I needed the rest of my army from Richmond, and I pleaded with President Davis to send it with all speed, but I pleaded in vain.

Having the weaker force, I decided to avoid a general engagement and to maneuver Pope away from McClellan by cutting Pope's communications and forcing him to retreat out of northern Virginia. I called on Jackson to execute another forced march like the ones he had performed so brilliantly in the Shenandoah last spring. He was to move around Pope's right flank, get far in his rear, and cut his supply line on the Orange & Alexandria Railroad. With Jackson in between Pope and Washington, Lincoln might react as he had during Jackson's valley campaign and rush troops back to defend the capital. Detaching Jackson, I admit, violated the canon that an army must remain intact against an enemy of equal or larger size; but we would never win the war if we followed canons.

On August twenty-fifth, Jackson set off with his twenty-three thousand men, telling them to "close up, men, close up! Push on, push on!" as they headed up the Rappahannock. I ordered Stuart to follow with his cavalry early the next morning. Longstreet meanwhile was to divert Pope's attention by threatening him in front, and then to follow Jackson as soon as he was sufficiently advanced. Later on the twenty-sixth Longstreet left his position opposite Warrenton Springs and marched to join Jackson. My staff and I rode with Old Pete.

On the way, I received an astounding dispatch from Jackson. Marching forty-eight miles in less than two days despite the heat, he had struck thirteen miles in Pope's rear at Bristoe Station, capturing two enemy trains. Stuart's cavalry had joined him. That night, a detachment of Jackson's force won an even bigger prize, capturing and burning the Federal supply depot at Manassas Junction on the Orange & Alexandria Railroad. Jackson caught up with the detachment the next morning.

This was the best possible news: General Jackson had done exactly what I wanted, had cut Pope's communications, destroyed his advance base, and now stood between Pope and Washington. I also received a welcome dispatch from President Davis saying that reinforcements from the Richmond defenses were on their way. "Confidence in you overcomes the view which would otherwise be taken of the exposed condition of Richmond," the president added.

We faced grave danger, however. My divided army was in the midst of perhaps 100,000 Federals, with thousands more on the way. To make matters worse, our reconnaissance revealed that Pope and part of McClellan's army had left their outflanked line on the

Rappahannock and were now marching for Manassas and Centreville, which meant that Jackson was in danger.

Trying to reach Jackson before the enemy did, Longstreet performed a brilliant forced march of his own, and without adequate cavalry. But when we reached Thoroughfare Gap in the Bull Run Mountains, at mid-afternoon of the twenty-eighth, we found it occupied by Federal troops disputing our way. Worse, we could hear the rumble of artillery to the east, probably the start of a battle. The Federals must have found Jackson—no way of knowing in what force. In desperation, Longstreet sent D. R. Jones's division to force the gap; but the enemy held the eastern end of the pass in large force and blasted the road with deadly artillery fire. I knew the country well and that night sent a division by a path over the mountain to get on the enemy's right flank. At dawn on the twenty-ninth, Longstreet reported that the pass was open. The flanking operation, I think, induced the enemy to withdraw.

Longstreet soon had his columns on the march again for Manassas. On the other side of Haymarket, Jeb Stuart rode up with news from Jackson. "He's fallen back from Manassas and is holding the enemy at bay along the Groveton-Sudley Road."

"We must hurry on and help him," I said.

The air was hot and thick with dust, and the smoke of battle could be seen on the horizon. Hood's Texans, leading Longstreet's columns, reached the Warrenton Turnpike about nine that morning, and soon after made the first contact with Jackson. By noon Longstreet had almost all his thirty thousand men into line on Jackson's right. Jackson held a strong defensive position on a timbered ridge just west of the Manassas battlefield. His men, finding natural trenches in the excavated grade of an unfinished railroad, had so far held off Pope's piecemeal assaults.

My instinct was to attack at once, and I said so to Longstreet. But, as was my way, I left it up to his discretion instead of ordering him to attack, and Pete wanted to reconnoiter the ground first. He reported that columns of dust in the direction of Mansassas could mean that Federal troops—maybe Porter's corps—were on the way. If he took the offensive now, he said, he would be vulnerable to a flank attack from that direction. I deferred to his judgment, but went to reconnoiter myself. Longstreet took another look, also, and both of us concluded that the enemy troops in the direction of Manassas— Porter's, it turned out—looked peaceable and not disposed to attack. I urged Longstreet to take the offensive immediately. But Pete thought it was too late in the afternoon for that. Instead he advised a reconnaissance in force to relieve Jackson and feel the enemy, and an all-out attack at dawn. Reluctantly I concurred.

Just after six that afternoon, Hood's Texans moved out to probe the enemy and were themselves attacked and became hotly engaged along the turnpike. Hood came to me that night and reported that the Federals were in our front in great strength and, aggressive fighter though he was, advised against a dawn attack. I was extremely disappointed—I wanted to punish those people, give the murdering Pope a beating he would never forget. But Pete was right: it was prudent to remain on the defensive, induce Pope to attack us, inflict as much punishment on him as possible, and look for a chance to counterattack. Defensive warfare was Old Pete's preference, and this day I deferred to him, though it frustrated me.

August thirtieth dawned bright and clear. The enemy massed his troops in front of Jackson and again renewed his attacks, and I followed the progress of battle from the top of a hill near Hood's Texans. A fierce and bloody struggle raged on Jackson's front; I learned later that some of his units ran out of ammunition and beat the enemy back with rocks. At one point, part of Jackson's line began to waver, and he called on Longstreet for reinforcements. Instead Longstreet ordered up his guns to enfilade the attackers, and the thunder of the cannon shook the hill. Shot and shell, hissing and shrieking, rained down on the attacking Federals in the valley, breaking up their supporting lines and driving them back through clouds of sulfurous smoke.

I saw that Jackson's troops had begun counterattacking. *Now* was the time to hit Pope with every man in the army, and I signaled Longstreet to attack with his entire command. But Longstreet had anticipated the order and in a brilliant display of generalship threw all five of his divisions forward in just half an hour. Thirty thousand screaming infantry fell upon Pope's weakened left flank, and our whole line, Jackson's men and Longstreet's, swept steadily on, inflicting great carnage upon the routed enemy, until rain and darkness ended the fighting and the pursuit at ten that night.

When the infantry had gone on the attack, I had followed on Traveller with members of my staff. When we reached Jackson's lead artillery position, I stopped to study the battleground with my glasses. Captain Mason of my staff pointed at a scruffy-looking young man leaning against a gun not five yards away.

"General," the captain said, "there is someone who wants to speak to you."

I looked at the scruffy soldier. "Well, my man, what can I do for you?"

"Why, General, don't you know me?"

It was my son Rob! I hadn't recognized him, as his uniform was ragged and filthy with red dust, and his hands and face black with powder.

"I'm glad to see you and glad you're well," I said.

Saying good-bye to my son, I rode on with my staff. That night we set up headquarters in a field, and I read dispatches from my victorious officers by firelight. General Hood rode up, looking tired but grinning with excitement.

"General Hood," I said. "What's become of the enemy?"

"They're lying thick as a bed of roses. We drove 'em across the field damn near at the double-quick. It was lovely to see our flags dancin' after 'em."

"God forbid," I said, "I should ever live to see our colors moving in the opposite direction."

At ten o'clock that night I wrote a dispatch to President Davis: "This army achieved today on the plains of Manassas a signal victory over combined forces of Generals McClellan and Pope. On the twenty-eighth and twenty-ninth each wing under Generals Longstreet and Jackson repulsed with valour attacks made on them separately. We mourn the loss of our gallant dead in every conflict yet our gratitude to Almighty God for His mercies rises higher and higher each day, to Him and to the valor of our troops a nation's gratitude is due."

33. LINCOLN

The routing of Pope depressed me so much I said we might as well stop fighting. Most of the Cabinet blamed McClellan for the fiasco at Bull Run. He'd been guilty of inexcusable delays in bringing his army to northern Virginia. When he finally reached Alexandria, he'd advised that we should either break through to Pope or defend

Washington and "leave Pope to get out of his scrape." That crack shocked and angered me. I thought McClellan was a little crazy, that he seemed to *want* Pope to be defeated. And what was wrong with Halleck? He was general in chief. Why didn't he order McClellan to hurry the movement of his troops to Pope? Had he done so, and had the entire Army of the Potomac in consequence been on the ground with Pope, we might have won a great victory, and I could have issued my preliminary emancipation proclamation. But Halleck became nervous and melancholy and was incapable of directing the two armies. I was reluctant to interfere and take over again, and as a result, the command system was in total chaos, just like our efforts on the battlefield.

On the day after the battle, I resolved to make some changes so that we could *hurt* the enemy, *whip* those people. I didn't care if the changes were unpopular—something had to be done about this military mess. Since McClellan and Pope refused to cooperate, one had to go and I decided it was Pope. I put McClellan in charge of the Washington defenses and ordered him to merge the remnants of Pope's forces with the Potomac Army. I tell you, I hated to put him back in charge after what he'd done, but I had to use the tools we had. There was nobody better at restoring morale and order to a whipped army. But I asked him bluntly: "Did you want Pope to fail? It seems to me you did." He swelled up, stuck his hand in his coat, and vehemently denied the charge. He was exultant, however, that I had named him and not Pope to command the capital's defenses.

The Cabinet, however, was on the verge of mutiny. In a stormy meeting, Stanton, Chase, Smith, Welles, and Attorney General Bates bitterly protested my naming McClellan to defend Washington and all demanded his removal.

"Gentlemen," I said, "I'm wrung by the bitterest anguish. I'm almost ready to hang myself. But McClellan knows the whole ground. His specialty is to defend. There is no better organizer. For disciplining and preparing an army for the field, he's superior to any of our generals."

Grudgingly, angrily, the Cabinet yielded to my decision, though Chase predicted it would prove "a national calamity," and Stanton griped about my "humiliating submissiveness."

In the privacy of my office, I sat down at my desk and stared at a blank piece of paper. I picked up a pen and wrote: "The will of God prevails. In great contests each party claims to act in accordance with the will of God. Both *may* be, and one *must* be wrong. God cannot be *for* and *against* the same thing at the same time. In the present civil war it is quite possible that God's purpose is something different from the purpose of either party—and yet the human instrumentalities, working just as they do, are of the best adaptation to effect His purpose. I am almost ready to say this is probably true—that God wills this contest, and wills that it shall not end yet. By His mere quiet power, on the minds of the now contestants, He could have either *saved* or *destroyed* the Union without a human contest. Yet the contest began. And having begun He could give the final victory to either side any day. Yet the contest proceeds."

34. DAVIS

When I received General Lee's dispatch announcing the signal victory of our arms at Second Manassas, I forwarded the telegram to Congress, which had convened in mid-August, and extolled our toil-worn troops for their gallant achievement. Northeastern Virginia was now freed from the presence of the invader, his forces having withdrawn to the entrenchments of Washington. Soon after the battle, we learned that hostile troops who had occupied Winchester in the valley had retreated north to Harpers Ferry. The war was thus transferred from the interior to the frontier, and the supplies of rich and productive farming districts were made accessible to our army. With Europe on the verge of recognition, I now had unflagging optimism in the ultimate success of our cause.

Our situation in the West had improved dramatically. Van Dorn had fortified Port Hudson, Louisiana, which gave us control of a 125-mile stretch of the Mississippi from Port Hudson northward to Vicksburg. That stretch of the river kept the supply and troop lines open to the Trans-Mississippi Department, which was now headed by General Theophilus H. Holmes. General Edmund Kirby Smith, a West Pointer (class of 'forty-five) and one of our ablest and purest officers, was in charge of Eastern Tennessee, a separate command from Bragg's Western Department. In late July and early August, Bragg had moved his Army of Tennessee to Chattanooga, within Smith's department; and he and Smith had held a cordial meeting at which Smith had agreed to place his troops under Bragg for the purpose of offensive operations.

We were ready to adopt a national strategy and carry the war into enemy territory in both theaters. My earliest declared purpose had been to feed upon the enemy and teach them the blessings of peace by making them feel the evils of war in its most tangible form, and the opportunity to do that was at hand. I wrote Smith that I wanted him and Bragg to crush the Yankee army under Buell and advance to the recovery of Tennessee and the occupation of Kentucky. Smith, however, proposed to invade Kentucky in an independent campaign while Bragg went after Buell. I agreed to Smith's proposal but cautioned both generals that I expected them to operate in concert.

In mid-August, while Lee pursued Pope, Kirby Smith moved across the Cumberland Mountains into Kentucky and marched north toward Richmond. On the twenty-seventh, Bragg also started north, passing to the rear of Buell in middle Tennessee, and out-marching him to the Kentucky border. To protect his communications, Buell retreated to Bowling Green, Kentucky. This was a brilliant piece of campaigning on Bragg's part, by which he maneuvered the foe out of the large and to us important territory of northern Alabama and middle Tennessee. Bragg entered Kentucky by the more westerly route and advanced on Munfordville while Kirby Smith, on the more easterly route, headed for Lexington. Bragg was confident that their two commands could unite on the Ohio for further conquest.

Meanwhile Van Dorn and Sterling Price had moved against Grant's Federal force at Corinth, Mississippi, to prevent it from pursuing Bragg, and Lee had crossed the Potomac into Maryland. Lee had suggested that he carry the war into Maryland to inflict "further injury" on the enemy, and I had readily agreed because the proposal accorded with my national strategy. East and West, a grand Confederate offensive was now under way, with more than 100,000 men advancing north across a six-hundred-mile front, and I followed the movements of our forces on a large map in my office. With armies of liberation upon their soil, the people of Maryland and Kentucky, I thought, would rise to join us, and that was how I justified to the public and to Europe the abandonment of a purely defensive policy in favor of invading enemy territory. We were driven, I said, to protect our own country by transferring the seat of war to that of the enemy.

35. LEE

On September fifth, with regimental bands playing "Maryland, My Maryland," the main body of the Army of Northern Virginia commenced crossing the Potomac by fords around Leesburg. The river was shallow here and a half mile wide, and long columns of infantry, cavalry, and horse-drawn artillery and wagons were splashing across the placid waters, which gleamed under the late-afternoon sun. The sight of the army moved me deeply: few of the men were dressed alike and all were covered with dust and grime, with shocks of hair protruding through holes in their caps and hats of felt or straw; they were lean from hunger and wracked with coughing, and many were barefoot, and yet they displayed such "magnificent morale," as Porter Alexander put it, that I believed them capable of anything.

I was sitting in an ambulance with both my hands in splints—one had a broken bone, the other was badly sprained, the result of a violent fall when I tried to seize Traveller's reins after he had been frightened. I turned to an aide and dictated a dispatch to President Davis. "This army is now entering Maryland," I said, "with a view of affording the people of that state an opportunity of liberating themselves. Whatever success may attend that effort, I hope at any rate to annoy and harass the enemy."

The invasion of Maryland carried with it certain risks. The army, numbering only fifty thousand men when we began the march, was not properly equipped for such an operation. It lacked much of the materiel of war, was feeble in transportation, the animals being much reduced, and the men were poorly provided with clothes, and in thousands of instances were destitute of shoes. It was also plagued by straggling, one of the greatest evils. Hundreds of men had fallen out of line, some because they were sick with diarrhea from too much green corn, others because they lacked discipline or objected to invading the enemy's territory. Straggling infuriated me. Nothing could surpass the gallantry and intelligence of the main body of the army, but there were individuals who, from backwardness in duty, tardiness of movement, and neglect of orders, did it no credit. On my orders, a provost guard followed in the rear of the army, arresting stragglers, punishing all depredators summarily, and keeping the men with their commands.

To make matters worse, the two wing commanders were also impaired. General Jackson had hurt himself when he fell from his horse; and General Longstreet had a painful blister on one heel and had to wear a carpet slipper. Worse still, General Jackson had placed tempestuous little Powell Hill under arrest; General Jackson believed that Hill had insufficiently enforced his orders for strict discipline, and Jackson had therefore relieved him of his command. Hill was furious and rode along at the back of the army, swearing at Jackson and demanding that he bring formal charges against him. This feud did not bode well for the army.

Despite all our difficulties, we could not afford to be idle. The Manassas area had been stripped of food and forage, and we could not rely on the overworked little supply train to bring enough provisions and stores from Richmond. We would find what we needed in bountiful Maryland and Pennsylvania, which had yet to feel the hand of war.

On September sixth, while the army was still crossing the Potomac, news came that Kirby Smith had defeated the enemy at Richmond, Kentucky, and I announced the victory in general orders to my army. "Let the armies of the East and the West vie with each other in discipline, bravery, and activity," I said, "and our brethren of our sister states will soon be released from tyranny, and our independence be established upon a sure and abiding basis."

My ambulance moved on with the infantry and on the seventh we entered Frederick, thirty-five to forty miles northwest of Washington. We found at Frederick a thousand pairs of shoes and some clothing for our troops. As column after column tramped through town, the citizenry was decidedly cool, flew no Confederate flags, and generally watched from behind closed windows.

I established my headquarters outside of town, in a grove of lovely oaks, near Longstreet's and Jackson's tents, and dictated dispatches to Richmond. Our intelligence indicated that McClellan had command of a regrouped Army of the Potomac, which included the remnants of Pope's routed army. I intended to lure McClellan out of his Washington defenses and attack and destroy his entire force. A victory on Union territory, I hoped, would induce Lincoln's government to sue for peace, or the British to intervene in the war. My plan, as I explained to John G. Walker, who commanded two brigades of reinforcements, called for the army to march to Hagerstown on the western side of South Mountain and there rest and reservice. "The short delay," I said, "will enable us to get up our stragglers—not stragglers from a shirking disposition, but from inability to keep up with their commands. We'll then have a very good army, one that will give a very good account of itself. We'll march into Pennsylvania, capture or destroy the Baltimore & Ohio Railroad, and then move to Harrisburg, the objective point of the campaign. You remember, no doubt, the long bridge of the Pennsylvania railroad over the Susquehanna, a few miles west of Harrisburg. I intend to destroy that bridge, which will disable the Pennsylvania railroad for a long time. After that I can turn my attention to Philadelphia, Baltimore, or Washington."

Walker looked incredulous.

"You probably think it's hazardous to leave McClellan practically on my line of communication, and to march into the heart of the enemy's country."

"Frankly, General Lee, I do think it's hazardous."

"Are you acquainted with General McClellan? He is an able general, but a very cautious one. His enemies among his own people think him too much so. His army is in a very demoralized and chaotic condition, and will not be prepared for offensive operations—or he will not think it so—for three or four weeks. Before that time I intend to be on the Susquehanna." I did not tell Walker so, but when and if McClellan gave pursuit, I intended to crush his army. To confuse him, I had Stuart divide his cavalry and threaten both Washington and Baltimore, giving the impression that I was behind him with my entire army.

On September eighth, I issued a proclamation to the people of Maryland, reminding them of all the evils the Lincoln Administration had visited upon them: the arbitrary arrests, the suspension of the writ, the occupation of Baltimore, the suppression of speech and press, and the unlawful arrest of members of the legislature, which had prevented it from voting to join us. "Believing that the people of Maryland possessed a spirit too lofty to submit to such a government, the people of the South have long wished to aid you in throwing off this foreign yoke, to enable you again to enjoy the inalienable rights of freemen, and restore independence and sovereignty to your State. In obedience to this wish, our army has come among you, and is prepared to assist you with the power of its arms in regaining the rights of which you have been despoiled."

That same day I wrote President Davis that the time had come to offer a peace proposal based on Confederate independence. "Such a proposition coming from us at this time," I pointed out, "could in no way be regarded as suing for peace, but being made when it is in our power to inflict injury upon our adversary, would show conclusively to the world that our sole object is the establishment of our independence, and the attainment of an honorable peace. The rejection of this offer would prove to the country that the responsibility of the continuance of the war does not rest upon us, but that the party in power in the United States elects to prosecute it for purposes of their own." The proposal of peace, I added, would enable the northern people to determine in their coming elections whether they would support the Republicans, who wanted to prolong the war, or the Democrats, who wished to end it.

36. LINCOLN

Lee's invasion of Maryland had Washington in hysteria—there was even talk of evacuating the government. Our latest intelligence put him at Frederick, from which place he could strike at Washington or invade Pennsylvania. I saw at once that this could be the last campaign—if Lee won a great victory on our soil, Great Britain would probably recognize the Confederacy and demand that we agree to an armistice and Confederate independence. In this critical hour, we needed fighting generals more than ever, needed to whip those people *now*. Yet all I had were McClellan and Halleck, and Halleck wouldn't command any longer—blamed himself for the Bull Run fiasco and lost his nerve, lost his pluck—and settled into a habitual attitude of demure. So *I* had to lead the military again, with Halleck acting as a first-rate clerk who gave me advice and wrote out my orders, but would not, could not, command.

The rebels were on the offensive in the West, too, but the most pressing danger was Lee's presence in Maryland. Who would lead the Potomac Army against him? Who else did I have but McClellan? I wasn't going to send our greatest army against Lee under a new and inexperienced field commander.

I went to McClellan's house and told him: "General, you will take command of the forces in the field."

He gave a flash of his old arrogance. "Your Excellency, I shall give Bobby Lee the drubbing of his life."

For two days, McClellan's army tramped across the bridges into Washington and swung along Pennsylvania Avenue to the beat of drums—column after column of blue-coated veterans marching by with bullet-torn flags, their rifled muskets slung across their shoulders, eighty-five thousand of them spreading out westward on various streets and roads. By September eighth, the army was marching northwest through Maryland in three parallel columns, followed by an enormous train of three thousand wagons in moving clouds of dust.

Watching McClellan ride off with his staff, I made a vow, a covenant with my Maker, that if McClellan won a victory, I would view it as an indication of divine will that God had decided the question in favor of the slaves and that it would be my duty to move forward in the cause of emancipation. That subject was on my mind, day and night, as I camped out in the little telegraph office, following McClellan's progress. My constant telegrams to the general attested to my acute anxiety. "How does it look now?" "What goes?" "How about our garrison at Harpers Ferry?" "Please," I said in reference to the enemy, "do not let him get off without being hurt."

37 · LEE

I had expected that my advance on Frederick would cause the enemy garrisons at Martinsburg and Harpers Ferry to evacuate, thus allowing me to shift my line of communications westward into the Shenandoah. But the two garrisons, though outflanked, had not retired, and it became necessary to dislodge the enemy from those positions before I could concentrate the army west of South Mountain for the move into Pennsylvania.

I sent for General Jackson and outlined a plan to overwhelm the enemy garrisons by sending three columns against them. Jackson was to drive the enemy from Martinsburg in Maryland and then to march his three divisions down the south side of the Potomac against Harpers Ferry. Meanwhile McLaws with his and R. H. Anderson's divisions of Longstreet's command would seize Maryland Heights on the north side of the Potomac opposite Harpers

Ferry, and Walker with his two brigades would take possession of Loudoun Heights on the east side of the Shenandoah where it unites with the Potomac. Walker and McLaws would thus be in position to intercept the enemy if he tried to escape. After reducing Harpers Ferry and clearing the valley of the enemy, so as to secure our supply line and our rear, these several commands were to rejoin the rest of the army at Boonsboro or Hagerstown.

It was a risky move, dividing the army into four separate columns in enemy territory. Yet we would be operating behind the barrier of South Mountain, and in any case Stuart reported that McClellan was moving ever so cautiously away from Washington, as I thought he would. I believed that Jackson could complete his operation and rejoin the army before McClellan posed a threat to us.

I distributed copies of my orders to all the commanders involved in the operation, and on September tenth they moved out on the National Road, with Jackson in overall command of the three columns. To my immense relief, Jackson released Powell Hill from arrest and restored him to command of his Light Division. Jackson would have need of that excellent soldier.

With D. H. Hill's detached division and Longstreet's remaining troops, I headed west to South Mountain, crossed it at Turner's Gap, and reached Boonsboro on the mountain's western side. Here we posted Hill's division to guard the mountain gap; he in turn sent one of his brigades, Howell Cobb's Georgians, down to hold Crampton's Gap. Stuart remained east of the mountain, watching and deceiving the enemy. Detaching Harvey Hill's division meant that the army was now divided into five separate columns.

Longstreet, who hadn't liked detaching Jackson, protested against further division of the army. "General," he said, "I wish we could stand still and let the damned Yankees come to us."

I told him that my faith in McClellan's overcautious nature made me confident that no disaster would befall us. On the eleventh we moved to Hagerstown and seized flour and stores that were being run off to Pennsylvania. A woman came up to me and sang "The Star-Spangled Banner" in an insulting manner. When she finished, I lifted my hat to her and rode on to find a spot for my headquarters. We could do nothing now but wait until Jackson returned. The next day I wrote President Davis that my first objective—drawing the mass of enemy troops north of the Potomac—had been accomplished. We then learned that with the approach of our troops, the enemy garrison at Martinsburg had fallen back to Harpers Ferry. No news came from Jackson on the thirteenth as to the status of Harpers Ferry, but I had every reason to believe it would fall shortly.

The thirteenth did bring alarming reports from Stuart and Hill that the enemy was pushing rapidly forward and was now approaching Turner's Gap in South Mountain on the National Road. Hill said that the Federals appeared to be at the base of the mountain "in force." McClellan's rapid advance was uncharacteristic of him, and it perplexed me. I found it difficult to believe that he, of all people, had taken the offensive with a demoralized army, but that was what the reports indicated. I did not know until later that a copy of my order directing the movement of the army from Frederick had fallen into McClellan's hands, disclosing to him the disposition of our forces.

A glance at my map revealed the danger we were in. If McClellan penetrated South Mountain at Turner's Gap, he could strike the rear of McLaws's troops on Maryland Heights and relieve the garrison at Harpers Ferry. McClellan might then attempt to destroy my army in detail.

What to do? If I called Jackson back before he could remove the enemy garrison at Harpers Ferry, it would upset my entire plan of operations. Not willing to let that happen, I resolved to hold South Mountain until Jackson could complete his mission. I sent orders back to Hill and Stuart to guard the passes in South Mountain and then went to Longstreet's tent, woke him up, and told him to march to Hill's support at first light. Longstreet objected, arguing that it would be better if our infantry and cavalry withdrew to better defensive ground at Sharpsburg near the Potomac. But this time I did not defer to him.

At dawn on the fourteenth, Longstreet put his divisions into motion, and I accompanied Old Pete on Traveller, despite my bandaged hands. It was unthinkable to ride into battle in an ambulance. As we approached South Mountain on the National Road, we could hear the noise of battle coming from Turner's Gap. A courier from Hill reported that he was under heavy attack and in desperate need of immediate reinforcements. Longstreet sent his troops rapidly forward and put them in position to shore up Hill's crumbling right. I must say, Harvey Hill fought well this day, repeatedly throwing off enemy attacks. A slim, erect man with a dark brown beard, Harvey had such a queer temperament I could never quite tell what to expect of him. But this day he held the enemy in check for five hours. Late in the afternoon, however, the Federals launched coordinated assaults at both of our flanks with greatly superior numbers. By nightfall their lines extended beyond both our right and left. I learned that another large body of Federal troops in the afternoon had forced their way through Crampton's Gap, knocking aside Cobb's Georgians, and were only five miles from McLaws's rear.

We could not hazard a renewal of the battle at Turner's Gap, since the enemy could now turn either flank there. With McLaws in peril, too, I had no choice but to abandon the campaign and order my scattered commands back to Virginia. I sent orders to McLaws to leave his position that night and find a way to cross the Potomac. But then a report came from Jackson that improved our prospects dramatically: he expected Harpers Ferry to fall next morning. I decided against retreating to Virginia and resolved at once to reconcentrate the army at Sharpsburg, Maryland. I sent word to McLaws and Walker to join us there.

Had the enemy not found the lost dispatch, and had McClellan continued his cautious movement for two or three more days, I would have had all my troops reconcentrated on the Maryland side of the Potomac, stragglers up, men rested, and *I would have attacked McClellan.* But the loss of that dispatch changed the character of the campaign, forcing me to assume the defensive.

Longstreet and Hill, accompanied by me and my staff, reached Sharpsburg about daybreak of the fifteenth, and I went out to reconnoiter. It was good defensive ground. The town was situated under one of a series of wooded ridges between the Potomac and winding Antietam Creek. The ground south of town consisted of timbered hills and ravines. The flatter ground to the north was a patchwork of woodlots and fields dotted with wood and stone farmhouses. The corn in some of the fields was as tall as a man. The creek itself was spanned by four bridges and was not wide, but it would impede the Federals unless they could capture one of the bridges.

I set up headquarters in a grove of trees just west of town and personally showed our dust-covered soldiers where to fall into line. "We will make our stand on those hills," I said, pointing to the high ground between Sharpsburg and the Antietam. If Mr. McClellan wanted a battle, we would offer it to him.

Soon after our arrival, I received intelligence from Jackson that Harpers Ferry had surrendered early that morning. Jackson said he would leave Powell Hill's Light Division to attend to the details of the surrender. "That is indeed good news," I said. "Let it be announced to the troops." I ordered Jackson to come to Sharpsburg promptly. McLaws and Walker should also be on their way.

At two that afternoon, our pickets reported the approach of the enemy army. I rode to the high ground along the Boonsboro pike and swept my glass along the long columns of Federal infantry and horse-drawn caissons. We had only eighteen thousand men in line, the enemy had several times that number, but my instinct told me that McClellan would not attack, that his aggressive behavior of the last few days had indeed been out of character and that he would now revert to the McClellan of old.

"There will not be a battle today," I said, "or tomorrow either. We'll have time enough to reunite the army."

The next day, Jackson and Walker arrived, and Jackson, wearing his soiled cadet cap pulled low over his eyes, found me with Longstreet, studying the Federals across the valley.

"Ah, General Jackson," I said, "it's good to see you."

He touched his cap. "General Lee, it's good to be here. A. P. Hill will leave Harpers Ferry tomorrow morning."

"Very well," I said. "When he and McLaws join us, the army will be united again."

We all turned to survey McClellan's powerful army, which our intelligence estimated at 80,000 to 100,000 strong, with several hundred pieces of artillery. Against them we had, today, but 26,500 men and 246 guns, and even if my soldiers were the best in the world, we might not have been able to withstand an attack all along the line. Still, I was right about McClellan: even with his vastly superior strength, he did not attack this day either.

When McLaws did not show up with his two divisions, I sent a courier to find them. Another courier set out for Harpers Ferry with orders for Powell Hill to march as early as possible tomorrow. As night fell, our defensive line extended around Sharpsburg from the north to the south. The campfires of Jackson's men glowed on our left, on the high ground around a little white church about a mile north of town. Stuart's cavalry was farther out, covering our left flank. Longstreet's campfires glimmered in the center and right of our line. Harvey Hill's boys were in the center, holding a sunken lane near the crest of a hill. Old Pete had placed more men and artillery on the hill just below town. Our extreme right was located on low hills overlooking a loop in the Antietam.

Late that night, as rain drummed at the roof of my tent, I sat on a campstool pondering our odds. I was sure that McClellan, having squandered two days, would attack tomorrow. Even if McLaws's two divisions came up during the night, we would have fewer than forty thousand men in line, with only Hood's division in reserve. But my blood was up. I was ready to give battle. Better to fight here than to retreat ingloriously with only the capture of Harpers Ferry to report to Richmond. There would be little honor in that.

At 3 A.M. on the seventh, intermittent firing sounded on our left. If McClellan meant to attack there, it was fine by me: he would be up against the two best combat divisions of the army—Hood's and Jackson's old division. I rose at four that morning and sent a warning to our reserve artillery to secure our line of retreat, just in case. The rain had stopped, but a heavy mist lay over the lines. I walked to command post hill, just behind the center of our line, where from a large rock I could get a clearer view of the fog-ridden countryside. As dawn broke in the mist, Federal artillery opened a furious cannonade on both sides of the Antietam. I had never witnessed such a murderous artillery barrage, most of it concentrated on Jackson's men in a cornfield and along the Hagerstown pike. The concussions of the big guns struck like continuous thunderclaps. Shell bursts lit up the fog and showered the ground with pieces of cornstalks, equipment, and men.

Around six in the morning the artillery died down and the Federals launched a massive infantry attack against Jackson's lines. The musketry was intense, smoke from the rifles obscured the ground even more. It was hard to tell what was happening over there. Presently a Jackson aide ran up to report that the enemy troops had broken through Jackson's flank and were now streaming down the Hagerstown road and through a woodlot near a little church! Hood's division was moving up to try to stop the attacking force, but Jackson needed reinforcements at once or faced disaster. As far as I could tell, McClellan had only attacked our left—our center and right were silent. Thank God it was not an attack all along the line— thank God for giving us McClellan to fight. I shifted three brigades from the right side of the line to reinforce Jackson. Meanwhile, McLaws and Anderson had arrived with their divisions, and I ordered McLaws up to reinforce Jackson and sent Anderson to support Harvey Hill, who held our center and was now engaged with his left in the air. These dispositions dangerously weakened the right of our line, leaving only seven brigades there to defend a mile and a half of ground—and only one, Toombs's sharpshooters, covering the lower bridge over the Antietam. I was gambling that McClellan would not launch an attack there while his right was engaged.

I set out for Jackson's front, heading through town on Traveller. An aide had to lead him, since my hands were still in splints. Shells from the Federal bombardment had struck the town, shredding trees and crashing into houses and other buildings. Several were on fire, and the streets were littered with shattered glass, bricks, and other debris. Stretcher-bearers carried the wounded into makeshift hospitals, and surgeons and attendants were already at their grisly work on the amputating tables.

North of town I met an artilleryman with an urgent message from Hood. "Without immediate reinforcements, sir, the day is lost."

"Don't get excited, Colonel," I said. "Go tell General Hood to hold his ground, reinforcements are on the way. Tell him I'm coming to his support."

"General," the colonel said, "your presence will do good, but nothing but infantry can save the day on the left."

When I reached the left, Hood filled me in on what had happened: his Texans and Law's brigade had plunged into the hole in Jackson's flank and struck the attacking Yankees with such force that it drove them back across the cornfield to the Miller farm where their attack had started. But then Hood had been hit by overwhelming columns of fresh enemy troops and driven back across the turnpike to the woods west of the little church, with enemy cannon raking his ranks with deadly blasts of canister and explosive shells. Our boys had fought the Yankees at close quarter with gun butts and bayonets, Hood said, both sides screaming in a frenzy of excitement and rage.

I supervised the posting of a reserve line of artillery on the high ground due west of the church and woods, and worried though I was about the left—I didn't know if it could hold or not—I rode to the center, anticipating an attack there. I was relieved to find that Anderson's four-thousand-man division had arrived to support Hill. I rode down the line, encouraging the men to ready themselves for an assault. The colonel of the Sixth Alabama yelled back: "These men are going to stay here, General, till the sun goes down or victory is won."

With Harvey Hill, I rode to command post hill near the Hagerstown pike and Pete Longstreet joined us, an unsmoked cigar in his mouth. Longstreet and I dismounted and Longstreet swept his glass over our left. The sun had burned the mist away by now, and we could see the ground clearly and the enemy guns across the Antietam.

I moved over to Hill, who was still mounted, and said something to him when Longstreet exclaimed: "Just saw a puff of smoke! There's a shot for you." A few seconds later a shell came whirling toward us, passed near me, and struck Hill's horse, blowing away its forelegs.

The roar of battle picked up again on Jackson's and Hood's front. It was another enemy attack in that sector—the third that morning. They broke through our line in the woods west of the church and threatened to roll up our flank, when suddenly McLaws's division and reinforcements from our right appeared in the front, flank, and rear of the attacking Yankees and delivered a counterattack that sent them reeling back with heavy slaughter. That ended the fighting in that sector. Couriers reported that the battleground along the Hagerstown turnpike was a hellish sight, dead and dying men everywhere, dead horses twisted in hideous positions, trees shredded, the corn in the field along the pike all mowed down as if by a giant blade.

Enemy cannon meanwhile raked the center of our line, and a solid mass of Yankee infantry struck Harvey Hill's position in the sunken road between the Hagerstown pike and Antietam Creek, but Hill's boys drove them back once, twice, three times. As I watched from command post hill, solid shot tore holes in that deadly ground; riderless horses bounded out of the smoke; and long lines of infantry swayed back and forth in hand-to-hand combat, their rifles blazing and clanging, their screams rising on the wind. Smoke and dust swirled up from the struggling mass until it obscured the sun. Harvey Hill never fought better, but the enemy gained the hilltop where they enfiladed his men in the sunken road and broke through with superior numbers, sending broken units fleeing into town.

I had no reserves to fill the hole; my center was collapsing. One more attack would shatter it and destroy the army. "We're badly whipped," Longstreet admitted. "The end of the Confederacy is in sight," said Porter Alexander of the artillery. In desperation I sent an order to Jackson to make a diversionary move against the enemy right flank. But McClellan never followed up his advantage—never launched a decisive final attack against our center that would have ruined the army. We were saved—by General McClellan and a merciful Providence.

While the attacks on the center and left of our line were taking place, the enemy made repeated efforts to cross the stone bridge on our far right, held by D. R. Jones's division. Jones's batteries and two regiments of Georgia sharpshooters under Brigadier General

Robert Toombs, who occupied the bluff above the bridge, repulsed five different assaults by a greatly superior force of enemy infantry. When the fifth attack began, I hurried to that sector of the field, only to find that the enemy had forced his way across the bridge, compelling Toombs and the rest of Jones's little division to fall back to the ridge south of town, where they were preparing to make a desperate stand. The Federals were massing down there in what appeared to be three-division strength. If they broke through Jones and seized Sharpsburg, it would cut off my line of retreat down the road leading to the one ford across the Potomac.

About two-thirty in the afternoon, as the Federals prepared to attack, I saw from the south a group of officers riding up at a gallop, their horses frothing and bathed in sweat. It was A. P. Hill from Harpers Ferry! I could tell by his red shirt, which he always wore into battle. His division, he said when he reined up, had marched at a killing pace, having covered seventeen miles in less than eight hours and losing almost half their number, but they were now at Boteler's Ford on the Potomac.

"Bring your division up at double quick," I said, "and put them in on the right there, in support of Jones. Hurry, General, time is of the essence."

It was indeed. If he did not arrive in time, the Federals would overwhelm Jones's 2,800 men. The Yankees, however, were slow to mount their attack—another godsend to us. At three o'clock they finally moved with their skirmishers thrown out, and the air was filled with hissing bullets and whirring canister. Solid shot whacked tree trunks and severed men's heads from their bodies or cut them in two. Overhead the sun shone blood red. Ambulances with blood dripping from their floorboards raced back into town, where Federal shells blew up buildings, filling the streets with more debris. I helped my junior officers try to rally broken units on our crumbling southern front, but enemy infantry broke through our thin line and were soon marching on the town. Once again the destruction of my army seemed at hand.

Then I saw, beyond the fighting, a distant cloud of dust. Soon a column of marching men came into view. A section of artillery rumbled by me, and I noticed that its commander, a lieutenant, had a telescope. I pointed to the column in the distance. "What troops are those?"

He offered me his glass.

"Can't use it," I said, and held up my bandaged hands.

The lieutenant peered through his telescope. "They are flying the United States flag," he said.

"Not those." I gestured at another column to the right. "*Those*."

The lieutenant focused again. "They're flying the Virginia and Confederate flags."

"It's A. P. Hill," I said, and if I didn't show it I felt immensely relieved and deeply grateful to him. For the second time that day, my army was saved. As we looked on, little Powell Hill hurled his reduced division against the flank of the advancing Federals, which surprised and confused them, and they fled back to the Antietam and the protection of their guns on the opposite shore.

That repulse ended the battle. Fewer than forty thousand men on our side had fought to a draw an enemy with twice that number and superior in guns and weight of metal. That evening, I assembled my weary officers at my headquarters in the grove west of town. Longstreet was not among them.

"Where is Longstreet?" I asked, suddenly fearful.

"I saw him at sundown," Major Venable said. "He was all right then."

"Look!" someone said. "There he is now." Longstreet rode up, the unsmoked cigar still in his mouth. He explained that he had stopped in town to help a family—some ladies—whose house was burning. As he dismounted, I walked over and took his hand with my bandaged ones. "Ah," I said, "Here is Longstreet. Here is my warhorse."

I hoped that the army could attack tomorrow and destroy the enemy. I asked Longstreet: "General, how is it on your part of the line?"

"Bad. My divisions suffered terrible losses. There's little better than a skirmish line left on my front."

Harvey Hill seconded Longstreet: his division had been cut to pieces. He had few troops to hold his line.

And Jackson? "Worst odds I ever saw," he said.

And Hood? How was his division? "I *have* no division, General Lee," he said with a trembling voice.

"Great God! General Hood, where is your splendid division you had this morning?"

"They're lying on the field where you sent them. My division has been almost wiped out."

No one yet knew how bad the day had gone for us. Total casualties, when they were finally known, amounted to more than ten thousand, with whole divisions wrecked; some brigades had lost fifty percent of their numbers. Hood's Texas brigade under Colonel W. T. Wofford had lost 560 of 854 men.

After Hood spoke, each general, one by one, expressed his fear that renewed enemy attacks tomorrow would destroy us, and each recommended complete withdrawal tonight.

I realized now that the army was hurt too badly to attack. But I believed it could defend its position if McClellan launched further attacks of his own. "Gentlemen," I said slowly and firmly, "we will not cross the Potomac tonight. You will go to your respective commands and strengthen your lines. Send two officers from each brigade toward the ford to collect your stragglers and get them up. If McClellan wants to fight in the morning, I'll give him battle again. Go!"

All the next day we lay in line, daring McClellan to attack again. But being McClellan, he declined to do so. The smell of death was in the air, and the surgeons toiling in the improvised hospitals in town were covered with bloody matter from head to foot. Across the Antietam battleground lay thousands of blasted and bloating bodies, broken equipment, and other debris of combat. Feeling that we had won a moral victory, I ordered my proud little army to retire across the Potomac that night. As we filed across the wide river, a band struck up "Carry Me Back to Old Virginnny."

38. LINCOLN

McClellan's telegrams from Antietam filled us with hope. "We are in the midst of the most terrible battle of the war, perhaps of history," he telegraphed on the seventeenth. "Thus far it looks well but I have great odds against me." And on the eighteenth: "The battle yesterday continued for fourteen hours. We held all we gained except a portion of the extreme left." And the nineteenth: "Last night the enemy abandoned his position leaving his dead & wounded on the field. We are again in pursuit. I do not yet know whether he is falling back to an interior position or crossing the river. We may safely claim a complete victory." Once again, the words "complete victory" sent our hopes soaring, Stanton's and mine. We had visions of McClellan catching Lee's army before it crossed the Potomac and *destroying it as a fighting force.* That's what complete victory means to me: the pursuit and annihilation of the enemy army.

But we forgot that this was McClellan. He next reported that he'd allowed Lee to get away to the safety of Virginia, to lick his wounds and fight again another day. McClellan didn't put it that way, of course. "The enemy is driven back into Virginia," he said. For him that was "complete" victory. He patted himself on the back for saving Maryland and Pennsylvania, and then went into camp on the Antietam battlefield and stayed there, exulting in his triumph.

At best Antietam was a drawn game. Still, Lee had *left the field.* It was the closest thing to a victory we were likely to get in the East, so I took the preliminary emancipation proclamation out of my desk, and on September twenty-second called the Cabinet together in the Executive Mansion.

"The time for the announcement of an emancipation policy can't be delayed any longer," I said. "Public sentiment will sustain it—many of our best friends and supporters demand it—and I promised my Maker I would do it."

Chase, who sat near me, asked: "Did I understand you correctly?"

"You did," I said. "I made a solemn vow before God that if Lee was driven back from Pennsylvania, I would declare freedom to the slaves." I then read my proclamation. When Congress convened in December, the document read, I would push again for gradual, compensated emancipation in the loyal slave states and continue my efforts at voluntary colonization on this continent or elsewhere. Then I turned to the insurgents. If they didn't stop fighting and return to the Union by January first, 1863—one hundred days from the date of the proclamation—I would free "thenceforward and forever" all slaves in the rebel states; and the executive branch of the government, including the army and the navy, would recognize and maintain the freedom of such people. On the same day I would announce which states or parts of states would be affected.

Now, the reason for the one-hundred-day interval was to give the rebels a chance to lay down their arms and return to the Union. They probably wouldn't do that, but even if they didn't, I could tell the North I'd given the rebels every opportunity before we laid a strong hand on their colored element and changed the entire nature of the war. If we were ever going to win it, we had to make it a war of subjugation. A remorseless, revolutionary struggle—the very thing I'd warned against last December. The old South, based on slavery, had to be destroyed and replaced by new ideas and propositions.

"I'll entertain criticism," I told the secretaries, "but no point in telling me not to issue this. It's going to be issued." After some discussion, the majority of the Cabinet supported me, and the next day, September twenty-third, I published the preliminary proclamation. The following day I put forth another proclamation suspending habeas corpus throughout the land and ordering military trials for all rebels and insurgents, their aiders and abettors, and all persons who discouraged volunteering in our armies or gave comfort to the rebels.

39. DOUGLASS

I sat in my newspaper office in Rochester, hardly able to believe the president's proclamation of emancipation that had come in over the telegraph. The words "forever free" leaped from the page. Could I dare believe that my words had helped move him to act at last? "We shout for joy that we live to record this righteous decree," I told my readers. "'Free forever! oh! long enslaved millions, whose cries have so vexed the air and sky, suffer on a few more days in sorrow, the hour of your deliverance draws nigh!'"

This noble act completely changed my opinion of the president. I told my friends, I told my readers, I told my neighbors: Abraham Lincoln might be slow, Abraham Lincoln might desire peace without removing our terrible national sore, to fester on for generations, but Abraham Lincoln was not the man to reconsider, retract, and contradict words and purposes solemnly proclaimed over his official signature. His torturous road to this decree was itself a guarantee against retraction. No, Abraham Lincoln would take no step backward. His word had gone out over the country and the world, giving joy and gladness to the friends of freedom and progress wherever those words were read, and he would stand by them and carry them out to the letter. If he had taught us to have confidence in nothing else, he had taught us to have confidence in his word.

Oh, it was a righteous decree indeed! This moral bombshell dropped on the Confederacy was more destructive than the bullets of 100,000 soldiers. By this act Lincoln reached out and seized *the moral high ground* in a vicious civil war. He recognized and declared the real nature of the contest, and placed the North on the side of justice and civilization, and the rebels on the side of robbery and barbarism. I predicted that Lincoln's act would disarm all purpose on the part of European governments to intervene in favor of the rebels and thus cast off at a blow one source of rebel power, and in that I was correct. In fact, Great Britain, which had seemed so close to recognition and intervention, backed away and remained neutral in the conflict. And so did the other European powers.

Now we abolitionists, blacks and whites, had work to do. During the interval between now and next January, I said in my paper, let every friend of the long-enslaved bondman do his utmost in swelling the tide of antislavery sentiment. By writing and speaking and agitating, let our aim be to make the North unite in favor of the president's policy. And when emancipation did come, I told my brethren, our work would really begin, for we must look after the welfare of the former slaves—must educate them that slavery had always been their direct calamity and curse and that free labor was honorable. Our work must be nothing less than a radical revolution in all the modes of thought which had flourished under the blighting slave system.

Yes, there were aspects of the preliminary proclamation I disliked. Lincoln should not have delayed making the proclamation permanent, but should have made it absolute and immediate, at once striking the death blow to the rebellion by striking a death blow to slavery. Second, as I've said before, I hated the very idea of colonizing free persons of color outside the country. In fact, I was deeply offended when Lincoln, back in August, had called leading black residents of Washington to the Executive Mansion and urged them to promote colonization among our people. I wrote at the time that Mr. Lincoln had assumed the language and arguments of an itinerant colonization lecturer, showing all his inconsistencies, his pride of race and blood, his contempt for Negroes and his canting hypocrisy. The only colonization scheme I would ever accept was the one put forth by Eli Thayer of Massachusetts: it called for blacks to be colonized on abandoned rebel lands in Florida on the free labor principle. This would introduce northern civilization in the place of southern barbarism.

Finally, the preliminary proclamation said nothing about colored soldiers. But I was certain that this would inevitably follow—that it was the next step in the revolution.

40. DAVIS

By such insane extravagance, the Lincoln government resorted to the most revolutionary measures for the emancipation of the African slaves and the enslavement of the free white citizens of the South. The cry of "war power" was the specious argument for this new usurpation. On September twenty-ninth the Confederate Senate took up Lincoln's proclamation, and some senators wanted to "*raise the black flag, asking and giving no quarter.*" Two days later resolutions were introduced in both houses demanding retaliation for "the barbarities" committed by Lincoln's proclamation. The Richmond papers rightly accused him of attempting to incite our slaves to insurrection. "Lincoln the fiend!" was what the *Dispatch* called him.

General Lee stood with us in condemning Lincoln's latest atrocities. "The military government of the United States," Lee wrote me, "has been so perfected by the recent proclamations of President Lincoln, which you have no doubt seen, and civil liberty so completely trodden under foot, that I have strong hopes that the conservative portion of that people, unless dead to the feelings of liberty, will rise and depose the party now in power."

41. LINCOLN

We were worried about the fall elections, no question about that. The Democrats made the ill-success of the war, the emancipation proclamation, and the military arrests the major themes of the canvass. They called me an abolitionist dictator, Lincoln the tyrant, Lincoln the nigger lover. Congressional Democrats damned the proclamation as blatantly unconstitutional and warned that any attempt to overthrow state institutions would be "a high crime"—in other words, an impeachable offense. That's right, they threatened to impeach me. "Lincoln's thunderbolt," yelped one Democrat, "leaves us all mute in amazement. Its suddenness, its utter contempt for the Constitution, its imperial pretension, the thorough upheaving of the whole social organization which it decreed, and the perspective of crime, and blood, and ruin, which it opened to the vision, fills every patriotic heart with astonishment, terror and indignation."

General McClellan, who made the proclamation possible with his (quote unquote) victory over Lee, let it be known how unhappy he was with my proclamation of freedom and my declaration of military law. He complained that I'd inaugurated servile war—that with a stroke of the pen I'd transformed our free institutions into a despotism. There were rumors that he would resign from the army before he would fight to free Negroes. He didn't resign, but he did issue an army order—and sent me a copy—in which he called attention to the proclamation of freedom and reminded his soldiers that "political error" could be corrected at the polls.

One Democratic paper, James Gordon Bennett's *New York Herald*, pointed out an underlying fear of northern whites: "The Irish and German immigrants, to say nothing of native laborers of the white race, must feel enraptured at the prospect of hordes of darkeys overrunning the Northern States and working for half wages, and thus ousting them from employment." To ease such fears was exactly why the Republicans advocated colonization. I let it be known that I was looking into the possibility of establishing a colony of repatriated blacks in the Chiriqui coal region of Central America.

Oh, we lost ground in the fall elections, all right. The North's five most populous states—Illinois, Indiana, Ohio, Pennsylvania, and New York, all of which had gone for me in 'sixty—sent Democratic majorities to Congress. The number of Democrats there rose from forty-four to seventy-five. The Republicans still controlled Congress, but only by a slim margin. New Jersey and New York both elected Democratic governors, and Indiana and Illinois elected Democratic legislatures. The Democratic papers had a field day. "The home of Lincoln condemns the Proclamation," they said. "Abolition slaughtered. The white race wins the Midwest." The *New York Times*, a Republican paper, conceded that the election results showed "a want of confidence" in my Administration.

I think several things told the whole story as far as the election was concerned. First, the Democrats were left in a majority by our friends going to the war. Second, the Democrats observed this and determined to reinstate themselves in power. Third, our newspapers, by vilifying and disparaging the Administration, furnished them all the weapons to do it with. Certainly, the ill-success of the war had much to do with this. And finally, the proclamation of freedom also played a big part. Yet I told a delegation of Kentuckians I'd rather die than take back a single word in it.

42. DAVIS

The results of the Federal elections caused rejoicing in Richmond and renewed hopes that it was the beginning of the end of Black Republican rule in the North. But I would not be forthcoming if I did not admit my great frustration with the results of our offensives in the East and West. I regretted that General Lee had been forced to retire from Maryland, but I did not share the criticism aimed at him by the croakers in Richmond. I wrote him: "I am alike happy in the confidence in your ability and your superiority to outside clamor, when the uninformed assume to direct the movements of armies in the field. In the name of the Confederacy I thank you and the brave men of your army for the deeds which have covered our flag with imperishable fame." I signed the letter: "Your friend, Jefferson Davis."

Meanwhile our western offensives had also run into difficulties. On October third, Van Dorn and Price, with Van Dorn in overall command, attacked part of Grant's Federal forces near Corinth and for two days launched one costly frontal assault after another. Then Van Dorn withdrew from the field and finally fell back to Holly Springs, having been thoroughly out-generaled and having gained nothing at all. It was such a mismanaged campaign, rife with bickering between the two commanders, that I replaced Van Dorn with General John C. Pemberton and charged him with the defense of the state of Mississippi. Above all, I told him, he had to safeguard Vicksburg, "the Gibraltar of the Mississippi."

Our invasion of Kentucky also fared badly. Bragg complained that Kirby Smith refused to cooperate with him in giving battle to the enemy army under Buell. Bragg had marched on Louisville, hoping to cut off Buell's supply line, but Buell beat him to that important city and secured his communications. Bragg also complained that "our prospects" in Kentucky were not what he had expected, that Kentuckians had not joined his force in anywhere near the numbers he had hoped for, and that he needed fifty thousand more men to hold the state. "Unless a change occurs soon," he warned us, "we must abandon the garden spot of Kentucky to its cupidity."

To stimulate volunteering, Bragg did install a Confederate state governor in Frankfort, but both he and the governor had to retreat when Buell's army, having marched down from Louisville, bombarded the city with artillery. On October eighth, at Perryville, Bragg fought Buell with part of his army—another part, I believe, was still around Frankfort. The Richmond papers reported that Bragg had won a victory, but in reality he withdrew to the southeast. Unable to hold Kentucky with the forces they had, Bragg and Kirby Smith both fell back into Tennessee.

The results in Kentucky were a bitter disappointment to me. But I was even more disturbed by the feud that broke out between Kirby Smith and Bragg. Smith blamed Bragg for the failure of the campaign and requested to be relieved of command if he had to continue serving under such a general. Alarmed, I called Bragg to Richmond for a long and candid interview. A thin, stooped man with beetle brows and a haggard countenance, Bragg was bothered by poor health, and for that he had my sympathy. Despite Smith's complaints, Bragg spoke highly of him, of his personal character and soldiering. Bragg explained in a direct and frank manner the circumstances of his Kentucky campaign and evinced the most self-denying temper in relation to his future position. I assured him of my confidence in him and fully approved of his plan to occupy and hold central Tennessee, where he hoped to secure desperately needed provisions.

After he left, I wrote Smith that another general might excite more enthusiasm than Bragg, but as all had their defects I did not see how to make a change with advantage to the public service. Bragg had displayed administrative capacity, had intimate knowledge of his troops, and the retreat from Kentucky was not so bad as Beauregard's flight from Corinth back in the spring. To recover from the distress caused by the failure in Kentucky, no move seemed better to me than to advance into middle Tennessee. If Buell came there, he would be weaker than in Kentucky, and I hoped would be beaten. But General Bragg, I warned Smith, could not succeed in middle Tennessee without Smith's support and cooperation. "You are now second in rank and possess to an eminent degree the confidence of the country. Your own corps could not be so usefully led by another commander. How then can I withdraw you?" I ordered him to assist Bragg with such part of his force as could be spared.

In November I decided to create a new Western Department that embraced all of Tennessee, Mississippi, and Alabama and the eastern part of Louisiana. The arrangement was intended to secure the fullest cooperation of our armies under Bragg and Smith in Tennessee and Pemberton in Mississippi, and to avoid delay in putting each of those commanders in direct correspondence with the War

Office. To head this new department, I chose Joseph E. Johnston, who had recovered from his wounds at Seven Pines and had reported for duty at the War Department.

In setting up this new command structure, I was aided by a new secretary of war, James A. Seddon. I had had nothing but trouble with Randolph in that post: he was too independent, abrasive, contentious in Cabinet meetings, and unrelentingly critical of me, accusing me of lacking "a system," of being "slow." When he offered his resignation, I accepted it gladly and named Seddon to replace him. Seddon was a great deal like me in appearance: emaciated and gaunt, with long hair and sunken eyes. One of his subordinates said he looked like a man who had been a month in his grave. We had another thing in common: he, too, was afflicted with neuralgia and poor health in general.

Meanwhile our leading problem in both theaters continued to be a want of manpower. General Lee himself insisted that conscription be extended to include all men between the ages of eighteen and forty-five, and I agreed with him. But when I proposed the measure to Congress, the malcontents in both houses put up a furious protest. Yancey accused me of being a dictator and declared that if he had to have a tyrant, he preferred Lincoln to me! Despite the opposition of Yancey and his kind, Congress extended the military age for conscription and also enacted a twenty-slave exemption rule for the benefit of planters and their wives and daughters. The fear was that conscription would deprive plantations of white men, leaving their women surrounded by Africans. To prevent that, the new legislation allowed the exemption of the owner or overseer on every plantation with twenty slaves or more. This, and the hiring of substitutes, produced cries among the poorer classes that it was "a rich man's war and poor man's fight," but they did not know what they were talking about.

Up to now, the states had enforced conscription under the guidance of the Confederate Adjutant and General Inspector's Office. But this unwieldy system failed to produce the necessary manpower. To make conscription more efficient, the Confederate government took charge of the system and established a Bureau of Conscription, which henceforth enrolled all troops east of the Mississippi and formed them into units for our armies. The bureau, of course, came under scathing attack from state-rights croakers like Joe Brown of Georgia.

By the fall of 1862, the anti-Administration clique in Congress had coalesced into an organized party of opposition. It included the lying

Foote, the drunken Toombs, the demagogic Yancey, the mulish Thomas Cobb, the turncoat Wigfall, and their diabolical ally, John Daniel of the *Richmond Examiner*. These bitter grumblers called me "an obstinate stupid fool," a "monomaniac," and kept up a constant sniping against my military appointments—particularly that of General Bragg, who had the misfortune of being regarded as my personal friend and was therefore pursued with malignant censure by men who were heedless of truth and whose want of principle rendered them incapable of conceiving that he was trusted because of his known fitness for command. The faultfinders also called me a despot when I found it necessary to ask Congress for, and received, the authority to declare martial law in threatened areas. Unlike Lincoln, I never declared martial law without congressional approval and authorization.

Varina, who had come back from Raleigh with the children, thought that the influence of these malcontents might have been weakened had we entertained more. At first we had tried to keep up numerous entertainments, but in every one of them, the death of someone's relative or dispatches from the front created intense excitement. If I had to eat under excitement, owing to my nervous dyspepsia, I was ill for days afterward.

"I can do one duty or the other—give entertainments or administer the government," I said, "but I can't do both. I believe I am expected to administer the government."

Thus, except for formal receptions and informal breakfasts and dinners, we stopped entertaining. Nor did I receive visitors in the evenings, for the simple reason that I was far too exhausted after a long day's work that had begun at or before dawn. The *Examiner,* of course, damned me for my "parsimony," and the incessant criticism from that paper and the clique of grumblers often made me ill.

"You're abnormally sensitive to criticism, Banny," Varina said. "And painfully sensitive to the fealty of friends. I know how much it hurts you to be misunderstood. The injustice of it makes you so *mortified* and *angry,* even *harsh.* It's because of your super-sensitive temperament and the terrible suffering it causes you to be misunderstood, that I didn't want you to be president. I want you to know that I love you and stand by you, but it hurts me to see how you let worry and conviction gnaw at your vitals in silence."

"If we succeed," I said, "we'll hear nothing of these malcontents. If we don't, then I shall be held accountable by our friends and our foes. I will do my best, dear wife, and God will give me strength to bear whatever comes to me."

43 · LINCOLN

I told Carl Schurz, a loyal Administration man and leader of the German-Americans, that if the war failed, I would be blamed for it, whether I deserved it or not. The only way the war would *not* fail was by winning victories on the battlefield. I said it again and again: "It's upon the progress of our arms that all else chiefly depends." But that was the problem: there was little progress of our arms. Almost a month after Antietam, McClellan was still encamped on the battlefield, offering excuse after excuse as to why he couldn't cross the Potomac and go after Lee. At one point I'd gone up there to see if I could light a fire under McClellan. I told him the country would not tolerate further delay. He *had* to move, *had* to strike a blow.

Then I came back to Washington and through Halleck *ordered* McClellan to cross the Potomac and strike after Lee. "Look at your map," I told him. "Lee's in the Shenandoah with an insecure base. You're closer to Richmond than he is. You must cross the river, and if he sets out for Richmond, you must press him closely, fight him if a favorable opportunity presents itself, and at least try to beat him to Richmond by the inside track. You must try to do this. If we never try, we'll never succeed. If Lee stands at Winchester, I would fight him there. If we can't whip him where he is now, we can never whip him if he falls back to the trenches around Richmond. Surely our men can march and fight as well as the rebels. It's *unmanly* to say they can't."

I'd been telling Buell the same thing, with about the same results. In fact, when the rebels invaded Kentucky and he retreated all the way back to Louisville, I ordered Halleck to relieve him, but Halleck begged me to give him another chance, and I did, against my better judgment. Yes, Buell fought the rebels to a drawn game at Perryville, and they ended up falling back into Tennessee. Buell followed them a ways and then wired us that he was heading off to Nashville to renew the advance against Chattanooga. Damn! I was furious that Buell had let the rebel army get away. It was Antietam all over again. When would our generals learn that the destruction of the rebel armies was the only way to win this war?

To make matters worse, Buell was no closer to East Tennessee than he was when he began campaigning months before. Through Halleck, I gave him an ultimatum: you must advance into East Tennessee before the autumn rains make the roads impassable. But Buell came down with a severe case of the "can't-do." He *can't* march on East Tennessee, he says, and he *can't* march on Chattanooga either. His supply problems, it seems, are insurmountable. Why, I groaned, can't we live as the enemy lives, march and fight as he does?

Delays in the West and the East and the people voting Republicans out of office in state after state—I'd had it with inert generals. On October twenty-third I relieved Buell and put William S. Rosecrans in command of the Army of the Ohio. Old Rosey had put up a good fight against the rebels in the battle of Corinth, and he had Grant's and Halleck's backing. He had an excitable streak and in a crisis sometimes lost his nerve, but maybe he would fight. No, he *had* to fight.

As for McClellan, he had an even worse case of the "can't-do" than Buell. He still hadn't gone after Lee as I'd ordered. Why? I asked him. Because, he said, my horses have got sore backs and are "broken down from fatigue." I telegraphed him: "Will you pardon me for asking what the horses of your army have done since the battle of Antietam that fatigue anything?" I won't bother repeating the answer he gave to that. But he did move, finally crossing the Potomac and inching southward at glacial speed, only to stop and complain about his supplies. I tell you, I was sick and tired of sticking sharp sticks under his ribs. I thought he was playing false and did not want to hurt the enemy. I promised myself: if McClellan lets Lee get between the Army of the Potomac and Richmond, I'll sack him. Lee must have read my mind, because he dispatched a wing of his army to Culpeper Court House, squarely between the Potomic Army and Richmond. With that, I relieved McClellan of command because I could no longer stomach his slows, could no longer tolerate a man with a special talent for a stationary engine.

On the same day, November fifth, I named Ambrose Burnside to command the Army of the Potomac. Old Burn sputtered that he wasn't fit to head a whole army, but who else did I have? Anybody, even Burnside, was better than McClellan. Burnside then advanced southeast to Fredericksburg on the Rappahannock, with plans to drive from there on Richmond. I didn't like the plan one bit and told Halleck so. Still, I chose not to interfere and told Burnside—through Halleck—that the plan would succeed only if he moved rapidly. But he forgot or neglected to take pontoon bridges with him, and while he waited for them to come up, Lee hurried down there to block his advance.

Rosecrans meanwhile spent an entire month in Nashville—
"building up my supplies," he told us. Damnit, I said, all this *impedimenta* is going to ruin us! I ordered Halleck to replace Rosecrans
with another commander, but Halleck begged me to give him another
chance. I'd been slow to replace McClellan and Buell because I'd
feared their replacements would do no better, and I'm sorry to add,
I'd seen little since to relieve those fears.

44 · LIVERMORE

In November, I accompanied a group of Sanitary Commission
women who called on Mr. Lincoln in the Executive Mansion. We
had been attending a Woman's Council in Washington, called
because the Sanitary Commission had found itself short of supplies
and needed to devise a more efficient and effective system of relief. It
was a time of great gloom and discouragement in the North. The
fruitless undertakings and timid, dawdling policy of General McClellan had perplexed and discouraged all loyalists and had strengthened
and made bold all traitors. Those of us who came from the more
sanguine Northwest listened in undisguised amazement to the open-
mouthed bitterness and treason of more than half the people we met
in the East. Our hearts died within us; and when the Woman's
Council adjourned, we were glad to accept an invitation to call on
the president in a group.

It was after dark, and the room in which he greeted us was
imperfectly lit by gas lamps. But I shall never forget the shock his
appearance gave us. Even in the flickering lamplight, his face was
ghostly pale. His introverted look and his half-staggering gait were
like those of a man walking in his sleep. He seemed literally bending
under the weight of his burdens. He took us each by hand mechani-
cally, in an awkward, absent way, until my friend Mrs. Hoge and I
were introduced.

"So you're from Chicago!" he said. "You're not scared by Washington mud, then. Chicago can beat us all to pieces in that department."

"Mr. President," we asked, "will you give us some word of
encouragement to take back to our homes?"

"I have no word of encouragement to give," he said. "The military situation is terrible and the country knows it as well as I do." He paused. "The fact is, the people haven't yet made up their minds that we're at war with the South. They haven't buckled down to the determination to fight this war through. They've got the idea into their heads that somehow we're going to get out of this fix by strategy. That's the word—*strategy*. General McClellan thought he was going to whip the rebels by strategy, and the army has got the same notion. They've no idea that the war has to be carried on by hard, tough fighting that will hurt somebody; and no headway is going to be made while this delusion lasts."

One woman disagreed. She pointed out that hundreds of thousands of men had rushed to arms to save the flag, that the army and navy had won spectacular victories in the West: Henry and Donelson, Pea Ridge, Shiloh, New Orleans.

"The people haven't made up their minds that we are *at war*, I tell you! One of the greatest wars the world has ever seen. The people, though, think there is a royal road to peace. The army does too. When you came to Washington, ladies, two weeks ago, few soldiers came on the trains with you, isn't that right?"

We agreed that it was.

"But when you go back you'll find the trains and every conveyance crowded with soldiers. Whole regiments have two-thirds of their men absent—a great many by desertion, and a great many on leave granted by company officers, which is almost as bad. General McClellan was all the time calling for more troops, more troops; and they were sent to him; but the deserters and furloughed men outnumbered the recruits. At Antietam, McClellan had the names of about 180,000 men on the army rolls, but 70,000 of them were absent on leave granted by company officers. Right now, furloughs and desertions are the most serious evil we have."

"Isn't death the penalty for desertion?" we asked.

"Yes."

"Why not enforce it, then? Before many soldiers had been executed, the wholesale depletion of the army would stop."

Lincoln shook his head. "No, no, that can't be done! It would be unmerciful, barbaric."

"But is it not more merciful to stop desertions and fill up the army, so that when a battle comes off it might be decisive, instead of being a drawn game, as you say Antietam was?"

"If I go to shooting men by the score for desertion, I'd soon have a worse hullabaloo than I already have. You can't order men shot wholesale. No, we must change the condition of things some other way. The army must be officered by fighting men."

The next day Mrs. Hoge and I called on the president again. If his face had looked haggard the night before, daylight revealed even more the ravages which anxiety and overwork had wrought.

"Mr. President," we said, "we were greatly depressed by the talk of last evening. You don't consider our national affairs hopeless, do you? Our country is not lost?"

"No, our country isn't lost, not by any means. We've got the right on our side. We didn't want this war, and we tried to avoid it. But we were forced into it. Our cause is just, and now it has become the cause of freedom." He admitted, however, that sometimes, when the woes of the country pressed most heavily on him, he envied the dead soldier sleeping in the cemetery. "Whichever way this war ends, I have the impression I won't last long after it's over."

Mrs. Hoge and I left with tears in our eyes and walked side by side up Pennsylvania Avenue, which was crowded with military vehicles. Ahead of us loomed the partially completed dome of the Capitol, surmounted by a scaffold and a towering crane, which moved against the clouds. We talked about our visit with Mr. Lincoln, and we believed that last night's meeting had had a salutary effect on all the women who were present. As women, we could not fight for the country. But the instinct of patriotism within our hearts now grew into a passion, and we returned to our various homes more inspired than ever to help save our government and our country.

When Mrs. Hoge and I were back in Chicago, a reorganization of the Chicago Sanitary Commission put us in charge—we were eventually called associate managers. We inherited a troubled organization, with only a hundred dollars in its treasury, only 250 auxiliaries, and only four boxes of stores coming in each day. Mrs. Hoge and I set about putting the Chicago branch on a secure footing and greatly enlarging its activities. I organized new Soldiers' Aid Societies and delivered public addresses to stimulate supplies and donations of money in the principal cities and towns of the Northwest; wrote letters by the thousand; and wrote the circulars, bulletins, and monthly reports of the Commission. Mrs. Hoge, a forceful woman and an excellent speaker, also presided over large meetings of potential donors—in fact, she ran them better than most men could have done. Soon we had two thousand auxiliaries across six northwestern states, which shipped us a hundred boxes of stores a day.

Every morning, after seeing my two daughters off to school, I rode the streetcar to the busy rooms of our Chicago depot, where the boxes from our affiliates were being unloaded. Our work women repackaged the items—socks, shirts, drawers, towels, blankets, jellies and jams, liquors, medical stores, and "comfort bags" containing things like pins, needles, combs, and dried fruit—in boxes stamped U.S.S.C. and shipped them by train and steamer to Mr. Lincoln's armies.

45. LINCOLN

Congress convened on December first and heard my message on the state of the Union in its trial by fire. The heart of my speech dealt with slavery, emancipation, and colonization. I pointed out that many free Negroes had applied to me for colonization as provided for by the recent acts of Congress, but the Chiriqui coal region of Central America was out as a colonization site because several Spanish-American republics protested against the sending of colonists to their respective territories. Liberia and Haiti were the only countries to which colonists of African descent from here could go with the certainty of being received and adopted as citizens. But the people contemplating colonization did not seem so willing to migrate to those countries as to some others. Still, I said, I believed ere long that there would be an augmented and considerable migration to both of those countries.

Much of this part of the address was aimed at northern whites who voted against us in the recent elections, out of fear that emancipated slaves would come rushing into their neighborhoods. I addressed that fear directly. "There is an objection urged against free colored persons remaining in the country, which is largely imaginary, if not sometimes malicious. It is insisted that their presence would injure and displace white labor and white laborers. If there ever could be a proper time for mere catch arguments, that time surely is not now. In times like the present, men should utter nothing for which they would not willingly be responsible through time and eternity." I denied that freed colored people would displace white labor. If they stayed in their old places in the South, they would jostle no white laborers; if they left their old places, they left them open to white laborers. "But it is dreaded that the freed people will swarm forth, and cover the whole land." How was this possible when there was but one colored to seven whites in the whole population? And in any case, why should emancipation south send the freed people north? People of any color seldom ran, I pointed out, unless they had something to run from. In the past colored people, to some extent, had fled north to escape slavery. But if slavery was removed, they would have nothing to flee from. Their old masters would give them wages until new homes could be found for the freed men in congenial climes and with people of their own blood and race.

As for removing slavery, I recommended several Constitutional amendments to accomplish that permanently. One amendment offered Federal funds to all states that abolished slavery any time before January first of 1900. Another guaranteed that all slaves liberated by the chances of the war would be forever free; it also compensated all loyal owners who had lost their slaves in the conflict. A third amendment authorized additional Federal funds for colonization.

"Among the friends of the Union," I said, "there is great diversity of sentiment and of policy in regard to slavery and the African race amongst us. Some would perpetuate slavery; some would abolish it suddenly and without compensation; some would abolish it gradually and with compensation; some would remove the freed people from us and some would retain them with us. Because of these diversities, we waste much strength in struggles among ourselves. By mutual concession we should harmonize and act together." These amendments, I said, were intended to embody a plan of such mutual concessions.

The amendments did not replace my emancipation proclamation. They were corollary moves, intended to push gradual emancipation in the loyal slave states and to offer the insurgents a choice. If they laid down their arms before January first, 1863, they could avoid the sudden derangement of Federally enforced emancipation and reap the benefits of my gradual, compensated program. But if the rebellion persisted beyond the above date, then I meant to issue my proclamation. The proposed amendments, if passed and ratified, would guarantee the permanency of the proclamation and the slave liberation sections of the confiscation acts. It was plain to everybody that presidential decrees could be rescinded by a subsequent administration, and that congressional laws could be overturned by a later Congress. And given the mood of the country, as demonstrated in the recent elections, this last was a real possibility. But I was committed to emancipation and meant to pursue it by every means.

I asked Congress—and the northern people—for their support. "The dogmas of the quiet past," I said, "are inadequate to the stormy present. The occasion is piled high with difficulty, and we must rise with the occasion. As our case is new, so we must think anew, and act anew. We must disenthrall ourselves, and then we shall save our country.

"Fellow citizens, *we* cannot escape history. We of this Congress and this Administration will be remembered in spite of ourselves. No personal significance, or insignificance, can spare one or another of us. The fiery trial through which we pass will light us down, in honor or dishonor, to the latest generation. We *say* we are for the Union. The world knows we do know how to save it. We—even *we here*—hold the power, and bear the responsibility. In *giving* freedom to the *slave*, we *assure* freedom to the *free*—honorable alike in what we give, and what we preserve. We shall nobly save, or meanly lose, the last, best hope of earth."

The world's last best hope, of course, was our system of popular government. Slavery had to be destroyed because popular government and its promise of the right to rise could not survive as long as some people were denied that right, were denied an unfettered start and a fair chance in the race of life.

While my message was being read, I stood at the window of my office in the Executive Mansion, as troubled as any man on earth. I didn't know if the amendments would ever be adopted, didn't know if the northern people would ever lay aside the prejudices of a lifetime and join me in thinking and acting anew. My old friend Orville Browning sure didn't. He stormed into my office and told me flat out that I was "hallucinating." He begged me to abandon my "reckless" emancipation schemes or they would wreck the party and destroy what remained of the country.

Sumner called, too, and I was glad to see him. He'd been away in Massachusetts when I issued the preliminary proclamation of freedom, and he told me now how "elated" he was with it and how it had scotched a so-called people's movement to unseat him, on the grounds that he was at odds with Lincoln's slavery policy.

"Your proclamation, Mr. President, fairly well assures me of reelection."

"Well, Sumner, it may have helped you in Massachusetts, but it may be my undoing in the rest of the country."

He stared hard at me. "Do I sense you're wavering on your promise of freedom?"

"Don't know how I can enforce a proclamation freeing slaves only in the rebellious states. It's like the pope's bull against the comet. Would my word free the slaves when I can't even enforce the Constitution in the rebel states?"

"Doesn't that miss the point?" he said. "Wherever our armies go, they will free the slaves. Our glorious flag, wherever planted on rebel territory, becomes the flag of emancipation. Conquering the rebel South and destroying slavery are one and the same." He continued to stare hard at me. "Mr. President, I'm going to be your conscience on this matter. I intend to make certain that you stand by your promise and issue a permanent proclamation on January first."

"Won't have to do it if the rebels stop fighting before then."

"Surely you don't expect that to happen."

"Nope, I don't."

46. LEE

I reached Fredericksburg in late autumn and established my headquarters at Hamilton's Crossing on the heights in back of town. Longstreet was drawn up on Marye's Heights with thirty-nine thousand troops, but Jackson was to remain in the valley, on Burnside's right flank, until I knew what that general intended to do. From the heights I kept a steady watch on the enemy army across the Rappahannock through my glass. They were there in great force: their fires and encampments and batteries stretched along the ridge as far as the eye could see. On our side of the river lay the old town of Fredericksburg, with its church spires and cobbled streets and its few great mansions. I hoped that this peaceable town might be spared the destruction of war and for that reason did not occupy it.

The day after I arrived, Burnside issued an ultimatum that I must surrender the town or he would reduce it by artillery fire. Such was the barbarity with which those people waged war. I advised the civilians to evacuate and they did so in a cold rain, whole families uprooting themselves and pulling out in wagons and on foot, their slaves following with their children tied to them by ropes. Long columns of refugees clogged the roads leading southward. Such was the nature of this war.

Burnside did not bombard the town on the day he threatened, and though greatly outnumbering us he remained strangely inactive. Still, I became satisfied from reports in the northern papers that he was concentrating here for an advance on Richmond, and I called Jackson from the valley with his thirty-one thousand men.

"I think Burnside will persevere in his present course," I wrote President Davis, "and the longer we can delay him and throw him into the winter, the more difficult will be his undertaking. It is for this reason that I have determined to resist him at the outset, and to throw every obstacle in the way of his advance."

Jackson reached our lines around the first of December. It had snowed, and some of his men were barefoot as they filed into position along the ridge to Longstreet's right. Still, Burnside did nothing aside from sending up his immense black balloons to peer down at us. We learned that Lincoln had been at Aquia Creek and told Burnside that he had to advance within two days. But he did not advance within two days, and then a snowstorm struck, freezing the water in the creek where I washed, and I worried about my men, who were poorly clad and barefoot.

In my tent, I tended to family matters, writing Mary in Richmond that she must thank lovely Miss Norvell for her nice cake, which I very much enjoyed. "But tell her I prefer kisses to cake. I had it (the cake) set out under the pines the day after its arrival and told the men it was a present from a beautiful young lady, and they did not leave a crumb." I told Mary how badly I needed a good servant. My boy Perry was willing and did his best, but was slow and inefficient and was very fond of his blankets in the morning. "I hope he will do well when he leaves me and gets in the service of some good person who will take care of him." As for his fate and that of the other Custis slaves, I intended to manumit all of them on December thirty-first, according to the stipulation in Mr. Custis's will, and had asked my son Custis to have the papers prepared for my signature.

As we continued to await Burnside's advance, I learned on the ninth that my little grandchild, the baby daughter of Fitzhugh and Charlotte, had died. I wrote Charlotte a letter expressing my deepest sorrow. "I was so grateful at her birth. I felt that she would be such a comfort to you, such a pleasure to my dear Fitzhugh, and would fill so full the void still aching in your hearts. But you have now two sweet angels in heaven. What joy there is in the thought! I can say nothing to soften the anguish you must feel, and I know you are assured of my deep and affectionate sympathy."

Two days later, before daybreak, the Yankees began throwing pontoon bridges across the Rappahannock. William Barksdale, a former congressman with flowing white hair, had his Mississippi riflemen drawn up along the riverfront buildings, and they opened a hot and steady fire on the Yankee bridge builders, preventing their advance. A carpet of mist lay over the town that morning—from the heights we could see nothing but the spires of churches floating above the mist. When the sun finally burnt it away, we could see artillery batteries and masses of infantry on the grounds of the Lacy Mansion and the broad plateau surrounding it. There might have been more than 100,000 enemy soldiers, standing in huge squares for three miles; behind them were seemingly endless parks of ambulances and white-topped wagons, arranged with precision in closed squares. All along Stafford Heights were the black muzzles of more than a hundred guns, and high overhead hung those two black balloons. "The most impressive exhibition of military force, by all odds, I've ever witnessed," said Porter Alexander, our young artilleryman.

About midmorning the Federal batteries on the heights opened fire on Fredericksburg, and shot and shell struck the lovely old town in a tornado of molten metal. Roofs blew off, walls and chimneys collapsed, buildings tore apart, timber and bricks exploded through the air, houses burst into flame, sending up columns of black smoke against the sun. When the bombardment ceased, enemy infantry crossed the river in pontoon boats and forced Barksdale's Mississippians to fall back to the heights, fighting almost every step of the way. When the bridges were complete, the enemy occupied the town in force and proceeded to pillage it. The destruction and sacking of this peaceable community attested to the savage spirit of an enemy who knew no honor.

The next day, General Stuart, on our far right, reported that the Federals were massing on his and Jackson's front as well. I was sure this was not a feint, that those people would attack on the morrow. Frankly, I could scarcely believe that Burnside meant to waste himself against our lines on the ridges. On our left, Longstreet held an all but impregnable position on Marye's Heights, with artillery and musketry commanding the open plain between here and the town. Across that plain the enemy must attack. Along the base of Marye's Heights, in a sunken road behind a stone wall, Longstreet had placed a brigade and a regiment of infantry, which, with artillery above them, were capable of delivering a murderous fire against assaulting columns. On Longstreet's right, Jackson held a lower ridge that was harder to defend, but even so it was a formidable position. My total force amounted to 78,000 men and 306 guns, including two thirty-pounder Parrott rifled cannon, which were in position near the parapet of my command post.

From that post, located to the right and behind Marye's Heights, I had a sweeping view of the entire ground. "I shall try to do them all the damage in our power when they move forward," I said.

The thirteenth of December dawned with a heavy fog obscuring the town and the battlefield. Longstreet, usually so reticent, was quite talkative this morning, for he sensed victory, as I did. My old warhorse wore a gray shawl over his shoulders and arms to guard against the cold. Jackson, stern eyed and thin lipped, had discarded his soiled cadet's cap and ragged uniform for a new one with rank marks, felt hat, and sword.

"I believe the uniform was some of my friend Stuart's doing," he said.

Jackson wanted to launch an attack forthwith, but I restrained him. "No," I said, "we hold the superior ground. We'll let those people vanquish themselves with suicidal assaults upon our lines. Then we'll counterattack."

As Jackson turned to go, Longstreet jested with him. "Jackson, what're you going to do with all those people over there?"

Jackson was not to be trifled with. "Sir, we will give them the bayonet."

As the mist burned away under the morning sun, we could see the smoke of the enemy's skirmish fire on our left, then came the popping noise of musketry. Presently the batteries of both sides opened fire with thunderous blasts that shook the very hills where we were standing. Then the enemy troops who had lain concealed in the streets of Fredericksburg charged out on both roads and rushed across the plain against Marye's Heights, yelling "Hi! Hi! Hi!" as they came. Now our guns on the hill and along the sunken road opened fire in a massive sheet of flame and smoke, and a whirlwind of bullets and missiles and canister struck the attacking columns, shredding men to pieces and severing heads from bodies, which ran on for a few steps with blood spewing forth until the bodies collapsed. On the Federals came, right into the muzzles of our muskets and artillery, their colors dancing in the smoke and dust, falling and rising and falling again. A shell from one of our thirty-pounder Parrotts struck a mass of running Federals and exploded with terrible force, and when the smoke cleared hardly a man was left standing.

Such murderous fire broke the Federal assault, and as the survivors fell back, one of my officers remarked: "It was magnificent, but it's not war."

I turned my glass to Jackson's front, where Federal columns were also massing for an assault. In the early afternoon they swept forward, up the wooded ridge against artillery and musketry fire from our lines. It was hard to see what was happening over there, and I sent couriers to find out. Suddenly, tremendous cheering came from the enemy: they had apparently pushed into a narrow neck of woods in Jackson's front across the railroad, from which our advanced batteries were pulling back. We could see figures in gray streaming to the rear of the Federals, in the direction of the Rappahannock. Prisoners! What did this portend? Was Jackson's line breaking?

I swung my glass back to our left, where the Federals had mounted another charge against Marye's Heights. It was an incredible spectacle. They came across the plain, rank after rank, stepping over the bodies and the debris, and as our artillery and musketry again crashed into them, they turned sideways, as if to breast a storm of sleet. Again we broke their charge and drove them back, their dead lying in heaps, their wounded writhing on the ground. When they reformed still again, I turned to Longstreet. "General, they are massing very heavily and will break your line this time, I'm afraid."

Longstreet shook his head. "Look to your right. You're in some danger there, but not on my line."

The reports from Jackson's front were not good: the Federals had driven between Lane's and Archer's brigades, and the screaming and firing from that direction indicated that a ferocious struggle was taking place. I couldn't tell what was happening, and the suspense of not knowing was excruciating. Meanwhile the enemy's big guns across the river were bombarding the whole length of our line. One shell struck under the parapet at my command post, right at my foot, but buried itself without exploding.

"That's the biggest shell I ever saw," said a young man on George Pickett's staff. "That thing must be six feet long and three feet in diameter and weigh two thousand pounds."

During the exchange of artillery fire, one of our two Parrotts exploded, sending fragments whirling near me and the officers standing at the command post, but by the grace of God nobody was hurt.

Suddenly, the wildcat screech of the rebel yell sounded on our threatened right. Jackson called that yell "the sweetest music I ever heard," and at this moment it was like music from heaven, for it meant that Jackson's men were counterattacking. Yes! we could see it now: Federals running back out of the woods with rebel infantry—the Carolinians!—charging after them. Down Deep Run to the open plain they drove the desperate Yankees, only to be stopped by fierce enemy fire. It was the most beautiful counterattack I'd seen thus far, and I turned to Longstreet with my heart pounding.

"It is well that war is so terrible," I said, "or we should grow too fond of it."

The fighting was finished on our right; Old Jack had held, *had held*. But on Longstreet's front the enemy tried yet another suicidal attack against Marye's Heights, with our men yelling "Come on, blue bellies! Come on!" and mowing them down in ghastly heaps seven or eight men deep. The Federals attempted a final assault at twilight, the spasm of a defeated army, and again the deadly fire of our muskets and artillery cut them down.

As night fell, an eerie silence descended on the battlefield. Then a strange light, a ghostly light, appeared on the horizon and spread across the sky in various hues of blues and reds; it seemed that the sky from here to Washington was on fire. One of our men had a ready explanation for this phenomenon. "The heavens are hanging out banners and streamers and setting off fireworks in honor of our great victory."

My spirits were soaring, too. I was certain those people would renew the assaults tomorrow at dawn and I was saving our men for the final struggle. When the Federals had thoroughly depleted themselves, I should be able to attack them with everything we had. Though the host covered the plain in our front and the hills beyond the river in numbers unknown to me, I felt confident we could stand the shock and inflict such casualties on the Army of the Potomac as to cripple it as a fighting force. But to my great disappointment, the enemy did not attack the next day, or the next.

"General," I told Longstreet, "I'm losing faith in your friend General Burnside."

On the night of the fifteenth, I had my suspicions that they might retire across the Rappahannock, but found it difficult to believe they would relinquish their purpose after all their boasting and preparations. That night a violent storm struck with rain and a terrific wind. The next morning the enemy army was safely on the north side of the Rappahannock. They had retreated as they had come, in the night.

Burnside's retreat distressed me, for it meant that we had won a Pyrrhic victory. I wrote Mary that had I divined that the battle of the thirteenth was to be Burnside's only effort, he would have had more of it. "They suffered heavily as far as the battle went," I told her, "but it did not go far enough to satisfy me. Our loss was comparatively light, about two thousand all told. The contest will have to be renewed now, but on what field I cannot say."

47. LINCOLN

The disaster at Fredericksburg gave me the worst case of the hypo since the war began. For days I was numb with grief and despair. "If there's a man out of perdition who suffers more than I do, I pity him," I said. "I would gladly change places today with the soldiers who died at Fredericksburg." Moderate and Radical Republicans alike blamed the disaster on me and Halleck and Stanton and our "weak and timorous policy." Senate Chandler croaked that I was "as unstable as water" and that I had sold out to "traitor" generals. A Cincinnati man wrote Sumner that I was "a cowardly imbecile." "I'm heartsick," said Senator Fessenden of Maine, "when I think of the mismanagement of our army. The simple truth is, there never was such a shambling, half and half set of incapables collected in one government before or since the world began." "God help us," declared the *New York Times*, "for man cannot."

Congressman John Cavode of Pennsylvania called and went on and on about the disaffection in the army and the public hostility toward the Administration.

"Cavode, stop!" I cried. "Stop right there! Not another word! I'm full, brim full, clear up to here"—I drew my finger across my neck.

"They want to get rid of me," I told Browning, "and I'm sometimes half disposed to gratify 'em. We're now on the brink of destruction. The Almighty seems to have turned against us, and I can hardly see a ray of hope."

The only ray of hope lay with our western armies. When Senator Trumbull of Illinois called, I told him we looked to Grant and Rosecrans, not to Burnside, to crush the rebellion and save the Union, and I asked him to convey that sentiment to Grant.

"If you'll leave him and Rosecrans alone," Trumbull said, "those two will soon clean out the Southwest and open the Mississippi."

"We'll leave 'em alone except to urge 'em forward. Rosecrans, you know, needs a lot of urging."

I was exceedingly anxious for our western forces to seize Vicksburg, because that river garrison was the key. The war could never be brought to a close until that key was in our pocket. "I'm acquainted with that region," I told a visitor, "and know what I'm talking about. We can take all the northern ports of the Confederacy, and still they can defy us from Vicksburg. It means hog and hominy without limit, fresh troops from all the states of the far South, and a cotton country where they can raise the staple without interference."

John McClernand, a war Democrat and an old friend and neighbor of mine from back home, proposed a shrewd plan to take Vicksburg. Slight, fidgety, and black bearded, he swept in here on leave from Grant's army and said let's talk about Vicksburg. He argued that the people of the Northwest were sick of the war; that it could not be won while the rebels controlled the Mississippi between Vicksburg and Port Hudson; and that the professional soldiers of the old army—the West Pointers—had failed to seize the river and drive to the Gulf. What he wanted to do, he said, was to raise an independent army of sixty thousand men, chiefly among war Democrats of the Northwest, concentrate them at Memphis, and then strike downriver against Vicksburg. After it fell he would move against Texas or Atlanta.

I thought the proposal was a good idea, especially the recruitment of loyal Democrats—Lord knows we needed their support. So I gave McClernand the go-ahead, even though Chase and Stanton both objected, on the grounds that McClernand wasn't fit for an independent command. I conceded that he was a tad overeager, but I wanted the Mississippi reopened, so why not give him a try. In the presence of Stanton and Halleck, I dictated a top secret order authorizing McClernand to raise troops in Illinois, Indiana, and Iowa, and when a sufficient force not required by the operations of General Grant's command had been raised, McClernand was to organize an expedition against Vicksburg "and to clear the Mississippi River and open navigation to New Orleans." When Halleck continued to protest, I added a final paragraph: "the forces so organized will remain subject to the designation of the general in chief, and be employed according to such exigencies as the service in his judgment may require." In short, McClernand's expedition would be independent *if* Halleck agreed to it and *if* Grant didn't need his troops.

McClernand then went off to Illinois and started raising soldiers and sending them to Memphis. Halleck telegraphed Grant that Memphis was to be "the depot of a joint military and naval operation on Vicksburg."

48. GRANT

Had my own plans for seizing Vicksburg by advancing down northern Mississippi by the railroad. But when I received Halleck's telegram and heard rumors that McClernand was to command the expedition from Memphis, I was in doubt as to what I should do. So I telegraphed Halleck asking if that movement was to be made independent of mine and if he expected me to push as far south as possible. He replied that all troops sent into my department would be under my control and that I was free to fight the enemy in my own way.

With that assurance, I moved into northern Mississippi by the Mississippi Central Railroad and seized Holly Springs and Oxford while Pemberton's rebel army fell back to a new line south of the Yalobusha River. At the same time, Sherman came down from Memphis with three divisions, and in early December we met at Oxford and worked out a plan to take Vicksburg that would keep McClernand out of the picture. I thought he was incompetent and unmanageable and didn't want him in command of any independent force within my department.

This was my plan: while I held Pemberton on the Yalobusha line, Sherman would go back to Memphis with one division and gather up all the troops there, including those McClernand had raised. With the help of the Mississippi squadron of gunboats under the command of David Dixon Porter, Sherman would then descend the Mississippi, make a lodgment up the Yazoo, and overwhelm the small garrison at Vicksburg from the rear. If Pemberton tried to reinforce Vicksburg with the main rebel force, I would follow him to its very gates and destroy him if possible.

I wired Halleck that Sherman, not McClernand, would command the expedition down the Mississippi while I advanced against

Pemberton on the Yalobusha. Halleck replied: "The president may insist upon designating a separate commander for the river expedition; if not, assign such officers as you deem best." He added: "Sherman would be my choice as the chief under you." Didn't know what Halleck meant: was Sherman in command of the river expedition or not? When I heard that McClernand, who was in Illinois, expected to go to Memphis in a few days, I telegraphed Halleck that Sherman had already gone there and that the entire enterprise would be far safer in his hands than in McClernand's.

That's where matters stood when I received word that Nathan Forrest's rebel cavalry had crossed the Tennessee River and was riding westward, straight for the Mobile & Ohio Railroad, which supplied my army in northern Mississippi from Memphis. Late that night, while I was worrying about Forrest, orders came from Halleck that riled me. I was to reorganize my army into four corps and give one to McClernand. "It is the president's wish that Genl McClernand's Corps shall constitute a part of the river expedition, and that he shall have the immediate command under your direction."

I resented the president's intervention—*Sherman* was the man for the job—but I did as I was ordered, and wrote McClernand to proceed to Memphis without delay and take command of the expedition. But before I could send the order, Forrest struck the Mobile & Ohio and cut my line of communications. It took two weeks to restore my telegraph communications—during that interval, I assumed that Sherman had proceeded downriver with the Memphis forces.

49. DAVIS

With Grant's huge force of forty thousand threatening to overwhelm Pemberton's beleaguered army of twenty thousand, fear gripped the state of Mississippi and her people fell into despondency. Governor John J. Pettus and Senator James Phelan both begged me to come out in person and bolster the confidence of the army and the people. Phelan even wanted me to take command of Pemberton's troops. "Plant your own foot upon our soil," he wrote me, "unfurl your banner at the head of the army, tell your own people that you have come to share with them the perils of this dark hour!" I was reluctant to leave Richmond—the battle of Fredericksburg had not yet been fought, but we knew that a great struggle between Lee and Burnside was imminent. If our situation deteriorated any further in the West, however, we faced certain disaster. I wired Lee that I was going west immediately with the hope that something might be done to bring out men not heretofore in the service, and to arouse all classes to a united and desperate resistance.

On December ninth, despite my sickly condition, I left Richmond in a special railroad car with a servant and a small traveling party; we departed in secret to avoid rumors that the capital was being abandoned. Our first destination was Murfreesboro, Tennessee, and Bragg's army. I found the troops in fine spirits and well supplied, and exhorted them to hold middle Tennessee at all hazards. From all that I could tell, the enemy in Nashville—this was Rosecrans's force—indicated only defensive intentions. This meant that Pemberton's was the more gravely threatened army, and I therefore ordered Johnston to transfer nine thousand men from Bragg's army to Mississippi. Johnston and Bragg both protested, Johnston arguing that this was "robbing Peter to pay Paul" and Bragg worrying that his weakened condition would encourage Rosecrans to attack him and seize middle Tennessee. I insisted that the order stand on the grounds that we could afford to lose middle Tennessee more than we could bear the loss of Mississippi and Vicksburg, which would be a catastrophe of incalculable proportions.

"You'll have to take your chances," I instructed Bragg. "Fight if you can, but fall back beyond the Tennessee if you must."

Then, with Johnston, I set out for Mississippi by a circuitous rail route with Lee's situation in Virginia weighing on me. At Chattanooga a telegram awaited me announcing that the enemy had attacked Lee at Fredericksburg, but reporting no details. You cannot imagine my anxiety. I wired Richmond asking for further information, but there was no immediate reply. If the necessity demanded it, I said, I would abandon my western trip and return to Richmond. A subsequent report, however, indicated that Lee had repulsed the attack and forced the enemy to withdraw across the Rappahannock.

"God be praised," I said, "for giving us General Lee."

As we rode across east Tennessee and north Alabama, the public sentiment was far from what I desired—there was hostility and much want of confidence in our cause. Senator Clement Clay of Alabama, an old friend, told me that the fear of traitors in the Huntsville area was so great that our friends looked around to see who was in earshot before speaking of public affairs.

We reached Jackson, Mississippi, on December nineteenth, and went on to Vicksburg, some forty miles due west. We spent two days inspecting the city's defenses, which now extended twelve miles along Chickasaw Bluffs, a range of ridges and hills overlooking the swampy bayous of the Yazoo River north and east of Vicksburg. Johnston complained that it would require a sizable army to hold this "immense, entrenched camp," and he also questioned Pemberton's competence. While I defended Pemberton, I feared that Vicksburg's defenses were not strong enough and wired Richmond of the immediate and urgent necessity for heavy guns and long-range field pieces at Vicksburg.

Johnston also argued that General Holmes should send reinforcements from Arkansas. "Banks is reported to be ascending the Mississippi from New Orleans in strength," Johnston said. "I think it will require an active army of forty thousand men to hold the state of Mississippi and the river against both Grant and Banks. No more troops can be taken from Bragg without enabling Rosecrans to move into Virginia or to reinforce Grant. Our great object is to hold the Mississippi. The country west of the river is as much interested in that object as that east of it. I respectfully suggest that the eight thousand to ten thousand men essential to the safety of Vicksburg and the state of Mississippi ought to come from Arkansas. With Holmes's and Pemberton's troops, I might be able to crush Grant. Then I could send Holmes into Missouri and with Pemberton, Bragg, and Kirby Smith, march to the Ohio River."

Persuaded by that argument, I wrote Holmes that it was essential for him to send Pemberton ten thousand men from the Trans-Mississippi Department. "To prevent the enemy from getting control of the Mississippi and dismembering the Confederacy," I explained, "we must mainly rely upon maintaining the points already occupied by defensive works; to wit, Vicksburg and Port Hudson. From the best information at hand, a large force is now ready to descend the Mississippi and cooperate with the army advancing from Memphis to make an attack upon Vicksburg. Large forces are also reported to have been sent to the lower Mississippi for the purpose of ascending the river to attempt the reduction of Port Hudson. If the enemy should succeed in possessing these two points, he will be then free to concentrate his forces against your department, and though your valor may be relied upon to do all that human power can effect, it is not to be expected that you could make either long or successful resistance. We cannot hope at all points to meet the enemy with a force equal to his own, and must find our security in the concentration and rapid movement of troops."

I did not order Holmes to send reinforcements to Mississippi, but left it up to his discretion. He declined to send the ten thousand men, on the grounds that Arkansas would be lost if he did. I did not entirely agree with him but deferred to his judgment, as he was a capable general and a loyal friend and more competent than Johnston or I of determining the needs of his department.

Johnston complained that I had not made my orders to Holmes peremptory. I had *made* Bragg send troops to Mississippi, he said, why didn't I do the same with Holmes? Johnston was blind to the obvious. Holmes did not belong to Johnston's new department, whereas Bragg and Pemberton did. I would order troops to move *within* a department, but not *between* departments, because that would violate our independent departmental organization.

While we were at Vicksburg, Pemberton reported that he had sent his cavalry under Van Dorn on a raid against Grant's advance supply base at Holly Springs. This was electrifying news. If the raid was successful, it could change the entire picture for our threatened forces on the Yalobusha.

50. GRANT

Van Dorn's cavalry surprised our garrison at Holly Springs—took 'em prisoner, burnt up a huge stockpile of stores, torched a train, blew up the armory, destroyed commissary warehouses and a large portion of the town's business district, and then skeedaddled. I'd warned the garrison commander, Colonel Murphy, to be on the alert for a possible cavalry attack, but he obviously hadn't heeded the warning. It was reprehensible. Made me furious. I sent my cavalry to drive Van Dorn from the country, but he managed to elude the patrols riding after him.

My army was now in danger—had no supplies and was cut off from our main base at Memphis by Forrest's destruction of part of the railroad. These accursed cavalry raids demonstrated the impossibility of maintaining a long supply line in hostile territory. Had no choice but to suspend the advance against Pemberton and order a retreat back to Holly Springs. Feared this would spell trouble for Sherman's river expedition, as the rebels were sure to reinforce Vicksburg by their interior lines.

As we were pulling out, the residents of Oxford smirked about the Holly Springs raid. Reckon they thought we would be starved into submission.

"What ya gonna do now without anything for your men to eat," they said.

Told 'em: "I ain't worried. I've sent out wagon teams to gather up all the food and forage they can find in a fifteen-mile radius from the railroad."

"What're *we* supposed to do for food?" they asked.

Told 'em we'd tried to feed ourselves from our own northern resources while visiting them; but their friends in gray had been uncivil enough to destroy what we had brought along, and they couldn't expect my soldiers to starve to death in the midst of plenty. I advised 'em to emigrate east or west fifteen miles and assist in eating up what we left. Tell you one thing: that stopped their smirking.

From the Yoknapatawpha to Holly Springs, our wagon details stripped the countryside of all the grain and beef cattle and fat hogs and plump chickens they could find. Surprised me how well stocked the farms and plantations were. It was a revelation—saw it was possible to subsist an army of thirty thousand men for two months on supplies drawn from the country.

I wrote Halleck that the raid on Holly Springs had forced me to change my plans. Meant to abandon the advance down the Mississippi Central, return to Memphis, and join Sherman's river expedition, probably after the New Year.

51. DAVIS

Two days before Christmas, Johnston and I reached Pemberton's army on the Yalobusha. Thanks to Van Dorn's daring raid, the enemy had retired from Pemberton's front and nothing was to be seen but their backs. We thought it probable that they had abandoned this line and intended to reinforce the heavy column now descending the river from Memphis. Vicksburg and Port Hudson were the real points of attack. Pemberton, however, could not abandon the Yalobusha line until we were certain of the enemy's intentions.

Because he was northern born, Pemberton had drawn a lot of criticism from overwrought patriots, but I believed he was completely loyal to our cause and agreed with Samuel Cooper, our adjutant and inspector general, that he showed "zeal and untiring efforts" in his defense of Mississippi. He was tall and slender, with a deeply lined face, black curly hair, and dark eyes. I was disturbed that Johnston thought so little of him and that they did not see eye to eye on how best to defend Mississippi. While Pemberton was confident that the state could be held with the troops from Bragg, Johnston was bitterly pessimistic and renewed his objection to the reinforcement of Pemberton at Bragg's expense; both armies, he complained, were too weak and too far apart to succeed against the superior foes they faced. That may be true, I told him, but regardless of the odds it was his responsibility to direct them with what they had.

While we conferred and reviewed troops, reports kept coming in about the menacing Federal force steaming down the Mississippi. Pemberton had already dispatched one brigade to Vicksburg; and on Christmas Eve he sent another. That same day, I left for Jackson and had Christmas dinner with my lovely niece, Ellen Anderson. The next day I called on Governor Pettus in his office in the statehouse. He was a tall, rough-hewn man who chewed tobacco and spit carelessly at the spittoon in his sparsely furnished office, whose carpet was tattered and whose windows were cracked and broken. Though he lacked grace and breeding, he was no obstructionist like Governor Brown, and for that I thanked him.

That same day I addressed an overflowing crowd in the house chamber of the legislature, with sunlight shining brilliantly through the high windows. Flanked by Pettus and Senator Phelan, I sought to rally my fellow Mississippians by warning them of the Yankees' evil designs. "You have been involved in a war waged for the gratification of the lust of power and of aggrandizement, for your conquest and your subjugation, with a malignant ferocity and with a disregard and contempt of the usages of civilization, entirely unequaled in history. Such, I have ever warned you, were the characteristics of the northern people. After what has happened during the last two years, my only wonder is that we consented to live for so long a time in association with such miscreants, and have loved so much a government rotten to the core. Were it ever to be proposed again to enter into a Union with such a people, I could no more consent to do it than to trust myself in a den of thieves.

"You in Mississippi have little experienced as yet the horrors of war. You have seen little of the savage manner in which it is waged by your barbarous enemies. It has been my fortune to witness it in all its terrors; in a part of the country where old men have been torn from their homes, carried into captivity and immured in distant dungeons, and where delicate women have been insulted by a brutal soldiery and forced even to cook for the dirty Yankee invaders; where property has been wantonly destroyed, the country ravaged, and every outrage committed.

"The issue before you is of no ordinary character. The question for you to decide is, 'will you be slaves or will you be independent?' Those men who now assail us, who have been associated with us in a common Union, who have inherited a government which they claim to be the best the world ever saw—these men, when left to themselves, have shown that they are incapable of preserving their own personal liberty. They have demonstrated their utter incapacity for self-government. And yet these are the people who claim to be your masters. These are the people who have determined to divide the South among their Yankee troops. Mississippi they have devoted to the direst vengeance of all. 'But vengeance is the Lord's,' and beneath His banner you will meet and hurl back these worse than vandal hordes.

"Immense navies have been constructed, vast armies have been accumulated, for the purpose of crushing out the rebellion. It has been impossible for us to meet them in equal numbers; nor have we required it. We have often whipped them when outnumbered three to one, and in the battle of Antietam, Lee whipped them four to one. We want public opinion to frown down those who come from the army with sad tales of disaster and prophecies of evil, and who skulk from the duties they owe their country. We rely on the *women of the land* to turn back these deserters from the ranks.

"We have expected recognition and sometimes intervention at the hands of foreign nations, and we have had a right to expect it. Never before in the history of the world has a people for so long a time maintained their ground, and showed themselves capable of maintaining their national existence, without securing the recognition of commercial nations. I know not why this has been so, but this I say, 'put not your trust in princes' and rest not your hopes in foreign nations. This war is ours; we must fight it out ourselves, and I feel some pride in knowing that so far we have done it without the goodwill of anybody."

Then, with Johnston, I rode the train back to Vicksburg, found Pemberton there, and learned that Federal gunboats and as many as forty-five transports full of enemy infantry were on the Yazoo. I was relieved to learn that Pemberton had already sent for a division of reinforcements from his army on the Yalobusha. Johnston and I conferred with several prominent military men at the Blake plantation on the Yazoo, from which we could see the Yankee gunboats. The question was whether our garrison of thirteen thousand men and twenty-nine guns could withstand the Yankee vandals at the gates.

5 2 . SHERMAN

I'll wager we scared the bloody shit out of every secesh who saw us descending the river. We had seventy transports filled with thirty-two thousand troops and escorted by seven or eight of Porter's gunboats. Before we left Memphis, I'd issued an order prohibiting all reporters from accompanying the expedition and warning that any who tried would be treated as spies. Goddamnit, they *were* spies because their publications reached the enemy and gave them direct and minute information of the composition of our forces. I didn't want my expedition jeopardized by the tribe of scribblers.

We bore down on Vicksburg and seized Milliken's Bend on the Louisiana side of the river. I left a division there and ascended the Yazoo to Walnut Hills, where enemy defenses protected Vicksburg on the northeast side. The Goddamned weather was awful—cold as hell, heavy rains—but we landed and moved across a bayou only to find ourselves on the bank of another. The damned country was a jungle of bayous and swamps—pure hell to campaign in. We forced our way through to Chickasaw Bayou, which ran from the Yazoo to near the foot of Walnut Hills. Now we faced a formidable abatis (sharpened tree limbs) and a plateau in front of the steep bluffs. I had every reason to believe that Grant would soon join us—heard from a nigger that there were Yankees in Yazoo City—thought that must be Grant.

The rebels were fortified on top of the bluffs—we could see cannon and rifle pits up there. My instructions did not contemplate my taking Vicksburg alone. The idea was that Grant and I would strike it with concerted blows. But we could hear the whistles of trains arriving in Vicksburg and assumed that the city was being heavily reinforced. I figured I had to act now—couldn't wait for Grant. On December twenty-ninth, I ordered a prompt and concentrated movement to break the center of the rebel line. Morgan's division was to lead the point of attack, the head of Chickasaw Bayou, with Steele's division in support. Once they gained a lodgment on the bluffs, it would open the door for my whole force to follow.

I pointed out to Morgan the place where he could pass the bayou, and he said, "General, in ten minutes after you give the signal I'll be on those hills."

The attack began with diversionary feints on both of my flanks. Then the real assault commenced. Morgan's lead brigade got safely across the bayou but took cover behind the bank and could not be moved forward. One of Steele's brigades under Frank Blair, the politician, also crossed the bayou and charged over the plateau, where they ran into a direct and enfilading crossfire from enemy artillery and musketry. Blair made it to the bluffs and launched an assault, but that Goddamned Morgan failed to send his other brigade to support Blair's troops and they had to fall back, leaving five hundred men behind, wounded and prisoners. The dead and wounded lay in the bushes and under the trees; some of the wounded tried to crawl back to our lines.

The attack failed. It failed because Morgan did not obey orders or fulfill his promise to me. Had he shown skill and boldness in support of Blair, they could have made a lodgment on the bluff, and the rest of the army would have driven through, breaking the rebel line.

I was certain that the enemy would reinforce the point we had attacked that day. Therefore I decided against further assaults at Walnut Hills and resolved to strike the bluffs farther up the Yazoo. But fog and heavy rains made operations impossible, so we reembarked and started back down the Yazoo.

As I passed near Porter's flagship, he shouted from the deck: "McClernand is at the mouth of the Yazoo waiting to take command of your army!" Goddamnit, I was mad as hell. McClernand was an unscrupulous old politician consumed by an inordinate personal ambition. On top of that he was wholly unfit to command an army. But there wasn't a Goddamned thing I could do about it because he ranked me. Can you imagine that? A *politician* ranking a professional soldier! Most idiotic Goddamned thing I ever heard of.

I ran down to the mouth of the Yazoo in a small tugboat and found McClernand on the steamer *Tigress*. You know what he had with him? His Goddamned *bride* and *bridal party*, for Christ's sake.

He was in a fit that I'd gone downriver with his troops and he thrust in my face his orders from the War Department to command the expeditionary force. He was a skinny bastard with a mangy black beard. I couldn't stand being around him: he was fussy as an old woman, fidgeted all the time, nervous as hell, a Goddamned *whiner*. But he had Washington behind him and I assured him, as graciously as I could, that he had my support.

I told him that the reinforcements pouring into Vicksburg must be Pemberton's army and that Grant must be near at hand.

"Grant's not coming," McClernand said. "Van Dorn destroyed his depot at Holly Springs and he fell back to Holly Springs and La Grange, Tennessee."

This explained how Vicksburg was being reinforced. I saw that any attempt on the city from the Yazoo was hopeless and with McClernand's approval we all came out of the Yazoo and rendezvoused at Milliken's Bend.

53 · DAVIS

With the situation improving in Mississippi, I left for Mobile by train near the end of the year. At Mobile I found a telegram from Bragg at Murfreesboro saying that "God has granted us happy New Year." Rosecrans had left his entrenchments at Nashville to attack Bragg's army; but when Rosecrans drew near, Bragg had struck first and the enemy had yielded his strong position and was falling back. "We occupy the whole field," Bragg said, "and shall follow him." This was excellent news! It confirmed my faith in Bragg and gave the lie to his shrill critics who accused him of incompetence and worse. I hoped that Bragg would mount a vigorous pursuit and recapture Nashville.

But on my way back to Richmond, I learned that Bragg, hearing that Rosecrans was being reinforced, had retreated to save his trains and supplies and had gone into winter quarters at Tullahoma, thus shielding Chattanooga to the southeast. The retreat was a disappointing turn of events, but Bragg had followed to the letter my orders to fight if he could, but fall back if he must. Besides, when I considered the superior numbers Bragg had faced and the fact that he had secured Chattanooga, I thought the battle of Murfreesboro was a victory for us.

When I reached Richmond, I felt better about our situation than I had when I had left for the West, for Vicksburg and Richmond, in addition to Chattanooga, remained securely in our hands. Though exhausted from my trip—I had traveled 2,750 miles and given many speeches—I nevertheless spoke to a crowd of serenaders at the Executive Mansion, where a band played "Mocking Bird" and other lovely airs. I praised our glorious Lee for his victory over Burnside and pointed out that our sacrifices, our anxieties, and our glory had made our people a band of brothers. "One year ago many were depressed and some despondent," I said. "Now deep resolve is seen in every eye, an unconquerable spirit nerves every arm. And gentle woman, too, who can estimate the value of her services in this struggle? With such noble women at home, and such heroic soldiers in the field, *we are invincible.*"

THE WINDS OF 'SIXTY-THREE

Mine eyes have seen the glory of the coming of the Lord:
He is trampling out the vintage where the grapes of wrath
    are stored;
He hath loosed the fateful lightning of his terrible swift
    sword:
His truth is marching on.

Shall fiends who basely plot our ruin,
Unchecked, advance with guilty stride
To spread destruction far and wide,
With Southron's blood their hands embruing?
To arms, to arms, ye brave!

1 . ABRAHAM LINCOLN

In the final days of 'sixty-two, I was preoccupied with my proclamation of freedom and the future of the black and white races in this country. Browning and Sumner took turns coming over here to pressure me—Browning begged me not to issue the proclamation, while Sumner demanded that I do my duty and put it forth. I told 'em both I would stand by my pledge.

"Then there is no hope," Browning said. "The proclamation will come. God grant it may not be productive of the mischief I fear."

The great question now was what to do with the liberated slaves. I'd made a lot of fuss about colonization, but I'll tell you the truth, I had my doubts about whether that was a workable solution to the adjustment of the races after emancipation. If, by divine miracle, we won this great war and four million southern blacks were freed, the cost of transporting that many people to other lands would be incalculable, not even counting what it would cost to provide 'em with shelter, food, and clothes to get 'em started in another land. In any event, Douglass and many other black leaders were hostile to colonization and warned us that the vast majority of Negroes would not apply for any colonization scheme of mine, on the grounds that their families had lived here for generations and that it was their home, where all their kin lived.

I appreciated that argument. The problem wasn't the logic or the justice of it. The problem was that most white people didn't want all those black people living among them in freedom. I'd tried to explain that to a group of Washington's colored leaders when I called them to the Executive Mansion last August.

"You and we are different races," I said. "We have between us a broader difference than exists between almost any other two races. Whether it is right or wrong I need not discuss, but this physical difference is a great disadvantage to us both, as I think your race suffer very greatly, many of them by living among us, while ours suffer from your presence. In a word we suffer on each side. Your race are suffering, in my judgment, the greatest wrong inflicted on any people. But see our present condition—the country engaged in war!— our white men cutting one another's throats, none knowing how far it will extend; and then consider what we know to be the truth. But for your race among us there could not be war." I repeated that. "Without the institution of slavery and the colored race as a basis, the war could not have an existence."

While that delegation of Negroes endorsed colonization and promised to recommend it to their people, I wasn't too hopeful, given the hostility of Douglass and other black leaders to the very idea of repatriation. So what to do? We couldn't eject the Negroes by force; once you start throwing people out of the country on the basis of color, then others would demand that you do it on the basis of religion and national origins. Coercion was out—didn't want that dangerous precedent set. Yet the blacks weren't going to leave voluntarily, not according to Douglass; and our white people weren't willing for free colored people to remain among them. It was as knotty a problem as I'd ever encountered, and I had no answer to it. Still don't.

Still, to keep my alternatives open and to pacify our whites, I signed a contract with white promoters to resettle five thousand black volunteers, if we could get that many, on Haiti's Isle of Vache. That way, when I issued my proclamation, I could show northern whites that a colonization program was under way. But I tell you, I'd pretty much decided that the fate of the liberated slaves would have to be worked out in the South. My general idea was that they could constitute a free work force and hire themselves out to their former masters for decent wages. Certainly this would keep 'em from migrating into the North, which was the chief reason our northern whites opposed emancipation. How to implement my idea—how to integrate whites and free Negroes without racial friction—that was the question, to which I had no answer.

But I did have an answer about able-bodied Negro men—northern free blacks and liberated slaves. I meant to enlist 'em in the army, as soldiers, and would say so in my proclamation. Sumner, Stanton, Chase, Douglass—all were right that I could no longer defer to the concerns of the border states. The plain fact of the matter was, we needed more troops to win the war. The colored population was the great *available* and yet *unavailed of* force for restoring the Union. And I aimed to avail myself of that force—to utilize the Negroes as soldiers, not combat soldiers, but as garrison troops, which would free up thousands of whites from garrison duty so they could fight. Even so, it was a radical move, a revolutionary move, to put a black man in a blue uniform and give him a gun. The repercussions of that could not be calculated.

Pondering all this, I couldn't help but think of a line in Julia Ward Howe's "Battle Hymn of the Republic": "He hath loosed the fateful lightning of his terrible swift sword." That was exactly what I would do this day, and it would turn the war into a remorseless revolutionary struggle that would change us and the country forever. I could only hope His truth *was* marching on.

On the last night of the year, I called at the War Department to check on military matters. I should have stayed in my office. Grant was retreating out of Mississippi and Sherman was repulsed before Vicksburg. If those two generals couldn't win victories, who could? Over in Tennessee, Rosecrans had been attacked at Murfreesboro and was apparently going down to defeat.

God help us.

I left the War Department and strode along the shadowy walkway back to the well-lit Executive Mansion. I got little sleep that night—couldn't get my mind off the lightning bolt I would hurl tomorrow, couldn't stop thinking about corpses on distant battlefields in Tennessee and Mississippi and silent troops lying in the rain and crowds of weeping people reading the death lists on the bulletin board at Willard's Hotel. Couldn't help thinking it was the supreme irony of my life that I who sickened at the sight of blood, who abhorred public unrest and physical violence, should be cast in the middle of a great civil war.

I lay in my chamber till the first gray light of morning spread through the windows. Tired and trembling, I made my way to my shop in my slippers and gown and there built a fire and lit the gas lamps. It was the dawn of the new year, and the war continued with no foreseeable end. To think that it had all begun as a ninety-day rumpus to restore the old Union with slavery. Now it had swelled into a vast vortex of destruction that covered two-thirds of the continent, with all of us whirling out of control in its winds and debris. Only God knew what it all meant and where it would all end.

At my desk I put the final touches to the emancipation proclamation and then read it over to make sure the words were right.

I, Abraham Lincoln, President of the United States, by virtue of the power vested in me as Commander-in-Chief, of the Army and Navy of the United States in time of actual armed rebellion against authority and government of the United States, and as a fit and necessary war measure for suppression of said rebellion, do, on this first day of January, in the year of our Lord one thousand eight hundred and sixty-three, do . . . order and designate as the states and parts of states wherein the people thereof respectively, are this day in rebellion against the United States, the following, to wit.

The proclamation then listed the areas I considered still in rebellion: Arkansas, Texas, Louisiana, Mississippi, Alabama, Florida, Georgia, South Carolina, North Carolina, and Virginia; and it exempted the occupied counties of Louisiana and West Virginia, and the forty-eight counties designated as West Virginia, which had broken away from the Confederacy and would soon be admitted to the Union as a new state. The proclamation did not mention the loyal border states or Tennessee, the western half of which we occupied and had under a military government headed by Andrew Johnson. East Tennessee was a pro-Unionist area with few slaveholders. The document went on:

> *And by virtue of the power, and for the purpose aforesaid, I do order and declare, that all persons held as slaves within said designated States, and parts of States, are, and henceforth shall be free; and that the Executive government of the United States, including the military and naval authorities thereof, will recognize and maintain the freedom of said persons.*
>
> *And I hereby enjoin upon the people so declared to be free to abstain from all violence, unless in necessary self-defense; and I recommend to them that, in all cases when allowed, they labor faithfully for reasonable wages.*
>
> *And I further declare and make known, that such persons of suitable condition, will be received into the armed service of the United States to garrison forts, positions, stations, and other places, and to man vessels of all sorts in said service.*
>
> *And upon this act, sincerely believed to be an act of justice, warranted by the Constitution, upon military necessity, I invoke the considerate judgment of mankind, and the gracious favor of Almighty God.*

You may wonder why I exempted the occupied areas and why the loyal border states were not mentioned. The proclamation had no constitutional or legal justification except as a military necessity. I exempted the loyal border states because they were not in rebellion and I couldn't use the justification of military necessity there. I exempted the occupied areas of Louisiana and Virginia for the same reason: military necessity didn't apply to localities where the rebellion had been put down. If I abolished slavery there, wouldn't I give up all footing upon Constitution or law? Wouldn't I be accused of absolutism? Would this go unnoticed and unresisted? Wouldn't it be seen that without any further stretch I might free the slaves in the loyal states of Delaware, Maryland, Kentucky, and Missouri, and even change the law in any state, even a free one? That is absolutism.

What's more, I was trying to organize loyal state governments in the occupied areas—reconstruct them under the direction of military governors and the army. We were already doing that in Tennessee, Louisiana, and Arkansas—and couldn't afford to alienate the fragile minority of white Unionists in those areas who would form the nucleus of any reconstituted state. But I would later make emancipation a mandatory part of the reconstruction process—in other words, the people who organized reconstructed governments would have to abolish slavery themselves—and I would push for a constitutional amendment permanently abolishing slavery everywhere in the country. That was the king's cure—a constitutional amendment. With an amendment in place, the freedom of all black folk would be guaranteed.

I would sign an official copy of the proclamation later in the day. Meanwhile I dressed in a black suit and blackened boots, ran a comb through my unruly hair, gave up on it, and went to fetch Mary for the usual New Year's reception. It was her first reception since Willie had died, and she was still in a bad way from our "furnace of affliction."

"Whew!" I said. "You do look pretty."

She was bejeweled with diamonds and was wearing a silver silk dress, with garlands in her hair and a black shawl around her head. Mary was happy about my proclamation—"an act of humanity," she called it. Thanks to the influence of Lizzie Keckley, her black seamstress, Mary was deeply involved in Keckley's Contraband Relief Association—even got me to donate $200 because, she said, "the cause of humanity requires it." In fact, Keckley and Sumner had made my little wife quite an abolitionist—she declared herself radically opposed to slavery and deeply concerned about "all the oppressed colored people." Pretty amazing for the daughter of a Kentucky slaveowner.

At eleven in the morning, we went down to the Blue Room to receive a long procession of well-wishers—the diplomatic corps, army and naval officers in order of rank, politicians, and the public. My mind kept drifting off to the war and the waiting thunderbolt— don't remember much about the reception except for the endless handshaking. But I did recognize young Noah Brooks when he came through the line. A Maine native who wore pince-nez glasses clamped to his nose, he was now Washington correspondent for a California newspaper and a frequent caller at the Executive Mansion. Mary and I liked him a lot—he reminded us of Ellsworth, our young friend who was gunned down in 'sixty-one.

As the procession wore on, Mary was growing unsettled and nervous. Heard her whisper to the commissioner of public buildings, "Oh, Mr. French, how much we have passed through since last we stood here." The strain was too much for her, and she left before the reception was over.

In the afternoon, Seward brought an official copy of the emancipation proclamation to my office and Cabinet room for my signature. We didn't make a big fuss about the signing—no official congregation, nothing like it. The Cabinet secretaries and government officials who happened to be in the Executive Mansion—under a dozen—casually gathered in the room. Seward spread the large sheet out on the Cabinet table; I dipped my pen in the ink jar and started to sign the proclamation, but my hand shook so badly that I laid the pen down.

"I've been shaking hands all day," I said, "and my right hand is almost paralyzed. I know I'm doing the right thing—my whole soul is in it. If my name ever gets into history, it will be for this act. I mean that. But if my hand trembles when I sign it, some will say 'he hesitated.'" I rested my arm for a minute, then seized the pen and slowly and firmly wrote out my full name. Then I smiled and handed the proclamation to Seward. "That'll do," I said.

Out the proclamation went to a divided nation. The reactions would come back soon enough. To tell you the truth, I wasn't too interested in what the papers would say or the people would write about it. I'd studied the emancipation problem so long I knew more about it than they did. Anyway, I knew it was going to do as much harm as good. We would lose a lot of Democrats over this and I feared the fires they would light in our rear.

Later that day, a great procession of blacks and whites gathered in front of the mansion and called for me. I went to a window and bowed. The colored people clapped and cried out in ecstasy, and one of 'em said: "Mr. President, if you'll come out of that palace, we'll hug you to death!" One excited man—think he was a preacher named Henry Turner—exclaimed over and over, "It's a time of times . . . *a time of times* . . . nothing like it will ever be seen again in this life."

2. DAVIS

Lincoln's so-called emancipation proclamation was the most execrable measure recorded in the history of guilty man. So I told Congress in my January message. The measure, I said, showed our whole people the complete and crowning proof of the true nature of the designs of the Black Republican Party, which elevated to power the present occupant of the presidential chair at Washington and which sought to conceal its purpose by every variety of artful device and by the perfidious use of the most solemn and repeated pledges on every possible occasion. I quoted from Lincoln's first Inaugural Address in which he had promised not to tamper directly or indirectly with slavery in the states where it existed. He had repeated that vow in official communications with England and France.

"The people of this Confederacy, then, cannot fail to perceive this proclamation as the fullest vindication of their own sagacity in foreseeing the uses to which the dominant party in the United States intended from the beginning to apply their power. They foresaw the approaching despotism and escaped it. This proclamation, moreover, would have a salutary effect in calming the fears of those who have constantly evinced the apprehension that this war might end by some reconstruction of the old Union. The proclamation affords the fullest guarantee of the impossibility of such a result."

It was by the slow and barely visible approaches of the serpent seeking its prey that the aggressions and usurpations of the United States government had moved on to this latest crime. Let us be clear as to what Lincoln intended by his infamous decree: he intended to invite our slaves to rapine and murder, to rise up and stab us in the backs, to violate our women and slit the throats of our children. I can assure you that it made every Confederate soldier and every Confederate woman struggle all the harder for victory, independence, and safety from the atrocities the usurper intended.

The southern press and people were virtually unanimous in their agreement with me. The *Examiner* called the proclamation "the most startling political crime in American history," warned that it was meant to inaugurate a "reign of hell on earth," and declared that we would have "war for life" against the North. In Congress, a legislator proposed that we "hoist the black flag against such people and show them no quarter."

I had already done something like that. In anticipation of Lincoln's decree and in retaliation against General Benjamin Butler and his reign of tyranny in New Orleans, during which he had tried to excite the African slaves to insurrection by every license and encouragement, had actually armed numbers of them for a war of merciless savagery, and had committed murder and numberless other atrocities against the white citizenry, and had all the while been fully supported by Lincoln's government, I had this past December issued my own proclamation:

I, Jefferson Davis, President of the Confederate States of America, and in their name, do pronounce and declare the said Benjamin F. Butler to be a felon, deserving of capital punishment. I do order that he be no longer considered or treated simply as a public enemy of the Confederate States of America, but as an outlaw and common enemy of mankind; and that in event of his capture, the officer in command of the capturing force do cause him to be immediately executed by hanging.

And whereas the President of the United States has, by public and official declaration, signified not only his approval of the effort to excite the servile war within the Confederacy, but his intention to give aid and encouragement thereto if these independent States shall continue to refuse submission to a foreign power after the first of January next, and has thus made known that all appeals to the laws of nations, the dictates of reason, and the instincts of humanity would be addressed in vain to our enemies, and that they can be deterred from the commission of these crimes only by the terms of just retribution;

Now, therefore, I, Jefferson Davis, President of the Confederate States of America, do order:

First. That all commissioned officers in the command of said Benjamin F. Butler be declared not entitled to be considered as soldiers engaged in honorable warfare, but robbers and criminals, deserving death; and that they and each of them be, whenever captured, reserved for execution.

Second. That the private soldiers and non-commissioned officers in the army of said Butler be considered as only the instruments used for the commission of the crimes perpetrated by his orders; that they therefore be treated, when captured, as the prisoners of war.

>   *Third. That all negro slaves captured in arms be at once delivered over to the executive authorities of the respective States to which they belong, to be dealt with according to the laws of the said States.*
>
>   *Fourth. That like orders be executed in all cases with respect to all commissioned officers of the United States, when found serving in company with armed slaves in insurrection against the authorities of the different States of this Confederacy.*

Since, by state law, it was a capital crime for African slaves to carry arms and for white people to incite them to armed insurrection, captured black soldiers and captured white officers in company with them would all be executed.

Nor did my retaliation against the degraded North stop there. On the fifth of January, 1863, I published in Richmond "An Address to the People of the Free States," which announced that on or after February twenty-second of that year, the Confederacy would enslave all its free blacks, numbering some 182,000, a third of them in Virginia; and that *all Negroes captured in the free states* would be reenslaved, "so that the respective normal condition of the white and black races may be ultimately placed on a permanent basis."

3. DOUGLASS

The emancipation proclamation made itself immediately felt. We can measure its significance by the hysterical reaction it produced in the traitor states and the threats of retaliation which fell from the poisonous pen of Jefferson Davis. Let them wage a war of the black flag. It would make us fight even harder to whip them and destroy their wretched experiment in nationhood based on the scarred and bleeding backs of my brothers and sisters in bondage.

On the platform in New York City, I told my people that in the hurry and excitement of the moment, it was difficult to grasp the full and complete significance of President Lincoln's proclamation. "The change in the attitude of the government is vast and startling," I said. "For more than sixty years the Federal government has been little better than a stupendous engine of slavery and oppression, through which slavery has ruled us, as with a rod of iron.

"I hail the proclamation as the doom of slavery in all the states. I hail it as the end of all that miserable statesmanship. At last the outspread wings of the American Eagle afford shelter and protection to men of all colors, all countries, and all climes, and the long-oppressed black man may honorably fall or gloriously flourish under the star-spangled banner.

"We are all liberated by this proclamation. Everybody is liberated. The white man is liberated, the brave men now fighting the battles of their country against rebels and traitors are now liberated. Henceforth January first, 1863, will take rank with the Fourth of July. Henceforth it becomes the date of a new and glorious era in the history of American liberty. I believe in the millennium—the final perfection of the human race—and hail this proclamation, though wrung out under the goading lash of a stern military necessity, as one reason of the hope that is in it. It is a *grand moral necessity*."

I said then—I said everywhere—that the proclamation now must be made iron, lead, and fire by the prompt employment of the Negro's arm in this contest. But we ran up against a wall of resistance. In January, I asked Governor Andrew G. Curtin of Pennsylvania to permit the formation of black regiments, but he refused. We asked the governor of New York if he would accept colored troops, and he said it was impossible. They did not know—few whites did—that there were already colored men in the army passing for white not much whiter than I, but by shaving their heads very closely had managed to get in. One from my own town had been promoted recently. I *knew* the colored men of the North, I said, I *knew* the colored men of the South. If northern governors would stop telling them they couldn't fight and tell them they *could* fight, they would fight and with vengeance. All we asked was to *give us a chance!*

It was Governor John A. Andrew of Massachusetts who first gave us the chance. He asked for, and received, authorization from the War Department to raise an elite black regiment as an "experiment." The success or failure of the regiment, as the first raised in the North in response to Lincoln's proclamation, would go far, Andrew said, "to elevate or depress the estimation in which the character of the colored Americans will be held throughout the world." Young Robert Gould Shaw, the blue-eyed son of an old Back Bay family and a soldier in the Second Massachusetts, would command the black regiment, which Andrew called "the most important to be organized during the whole war."

There were not enough colored men in Massachusetts to fill up the regiment, so Andrew enlisted George Luther Stearns, the Boston merchant and one of John Brown's secret backers, to head a team of recruiters who would raise volunteers across the North. In late February, Stearns stopped in Rochester and asked me to be one of the recruiters, and I agreed with alacrity. Had I been asked, I would have served as colonel of a colored regiment, but the army in its *wisdom* allowed only white officers to command Negro regiments. I had no desire, at forty-five, to fight as a common soldier myself, but I was eager to use my voice and pen to call young black men of the North to arms.

"Action! Action!" I told them in a broadside published in the leading papers. "We can get at the throat of treason and slavery through the state of Massachusetts. She was the first in the War of Independence; first to break the chains of her slaves; first to make the black man equal before the law; first to admit colored children to her common schools; and she was first to answer with her blood the alarm cry of the nation. The iron gate of our prison stands half open. One gallant rush from the North will fling it wide open, while four millions of our brothers and sisters shall march out into liberty. Remember Denmark Vesey of Charleston; remember Nathaniel Turner of Southampton; remember Shields Green and Copeland, who followed noble John Brown. The case is before you. This is our golden opportunity. Let us accept it and forever wipe out the dark reproaches unsparingly hurled against us by our enemies."

My first recruit, I'm proud to say, was my youngest son, Charles, aged nineteen, whose bright black eyes shone with pride and militancy. My son Lewis, aged twenty-two, brown skinned and brown eyed, also joined up and went on to become the regiment's first sergeant major. Their beaming father was certain they would set a gallant example for our race.

My goal was to raise one hundred men, and I set off across New York summoning black audiences "to arms! to arms!" But many Negroes resisted my appeals. "Why should we fight in a white man's army for a white man's war?" they demanded. "Because," I told them, "he who looks upon a conflict between right and wrong, and does not help the right against the wrong, despises and insults his own nature, and invites the contempt of mankind.

"You should enlist," I told them, "because every Negro-hater and slavery-lover in the land regards the arming of Negroes as a calamity and is doing his best to prevent it. You should enlist because the only way open to any race to make their rights respected is to learn how to defend them. You should enlist because you are a member of a long enslaved and despised race. Men have set down your submission to slavery and insult to a lack of manly courage. They point to this fact as demonstrating your fitness only to be a servile class. You should enlist and prove the slander wrong and wipe out the reproach.

"Enlist for your own sake. Decried and derided as you have been and still are, you need an act of this kind to recover your own self-respect. In defending your country against rebels and traitors you are defending your own liberty, honor, manhood, and self-respect.

"Enlist to prevent the country from drifting back into the whirlpool of proslavery compromise at the end of the war. Enlist to help liberate our own enslaved people. Can you ask for a more inviting, ennobling, and soul-enlarging work than that of making one of the glorious band who shall carry liberty to them? Enlist and you make this your country in common with all other men born in the country or out of it. To fight for the government in this tremendous war is to fight for our *citizenship*, for a place with all other classes of our fellow-citizens. Enlist, therefore, enlist without delay, enlist now, and forever put an end to the human barter and butchery which have stained the whole South with the warm blood of our people. Enlist and not only win for yourselves a name and a place among men, but secure what is infinitely more precious, the fast dropping tears of gratitude of your kith and kin marked out for destruction."

I signed up one hundred recruits and sent them to Reading, the muddy rail town near Boston where the regiment was being assembled. Soon they were a thousand strong, and Governor Andrew told Colonel Shaw, "I know not, Mr. Commander, when, in all human history, to any given thousand men in arms there has been committed a work at once so proud, so precious, so full of hope and glory as the work committed to you. I stand or fall with the rise or fall of the Fifty-Fourth Massachusetts." In fact, there were so many volunteers that another colored regiment, the Fifty-Fifth Massachusetts, was formed with the surplus.

The destination of the elite Fifty-Fourth was Port Royal, South Carolina, the base of the South Atlantic Blockading Squadron and the staging area for army-navy operations against Charleston and the rebel mainland. I was in Boston on the day of departure—was one of the "distinguished dignitaries" invited to witness the spectacle. I saw the regiment step off the train from Reading and set out for the statehouse in perfect formation, with the national flag and state and regimental colors snapping overhead. I followed it through the narrow, winding streets, past throngs of spectators who stood at the windows and on balconies and sidewalks and cheered and waved handkerchiefs and Union flags as the swaying lines swept by. As the regiment swung by Wendell Phillips's house on Essex Street, William Lloyd Garrison was standing on the balcony with a hand resting on a bust of John Brown. From the statehouse, I followed the regiment to the Common, where it passed in review before the governor and Senator Henry Wilson and a crowd of twenty thousand. Then it was off to Battery Wharf, with a band playing "John Brown's Body" and the soldiers singing as they marched:

> John Brown's body lies a-moldering in the grave,
> John Brown's body lies a-moldering in the grave,
> John Brown's body lies a-moldering in the grave,
>   As we go marching on.
> Glory, glory, hallelujah!
> Glory, glory, hallelujah!
> Glory, glory, hallelujah!
>   His soul is marching on.

My son Charles was sick and back in Readville; but Lewis was in the ranks this day, and I boarded the troop transport with him and rode till we were well down the harbor, and then got off and returned to shore on a tug.

The day the Fifty-Fourth marched through Boston, composed of well-drilled, well-uniformed, well-armed, well-appointed colored soldiers, under the ample folds of the Star-Spangled Banner, lifting their high and orderly footsteps to the inspiring notes of "John Brown's Body," singing those words with a spirit and meaning with which they were never sung before, was the proudest and happiest day for the colored race ever witnessed in the United States.

4 · LINCOLN

Just as I feared, the proclamation of freedom destroyed what was left of our bipartisan war coalition. Northern Democrats by the thousands declared themselves in open revolt against my new "revolutionary" policy and the "radical clique" surrounding me. Young Hay and Stoddard showed me samples of what the Democratic papers were saying, and it was pretty frightening. "A wicked, atrocious, and revolting deed," they said of the proclamation. "It means a war for the liberation of three million negro barbarians and their enfranchisement as citizens." "The North will be flooded with savages." "This monstrous, impudent and heinous Abolition proceeding is as insulting to God as to man, for it declares those 'equal' whom God created unequal." With leading Democrats up in arms, a storm of Negrophobia rolled over the land. In Detroit, a white mob invaded the Negro section, killing blacks and burning their homes down. Nobody hated riots worse than I did, and there would be more of 'em in the months ahead.

There was a backlash in the army, too. Correspondents reported that hardly one soldier in ten approved of emancipation, and that white soldiers cussed niggers with "an unreasoning hatred" and talked about how hordes of niggers would now invade the free states, and they vowed to throw down their weapons before they would fight to free them. Some officers from the Northwest did resign in protest. Other officers reported that the proclamation definitely hurt the morale of the army.

The hostile reaction shocked and scared Republicans. "These are dark hours," Sumner said. "There are senators full of despair—not I." "We've made a terrible mistake," said Hale of Connecticut. "We should've stayed clear of the Negro." Conservative Republicans like Browning, Doolittle, and Ewing thought we were near the apocalypse. "We all agree," Browning told me, "that we're upon the brink of ruin, and see no hope of an amendment in affairs unless you change your policy and withdraw or greatly modify your proclamation." My oldtime friend from home, David Davis, whom I'd appointed to the U.S. Supreme Court, agreed with Browning. Davis tromped in here, all three hundred pounds of him, and told me: "Lincoln, the situation is alarming. You've got to reorganize the Cabinet and change your policy at once. It's the only way to save the country."

"The proclamation of freedom is a fixed thing," I said.

"Then our cause is hopeless," he said.

I didn't think so. Given time, I had to believe, the army and most of the people would see as I saw, think as I thought. In any case, I may be a slow walker, but I never walk back. Oh, I worried about the fire in the rear, don't get me wrong. But I'd made up my mind to destroy the cornerstone of the rebellion and avail myself of my "strong black arm," to use Douglass's words, and all the protest and discontent—all the riots and the threats of disunion from disgruntled Democrats—all the dire warnings from Browning and Doolittle and Davis—were not going to change my mind. To use a coarse but expressive figure, broken eggs cannot be mended. I had issued the proclamation, and could not retract it.

Anyway, Charles Francis Adams, our minister in England, reported that the proclamation was having a salutary effect there. "It has rallied the sympathies of the working classes and has produced meetings the like of which, I am told, have not been seen since the days of the corn laws." Reckon the proclamation impressed the British government, too, just as Sumner claimed it would, because Great Britain has not recognized the Confederacy and remains neutral in our great war.

Meantime Stanton and I worked out the specifics of how the War Department would utilize colored soldiers. As a concession to the prejudices of our white people, we agreed that Negro troops would serve in segregated units under white officers and would get less pay than whites—the wages for white privates was thirteen dollars a month; black privates would get ten dollars a month—the same pay as black laborers. Even so, I had high hopes that tens of thousands of Negroes would fill up our ranks. I argued that the bare sight of fifty thousand armed and drilled black soldiers on the banks of the Mississippi would end the rebellion at once.

To organize and coordinate the enrolling of Negro soldiers, we installed a Bureau of Colored Troops in Washington and directed Union commanders in the occupied South—inside Union lines in Tennessee, Mississippi, Louisiana, Virginia, and the Sea Islands—to enlist Negro men who'd come to them from the Confederacy. Stanton and I also agreed that Adjutant General Lorenzo Thomas ought to go to the Mississippi Valley and supervise and facilitate the recruitment of former slaves there. He would also deal with another problem. Since the proclamation, slaves were escaping to our lines in greater numbers than ever, and Grant and Rosecrans and our other commanders were all complaining about the masses of refugees congesting their camps. What we worked out was this: Thomas was to install a refugee system in the Mississippi Valley and then in other occupied areas of the South. He would, as I said, enlist the able-bodied black men in the army; he would employ other liberated slaves as military laborers and put the rest of the adults to work on confiscated farms and plantations for wages set by the government. This would serve a twofold purpose: it would keep blacks in the South, and it would give them jobs, helping them to help themselves.

I thought this was a good program and a sound alternative to colonization. The plain fact was, by the spring of 'sixty-three the Haitian project was in trouble—the damned promoters proved to be inept or dishonest and northern Negroes were generally hostile to the whole idea. Only 450 had volunteered to leave, and there was little hope that any more would join them. When the colonists moved to Haiti in May, it became a terrible nightmare: white management was corrupt, facilities were terrible, the colonists were plagued by smallpox, starvation, and mutiny, and the Haitian government was hostile to the whole enterprise. In the end, I had to send a warship down to bring the survivors home. After that Congress canceled the appropriations it had made for colonization purposes, and that put an end to that.

I'd pretty much crossed off colonization before the blacks had even left for Haiti. Never brought it up in public again. I mean hell, if the free Negroes refused to cooperate, it would never work. So we turned to Thomas's refugee program, which would be put into place in the wake of our advancing armies. We hoped that the program would convince our white people that there would be no black exodus into the North. We told 'em—Republican campaigners and papers did—that the Negroes were being prepared to work and live as freemen in Dixie.

Even though colored men were joining up in the North and in occupied Dixie, we still suffered a shortage of combat troops, and it was going to get worse unless we did something drastic: the enlistment of 130 regiments would be up in the spring and summer of 'sixty-three. We had no choice but to start conscripting men into the service. It was a severe war measure, but almost every Republican in Congress favored it, and so did Stanton and I. Congress enacted the conscription bill, and I signed it into law in March. The idea was to stimulate men of military age to volunteer and receive a bounty. If they refused, they would be drafted without a bounty. A Provost Marshals Bureau in the War Department enforced the law by detailing provost marshals to every congressional district for the purpose of enrolling every male citizen between the ages of twenty and forty-five and then assigning each district a quota for an upcoming draft.

There was a way out, since conscripted men could hire a substitute or buy an exemption for three hundred dollars.

Even so, Stanton and I saw to it that the law was rigorously enforced, not only to get the needed soldiery, but also to win back the loyalty of white soldiers already in the field, by demonstrating that the government intended to send 'em reinforcements and sustain the armies no matter how unpopular the war was back home.

For disaffected Democrats, the second conscription act was the last straw. In their eyes, the emancipation proclamation was evil enough; now white men would be *coerced* into fighting a nigger war. That spring, they launched a so-called peace movement to throw "the shrieking abolitionist faction" out of office and negotiate a peace treaty with the Confederacy on the basis of the old Union with slavery preserved. The lower Northwest—Ohio, Indiana, and Illinois— was the hotbed of the antiwar movement. Whole battalions of peace Democrats stumped the region, holding shrill rallies and calling me an abolitionist dictator and damning me to eternity for my half-witted efforts to bring about nigger equality. They held secret meetings, too, and plotted and schemed ways to obstruct the draft and otherwise undermine the government. Republican agents, editors, politicians, and military commanders across the North sent us alarming reports about the Peace Democrats: they discouraged enlistment, raised guns and money for the rebel government, murdered provost marshals, and battled government agents who tracked 'em down.

I told Sumner I feared the fire of the Copperheads—our name for those sneaking traitors—even more than our military failures, and Stanton and I did everything within our power to suppress 'em. It was either that or lose the war from within. With my support, Stanton had the provost marshals and army officers imprison anybody who interfered with conscription, discouraged volunteering, or otherwise helped the enemy. Stanton organized a system of police chiefs, state militia, home guards, and volunteers to help the provost marshals and army officers ferret out traitors and put 'em in jail. We got right at thirteen thousand of 'em all told.

Of course, that made the outcry against us even worse. Arbitrary arrests—that's what the Copperheads called 'em. Don't care what they said. We went out of our way to prevent excesses; Stanton had people who were unwarrantably arrested speedily released; and I spent a good part of my day writing pardons for imprisoned civilians.

The most controversial case involved Clement L. Vallandigham, an Ohio congressman and a notorious Copperhead. Valiant Val, his supporters called him. In the House and on the platform, Valiant Val raged at me for converting a war for the Union into a crusade for niggers in which the white people were to be enslaved. "I see nothing before us," he cried, "but universal political and social revolution, anarchy and bloodshed, compared with which the Reign of Terror in the French Revolution was a merciful visitation." On the stump in Ohio that spring, he denounced abolition, the war, and the despotism of "King Lincoln" and demanded a truce with the Confederacy. During one of his performances, an army officer in civilian dress took notes while leaning against the platform. Three days later an infantry column broke into Vallandigham's Dayton home at midnight and hauled him off to jail in Cincinnati. This caused another riot, this time in Dayton. A military commission went on to convict Vallandigham of undermining government efforts "to suppress unlawful rebellion" and sentenced him to prison for as long as the war lasted.

What a howl of protest that brought from the Democrats! When a group of 'em censured me for violating the Constitution, I made a public reply in which I defended martial law and military arrests on the grounds of military necessity. In this clear, flagrant, and gigantic case of rebellion, when combinations in the North obstructed conscription and assassinated loyal officers and when the insurgents maintained a most efficient corps of spies, informers, and aiders of their cause in a thousand ways, it was perfectly legal for me to suspend the writ of habeas corpus, declare martial law, and arrest the offenders. They could not claim the cover of liberty of speech, liberty of the press, and habeas corpus to carry on their treasonable activities.

Now, I said, I had a reverence for the guaranteed rights of individuals and I was slow to adopt the strong measures I'd been forced to regard as being within the Constitution and as indispensable to the public safety. Military arrests of civilians had been made to prevent injury to the Union war effort, without which there would be no Union. The government could not always wait until defined crimes had been committed. At the beginning of the rebellion, if we'd arrested Robert E. Lee, Joseph E. Johnston, John B. Magruder, and Simon B. Buckner, who were nearly as well known to be traitors then as now, the insurgent cause would be much weaker now.

Those who censured me claimed that Vallandigham had been arrested only because he'd criticized the Administration at a public meeting. That, I told 'em, was not the case. He was arrested because he was laboring, with some effect, to prevent the raising of troops, to encourage desertions from the army, and to leave the rebellion without an adequate military force to suppress it. He was warring upon the military; and this gave the military authority constitutional jurisdiction to lay hands on him. Long experience, I went on, had shown that armies could not be maintained unless desertion was punished by the severe penalty of death. "Must I shoot a simple-minded soldier boy who deserts," I asked, "while I must not touch a hair of a wily agitator who induces him to desert? This is none the less injurious when effected by getting a father, or brother, or friend, into a public meeting, and there working upon his feelings, till he is persuaded to write the soldier boy, that he is fighting in a bad cause, for a wicked Administration of a contemptible government, too weak to arrest and punish him if he deserted. I think that in such a case, to silence the agitator, and save the boy, is not only constitutional, but a great mercy."

So I silenced the agitator, Vallandigham, and instead of leaving him in prison, I banished him to the Confederacy, where he belonged. I made it plain to the enemy in the rear that I meant to keep the military courts and suppress treason just as I meant to enforce the draft and the proclamation of freedom to the slaves.

Victory over the enemy in the front, of course, would only come with the triumph of our arms. But that would never happen as long as family feuds kept plaguing our armies.

5 · GRANT

When I arrived at Milliken's Bend to take command of the Vicksburg expedition, McClernand sent me a bitter protest. "As I am invested, by order of the secretary of war, endorsed by the president, and by order of the president communicated to you by the general in chief, with the command of all the forces operating on the Mississippi River, I claim that all orders affecting the condition of operations of those forces should pass through these headquarters. If different views are entertained by you, then the question should be immediately referred to Washington, and one or the other, or both of us relieved. One thing is certain. Two generals cannot command this army."

'Course it made me mad. Horse-faced McClernand was nothing but trouble—insubordinate, contentious, arrogant. But I couldn't afford to quarrel with a man I was obliged to command. So I simply had Rawlins issue General Orders No. 13 announcing that I assumed immediate command of the army and that all corps commanders would now resume command of their respective corps. McClernand demanded a clarification. Was it my aim, he asked, to relieve him from all or any portion of the forces making up "the Mississippi River expedition?" "The intention of Gen. Orders No. 13," I told him, "is that I will take direct command of all the Mississippi River expedition, which necessarily limits your command to the 13th army corps."

McClernand replied that he would "acquiesce" in my order in order to avoid a conflict of authority, in the presence of the enemy, but he requested that my order and his "protest" be sent to Washington. I obliged him, with a cover letter pointing out that I had no confidence in McClernand's ability as a soldier to conduct an expedition of the magnitude of this one successfully. But if the president or General Halleck disagreed, I said, I would cheerfully submit to their decision. They didn't disagree.

But they disagreed when I tried to solve another troublesome problem: the excessive number of fugitive slaves coming to our lines. Many of 'em were old and very young, and I was concerned about what would happen to 'em when we left, where they would get shelter and food and transportation. As a consequence, I issued an army order positively forbidding any more Negroes to leave their homes and come to our lines.

Halleck overruled me. "It is the policy of the government," he said by telegram, "to withdraw from the enemy as much productive labor as possible. Every slave withdrawn from the enemy is equivalent to a white man put *hors de combat*. They can be used with advantage as laborers, teamsters, cooks. And it is the opinion of many who have examined the question without passion or prejudice, that they can also be used as a military force. It is expected that you will use your official and personal influence to remove prejudices on this subject, and to fully and thoroughly carry out the policy now adopted by the government. That policy is, to withdraw from the use of the enemy all the slaves you can, and to employ those so withdrawn, to the best advantage against the enemy."

He added: "The character of the war has very much changed. There is now no possible hope of reconciliation with the rebels. We must conquer them or be conquered by them. The North must destroy the slave oligarchy, or be itself enslaved."

I wired Halleck that they could count on me. I agreed with him and the president that slavery was doomed and had to go. I rescinded my order excluding contrabands and urged all Negroes, particularly able-bodied males, to come to our lines. When Adjutant General Thomas came down in the spring to install the president's refugee system, I made certain the army cooperated. Thomas also read us the president's order to arm Negro men, and I told him I fully approved. I instructed my commanding officers to "exert themselves in carrying out the policy of the Administration, not only in organizing colored regiments and rendering them efficient, but also in removing prejudice against them."

Many of our officers and men didn't agree with the policy of arming the Negroes, said this was a white man's war and the coloreds should have been kept out of it. Sherman was the most outspoken against the president's new policy. "They're not ready for freedom," he said of the coloreds, "will only abuse it, and they sure ain't fit for soldiering. With my opinion of niggers and my experience, and yes my prejudice, I don't trust a nigger with a gun in a position of danger and trust. Grant, it's the height of folly to send a recruiting officer like Thomas into slave territory. Don't like that bastard anyway, coming down here in his glittering uniform and sword and telling us what to do. I'll never forgive the son-of-a-bitch for his role in the insanity charge against me in 'sixty-one.

"But the new conscript law is all even I could ask for. It's the first real step toward a war of conquest. If Lincoln will ignore popular clamor and use the power it confers, we might at last have an army approximating the vast undertaking which was begun in utter, blind, and willful ignorance of the difficulties and dangers we faced. I like the new law because it makes Lincoln a monarch—I'm a monarchist, remember?—and if he don't use the power, somebody else ought to."

I don't know about the monarchist stuff, but I liked conscription too—showed the government was behind the man in the field—and I was anxious to get on with the vast undertaking of winning the war. But we were stalled because of inclement weather: heavy rains in the late winter and early spring swelled the Mississippi and flooded our camps at Milliken's Bend and made campaigning impossible. Sherman was right, you couldn't pick up a paper that didn't report our situation here, an army of fifty thousand men immobilized by rains and knee-deep mud and ravaged by dysentery, fever, and smallpox. The *New York Times* correspondent, before he left, reported that "Grant is stuck in the mud in northern Mississippi, his army of no use to him or anybody else." The *New York World*, a Copperhead paper, told the North that "the confidence of the army is greatly shaken in Gen. Grant, who hitherto undoubtedly depended more upon good fortune than upon military ability for success." It said worse things about Sherman: "He hates reporters, foams at the mouth when he sees them, snaps at them, sure symptoms of a deep-seated mania." No wonder he hated journalists like he did. Even had one arrested and court-martialed.

6. SHERMAN

Thomas Wallace Knox was his name. A sarcastic young prick from New England who worked as a reporter for the *New York Herald*. He'd violated my orders prohibiting correspondents and all other civilians from accompanying my expedition to Chickasaw Bayou last December. The son-of-a-bitch hitched a ride on Frank Blair's headquarters steamer, a blatant violation of my orders, but Blair was a Goddamned political general who liked to talk about himself to reporters. This was all bad enough, but then Knox mailed a dispatch about the expedition to his paper; it was in a fat envelope with maps, which was intercepted in Cairo by our mail agents and sent back to me. Knox's dispatch made the red hair on the back of my neck stand up. He blamed me for the failure of the expedition, attributing it to my "sad mismanagement" and "criminal oversight" and abusing and libeling some of my officers as well. He even said I was "so exceedingly erratic" that it revived the question of my sanity. The *gall* of that Goddamned turd!

I called him to my headquarters and showed him my orders and instructions and the official reports of my officers, which proved how wide he was of the truth. He tried to talk his way out of his crime, admitting that he'd made "repeated errors" in his report and that he was satisfied now that neither I nor my officers could be blamed for the failure of the expedition. But he said his trade was to collect news. He had to furnish reading matter for the public—true, if possible; otherwise, whatever he could get.

I had no sympathy for the insolent bastard and the whole class of vultures he belonged to, and I had him arrested and tried by court martial as a spy and informer. I wrote Ellen: "I will never again command an army in America if we must carry along paid spies. I will banish myself to some foreign country first." I explained to Mr. Ewing, my stepfather: "No army or detachment moves or can move that is not attended by correspondents of hundreds of newspapers. They encumber our transports, eat our provisions, swell the crowd of hangers-on, and increase the impedimenta. They publish without stint positive information of movements past and prospective, giving organizations, names of commanders and accurate information, which reaches the enemy with as much regularity as it does our people. They write up one class of officers and down another, and fan the flames of discord and jealousy. Being in our midst, catching every word of officers, clerks, and orderlies, and being keen, expert men they detect movements and give notice of them, so that no matter how rapidly we move, our enemy has notice in advance." I told my brother John: "Who gave notice of McDowell's movement on Manassas, and enabled Johnston to reinforce Beauregard so that our army was defeated? The press. What has paralyzed the army of the Potomac? Mutual jealousies kept alive by the press. What has enabled the enemy to combine so as to hold Tennessee after we have twice crossed it with victorious armies? The press. And who gave notice of the movement on Vicksburg? *The press.*"

After a week of trial, the court exonerated Knox of the charge of spying and informing the enemy. It found him guilty of violating my order—but attached "no criminality thereto"—and for violating War Department General Orders of August, 'sixty-one, which required correspondents to get the permission of the general in command before filing reports of military operations. As punishment, he was banished from Grant's army and warned that he would be imprisoned if he returned.

I was so Goddamned furious I threatened in my letters to Ellen and John to quit the army. Ellen begged me not to. "I implore you by all you hold sacred and dear do not encourage the thought one moment. You would be abandoning your country in her hour of peril. You would be giving your enemies—the correspondents—the thing they wish—*they will have written you down.*"

I didn't quit, but I came that Goddamned close when Knox took his case to the president and came back in March with a memo from Lincoln saying that Knox's offense was "technical" rather than willful wrongdoing and ordering the sentence to be revoked and Knox returned to Grant's army as long as Grant gave his consent. Good old Grant chewed Knox out, accused him of trying to undermine my influence with the soldiers, and said he could stay only if I agreed to it.

"Never!" I said.

I told Grant: "If the press is allowed to run riot and write up and write down at their pleasure, it means the end of constitutional government in America and anarchy will result." So Knox was banished again—the last we heard, he'd quit journalism, which meant that one lying tongue was silenced. So were two more when the correspondents for the *New York World* and *New York Times* left the Vicksburg front, in what I felt was a major blow for military security. Now we needed to get on with the business of seizing Vicksburg and winning the war.

7. GRANT

How to get at Vicksburg. That was the troublesome question. Had long and sometimes heated talks about that on board my headquarters steamer. Porter was there, Sherman, and my other commanders. We would go at it late into the night, leaning over maps and smoking cigars. Sherman lobbied for a return to Memphis and an advance back down the railroad to the Yalobusha or Jackson, and for using one of them as a base of operations to drive against Vicksburg from the east. I objected to that, because it would look to Washington and the North that we'd retreated. The off-year elections had gone against the Republicans, I said, and volunteering had fallen off and many strong Union men thought the war was lost. A retrograde movement from Vicksburg would further damage the government and undermine faith in the war effort. No progress was being made on any other field. The problem for us was to move forward to a decisive victory from where we were, or the cause was lost.

But how did we move forward from where we were? Sherman and Porter argued against a direct attack from the north. They'd tried that, by the only route where a landing could be made, and had failed. The rebels were too strongly fortified on Walnut Hills, they said, for a breakthrough from that direction. We couldn't undertake an amphibious assault directly across the river and storm the bluffs on the city's waterfront. The enemy's heavy water batteries—thirty-seven big guns and thirteen field pieces—would annihilate my army.

The other option was to move downriver on the Louisiana side, cross to the eastern shore, and operate against Vicksburg from below. But that move was fraught with danger: the rebels would surely see us as we marched south and would likely move to meet the threat. Certainly our supply line back to Milliken's Bend would be vulnerable to attack. Also, the transports and gunboats would have to run past the city's powerful water batteries in order to carry us from the west to the east side of the river.

I liked the downriver option despite the dangers. But I resolved to explore all possible choices before committing myself to a definite plan of operations. We couldn't do any campaigning anyway until the foul weather ended. So I began a series of experiments to consume time and divert the attention of the enemy and the public. Never felt much confidence that any of the experiments would prove successful, but they kept my men occupied.

We tried digging a canal across the peninsula in front of the city. This would turn the course of the river, creating a new channel through which our fleet could get around the city's river batteries. But the rebels discovered the project and erected a battery that could blast the canal's entire length, so we abandoned the project. We also sent expeditions back up the torturous Yazoo and explored its waterways with their heavy overhanging trees and manmade obstructions, to see if there was any point where we might get at Vicksburg from the east, but all the expeditions failed.

Halleck warned me that the president was frustrated with our lack of success, and I could appreciate that. I was frustrated, too. As if the endless rains weren't bad enough, an outbreak of scurvy in March threatened to prostrate the army. At one point a third of my troops were down sick, most of 'em scurvy victims. Terrible, debilitating disease, scurvy. More deadly to an army than bullets and shells. Turns the color of your skin a sickly green. Your hair falls out. Legs and arms swell up. Body breaks out in purplish sores. Gums bleed and puff up. You feel awful, no strength, no spirit. And finally you die. The terrible disease threw a scare into us, because we were desperately short of anti-scorbutics—fruits and vegetables—to fight it. Government didn't have any to send. Don't know what would have happened if Mary Livermore and the Chicago Sanitary Commission hadn't come to our aid. I liked Mrs. Livermore. Tall. Confident. Straightforward. Good patriot. Good friend to my army.

8. LIVERMORE

As soon as we learned of the scurvy outbreak at Milliken's Bend, our Chicago office telegraphed "an appeal" to towns across the North-west, urging local committees to rush forward anti-scorbutics to put down the scurvy in Grant's army. The committees went in wagons from house to house and farm to farm, in rain and mud, begging for fruits and vegetables. Soon a steady flow of anti-scorbutics came to the Chicago office from Michigan, Wisconsin, and Iowa. As rapidly as the supplies arrived, we shipped them by rail and boat to Grant's army: onions, potatoes, pickles, sauerkraut, fruit—as many as 150 barrels and boxes a day—rolled down the Central Railroad and sailed down the Mississippi to Milliken's Bend. From January to July, our office sent Grant's army more than eighteen thousand bushels of vegetables, more than sixty-one thousand pounds of dried fruit, three thousand cans of fruit, and three hundred and ninety packages of pickles. The rush of anti-scorbutics ended the scurvy epidemic and saved the army.

At the same time, relays of nurses—male and female—went to Milliken's Bend to help in the field hospitals there. The Chicago office also sent supplies by visiting committees or delegations, for we believed that they could stimulate contributions by furnishing eye-witness descriptions of what they found.

In March I accompanied the third relief expedition to Milliken's Bend. Our goal was to supply every hospital between Cairo and there. From Cairo we took a little, rickety, wheezy, crowded, unsafe craft, which poked along down the river, towing several barges loaded with potatoes, sauerkraut, onions, oranges, and lemons, for scurvy victims, with farina, hay, corn starch, extract of beef, codfish, jellies, canned fruits, condensed milk, ale, small amounts of high-quality brandy, plus hospital clothing, bandages, lint, sheets, socks, and drawers, not to mention five hundred private boxes marked for specific units or individuals. Several musicians were on board, too, and the boat rang with patriotic music all the time. As we approached the landing of a military post, the musicians on deck would play and sing "Rally Round the Flag, Boys!"

It must have been early April when we reached Milliken's Bend and found the army encamped in a great mass of smoky white tents in pestilential swamps and bottomlands, which were drenched from the protracted spring rains. Here and there levees had broken and flooded the countryside. The tents were pitched on little islands of dry ground and were surrounded by deep mud or standing water.

Our first order of business was to call on General Grant and explain our mission. We found him on his headquarters boat, tied up downriver at Young's Point, and the interview was brief and on the part of the general, laconic. *We* talked; *he* listened. He was a slender man in his forties, with clear blue eyes and light brown hair. He was very uncomfortable and did not seem to know what to do with his right hand. He stroked his beard with his left hand and raised and lowered the right, then placed it on his knee, then raised and lowered it again. When we finished, though, he appeared to approve of our errand. As we rose to go, he assigned a staff officer to arrange an escort, passes, ambulances, and transportation for us.

This interview decided two points we had often discussed on our trip downriver. One was that General Grant was not a garrulous man. All the way down from Chicago, we had heard constantly of General Grant's alleged boasting of how he would take Vicksburg in so many days if it cost him three-fourths of his army. Our faith in all this twaddle had been feeble to begin with. But after the first five minutes of our interview, we learned, by some sort of spiritual telegraphy, that reticence, patience, and persistence were the dominant traits of General Grant. We would as soon have undertaken a tête-à-tête with the Sphinx itself as with this quiet, repressed, reluctant, undemonstrative man.

The other point was that General Grant was not a drunkard. That was immediately apparent to us, and we breathed easier. We had seen enough on our way here, at the different headquarters where we had called, to make us anxious beyond measure lest our brave army should be jeopardized by the intemperance of its commander. But the clear eye, clean skin, firm flesh, and steady nerves of General Grant gave the lie to the universal stories concerning his intemperate habits.

We set off to visit the hospitals, which were clusters of white tents situated on high ground, surrounded by water and mud; many of them could only be reached by boat. Of the thousands and thousands of patients we saw, only a few suffered from wounds, all the rest were sick. Many were homesick and longed for a wife, mother, sister, or friend. What they needed, I decided, was some encouragement and cheerful talk. I went from bed to bed offering each soldier a word of sympathy that often brought tears to his eyes. If the patients wanted messages or letters sent home, I copied down the information in a memo book and wrote the missives myself.

At a Wisconsin regimental hospital, I found about two hundred men, all of them very sick with measles, mumps, diarrhea, dysentery, and fever, lying in their uniforms on the bare board floor, with their knapsacks for pillows, with no food but army rations, no nurses but convalescent soldiers, themselves too sick to move except on compulsion. The sick men were covered with vermin, tormented by flies during the day, and devoured by mosquitoes at night—and their surgeon was dead drunk in bed. I took the hand of one very sick man and said, "My poor boy, I'm very sad to see you in this dreadful condition." From an ambulance outside, I gave him and the other patients all the crackers, tea, condensed milk, and sugar I had.

Then I went directly to medical headquarters and complained to Surgeon General Wolcott of Wisconsin about the conditions of that wretched place. He ordered the hospital closed, the surgeon sent home in disgrace, and the patients transferred to a huge hospital boat, the *Nashville*. A converted barge that was three stories high and fitted up with cooking apparatus, bathrooms, laundry, and cots, the *Nashville* was towed from landing to landing, taking on sick soldiers until the hospital steamers could carry them north.

At Young's Point there was a large field hospital made by pitching tents lengthwise, one beside and opening into the other. Some two hundred chronically sick men lay in this miserable place, waiting for the *City of Memphis*, a hospital steamer, to evacuate them to St. Louis, when the hospital was to be closed. The poor fellows had only army rations for food, and I persuaded the surgeon in charge to let me arrange a special diet for them. The colored men made a huge fire of cottonwood logs sufficient to roast an ox, and I saw to it that water was put into the boilers to heat. The cooking took place in the open air, where smoke and ashes covered both the cook and the food.

Inside the leaky tents, the air was dense with gnats, small flies, and every other variety of winged insect. The place swarmed with large green flies, and their buzzing was like that of a beehive. The men were hushed to the stillness of death. They had been sick a long while and had utterly lost heart and hope. Many of them did not even lift their hands to brush away the flies that swarmed into their eyes, ears, noses, and mouths.

I resolved to cheer them up. "Boys!" I said from the center of the tents. "This hospital is to be broken up. Day after tomorrow, you are going to St. Louis and perhaps the Chicago hospitals. The *City of Memphis* is on its way down here for you. By next Saturday at this time you'll almost be home. Isn't that tiptop news?" That got their attention. "Now, boys, I expect to stay till this hospital is broken up. And if you would like to have me, I'm going to stay here with you. I've got lots of good things for you. The folks at home have sent me down here with everything you need: eggs, tea, crackers, white sugar, condensed milk, lemons, ale, everything—and your surgeon wants you to have them."

I had got into business now. The cry of "Tea! tea! tea! with white sugar and milk in it!" came from every bed. For nearly three days I made tea for all who wanted it in a three-point teapot over an alcohol lamp. And I made them soup of condensed extract of beef and desiccated vegetables—the men called them desecrated vegetables because they were inedible unless served up in soup. And three days later, just as I promised, the *City of Memphis* steamed up to the point and took all the patients away, and I went on board to tell each man good-bye.

As I visited the hospitals and posts, I got many requests to have wrongs righted. Only one request I considered important enough to command General Grant's attention: the cases of twenty-one sick soldiers declared by the surgeons to be incurable. These poor fellows were of no use to the army and ought to be discharged and sent home. So I went to General Grant's steamer to plead their case. I found him in an apartment on his boat, sitting at the table, wearing his hat, a cigar in his mouth, one foot on a chair, and buried to his chin in maps, letters, reports, and orders. When he saw me, he was discomposed. For a moment he seemed the most bashful man I'd ever seen. He rose, begged me to sit down, took his hat off and removed his cigar from his mouth, and then replaced both. Then he sat down and heard my story.

"These are matters that should be laid before my medical director," he said.

"I understand. But it's necessary for someone to 'cut red tape' boldly and promptly, and everyone I've talked to said that only you can do that. Please, General, release these men so they can go home to their families."

He said he would let me know what could be done. That evening an aide brought word from Grant that the twenty-one men would be discharged and could go home tomorrow. He made those men, and me, supremely happy.

There were ladies of our party who played the piano and sang well, and one evening General Grant's chief of staff, Mr. Rawlins, invited us to spend an hour or two on board the headquarters boat. After an hour of music, we drifted into a conversation on various topics, and General Sherman's name came up. I noticed that General Grant listened intently. General Sherman at that time was under a cloud; the papers had pilloried him for his Chickasaw Bayou expedition, calling him a poor general. One of our party repeated that. "It's very evident that General Sherman has been much overrated in the past."

"You're mistaken," Grant said, quietly but firmly.

Another of our party said: "The country would place you before General Sherman in soldierly ability."

"The country does General Sherman a great injustice," Grant said. "I'm not his superior as a soldier. If I surpass him anywhere, it may be in the planning of a campaign. But what's the value of the best-planned campaigns, if there aren't great soldiers like General Sherman to execute them?"

My party soon left Milliken's Bend on the *Maria Denning*, an uncouth and lumbering three-decker. It was loaded with us on the top deck, three or four hundred condemned government horses and mules on the lower deck, and the sick and wounded soldiers and the twenty-one discharged men on the deck in between. Also on the second deck was a group of colored refugees bound for St. Louis. My heart went out to them. They were subdued, impassive, and solemn, with hope and courage now and then lighting up their sable faces. Mothers carried their babies in one arm and led little children with the other. Old men and women, gray, nearly blind, some of them bent almost double, bore on their heads and backs the small plunder they had toted from their homes on the plantation, and the bread and meat furnished them by some friendly authorities. They were all going forth, like the Israelites, "from the land of bondage to they knew not." What a freight of living misery our boat bore up the river!

9. LINCOLN

I admit it, I was all out of patience with Grant. That canal business had me buffaloed. Why would a sensible man like him try such a foolish thing? Why didn't he just march down the Louisiana side of the Mississippi and operate on Vicksburg from below? I told Admiral Dahlgren that Grant was doing nothing down there. Maybe bad weather was a factor, as Grant said, but why was it the damned rebels could fight in bad weather, but we couldn't?

To make matters worse, the stories about Grant's drinking had resurfaced. Chase showed me a letter from a Cincinnati editor, who called Grant "a poor drunken imbecile who is wasting our noble army of the Mississippi." Reports like that and Grant's lack of progress worried us, so Stanton and I decided to send Charles Anderson Dana, a special commissioner of the War Department, down there to size Grant up and report back to us.

I kept track of Grant's whereabouts and the whereabouts of all our other armies on a large framed map on the wall of my study and Cabinet room. Pins stuck in the map—red for the enemy, blue for us—marked the disposition of the forces in the field, from Virginia to Louisiana. By the way, Nathaniel Banks of Massachusetts was now in command in Louisiana; Ben Butler had been relieved in December and had come to Washington on leave and was often in the company of Sumner and Henry Wilson. I liked Butler and had him to dinner. I thought he had ability and fidelity and deserved well of the country, and was giving some thought of making him my running mate in 'sixty-four. He's a stout fellow with very white teeth and a receding hairline, and he squints his eyes badly, but he isn't the monster the insurgents make him out to be.

I kidded him: "Don't let Davis catch you. He's put a price on your head. He'll hang you sure."

"That's a game two can play. If I get him, I'll give him time to say his prayers and then give him the law of the outlaw."

Spunk, that's what Butler had, and I liked it.

I mentioned a while ago that I was impatient with Grant. Impatience is not the word for how I felt about the Army of the Potomac and its commanders. Burnside was out now, on account of the mud march. What a sorry tale that is. In January he'd sent the army forward again with the idea of crossing the upper Rappahannock and turning Lee's left flank. But a severe storm wrecked the advance, turned the roads into rivers of mud and mire, which the entire army sank into—men, artillery and caissons, ambulances, supply wagons, horses, mules, the whole works. As if that wasn't bad enough, Burnside had whiskey issued to the ranks, and a lot of the men got drunk and started fights. The rebels across the river whooped and pointed at the drunken brawlers and held up signs that read, THIS WAY TO RICHMOND.

Back in camp at Falmouth, the army rocked with recriminations—everybody pointed a finger at everybody else. Hooker, a corps commander, told a reporter and some senators that Burnside was hopelessly inept, Lincoln was "a played-out imbecile," and said what we needed was a dictator. When Burnside tried to relieve Hooker, I stepped in and relieved Burnside. It was either that or face a complete breakdown of army command. Without consulting Halleck, Stanton, or anybody else, I named Hooker to head our abused and misused Potomac Army. Yes, yes, he was a loudmouth and a braggart and a little too fond of his glass, but that man could fight. His nickname was Fighting Joe. And anyway, what other choice did I have?

I called him to the White House and gave him a good looking over. He was forty-four then, tall, with wavy brown hair, blue eyes, and a florid complexion. I handed him a letter I'd written to him.

> I believe you to be a brave and a skillful soldier, which, of course, I like. I also believe you do not mix politics with your profession, in which you are right. You have confidence in yourself, which is a valuable, if not an indispensable quality. You are ambitious, which, within reasonable bounds, does good rather than harm. But I think that during Gen. Burnside's command of the Army, you have taken counsel of your ambition, and thwarted him as much as you could, in which you did a great wrong to the country and to a most meritorious and honorable brother officer. I have heard, in such a way as to believe it, of your recently saying that both the army and the government needed a dictator. Of course it was not for this, but in spite of it, that I have given you the command. What I now ask of you is military success, and I will risk the dictatorship.
>
> And now, beware of rashness. Beware of rashness, but with energy, and sleepless vigilance, go forward, and give us victories.

"Mr. President," he said. "You can depend on me. If the enemy doesn't run, God help him."

He returned to the army on the Rappahannock, but of course did not go forward to victory because winter storms dumped snow on northern Virginia and Washington. Young Nicolay got it right: "The Army of the Potomac is for the present stuck in the mud, as it has been during nearly the whole of its existence."

When the spring came, I decided to pay Hooker a visit and find out what he planned to do with the army. It was early April when I left on a little steamer, with Mary, Tad, a couple of friends—young Noah Brooks, the California journalist with the pince-nez glasses, and Dr. Anson Henry—and of course the crew. But we hadn't got very far when a snowstorm struck, and we huddled around the fire in our cabin. It was still snowing the next morning when we reached Aquia Creek, thirty-five miles downriver, and docked at the wharf of the army's busy supply base. Steamers and whistling tugs were chugging about in the harbor, and there was great activity at the long rows of unpainted wooden storehouses on the shore. The wharf was crowded with military workers and soldiers, some sick and others on furlough, waiting for transportation back to Washington.

From Aquia Creek, we took a rattling military train down to Falmouth. We rode in a freight car equipped with wooden benches, staring out at a desolate wintry countryside, the consequence of two years of unrelenting warfare. I'd read that this had once been a fertile farm and plantation region, but now many of the mansions were wrecked or burnt; cabins, barns, and fences had been torn down for firewood; and all the livestock eaten or driven off.

When we reached Falmouth Station, a mile or so east of the Rappahannock, we looked out over a sprawling tent city that stretched from the hilltop mansions in back of the station to the riverfront village of Falmouth, a mile or so to the northwest. This was the great camp of the Potomac Army, officially 130,000 strong, but a good deal less than that when you subtracted the sick, the furloughed men, and the deserters. There were long lines of wagons and ambulances, droves of cattle and horses, and soldiers everywhere, sitting or standing beside campfires whose smoke filled the air with the odor of burning pine. Over it all hovered Hooker's giant observation balloons, three of 'em, watching rebel troop movements across the river.

On the opposite shore lay Fredericksburg with its steeples and houses, and beyond that the heights our troops had assaulted last December, which were covered with enemy tents and fortifications with rebel flags floating overhead. We could see the smoke from rebel campfires rising in a thousand columns and drifting with the wind.

I went down to the picket lines along the river and looked at Fredericksburg through a field glass. Saw burnt and shattered homes and loose sheets of tin flapping from a church steeple. A blackened chimney stood by itself near the riverbank, and a couple of rebel pickets huddled around a fire on the hearth, warming themselves in the cold. Our own pickets said they often talked to the rebel sentinels and even traded with 'em, exchanging Yankee coffee for rebel tobacco.

We stayed five days at Falmouth—lived in three large hospital tents with plank floors and often visited with the wounded in the hospital tents nearby. I spent a lot of time reviewing troops and attending parades with fine bands of fifes and drums playing military airs. Between reviews, I rode around camp in a mule-drawn ambulance and visited with the soldiers. Fine men, brave men, ready to die for our cause.

My driver was something else. Cussed everything with gusto— the mules, the raw weather, the mud, the wagons and cavalry sloshing past.

I tapped him on the shoulder. "Excuse me, friend, are you an Episcopalian?"

"No," he said. "I'm a Methodist."

"Well," I said, "I thought you must be an Episcopalian, because you cuss just like Governor Seward, who's a churchwarden."

Yes, I was impressed with this volunteer army (the first draft hadn't been held yet). Hooker called it "the finest army on the planet," as he showed me around. He'd done a fair amount of reorganizing, and what I liked was that the cavalry was now a separate corps. Good, I said, now the cavalry can fight like the enemy fights, can ride and raid and destroy communication like the enemy cavalry did with such alarming skill.

Hooker himself troubled me—bragged constantly about what he was going to do after he captured Richmond. I told young Brooks that all the talk about the rebel capital was the most depressing thing about Hooker. Seemed cocky and overconfident, too much like McClellan to suit me. Besides, as I kept telling Hooker, his objective was not Richmond, but Lee's army across the river. We would never win the war by capturing cities and capitals, that much I'd learned. We would win it when we wiped out the rebel armies.

I asked Hooker what his plans were, and he said he intended to take the offensive when the weather cleared, maybe try to get around Lee's left flank, but the big question was where to cross the Rappahannock. He promised to let me know when he had things worked out, and I told him and his corps commanders: "Gentlemen, in your next battle *put in all your men*." Then we left for Washington. It had been a great relief to get away from the capital and the politicians, I said, but nothing touched the tired spot.

10. LEE

We could surmise the reason for the visit of the enemy president. It was to urge the savage and brutal policy he had announced in his emancipation proclamation, which would destroy our social system and dishonor our families with pollution. To accomplish that, the Federal Congress had put the whole power of their country into the hands of their president, appropriating $900 million and providing for three million men through conscription. In view of the vast increase of the forces of the enemy at every strategic point, and of the ruthless war of emancipation and extermination he intended to wage, I believed that every means must be employed to increase and maintain the ranks of our armies, and I told the government of the absolute necessity of putting fresh troops into the field at once. "Let the Confederate people hear the appeal of their defenders for help," I wrote War Secretary Seddon, "and drive into the ranks, from very shame, those who will not heed the dictates of honor and of patriotism. Let the state authorities take the matter of conscription in hand, and see that no man able to bear arms be allowed to evade his duty."

What had our Congress done to meet the extremity we faced? As far as I knew, it had concocted bills to excuse certain classes of men from taking service, and it made me furious. The enemy across the Rappahannock, thanks to heavy reinforcements (we had seen them arriving by train all through the winter), greatly outnumbered us. But instead of increasing the size of my army, Richmond felt the necessity of detaching troops to defend points it considered more immediately threatened. D. H. Hill's division went to North Carolina after an enemy raid there alarmed the Administration. In February, enemy troopships were spotted sailing down the Chesapeake, and Richmond feared that they were on their way to the James to attack the capital from below. To counter the new threat, I had to dispatch Longstreet with two of his divisions to guard Richmond and the area south of the James. Our understanding was that Longstreet would be returned to me should I become engaged.

That left me with only sixty thousand men and 170 guns on the Rappahannock line, facing a host of three times that size. Inferiority of numbers, however, was not our only problem. We suffered terribly from a want of rations. The daily ration for my men was eighteen ounces of cornmeal and a quarter pound of bacon, which was often rancid, plus a little rice every third day and occasionally peas and dried fruit when available. Starving, ravaged by disease, weakened by desertion, my army was in no condition for active campaigning, and in mid-March I went to Richmond to plead personally for the relief of my suffering men and to discuss our military situation.

To solve the shortage of food, the president and I agreed that General Longstreet should gather bacon and other commissary stores for my army in southern Virginia and western North Carolina, which had been largely untouched by the war. The president did not look well, was exceedingly thin and pale, cheeks sunken, his one good eye inflamed. Despite his poor health, though, he remained confident that we would win the war soon. I did not share his optimism.

"The enemy will make every effort to crush us between now and June," I said, "and it will require all our strength to resist him."

11. DAVIS

I assured General Lee that the government was doing all in its power to sustain his army. But owing to the ruthless Yankee blockade and the enemy occupation of much of our fertile croplands, shortages of food and supplies of every description plagued all our armies. The capture of many of our railroads made it difficult to distribute what we did have. To properly supply and equip our forces, Congress, at my urging, approved the impressment act in March. It authorized the quartermaster and commissary departments to seize private property from our civilians—foodstuffs, horses, livestock, equipment, and anything else of military value—in return for certificates of credit. The same measure also authorized the impressment of slaves for military labor. In practical application, those who sacrificed most were the ones who lived in the areas where armies were fighting; elsewhere our people suffered not at all. I conceded that impressment was so unequal in its operation, vexatious to the producer, injurious to the industrial interests, and productive of such discontent among the people as only to be justified by the existence of an absolute necessity. Alas, the necessity never ended, and our civilians complained bitterly.

A related problem was our finances. Thus far, we had in the main funded our war effort and the other operations of the government, not by comprehensive taxation, but by issuing non-interest-bearing treasury notes that were not backed by gold. I admit that repeated issues of paper currency led to escalating prices. By March of 1863, turkeys sold in Richmond for $30 each, a barrel of flour for $30, and a pound of butter for $3. Secretary of the Treasury Christopher Memminger, to whom I left the handling of our finances while I concentrated on the war, reported that it now cost five times as much for a southerner to live as it had in 1860.

To correct this evil, we persuaded Congress to enact a stringent new tax law, which among other things levied a 10 percent tax-in-kind on agricultural produce and livestock, an 8 percent ad valorem tax on farm products, a 10 percent tax on profits earned from the sale of clothes, iron, and foodstuffs, and a graduated income tax of 1 percent on income under $500 per annum and 15 percent on income above $10,000 per annum. "Tax-in-kind" men then went across the Confederacy to enforce the law and collect the crops for the government. This severe war measure produced howls of protest from all quarters—cries of consolidated government and despotic infringement on the rights of the people, but it was justified by absolute and pressing necessity. Only by an exertion of national power, I maintained, could we survive against our ruthless foe.

Perhaps impressment and taxation did work a great hardship on our people, but they had to be made to understand that our salvation required enormous sacrifice. Some of them, alas, did not understand. In early April, complaining of a shortage of bread and other food, several hundred Richmond women rioted in the streets. Policemen and state troops rushed to the scene of disturbance, but were unable to restore order. The mayor of the city and Governor Letcher came to me in alarm, and I went at once to see what I could do.

Most of the rioters were gathered on a side road off Main Street and were under the direction of a huge woman with a white feather in her hat. Several men and boys had joined them. A dray, stripped of its horses, blocked the main avenue. The rioters were crying: "We are hungry and need bread." But if that was true, why had they bypassed bakeries and provision stores and completely looted a jewelry store and some millinery and clothing shops in the area? It was clear to me that plunder was what they wanted.

As I made my way through the crowd, some of the boys threw bread crusts at me. I mounted the dray, reached into my pockets, and took out what money I had. "You say you are hungry and have no money," I shouted. "Here is all I have; it's not much, but take it." I flung the money at them. "We do not desire to injure anyone," I said, "but this lawlessness must stop. I will give you five minutes to disperse, otherwise you will be fired upon." No one moved. I took out my watch and waited. When five minutes had elapsed, I turned to the soldiers. "Load!" The soldiers did as they were told and aimed their weapons. The rioters dispersed immediately.

A few days later, I issued a proclamation to rally the people to the support of our suffering armies. "Your country appeals to you to lay aside all thought of gain and to devote yourselves to securing your liberties, without which those gains would be valueless. Let fields be devoted exclusively to the production of corn, oats, beans, peas, potatoes, and other food for man and beast; let corn be sown broadcast for fodder in immediate proximity to railroads, rivers, and canals, and let all your effort be directed to the prompt supply of these articles in the districts where our armies are operating. Let us all unite in the performance of our duty, each in his sphere, and with concerted, persistent, and well-directed effort we shall maintain the sovereignty and independence of these Confederate States."

It was argued that the ruling class lived in relative opulence while our less fortunate classes suffered. I received many complaints that I entertained lavishly while the poor did not have bread. But that was not true. We made our own sacrifices and suffered without complaint when some of our slaves ran away and a thief stole one of my horses.

Of course, we had guests for dinner in the Executive Mansion. The Chesnuts were back in Richmond and were our frequent companions. But I repeat what I said before: I was far too occupied with the war and my health far too feeble to hold lavish state dinners and functions at the expense of the people.

12. CHESNUT

Last year, James had resigned his position on the Executive Council in Columbia after a bitter disagreement with the other councilmen. Until he decided our next move, I had gone back to Mulberry, in exile again, where those *good* people, old Mr. and Mrs. Chesnut, had no end of creature comforts. Had their good tea and coffee and plenty of plantation poultry, beef, mutton, cream, and butter. The war had not reached here. I pined after a certain James Chesnut, Jr., who was toiling and moiling in Columbia, until winter came and James fetched me and took me north with the delightful news that Jefferson Davis had made him a colonel and had called him back to Richmond as his personal aide. I was so *excited* to be back in the social whirl of Richmond—you just can't know. On our very first night in town, there was a party at Mrs. Ives's.

For our personal quarters, we rented one floor of a house at Twelfth and Clay Streets near the Confederate White House. Our floor consisted of a drawing room, a dining room, a chamber, and two rooms for our servants, Lawrence and Molly. Not long after, those two irresistible young delights, Sally Buchanan Preston—we call her Buck—and Mamie Preston came up from Columbia to stay with us. The Prestons were a lovely family, our dear dear friends. They were all so curiously candid, so utterly without guile. But it was those two girls who touched me the deepest. Even though we were crowded and had to convert the dining room into a bedroom for them, I *relished* their company. They were such *beautiful* girls, and so intelligent. They had been schooled in France and often declaimed for us in French.

Before a week was out, a long line of male admirers professed to be in love with Buck. She was a flirt, that one was. And Mamie attracted the attentions of John Darby, a friend of mine and a surgeon attached to Hood's division. Darby taught the girls to play casino and it became their favorite game. We made an immense amount of taffy and were so *happy*.

And my, how we entertained, my girls and I. Yes, there were terrible shortages—bread riots in the city. But for Lawrence there was no such word as fail. "You give me the money," he said, "I'll find everything you want." He kept us plentifully supplied with turkeys, and we had sent from Mulberry wine, rice, potatoes, hams, eggs, butter, pickles—once a month a man came on with all that the plantation could furnish us.

The days were beautiful. Our poor drawing room served as parlor and dining room, and it was crowded to capacity every night. We danced to the music of an old ramshackle piano and had a good time generally. We received there all that the Confederacy had of good and great, from Mr. and Mrs. President Davis, the Lees, Mr. Hunter, down to the humblest private, who was often our nearest friend or relative. I was especially glad to receive President Davis in our home. When he entered, my girls and I stood to show our respect.

In addition to our parties, my young charges and I attended rounds of delightful teas and splendid dinners with the best people. Once, when Varina was out of town, the president himself gave a breakfast for us. He was so kind and so amiable and agreeable, we were all charmed, and Buck came away in a very ecstasy of loyalty. As we got to lonely Clay Street, she hurrahed for Jeff Davis and professed her willingness to fight to the death for him.

13. DAVIS

I stood at a map in my office in downtown Richmond, pondering our innumerable difficulties. Threatened on every strategic point by armies greatly superior in numbers and arms, our scattered, underfed, and undermanned forces were obliged to adopt a defensive posture and await the enemy's moves. Inclement weather and muddy roads kept Hooker inactive on the Rappahannock and Rosecrans within his fortifications in Nashville, but in Louisiana Federal forces under Banks had moved from New Orleans to Baton Rouge, probably to operate against Port Hudson. I had removed Holmes and placed Kirby Smith in command of the Trans-Mississippi Department, warning him that his main objective was to aid in the defense of the lower Mississippi and to keep the great artery of the West effectually closed to northern occupation or trade.

Our greatest danger came from Grant in front of Vicksburg. General Pemberton, directing the defense of that city from his headquarters in Jackson, kept me informed of Grant's activities—the canal, the expeditions up the Yazoo—and at my request sent me all the pertinent information about the city's defenses. When a letter came condemning me for appointing Pemberton to command in Mississippi, I replied that he had been assigned to that post because he was the best qualified officer then available, and that I had since found no reason to change my opinion. He had, thus far, foiled every attempt of the Federals to take possession of the Mississippi.

In mid-April, the strains of the war again prostrated me with neuralgia, which caused spasms of sharp pain in my face and threatened the sight of my remaining eye. To compound our difficulties, we learned that General Lee himself was ill, and it caused much anxiety in Richmond lest our greatest commander not be fit when the fighting resumed.

14. LEE

Since my return from Richmond, I had not felt well. I was unable to attend church services and offered my poor prayers in the solitude of my tent. *In Him is our only salvation. He alone can give us peace and freedom and I humbly submit to His holy will.* The sickness had begun with a heavy cold and a pain in my throat; then the cold turned violent, with a good deal of pain in my chest, back, and arms. It came on in paroxysms and was quite sharp. I wrote dear Mary that the physicians feared I suffered from a malady which must be dreadful if it resembled its name, which I couldn't recall. They bundled me up and took me to Mr. Yuby's, where I had a comfortable room with Perry attending me.

"I am enjoying the sensation of a complete saturation of my system with quinine," I wrote Mary. "The doctors are very attentive and kind and have examined my lungs, my heart, circulation, &c. I believe they pronounce me tolerable sound. They have been tapping me all over like an old steam boiler before condemning it. I am about a mile from my camp and my handsome aides ride over with the papers after breakfast which I labor through by 3 P.M., when Mrs. Neal sends me some good soup or something else which is more to my taste than the doctors' pills. I am in need of nothing. I have tea and sugar and all that I want. Some of my brother officers have sent me apples, some butter from the valley, others turkey, tongue, hams, sweet potatoes. So it seems to me I had better remain sick. I think I shall be well soon and in the meantime must suffer. Soldiers you know are born to suffer and they cannot escape it."

As I lay abed, my thoughts were much on my scattered family. What a cruel thing is war. To separate and destroy families and friends and mar the purest joys and happiness God has granted us in this world. To fill our hearts with hatred instead of love for our neighbors and to devastate the fair face of this beautiful world. Ah, may God forgive us our blindness and our many sins.

By mid-April, I felt better and was able to ride out to inspect my lines. The snows had melted and warmer weather was at hand, and I hoped I would recover all my strength. My pulse was still about ninety, the doctors said, which was too quick for an old man, but I hoped the fresh air and exercise would reduce it soon.

I studied the Federal camps across the river and told my staff that if Mr. F. J. Hooker was going to do anything we should hear from him soon. He was reported to be all ready for campaigning, and I wished I could say the same for us. We were scattered, without forage and provisions, and even if united could not remain long together because of the continued shortage of food for our ranks.

Richmond seemed more alarmed about Bragg's situation in Tennessee than about mine on the Rappahannock. Secretary of War Seddon even asked me about the possibility of sending part of Longstreet's forces to reinforce Bragg. I replied that the best way to relieve the pressure on Bragg and Johnston in the West was for me to invade Maryland, but that I could do nothing until Longstreet returned with the provisions he was gathering for my troops. Of course, Hooker might take the offensive before Longstreet got back—that was the risk we were taking. If the enemy did not move before May first, I hoped to reunite my army and take the offensive myself. I would first drive the enemy from the Shenandoah and then once more carry the war into enemy territory.

I was not insensitive to our situation in Tennessee and at Vicksburg. I told Richmond that I had reflected with great anxiety on the state of affairs in that region, but could not arrive at a satisfactory conclusion with regard to reinforcing the troops in the Western Department. Since the enemy outnumbered us in every department, it was difficult to say which troops could be safely spared. But if the statements I saw in the papers were true, General Grant appeared to be withdrawing from Vicksburg, and would hardly return to his former position there this summer because of the excessive heat. "The president from his position, being able to survey all the scenes of action, can better decide than any one else," I said, "and I recommend that he follow the dictates of his own judgment."

15. DAVIS

What the northern papers said appeared to be true. General Pemberton reported that Grant was withdrawing from Vicksburg and was likely on his way to join Rosecrans for a joint operation against Bragg. At my urging, Johnston, in command of the Western Department, ordered Pemberton to send help to Bragg from Mississippi. Pemberton thereupon dispatched eight thousand men, including Van Dorn's cavalry, to reinforce the Army of Tennessee.

I dictated outgoing dispatches and had incoming ones read to me in my sickroom at the Executive Mansion. My remaining eye pained me so much that my doctors feared total blindness. But I worked on, refusing all callers except the couriers who brought me dispatches from Lee, from Bragg and Johnston, from Kirby Smith and Pemberton. Anxious though we were about the situation in Tennessee, we were relieved that the threat against Vicksburg appeared to have ended.

16. GRANT

We weren't withdrawing. I'd sent a detachment upriver to threaten Greenville and make Pemberton think I was calling off the Vicksburg operation. My plan was to march down the Louisiana side of the river, seize Grand Gulf, and dispatch a corps to help General Banks capture Port Hudson, Louisiana. This would open the river to New Orleans, which would then serve as my supply base. With Grand Gulf as a starting point, Banks and I could move our combined forces against Vicksburg from the south and southeast.

Meanwhile, as we marched from Milliken's Bend, a column of 1,700 picked horsemen under Colonel Benjamin H. Grierson, a former music teacher from Illinois, would leave Tennessee and raid southward through central Mississippi, burning depots and wrecking railroads. I hoped that Grierson's raid would cut Mississippi's communications with the eastern Confederacy and divert the enemy's attention away from my movement south.

I communicated all this to Mr. Dana, sent by the president and Secretary of War Stanton to spy on me, find out if I was sober. I'd talked with my staff and other officers about how to deal with him. My artillery chief, Colonel Duff, wanted to throw Dana in the river. But Rawlins and Wilson of my staff advised me to treat him with respect—take him into my confidence and explain my plan of operations in full—which is what I did. Paid off, too. In conveying my plan to Washington, he expressed his full confidence in me, told 'em I was indispensable if Vicksburg was to be taken. I liked Dana, liked to listen to him—he was a talker like Sherman, had a great memory, could quote prose and poetry from all times and discourse on history, romance, and life.

McClernand was generally enthusiastic about the plan of operations, but Sherman continued to object, came to my boat and paced back and forth. Ran his hands through his hair. Puffed on his cigar. Said: "See here, Grant, you're going into enemy country, with a large river behind you and the rebels holding points strongly fortified above and below. It's an axiom of war that when any great body of troops moves against an enemy they should do it from a secure base of supplies, which they would guard as they would the apple of the eye. Moving downriver like you propose could cut you off from the North and all its supplies. It's too big a risk. You won't have a secure base until Banks takes Port Hudson, if he can do it at all. The best campaign would be to go back to the line of the Yalobusha in northern Mississippi, use that as your advance base, and operate against Vicksburg along the railroads, from the northeast and east."

"I would have to go back to Memphis to do that."

"Exactly. That's what I mean."

"I told you before. It would look like a retreat and would be disastrous to the country. I won't take a backward step. Don't care about axioms and textbook warfare. To win a real war you've got to take risks. We're going south."

Sherman didn't like it, but he knew better than to keep arguing. "Who's going to lead the advance?" he asked.

"McClernand."

"McClernand! He's a Goddamned *politician*. No skill as a soldier. Rude and insubordinate as hell."

"He's senior corps commander. A favorite of Lincoln's. And he likes the plan of operations and wants to lead it. I'm going to give him the chance."

McClernand's Thirteenth Corps, one division after another, moved south by a winding narrow road and by mid-April had established an advanced staging area at a plantation near New Carthage on the Louisiana side of the river, about thirty-five miles south of Milliken's Bend.

On the sixteenth, as the other corps made their preparations, my wife, Julia, and our other children arrived in camp for a short visit—our twelve-year-old, Fred, had come down earlier. Glad to see them all. Buck, Nellie, little Jesse. But especially dear Julia. She was a good wife, loving, nicely plump, not much chin, hair worn in a bun. I had some painful boils and she doctored 'em with some remedies from the physician. Wished she could stay with me. My best friend, kept me steady. Could talk to her. Talked about the army, the upcoming campaign, Lorenzo Thomas and the colored regiments. His name alarmed her. She thought Thomas was just a mouthpiece to Lincoln and that he'd been sent down here to relieve me.

"The president," I said, "has sent General Thomas here to arrange a plan for taking care of the freed slaves. They're in a sad condition. Had an interesting talk with Thomas about them. He and I are in sympathy." Julia was listening intently, but I changed the subject: "You got here just in time to see the gunboats and transports run the river batteries at Vicksburg. Going to do it tonight. The boats will drop silently down the river and then put on all steam and sail past Vicksburg and its batteries to where I want to use them."

We ate supper with a few officers and ladies, and after dark Julia and I and the children, with Dana and Lieutenant Colonel Wilson of my staff, gathered on the hurricane deck of my headquarters boat, the *Henry Von Phul*, which was anchored near the western shore of the river. Presently we saw 'em in the moonless night—seven iron-clad gunboats and three river steamers, formless black masses moving silently in the currents, no lights, no engines running. They slid past us, the side-wheel steamers towing barges filled with coal, supplies, and ammunition.

The children were so excited they couldn't stay still. I sat there smoking a cigar, trying to make out what was happening in the gloom. Suddenly a bonfire flamed up in the darkness, then another. That must be the rebel pickets on the point. The fleet had been spotted. The ships picked up steam now and moved past the ghostly fires and then the enemy's huge guns opened up with thunderous blasts that made the children put their hands over their ears. From the sounds of it, the rebels had some big stuff over there—thirty-two–pounders, sounded like, and ten-inch Columbiads, some Whitworths. The gunboats steamed in under the bluffs and returned the fire, and the flaming guns and bonfires lit up the night. We could see the rebel gunners at work and people running through the streets of the city.

The enemy fire was heaviest when the fleet was abreast of the courthouse: a whirlwind of projectiles swept over the ships, crashed into their bulwarks, cut their ropes and chimney-guys, exploded in their machinery and pilothouses. One steamer, the *Henry Clay,* burst into flame and drifted out of control. But the other boats sailed on and finally disappeared in the darkness. Then the rebel batteries fell silent, and only the blazing hull of the *Henry Clay* remained to remind us of the battle.

The next day, if all was going according to plan, Grierson commenced his cavalry raid south through Mississippi. I said good-bye to Julia and the younger children and with Fred and my staff and a cavalry escort rode down to New Carthage to check on Porter and McClernand. Porter's fleet was anchored above New Carthage and I was relieved to learn that with repairs the surviving vessels would be fully operational.

There was a problem at New Carthage. The levee had broken and flooded the roads and countryside, rendering transportation through there to Grand Gulf all but impossible. So we located an alternate route round by Perkin's plantation to the south. Then I rode back north to get James McPherson's corps. Sherman's Fifteenth Corps would stay at Milliken's Bend and make diversions until we'd crossed to the Mississippi side of the river. I hoped Sherman's activities would confuse the rebel commander in Mississippi, make him uncertain where and when we meant to strike.

McPherson's corps moved south with a ten-day supply of rations and ammunition. I liked McPherson as much as I did Sherman. He was a dignified man, tall and lean, with dark eyes, dark brown hair, and a flowing beard. A man of good sense, winning manners, an ability to harmonize all parts of his command. In him and Sherman I had a host. They were worth more than a full brigade each.

On the night of April twenty-second, six more steamers and twelve barges full of supplies ran past the Vicksburg batteries and joined Porter's fleet. Meanwhile I rode back to Perkin's plantation with my headquarters staff and put the army into motion to Grand Gulf with McClernand in the lead. My intention was for Porter's ironclads to reduce the enemy batteries at Grand Gulf. Then my infantry would cross the river and seize the heights. Possession of

Grand Gulf, on the eastern side of the river, I looked upon as virtual possession of Vicksburg and Port Hudson and the entire Mississippi.

Porter, however, told me he'd reconnoitered Grand Gulf and found it a formidable garrison on a high bluff overlooking the river. "They are throwing in reinforcements from Vicksburg," Porter said. "There are four forts in all, well placed, and mounting twelve large guns. I don't think a direct attack will work."

Next day, the twenty-fourth, we steamed down to Grand Gulf, and looking it over through my glass, I remained convinced that a gunboat attack would work if it could be made within the next two days. Porter agreed to try. To stop the enemy from sending further reinforcements to Grand Gulf, I ordered Sherman to make a reconnaissance in force up the Yazoo and threaten the enemy fortifications on Snyder's Bluff northeast of Vicksburg. That would confuse the rebels as to where we were mounting our main attack.

17. DAVIS

Pemberton insisted that the enemy thrust downriver was a diversion, that the presence of a large body of Federal troops at Milliken's Bend and on the Yazoo indicated that the attack on Vicksburg, if there was to be one, would again come from the north. But what alarmed Pemberton the most was the enormous force of enemy cavalry rampaging through central Mississippi. He had relatively few cavalry to throw against the raiders—most of his horsemen had been shifted to Tennessee—and he begged us repeatedly for more cavalry. I implored Johnston to return some of Pemberton's horsemen, but Johnston argued against that because he was still convinced that Grant intended to reinforce Rosecrans for a joint campaign in Tennessee. I suggested that Pemberton call on Kirby Smith for reinforcements, but when Pemberton did so, Smith argued that he had his hands full with the Federal threat in Louisiana and could not spare any troops.

From Richmond, with only Pemberton's dispatches to guide us, it was impossible to know what Grant intended to do. Whatever it was, General Pemberton's instructions were to hold Vicksburg at all cost. General Lee himself had warned that the city must be saved even if it meant fighting from house to house and street to street, and I agreed. I could only hope that Pemberton would find the resources to hold the city and the river, and yet I could find little reassurance from the consternation and confusion that inhabited his dispatches. I wasn't so sanguine as he was that the movement of enemy troops downriver was a mere diversion. The commander of our small garrison at Grand Gulf, south of Vicksburg, reported that enemy gunboats and transports and a huge body of troops were massing in his front.

18. GRANT

The success of the attack on Grand Gulf depended on McClernand's getting his corps aboard his transports in time, so that he could cross the river and carry the forts by storm the moment the batteries bearing on the river were silenced. But McClernand was slow and inefficient in putting his divisions forward and concentrating his steamers and barges to cross the river. Yes, the roads were narrow and muddy, but still no excuse for such sorry marching. It threw the attack behind schedule by three days. Frustrated and disgusted me. I rode up and down McClernand's disorderly lines, untying traffic jams and urging the men: "Come on, keep it moving, push right along, close up fast." Was so fed up I wrote McClernand a severe letter of rebuke, but didn't send it when I learned he'd finally gotten his boats in place during the night and his troops were starting to board.

We finally attacked Grand Gulf on the twenty-ninth. While Fred and I watched from the deck of a tug in the middle of the river, with ten thousand men waiting on steamers and barges closer to shore, Porter's gunboats, four of 'em the massive flat-backed Turtles, steamed into battle. It was a mistake, should never have tried it. The enemy batteries were too high—gunboats couldn't hit 'em. The ironclads would pass the fortifications in a line, turn and pass again, firing all the while in a vain attempt to hit the elevated batteries. The enemy guns, however, laid down a deadly fire on the gunboats, and they finally withdrew.

I went on board Porter's flagship, the *Benton*, and saw that a shell had struck its side, exploding between the decks where the sailors manned the guns. The sight of all those mangled and dying men made me sick. Porter himself had been wounded in the back of his head, and his face showed his agony.

"It's no use, General," he said. "The thing has failed."

"Then we'll bypass Grand Gulf. If you can attack again after dark tonight and keep the enemy guns occupied, the transports can run safely by. I'll march the soldiers downriver opposite Rodney or Bruinsville where we can cross and take Grand Gulf in the rear."

That's what we did. The gunboats and transports ran past the batteries and met us at a point on the river opposite Bruinsville. McClernand's corps was up and McPherson's was close behind. I sent a courier with orders for Sherman to march south as fast as possible, so that we could unite the army.

On April thirtieth the transports and gunboats ferried McClernand's entire corps and McPherson's lead division across the river—twenty-two thousand men in a single day. Couldn't have done it without Porter's cooperation. When I asked him if we could use his gunboats as ferries, he agreed without hesitation. He wasn't a touchy admiral, wasn't jealous of his rank. I rate him as great an admiral as Lord Nelson.

On May first I moved at once on Port Gibson, ten miles inland and six miles southeast of Grand Gulf. Once I had Port Gibson, the enemy garrison up at Grand Gulf would be outflanked and forced to evacuate. We had only three-days' rations with us and lacked a supply line, but it didn't bother me none. I remembered the lesson of Holly Springs: an army campaigning in Mississippi could live on the abundance of the countryside. On the march, we relieved enemy homesteads of their cornmeal, bacon, vegetables, beef, and mutton. Had a shortage of wagons, too, so we took every four-wheeled vehicle and all the draft animals we came across.

As we approached Port Gibson, we found an enemy force from Grand Gulf drawn up on the ridges west of town, prepared to dispute our advance and prevent us from flanking their garrison. The country was the most broken and difficult I'd ever seen: the ridges were narrow and divided by deep ravines full of heavy timber, undergrowth, and cane. My infantry went forward on the attack, but it was impossible to throw in a considerable force of 'em at any one time, and the battle raged piecemeal along the ridges and ravines for almost eighteen hours before the rebels finally retreated up the road to Grand Gulf.

Port Gibson was ours. From enemy prisoners we learned that the rebel commander had hoped to get five thousand reinforcements from

Vicksburg, but we'd moved too fast and routed him before most of 'em had arrived. Dana and my boy overtook us at Port Gibson, riding two fat old horses. Funny sight. I'd left the river in such a hurry that I didn't have my mess chest. Only baggage I carried was my toothbrush.

Next day, our reconnaissance learned that the rebel garrison, now outflanked, had abandoned Grand Gulf and retreated north across the Big Black River. Our move to Bruinsburg and Port Gibson had undoubtedly taken the enemy commander in Grand Gulf by surprise. When we occupied the place on the third, I discovered that the entire rebel command in Mississippi was confused and filled with apprehension by the various moves of our forces, especially Grierson's cavalry raid. From rebel papers and informants, we learned that Grierson and his horsemen had plunged southward through Mississippi, breaking up railroads and spreading fear across the state. They had struck the railroad east of Jackson, cut the telegraph, burnt railroad cars, blown up locomotives, and wrecked bridges, trestles, and track. This, i hoped, had severed Vicksburg's and Jackson's communications with Meridian and the eastern Confederacy. With the rebels in northern Mississippi concentrating to capture him when he headed back to Tennessee, Grierson fooled 'em by racing south for Baton Rouge. That drew off two infantry divisions by railroad from Jackson, but Grierson eluded 'em and continued to wreak such havoc that he seemed to be everywhere at once, burning and wrecking everything in his path. Fine job of soldiering. Grierson more than accomplished his mission of drawing attention away from me. He "knocked the heart out of the state," as my informant said.

19. DAVIS

The news from Mississippi aggravated my sickness so badly that at one point I could not speak. While Pemberton dispatched troops to pursue the marauding enemy horsemen, he had left his southern flank vulnerable, and now we had lost Grand Gulf. To make matters worse, the leaders and the citizens of Mississippi bombarded Richmond with complaints. We had stripped the state of its cavalry defenses, they said. We had made the Federal raid possible. And of course they demanded that I relieve Pemberton of command on the grounds of incompetence.

I still had faith in Pemberton and wired him that he could expect whatever was in my power to do. I had already sent him what few reinforcements I'd found at inactive outposts, but warned him that this was all I could do. I also advised him that he needed to repair his relations with the people of Mississippi. "In your situation, much depends on the goodwill and support of the people. To secure this, it is necessary to add conciliation to the discharge of duty. Patience in listening to the suggestions which may not promise much, is sometimes rewarded by gaining useful information. I earnestly desire that, in addition to success, you should enjoy the full credit of your labors."

Meanwhile we had reports from Lee that the enemy was taking the offensive on his front. A strong column of enemy cavalry crossed the upper Rappahannock and the Rapidan and began operating on Lee's communications and threatening Richmond. The tocsin sounded the alarm, and Varina rushed out of the Executive Mansion and returned with Mary Chesnut. The Yankees were within three miles of the city, they said, and young boys and old men were mustering by the thousands in Capitol Square and rushing with muskets to man the trenches protecting the city. Sick though I was, I came down from my chamber, took two loaded pistols from James Chesnut and Custis Lee, and rode to the outer works in a carriage, with Chesnut and Lee following on horseback. The Yankee cavalry, however, did not attack, and that night reinforcements arrived from Petersburg, which ended the danger.

The cavalry raid was but a diversion from the real enemy thrust, which was against Lee on the Rappahannock. A dispatch from the general reported that Federal infantry was on the move above and below Fredericksburg and that he was preparing to meet them wherever they struck. I prayed that God would be with General Lee in the coming battle.

20. LEE

On April twenty-eighth and twenty-ninth, enemy infantry crossed the Rappahannock below Fredericksburg in large numbers and took position under the bank of the river. In a swirling fog, I rode to my command post on the ridge in back of town and studied the enemy position through rifts in the mist. Might be a corps on this side of the river, I thought, but they seemed content to remain within their lodgment. They had the cover of heavy artillery and a powerful supporting force on the opposite shore.

On the twenty-ninth, an alarming dispatch came from Stuart, who was covering our far left. Three enemy corps were moving along the upper Rappahannock north of Fredericksburg. At first I believed they were heading for the railroad, but then Stuart reported that they had crossed the Rappahannock and were marching south for Germanna and Ely's Fords on the Rapidan. I knew that country well: the roads from the fords led to Chancellorsville, nine miles west of Fredericksburg, in the dense thickets of the Wilderness. So that was it: those three corps were trying to get on my left flank.

That night I shifted Anderson's division to Chancellorsville to cover my left, and pondered the intentions of Mr. F. J. Hooker. Was the move on my left a diversion or the main attack? Hooker had left an imposing force below and in front of Fredericksburg—still had powerful guns on Stafford Heights. Perhaps he wanted me to move to my left so that he could mount his main attack from this front. Either way he was obviously trying to trap me between the two wings of his giant army.

Next morning, I swept my glasses over the enemy lines below Fredericksburg and across the river and decided that they looked too peaceable to be contemplating an offensive movement.

"The main attack will come from above," I said, snapping my glasses in their case.

That same morning Anderson reported from Chancellorsville that enemy infantry was advancing on him in strong force. I ordered him to fall back to a new defensive line on the Orange Plank Road near Tabernacle Church. That day, according to our reconnaissance, three enemy corps reached Chancellorsville, which consisted of one chimney mansion of brick and timber, the Chancellor House, which stood in a large clearing. By late afternoon, Hooker himself had arrived and established his headquarters in the mansion. Soon a fourth corps came up, with another on the way. In a short time, Hooker would have seventy to eighty thousand men poised on my left flank, with only one division, Anderson's, opposing them. No question now that the main attack would come on my left. Hooker meant to get across my communications and force a general battle or try to beat me to Richmond.

We had two alternatives: retreat or fight at Chancellorsville. I elected to fight. Had to do it without Longstreet and three of his divisions, too. I would have felt safer if Old Pete had been with me, but there was no time to belabor that. I would also have to divide my under-manned army in the face of a superior enemy. It was a violation of the canons of warfare, but I say again, we could never win unless we were audacious and took risks.

To check the enemy force around Fredericksburg, I left ten thou-sand men under Jubal Early on the heights in back of town. Then I moved the rest of the army, about fifty thousand, west to Anderson's position on the Plank Road.

On May first, with McLaws's division in the lead, the army moved forward on both the Orange Plank and the Orange Turnpike roads, probing for the enemy in the dense woods and tangled under-growth. I was with Jackson when spirited musketry fire broke out on our front, which meant that our skirmishers had encountered the enemy as he moved east from Chancellorsville. I wondered if Hooker had the spirit to bring on a full engagement. He didn't. After a single attack on McLaws, which failed, Hooker's infantry retreated rapidly back to Chancellorsville and took up a defensive position.

Mr. F. J. Hooker offered me the initiative, and I took it. We would attack. My army may have been outnumbered two to one, but I meant to crush the Army of the Potomac once and for all and gain for us our independence. This, I hoped, would be the last battle.

Before dark, I reconnoitered the enemy position and found it a great natural one surrounded on all sides by thick woods choked with vines and brambles, in the midst of which the Federals had con-structed log breastworks, with trees felled in front so as to form an impenetrable abatis. Enemy artillery commanded the adjacent woods and swept the few narrow roads by which we might assault from the front.

A frontal assault, then, was out of the question. So I rode over to Hooker's left flank, hoping that I could attack him there and cut him off from the Rappahannock. But I saw that his flank extended to the river and could not be turned. That left Hooker's right. Dark closed before we could ascertain the extent and strength of that part of his line.

That night, as my army formed in line of battle in front of Chan-cellorsville, I met Jackson in the woods off the Orange Plank Road, and we sat down on a log to decide what to do. The moon was out and cast the woods in deep shadows. I asked what Jackson knew about the enemy right, and he said it didn't matter. He believed that Hooker's abrupt halt and retreat that day pointed to an early withdrawal back across the Rappahannock, but I did not believe he would give up so easily.

While we talked, Jeb Stuart rode up, dressed in a plumed hat, a red cape, and a glittering new uniform decorated with gilt buttons and gold lace. So far, his undermanned cavalry had done a brilliant job of tracking enemy movements, and I was proud of him. Two of his regiments, under my son Rooney, were off tracking the enemy cavalry operating in our rear. Stuart saluted and begged to report that Hooker's right flank west of Chancellorsville was in the air and wide open to an attack.

This was astounding news. "Then we will attack there," I said, "though it means dividing the army again. General Jackson, you will take one wing of the army, assault the enemy's exposed flank, and get into his rear. I will remain in his front to keep him in check and conceal your movement. General Stuart will cover you with his cavalry. I leave the route and execution of your march to your discretion."

He stood and touched a finger to his cap. "My troops will move at four o'clock."

During the night, my topographical engineer and Jackson's chaplain, who had once lived in the area, inspected the routes Jackson might take and discovered an obscure track in the forest that would allow him to get into position out of the enemy's sight. Early the next morning, Jackson prepared to march.

"General Jackson," I said, "what do you propose to make this movement with?"

"My whole corps," he said.

That meant about thirty thousand men. "What will you leave me?" I asked, though I knew the answer.

"The divisions of Anderson and McLaws," he said.

In other words, about fourteen thousand men to hold perhaps fifty thousand Federals in check along a three-mile front. Still, I did not believe Hooker would attack me. He seemed to have suffered a failure of nerve.

"Very well," I said.

As I watched Jackson ride away with his cap down over his eyes, I felt great affection for this man who was my right arm. Such an executive officer the sun never shone on. I had but to show him my design and knew that he would do it. Straight as the needle to the pole he advanced to the execution of my purpose.

Jackson's corps began marching at seven o'clock. All we could do now was wait. It was crucial that Jackson move rapidly by his roundabout route and make his attack while plenty of daylight remained. If he had to delay the attack till next morning, he would lose the element of surprise. Finally, about five-fifteen in the afternoon, the rumble of artillery sounded to the west. "That's Jackson," I said. But barely an hour and a half of daylight was left, and I was concerned that darkness might stall the attack.

Quickly I ordered my line forward to engage the enemy in front of Chancellorsville and prevent men there from being shifted to fight Jackson. Our troops rushed up to the enemy's entrenchments and several of our batteries played with good effect upon his lines until darkness fell. That day, I'm proud to say, fourteen thousand of my soldiers held four times that many Federals in their works.

On Jackson's front, the battle raged furiously until well after dark. The entire horizon over there seemed to be on fire. I wrote a detailed message to President Davis and then fell asleep on the ground, from exhaustion. In the early morning hours, Jackson's signal officer, Captain Wilbourn, woke me to report what had happened on Jackson's front. Jackson had found the exposed enemy corps north of the turnpike and had attacked on a two-mile front, three divisions deep, while the Yankees were cooking supper with their arms stacked. He had routed them and rolled up the entire Federal flank for two miles before the enemy's massed guns finally stopped him at Hazel Grove.

"It's a magnificent victory, sir," Wilbourn said. "General Jackson said that if he'd had another hour of daylight he would have completely destroyed the Federal army." He paused. "General, I also have some bad news to report. After dark, when the moon was up, General Jackson went forward with his staff to reconnoiter the front. On their way back, some of our skirmishers mistook them for the enemy and opened fire. Killed several officers and wounded General Jackson in the arm. He turned the command over to General Stuart and was taken to a field hospital near Old Wilderness Tavern. Dr. McGuire does not think the wounds are serious."

"Captain," I said, "any victory is dearly bought which deprives us of General Jackson's services, even for a short time." The captain started to describe Jackson's wound and the pain he was in, but I stopped him. "Don't talk about it. Thank God it's no worse." I remembered that today was Sunday. Strange that Jackson, one of the most devout men in the army, should be shot on the Sabbath. I rose and told my staff: "These people must be pressed today."

On the second day of battle, Stuart and I attacked the enemy right and center, respectively, and united our army at Hazel Grove after Hooker had abandoned it. This position was the key to the battleground. From it our guns blasted the enemy works around Chancellorsville with deadly enfilading fire, and then my incomparable infantry rushed forward in an all-out attack. Forty thousand screaming Confederates drove seventy thousand Yankees from Chancellorsville, forcing them to retreat to a new defensive line near the Rappahannock. By ten that morning, we were in full possession of the field. When I rode up to Chancellor's House, which was on fire and billowing smoke, my victorious soldiers broke into tumultuous cheering that rang across the clearing. I had never heard them cheer so exultantly.

A message came from Jackson congratulating us for our great victory. The courier reported, however, that Jackson's wounded left arm had been amputated. I frowned in anguish. "Send this to General Jackson," I told a staff officer, and then dictated a reply. "Could I have directed events, I would have chosen for the good of the country to be disabled in your stead."

I told my officers we must complete our work now. I meant to launch a final attack and destroy the Army of the Potomac while it had its back to the river. But before we could deliver a final blow a courier brought dismaying news from Early. The Federals under General Sedgwick had assaulted his lines on Marye's Heights, broken through, and sent him fleeing southward. The victorious Federals were now marching due east on the Plank Road—right into my rear.

This forced me to postpone the attack on Hooker until I could dispose of the new enemy threat. I sent McLaws's division to slow the Federal advance near Salem Church and ordered Early, who had stopped when he found he was not pursued, to move against Sedgwick's left. The next day, I dispatched yet another division against him from Chancellorsville. This left only twenty-eight thousand men to hold the Federal main body, but Hooker showed no sign of doing anything. Leaving Stuart in command at Chancellorsville, I rode back down the Plank Road to direct the attack against Sedgwick myself.

Owing to the broken and irregular nature of the ground, it was almost dark before my troops were in position and launched the attack. They drove the Federals rapidly before them across the Plank Road toward the Rappahannock. But darkness and a dense fog prevented a successful pursuit. The next morning, we found that Sedgwick had escaped across the river.

We returned to Chancellorsville in the midst of a violent storm, and on the sixth, our skirmishers went forward to renew the attack against Hooker. I was preparing to order a general advance that would smash the Army of the Potomac and make our victory complete when General Pender galloped up.

"Hooker's gone," he said. "His works are empty."

I was so frustrated I lost my temper. "That is the way you young men always do. You allow those people to get away. I tell you what to do, but you don't do it!" Pender said nothing. "Go after them," I said bitterly, "and damage them all you can."

But it was too late. Hooker's entire army had escaped across the river during the storm of yesterday and the darkness of the night. Furious that we had not destroyed the Army of the Potomac, I led my forces back to the heights of Fredericksburg in a heavy rain. There I wrote President Davis a report of the battle, but did not mention that it was a victory. That was how unhappy I was.

I did not know the enemy's casualties, but assumed they were very high. Still, he could replace his losses from the endless supply of manpower available at the North. We would have far more difficulty replacing ours. More than 1,500 of our men lay dead, and 11,500 more were wounded or missing. Twenty-two percent of my men lost in a single battle! I hoped the government and the people would understand that *this* was the price of winning victories with an understrengthed army.

I was most anxious about General Jackson. An ambulance had borne him to Tuiney Station, where his wife, Anna, and his child joined him. Doctor McGuire feared that he had pneumonia and was not optimistic about his chances. This news threw my headquarters into gloom. I told a courier: "Give General Jackson my affectionate regards, and tell him to hurry and get well, and come back to me as soon as he can. He has lost his left arm, but I have lost my right." Surely, I thought, General Jackson will recover. God will not take him from us, now that we need him so much.

A few days later, as I was pondering a dispatch from Richmond, word came that Jackson had died. "It is a terrible loss," I wrote Custis. "I do not know how to replace him. Any victory would be dear at such a cost. But God's will be done."

* * *

The dispatch from Richmond concerned Vicksburg. Pemberton was in trouble and in desperate need of reinforcements, and Seddon, the secretary of war, wanted me to send him one of my divisions. I wrote Seddon that if I did so the division would not reach Pemberton until the end of May. If anything was to be done in that quarter, I said, it would be over by that time, since the climate in June would force the enemy to retire. The uncertainty of the arrival of my division and the uncertainty of its application argued against sending it. There was another reason not to detach it. From reports in the northern papers, I calculated Hooker's aggregate force at more than 159,000 men. "You can see the odds against us," I said, "and decide whether the line of Virginia is more in danger than the line of the Mississippi."

I wrote a similar letter to President Davis, informing him that from the northern papers it appeared that the administration at Washington intended to reinforce Hooker by 18,000 men. "It would seem that Virginia is to be the theater of action," I said, "and this army, if possible, ought to be reinforced."

21. LINCOLN

For me, the days surrounding the battle of Chancellorsville were the most anxious days of the war to date. I spent most of my time in the telegraph office, snapping up dispatches as they ticked in from Hooker's headquarters. The telegraph that alerted me to another possible defeat came on May third, saying that a great battle had been fought and that there was "no success for us" and "if only Sedgwick could have gotten up here." I was pretty sure Hooker had been licked, and I was nervous and harassed beyond words to describe. My hunch proved right. On the sixth Hooker reported that he'd lost the battle and was back at Falmouth.

Back at the Executive Mansion, I showed the telegram to young Brooks and walked up and down the room with my hands locked behind my back. "My God, my God. What will the country say? What will the country say? I don't know what condition the army is in. Don't know if it's safe. Halleck's coming with a carriage—we're going down there. My God, my God."

We went down to Falmouth and looked the army over. It was all in one piece and looked safe, and anyway a heavy rain made it impossible for Lee to attack right away. With Hooker absent, I had a candid talk with his corps commanders in the mansion that served as his headquarters. John Reynolds was there, Sumner, Darius Couch, Dan Sickles, George Meade, O. O. Howard, John Sedgwick. Several of them urged me to sack Hooker. Said he was unfit, said he'd lost his nerve at Chancellorsville and given up the initiative—virtually handed it to Lee. Said he'd been knocked senseless on the second day, when a shell struck his headquarters and part of a roof had fallen on him. When he came to, he ordered a retreat when most of the corps commanders wanted to stay and fight. I heard 'em out and talked to Hooker, and decided that nobody could be blamed for the defeat and left him in command. But its effect at home and abroad, I said, would hurt us more than any other defeat.

When we returned to Washington, hospital steamers were tied up at the crowded docks, unloading the wounded from Chancellorsville. I couldn't bear to look at those torn and bleeding men. I didn't know what our total casualties were—knew they were high—and for what purpose? to what end? Back at the Executive Mansion, I told Mary it was dark, dark everywhere.

For days, the capital crawled with rumors. I heard people talking on my way back and forth to the telegraph office. "You hear the news?" they said. "Stanton's resigned. Halleck's been arrested." "I heard McClellan's been put back in command. Coming down on a special train from New York." Had that been true, it would have pleased the Copperheads.

What to do with the Potomac Army now? At first I thought a renewal of the offensive might restore its morale, but then changed my mind. Wrote Hooker I wouldn't complain if he did no more for a time than to keep the enemy at bay and out of mischief, by menacing him with occasional cavalry raids. "Still, if in your own clear judgment, you can renew the attack successfully, I do not mean to restrain you." I added: "Bearing upon this last point, I must tell you I have some painful intimations that some of your corps and division commanders are not giving you their entire confidence." To tell you the truth, I didn't have full confidence in Hooker either. But I wasn't going to throw a loaded gun away because it had failed to fire the first time. I was going to give it a second chance.

The man I had full confidence in was Grant. Dana's reports from the Mississippi convinced me Grant was not only sober, but the best

general we had in the field. I haven't talked much about his campaign—too busy going on about Hooker and the Army of the
Potomac, which caused me the most anxiety. I tell you now, I was
happy when Grant marched downriver—it was what I wanted him
to do all along. Now that he had Grand Gulf, I thought he ought to
move south and connect with Banks for a joint operation against
Port Hudson, the other rebel stronghold on the Mississippi. Once we
controlled the Mississippi above and below Vicksburg, the city would
fall in due course.

22. GRANT

My original plan was to send one of my corps to cooperate with
Banks against Port Hudson. Then Banks's force would join me in the
campaign against Vicksburg. But I figured it would take a month for
my corps to go down there, help take Port Hudson, and get back. To
wait a month would cost me the element of surprise. Give the enemy
time to gather his scattered forces and mass 'em against me. I
couldn't lose the time. So I canceled the Port Hudson operation and
resolved to operate against Vicksburg as soon as Sherman was up.

Once Sherman joined us, we'd have forty-three thousand men
and 120 guns. The country would provide all the forage and fresh
beef and mutton we'd need. Other supplies—hard bread, coffee, and
salt—would come from Milliken's Bend through Grand Gulf, which
would serve as my advance base. This was a long and precarious
route, but I was confident that between the country and the trains
we would have enough supplies to campaign.

On May seventh Sherman crossed the river with two of his divisions and moved to Hankinson's Ferry, where he linked up with
McClernand's rear troops. Sherman's third division, under Frank
Blair, was on its way with a train of two hundred wagons loaded
with supplies. Blair and the train would follow in the rear of the
advancing army, and the wagons would return to Grand Gulf for
bread, coffee, and salt when we needed them. I was so eager to get
going that I already had the rest of the army on the march, heading
northeast for Edwards Station, on the Jackson-Vicksburg railroad
east of the Big Black River.

According to our intelligence, Pemberton had moved his headquarters from Jackson to Vicksburg and had his army out on the railroad to Jackson, holding a line west of the Big Black, which ran southwest-northeast across the railroad. He was trying to cover Jackson and defend Vicksburg at the same time. I aimed to concentrate at Edwards Station, east of the Big Black, attack and defeat him there, then capture or invest Vicksburg. But to confuse Pemberton as to our true destination, my two lead corps marched on separate routes, McClernand hugging the Big Black, while McPherson marched directly toward Raymond, farther to the east, in the direction of Jackson. That would keep Pemberton guessing as to whether we were heading for Jackson or his line on the Big Black.

I rode with Sherman behind McPherson and McClernand. Fred was with me and having the time of his life. As our columns moved inland, foraging parties swept the countryside on both sides of the line of march. They ransacked every farm and plantation, every flour mill and storehouse, and returned with an abundance of corn and cornmeal, hogs, sheep, goats, cattle, turkeys, geese, ducks, and chickens. Many Mississippians fled before our advancing army, and their Negroes swarmed to us on foot, on horseback, and in all manner of conveyances abandoned by their masters. We didn't want the Negroes to slow us down and discouraged them from following us.

From the field, I sent dispatches to Banks and Halleck explaining my change of plans. Asked Banks to join me or send me all the force he could spare. Told Halleck: "I shall communicate with Grand Gulf no more except it becomes necessary to send a train with heavy escort. You may not hear from me for several days."

23. DAVIS

Pemberton informed us that Grant might strike at Jackson first and then turn west to attack Vicksburg along the railroad. "If the enemy moves on Jackson," Pemberton said, "I will advance to meet them." In anticipation of such a move, Pemberton sent a brigade to Raymond. But he was pretty sure that Grant's column advancing toward Raymond was a diversion and that the main attack would be made against Pemberton's line on the Big Black. He insisted he was badly outnumbered and begged us for reinforcements.

We asked Lee if he could spare a division, but of course he said he could not and himself called for reinforcements. All our commanders were crying for more men, more men, as if the Conscription Bureau were not doing everything in its power to provide them. To help Pemberton, I wired Governor Pettus of Mississippi requesting him to use all practicable means to get every man and boy capable of aiding their country in its need to turn out, mounted or on foot, with whatever weapons they had, to aid the soldiers in driving the invader from our soil.

Pemberton's dispatches left me in doubt as to Grant's objective, the size of his force, and the efficiency of Pemberton's measures to meet him. Since Grant was moving into the interior, his supply line must be long and vulnerable, and I suggested that Pemberton try to cut it. Of course he lacked sufficient cavalry—the sending of Van Dorn to Tennessee had been a blunder—but even infantry ought to be able to break Grant's extended communications.

What alarmed me, even more than Pemberton's dispatches, was Johnston's inaction. He remained at his headquarters in Tullahoma, Tennessee, in apparent unconcern for Pemberton's danger in Mississippi except for an occasional vague order. Johnston was the departmental commander—he ought to be on the ground in Mississippi, directing operations himself. His behavior caused me intense anxiety, and that and my worries about Pemberton brought on coughing spells that left me gagging. Worse still, we received reports that prejudice and malignity had so undermined the confidence of the troops at Vicksburg in their commander as to threaten disaster. By the ninth, I could tolerate it no longer. I ordered Johnston to go to Mississippi at once, join Pemberton, and assume chief command of all the forces in the field. I authorized him to take three thousand men from the Army of Tennessee and five thousand from Charleston. Another four thousand would follow soon, I said, but I feared no more could be spared to him.

But the situation in Mississippi threatened to deteriorate before Johnston could get to Jackson by rail. On May twelfth, the commander of our force at Raymond reported that he had been fighting a large body of enemy infantry all day and that he was retreating to Jackson. What did a large body of infantry mean? Was it possible that Pemberton was wrong and that Grant's objective was Jackson and not Pemberton's line on the Big Black? If so, and he reached Jackson first, it would prevent Johnston from effecting a junction with Pemberton. We awaited news from Mississippi in a state of growing alarm.

24. GRANT

Didn't like it when the rebels in Raymond fell back to Jackson. Seemed to me they were concentrating a considerable force there. We learned from prisoners and our scouts that reinforcements were arriving in Jackson every day. Heard, too, that Joe Johnston was on his way to assume command. I knew Johnston, had respect for him as a soldier. All this put things in a new light. If I attacked Pemberton on the Big Black, Johnston would have a force of unknown strength in my rear. Course, if I advanced against Jackson, Pemberton could attack my left flank. But I didn't think much of Pemberton. Seemed to me he was committed to the defensive and wouldn't do anything if I moved rapidly against Jackson. So I canceled the plan to concentrate at Edwards Station and ordered the entire army to march on Jackson at once. I aimed to destroy the enemy forces there before Pemberton could react, then turn and whip him.

That night I did something I seldom did during a campaign. I was dead tired and remembered that Colonel Duff of my staff had half a barrel of whiskey from Governor Yates. Went to Duff's tent and asked for a shot. He handed me a canteen full of whiskey, and I poured a cup, downed it, and poured another. If Rawlins had found out, he would've cussed me from one end to the other. Duff poured some whiskey for himself and proposed a toast.

"Success to our campaign, and confusion to the whole Confederacy."

Next day, Sherman marched directly toward Jackson while McPherson advanced by way of the railroad, wrecking track and burning bridges as he went. He also captured a dispatch that confirmed what I'd thought about Pemberton: he'd ordered one of his commanders to assume a defensive position at Edwards Station just east of the Big Black. To keep Pemberton on the defensive and out of the coming battle, I ordered McClernand, who was bringing up our rear, to keep up the appearance of moving toward Edwards Station.

On May fourteenth Sherman and McPherson converged on Jackson in the rain and prepared to launch a coordinated assault against the enemy entrenchments southwest and west of town.

25. DAVIS

"*I am too late.*" That was what Johnston reported when he reached Jackson on May thirteenth and found the invaders between him and Pemberton and advancing rapidly on the capital. He ordered Pemberton to attack the enemy from behind, "if practicable," and Pemberton answered that he would move at once with his "whole available force, about sixteen thousand." I wired Johnston: "Anxiously wait for further information as to dispositions against the enemy. Have the reinforcements arrived?"

The next day, I was seriously thinking about rushing part of Lee's army to Mississippi when the general himself arrived in Richmond for a conference with me and Secretary of War Seddon. I had called Lee down so that we could discuss the military situation, and as we met in the Cabinet room of the White House, he looked pale and thin, the result, I supposed, of his illness before Chancellorsville. I personally congratulated him for that magnificent victory in defiance of all odds. Then I explained the critical situation in Mississippi and raised the question of sending part of his army there, which I knew was a touchy subject with him.

"Your Excellency," he said, "may I propose something else. If my army can be strengthened by the return of all my detached units and by additional reinforcements, I could invade the North again and campaign in Pennsylvania. You know, your Excellency, that my troops are desperately short of rations. A campaign in Pennsylvania would allow us to subsist on the enemy countryside. It would draw Hooker out of Virginia and cause panic in Washington. It would break up their plans to renew the fighting on the Rappahannock. I see an offensive in Pennsylvania as an aggressive application of our defensive system. I've talked with Longstreet about the plan, and he agrees with me."

"I spoke to General Longstreet just over a week ago," Seddon said, "and he agreed with us that troops from your army ought to be sent west."

"That was before I saw him and explained my plan of operations. He said that plan changed the aspect of things as far as he was concerned."

"Do you propose to give battle in Pennsylvania?" I asked.

"Not a general battle, if I can avoid it. But if I have to fight, I will. Mr. President, the most important aspect of the campaign is its political repercussions. I believe it will strengthen the northern peace party and discredit the Republican leaders. Shake northern confidence in them so badly that they will be forced to sue for peace. In short, Mr. President, the campaign could very well win the war for us."

"When could you start such a campaign?" Seddon asked.

"Early June."

"We could lose Vicksburg before then," I said. "If we lose Vicksburg, we'll lose the Mississippi and probably the war."

"That is the risk we take, Mr. President. But if you send part of my army to Mississippi, I shall be forced to fall back to the defenses of Richmond. Hooker would follow and put the capital under siege. If that happens, it would be a matter of time before the capital would fall."

I had serious reservations about General Lee's proposal, still thought that sending reinforcements from his army to Mississippi was the wiser move. But General Lee's confidence and fighting mood were difficult to ignore. The next day, I presented his plan to the Cabinet, and all of the secretaries but one were enthusiastic about an invasion of the North. I think they were in awe of Lee and believed he could not possibly fail after the miraculous victories he had won for us.

The sole dissenter was Postmaster John Reagan of Texas. With great passion, he proposed that Lee only threaten to invade the North, then dispatch twenty-five to thirty thousand of his men to Mississippi. Our augmented forces there would crush Grant and then drive the invader from Tennessee. I thought this idea had considerable merit, but could not bring myself to reject Lee and therefore sided with the majority of the Cabinet. General Lee would invade the North.

That same day, the fifteenth, we heard that the Yankees had occupied Jackson, and dispatches from Mississippi the next day confirmed it. Johnston had abandoned the capital on the fourteenth and retreated northeast to Canton. He had given Jackson up just one day after he had arrived! *One day!* I was furious that Johnston had not even attempted a junction with Pemberton and damned that accursed tendency of his to retreat, always retreat. I sent Johnston an angry telegram: "Do not perceive why a junction was not attempted, which would have made our force nearly equal to the estimated strength of the enemy, and might have resulted in his total defeat."

Johnston's behavior convinced me that I had made the correct decision in not sending him part of Lee's army. If our fate had to rest on one of the two generals, I preferred that it be on Lee.

Pemberton meanwhile had not carried out Johnston's orders to attack the invader in the rear. Instead he had crossed the Big Black and moved east to Edwards Station, with plans to march south of the railroad and cut the enemy's line of communications, as I had earlier suggested that he do. "The object," he explained, "is to force him to attack me, as I do not consider my force sufficient to justify an attack on the enemy position, or to attempt to cut my way to Jackson."

In this Pemberton was entirely correct. Cutting the invader's supply line was the best way to drive him back. Still, it filled me with the most intense anxiety that Johnston was off to the northeast, doing nothing, while Pemberton moved to the southeast, alone, in hopes of inducing the enemy to attack with his superior numbers. I prayed to God in heaven that disaster was not about to befall us in Mississippi.

26. GRANT

Amazed me that the rebels gave up Jackson so easily. Halfhearted ain't the word for the resistance they put up. Some desultory fire and then they skeedaddled. As I rode into the city with Fred and my staff, we saw white flags hanging out of civilian houses and a large rebel flag floating over the statehouse. Fred said he wanted to capture the enemy flag and trotted ahead. Our troops whooped it up in the streets, and crowds of happy Negroes danced around and shouted with joy and told us how glad they was to see us. We came to a hotel whose original name had been the United States Hotel, but the owner had painted "Confederate Hotel" over the sign.

We dismounted and went inside and found a bunch of scared civilians who begged me not to destroy Jackson. Told 'em I had to destroy everything that belonged to the Confederacy and all stores that could be used by the enemy army, but I would try to protect private property. In a minute Fred came running in, so excited he couldn't stand it. Didn't have the flag, a cavalryman got it first, but he had a pipe he'd confiscated from the governor's room.

In the hotel, I conferred with Sherman and McPherson about our next move. We'd learned from prisoners that Johnston was twenty miles northeast of us, at Canton. I was glad he hadn't retreated northwest—would have made it easier for him to join Pemberton.

"I figure Johnston and Pemberton will try to link up north of us, cross the Big Black, and beat us into Vicksburg," I said. "We can't let that happen. McPherson, you will move against Pemberton as early tomorrow morning as possible. McClernand will march up from Raymond and connect with you at Bolton on the railroad. Sherman, you will stay behind and destroy Jackson as a rail and manufacturing center and then follow us. Burn the depot, the railroads, bridges, workshops, arsenals, factories, and anything else that might be used to support enemy forces. The government wants us to wage a harsh war. I aim to oblige."

"It'll be a Goddamned pleasure," Sherman said. "Time we broke the spirit of these people."

That night I slept in the room Johnston was said to have occupied during his one night in town. Kept waking up from the noise in the streets. Negroes and poor whites were vandalizing stores and abandoned homes, and making off with all the goods they could carry. Sherman said some of our troops were involved in the pillaging, and he stopped it.

Next day, McPherson moved west along the railroad, and I followed with Fred and my headquarters staff. Behind us, columns of smoke rose over Jackson, indicating that Sherman was at his work. Next morning, we came across two employees of the railroad who said they had passed through Pemberton's army during the night, at Edwards Station. That put him east of the Big Black. I sent word of the enemy position to McClernand, who was converging on the railroad ahead of us. Told him to feel the enemy but not to bring on a general engagement until the entire army was up. Sent a courier back with instructions for Sherman to join us with all possible speed.

We rode ahead and overtook McPherson's advance, which was stalled behind the wagon train of McClernand's lead division. I yelled at the drivers, "Get your teams off the road," and then heard gunfire ahead of us. We hurried to the front and saw McClernand's lead division drawing up in line of battle. Commander was A. P. Hovey, an Indiana lawyer in his forties, nervous man, irascible. He pointed and said the rebels were drawn up there, on a narrow ridge south of the railroad, place called Champion Hill. I took out my glass and saw that it was very strong ground: steep, with thick woods on the crest. Maybe twenty thousand rebels up there. Hovey was itching to get after 'em, but I held him back. McClernand was only two miles away with his other three divisions, and McPherson was marching up fast. We would wait for them.

McPherson and his lead division, Logan's, soon joined us, and we waited for McClernand. I sent him orders by courier to push forward at once and attack, but he didn't show. Time was wasting and it irritated me no end. "How long does it take to march two miles?" I asked in disgust. Gave tactical command to McPherson, and rode over to the first spur of Champion Hill, lit a cigar, and watched as two of our batteries lay down an enfilading fire and ten thousand troops rushed the ridge, yelling infernally. Rebel guns on the crest exploded in answer, and fighting broke out all along the line.

The battle seesawed back and forth—we'd drive the rebels from the crest, they'd counterattack and retake it. When more of McPherson's troops arrived on the field, I sent 'em forward myself and shifted other units to reinforce a threatened part of our line. Was under fire myself. Leaned against my horse and smoked under fire. Finally, two of McClernand's divisions appeared on the enemy's southern flank, and McPherson's infantry struck the crest again. Routed the rebels this time. Sent them in headlong retreat back toward the Big Black.

I saw McClernand on the next ridge with one of his divisions and rode over to him. "Since your troops are fresh," I told him sarcastically, "you will lead the pursuit." McClernand's boys chased 'em clear to Edwards Station before darkness stopped the pursuit. Here they found huge quantities of abandoned rebel stores and a train of cars loaded with ammunition, which was on fire. The fleeing rebels had put the torch to it and to a cotton gin, and the flames lit up the night.

My staff and I were with the pursuit, and in the excitement of victory we somehow got ahead of the lead troops, were out there by ourselves in the direction of the Big Black, and had to double back to where the advance was making camp. We were all happy that night, felt we had won a tremendous victory, thought the battle of Vicksburg had been fought. No way now that Johnston and Pemberton could unite—we were between 'em, and had Pemberton on the run back toward Vicksburg. My plan now was for McClernand and McPherson to advance on the city from the east while Sherman marched north of us, crossed the Big Black at Bridgeport, seized Walnut Hills northwest of Vicksburg, and opened up the Yazoo so we could bring in supplies from Memphis.

At dawn on the seventeenth, we resumed the pursuit and found the rebels in force at the railroad bridge on both sides of the Big Black, where it bent around like a horseshoe. On the east side of the river, facing us, they had rifle pits and an infantry parapet. It was a strong position, but I was confident my army could carry it and drive the enemy so closely that he would not be able to destroy the bridge.

While our troops were coming up and forming into line, an officer rode up, introduced himself as William Dwight of General Banks's staff, and handed me a telegram from Halleck. I think Dwight had come up to Memphis by the river and got the telegraph there. Anyway it was addressed to me. "If possible the forces of yourself & of Genl Banks should be united between Vicskburg & Port Hudson so as to attack these places separately with the combined forces. The same thing has been urged upon Genl Banks."

"It's too late," I told Dwight. "If Halleck knew I was here, he wouldn't have given the order." Dwight argued that I had to obey the order, wouldn't let up on it. I told him it was ridiculous; we had Pemberton on the run and Port Hudson was now an easy target. I wasn't going to call off the campaign now. "Go right ahead with Port Hudson," I told him, "and I'll send five thousand men after I get Vicksburg."

While we were arguing, cheering broke out on our right. I turned and saw Lawler forming his brigade for an attack while newly arrived troops urged him on. Lawler's a big Irishman from Shawneetown, Illinois, a three-hundred-pounder, so big around the belly he had to wear his sword across his shoulder. When it comes to plain hard fighting, I would rather trust Mike Lawler than any of 'em.

"Let's go, boys!" he cried, and more than a thousand men rushed forward to assault the rebel parapet. Stirring sight. Inspired the other troops. One officer cried: "Let's get the damned rebels!" And they surged forward after Lawler. I mounted my horse and rode in the direction of the attack. Saw no more of the officer who'd delivered the dispatch from Halleck.

By the time I got to our right, Lawler's boys had carried the enemy works and driven the rebs across the river. They set the bridge on fire and fled down the road to Vicksburg, leaving behind near two thousand prisoners and eighteen guns. We'd won another victory and it was all Lawler's. He made that attack on his own, no orders from me or anybody else. Saw the enemy and went after 'em. Mike Lawler was my kind of soldier.

My engineers built three pontoon bridges across the Big Black, and by the eighteenth McClernand's and McPherson's divisions were filing across the river and heading for Vicksburg. Meanwhile, to the

north, Sherman had reached Bridgeport and was poised to march on
Walnut Hills. I rode up there on the seventeenth, and that night we
sat on a log together and watched as his troops crossed the river on
a pontoon bridge by the light of bonfires.

Next day, we rode toward Vicksburg in advance of the troops.
My first concern was to secure a base of supplies on the Yazoo River
above Vicksburg. Sherman's line of march led to the very point on
Walnut Hills occupied by the rebels last December, when he'd been
repulsed. We were so impatient we rode well up ahead with the
advanced skirmishers, and found that the rebels had abandoned
their fortifications on Walnut Hills save for some detached works
along the crest of the hill. Enemy infantry there fired on our party
and bullets whistled about us pretty thick for a short while, but the
Johnnies lit out when the body of Sherman's troops approached.
Sherman and I lit cigars and rode over to the edge of the bluff, which
overlooked the thickly wooded swamplands of Chickasaw Bayou.
Sherman had the pleasure of looking down from the very spot he'd
tried to take by assault last December.

He turned to me and said: "Until this moment I never thought
your expedition a success. I never could see the end clearly till now.
But this is a campaign, Grant. This is a success if we never take the
town."

In nineteen days, we'd marched near two hundred miles, fought
and won five battles, captured and burnt Jackson, divided Johnston
and Pemberton, driven Pemberton into the defenses of Vicksburg,
and opened up the Yazoo as our supply line to Memphis. We'd
killed and wounded several thousand rebels and captured more than
6,000 prisoners and sixty-one field pieces and twenty-seven heavy
cannon. My total casualties came to about 4,500.

Now I meant to take Vicksburg. McClernand and McPherson
had also arrived, and by the next day, May nineteenth, we had the
city nearly invested with forty-three thousand men. They were in
high spirits and raring to finish off the battered rebel army, which
occupied a line of fortifications seven or eight miles long on the
ridges east of town. Their works bristled with muskets and artillery
that commanded the narrow hollows in their front, and abatis—the
sharp points of felled trees—guarded the whole length of their line.

Strong works, but I thought the rebels were stunned and demoralized, so I ordered an immediate frontal assault by the whole army.
At the cry of bugles, the infantry swept forward across the broken
ground, a regular outfit out in front with banners streaming in the

wind. This was the First Battalion, Thirteenth U.S. Infantry, in Giles Smith's brigade of Sherman's corps. They dashed through a storm of canister and shell, men falling and flying apart, arms and legs spinning in the air, and reached the rebel works first and planted the first Union flag on the parapets. But the assaults were poorly organized and coordinated, and enemy fire was deadly all along the line, and the attacking columns fell back, repulsed. The regular outfit lost almost half its men that day, in a charge that Sherman said was "unequaled in the army." They were so proud of what they'd done that they sewed FIRST AT VICKSBURG on their flags.

I wanted to avoid a siege because it would give Johnston time to gather reinforcements and march to the relief of Vicksburg. Meant to take the city by assault and then drive Johnston from the state. Over the next two days, we strengthened our positions, scouted the enemy works for weak points (didn't find any), and opened communications with Porter's river flotilla. At my request, Porter took his gunboats and floating mortars down the Mississippi and at noon on the twentieth he started shelling Vicksburg and its river batteries with one hundred guns.

The army was now ready to attack from the east. I ordered simultaneous assaults on all parts of the line on May twenty-second, to commence with an artillery bombardment at ten o'clock in the morning. To ensure a coordinated attack, all three corps commanders set their watches by mine. I took a position on a high point in the center of our line, near McPherson's front, where I had a commanding view of the battleground. Across the way I could see Vicksburg, smoking and blazing from Porter's bombardment.

At ten o'clock, the signal gun sounded and my two hundred guns opened fire on the rebel works while Porter's mortars and gunboats blasted away from the river. The rebel artillery returned the fire, and the roar of the guns rolled across the ridges like constant thunder. The air was filled with missiles of every description, shrieking and hissing as they fell on the rival lines. At the prescribed hour, our guns fell silent and bugles sounded the attack. Thousands of blue-clad infantry, formed into storming columns, charged forward at quick time with fixed bayonets, Sherman's boys attacking north along Graveyard Road, McPherson's assaulting in the center and McClernand's to the south. A continual sheet of flame danced along the enemy parapets, and musketry and deadly canister ripped the assaulting columns to pieces. The enemy fire was so hot—some men said it was the hottest they'd ever faced—and the ground so hard to cross that many of the troops took cover under the brows of the hills. Here and there in the smoke and thunder of the guns, formless groups of our infantry made it across the ditches in front of the enemy bastions and succeeded in planting their flags on the outer slopes. A few even reached the summit, where they were shot or pulled down as prisoners. All along the line, the assaults wavered and broke under that merciless fire, and the survivors took shelter in the ditches in front of the enemy bastions.

We'd failed. The rebel works were too strong to be carried. I was prepared, reluctantly, to settle for a siege when a series of strange messages came from McClernand. He stated "positively and unequivocally"—I quote him—that his troops had seized and still held two of the enemy's forts. He thought they could break through, but they were hard-pressed and needed support, so he asked me to have Sherman and McPherson renew their assaults as diversions from his own.

This amazed me. I'd watched McClernand's attack and thought his entire line had been repulsed. From where I stood, I had a good view of his front—better than he had himself—and I couldn't see that his men had possession of any forts. But suspicious as I was, I couldn't ignore McClernand. Couldn't overlook any possibility to seize the enemy works and carry the day. So I sent one of McPherson's divisions to reinforce McClernand. Then on my orders Sherman and McPherson mounted vigorous assaults as diversions.

Turned out McClernand's men hadn't seized any forts at all. Horse-faced bastard made me mad as a hornet. His wild claims had needlessly prolonged the battle and the killing. Our losses, which came to about three thousand dead, wounded, and missing, would have been a good deal less if McClernand had kept his senses. I wrote Halleck that McClernand was entirely unfit as a corps commander both on the march and the battlefield, and the next month I relieved him. Didn't care if he was a friend of the president's.

So we settled for a siege. Completed the investment, built our own fortifications, and brought down reinforcements and field and siege guns from Memphis till we had more than seventy thousand men and eighty-nine batteries. Had the guns arranged so they could lay down a converging, direct, enfilading, and reverse fire on the opposing line. The guns shelled the city and the enemy works day and night. To guard against a relief effort from the east, Sherman took thirty-five thousand men and set up a defensive line that stretched from the Big Black railroad bridge to Haynes Bluff on the Yazoo.

I wrote Halleck that the fall of the city and the capture of the garrison was only a question of time.

27. LINCOLN

A question of time? How long would that be? I tell you, I was apprehensive about Vicksburg. We'd been through too many campaigns when we seemed on the verge of victory, only to lose it all. I assured myself that this was Grant, not McClellan, not Buell, not Burnside or Hooker. Told myself, Grant had just conducted one of the most brilliant campaigns in the world and now had hold of Vicksburg with bulldog grip and would not let go.

But I remained apprehensive. I longed for complete victory at Vicksburg, so that I could tell the country: *here at last is a real triumph, the fall of a mighty river garrison and the destruction of an enemy army, which puts the key of the Mississippi in our pocket. We're on the way now. We can win. There is hope.*

On the map in my office, blue pins surrounded Vicksburg and Port Hudson, Louisiana, which Banks also had under siege. Up in Tennessee a blue pin was stuck in Nashville. It hadn't moved since I put it there in January. That pin was Rosecrans. He was also showing the peculiarities of a stationary engine. I couldn't figure out what was wrong with him. He should've cooperated with Grant by clearing the rebels out of middle Tennessee and Chattanooga. That hadn't happened. While Grant was running all around Mississippi, beating up every rebel force that got in his way, Rosecrans sat in Nashville, complaining to reporters that somebody in Washington— meaning Stanton and Halleck—was out to destroy him. Oh he professed only the highest respect for me, but Halleck and Stanton, he said, were his bitter enemies. Meanwhile he bombarded us with demands for more men and supplies and even accused the government of deliberately withholding them.

Finally, I'd had a bellyful and told him in so many words, through Halleck: *If you don't move, the rebels will shift troops from Tennessee to break Grant's siege. Move and fight the enemy in your front, or part of your force will go to Grant.* Back came an unctuous reply that it was dangerous to fight two battles at the same time—it violated a cardinal maxim of war—and that he would wait for the business of Vicksburg to be settled before he took the offensive. Halleck reminded him that the maxim applied to one army, not two. But Halleck refused to order him forward if he wasn't ready, so I stepped in. Through Halleck, I sent Rosecrans an ultimatum: *Are you going to advance immediately? Yes or no?* Eight days later he moved out of Nashville and fought the rebel Army of Tennessee at Middleton and Big Springs Ranch. On that day, Grant's guns were still shelling Vicksburg.

28. DAVIS

The disastrous turn of events in Mississippi and the behavior of General Johnston left us in the blackest despair. When Pemberton fell back inside Vicksburg, Johnston advised him to abandon the city in order to save the troops. "No!" I cried when I read that dispatch. "*Vicksburg must not be abandoned.*" I was relieved when Pemberton declared Vicksburg "the most important point in the Confederacy," which it was, and vowed to hold it as long as possible against the investing army.

The invaders then subjected the city and its civilian population to the most brutal and merciless artillery bombardment. To shelter the civilians, caves had to be dug in the hills on which the city is built, and many of the women and children lived in them throughout the siege. They were forced to eat horse and mule meat and spoiled bread. From these places of refuge, heroically facing the danger of shells incessantly bursting over the streets, gentlewomen hourly went forth to the many hospitals to nurse the sick and the wounded and to soothe the dying.

The only hope for Vicksburg was for Johnston, who was still at Canton, to attack the invading army from the rear while Pemberton attacked from the front. Johnston, however, could not do that without reinforcements, and we exhorted the people of Mississippi to join him for the relief of Vicksburg, but to our dismay they failed to come forth. We did reinforce Johnston from other points more heavily than we considered altogether safe, which brought his force to twenty-three thousand effectives. But he argued that this was not enough, that he must have seven thousand more men in order to carry out a successful attack. I wired him that we could not hope for numerical equality and that he must move without delay with the force he had.

I was in such anxiety about the fate of Vicksburg that I wanted to go out there and take the field myself. But my health would not permit it. My anxiety rose higher still when Johnston reported, in mid-June, that reinforcements estimated at thirty thousand were moving downriver to join the invading army, and that an attack by him was impossible without heavy reinforcements.

The situation in Mississippi was so desperate that we urged him to draw troops from Tennessee in his capacity as departmental commander, but Johnston refused. "I have not considered myself commanding in Tennessee since assignment here," he telegraphed, "and should not have felt authorized to take troops from that department after having been informed by the Executive that no more could be spared. To take from Bragg a force which would make this army fit to oppose Grant, would involve yielding Tennessee. It is for the government to decide between this state and Tennessee."

This was stupefying. How in God's name could Johnston believe himself *not* in command in Tennessee? I telegraphed him that his transfer to Mississippi had not relieved him of command in Tennessee and asked him when had I ever written him that no more troops could be removed from there. When he did not respond, I asked the question again. He replied that he had meant the secretary of war, that Seddon had told him that. I did not believe it and to prove Johnston wrong I had all the correspondence with him brought to me from the War Office. I ran my inflamed eye over each of them, and then wired Johnston that there was nothing in the correspondence that could possibly give him the impression that he was no longer in command in Tennessee.

Johnston telegraphed us that saving Vicksburg was hopeless. "My God," I cried, "is the man a coward?" At my instruction, Seddon replied: "Your telegram grieves and alarms us. Vicksburg must not be lost, at least without a struggle. The interest and honor of the Confederacy forbid it. I rely on you still to avert the loss. If better resources do not offer, you must hazard an attack. It may be made in concert with the garrison, if practicable, but otherwise without. By day or night, as you think best."

Seddon followed that telegram with a letter. "Only my conviction of almost imperative necessity for action induces the official dispatch I have just sent you," he told Johnston. "On every ground I have great deference to your judgment and military genius, but I feel it right to share, if need be to take, the responsibility and leave you free to follow the most desperate course the occasion may demand. Rely upon it, the eyes and hopes of the whole Confederacy are upon you, and the full confidence that you will act, and with the sentiment that it *were better to fail nobly daring, than, through prudence even, to be inactive.* I rely on you for all possible to save Vicksburg."

But it was all in vain. Shortly afterward, the enemy army in Tennessee took the offensive against Bragg, which meant that no more troops could be drawn from him in any event. And without reinforcements, Johnston adamantly refused to attack Grant.

The only hope for Vicksburg was the success of General Lee. But we were having difficulties with him as well, for he also asked for reinforcements, even to the point of stripping the defenses of Richmond. We sent him what could be spared, but with the strong Federal presence at Yorktown and other places on the Virginia and North Carolina coasts, we could not afford to deprive Richmond of adequate defense. The loss of Richmond would negate anything Lee might achieve in the North. Still, I fully appreciated the value and magnitude of Lee's plan of operations, and I told him I was sorry that we lacked the means that would make it safe to attempt all that we desired.

29. LEE

President Davis and I had a fundamental disagreement about military strategy. I believed that we should concentrate all our available forces and strike at a vital point, in this instance, Pennsylvania. The president, far more wedded to the defensive than I, desired to protect all strategic points—Vicksburg, Port Hudson, middle-Tennessee, Charleston, Richmond—with the limited forces available. He and Seddon were especially touchy about the safety of Richmond. I could appreciate that—I cared about the capital, too. But I tried to convince the president to take a risk and give me all possible troops, so that I could apply maximum pressure upon the enemy in Pennsylvania. If we could invade Federal soil with 150,000 men, as Longstreet said, we could force Lincoln to declare his purpose to the world:

either give us peace according to Christian principles, or fight a war of extermination, in which case we would "play a little of that game" ourselves.

Longstreet's two divisions—Hood's and most of Pickett's—were returned to the Army of Northern Virginia. But despite all my pleading with the president, one of Pickett's brigades and three of my veteran brigades sent southward the previous winter remained on detached duty. In their place, Richmond sent me two untried brigades—one of them commanded by the president's nephew, a lawyer with little battlefield experience. All told, with modest reinforcements from elsewhere, the army would campaign with 77,500 men of all arms.

It was a reorganized and more efficient army that prepared to move north in June. Because Hooker had put his cavalry into one large corps, I added two brigades to Stuart's force, which gave him almost ten thousand horsemen to contend against the enemy cavalry. Had the army retained its old organization, the infantry would have been divided into two large corps of about thirty thousand fighting men in each, which I thought was more than one man could properly handle and keep under his eye in battle. Therefore, with the president's permission, I reorganized the infantry into three corps of three divisions each. Longstreet had the First Corps. Dick Ewell had the Second Corps, comprising the bulk of Jackson's former troops. And little Powell Hill had the new Third Corps, which consisted of one division from each of the other corps and a new third division.

Only Longstreet, my stolid warhorse, was a veteran corps commander. Powell Hill, a feisty soldier with his red battle shirt and auburn hair, had been a brilliant divisional commander, the best of that grade with me, and I hoped he would prove himself equally fit as a corps commander. The big question was Dick Ewell, whom I had known from the old army. Odd-looking soldier—had a bald head, large nose, and face like the president's, drawn and sickly. He'd lost a leg at Second Manassas—amputated above the knee—and now wore a wooden leg. He was an honest, brave soldier, had always done his duty well, but he suffered quick alterations of mood from elation to despondency and sometimes showed a want of decision. I had a long and earnest talk with him and hoped he had gotten over those deficiencies when I assigned him to command Jackson's old corps. We still grieved for Jackson and sorely missed him. But his spirit was with us, and I hoped it would raise many Jacksons in our ranks.

Even without Jackson, it was a magnificent army. An *invincible* army if properly officered. Most of the men now carried Enfield or Springfield rifled muskets and had enormous confidence in their superiority over the Army of the Potomac. They could march fifteen or twenty miles in a day and had no equals in battle. No equals. There never were such men in an army before. I had absolute faith that they could do anything if properly led.

In my headquarters tent on the ridge above Fredericksburg, I studied my maps and refined my plan of operations. The more I thought about it, the more convinced I became of the value of drawing Hooker into battle. Yes, a final battle that would determine the outcome. I was so very tired, had pains in my chest and had trouble sleeping. In the sanctity of my tent, I prayed to a kind Providence that this would be the last campaign, that He would watch over us and despite our weaknesses and sins would yet give us a name and a place among the nations of the earth.

Colonel Long of my staff suggested that it might be advantageous to draw Hooker into battle near Manassas. But I shook my head. No decisive value to our cause would derive from a victory in that area. The best course, I said, pointing at the map, was to invade Pennsylvania in the direction of Chambersburg, York, or Gettysburg, giving battle at one or other of these places as circumstances dictated. I believed that my magnificent army could crush the Army of the Potomac in a pitched battle and send its disorganized remnants in pell mell retreat across the Susquehanna. We would then have control of Maryland and western Pennsylvania, and it would very likely cause the fall of Washington and the flight of Lincoln's government.

Later, a story got around that I had promised Longstreet and my other commanders not to fight a general battle in Pennsylvania, that I had committed myself to the tactical defensive. The story was attributed to Longstreet, but I do not believe he ever said that. The idea is absurd. I never made any such promise, never thought of doing any such thing.

In early June I concentrated Ewell's and Longstreet's corps at Culpeper Court House, leaving Hill's new corps on the Rappahannock to deceive the Federals. On the eighth I rode with my staff to nearby Brandy Station, Stuart's headquarters, to review his cavalry. General Stuart met us with a wreath of flowers around the neck of his horse.

"A gift from the young ladies of Culpeper," he said, grinning.

I teased him: "Take care, General Stuart. That is the way General Pope's horse was adorned when he went to the battle of Manassas."

I rode down the first line of cavalry and back up the second, and then General Stuart formed them into columns, nearly ten thousand strong, and led them by us at a gallop with his saber blade at *tierce point*. It was a splendid sight—General Stuart was in all his glory. My sons Rooney and Custis, and three of my nephews, were in Stuart's cavalry, and they looked well and flourishing.

My teasing remark to Stuart turned out to be strangely prophetic. The very next day nearly eleven thousand Federal horsemen with infantry support, having crossed the fords of the Rappahannock, fell on Stuart at Brandy Station. Caught him completely by surprise. It developed into a fourteen-hour running battle, the biggest cavalry engagement of the war, fought with sabers and revolvers in clouds of dust and smoke around Fleetwood Hill until the enemy finally withdrew.

When I learned that a battle was under way, I rode to Brandy Station and found Rooney being carried from the field, wounded. We decided that he should be taken to Hickory Hill, twenty miles from Richmond, and that my son Rob, a gunner in the artillery, should go with him. Back at Culpeper, I wrote Rooney that I hoped he was comfortable and that I wished I could see him. "Take care of yourself," I said, "and make haste and get well and return. Though I scarcely ever saw you, it was a great comfort to know that you were near and with me. Kiss Chass for me. Tell her she must not tease you while you are sick, and let me know how you are." I wrote Mary, my dear Mim, that Rooney had been wounded but assured her that he was young and healthy and would soon be up again. "I grieve I fear too much over my separation from you, my children, and friends," I told her. "Kiss Agnes and Mildred for me."

On June tenth, Ewell's Second Corps set out for Winchester, west of the Blue Ridge, with orders to clear the Federals out of the valley. The campaign into Pennsylvania had begun. Perhaps, God willing, it would indeed be the final campaign of the war. A few days later, our scouts reported that the enemy army was moving up the Rappahannock, which meant we had been discovered. I believed those people were mystified as to our movements until the Richmond papers published my dispatch to the secretary of war concerning the cavalry fight at Brandy Station. That and the comments and assertions in the papers had alerted the Federals that we were on the move.

On the fifteenth word came from Ewell that he had driven the Federals out of Winchester and was now marching north to the Potomac. That same day, Longstreet's corps followed Ewell, heading northward on the eastern side of the Blue Ridge, with Stuart's cavalry screening his right. Next day I ordered Hill up from Fredericksburg, and then left Culpeper myself, worried that my army was now strung out for almost one hundred miles. I would not rest easy until it was reunited.

30. Lincoln

The news that Lee was heading north again threw all Washington into alarm. On June fourteenth our outposts reported that his advance was threatening Martinsburg, West Virginia. There were scary rumors that his objective was Pennsylvania. Halleck, Stanton, Welles, Meigs, and I gathered around the ticking telegraphs at the War Department to stay on top of events as they unfolded. Hooker reported that he was tracking Lee's army, moving northwest through Virginia on a roughly parallel course, taking care to keep the Potomac Army between Lee and Washington.

"Our scouts report the rebel army is stretched out for a hundred miles," Halleck said.

"If his head is at Martinsburg and his tail is back in Virginia," I said, "the animal must be very slim somewhere. Can't Hooker break him?" I asked Hooker the same thing by telegraph, but he said he didn't want to risk an attack until he was satisfied about Lee's whereabouts.

The next day, I called out 100,000 militia to meet the invasion, and again urged Hooker to break Lee's long, thin line. To relieve the tension in the crowded telegraph office, I talked about the humorist, Orpheus C. Kerr, whose wicked satire gave me much pleasure.

"Who's he?" Meigs asked.

"You haven't read his books?" I asked, pretending amazement. "Anyone who hasn't read 'em must be a heathen. I enjoy him immensely, except when he plays his wit on the president, which isn't too successful. But how I enjoy Kerr's hits on Chase and Welles. I think my favorite is his poem about McClellan. It presents him as a monkey who fights a serpent representing the rebellion. The monkey keeps calling for 'more tail,' 'more tail,' which Jupiter gives him." I laughed until tears came to my eyes.

The next dispatches were no laughing matter, I tell you. They reported that the head of the rebel army was advancing into Pennsylvania and that panic gripped the state, people were in flight. Nobody could tell where Lee was heading—Harrisburg? Philadelphia? Washington? The news plunged the War Department into gloom. As we awaited news, insects swarmed around the room. Stanton squinted behind his tiny spectacles, Welles tugged on his beard, Halleck stared blankly, and I paced back and forth with my hands locked behind my back.

31. LEE

My staff and I were riding with Longstreet's corps. On the eighteenth we reached Berryville, near Winchester in the Shenandoah, and the next day connected with Hill's corps, which had made a killing march up from Fredericksburg. Both corps then marched north for the Potomac, with Hill in the lead. We were in magnificent farm country, with undulating fields and the Blue Ridge mountains in the background. In all directions we saw burnt-out farmhouses with only the chimneys left standing—evidence of the ruthless war waged by the enemy.

General Stuart's role in the campaign was to operate on our right flank and keep me informed of Hooker's movements, in addition to protecting our communications. General Stuart, however, proposed a more ambitious move. He would ride to the rear of the enemy and damage and delay him if he tried to cross the Potomac. I agreed in principle but warned Stuart that if Hooker did cross the river, which was what I wanted him to do, Stuart must immediately cross the river himself and take his place on our right flank, to screen our movement and observe the enemy's, which was his primary function.

The next day, our scouts reported that Federal troops had reached Edwards' Ferry on the Potomac. I thought: it will take a long time for Hooker's huge army to come up and cross the river. No reason why Stuart can't ride around them, cross the river east of Edwards' Ferry, and rejoin us in Maryland before Hooker got close. Accordingly I wrote Stuart a final directive giving him discretionary orders. "You will be able to judge whether you can pass around their army without hindrance, doing them all the damage you can, and cross the river east of the mountains." I made it plain that after crossing the river, he was to move on and feel the right of Ewell's troops, collecting information as he went. In short, Stuart was not to embark on one of his glory rides around the enemy army if it prevented him from screening our army and keeping us informed about the Federals.

On the twenty-fifth, Stuart set out with his three best brigades. That left me with his other two brigades and two additional cavalry outfits. But I had little confidence in their ability to gather accurate intelligence. I relied on Stuart for that—had great faith in his ability and judgment—and was sure he would not let me down.

That same day Longstreet's corps began crossing the Potomac in a heavy downpour—Hill's troops had already gone across. Frequent rains had swollen the river, and the troops had to wade across in shoulder-high water, holding their rifles overhead. But it didn't dampen their spirit—they sang "Dixie" and "The Bonnie Blue Flag" as they crossed the river, and the sight of them moved me deeply. I thought again what splendid soldiers they were.

We marched rapidly north to Chambersburg, Pennsylvania, located west of South Mountain and forty-five miles southwest of Harrisburg. As our soldiers filed into Chambersburg in the rain, the citizenry defiantly waved Union flags. Four elderly women and some young girls stood in line, blocking the street while singing "John Brown's Body." My men simply marched around them on the sidewalk.

Not all the citizens were hostile. When a group of women surrounded me, one young lady asked for a lock of my hair. "My hair's too thin already," I said. "You'll want a lock from a younger officer." We rode on through town and set up headquarters in a grove on the road to Gettysburg.

We stayed a few days at Chambersburg so that the army could gather supplies. This was a region of prosperous Dutch farms, with well-stocked barns, well-fed cattle, verdant vegetable fields and fruit orchards as far as the eye could see. Our foraging parties found food in an abundance undreamed of in war-ravaged Virginia—butter, eggs, fresh pork, bacon, beef, chicken, molasses—which we took in exchange for Confederate scrip of credit. We also took horses, cattle, hogs, shoes, and clothing, again in exchange for Confederate credit. When one farm woman protested the seizure of her hogs and cattle,

Longstreet replied: "Yes, madam, it's very sad, very sad, and this sort of thing's been going on in Virginia for two years. Very sad."

While we subsisted on the country, I wanted to avoid the vandalism and atrocities committed by the enemy in desolating our country and distressing our innocent women and children. I wanted to show the world that we southerners waged honorable warfare. Accordingly, I issued orders to the army that forbade pillaging. "The commanding general considers that no greater disgrace could befall the army, and through it our whole people, than the perpetration of the barbarous outrages upon the unarmed and defenseless and the wanton destruction of private property that have marked the course of the enemy in our own country. It must be remembered that we make war for the wrongs our people have suffered without lowering ourselves in the eyes of all whose abhorrence has been excited by the atrocities of our enemies."

I had another reason to practice restraint: I hoped to encourage the rising peace party in the North, which had commanded my attention for some time now. True, as I had told the president, they professed to want reunion as the objective of peace negotiations, while we regarded independence as the object. But it would not hurt to encourage such reunion sentiment—it might undermine northern support for the war, and that after all was what we were interested in bringing about

We did destroy legitimate military targets, such as the railroad north and west of town. Ewell meanwhile was conducting his own commissary raid as he advanced on Harrisburg, on the Susquehanna, which was the army's destination. One of his columns under Jubal Early had swept to the east, burning an ironworks on the road to Gettysburg, requisitioning shoes, hats, and provisions there, and then marching on to York.

On June twenty-seventh, I had a conversation with General Trimble at my headquarters. He was still a splendid soldier at sixty-one and wore a flamboyant black army hat with its cord and sweeping feathers. I said that thus far our army was in good spirits, not overly fatigued, and could be concentrated on any one point in twenty-four hours or less. "I haven't heard that the enemy has crossed the Potomac," I said, "and am waiting to hear from General Stuart. When the Federals hear where we are, they will make forced marches to interpose their forces between us and Baltimore and Philadelphia. They will come up, probably through Frederick, and will be broken down with hunger and hard marching, strung out on a long line and much demoralized when they come into Pennsylvania. I mean to throw an overwhelming force on their advance, crush it, follow up our success, drive one corps back on another, and by successive repulses and surprises, before they can concentrate, create a panic and destroy the enemy army."

"General Lee, it can be done," Trimble said. "The morale of the army has never been higher."

"That, I hear, is the general impression." I directed Trimble's attention to a map and pointed at Gettysburg, a little market town twenty miles east of South Mountain, where the roads converged from all directions like spokes on the hub of a wheel. "Hereabouts we shall probably meet the enemy and fight a great battle," I said, "and if God gives us the victory, the war will be over and we shall have our independence."

I was concerned, though, that I had not heard from Stuart. The success of the coming battle depended on his supplying me with accurate information on the movements of the enemy army, which I assumed was still in Virginia. Had Hooker crossed the Potomac, Stuart would surely have reported it to me.

32. LINCOLN

The latest dispatches indicated that the rebel cavalry was on a raid, riding south and east of Hooker's army as it was crossing the Potomac. This was astounding news. It meant that Lee's eyes were gone—he could not know where Hooker was.

"If Hooker has generalship," I said in the telegraph office, "now is his chance to prove it. Lee's stumbling along blind without his cavalry. Hooker can't help but beat him now and destroy his army."

But instead of attacking the blind rebel army, Hooker raised the old McClellan cry. "I'm outnumbered!" he said. "Send reinforcements!" he said. "Send all the troops defending Washington!" he said. When Halleck refused to do that, Hooker took umbrage and offered his resignation, which I accepted. In the crisis unfolding, we didn't want another McClellan in command of our army. I had no ill will toward Hooker—told young Brooks I had the same regard for Hooker as a father had for a crippled son: his love for the boy grew when he realized the son would never be a strong or successful man.

My first choice to command the army was John Reynolds, head

of the First Corps, a hard-fighting general who stayed out of army politics, which I liked. I'd actually offered him the command three weeks ago, but he'd turned the offer down on the grounds that there was too much interference from Washington, which didn't set well with us. Now, in conference with Stanton, I chose George Gordon Meade, head of the Fifth Corps, who accepted the offer, even though he thought Reynolds was the better choice to head the army. I remembered Meade as a stern-faced six-footer with a bad temper— his men called him "a damned old goggle-eyed snapping turtle." He was a good fighter, Meade was, and we trusted him to chase down and destroy the invading army. Through Halleck, I assured him we would not hamper him with a lot of minute orders. "But remember," Halleck cautioned him, "you're defending the capital as well as covering the enemy army."

The rebels meanwhile were raising all billy hell in Pennsylvania, pillaging and plundering the countryside. We had reports that they'd made forced requisitions of money from banks and businesses, looted houses, and confiscated medical stores and all the food and livestock they found in return for worthless IOUs. They also seized free Negroes, scores of 'em, and sent 'em south into slavery. Thus did they carry out Jefferson Davis's proclamation of last January, that "*all Negroes captured in the free states*" would be reenslaved, so that "the respective normal condition of the white and black races may be ultimately placed on a permanent basis." This was the kind of *honorable* warfare Lee and Davis waged.

33 · LEE

On the morning of June twenty-eighth, Henry Harrison, a Mississippian and one of Longstreet's spies, called at my tent on the Gettysburg road. I had no confidence in a spy, but General Longstreet thought a good deal of Harrison. So I had him shown inside. He said he had been in Washington and heard there that Hooker had crossed the Potomac. To check the story, he rode to Frederick and found two corps of Union infantry there. On the way here, he said, he saw two more Union infantry corps near the east side of South Mountain.

I thanked and dismissed Harrison, then turned to my map. The nearness of the enemy alarmed me. Where the devil was Stuart? I needed him now to track the Federal army and couldn't believe he had disappeared. I had no cavalry at Chambersburg—two brigades were on guard duty far in the rear and another was with Ewell—and therefore had no way of knowing where the Federal army was.

Determined to reunite my army, I sent orders to Ewell to rejoin us on the east side of South Mountain at Cashtown or Gettysburg as circumstances required. On the twenty-ninth, Hill started for Cashtown, fifteen miles away, and Longstreet followed the next day with the divisions of McLaws and Hood. Pickett's division of Longstreet's corps remained in Chambersburg to guard our rear until Imboden's cavalry came up to relieve him. I rode with Old Pete that day, the thirtieth, and sensed that battle was imminent somewhere on the Chambersburg-Gettysburg pike.

We encountered no Federals on the pike, but I was increasingly irritated with Stuart. We had great need of him now to screen our advance as well as to report on the exact whereabouts of the enemy. At some point, we learned that Meade had replaced Hooker as commander of the enemy army. This was disappointing news—I had little regard for Hooker's generalship, thought we could depend on his suffering another failure of nerve. But Meade was a different matter.

"General Meade will commit no blunder in my front," I said, "and if I make one he will make haste to take advantage of it."

We camped that evening at Greenwood, on the western slope of South Mountain. Later in the evening we received disturbing news from Hill, who was five miles ahead of us, at Cashtown. That day, one of his brigades had gone ahead into Gettysburg in search of shoes, only to find Federal cavalry there in unknown strength. Hill reported that Heth's division would march there tomorrow to find out what was in their front.

Next morning, July first, I felt cheerful despite Stuart's absence. With our staffs, Old Pete and I rode up South Mountain past long lines of infantry and horse-drawn artillery of every description—Parrotts and Napoleons, smoothbores and rifled cannon. Suddenly we heard the rumble of artillery in the direction of Gettysburg. Harrison, who had joined us, warned that there was "a pretty tidy bunch of blue bellies in or near Gettysburg."

Alarmed, I rode ahead to Cashtown and found Hill looking pale and sick. "I don't know what's happening," he said. "At daybreak I sent Heth to reconnoiter Gettysburg but warned him not to force an action until the whole army was up. As a precaution I dispatched Pender's division to support him. I'm going ahead now to find out what's going on."

The sound of fighting to the east was louder and continuous now. The situation was getting out of control and it made me anxious and impatient. This was Stuart's fault: at the beginning of every previous battle he had furnished me with a detailed appraisal of what was taking place. But on this campaign I had been kept in the dark ever since crossing the Potomac.

"I cannot think what has become of Stuart," I said. "I ought to have heard from him long before now. He may have met with disaster, but I hope not. Without reports from him, I have no idea what is in front of us. It may be the whole Federal army."

A courier rode up to report that Ewell's lead divisions—Early's and Rode's—were coming down on Gettysburg from the north. I asked the courier if Ewell had heard from Stuart. "No, sir. Nothing for three days."

With my staff, I hurried toward Gettysburg. When we came to open country west of town, Heth's division, supported by Pender's, was forming on a mile-long front along Willoughby Run. Through my glasses I saw enemy guns in the run and enemy troops on the ridge in back of it, but in what strength I could not discern. I learned from several officers what had happened: Heth's two lead brigades had run into enemy cavalry on Herr Ridge. The Federals had fought dismounted behind trees and fences—fought better than anyone could have expected, but Heth's troops had mounted a vigorous attack and driven them back, only to run into Federal infantry in force. The Federals had counterattacked and forced Heth to retreat, but he was now reforming his men for another thrust.

This was not good. On a simple expedition to get shoes, Heth had stumbled into a battle he could not break off. Anxious not to bring on a general engagement until the entire army was up, I told Heth not to attack. But the timely arrival of Rodes and then Early from the North changed the aspect of things. When, one after the other, they formed on Heth's left, nearly at right angles with his line, and fell upon the enemy flank, I saw an opportunity to rout the Federals then on the field, and I ordered Heth to attack as well. In just forty-five minutes, their combined assaults broke the Federals and sent them fleeing through Gettysburg to Cemetery Ridge south of town. From prisoners we learned that two enemy corps had been on the ground that day and that one of the corps commanders, Reynolds, had been killed.

With my staff, I rode to Seminary Ridge, to a point near the Lutheran Seminary, and swept my glasses over Cemetery Ridge. The two ridges ran parallel with one another. Cemetery Ridge was the higher ground and was shaped like a fishhook, with two hills on the south end and Cemetery and Culp's Hill on the hook-shaped north end. On Cemetery Hill, just south of town, I could see masses of infantry in great confusion and disorder. I thought: *if we can push those people off and take that hill at once, before the rest of the enemy army comes up, we can command the entire position.* Hill's troops were too exhausted and disorganized to fight any more that day. So I sent orders for Ewell to take that hill, if practicable, without committing the entire army to battle.

When Ewell showed no sign of advancing, I rode into town to find out what the trouble was, and found Ewell at his headquarters with Rodes and Early. Ewell explained that his two divisions had lost a lot of men that day and he had decided to wait for Anderson's division, which was marching down from Carlisle with Ewell's trains. "Well," I asked, "can you attack the hill tomorrow?" Ewell did not reply, and I sensed an indecisiveness in him that troubled me.

Early spoke up in his stead. Old Jube, as his men called him, was tall but stooped from rheumatism, with flashing black eyes. An attack against the hill would be costly, he said in a rasping voice, and would probably fail. The ground to the south was more favorable for an attack.

"Then perhaps I had better draw you around toward our right," I said. "The line will be very long and thin if you remain here. The enemy may come down and break through."

"A retreat would be bad for morale," Early said. "Our boys fought hard for this position. We ought to hold it." Ewell and Rodes said they agreed.

"If I attack from my right," I said, "Longstreet will have to make it. He is a very good fighter, but it will take him all night to get into position and get everything ready."

I was upset. Where was the vaunted aggressiveness of my officers? I rode back to Seminary Ridge where Hill's corps was posted, and found Longstreet with his staff. I told him to bring up McLaws and Hood for a possible attack tomorrow, and he left at seven that evening to expedite their march. Anxious about my long, perilous line, I had second thoughts about leaving Ewell at Gettysburg and sent word for him to move around and reinforce our right flank. But Ewell came over in person to argue against the move. His scouts, he said, had found that Culp's Hill, which overlooked Cemetery Hill, was unoccupied. "If we take Culp's Hill," he said, "the whole Yankee line will be untenable." Ewell's information was old by several hours, and I doubted that the Yankees would leave Culp's Hill and their right flank uncovered. But encouraged by Ewell's show of aggressiveness, I told him to seize the hill as soon as practicable. When he sent a division to occupy the hill, after midnight, the enemy was there in force, as I thought he would be.

In camp that night on Seminary Ridge, I was anxious about the army and suffering from the old soldier's disease, diarrhea. After a fitful sleep, I rose before daybreak, July second, and dressed in my full uniform, blue trousers tucked into Wellington boots, gray jacket buttoned to my neck, and a black felt hat, and then buckled on my sword. I took breakfast under the trees of an apple orchard, and sent my engineer and then two aides to scout the Union left flank. As the sun was rising a brilliant red, I rode to an overlook near the seminary, which afforded a commanding view of the opposite ridge. As far as I could make out, the ridge south of Cemetery Hill was unoccupied, which made a flank attack promising.

Shortly after daybreak, Longstreet joined me. I pointed to the enemy position on Cemetery Ridge and told him I meant to attack. Old Pete studied the ridge through his glasses, frowning.

"Don't like it," he said. "They've got the higher ground, just as they did at Malvern Hill. Instead of fighting here, we ought to throw the army around by their left and get between them and Washington. We can choose the best ground, let them attack us, and beat them as we did at Fredericksburg. Once we've destroyed the enemy army, we can march into Washington and dictate our terms."

I disliked even the idea of a retreat. We had routed the enemy yesterday, and the spirit of the army was soaring. A retreat would hurt our morale—cost us the initiative—and would be dishonorable on the face of it. Besides, what route could we take? Not the pike to Chambersburg—it was clogged with troops and trains. A shift to our right, as Pete suggested, meant moving into the unknown. Without Stuart, we had no idea whether the enemy was out there, and if he was, in what strength.

"No," I told Pete, pointing to Cemetery Ridge, "the enemy is there, and I'm going to attack him there."

"If he's there," Longstreet said, "it's because he wants us to attack him. A good reason, in my judgment, not to do it."

I felt a flush of anger. "General, your proposal is impracticable under the circumstances. We're going to attack the enemy where we find him."

I had not intended to fight a general battle so far from our base unless attacked, but my blood was up. I wanted to strike the Federal army a fatal blow, here, on this ground. Yes, I thought, let this be the final battle. Let the war end here.

Before long, Hill and Hood joined us, and we sat on a log and studied a map. Hood and Longstreet whittled sticks as we talked. The troops of Hood and McLaws were up now and posted on Herr Ridge to the west of us. Later in the morning, my engineer returned from his scout. Pointing at the map, he said that he had explored a peach orchard along Emmitsburg Road and the two hills—Little Round Top and Round Top—at the southern end of Cemetery Ridge and had seen no Yankees there. This was confirmed by my two aides when they returned. I was confident now that an oblique attack north of the Round Tops would envelop the Union left flank and roll it up toward the town, and that Longstreet should make it.

"Gentlemen," I said, "we will attack by the Round Tops. General Longstreet, you will place McLaws and Hood on the right of General Hill and drive in the enemy left. General Hill, you will threaten the enemy's center, to prevent reinforcements from being drawn to either wing, and cooperate with your right division in Longstreet's attack."

Longstreet again objected to fighting here, again argued in favor of throwing the army between the enemy and Washington. Struggling to control my temper, I walked off and stood alone under the trees, staring at the Federal position. Then I turned to Longstreet and suggested that he put his divisions into motion.

I rode around to our left and told Ewell that he was also to cooperate in the attack on our right, by assaulting the two hills in his front when he heard Longstreet's guns. This would prevent the enemy from shifting troops to the south. From the cupola of an almshouse, I saw that the Federals had used the night to improve their position on Cemetery and Culp's Hills. They had the advantage of a short and inside line, and we were too much extended. Because we had failed to pursue our advantage yesterday, the enemy was now in a good position on the north end of the ridge.

I rode back to the overlook on Seminary Ridge and was furious to find Longstreet still there. He had not deployed his artillery or infantry. When I asked him why, he said that Pickett was coming up and he was waiting for him—said he never liked to go into battle with one boot off. Chafing with impatience, I ordered Longstreet to advance with the men he had on the field. Bitterly resigned to the task I had given him, Longstreet put Porter Alexander, a thin, erect young man of twenty-eight, in command of three battalions of artillery, which were to cover the attack. Then Longstreet went off to get his two infantry divisions into position.

I checked on other parts of our line and then returned to the overlook to watch the attack with Hill and members of my staff. Through my glasses, I could see Rode's division waiting in Gettysburg and thousands of blue-clad Federals and scores of field guns on the Cemetery Ridge south of town. In front of the southern end of the ridge, near Emmitsburg Road, I could see the peach orchard and what appeared to be Federal infantry. I hoped not, because I intended for Longstreet to occupy that ground. Beyond the orchard the timbered crest of Round Top shimmered in the afternoon heat and still looked deserted. To the left of that hill, on Little Round Top, Federal signalmen were wigwagging messages. It was impossible to tell how far the enemy's lines extended toward the two Round Tops, but from what I could see of them, his front was longer and more menacing now than it had been at daybreak.

I sat down on a tree stump and waited impatiently for the attack to commence. Owing to unaccountable delays, Longstreet did not get into position until around four in the afternoon. At last the roar of his artillery sounded on our right, and I rose and walked to the overlook. Soon guns were blazing along our entire line, and dense clouds of smoke drifted overhead with little wind to blow it away. An English observer was with us, James Arthur Lyon Fremantle, and he took extraordinary delight in the cannonade, exclaiming that the air was jolly well full of shells, each with a different style of going and a different explosion when it struck the Federal lines. At the height of the bombardment, one of our bands, in a nearby ravine, began to play waltzes and polkas, and Fremantle said it was curious music accompanied by the hissing and bursting of the shells.

Meanwhile I had my glasses trained on the southern end of Cemetery Ridge and the Emmitsburg Road, looking for a sign of Longstreet. But it was difficult to see much from where I stood. Around four-thirty I caught a glimpse of small gray figures running forward under a cloud of smoke. That would be Law's brigade, leading the attack. If all was going as planned, each of Longstreet's divisions was formed in double line of battle, two brigades in front and two in the rear, and were sweeping forward *in echelon* from right to left on the Emmitsburg Road. Only about three hours of daylight remained, and I hoped it was enough time for my warhorse to roll up the Federal flank and carry the day.

A burst of gunfire sounded from Round Top, which meant that Laws's Alabamians under William C. Oates were charging over its shoulder and would soon be clambering up the slope of undefended Little Round Top. If we could get artillery up there, we could enfilade the enemy line on the ridge. West of the Round Tops, I could see more small gray figures charging with flags and banners unfurled. Those would be Hood's Texans and Georgians, attacking a rocky area known as Devil's Den. As far as I could see, Hood's brigades were not moving up the Emmitsburg Road as I'd instructed, but were attacking the ridge directly.

As the battle swept northward, I could see Lafayette McLaws's division going into action in the area of a wheat field and the peach orchard. Those were William Barksdale's Mississippians charging into the orchard—they told me later that Barksdale was out in front with his white hair streaming in the sun. McLaws's boys routed the Federals in that sector and advanced toward what appeared to be a gap in the enemy line, but Federal artillery held them off with blasts of canister until reinforcements came up.

The last division to join the attack was R. H. Anderson's of Hill's corps, which was to come in on McLaws's left. Anderson formed in line of battle in front of us, moved forward across open ground, and bore down on enemy infantry on the Emmitsburg Road. Though exposed to deadly artillery fire, Anderson's brigades knocked aside the enemy skirmish line and drove the Federal infantry back to the cover of a ravine and a line of stone fences at the foot of Cemetery Ridge. There was savage fighting on that line until the Federals broke and retreated up Cemetery Ridge. Wilcox's Alabama brigade reached the foot of the ridge, and Wright's Georgia brigade gained the crest itself, breaching the main Yankee line. But enemy infantry struck them in front and on both flanks, and without support and separated from McLaws, they had to fall back.

I swung my glasses to the right and saw that McLaws was also pulling back. It was now nearly dark, and I was exceedingly frustrated with Ewell. As far as I knew, he had done nothing all afternoon beyond firing his artillery. To my dismay, he finally launched his attack against Culp's and Cemetery Hills at eight o'clock, after the battle to the south was over. I learned later that two of Early's brigades actually gained the crest of Cemetery Hill and captured the enemy batteries, but Federal reinforcements counterattacked in the dark and drove them off. Early complained bitterly that Rodes, who was supposed to support him, did not even have his troops in position. Had Rodes supported Early as he was supposed to do, Early might have turned the captured guns on the enemy, enfilading the ridge south of the hill and forcing the Federals to abandon their entire position.

We had failed to carry Cemetery Ridge that day because of a want of coordination, of concert of action. Still, we had achieved partial success, had seized Devil's Den, the peach orchard, and the wheat field, had held Cemetery Hill briefly, and had almost turned the enemy flank on Little Round Top, where the timely arrival of Union infantry had prevented Oates from seizing that eminence. Fierce and repeated attacks by his Alabamians had failed to dislodge the enemy, who fought with a tenacity uncharacteristic of the Federal army.

The cost of our partial success was high—almost six thousand killed, wounded, and missing. General Hood, I was sad to learn, had been badly shot in the arm, and Barksdale, my brave Mississippian, had been shot down at a farm north of the peach orchard, fallen into enemy hands, and died in an enemy hospital. One of our colonels, stricken with a mortal wound, had written on a piece of paper, "Tell father that I died with my face to the enemy." That spoke for all our gallant dead that day.

Just before sunset, General Stuart reported to me on Seminary Ridge. "Well, General Stuart," I said, "you are here at last." He knew from the tone of my voice and the look in my eye that I was angry at him. He had indeed gone on a joy ride, had moved around the rear of the enemy army, raced north between it and Washington, overtaken a Union supply train and captured 125 wagons, and then had ridden to Carlisle more than thirty miles north of Gettysburg. Longstreet and some of our other officers were furious with Stuart and thought I should have censured him, but I could not bring myself to do it. He realized he had made a grievous mistake—I was confident he would not repeat it.

It was a hot, sultry, moonlit night. Sitting with my staff at my headquarters in the apple orchard, I resolved to renew the attack tomorrow, but to avoid the breakdown of coordination that had impaired our efforts today. I sent directions to Longstreet that his corps, reinforced by Pickett's division, was to renew the attack against the enemy's left flank at daybreak. I ordered Ewell to assault the enemy right at the same time. The spirit of the army was still very high, and I was confident that on the morrow my infantry would crush the Army of the Potomac, for which we had nothing but contempt.

I was tired, had never felt so tired. I tried to sleep, but the old soldier's disease kept me awake most of the night. Before dawn, July third, I dressed and rode to Longstreet's headquarters in the dark, hoping and praying that today would be the last battle, that it would all end today, one way or the other. Far off to our left, on Ewell's front, a furious cannonade broke out, but I could not tell whether it was our artillery or theirs. When I reached Longstreet's headquarters, I saw no sign of Pickett or any preparations for an attack.

"What is the meaning of this?" I asked Longstreet.

"General," he said, "the enemy is too strong on his southern flank for a direct attack to be successful. I've had my scouts out all night, and they report that there are no organized forces guarding the enemy rear. I aim to move south of Round Top and fall on the enemy left by flank and reverse attack."

"Your orders," I said, "were to attack the enemy flank on Cemetery Ridge at dawn in concert with Ewell. The movement you propose will consume far too much time and destroy any chance for simultaneous attacks on both enemy flanks."

There was no hope for that anyway, since Longstreet had not prepared for a dawn attack and admitted that he had not called Pickett up until an hour or so ago. Longstreet's lack of confidence in a renewed attack against the enemy left angered and troubled me. I was certain that the army could take that ridge, but the question now was where, at what point, to launch a decisive attack. With Old Pete and some staff officers, I rode back to my observation point on the eastern slope of Seminary Ridge, so that I could study Cemetery Ridge in the reddening light of early dawn. The thunder of artillery and the rattle of small-arms fire in the direction of Cemetery Hill meant that Ewell was already engaged. But without a concerted attack at the other end of the Federal line, Ewell, I feared, stood little chance of success.

As I looked over the Federal line on Cemetery Ridge, I thought: *We struck both enemy flanks yesterday and pinned down troops there. Therefore it seems safe to assume he is weakest in his center.* That, I decided, was where we would hit him, at a bare spot that afforded little cover for infantry and artillery. An assaulting force would approach that point across a mile of open field, which meant it would be vulnerable to raking fire from enemy cannon and musketry. To reduce the risk, our guns would open with a preliminary cannonade along the entire length of the enemy line, a massive converging fire that would destroy his artillery and damage and demoralize his infantry.

The difficulty was not getting to Cemetery Ridge—Wright had shown yesterday that the enemy line could be breached. The difficulty was staying there. This time I would concentrate an overwhelming force at the weak point in his center. The assaulting columns would converge on a clump of trees there shaped like an umbrella, break through the line, and then turn and attack Cemetery Hill from the flank and rear. This would neutralize the Federals on the southern end of the ridge: they could not fire without hitting their own people. Before the day was done, the Army of the Potomac would cease to exist.

Powell Hill had joined us, and I explained the new plan to him and Longstreet. "I want you to make the attack," I told Longstreet, "with Pickett's fresh division and two of Hill's divisions, which were not engaged yesterday. About fifteen thousand men in all."

Longstreet frowned and shook his head. "General Lee, I've been a soldier all my life and I know what soldiers can do. In my opinion there never was a body of fifteen thousand men who could make such an attack successfully." He was wrong. At Solferino in 1859, Napoleon III had broken through the Austrian center with a frontal assault after an intense artillery bombardment. "The Federals are concentrated on a far shorter line than ours and on the higher ground," Longstreet went on. "The strength of their position, as one of my officers says, is frightening. They have batteries on Round Top which can make a raking fire against troops attacking their front. In my opinion, we ought to move around—"

I struck the air. "The enemy is *there*," I said, "and I'm going to *hit* him there." Longstreet stopped arguing, but as we worked out the details of the assault he looked as sad and weary as I had ever seen him. I was not at all daunted by the Federal position and had complete confidence in my infantry, which I believed could do anything I asked them to do.

The assaulting force assembled under cover of the woods and a hollow behind the line of guns along Seminary Ridge. I rode the length of the attacking columns three times to make certain every brigade was in place and every commander understood what he was expected to do. Pickett's brigades constituted the right side of the attacking force and were formed in double lines, two brigades in front and one in the rear. George Pickett was so excited he was quite beside himself. Not yet forty, he was a slender, dapper man with a drooping mustache, a curly beard on his chin, and shoulder-length auburn hair, which he wore in perfumed ringlets. He had graduated last in his class at the Academy and was the butt of many jokes, but he had been the first American soldier over the walls of Chapultepec in the Mexican War and was a brave and reliable brigadier.

Four brigades of Heth's division under Pettigrew, followed by two brigades of Pender's division under Isaac Trimble, would march on Pickett's left. Two other brigades would follow Pickett to protect his flank and rear from counterattack. All told, eleven brigades numbering about fourteen thousand men would make the charge. I believed that the sight of that many infantry bearing down in perfect formation, confident and deliberate in every step, would look irresistible and further demoralize the Yankee defenders, who would already be reeling from the massive cannonade. Once the breach in the enemy line was secured, I intended to throw in an additional ten thousand men. While the infantry struck from the front, Stuart was to ride around behind Cemetery Ridge and attack the Federals from the rear.

My artillery was in position now, 159 guns stretching in an almost unbroken mass from the peach orchard to a point opposite the town: twelve-pounder smoothbore Napoleons, twelve-pounder howitzers, three-inch ordnance rifles, ten- and twenty-pounder Parrotts, twenty-four-pounder howitzers, and two British Whitworths stood ready to pulverize Cemetery Ridge. I returned to my observation point, and at about ten minutes past one o'clock in the afternoon, the boom boom of two signal cannons sounded from the peach orchard. The guns all along our line erupted in a solid sheet of flame, and shells of every form and size screamed, moaned, fluttered, hissed, whined, and whistled in flight and exploded on the opposite ridge in intense flashes of dust and shrapnel. Round shot struck the earth with a terrific thud and bounced crazily in their paths of destruction. The long steel bolts from the Whitworths howled through the air and pounded and ricocheted over the enemy lines. Sulfurous clouds of smoke obscured the sky and drifted over the ridge and into the valley. Soon the acrid smell of gunpowder was so strong it was difficult to breathe.

Now the enemy guns were firing back, and the roar of all that artillery was so loud that I had to clamp my hands over my ears. It was like being in the center of a ferocious thunderstorm. The earth vibrated so violently that loose grass, leaves, and twigs rose a good eight inches off the ground. Shells crashed into the woods on Seminary Ridge in a tornado of destruction. Guns flew from their carriages. Ammunition chests exploded. Haversacks, rifles, swords, human bone and flesh spun through the air.

Just before three o'clock, our guns stopped firing, and the enemy fire also faded away. The silence was almost as deafening as the thunder of the guns had been. When the smoke cleared, I swept my glass over Cemetery Ridge to assess the damage. Alas, too many of our gunners had fired high and overshot the Federal position. The batteries on Cemetery Hill and elsewhere appeared to be intact. Even so, I remained confident in the ability of my infantry to break through at the copse of trees in the center.

The assaulting brigades moved past our guns now, out into the open, and dressed their lines while a band played. Pickett rode jauntily at the head of his Virginians, his cap pulled over his right ear. Dick Garnett, so ill he couldn't walk, rode a great black horse in front of his brigade. Kemper was also mounted at the head of his regiments. Pettigrew and his Carolinians were on Pickett's left, a gap of two hundred yards between them, and the sight of the bandages on the arms and heads of some of those brave boys brought tears to my eyes. The attacking force formed a mile-wide front, with battle flags snapping and fluttering and bayonets and rifles flashing in the sun. It was the most magnificent spectacle I have ever seen.

They went forward in near perfect formation, with a line of skirmishers out in front, Pickett's division marching at left oblique so as to converge with Pettigrew's and create a wedge that would hammer through the point of assault. Across the undulating field they went, the hopes of an entire people riding on their muskets. They had not gone two hundred yards, however, when enemy artillery opened on them with terrible fury. Gaps appeared in their lines; flags bobbled and went down, only to rise again. When they reached the Emmitsburg Road, enemy guns on top of Little Round Top opened fire, enfilading the entire line. Young Porter Alexander, Longstreet's artillery chief, ran down his line of guns and got two out of every five to move forward after the attacking columns, which were starting to falter under the relentless pounding of the enemy cannons and musketry. Soon there was little to see but smoke, flashes of gunfire, shell bursts. But now and then, through rifts in the smoke, I could see our men still going forward, their tattered lines converging now and charging the copse of trees, only to disappear in the smoke and then emerge again before a stone wall ablaze with enemy musketry. Dear God, I whispered, they are going to make it, *they are going to make it.*

Were they over the wall? I thought they were over it. Thought I saw our flags go over it. Blast it, if I could only tell what was going on. But all I could see along the stone wall was a smoke-covered mass. Then my heart sank. Our men appeared to be falling back, out of the pall of smoke.

"Are they retreating?" I asked one of my staff.

"Yes, sir, I fear they are."

Some had converted rifles to crutches and were hobbling back. Others who had their feet or legs shot off were crawling down the slope. Still others helped those who could not walk or crawl. The attack had failed, *had failed*, and it caused a hurt I cannot describe.

I mounted Traveller and rode out to rally the survivors in case of an enemy counterattack. "It's all my fault," I told them. "I've lost this fight, and you must help me out of it the best way you can. Form your ranks again when you get back to cover. We want all good men to hold together now. "

Colonel Fremantle rode up. "This has been a sad day for us," I said, "a sad day. But we can't always win victories."

"Don't you worry none," cried one soldier. "Uncle Robert will get us into Washington yet. You bet he will."

I spotted General Pickett and rode over to him. He looked stunned. "General Pickett," I said, "place your division in the rear of this hill, and be ready to repel the advance of the enemy if they follow up their advantage."

"General Lee," he said, "I have no division now. Armistead is down, Garnett is down, Kemper is mortally wounded."

"This was my fight," I said. "I must shoulder the blame for what's happened. The men and officers of your command wrote the name of Virginia as high today as it has ever been written."

There was Longstreet, Old Pete, also trying to rally the men. I rode over to him. "It's all my fault," I said. "I thought the men were invincible. Let us do the best we can in saving what is left."

The Federals cheered and cheered along the entire length of their line, but showed no signs of launching a general counterattack. Well, I thought, we must be thankful for that anyway. General Stuart reported that he had attempted to get around the flank of the enemy in order to attack him in the rear, but Union cavalry had met him three miles east of Gettysburg and after a fierce hand-to-hand fight in the open fields Stuart had withdrawn. So the battle was over. No success that day on any part of the line.

I rode back to my headquarters under the apple trees and issued orders for the army to prepare to retreat. The severe loss sustained by the army and the reduction of its ammunition rendered another attempt to dislodge the enemy inadvisable, so there was no choice but to withdraw. The loss had indeed been severe. Of the fourteen thousand men who made the assault, almost half had fallen. Officially, I reported that total casualties for the three-day battle would not fall short of twenty thousand, but they may have been higher.

I sent for Imboden, who commanded an independent cavalry brigade. "It's been a sad, sad day for us," I said. "But I tell you, I never saw troops behave more magnificently than Pickett's division of Virginians did today in that grand charge against the enemy. We must now return to Virginia. As many of our wounded as possible must be taken home. I've sent for you, because your men and horses are fresh and in good condition, to guard and conduct our train back to Virginia. I'm entrusting the transportation and care of our wounded to you. The duty will be dangerous—I'm afraid you will be harassed by enemy cavalry. I can spare as much artillery as you require, but no other troops. I'll need all I have to return safely by a different route. You will recross the mountain by the Chambersburg Road, and then proceed to Williamsport by any route you deem best, but don't halt till you reach the river. Rest there long enough to feed your animals; then ford the river and don't halt again till you reach Winchester. I'll communicate with you there."

The next day, July fourth, a vicious storm struck, with thunder, lightning, roaring wind, and blinding sheets of rain. The storm delayed the departure of our supply and ambulance train, which stood in the fields along the Cashtown road. The canvas tops of the wagons offered no protection against the storm's fury, and the rain drenched the poor wounded who lay on the boards inside the ambulances. Imboden finally got the train under way late in the afternoon, and the next day, with rain still falling in torrents, the army itself commenced a general withdrawal along the muddy roads back to Cashtown and Chambersburg.

When we reached the Potomac on the seventh, the river was so swollen from the rains that it could not be forded. Here I learned that enemy cavalry had raided Hickory Hill, seized my son Rooney, and taken him to Fort Monroe as a prisoner. I wrote Mary what had happened and told her we must bear this additional affliction with fortitude and resignation. "You will have learned before this reaches you that our success at Gettysburg was not as great as reported," I said in a second letter. "In fact, we failed to drive the enemy from his position, and our army withdrew to the Potomac. I trust that our merciful God, our only help and refuge, will not desert us in this our hour of need, but will deliver us by His almighty hand, that the whole world may recognize His power and all hearts be lifted up in adoration and praise of His unbounded loving kindness."

I wrote President Davis that though much reduced in numbers by hardships and battles since leaving the Rappahannock, the army was still in good condition and its confidence unimpaired. Our scouts, I told him, reported enemy troop movements approaching in this direction. "If these reports be correct, it would appear to be the intention of the enemy to deliver battle, and we have no alternative but to accept it if offered."

34 · LINCOLN

We hovered over the telegraphs in the War Department, sweating from the oppressive heat and hanging on every fragmentary message from Gettysburg: *heavy fighting all day ... all our forces engaged ... severe losses on both sides ... rebel frontal assault repulsed ... enemy army apparently in retreat.* We broke into cheers when we read that!

"Now Meade can pitch in and annihilate Lee's army," I said.

Then Meade's congratulatory order came ticking in over the wires. "Our task is not yet done," it said. "We must drive from our soil every vestige of the presence of the invader."

I couldn't believe this. "Drive the invader from our soil," I cried. "My God! Is that *all*? Meade's supposed to *destroy* Lee's traitor army, not drive him out. If Meade would only attack and destroy him now, it would end the war. Lee's heading for the Potomac, unhindered, and I fear will escape again. Isn't this reminiscent of McClellan? Son-of-a-bitch! When will our generals learn: the destruction, I mean the *total destruction*, of the rebel armies is our objective."

I was even more anxious to destroy Lee when we learned of the staggering casualties: the Potomac Army had lost twenty-three thousand men of ninety-three thousand on the field, but the rebels had lost thirty thousand, more than a third of their army. Lee was badly crippled and ripe for a death blow. Meade's men, I said, had expended all the skill and toil and blood to plant an enormous crop. Now they *must* harvest it.

On July seventh Welles came to the Executive Mansion with a dispatch from Admiral Porter on the Mississippi. Vicksburg, he reported, had surrendered to Grant on July fourth and the Union flag was now flying over the city.

"God bless Grant and his army," I said. "And his victory came on the glorious old fourth." I seized Welles's hand and almost hugged him. "What can we do for the Secretary of the Navy for this glorious intelligence? He's always giving us good news. I can't tell you my joy." I grabbed my hat and headed to the war office to telegraph the news to Meade. "Now," I told Halleck, "if General Meade can complete his work and destroy Lee's army, the rebellion will be over."

Halleck telegraphed Meade: "The president is urgent and anxious that your army should move against the enemy by forced marches." But Meade made no forced marches, pleading the problem of torrential rains. "Lee executed a forced march in the rain," I cried. "Why can't Meade?" Now Lee was sitting on the swollen banks of the Potomac, with the river at his back, a prime target for destruction. Why didn't Meade move? I had dreaded and expected this, knew something like it would happen. I said I ought to go up there and take command of the army myself. But it was too late for that. At noon on July fourteenth came the distressing news that Lee had crossed safely into Virginia.

"We had them in our grasp," I groaned. "We had only to stretch forth our hands and they were ours."

Young Brooks called. He had been to the front and had seen Lee's escape—had seen his army crossing on pontoon bridges without a challenge. I paced back and forth, my fists clenched behind me. "If I had gone up there," I said, "I could have whipped them myself. There is bad faith somewhere."

Halleck wrote Meade of my "great dissatisfaction" that Lee had gotten away. Meade was offended and offered his resignation. I wrote him a blunt letter: "My dear general, I do not believe you appreciate the magnitude of the misfortune involved in Lee's escape. He was within your easy grasp, and to have closed upon him would, in connection with our other late success, have ended the war. As it is, the war will be prolonged indefinitely. If you could not safely attack Lee last Monday, how can you possibly do so south of the river? Your golden opportunity is gone, and I am distressed immeasurably because of it."

When I calmed down, though, I decided not to send the letter. I directed Halleck to decline Meade's resignation and told Hay that while Meade had made a terrible mistake, I was grateful to him for the great service he did at Gettysburg. And he finally did move, crossing the Potomac east of the Blue Ridge, which forced Lee to fall back into middle Virginia, south of the Rapidan.

I was far more grateful to Grant for his brilliant campaign. Once Vicksburg fell, Port Hudson could no longer hold out and surrendered to General Banks. Thanks to Grant, the father of waters now ran unvexed to the sea. On my military map, I put blue pins down the full length of the Mississippi. I also stuck blue pins in middle Tennessee. After I'd made Rosecrans advance, he'd successfully driven the rebels out of there and was preparing—or so he said—to move against Chattanooga.

At my desk, meanwhile, I sat down and wrote Grant a personal letter of thanks.

My dear General: I do not remember that you and I ever met personally. I write this now as a grateful acknowledgment for the almost inestimable service you have done the country. I wish to say a word further. When you first reached the vicinity of Vicksburg, I thought you should do what you finally did—march the troops across the neck, run the batteries with the transports, and thus go below; and I never had any faith, except a general hope that you knew better than I, that the Yazoo Pass expedition, and the like, could succeed. When you got below, and took Port Gibson, Grand Gulf, and vicinity, I thought you should go down the river and join Gen. Banks; and when you turned Northward East of the Big Black, I feared it was a mistake. I now wish to make the personal acknowledgment that you were right, and I was wrong.

Yours very truly,
A. Lincoln

Inevitably there were stories about Grant's drinking. One claimed that he got so drunk during the siege that he rode hysterically through the camp at night. I don't put much stock in stories like that. Grant's performance on the battlefield and that alone was what concerned me. And so far he had no equal in either army when it came to fighting. His Vicksburg campaign, which he fought without once demanding reinforcements, stamped him as the greatest general of the age.

Another story got around that a delegation of politicians came to me and demanded that I fire Grant because he drank too much. I supposedly told them that if they could find out Grant's brand, I would send every general in the field a barrel of it. When a telegraph operator in the War Department asked me if the story was true, I laughed. "That would have been very good if I'd said it. But I reckon it was charged to me to give it currency."

Meanwhile we were getting reports of terrible suffering in the battlefield hospitals at Gettysburg because of a lack of sufficient medical personnel. There were something like 14,500 of our wounded up there, plus 6,000 rebel wounded Lee had left behind. When the Army of the Potomac set off for Virginia, Meade's medical director moved with it, leaving only 106 doctors at Gettysburg to care for 20,000 wounded men. A formal call had already gone out for volunteers: "Nurses, matrons, lady superintendents, all females qualified for usefulness in this emergency, are asked to report at once to the headquarters of their aid societies or to the headquarters of the United States Sanitary Commission or the Christian Commission."

35 · CORNELIA HANCOCK

My brother-in-law, Dr. Henry T. Child of Philadelphia, had promised that he would contact me when he thought I could be of use. After my only brother and every male relative and friend that we possessed had gone to war, I deliberately came to the conclusion that I, too, would go and serve my country, and I told the doctor so. There followed anxiety, woe, and endless waiting till just after the great battle at Gettysburg, when the good doctor's horse and carriage came to our house, five miles from the little village of Hancock

Bridge in southern New Jersey. The carriage had come down on an excursion boat that was returning to nearby Salem.

"Oh, what has happened?" asked my mother, alarmed.

"Nothing, Mother," I said. "Doctor has sent for me to go to war!"

Off I went to Philadelphia brimming with joy. The city was wild with excitement over the news of the battle. The rebel army was at first supposed to be on its way to Philadelphia. Every hour brought tidings of the awful loss of life on both sides, and the doctor and a number of other physicians were to leave for the battlefield that night by train. Miss Eliza Farnham and many other ladies of suitable age were going with them as volunteer nurses and all had passes from General Robert Schenck, commander of the Middle Department with headquarters in Baltimore. The ladies were all many years older than I was, and so I was put under the special care of Miss Farnham.

Thee may wonder, who am I? Suffice it to say that I am a Quaker, twenty-three years of age, with rosy cheeks and a sunny countenance—there are those who say I'm pretty—as yet unmarried and a schoolteacher. I am ambitious and impatient and suppose I inherited those traits from my maternal grandmother, who, my father said, got annoyed waiting for the teakettle to boil. My father voted for Frémont in 1856, but for the most part our neighborhood is conservative: one of my aunts was a secessionist sympathizer, and my Uncle William a hater of Negroes. The war had been a hideous reality for two years now, and I had waited, chafing with impatience, for an opportunity to get involved. Thee can understand why I was so excited when our train left Philadelphia late on the night of July fifth, bound for Baltimore and Gettysburg.

When we reached Baltimore, trouble loomed instantly in the form of Miss Dix, who met the train at the depot. As head of the War Department's corps of female nurses, she had imposed a strict rule that no woman who was pretty and under thirty need apply, and she was standing guard in the Baltimore depot, screening applicants for nursing duties at Gettysburg. In her sixties, I would say, she had abundant dark hair, coiled on top of her head save for twin locks in front. Her dress was severely plain, and she wore no jewelry. She looked us over and pronounced everyone suitable except me. She objected to my going on the grounds of my "youth and rosy cheeks," to quote her. In those days, thee must remember, it was considered indecorous for angels of mercy to appear otherwise than gray-haired and spectacled. Such a thing as a hospital corps of comely young maiden nurses, possessing grace and good looks, was then unknown. Miss Farnham and the other women of our party argued with Miss Dix on my behalf, and while they did so I slipped aboard the Gettysburg train and quietly took my seat. Miss Dix apparently forgot about me in all the commotion of the crowded depot. I must admit that none of us would have gotten through to Gettysburg had it not been for her. The military authorities in Baltimore ignored Shenck's passes and refused to let civilians through, but Miss Dix persuaded them to allow our party to proceed.

The train crawled westward, past fields with fences torn down—someone said that in one of them our cavalry had fought the rebel cavalry. We stopped where the railroad bridge was being repaired and walked the remaining two miles to Gettysburg. The detritus of war was visible everywhere in the town. Discarded muskets, haversacks, caps, wrecked caissons, and wagon wheels littered the streets. Some of the homes and buildings were battered with great holes through them and windows shot out. A steady line of wagons loaded with coffins rolled through Gettysburg from the battlefield. Houses and churches in all directions had been converted into hospitals, with small red flags hanging from their upper windows.

We proceeded to a church hospital and found hundreds of severely wounded soldiers stretched out on boards laid across the high-backed pews. On them the soldiers were packed closely together. There were a dozen amputation tables in one room alone, and the physicians who worked at them were covered with blood. Chloride of lime had been spread freely over the floors and on the streets outside.

Next morning, accompanied by Dr. Child, I set out for the field hospital of the Third Division, Second Corps, which included the Twelfth New Jersey, my brother's unit, some five miles from town. The roads and fields were covered with dead horses and corpses, and groups of people roamed among the dead soldiers, searching for relatives or friends.

The Second Corps field hospitals, consisting of clusters of tents organized by divisions, was situated on the high ground southwest of the Emmitsburg Road. As we approached, we smelled a sickening, overpowering, awful stench from the unburied dead, on which the July sun was mercilessly shining, and at every step the air grew heavier and fouler. The dead, swollen and disfigured, lay in piles everywhere. The nauseating atmosphere robbed the battlefield of its glory, the survivors of their victory, and the wounded of what little chance of life was left to them.

When we reached a belt of timber where the Third Division hospital was located, we saw lying on the ground a collection of semiconscious human forms, all of whom had been shot through the head and were considered hopeless and left to die. In the woods stood a long operating table, where surgeons and attendants were sawing on poor victims who screamed in unimaginable agony. A wagon standing nearby was rapidly filling with amputated legs, arms, feet, and hands. There were so many wounded and so few surgeons and nurses that I felt numb. Action of a kind hitherto unknown to me was desperately needed here.

I spotted some wagons arriving with provisions and helped myself to a loaf of bread and a jar of jelly, but lacking spoons or utensils of any kind, I spread the jelly with a stick and offered it to the wounded on a shingle board. The tents had been erected in rows in the woods and were crowded with patients who were glad for the little nourishment I could offer them. From the hospital, one could see the battlefield—Culp's and Cemetery Hills and Round Top, reminders of what had caused such rampant misery.

The Second Corps, I learned, had received the brunt of Pickett's charge and repulsed it on the third day of battle and had suffered about two thousand casualties. The First Minnesota bore the first honors for losses: the colonel, lieutenant colonel, major, and adjutant had all been wounded, and four captains killed. Of the 384 men who had gone into battle, 234 had fallen on that deadly ground.

I was the first female to reach the Second Corps hospitals—I don't think there was another woman within half a mile. The need was so great there was no further cavil about my age, and the surgeon in charge allowed me to go everywhere in the corps. Everyone from privates to officers was exceptionally polite to me. They said they liked my name, Hancock, because that was the name of their commander, Winfield Scott Hancock, who was the best soldier in the entire army. He had suffered a groin wound on the third day of battle and had gone to Philadelphia to recuperate.

On my first full day as a nurse at Third Division hospital, July seventh, I discovered that there were no words in the English language to express the suffering I witnessed. The men lay half naked on the ground, their clothes having been cut off to dress their wounds. They had nothing to eat but hardtack provided by the Sanitary Commission and Christian Commission. Four surgeons, none of whom were idle fifteen minutes at a time, were busy all day amputating legs and arms. I gave to every man that had a leg or arm off a gill of wine, to every wounded man a single glass of lemonade, some bread and preserves, and tobacco—as much as I am opposed to the latter, they needed it so much, they were so exhausted.

What impressed me was how high their spirits remained. What was an arm or leg, they said, compared to whipping Lee out of Pennsylvania? I would get on first rate had they not asked me to write to their wives; that I couldn't do without crying. I didn't mind the sight of blood a bit, saw arms and legs both sawed off and was not sick at all. But it was distressing that so many of the amputees contracted gangrene and died of that foul-smelling greenish poison that got into their wounds.

It had taken three days to fight the battle. It took nearly five days for some three hundred surgeons to perform the amputations that occurred there, during which time the rebel wounded lay in a dying condition with scarcely any food and without their wounds being dressed. One surgeon said that he worked at the outdoor operating tables for four straight days—"until my legs were swollen and painful, my arms and hands immersed in blood and water so long that it became difficult to hold the knife. My muscles cramped, eyes burned from the sun, sweat, and dust, and flies over it all, covering the gore that lay everywhere, the pile of severed limbs nearby that grew with each passing hour."

I witnessed so many amputations that I became inured to them. I could have stood by and seen a man's head taken off, you got so used to it. After two days in the field, I wrote my sister, I felt assured I should never feel horrified at anything that might happen to me hereafter. "There is a great want of surgeons here," I told her, "and hundreds of brave fellows who have not had their wounds dressed since the battle." Uncle Sam was very rich, but very slow. Thank God for the Sanitary and Christian Commissions, which provided us with what provisions and medical stores we had. We gave the men toast and eggs for breakfast, beef tea at ten o'clock, ham and bread for dinner, and jelly and bread for supper.

I had eight wall tents full of amputated men whose cries of agony no longer upset me the way they had at first. The most painful task we had to perform was ministering to the people who came from home and saw their relatives and friends all mangled up. I hated to see the people from home. Soldiers took everything as it came, but the citizens were shocked at the horrible sights and smells.

I thrived on my work. I was black as an Indian and dirty as a pig and as well as I ever was in my life. I had a nice bunk and tent about twelve feet square, where I slept on a bed made of four crotch sticks and some sticks laid across and pine boughs laid on that with blankets on top. I felt like a new person, ate onions, potatoes, cucumbers, anything that came up, walked as straight as a soldier, and felt life and vigor which I'd never felt at home. I could go steadily from one task to another from half past six in the morning until ten o'clock at night, and felt more like work at ten than when I got up in the morning. So much for the notion of the weaker sex!

I wrote my cousin that women were needed here very badly, and within a few days several did show up. Among them was Anna Holstein of Montgomery County, Pennsylvania; she and her husband arrived on July tenth or so. When she'd gone through her first hospital, at the Antietam battlefield, she'd said, "This is the work God has given me to do in this war." I felt the same way, told everyone I liked to be here very much and was perfectly used to the suffering and the work just suited me. The only problem was that I had no dress now except the nursing suit provided by Uncle Sam, which was threadbare. I wrote my sister, asking her to make a new dress for me. The hospital steward, a funny fellow, was going to New York with some wounded and said he would bring me a calico dress.

I cared deeply for my boys and they liked me, too. One soldier named William told me I was very popular because I was such a contrast to Miss Dix's nurses. The boys called me Cornelia and presented me with a silver medal with an inscription on one side: "Miss Cornelia Hancock, presented by the wounded soldiers 3rd div 2nd Army Corps." The other side read: "Testimonial of regard for ministrations of mercy to the wounded soldiers at Gettysburg, Pa.—July 1863." They begged me never to leave them, and I assured them I never wanted to. But so many of them died, and those who survived went home when they were able to travel. I intended to stay with all my patients until they were started on the road to heaven or home.

In late July and early August, the field hospitals were closed and all the patients too injured or too sick to travel—about four thousand of them—were concentrated at Camp Letterman, set up in a field east of town, near a fresh spring and the railroad. Fourteen of my boys and I relocated there, and we had the first four tents abreast of the cook house. The new hospital contained some four hundred tents in six double rows, each holding twelve patients. By now there must have been thirty female nurses working in the hospital, and I did not know what my fate would be. "I look at it in this way," I wrote my niece, "I am doing now all a woman can do to help the war along. I have no doubt that most people think I came into the army to get a husband. It is a capital place for that, there are very many nice men here, and all men are required to give great respect to women here. There are many good-looking women here who gallivant around in the evening and have a good time. I do not trouble myself much with the common herd."

Oh mercy, the suffering continued! All the worst wounded and worst sick were dying rapidly. I saw one of my best men die after he wore away to skin and bone. He had been so anxious to recover, but it was not to be for him, and he prayed to be taken from his suffering. He said if there was a heaven he hoped he would meet me there. They removed him from my ward, and I went over in time to be with him and hold his hand when he died.

I did not read the papers very often—thought I was doing all I could and left the issue to God. But I will say this: from what I saw in the hospitals at Gettysburg, I think war is a hellish way of settling a dispute. When Dr. Child decided he'd done enough and left for home, I went with him. The hospital had gotten so full of women that one had to sit down while the others turned around, so I thought the most patriotic woman was she who took leave of Uncle Sam until there was greater need for her services. I did know this: as soon as there was another battle I would go to the front again. The doctor said there would be another contest soon, that the proud and arrogant rebels would look to avenge their defeat at Gettysburg.

36. LEE

Not long after establishing my headquarters at Orange Court House, south of the Rapidan, we heard that there was much despondency in Richmond about the recent campaign in Pennsylvania, and in fact some papers were harshly critical of what they claimed was a terrible and ignominious defeat. I wrote dear Mary that the army had labored hard, endured much, and behaved nobly, and it had accomplished all that could have been reasonably expected. It ought not to have been expected to perform impossibilities or to have fulfilled the anticipations of the thoughtless and unreasonable.

I have only contempt for the criticism—the critics talked much of what they knew little about. I had fought honestly and earnestly to the best of my knowledge and ability for the cause and never allowed my reputation to come into consideration. I cared nothing for that—*success* was the great object. And we *did win a success at Gettysburg*, if not a victory. We broke up the Federals' summer campaign and inflicted such heavy casualties on the Army of the Potomac that for the next six months it was as quiet as a sucking dove.

I say again what I've said before: if I had had General Jackson with me, I should have won a great victory at Gettysburg. And I feel confident that a complete success there would have won for us our independence.

General Pickett filed a report in which he complained of a want of support during his charge on the third day of battle. I returned the report to him, saying, "You and your men have covered yourself with glory, but we have the enemy to fight and must carefully, at this critical moment, guard against dissension which the reflections in your report would create. I will, therefore, suggest that you destroy both copy and original, substituting one confined to casualties merely. I hope all will yet be well."

But when alone in my tent with the privacy of my thoughts, I accepted what had happened at Gettysburg as the decision of Almighty God for my own faults and failings. I prayed that God in His mercy might pardon my many and long-standing sins and allow me once more to gather around me my wife and dear children and grant me a little time with them before I went hence and was seen no more. How great was my remorse at having thrown away my time and abused the opportunities afforded me. Now I was unable to benefit either myself or others, and was receiving in this world the punishment due to my sins and follies. I felt so very tired and realized that my bodily strength was fading and that I had not recovered from the illness that had struck me before Chancellorsville.

In early August, I sat down at my camp table and wrote President Davis asking to be relieved of command. "We must expect reverses, even defeats," I told him. "They are sent to teach us wisdom and prudence, to call forth greater energies, and to prevent our falling into greater disasters. Our people have only to be true and united, to bear manfully the misfortunes incident to war, and all will come right in the end." I thought about that for a moment, then resumed writing. "The general remedy for the want of success in a military commander is his removal. I have been prompted by these reflections more than once since my return from Pennsylvania to propose to Your Excellency the propriety of selecting another commander of this army. I have seen and heard of expression of discontent in the public journals at the result of the expedition. I do not know how far this feeling extends in the army. My brother officers have been too kind to report it, and so far the troops have been too generous to exhibit it. It is fair, however, to suppose that it does exist, and success is so necessary to us that nothing should be risked to secure it. I therefore, in all sincerity, request Your Excellency to take measures to supply my place. I do this with the more earnestness because no one is more aware than myself of my inability for the duties of my position. I cannot even accomplish what I myself desire. How can I fulfill the expectations of others? In addition I sensibly feel the growing failure of my bodily strength. I have not yet recovered from the attack I experienced the past spring. I am becoming more and more incapable of exertion, and am thus prevented from making the personal examinations and giving the personal supervisions to the operations in the field which I feel to be necessary. I am so dull that in making use of the eyes of others I am frequently misled. Everything, therefore, points to the advantages to be derived from a new commander, and I the more anxiously urge the matter upon Your Excellency from my belief that a younger and abler man than myself can readily be attained."

37. DAVIS

I answered General Lee: "Suppose my dear friend that I were to admit, with all their implications, the points which you present, where am I to find that new commander who is to possess the greater ability which you believe to be required? To ask me to substitute you by someone in my judgment more fit to command, or who would possess more of the confidence of the army or of the reflecting men in the country is to demand of me an impossibility."

As for the battle of Gettysburg, I believe that had Lee been able to compel the enemy to attack him in position, we would have had a complete victory resulting in our independence. Had there been a concentrated attack at sunrise on the second day, with the same gallantry and skill exhibited in the partial assaults, it may reasonably be assumed that the enemy would have been routed. These assaults having failed from whatever cause, and Meade having occupied in force the commanding position of Round Top, I must concede that it would have been better to withdraw than to have renewed the attack on the third day. The high morale and discipline of our army, together with the unqualified confidence of the men in their commanding general, excluded the supposition that they would have been demoralized by retreat.

I am not saying that our army was defeated at Gettysburg. The enemy's claim to a victory is refuted by the fact that, when Lee halted on the banks of the Potomac, Meade did not attack, as a pursuing general would a defeated foe, but halted also and commenced entrenching. General Lee again proved himself the better general by putting such fright into Meade that he entrenched while Lee awaited battle, with his back to a swollen river. The fear he instilled in the enemy was why General Lee was irreplaceable. We could not survive without him.

I could not say the same for General Johnston. Upon his shoulders I placed the responsibility for the fall of Vicksburg. When Josiah Gorgas of the Ordnance Bureau said that Vicksburg had surrendered because the garrison was starving, I replied: "Yes, from want of provisions inside and a general outside who wouldn't fight." The loss of Vicksburg and the Mississippi, which severed the Confederacy, plunged me into the depths of gloom. The endurance of our people, I said, was to be severely tested. We were now in the darkest hour of our political existence. Gorgas expressed what many were thinking: "It seems incredible that human power could effect such a change in so brief a space. Yesterday we rode on the pinnacle of success—today absolute ruin seems to be our portion."

We received alarming reports of disaffection and peace movements in parts of North Carolina and Alabama. There were one hundred peace meetings within eight weeks in North Carolina, and several avowed peace candidates won office in the state elections there. This was an excruciating development because we needed unity now more than ever, if we were to survive the crisis of the hour. Governor Vance feared that the cost of independence would be more bloodshed and misery and said that his people would not pay the price, but he promised to fight the peace movement because for North Carolina to negotiate a separate peace, he said, would be "a mark of intolerable shame."

Our people, I said, must understand that *we must fight on*, that nothing could be hoped for from our brutal enemy. We could only expect such degradation as to a free man would be worse than torture at the stake. Could anyone not wanting to be a slave think of passing under the yoke of the Yankees, who had shown themselves to be evil beyond description by their vicious conduct of this war?

Nothing was more vicious than their arming and employment of our slaves, who were now appearing in battle and *killing our white soldiers*. This was intolerable, niggers in blue uniforms killing white men, and it provoked furious speeches in Congress. In response to my proclamation of December last, Congress formally authorized me to retaliate by ordering the execution, when captured, of white commissioned officers in command of Negro troops and by having captured Negro soldiers turned over to the states for hanging as insurrectionaries. Our armies also sold back into slavery captured black teamsters and laborers employed by the enemy army. This was a proper response to the heinous attempt of the enemy government to excite our slaves to insurrection, rapine, and murder.

38. DOUGLASS

Through the spring and early summer of 1863, I continued to recruit Negro soldiers for Mr. Lincoln's armies, calling colored men to action on behalf of our race. I was ecstatic when black soldiers brought pride to themselves and to the race in three successive battles that year, which, alas, were overshadowed by the successes of Union arms at Vicksburg and Gettysburg.

Colored soldiers first proved themselves in battle at Port Hudson, Louisiana. When Banks moved against that river bastion, his forces included the First and Third Louisiana Native Guards, consisting of many prominent free Negroes of New Orleans. On May twenty-seventh, the two black regiments repeatedly charged the enemy fort with a reckless courage that impressed General Banks, General Halleck, and many others. The *New York Times* reported: "Those black soldiers had never before been in any severe engagement. They were comparatively raw troops and were yet subjected to the most awful ordeal that even veterans ever had to experience— the charging upon fortifications through the crash of belching batteries. It is no longer possible to doubt the bravery and steadiness of the colored race, when properly led."

A month later, while Grant was sieging Vicksburg, a garrison of mostly ex-slaves distinguished themselves in battle at Milliken's Bend, where they were protecting blacks who were laboring at plantations along the river. A rebel brigade, screaming "no quarter," attacked the garrison, and the battle turned into fierce close-quarter combat with bayonets and rifle butts. Several times the Confederates attempted to drive the colored men back into the river, but they repulsed each assault and finally drove the rebels off with the help of Union gunboats on the river. Grant himself said that the colored soldiers had done well for raw troops. Assistant Secretary of War Dana, who was with Grant's army, was more emphatic. "The bravery of the blacks completely revolutionized the sentiment of the army with regard to the employment of negro troops. I heard prominent officers who formerly in private had sneered at the idea of negroes fighting express themselves after that as heartily in favor of it."

Two weeks after Gettysburg, the elite Fifty-Fourth Massachusetts brought more glory to our race on Morris Island at the mouth of Charleston Harbor. The regiment led a frontal assault against Fort Wagner in one of the greatest displays of heroism of the war. Led by their gallant Colonel Shaw, the colored soldiers charged across open sand through a terrific storm of musketry and canister, leaped a ditch at the base of the fort, and scaled the blazing parapets, where they planted both the regimental flag and Old Glory. My son Lewis participated in that attack and stood on the walls of Wagner with Colonel Shaw before the colonel fell, his sword pointing skyward, in a whirlwind of iron and lead. The black soldiers engaged the rebels in ferocious hand-to-hand fighting along those deadly parapets. Some of the colored men leaped inside the fort, only to run into a murderous fire by the rest of the garrison troops, who had survived a day-long artillery bombardment by hiding inside the fort's bomb-proof shelters. Without effective support from the white regiments, the Fifty-Fourth was forced to retreat, having lost 272 of the 600 men engaged. Lewis wrote that he had escaped unhurt from that "perfect hail of shot and shell" and that if he was killed or wounded in the next fight, he wanted to fall with his face to the enemy.

After Fort Wagner, we heard no more of sending Negroes to garrison forts and arsenals, to fight only miasma, yellow fever, and smallpox. Talk of their ability to meet the foe in the open field, and of their equal fitness with the white man to stop a bullet, began to prevail. We were enraged, however, to learn that several blacks who tried to surrender at Fort Wagner were murdered and mutilated, and that others were sold back into slavery. This was a scandalous outrage, and yet Mr. Lincoln and the War Department said nothing in response.

That was not the government's only sin against its colored fighting men. Black soldiers got no enlistment bounties, had no commissioned officers of their own race, and had to fight too often with poor arms and equipment. Worse, the War Department had arrogantly reduced them to the status of army laborers and paid Negro soldiers what the workers earned, $10 per month, rather than the $13 per month white privates received. The men of the Fifty-Fourth Massachusetts and Fifty-Fifth Massachusetts regiments were so indignant that they refused to accept any pay at all.

The meanness, ingratitude, and cruelty of the government made it exceedingly difficult to recruit black soldiers. Why should we enlist when the government treats us like dirt? was the constant question thrown at me. Bitterly disillusioned, I quit recruiting for the government and wrote George Luther Stearns, who'd headed the team that recruited the Fifty-Fourth and Fifty-Fifth regiments, an angry letter in which I set forth my reasons. "I owe it to my long-abused people, and especially those already in the army, to expose the wrongs committed against them and plead their cause. I cannot do that in connection with recruiting. When I plead for recruits, I want to do it with all my heart, without qualification."

What disturbed me most about Mr. Lincoln, I told Stearns, was the president's silence about the treatment of colored prisoners. When he began employing black troops, I had been confident that he would see to it that they would be guaranteed their rights as legitimate prisoners of war if captured by the rebels. The piratical proclamation of President Davis announcing slavery and assassination to colored prisoners was before the country and the world. But I had faith in Mr. Lincoln and believed his silence suggested that being a man of action rather than words, he was only waiting for a case in which he should be required to act. This faith in the man had enabled me to speak with warmth and effect in urging enlistments among colored men.

But that faith, I told Stearns, was now nearly gone. No word had come from Mr. Lincoln or the War Department sternly assuring the rebel chief that atrocities against black prisoners would not go unpunished. No word had come when black teamsters were slaughtered by the rebels at Murfreesboro. The same crushing silence had reigned when brave black men who planted the Stars and Stripes on the fiery ramparts of Fort Wagner were captured and killed in cold blood or returned to slavery. I asked Stearns: "How many Fifty-Fourths must be cut to pieces, its mutilated prisoners killed and its living ones sold into slavery, to be tortured to death by inches, before Mr. Lincoln says: 'Hold, enough!'"

Stearns replied by sending me a copy of Lincoln's "Order of Retaliation," issued the day before I wrote Stearns. This was the first I'd seen of it.

> *It is the duty of every government to give protection to its citizens, of whatever class, color, or condition, and especially to those who are duly organized as soldiers in the public service. . . . To sell or enslave any captured person, on account of his color, and for no offense against the laws of war, is a relapse into barbarism and a crime against the civilization of the age.*
>
> *The government of the United States will give the same protection to all its soldiers, and if the enemy shall sell or enslave anyone because of his color, the offense shall be punished by retaliation upon the enemy's prisoners in our possession.*
>
> *It is therefore ordered that for every soldier of the United States killed in violation of the laws of war, a rebel soldier shall be executed; and for every one enslaved by the enemy or sold into slavery, a rebel soldier shall be placed at hard labor on the public works and continued at such labor until the other shall be released and receive the treatment due to a prisoner of war.*

Well, I thought, it's about time! "What ought to have been done at the beginning, comes late, but it comes," I said in my newspaper. "The poor colored soldiers have purchased this interference dearly. It really seems that nothing of justice, liberty, or humanity can come to us except through tears and blood." In my paper and on the platform, I demanded that Lincoln stand by his order and exact an eye for an eye. For our government to do less, I argued, was to deserve the indignation and the execration of mankind.

Stearns urged me to go to Washington and plead the cause of the colored soldier in person, and I decided to do that. It would be my first trip to the capital of the nation. I had not gone there before because until 1862 it had been a slave-owning city and could only be reached across a slave-owning state, and I had feared for my freedom and even for my life. Maryland was still a slave state in 1863, but the Federal government's commitment to emancipation emboldened me to make the journey.

When I arrived at the president's mansion, the stairway was crowded with white office seekers and other visitors. Since I was the only dark spot among them, I expected that I would have to wait half a day to see Mr. Lincoln—I had heard of some men waiting a week. But two minutes after I sent in my card, the messenger came out and respectfully invited me into the president's office. As the eager multitude on the stairway saw me pressing and elbowing my way past them, someone remarked in a despairing voice, "Damn it, I knew they would let the nigger through."

When I went in, the president was seated in a low armchair with his huge feet in different parts of the room. He rose and kept rising until he stood over me. I started to introduce myself, but he interrupted. "I know who you are, Mr. Douglass. Mr. Seward has told me all about you. Sit down. I'm glad to see you."

That put me at ease, and I sat down. I noticed a large map on the wall with red and blue pins in it, and stacks of weapons of every description along another wall.

"Well, Mr. Douglass," he said. "I seem to recall a speech you gave somewhere in New York that got into the papers. I believe you said that 'the tardy, hesitating and vacillating policy of the president of the United States is the most disheartening feature of our present political and military situation.' Well, you're right, I'm slow, but I've never vacillated. I think it can be shown that once I've taken a position, I've never retreated from it. Now tell me, Mr. Douglass, what brings you here?"

I explained that I had been engaged in raising black troops in the North, that it had been successful at first, but that now it was hard to induce Negro men to enlist because they felt that the government did not deal fairly with them. Lincoln asked me to be specific.

"You must reverse your discriminatory policies," I said. "First, you must grant colored soldiers equal pay with white soldiers. Second, you must promote them like whites for bravery in the field. Third, you must force the Confederacy to treat captured black soldiers as prisoners of war and retaliate in kind when it murders colored prisoners in cold blood."

The president was attentive and sympathetic. He spoke of the opposition to employing Negroes as soldiers at all, of the prejudice against our race, and of the advantage to colored people that would result from being employed as soldiers in defense of their country. As to unequal pay, we had to make some concession to prejudice, he said. There were threats that if we made soldiers of blacks at all, white men would not fight beside them. Unequal pay, he said, was a necessary concession in order to achieve the higher goal of getting blacks into the army.

"But I assure you, Mr. Douglass, that in the end they will have the same pay as white soldiers."

He admitted the justice of my demand for the promotion of colored soldiers for good conduct in the field. On the matter of retaliation, he said that he had been somewhat slow in issuing his retaliatory order because most whites would not accept reprisals against white prisoners, and that the country needed talking up to on that point. "Remember this, Mr. Douglass: remember that Milliken's Bend and Fort Wagner are recent events. They were necessary to prepare the way for my order of retaliation."

"Then you will retaliate, just as your proclamation states?"

He hesitated. "It's a terrible remedy," he said. "Once begun, I don't know where it would end. If I could punish the soldiers who actually committed atrocities, I would do it. But hanging innocent men for the crimes of others is a revolting idea. I think—I hope—the threat of retaliation will convince the rebels to stop waging barbaric warfare. We've recently received information that in some instances, black prisoners have been treated as prisoners of war."

Despite our differences over reprisals, I was deeply impressed with the president's honesty, sincerity, devotion to the country, and determination to save it at all hazards. I was equally impressed with his entire freedom from popular prejudice against colored people. He was the first great man I talked with in the United States freely, who in no single instance reminded me of the difference between himself and myself, of the difference of color. I felt as though I could go and put my hand on his shoulder. I felt *big* in his presence.

My interview with the president did much to reassure me of the antislavery integrity of the government and of its commitment to deal fairly with black soldiers, if not now, certainly when Lincoln thought the white citizenry would allow it. From the genuine abolitionist view, Mr. Lincoln may have seemed tardy, cold, dull, and indifferent. But measuring him by the sentiment of the country—a sentiment he was bound as a statesman to consult—he was swift, zealous, radical, and determined.

39. LINCOLN

I saw a lot of myself in Fred Douglass. There was a similarity in how we'd had to fight our way up, we both starting off at the lowest rung of the ladder. When you consider the condition he rose from and the prominence he's attained, he's one of the most meritorious men in America. And I don't mind saying so: Douglass had a lot to do with nudging me forward in the matter of emancipation and colored troops.

I meant what I told him about equal pay for our black soldiers. What Judge Advocate General Holt told Stanton pretty much summed up my view: "The tenacious and brilliant valor displayed by troops of this race at Port Hudson, Milliken's Bend, and Fort Wagner has sufficiently demonstrated to the president and to the country the character of the service of which they are capable." At my urging, Stanton requested in his report for 1863 that Congress equalize pay for blacks, and the following year it was done.

Now that we had control of the Mississippi, I wanted Grant to help Adjutant General Thomas recruit soldiers among the liberated slaves in all the occupied territory in the Mississippi Valley. I wrote Grant: "I believe it is a resource which, if vigorously applied, will soon close the contest. It works doubly, weakening the enemy and strengthening us. We were not fully ripe for it until the river was opened. Now, I think at least a hundred thousand can, and ought to be rapidly organized along its shores, relieving all the white troops to serve elsewhere." I added: "Mr. Dana understands you as believing that the emancipation proclamation has helped some in your military operations. I am very glad if this is so."

Grant's reply increased my admiration for him. "I have given the subject of arming the Negro my hearty support," he said. "This, with the emancipation proclamation, is the heaviest blow yet given the Confederacy." He said I could rely on it, he would give Thomas all the help he could. He went on: "I would do this whether the arming of the Negro seemed to me a wise policy or not, because it is an order that I am bound to obey and I do not feel that in my position I have a right to question any policy of the government." I tell you, I love that man. With his unqualified support, I agreed with my friend Hurlbut that "soon the banks of the great river will bristle with the bayonets of colored regiments taken from the former slaves of the soil."

While our prospects were looking brighter on the battlefronts, the fire in the rear had grown ominous by the summer of 'sixty-three. In the Northwest white mobs protested my emancipation policy by beating and murdering conscript officers. At the same time, draft riots erupted in several northeastern cities, where whites who couldn't afford to buy exemptions or hire substitutes took to the streets to protest against being conscripted to fight with "nigger" soldiers for "nigger" freedom.

The worst riot broke out in New York City about a week after Gettysburg. An Irish mob burned down the draft office, looted stores, beat up policemen, attacked the mayor's house, and then stormed into the black section of town, where they set an orphanage on fire, lynched Negroes from lampposts and incinerated them, clubbed and whipped others to death, and shot policemen who interfered. The rioting went on for three days and upwards of five hundred people died. Finally, Federal troops had to be sent in to restore order. Fred Douglass was right, these antidraft, anti-Negro riots were something worse than civil disorders: "they are part of the rebel military force, without the rebel uniform, but with all its deadly hate."

An army report claimed that there existed "a widespread and organized determination" to resist conscription, in large part because of the Negro question. After the riot in New York City, Governor Seymour—an anti-Administration Democrat—begged me to suspend the draft there. But I refused to do it. "We're fighting an enemy," I said, "who forces all available men into his ranks very much as a butcher drives bullocks into a slaughter pen. We *need* men. I *won't* make an exception."

We had information that certain judges were obstructing conscription by discharging draftees under habeas corpus, and I was determined to put a stop to it. I told the Cabinet that if I had to, I would banish the mischievous judges to the Confederacy, like I'd done with Vallandigham. Men like him and Seymour claimed that conscription was unconstitutional, but they were wrong. Not only was it constitutional, I told the Cabinet; it also had historical precedent—our fathers had used it in the Revolution and the War of 1812. "Are we not now to use what our own fathers employed?" I asked. "Are we degenerate? Has the manhood of our race run out?" Instead of banishing the obstructionist judges, I issued a proclamation suspending habeas corpus for draftees.

A related worry of mine was the state elections coming up in the fall. In my view, they would be a test of my war policies, of whether we Republicans had convinced the voters of the necessity for martial law, emancipation, colored troops, and conscription. The Copperheads had already taken the stump, begging the voters to throw the Black Republicans and abolitionists out of office. Clement Vallandigham, who was now in Canada, was running for the governorship of Ohio in absentia and showering the state with letters and written speeches which damned my arbitrary power and insisted that the rebels would discuss reunion as soon as the fighting stopped.

In response to the Copperheads, Republican campaigners and newspapers stressed our brilliant successes at Vicksburg and Gettysburg and played up the refugee system, pointing out that this put the emancipated blacks to work for government wages and *kept them in the South*. In an effort to broaden our appeal, Republicans counted war Democrats in our ranks and designated ours as the Union party, a shrewd move, I think, because it plainly implied that the Peace Democrats were not Unionists, which they weren't. I'll tell you what: if they gained control of the North, it would be the *end* of the Union.

To combat Copperhead sentiment, I wrote a public letter in which I spoke rhetorically to Democrats who were dissatisfied with me. You say you are for the Union, I told 'em, yet you are against me on the grounds that I use too much force to restore the Union. "If you are not for force," I said, "nor yet for dissolution, there only remains some unimaginable *compromise*. I don't believe any compromise, embracing the maintenance of the Union, is now possible. I assure you that no word or intimation from the rebel army, or from any of the men controlling it, in relation to any peace compromise, has ever come to my knowledge or belief.

"But, to be plain, you are dissatisfied with me about the Negro. Quite likely there is a difference of opinion between you and myself upon that subject. I certainly wish that all men could be free, while I suppose you do not. You dislike the emancipation proclamation and want it retracted. Yet some of the commanders of our armies in the field who have given us some of our most important successes, believe the emancipation policy and the use of colored troops constitute the heaviest blow yet dealt to the rebellion.

"You say you will not fight to free Negroes. Some of them seem willing to fight for you; but, no matter. Fight you, then, exclusively to save the Union. I issued the proclamation on purpose to aid you in saving the Union. I thought that in your struggle for the Union, to whatever extent the Negroes should cease helping the enemy, to that extent it weakened the enemy in his resistance to you. Do you think differently? I thought that whatever Negroes can be got to do as soldiers, leaves just so much less for white soldiers to do, in saving the Union. Does it appear otherwise to you? But Negroes, like other people, act upon motives. Why should they do anything for us, if we will do nothing for them? If they stake their lives for us, they must be prompted by the strongest motive—even the promise of freedom. And the promise being made, must be kept.

"The signs look better. The Father of Waters again goes unvexed to the sea. Thanks to the great Northwest for it. Nor yet wholly to them. Three hundred miles up, they met New England, Empire, Keystone, and Jersey, hewing their way right and left. The sunny South too, in more colors than one, also lent a hand.

"Peace does not appear so distant as it did. I hope it will come soon, and come to stay; and so come as to be worth the keeping in all future time. It will then have been proved that, among free men, there can be no successful appeal from the ballot to the bullet, and that they who take such appeal are sure to lose their case, and pay the cost. And then, there will be some black men who can remember that, with silent tongue, and clenched teeth, and steady eye, and well-poised bayonet, they have helped mankind on to this great consummation; while, I fear, there will be some white ones, unable to forget that, with malignant heart, and deceitful speech, they have strove to hinder it."

That letter was widely published in the newspapers and read aloud at a big Union rally back home in Springfield. "It's a great thing, Mr. President," young Hay said of the letter. "You can snake a sophism out of its hole better than all the trained logicians of all schools." I liked that. Sumner called it "a true and noble letter" and said it could not be answered. Still, I was nervous about the state elections, more so than I'd been about the national election in 'sixty. I spoke with a good deal of emotion about the likes of Vallandigham and the possibility that the voters might hand us another defeat.

I asked Stanton about the soldier vote, and he said he was certain that most soldiers hated the Copperheads and would vote for Union candidates. So with my approval, Stanton furloughed soldiers home to vote in Delaware, New York, Kentucky, and other states, especially Ohio. It paid off, too. In the Ohio elections, Union candidate John Brough won forty thousand soldier votes and wound up whipping Vallandigham by more than one hundred thousand ballots. I wired Brough: "Glory to God in the highest, Ohio has saved the nation." When all the returns were in, Union candidates had carried every northern state save New Jersey. This, I said, was the dawn of a new era and proof that we had convinced the people of the necessity of a tough war policy. I told Zach Chandler, the Radical senator from Michigan, I was glad I had not, by my native depravity, or under evil influences, done anything bad enough to prevent the good result.

In mid-October, I received a request from Mary Livermore, the tall lady who headed the Northwest Sanitary Commission, asking me to donate the original manuscript copy of the emancipation proclamation to a sanitary fair they were getting up for the end of the month. My friend Isaac Arnold of Chicago called in person to plead their case. "They mean to auction off everything from farm machinery to pocket watches and think they can net up to $50,000 in behalf of our soldiers. If you gave them your proclamation, they think there would be great competition among buyers to get hold of it. They would make arrangements for a permanent home for the document at the state or the Chicago historical societies. I think they can make a good thing of it." On his endorsement, I wrote Mrs. Livermore that I was happy to oblige.

40. LIVERMORE

Jane Hoge and I conceived the idea for a grand fair to raise funds to replenish the treasury of the Northwestern Sanitary Commission. But when we consulted the men of the Sanitary Commission, they laughed incredulously. The very idea of women organizing and holding a huge fair was beyond their comprehension. But we were determined to bring it about and involve every one of our affiliated Soldiers' Aid Societies. In September we held a women's convention in Chicago to work out a plan, and it was a resounding success, with 1,400 female delegates from across the Northwest in attendance. Mrs. Hoge gave the keynote address: "Ladies! Our soldiers *must* be cared for!" We agreed that the fair would open in Chicago on October twenty-seventh and arranged to use four of the city's great halls.

The next step was to gather articles to be sold at the fair. We mailed out twenty thousand circulars listing the items we wanted and held fair meetings in every principal town in the Northwest. In response, farm folk contributed pianos, watches, oats, corn, bulls, and other livestock. Six young girls brought us five barrels of potatoes they had grown themselves. An elderly black woman, who had escaped from slavery in Alabama, contributed a sheet she had stitched to be sold for the benefit of our soldiers. Before long, our city men caught the fair mania and offered donations of merchandise, and manufacturers donated an impressive array of machinery—mowers, threshing machines, reapers, pumps, and drills for sowing wheat.

This first sanitary fair was an experiment and preeminently an enterprise of women, receiving no assistance from men in its early beginnings. The city of Chicago regarded it with indifference, and the gentlemen members of the Sanitary Commission barely tolerated it. To stimulate interest in the fair, Mrs. Hoge and I went east, Mrs. Hoge traveling to Pittsburgh and I to Hartford. We told everyone that the fair was more than merely an attempt to raise money for the relief of our soldiers; it was a women's demonstration in favor of the Union war effort, an endorsement of the government and its war policies. That is what prompted us to ask President Lincoln for the original manuscript of the emancipation proclamation. "There would seem great appropriateness in this gift to Chicago for the benefit of our Western soldiers, coming as it would from a western President," I wrote Mr. Lincoln. We were so *delighted* when he came through for us. Then I knew the fair was going to be a great success.

So many machines had been contributed that we found it necessary to erect a temporary wooden hall next to Bryan's Hall to house them all. Accordingly, Mrs. Hoge and I secured a building permit from the city authorities, and a benefactor donated the lumber. Next we sought out a builder. The plan was drawn, the bargain made, the contract written, and we both signed it.

"Who endorses for you?" asked the builder.

"We wish no endorsers," I said. "We have the money in the bank, and will pay you in advance. We have more faith in you than you have in us."

"It isn't matter of faith at all, but of law. You're married women. By the laws of Illinois, your names are good for nothing, unless your husbands write their names after yours on the contract."

"We'll pay you in advance. We have money of our own earning and can settle your bill on the spot. Instead of a contract, give us a promissory note, like this: 'In consideration of _____ dollars, I promise to build for Mrs. Hoge and Mrs. Livermore a hall of wood.' Can't you do that?"

"By the law, the money of your earning belongs to your husbands. The wife's earnings are the property of the husband in this state. Until your husbands give their written consent to your spending your earnings, I can't give you the promise you ask. The law must be respected."

Here was a revelation. We two women were able to enlist the whole Northwest in a great philanthropic, money-making enterprise in the face of great opposition, and had the executive ability to carry it forward to success. We had money of our own in the bank, twice as much as was necessary to pay the builder. But by the laws of the state of Illinois, our individual names were not worth the paper on which they were written. Later in the conversation, we learned that we had no legal ownership in our minor children, that they too were the property of our husbands. I vowed then and there that when the war was over I would take up a new work—the work of making law and justice synonymous for women.

The signing of the contract was delayed till our husbands could give legality to it, by signing with us. Then the builder erected the wooden hall, and the planning for the fair moved rapidly forward. On opening day, October twenty-seventh, all public offices and business closed for the day, and an inaugural parade three miles long moved through Chicago with drums beating, bands playing, and banners snapping overhead. One carriage sported captured rebel flags, and children in a line of carriages and omnibuses sang "John Brown's body lies a-moldering in the grave!" A delegation of farmers brought up the rear of the parade, driving one hundred flag-draped wagons pulled by flag-covered horses and loaded with vegetables and barrels of cider.

At noon, the fair opened at Bryan's Hall and five other great halls, plus the temporary wooden building that housed the heavy machinery. We had arranged for the railroads to run daily excursion trains at discounted rates from various parts of the country, and every day six thousand people crowded the great halls, moving from booth to booth and buying articles from fair saleswomen while bands played lively patriotic tunes. In the wooden building, dubbed

Manufacturers' Hall, we auctioned off corn shellers, corn planters, straw cutters, fanning mills, millstones, washtubs, Saratoga trunks, chairs, axles, hub and buggy spokes. The item that attracted the most attention was a beautiful ten-horsepower upright engine made and presented by the generous employees of the Chicago Eagle Works, every member of the establishment contributing to it.

The item that fetched the most money, however, was Mr. Lincoln's emancipation proclamation. Thomas B. Bryan, president of the Chicago Soldiers' Home, bought it for $3,000 and donated it to the home. I wrote the president: "During the progress of the Fair, Mr. James H. Hoes, Jeweler of Chicago, a most loyal and liberal man, after giving very largely himself, in order to stimulate donations from others, proposed through the columns of the *Tribune*, to give a gold watch to the largest contributor to the Fair. 'Thou art the man.'" And I enclosed the watch.

On the last day of the fair, there was a grand dinner for the soldiers stationed at Camp Douglas, and six hundred of them showed up to partake of the food and hear a mesmerizing address by the famous orator and abolitionist Anna Dickinson, a lovely young Quaker with curly chestnut hair and a gift of eloquence. Afterward the whole crowd gave a cheer for Abraham Lincoln. Then the boys gave a cheer for the ladies, after which the ladies gave a cheer for the boys. Then the boys shouted a lusty battle cry, and then the band played and the assembly sang together one patriotic song after another until we were all quite exhausted. After the soldiers left the hall, the women who had organized and staged the fair held a concluding dinner, and the gentlemen volunteers donned aprons and the uniformed caps of the ladies and to our very great delight proceeded to serve us.

The great sanitary fair of Chicago raised nearly $100,000 and became the model for similar fairs in Cleveland, Boston, Pittsburgh, St. Louis, New York City, Philadelphia, and Washington, D.C. The fair mania that swept the North raised a grand total of $2,738,869 for the relief of Union soldiers. When Mrs. Hoge and I gave the funds we had raised to the men on the executive committee of the Northwest Sanitary Commission, they voted the two of us a resolution of thanks. They never laughed at us again.

As the originators of the sanitary fair, Mrs. Hoge and I found ourselves nationally famous, so much so that we were invited to give public lectures across the North. During my travels, I was amazed at how much the women of the war were breaking down the barriers that restricted them to domesticity and were expanding the boundaries of what was possible for them. When male workers went into the service, women took their places as counters in the Treasury Department, as clerks in mercantile stores, as laborers in war-related industry, and as farmers in the fields. Frequent calls of business brought me into Wisconsin and Iowa, and as the train sped along, I noticed a great increase in the number of women engaged in outdoor work, especially during the times of planting, cultivating, and harvesting. Women were in the field everywhere, driving the horse-drawn reapers, binding and shocking wheat, and loading grain. At first the sight displeased me, and I turned away in aversion. By and by, I observed how skillfully these women drove the horses round and round the wheat fields. There were men at work, too, and though the women did not quite keep up with them, their work was done with more precision and nicety, and their sheaves had an artistic finish that those made by the men lacked. I told myself: "They are worthy women, and deserve praise. They have given themselves to this work and they are doing it superbly. Good wives! Good women!"

41. LINCOLN

I tell you, there were many amazing developments in this extraordinary war not seen in former contests, and none of them was more remarkable than the fairs got up by our women for the relief of suffering soldiers and their families. Now I have never studied the art of paying compliments to women, but I must say that if all that has been said by orators and poets since the creation of the world in praise of women were applied to the women of America, it would not do them justice for their conduct during this war. All I can say is, God bless the women of America.

Now, let me tell you about the military picture in the late summer. As I've said over and over, the war would be won or lost on the battlefield. As I scanned the whole military picture, I tried to get my generals to conduct the kind of concerted operations in the East and West I'd wanted since 'sixty-one. But Meade seemed in no hurry to resume the contest with Lee. Oh, Meade did wire us that he might be able to make Lee fall back, but doubted that the Army of the Potomac was strong enough to follow him to Richmond and besiege it.

"Besiege Richmond!" I said. "That's the problem with Meade. He can't get it into his head that his target is *Lee's army*, not Richmond." I told Halleck that fighting Lee back to Richmond was an idea I'd been trying to repudiate for a year—since the peninsula campaign, in fact. "If our army can't whip the enemy where he is," I said, "it can't do it if he falls back to the trenches of Richmond." Halleck explained that to Meade and urged him to strike Lee where he was. But Meade replied that he didn't know where Lee was for sure. "Why don't you attack and find out?" Halleck asked. But Meade wouldn't budge until he knew Lee's exact location.

"It's the same old story with this Army of the Potomac," I told Welles. "Imbecility, inefficiency, don't want to *do*. It's terrible, terrible, this weakness, this indifference of our Potomac generals, with such an army of good and brave men. What can I do with such generals? Who among them is any better than Meade? The thing gives me the hypo."

At least there was movement in Tennessee, where Union forces at my urging mounted something of a joint offensive. Rosecrans moved south through the mountains and threatened Chattanooga while Burnside led a small army into East Tennessee and seized Knoxville, liberating our Unionists friends there—something I'd wanted as though my own home and family were in Knoxville. I sent Burnside a thousand thanks for his successful campaign and urged Rosecrans to destroy the enemy army holding Chattanooga.

42. DAVIS

Chattanooga was a vital industrial and railroad center and our last possession in Tennessee. Should the Federals capture Chattanooga, they would have a base from which to invade the Deep South. I asked Bragg by telegram: can you not cut Rosecrans's communications and force him to retreat? I was convinced that Rosecrans meant to effect a juncture with Burnside after seizing Chattanooga. I told Bragg that his success depended on his fighting the two enemy forces in detail, before they could unite.

General Lee was with me at this time: I had called him to Richmond to have the benefit of his counsel regarding the deteriorating situation in Tennessee. I proposed that he go to Tennessee at once and assume command of the Army of Tennessee before disaster befell us.

"I'll go if you truly wish it," Lee said. "But I believe the officers already out there can run that army better than I could. I am hopeful, Your Excellency, of rebuilding my depleted army so that I can take the offensive and crush Meade."

I persuaded him that Tennessee now demanded our most strenuous efforts or we risked losing the war in the West, and he agreed to send Longstreet with two of his divisions—Hood's and McLaws's, some eleven thousand men—to Tennessee. They left by train on September ninth, crowded into mail, box, passenger, coal, and flat cars. But they were too late to save Chattanooga—on the very day they left we learned that Bragg had abandoned the city and retreated across the border to Chickamauga Creek in Georgia. I was extremely disappointed with General Bragg.

"I can only hope," I told General Lee, "that with the large army which General Bragg will soon command, he will recover by force the country the enemy has maneuvered him out of."

My faith in Bragg should not have faltered. His retreat, it developed, was a masterfully conceived plan to lure Rosecrans out of Chattanooga so that Bragg could attack and destroy his army. Rosecrans did follow Bragg, and on the nineteenth of September, reinforced by the first of Longstreet's divisions, Bragg fell upon the unsuspecting foe at Chickamauga Creek. The next day, with Longstreet's other division up, Bragg renewed the attack. We learned of the results on the twenty-first, when we received a report from Bragg. "After two days' engagement," he said, "we have driven the enemy, after a desperate resistance, from several positions. We hold the field, but the enemy still confronts us." Late that night a courier brought me another dispatch from Bragg. "The victory," he said, "is *complete*," which encouraged me to believe that Rosecrans's army had been thoroughly crushed and that our flag was again flying over Chattanooga.

43. LINCOLN

For two days I stood at my battle station in the telegraph office, awake and watchful. I felt something bad was happening out there, could feel trouble in the air. Sure enough, the next report from Rosecrans told of an awful fight and admitted "a serious disaster, extent not yet ascertained." This news shocked me and everybody else in the War Department. I telegraphed Burnside: "Go to Rosecrans with your force, without a moment's delay." Then to Rosecrans: "Burnside is on the way. Be of good cheer. We have unabated confidence in you." But another telegram from Rosecrans confirmed my worst fears: he'd suffered a terrible defeat at Chickamauga, an Indian word meaning river of death. After two days of the heaviest fighting he'd ever seen, Rosecrans said, his right and center were beaten by a rebel force that had been reinforced by troops from Lee's army. Charles A. Dana, sent by the War Department to report on Rosecrans, wrote in detail what had happened: "Chickamauga is as fatal a name in our history as Bull Run. The battle began late this morning. The rebels massed a murderous attack on the Federal left and turned it; then the fire suddenly burst in enormous volume upon our center. Never in any battle I have witnessed was there such a mass of cannon and musketry. They came through with restless impulse, composed of brigades formed in divisions. Before them our soldiers turned and fled. It was wholesale panic. Vain were all attempts to rally them. They retreated directly across two lines of considerable ridges running parallel to our line of battle, and then most of them made their way over Missionary Ridge and are coming here by the Chattanooga Valley road." The only light in this dismal story was that General George Thomas, commanding the Federal left, had held his ground, which earned him a nickname, the Rock of Chickamauga.

I wired Rosecrans: "Please relieve my anxiety as to the position and condition of your army up to the latest moment." He replied that he'd pulled his troops back to Chattanooga, but the rebels had the city invested and were threatening him across his whole front. Burnside, he said, would be too late to help. "We are brave and determined," he concluded, "but our fate is in the hands of God."

"Good God!" I said. "Where's Burnside now? Can he get there in time?" It turned out that he was marching not toward Chattanooga but away from it, in the direction of Jonesboro, because he'd heard that the rebels were in full retreat. This news made me doubt whether I was awake or dreaming. It was incomprehensible. "Damn Jonesboro!" I cried. "He's further from Chattanooga now than when he began."

On the twenty-third, Rosecrans telegraphed that he'd secured Chattanooga and thought he could hold out unless attacked by a superior enemy force. Now we didn't know what to think, didn't know if the danger had really passed or if Rosecrans was too confused to tell. That night I rode out to the Soldiers' Home, where we were staying—I was trying to get a little sleep there, had had very little in the last three days. But during the night young Hay woke me— he'd ridden up from Washington—and said that Stanton had called an emergency conference at the War Department. I was exceedingly disturbed—it was the first time Stanton had ever called me from sleep—and got dressed in a hurry.

We rode back to Washington through brilliant moonlight. At the War Department, Stanton, Halleck, Seward, and Welles greeted me when I walked in. Stanton wore a grave look.

"Tell me," I said.

"The reports are that Rosecrans ran away from the battlefield," Stanton said. "He and two of his officers abandoned the army and ran thirteen miles back to Chattanooga. Then he ordered Thomas to fall back too."

We talked about what to do till dawn. We agreed that Chattanooga must be held at all cost—it was the hub of two vital railroads and the gateway to the Deep South. We decided to detach twenty thousand men under Hooker from the Army of the Potomac, which wasn't doing anything anyway, and rush 'em to Tennessee by rail. We asked Grant to send all the men he could spare, and he wired us that he'd dispatched four divisions under Sherman. I telegraphed Rosecrans to hold on to Chattanooga, help was on the way. Once Chattanooga was secure, we could decide what to do about him.

Thanks to Stanton, who commandeered trains and broke down military red tape, Hooker's huge force reached Tennessee in eleven days and took up a position to protect Rosecrans's railroad lifeline to Nashville. Meanwhile a report from Dana warned us that Rosecrans's army had no faith in him and that the general was "greatly lacking in firmness and steadiness of will."

"Since Chickamauga," I said, "he's acted confused and stunned like a duck hit on the head."

In mid-October, I consolidated the departments and armies of the Tennessee, the Cumberland, and the Ohio into the Military Division of the Mississippi and put Grant in charge of the whole works, with the authority to relieve Rosecrans if he was so disposed. Stanton himself met Grant at Indianapolis to explain the new command organization and rode with him to Louisville. There Stanton wired us that Grant had relieved Rosecrans by telegram and put George Thomas in command of the forces in Chattanooga. I tell you, I admired the way Grant took charge.

The southern papers derided the command changes, saying, "Lincoln supplanted one hero—Rosecrans—with two fools—Grant and Thomas." I laughed. "With one more fool like Grant, we'll make short work of 'em."

44. DAVIS

No sooner had the guns fallen silent after Chickamauga, than poisonous bickering broke out between Bragg and his subordinate officers. Longstreet sided with the subordinates, writing Secretary of War Seddon that Bragg had done nothing right and that Lee ought to be sent out to replace him. General Polk, commander of a corps in Bragg's army, wrote me the same thing. Then a letter came from Bragg accusing the malcontents of deliberately disobeying his orders —in short, of rank insubordination. The worst offender, he said, was Polk, whom Bragg relieved of command over Polk's bitter protest.

All this from a *victorious* army! It made my face burn to read these quarrelsome dispatches. I wrote General Bragg: "The opposition to you both in the army and out of it has been a public calamity in so far that it impairs your capacity for usefulness, and I had hoped the great victory which you have recently achieved would tend to harmonize the army and bring to you a more just appreciation of the country."

Despite continued poor health, I decided that I should make another trip to the West, to restore harmony to the Army of Tennessee and appeal to the people, warning them of the danger of the peace movements and of an alarming rise in desertions. The War Department estimated that more than 100,000 soldiers were absent without leave or otherwise evading duty, an appalling figure for our already depleted armies.

On October sixth I left Richmond on a private train with a military escort that included my friend and personal aide, Colonel James Chesnut. At Atlanta, I had a long talk with General Polk, and it convinced me that General Bragg was not justified in relieving him. When we reached Bragg's army on top of Missionary Ridge, which overlooked Chattanooga, I studied the city through a glass and saw dead mules lying in the streets. They had apparently starved to death, the result of Bragg's investment.

I had a long and candid private talk with Bragg, and he said he regretted the disharmony that plagued his army and offered to resign. He was exceedingly thin and stooped, with a sickly look in his eyes. I assured him that his resignation was not what I desired and that I remained his friend. But I did call a meeting with Longstreet and the four senior generals in Bragg's army, hoping that their reported hostility toward him was greatly exaggerated. To my despair, it was not. Longstreet frankly stated that Bragg "would be of greater service elsewhere than at the head of the Army of Tennessee," and the other generals agreed.

This created an excruciating dilemma: if I relieved Bragg, it would be giving in to insubordination. If I did not relieve him, the poisonous feuding would likely continue. Still, there was in my judgment no better general to command this army. Bragg, therefore, must stay, but I had to persuade him to do so.

The next day I addressed Bragg's veterans. "United as you are in a common destiny," I said, glancing at Bragg's subordinate officers, "obedience and cordial cooperation are essentially necessary. He who sows the seeds of discontent and distrust prepares for a harvest of slaughter and defeat. As far as General Bragg is concerned, he has borne bravely the shafts of malice hurled at him, and the bloody field of Chickamauga plainly stamps him as a military commander of the first order."

Then I left for Bridgeport, Alabama. There, on the seventeenth, I learned that Lincoln had called for 300,000 more volunteers for three years or the duration of the war and that the U.S. and state governments were offering them liberal bounties. "The empty Confederate Treasury cannot afford to offer bounties," I thought bitterly, and wired Bragg: "You must not allow time to Lincoln. You must hit Rosecrans before Lincoln can send him heavy reinforcements of volunteers and conscripts." Then we went to Selma, where, from the balcony of a hotel, I told a crowd of civilians that a little more sacrifice by our people this spring would see the invader driven from our borders. A few days later, en route across Alabama, I learned that Grant, Lincoln's most savage and ruthless general, had been put in charge of all enemy armies in the West and was on his way to Chattanooga to take command.

45 · GRANT

Situation in Chattanooga was terrible—rebels had practically encircled the town, which gave 'em control of the river, the railroad, and the wagon roads from Bridgeport, Alabama, to the southwest. Thomas already had his troops on half rations and now faced starvation. Only way to get supplies to him was by railroad from Nashville to Bridgeport, then by wagon train up the Sequatchie Valley and across a rough mountain road to Chattanooga. It took eight days for a wagon train to make that dangerous trip, and Thomas had only five days of rations on hand. Stanton and Lincoln were afraid he might abandon Chattanooga. Decided I had to go there myself and break the rebel siege.

"Hold Chattanooga at all hazards," I wired Thomas. "I will be there as soon as possible."

Staff and I took the train to Sevenson, Alabama, which was near the river and about thirty-five miles southwest of Chattanooga. Hooker had one corps here—the other was at Bridgeport, the railroad terminus near the river. The troops were guarding the railroad and the trains bringing supplies from Nashville. Hooker called at my car to pay his respects. So did O. O. Howard—they called him "the Christian general." Had lost an arm during the peninsula campaign. Hit it off with him right well.

Same night went on to Bridgeport. Next day, Rawlins lifted me on my horse for the ride up the valley and over Waldron's Ridge to Chattanooga. Month before, I'd hurt my leg during a visit to New Orleans and was still on crutches. Wild charger took off on me, got spooked by the shriek of a train whistle, slammed into a carriage, and fell on my hip and leg. Put me in bed for three weeks, leg swollen almost to the point of bursting, and pain clear up to my armpit. Couldn't even turn over without help.

Anyway, we started up the valley in a terrific storm—cold rain and a howling wind. Next day, when we turned right across Waldron's Ridge, rain fell in torrents and rolled down the mountainside a foot deep, washing deep gullies into the road. I had to be lifted from my horse and carried across the gullies. Road was nothing but mud, knee deep in places, and littered with broken-down wagons and the carcasses of thousands of starved mules and horses. We struggled along that winding narrow road and skirted overhanging precipices. At one place my horse slipped and fell on my bad leg—pain almost blinded me. We met a long line of refugees, pro-Union families driven from their homes, mothers carrying little children, all wet and shivering from the driving rain and cold.

"I've seen a lot of human misery caused by this war," Rawlins said, "but never anything so distressing as that."

Just before nightfall, we reached Chattanooga in the rain and went straight to Thomas's headquarters in a one-story wooden house. Rawlins lifted me off my horse and I hobbled inside on crutches. Thomas is tall and more taciturn than I am, has what Wilson of my staff calls "a lofty bearing." Wasn't at all friendly. We sat in front of a fire, and his silence was embarrassing. Couldn't tell by his behavior that I was his commanding officer. I sat there ill at ease, my drenched uniform steaming from the heat. Rawlins was so mad he swore under his breath.

Finally Wilson spoke up: "General Thomas, General Grant has been on the road two days. He's wet and suffering from a bruised leg. He's also tired and hungry. Can't you get him some dry clothes from one of your staff and order some supper?"

That jarred him. "Of course I can," he said, and he did get some dry clothes and ordered some food. But none of us would forget his chilly behavior—think he was jealous of me. Frankly, I preferred Sherman and McPherson, thought them better generals. Thomas was an inert man, slow, overly meticulous. Old army joke said he was too slow to move, too brave to run away.

Talked that night with General W. F. "Baldy" Smith, Thomas's chief engineer. Known him since West Point, a Vermont man, wore a Vandyke beard, had a bald spot on his head—reason for his nickname—but while an able officer, was obstinate and likely to condemn whatever was not suggested by him. He painted a dismal picture. I questioned him and other generals who came in. Told 'em I aimed not only to open the supply line and break the siege, but to attack and whip the rebel army.

Next day my staff and I took stock of what we faced. Smith had described the pitiful conditions here, but they had to be seen to be believed. Hundreds of dead mules lay chained to trees or abandoned wagons, where they'd starved to death. In their hunger they'd gnawed almost clean through the trees or chewed off the softer parts on the gears of the wagons. Soldiers wandered aimlessly in the streets, stopping long enough to pluck from the sandy street a grain of corn or oats that had fallen out of a supply wagon. The officers and men we met were despondent, short of ammunition, blankets, overcoats, rations. Said they didn't think they could hold out much longer against the big rebel army, which was fortified on what looked like impregnable ridges overlooking Chattanooga.

I trained my glass on Missionary Ridge, which ran east and south of town. You could see a line of entrenchments stretching across the length of the ridge and enemy troops moving around. That day and the next, I made a full reconnaissance of the enemy lines, which extended from Chickamauga Creek on our left across the ridge and through an adjacent valley to Lookout Mountain to the west. The rebel picket line, not a hundred yards from ours in places, extended across the valley from the river east of town all the way around to Brown's Ferry west of town and from there north along the river. Result was, enemy troops commanded the Tennessee, the railroad, and the wagon roads on both sides of the river that connected Chattanooga to Bridgeport. Had us boxed in, all right, with the river at our backs.

My first objective was to open our supply line, by a plan conceived by Baldy Smith—I'd transferred him to my staff as chief engineer. I ordered Hooker, at Bridgeport, to cross to the south side of the river and march to Brown's Ferry with Howard's corps and two of Slocum's divisions. On the twenty-seventh a brigade chosen by Smith floated downriver on pontoon boats and drove off the rebel pickets at the ferry. Smith brought a second brigade across the peninsula between a curve in the river and threw a pontoon bridge across it at the ferry. Next afternoon Hooker arrived in Lookout Valley, beat off a rebel attack, and secured the valley. That opened the supply route from there back to Bridgeport. Soon steamers were bringing ammunition and supplies—including hardtack, why the soldiers called it "the cracker line"—from Bridgeport to Kelley's Ferry; Hooker's wagons then carried the supplies and ammo around to Brown's Ferry and into Chattanooga. Within a week, the soldiers were on full rations and Chattanooga was secure. It put a spark back into Thomas's army I was glad to see.

Had my headquarters in a two-story brick house on a bluff over-looking the river. Heard the house had belonged to a leading seces-sionist. Wrote Julia the hard ride over the mountain and the exercise since to gain a full knowledge of the location, instead of making my leg injury worse, had almost entirely cured it. I now walked without the use of a crutch or cane and mounted my horse without difficulty. Told her this was one of the wildest, most out-of-the-way places you ever saw.

Next goal was to drive the rebel army off the overlooking ridges. While we were working on offensive plans, we learned from a rebel deserter that two enemy divisions under Pete Longstreet had been detached from Chattanooga and sent to drive Burnside out of east Tennessee. Longstreet was Julia's cousin and an old friend of mine. Spent three years together at the Academy and fought in Mexico together, and he attended our wedding. A fine soldier. Bragg I also knew from the Mexican War, smart man, professional soldier, but contentious, irascible. We learned that Jefferson Davis had visited Bragg's army before I came to Chattanooga and that Davis had planned and ordered Longstreet's expedition into east Tennessee. That was good for us because it weakened Bragg.

Course, Washington bombarded me with demands that I relieve Burnside—president was anxious not to lose Knoxville. But I told 'em the best way to help Burnside was for me to attack Bragg's weakened army, knock him clean back into Georgia, and then send a column to relieve Knoxville. So I ordered Thomas to attack the enemy flank at the north end of Missionary Ridge and then fall on his line of communications.

"The movement," I told him, "should not be made one minute later than tomorrow morning."

But Thomas said he had no horses to pull his guns and couldn't move against Bragg or help Burnside. Found out he was right, and it was a great disappointment. I felt restless beyond anything I'd expe-rienced before in the war, at my inability to either move to reinforce Burnside or to attack the enemy at Missionary Ridge. I was forced to leave Burnside to contend alone against Longstreet's force until Sher-man could arrive with his men and means of transportation.

Sherman had been marching slowly eastward from Memphis with four divisions of my old army, which he now commanded, repairing the railroad as he moved so as to maintain our supply line. On November eleventh I wired him to come to Chattanooga, by way of Bridgeport, as fast as possible. "I want your command," I told him, "to aid in a movement to force the enemy back from their present position and to make Burnside secure in his."

46. SHERMAN

I was Goddamned glad to get Grant's order. I hated the tedious business of repairing the railroad and hated to leave troops in the towns along the road to hold it. It deprived me of good men. Besides, the damned railroad lay parallel to the rebels' country and they could break it whenever they pleased, but Halleck demanded that the railroad be held. Grant's order unchained me from the Goddamned thing and I lit out for Chattanooga with my troops.

Personally, it was a rough time for me—I was still hurting from the passing of my boy, Willy. In August, Ellen and the children had come down to stay with me while my corps was encamped on the Big Black. Nine-year-old Willy was a favorite of the soldiers and loved the parades and scouts and the guns—he even learned the manual of arms. A fearless boy, rode everywhere and engaged in manly conversation with anybody. He was named after me and was my favorite child, my alter ego. I'd followed his growth and development since his birth in San Francisco, and he seemed to take far more interest in my profession than the other children. God, he was a smart kid. One day at our mess table in the bungalow, I mentioned a ship listing to windward, and he asked me how can the wind blow a ship toward itself? A question that not one educated man in a thousand can explain. I had to tell him that it resulted from mechanical laws that would require a great deal of study for him to understand.

I thought it was perfectly safe and healthy on the Big Black—beautiful countryside, comfortable camp. I don't know, maybe Willy's nervous system was too sensitive for the intense excitement he experienced at Big Black. Anyway, when Grant ordered me to march to Chattanooga with four divisions, I put the troops in motion and then bundled the family up and went to Vicksburg, where we took passage to Memphis on the steamer *Atlantic*. Willy was dressed in his sergeant's uniform, which he loved, and carried a double-barreled shotgun.

As we stood on the guardrails to see our old camps at Young's Point and Milliken's Bend, I said that Willy didn't look well, and he admitted he felt sick. His mother put him to bed and consulted Dr. Roler of the Fifty-Seventh Illinois. He found symptoms of typhoid fever and told me Willy's life was in danger—we had to get him to Memphis. But the river was low and the steamer made slow progress. We finally got there on October second and carried Willy up to the Gayoso Hotel and found the most experienced physician in town to assist Dr. Roler. But Willy sank rapidly and a priest came and administered extreme unction, telling the boy he might die. Willy whispered he was ready if that was God's will, but he hated to leave his father and mother. It just broke my heart, it was all so sudden and unexpected, and I cursed myself for bringing my precious boy down to that sickly region in the summer. After the priest left, we all gathered around Willy's bed—Ellen and me, Tom, Lizzie, and Minnie—and, helpless and overwhelmed, watched him die. The child that bore my name and had such a future before him lay lifeless on the bed, and I turned away in my grief, wondering why, God, why did he have to die so young.

Ellen and the other children soon left for Ohio with dear Willy's remains, and I tried to compose myself enough to work. But asleep or awake I saw little Willy as plain as life. I could see him stumbling over the sand hills on Harrison Street in San Francisco, could see him sitting at the table in Leavenworth, could see him running to meet me with open arms at Big Black River. And last, I could see him moaning as he died. Before I left Memphis with my command, I saw ladies and children playing in the room where Willy left us, and it seemed a sacrilege. I followed Ellen in my mind and almost estimated the hour when all Lancaster would be shrouded in gloom in honor of Willy Sherman. Ellen wrote me, "The body of our little Saint rests in the grave, he is not lonely and I know he is blessed." She had this incredible Catholic faith that allowed her to cope with his passing better than I could. Why, I asked, couldn't I have been killed at Vicksburg in Willy's place, and left him to grow up to care for Ellen? God knows I exhausted human foresight and human love for that boy. Then feelings of reproach would crawl over me again for my want of judgment in bringing my family to that dread climate—it nearly killed me when I thought of it. I tried to console myself that I'd done so because it was the only lull I could foresee in the long bloody war ahead of us.

The slow going along the railroad left me too much alone with such thoughts, and I was damned glad when Grant ordered me to come on to Chattanooga as soon as possible. I reached Bridgeport in mid-November with seventeen thousand men and there found a dispatch from Grant to come ahead in person. I reached Chattanooga on the fourteenth and reported to Grant at his headquarters. I bounded in and shook his hand warmly, and he gave me a cigar and pointed to a rocking chair.

"Take the chair of honor, Sherman."

"Oh no," I said, "that belongs to you, General."

"Never mind that," he said. "You're older'n me, and I always give precedence to age."

"Well, if you put it on that ground, I accept," I said with a grin. I sat down and lit a cigar and puffed on it as he explained his plan of battle against Bragg. "Reconnaissance," he said, "shows that the north end of Missionary Ridge is poorly guarded. The bank of the river from the mouth of Chickamauga Creek westward is watched only by a small cavalry picket. Want you to bring your forces from Bridgeport across Brown's Ferry and up the north side of the river, behind the range of hills, to near the mouth of Chickamauga Creek, keeping your men concealed from the enemy. As soon as they're all up, throw them across the river on pontoon bridges and attack Bragg's exposed flank. Tomorrow we'll go over the ground and I'll explain the plan in more detail."

The next day we walked out to Fort Wood. From its parapet we had a magnificent view of the whole panorama. Lookout Mountain, with its rebel flags and batteries, stood out boldly, and an occasional shot fired toward Wauhatcheee or Moccasin Point gave life to the scene. All along Missionary Ridge were the tents of the rebel beleaguering force; the lines of trenches from Lookout up toward the Chickamauga were plainly visible, and rebel sentinels, in a continuous chain, were walking their posts in plain view.

"General Grant," I said in mock surprise, "you're besieged."

"Yep," he said, and pointed to a house on top of Missionary Ridge. "Bragg's headquarters," he said. "Aim to drive him off that ridge. Real problem is Washington. Halleck says I've got to send reinforcements to Burnside, else he and Lincoln think Burnside will abandon Knoxville. I told 'em Burnside could detain Longstreet until we can take care of Bragg, but Halleck says 'immediate aid from you is now of vital importance.' That's why it's crucial for you to get your troops here and into position as soon as possible, so you can make the main attack against Bragg's exposed left while Thomas and Halleck cooperate. I want to move by November twenty-first. Whip Bragg, relieve Burnside, and get Washington off my back."

47. LINCOLN

Sure, we were anxious about Burnside's situation in Knoxville—this was Burnside, you know, and he was threatened by veteran troops from Lee's army. With the situation there far from certain, I left for Gettysburg on November eighteenth, to say a few words at a memorial celebration commemorating a new National Soldiers' Cemetery on the battlefield. Fellow by the name of David Wills, a go-ahead young lawyer of the town, had thought up the idea, got Pennsylvania and eighteen other states to cooperate, lined up Edward Everett of Boston to be the featured speaker, and invited me to say something, too. I was so busy with the war that I turned down other invitations to speak, but this one I accepted, saw it as an opportunity to talk about the meaning and higher purpose of this great conflict at the sight of its greatest battle so far.

I gave a great deal of thought to what I would say, and when an idea came to me I'd write it down on a slip of paper and stick it in my stovepipe hat. In between goading Meade to attack Lee and keeping track of the situation in Tennessee, I managed to get about half of a draft down on executive stationery. Everett sent me an advance copy of his speech—it was learned and long. I told young Brooks my speech was going to be "short, short, short."

Stanton promised to keep me posted on developments in Tennessee, and a special escort he'd assigned to go with me called at the White House and said I'd better hurry.

"Well," I said, "I feel about that as the convict felt about going to the gallows. There won't be any fun till I get there."

We boarded a special train with three of my Cabinet secretaries—Seward, Monty Blair, and John Usher—plus Nicolay and Hay and my colored valet, William. We took our seats in the last car, a special coach generally used by the railroad's board of directors. I tell you, I hated to leave and not just because of the situation in Tennessee. My boy Tad was sick and Mary was nervous and apprehensive. "But what if he dies? *What if he dies like Willie?*" she cried over and over. I was worried, too, but told Mary I'd given Wills and his people my word and had to go.

It was after dusk when the train pulled into Gettysburg, a peaceful-looking village surrounded by fields and orchards, stone walls and white fences. Thousands of people were already on hand for the festivities. Most, I learned later, were relatives of soldiers who'd fallen here. Young Wills and Ward Lamon met us at the depot; Lamon is marshal of Washington and my old friend from back home, a big, burly, boisterous fellow who plays the banjo and enjoys his glass. They took us to Wills's home on the town square and that evening we sat down to a dinner for twenty-four people, including Everett. First time I'd met him. He'd had a long and distinguished career as a Boston minister, a professor of Greek, president of Harvard, governor of Massachusetts, U.S. senator, minister to England, secretary of state—hard to believe he'd done all that in one lifetime. He was almost seventy now, with white hair and puffy eyes, and he suffered from a kidney ailment, which obliged him to make frequent trips out back. He said he'd spent six weeks preparing his address, and had come here two days ago to get a feel for the battlefield. In fact, he'd just returned from a tour and spoke sadly of the shallow graves with wooden markers and the southern corpses covered with rocks at Devil's Den.

Outside a military band struck up a serenade for me and called for a speech. I went out to tell 'em howdy, but refused to say anything formal. "In my position," I said, "it's important not to say anything foolish." After dinner, I went up to my room to work on my speech. William was with me and I read the speech aloud, as was my practice, so as to bring two senses into play at the same time. "William," I asked, "now how does that sound?"

"Just fine," he said.

Around eleven that night I went next door where Seward was staying to get his advice about my speech. Outside we could hear revelers yelling and calling my name, and the Baltimore Glee Club singing "Our Army Is Marching On" and "We Are Coming, Father Abraham." Seward suggested a word change in the opening line of my speech, and I thanked him and went back to Wills's and resumed work on the speech, but without changing the word. A military sentry brought me some telegrams just in from Washington. Stanton reported that all was quiet in Tennessee and the other battlefronts, and added, "Mrs. Lincoln informs me that your son is better this evening." I was so glad I opened the door and told the army sentinel—startled him, I think—that my little boy was better.

By the next morning, people on horseback and in wagons and carriages clogged Gettysburg in all directions, and artillery salvoes thundered at Cemetery Hill just south of town. I made a new copy of my address, crossing a few words out and adding some final thoughts. Just before ten I rolled up the two pages of writing and stuck 'em in my coat pocket. I guess I'd said what I meant to say as well as I could.

Then I went outside to join the parade and mounted a horse that was too short for me—my feet almost touched the ground. It took an hour for Lamon to get everybody in place, but finally the procession lurched forward to the measured beat of drums, with brass bands playing slow dirges for the dead. Flags flew at half mast that day and soldiers saluted as I passed, followed by a column of Gettysburg veterans, some of 'em still bandaged and on crutches. Along the way, children sold bullets and shell fragments at little stands. I noticed some signs of the battle that had swept through the town: some of the buildings had bullet holes and some of the trees were splintered and cut in two.

When the procession reached the top of Cemetery Hill, I took my place on a small wooden platform, sitting near a special area reserved for the press. From here, I could see the bloated corpses of thousands of horses rotting on the battleground. They filled the air with a sickeningly sweet odor. I could see coffins lying in silent formations under the trees and in the clearings, and souvenir hunters prowling over the fields. Everett, the orator of the day, was late—somebody said he was out on the battlefield, trying to get inspired—but we learned later that he'd gone to visit the latrine. At last, he returned and took his place on the platform.

Birgfeld's Band of Philadelphia opened with a dirge, and Rev. Mr. T. H. Stocktown, chaplain of the U.S. Senate, uttered a prayer. Everett was much agitated about something, and I found out what it was when I glanced over the program. It had failed to include his name after the oration. The next line gave full billing to me, "Dedication Remarks by the President of the United States," but nowhere was Everett mentioned. He was so mad he crossed out Lamon's name on his copy of the program.

When Everett rose to speak, there must've been fifteen to twenty thousand people milling about the hilltop. Everett spoke for almost two hours, describing the three-day battle in detail and drawing lessons from European history. When he finished, I rose and shook his hand during the applause, and somebody put a blanket over his

shoulders. After another dirge, Lamon stood at the front of the platform and introduced the president of the United States. I removed a
gray shawl from around my shoulders, donned my wire-rimmed
spectacles, took out my scroll, rose slowly to my full height, and
stepped to the front of the platform in my flat-footed gait. I surveyed
the vast throng and started to speak.

Voices rang out, "Down in front!" "Quiet, please!" The people
in the front rows strained to listen but there was a steady muffled
din from the huge crowd that made it hard to hear. Others were distracted by a photographer right in front of the stand who was fidget-
ing under a big black cloth, trying to get me into focus. I was sure
that those strolling about on the fringes of the crowd, where local
entrepreneurs hawked cookies, cakes, lemonade, and battlefield
relics laid out on tables, couldn't hear anything at all.

I ought to mention that my voice is peculiar, high-pitched, nasal.
When I first begin a speech, it's shrill, almost squeaky, but once I get
going it settles into a little lower and some would say not unpleasant
tone. I held the speech out at arm's length but spoke from memory.
Only looked at it once, brought it to my face, then held it back out
again.

"Four score and seven years ago," I said, "our fathers brought
forth upon this continent a new nation, conceived in liberty and dedicated to the proposition that all men are created equal.

"Now we are engaged in a great civil war, testing whether that
nation—or any nation, so conceived and so dedicated—can long
endure.

"We are met on a great battlefield of that war. We are met to
dedicate a portion of it as the final resting place of those who have
given their lives that that nation might endure.

"It is altogether fitting and proper that we should do this.

"But, in a larger sense, we cannot dedicate, we cannot conse-
crate, we cannot hallow, this ground. The brave men, living and
dead, who struggled here, have consecrated it, far above our power
to add or to detract.

"The world will very little note nor long remember what we say
here"—when I said that, my lips trembled and my voice almost
broke, but I steadied myself and went on—"But it can never forget
what they did here. It is for us, the living, rather, *to be dedicated*,
here, to the unfinished work that they have thus far so nobly carried
on. It is rather for us to be here dedicated to the great task remaining
before us; that from these honored dead we take increased devotion

to that cause for which they here gave the last full measure of devotion; that we here highly resolve that these dead shall not have died
in vain; that the nation shall, under God, have a new birth of freedom, and that government of the *people*, by the *people*, for the *people*, shall not perish from the earth."

It took about two minutes to give the address—I was done
before the photographer got his picture—and there was only a patter
of clapping as I returned to my seat. Most people, I think, were confused, bewildered even. If Everett had gone on for two hours, they
probably expected the president to speak for the rest of the day.

"Is that all?" a reporter asked me.

"Yep," I said, and sat down.

I had a bad headache and was glad to get away from that
crowded hill and back to Wills's house. Feeling sicker by the minute,
I went to a local church for another ceremony, walking arm in arm
with old John Burns of Gettysburg, who'd fought in our ranks
armed only with a squirrel rifle. When we finally got away by train
at six-thirty that evening, I lay stretched out on the seats with a cold
towel across my forehead. I'd gone to Gettysburg, to say my mite
about the central idea of this vast and terrible war and why our honored dead will not have died in vain: they had sacrificed themselves
for the survival of the world's last best hope, popular government,
and the proposition that *all* men are created equal, that *all* enjoy
equal opportunity in the race of life. I'd called that day for a new
birth of freedom that included the black man, and a new crusade to
save the best political system the world ever saw, the beacon of hope
for oppressed people the world over and for all future time.

Maybe it should have been a longer speech—there were reporters
and politicians who said it should have been. I tell you, some of the
papers were downright hostile. One dismissed my speech as "silly,
flat, and dishwatery," another said it was "an insult to the memory
of the dead." A Copperhead paper said "it spouted odious abolition
doctrines," which indeed it did. There were sympathetic notices, of
course, but the one I most prized came from Edward Everett. "I
should be glad," he said, "if I could flatter myself that I came as near
to the central idea of the occasion in two hours as you did in two
minutes." I replied: "In our respective parts yesterday, you could not
have been excused to make a short address, nor I a long one. I am
pleased to know that, in your judgment, the little I did say was not
entirely a failure."

Back in Washington, the doctors said I had varioloid, a mild strain of smallpox. "Where are the office seekers?" I said. "Now I've got something I can give everybody." As I lay in my chamber, I set to work on my upcoming message to Congress, which would announce a reconstruction program—my little talk at Gettysburg was a kind of prologue to it. I was writing in bed when Stanton hurried into the chamber with a handful of dispatches from Tennessee.

48. GRANT

Wanted to attack Bragg on November twenty-first, but the rains were so heavy they slowed Sherman's march from Bridgeport. He made almost superhuman efforts to get his divisions up, but his men and guns bogged down in the mud, and the river was so high it threatened to break the bridge at Brown's Ferry. On the twenty-first Sherman got two divisions across the ferry in the rain, but the raging currents swept the bridge away and his men had to work all day and night to retrieve it and get it back in place. Sherman told me he couldn't possibly get into position before the twenty-third, and it frustrated me no end, since Thomas kept insisting he had to borrow teams from Sherman to move his artillery into place. I wired Halleck I'd never felt such restlessness before as I had at the fixed and immovable condition of Thomas's Army of the Cumberland. To make matters worse, we learned that Longstreet had attacked Burnside and blockaded the roads leading into Knoxville, cutting off my communication with him.

On the night of the twenty-second a rebel deserter brought us the disturbing news that Bragg had sent a division to reinforce Longstreet and that Bragg was retreating from Missionary Ridge with the remainder of his army. "That does it," I said. "Can't wait any longer—have to begin the offensive with only the Army of the Cumberland or risk letting Bragg get away." I ordered Thomas to make a demonstration the next day to ascertain the truth or falsity of the prisoner's report.

Next day, while Thomas, myself, and other officers looked on from the parapet of Fort Wood, a big redoubt in the Union line west of town, three divisions of the Cumberland Army lined up in perfect formation, with flags flying and officers shouting commands and the sun reflecting off ten thousand polished bayonets. At two that afternoon the boom of artillery signaled the advance, and Thomas's troops moved out from their works, drove in the enemy pickets, and seized a small ridge and adjacent Orchard Knob, a small timbered hill overlooking the plain below Missionary Ridge. The rebels fought back vigorously and at sundown tried to blast Thomas's men off the knob with a ferocious artillery barrage from Missionary Ridge— their guns thundered and lit up the twilight like lightning. The cannonade proved the prisoner was wrong, Bragg hadn't retreated at all.

Thomas's troops held on to the ground they had gained, and their performance surprised me. Wired Halleck that they had moved under fire with all the precision of veterans on parade. They would entrench, I said, and hold their position and at daylight Sherman would join the attack from the mouth of the Chickamauga and the decisive battle for Chattanooga would be fought.

My final orders called for Sherman to make the main attack against the enemy right flank and roll it up while Hooker demonstrated against Lookout Mountain and seized it if that was practicable. At the same time, Thomas would assault Bragg's center to prevent him from shifting troops to either flank, and then link up with Sherman, who would get across the railroad in Bragg's rear and cut his communications. Hooker would move to Rossville, where he would be in a position to cut Bragg off if he tried to retreat. I had complete confidence in Sherman to lead the attack and was certain my forces would crush Bragg. I had sixty thousand men to perhaps forty thousand rebels, but their inferiority in numbers was offset by their allegedly impregnable positions. We would see how impregnable they were tomorrow.

November twenty-fourth came in with a cold rain and dark, low-hanging clouds. I took up my place on the parapet at Fort Wood, with Thomas, Baldy Smith, General Granger, Rawlins, and many other staff officers, plus Quartermaster General Montgomery Meigs, a tall, stern soldier who was visiting my headquarters. The spectacle was grand beyond anything I'd ever seen on this continent. It was the first battlefield I'd been on where you could see the entire length of the front, which was fifteen miles long, and watch a plan of battle unfold from one spot.

The battle commenced on our right when Hooker's divisions, reinforced with Sherman's rear division, crossed Lookout Creek, captured the rebel pickets, and fought their way up the rugged western slope of Lookout Mountain. The low-hanging clouds and mist obscured the fighting, but we could hear gunfire and men yelling. Gun flashes lit up the clouds hugging the mountainside, and the smoke of musketry and cannon enveloped all the troops in a thick, impenetrable fog. Meigs had never seen combat before and was as excited as a kid. He called it "the battle above the clouds." Wilson of my staff said the flash of small arms looked like fireflies in the bank of clouds and mist.

I swung my glasses around to our left. Where was Sherman? Ought to have made his attack on the enemy's right flank at the same time that Hooker had advanced against his left. But there was no sign of battle on Sherman's front. Worse, we could see enemy troops moving in his direction on top of Missionary Ridge. I sent him a message: "Thomas's forces are confronting enemy's rifle pits which seem to be weakly lined with troops. Considerable movement has taken place on top of the ridge toward you. Until I hear from you I am loath to give any orders for a general engagement. Hooker has been engaged for some time but how I have not heard. Does there seem to be a force prepared to receive you east of the ridge? Send me word what can be done to aid you."

Finally a courier brought word that Sherman had moved forward from the river in three columns. Good. I turned back to Lookout Mountain. Around one in the afternoon a strong gust of wind made a rift in the clouds and smoke, and we could see enemy troops fleeing White House plateau. Around the slope came men in blue, rank after rank of 'em with Old Glory and unit colors snapping in the wind. At sight of them, the Army of the Cumberland, which lay on their arms on Orchard Knob and the adjacent ridge, broke into cheer after cheer. But the clouds and smoke soon closed in again, cutting Hooker off from view.

I looked back to Sherman's front and saw his troops advancing against the northern end of Missionary Ridge. Soon a courier from Sherman reported that he'd taken Tunnel Hill, so called because the railroad ran through it, at the north end of the ridge, and that he was now fortifying. Seizing Tunnel Hill was his first objective and it put Sherman in a perfect position to carry the ridge tomorrow. To ease Washington's anxieties, I wired Halleck: "The fight today progressed favorably. Sherman carried the end of Missionary Ridge and his right is now at the Tunnel and his left at Chickamauga Creek. Troops from Lookout Valley carried the point of the Mountain and now hold the eastern slope and a point higher up."

That night a heavy fog settled over the ridges and the town, but after midnight the sky cleared away and a full moon shone on the battlefield. At my headquarters, I drew up battle orders for tomorrow to sweep the enemy from the field. Sherman was to attack at early dawn and Thomas was to cooperate with a simultaneous advance against the enemy rifle pits directly in his front. Hooker was to carry the top of Lookout Mountain and attack Missionary Ridge from the west, but if that was not practicable he was to move up Chattanooga Valley and ascend the ridge by the first practicable road.

Dawn broke with a brilliant sunrise but the air was cold and raw. We moved our command post to Orchard Knob, which gave us a closer view of the panoramic battlefield, the Cumberland army lying under arms all around us. I swept my glass along the ground in our front and saw a cotton field Thomas's troops would have to cross to reach the line of rebel rifle pits at the base of Missionary Ridge. Saw even clearer the second line of rifle pits along the face of the ridge about halfway up, and the earthworks on top, which bristled with heavy artillery. Saw rebel battle flags fluttering overhead, and troops moving about and enemy officers looking at us through their glasses. Bragg's headquarters stood in plain view, with staff officers coming and going. Then I looked farther to the right, across Chattanooga Valley, and focused on Lookout Mountain.

"Look at that," I said, pointing at a Union flag flying on the mountaintop. "The Johnnies must have retreated during the night." But we hardly had time to enjoy the sight 'cause rebel gunners on Missionary Ridge opened fire on me and the other generals, and shells burst all around us. We could see the solid shot coming, and Meigs and most of the others ducked when the shot sailed overhead and struck the ground and bounced rearward. I didn't duck and neither did Thomas or Granger.

I moved to our left to get a good fix on Sherman's position at the northern end of Missionary Ridge. Couldn't figure out why he hadn't attacked at dawn. I looked again—and couldn't believe what my eyes told me. Sherman didn't occupy Tunnel Hill at the northern end of the ridge—the rebels did. Were there in force, with artillery, and more columns were on the way there across the ridge—we could see 'em. Sherman, to my horror, had seized an unattached hill to the east. I was stunned. Knew Sherman was, too. Explained why he hadn't attacked. He was trying to figure out what to do.

Damn it all to hell, I muttered to myself. I'm not a cussin' man, but this riled me—couldn't help myself. Turned to Thomas and can-

celed his attack. Then sent a dispatch to Hooker by courier—told
him to advance at once down the eastern slope of Lookout Mountain and attack the southern end of Missionary Ridge. When he
struck the enemy left there, it would be the signal for Thomas to
assault the enemy's center.

I fretted with impatience, fought down a surge of anger toward
Sherman. Looked at his front: no movement at all. Looked back at
Hooker: he was in motion down the side of Lookout Mountain and I
watched as his men advanced without resistance across Chattanooga
Valley, which ran between the mountain and Missionary Ridge. But
still no sign of an attack on Sherman's front. Figured he must need
help, so I sent him Carl Schurz's division. Finally, late in the morning,
we saw Sherman's men descend their hill in brigade strength, cross an
open space, and assault the strong enemy position on Tunnel Hill,
which exploded with musketry and artillery fire. Repulsed, Sherman's
brigade fell back across the open space with heavy casualties. A second brigade attacked the hill, but enemy gunfire blasted it to pieces,
pinning the survivors down with deadly fire. Through my glasses, I
could see the enemy gunners on Tunnel Hill working their cannons,
which puffed with smoke. In back of 'em other batteries moved up,
unlimbered, and let loose on Sherman's boys. Our own guns were firing behind us and the shells screamed overhead and exploded on the
enemy lines. Now a third Federal brigade advanced on Tunnel Hill,
only to meet the same fate as the others.

I dropped my field glasses and said to Sylvanus Cadwallader, the
one reporter I trusted and allowed a place at my headquarters:
"Driving our boys quite lively, aren't they?"

"Yes, driving them back badly."

"You see the signal flag beyond and a little to the right?" He
nodded. "That's where Sherman is posted. He'll soon make it all
right."

About two-thirty that afternoon I saw another brigade of Sherman's men charging toward the summit of Tunnel Hill, and for a
fleeting moment I thought he was going to make it all right. But a
rebel counterattack drove 'em back off the hill.

It was plain to me and everybody else at the command post that
Sherman couldn't take the hill. I looked to our right, trying to make
out what Hooker was doing. Couldn't see him and hadn't heard a
thing from him since one o'clock. What to do now? Sherman's situation was critical, but I thought: Bragg had weakened his center to
reinforce his right. Hooker's attack on Bragg's left was supposed to

be the signal for Thomas to attack, and I expected at any minute to see Hooker's column moving north on the ridge. Why wait? I suggested to Thomas that he make his demonstration at once against the rebel rifle pits at the foot of the ridge. That would force Bragg to withdraw troops from his right and relieve the pressure on Sherman. Thomas just stood there, silently studying the enemy position on the ridge through his glass. You see why I call him an inert man. When Slowtrot remained inert and silent, I turned on him with my face full of anger and *commanded* him to order his troops to advance and take the enemy's first line of rifle pits, and then to reform his lines with a view to carrying the ridge.

An hour elapsed with no word from Hooker and no movement by Thomas's army. I saw General Tom Wood, one of Thomas's divisional commanders—my roommate back at the Academy—and asked him: "Why aren't your men moving forward?" He said he hadn't received any orders to attack. *Jesus Christ!* I thought. Went back to General Thomas and demanded to know why my orders hadn't been carried out.

"I gave the order to General Granger an hour ago," Thomas said, referring to the commander of the four infantry divisions that were to make the charge. Where was Granger? I asked. Thomas said he didn't know.

You know where he was? Back directing the artillery! Made me mad as a hornet. I went to him and told him if he would leave that battery to its captain and take command of his corps, it would be a sight better for all of us.

Finally, about four in the afternoon, six signal guns on Orchard Knob fired in rapid succession, and the Army of the Cumberland moved forward on the attack three lines deep, twenty-three thousand officers and men, yelling and cheering with flags flying and drums beating. They drove the enemy skirmishers out of the cotton wood timber and into the cottonfield and chased 'em on the run under heavy musketry fire back to the first line of rifle pits. From the summit, rebel gunners fired volleys of shell and grape and canister from near thirty pieces of artillery, but luckily for us the enemy gunners tended to overshoot Thomas's troops. Men around me were cheering now as our infantry carried the first line of rifle pits, drove the rebels out, and planted the colors all along the line. But they didn't stop there. They started climbing the face of the ridge, which was five hundred feet high, its sides almost denuded of timber. They were yelling and cheering as they went up.

This was contrary to my orders. I meant to reform the lines and then launch the assault. I growled at Thomas: "Who ordered those men up the ridge?"

"I don't know," he said. "I didn't."

"Did you order them up, Granger?"

"No," he said. "They started up without orders. When those fellows get started, all hell can't stop 'em."

I bit down on my cigar and watched 'em scale the face of the ridge, thousands of 'em climbing and pulling and clawing their way up with their flags in hand. They assaulted the second line of rifle pits halfway up the ridge, routed the enemy troops there, and swarmed up until flag after flag reached the crest. As they went over the top, they screamed, "Chickamauga! Chickamauga! Chickamauga, Goddamn you!" The rebel army disintegrated under all that Yankee fury and flew to the rear in all directions, and everybody at the command center broke into cheers, including me. Charles Dana, the War Department man Stanton and Lincoln had sent out to accompany my army, telegraphed Washington: "Glory to God! the day is decisively ours. Missionary Ridge has just been carried by the magnificent charge of Thomas's troops, and the rebels routed."

"I'm going up there," I said. Found my horse and rode up to the summit so I could consolidate our victorious forces and organize a pursuit. When I reached the top, some of the men recognized me, and soon hundreds of troops were gathered around me, cheering and shouting. "Now we have a general!" one of 'em said. "We paid them back for Chickamauga. All we needed was a leader." I sent 'em in pursuit of the fleeing rebels—fact, I chased 'em myself for a couple of miles. But darkness and our ignorance of the roads put an end to the chase.

Back at my headquarters in Chattanooga, I wired Washington: "I believe I am not premature in announcing a complete victory over Bragg. Lookout Mountain top, all the rifle pits in Chattanooga Valley, Missionary Ridge entire have been carried and are now held by us."

Lincoln himself telegraphed back: "Well done. Many thanks to all. Remember Burnside."

How could I forget Burnside with Washington constantly reminding me? But before I sent a column to relieve Burnside, I aimed to destroy Bragg's beaten army. On the twenty-sixth Sherman chased the enemy clear back to Chickamauga Station in Georgia, and Hooker advanced to Rossville in the direction of Ringgold in hopes of cutting Bragg off. But it was not to be. Next day, with Hooker's advance bearing down on Ringgold, Bragg escaped through Ringgold Gap. Hooker's men attacked the rebel rear guard there, but it held long enough for the rebel trains and artillery to get through after the infantry. I rode to Ringgold, on the enemy railroad, and saw unmistakable signs of rout: the roads were strewn with wagons, caissons, small arms, ammunition, and provisions. Tell you what: if I hadn't had to relieve Burnside, I would have chased the broken and demoralized Johnnies for as long as supplies could've been found in the country. But I was told Burnside would run out of supplies in a few days, so I called off the pursuit so as to rescue Burnside. Still, we'd won a considerable victory—had more than six thousand prisoners and forty captured guns, at a loss of about six thousand total casualties to our arms in the three days of fighting. We'd not only raised the siege of Chattanooga and driven the Johnnies clear back to Rome, Georgia, but we stood between Bragg and Longstreet and had a secure base for a drive into the enemy heartland.

Wilson of my staff was hypercritical of Sherman for his failure to seize Tunnel Hill, but Rawlins and I both pointed out that Sherman had run into unexpected resistance. In my official report of the battle, I praised General Sherman for vigorously pressing his attack all day, which forced the rebels to mass against him and weaken their center. Sherman's operations, I said, made Thomas's breakthrough possible.

Next goal was to relieve Burnside and ease the president. I gave the job to Sherman, even though he and his men were exhausted, had had only two days' rations in five days, had endured the cold without enough blankets or overcoats, and had no provisions beyond some confiscated rebel bread and whatever they could gather from the countryside. Without complaint, Sherman marched eighty miles in four days, only to discover that Burnside was well fortified with two weeks' worth of supplies on hand. If anything, Longstreet's sieging force was in worse shape—was campaigning in hostile territory without a supply line. When Sherman approached, Longstreet fled northeast into the mountains, heading toward the Virginia border. Now virtually all of eastern Tennessee was in our hands.

49. LEE

Longstreet wrote Seddon that I ought to be sent west to help recover Tennessee, but I was not about to relinquish command of the Army of Northern Virginia and be transferred to an area of the war I knew little about. With the Army of the Potomac weakened by the detachment of two corps that went to Tennessee, I resolved to attack Meade and relieve the pressure on our forces in the West. Meade's lines then extended from Culpeper Court House to the Rapidan, and I crossed that river with my army in an attempt to turn the enemy's flank. This maneuver forced Meade to fall all the way back to Centreville. We caught his rear guard at Bristoe Station and should have destroyed it, but a want of concert of action as at Gettysburg allowed the enemy to escape.

My officers and I were appalled to see the wanton destruction of the property of citizens by the enemy. Houses were torn down or rendered uninhabitable, furniture and farming implements broken or destroyed, and many families, most of them in humble circumstances, stripped of all they possessed and left without shelter and without food. I have never witnessed on any previous occasion such entire disregard of the usages of civilized warfare and the dictates of humanity. Unable to maintain the army in this war-desolated region, we retired to the south bank of the Rapidan, so as to maintain our railroad supply line to Richmond, and entrenched. Here we could fight a general battle on more favorable terms.

Deprived of the two divisions under Longstreet and plagued by appalling desertions, the army was dangerously weak, and I wrote Richmond that something must be done to replenish our ranks. As punishment for my sins and failings, I was ill again with rheumatic pains so severe that I had to be hauled about camp in a wagon. I wrote Longstreet that I missed the counsel of my old warhorse and conceded that if I had only taken his advice on the third of July, and moved around the Federal left, how very different it all might have been. In moments alone, contemplating our calamitous defeats in Tennessee and facing the future, I had glimpses of where this was all going to end, and it pained my heart.

On the first day of December, Captain W. W. Blackford brought me news that the Army of the Potomac was on the move across the Rappahannock. My headquarters was in a small frame house on the roadside, and though it was long before dawn, I was already up and partly dressed. As Blackford made his report, I walked back and forth before a crackling fire, brushing my beard and hair. When he finished, I stopped pacing and asked him: "Well, Captain, what do you think those people are going to do?"

"I think they're going to attack, sir."

"Where do you think they will make the attack?"

"Our right flank, sir, at Mine Run. They'll try to turn it."

"Why do you think that?"

"The ground on that flank is the only part of our line where they can possibly hope for success; it's leveler and more favorable in every way."

I resumed walking and brushing my hair, then faced Blackford again. "Captain, if they don't attack us today we must attack them," I said and struck the palm of my left hand with the brush. "*We must attack them, sir!*" I said, slapping the brush against my hand more sharply and stamping the floor with my foot. "And you young men must exert yourselves! *You must exert yourselves, sir!*"

But instead of attacking, Meade withdrew and took up winter quarters between the Rapidan and the Rappahannock. I was bitterly disappointed. "I'm too old to command this army," I told my aides. "We should never have allowed those people to get away." With the onset of cold weather, we had no choice but to go into our own winter quarters near Orange Court House.

50. LINCOLN

Don't get me started on the "can't do" of the Army of the Potomac. All fall it had done nothing but maneuver and retreat, maneuver and retreat—not a single battle after Gettysburg for the rest of the year. But God bless General Grant. He'd gained both of my two great strategic objectives in the West—opening the Mississippi and liberating east Tennessee. I sent him and all in his command my profoundest gratitude.

While Grant was whipping Bragg and Meade was watching Lee, I propped myself up on two pillows—was still sick in bed with varioloid—and worked on my message to Congress, which was scheduled to convene on December eighth. Much of my message dealt with one of the thorniest problems I've ever faced: how to recon-

struct a captured insurgent state, how to create a loyal civilian government and restore it to the Union. I believed the job belonged
properly to the Executive branch, to be carried out swiftly and efficiently by the War Department and the army. Now that we'd liberated Tennessee and occupied large areas of Arkansas, Louisiana, and
Virginia, I was anxious to get reconstruction started there along the
right lines, because I had no idea whether I'd be reelected in 'sixty-
four. I was hardly a popular president and might well be thrown out
of office, so time was crucial.

I'd already tried to reconstruct occupied Tennessee, North Carolina, Louisiana, and Arkansas by appointing military governors in
them with instructions to build loyal state governments around the
minority of white Unionists—men who'd opposed secession and
refused to participate in the rebel war effort, many of 'em former
Whigs. I'd installed Andy Johnson as military governor of Tennessee
and warned him that Tennessee must be controlled and reconstructed
solely by loyal Union men, and that all others must be excluded. Told
him to use whatever powers were necessary to set up a loyal Unionist
government, because if the state fell into the hands of our enemies, all
we'd fought for there would be lost. I was glad, I said, that he'd
declared in favor of emancipation and colored troops, and told him to
see to it that emancipation was written into a new state constitution.

I'd given similar instructions to General Banks, military governor
of Louisiana, but his reconstruction efforts had faltered because of
an obstacle that always bedeviled us: family quarrels. From the start,
the loyal Unionist minority split into feuding factions, with the "conservatives" declaring in favor of the old state constitution, which
guaranteed slavery, and the "radicals" demanding a new constitution that would outlaw slavery. No choice as far as I was concerned:
I sided with the radicals. Through Banks, I told the Louisiana Unionists they must not only support the emancipation proclamation and
the slave-liberation sections of the confiscation acts, but must also
write a constitution that abolished slavery throughout the state,
including the parishes I'd exempted. But I told 'em I would be flexi-
ble about the relations between the races: I wouldn't object if some
temporary practical system of labor were adopted so that the two
races could gradually live themselves out of their old relation to each
other, and both be better prepared for the new, so long as the system
did not impair the permanent freedom of the former slaves. Whatever system Louisiana came up with, I added, it ought to provide for
the education of young blacks.

Now get on with it, I told Banks: call a convention to write a new constitution and hold elections. But I warned him: if Louisiana Unionists drafted a constitution that rejected emancipation, I would repudiate their work. To my bitter disappointment, delays and factional feuds continued to impede reconstruction in Louisiana. I worried, too, because the fractious Unionist minority was surrounded by a large majority of hostile rebel sympathizers.

My reconstruction efforts had also run into a formidable opponent on Capitol Hill. My good friend, Sumner, argued that Congress and not the president had constitutional jurisdiction over reconstruction. He based that argument on the theory that the insurgent states had committed suicide as states and had reverted back to the status of territories, which were the creatures of Congress and could only be administered and readmitted to the Union by Congress. Sumner also doubted that southern whites could ever be loyal, and he objected to their participating in the reconstruction process. The blacks, he said, were the only Unionists in Dixie, and he wanted Congress to grant them full citizenship, including the right to vote.

Sumner's program gave conservative Republicans fits. If the former slaves became citizens with the right to vote, the conservatives cried, they could also run for office, and the next thing you'd know, they'd be sitting in Congress and influencing the destiny of the Republic. Another fear was that rebellious whites would gain control of the Negro vote and would have more power than ever. Postmaster Monty Blair of Maryland summed up the views of this class of Republicans when he said in a speech in Maryland that Sumner and his followers were scheming to bring about racial equality and amalgamation, that this was the whole purpose of Sumner's approach to reconstruction.

I tried not to make anything out of the Blair-Sumner split. The controversy between them and the two sets of men they represented, I told young Hay, was one of form and little else. "I don't think Blair wants the states in rebellion to be permitted to come at once into the political family and renew the very acts that have so bedeviled us. I don't think Sumner would insist that when the loyal people of a state gain control and are ready to assume the direction of their own affairs, that they should be excluded. I don't believe Blair wants Jefferson Davis to take his seat in Congress, and I don't believe Sumner wants the Virginia Unionist, John Minor Botts, to be excluded from Congress. As far as I understand Sumner, he wants Congress to take from the Executive the power over insurrectionary districts. But as to the vital question of the right and privilege of the people of these states to govern themselves, I think there will be little difference among loyal men. The great practical problem we face is how to keep the rebellious populations from overwhelming and outvoting the loyal minority and returning the old southern ruling class to power."

My message to Congress addressed that problem and offered a solution to it. When Congressman Elihu Washburne called in early December, I decided to try the message out on him. He's a gray-haired, broad-shouldered fellow with an ample belly and thin legs—walks with a limp, because of a problem in his hip. His district in Illinois included Galena, Grant's home, and he was Grant's greatest supporter and champion. Can't count the number of times he's stood here in my office and argued Grant's case. I wanted Grant to have a gold medal for his great achievements in the field and entrusted Washburne with the task of getting congressional approval.

"Mr. President," he said, "I want to thank you for your unwavering support of General Grant. When newspapers and politicians attacked him and Sherman after Shiloh, you stood like a wall of fire between them and their critics, and I know Grant appreciates it, as I do. It will be an honor to get the medal for him."

"Sit down, Washburne. I've got something I want to read you. My message to Congress. Nobody else has heard it. I want your opinion on the sections that deal with emancipation and reconstruction." Walking back and forth in my office, I read the message:

"The policy of emancipation and of employing black soldiers gave to the future a new aspect," I said, "about which hope, and fear, and doubt contended in uncertain conflict. According to our political system, as a matter of civil administration, the general government had no lawful power to effect emancipation in any state, and for a long time it had been hoped that the rebellion could be suppressed without resorting to it as a military measure. But the necessity for it came, and as was anticipated, it was followed by dark and doubtful days. Eleven months having now passed, we are permitted to take another review. The rebel borders are pressed still further back, and by the complete opening of the Mississippi the country dominated by the rebellion is divided into distinct parts, with no practical communication between them.

"Of those who were slaves at the beginning of the rebellion, full one hundred thousand are now in the United States military service, thus giving the double advantage of taking so much labor from the insurgent cause and supplying the places which otherwise must be filled with so many white men. So far as tested, it is difficult to say they are not as good soldiers as any. No servile insurrection, or tendency to violence or cruelty, has marked the measures of emancipation and arming the blacks. These measures have been much discussed in foreign countries, and contemporary with such discussion the tone of public sentiment there is much improved. At home the same measures have been fully discussed, supported, criticized, and denounced, and the annual elections following are highly encouraging to those whose official duty it is to bear the country through this great trial. Thus we have the new reckoning. The crisis which threatened to divide the friends of the Union is past."

Then the message turned to reconstruction. "Looking to a resumption of the national authority within the insurgent districts, I have thought fit to issue a proclamation, a copy of which is herewith transmitted." I then read the Proclamation of Amnesty and Reconstruction, which offered a solution to the problem of how to prevent the rebellious majority of a conquered state from overwhelming and outvoting the loyal minority. The proclamation offered a full pardon to all persons who had directly or by implication participated in the rebellion, with the restoration of all rights of property except as to slaves, on the condition that every such person should take and subscribe to the following oath of allegiance, which would be inviolate:

"I _____ do solemnly swear, in presence of Almighty God, that I will henceforth faithfully support, protect and defend the Constitution of the United States, and the Union of the states thereunder; and that I will, in like manner, abide by and faithfully support all acts of Congress passed during the existing rebellion with reference to slaves, so long and so far as not repealed, modified or held void by Congress, or by decision of the Supreme Court; and that I will, in like manner, abide by and faithfully support all proclamations of the President made during the existing rebellion having reference to slaves, so long and so far as not modified or declared void by decision of the Supreme Court. So help me God."

In my message proper, I explained why I'd come up with this particular oath. "There must be a test by which to separate the opposing elements so as to build only from the sound; and that test is a sufficiently liberal one, which accepts as sound whoever will make a sworn recantation of his former unsoundness. But if it be proper to require, as a test of admission to the political body, an oath of allegiance to the Constitution of the United States, and to the

Union under it, why also to the laws and proclamations in regard to slavery? Those laws and proclamations were enacted and put forth for the purpose of aiding in the suppression of the rebellion. To give them their fullest effect, there had to be a pledge for their maintenance. To now abandon them would be not only to relinquish a lever of power, but would also be a cruel and an astounding breach of faith. I shall not attempt to retract or modify the emancipation proclamation; nor shall I return to slavery any person who is free by the terms of the proclamation or by any of the acts of Congress. For these and other reasons it is thought best that support of these measures shall be included in the oath; and it is believed the Executive may lawfully claim it in return for pardon and restoration of forfeited rights." In other words, I explained to Washburne, emancipation was a mandatory part of the reconstruction process, unless modified or abrogated by congressional legislation or supreme judicial decision.

I flipped back to the appended proclamation, which declared that the following classes of persons would not be pardoned and thus would not be permitted to participate in the reconstruction process: "all who are, or shall have been, civil or diplomatic officers or agents of the so-called confederate government; all who have left judicial stations under the United States to aid the rebellion; all who are, or shall have been, military or naval officers of said so-called confederate government above the rank of colonel in the army, or of lieutenant in the navy; all who left seats in the United States Congress to aid the rebellion; all who resigned commissions in the army or navy of the United States, and afterwards aided the rebellion; and all who have engaged in any way in treating colored persons or white persons, in charge of such, otherwise than lawfully as prisoners of war, and which persons may have been found in the United States service as soldiers, seamen, or in any other capacity."

The proclamation went on to proclaim that whenever, in any of the insurgent states, a number of qualified voters equal in number to one-tenth (or 10 percent) of those who'd cast ballots in the 1860 presidential election had taken the oath of allegiance, they could proceed to reestablish a state government, which should be republican in form, and the state would then receive the full protection of the Federal authority. The proclamation also repeated what I'd told Banks and the Unionists of Louisiana: "any provision which may be adopted by such state government in relation to the freed people of such state, which shall recognize and declare their permanent freedom, provide for their education, and which may yet be consistent, as a temporary arrangement, with their present condition as a laboring, landless, and homeless class, will not be objected to by the national Executive."

In both the proclamation and the message proper, I said I was offering a mode in and by which loyal state governments might be reestablished within the states where the national authority had been suspended; and while the mode presented was the best the Executive could suggest at present, it must not be understood that no other possible mode would be acceptable. And in saying that certain classes would be pardoned, with their rights restored, I was not saying that other classes, or other terms, would never be included.

Washburne said he liked the message and thought it would be well received by all classes of Republicans.

"I hope you're right," I said.

The message was read to a joint session of Congress on December ninth. Afterward young Hay and young Brooks circulated among Republicans in both houses, collecting opinions. Turned out, Washburne's prediction was right. Hay reported that Republicans in both houses "acted as if the millennium had come." In the Senate, Chandler praised the message and the proclamation, and Sumner said he was "not displeased," said my proclamation satisfied his idea of a correct approach to reconstruction in the absence of a congressional plan for now. Conservatives like Dixon and Reverdy Johnson also declared the proclamation "highly satisfactory."

In the House, Owen Lovejoy, who was the best friend I had on the Hill, was overjoyed and said that he would actually live to see slavery dead in America. One Michigan congressman actually called me "a great leader" and said I saw "more widely and clearly than anybody." Newsman Forney said: "We only wanted a leader to speak the bold word. It is done and all can follow."

"This proves that there is no essential difference between loyal men on the subject of reconstruction," I said.

Well, I was wrong. Reconstruction split the party badly. Louisiana was what did it. I'd made General Banks sole master of the reconstruction process there, and he installed a freedmen's labor system like the one Thomas had established in the Mississippi Valley. Under Banks's system, Federal agents hired out former slaves to white planters or government "lessees"—men who managed abandoned rebel estates—at government-regulated conditions and wages. I approved of the system, so long as the colored people were paid and treated fairly. Under Banks's supervision, Louisiana loyalists also elected a governor and chose delegates to a state constitutional convention. Before the convention met, I received petitions from prominent colored men of New Orleans, who belonged to a relatively well-educated and outspoken free black community; they implored me to grant them the right to vote, and I was sympathetic. I wrote the newly elected governor: "I barely suggest for your private consideration, whether some of the colored people may not be let in on the electoral franchise—as, for instance, the very intelligent, and especially those who have fought gallantly in our ranks. They would probably help, in some trying time to come, to keep the jewel of liberty within the family of freedom." Now this was just a suggestion, not an order. Negro suffrage was exceedingly controversial—blacks couldn't even vote in most of the North, and most Republicans did not support that right. If I tried to force it on the white Unionist minority in Louisiana, it would alienate 'em entirely and Louisiana would never be reconstructed.

Turned out, the Louisiana convention, when it met, rejected my suggestion and denied the suffrage to the former slaves. Banks and I did persuade the convention delegates to agree to a compromise: the constitution they drew up did not enfranchise Louisiana blacks, but it did authorize the legislature to grant 'em the vote. Louisiana's white voters ratified the constitution by a margin of more than four to one and elected state and national representatives. I accepted reconstruction in Louisiana as the best that could be accomplished and took similar steps in reconstructing Arkansas.

Okay. The all-white government in Louisiana *was* imperfect, but it was a hell of a lot better than no government at all. In the passage of time, when prejudice and passions subside, its worst defects can be corrected. It's a foundation to build on for whites and colored people.

51. DOUGLASS

I hated Lincoln's approach to reconstruction. His 10 percent plan, as his program was popularly called, was a fraud, an entire contradiction of the constitutional idea of Republican government. Senator Sumner was right: how could *military power* create a *free civilian government*? What really enraged me was Banks's reconstruction regime in Louisiana. The labor system installed there for the freedmen was a *swindle* that practically reestablished the hateful system of slavery. The rate of pay for plantation workers—ten dollars a month—was too low, lower than what free Negroes in the South had earned before the war. There were reports that some white employers were abusing and exploiting their black workers. How had conditions materially improved for them? What the blacks needed was land, which would give them economic independence, a way to sustain themselves. *Self-help*, that was what we wanted for them.

What they absolutely had to have was full citizenship and the *right to vote*. Without that and without economic security, they would be at the mercy of their former masters. They would not have a single element of strength to shield themselves from the vindictive spirit sure to be roused against the whole colored race. How could Lincoln endorse the evil system in Louisiana? It rocked my faith in him to the foundations. He no longer had my vote. I wanted the nomination and election of a man to the presidency of more decided antislavery convictions and a firmer faith in the immediate necessity and practicability of justice and equality for all men, than had been exhibited in the policy of the present Administration.

52. DAVIS

Lincoln's plan of reconstruction was a constitutional atrocity. He told us that we could only expect his gracious pardon by emancipating all our slaves, dissolving the Confederacy, disbanding our armies, swearing allegiance and obedience to him and his proclamations, and becoming in point of fact the slaves of our own niggers. Lincoln's own partisans at the North avowed unequivocally that his purpose in his message to Congress and his Proclamation of Amnesty and Reconstruction was to shut out all hope that he would ever treat with us on any terms. In order to render his proposals so insulting as to secure their rejection, he joined to them a promise to support with his army one-tenth of the people of any state who would attempt to set up a government over the other nine-tenths, thus seeking to sow discord and suspicion among the people of the several states, and to excite them to civil war in furtherance of his ends. The oath in his proclamation required the voter to swear allegiance to the U.S. Constitution. Thus to invoke the Constitution was like Satan quoting Scripture.

With only his usurped war power to sustain him in the work of destruction, Lincoln went imperiously forward, trampling under foot every American political principle and breaking through every constitutional limitation. As I told Governor Vance of North Carolina, we had to fight on for our great cause of liberty and independence. Peace on any other terms was impossible. The struggle had to continue until the enemy was beaten out of his vain confidence in our subjugation. Then and not until then would it be possible to treat for peace.

Meanwhile I was preparing my message to Congress and debating what to say about the incomprehensible and excruciating disaster that had befallen Bragg at Missionary Ridge and Lookout Mountain. The Federal forces in Chattanooga ought to have been wiped out or starved into capitulation, but neither had happened, and positions of great strength had been inexplicably abandoned. At least Bragg spared me the ordeal of dismissing him from command of the army; he asked to be relieved, and I obliged him. General Hardee assumed temporary command and was the logical choice to succeed Bragg, but Hardee informed us that he did not want permanent command. On December sixth, I again asked Lee if he would take charge of the Army of Tennessee. But Lee again declined the offer, arguing that the subordinate commanders would not cooperate with him. "I can see no good that will result," he said. That left me with either Johnston or Beauregard, the ranking full generals, and either of them would be a bitter pill to swallow.

Congress convened on December seventh, and my message was read to a joint session of both houses. In my message, I conceded that grave reverses had befallen our arms at Vicksburg and Port Hudson. But the determined and successful defense of Charleston against both land and naval forces demonstrated our ability to repel an enemy ironclad fleet. As for Gettysburg, the able commander who led the Army of Northern Virginia resolved to meet the threatened enemy advance against Richmond by forcing the enemy army to cross the Potomac and fight in defense of the northern capital and northern homes. He succeeded in forcing the enemy to abandon Virginia and in the hard-fought battle of Gettysburg inflicted such severity of punishment as disabled the Federals from an early renewal of the campaign as originally projected.

As for the West, I praised the Army of Tennessee for winning on the battlefield of Chickamauga one of the most brilliant and decisive victories of the war. That victory forced the invader to fall back into Chattanooga, which had the salutary effect of relieving the pressure of invasion at other points because the enemy was compelled to concentrate large bodies of troops to relieve the besieged force at Chattanooga. The combined enemy forces, which greatly outnumbered our own, attacked and after a long and severe battle, in which great carnage was inflicted on the invaders, some of our troops inexplicably abandoned a position of great strength, and by a disorderly retreat compelled the commander to retreat with his whole army. Had the troops who took flight fought with the gallantry displayed on previous occasions, I said, it was believed the enemy would have been repulsed with very great slaughter.

Our enemy, I went on, continued to wage war with savage ferocity against our people. These pretended friends of human rights and liberties also perpetrated *unrelenting warfare* against the unfortunate Negroes. Whenever possible, the invaders had seized and forced into their military ranks every able-bodied slave and had left old men, women, and children to starve, or had gathered them into camps where they suffered frightfully. Without clothing or shelter, often without food, incapable without supervision of taking the most ordinary precautions against disease, these helpless dependents, accustomed to having their wants supplied by the foresight of their masters, were being rapidly exterminated wherever brought in contact with the invaders. By the northern man, on whose deep-rooted prejudices no kindly restraining influence was exercised, the Negroes were treated with aversion and neglect. These facts, I pointed out, derived from our own observations and from the reports of Negroes who had succeeded in escaping from the enemy, and were fully confirmed by the northern press.

Having begun the war in direct violation of their Constitution, which forbids the attempt to coerce a state, our northern enemies had been hardened by crime until they no longer attempted to veil their purpose to destroy the institutions and subvert the sovereignty and independence of these states. *We now know that our only reliable hope for peace is in the vigor of our resistance.*

While my message was being read, I steeled myself for the attacks to which I knew I would be subjected. The next day bitter-tongued Henry Foote took the floor in the House and demanded an investigation into the loss of his adopted state of Tennessee, which, he said, lay bleeding under the heavy boot of the invader. He blamed me for our disasters there, saying that I was "guilty of gross incompetence" and "kept unworthy and incompetent men in command," by which, of course, he meant General Bragg. Why, he demanded, was I equivocating in appointing a new commander for the Army of Tennessee? "Why is Johnston not now appointed? Why isn't Beauregard?"

I was not equivocating! I was understandably reluctant to turn our second most important army over to the likes of Johnston or Beauregard. On the ninth I called Lee to Richmond for a series of talks with him and my Cabinet, hoping that I could persuade him to go to Dalton and take command of the Army of Tennessee. But General Lee remained adamantly opposed to such a move, insisting that his heart and his fate lay with the Army of Northern Virginia. He preferred that the western army be given to Johnston, and Seddon and most of the other Cabinet secretaries agreed that I ought to give Johnston another chance.

With great reluctance, I gave in and reinstated General Johnston—I had no other choice. In hopes of assuaging the bad feeling between us, I sent him a letter urging him to communicate fully and freely with me and promising that I would support him to the fullest. With my enemies in Congress crying for my head, I beseeched Johnston to take the offensive and regain the territory Bragg had lost. Johnston replied that he would like to do that, but that "difficulties appear to be in the way." I groaned when I read that. Throwing the dispatch aside, I rose from my desk, went to the window, and stared at the rain falling outside.

53 · CHESNUT

When the Wigfalls called on us that December, Louis began by talking virulent nonsense, saying he wanted to hang Jeff Davis. James managed him beautifully and then took me aside and blamed me for Wigfall's outburst. "You looked to be keenly interested in what he was saying. Don't let him catch your eye! Look into the fire." I laughed hysterically, so sudden, violent, and unlooked for was my husband's attack. But as an obedient wife I returned to my seat and stared into the fire.

One Sunday evening in mid-December, I called at the president's mansion and had tea with Varina and her sickly, careworn husband. I believe he hated to put our western army into the hands of General Johnston, who was such a horrible failure. For a day of Albert Sidney Johnston out west! And Stonewall, could he only come back to us! While Varina and I chatted, little Joe Davis rushed in clad in his nightclothes and insisted on saying his prayers at the president's knee. The president patted him on the head and kissed him good night. He was so *sweet* to his children, so kind and gentle. The picture of Jefferson Davis as a cold, aloof, unfeeling man is all wrong.

He was such a gentleman in every respect and claimed to enjoy my company immensely. Once he walked me home after church, but his gait was so fast that I had no breath for talk. The truth is, I was too much afraid of him to say very much when there was just the two of us. He was so sick so much of the time, you just can't imagine his suffering. When Varina gave her "luncheon to ladies," as she called it, she spoke of the president's poor health as we dined on gumbo, ducks and olives, supreme de volaille, chickens in jelly, oysters, lettuce salad, chocolate jelly cake, claret soup, and champagne. In addition to neuralgia, the president had dyspepsia and had such an aversion to food that Varina often had to fix a lunch, take it to his office on a tray, and stay to see that he ate.

With the onset of winter, Richmond seemed to be full of generals and officers on leave from their commands. One Sunday I saw General Lee in church, making his way down the aisle, bowing royally right and left. When he looked my way, he bowed low and gave me a smile of recognition. I was ashamed of being so pleased. I blushed just like a schoolgirl. By all odds, General Lee was the handsomest man in the entire Confederacy.

But oh his poor wife! When I visited her in her little place in Richmond, she was so crippled from rheumatism. She couldn't walk and rolled about her rooms in a wheel-chair. She called herself a poor lame mother, useless to her husband and her children. I felt so *sorry* for her and her family, all the suffering they endured. Her son Rooney was still a Yankee prisoner—they said he was at Fort Lafayette in New York Harbor. Rooney's wife, Charlotte, died that winter; she was only twenty-three. One of her babies also died.

Constance Cary said, "If it would please God to take poor Cousin Mary Lee away—she suffers so—wouldn't the Richmond women campaign for Cousin Robert's hand?" Wherever her Cousin Robert went in the city, adoring females surrounded him, yet he held all at arm's length. One day, James told me that General Lee had come to his office to pay his respects and have a talk. I said that this was a wonderful compliment from the very first man in the world.

General Hood, the wounded knight, was also back in town. He had lost a leg at Chickamauga—an exploding bullet had shattered the bone in his right leg and the surgeons had to amputate it above the knee. The men of the Texas Brigade contributed some $3,000 with which to buy him a cork leg. When he called on us, Henry Brewster had to lift him out of the carriage and carry him inside to our sofa, where he lay with a blanket over him.

Our poor Sam! He was about thirty-two then, a shy, rustic-looking man with a long face, a large nose, and sad eyes. Back in the summer, when he was recovering from a nasty arm wound at Gettysburg, he had come to our house for tea and had fallen madly in love with Sally "Buck" Preston, my beautiful charge, who had a knack of being "'fallen in love with' at sight, and never being 'fallen out of love with.'" Later Buck and her sister Mamie had gone home to South Carolina, and in November all the Prestons had come to Richmond, and each of the girls brought a friend. How I loved and enjoyed those four young people, but blue-eyed Buck remained my favorite, she had such a wonderfully sweet smile and a clear, ringing, musical voice.

While Buck and Mamie lived with their parents, our house remained their headquarters, which was why Sam Hood came calling on us that December, minus a leg. The Preston girls were due back that very day from Petersburg, and he kept watching the door wistfully. Other visitors called that day—the Wigfalls, Mrs. Mallory, Mrs. Randolph. They lavished sympathy on Sam, were all condolence and tears. Mrs. Mallory proclaimed him a martyr to the country.

"I don't aim to become a recluse," Sam said. "I aim to be as happy a fool, well, as a one-legged man can be. Send me off now. So many strangers scare me. I can't run now like I did before."

There was such sighing and wringing of hands when Mr. Brewster carried him away. When Buck arrived from Petersburg, she acted very strange about Sam—it was hard to know where matters stood between them. A few nights later, at a dinner party at our house attended among others by Howell Cobb, R. M. T. Hunter, Custis Lee, and the ever-welcome Lieutenant Colonel Charles Venable of General Lee's staff, Buck flirted shamelessly. Colonel Venable said she couldn't help herself, it was in her nature to flirt. "As for Sam Hood," he said, "she doesn't care for him as a man. It's sympathy with the wounded soldier, helpless Hood, that she cares about."

At the table, the principal topic of conversation was Lincoln's Proclamation of Amnesty and Reconstruction, which denied clemency to our military officers, Confederate officials, and politicians who had held office in the Union before the war. Mrs. Benjamin Huger said she was delighted that her husband was one of those not pardoned. "I would be ashamed if he was not among those Lincoln threatened to hang," she said.

A few days before Christmas, Sam took Buck for a ride in his carriage, and I went along as her chaperone, with Mr. Brewster driving. Buck was dressed in black velvet and ermine and looked just queenly. It was very cold out, and the rest of us were well wrapped in rugs and furs. As we rode back from the fairgrounds, Sam, the wounded knight, asked Bewster: "What are the symptoms of a man's being in love? I once fancied myself being in love, when I was seventeen, but that was a long time ago."

Brewster said: "When you see her, your breath is apt to come short. If it amounts to mild strangulation, you've got it bad. You're stupidly jealous and have a gloomy fixed conviction that she likes every fool she meets better than you."

"I haven't felt any of that so far," Hood said. He was quiet for a moment. "You know what they're saying, don't you?" he asked. "They say I'm engaged to four young ladies."

"Who?" Buck asked.

"Miss Wigfall is one," Sam said. "And Miss Sally Preston is another."

Buck didn't bat an eye, kept her gaze on the horses.

"Are you annoyed at such a preposterous report?" he asked.

"No," she said. "You know what they say about me? They say I'm engaged to *two* young men."

"I think I'll set a trap near your door and break some of those young fellows' legs," Sam said. I thought he had one of Brewster's symptomatic strangles, but I said nothing, since it was none of my business.

We invited Sam and Alex Haskell, who had lost an eye, to share Christmas dinner with us, a rather simple fare of oysters, ham, turkey, partridges, and wine. While Alex and James were chatting, Sam took me aside and said that he had called on Buck last night and that he hadn't been able to sleep after that. "Hardest battle of

my life," he said, "and I lost it. She told me there was '*no hope*'—
that ends it. You know, at Petersburg, on my way to the western
army, I asked for her hand, and she half-promised me to think about
it. She didn't say yes, but she didn't say no, that is, not exactly. At
any rate, I went off, saying, I'm engaged to you, and she said, I'm
not engaged to you. After I was so fearfully wounded, I gave it up.
But then, since I've been back—"

"You mean you'd already proposed to her when you asked
Brewster about the symptoms of being in love?"

"Oh, she understood," Sam said, "but it's all over now. She says
no."

Sometime after that, at a dinner party at our house that featured
terrapin stew, oysters, and Rhine wine, Sam told Buck and me that he
was going to be promoted to lieutenant general and given command
of a corps in the Army of Tennessee. His eyes blazed as he said this.
"When I'm gone," he said to me, "it's all over. I'll not come back."

"Aren't you threatening the wrong end of the sofa?" I said.

Sam laughed and turned his back on Buck. "Will she care?"

"How do I know?" I asked and moved away.

When the party was over and Sam was making his leave, I
noticed that the diamond star was missing from the front of his hat.
Later that night, I asked Buck about it, and she was all giggle and
blush. *She* had his diamond star. So it wasn't over after all.

Sam and the president saw a good deal of one another that winter. Once Sam was able to sit a horse by strapping himself into the
saddle, he accompanied the president on his afternoon rides around
Richmond. Sam became a friend of Varina's, too, and of their children, and one Sunday he joined the first family in the president's
pew in St. Paul's Episcopal Church. Varina spoke highly of Sam and
said that her husband very much liked his company. I think Sam was
a good listener to the president's many woes.

When the president was too ill to take Varina to a dinner party
at our house, Sam escorted her himself. As they sat talking, we could
all hear Buck's clear, musical voice in the next room, where she was
flirting with a young man. "Absurd!" she said. "Engaged to that
man! Never!" Varina told Sam what General William N. Pendleton
once said: "If he had been so often hit, he would wince and dodge at
every ball." Sam said: "Why wince—when you wished to God for a
ball to go through your heart and be done with it all?" Varina later
told me: "This is high tragedy, for there was the bitterness of death
in his tone."

A few days later, Sam took Buck for a ride in his carriage. He had a wooden leg now and was able to get about fairly well. When Buck returned, she told me he had proffered his hand to her. "I told him, don't do that!" she said. "I told him, 'You know I like you. You want to spoil it all.' 'Say yes or say no,' he said. 'I won't be satisfied with less. Yes or no.' Well, Mrs. Chesnut, he kept holding out his hand. What could I do? So I put mine in his and heavens, what a change came over his face. I had to *pry* my hand loose from his. He is such a wretch! He said at once: 'Now I will speak to your father. I want his consent to marry you.'" Buck gave a deep sigh. "I said okay, which I suppose means we're engaged. Did you ever know so foolish a fellow? Now do you believe I like him?"

"No," I told her frankly. Later I wrote in my diary: "So the tragedy has been played out, for I do not think *even now* that she is in earnest."

Sam was indeed transformed. "I'm so proud, so grateful," he said when I next saw him. "The sun never shone on a happier man! Such a noble girl—a queen among women." He told everybody that he and Buck were engaged, and notices about it appeared in the newspapers. The Richmond correspondent to the *Charleston Mercury* reported: "Gossips say General Hood has been captured, and even completely subjugated, by a fair daughter of South Carolina, and a representative of one of its most honored families. It is believed that he will soon take the oath of allegiance, but the date of the swearing has not been stated."

The reason it had "not been stated" was the strenuous opposition of Buck's parents to the engagement, which they thought was appalling. John Preston refused to give his consent, and Caroline Preston was in a dreadful state that her daughter would even think of betrothing "that uncouth Texan." Buck herself was offended by Sam's "rough way of wooing," as she put it. "A few days ago," she told me, "as I was standing beside the fender of his carriage, warming my feet, he seized me around the waist with his good arm and kissed my throat. It was perfectly horrible. When he saw how shocked I was, he was frightened and humble and full of apologies. He told me my throat was so soft and white he couldn't help himself. I drew back, turned away, and told him I was offended. In a moment I felt a strong arm so tight around my waist I couldn't move. He said I should stay until I forgave his rash presumption, and he held me fast. He said my promise to marry him made all the difference in the world, but I told him I was still offended and made him let me go."

When I asked if the engagement was still on, Buck just shrugged.

Just before Sam left for northern Georgia and the Army of Tennessee, he told me that the president had been finding fault with some of his commanding generals. Hood said to him: "Mr. President, why don't you come and lead us yourself. I would follow you to the death." I told Sam if he remained in Richmond much longer, he would become a courtier. Two days later, our gallant Sam was gone. Honestly, I think Buck was relieved to see him go.

The rain and mud kept all the armies quiet for now. Beneficent mud! No killed or killing on hand. No rumbling of wagons laden with the dead and the dying. We enjoyed this reprieve, this brief interlude of comparative peace. But we knew it would not last—knew that with spring the dreadful work of death would begin again, with endless funeral marches and untold suffering throughout our embattled Confederacy.

THE WINDS OF 'SIXTY-FOUR

Bring the good old bugle, boys, we'll sing another song—
Sing it with a spirit that will start the world along—
Sing it as we used to sing it, fifty thousand strong,
While we were marching through Georgia.

Hurrah! Hurrah! we bring the jubilee,
Hurrah! Hurrah! the flag that makes you free!
So we sang the chorus from Atlanta to the Sea,
While we were marching through Georgia.

Now the dangerous storm is rolling,
Which treacherous brothers madly raise,
The dogs of war let loose, are howling,
And soon our peaceful towns may blaze
And soon our peaceful towns may blaze.

1. SHERMAN

The rebels still maintained a considerable force of infantry and cavalry in Mississippi, which threatened the great river and kept the railroad open to the eastern Confederacy, so that supplies could be sent there from the eastern part of the state. I thought I could check this and got permission from Grant to take twenty thousand men and march through eastern Mississippi as far as Meridian, breaking up the Mobile & Ohio Railroad and cutting a swath of destruction so as to punish the hostile civilian population. I aimed to make the rebellious southern people understand that they had caused this contest and thus invited the war of conquest and ruin we were now obliged to wage against 'em.

We could not change the hearts of these people of the South, could not make them love us, but we could make the monster of war so terrible that they would dread the passage of our armies and realize the futility of having ever appealed to it. I believe that many of their ruling class, the rich slaveholders, by skillful political handling had involved the whole South in fighting this war for their Goddamned benefit. Some of that class hated the Union so much that nothing but death and ruin would ever extinguish them.

One of my objectives was the destruction of Nathan Forrest's irregular cavalry, which was constantly threatening Memphis and the river above it, as well as our railroad supply routes in middle Tennessee. I hated the Goddamn irregulars and guerrillas because they struck our columns and trains at night, murdering and bushwhacking, and then melted back into the civilian population by day like the Goddamned cowards they were. I placed under Brigadier General Sooy Smith, at Memphis, a cavalry force of about seven thousand and told Smith I wanted that fucking Forrest wiped off the face of the earth. I ordered Smith to march straight from Memphis to Meridian, starting February first. I also directed General A. J. Smith at Columbus, Kentucky, to move his force into western Tennessee, to cooperate with me. Smith was to punish the hostile civilian inhabitants for permitting Forrest's irregulars and other guerrillas to hide among them. Smith was to take freely their horses, mules, and cattle and let them all understand that if from design or weakness they permitted their country to be used by the enemy they must pay the Goddamned price.

I went to Vicksburg and there found a spy who had been to Meridian and who reported that the enemy commander there, Bishop Polk, had four divisions—two infantry and two cavalry—posted in the area. At Vicksburg, I concentrated two of McPherson's divisions and two of Hurlbut's and on February third we started east along the railroad in two columns. Once across the Big Black, we abandoned our supply line and lived off the country, confiscating from homesteads and plantations all we needed to eat and storing the food in our wagons. On the march eastward to Meridian, we destroyed a full hundred miles of railroad and left a swath of desolation fifty miles broad across the state which the present generation of Mississippians would not forget. We seized cattle and livestock and farm produce and burned and destroyed everything the rebels could use to make war.

As we approached Meridian, Bishop Polk was scared clear out of his senses, and he fled, leaving behind immense piles of stores and weapons. We entered Meridian on the fourteenth and the next day commenced burning its depots, arsenals, storehouses, offices, and hotels, ripping up the railroads east and west, and north and south, with axes, crowbars, clawbars, and sledges. We stayed there five days and I am proud to say that when we finished the task of destruction, Meridian had ceased to exist as a place that could support the rebel forces. The railroads were so badly wrecked they could not be used again for hostile purposes.

We expected every hour to hear of Sooy Smith, but we heard no tidings from him whatever. I even sent my own cavalry out to search for him—they rode all the way to Louisville, in northern Mississippi, but found no sign of him. Finally, we gave up on Smith and headed back to Vicksburg, followed by a column of nigger refugees ten miles long. At Vicksburg, I learned that Smith had bungled his orders and had started from Memphis ten days late. When he ran into Forrest, the Goddamned coward turn tail and fled, and Forrest overtook and whipped him with an inferior force.

The Meridian raid taught the southern people what kind of war they could expect from now on. We would make them so sick of war that generations would pass away before they would again appeal to it. The raid taught me something, too. Because we'd met so little opposition, it convinced me that the interior of the Confederacy was a hollow shell. Once we pierced the enemy's defensive lines, we could march all over the Goddamned interior, wrecking everything in our path.

2. DAVIS

Sherman's barbaric punitive raid against innocent civilians in Mississippi, which our undermanned forces were powerless to stop, convinced me of the absolute need to conscript into the service every man of military age, which, in accordance to a new conscription law, now included everyone between the ages of eighteen and fifty-five for the duration of the war. In the War Office, I remarked that if desertions and manpower shortages got worse, we might have to take twelve- and thirteen-year-old boys. In response to my plea that no effort must be spared to add largely to our effective force, General Patrick Cleburn, at a secret meeting of the general officers of the Army of Tennessee, proposed the radical step of enlisting slave soldiers as the Yankees were doing. He argued that if we resorted to slave soldiers it would win the Negro and world opinion back to our side.

His proposal was forwarded to me by General W. H. T. Walker, who thought it incendiary and even treasonable. I agreed. This dangerous proposition, if it became known, would create a horrendous controversy that would divide our people at a time when we most needed unity. Therefore I had Seddon inform General Johnston, commander of the Army of Tennessee, that he must keep Cleburn's proposal a secret and see to it that it did not find its way into the public journals.

At my urging and that of Secretary of War Seddon, Congress did authorize the Administration to impress twenty thousand slaves to function as cooks, teamsters, and laborers on fortifications. Up to now, the government had relied on masters to voluntarily hire their slaves to the government, but that policy had failed. Hence the resort to the new coercive measure, with a compensation of $11 per month to the master of each slave impressed.

Meanwhile Governor Vance sent me troubling reports about the extent of disloyalty in North Carolina, where the *Raleigh Press* and traitorous groups were urging peace at any price. Vance warned that disaffection was so widespread in North Carolina that it could not possibly be removed save by my negotiating with the enemy.

"We have tried three times to communicate with the authorities in Washington, without success," I replied. "To attempt again to send commissioners or agents to propose peace, is to invite insult and contumely, and to subject ourselves to indignity without the slightest chance of being listened to. No true citizen, no man who has our cause at heart, can desire this, and the good people of North Carolina would be the last to approve of such an attempt, if aware of all the facts. And what if we did get an interview with Lincoln? That contemptible despot has already apprised us that his terms for peace include the emancipation of all our slaves, a declaration of our allegiance and obedience to him and his proclamations. Can there be in North Carolina one citizen so fallen beneath the dignity of his ancestors as to accept, or to enter into conference on the basis of these terms? That there are a few traitors in the state who would be willing to betray their fellow citizens to such a degraded condition may be true. But I do not believe that the vilest wretch would accept such terms for himself."

I made it plain that I would *not compromise* my condition for peace. That was the permanent independence of the Confederate States of America.

I was so alarmed by the so-called peace movements in North Carolina and elsewhere that I asked Congress for the authority to suspend the writ of habeas corpus as a means of suppressing disloyal meetings and secret peace societies. If something were not done, I warned, we could not retain men already in the service. "Desertion, already a frightful evil, will become the order of the day. And who will arrest the deserter, when most of those at home are engaged with him in the common cause of setting the government at defiance? Organized bands of deserters will patrol the country, burning, plundering, and robbing indiscriminately, and our armies, already too weak, must be still further depleted at the most imminent crisis of our cause, to keep the peace and protect the lives and property of our citizens at home."

I received the authority to suspend the writ and promptly did so in the disaffected areas, so that the traitors to the cause could be imprisoned and silenced. This provoked violent protests from Governor Brown of Georgia and Alexander Stephens, my alleged vice president, who had long since gone home to his Georgia plantation. They complained bitterly to the state legislature about the suspension of the writ. Brown ranted that it would lead to "illegal and unconstitutional arrests," and Stephens raged that it was a menace to liberty and a vicious wrong. Senator Herschel Johnston told Stephens bluntly: "You are wrong in view of your official position as vice president; you are wrong because the whole movement originated in a mad purpose to make war on Davis and Congress. You are wrong because the movement is joyous to the enemy, and they are already using it in their press."

We heard disturbing rumors that the Georgia legislature would attempt to negotiate a peace with the Union. The legislature did adopt resolutions calling for peace, but not before our loyal friends added an amendment that pledged the state's support for the war until we won our independence.

To help me coordinate our far-flung military operations, I called Braxton Bragg to Richmond as my military adviser. The croakers of course put up a vicious howl, accusing me once again of favoritism, but I had need of Bragg's skill as a military administrator in the great battles that lay ahead when warmer weather returned.

On March first, while I was in my office, I heard the boom of artillery off to the north. Now what? Couriers from the country announced that a powerful force of some five thousand enemy cavalry was approaching the city's outer fortifications, and Colonel Chesnut and I rode out to inspect them. On the way, we passed an ambulance of wounded men, who cheered when they recognized me. Mrs. Chesnut was right: "It is not the army but civilians only who hate Jeff Davis."

Our defenses repelled the main body of the invaders and our cavalry chased them down the peninsula to Fort Monroe. A second column of enemy horsemen managed to break through our lines north of the city, but our home guard forces, reinforced by a detachment of Virginia cavalry and some furloughed horsemen from Lee's army, surprised and attacked the second column, capturing prisoners and killing the leader, Colonel Ulrich Dahlgren, who turned out to be the son of a prominent Yankee naval officer and a friend of Lincoln's. Our troops found on Dahlgren's body orders and instructions that called for the liberation of the Yankee prisoners on Belle Isle in the James River and the burning of Richmond. One appalling document, apparently a speech Dahlgren made to his men, declared that "Jeff. Davis and Cabinet must be killed on the spot. The men must keep together and well in hand, and once in the city it must be destroyed and Jeff. Davis and Cabinet killed."

I caused the documents to be published in the press so that our people and the whole world would see the character of the war the evil Yankees were waging and the assassinations and indiscriminate slaughter they plotted against us. The *Richmond Sentinel* demanded retaliation against the Yankee efforts at massacre and conflagration. "The hostilities which the Washington authorities carry on are not war, but military execution and coercion. What would we suggest?

First to put to death all 'raiders' caught in the act, secondly, to insist upon the most scrupulous carrying out of retaliation for murder, robberies, and other outrages, with the most punctual exactitude."

Seddon sent General Lee photographic copies of Dahlgren's papers, and Lee was furious. "I presume," he replied, "that the blood boils with indignation in the veins of every officer & man as they read the account of the barbarous & inhuman plot." But he advised against executing the captured raiders. Dahlgren's papers only showed his intentions, Lee argued; they did not reveal how many of his men knew about them, or that the enemy government had sanctioned them. It was best to be prudent, he said, "to do right, even if we suffer in so doing, than to incur the reproach of our consciences & posterity."

General Lee did send a note to Meade demanding to know if the captured papers were authentic. Meade answered that General Kilpatrick, the leader of the cavalry raid, denied that assassination had been its goal. Meade also denied that he or the government desired the murder of Confederate civilian leaders.

Officially, we accepted Meade's denial. But in private Seddon, I, and several other government officers believed beyond doubt that Lincoln himself had ordered our assassination and the burning of Richmond. Dahlgren, we believed, would never have planned to burn Richmond and murder me and my Cabinet without the approval of the highest Federal authorities. Accordingly, in mid-March I held a conference with Lee, Longstreet, and other leading officers to discuss the military situation and how we ought to respond to Dahlgren's raid. One mode of retaliation was to conduct raids into the North against enemy cities and liberate our prisoners. Another was to strengthen the Peace Democrats of the North and even incite them into open revolt. The enemy's presidential election was to take place in 1864, and the issue to be decided was peace or war. If we could help defeat Lincoln and elect a Peace Democrat, we believed we could achieve our independence.

We also discussed aiding a secret political organization in the Northwest. A certain individual who came to Richmond from Missouri informed me that he was active in that organization and that its objective was to form Michigan, Minnesota, Wisconsin, Iowa, Illinois, Indiana, and Ohio into a Northwest republic that would protect state rights and establish friendly relations with the Confederacy. The man claimed that the organization had almost fifty thousand members and had already destroyed Union ships and factories.

To cooperate with that secret society and to aid the Peace Democrats, I sent two commissioners to Canada with orders to intensify our clandestine activities from there. Two agents—Beverly Tucker, a former Virginia judge, and George Sanders of Kentucky—were already conducting secret service operations in Canada. The two commissioners who joined them that spring were my fellow Mississippian Jacob Thompson and my friend and longtime political associate Clement C. Clay of Alabama. They had $1 million in secret service money with which to encourage and cooperate with the Peace Democrats, assist the secret society plotting to establish a Northwest republic, and carry out punitive raids against northern cities, which was Sanders's specialty.

There were other forms of retaliation aimed at Lincoln himself. I am not at liberty to discuss the details, but I will say that they involved the kind of punishment which that crude usurper deserved for sanctioning the assassination of me and my Cabinet and for waging savage and relentless warfare against innocent civilians.

3 · JOHN WILKES BOOTH

I loved peace more than life, loved the *old Union* beyond expression. For four years I waited, hoped, and prayed for the dark clouds of civil war to break and for a restoration of our former sunshine. Wherever I played on the stage, as Richard the Third, as Pescara, as Raphael and Phidias, as Hamlet, Romeo, and Brutus in the North's great cities, with beautiful young women crowding the stage door to get a glimpse of the greatest tragedian in the land, swooning at his spectacular leaps and swordplay, at his matchless and musical voice reciting his lines to perfection, I kept a record of Caesar's vile deeds: the *war* upon southern rights and institutions, the *freeing* and *arming* of the niggers, the wholesale destruction of *home* and *hearthside*, the brutal *battles* and the killing of the *cream* of southern manhood, the *criminal arrests* in the North, the suave pressing of hordes of *ignorant foreigners* to swell his armies, the attempted *assassination* of Jefferson Davis and his Cabinet, so that there was no turning back, the old Union was dead and gone forever. Ah Caesar, you despicable tyrant! I played before you once, on the stage of Ford's New Theater, in the duel role of Raphael and Phidias in *The Marble*

Heart—the first actor in America to do that—and there you sat, in the presidential box just above the stage, with a couple of young men and a fat little woman I took to be your wife. Afterward, someone told me you had applauded my performance. *I would rather a nigger had applauded me,* I sneered.

As long as I can remember, my heart and all my sympathies have ever been with the South. I am a Marylander, the son and ninth child of the immortal Shakespearean Junius Brutus Booth, dead now, long live his name, and raised on a slaveowning farm not far from Bel Air, where my sisters, my beloved mother, my brothers, and all the niggers knew me as Johnny. When I attended St. Timothy's Hall, a military academy at Catonsville, I befriended southern cadets and shared their views of slavery and the heroic Cavaliers who ruled Dixie. How I *thrilled* my comrades when I proclaimed that *a name in history* was what I wanted, as I stood before the door-length mirror, admiring the reflection I saw of a handsome lad with wavy black hair, dark flashing eyes, and an exquisite mouth that made girls weep with longing.

I know I have not a long life to live, for an old wrinkled Gypsy said so when she read my palm. "Ah, you've a bad hand," she said in a hoarse voice. "The lines all crisscross. It's full enough of sorrow—full of trouble—trouble in plenty, everywhere I look. You'll break hearts." Aye, I *have.* "You'll die young, but you'll be rich, generous, and free with your money." Aye, true, true. "You're born under an unlucky star. You've got in your hand a thundering crowd of enemies—not one friend—you'll make a bad end, and have plenty to love you afterward. You'll have a fast life—short, but a grand one. Young sir, I've never seen a worse hand, I wish I hadn't seen it, but every word I've said is true by the signs. You'd best become a missionary or a priest to escape it."

A missionary or a priest—Ha! An *actor* is what I became—it was in my blood, my birthright—and when before the war I played on the Richmond stage, before full audiences of well-dressed gentlemen planters and their beautiful wives and daughters who fanned themselves and smiled at me when my eyes touched theirs, I fell in love with the South, with its magnificent plantations and its rural traditions, and ever since the clouds of war broke over our poor land I have always thought of myself as a son of Dixie.

"If you feel that way," said my brother Edwin, a fellow actor and a Union man, "why don't you join the rebel army?"

"I promised Mother I would keep out of the quarrel," I said, "and I'm sorry I said so."

"You're crazy," he said. "All this patriotic froth about the secesh when you know good and well they're traitors."

"Traitors! *You* are the traitors, you of the North!"

He would shake his head and wave me off. How the words of Caesar had poisoned his mind!

My mother, the sweet woman who gave me birth, also disagreed with my sentiments, as did my sister Asia and her husband, a Lincoln-loving wretch named James Clarke. Once when he had the temerity to criticize Jefferson Davis, I seized the rascal by the throat and hissed in a tempest of rage: "*Never*, if you value your life, *never* speak in that way to me again of a man and a cause I hold sacred."

Early in 1864, when the war was going badly for us, I spoke with my sister Asia, in the parlor of her home in Philadelphia. "If the North conquer us," I said, "it will be by numbers only, not by native grit, not pluck or devotion."

"If the North conquers us," she cried. "We *are* of the North."

"Not I, not I! So help me holy God! My soul, life, and possessions are for the South."

"Why not go fight for her then? Every Marylander worthy of the name is fighting her battles."

I stared at her until she said she was sorry. "I have only an arm to give," I said. "My brains are worth twenty men, my money worth a hundred more. I have a free pass everywhere, my profession, my name, is my passport. My knowledge of drugs is valuable, and my money is one of the means by which I serve the South. Mr. U. S. Grant has given me freedom of range without knowing what a good turn he's done for the South. Not that the South cares a bad cent about me, mind—a mere peregrinating play-actor."

She said in a low voice: "A man called the other day and asked for 'Doctor' Booth. What does that mean?"

"All right, I am he, if to be a doctor means a dealer in quinine and morphine."

"The drugs the South is so desperate for?"

"Yes."

"*You* send them! How?"

I laughed. "Horsecollars, seats of wagons, and so forth." I did not tell her so, but I ran the drugs from Washington to Richmond along a secret line maintained by the rebel signal corps. The line, called "the corridor," ran through southern Maryland where "safe houses"—those owned by men sympathetic to the Confederacy—afforded shelter for a night. The corridor ran across the Potomac and down the Northern Neck to Richmond. A clandestine traffic of rebel couriers, dispatch bearers, secret service agents, bearers of northern newspapers and foreign mail traveled "the corridor," always taking care to elude enemy gunboats when crossing and recrossing the Potomac.

Asia was looking at me with horror in her eyes. "You're a, a rebel *agent,* a *spy?*"

I started to tell her that I even had the secret cipher that furnished the key to ciphered rebel dispatches between Canada and Richmond, but thought better of it. I did not want to implicate her unduly

During my trips along the corridor, I heard other agents and spies in the safe houses talk of secret plots against the tyrant all of us hated. I thought he would *never* rule as the Caesar of history did, as emperor of a subjugated land, if even one of these were hatched against him.

4. LINCOLN

Sure, I heard the rumors. Francis Carpenter, a New York painter who'd come to the White House to do a portrait of the signing of the emancipation proclamation, told me that a recent number of the *New York Tribune* reported a conspiracy was afoot to murder me.

"According to the paper," he said, "a correspondent within rebel lines uncovered an elaborate conspiracy, matured in Richmond, to abduct you or, if that isn't practicable, to assassinate you. A secret organization of five hundred or a thousand men solemnly swore to accomplish the deed."

"Well, even if the story is true," I said, "I don't see what the rebels would gain by killing or getting possession of me. I'm just one individual, and it would not help the rebel cause or make the least difference in the progress of the war. Everything would go right on just the same."

I told Major Charles Halpine of Halleck's staff the same thing. "Do you think the Richmond people would like to have Vice President Hamlin here any better than me? And besides if there was such a plot, and they wanted to get at me, no amount of vigilance could stop them."

Stanton and my old Illinois friend Marshal Ward Hill Lamon worried constantly about my safety, and Stanton had the habit of detailing soldiers to accompany me on my trips to the telegraph office and the Soldiers' Home. I tell you, I hated military escorts— made me feel like a damned emperor—and I often sneaked out with- out 'em and walked to the War Office or rode to the Soldiers' Home alone. When a cavalry guard was posted at the White House gates, I worried until I got rid of it. At one point, General Wadsworth detailed a cavalry escort to accompany me on my afternoon carriage rides. But the clatter of their sabers and spurs was so loud that Mary and I couldn't hear ourselves talk, so I urged the driver to outrun 'em, and off we went, the carriage careening down country roads with the cavalry pounding along in pursuit. Beat 'em, too, to my sat- isfaction.

Carpenter often accompanied me through the streets of the capi- tal at a late hour of the night, without an escort. When he ques- tioned the wisdom of this, I told him I thought a good deal about coming to a sudden and violent end, but there wasn't much I could do about it. I mean, what can I do? I see hundreds of strangers every day, and if anybody wants to kill me he'll find a way. To be abso- lutely safe, I'd have to lock myself up in a box.

The truth is, I told Carpenter, I'm a great coward physically and would make a poor soldier and would probably run at the first sign of danger. I was sporting, of course, and added seriously, "Moral cowardice is something I think I never had."

That winter, a constitutional amendment abolishing slavery everywhere in America—the Thirteenth Amendment—was up before Congress. I wanted that amendment in the worst way because it would guarantee the permanency of the emancipation proclamation. Congressman Arnold, my longtime friend, told me: "I hope, Mr. President, that on New Year's day of 'sixty-five I may have the plea- sure of congratulating you on three events which now seem very probable. First, that the war may be ended by the complete triumph of the Union forces. Second, that slavery may be abolished and pro- hibited throughout the Union by an amendment of the Constitution. Third, that Abraham Lincoln may have been reelected president."

"I think, my friend, I would be willing to accept the first two by way of compromise," I said.

The Senate approved the amendment overwhelmingly, but it faced powerful Democratic opposition in the House. Arnold fought hard for its passage there, arguing that "slavery is the soul, body, and spirit of the rebellion. We can have no permanent peace while slavery lives." But the amendment failed to muster the requisite two-thirds majority, and that spring went down to defeat.

"I'm exceedingly disappointed," I said. "Don't our opponents in the House see the writing on the wall? Slavery in this country is done for. The war has doomed it. This amendment merely ratifies what the war has done."

"As Henry Clay once told some Kentucky hunters," Arnold said, 'We must pick our flints and try again.'"

"Right," I said. "After the fall elections. Maybe enough Union candidates will get elected to the House to get the thing passed."

This was a presidential election year, and people were hounding me to distraction about my intentions. Would I seek a second term or not? No president since Andy Jackson had served more than four years, and one term had become something of a tradition. But that was in peacetime. The war changed all that as far as I was concerned. *Of course* I wanted to be reelected, to prove to our enemies that the people approved of my war policies. I told young Brooks that a change of administrations would be virtually voting me a failure.

In private, I had mixed feelings about staying in office. "This war is eating my life out," I told Congressman Owen Lovejoy, a Radical Republican and a great friend. "I've got a strong impression I won't live to see the end." Lovejoy knew I had to remain in office, to vindicate myself and my work, and he put out word that he supported my bid for a second term. "If he is not the best conceivable president," Lovejoy said, "he is the best possible."

A lot of Republicans disagreed. In fact, there was strong opposition to a second Lincoln term throughout the party, as conservative Republicans thought I was too radical and Radical Republicans viewed me as a complete failure. "This vacillation and indecisiveness of the president," said a Republican pamphlet, "has been the real cause why our well-appointed armies have not succeeded in the destruction of the rebellion. The cant about 'Honest Abe' was at first amusing, it then became ridiculous, but now it is absolutely criminal." The Washington correspondent of the *Detroit Free Press* reported that not a single U.S. senator favored my reelection.

Horace Greeley and a number of Radicals made it plain that they wanted Chase for President. Well, I said, Chase was a pretty good fellow and an able secretary of the treasury. His only trouble was, he had the White House fever a little too bad. In January he declared

himself "available" for the Republican nomination, and took pleasure in running me down, telling his Radical friends I was ignorant
about fiscal matters and ticking off my blunders. If elected, he
promised to run a far more efficient administration than I'd done. By
February, Senator Samuel Pomeroy of Kansas headed a Chase central committee, and Chase clubs were springing up across the North.
My friends told me I ought to boot that scheming rascal out of the
Cabinet, but I refused. Sure, Chase was a little insane about the presidency, but I meant to keep him in the Cabinet as long as he continued to run the Treasury skillfully.

In late February, a letter written by Pomeroy appeared in the
public prints. I didn't read the thing, but my secretaries did and said
it was pretty damned hostile to me and urged the party to replace me
with Chase. Chase burst in here, declared himself "mortified,"
insisted he knew nothing about the letter, and offered to resign. I
rejected the offer. "Chase," I said, "neither of us should be held to
account for what our friends do without our consent. Now go and
say no more about this Pomeroy business."

Turned out, the Pomeroy Circular caused the Chase boom to
collapse. The circular's virulent tone offended my friends and many
of my foes. In one state after another, Union leagues and local conventions announced in favor of my reelection. Chase even lost the
support of his home state, Ohio. Indignant over the Pomeroy business, a caucus of Ohio Republicans rejected their favorite son and
came out in support of me. In early March my able but scheming
secretary of the treasury withdrew his candidacy. Not long after
that, the Republican National Committee came out for me, which
pretty much assured my renomination, but a lot of Radicals were
still unhappy with me and my alleged ineptitude.

Because of Grant's great popularity, we heard a good deal of talk
about his running for president as a war Democrat. To tell the truth,
I worried that Grant had the presidential bug, and when Congress
debated Washburne's bill reviving the rank of lieutenant general,
which was sure to pass, I was reluctant to appoint Grant to the job,
even though he was the obvious choice, because of his possible political ambitions. To find out more about his ambitions, I invited his
friend J. Russell Jones of Chicago to the White House. Jones showed
me a letter Grant had sent him that put my worries to rest. In it,
Grant said he'd received a great many letters from war Democrats
urging him to run for president, but he threw them all in the waste-
basket. "I already have a pretty big job on my hands, and my only

ambition is to see this rebellion suppressed. Nothing would induce me to think of being a presidential candidate, particularly so long as there is a possibility of having Mr. Lincoln re-elected."

I tell you again, I loved that man. A lot of military heroes turned their battlefield victories into political gain, but not Grant. He knew his duty was to the army, and he wouldn't be satisfied until he finished his job. When the lieutenant general bill passed, I sent his nomination forthwith to the Senate, and it was confirmed on March third. Only two other officers had ever held the rank of lieutenant general—George Washington and Winfield Scott. As lieutenant general, Grant would command all our armies in the field, and Halleck would function as nothing but a staff officer. I ordered the new general in chief to report to Washington at once, so that we could get acquainted and talk about the war.

5 . GRANT

My promotion to lieutenant general fell on me like a wet blanket. Feared the president aimed to fire Halleck and put me in his place, take me from the field and stick me behind a desk in Washington. I was sick just thinking about it. Told Rawlins if I could be of service to the government in any place it was in command of an army in the field. Rawlins passed that sentiment on to Congressman Washburne, who undoubtedly relayed it to Lincoln.

Wrote Sherman from my Nashville headquarters that I owed my success in this war to the energy and skill of my subordinate commanders. "I want to express my thanks to you and McPherson as the men to whom, above all others, I feel indebted for whatever I have had of success." Sherman replied: "You do yourself an injustice and us too much honor in assigning to us so large a share of the merits which have led to your high advancement. You are now Washington's legitimate successor and occupy a position of almost dangerous elevation, but if you can continue to be yourself, simple, honest, and unpretending, you will enjoy through life the respect and love of friends, and the homage of millions."

Anxious about what lay in store for me, I set out for Washington with my son Fred. Got there in the evening of March eighth and went to Willard's Hotel. The clerk at the desk didn't recognize me till I registered for a room. I wrote: "U.S. Grant and son, Galena, Ill." The fellow was astounded. Said they had an excellent room already reserved for us. We went upstairs and washed up and came down to the dining room for supper. People stared and whispered, "That's Grant!" Somebody announced it to the entire room, and the crowd of diners cried, "Grant! Grant! Grant!" Embarrassed me, face turned beet red. Someone else mounted a chair and called for "three cheers for Lieutenant General Grant." The diners cheered and pounded their tables and kept calling my name. Finally I stood, dabbed my mustache with my napkin, bowed, sat down and tried to eat, but I could feel all those eyes staring at me as I dabbed at my plate.

Later that evening had to attend a public reception in the Blue Room of the White House. The president had arranged it "in my honor." When I entered the Blue Room, it created a commotion. The president said over the din, "Why, here's General Grant!" He strode over and took my hand firmly. "Well, this is a great pleasure, I assure you," he said. He towered over me a good eight inches and wore a turned-down collar that was way too large for his neck. He had the saddest face and saddest gray eyes I ever saw. I'd never met him, but I'd heard officers in the West who knew him and spoke highly of him. I'd read the Lincoln-Douglas debates of 'fifty-eight, and though by no means a Lincoln man at that time—I was a Douglas Democrat—I did recognize Lincoln's great ability. Was a Lincoln man now, though.

Lincoln introduced me to Secretary of State Seward, who had a beaked nose like a buzzard's and jabbered so fast I couldn't catch everything he said. He took my arm and steered me over to meet Mrs. Lincoln, who smiled radiantly. "It's such a *pleasure* to meet you," she said. Then Seward took me into the East Room, where an even bigger crowd was gathered. When they started crying, "Grant, Grant, Grant!" Seward urged me to stand on a sofa so they could all see me. I did it, but my face burned with embarrassment. Felt like an idiot at a circus, standing on the sofa with everyone staring at me and yelling my name.

Then friendly hands steered me away to a small drawing room where Lincoln and Seward were waiting. We talked for a little while and then I left. Never so glad to get away from a place in my life. Next day had to go back to the White House, so the president could officially present me with my commission in front of the Cabinet. Afterward had a talk with Stanton and Halleck. Struck me as ironic that I now ranked Halleck—that the man I'd served under and who'd made me so miserable earlier in the war now took orders from me.

Next day I took a military train south to General Meade's headquarters near Brandy Station on the Orange & Alexandria Railroad, some seventy miles southwest of Washington. The train, trailing a plume of black smoke, roared through a region desolated by constant warfare: fences torn down, fields uncultivated, homes in ruins. Some places only fire-scarred chimneys remained. As I stared out the window, the train sped past Bull Run and Manassas Junction, where the Eastern Army had twice been routed; past Bristoe Station and Rappahannock Station, and finally steamed to a stop at Brandy Station in a heavy rain. Even so, brass bands struck up a welcome by playing martial tunes. I don't have an ear for music—recognize only two tunes. One's "Yankee Doodle" and the other isn't.

Meade had a bad cold, so his chief of staff met me at the station and took me out to Meade's headquarters. We had a long interview in his tent, both of us smoking cigars. I'd known him slightly in the Mexican War, but hadn't seen him since. A tall, spare, restless man with blue eyes and a full beard. Wore a slouched gray hat with the rim turned down. I'd heard he had a terrible temper. If he did, he didn't show it with me—we got along right well. But he was obviously nervous 'cause his hands shook.

"General Grant," he said, "it occurs to me, you might want to put another officer in command of the Army of the Potomac. Sherman or somebody else who served with you in the West. I ask you to remove me at once, if it suits your plans."

"General Meade," I said, "I've no intention of replacing you with Sherman. Sherman's needed in the West. I'll be frank, though. When I came east, I assumed the Administration wanted another commander for the Army of the Potomac—newspapers kept saying so—but the subject never came up while I was in Washington."

He was very grateful that he would continue to command the army—he called it "my people"—and asked where I intended to make my headquarters. "At first I meant to stay in the West," I said, "but when I got to Washington and saw the situation, it was clear that I ought to be in the East. Because of the overriding importance of the Virginia theater and because Lee's army is the best the Confederacy has."

"You'll be in Washington then," he said a little too hopefully.

"Nope. Hate that place. Ain't a desk general. I'll make my headquarters and travel with your army." I left unsaid that I aimed to instill some boldness and tenacity in Meade's "people," to prod them to fight like our western soldiers.

Next day I rode the train back to Washington. The president invited me to supper at the White House, but I begged off on account of I was fed up with this show business that made me an object of curiosity. Told the president I couldn't stay over, couldn't lose a day in reorganizing my vast forces, and left that night for Nashville. Had already wired Sherman to meet me there.

At my Nashville headquarters, I officially named Sherman to replace me as commander of the Military Division of the Mississippi. When I told him I aimed to move my headquarters to the Virginia theater, he was horrified.

"Goddamn it, Grant, the fucking politicians will eat you alive. Halleck's better qualified than you to stand the winds of intrigue and interference. Let him run the show there. You're at home here in the West. You know your ground and you've tested your subordinates. You know us, and we know you. Here you're sure to succeed." He was pacing back and forth, gesturing with a cigar and running his hand through his red hair. "At the East, you'll start new campaigns in an unfamiliar field, with troops and officers you've not tested or led to victory. They can't feel toward you what we do. Stay here where you've made your fame, where you can lead us to more victories."

I shook my head. "I appreciate what you say, Sherman. But my duty calls me to Virginia. Only in Virginia can I achieve my principal object as general in chief: *the constant use of all the troops in every direction at the same time.*"

Julia met me in Nashville and accompanied me on the train back to Washington. Six-year-old Jess, our youngest, was with us; the other children were with Julia's cousins in St. Louis, where they were in school.

Sherman rode with us as far as Cincinnati, and we discussed my grand plan for the upcoming campaigns while studying topographical maps. "Johnston's army at Dalton in northern Georgia is your first objective," I told Sherman, "and the important railroad center, Atlanta, is the second. General Banks has already launched his big campaign up the Red River, with something like forty thousand troops, including the ten thousand you sent him, in hopes of seizing the rest of Louisiana, threatening Texas, and capturing a great deal of valuable rebel cotton. Myself, I think the campaign is strategically absurd, but Lincoln and Halleck are all in favor of it. I hope Banks will finish that operation in time to cooperate with you and the armies in the East.

"Here's how the grand plan will work. Banks will advance overland from Louisiana and seize Mobile while you'll move south from Chattanooga, destroy Johnston, and take Atlanta. Then you and Banks will establish a line from Atlanta to Mobile, which will cut the Confederacy in two from Chattanooga to the Gulf. I've argued a long time for a Mobile-Atlanta campaign that would give us the entire states of Alabama and Mississippi and part of Georgia, which would force Lee to abandon Virginia and North Carolina. Told Washington last winter that the enemy didn't have army enough in the West to resist the forces I would field on such a campaign. But Halleck wanted me to clear all the rebel forces out of east Tennessee before embarking on such an operation, and it was shelved. Now I'm reviving the Mobile operation and entrusting it to you and Banks. You two will launch your respective campaigns at the same time that the Army of the Potomac goes on the offensive in Virginia."

"We'll make the rebel people Goddamned sorry they were ever born," Sherman said. He left us at Cincinnati, and Julia, Jess, and I went on to Washington by train. I called at the White House and spent an entire evening alone with the president. We had a free and candid discussion about what I could expect from him in my new capacity as general in chief.

6. LINCOLN

I told Grant I'd never professed to be a military man or to know how campaigns ought to be conducted, and never wanted to interfere in them. "But the procrastination of previous commanders," I said, "and the pressure from the people at the North and from Congress, which was constantly on me, forced me to issue a series of military orders, telling my generals what to do. Some of those orders were wrong, but they came from patriotic motives. All I've ever wanted was someone who would take responsibility for military operations and *act*, and call on me for all the assistance he needed from the government. Now, in you, I've got the man for the job, and

I return the authority of directing our armies to the hands where it properly belongs. I promise you my full support. You'll have the same promise from Stanton."

I told Grant that I did not want to know the details of his plan of operations, because I trusted him more than any of my previous commanders. But that didn't mean Grant had a free hand in conducting the war. I *did* want to know about his *strategical planning*. When he said that all our armies would advance simultaneously on all fronts, I smiled and nodded in agreement, because that was precisely what I'd been advocating since 'sixty-one. Finally, I had a general in chief who understood that concert of action in all theaters was *the* way to defeat the rebels with our superior numbers.

"I aim to make all the line useful," Grant added. "Those not fighting can help by advancing."

I chuckled and said: "Those not skinning can hold a leg."

"Yep. Exactly."

"What do you intend to do against Lee?" I asked.

"Invade North Carolina and wreck the railroads that supply Lee's army from the Deep South," Grant said. "It will force Lee to abandon Virginia."

I didn't like it. "I must remind you, General Grant, that your primary objective in Virginia is the destruction of Lee's army, the capture of Richmond, and the protection of Washington."

He mumbled "of course" and dropped the idea of a North Carolina invasion.

We also discussed the presidential election in November. "A terrible war weariness has set in across the North," I said, "a sense that we can't win the war on the battlefield. You must give us victories before the election, or the Union party in all probability will be defeated at the polls. A Peace Democrat will replace me, and the cause will be lost. The rebels are pinning their hopes of victory on just such an outcome. They're looking to a disillusioned Union electorate to throw the war party out of office and hand the Confederacy her independence."

"I'm well aware of that, Mr. President. I'll try not to let you down. Your defeat and the defeat of the war party in November would be a disaster. The war would be lost and the country with it."

I walked him to the door. "Good to talk to you, Grant. I think we understand each other."

"Believe we do, Mr. President."

When he left, I told young Stoddard I hardly knew what to think of the general. "He's the quietest little fellow you ever saw. Never makes a fuss. Couple of times he's been in this room a minute before I knew he was here. It's about the same all around. The only evidence you have that he's in anyplace is he makes things git!"

I thought to myself: *that unassuming little man has the most awesome responsibility of anybody in the country. On his slumped shoulders rest all our hopes for the defeat of the insurrection, the destruction of slavery, and the salvation of popular government.*

7 . GRANT

Meade met me at the railroad station at Culpeper Court House, about ten miles southwest of Brandy Station, and took me to my headquarters—a brick house with tents erected in the yard. The Army of the Potomac was encamped along the railroad between the Rapidan and the Rappahannock rivers—thousands of white tents as far as the eye could see, with smoke curling up from campfires. The War Department had reorganized the army the day before I arrived, consolidating its five infantry corps into three—the Second, Fifth, and Sixth—with an average strength of twenty-five thousand men each. Burnside's Ninth Corps had been brought east from Tennessee and was concentrated at Annapolis with more than twenty thousand men. It was an independent command I would personally direct in the coming campaign.

With Rawlins and the rest of my staff, I took a look around the old town and the surrounding countryside. Lieutenant Colonel Adam Badeau of my staff said it was once rich farm and plantation country, but three years of unrelenting warfare had left it pretty desolate. Here and there a busted cistern or a stack of chimneys marked where a homestead had been. Couldn't see a house or a fence for miles around, and the hills had been stripped of all their trees. Off to the west rose the skyline of the Blue Ridge—real pretty to look at. Beyond it lay the Shenandoah Valley, the so-called breadbasket of the Confederacy.

We rode up to Mt. Pony and trained our glasses on the country south of the Rapidan, where Lee's army was fortified along a line from the railroad east to Mine Run. We could see a rebel signal station on top of Clark's Mountain on the south side of the river. When we got back to town, some of my staff officers joked about Lee. Weren't in awe of him like the officers of Meade's army. I didn't like their fear of him and his so-called superior ability. My staffers heard some of 'em say, "Well, Grant has never met Bobby Lee yet." Nope, I hadn't. Itching to, though. Thought he fought best on the defensive, but had no great admiration for his offensive operations.

During the next few days, Meade took me around to meet his three corps commanders. Winfield Scott Hancock, head of the Second Corps, was the best of 'em, but still suffered from a painful wound in the groin he'd gotten at Gettysburg. A good-looking man, tall and soldierly, with a firm jaw and light brown hair. Always perfectly dressed in a spotless uniform and clean white shirt.

Gouverneur Warren, commander of the Fifth Corps, was only thirty-four but smart as all get out. Second in his class at the Academy, taught math there. Loved limericks, tickled everybody the way he told 'em. He had little piercing dark eyes, one a little bigger than the other, and hair combed straight back over his head.

The commander of the Sixth Corps was John Sedgwick—men called him Uncle John. He was a short and stocky bachelor, had curly brown hair. Liked to play solitaire in his off hours.

Early in April Phil Sheridan arrived to take command of the cavalry corps of the Potomac Army. I had no regard for that cavalry, thought it had done little in the war, and said so to Lincoln and Halleck on my first trip back to Washington. "I want the very best man in the army for that command," I said, and Halleck mentioned Sheridan. "The very man I want," I said.

When he joined us at Culpeper, Sheridan looked exhausted and skinnier than I'd ever seen him. Couldn't have weighed much more than 110 pounds. Funny-looking fellow—short, about five feet five, with coarse black hair, a ruddy face, and a bullet-shaped head. But the best cavalry commander in the war.

When I next saw the president in Washington, he said: "The officer you brought from the West was through here the other day. He's a brown, chunky little chap, with a long body, short legs, not enough neck to hang him, and arms so long that if his ankles itch he can scratch them without stooping. Isn't he rather a little fellow to handle your cavalry?"

"You'll find him big enough before we get through with him," I said.

By April fourth, I'd worked out the details of my plan to concentrate all the force possible against the Confederate armies in the field. The plan called for simultaneous offensive operations against rebel armies in the East and the West, with the goal of destroying them completely. The main thrusts would be against Lee in Virginia and Johnston in Georgia, with cooperating columns in each theater. I meant to hammer continuously at the enemy's military forces and his resources, until by mere attrition, if in no other way, there would be nothing left to him but total submission. Up to now, our armies had acted without concert, like a balky team, no two ever pulling together. This time all the armies were to move together toward a common center.

I wrote Sherman that he was to attack Johnston's army, break it up, and get into the interior of the enemy's country as far as he could, inflicting all the damage he could against their war resources. I sent a private messenger to Banks with instructions to finish up his Red River expedition with all dispatch, return Sherman's ten thousand men to him, and with eight thousand troops called up from Arkansas, to operate against Mobile as soon as possible in support of Sherman.

I wrote Meade that Lee's army was his objective point. Wherever Lee went, there Meade would go also. Burnside's corps, which included a new colored division under General Edward Ferrero, would march down from Annapolis and support the Army of the Potomac. Two political generals would also operate in support of Meade. Franz Sigel would advance up the Shenandoah with a force of twenty-six thousand and seize Staunton on the Virginia Central Railroad, thus preventing Lee from bringing reinforcements from the valley by that route. At the same time that Meade attacked Lee, Benjamin Butler's Army of the James, based at Fort Monroe and numbering thirty-three thousand, would advance up the James River and operate against Richmond from the south. In a personal meeting with Butler at Fort Monroe, I pointed out the importance of first getting possession of Petersburg, a crucial railroad junction south of Richmond, and destroying railroad communications as far south as possible. That would cut off both cities from their supply sources in the rebel interior. Then Butler was to invest Richmond on the south side and attack it vigorously. If he could not carry the city, he would at least detain as large a force there as possible and deprive Lee of reinforcements.

As for Lee, the big question was which way to attack him. All of us ruled out a frontal assault because his line of works was impregnable. I weighed very carefully the advantages of moving against

Lee's left or moving against his right. If I moved around his left into more open country, it would prevent him from raiding north against Washington, but it would also separate us from Butler and deprive us of easy communications with a base of supplies on the Potomac. We would have to carry a large amount of ammunition and rations in a huge wagon train and detach a great many troops to guard it. A move by Lee's left presented too many serious difficulties. When I considered the sufferings of the wounded in being transported long distances overland, instead of being carried by short routes to water where they could be comfortably moved by boats, I no longer had any hesitation in deciding to cross the Rapidan below Lee's army and move around his right flank. The army would then be supplied by a shorter overland route from the Potomac. This plan would also enable us to cooperate with Butler's forces.

There was one big drawback to the plan: the huge Army of the Potomac would have to pass through the Wilderness, a jungle of cut-over woodland lying south of the Rapidan, some ten miles deep and fifteen miles wide, with poor roads. Had no intention of fighting a battle in the dense woods of the Wilderness. If we set the whole army in motion at midnight, when Lee's signal station on Clark Mountain couldn't see us, we could move so far beyond the Rapidan the first day that we would *pass out of the Wilderness* and turn Lee's right flank south of Mine Run. This would force him to abandon his Rapidan line and fight for his communications or fall back. If I could flush him into open battle, outside the Wilderness, I meant to destroy his army. If he retreated to Richmond to fight from behind its fortifications, we would follow, connect with Butler, and put Richmond under siege. I looked at the map on the wall of my head-quarters and described an arc around Richmond and Petersburg with my finger. *When my troops are there,* I thought, *Richmond is mine. Lee must retreat or surrender. If he retreats, we'll chase him down and destroy him, which is the objective of the campaign.*

While I worked on the details of this flanking movement, I received word from Sherman of a massacre at Fort Pillow on the Mississippi. On April twelfth, a rebel force under Nathan Forrest attacked and captured the Union garrison there, which consisted mainly of Negro soldiers. "Fifty white soldiers killed and one hundred taken prisoners," Sherman reported, "and three hundred blacks murdered after captured." Stanton sent me other reports about the slaughter of our Negro troops. I was furious. "If our men have been murdered after capture," I wrote Sherman, "we must retaliate promptly." The Administration, however, decided against executing an equal number of rebels held prisoner at the North. The president decided instead to punish the men who'd committed the atrocities, if they were captured, and to suspend the cartel and the exchange of prisoners until the rebels treated black prisoners according to the rules of war. I fully endorsed that suspension because I wanted justice for our black soldiers and because the exchange of prisoners helped the rebels, who were desperately short of troops. As soon as we exchanged rebel prisoners, they turned up at the front to fight us again.

Sherman, meanwhile, relayed a telegram from the Union commander at Cairo, who reported that Banks had met with disaster in Louisiana. "Banks," he said, "was attacked by Kirby Smith near Mansfield, Louisiana, on the eighth and retreated to Grand Encore à la Bull Run." I wrote Sherman that I'd always feared that Banks would fail in his foolhardy expedition up the Red River and that the forces Sherman had sent to Banks would be lost for our spring campaign, which, in fact, they were. Now Banks would not be able to operate against Mobile in concert with Sherman, as I'd hoped, and I cursed the day political generals like him were ever allowed into the army. Later I urged the president to replace Banks with General E. R. S. Canby, a professional soldier, and Lincoln did so.

April twenty-seventh was my forty-second birthday. Wrote Julia, who'd gone to New York with Jess: "Getting old am I not? I am still very well. Don't know exactly the day when I will start or whether Lee will come here before I am ready to move. Would not tell you if I did know. Kisses for yourself and Jess. Ulys."

Two days later I telegraphed Halleck that the concerted advance in the East and West would begin May fourth and fifth. Not long after that, I received a letter from the president: "Not expecting to see you again before the spring campaign opens, I wish to express, in this way, my entire satisfaction with what you have done up to this time, so far as I understand it. The particulars of your plans I neither know, or seek to know. You are vigilant and self-reliant; and, pleased with this, I wish not to obtrude any constraints or restraints upon you. While I am very anxious that any great disaster, or the capture of our men in great numbers, shall be avoided, I know these points are less likely to escape your attention than they would be mine. And now with a brave Army, and a just cause, may God sustain you."

I wrote him back: "Should my success be less than I desire, and expect, the least I can say is, the fault is not with you."

8. CHESNUT

We were certain the Yankees were coming to lay siege to Richmond, and it made us all utterly depressed. To make matters worse, old Mrs. Chesnut had died, and James was anxious to return home, to be near his aged father. The president obliged by promoting James to brigadier general and giving him command of the South Carolina Reserves. Which meant that we were leaving Richmond for the lonely confines of Mulberry Plantation. My Richmond friends all grieved that I had to leave; but not half so much as I grieved. We called to tell the president and Varina good-bye, and the president looked terrible, worn down by labor and anxiety about the coming battles.

"When the Yankee siege begins," Varina said, "I hope to send our children to you. They'll be safe at Mulberry."

"We would be proud to take care of them," said I, the childless wretch. "But you must come to us, too."

"It depends on Jeff's health," she said.

On the eve of our departure—it was late April—we received word that five-year-old Joe Davis had been killed. Maggie Howell, Varina's younger sister, was with us, and she began sobbing hysterically. Faint, bewildered, I rushed her to the presidential mansion in a carriage, thinking what a terrible, unthinkable tragedy this was, oh that poor little boy, his father's favorite child. When we reached the mansion, all three floors were lit up, all the doors and windows seemed wide open, and a gusting wind tossed the curtains eerily about. Mr. Burton Harrison met us at the door, and Mrs. Semmes and Mrs. Barksdale, wife of the attending physician, were also there. I sat in the drawing room, listening to the tramp of Mr. Davis's step as he paced up and down the room above, crying: "Not mine, oh, Lord, but thine." The mansion was silent as death save for the sound of the president's footsteps. With curtains flapping in the wind and a gas lamp flaring nearby, I sat numb—stupid—half-dead with grief and weeping.

At midnight I went to get James, and both of us took up a vigil in the drawing room. Mrs. Semmes was still there, but we saw nobody else. We thought some friends of the family ought to be there, so we stayed the night. I said all the prayers I knew. Poor little Joe was the good child of the family, so gentle and affectionate; he used to run in to say his prayers at his father's knee. Now he was laid out somewhere in the mansion—crushed—killed.

Mrs. Semmes said he had fallen from that high north balcony upon the brick pavement thirty feet below. Varina and the president had hurried to his side, but he passed on a few minutes later. The grief of both parents was beyond words to describe. Varina later told me that, shortly after the accident, a courier brought a dispatch to the mansion, and the president held it for a moment and then tried to write a reply, but gave up.

"I must have this day with my little child," he said.

Varina recalled: "Somebody took the dispatch to General Cooper and left us alone with our dead."

In the drawing room, we heard Mr. Davis's step as he walked the floor all the livelong night. When James and I left the mansion early in the morning, I saw little Joe lying there, white and beautiful as an angel and covered with flowers, his weeping Irish nurse lying flat on the floor by his side. Outside we met a child who offered me a handful of snowdrops and asked me to put them on little Joe. Walking home, I kept seeing the heartbroken parents, and hearing Mr. Davis's footsteps on the floor above.

We stayed in Richmond an extra day to attend the funeral. There was an enormous crowd, including thousands of children, each with a green bough or flowers to throw on little Joe's grave. The funeral procession wound among those tall white monuments up the hillside where the cemetery was located. The James River tumbled about below, over rocks and around islands. I'll never, never forget the Davises. That poor old gray-haired man stood bareheaded, straight as an arrow, clear against the sky, by the open grave of his son. Varina stood back in her heavy black wrappings, and her tall figure drooped. Those two dark, sorrow-stricken figures created a haunting image.

James and I returned to Mulberry, which is lovely in the spring, with its primeval oaks, water oaks, live oaks, willow oaks, violets, roses, yellow jasmine, popinacs—the air is laden with perfume. We enjoyed plenty of creaturely comforts—green peas, asparagus, strawberries, spring lamb, spring chickens, fresh eggs, rich yellow butter, clean white linen for one's bed, dazzling white damask for one's table. Such a contrast to Richmond—where I wished I was.

My thoughts often turned to General Lee and the battles for our survival he would have to wage against our all-powerful foe. His son Rooney had been freed before the suspension of the prisoner exchange. I saw the general and his daughters at the Capitol grounds when the prisoners arrived. General Lee had tears in his eyes when he spoke of his dead daughter-in-law, Rooney's wife. Then a few days later he was gone again, back to the Rapidan line northwest of Richmond.

News reached us that the horrible work of death was beginning again, to end in the killing of thousands more of our brave young men and countless fresh graves on the hillside in Richmond. I remembered all the true-hearted, the laughing, singing, dancing young fellows I had seen go off to war in the last three years—I had looked into their brave young eyes and helped them every way I could, and then saw them no more forever. They lay stark and cold, dead upon the battlefield or moldering away in hospitals or prisons—which was worse? When I considered the long array of those bright youths and loyal men who had gone to their deaths almost before my eyes, it seemed my heart might break.

Is anything worth it? I asked my diary. This fearful sacrifice—this awful penalty we pay for war—*is it worth it?*

9. LEE

On May second our signal station on Clark's Mountain reported increased activity in the Union camps north of the Rapidan. I went up to the mountaintop with my generals and staff to have a look. The corps commanders and their staffs were there—Old Pete, little Powell Hill, Stuart, and Dick Ewell with his artificial leg. Eight divisional commanders were also present. Through our glasses, we saw enemy bands playing and soldiers hurrying about the Federal camps in obvious preparation for something, probably the move across the river we had been expecting.

I was bitterly disappointed that our shortage of troops and want of provisions for men and animals prevented me from taking the initiative and attacking the huge Federal army first. Had I been able to attack and had God given us a crowning victory, all the enemy plans would have been dissipated, and Burnside's force, which we knew had reached Alexandria, would have been detained to protect Washington. I had actually proposed such an attack to Richmond if Longstreet's corps were returned to me and if supplies were sent forthwith. Richmond did allow Longstreet to rejoin us from Tennessee. But the continued shortage of provisions and supplies made offensive warfare north of the Rapidan impossible. I would have to remain on the defensive, fighting at the time and place of the enemy's choosing.

"And we *will fight*," I told my staff. "We must destroy Grant's army before it gets to the James River. If he gets there, it will be a mere question of time."

There was a good deal of discussion among my generals about Grant, whose promotion to general of all the enemy armies had not surprised me. Some of my officers, however, impugned Grant and scoffed at his record. "His western laurels will wither in the climate of Virginia," they said. "Sidney Johnston outgeneraled and badly beat him at Shiloh, where he was saved only by Buell. Vicksburg and Chattanooga, which made his reputation in the North, did not come from any great ability on his part, but from weak Confederate forces and inept Confederate generalship. Wait till he comes up against the audacity and cunning of General Lee! He'll whip him with ease."

Old Pete frowned. "Do y'all know Grant?" he asked the officers. "No."

"Well, I do. I was in the corps of cadets with him at West Point for three years, I was present at his wedding, I served in the same army with him in Mexico, I have observed his methods of warfare in the West, and I tell you we can't afford to underrate him and the army he now commands. We must make up our minds to get into line of battle and stay there, because that man will fight us every day and every hour till the end of this war. In order to whip him we must outmaneuver him, and husband our strength as best we can."

It was a long speech for my laconic old warhorse, and I patted his shoulder affectionately. "You may be right about Grant," I said. "But I have faith in this army and its ability to inflict terrible casualties on those people and throw them back across the Rapidan. President Davis and I both hope that the terrible cost of fighting us will wear down the Union resolve to fight and strengthen antiwar sentiment at the North. If they attack again, we'll defeat them again, and in November the war-weary North will throw Lincoln out of office and put a Peace Democrat in his place. Then we shall have our independence."

On top of Clark's Mountain, I swept my glass over the bustling Federal camps, then looked to the country to the left and that to the right, trying to predict what Grant would do. Would he attack us straight on to get at Richmond? Or would he try to outflank us? I doubted that he would attempt a frontal assault against our strong fortifications. That left a flanking maneuver. The logical approach was the western end of our Rapidan line around Orange Court House on the railroad: it was open farm country, good for maneuvering a huge army. But moving that way would create supply problems for Grant: he would have to protect his extended communications back to Alexandria. To the east lay the dense jungle of the Wilderness and Fredericksburg on the Rappahannock. The Wilderness created problems of maneuver for Grant, but if he moved in that direction he could bring supplies down from the Potomac. Still looking east, I focused my glass on the Rapidan and studied Germanna Ford and Ely's Ford in the heart of the Wilderness. *Yes, I* thought, *that is where he will go, and it affords us an excellent opportunity to strike him with a counterblow*.

"Gentlemen," I said, pointing to the fords. "Grant will cross the river, on our right, at Germanna or Ely's ford. When he does, we will attack him in the Wilderness. Gentlemen, we've *got* to whip him—we're *going* to whip him—and it's already made me feel better to think of it."

10. GRANT

Had considerable apprehension about crossing the Rapidan in the face of an active and ably commanded enemy army. Also worried about how we were going to bring Meade's huge trains of more than four thousand wagons through hostile country and protect 'em. Meade's chief of staff, Andrew Humphreys, a bowlegged little soldier with iron gray hair and mustache, worked out the details of the army's advance: the right wing would cross Germanna Ford, advance to the Catharpin road, and turn west there. The left wing would cross Ely's Ford, march through Chancellorsville to the Catharpin-Pamunkey "corridor," and also turn west. By hard marching, the united army would be on Lee's flank before dark on May fourth. By the next day we would be in a position to turn his flank and strike him from the rear. Speed was the key to victory, but Humphreys had to sacrifice speed to accommodate the huge supply train. As a consequence, Meade's headquarters elected to stop the army in the Wilderness on the afternoon of May fourth and move on Lee's flank the next day.

Just after midnight, May fourth, the three infantry corps set out for the fords on the Rapidan with two divisions of Sheridan's cavalry in the lead. Warren followed by Sedgwick crossed at Germanna Ford while Hancock crossed at Ely's. The army numbered near 100,000 men of all arms and had 274 guns. Burnside's Ninth Corps, more than 19,000 strong with 80 guns, was at Rappahannock Station and would bring up the rear.

Next morning, my staff and I followed the infantry. It was a fine May morning, birds singing in the trees. Dogwoods and other flowers were blooming and gave off a sweet smell. I wore knee-length top boots, spurs, a sash, a black felt slouch hat, an unbuttoned coat, and a pair of gloves. Meade and his staff and Congressman Washburne, who'd come down a few days earlier, rode with us. Since Washburne wore a silk hat and long-tailed black coat, the men thought he was an undertaker I'd asked along to bury Jeff Davis.

As far as the eye could reach, the narrow road was filled with marching troops, their rifles gleaming in the brilliant sunlight, their bullet-riddled battle flags snapping overhead. Corps, divisions, brigades, trains, batteries, and cavalry squadrons moved on in endless waves of blue, men were cheering, drums rolling, bands playing. Just before noon, our party trotted across the pontoon bridge at Germanna Ford and rode to the crest of a bluff overlooking the Rapidan where we established my headquarters in a deserted old farmhouse with a table and two chairs inside. I sat on the steps, smoking a cigar and watching the men of Sedgwick's corps crossing the pontoon bridge and marching into the darkened Wilderness.

"Well," I said, "so far, so good. We've seized the fords and crossed the river without delays. By this time, Lee probably knows what roads we're advancing on, but he might not realize the full extent of the movement. We'll probably get some indications soon as to what he intends to do."

By early afternoon, the army's left wing, Hancock's corps, was at Chancellorsville, its designated halting place, and reported unburied skeletons lying in the thickets there. The army's right wing—Warren and Sedgwick—were also where they were supposed to be. Warren's corps was at Old Wilderness Tavern at the junction of the Germanna Road and Orange Turnpike, with one division, Griffin's, stationed a mile out on the pike. Sedgwick's Corps was behind Warren on the Germanna Road. Pleased me that Hancock and Warren had both marched over twenty miles that day.

Early that afternoon, Meade handed me a report from our signal officers on Stony Mountain. It was a deciphered message to the enemy general Dick Ewell. "We are moving. Had I not better move D. and D. toward new Verdiersville?" I looked at the map and saw that Verdiersville was on the Orange Turnpike east of Orange Court House.

Said: "That's just the information I wanted. Shows that Lee's drawing out from his Rapidan line and pushing east to meet us." We had no information as to how fast he was moving, but Meade was sure he would take up a position at his old fortifications on Mine Run, which ran south from the Rapidan across Orange Turnpike about five miles west of our location. I sent a telegram to Burnside to move at once and make a forced march to reach us. Then a quick message to Washington: "Forty-eight hours now will demonstrate whether the enemy intends giving battle this side of Richmond."

That evening, staff and me ate supper under the fly of a big hospital tent pitched near the farmhouse. Then Meade came over from his headquarters, and we sat in folding camp chairs by a crackling fire and smoked cigars. We'd been told that the huge wagon trains had commenced crossing the Rapidan—would take two entire days to complete the crossing. While we smoked, a staff officer brought telegrams from Washington reporting that Sigel, Butler, and Sherman were all on the move, too. So far, everything seemed to be going exactly as planned.

11. LEE

When our flags on Clark's Mountain wagged that Grant's army was on the move, heading for the fords to our right, as I expected, I thought he would do one of two things: push rapidly to the southeast and get between me and Richmond, or turn southwest and attack my Rapidan works from the flank and rear. I resolved at once to march my army into the Wilderness and try to surprise him with an attack on his own flank. It was a "desperate gamble," as someone said, for I had only 64,500 men of all arms to contest Grant's superiority in numbers and in artillery. If I failed, the huge Federal army would stand between me and Richmond, and I would be obliged to give battle for my communications. Still, I knew the

Wilderness and its roads very well and thought the dense thickets would neutralize Grant's superior force of men and render his guns useless. If we struck him hard enough, inflicted crippling casualties, he would likely retreat across the river, as all the others had done before him.

I sent Dick Ewell's corps eastward on the Orange Turnpike and two divisions of Powell Hill's corps eastward on the Orange Plank Road, which ran parallel to the pike a little south of it. Hill's third division, under General Anderson, stayed in the rear to scout the Rapidan. Stuart and his cavalry were out in front of Ewell and Hill, screening their columns and reconnoitering the enemy, at which Stuart excelled. Old Pete, at his own suggestion, marched farther south, intending to get on the Catharpin Road and try to cross Grant's southern flank.

My staff and I rode with Hill at the head of his magnificent infantry. When we halted for the night, May fourth, I sent an urgent message to President Davis that the long-threatened effort to take Richmond had begun, that we were inferior in numbers, and that all my detached troops—Pickett's Division and Hoke's old brigade— must be returned to me. The president telegraphed that I would get them in four days. But a second wire reported that a substantial enemy force had ascended the James and landed at Bermuda Hundred south of Richmond, which forced the president to detain two of the brigades intended for me. Another message, this one from the Shenandoah, reported that a third enemy army was moving against our forces under Breckinridge in the valley, on my left flank. I had anticipated both thrusts, whose aim was to prevent me from getting reinforcements from Richmond or the Shenandoah. Very well: we would fight Mr. U. S. Grant with what we had.

Next morning I rose before daybreak and breakfasted with my staff in their tents. Soon General Stuart, wearing his cape and gray hat with an ostrich feather pinned to its crown, rode up to report the latest intelligence from his scouts. Grant's army was encamped in the Wilderness, at Chancellorsville and the Wilderness Church area. There was no sign of his moving southeast. In fact, the heads of his columns had turned southwest, in the direction of Orange Court House, before encamping. This was proof that Grant was not hurrying toward Richmond. No, he intended to march southwest through the Wilderness and try to turn my right flank.

"We will surprise him," I said. "He won't expect us to be on *his* flank, since we didn't dispute his crossing of the Rapidan."

My plan of battle called for Ewell and Hill to engage Grant and pin his army in the Wilderness all day, May fifth, while Longstreet, marching farther south on the Catharpin Road, came up on Grant's left flank. By his own timetable, Pete should reach that point sometime in the afternoon. The next morning, the sixth, Longstreet would launch a flank attack that would roll the Federal army up, sweeping it back to the Rapidan. It was similar to the plan that had worked so well for us at Chancellorsville.

Yes, it was risky: we would have five undermanned divisions to hold the massive enemy army in check while we waited for Old Pete to get around on Grant's left. Still, I was optimistic and in a cheerful mood.

"I'm surprised that Grant has placed himself in the same predicament as Mr. F. J. Hooker did last year," I told my staff. "I hope the result will be even more disastrous to Grant."

Ewell and Hill put their corps in motion, Ewell marching east on the Orange Turnpike with the river protecting his left flank while Hill moved down the Plank Road with Stuart protecting his right flank. My orders to Ewell, who was on the shorter route to the Wilderness, was to pace his march with Hill's and not bring on a general engagement until Longstreet was in position.

I rode with Hill's troops on the Plank Road, with Heth's division in the lead. It was a warm, foggy morning, and the men were in fine spirits. "General Lee," a staff officer said, "the men are saying, 'Marse Bob is *going* for them this time.'" I was indeed, and I prayed to merciful God to give me strength for the coming battle. If we were defeated, I thought, nothing would be left for us to live for. But if we were victorious, we would have everything to hope for in the future. My whole trust was in God, and I was ready for whatever He might bring.

1 2. GRANT

Five next morning, May fifth, the army was in motion again. Our march out of the Wilderness would be along three roughly parallel roads. Sedgwick, following Griffin's division of Warren's corps, would march on the Orange Pike, on our right; Warren's corps would move down and march on the Plank Road, in our center; and Hancock's corps would march on the Catharpin Road, on our left.

Wilson's cavalry division would reconnoiter in Hancock's front while Sheridan's main body of horsemen guarded the huge wagon train, still crossing the Rapidan in our rear.

Meade and his staff rode on ahead to join Warren at his headquarters at Old Wilderness Tavern. I stayed behind, waiting for Burnside. This was Meade's army and he was in charge of the advance, and I didn't want to interfere with him, unless the army balked at fighting. Assigned myself the job of coordinating Burnside's march with Meade's.

Just before eight-thirty that morning, a courier rushed up with a dispatch from Meade. "The enemy have appeared in force on the Orange Pike and are now reported forming line of battle in front of Griffin's division of the Fifth Corps—I have directed General Warren to attack them at once with his whole force. Until this movement of the enemy is developed, the march of the corps must be suspended. I have therefore sent word to Hancock not to advance beyond Todds Tavern for the present. I think the enemy is trying to delay our movement & will not give battle but of this we shall soon see."

This was an unexpected turn of events. Meade had been confident that Lee would occupy his old works on Mine Run, not give battle in the Wilderness. I scribbled a quick reply to Meade that Burnside's advance division was now crossing the Rapidan—I would send it along at once and urge Burnside to speed up his march and would go forward the minute I saw him. I added: "If any opportunity presents itself for pitching into a part of Lee's army do so without giving time for disposition."

I was annoyed and impatient. A battle could be developing and here I was, stuck in a farmhouse waiting for Burnside. Chewed cigars and whittled sticks and chafed with impatience. Finally couldn't stand it any longer. Sent a message to Burnside to close up with Sedgwick's rear as rapidly as possible, and with my staff set out for Wilderness Tavern at a jingling trot. Dark as night in this thick jungle—scrub pine and oak, looked like, with interlocking limbs and tangled undergrowth of thorny vines and creepers. Terrible place to fight a battle—almost no way to use artillery.

As we rode along through the dark woods, a courier galloped up with another message from Meade. "General Meade directed me to tell you that rebels are moving down the Plank Road and the Turnpike." This was serious. Rebel troops on both roads! Meant Lee's whole army was coming up. We spurred our horses faster and soon reached the intersection of the Germanna Road and the Orange Pike. Meade and Sedgwick were standing by the roadside, not far from the Wilderness Tavern, which was deserted.

"Enemy infantry and cavalry are on the Orange Plank Road," Meade said. "No doubt about it. Lee means to fight us here, in the heart of the Wilderness."

"If he's got troops on the Plank Road, it means he's trying to turn our flank," I said. "Tell your boys to pitch right into 'em."

Couriers galloped off to give the commanders their battle instructions: Warren, called back to the Orange Pike, would pitch into the Johnnies there. Sedgwick would go back up the Germanna Road, turn down the Spottswood Road, which ran southwest to the Orange Pike, and support Warren in sweeping the Johnnies out of the turnpike sector. Getty's division of Sedgwick's corps would hold the junction of the Brock and Orange Plank Roads. Hancock would march double quick, fall in on Getty's left, and crush the rebels on the Plank Road.

Meade and I set up our headquarters on a piney knoll near the crossroads. The knoll was the only place where we could see the wild, rugged country to the west. There were a few houses with a little open ground around them, but all the rest was a tangled mass of trees with a thick undergrowth of shrubs. Dang near impenetrable, I thought. I sat on a tree stump and smoked cigars and whittled sticks with my penknife, waiting for the opening sound of the guns.

An hour or two passed with no sound of fighting on Warren's front. Just before noon, he rode back to talk to us. He didn't want to attack—thought the force in his front stronger than Meade and I did. Warren was afraid he'd be repulsed. Meade told him to get back to the front and launch his attack.

"The army seems reluctant to start a fight," I said.

"They'll fight," Meade said, "or there'll be thunder to pay."

13. LEE

A ways ahead, we could see the Orange Plank Road disappearing in the gloom of the Wilderness. Hill, I, and our staffs were riding along in front of the main body of his corps. General Heth's division was ahead of us with his skirmishers thrown out. In a moment, a courier rode up with a message from Ewell on the Orange Turnpike to the north of us. He had reached Saunders' Field, on elevated ground, and could see Yankees in his front. What were his orders?

I said to the courier: "Tell General Ewell not to advance too fast or he'll run right into the enemy when he's out of reach of Hill. He must keep pace with Hill in the center. *He must not bring on a general engagement until Longstreet is in position on the enemy flank.*"

The courier galloped away, and we moved forward again and entered the Wilderness. Trees and underbrush were so thick you couldn't see a man twenty yards away. We hadn't gone too far when we heard firing from Ewell's front, off to the northeast.

"That's rifle fire!" I said. "I fear that General Ewell has engaged."

Worse still, the two roads had begun to diverge, so that the gap between Ewell and Hill had widened perilously. I feared that Grant would discover the gap and throw Federal infantry into it, in an attempt to divide my army and destroy it in detail.

At noon, we came across Heth's division at a farm owned by the Widow Tapp. Heth had deployed his artillery on an elevated field so as to command the Plank Road, which intersected with Brock Road about a mile distant. Brock Road ran north to the Turnpike and south to Catharpin Road, on which Old Pete was marching. Brock Road had to be secured for his flank attack from the south. We sent Heth's infantry to secure the intersection and develop the enemy's strength, but not to bring on a general engagement.

Meanwhile the rattle of musketry to the north had grown more intense, indicating that Ewell was in a battle beyond my control, and it disturbed me. So did that gap between Hill and Ewell. If only I had more information about the enemy's strength and whereabouts. Couldn't ask Stuart to reconnoiter—he had his hands full, skirmishing with Federal cavalry while trying to guard Hill's right flank and keep the Catharpin Road clear for Longstreet.

When Wilcox's division reached the Tapp farm, I sent it to fill the gap between Hill and Ewell. Now the two corps presented a united front against the enemy.

14 . GRANT

Warren himself came back to report that he'd driven the rebels almost a mile along the turnpike, but then had to fall back to restore the order of his divisions. I rode to the front with him to see the terrain of battle. The pike was nothing but a narrow little road running through a thick growth of trees and thickets. Ahead we could see infantry struggling in the timber and wounded men lying on the roadside, with thick clouds of smoke hanging above the trees. Apparently the enemy had thrown up partial works in a field south of the road where the hottest fighting had taken place. The gunfire had set the works on fire, and the flames had spread rapidly across the battleground, fed by a thick blanket of dead leaves. A wounded Indiana soldier said the burning ground was strewn with dead and wounded. All the Union men who could move tried to get back across the pike and away from the flames. But the fire overtook many of the wounded and burned them to death. Their screams, he said, made his blood curdle.

I rode back to headquarters and learned that Getty had reached the crucial junction of the Brock and Plank Roads, but a large force of the enemy was in his front and coming up fast on the Plank Road. Seemed clear now that Lee was aiming to strike our left flank before we could put the army into line of battle. Made me impatient as all get out. Wanted a coordinated attack against the two rebel columns. At my urging, Meade sent orders to Hancock: "The commanding general directs that Getty attack at once and that you support him with your whole corps." Finally, late in the afternoon, a blast of musketry to the south announced that fighting had begun on Getty's front.

15 . LEE

I was wondering what Heth had found at the Brock–Plank Road intersection when an explosion of musketry sounded in his direction and grew increasingly louder. "What the devil is going on?" I said. "I must have information!" I was just about to send a courier to find out when a member of Heth's staff galloped up.

"General Lee, sir," he said. "All hell's broke loose up there. The blue bellies have attacked Heth on both sides of the Plank Road in overwhelming numbers. Worst musketry I've ever seen, sir. A perfect hurricane of fire on both sides of the road. Heth's troops are falling back this way."

I was certain it was an all-out attack to smash Heth and turn our flank. So I recalled Wilcox's brigades and dispatched them up the Plank Road to reinforce Heth. Powell Hill went with them. I sat on Traveller in the elevated clearing on the Tapp farm, looking at the battlefront through my glass. The roar of musketry rolled through the forest like a terrible windstorm. But it was impossible to see much in the dense woods and boiling smoke. Only by couriers did we know what was happening. Heth and Wilcox mounted a furious counterattack and drove the enemy back to the Brock Road intersection. But the Federals regrouped and charged our lines again and again, fighting as hard as we had ever seen them fight. From the clearing, Heth's artillery blasted the enemy on the road with explosive shells and solid shot. The solid shot too often went over their heads and ricocheted from the road's hard surface into the thick underbrush. One shell, however, exploded in the enemy ranks, showering the survivors with entrails and blood, and the torn whirling body of one man rose high into the air, paused for a second, and then fell limply to the ground.

The battle seesawed until dusk, when it ended in stalemate. Hill's two gallant divisions, led by little Powell himself, had fought hard and well that day but were too exhausted and too few in number to hold off the masses of enemy infantry when the battle renewed on the morrow. I therefore revised my battle plan. I would shift Hill's men into the gap on our left and bring up Anderson's division from the rear and Longstreet's corps from the Catharpin Road to carry the battle tomorrow morning on the Plank Road.

I sent Colonel Venable to find Old Pete. "Tell him to cancel his flank attack from the Catharpin Road," I said, "and march across country to Hill's position. Tell him to reach us as soon as practicable tomorrow morning."

That night I received a report from Ewell concerning the day's action on the turnpike. He'd been attacked by elements of two entire Federal corps, first Warren's and then Sedgwick's, but had repulsed their wild charges. I sent General Ewell my compliments and told him that the enemy was shifting his strength to our right. If practicable, I said, he was to attack the enemy right at dawn and cut him off from the Rapidan. If that was not practicable, he was to reinforce our forces on the Plank Road. Then I sent a message to Longstreet, urging him to strain every nerve to reach our lines before daybreak. Old Pete sent word that he would be there.

16. GRANT

That night Meade came over to my headquarters and we sat down by the fire to talk about the day's fighting. Could hear the sounds of both sides entrenching—clang of axes, thump of falling trees. Fires still glowed in the night and filled the air with the odor of burning leaves and timber. I was anxious about the wounded who lay out there, screaming in agony. It had been hard enough to get 'em in during the day; almost impossible at night. Every time the ambulance men showed a lantern, it attracted enemy fire.

Frustrated me that the Army of the Potomac couldn't mount coordinated attacks against the Johnnies on the turnpike and the Plank Road. Hancock was supposed to be the best general in the army—they called him Hancock, the superb—yet he'd thrown his brigades into battle piecemeal. That's why the rebels had held on the Plank Road. So it was a drawn battle. Still, I was relieved that Meade's army had foiled Lee's attempt to attack them in flank before they could be put into line of battle. Next day I meant for the army to seize the initiative and smash Lee with coordinated attacks.

From prisoners that night we learned that Longstreet was due up in the morning and planned to assault our left with twelve thousand men. I aimed to ruin that plan—would have Hancock and Getty crush the enemy on the Plank Road before Longstreet came up. Ordered Meade to launch the attack at four-thirty in the morning, May sixth, and sent word for Burnside to march up and fill the gap between Hancock and Warren. Burnside was to strike the flank of the enemy on the Plank Road at the same time that Hancock and Getty attacked his front. Warren and Sedgwick meanwhile would assault the rebels on the turnpike, preventing them from sending reinforcements to Longstreet.

But Meade didn't think the troops could be put into position to attack at four-thirty on account of their exhausted condition and the difficulty of maneuvering in the accursed Wilderness. He wanted to attack at six. I told Meade the rebels *must not take the initiative*, and I ordered an attack all along the line to commence no later than five the next morning.

Slept in my tent that night. Sound of marching troops woke me at four. Porter said it was Burnside's men, hurrying to connect with Warren's left. I had breakfast—cup of strong coffee and a sliced cucumber with vinegar. Lit a cigar and stuffed couple of dozen others in my pockets. Before the scheduled attack, heard firing on the turnpike front: the Johnnies, turned out, had attacked Sedgwick before he could begin his assault. *Useless*, I thought. Fifteen minutes later the din of battle sounded from the south. That ought to be Hancock hitting Hill with everything he had.

17. LEE

The Yankees struck Hill's exhausted infantry with a full corps of twenty-five thousand troops and caused what one of our men called "one of the worst stampedes I ever saw." Before long our infantry came streaming back to the Tapp farm, pursued by a mass of Federals on the road and in the woods on both sides of it. I spotted our General McGowan, whose brigade had fought with valor the day before.

"My God, General McGowan," I cried, "is this your splendid brigade, running like a flock of *geese*?"

"General," he said, "these men are not whipped. They just want a place to reform and they are ready to fight as well as ever."

As they retreated into the cleared field where our artillery was deployed, other broken units came streaming back. I was sitting Traveller just behind the line of howitzers, under the command of Colonel William Poague. At that moment his sixteen guns and three hundred gunners were all that stood between the Army of Northern Virginia and utter disaster. There was no supporting infantry, no line of retreat. In desperation, Poague's gunners opened fire with canister and short-range shells, firing over the heads of our retreating soldiers and blowing holes in the ranks of the advancing Federals at point-blank range. Behind me, officers tried to rally our infantry, yelling and waving their swords overhead. But it appeared that the Federals would overwhelm us.

Then somebody yelled: "Look. It's Longstreet! The old warhorse is here!"

I whipped around in my saddle and saw Longstreet's advance troops trotting up the Plank Road and into the field.

"What troops are you, boys?" I asked.

"Texas boys," they said.

It was Hood's old Texas Brigade, now commanded by General John Gregg. They had been my favorite troops since the Seven Days campaign of 'sixty-two. I waved my hat and shouted, "Hurrah for Texas. Now we'll show those people how to fight." I rode out in front of the brigade—my blood was up, I intended to lead them on a counterattack myself. But they protested. "Go back, General Lee, go back. We won't go unless you go back!" A sergeant had just seized my reins when Colonel Venable rode up. "General, you've been looking for General Longstreet. There he is, over yonder."

Reluctantly, I rode over to him. "General," I said, "it is good to see you."

He saluted and smiled. "General Lee, you can go to the rear now."

As was my practice, I let Old Pete assume tactical command of the battle, and rode back a ways. Meanwhile the Texans threw themselves against the onrushing Yankees, and with the help of Poague's gunners they broke the force of the enemy attack. I was proud of my Texans—the enemy never saw their backs. Then Longstreet flung his other brigades forward in an all-out counterattack on both sides of the road. As they went forward they broke into the rebel yell. I had never been happier to hear that yell than I was at that moment.

What magnificent infantry they were! Two divisions charging against five victorious enemy divisions! Even in those impenetrable woods, they swept the Federals back a considerable distance. But the enemy rallied, and again the battle swayed back and forth, neither side able to gain the advantage in the woods and thickets, which were filled with sulfurous white smoke.

Longstreet rode back to confer with me. Both of us thought a surprise flank attack would break the deadlock. Old Pete's aide, Moxley Sorrel, and Pete's chief engineer rode off to reconnoiter and reported back that the enemy's flank was in the air and that they had discovered a route for a flank attack, by way of a railroad cut through the woods south of the Plank Road. Longstreet sent twenty-six-year-old Sorrel, who had never led troops in battle, with a makeshift force of four brigades to execute the surprise attack.

There was a lull in the fighting along the Plank Road as both sides tried to regroup. It was getting toward late morning when we heard firing off to our right. "That must be Sorrel," I said. Sure enough, a courier brought word that Sorrel's brigades had fallen on the enemy's exposed left flank and were now rolling up the Yankee line toward the Plank Road. This forced the enemy in our front to fall back in great disorder. The rest of Longstreet's infantry charged after them, filling the woods with the high-pitched screech of the rebel yell.

"We've got another Bull Run on them," Longstreet said and with his aides trotted after his troops, heading east on the Plank Road. My aides and I rode forward as well, sensing a tremendous victory in the making. Longstreet had the opportunity to rout the whole Federal army by rolling up Hancock and then the other Union corps. If we could drive them back to the Rapidan, the river would be at their backs and we would destroy them as an army.

Presently we saw someone riding toward us at a gallop. It was Moxley Sorrel.

"General Lee, sir," he said when he reached us. "It's General Longstreet. He's been shot."

"No!" I cried. "Not General Longstreet." The news filled me with dread—it was just like Chancellorsville, when General Jackson was shot down near the very pinnacle of victory. "Is the wound mortal?"

"Don't think so, sir. But he is coughing up blood."

"How did it happen?" I asked.

"He'd ordered Kershaw's division to push straight toward the Brock Road and connect with my force driving up from the south. My men had reached the Plank Road, and I rode west and met General Longstreet and General Kershaw. We followed Kershaw's troops when all of a sudden gunshots rang out from the woods. It was our own men. In all the confusion in the damned thickets, they thought we were Yankees. Kershaw galloped ahead screaming 'Friends! Friends! We're friends!' But it was too late: a bullet struck Longstreet in the throat and passed through his right shoulder. The force of it lifted him clean out of his saddle. General Micah Jenkins was shot, too, in the head. He's incoherent. The bullet's in his brain. No chance he can survive."

We rode forward and met the ambulance carrying Old Pete to the rear. I peered inside, and the sight of my great warhorse, bandaged and prostrate, moved me to tears. He made a futile gesture with his hand and then the ambulance bore him away. General Charles Field, a native of Kentucky, assumed field command of Longstreet's troops. By now, they were so badly disorganized and separated that the attack could not continue until General Field and I got them realigned. Finally, at four in the afternoon, they charged forward again and drove the Yankees clear back to their reserve line—their works along the Brock Road.

The works were strong, made of dirt and logs as high as a man's chest, and bristled with artillery, but I sensed that the enemy was demoralized and confused, while the morale of Longstreet's men was soaring. My instinct was to attack—carry the Federal line by a frontal assault—and I ordered Field and Kershaw to launch it. With a blast of bugles, Field's division attacked north of the Plank Road and Kershaw's south of it. But the woods and undergrowth made it impossible for them to put all their troops into the assault, and the enemy guns and musketry repulsed it, leaving the parapets littered with our wounded and dead. During the fighting, the woods caught fire, and the wind fanned the flames into a furious mass that suffocated or burned alive hundreds of wounded men on both sides.

To the north, meanwhile, one of Ewell's brigade commanders, young John B. Gordon, whose aggressiveness I very much liked, mounted a dusk attack against the enemy right north of the turnpike, only to fall back after he encountered enemy trenches.

When night closed on the Wilderness, our situation was critical. Hill had connected with Ewell to form a unified front, but we had lost a great many casualties and had no fresh troops and no reserves. Without them, it was impossible to mount a decisive attack the next day. To my dismay and frustration, I had no choice but to go on the defensive, and I ordered the army to construct strong fieldworks during the night. At daybreak, I expected the Federals to attack us all along the line. I meant to make them pay dearly for it.

18. GRANT

Most confusing and frustrating battle I ever took part in. Near impossible to maneuver a large army in that jungle. Army of the Potomac was inept anyway. Meade couldn't coordinate his corps commanders, get them to attack in concert. Warren was overcautious—acted like a scared old woman in the face of the enemy; Sedgwick had fought without spirit, had failed to attack the enemy flank or to protect his own flank. Hancock had fought well for a while, but had left his flank exposed to a rebel assault, and his corps broke and according to one report "ran like sheep." Burnside got lost in the swamps and thick underbrush, halted his two divisions to have dinner, and failed to launch his attack in support of Hancock until after that superb general was stampeded. Just terrible generalship all around. No excuse for it. Don't care how bad the Wilderness was to fight in.

On top of it all, the Johnnies nearly overran my headquarters on the knoll near Old Wilderness Tavern. Happened after General Wadsworth of Warren's corps was killed and his division collapsed. I was sitting on a tree stump, smoking a cigar and whittling a stick, when the Johnnies appeared. I stood up slowly and watched the fighting.

An officer said, "General, wouldn't it be prudent to move headquarters to the other side of the Germanna Road till the result of the present attack is known?"

"It would be better to order up some artillery and defend the present position," I said. A battery of guns came up and drove the rebels away.

At sundown the Johnnies attacked Sedgwick's corps in the turnpike sector. Could hear the hellish screech of the rebel yell—sounded like a bunch of wildcats with their tails caught. A courier reported that Sedgwick's right flank had been turned and his entire line had given way. Sent my aides up to there to assess the damage—they came back with wild reports, hysterical reports, that Sedgwick's entire corps had been routed and Sedgwick and the wagon train had been captured. I didn't believe it. Questioned the aides till I had a pretty good picture of what had really happened, which was no more than a feeble attempt to turn our right flank, which had failed. Then I sent reinforcements to help Sedgwick form a new line. When the fighting ended after dark, I'd whittled so many sticks my gloves had holes in the fingertips.

An officer followed me to my tent, where I lit a cigar. "General Grant," he said, "we face a serious crisis. I know Lee's methods well from past experience. He'll throw his whole army between us and the Rapidan and cut us off completely from our communications."

Took my cigar out of my mouth and told him: "I'm tired of hearing about what General Lee's going to do. Some of you seem to think he's going to turn a double somersault and land in our rear and on both of our flanks at the same time. Go back to your command and try to think what we're going to do to Lee, instead of what he's going to do to us."

Tried to get some sleep but couldn't because the wind was howling outside. The wind stoked the fires raging in the Wilderness. Thought I could hear the wounded screaming in the flames—made me sick. Then I heard musketry and got up and went outside; my aides had come out of their tents too. But the musketry died out and they went back to bed. I sat down in an army chair by the campfire, pulled my hat down over my face and the collar of my army coat over my ears, and stared at the fire, thinking about the drawn battle. Terrible battle. Worse than Shiloh, worse than any fighting I'd ever seen. Lee had made us fight on a field he'd chosen, and we'd probably lost far more men than he had and without gaining any advantage. I blamed that on the incompetence of our commanders, and vowed that night to take a more direct hand in leading the Potomac Army.

19. LINCOLN

We'd heard nothing from Grant for two days and I tell you, the silence was nerve-racking as Stanton, Halleck, and I all paced around each other in Stanton's office. Oh, sure, I tried to joke about it. "Grant has gone into the Wilderness, crawled in, drawn up the ladder, and pulled in the hole after him. We'll have to wait till he comes out to know what happened." Finally at about noon on May sixth Halleck received a telegram from Grant. "We have engaged the enemy in full force since early yesterday," Grant said. "So far there is no decisive result, but I think all things are progressing favorably. Our loss to this time I do not think exceeds eight thousand."

That report eased the tension some: Grant may not have won a decisive battle yet, but he hadn't lost one either. When nothing else came from him that day, we became anxious again, fearing the worse was taking place down in the Wilderness. That night I went back to the Executive Mansion, but I couldn't sleep, and paced up and down the corridor with my hands folded behind my back. Finally I went back to the War Department and summoned Charles Dana, the fellow who'd checked on Grant for us at Vicksburg.

"We've been pretty much in the dark for three days since Grant moved," I said. "We're very much troubled and have decided to send you down there to find out what's going on. How soon can you start?"

"In half an hour," he said. Soon he was on his way to the front by train with only his toothbrush for baggage and a cavalry escort. I wouldn't get any sleep until we heard from Dana or Grant.

20. GRANT

Rose at dawn on the seventh. Fog and smoke hung thickly in the woods as an aide built a fire. Looked over and saw General Ferrero's division of Negro soldiers massed in a nearby hollow. They'd been assigned to guard the trains—we heard they'd fought well in driving off enemy cavalry attacks.

A little later, Meade's patrols reported that Lee's entire line had pulled back three-quarters of a mile and entrenched. So he'd gone on the defensive, was waiting for us to attack him behind his works. Had no intention of assaulting him there; he'd have all the advantage. No, I meant to march the army by our left to Spotsylvania Court House, twelve miles to the southeast on the direct road to Richmond. Thought this would in all probability force Lee to try to throw himself between us and Richmond; if so, I hoped to attack him in more open country, outside his breastworks.

All that day, May seventh, our stretcher bearers brought seven thousand of our wounded into the tent field hospitals. Grotesque sights in the field hospitals—piles of arms and legs from amputations. Can't bear to talk about it. More than eight hundred ambulances and wagons collected the wounded and set out that night for the rear, escorted by 1,300 cavalry. Since the army aimed to move by our left, the medical director routed the huge train to Fredericksburg on the Rappahannock, which became our evacuation hospital. The cavalry rode ahead to clear out any rebels that might be there.

That night the army set off for Spotsylvania with Warren in the lead and Hancock in the rear. The men cheered when we headed south. Said ole Grant was different—didn't retreat like all the other commanders had done after fighting a battle.

Next morning, we reached Piney Branch Church, where we set up my marching headquarters. Charles Dana of the War Department joined us there—the president had sent him to check on me and the army. Told him what had happened, which he no doubt relayed to the anxious president.

Later that morning we heard firing in the direction of Spotsylvania.

"Hope it's not a bad omen for us," said Lyman of Meade's staff.

2 1 . LEE

Unlike many of my officers, I didn't think Grant would retreat without fighting another battle. When he did not attack our works on the seventh, I decided he intended to march around my right and head for Hanover Junction, where the Virginia Central and the railroad from Richmond intersected. If he seized that junction, it would cut off my supply line and force me to come out and fight or retreat to Richmond. To get to Hanover Junction, Grant would have to pass through Spotsylvania Court House. I meant to beat him there by a shorter interior route and ordered Longstreet's corps, now under Richard Anderson, to start marching for that place no later than three in the morning, May eighth. With commendable foresight, General Anderson set his columns in motion at eleven that night, May seventh, with Stuart reconnoitering the roads on Anderson's right and supplying him with accurate information concerning the enemy's movements.

I rose early on the morning of the eighth and learned from our outposts that the enemy was gone. Then word came from Wade Hampton's cavalry: one of his scouts had seen a large body of Federal troops heading for Todd's Tavern on the road to Spotsylvania. *Ha!* I thought. *This old gray fox still has a knack for anticipating what those people will do.*

Quickly I put Ewell and Hill in motion and with my staff rode out ahead of Ewell's columns. A messenger reported that Powell Hill was sick, so I put Jubal Early in temporary command of the Third Corps. About two-thirty in the afternoon, my staff and I reached the Spotsylvania neighborhood and saw our troops behind works there. We had beat Grant in the race for Spotsylvania! Stuart, we learned, had brilliantly screened Anderson's infantry while fighting a series of running skirmishes with the enemy cavalry. Stuart had reached Spotsylvania first, had erected works and held the town against Federal cavalry attacks until Anderson's lead brigades came up. They did so just as the head of an enemy infantry column appeared not a hundred yards away. That was how close the race to Spotsylvania was.

The Federal infantry mounted an attack against our works, but Anderson's boys repulsed them with heavy slaughter. Elated, I wired Richmond that the Army of Northern Virginia was planted squarely across the road to Richmond, blocking Grant's way.

I was certain that the enemy would attempt another frontal attack that day, so I ordered Ewell to move up at once and support Anderson. The enemy did attack again late in the afternoon—it was the biggest assault of the day—but Ewell arrived just in time to support Anderson, and together they handsomely drove the enemy back.

Next morning, May ninth, I ordered Early up and set the army to constructing the most intricate fieldworks thus far in the Virginia theater. The men piled stones, logs, and fence rails along a line that ran for three miles; then they dug a trench behind that line with bayonets, which resulted in a barricade high enough to protect a man kneeling with a rifle. The line of works formed a semicircle around the northern side of Spotsylvania, with streams protecting each flank. In the center of the line was a salient, which the men called the mule shoe; it was manned by Edward Johnson's division of Ewell's corps. Anderson was to Ewell's left and Early to Ewell's right.

I chafed at not being able to attack the enemy—my instinct was to hit him while he was confused and uncertain. But his superior numbers forced me to refrain from undertaking a bold adventure like that at Chancellorsville and to remain on the defensive, inviting Grant to attack our superior works in hopes of inflicting severe casualties on him. Once we wore Grant's army down to a roughly equal size as ours, an attack by us would stand some chance of success.

22. GRANT

Angered me that the enemy had beat us to Spotsylvania, and that Warren and Sedgwick had failed to dislodge him on the eighth. The two hadn't attacked till late in the day, and Warren could only get one division into action and Sedgwick about half his force. No excuse for such poor generalship.

Next day Meade and I rode out to inspect our lines and the enemy's. I was on a black pony named Jeff Davis, on account of his having been captured at Joe Davis's plantation in Mississippi. The country around Spotsylvania was rolling and heavily wooded, with occasional patches of cleared land where artillery could be employed. A succession of parallel ridges described the terrain—our lines ran east and west on a high, curving ridge a mile and a half north of the cluster of houses known as Spotsylvania. Through our glasses, we studied the line of rebel works south of us. It extended along a wooded, irregular ridge which separates the Po and Ny, and it formed a semicircle that nearly enclosed the little town and covered all the roads that passed through there.

"He's across the road to Richmond," Meade said of Lee. "He means for us to attack his works."

"Then we'd better oblige him," I said. "We'll hit him tomorrow. All along the line."

We rode to Sedgwick's part of the line and conferred with him about tomorrow's attack. Then we rode on. A bit later I sent Colonel Porter back for more discussion with Sedgwick. But Porter returned with terrible news. Sedgwick, he said, had been killed by a rebel sharpshooter using a telescopic sight.

I couldn't believe it. Couldn't say a word.

"He noticed a soldier dodging bullets," Porter went on. "He asked the soldier: 'Why are you dodging? They can't hit an elephant at that distance.' Just as he said 'distance,' he fell with a bullet in his brain.'"

I put Brigadier General Horatio Wright in command of Sedgwick's Sixth Corps and informed him that he would lead tomorrow's assault. Good-looking fellow, Wright. In his forties, curly hair and curly beard. Had helped organize the expedition that captured Port Royal and Hilton Head.

That same day, May ninth, Sheridan set out on a crucial raid with his powerful corps of cavalry, ten thousand strong. His orders were to ride around Lee's left, defeat Stuart's cavalry, and cut the railroad from Richmond. "I'll whip that son-of-a-bitch and all the traitorous bastards that ride with him," Sheridan said before he left.

At noon on the ninth, dispatches arrived from Washington. Sherman was threatening Reseca in northwest Georgia, and Butler was at City Point on the James. He'd reported on May sixth and seventh that his troops were on their way to seize the railroads at Petersburg. If Butler could take those roads, it would cut off Lee's railroad supply line from Petersburg to the southern interior.

Next morning, I telegraphed Halleck that the enemy held our front in force and evinced a strong determination to interpose between us and Richmond to the last. I would take no backward step, I said, and instructed Halleck to send to us by way of Belle Plain all the infantry he could rake and scrape together. Belle Plain, a landing on Potomac Creek that emptied into the Potomac River, was our new supply base. Wagons taking the wounded to Fredericksburg would go on to Belle Plain, twelve miles to the northeast, pick up supplies brought downriver by transports, and haul them overland to the army.

I aimed to hit Lee's works with combined simultaneous assaults. Hancock had already threatened Lee's left, but found that part of his line too well fortified to carry by assault. Wright, however, reported that one section of Lee's line was "vulnerable to a systematic, resolute attack." That was the apex of the salient to the right of center. I ordered Wright to attack there at five that afternoon while Burnside probed Lee's extreme right, preventing him from shifting troops to the center. "Reconnoiter the enemy's position," I told Burnside, "and if you have any possible chance of attacking their right do it with vigor and with all the force you can bring to bear. Make all the show you can, as the best cooperative effort."

Wright chose Colonel Emory Upton to make the attack with twelve regiments numbering near five thousand men. Mott's division of Hancock's corps would support Upton. While the assaulting units were moving into position, I sat down on a fallen tree to write orders. A shell burst right in front of me. I looked up and then resumed writing. Soldier in the Fifth Wisconsin was standing nearby. Heard him say, "Ulysses don't scare worth a damn." Nope, I don't.

We rode over to Warren's position to watch the combined assault. Didn't know it, but somebody at Meade's headquarters had changed the time of attack to six that afternoon. Mott apparently didn't get the word and moved out at five and was promptly repulsed by a heavy enfilading fire. Upton's support had already collapsed before he made his attack.

"Damn it all to hell," I muttered to myself.

At six our artillery opened fire on the salient in the enemy line, and bursting shells and solid shot kicked up columns of dirt and debris along the rebel works. At the same time, Upton's main assaulting force moved up near the edge of the forest, within two hundred yards of the enemy fortifications. Then our guns fell silent, and Upton's boys, yelling infernally, rushed forward four lines deep in a classic column assault: the first line, with bayonets drawn, scaled the parapet in the face of murderous musketry and artillery fire from the front and flank. Didn't stop 'em. They drove the rebels back in hand-to-hand combat while the next two lines fanned out and seized part of the works on each side. The last line rushed in to reinforce the lead line. Then they went forward in column again and captured the enemy's second line of works with a battery. We all burst into cheers. Upton's boys had broken Lee's line completely.

While we watched the battle through field glasses, a piece of shell struck my orderly's horse, shearing part of its head off. The poor animal went berserk, plunged wildly about—panicked the other horses—finally died. I kept my glasses trained on the battle inside the salient. Upton had stopped now to wait for Mott to reinforce him. 'Course Mott never showed. Burnside, too, failed to provide support. When the rebels mounted a furious counterattack, which put Upton in peril, I ordered him to withdraw under cover of darkness.

Told Meade that Upton would have won a great victory if he'd been vigorously supported by Mott and Burnside and if the combined assaults had begun at five as planned. Still, Upton's attack gained us useful information about the bulge in the right center of Lee's line. That was Lee's weak point, all right. I meant to hit that point with an overwhelming force and divide and crush Lee's army.

Next morning, May eleventh, I sent a report to Washington.

> *8:30 a.m.*
> *Near Spotsylvania C. H. Va.*

> *We have now ended the sixth day of very heavy fighting. The result to this time is much in our favor. But our losses have been heavy as well as those of the enemy. We have lost to this time eleven general officers killed, wounded or missing, and probably twenty thousand men. I think the loss of the enemy must be greater we having taken over four thousand prisoners, in battle, whilst he has taken from us but few except stragglers. I am now sending back to Belle Plain all*

my wagons for a fresh supply of provisions and ammunition,
and propose to fight it out on this line if it takes all summer.

That last line made bold headlines in the papers—they say it delighted Lincoln and electrified the North. Meantime I wrote a similar letter to Julia, told her I'd never felt better in my life. Worked on my plan of attack most of the day. There was a cloudburst that afternoon, but I told the army there would be no postponement on account of the storm. Gave Meade my final instructions for tomorrow's battle: Hancock's fresh corps would mount the main attack against the salient in the enemy's line. His attacking column would consist of two divisions with a third going forward in support. Tell Hancock, I said, to move with "utmost secrecy" during the night, take up a position between Wright and Burnside, and assault the angle at precisely four in the morning. At the same time Burnside would attack the enemy's right. Warren and Wright would move in close to the rebel line and take advantage of any opportunity to launch diversions to prevent the enemy from shifting troops to Hancock's front. That night I sent my adjutant, Anthony Comstock, to stay with Burnside and impress him with the importance of a prompt and vigorous attack at precisely 4 A.M.

Next morning, May twelfth, I was up before dawn. Terrible weather for a battle: it was raining, with a strong wind and heavy ground fog. Staff and I moved my headquarters to a thickly forested dell closer to the front. Couldn't see any part of the battlefield from there, but all the corps commanders could reach me easily at that point. Aides built a fire and I stood by it in the rain, issuing orders and receiving reports. But shut in by the dripping woods, we were completely cut off from the movements of the army.

Colonel Porter came up. He'd been with Hancock, said he'd made a hard night march to get into position. As Porter spoke, the thunder of artillery sounded off to the Federal left. That was Burnside! Moments later we heard loud cheering and musketry in Hancock's direction, indicating his assaults had begun against the salient.

23. LEE

I rose at three that morning, ate breakfast by candlelight in my tent, and started out on Traveller to visit the front. It was cold, rainy, and foggy—visibility was only about fifty yards. Suddenly I heard heavy gunfire from the direction of the mule shoe, held by Stonewall Jackson's old division, some four thousand men under Edward Johnson. Alarmed, I spurred Traveller to a gallop and found the open end of the salient full of routed Confederate soldiers running to the rear.

I was furious. "Hold on!" I cried. "We're going to form a new line. Your comrades need you. Stop! *Stop!*" A few did stop, but the others kept running. "Shame on you men," I yelled after them. "*Shame on you.* Get back to your regiments. *Back to your regiments!*"

I spotted a member of Johnson's staff riding out of the fog-covered salient. "General Lee," he said, "the line is broken at the angle in General Johnson's front! They hit us with an overwhelming force. Must be an entire corps."

This meant they had broken through the very center of my line, had cut the army in two, and were now moving to destroy it. I didn't wait for a full report and set off for the rear, where General Gordon's division was in reserve. I came across his Virginia brigade heading for the salient—Gordon had sent them ahead when he heard the gunfire. "Go Virginia!" I cried, and rode on. In a few minutes I saw in the fog and rain Gordon coming up with his other two brigades, heading toward the mule shoe. As I rode up to Gordon, bullets struck the trees nearby; one bullet nicked his coat as he formed his brigades for an attack. I fell into line with him—I meant to lead them myself.

"General Lee," Gordon yelled, "this is no place for you. Go to the rear, General. We'll drive 'em back. These are Virginians and Georgians. They've never failed. They never will. Will you boys?"

They cried, "no, no" and "General Lee to the rear." But I refused to look at Gordon; my eyes were fixed on the fog ahead where masses of unseen Yankees were sweeping toward us. When they were almost upon us, Gordon rode in front of me to block my way, and a Virginia sergeant seized Traveller's reins and pulled us a little ways to the rear. Gordon cried, "Forward! Charge!" And his two brigades plunged into the gloom. I could no longer see them in the fog, but I heard gunfire and the rebel yell, which meant they had struck the enemy in the mule shoe. *God give them strength,* I whispered.

In a short while a courier rode up with a message from General Rodes, whose division held the left side of the mule shoe. One of his brigades had struck the attacking Yankees with a gallant charge and had driven them back beyond the front line of works, only to be assaulted by a fresh Yankee division. Rodes had to have help or he would be overwhelmed.

I dispatched Colonel Venable to bring up Anderson's old division, now under little Billy Mahone, which had moved into town from our far left. I sent word to Rodes, "Hold your line! Reinforcements are on the way!" Then I rode back to hurry them up. On the courthouse road, just behind the open end of the salient, I met Nat Harris's Mississippi brigade moving forward with young Venable. I turned and rode at the head of the column with him and Harris. Suddenly artillery shells exploded around us. Traveller reared; as he did so a solid shot passed under his upraised hooves. Had Traveller not reared, I would in all likelihood have been killed.

The men yelled: "Go back, General Lee! For God's sake go back."

"If you promise to drive those people from our works, I'll go back."

"We promise!"

As I looked on, they went forward to support Rodes. Another of Mahone's brigades came up to reinforce Gordon, and their combined forces smashed the Yankees' assault and drove them out of the mule shoe. They clung to the other side of our works, however, with a maddening tenacity that enraged me. But we lacked the strength to drive them away. In an attempt to break the deadlock, I directed Heth's division to mount an attack on our far right, but the Federals there attacked first, only to be repulsed by blasts of canister from our artillery.

I realized that our position was now untenable: we had to abandon the salient and fall back to a new line of fortifications at its base. While our rear soldiers set to work on the new works, I ordered my officers to hold the parapet at all costs. Fierce hand-to-hand combat broke out between the enemy outside our works and our men inside of them. Our troops rose, fired over the parapet, and ducked back into a ditch that oozed with blood and mud. The Federals fired and stabbed their bayonets through openings in the parapet, even climbed on top and threw bayoneted guns like spears at the heads of our men. Our artillery blasted the enemy with double shots of canister at point-blank range until the dead lay three and four deep in many places. Yankee artillery from a nearby ridge pounded the inside of the salient with shot and shell. The rifle fire alone was so intense that bullets stripped the bark away from the trees and cut down one large oak measuring twenty inches in diameter. Many of the dead were hit hundreds of times, so completely riddled with bullets that their bodies turned to mush.

In the midst of the violent deadlock along the mule shoe, I received a report from General Stuart's cavalry. General Stuart had given battle to the Yankee cavalry at Yellow Tavern just a few miles north of Richmond. He had fallen with a mortal wound. "General Stuart has been shot," I said with a quavering voice. "A more zealous, ardent, brave, and devoted soldier the Confederacy did not have." Early that evening General Stuart died. When I heard the news, I could not speak. I went alone to my tent. I could scarcely think of that fine young man without weeping.

To compound our difficulties, the Yankee cavalry had severed the railroad to Richmond, thus cutting off our supply line and forcing us to fight on short rations. The battle of the salient meanwhile raged on into the night. The flash of the guns lit up the clouds. At last, around four in the morning, the new fortified line was complete, and our brave and exhausted troops fell back to it, abandoning the mule shoe in which so much blood had been spilled. Ironically, the enemy also withdrew. The battle over those parapets and traverses had gone on for nearly twenty-three straight hours in fog, rain, and mud. Our losses came to five or six thousand. Major General Johnson had been wounded and seven brigadiers had been wounded or killed.

One of our officers expressed a widespread feeling in our army about Grant. "He's the most obstinate fighter we've ever met. He's resolved to lose every man rather than retreat, which he knows is equivalent to our independence. He gives his blue bellies whiskey before every fight and then sends them out to meet their death in a furious state of intoxication. To all who engage in their reckless charges against our works, he gives a $50 bounty. Can you conceive of people who'll take money to do such work in such a cause?"

We waited behind our works for Grant to make his next move.

24. GRANT

Hancock and his corps fought well in the battle of the salient. His aggressiveness was what I liked to see in a field general. Wright also did well: threw two divisions against the rebel works on Hancock's right; got himself wounded in the desperate fighting there but would not leave the field. "A sterling soldier he is," said Lyman of Meade's staff. I agreed. Burnside and Warren, however, were wholly inept. Even with my adjutant spurring him on, Burnside was slow to mount his diversionary attack against the enemy right. Had to *order* him to do it. He finally went forward late in the morning, but hadn't bothered to scout the terrain before him even though I'd told him to. His diversionary attack was ineffectual.

As for Warren, I'd ordered him to attack the enemy left by eight that morning to relieve Hancock's troops fighting in the salient and prevent Lee from shifting troops there. But eight came and went and Warren didn't budge. Made me lose my temper. Sent word to Meade that Wright hadn't made the attack and was not inclined to make it. Meade sent him peremptory orders to attack. But he still didn't move. By then I'd had a bellyful. Told Meade: "If Warren fails to attack promptly, send Humphreys to command his corps, and relieve him." Meade didn't relieve Warren of command, but he did relieve him of two of his divisions, giving one to Wright and the other to Hancock. By doing that, Meade abandoned operations on our right. Had Warren on the right and Burnside on the left made vigorous assaults in support of Hancock and Wright, the Army of the Potomac might have won a great victory at Spotsylvania. Instead it had to settle for another drawn battle.

When Lee abandoned the salient early the next morning, May thirteenth, Meade and I thought the rebel army was in full retreat. Then we discovered that Lee had just fallen back to another heavily fortified line at the base of the mule shoe. I told Meade I didn't want to attack him in his works like we'd done yesterday.

"We must get by his right flank for the next fight," I said.

During the fighting yesterday I'd ridden back and forth along the entire line of battle. Saw the terrible hand-to-hand fighting on the parapet at the top of the mule shoe. Today, Colonel Porter of my staff rode over to look at the battleground and reported what he saw. "Our own wounded are scattered over a large space near the 'angle,'" he said. "The enemy's dead appear to be far greater than ours, and are piled on each other in front of the captured breast-works. The corpses are terribly mutilated and decaying fast, but among them we saw arms and limbs twitching convulsively, which meant that there were wounded men still alive and trying to extri-cate themselves from the heap. Some of our ambulance men tried to rescue them, but in too many cases they were too late. The soldiers call it, aptly, 'Bloody Angle' or 'Hell's Half-Acre.'"

Alone in my tent later that day, I wrote a letter to my dear Julia. "The ninth day of battle is just closing with victory so far on our side. But the enemy are fighting with great desperation entrenching themselves in every position they take up. We have lost many thou-sands of men killed and wounded and the enemy have no doubt lost more. We have taken about eight thousand prisoners and lost likely three thousand." The capture of so many enemy prisoners was why I thought the Johnnies had been outfought. "I am very well and full of hope," I went on. "I see from the papers the country is also hopeful. The world has never seen so bloody or so protracted a battle as the one being fought and I hope never will again. The enemy were really whipped yesterday but their situation is desperate beyond anything heretofore known. To lose this battle they lose their cause. As bad as it is they have fought for it with gallantry worthy of a better cause."

Later that day another immense train of wagons and ambulances filled with 3,560 of our wounded set out on the road to Fredericks-burg. An earlier train had already carried 2,500 wounded men up there.

25. HANCOCK

Once again the Medical Department found itself desperately short of physicians and nurses to treat the vast number of wounded men at Fredericksburg, and it had to issue another call for volunteers. I went to Fredericksburg as the assistant of my brother-in-law, Dr. Henry Child, who was associated with the Sanitary Commission. We arrived on May twelfth, and I saw at once that I was the first Union woman there. Some of the medical men again remarked that I didn't look at all like the nurses of Miss Dix, for I was young and pretty, had rosy cheeks, and wore a fashionable dress, a breast pin, gum shoes, and leggings. But I had nursed the wounded at Gettysburg and the sick at Brandy Station, and thought of myself as a veteran.

An ambulance train from Spotsylvania, carrying 2,500 wounded men, arrived in Fredericksburg on the same day that I did, but the town was already overflowing with 14,000 wounded and dying soldiers brought here from the Wilderness battles. The train left the 600 worst hurt men in Fredericksburg and took the rest directly up to Belle Plain, where they were to be evacuated to Washington by water. Another train from Spotsylvania arrived a day or so later, this one filled with 3,560 wounded men. Since there was no place to put them, they had to lie in the wagons all night without food or water. Many of them died, and their companions threw their bodies in the street, where they still lay the next morning while buzzards circled overhead. A bloody spot in the mud below many of the wagons told how the life of some poor soldier had dripped out during the night. Not long after daybreak, the train set out on the twisting muddy road up to Belle Plain, where the wounded would have to lie in the wagons and ambulances, no telling how long, while the steamers that would evacuate them unloaded supplies for Grant's army.

The conditions in Fredericksburg paralyzed all of us who had come there as medical volunteers. Churches, warehouses, private dwellings, filthy stores, old blacksmiths' shops, crude stables—all had been converted into makeshift hospitals. Dozens of shattered men lay on the cold, broken floors of ruined buildings. Hundreds of others lay in the debris-ridden streets, waiting to take the places of those who died inside or were removed to Belle Plain. Some of the poor fellows outside had died from lack of care, and their maggot-infested bodies were rotting in plain sight. The stench was just awful.

Since I had nursed in the Second Corps hospital at Gettysburg, I went to the same hospital at Fredericksburg, accompanied by two prominent New York surgeons, Dr. Detmold and Dr. Vanderpool. What we found in the churches that functioned as the Second Corps hospital left us dumb with shock. The injured lay crowded together on the floors, some with their faces blown away, others with arms and legs shot off, still others with intestines hanging out. The victims of the explosive shells were the worst hurt: their bodies were mangled almost beyond recognition. The poor wretches had no blankets or pillows, and were crying out for water and food. Many had not eaten for three or four days.

To make matters worse, rain leaked through bullet holes in the roofs and the wounded lay in pools of water turned red by their injuries. The two doctors gazed in horror and seemed not to know where to take hold. My Gettysburg experience enabled me to start right in. I set about preparing hot soup and passing it out to the poor fellows lying on the floor.

The next morning Dr. Vanderpool and Dr. Detmold opened a better hospital in a Methodist church, and at their invitation I went with them. We brought 120 wounded men there, had the pews knocked to pieces and cleats put under the backs and seats, and made little beds to raise the wounded from the floor and the rain puddles. The amputating table was improvised under a tree in the church yard where those two good surgeons worked tirelessly until their clothes were soaked in blood.

The men awaiting amputation lay in a long line in the yard. Skilled surgeons like Dr. Vanderpool and Dr. Detmold could perform an amputation in a few minutes. Attendants would place the patient on the table and the surgeon would put him to sleep with chloroform or ether. When we ran out of those, the patient would get a shot of whiskey or a slab of leather placed in his mouth, so that he could bite down on it when he began screaming. The surgeon would slice through the flesh with a sharp knife, saw through the bone with a sharp-toothed saw, and snip off bone ends with pliers. Then he would close the bleeding arteries with a clamp, tie them with silk thread, apply a styptic, and dress the bloody stump, hoping it would not turn gangrenous. Then the surgeon would cry, "Next!" and the attendants would put another patient on the table. On it went hour after hour, until there were grotesque piles of bloody limbs on both sides of the table.

I had become inured to such sights at Gettysburg. But I never became used to the terrible screaming of the patients as the surgeon sawed off a leg, an arm, or a hand. Trying to put their screams out of mind, I made beef soup and distributed it to the poor hungry men inside the church. They were so thankful! It just made you want to cry the way they thanked you over and over for a little cup of hot soup. For the dying, I sat by their sides and tried to soothe them in their last moments. I wrote letters to their families for them and closed their eyes when they died.

The day we opened the Methodist church hospital, a Dr. Miller sought me out with a message from my dear friend, Dr. F. A. Dudley of the Fourteenth Connecticut, who was at the front. "He wants you to know he's all right," Dr. Miller said. Oh how that relieved me! I had met Dr. Dudley in the hospital at Brandy Station. He was smart, a Yale graduate, and yet not at all enlightened about politics. He was not *pro*slavery, that is, he did not wish for slavery to exist, but he thought nothing of the black man himself, thought the black man was nobody and ought to remain nobody. I always spoke my mind to him, and he listened with respect, for which I was grateful. Though he could not have been more than twenty-three years old, he was a major surgeon in charge of the Third Division hospital. I greatly enjoyed his company and worried so about him when the fighting began.

I'd burst into tears when I saw Dr. Miller; he reminded me of a lieutenant I had known and admired, who had died. What Dr. Miller said about my friends at the battlefront shocked me. Almost everyone I knew had been shot dead except Dr. Dudley. Some of my friends had been taken prisoner, and the battle was still raging. There was terrific firing this day—it sounded like continuous thunder just over the southern horizon.

During the next few days, the famous Clara Barton and several other women volunteers arrived in Fredericksburg to help nurse and feed the wounded. Among them was Miss Georgeanna Woolsey of the Sanitary Commission. Miss Woolsey had nothing but horror tales to report about Belle Plain. "The mud is frightful and the rain keeps coming down," she said. "Nothing I've ever seen equals the condition of the wounded there, who were waiting to be evacuated. They'd been two or three days in the ambulance train, without food. We worked with them from morning till night without ceasing, filling one boat, feeding the men, filling another, and feeding them. They ate as if they were starving. The wounded arrive in ambulances, one train a day, but the trains are miles long, plunged in quagmires, jolted over corduroyed roads, without food, and filled with fainting, filthy, frightfully wounded men. Arms gone to the shoulder, horrible wounds in the face and head. I would rather a thousand times have a friend killed on the field than suffer this way. It's worse than what I saw at Gettysburg. We found thirty-five dead men in the ambulances yesterday, and five more died on the stretchers while being put on the boat. Mules, stretchers, army wagons, prisoners, dead men, and officials all tumbled and jumbled on the wretched dock, which falls in every little while and keeps the ambulances waiting for hours. To make matters worse, the neighborhood is infested with guerrillas."

The hospitals at Fredericksburg still suffered terrible shortages of food and medical supplies, since the wagon trains were mostly taken up carrying forage, supplies, and ammunition to the front. I'd had nothing but hardtack and tea since I'd come here. Ten huge wagons bursting with supplies did arrive from the Sanitary Commission; I don't know how we would have survived without the heroic labors of that organization.

One day, venturing into a dark, loathsome stone house whose floor was smeared with molasses, I found about twenty wounded men who had not had their wounds dressed for twenty-four hours. Oh God! such suffering it never entered the mind of man or woman to think of. I wrote my sister that there was no end to the wounded: they arrived anytime, night or day, and we only had coffee and hardtack to give them, the supplies of the Sanitary Commission having been consumed. I told my sister that the public must know that Fredericksburg was one vast hospital requiring all the muscle and supplies the North could send down. The public must know that the groans of the wounded and dying rose from every building. It was worse than at Gettysburg because now the army fought every day without letup. I hoped that Grant was doing something at the front, because he was making terrible suffering in the rear. In all honesty, I did not see that Grant had accomplished much, yet he fought straight ahead whether he won any advantage or not.

Despite the indescribable suffering I witnessed every wakened hour, I was glad to be in Fredericksburg. "I never was better in my life," I wrote my sister. "I'm certain I am in my right place."

Orders came to remove all the wounded from Fredericksburg and take them to Washington. Grant was preparing to move south again, and the evacuation hospital was to relocate closer to the fighting front.

26. DAVIS

The evil foe meant to destroy us by fighting a war of attrition all across the Confederacy, putting an immense strain on our limited resources in soldiers and supplies. To resist Beast Butler's advance up the James, we called Beauregard and his command up from Charleston to Petersburg, and ordered every organized brigade in the Department of South Carolina and Georgia to go there as well. But for a time all we had between the Yankees and that vital railway center was five thousand troops and government clerks serving as militia. Fortunately for us Beast Butler did not attack Petersburg, perhaps because I had declared that cowardly wretch an outlaw for his atrocities against our people in New Orleans in 1862.

Lee meanwhile begged us for reinforcements so that he could hold Grant's hordes in check at Spotsylvania. I informed him that it was impossible to spare a single man from the Richmond front at this time, since Beast Butler's huge force was threatening the capital from the south. Having heard reports that General Lee had exposed himself in the fighting, I begged him to stay in the rear. "The country can not bear the loss of you," I said.

Meanwhile another Yankee force was advancing on Staunton in the Shenandoah, from which Lee was getting some of his meager supplies. A makeshift force of five thousand men under former Vice President John C. Breckinridge attacked and routed the Federals at New Market, which secured the valley for now.

On May fourteenth, we heard the heavy boom of artillery to the south. That was Beast Butler's army, ascending the James to attack our garrison at Drewry's Bluff. If that fell, the Yankees would take Richmond by its "back door." That afternoon I rode down to watch the battle and was shocked to see that Beauregard's troops were not in their entrenchments. Finding Beauregard in a nearby house, I asked him why his entrenchments had been abandoned. I could not stand this arrogant and insufferable officer, whose hatred of me showed in his bloodhound eyes. He rose to his full height and said stiffly that he intended to concentrate his troops against Butler.

"But there is nothing to stop Butler from turning your position," I said.

"If he does, I'll fall on him and cut him off from his base."

It was my uniform practice never to make more than a suggestion to a general commanding in the field. But affairs here were critical. I told Beauregard I wanted him to *attack* Butler, and I offered to give him the field force under General Ransom now defending Richmond. When Beauregard protested, I glared at him. "General," I said, "you are *ordered* to make the attack."

Two days later, with me looking on, Beauregard and Ransom attacked Beast Butler at Drewry's Bluff with a hastily assembled force of eighteen thousand men. The weather was inclement, with dense fog and rain, but our soldiers pitched into the larger enemy force with great élan. There was much confusion in the roar of artillery and crack of muskets, and shells exploded close to me. One burst only five feet away, taking off a man's arm. I had no intention of leaving, not when the battle was going in our favor. To my bitter disappointment, however, Beauregard allowed Butler to escape back to his entrenchments on Bermuda Hundred, a peninsula at the confluence of the James and Appomattox Rivers. I wanted Butler's force destroyed and Butler captured and hanged. But at least he was "cooped up" on Bermuda Hundred with our troops entrenched in his front and the rivers at his back. He was not likely to threaten Richmond again.

Soon after the battle of Drewry's Bluff, Beauregard addressed to me an outrageous communication. He proposed that he be heavily reinforced from General Lee's army—he wanted an entire corps—so that he could crush Butler in his entrenchments. Then, with the main body of his own force and the corps from the Army of Northern Virginia, he proposed to join General Lee, overwhelm Grant, and march on Washington.

I thought Beauregard had gone mad. General Lee confronted an army vastly superior to his in numbers, fully equipped, with inexhaustible supplies and reinforcements and a persistence in attacking. I knew that General Lee would never consent to Beauregard's crazy proposal. Still, as a matter of courtesy, I forwarded it to General Lee. His opinion of the plan was shown by his instructions to Beauregard. *You will straighten your line so as to reduce the requisite number of men to hold it and send the balance to join the army north of the James.* I wish I could have seen Beauregard's reaction when he read that.

Dispatches from Georgia, meanwhile, filled me with foreboding. Sherman had flanked General Johnston's strong position at Dalton in northwest Georgia. That hapless general had fallen back to Resaca on the north bank of the Oostanaula River. I was profoundly upset that Johnston had abandoned the Dalton line without a fight. I fully expected him to retreat no farther than Resaca, but to turn and give battle to Sherman north of the Oostanaula. I counted on a decisive battle that would eliminate the enemy threat in Georgia.

27 . SHERMAN

When we left Chattanooga and entered Georgia, I had right at a hundred thousand men and 254 guns in three separate armies—the Army of the Tennessee under McPherson, the Army of the Cumberland under Thomas, and the Army of the Ohio under John M. Schofield—plus a consolidated corps under Hooker. I thus commanded a vast machine whose life and success depended on our supply line back to Nashville, a single thread of rails that for nearly five hundred miles lay within a hostile country. My forces required 1,300 tons of stores a day, which were carried to us by rail on 130 cars. Against me, Joe Johnston had, I reckon, about fifty thousand men. Now I admired Johnston as a soldier, and it made me damn proud when we turned his flank at Dalton and forced him to fall back eighteen miles to Resaca.

There he put up a strong line of entrenchments. So did we, enveloping the town to the north and west. I rode down my lines saying, "Take it easy today, boys, you'll have work enough tomorrow." Next day, the fifteenth of May, we pressed at all points, and the roar of cannon and musketry rose to the dignity of battle. Turned out, Johnston's works were too strong for a direct assault, so I sent McPherson on another flanking maneuver. His boys got a bridge across the Oostanaula and threatened Johnston's railroad supply line back to Atlanta, which caused him to retreat again, burning the railroad bridge across the river as he went. We quickly repaired the bridge and chased the rebs clear to Kingston, fighting all the way. At one point I was near the head of the lead column, studying the enemy's position from an elevation in an open field. My party attracted the fire of an enemy battery. A shell passed through our group and burst just beyond, which scattered us promptly. My Goddamn name could've been on that shell—I thanked the fates it wasn't.

Our difficulties increased as we proceeded deeper into Georgia, for I had to drop men off to guard the Goddamned railroad in our rear while Johnston gathered his guards and collected other reinforcements as he retreated. My objective was to cross the Etowah and Chattahoochee and threaten Atlanta—if I could break up the railroads there it would be one hell of an achievement. I had no doubt that we would have to fight a terrific battle at some point near the Chattahoochee River, just north of Atlanta. We had reports of

Grant's battles in Virginia: they were fearful, but the immense slaughter was necessary to prove that our northern armies could and would fight.

At Kingston I issued a circular banning all reporters from traveling with my forces. I hated those fucking leeches worse than ever. Too cowardly to take up a musket and fight, they followed us just to pick up news for sale, which was dangerous to our army and our cause. The pack of scribblers deliberately bolstered up idle and worthless officers instead of noticing the hardworking and meritorious who scorned the cheap flattery of the press. The Goddamned scribblers howled and ranted about freedom of the press, quote, unquote, but I didn't give a shit. Told 'em liberty of the press, like that of individuals, had to be restrained to just limits consistent with the good of the whole, and fools must not be allowed to print and publish falsehood and slander as they pleased. If the fools didn't like it, they could go to hell.

Thomas, whose army was in the lead, sent word back that he'd found the rebels drawn up on extensive, open ground about halfway between Kingston and Cassville, apparently prepared for battle. I rode forward over some rough gravel hills and found Thomas's army deployed. The rebels, however, had fallen back yet again, this time to Cassville. The enemy newspapers, which we found, were loud in denunciation of Johnston's constantly retreating before us without attempting to fight a serious battle. But his friends proclaimed it was all strategic, that he was deliberately drawing us further and further into the meshes, further and further from our base of supplies, and that in due season he would not only halt for battle, but assume a bold offensive. It was my aim to bring him to battle as soon a possible, when our numerical superiority was at the greatest.

We chased the rebel army and found 'em behind fresh-made earthworks on a high range of hills in back of Cassville. Night was closing in, but Thomas's artillery laid into 'em with thunderous fire. Meanwhile Thomas and I went forward with his skirmishers. We were approaching a seminary in dense woods when all of a sudden enemy musket balls struck the trees, showering us with leaves.

"This ain't no place for the two senior officers of our armies," I said, and Thomas and I rode back to one of his batteries, where we spent the night. As usual, I slept little. I liked to visit with the pickets, smoke cigars, listen to what the enemy was doing at night, plan the next day's action. One time I stayed up all night, only to fall asleep sitting on a log with my back against a tree. Woke up when some soldiers marched by.

One said, in reference to my prone position, "A pretty way we're commanded."

I jumped up. "Listen, man, while you were sleeping last night I was planning for you. Now I'm taking a Goddamned nap." Both men lit out.

Don't get the wrong idea: my men loved me. Called me Uncle Billy. On the march I like to stop and talk to 'em, tell 'em what we were going to do to the Goddamned rebels if they ever stood and fought.

I ordered McPherson, Hooker, and Schofield to attack the rebel works at Cassville at dawn, but when daylight came the enemy was gone. We found a long line of fresh entrenchments on another hill, which convinced me that the enemy had been preparing for a grand battle. I was certain that the whole of Polk's corps had joined Johnston from Mississippi, and that he had in hand three full corps under Hood, Polk, and Hardee, numbering about sixty thousand men. I couldn't imagine why Johnston had declined to give battle. Instead he'd fallen back across the Etowah River and retreated to a new defensive line in the Allatoona range. That left us masters of all the country above the Etowah.

I knew the mountainous country south of the Etowah—I'd crossed it on horseback in 'forty-four when I was sent there on old army business. Allatoona Pass was very strong, would be hard to force, so I resolved not even to attempt it, but to break loose from my railroad supply line and make another wide flanking movement around Johnston's left, heading for Dallas in the piney woods off to the southwest. Possession of Dallas would pose a threat to Marietta and Atlanta, just twenty-four miles to the south, and would force Johnston to retreat again.

From my tent in the field, I wrote a quick letter to Ellen: "Tomorrow we start for Atlanta. I think I have the best army in the country, and if I can't take Atlanta and stir up Georgia considerably I am mistaken. Our next step is to force the enemy behind the Chattahoochee, and last to take Atlanta and disturb the peace of central Georgia and prevent reinforcements from going to Lee."

28. DAVIS

When Johnston retreated all the way to Allatoona, calamity seemed at hand. The reports from his army were alarming: the men were discouraged, the subordinate commanders were feuding, nobody had any confidence in Johnston. The people of northern Georgia had taken to the roads as refugees, all heading south and dragging their slaves with them. Delegations of Georgians came to me in hot haste, demanding that I remove Johnston and put a general in command of the Army of Tennessee who would fight Sherman, the North's Attila the Hun.

"Johnston has fulfilled all our predictions about him," said Josia Gorgas. "He'll be falling back as fast as his legs can carry him. He will fall back behind the Chattahoochee and I fear will give up Atlanta. Where he'll stop heaven only knows."

Mary Chesnut was correct in calling Johnston "the Great Retreater." He seemed to lack the will to fight, and it filled me with anxiety, as bad as it had ever been during the Vicksburg and Gettysburg campaigns. I too feared that Johnston might retreat through Atlanta and give the city to the enemy. An intolerable thought! Plainly Johnston had to be replaced. But by whom? Not by Beauregard—that arrogant Creole was no better than Johnston. General Hardee was the obvious choice, but he had made it clear he was not interested. That left Sam Hood, who had complained to us about Johnston's cowardly retreats. One thing I knew for certain: Sam Hood would fight. I even thought briefly about going out there and leading the Army of Tennessee myself. But I couldn't do that with Grant's army threatening Richmond from the north. Reminding myself that it was dangerous to remove the general of an army in the midst of a campaign, I left Johnston in command, but with blunt instructions to stop his infernal retreating, to stand firm at Allatoona and destroy the infidel invaders.

29. SHERMAN

My forces set out for Dallas on May twenty-third, with Hooker in the lead. We were marching in desolate country with occasional deserted farms here and there. The roads were few and terrible and meandered through dense woods and underbrush. Our skirmishers cleared the way by hacking with their bayonets. We plunged into deep gorges and struggled up hills whose soil was shifting and loose. The area abounded in small streams and lagoons bordered by treacherous quicksand. On the twenty-fifth, heavy rains came and turned the roads into oozing mud. The soldiers became so bespattered with mud they looked inhuman.

Just four miles from Dallas, our lead division struck a heavy enemy infantry force marching down from Allatoona toward Dallas. The Goddamned rebs were trying to beat us there! According to my map, we were at a crossroads called New Hope, so called because of a Methodist meeting house there by that name. I ordered Hooker to secure the crossroads that night, but before he could bring up his other two divisions the enemy was greatly reinforced. The woods were so Goddamned dense and the resistance so spirited that Hooker could not carry the position.

It rained hard that dark night, and whole units became confused and mixed up as the rest of the army began arriving. I resolved to renew the battle of New Hope Church at first light, but morning revealed a strong line of enemy entrenchments facing us, manned by a heavy force of infantry and artillery. Convinced me that Johnston was at New Hope in person with all his army. Since New Hope was nearer to the railroad than Dallas, I decided to fight Johnston here and ordered my men to entrench. They cut down trees and laid the trunks on top of one another until they had a line of works three feet high. Then they dug a ditch behind the log works two feet deep and laid head logs on top of the works with rifle holes to shoot out of.

The battle broke out again between the rival works and went on for a week. The musketry and cannon resounded day and night, and was so fierce and frightening that the men called it Hell Hole. Occasionally one party or the other would make a dash against the enemy works, but usually it was repulsed with great loss of life.

I personally visited all parts of our lines nearly every day and was constantly within musket range. At one point, under heavy artillery fire, I spotted one of my soldiers cowering behind a tree and crying out every time a shell burst: "Oh God! Oh God! If I get out of this, I'll never be caught again. Dear God, I know I'll be killed." I couldn't stand the sight of the cowardly son-of-a-bitch, so I started throwing rocks against his tree.

"My man," I said, "those Goddamned shells hit hard."

"Hard!" he cried. "It's terrifying. I think thirty shells have struck this tree while I've been here." Suddenly he recognized me. Scared the little shit out of his wits. Took off and didn't stop running till he reached his regiment. I issued orders forthwith, threatening instant death or the harshest labor to all skulkers like him.

Hell, the battle was a Goddamned stalemate, any fool could see that. So I extended our strong infantry lines to the left toward Acworth, on the railroad about four miles south of Allatoona. When Johnston saw I was making for the railroad around his right flank, he abandoned his works and retreated south again.

Told my officers: "Johnston might fight us at the ridge of hills just this side of Marietta, but I think we can dislodge him and force him to fall back to the Chattahoochee. That will leave the great battle to be fought on or near the river, because Johnston can't afford to let us cross it. He's got a strong, well-disciplined army, but I think I can lick him on anything like fair terms in an open fight. So I won't run hotheaded against any works he's prepared for us. That's what he's wanted me to do since the campaign started. So he can inflict heavy casualties on us a long way from our base. No way I'm gonna do that. We'll keep fighting an Indian war and turn his flank."

I stabbed out a cigar and lit another. "As long as we press Johnston close and prevent him from sending anything to Lee, we fulfill our part of the grand plan. Meantime Grant will give Lee all the fighting he wants until he's Goddamned sick of it. Every man in the North ought to be in uniform now. Every man who won't fight ought to be put in petticoats and deprived of the right to vote, Goddamn 'em."

30. GRANT

I was proud of what Sherman was doing in the West, driving Joe Johnston back toward Atlanta in a brilliant campaign of maneuver. But in the East Sigel and Butler were bungling incompetents who threatened the success of the grand plan. Instead of advancing on

Staunton in the Shenandoah, Sigel got himself whipped by a rebel force and retreated clear back to Cedar Creek. Halleck wired me that Sigel would "do nothing but run" and said that Stanton proposed to put General Hunter in his place. I told Halleck to do it, and he did.

Butler was even worse than Sigel. Instead of harassing Richmond and detaining ten thousand troops there, he'd retreated to his works on Bermuda Hundred and allowed the rebels to entrench all along his front. His Army of the James was as completely shut off from further operations directly against Richmond as if it was in a bottle strongly corked. On top of that, he'd also failed to capture Petersburg. Made me madder'n all get out. Rebels still had control of the city and all the railroads running through it. A disaster, was what it was. I couldn't relieve Butler because he was a friend of the president's. But I did order Baldy Smith's corps of Butler's army to come up and reinforce the Army of the Potomac.

Told my staff: "Lee will undoubtedly reinforce his army by bringing Beauregard's troops from Richmond, now that Butler has been driven back, and will call in troops from the valley, since Sigel's defeated forces have retreated to Cedar Creek. Lee's army will be materially strengthened. I thought the other day they must feel pretty blue in Richmond over the reports of our victories in the East and the West. My goal now is to draw Lee out of his works and fight him in the open field, instead of assaulting him behind his entrenchments."

I therefore ordered the army to move out again by the left flank, heading into more open country with cultivated fields and wide roads. Our line of march, with Hancock in the lead, took us southeast toward Hanover Junction, located between the North and South Anna Rivers, about twenty-five miles north of Richmond. I aimed to cross the North Anna and get in Lee's rear and across his communications with Richmond, which would flush him out of his works.

About noon on May twenty-third, Hancock's lead columns reached the North Anna at the Telegraph Road bridge and found rebel troops already there. Hancock's boys drove 'em off and started crossing the river. That afternoon, I stopped at a house near the river and learned from the inhabitants that Lee had stayed in this very house the day before and that he had his entire army on the other side of the river ahead of us.

"Damn it all to hell," I muttered to myself. "They've beat us again."

Same day Burnside's Ninth Corps reached Ox Ford on the North Anna, two miles up from Hancock, and found the enemy in force on the opposite side. Warren also reached the river at Jericho Ford, seized the pontoon bridge there, and had his troops across by late afternoon. A rebel force attacked him there, but he repulsed 'em in an uncharacteristic show of pluck.

Next day Sheridan and his cavalry corps rejoined the army, and Sheridan reported the details of his raid in his animated style: he'd ridden around the right flank of Lee's army, crossed the North Anna, wrecked ten miles of the Virginia Central Railroad and burned cars, locomotives, and army supplies; he'd crossed the South Anna, destroyed the depot at Ashland and wrecked a train and many miles of the Fredericksburg railroad; he'd fought Stuart's cavalry at Yellow Tavern just seven miles north of Richmond, and mortally wounded Stuart. Sheridan had then intended to link up with Butler just south of Richmond, so that their combined forces could seize the enemy capital. But when Sheridan struck Richmond's outer defenses, Butler had skeedaddled back to Bermuda Hundred; so Sheridan had to call his raid off. Another opportunity missed. If Butler and Sheridan had seized Richmond, it would have forced Lee to retreat, probably into southwestern Virginia, where Meade's and Butler's armies could have destroyed him.

Same day Sheridan rejoined us, a cipher dispatch came from Sherman. Charles Dana of the War Department read the dispatch before Meade, me, and other officers. Sherman said that the Army of the West had proved its fighting ability. Now, he said, if I could inspire the Army of the Potomac to do its share, our efforts would be crowned with success.

Pardon the expression, but it pissed Meade off. Eyes bulged with rage. "Sir!" he snarled, "I consider that dispatch an insult to the army I command and to me personally. The Army of the Potomac doesn't require your inspiration or anybody else's inspiration to make it fight!"

Meade fumed about Sherman's dispatch all day. At dinner he called the Western Army "an armed rabble." I told him I didn't share Sherman's low opinion of the Army of the Potomac. Said the fighting in the present campaign threw in the shade anything I'd ever seen, said I'd never anticipated such fierce resistance on the enemy's part. To reassure Meade of my good opinion of him and his army, I assigned him the Ninth Corps, which made Burnside his subordinate. The two men had no liking for each other, but to his credit Burny took the assignment without complaint.

When my staff and I reached the North Anna and studied Lee's position on the opposite shore, I had to admire his cunning. Plain to me he meant to make a stand. Had his army entrenched in a V-shaped line, with the point of the V resting on the river at Ox Ford, contesting Burnside on the opposite bank. Hancock was across the river on Lee's right, and Warren and Wright were on his left. His line had split the Army of the Potomac in two. A trap, is what this was. No way I was going to attack Lee here. It would cause a slaughter of our men that even success couldn't justify. So I pulled the army back across the river and sent it on another flank march, intending to cross the Pamunkey River at Hanover Town and try to turn Lee's right. Meanwhile I shifted our base of supplies and evacuation hospital to White House Landing on the Pamunkey, farther to the east.

I explained all this in a wire to Halleck. "Lee's army is really whipped," I said. "The prisoners we now take show it, and the actions of his army show it unmistakably." By that, I meant that Lee was too weak to take the offensive, and could only fight behind his works. "A battle with them outside of entrenchments cannot be had," I said. "Our men feel that they have gained morale over the enemy and attack with confidence. I may be mistaken but I feel that our success over Lee's army is already insured."

31. LEE

I was ill with intestinal cramps and the old soldier's disease, but gritted my teeth against the pain and kept to my duties. I was also frustrated with the campaign. I detested fighting defensively behind earthworks. I intended to destroy Grant, I mean *destroy* him. I meant to mount a counteroffensive. "We must strike them a blow," I told Colonel Venable. "We must never let them pass us again—we must strike them a blow. If I can get one more pull at Grant, I will defeat him."

But to my chagrin they passed us again, pulled back across the North Anna and headed southeast to Hanover Town, where they crossed the Pamunkey and set out for Totopotomoy River, in yet another attempt to turn my right flank. I put the Army of Northern Virginia in motion, too, trying to keep it between Grant and

Richmond, and had cavalry scouts out to keep me posted on Grant's whereabouts. I myself was too sick to ride my horse and traveled in a carriage.

I poured out my frustration in a dispatch to Powell Hill. "The time has arrived when something more is necessary than adhering to defensive positions. We shall be obliged to go out and prevent the enemy from selecting such positions as he chooses. If he is allowed to continue that course, we will be obliged to take refuge behind the works of Richmond and stand a siege, which would be but a work of time. We must be prepared to fight him in the field, to prevent him from taking positions such as he desires."

By now, my poor troops were in desperate need of rations. On the march from Spotsylvania, many units had gone for two days without food. Then each man had received but one thin slice of fat pork and three hard biscuits. Then two more days without rations and then each man got only one cracker.

Since we were outnumbered two to one, I kept begging President Davis to send me Beauregard's force and whatever troops could be spared from the defenses of Richmond. But on May twenty-ninth, General Beauregard called on me and said that Butler had been reinforced and that he, Beauregard, had only twelve thousand men and could not spare any of them. This was depressing news, as was the silence from the president about reinforcements from Richmond.

"Very well," I said, slapping my fist against my other palm. "If Grant advances tomorrow, I will engage him with my present force."

But Grant did not advance against us. Instead he began crossing the Totopotomoy to the east—my best scout believed that Grant was on the road to Old Cold Harbor. So I sent Fitz Lee's cavalry to hold that crossroads. By nightfall, other scouts had reported terrible news: an entire corps from Butler's Army of the James was disembarking at White House Landing! Perhaps sixteen thousand men, and they would be with Grant by tomorrow. This was a calamity in the making. I wired Beauregard directly to send me Hoke's division of seven thousand men at once. But Beauregard replied that my request must go through the War Department. I was enraged at him—uttered an oath—then I wired the president, pointing out that this delay would be a disaster. Before midnight, a telegram came from His Excellency that Hoke's troops were on the way by train and would reach me by tomorrow.

I was so ill that I had to draw on all the will and strength I had to remain in the field. "Sir," Colonel Venable said, "you are the head and front, the very life and soul of this army."

Next day, May thirty-first, our scouts reported that Grant was indeed heading south on the road to Old Cold Harbor. Unfolding my map, I studied Old Cold Harbor and tried to think like Grant. Seemed to me he would do one of two things: either make me stretch my line so thin as to create a vulnerable point, which he could attack, or concentrate his entire army at the little crossroads for an overwhelming attack against my flank. I believed he would do the latter.

I resolved therefore to attack him before he could attack me. I would strike the head of his army at Old Cold Harbor and roll it back over the other marching columns until it became a rout and ended in the destruction of his army. I dispatched Anderson's corps to Old Cold Harbor to make the attack. When Hoke's division arrived, I sent it to support Anderson. But before Anderson's two divisions could reach Old Cold Harbor, alarming reports came from Fitz Lee: enemy cavalry had driven him from Old Cold Harbor, and enemy infantry was coming up fast. That meant we were in a race for Old Cold Harbor.

Anderson managed to get there ahead of the enemy infantry, but instead of throwing both his divisions against the enemy cavalry holding the crossroads, he undertook a reconnaissance in force with only one division, with a green South Carolina regiment in front! The enemy cavalry, two divisions strong, repulsed the attack with rapid-fire carbines. Hoke failed to come up in support, and the South Carolinians broke and ran and so did the supporting units.

Late that afternoon I hurried to Old Cold Harbor to take command and ward off disaster. I was glad of one thing: Anderson had had his men construct defensive works across the road between Old Cold Harbor and New Cold Harbor. It was well that he had. On June first the Federal infantry counterattacked, driving between Anderson and Hoke and imperiling Anderson's entire corps. The Federals did withdraw that night, but a dangerous gap remained between Hoke and Anderson, and Anderson was crying for reinforcements. I had already ordered Breckinridge's force to join us from the Shenandoah and now brought up the rest of the army, putting Hill's corps to the right of Anderson and Ewell's corps to his left. We currently held a defensive position between Grant and Richmond, which was only nine miles behind us. And we had no reserves. I chafed bitterly at being thrown again on the defensive. It was not at all what I wanted.

Through my glass, I could see the huge Yankee army concentrating around Old Cold Harbor, just as I had thought it would do. I was certain that Grant would try to break our line by frontal assault. Accordingly, at my orders, the army dug a strong series of interlocking trenches, which abounded with muskets and artillery.

32. GRANT

The Johnnies were there, all right, blocking the road to Richmond. Were furiously throwing up works, preparing to make another desperate fight as long as they could get a respectable number of men to stand. Aimed to whip 'em before they could complete their trenches, and ordered Hancock, the best general with the best corps in the army, to swing from the far right of our line to the far left, and launch an attack at five the next afternoon, June second. The rest of the army would attack, too, all along the line. Hancock reached his new position at Old Cold Harbor the next morning, but claimed his men were too exhausted from their night march to fight that day.

Frustrated me. If Hancock couldn't fight after a night march, who in this army could? Told Meade: "We ought to be able to eat the Johnnies up. They've placed themselves in such a position to be eaten up."

But it was the Johnnies who ate us up that day: assaulted and battered a division of the Fifth Corps. Colonel Lyman of Meade's staff went on and on about the prowess of the rebels. "They're sharp as steel traps. We can't shift a hundred yards but presto! skirmishers forward! and they come piling in, *pop, pop, pop*; with reserves close behind and a brigade or two hard on the reserves all poking and probing."

Moved my headquarters near Bethesda Church, closer to the center of our line, and rode forward to study Lee's position. Hated to give him this extra day to prepare his defenses, but nothing could be done about that now. Lee's line extended more than six miles—I thought it must be weak somewhere. Terrible ground: thick woods and thickets, swamps here and there. The ground sloped upward to a series of flat hills where Lee's men had dug their trenches in a zigzag fashion. Formidable log and earthworks protected the trenches from the front, with abatis—slashed trees with sharpened branches—sticking out to impede assaulting infantry. Lee's right was at Old Cold Harbor, with earthworks thrown up there behind a sunken road and his flank protected by what looked to be an impassable swamp. His left was strong, too, protected by swamps and dense thickets. As for the rest of his line, the broken terrain and dense copse wood obstructed my view. Impossible to tell where the line was soft save by actual attack.

Knew an attack would be costly. My other option was to strike out for the James, seize Petersburg, and sever Lee's railroad lifelines to Wilmington and the rebel interior. But transferring the scene of battle to the James meant prolonging a conflict that was already costing a war-weary North $4 million a day. No, I decided, I would crush Lee where he was. Try to win the war here, now. Consequently, I ordered Meade to attack all along the line at 4:30 A.M., June third. His corps commanders would choose their own points of assault.

That night a severe rainstorm struck, and I lay awake in my tent, listening to the rain pounding on the roof and the terrible thunder that rent the sky. The storm passed, and a few hours later the man-made storm began with a massive artillery barrage against the enemy's fortifications. The roar was so violent, they say, that it rattled window-panes in Richmond. I was already up, smoking cigars and whittling sticks. Worried about the mist hanging in the woods and swamps; men would have to charge through the mist over difficult terrain.

At exactly four-thirty, bugles blared and the assault began on our right and spread across the entire front. I stayed at headquarters, letting Meade direct the battle, since it was his army. Didn't see the fighting myself, but the terrible noise, far worse than the thundering of last night, told me it was savage. Brutal. Shells hissed and shrieked across the heavens and exploded in the field where our infantry was attacking. Couriers reported that the field was a boiling whirlwind of dirt, sand, and smoke, and that musketry lit up the enemy works as far as the eye could see. Could only imagine what all that deadly fire, especially the whirling blasts of canister, was doing to our ranks.

Turned out, the battle was over in a matter of minutes. One officer said he'd led his brigade across that deadly field swinging his ramrod for a sword, but when he looked back there was no brigade to be seen. All told, more than seven thousand Union boys lay dead or wounded in front of the rebel works. The survivors fell back from fifty to two hundred yards and entrenched. When Meade ordered the assaults to be resumed, a captain cussed the generals who had ordered this suicidal charge, and the men all down the line refused to move. Don't like reporters, but one of 'em, William Swinton, got it right: "The immobile lines," he said, "pronounced a verdict, silent yet emphatic, against further slaughter."

At eleven o'clock that morning, I rode along the lines to confer with the generals. They didn't think it was possible to break through Lee's lines, so I ordered Meade to suspend the battle. For us, it was a disaster. No other way to put it. Told my staff that night: "I regret this assault more than any I've ever ordered. Gained no advantage whatever to justify our heavy losses. I'd hoped to end the war here, but the war will go on."

33 . HANCOCK

With General Grant marching southward, the hospital corps of surgeons, attendants, and women volunteers moved with all our medical stores to White House Landing on the Pamunkey, which was closer to the front and was also Grant's new base of supplies. When we arrived, supply boats were plying their way up the dark, muddy river with its low marshy banks. White House, we learned, had once belonged to Mary Custis Washington and more recently had been the property of one of General Lee's sons. Since the war started, fire had destroyed the house, all the trees had been felled, and the outbuildings torn down. All that remained of the mansion was two blackened chimneys. A row of crude slave huts made of hewn logs still stood on the brink of the river.

The fighting broke out again to the south of us. We heard the firing night and day, a continuous belching forth of artillery and musketry. To accommodate the next shipment of mutilated men, we started putting up hospital tents on the vast grounds of White House Landing. But the ambulance trains began arriving before we had the tents up, and the wounded were laid out on the grounds under a searing sun. I felt so *sorry* for them. The poor wretches hardly looked human. There were not surgeons near enough who were willing to stay in the sun and attend to the men, and it was too awful to leave them uncared for, so I went out and dressed their wounds. Just for one moment consider a shattered arm having been left three days without dressing, and the poor wretch having ridden two days in an army wagon with little food.

All that day and night the trains came with their freight of suffering. There were far too many wounded for the small number of tents we had on hand. By next day some eight thousand men from the recent battles at North Anna and Cold Harbor lay under the glaring sun on the vast acres of White House Landing. The scene was very strange. Black army laborers were loading up supply wagons while their teams of mules, still in harness, knelt on their knees. Several hundred Negro contrabands, both men and women, old and young, stood off to one side, unsure of their place, vacant looks in their eyes. Several hundred prisoners came marching by, guarded by squads of soldiers.

Sophronie Bucklin of Auburn, New York, shook her head as we looked over the thousands of wounded men lying around us. "It makes you want to cry," she said "Just look at them. Disfigured with powder and dirt. Blood oozing from their torn flesh. I saw some fellows, over there, with worms literally covering their festering wounds. They're dying from thirst, starving for food, groaning in delirious fever, praying to die. This is one vast plain of agony, and the sun adds to the torture. I can hardly stand it—the groans and cries for help—the pleading and glassy eyes of dying men who can no longer speak in their delirium." She paused for a moment, then looked at me. "You don't want to see the amputation tent. Large piles of human flesh—legs, arms, feet, and hands—all around it. They're strewn about. When I was there, I noticed an amputated hand lying under my feet. It was white and bloody, and the stiffened fingers seemed to be clutching at my clothing."

All around us men cried out, "Something to eat—please, *something to eat.*" We gave them what we had, and when the transports arrived we helped load the poor wretches on board, packing them on the decks and in the cabins so closely that you had no room to turn.

On June seventh, I rode an ambulance to the front with Arabella Barlow, whose husband was a general in the army. She had worked as a Sanitary Commission nurse at Harrison's Landing, at Antietam, and at Gettysburg, where her husband had been wounded and she had taken care of him. She was so full of energy and such a *talker*—it wore me out just to listen to her.

We found the field hospital of the First Division, Second Corps, situated in a Virginia mansion at the extreme front. Dr. Dudley was here! When he saw us, he came up and bowed. He was such a nice-looking gentleman.

"I'm so glad to see you, Cornelia," he said. "Still lovely and well dressed as ever, even in the field."

I blushed. "Thee are too kind."

I was so glad to find him well and in good spirits. The only trouble I had with him was that he would go up on the breastworks to see how things were going. There was constant sniper fire, and I feared that one of these times Dr. Dudley would be brought in dead or wounded. If a soldier tried to leave his rifle pit for water, he was shot at. They told me that an average of six men a day were shot down as they went for water.

I stayed a week at Dr. Dudley's hospital, hoping to be of service, but the practice here was to operate on the wounded men at once and send them back to White House Landing, so there was little opportunity for a lady to be of much service. I bade Dr. Dudley good-bye and returned to White House Landing, only to find that all the wounded had been evacuated and that the Pamunkey was full of transports carrying troops somewhere.

"The hospital is being moved to the James," a Sanitary agent told me. "All the surgeons and nurses are on the transports. You'll have to go with our wagon train."

34 . GRANT

Saw I couldn't whip Lee north of Richmond as long as he fought defensively behind strong breastworks. So I took my alternative—I would starve him into submission by cutting off his supply lines to the Shenandoah and the southern interior. Sheridan's cavalry would break up the railroads connecting Richmond with the granaries of the Shenandoah. At the same time, Hunter would advance up the valley with eighteen thousand men, cross the Blue Ridge, and destroy the huge rebel supply depot at Lynchburg. Then he would move east toward Richmond, wrecking the railroads as he went. If practicable, Sheridan was to join Hunter, and together they would destroy the canal that connected Richmond to Lynchburg through the James valley. All of this, if successful, would utterly wreck the enemy's lines of supply on the north side of the James.

Once Sheridan was away, the Army of the Potomac would move to the James, seize Petersburg, and cut off Lee's railroad supply lines to the south. Celerity and surprise were the key to the success of the move: we had to get to Petersburg before Lee realized what was happening and beat us there on a shorter route across his interior lines. Yep: was risky, withdrawing a large army from the front of an enemy and moving past his flank while keeping him in the dark. But I was in excellent health—never felt better in my life—and confident that I could execute the maneuver successfully.

June seventh, Sheridan with two cavalry divisions crossed the Pamunkey and rode west to destroy the railroads connecting Richmond to the Shenandoah. When word came that Lee had sent his cavalry in pursuit of Sherman, I slapped my knee happily. Lee had just blinded himself. Without sufficient cavalry, he would not be able to track our movement to the James.

35 · LEE

Wade Hampton and Fitz Lee, my nephew, took most of my cavalry, some 4,700 all told, to counter Sherman and prevent him from connecting with Hunter. That left me with a force of 45,000 men to fight Grant's more than 100,000, and it deprived me of sufficient cavalry to reconnoiter his army if it moved out again. While our pickets kept Grant's lines under constant surveillance, bad news arrived from the Shenandoah. Hunter was doing us great evil in the southwestern end of the valley: he had occupied Lexington, torched the Virginia Military Institute, and burnt the town. Now he could march east across the Blue Ridge, attack our supply base at Lynchburg, and even join Grant. Together they could destroy our railroad communications with the valley. To prevent that, I sent Early to the valley with eight thousand infantry and a fair number of guns. His orders were to destroy Hunter and then demonstrate against Washington. This would cause Grant to do one of two things: either attack me in an effort to force me to recall Early, or detach a sizable force to deal with Early. If Grant did the latter, I would attack and destroy his weakened army.

We were playing a deadly game of maneuver with the Yankees, and the risk was extremely hazardous. Early's departure left me with a force of just under 30,000 men of all arms. Richmond, just nine miles in our rear, had only 6,400 men. My reduced numbers forced me to remain on the defensive.

The next move was Grant's.

36. GRANT

June twelfth the army was ready to march. So far I'd confided my plan of operation only to the officers involved in preparing it. Now my aides delivered my marching orders to the commanders in strict secrecy. That night, Smith's corps headed back to White House Landing on the Pamunkey, where it would embark on transports for the James and Butler's line on Bermuda Hundred. At the same time, the four corps of Meade's army headed south for the James in brilliant moonlight, with Wilson's cavalry in the lead, and my staff and I following. The artillery and tramping soldiers raised so much dust that it was hard to see. Glad to be leaving the swampy country around Old Cold Harbor—lucky half the army didn't have malaria.

Reached Wilcox Landing on the James next evening. Hancock's corps, marching at a killing pace, was already there. Rest of the army came up the next day. While ferryboats started hauling Hancock's men to the south shore, our engineers set to work building a two-thousand-foot pontoon bridge across the river. I took a steamer upriver to Bermuda Hundred to confer with Butler about the impending move against Petersburg, which we believed was largely undefended. Facing Butler on Bermuda Hundred was a rebel force under Beauregard. Butler said he'd seen no sign of enemy troop movements south to Petersburg.

"Porter says we've stolen a march on Lee," I told Butler. "Smith's on his way by boat from White House and will reach you tonight. Send him immediately against Petersburg with all the troops you can give him without sacrificing your position here. Hancock's corps is now crossing the James and will come up in support tomorrow."

Before I left Bermuda Hundred, I sent a telegram to Washington: "Our forces commence crossing the James River today. The enemy shows no signs of having brought troops to the south side of Richmond. I will have Petersburg secured if possible before they get there in much force. Our movement from Cold Harbor to the James River has been made with great celerity."

Then I sailed back to Wilcox Landing. By dawn the next day, the fifteenth, Hancock's corps was across the river and heading up the road to Petersburg to join Smith for the attack on the city. They had forty thousand men between them, and I was confident they would seize Petersburg and its vital railroads with little difficulty.

Meanwhile the engineers had completed the pontoon bridge across the James, and my staff and I stood on a bluff on the north side of the river, watching the rest of the army cross the huge bridge to the other side. Awesome sight: endless columns of troops tramping across to the beat of drums, with brilliant banners flapping in the river breeze and bright sunlight gleaming off burnished rifles. Bands, generals and their staffs, groups of camp followers, wagons with their teams, horse-drawn artillery, heavy guns, and hundreds of ambulances flowed across. I threw away my cigar and watched in silence, my hands clasped behind my back.

A courier brought me a dispatch from the president. "Have just recd. your dispatch of 1 P.M. yesterday—I begin to see it. You will succeed—God bless you all. A. Lincoln."

"Better get going," I told my staff. We mounted, rode across the bridge, and headed up to City Point, a bluff overlooking a wide crook in the James where it met the Appomattox. Petersburg lay on the banks of the Appomattox about eight miles to the southwest. Could see Bermuda Hundred just across the James to the north. I established my headquarters at City Point and sent a message to Butler: "Have just arrived. Have you any news from Petersburg?"

Butler's chief of staff wired back: "Genl Butler at lookout. Nothing heard from Smith."

37. LEE

Our pickets reported that the enemy trenches at Old Cold Harbor were empty—had been abandoned during the night. Our pickets had heard nothing, not a sound. We found this difficult to believe. Worse still, we had no idea where Grant was heading—blast this lack of adequate cavalry. I was virtually blind, as I was during the Gettysburg campaign. But then a dispatch arrived from General Hampton:

he and Fitz Lee had intercepted Sheridan at Trevilian Station, near Gordonsville, and defeated him with heavy loss.

I was elated. "Sheridan's handsomely whipped," I told my staff. "Now he can't join Hunter for a joint campaign against our communications north of the James."

On June fourteenth I wired Richmond that Grant could be heading for the fortifications at Harrison's Landing, where, with the added protection of his gunboats, he would have a strong position. "I do not think it would be advantageous to attack him in that position," I said. "I apprehend that he may be sending troops up the James River with the view of getting possession of Petersburg before we can reinforce it. We ought therefore to be extremely watchful and guarded."

That same day we learned that Grant had broken up his depot at White House on the Pamunkey, which meant that he had no intention of remaining on the north side of the James. That night word reached us that the enemy army was indeed on the James. Fearful that Grant was heading for Petersburg, I dispatched Hoke's division to General Beauregard on the Bermuda Hundred line.

Next morning, June fifteenth, Beauregard reported gunfire in the direction of Petersburg. I still wasn't certain whether Grant's objective was Petersburg or Richmond: moving up the James, he could attack either place. I decided that my army should fall back to the exterior defenses of Richmond, but reports of enemy cavalry on the north side of the James cautioned me not to move too far back.

38. GRANT

At City Point that day, the fifteenth, we could hear firing in the direction of Petersburg. Hoped it meant that Smith was attacking the city and would capture it before Lee or Richmond could recover and dispatch reinforcements south by the railroad. I sent word to Hancock to hurry his corps forward.

Finally heard from Butler at midafternoon. "I have been watching the progress upon Petersburg at the lookout. There has been pretty sharp fighting and I could see the enemy withdrawing on one part of the line and our forces advancing, but further I could not see."

Made me fidgety, not knowing what was happening. Paced and smoked like Sherman. That evening another wire came from Butler: "A train of eleven cars loaded with troops has just passed toward Petersburg."

"Is it Lee's army or troops from Richmond's defenses?" I asked. "Smith has got to carry the city before any more rebels get there."

An hour later another dispatch came from Butler: "Hancock seems to be driving them slowly. The fight has been raging with great violence for half an hour near Harrison's Creek. A train of fourteen cars loaded with troops just passed toward Petersburg. They also appear to be sending troops on the roads west of Petersburg. Another train of twenty-two cars has just passed toward Petersburg loaded with troops."

This was terrible news. Frustrated me. Showed in a message I sent to Hancock: "The enemy are now seen to be reinforcing Petersburg by rail and by troops marching. If Petersburg is not captured tonight it will be advisable that you and Smith take up a defensive position and maintain it until all the forces are up. It was hoped to be able to carry Petersburg before the enemy could reinforce it."

Later I learned what had happened this day before Petersburg. Smith had reached the enemy lines before daylight and driven in the enemy pickets. But for some reason I couldn't understand, Smith didn't get ready to assault the main enemy line until near sundown. I'd bet the enemy had no more than 1,500 troops in that line, while Smith had about 16,000 thousand men. He finally made the assault with only part of his command and carried the line northeast of Petersburg from the Appomattox River, for a distance of more than two and a half miles. There were no other enemy works between Petersburg and the lines Smith had captured. The reinforcements had not yet arrived. The city lay there for the taking, but Smith didn't move. Right after dark, Hancock came up and offered his corps to Smith if he wanted to attack that night. The moon was shining brilliantly, so the men could see well enough to fight. But Smith didn't want to attack. Smith's defenders say he wasn't himself—was suffering from malaria. Also was afraid a full frontal attack would end up like Cold Harbor. But that sounds like an excuse for incompetence or cowardice.

The next morning, June sixteenth, Butler informed us that the enemy troops on Bermuda Hundred had evacuated their lines and gone to Petersburg. A division from Lee's army was also on the way. This was terrible news. I ordered Meade to hurry Warren up by the nearest road and to come up himself by steamer and take command of the army in person. Then I took a steamer up the Appomattox to see the front for myself. By the time I arrived, the enemy was there, apparently in considerable force. He'd thrown up works during the night, which formed a semicircle around east of Petersburg with the left flank on the Appomattox.

As we surveyed the enemy lines with our glasses, we could see the church spires of Petersburg in the hazy sunlight. Smith said that his black troops had led the sundown attack yesterday and had fought harder and more magnificently than any of his other troops. They kept shouting, "Remember Fort Pillow!" I thought: *if you'd fought like the Negroes, Petersburg would be ours now.*

While we talked, Burnside's lead troops came onto the field. I sent him an order to mass his corps on Hancock's left, then told Smith they must attack the enemy works as soon as Burnside was in position. Then my staff and I set off down the road to City Point and met Meade and his staff on their way to Petersburg. Told Meade: "General, Burnside should be into position by 6 P.M. I want a vigorous assault made by him, Smith, and Hancock at that time. If possible, I want you to drive the enemy across the Appomattox."

We rode on to City Point, where I could keep an eye on Butler, just in case the enemy tried to attack him and get into the rear of the Army of the Potomac. At six that evening, June sixteenth, firing broke out in the direction of Petersburg, which meant that Meade had launched his assaults. The powder smoke from the batteries and the smoke from exploding shells drifted across the setting sun.

About seven-thirty or so, Butler forwarded a message from one of our naval officers: "Large bodies of troops, estimated by the gunboats at from forty thousand to fifty thousand, seen passing Deep Bottom from Malvern Hill toward Richmond this afternoon."

"That must be Lee's army," I said. "It means the enemy is not yet on the south side of the James River in great force." I sent the intelligence on to Meade, hoping it would inspire his troops to fight harder as they assaulted the rebel works.

39. LEE

When Beauregard took his force to Petersburg, the Federals under Butler advanced and occupied Beauregard's works on Bermuda Hundred. I dispatched a division to recover the works, and they drove the enemy from the second line of fortifications, but not from the first. I did not know whether Grant's army was holding this line or whether it was in front of Petersburg. I could not learn from Beauregard what force opposed him there. Since I did not know the position of Grant's army, I told Beauregard, I could not strip the north bank of the James River of its defenders. Did he not have force sufficient to hold Petersburg? He replied that he did, which eased my anxiety about that. "Hope you will drive the enemy," I telegraphed. "Have not heard of Grant's crossing the James River. Has Grant been seen crossing the river?"

That night, units under my personal direction assaulted and recovered Beauregard's first line of works on Bermuda Hundred. We learned from prisoners that the troops in our front belonged to Butler's army, not Grant's. Early the next morning, June seventeenth, Beauregard reported that the enemy had assaulted his works twice but that his men had thrown them back. I wired him that I was delighted and asked him if he could ascertain anything of Grant's movements. Until I could get more definite information about Grant, I did not think it was prudent to draw more troops to the south side of the James.

40. GRANT

I knew nothing about the result of Meade's assaults, which finally broke off at six in the morning of the seventeenth, till Meade's report came in. The army had captured some of the main works of the enemy to the right of those previously seized by General Smith, and Meade promised that this advantage would be pushed. "The men are tired," he added, "and the attacks have not been made with the vigor and force which characterized our fighting in the Wilderness. If they had been I think we should have been more successful. I will continue to press."

The men were tired! No excuse for such poor fighting yesterday. Well, this day, June seventeenth, was the anniversary of Bunker Hill. Hoped it would inspire the Army of the Potomac to fight like our western army and take Petersburg before Lee got there.

Heavy firing—artillery and musketry—all morning. I was on edge, whittled sticks and smoked cigars to stay calm. Thought we still had the jump on Lee and didn't want to lose a great opportunity that could very well end the war. A midmorning dispatch from Meade said that Burnside's Ninth Corps had attacked earlier that morning after having marched all yesterday and all the night before. Had captured two redoubts and 450 prisoners and four guns. Burnside, Meade said, was preparing to renew the attack, and Warren was moving into position to protect the army's left flank. Meade said he expected an attack there "so soon as Lee's army gets up." I didn't like the sound of that at all. I wanted the enemy lines carried and Petersburg captured *before Lee got up*.

By day's end Meade's army had captured most of the rebel line, and I clung to some hope that victory would be ours when we resumed the assaults next day, June eighteenth.

41. LEE

Beauregard's messages on the afternoon of the seventeenth grew more and more frantic. He now reported two Federal corps were in his front: Smith's and Hancock's. "We greatly need reinforcements to resist such large odds against us. The enemy must be dislodged or the city will fall." Another telegram from Beauregard reported that prisoners captured that day admitted that they were from the Yankee Second, Ninth, and Eighteenth Corps, and that the Fifth and Sixth Corps were coming up. This was shocking news. It meant that Grant had deceived us: he had gotten his entire army across the James and was attempting to seize Petersburg by a *coup de main*, as Colonel Venable expressed it. Unless I acted quickly, calamity was at hand. I ordered most of the army to move to Petersburg at once. They began arriving at seven-thirty on the morning of the eighteenth. I explained the move in a dispatch to the president and said I too was going to Petersburg.

42. GRANT

At dawn on the eighteenth, the Army of the Potomac again charged the rebel works, only to find them empty. I was on edge again. Piecemeal reports from the front made it worse. Finally got Meade's full report that night. "Our whole line advanced and in a short time found the enemy in force in a new interior line about one mile from Petersburg. I meant to force the rebels across the Appomattox and ordered strong columns of assault to begin at noon. About 2 P.M. Warren and Burnside advanced a considerable distance but failed to find contact with the enemy. Birney and Martindale both attacked but were repulsed. Both reported the enemy in very strong force with heavy reserves masked in the rear from which I inferred that Lee had reinforced Beauregard. It is a source of great regret that I am not able to report more success but I believe every effort to command it has been made."

Hadn't either. Terrible performance all the way around. Couldn't figure this army out, why its corps commanders couldn't attack in concert. *Lackluster*'s the word for that army, botching up a great opportunity to take Petersburg and its railroads. Reports from every corps, division, and brigade commander pointed out that the men no longer fought with the spirit they'd shown at the start of the campaign and that morale was dangerously low. Some officers attributed it to the failed assaults at Cold Harbor.

Reckon we'd lost more than sixty-four thousand total casualties since the start of the campaign. Feared that would have a bad effect on public morale in the North. Still, we'd been heavily reinforced and were plenty strong enough to hold against a rebel attack. We hadn't destroyed Lee, which was the goal of the campaign, but we had him pinned down now, which eliminated his mobility. Also kept him from sending reinforcements out to Joe Johnston in his struggle against Sherman.

I wired Washington that Lee's whole army had arrived at Petersburg and taken advantage of the country's topography to create strong works. Told 'em I would make no more assaults, but would have the men throw up works all along our line east of Petersburg and settle for a partial siege. Success, I said, really was just a question of time. We would look to extending our line to the south, with a view to cutting the two railroads that fed Lee's army and Richmond. One was the Petersburg & Weldon Railroad, which ran south to Wilmington, North Carolina, the enemy's most important block-ade-running port. The other was the Southside Railroad, which ran to Lynchburg, the big rebel supply base. Sheridan should be break-ing the railroad supply lines north of the James. Once Lee's commu-nications were cut, he would have to abandon his works and retreat into the open. When he did, we'd jump him.

About a week later Sheridan crossed the James and rejoined the army. Had bad news to report about his campaign. He'd damaged one of the railroads and fought the rebel cavalry at Trevilian Station, but had failed to link up with Hunter. Hunter, turns out, had crossed the Blue Ridge and advanced to Lynchburg, but the Johnnies under Breckinridge and Early were there in force. So Hunter high-tailed it west into the mountains of West Virginia, which took him out of the war for weeks and left the valley in enemy hands. Couldn't believe what Sheridan was telling me. Lee's supply lines to the Shenandoah were still intact. Valley campaign was a complete failure.

"Can't anybody besides you fight in the eastern theater?" I asked Sheridan.

Still, I was fairly optimistic. The enemy had the bulk of his forces concentrated in two grand armies, Lee's and Johnston's, and neither could stand a single battle outside its fortifications. The last man in the Confederacy was now in the rebel army. The Johnnies were becoming discouraged, their men deserting and being killed and cap-tured every day. We lost men too, but our losses could be replaced. Only thing I feared was the people of the North would lose heart. "If the rebellion is not perfectly and thoroughly crushed," I wrote a friend of mine, "it will be the fault and through the weakness of the people of the North. Be of good cheer and rest assured that all will come out right."

43 · SHERMAN

As my combined armies moved southeast toward Atlanta, all the people fled before us and there was nothing but desolation behind. We burned all the factories and shops in northwest Georgia that made cloth and other things for the rebel government. About four hundred young women worked in one of the factories we destroyed, and it was damned near impossible to keep them in line or to keep our men away from them, so I had them removed. They put up a huge howl, called me a barbarian, a vandal, a monster, and worse, but I didn't give a damn. I'd rather try to guard the whole rebel army than those snarling young shrews.

"To realize what war is," I wrote Ellen, "one should follow our tracks. I know the country swarms with thousands who would shoot me, and thank their God they had slain a monster. Yet I've been more kindly disposed to the people of the South than any general officer of the whole army."

On June tenth we passed through Big Shanty on the railroad and found the whole rebel army a few miles south of there, drawn up on three hills called Kennesaw Mountain, Pine Mountain, and Lost Mountain. With the naked eye, we could see signal stations and fresh lines of parapets manned by heavy masses of infantry on all three hills. Johnston had chosen his ground well and was prepared for battle. But his line was ten miles long—too long, I thought, to be defended successfully.

My forces moved into position, McPherson on the left, Thomas in the center, Schofield on the right. But it was raining so hard it impeded our deployment. Never saw any country where it rained so Goddamned hard as it did in Georgia. Left a regular Noah's flood to try to maneuver in. The rain did slacken in a few days, and I rode to my advanced line and from a hill ran my glasses over Pine and Kennesaw, looking for a point where we could move between them. Then I saw, not eight hundred yards away, three Confederates looking at me through their glasses.

"Goddamned saucy," I said, and turned to General Howard, pointing at the three rebels. "Make 'em take cover. Have one of your batteries fire three volleys into 'em." At Howard's orders, Captain Hubert Dilger, a Prussian and maybe the best artilleryman in the West, sighted his cannons on the three rebels and told his gunners, "Shust teeckle them fellows." I rode off, but should've stayed to watch the show. The shells exploded near the rebels and scattered two, but the third just stood there. I learned later that they were none other than Joe Johnston, Hardee, and Polk. Can you believe that? Well, it was Johnston and Hardee who took cover and fat old Bishop Polk who stood his ground because he didn't want to give his men a bad impression. But the fire was so hot that he finally took cover. When he came to a clearing, he stopped to look at the battery, and a cannonball smashed into his stomach and tore him to pieces.

Couldn't have been much left of him to bury. A legend spread among the rebs that *I'd* sighted the cannonball that killed Bishop Polk. Wish to hell I had.

Next day we began advancing our lines with the idea of attacking any weak point we discovered in the long enemy position. In a smart move, Joe Johnston abandoned Pine and Lost mountains so as to concentrate his army on Kennesaw Mountain, just northwest of Marietta on the railroad. He now had an unusually strong defensive position, with his flanks retired to cover the town and the railroad behind it. To make matters worse, the Goddamned heavens erupted—it was raining in torrents again, which made the roads impassable, turned the woods and fields into quagmires, and greatly hampered our efforts to extend our lines around the enemy's. By June twenty-sixth my lines were ten miles long

Somehow I had to make Johnston let go of Kennesaw Mountain, which was the key to the whole surrounding country. I consulted with my three army generals and we all agreed that we couldn't stretch our lines any more on this hilly, wooded, muddy ground. All agreed that there was no alternative but to attack the enemy's fortified lines, which we'd carefully avoided up to that time. For me, there was another reason to make the attack: our officers and men had become convinced that I wouldn't assault fortified lines and always tried to outflank the rebs. I wanted, *for the moral effect,* to make a successful assault against the enemy behind his breastworks. A third reason was Slowtrot Thomas's Army of the Cumberland, which moved with the speed of a Goddamned snail and used any excuse, even a fresh furrow in a plowed field, to stop and start throwing up entrenchments. Again and again I'd tried to impress on Thomas that we had to *assault* and not *defend.* We were on the offensive, and yet it seemed that the whole Army of the Cumberland from the commander to the lowest private was so habituated to the defensive that I couldn't get it out of their Goddamned heads. At Kennesaw, I meant to *get it out.*

"If we can make a breach anywhere near the rebel center," I told my generals, "and thrust in a strong head of column, then half our army can sweep in flank and overwhelm half the enemy's army, while the other half of ours holds the other half of his in check."

The assault took place on June twenty-seventh—about a week after the Army of the Potomac had assaulted the enemy works in front of Petersburg. So that I could oversee the attack on Kennesaw, I had a place cleared on top of a hill behind Thomas's center and had telegraph wires laid to it. Our batteries opened fire along the entire line and pounded the side of the mountain with a furious barrage of solid shot and exploding shells until white smoke drifted over the landscape. Then the infantry went forward with a blast of bugles and flags and banners visible here and there in rifts in the smoke. McPherson's attacking column fought up the face of Kennesaw but could not reach the fiery summit. About a mile to the right, Thomas's assaulting column reached the rebel parapet, but lethal salvos of canister and musketry repulsed the attack. When the smoke cleared, several valuable officers and 2,500 of our men lay dead or wounded on the slopes of Kennesaw Mountain. It made my heart bleed to see the carnage of that wretched battle.

I telegraphed Halleck: "The assault I made was no mistake; I had to do it. The enemy and our own army and officers had settled down into the conviction that the assault of lines formed no part of my game, and the moment the enemy was found behind anything like a parapet, why, everybody would deploy, throwing up counterworks and taking it easy, leaving it to the 'old man' to turn the position."

I don't apologize for Kennesaw Mountain. But I will say this: it satisfied me that attacking entrenched lines was too Goddamned costly. So I sent McPherson on another flanking movement, which forced Johnston to abandon Kennesaw and Marietta and flee southward toward the Chattahoochee. I ordered every part of the army to pursue vigorously. I was certain that Johnston would try to cross the river—he was too smart to invite a battle with the Chattahoochee at his back. I hoped to strike him a decisive blow in the confusion of his crossing the river, which was broad and deep. But our cavalry and the head of our infantry made a piss-poor excuse of a pursuit, and it made me so Goddamned mad I was ready to chew nails. With me pushing him on, Slowtrot Thomas finally closed up against the retreating rebels, only to meet heavy and severe fire. I ordered Thomas to assault 'em fiercely, supposing that they were just opposing us to gain time to get their trains and troops across the river. But when I made a personal reconnaissance with my staff, I saw that Johnston had drawn his entire army into an entrenched camp, prepared in advance by his engineers, on *our side* of the Chattahoochee, in the nature of a *tête-de-pont*, or bridgehead. It was one of the strongest pieces of field fortification I'd ever seen.

"I'll be Goddamned if I'm going to assault those lines," I told my staff. "If we can cross the river and once again threaten his flank and rear, Johnston can't remain on this side of the river."

When I raised my glasses, I could see the spires and domes of Atlanta, glittering in the sunlight only 9 miles away. How far we'd come! In less than two months of campaigning, I'd brought an army of a hundred thousand 120 miles across hostile territory; driven a well-commanded army of sixty thousand from fortified positions at Dalton, Resaca, Cassville, Allatoona, and Kennesaw; had seized the enemy's only niter country (niter being a white salt used to manufacture gunpowder), his vast ironworks and lodes of ore, and the most extensive cotton and woolen manufactories of Georgia. I don't think ten men in the North appreciated the vast labor of mind and body expended in accomplishing all this. Maybe I was at fault for discouraging flattering descriptions of us in the Goddamned press that would satisfy the greedy curiosity of a gaping public. Still, as I stood there looking at Atlanta through my field glass, I was proud of what we'd done. Man oh man, I could *taste* victory.

Instead of assaulting Johnson's fieldworks, I aimed to feint to our right and then cross the Chattahoochee by the left. Schofield found a good place just below the mouth of Soap's Creek. He crossed there on July ninth and by nightfall was on the high ground beyond, strongly entrenched, with two good pontoon bridges thrown across the river. We'd outflanked Johnston again. That night he evacuated his trenches, crossed the Chattahoochee, and fell back to Atlanta. My entire force then crossed the river and set out to whip Johnston and seize the queen city of the Deep South. When I galloped past, the troops cheered for Uncle Billy and promised to wipe the enemy army from the face of the earth.

As we approached Atlanta's outer defenses, a staff officer brought me a citizen, one of our spies, who'd just come from the city. He showed me a newspaper, which had Johnston's order relinquishing command of the rebel forces in Atlanta to General Hood. There'd been such a popular outcry against Johnston that Jeff Davis had been forced to remove him. I was damned glad I'd beaten Johnston because he had an exalted reputation in the old army as a strategist. No question who was the better strategist now.

So Sam Hood was my new opponent—heard he'd lost a leg at Chickamauga and the use of an arm at Gettysburg. McPherson and Schofield had been in the same class with him at West Point and said Hood wasn't all that smart, but he was a fighter, rash and reckless with the lives of his men. We all agreed we would have to be vigilant in maneuvering against him.

On July nineteenth, our armies converged on Atlanta against

such feeble resistance that I thought the enemy intended to evacuate the city. But next day the Johnnies made a furious sally while Thomas's troops were crossing Peach Tree Creek some three miles north of the city. The rebs came pouring out of their trenches and leaped on Thomas's columns howling like hyenas. It was a furious fight, in many places hand to hand, but several of our batteries found good ground on the north side of the creek and poured murderous volleys into the enemy troops, driving them back to their trenches. *So this is Hood's game,* I thought: *the furious sally. Well, Mr. Sam Hood, we've repulsed the first one handsomely.* I sent congratulations to Thomas, who'd fought Goddamned well for a change, but warned him and my other two commanders to be on the alert for a Sam Hood sally.

Our reconnaissances found that the rebels had strong outer entrenchments in the form of a square around Atlanta. From our position north of the city, we could see the formidable parapets, with *chevaux-de-frise,* which are obstacles bristling with spikes, and abatis, which are sharpened tree branches, sticking out all along the front. Like I said, I had no intention of assaulting fortifications and settled for a siege. Didn't have enough troops for a full investment—we would make do with a half-circle investment north and east of Atlanta. We'd already cut the railroad that ran north to the Chattahootchee. I aimed to destroy the Georgia Railroad connecting Atlanta to Decatur and Augusta to the east, then withdraw troops from the left flank and add them to the right and keep doing that till we'd cut the other railroad running south to East Point.

While we were forming our lines and selecting positions for our batteries, I met with McPherson and his staff in the Howard House on the Decatur Road east of Atlanta. It was July twenty-second, and McPherson's Army of the Tennessee held the extreme left of our line, with Schofield in the center and Thomas on the far right. McPherson and I sat on the steps of the house, discussing Sam Hood and wondering when he would try another furious sally. Presently we walked down the road a short distance and sat by the foot of a tree, where I pulled out my map and explained how I wanted to extend our lines to the west. All of a sudden lively skirmishing broke out down about the distillery, then round shot from twelve- and twenty-four-pounder guns crashed through the trees. In a minute, we could hear the crack of musketry and explosion of artillery all along McPherson's front.

"Sounds like Hood's attacking," I said.

McPherson called for his staff and orderlies and told me he would ride out to investigate and would send me a report. As he rode away, I thought what a handsome officer he was, over six feet tall, and impeccably dressed in his general's uniform with his pants stuck in his polished boots. In his mid-thirties, he was in his prime, universally liked, the best officer I had.

I went back to the Howard House and was walking up and down the porch smoking a cigar when one of McPherson's staff officers galloped up, his horse lathered in sweat.

"Sir," he said, "the rebs have attacked Blair's corps, came out of the dense woods, masses of 'em, and drove his men back in great disorder. But there's worse, sir. General McPherson's been killed. He was arranging troops and bringing up units and ran into an ambuscade with only Colonel Strong with him. Strong said the rebs cried, 'Halt, halt, you sons-of-bitches.' General McPherson raised his hat, as if to salute them, then turned his horse and tried to get away, when they shot him. That's what Colonel Strong said."

Within an hour, with the battle raging more and more furiously, an ambulance bearing McPherson's body came up to the Howard House. I had it carried inside and laid on a door wrenched from its hinges. While we examined McPherson's body—he'd been shot in the chest—bullets pattered on the roof and struck the outside walls of the house, and shells exploded in the woods. I marched back and forth barking God knows what at my orderlies, then I turned and looked at the pale face of my friend, tears streaming down my cheeks. God, his death hurt, almost as bad as the death of my Willy.

Couriers brought terrible news from the front: McPherson's Army of Tennessee was surrounded and faced annihilation unless heavily reinforced. I refused to believe it. McPherson's army had always won and would do so again. Sure enough, his men, though sorely pressed, rallied and repulsed the Johnnies with great loss. That night Hood fell back to the entrenchments of Atlanta itself, which were in a general circle. We remained masters of the ground outside the city.

I wired Washington that General McPherson had fallen in the Battle of Atlanta, booted and spurred, as the gallant knight and gentleman would wish. "History tells us of but few who so blended the grace and gentleness of the friend and the dignity, courage, faith and manliness of the soldier," I said. I missed him fiercely, had to wipe tears away. Who could ever replace him? Finally chose one-armed O. O. Howard to command the Army of Tennessee. A good man, brave and pious. That appointment pissed off Hooker, and he asked to be relieved of command of the Twentieth Corps. Hooker was envious, imperious, and a Goddamned braggart—I didn't regret obliging him. I gave command of the Twentieth Corps to General Henry W. Slocum. He was in his late thirties with a bushy gray mustache, a receding chin, a huge nose, bulging eyes, and thick gray hair. Had a reputation of being a harsh disciplinarian. When one of his soldiers blundered, he gave 'em one hell of a tongue-lashing.

A warning came from Grant, then investing Petersburg and Richmond, that the rebel government had become aroused to the critical situation in Atlanta, and that I'd better look out for Hood's being greatly reinforced. I resolved to push matters here and at once transferred the whole Amy of Tennessee to our right flank, leaving Schofield to stretch out so as to rest his left on the railroad to Augusta, now torn up for thirty miles.

I dashed off a note to Ellen: "We have Atlanta close aboard, as the sailors say, but it is a hard nut to handle. These fellows fight like devils and Indians combined, and it calls for all my cunning and strength. Instead of attacking the forts which are really unassailable I must gradually destroy the railroads which feed Atlanta. This I have partially done, two out of three are broken and we are now maneuvering for the third."

44 · LEE

President Davis called me to Richmond for a conference about General Hood and the troubling situation in Atlanta. Though Mrs. Davis had recently given birth to a baby girl, the president was without cheer and looked more sickly than any time I could remember. His thin body was badly stooped and his haggard face twitched. He said he liked General Hood's aggressiveness but was alarmed that he had not been able to break the Federal investment of Atlanta. I feared His Excellency would ask me to take command there, as he'd asked me to go to Vicksburg the year before. I already had a speech made up in which I declined to leave my army and my state, but the president, to my very great relief, did not ask me to go.

"I was most reluctant to remove General Johnston," he said. "But his penchant for retreating caused a disastrous loss of territory, and the terrible consequences likely to result from his policy filled me with apprehension: the destruction of the railroads which Petersburg and Richmond depend on for indispensable supplies from the Deep South. The enemies of General Johnston, including a distressed delegation of Georgians, came here in hot haste to demand Johnston's removal, and I concluded, with great reluctance, that he had to go. General Bragg and the Cabinet members unanimously favored Hood to replace Johnston. It was a sad alternative, but the case seemed hopeless in Johnston's hands."

He tugged at his goatee thoughtfully, then said: "What I really want, General, is to take command in the West myself and cooperate with you in one great battle which would win the war for us. But that is utterly impossible—I am needed here."

On my way back to Petersburg, I thanked merciful Providence that General Hood had attacked the Federals at the gates of Atlanta, otherwise President Davis would surely have raised the question of my going out there. Then came the news that Hood had abandoned his outer fortifications and retreated inside Atlanta. I worried each time a telegram came from Richmond, for fear that it was from the president *ordering* me to Georgia, which I feared might already be lost.

I was also pessimistic about our chances at Petersburg. I had said repeatedly that if Grant made it to the James and put us under siege, it would be a mere question of time before we lost. Young Alexander of our artillery said so, too. "However bold we might be, however desperately we might fight, we're sure in the end to be worn out."

Perhaps we all knew it after both armies had fashioned works that were all but impregnable to assault. Our fortifications formed a defensive perimeter around the eastern side of Petersburg, facing a line of Yankee works extending from the Appomattox above the city toward the south. The two armies shelled one another relentlessly, day and night, until the landscape was wholly denuded and shell torn. Sometimes I sat on the porch of the house that served as my headquarters, and watched the blazing fuses of the shells as they arced overhead and then plunged to earth, exploding in brilliant bursts of red and yellow.

Meanwhile Grant's army, growing ever larger with reinforcements, extended its flank farther and farther to his left against our railroad lifelines to Wilmington and Lynchburg. This forced us to extend our line to cover our right and our railroads, which stretched my undermanned army thinner and thinner. I feared that Grant's tactic would seal our fate unless we found a way to break his grip on us at Petersburg.

One way, of course, was for us to leave our works and attack his huge army in its entrenchments. This I hesitated to do, as a want of success would be fatal to us. A better way to break Grant's siege, I thought, was a valley campaign like the one General Jackson had brought off so successfully in the spring of 'sixty-two. Accordingly, I instructed General Early to drive down the Shenandoah, cross the Potomac, and threaten Washington. If the Lincoln government panicked, as it had in the spring of 'sixty-two, it might recall a sizable part of Grant's army, and I could break the siege.

General Early carried off his mission with a daring worthy of General Jackson. He marched his force of fifteen thousand infantry and cavalry through the Shenandoah with great speed, crossed the Potomac on July sixth, routed an enemy force east of Frederick, and marched on Washington, throwing that city into a panic. By July eleventh, Early's guns were bombarding the defenses of Washington itself. I hoped the enemy president was so frightened that he was already telegraphing Grant to break off from Petersburg and come to the relief of Washington.

45. LINCOLN

I was incredulous and exceedingly irritated that a large enemy army, said to be thirty to forty thousand strong, could invade Union soil when the rebels were supposed to be disastrously short of troops in every theater. With the rebel raiders bearing down on Washington, Mary and I and the boys had to rush in from the Soldiers' Home in a carriage sent by Stanton. Farmers who lived in the raiders' path fled to Washington with terrible stories to tell. The rebels had destroyed bridges, burned farms, torched the home of the governor of Maryland and Monty Blair's home too, and spread terror in every direction.

Washington's defenses were badly depleted because we'd sent heavy reinforcements to Grant, and there was much censure of Stanton, Halleck, and Yours Truly for the near defenseless condition of the capital. We wired Grant that we had absolutely no force fit to take the field and that the city would fall unless he came up with a good part of the Potomac Army. Grant replied that he wasn't coming himself, but one entire corps, two divisions of another corps, and three thousand dismounted cavalry were on their way, but we feared they wouldn't get here in time. The teamsters and other government employees took up arms and organized regiments, invalids and hundred-day men formed other outfits, and the streets were full of marching troops on their way to the girdle of fortifications that surrounded and protected the city.

When the rebel army approached from the north, I rode out to the forts to escape my tormentors, and saw the enemy guns blast our parapets with round shot and explosive shells. I went back to the White House and from the roof kept my spyglass trained on the Potomac, looking for a sign of the troop transports from City Point. I tell you, I let out a whoop when I spotted 'em steaming upriver. I strode down to the wharf and told 'em: "Howdy, howdy. I'm mighty glad to see you."

I followed 'em out to Fort Stevens and stood on the parapets and watched through a field glass as the rival pickets banged away at one another. A group of rebel sharpshooters had occupied a large mansion and you could see white puffs of smoke in the windows as they shot at us. Their bullets struck the fort and whistled near my head, and an officer fell mortally wounded at my side. Another officer yelled at me: "Get down, you fool!" But the fool kept watching as one of our batteries shelled the mansion until it went up in flames. Then our infantry went forward in the shimmering heat and attacked the rebels on Silver Springs Road. The enemy lines faltered and broke, and we could see gray-clad figures, many of 'em barefoot, running back across the fields and seeking the shelter of the woods on the sides of the opposite hills.

It was near dark when I left with Secretary of Navy Welles, Senator Ben Wade, and several others. "A grand spectacle," Welles said of the day's battle. "Did you see the rebels run? Made my heart pound."

Next day, the raiders disappeared from in front of Washington. Our scouts reported 'em retreating northwest away from the city. I thought we ought to push our whole force straight up the River Road and cut off as many of 'em as possible, but nobody was in overall command of the hodgepodge of forces in the Washington area. The officers stood around waiting for orders, and the rebels escaped. By July fourteenth, they were safely back in Virginia, ready to attack again when they regrouped and got reinforcements.

If the raid was meant to break Grant's siege of Petersburg, it was a failure, a flat failure. The great thing about Grant is his coolness and persistency of purpose. He isn't easily excited, which is a great element in an officer, and he has the grip of a bulldog. Once let him get his teeth in and nothing can shake him off. Well, let me tell you, he kept his bulldog hold on Petersburg, and I issued a call for 500,000 more volunteers to strengthen our depleted armies, even though the call added fuel to the popular outcry against the Administration. William Dole, Commissioner of Indian Affairs, groaned that the call was an admission of defeat and utterly ruined my chances for reelection.

"It doesn't matter what happens to me," I said. "We must have the men. If I go down, I mean to go down like the *Cumberland*, with my colors flying."

I admit, it was an exceedingly difficult time for me. Frémont had broken with the Administration and was running for the presidency with the support of disgruntled Republican Radicals. The Frémont men damned me as a failed president running a failed war effort and promised to put us back on a winning track when Frémont occupied the White House.

I still had the support of the regular Republicans and the war Democrats, who, if you'll remember, had joined together as the Union party, so-called to contrast our differences with the Copperheads, who would sacrifice the Union, emancipation, popular government, everything worth fighting for. The Union party met in Baltimore and nominated me for a second term, with Andy Johnson of Tennessee as my running mate. At my urging, the party included a plank in the platform calling for the passage of the Thirteenth Amendment, which would eradicate slavery everywhere in the country and prevent the emancipation proclamation from ever being overturned. This was the amendment that had passed the Senate but failed in the House. I was anxious to put the amendment before the electorate with the emphatic support of my Administration.

William Lloyd Garrison, the fire-and-brimstone abolitionist, called at the White House and praised the amendment and offered to support me in my bid for reelection. I thanked him and we had a long chat. The bald-headed little fellow was so polite and cheerful that I had a hard time believing he was Garrison. Harriet Beecher Stowe also gave me her support and wrote a kind piece about me in the Boston prints. I'd met her earlier in the war and said jokingly: "So you're the little woman who wrote the book that made this great war." I told her that whichever way the contest ended, I didn't think I would live long after it was over.

For a while there, I didn't think I'd live through the summer. By late June things were so strained between me and my troublesome secretary of the treasury that we communicated only through icy notes. When I overrode one of his Treasury appoints, on account of it would've offended New York Senator Edwin Morgan, Chase blew up. Accused me of violating the integrity and independence of his office, and once again offered his resignation. This time I accepted it. "Of all I've said in commendation of your ability and fidelity," I wrote him, "I have nothing to unsay; and yet you and I have reached a point of mutual embarrassment in our official relationship which it seems can not be overcome, or longer sustained, consistently with the public service."

That move enraged Chase's Radical friends in Congress. William Pitt Fessenden and the Finance Committee stormed in here and demanded to know why I'd removed Chase. I told 'em why and added that if the Senate didn't like what I'd done, it could have *my* resignation and have Hannibal Hamlin as president. That night, I lay on the sofa in the library, trying to figure out a way to appease the Radicals and prevent any further defections to Frémont. It suddenly occurred to me that I ought to make Fessenden himself Treasury secretary. As chairman of the Finance Committee, he knew the ropes thoroughly. Also had a national reputation and was popular with the Radicals, but without the petulance and impatience of many of that ilk. The idea of Fessenden as Treasury secretary, I thought, was proof that the Lord hadn't forsaken me yet.

Fessenden's always impressively dressed in black jackets and black silk ties. He'd made his reputation in verbal duels with Judge Douglas before the war. Don't want to sound like a gossip, but Fessenden's illegitimate, and the unspoken shame that goes with that stigma made him proud and exceedingly sensitive to slights. He and Sumner had once been friends and used to enter the Senate chamber arm in arm, but Fessenden had taken umbrage at Sumner's condescending airs, and their friendship had degenerated into mutual animosity. Fessenden was still old friends with Wade and Chandler, and I hoped his appointment as Treasury secretary, which I announced on July first, would forestall further rifts with the Radical wing of the party, but it didn't.

In July, I lost more Republican support over the congressional reconstruction bill, promoted by Winter Davis of Maryland. A pale and contentious man with a drooping mustache and a ringing voice,

Davis was the bitter foe of the Blairs for control of Maryland politics. He and I had skirmished over something or other involving the
Maryland patronage, and he vowed to have no further intercourse
with me. He declared war on my 10 percent plan for restoring rebel
states and promoted a reconstruction scheme of his own, which he
guided through the House and Wade pushed through the Senate.
Supported by nearly every Republican on the Hill, the Wade-Davis
bill prohibited slavery in every reconstructed state. It threw out my
10 percent test and the free-state governments of Louisiana and
Arkansas that had been created under it. In place of the 10 percent
test, the bill required that a majority of voters in a conquered rebel
state had to take the oath of allegiance before they could establish a
new state government. Like my proclamation of last December, the
bill disqualified all southerners who'd held important military and
civil posts in the Confederacy. The bill also restricted the southern
vote to whites only.

On principle, I didn't disagree with the majority test section of the
bill. What I objected to was the part that vanquished slavery in the
states. That was something Congress had no authority to do. We'd
always said so. I didn't see how we could deny and contradict what
we'd always said. Maybe Congress could provide for the confiscation
of property in slaves during wartime. But it had no constitutional
authority to abolish slavery as a *state institution* by ordinary statute.
So I pocket vetoed the Wade-Davis bill, and it infuriated damn near
every Republican in Congress.

"I am inconsolable," Sumner said.

"Goddamn that Lincoln," cried Winter Davis. "There'll be civil
war in the North if we Republicans don't rebel against his nomination."

To mollify my congressional critics, I issued a proclamation
explaining why I'd rejected the Wade-Davis bill. I was, I said, unprepared to be inflexibly committed to any single plan of reconstruction, and was also unprepared to declare that the free-state governments already installed in Louisiana and Arkansas should be set
aside and held for naught, or to declare a constitutional competency
in Congress to abolish slavery in the states. Now I was fully satisfied
with the system for restoration contained in the bill, as one very
proper plan for the loyal people of any state choosing to adopt it,
and I was ready and willing to give aid and assistance to any people
that did adopt it, once our military forces had suppressed the armed
insurrection in the South.

My proclamation did not have the desired effect. It made my congressional opponents madder than ever. "This Goddamned thing is infamous," said Thad Stevens. "What audacity the president has! He rejects a bill and then issues a Goddamned proclamation about how far he'll conform to it!" Sumner complained that what this country needed was "a president with brains, one who can make a plan and carry it out." In response to my proclamation, Davis and Wade drafted a blazing manifesto that appeared widely in the public prints. "Good Republicans," they said in effect, "owe their allegiance to a cause and not a usurper. The president has defied Congress and exercised dictatorial usurpation in creating shadow governments in Louisiana and Arkansas so as to get their electoral votes in the forthcoming election. His recent proclamation is the most studied outrage ever visited on Congress. If he wants our support, he should devote himself to suppressing the rebellion and leave political reconstruction to Congress."

The New York Times called the manifesto "the most effective Copperhead campaign document" thus far. It was so severe, in fact, that some Radical Republicans refused to endorse it. I told a friend it reminded me of an old acquaintance who bought a microscope for a son of a scientific turn. The boy went around experimenting with his glass on everything he found. One day, at the dinner table, his father took a piece of cheese. "Don't eat that, father," the boy said. "It's full of wrigglers." "Son," replied the old gentleman as he took a huge bite, "let 'em wriggle; I can stand it if they can." Still, I admit the manifesto hurt. "To be wounded in the house of one's friends," I told young Brooks, "is the most grievous affliction that can befall a man."

During the Wade-Davis fight, Horace Greeley of the New York Tribune wrote me that rebel emissaries, "duly commissioned and empowered to negotiate for peace" by Jeff Davis himself, were at Niagara Falls in Canada and wanted to confer with me or any emissaries I might appoint with a view to ending hostilities. "I am sure," Greeley said, "that this is evidence of the anxiety of the Confederates everywhere for peace. And thereupon I venture to remind you that our bleeding, bankrupt, almost dying country also longs for peace— shudders at the prospect of fresh conscriptions, of further wholesale devastations, and of new rivers of human blood. And a widespread conviction that your government is not anxious for peace and does not improve proffered opportunities to achieve it, is doing great harm now, and is morally certain, unless removed, to do far greater harm in the approaching election. Mr. President, I fear you do not realize how intently the people desire any peace consistent with the national honor and integrity. I do not say that a just peace is now attainable, though I believe it to be so. But I do say, that a frank offer of terms by you to the insurgents will prove an immense and sorely needed advantage to the national cause; it may save us from a northern insurrection. I beg you to invite those now at Niagara to exhibit their credentials and submit their ultimatum."

I didn't like it. Could be a trap, calculated to embarrass me with the electorate and further damage my chances for reelection in November. Then I got another letter from Greeley. Turned out, the so-called commissioners were not empowered by Davis or anybody else in Richmond to negotiate for peace. They did claim to be employed by the rebel government and to know its wishes on the subject of peace, and said that if the circumstances discussed in their correspondence with Greeley were communicated to their government, they would be authorized to come to Washington with the object of ending the war.

I gave 'em an answer on July eighteenth—the same day I called for 500,000 more volunteers. The answer was in the form of a public letter addressed "To Whom It May Concern," which was widely published in the public prints on both sides. "Any proposition," I said, "which embraces the restoration of peace, the integrity of the whole Union, and the abandonment of slavery, and which comes by and with an authority that can control the armies now at war against the United States will be received and considered by the Executive of the United States."

That made my conditions plain enough, and I repeated 'em every time I had the chance. The rebels could have peace if they laid down their weapons, disbanded their military forces, and recognized the restoration of the Union and the end of slavery. Until they did all of these, I aimed to fight on as long as I was in office.

46. DAVIS

Lincoln's terms for peace amounted to unconditional surrender of everything we were fighting for. I told our people that Lincoln's terms showed us that peace was not possible with him in command and that we must fight the Yankee invader all the harder. I placed great hopes on the peace party at the North, and believed that the issue to be decided in the North's presidential contest was the continuance or cessation of the war.

I had my own conditions for peace, which I explained to two northerners who called on me in Richmond. "The war can be stopped in a simple way," I said. "Withdraw your armies from our territory, and peace will come of itself. We do not seek to subjugate you. We are not waging an offensive war, except so far as it is offensive-defensive—that is, so far as we are forced to invade you to prevent you from invading us. Let us alone, and peace will come at once."

One of the northerners said he did not see how we could resist much longer, given the North's vast superiority of numbers on the battlefield. "If you continue to resist," he warned, "you will only deepen the radical feeling of the northern people. Let them once really *feel* the war, and they will insist on hanging you and all your other leaders."

"There are some things worse than hanging or extermination," I said. "We believe that giving up the right of self-government is one of those things."

"By self-government you mean disunion—southern independence?"

"Yes. Absolutely. I desire peace as much as you do. I deplore bloodshed as much as you do. But I feel that not one drop of blood shed in this war is on my hands. I can look up to my God and say this. I tried everything in my power to avert this war. I saw it coming, and for twelve years I worked night and day to prevent it, but I could not. The North was mad and blind. It would not let us govern ourselves, and so the war came, and now it must go on till the last man of this generation falls in his tracks, and his children seize his musket and fight our battle, unless you acknowledge our right to self-government. We are fighting for independence, and that, or extermination, we *will have*, one way or another."

47. LINCOLN

General John A. Dix, commander of the Department of New York, called at the White House with disturbing intelligence. I sat in my chair, rubbing my elbow, while he described what he'd heard from Ambrose Stevens, the head of Dix's Secret Service Bureau.

"Before you issued your 'To Whom It May Concern' letter," Dix said, "Stevens heard rumors that something of the highest importance to the southern cause was afoot in Niagara Falls. He took the express train up there and checked into the Hilton House. The place was mobbed with rebel agents and northern Copperheads, talking about the upcoming election. The rebel peace commissioners arrived. You issued your public letter. The commissioners stayed on. One of them, a man named George Sanders, saw Stevens sitting at a table. Before the war, Stevens had been a Democrat with many southern friends. Sanders still considered him an old party friend and invited him to his room. There he spoke of his hatred for you and revealed the real nature of the peace commissioners: *your assassination.* All the talk about peace negotiations was a blind. The plot has the backing of certain northern Copperheads, who helped to make the arrangements in Washington to take your life."

According to Stevens, Sanders then said: "Our object is not so much to put Lincoln out of the way as to elect McClellan, for he will bring us peace. But we are satisfied that the only way we can insure McClellan's election is to kill Lincoln. The deed will be done in the afternoon or evening of the day before the election. The news will be telegraphed all over the North the same night and every voter will know of it the next morning. The Republicans will be panic-stricken. In all the confusion thousands of them will refuse to vote in the upcoming election, and a large majority of McClellan electors will be chosen in the Electoral College. If somehow the Republicans win a majority of the electors, they will be disorganized over Lincoln's murder. The whole North will be filled with strife and turbulence, and the gravity of the crisis will soon compel the choice of McClellan."

I called the Cabinet to hear the story, and when Dix finished saying what he'd told me, they all wanted to disclose the plot to the papers, thinking it might discourage the ringleaders and benefit the Union cause. I vetoed the idea.

"It would do us more harm than good," I said. "It would discourage the weak-kneed and shaky, and encourage the Copperheads. No, this little secret will keep."

I wasn't sure I believed the story anyway. Then somebody took a shot at me. Happened one night that summer when I was riding out to the Soldiers' Home on Old Abe, as the boys called my horse. When I reached the foot of a hill on the road to the home, I was riding at a slow gait immersed in thought, wondering what else would happen in the unsettled state of things, when the report of a rifle aroused me—I should say lifted me out of my saddle and out of my wits. The shot spooked Old Abe, and in a reckless bound he separated me from the company of my eight-dollar plug hat. Then he took off at full gallop and didn't stop till we reached the Soldiers' Home. I told the guards what had happened, and they went back and found my hat with a bullet hole in the crown. I tried to dismiss the episode, arguing that the bullet was probably intended for somebody else. But I tell you what, I stopped riding alone after that.

48. BOOTH

I read on the front page of a newspaper Caesar's letter addressed "To Whom It May Concern." It announced his policy of *total destruction* of the South and the most beautiful way of life God has ever created. I read and reread the tyrant's letter in the dim light of my hotel room and then I crumpled the paper and threw it to the floor. That letter convinced me it was time to act. I had heard and shared much talk in the safe houses along the corridor about slaying or abducting Caesar. A Confederate partisan had a scheme to kidnap Lincoln at the Soldiers' Home, and I had formulated plans of my own. I was twenty-six, in the *prime* of manhood, and ready to put my plans into action. I wanted the world to know what impelled me to act, so I wrote a reply to Caesar, addressed to a northern friend:

1864

Dear Sir:
    You may use this as you think best. But as some may wish to know when, who and why, I give it (in the words of your master)—"To Whom It May Concern."
    Right or wrong, God judge me, not man. For be my motives good or bad, of one thing I am sure, the lasting condemnation of the North. All hope for peace is dead. My prayers have proved as idle as my hopes. God's will be done. I go to see and share the bitter end. I have ever held the

South were right. The very nomination of Abraham Lincoln, four years ago, spoke very plainly of war, war, upon southern rights and institutions. In a foreign *war I too could say "country right or wrong." But in a struggle* such as ours *(where the brother tries to pierce the brother's heart) for God's sake choose the right. When a country like this spurns* justice *from her side, she forfeits the allegiance of every honest freeman and should leave him to act as his conscience may approve.*

The country was formed for the white, not for the black man. And looking upon African slavery from the same standpoint held by the noble framers of our Constitution, I for one have ever considered it one of the greatest blessings (both for themselves and us) that God ever bestowed upon a favored nation. Witness heretofore our wealth and power. Witness their elevation and enlightenment above their race elsewhere. I have lived among it most of my life, and I have seen less harsh treatment from master to man than I have beheld in the North from father to son. But Lincoln's policy is only preparing a way for their total annihilation. The south are not fighting for the continuation of slavery. The first battle of Bull Run did away with that idea. Their causes for war have been as noble and greater far than those that urged our fathers on.

But there is no time for words. I write in haste. I know how foolish I shall be deemed for taking such a step as this, where on the one side, I have many friends and many things to make me happy, where my profession alone has gained me an income of more than twenty thousand dollars a year, and where my great personal ambition in my profession has such a great field for labor. On the other hand, the South have never bestowed upon me one kind word: a place where I must become a private soldier or a beggar. To give up all the former *for the* latter, besides *my mother and my sisters, whom I love so dearly (although they so widely differ from me in opinion), seems insane: but God is my judge. I love justice more than a country that disowns it, more than fame and wealth; more (Heaven pardon me if I am wrong), more than a happy home.*

O my countrymen, could you all see the reality *or* effects *of this horrid war as I have seen them I know you would think like me, and would pray the Almighty to create in the northern mind a sense of right and justice and that He would dry up the sea of blood between us which is daily growing wider. Alas, my poor country. Is she to meet her threatened doom?*

Four years ago I would have given a thousand lives to see her remain powerful and unbroken. Oh, my friends, if the fearful scenes of the last four years had never been enacted, or if what has been was a frightful dream from which we could now awake, with what flowing hearts could we bless our God. How I have loved the old flag can never be known. A few years since and the entire world could boast of none so pure and spotless. But I have of late seen and heard of the bloody deeds of which she has been made the emblem. Oh, how I have longed to see her break from the mist of blood that circles round her folds, spoiling her beauty and tarnishing her honor. But no, day by day, has she been dragged deeper and deeper into cruelty and oppression till now (in my eyes) her once bright red stripes look like bloody gashes on the face of heaven. I look now upon my early admiration of her glories as a dream. My love (as things stand today) is for the South alone. Nor do I deem it a dishonor in attempting to make for her a prisoner of this man to whom she owes so much misery.

A Confederate doing duty on his own responsibility.

J. Wilkes Booth

Late in July I'd met with rebel secret service agents in the Parker House in Boston, and we talked about my mission. They planned to raid northern prisons to free rebel captives, and had various plots of their own against Caesar, and we agreed to coordinate our efforts. Then I headed south again, stopping in Philadelphia long enough to visit Asia.

She begged me: "Don't go South again, my poor brother, don't go."

"Why, where should I go then? Do you not understand the danger, dear sister? This is a presidential election year, this is the year when Lincoln runs for reelection." I then sang a parody, ending with, "1865 when Lincoln shall be king.'"

"Oh, not that," she said, "that will *never* come to pass."

"No, by God's mercy, never *that*!" I spit the words out in a rage. "That sectional candidate should *never* have been president, the votes were *doubled* to seat him, he was smuggled through Maryland to the White House. Maryland is true to the core—every mother's son. Look at the Yankee cannon on the heights of Baltimore. It needed that to keep her quiet. Lincoln's appearance, his pedigree, his coarse low jokes and anecdotes, his vulgar similes, and his frivolity, are a disgrace to the seat he holds. Other brains rule the country. He is made the tool of the North to crush out slavery, by robbery, rapine, slaughter, and bought armies. He is walking in the footprints of old John Brown, but no more fit to stand with that rugged old hero—Great God, no! I loathed Brown's cause, but he was inspired—the audacity of his lone-handed blow! He is the grandest character of this century! But Lincoln! In one great move he overturns this blind Republic and makes himself a king. This man's reelection will be a reign! The bastard subjects of other countries who fight in his armies, they are eager to help him overturn this government. You'll see—you'll see—the *reelection* means *succession*. Trust the songs of the people—they are the bards, the troubadours. I hear what they sing in the taverns in Baltimore, New York, Pittsburgh, Washington. They hate the bloody tyrant and make heroes of those who bring him down. Who make these songs if not the people? 'Vox populi' forever! The false-hearted, unloyal foreigners would glory in the downfall of the Republic—and that by a half-breed too, a man springing from the ashes of old John Brown, a false president yearning for kingly succession as hotly as Ariston ever did."

"John, *please*—" But I stormed out and headed south by horse. I had two old friends to see in Baltimore, men who were with me in sentiment. When I reached the city, I checked into Barnum's City Hotel and sent for Samuel Arnold and Michael O'Laughlin. I read in the newspapers that day that heavy reinforcements were on their way to Grant, which meant that something big was afoot at Petersburg. We had to move swiftly.

49. GRANT

Burnside proposed a scheme that might win the war for us. A regiment of Pennsylvania miners in his corps came up with the idea of digging a mine twenty feet deep and five hundred feet long right under the rebel fortifications, and load it with nine thousand pounds of gunpowder. The explosion would blow a huge hole in the rebel defensive line and throw Lee's entire army into confusion. Burnside's infantry, led by Ferrero's black division, would swarm around the hole, charge into Petersburg, and seize the city. Burnside took the proposal to General Meade, and Meade brought it to me. We discussed it in my headquarters tent at City Point.

"I think it's a crackpot idea," Meade said, frowning irritably. "But I don't see any harm in letting 'em try. So I gave it my tentative approval as long as white troops lead the assault. It would be a God-damned disaster if the nigger troops led it. They're untested in battle. And for my money are poor soldiers."

"Burnside thinks highly of 'em," I said. "Claims they have the best morale in his corps, well trained, disciplined, eager to prove themselves."

"I don't give a damn what Burnside says. You can't trust his judgment."

I upheld Meade's decision about the colored troops—it was his army and I had to respect the chain of command. Without it, the army would disintegrate. I was more optimistic than Meade about the mine, though. Burnside was right: if we took the initiative and won a decisive victory, it would ensure Mr. Lincoln's reelection in November.

So the miners dug the tunnel—brilliant job of engineering, longest tunnel ever dug up to then—and loaded it with 320 kegs of gunpowder. Around four-forty-five on the morning of July thirtieth they blew the mine. Sent a huge column of reddish earth about two hundred feet into the air with flashes of fire in it all mixed up with parts of men and guns, splintered timber, and all kinds of debris whirling and spreading, and then it all fell to earth with a great roar. Then our artillery—110 guns and 44 mortars—opened up along the entire two-mile line. Concussions were so deafening we had to hold our ears back at City Point. The smoke of the guns and the dust from the explosion drifted upward against the rising sun—turned it blood red. Then Burnside's infantry poured out of their lines, with

James Ledlie's white division in the lead, two other white divisions and the black division in support. Worst mistake Burnside ever made, letting that drunken fool Ledlie lead the assault. Heard Burnside couldn't decide which of his three white divisions ought to lead the attack, so he had the three commanders draw blades of grass and Ledlie got the short one. Had the worst troops in the army, terrible morale, poorly trained. Instead of going around the huge crater, they rushed *into* it while Ledlie stayed behind in his bombshelter, getting drunk. The support divisions also pitched into the smoking crater until it became a writhing mass of men. The Johnnies regrouped, ran up to the rim, and opened fire on the trapped Federals, raking the hole with musketry and lobbing mortar shells on top of 'em. The Johnnies shot our colored troops in cold blood when they tried to surrender. A disaster, is what it was. Rode down there and saw it for myself. More than five hundred of Burnside's men, white and colored, died in that pitiful crater, more than three thousand others were wounded or missing. By the time Lee finally agreed to a truce three days later, the corpses were so black and bloated that the only way you could tell coloreds from whites was by their hair.

I admit it: the colored troops should've led the charge—they were highly trained for it. Meade and I were wrong in not letting 'em go first. A missed opportunity, makes my head hurt to think about it. Think Meade's contempt for Burnside clouded his judgment. Still, Meade was the head of the Army of the Potomac—I couldn't relieve him. So I relieved Burnside instead, him and Ledlie. And the siege and the war went on with no end in sight.

The wounded from the Crater and from daily bombardments and sniping along the trenches were taken back to Depot Hospital on the banks of the Appomattox about a mile around the bend from my headquarters. Impressive place—huge complex of white tents, best field hospital of the war. I went down there once and saw how dense clouds of dust settled on the wards from constant wagon trains and troops passing on the main road and from the unpaved streets of the hospital. Dust everywhere inside the tents, covered the men's clothes and bedding and got into their food.

"These men have to be better cared for," I said. "The streets have to be watered." A minister of the Christian Commission recommended a fire engine. I liked the idea and sent a man to Baltimore to get one. Later we added a second fire engine and installed sprinkling carts, and that settled the dust.

50. HANCOCK

I thought we should all *die* of breathing dust—it was shoe-top deep and drifted over the hospital like a heavy brown fog. We were so *happy* when General Grant brought in fire engines and sprinklers to settle the dust—you just don't know. If only he could have done something about the weather. It was excessively hot and depressing, the sun beat down on us relentlessly, and the smell was almost intolerable.

Depot Hospital was divided into divisions and laid out with streets and avenues just like a city. It had some twelve hundred tents that could hold up to ten thousand patients at a time. Gettysburg was a skirmish comparatively speaking. The wounded and sick stayed with us until they were well enough to be evacuated to the North. Across the main thoroughfare was Agency Row, which consisted of the stations of the U.S. Sanitary Commission and the tents of the state relief agencies. The black troops had a separate hospital run by Miss Helen Gilson, who was a few years older than I and so sweet. When she passed through her wards, the men would follow her with adoring eyes. She used colored women as cooks, assistant nurses, and laundresses, and made her diet kitchen a model for the rest of the hospital.

I was in charge of the Sanitary Commission's Second Corps diet kitchen, had a good cook and plenty of stores, and sent things up to the rifle pits to men I knew. By August 1864 I was caring for 360 men and had a first-rate work squad consisting of a soldier, an Irish woman, a contraband woman from the floods of Negro contrabands coming in. A jewel of a little Negro boy ran errands for me. I lived in a large hospital tent and worked all day long and at night fell right down to sleep.

There were many women at Depot Hospital, serving as managers of diet kitchens, nurses, and laundresses, and most wore plain gray flannel gowns, but not me: I had a reputation to uphold. I wore stockings, corsets, dresses, a hood, and a nice plain black net. I believe I had the confidence of more people than almost any lady in the army.

One of my patients, Captain Charles H. Dod, said he couldn't get over how well dressed and very pretty I was. It was such a nice compliment. The poor man was in so much pain that we had to keep him on quinine and opium. I took down a letter he dictated to his mother; he said I was "as well known and as much loved in the Second Corps as Florence Nightingale was in the British Army." Oh dear, how that made me blush! But my poor captain soon became delirious. I took him to my tent and put him in my bed, where he lay dying. I did everything I could for him, bathed his face and begged him not to die, but it was no use. I wrote his mother about his condition, and she came to the hospital and was at his side when he died in my bed. We fixed him up nicely, as if he were at home. My dear, brave captain—there were so many like him, it just broke my heart.

The cannonading at the front was severe by day and by night and brought us endless shipments of mutilated men. Sophronie Bucklin said that a shell had partly blown the head off of one poor fellow taken to her hospital: one eye, one ear, and part of his forehead were gone. "His brains oozed out of the gap," she said. "He lay with a squad of men, on the ground, so close that they could scarcely be placed straight, and with their feet toward the center of my tent. When I passed him, he caught at my dress with his hands, and made a noise, vainly endeavoring to articulate a word. He lived for several days without taking a bit of nourishment, and then died."

One day I fell sick, which was rare for me. I felt miserable, but at least I survived: the same could not be said for my friend Arabella Barlow. One day she fainted at her work, tried to keep going, only to faint again. It turned out that she had the fever really bad and just wasted away. At last she had to be evacuated to Washington, where she died. It just made me so *sad* to lose such a lovely, vital friend and such a competent nurse.

I wrote my mother that I was lucky to come off with one day's sickness in this hot and smelly place. "It is really awful here," I said. "The cannons boom along the line all the time, the heat is intense and the day of the explosion and the Battle of the Crater it seemed like what we read about hell. Our ladies in camp are being reduced considerably by sickness and an indisposition to stay. I pray for health. I can stand all other hardships but sickness."

Dr. Dudley, the young surgeon and Yale graduate I mentioned earlier, came to see me, and that cheered me up. He is so practical, so down-to-earth. "You know what I want, Cornelia?" he said. "I want this terrible war to end, the rebels whipped for good, and peace restored in the land, so we can all go home and stay at home in peace and contentment. I have my own mark to make in the world and must get out of the war and get at it. I've a dim hope that we can finish the war this coming winter."

Dr. Dudley ran a flying hospital close to the front. In August he went with the Second Corps on a raid at Deep Bottom on the James, and they had a fight on a terribly hot day. You could hear the cannons belching forth with double venom, and word came back that we were repulsed. Poor Dr. Dudley was almost sunstruck and gave out; they had to put him on a stretcher, and I looked for him at Depot Hospital; but he never came. When he was well again, he fetched me and took me to the front to see Petersburg. You could see the city's church spires shimmering in the heat. Our soldiers lived in the trenches and little bombproof huts and were covered with dust and grime—one soldier said they looked like "troglodytes." The flies and mosquitoes were perfectly awful. The shells were flying pretty lively and exploding in whirlwinds of dirt and dust. One man was killed while I was there.

We came back to City Point to get supplies for our hospitals. The Union base there was a vast military city, with seven wharves that serviced up to two hundred ships a day. The ships brought supplies and ordnance from the North, which were stored in warehouses along the waterfront. A huge bakery cooked a hundred thousand loaves of bread a day for Grant's sieging army. There were army repair and blacksmith shops, a post office, slaughterhouses, and coffin shops and parlors for embalming. The construction corps rebuilt the City Point railroad track, and whistling military trains rolled right up to the wharves on railroad spurs, so that the army's colored workers could load supplies on boxcars and flatcars for the troops at the front.

General Grant's headquarters tents were situated on the east lawn of Appomattox Manor, which overlooked the James River. It had once been the big house of a plantation with almost 130 slaves, but that was all gone now. We could see General Grant sitting under the flap of his tent, with orderlies and staff officers coming and going briskly, and we hoped the general was preparing a campaign that would finally end this terrible war.

51. GRANT

The president wired me to meet him at Fort Monroe. Went there the day after the Crater. We talked in his stateroom on board the *Baltimore*. The pressing problem, he said, was the need for a unified command in Maryland and Pennsylvania to deal with Early's force if it invaded the North again. We discussed possible commanders and the name of McClellan came up. He was sure to be the Democratic nominee for president, and a couple of prominent Republicans wanted to give him the military assignment to get rid of him politically. The president didn't think much of the idea, though. Before we parted, I told him about the disaster of the Crater, and the disappointment showed in his eyes.

Next day Lincoln left for Washington, and I wired Halleck that Phil Sheridan was my choice for commander of the upper Potomac. Told Halleck I wanted all the forces there concentrated under Sheridan, with instructions that he should put himself south of the enemy and follow him to the death. Halleck and Stanton both objected on the grounds that Sheridan was too young. But the president agreed with me. He wired me that he'd seen my dispatch with my instructions for Sheridan. "This, I think, is exactly right as to how our forces should move," he said. "But there is no idea in the head of anybody in Washington of putting our army *south* of the enemy or of following him to the *death* in any direction. It will neither be done nor attempted unless *you* watch it every day, and hour, and force it." In short, I had to go up there myself and see that it was done.

Went to Washington and then to the Federal camp on the Monocacy River, where General Hunter, commander of the Department of West Virginia, had some twenty-five to thirty thousand men. Hunter was senior in rank to Sheridan, and that might've been a problem. Solved it by leaving him in command of the department and ordering him to remove his headquarters to Baltimore, where he was out of the way. Sheridan was to have supreme command of all troops in the field.

When Sheridan arrived from Petersburg, I told him: "You will take orders from nobody but me. Your job is to find the enemy and attack him. As you push southward up the Shenandoah, you should leave nothing to invite the enemy to return. Take all provisions, forage, and stock wanted for the use of your command. Carry off the Negroes so as to prevent further planting. Destroy what you can't use. Don't destroy buildings, but wreck all the railroads and burn the fields and crops. In other words, eat out Virginia clear and clean as far as you go, so that crows flying over it for the balance of this season will have to carry their provender. If the war is to last another year, we want the Shenandoah Valley to remain a barren waste."

52. LINCOLN

I approved Grant's orders to Sheridan: burn the Shenandoah from one end to the other so the rebels could no longer feed off it or use it to launch raids against the North. Was this cruel to civilians? Yes. But they had to be told that as long as an army could subsist among 'em, the enemy raids would go on, and we aimed to stop 'em. Permanently.

August brought glimmers of hope from the far-flung battle fronts. First, Admiral Farragut ran his fleet past the rebel forts protecting Mobile Bay, and closed it as a blockade-running port. Then, on Grant's orders, the Potomac Army extended the southern end of its siege line and captured a mile-long stretch of the Weldon Railroad, which ran south from Petersburg to Wilmington, Charleston, and Savannah. Now Lee and Davis could no longer draw supplies by that route.

But for the northern public these victories were not nearly enough. From their view, the war remained stalemated, with both our principal armies locked into protracted sieges, and no *decisive* victories anywhere. The people were weary of the war, weary of the death lists in the papers, and sick and tired of me. My hate mail was piling up—I couldn't bear to look at the stuff. On the day I'd set apart for fasting, humiliation, and prayer across the North, my old Democratic adversary, the *Illinois State Register*, probably spoke for thousands when it ridiculed "Massa Linckum's" proclamation. "As the *Register* thinks the nation has ample reason for fasting, because Lincoln has made food so high; for humiliation at the disgrace his miserable, imbecilic policies have brought upon us; and for prayer that God, in his goodness, will spare us a second term of such a president, the day will be observed by the employees of this establishment."

With defeatism spreading across the country, Republicans were sure I couldn't be reelected. "I find everywhere a conviction that we need a change," said one Republican, "that the war languishes under Mr. Lincoln and that he *cannot* and *will not* give us peace." Another Republican said flatly: "There are no Lincoln men." Thurlow Weed, Seward's New York crony, bluntly told me I was going to lose; Henry Raymond of the *New York Times* agreed; and so did my old Illinois friends Leonard Swett and Orville Browning.

I tell you, I was at the bottom of the tub. It looked like I was going to be beaten in November, and unless some great change took place, *badly beaten*. The election would be the most critical this country's ever had—the weal or woe of our great nation would be decided then. McClellan was sure to be the Democratic nominee, and if he won, as everybody seemed to think, the country was doomed.

When Judge J. T. Mills and former Governor Randall, both of Wisconsin, called on me at my summer retreat up at the Soldiers' Home, I told 'em: "There is no program offered by any wing of the Democratic Party that wouldn't result in the permanent destruction of the Union."

"But Mr. President," the judge said, "General McClellan is in favor of crushing out the rebellion by force."

"The slightest knowledge of arithmetic," I said, "will prove that the rebel armies cannot be destroyed by Democratic strategy. There are now nearly two hundred thousand able-bodied colored men in the service of the Union, most of 'em under arms, defending and acquiring Union territory. Democratic strategy demands that the colored forces be disbanded, and that their former masters be conciliated by returning them to slavery. The experience of the war proves that the rebels will win the war if you fling the compulsory labor of millions of black men onto their side of the scale. But that's exactly what the Democrats mean to do. How can you give the rebels a military advantage that will ensure their success, and then rely on coaxing, flattery, and concessions, to get 'em back into the Union? I tell you, it won't work. If we take two hundred thousand black men from our side and put 'em in the battlefield or the cornfield against us, we would be forced to abandon the war in three weeks.

"Do you know there have been men who've urged *me* to return our black warriors to slavery? If I did, I'd deserve to be damned in time and eternity. No human power can subdue this rebellion without the emancipation policy, and every other policy calculated to weaken the rebels' moral and physical forces. Freedom has given us two hundred thousand men raised on southern soil. It will give us more yet."

Still, in the privacy of my office, I admitted it was just about the end of the line for me. In a week or so, the Democrats would nominate McClellan. That he would likely whip me and become the next president was a humiliating irony, but I resigned myself to that probability. I sat down at my desk, took out a sheet of stationery, and dated it August twenty-third, 1864. "This morning, as for some days past, it seems exceedingly probable that this Administration will not be reelected. Then it will be my duty to so cooperate with the president elect, as to save the Union between the election and the inauguration; as he will have secured his election on such ground that he cannot possibly save it afterwards."

I stared at the paper, pondering what I would tell McClellan when that day came. "General," I would say, "the election has demonstrated that you are stronger, have more influence with the American people than I. Now let us together, you with your influence and I with all the Executive power of the government, try to save the country. You raise as many troops as you possibly can for this final trial, and I will devote all my energies to assisting and finishing the war."

I signed the memorandum, folded and sealed it. Later I asked all my Cabinet secretaries to sign their names on the back of the document, but did not tell them what it said. Then I put it in my desk.

One of my most outspoken opponents in 'sixty-four was Frederick Douglass. He'd declared his support for Frémont, and that hurt. A mutual friend told me that Douglass was furious about my reconstruction efforts in Louisiana, my failure to support black suffrage and protect our colored soldiers from rebel atrocities. I was concerned about his feelings. I told our mutual friend I wanted to see Douglass, and the friend arranged an interview.

I'll be honest: at this time, late August, I'd begun to waver about emancipation. Asked myself, *how can I commit the country to an abolition war, when the country obviously doesn't want it?* So I drew up a letter in which I offered to stop the fighting if the rebels would return to the Union and recognize the national authority. Slavery and all other questions would be left for adjustment by peaceful means. Raymond of the *Times* would take the letter to Jeff Davis. If he rejected it, Raymond was to find out what terms Davis would accept.

When Douglass called for our interview, I read him the letter. The anguish I felt had to have shown on my face. "What do you think, Douglass. Should I send the letter?"

"Absolutely not," he said. "It would be taken as a complete surrender of your antislavery policy and hurt you irreparably among the people who count."

"Don't get me wrong, Douglass. I hate slavery just as much as you do. Personally I'm still committed to emancipation and justice for black people. This comes from a deep moral conviction, not merely from necessity. I'm convinced no lasting peace can be achieved short of absolute submission by the rebels, but I might be forced to end the war by a negotiated peace. The low morale in the North, the pressure from Greeley and others, the increasing opposition to the war because I've converted it to an abolition war—all make me apprehensive that a peace might be forced on me which will leave enslaved all Negroes who haven't made it to our lines."

Douglass was incredulous. "You mean you only have faith in the proclamation of freedom *during* the war? Afterward, it will cease to operate? If slavery and the master class based on it survive, what will the war have been about except a lot of killing?"

"It's not my wish, but it may happen. What we might have to do is to send a band of black scouts into rebel territory and smuggle as many slaves as possible to Union lines. You could be the leader."

Douglass thought my idea had merit, and when he left, he promised to discuss it with "trustworthy" and "patriotic blacks." But the plan turned out not to be necessary because I changed my mind about sending the letter to Davis with its modified terms for peace. Douglass was right: what would the war have been about if slavery and the southern master class survived it? How would that save the Union, our experiment in popular government? Besides, I could never live with myself if I broke my promise of freedom to the slaves. Next day, with awakened resolution, I told the Cabinet about my decision. The stronger members supported me. A peace overture would be worse than losing the election, they said. "It would be ignominiously surrendering it in advance."

As we expected, the Democratic convention, which met in Chicago, nominated McClellan on a platform charging that my "experiment of war" had failed. The platform promised that slavery would be preserved by maintaining "the rights of the states unimpaired." A peace plank demanded that hostilities end immediately, and that a convention of the states should ultimately meet for the purpose of restoring peace on the basis of "the Federal Union of the states." In other words, the Democratic platform made peace through an *unconditional* armistice the first objective, the Union second. This was too much even for McClellan, and he publicly repudiated the peace plank, saying he couldn't look his former comrades in the eye if he didn't. "The *Union* is the one condition of peace," he said in his acceptance speech, "we ask no more." This gave the voters a clear choice between his one condition for peace, the Union, and my two conditions, the Union *and* emancipation.

McClellan also promised to "guarantee for the future the constitutional rights of every state," meaning the right to own slaves. If he won the presidency, he meant to abandon emancipation, to preserve slavery as a state institution, and return our colored soldiers to bondage—and surely lose the war. Yet the North would probably vote for that disastrous policy.

Some men begged me to cancel the election, even declare myself a dictator, rather than let the government fall into McClellan's hands. I told 'em no, a thousand times no. "The election is a necessity," I said. "We can't have a free government without elections. If the rebellion could force us to cancel or even postpone a national election, it might fairly claim to have already conquered us."

"I mean to hold my ground," I told visitors to the White House. "To agree to an armistice would be the end of the struggle and the loss of all that Union men have fought and died for. Keep my war policy, and you can save the Union. Throw it away, and the Union goes with it. As long as I'm in office, I will not violate my promise of freedom to the Negroes. I will accept no measure that reenslaves them. It can *not* be."

We have an even greater obligation to fight on to victory. It's to preserve the central idea of the war, the thing that lies at the heart of the American promise. I tried to explain that to the men of the 148th Ohio when they called at the White House. "I look upon the war as an attempt on the one hand to overwhelm and destroy the national existence, while on our part, we're striving to maintain the government and institutions of our fathers, to enjoy them ourselves and transmit them to our children and our children's children forever." I got closer to what I meant in a speech to the 166th Ohio: "I happen temporarily to occupy this big White House. I am a living witness that any one of your children may look to come here as my father's child has. It's in order that each of you may have through this free government which we've enjoyed, an open field and a fair chance for your industry, enterprise and intelligence; that you may all have equal privileges in the race of life, with all its desirable human aspirations. It is for this the struggle should be maintained, that we may not lose our birthright. The nation is worth fighting for, to secure such an inestimable jewel."

The end of August brought another blow to my chances. A worried group of Republicans issued a call for a new convention to meet at Cincinnati at the end of September and nominate another candidate. Horace Greeley, Winter Davis, Smiler Colfax, and Ben Butler were behind the "Cincinnati call," and there was talk that Butler would be the new candidate. Wade and Sumner thought I would be defeated, too, but held back from endorsing the Cincinnati convention. Sumner said I ought to resign voluntarily, not be forced out. The Copperhead *New York World* said it was hard to tell what hurt me most: the frontal blows from my "manly opponents," or the stabs in the back from my friends.

On that unhappy note, the campaign of 'sixty-four got under way. It was a bitter, nasty contest. The Republican press denigrated McClellan as "a cowardly traitor" and claimed that the Democratic platform had been written in Richmond. The Democratic prints, on the other hand, damned me as Dictator Lincoln, claimed I was the bastard son of one "Inlow," and distributed a broadside showing white Republican men and black women at "the Miscegenation Ball." A Democratic pamphlet warned voters what they could expect under a second Lincoln Administration: a cover sketch showed a thick-lipped Negro man kissing a young white girl. One Democratic paper in Wisconsin said that if I was elected to "misgovern" for another four years, it hoped that some brave soul would stab me in the heart "for the public good."

53 · BOOTH

When Sam Arnold joined me in my room at Barnum's City Hotel in Baltimore, we celebrated our reunion with wine and cigars. I had not seen him since our school days together at St. Timothy's Hall. He was around thirty, four years my senior, and was as carefree and gay as he had been at St. Timothy's. *Pleasure* was his byword. "I have no wish of the heart that hasn't been gratified," he said with a merry sparkle in his eye. He said he'd served off and on in the Confederate Army and had worked in the Confederacy's Office of Niter and Mining Bureau in Tennessee, but owing to his mother's ill health he had returned to Baltimore early in 1864. At the time, he said, he was broken down, in ill health himself, and had to endure persecution from Unionist neighbors because of his devotion to the Confederacy. I was appalled that there were *Unionists* in Baltimore, but Arnold thought they were an impotent minority.

"You'll find that plenty of the best people share our views," he said.

There was a knock at the door. It was my old boyhood friend, Mike O'Laughlin. I introduced him to Arnold, and offered him a cigar and a glass of wine. I asked him what he had done in the war, and he said he'd fought in the rebel army—the First Maryland Infantry, C.S.A.—but had left it at the time of Antietam, in poor health, and had returned to Baltimore, where he worked for a while in his brother's feed and produce business and lived with his widowed mother in a house on North Exeter Street owned by my mother. He was an amiable fellow, around twenty-four years of age, and shared our love for the Confederacy. We talked about the war and the dire condition of the Confederacy, and then I broached the subject for which I had summoned them.

"Since Lincoln canceled the prisoner exchange, there is a great surplus of prisoners in the hands of the Union. I have a plan to get them released so that they can fight again for the Confederacy and turn the tides of war back in her favor. It involves kidnapping Lincoln. Rebel agents who've watched his movements say he often goes alone and unguarded out to the Soldiers' Home in the country. We can easily seize him, tie him up in the bed of a wagon, and take him through southern Maryland, where there are plenty of people who will help us, and then smuggle him across the Potomac by boat. We'll stretch ropes across the road behind us to trip the horses of any pursuit. Then we'll take Caesar to Richmond and turn him over to the Confederate government, which will offer to exchange him for all the prisoners in Federal hands." I paused, studying my two friends. "This, my friends, is a legitimate act of war. It's our chance to strike a decisive blow for the South, a blow that will enable it to fight on to victory. Think of it! *Our names will go into history!*"

I did not tell them that the plan had the approval of authorities at the highest level in Richmond, or that it was to be coordinated with similar schemes of the rebel secret service. That I kept to myself.

"Are you with me?" I asked.

"We're with you," they said in unison.

"Swear an oath to secrecy and good faith," I said.

"I swear it," said Arnold.

"So do I," said O'Laughlin.

"I have some matters to take care of in Pennsylvania and Canada. I should be back in a month. Remember your oath. Not a word to anybody."

54. LINCOLN

Just when it looked the worst for me, Sherman sent an electrifying telegram from Georgia. He'd gotten across Hood's railroad lifeline southwest of Atlanta, which forced Hood to come out and fight for his communications. But the rebel attack was a failure. Hood now had no choice but to evacuate Atlanta, and on September second, Sherman occupied the city. "God bless General Sherman!" I cried. "This is a *decisive* victory. Old Glory now flies over Atlanta, strategic railroad center, symbol of deep southern resistance, queen city of the cotton states. Glory hallelujah! *Glory hallelujah*!" I declared the fall of Atlanta a gift from God, designated Sunday as a national day of thanksgiving, and caused one-hundred-gun salutes to be fired in Washington and Baltimore, in Philadelphia and Pittsburgh, in New York and Boston, in St. Louis and New Orleans. Let news of Atlanta sweep the country from ocean to ocean. Let it ring forth in the public prints, ring forth in a thousand telegraphs in every city in the North: this Administration was *not whipped yet*, our armies were *winning again*.

55. DAVIS

It began as an ugly rumor on the streets: *Atlanta has fallen.* Then we received Hood's dispatch that confirmed the rumor: Atlanta was indeed in Sherman's hands, and Hood had retreated to Palmetto southwest of the city. There was a sound reason why he had gone there: owing to the obstinately cruel policy which the Lincoln government was pursuing, of refusing on any terms to exchange prisoners, upward of thirty thousand Yankee prisoners were at Andersonville in southwest Georgia. To guard against the release and arming of these prisoners, Hood thought it necessary to place our army between them and the enemy.

The fall of Atlanta was one more calamity in a long list of woes. What remained of our inadequate rail system would suffer a fatal blow if the situation in Georgia were not reversed. To compound the misery Sherman had visited on us, he expelled all the civilians living in Atlanta. Since Alva's atrocious cruelties to the noncombatant population of the Low Countries in the sixteenth century, the history of war records no instance of such barbarous cruelty as what this order was designed to perpetrate. It involved the immediate expulsion from their homes, and the loss of their only means of subsistence, of thousands of unoffending women and children, whose husbands and fathers were either in the army, in northern prisons, or had died in battle. This was unsurpassed cruelty from the North's Attila the Hun.

General Hood sent Sherman a furious protest: "You came into our country with your army, avowedly for the purpose of subjugating free white men, women, and children, and not only intend to rule over them, but you make negroes your allies, and desire to place over us an inferior race, which we have raised from barbarism to its present position, which is the highest ever attained by that race in any country, in all time. We will fight you to the death! Better die a thousand deaths than submit to live under you or your government and your negro allies!"

56. SHERMAN

My reply to Hood was Goddamned succinct: "We have no 'negro allies' in this army; not a single negro soldier left Chattanooga with this army, or is with it now." And for good reason: I didn't agree with Grant or the Administration that niggers could make good soldiers, but I didn't tell Hood that. "This is the conclusion of our correspondence," I said, "which I did not begin, and terminate with satisfaction."

The mayor of Atlanta and two city councilmen begged me to revoke my expulsion order, but I refused. "You cannot qualify war in harsher terms than I will," I wrote them from my headquarters in the Lyons House. "War is *cruelty*, and you cannot refine it; and those who brought war into our country deserve all the curses and maledictions our people can pour out. You might as well appeal against the thunderstorm as against the terrible hardships of war. They are inevitable, and the only way the people of Atlanta can hope once more to live in peace and quiet at home, is to stop fighting, admit that you cannot have a division of our country, return to the Union, and acknowledge the authority of the national government."

Yep, the people of the South made a big howl about my expelling the families of Atlanta, but I would have been a God-damned fool to take a town at such cost and leave it occupied by a hostile people. If Jeff Davis and Hood didn't like it, fuck 'em.

57. DAVIS

At the time Atlanta fell, 121,000 of our troops were reported to be absent without leave, and Hood and Lee were both complaining about their severe shortage of troops. "We need every man possible for field duty," Lee wired me: "every white man liable for military service must be pressed into the ranks immediately. So should all able-bodied white cooks, teamsters, mechanics—all male soldiers. Negroes should take their places. It seems to me that we must choose between employing Negroes ourselves or having them employed against us."

At Lee's urging, we intensified conscription—farmers who visited Richmond found themselves drafted into the army—and we searched every corner of the Confederacy for troops. I wired Governor Brown that we needed the help of Georgia men now more than ever, but that scoundrel threatened to recall all Georgia regiments in Lee's army in order to save the state from Sherman. He had already withdrawn ten thousand Georgia militia temporarily given to Hood during the struggle for Atlanta. I wrote Brown that Atlanta could be *recaptured* if he returned the militia to Hood and gave him the temporary use of the fifteen thousand other Georgians exempted from the draft on the grounds that they were so-called state officials. With that many fresh troops, I informed Brown, Hood could drive Sherman's army from the state, perhaps utterly destroy it.

On September twentieth, a rumor reached Richmond that Sherman had invited Brown and Senator Herschel Johnson, one of my bitterest critics, to discuss peace terms and the return of Georgia to the Union. From subsequent reports we learned that Sherman had indeed asked them to negotiate, but they had declined. Nevertheless, the crisis in Georgia was so grave that I resolved to go there at once, to work out a sound military strategy with Hood, rally the people to the cause, coax deserters back into the ranks, and persuade Brown to cooperate.

I left by train and reached Hood's headquarters at Palmetto, southwest of Atlanta, toward the end of September. I was happy to see Sam Hood again—he was a loyal friend and I trusted him implicitly. He invited me into his headquarters, and I observed that he walked well with his wooden leg.

"Sherman won't stay inactive long," he said. "He's collecting recruits and supplies in Atlanta so fast he's probably thinking about a movement farther south, with Atlanta as his secondary base."

Pointing at a map on the table, I proposed that Hood march north and tear up Sherman's railroad supply lines back to Chattanooga and Nashville. "That would blight all of his campaign in Georgia," I said. "He would have to abandon Atlanta and move north to recover his communications. If he tries to attack you in position, which is probable, you should give battle. Otherwise you should retreat to Gadsden, Alabama, here, on the dividing line between that state and Georgia. At that point, the largest number of militia and home guards of both states can be assembled as an auxiliary force, and there a final stand can be made for a decisive battle. If you are victorious, Sherman cannot retreat through the wasted country behind him, and would have to surrender or disperse. If he does not pursue you to Gadsden, but returns to Atlanta and sets out for the seacoast, you will pursue him and fall on his rear. With the advantages of a better knowledge of the country, of a devoted population, and our superiority in cavalry, we can reasonably hope that retributive justice might overtake the ruthless invader." But I cautioned Hood. "If Sherman should move southward from Atlanta, do not consider any operation that would place your army beyond striking distance of him."

I wanted to coordinate the operations of Hood's army with Richard Taylor's forces in Mississippi. To do that effectively required a unified command in the West such as General Johnston had had the year before. Though I detested Beauregard's pompous arrogance, I had him in mind for that vital role, and I telegraphed General Lee to discover if Beauregard would accept the command. Lee replied that he would. I then telegraphed Beauregard to leave Virginia and meet me in Augusta.

One of my objectives was to persuade Brown to give us the twenty-five thousand men he was withholding from national service. He sent a distempered letter to the War Department, the substance of which was relayed to me, that he absolutely would not respond to my call for the militia. He said he would not cooperate with my "ambitious projects" by giving me control of all that remained to safeguard the rights of his state. Damn that blackguard. That sort of narrow-minded and selfish enslavement to state rights was going to destroy us!

I set off across Georgia to raise civilian morale and to bring the absentees and deserters back to the ranks. At Macon, I addressed a crowd from the back of the train: "Our cause is not lost. Sherman cannot keep up his long line of communication and must retreat sooner or late. Our cavalry and our people will harass and destroy his army as the Cossacks destroyed Napoleon, and like him, the Yankee general will escape only with a bodyguard. How can this be achieved? By every man, old and young, taking up the musket. By the absentees of Hood's army returning to their posts.

"Citizens, hear me well! More than a third of our men are absent—some sick, some wounded, but most of them absent without leave. The man who repents and returns to the army makes a strong case for presidential clemency. I urge every citizen to pressure deserters to return to the Army of Tennessee. If one-half the men now absent without leave will return to duty, we will defeat the enemy and win our independence. With that hope, I am going to the front. I may not realize this hope, but I know there are men there who have looked death in face too often to despond now. Let no one despond. Let no one distrust, and remember that if genius is the beautiful, hope is the reality."

I gave similar speeches at Montgomery, Columbia, and Augusta. "The time for action is now at hand," I said. "There is but one duty for every southern man. It is to go to the front. Remember what we are fighting for. On our success depends the existence of constitutional liberty in the world. We are fighting for that principle—upon us depends its last hope. Let me say to you, there can be no reconstruction with the Yankee. What does he offer as terms? Acknowledge your crime, lay down your arms, emancipate your slaves, turn over your leaders—as they call your humble servant—to be punished, then you will have permission to vote with your niggers upon the terms Lincoln has graciously allowed you to live as part of his nation. If there are those who still hope to win peace and independence by electing a peace candidate in the North, they deceive themselves. *Victory* is the surest element of strength to a peace party. Let us *win battles* and we shall have overtures soon enough.

"And you, my fair countrywomen. You have done your duty. You have sent your husbands, your fathers, your sons, to the army.

But you must do more. You must use your influence to send all to the front, and form a public opinion that shall make the skulker a marked man, and leave him no house where he can take shelter. And you, young ladies who are yet to marry, let me tell you that when the choice comes between a one-armed soldier and one who has grown fat on extortion at home, choose to cling to the armless sleeve."

On October second, I met with Beauregard in Augusta, and told him about the plan of operations I had worked out for Hood. Beauregard said he approved. I then appointed him as overall commander of Hood's and Taylor's armies. "Wherever you are present with an army in the field," I said, "you will exercise immediate command of the troops."

By then, Hood had moved north and put his army across the railroad in Sherman's rear. Certain that victory was within Hood's grasp, I left for Columbia, where I enjoyed a reunion with James and Mary Chesnut. They held a reception in my honor at their town cottage, and the crowd shook my arm so hard I feared it might fall off. Neighbors sent elegant dishes for the president's dinner: stuffed peppers, stuffed tomatoes, and a boned turkey filled with truffles, along with a sixty-year-old Madeira from Mulberry, the Chesnuts' plantation. Miss Preston was present, and when I defended Hood she said she could kiss me for that. Then, to my embarrassment, she did kiss me.

Mary told me later: "When she kissed you, you were smoothing her down on the back from the shoulders as if she were a ruffled dove." She laughed her charming laugh. Then she grew solemn. "Your aide, Custis Lee, spoke candidly and told me many a hard truth about the Confederacy and the bad time that's at hand."

"We will *reverse* the military situation," I assured her, "and one day plant our banners on the banks of the Ohio, where we shall tell the Yankees to shut up or we shall teach them a hard lesson."

When it was time to go, I kissed her hand. "Mary, the best hams—the best Madeira, the best coffee, the best hostess in the world, has made Columbia a delight. Thank you."

By October sixth I was back in Richmond, having done all I could to warn our people that disunity within one's own ranks makes deeper wounds than the enemy's sword. Then I hastened to the War Office to find out what had happened in Georgia.

58. SHERMAN

That Goddamned Hood was afraid to fight me on open ground and therefore moved around and north of Atlanta to try to break up the railroads that supplied my army from Chattanooga and Nashville. He had three corps, about forty thousand men, and swung around by Dallas and broke the road at Big Shanty to Kennesaw. He stole a march on me of one day, and his men, disencumbered of baggage, moved faster than we did when we gave pursuit. When I got to Kennesaw Mountain, I had a superb view of the vast panorama to the north and west: I could see the smoke of Hood's campfires at Dallas. He was after our big supply depot at Allatoona, where we had a million rations of hardtack and nine thousand head of beef guarded by fewer than a thousand troops. At my orders, our signal man wig-wagged to Brigadier General John Corse at Rome, telling him to take his division to reinforce Allatoona. Then we saw smoke rising over Allatoona—the rebs were attacking! Looked like Corse would be too late. The smoke of battle obscured Allatoona so badly we couldn't see our signal men over there.

Finally my signal officer spotted a signal man. "He's signaling C,R,S,E,H,E,R," he said. "I can't make sense of it."

"Hell, I know what it means. It means 'Corse Here.' Hot damn, the son-of-a-bitch made it!" Later we got a wire from him: "I am short a cheek-bone and an ear, but am able to whip all hell yet." He whipped 'em all right and held the fort, and when we reached Allatoona I looked at Corse's ear and cheekbone and said: "Why, Corse, they damned near missed you, didn't they?"

So we'd saved our supply depot. Even so, we found that Hood had struck our railroad a heavy blow, burning every tie and bending every rail for eight miles, which took ten thousand men seven days to repair.

I didn't like chasing Hood and trying to guard the railroad, and I told Grant so by telegram. It was a physical impossibility to protect the railroads, I said, now that Hood, Forrest, Wheeler and the whole batch of devils were turned loose without home or habitation to wreak havoc on the roads.

I proposed that my army break up the railroad from Chattanooga to Atlanta and strike out for Milledgeville, Millen, and Savannah, living off the country and utterly destroying Georgia's railroads, cotton gins, foundries, machine shops, plantations, and farms. This would cripple Georgia's military resources and break the morale of its hostile population. "I can make this march," I said, "and make Georgia howl!"

Grant didn't agree. "If you cut loose, I do not believe you would meet Hood's army but would be bushwhacked by all the old men, little boys, and railroad guards still left at home." Grant thought Hood would strike north for Nashville, where I'd sent Thomas with a powerful force. "If there is any way of getting at Hood," Grant said, "I would prefer that."

But there was no way to get at Hood. The lightness and celerity of his army prevented me from catching him on a stern chase. I told Grant this and said I still preferred to move through Georgia, smashing things to the sea. This would force Hood to follow me. Instead of being on the defensive, I told Grant, I would be on the offensive. Instead of my guessing what Hood meant to do, he would have to guess what I intended to do.

That brought Grant around. "On reflection," he said in a wire in mid-October, "I think better of your proposition. It would be better to go south than to be forced to come north." President Lincoln, however, felt "much solicitude" about my proposed march, worried that "a misstep" by me would cost me my army. But Grant wired the president that "Sherman's proposition is the best that can be adopted. Such an army as Sherman has, and with such a commander, is hard to corner or capture." Stanton then telegraphed me that I had the government's full support and confidence in my plan to march to the sea.

I sent the Fourth Corps to General Thomas in Nashville, which, with the garrisons and new troops, would give him a force of eighty thousand men to defend the line of the Tennessee River and pulverize Hood if he was fool enough to invade Tennessee. I explained to Halleck that my big raid to the sea would illustrate the vulnerability of the South and make its inhabitants feel that war and individual ruin were synonymous terms. The rich planters had no idea what war meant, but they sure as hell would when they saw their fences and corn and hogs and chickens and calves and sheep vanish before their eyes, their railroads wrecked, their barns and fields burned away. "I'm going into the very bowels of the Confederacy," I wrote Thomas, "and mean to leave a trail that will be recognized fifty years hence." If there was to be any hard fighting, I said, Thomas would have to do it, since there was no adequate force in Georgia to slow my march. "It's a big game," I told a staff officer, "but I can do it—I *know* I can do it."

But as I was planning to return to Atlanta, Grant changed his mind again when Hood went north across the Tennessee River. This was toward the end of October. "Do you not think it advisable now that Hood has gone so far north to entirely ruin him before starting on your proposed campaign?" Grant asked. "With Hood's army destroyed, you can go where you please with impunity. Now that he is so far away he might look upon the chase as useless and he will go in one direction whilst you are pushing in the other. If you can see a chance of destroying Hood's army attend to that first and make your other move secondary."

I wired Grant that Thomas had a force strong enough to prevent Hood from reaching any country in which we had an interest. "No single army can catch Hood," I said, "and I am convinced that the best results will follow from our defeating Jeff Davis's cherished plan of making me leave Georgia by maneuvering. I regard the pursuit of Hood as useless." That brought old Grant back around. "I say, then, go on as you proposed," he wired me.

I started my army back to Atlanta and wired Grant that if we could march a well-appointed army right through Jeff Davis's territory, it would demonstrate to the world that we had a power Davis could not resist.

"I'll be ready to march as soon as the presidential election is over," I told Grant.

"I believe you will be eminently successful," he said.

59. LINCOLN

Grant convinced me not to worry about Sherman—what he proposed to do would likely shorten the war. Meanwhile the situation in the Shenandoah was turning in our favor too. In late September Sheridan struck Early at Berryville, whipped him at Winchester, and beat him again at Fisher's Hill. I tell you, after the gloom we'd gone through, I was *elated*. But I worried that Lee might send reinforcements to Early, and I telegraphed my fears to Grant. "I am taking steps to prevent Lee from sending reinforcements to Early by attacking him here," Grant replied. On September thirtieth, Butler's Army of the James struck the defenses of Richmond; his cavalry rode clear to the outskirts of the city and fired on it with artillery. At the same time, the Army of the Potomac attacked Lee's far right flank southeast of Petersburg and stretched the Federal siege line ever closer to the South Side Railroad, Lee's vital supply line to Lynchburg and the rebel interior. That move forced Lee to extend his line, too, and stopped him from reinforcing Early, whose defeat gave our war-weary people another reason to cheer.

Our military victories took all the wind out of the Cincinnati call and gave me renewed hope. I tell you what, I owed a lot to Zach Chandler, the Radical senator, who'd often been one of my worst critics. But now he was doing his best to unify the party behind me. "I may not accomplish anything," he said, "but Goddamn it, I'd prefer the traitor Jeff Davis to the equal traitor McClellan for president." Chandler persuaded me to strike a deal to win back the Frémont men: if I would remove contentious Monty Blair, the sworn enemy of Republican Radicals, as postmaster general, Chandler would get Frémont to withdraw. Turned out, Frémont quit unconditionally, not to help me—in his eyes I remained a military and political failure—but to prevent the election of McClellan. A couple of days later I replaced Blair with William Denneson of Ohio. Blair complained that he'd been decapitated, but he was too caustic and divisive to keep.

With the military picture looking brighter, Republicans of all stripes closed ranks behind me as their candidate. Greeley declared that Grant, Sherman, Sheridan, and Farragut were the only successful peace commissioners. "I'll fight like a savage in this campaign," he told young Nicolay. "I hate McClellan." Greeley's *New York Tribune* announced that despite my faults I was ten thousand times better than McClellan. "We must reelect Lincoln," the paper said. "And God help us we will." At Union rallies, men who'd favored the Cincinnati call now defended my candidacy. Frederick Douglass also supported me, on the grounds that a McClellan victory would be "the heaviest calamity of these years of war and blood." Other abolitionists actually took the stump in my behalf. Young Anna Dickinson lent her great voice to the Lincoln cause. Editor Theodore Tilton campaigned so hard for our ticket he collapsed from exhaustion. Gerrit Smith, a backer of John Brown and a former presidential candidate of the Radical Abolition party, spoke for my candidacy almost every day for five straight weeks in upstate New York. Strange days, wouldn't you say?

In October, both parties looked to the early state elections in Indiana, Ohio, and Pennsylvania as barometers to the presidential race. If we lost, I feared it would go far in bringing down the entire

Union cause. Our strong suit lay with the soldier vote—Republican campaigners insisted that most of our troops favored my conditions for surrender and would stand with their commander in chief. Ohio and Pennsylvania allowed their soldiers to vote in the field, but not Indiana. Sherman had a lot of Indiana soldiers in his army, and I wrote him that anything he could safely do to let 'em go home and vote in the state election would be greatly appreciated. But they didn't have to stay until the presidential election, I told Sherman; they could return to him at once. To my great relief, Sherman granted wholesale furloughs to the twenty-nine Indiana regiments serving in his army, which convinced me that the mercurial general supported me, too. I knew I had the unequivocal support of Grant: he'd told his chief backer, Congressman Washburne, that Lincoln was his man.

October eleventh was election day, and young Hay and I went to the War Department to watch the dispatches, but found the building locked. We spotted a messenger pacing in the moonlight, and he let us in by a side door. I tell you, I had a bad case of nerves as we waited in front of the telegraphs with Stanton. When all the returns were in, Union candidates had narrowly carried Pennsylvania, but had won impressive victories in Ohio and Indiana. The soldier vote had swelled Union majorities in those crucial states, for which I was eternally grateful. The soldiers understood better than anyone why we must fight on. Reports from the hospitals and camps in the Washington area showed that the Ohio troops went for us by ten to one, the Pennsylvania men about three to one. The returns from Carver Hospital, which Stanton and I passed every day on our carriage rides, registered the largest opposition vote.

I chuckled. "That's hard on us, Stanton. They know us better than the others."

Every Republican was excited about the state elections, but I was still apprehensive about the presidential contest. After all, everything hinged on the progress of our arms. What if we suffered a disastrous defeat? A week after the state elections, that seemed to be a distinct possibility. While Sheridan was on his way back from a conference in Washington, Early surprised and routed Sheridan's forces at Cedar Creek. Sheridan raced to the battlefront, rallied his men, and smashed Early, turning certain disaster into a stunning victory. Sheridan then renewed his campaign of destruction in the Shenandoah, burning fields and driving off livestock to help starve the rebels into submission. Before he was through, he'd cut a path of destruction nearly a hundred miles from Winchester south to Staunton. In the White House I joked that it was a good thing Sheridan was a little fellow: no telling what he would do to the rebels if he was bigger.

60. DAVIS

What manner of warfare was this? What kind of people would burn the farms and fields of hungry civilians and send them fleeing south? I felt no remorse when Confederate partisans shot Sheridan's medical inspector, slit the throat of one of his aides, and killed a Yankee officer after he had surrendered. Was this not justified by the burning of the Shenandoah, which was reduced to a smoking wasteland?

It became clear now that the aim of the Yankees was to starve us into submission by seizing the railroads around Petersburg and burning the Shenandoah. The destruction of Georgia's railroads was part of this savage strategy. Starving innocent civilians, women and children, did not trouble the consciences of Lincoln and his generals: they had no consciences; they were inhuman.

Hood, meanwhile, had devised a new plan for dealing with Sherman in Georgia, and Beauregard explained it in a telegram to me, saying he had approved it. Sherman, Beauregard said, had turned back to Atlanta. Instead of hanging on his rear, and harassing him on his march, Hood had decided to let Sherman go and to continue his march into Tennessee. He planned to defeat Thomas, capture Nashville, and then strike north across Tennessee and Kentucky to the Ohio River. This would likely force Sherman to follow him there, and with the twenty thousand new recruits Hood expected to pick up along the way, he would be strong enough to crush Sherman, too. Hood would then march eastward into Virginia and attack Grant in his rear at Petersburg and destroy his army. If Sherman did not follow Hood north but remained in Georgia and set out for the sea, Hood would send Wheeler's cavalry to harass him. Once Grant was crushed, Hood and Lee would unite and dispose of Sherman wherever they found him. "Should he move south from Atlanta," Hood said in a telegram to me, "I think it would be the best thing that could happen for our general good."

I objected to the change of program. This was not at all like the plan of operation I had devised for him at Palmetto. I wanted Hood to pursue Sherman if he set out for the coast. In that case, I explained to Beauregard, he and Hood could concentrate their forces on Sherman and reduce his army to such a condition that it would be ineffective for further operations. As for Hood's plans to capture Tennessee and Kentucky, I said I thought Sherman and Grant would regard that as of minor importance.

Still, since Beauregard had endorsed Hood's new proposal, I reluctantly approved. But I stressed the urgent need for Hood to defeat Sherman *before* he could reunite or reinforce his army. If a large part of Sherman's army did indeed move south, I said, Hood should first beat him in detail and subsequently, without serious obstruction or danger to the country in his rear, advance to the Ohio River. Alas, that was not what Hood did.

The North's presidential election was approaching. I had been hopeful that peace was near at hand when the Democrats nominated McClellan—I thought I could negotiate with him, with the view of his recognizing our independence. I was therefore profoundly distressed when McClellan *repudiated* the peace platform of his own party and made the Union his condition for peace, which of course *we would never accept*. We had to look to ourselves for our own salvation by every possible means.

61. BOOTH

After parting with Arnold and O'Laughlin, I went to the Pennsylvania oil fields to close out some investments I had there and then hurried up to Montreal with my trunk of clothes and checked into the St. Lawrence Hall, which served as a secret rendezvous for rebel agents operating in Canada. I drank and spoke at length with one of them, George Sanders, and was delighted to find that he loathed Caesar as much as I.

"We now think Lincoln's reelection in November is certain," he said. "If he wins and his armies are victorious, we'll never get recognition from Europe, not to mention any military aid. Maybe the only way to save ourselves is to kill him."

"I have a way to turn the war in our favor," I said, and told him about the abduction scheme. He promised to help.

I also had extensive discussions with Patrick C. Martin, a rebel blockade runner who was connected with the right people in southern Maryland. He gave me a letter of introduction to Dr. William Queen, a Confederate sympathizer who, Martin said, would help me chart an escape route and secure the support of Dr. Samuel Mudd and other neighbors. Martin and I talked about the upcoming election when Lincoln would be made king, and Martin said he and other rebel agents in Canada had talked about killing him on the day of his second inauguration.

I shipped my trunk to Richmond by schooner, deposited $450 in the Ontario Bank, and bought a bill of exchange worth $300 in U.S. gold. Then I went south to Baltimore and met again with Arnold and O'Laughlin. I told them we needed more recruits and weapons before we could make our move, and that I knew where to find new good men. "Stay here," I said. "I'll signal you when I'm ready." Then I took the train to Washington. It was the day of the presidential election.

62. LINCOLN

On election day, November eighth, it rained hard in Washington and rivulets of water ran through the streets. My young California friend with the pince-nez glasses, Noah Brooks, joined me in my office, and we talked about the election while rain drummed against the windows. "I'm just enough of a politician to know that there wasn't much doubt about the Baltimore convention," I said, "but about this thing I'm far from being certain. I wish I were certain. I think our papers have done a good job of stressing the refugee system Adjutant General Thomas installed in the Mississippi Valley and other occupied territory. That ought to ease northern fears that the liberated slaves will invade the North. But we can't know for sure until the votes are all counted."

To break the tension, I told Brooks a story about Jack, Tad's pet turkey. The year before, Tad had rescued him from a destination for our table. "Well, a few days ago," I said, "Tad broke into the office and pulled me to a window. 'Papa-day, look,' he said and pointed at the White House lawn, where a company of Pennsylvanians that guarded us were camped. 'They're all voting,' Tad said, 'for Lincoln and Johnson.' I saw Tad's turkey walking and fluttering among the soldiers. 'Does he vote?' I asked. 'We need all the help we can get.' 'No, Papa-day,' Tad said, 'Jack's not of age.'" I thought it was a very funny story.

At seven that evening, Brooks and Hay went with me to the War Office to watch the returns. It was a dark, rainy night and our breath turned to steam as we crossed the wet grounds and approached the side door of the War Department. A soaked army sentinel stood guard there, huddled up in a rubber cloak. We climbed the stairs to the telegraph office, where a clerk handed me a wire. We had a ten-thousand-vote majority in Philadelphia. Another telegram put us ahead in Baltimore, *of all places*, where in 'sixty-one a cabal of secessionists had plotted to assassinate me and a mob of plug-uglies had rioted against the Sixth Massachusetts.

"You're ahead in Maryland, too," a clerk said.

"That is superb," I said. I thought the war had gone far to redeem Maryland, whose voters had recently ratified a new state constitution that outlawed slavery. I like to think I contributed my mite to the outcome: I'd sent a letter to the constitutional convention, emphatically endorsing the emancipation provision. "I wish all men to be free," I said. "I wish the material prosperity of the already free which I feel sure the extinction of slavery would bring. I wish to see, in process of disappearing, that only thing which ever could bring this nation to civil war."

While we were talking about Maryland, Gustavus Fox of the Navy Department reported that my bitter opponent, Congressman Winter Davis, had gone down to defeat there. "It serves him right," Fox said. "He's been really vicious toward us. You especially."

"Well," I said, "you've got more personal resentment than I have. Maybe I've got too little of it, but I never thought it paid. A man hasn't got the time to spend half his life in quarrels."

The telegraph was ticking again, reporting that we'd won a great triumph in Indiana and enjoyed steady gains all over Pennsylvania and other crucial states. Around midnight Major Eckert of the telegraph office brought supper into the crowded room, and I set to work, a bit awkwardly, shoveling fried oysters onto everyone's plate. Later returns from the West gave us Michigan and maybe Missouri. "That's about it," I said, and went back to the White House in the rain.

Mary was still up, and I told her I was pretty sure we'd carried the election. She looked even more relieved than I did. On my way to my room, I overheard her tell her black seamstress, Lizzy Kecklie:

"Now that we've won, I almost wish it were otherwise. Poor Mr. Lincoln is looking so broken-hearted, so completely worn out, I fear he will not get through the next four years."

I think that was what prompted me to tell young Brooks about the looking-glass episode. It had happened one day after the election of 'sixty. The news had come in thick and fast all that day, and I was well tired out and went home to rest, lying down on a couch in Mary's sitting room. Opposite where I lay was a bureau with a swinging glass on it. When I looked into the glass, I saw myself reflected nearly at full length. But my face, I noticed, had two separate and distinct images. Startled me. I got up and looked in the glass, but the illusion vanished. I lay down again and saw it a second time, clearer than before. I noticed that one of the faces was paler than the other—a ghostly pale. I got up and the thing disappeared. I went off, and in the excitement of the hour tried to forget about it. But now and then I would remember the ghostly image and feel a little pang, as if something uncomfortable had happened.

A few days later I told Mary about the ghost and tried to show it to her, but I never succeeded in bringing it back. I probably shouldn't have told Mary because it upset her pretty bad. She thought it was a sign that I was to be elected to a second term. The healthy face indicated I would survive the first four years. But the ghostly pale face, she feared, was an omen that I wouldn't live through my second term.

When the final election returns were in, I'd defeated McClellan by almost half a million popular votes out of some four million cast and had carried every Union state save Delaware, New Jersey, and Kentucky. More than 250,000 soldiers had voted, and a large majority of 'em had gone for me and Johnson. Grant wired us that the Army of the Potomac had given me a majority of 8,208 votes—even the Maryland soldiers in the army voted for the Union ticket by an overwhelming margin.

As far as I'm concerned, the election showed that he who is most devoted to the Union, and most opposed to treason, can receive most of the people's votes. More important, the victory was a popular mandate for my policy of emancipation and reunion. The voice of the people, for the first time, was heard on that question.

The election demonstrated something else, which I pointed out to a group of serenaders. "It has long been a grave question, whether any government not *too* strong for the liberties of its people can be strong *enough* to maintain its own existence in great emergencies. On this point, the present rebellion brought our republic to a severe test. Yes, the election was full of strife, but it has done good, too. It has demonstrated that a people's government can sustain a national election, in the midst of a great civil war. Until now it has not been known to the world that this was a possibility. It shows also how *sound*, and how *strong* we still are."

63. BOOTH

"The King will not be crowned," I cried. "Damn his black soul! So help me God, we'll get Caesar to Richmond before March fourth, next, and President Davis will make him the laughing stock of the civilized world. The day that Caesar is held for ransom will be the proudest day of my twenty-six years."

The day after the election, I rented room No. 20 in the National Hotel, a fashionable Victorian hostelry and a favorite of Baltimore's finest when they were in the city. New Hampshire Congressman John P. Hale and his family lived here, and I knew them well and often escorted Hale's daughters, Lucy and Elizabeth. I told people I was looking to buy land and horses from profits I'd made from my oil investments, but that was my cover. I started stalking Lincoln, observing from doorways and behind trees the time and route of his outings.

I learned that another Confederate agent was in town and was also spying on Lincoln. This was Thomas Nelson Conrad, who had devised a similar kidnapping scheme to mine. He had operated a signal station on the Potomac, had often visited Washington, and thought up his scheme when he saw Lincoln riding alone to the Soldiers' Home. The word was, Conrad had gone to Richmond and won the backing of President Davis and Secretary of War Seddon. I understand that they advanced him $400 in gold to carry out his plot. I didn't ask for money, since I had plenty of my own to use for the southern cause. The next I heard of Conrad, he'd abandoned his mission and left the city, for reasons that were not clear.

On November eleventh or so, I took the train to Charles County in Lower Maryland to meet Dr. Queen and Dr. Mudd, Confederate sympathizers whose knowledge of the country I would need in charting an escape route. I spent two or three days with Dr. Queen at his farm near Bryantown. I showed him my letter of introduction from Martin in Montreal and said I wanted to buy land and horses. I asked him and his son-in-law about the price of land in the area and what roads led from Washington City to the landings on the Potomac. On Sunday I went to church with them, and Queen's son-in-law pointed to a man standing in front of the church and said it was Dr. Samuel A. Mudd. He was a big man, six feet tall, with florid complexion. The son-in-law introduced us, and Mudd and I talked.

"I'm interested in buying land and horses," I said. "Do you know a neighbor who has horses and will sell them cheap?"

"Gardner," he said. "He's got some horses that are good drivers."

"I'll be back," I said.

The next day I returned to Washington where I deposited $1,500 in the bank.

A couple of weeks later, I went to New York City, where my two brothers and I appeared in *Julius Caesar* in the Winter Garden Theater. I preferred the part of Brutus, a sympathetic assassin, but this time I played Marc Antony, Edwin was Brutus, and Junius Brutus was Cassius. Mother and Asia were present, watching us perform from a private box. When the curtain fell to a resounding ovation from the audience, we bowed side by side, and Mother and Asia smiled and waved handkerchiefs at us.

On that same day, rebel agents tried to burn down New York by setting fire to three hotels and Barnum's Museum. One of the hotels was in the same building as the Winter Garden Theater. Fire broke out in the hotel while the play was under way and fire engines rushed to the scene with clanging bells and managed to put the flames out before they could spread to other buildings. The other fires were also extinguished before they could spread, which was rotten luck for us: if New York had gone up in an inferno of fire and smoke, it would have been a glorious victory for Jefferson Davis and his government.

A day or so later I walked along Broadway with a friend and fellow actor, Samuel Knapp Chester. We met several of my other friends. I told them about my recent visit to the oil fields, and they joked about my oil speculations. When Chester and I left, I told him: "I have a better speculation than that, and one they won't laugh at." I told him what it was and invited him to go in with me. He pleaded that he couldn't because he didn't have the means. "I've always liked you, Chester," I said. "I'll *furnish* the means."

Then, wearing a worn hat and thigh-high boots with pistol holsters strapped to them, I headed for Philadelphia to give a package to Asia. I think it was there she told me that Edwin had voted for Lincoln—the only vote he had ever cast—and it filled me with a rage so great I could hardly speak.

"John," she asked a while later, "whatever became of your old friend Michael O'Laughlin? We heard he was in Beauregard's army."

I looked at her with a start. "Michael!" I said. "Why, what possessed you to—to ask about *him*?" I tried to calm down. "He's home, on leave."

"Home on leave, not in the hospital?"

"No. Listen to me, Asia. Forget his name, don't talk about him!"

I changed the subject, pointing out that I had a great carbuncle on my neck that was terribly painful. Asia summoned a physician to examine it. He said it would have to be lanced and laid his instruments on the table. Asia removed the lamp shade to provide more light, and when she did the gas flame caught part of the shade on fire, and I crushed the flames out with my bare hands and then bound my hands with some dress braid. The physician then lanced my neck—it felt as if he had stabbed me with a red-hot poker. Asia took my hands to see how badly they were burned.

"Your palms are so rugged and hard," she said.

"From nights of rowing," I said.

Before I left, I gave her a packet of my letters and asked her to keep the packet for me. In it was my answer to Lincoln's "To Whom It May Concern" letter, giving the reasons for the abduction plot, and a letter to my mother, telling her I was now devoted to a noble duty for my country, by which I meant the Confederacy.

"Lock this in your safe for me," I said. "I may come back for it, but if anything should happen to me, open the packet by yourself and send the letters as directed." I kissed her good-bye many times and left. But in a moment I came back.

"Let me *see* you lock up the packet," I said. Together we opened the heavy iron door of the safe, placed the packet inside, and locked the door. Then I kissed her again.

"God bless you, sister. Take care of yourself and try to be happy."

"Oh, my boy, I shall never be happy till I see your face again."

I took the train back to Washington. The car was full of talk about Sherman. The papers reported that he had burnt Atlanta. That barbaric Hun! I hoped to God some Confederate sharpshooter would get the blackguard in his sights and blow his head off. The atrocities he had visited on Georgia could only have come on Caesar's orders. The thought of that low-born tyrant urging Sherman on made me furious. I gritted my teeth and trembled with rage. There would be a *reckoning* for the crimes they were committing in Georgia!

64. SHERMAN

I'd grouped the four corps of my army into two wings—one under O. O. Howard, the other under Henry Slocum—plus a cavalry division led by Hugh Judson Kilpatrick. I'd made every effort to purge the army of noncombatants, the sick, the feeble, and the faint-hearted. That left me with about sixty-two thousand hardened combat veterans—I called 'em my little devils—who were raring to make Georgia howl. Also had a regiment of Alabama cavalry made up of white Unionists from the hill country. Southern Yankees, is what they were, nonslaveholders who were ready to put the Goddamned slaveowners out of business. Since we planned to live off the country, we had 2,500 mule-drawn wagons and 600 horse-drawn ambulances, all loaded with essentials.

In my orders to the army, I said we would cut loose from our base and forage liberally on the countryside. This wasn't rash. Hell, I read the census statistics: we were going to march through a God-damned *Garden of Eden* that hadn't felt the cruel hand of war, that had plenty of livestock, corn, grain, sweet potatoes, and other vegetables. According to my orders, each brigade commander would organize a foraging party to gather food from plantations and home-steads along the line of march. Cavalry and artillerymen, I said, could also take horses, mules, and wagons. I cautioned the soldiers, however, that they were not to enter the homes of civilians or to lift personal belongings—jewelry and the like.

I also told the army not to take any nigger refugees. Grant had urged me to "clean the country of Negroes," but I wasn't going to do that: would just slow us down. Only niggers I wanted were able-bodied men to work as army laborers.

Just before the army started, General Howard—we called him "Old Prayer Book" because of his piety—called at my headquarters while a servant was massaging my right arm, which was hurting from an attack of rheumatism so Goddamned bad I couldn't write. Howard said he understood that he was to be second in command and wanted to know my objectives in full. I went to a map and with a finger traced the route the army would take to the sea and up through South Carolina to Goldsboro, North Carolina. "I believe we can go there," I said, pointing to Goldsboro. "When we reach there, Lee will have to leave Virginia, and Grant and me will whup him."

The army started marching on November fifteenth, leaving the Fourteenth Corps to bring up the rear. Under my orders, Colonel O. M. Poe of the engineers and two Michigan regiments systematically destroyed everything in Atlanta the rebels might be able to use. They wrecked and burned all shops, factories, foundries, warehouses, machine shops, and mills. They leveled the great railroad depot and torched the stacks of bedding and tents and the broken-down wagons stored in it. The Johnnies had used one machine shop as an arsenal, and there were stacks of round shot and explosive shells in it. When the building was set on fire, the shells exploded with spectacular effect, and fragments came Goddamned close to Judge Lyon's hilltop mansion where I had my headquarters. A great firestorm roared out of depot square and swept over a block of stores, hotels, theaters, slave markets, and Washington Hall.

I stood at a window of Lyon's house and watched as the heart of Atlanta burned. Immense fires lit up the sky and could probably be seen at Griffin, fifty miles away. Bursts of dense, black smoke with tongues of flame rolled up toward the heavens. The skeletons of great warehouses blazed eerily against the night.

As I stared at the blazing city, I rubbed my hair with both hands, drummed my fingers on the windowsill, lit a cigar, and blew smoke furiously from my mouth and nostrils. "Atlanta," I told my staff. "I've been fighting Atlanta all this time. It's done more to keep up the war than any other city—well, except Richmond. All the guns and wagons we've captured along the way—all were marked 'Atlanta.' They were made here. They've done so much to destroy us, we've got to destroy Atlanta—at least enough to stop any more of that."

Next morning I left Atlanta with the Fourteenth Corps, which brought up the rear of Slocum's left wing. Slocum was marching along the Georgia Railroad, heading east in the direction of Decatur and Augusta. Howard's right wing was moving south toward Jonesboro and Macon, tearing up the Macon & Western Central Railroad as it went. The divergent lines of march were designed to threaten both Macon and Augusta and confuse the rebels as to where we were heading. Our rendezvous point was Milledgeville, the state capital, a hundred miles to the southeast.

I was riding Little Sam, my favorite mount, with my broad-brimmed black hat pulled down over my ears. The road as far as the eye could see was full of marching troops, kicking up clouds of dust as they tramped along. When we reached the hill just outside the old rebel works, we paused to look back on the scenes of our past battles. We could see the copse of wood where McPherson had fallen. Behind us lay Atlanta, smoldering and in ruins, the black smoke rising high in the air and hanging like a pall over the remains of the city. Away off in the distance, on the McDonough Road, were the rear troops of Howard's column, their gun barrels glistening in the sun, the white-topped wagons stretching away to the south. And right before us, the Fourteenth Corps marched steadily and rapidly, with a cheery look and a swinging pace that made light of the thousand miles that lay between us and Richmond. A band struck up the anthem, "John Brown's soul goes marching on." The men caught up the refrain and never before had I heard the chorus of "Glory, glory hallelujah!" done with more spirit. Then we turned our horses to the east. Atlanta was soon lost behind a screen of trees and became a thing of the past.

One of our main goals was to destroy the railroad communications between the Deep South and the rebel army and government in Virginia, and both wings set about that task with a "devil-may-care" spirit. By means of large iron hooks and crowbars, they pried up the rails and piled 'em on bonfires made of rail ties. When the rails were red hot, the men twisted 'em around tree trunks or telegraph poles— they called 'em "Sherman's neckties." At every milepost, the wrecking crews left rails twisted in the form of "US."

My staff and I camped the first night by the roadside near Lithonia. Stone Mountain, a mass of granite, was in plain view, cut out in clear outline against the sky. The whole horizon was lurid with bonfires and flames of burning buildings, which marched steadily eastward all that night. I smoked cigars and slept little, and next day, in the saddle again, we saw two cotton gins burned to the ground and foraging parties at work on farms and plantations, where whites stared sullenly from behind closed windows. A brigade's foraging party usually numbered fifty men; they went off before daylight and foraged on farms and plantations out on our flanks, where they served all the military uses of flankers. They would liberate a wagon or family carriage, load it with bacon, cornmeal, turkeys, chickens, and ducks, then return to the main road and deliver their supplies to the brigade commissary when it came up. I often passed foraging parties at the roadside waiting for their wagons to come up and was amused at their strange collection of mules, horses, and cattle. They were packed with old saddles and loaded with ham, bacon, bags of cornmeal, poultry of every description, and fine sweet potatoes.

Wasn't long before we reached the handsome town of Covington, just south of the Georgia Railroad, where soldiers closed up ranks and color bearers unfurled their flags, and the bands struck up patriotic airs. White people, despite their hatred of the Yankee invaders, came out of their houses to stare at the sight, and the niggers were frantic with joy. Whenever they heard my name, they clustered about my horse, shouted and prayed in their peculiar style. I saw one poor girl, in the very ecstasy of the Methodist "shout," hugging a regimental banner and jumping up to the "feet of Jesus."

Beyond Covington, we came across a group of soldiers who were plundering a homestead, chasing after chickens and pigs in the yard. These were stragglers, men who'd dropped out of the ranks to reap the riches of the countryside, despite my orders against plundering. An old woman ran out to me and begged me to save her something, even post a guard to protect her property, but I told her I couldn't do that and rode on.

I told my staff, "I'll have to harden my heart to these things. That poor woman—how could I help her? The soldiers will take all she has. I don't like straggling, but to stop it I'd have to post a Goddamned guard at every house. We can't do that."

The stragglers became too numerous to control. They roamed far and wide and were often gone for days at a time. We called 'em "bummers," but that name became associated with all foragers. The stragglers committed outrages, won't deny it: pillaged and robbed homesteads, put the inhabitants to flight, carried off their silver and gold coin, plates, carpets, satins and silks, and burned down their houses.

"For the first two years of the war," I told my staff, "no man did more than I did to try to stop straggling and plundering. I personally beat and kicked men out of yards and houses—but it was hopeless. Goddamn it, an army is a terrible engine and hard to control." This one certainly was: we were cutting a sixty-mile swath of destruction through the heart of Georgia, leaving wrecked railroads, fire-scarred chimneys, the ruins of barns and cotton factories in our wake. "Blame all this on Jefferson Davis and the other sons-of-bitches who led the South into war," I said. "Maybe they'll look back to the day when, as a stranger in Louisiana, I begged 'em not to secede, warned 'em it would be fatal, the death of everything they held dear."

Frankly, I had no qualms about bringing the war to the civilian population. We were not only fighting hostile armies, but a hostile people, and must make old and young, rich and poor, feel the hard hand of war. My aim was to *humble* their pride, make 'em *fear* and *dread* us. The more awful you make war, I said, the sooner it will be over. War is *hell*. No other way to describe it. Sure, they called me a monster, but the real monster was war itself, and now it had come to feed on the fair face of Georgia.

Still, this campaign was different. It had no great pitched battles, no frontal assaults against fortifications, no horrendous casualties. Compared to Shiloh, Missionary Ridge, and Kennesaw Mountain, there was minimal loss of life. One of our brigades did fight about four thousand raw Georgia militia at Griswoldville and routed 'em with repeating rifles, with a loss of three hundred dead on their side and only thirteen killed and seventy-nine wounded on our side. Wheeler's rebel cavalry harassed our front and rear, skirmished with Kilpatrick's boys, and bushwhacked our bummers, but that and the tussle at Griswoldville was the extent of the fighting. We were making war, not against an organized enemy army, but against the *enemy's war economy*, destroying its ability to support rebel military forces and the traitor government in Richmond. For that, the rebels called me the Attila of the West. Fuck 'em. I didn't give a shit what they called me.

We camped that night on Judge Harris's plantation eleven miles out from Covington. An advanced guard was already there, sitting along the road, sipping sorghum molasses from cups and canteens. A soldier passed me with a ham on his musket, a jug of sorghum molasses under his arm, and eating a big piece of honey he was holding in his hand. When he saw me glaring at him, he said: "Just foraging liberally on the country, sir." Everybody laughed except me.

"Soldier," I said, "foraging is restricted to the regular parties properly detailed for that purpose."

"Yes, sir," he said and sauntered on with his plunder.

When my staff and I reined up in the yard, four or five stout slave men came up to us, said they had skeedaddled from their masters four or five miles off to go with us. Major Henry Hitchcock of my staff asked 'em if they knew how we treated Negroes.

"White folks tole us you burned the men in the houses," one said, "and drowned the women and children."

"Did you believe it?"

"No, sir! We didn't believe it—we has faith in you."

A coal black young man said: "White folks here, they don't think nothin' 'bout tying up a feller and givin' him two hundred or three hundred strokes with the strap."

That evening I had a long talk with a gray-haired old colored, with as fine a head as I ever saw. "Well, now, old man," I said, "what do you think about the war?"

"Well, sir, I've thought a lot about it, till I hardly knows what to think."

"But you do think about it," I said. "Come now, tell me just what you think. Don't be afraid. We're friends."

"Well, sir, what I think is this—it's mighty depressin', this war, but it 'pears to me like *the right thing couldn't be done* without it. Abolishin' slavery, I mean. I know you say you's fightin' for the Union, but I 'spect it's all about slavery—and you're gonna set us free."

The old fellow got it just right. "Do all slaves understand that?" I asked.

"Sholy does."

"You must stay where you are and not load us down with too many extra mouths to feed. You'd eat up all the soldiers' food. If we win the war, you're free. We can take along some of the young, strong men, but if you swarm after us, old and young, feeble and helpless, you'll just cripple us."

I said the same thing to other slaves, but it did no good: vast numbers of 'em, up to twenty-five thousand at a time, attached themselves to the rear of the army. "They think it's freedom now or never," said one of my soldiers. They followed us on foot, in carts and buggies, on horses and mules, dressed in all manner of patched-up garments, and I cussed the Goddamned extra mouths we had to feed. An extraordinary number of 'em were women with babies in their arms and older children clinging to their ragged skirts. One mother hid her two boys in a wagon—I guess she wanted 'em to make it to freedom even if she didn't. Mothers on mules told their babies to hold on tight behind 'em, but many of 'em fell off and drowned in the swamps. Along the roadside mothers were crying for lost children, and lost children were crying for their mothers.

At night, the blacks gathered in gypsy camps on the fringes of our bivouacs. They lived on the charity of my men and what they could find in the wake of our foragers. Around their fires, they played banjos, fiddles, and homemade drums, rattled bones, and danced and sang and juggled. Many of my soldiers, I'm sorry to say, eyed the pretty slave girls, especially the octoroons, and visited 'em at night for carnal purposes. During the day the girls would walk with the soldiers, carrying their rifles and cooking utensils. I saw a group of 'em riding in some baggage wagons and made 'em get out and get the hell back to the rear where they belonged.

We reached Madison on November nineteenth, and the mayor met Slocum outside of town and begged him not to burn their God-damn town. Niggers thronged the street and shouted at the top of their lungs when Slocum burned the depot, the courthouse, and the slave pen. Behind us, for seventy miles, the railroad back to Atlanta was thoroughly destroyed. Beyond Madison, Slocum's columns turned southward for Milledgeville, and I heard the soldiers talk as I rode by: "There goes the old man. All's right."

Three days later we camped for a day on the plantation of How-ell Cobb, a major general in the rebel army and one of the "head devils" of the Confederacy, as Major Hitchcock of my staff described him. The place had six thousand acres and a hundred slaves at its peak, but only forty were there now, the old, the decrepit, and the young. We confiscated Cobb's property, finding it rich in corn, beans, peanuts, and sorghum molasses.

"Come on!" I told the slaves. "We're your friends. You needn't be afraid of us. All this is for you—corn, wheat, molasses."

A woman said: "Our white folks tole us you would string us up, every one. They said you put black folks out front in the battles and killed 'em if they didn't fight. They said you threw women and chil-dren into the Chattahoochee River and roasted 'em in the Atlanta fire." I assured 'em this was all hateful rebel propaganda—not a word of it was true. Then I told my soldiers: "Let the coloreds have what they want here, then confiscate or burn everything else of value." That would teach Mr. Howell Cobb the price of treason.

As we bore down on Milledgeville, we heard that the rebel legis-lature was in session. When we entered the capital on the eighth day out from Atlanta, Governor Brown, other state officers, and the leg-islators all ignominiously fled, in the utmost disorder and confusion, some by rail, some by carriage, and many on foot. As Slocum's columns streamed into town, I occupied the governor's mansion and raised Old Glory over it.

"First act of the drama well played, General!" said Major Hitch-cock.

"Yes, sir, the first act is played."

This was a pretty, tree-shaded little town, with fine homes, a hotel, a statehouse, an arsenal, and an insane asylum, where the leg-islators no doubt stayed. Some of Slocum's officers gathered in the vacant Hall of Representatives in the statehouse, elected a speaker, and declared themselves the legislature of the state of Georgia. Inspired to mischief by generous tugs on the bottle, they repealed the secession ordinance (it was "a damned farce"), voted the state back into the Union, and appointed a committee to kick the asses of Jeff Davis and Governor Brown. While they engaged in hilarious, besot-ted debate, soldiers ran into the hall crying, "The Yankees are com-ing!" The "members" fled in bedlam, as the real legislators had done, and the soldiers proceeded to plunder the statehouse. They found piles of worthless Confederate bank notes and used 'em to make campfires. They also discovered stands of cutlasses and medieval pikes with which, for want of firearms, the sons of Georgia intended to turn back the evil invader.

On Thanksgiving day, escapees from Andersonville prison stag-gered into town, and soldiers celebrating in the streets stopped to stare at them. The scarecrows had walked almost a hundred miles with rebel patrols and bloodhounds on their trail, and their eyes had the look of wild animals. The stories they told of Andersonville—of starvation, torture, scurvy, and murder, of deaths by the hundreds each day—sickened and enraged us all.

So did Davis and Beauregard, who exhorted Georgia civilians to fight a guerrilla war against us. It was all in the papers we found in Milledgeville. They urged civilians to burn bridges and forage in our front, to throw fallen trees across the roads and bury shells under the surface which would explode when we stepped on 'em. One paper printed Beauregard's appeal to the citizens of Georgia from Corinth. "Arise for the defense of your native soil! Obstruct and destroy all the roads in Sherman's front, flank, and rear, and his army will soon starve in your midst."

I felt justified in calling, henceforth, for a devastation more or less relentless. The two wings of the army united at Milledgeville and then diverged again, with plans to rendezvous at Sandersville on the Georgia Central Railroad. Our only opposition was Wheeler's cav-alry, which got in front of us and tried to cover all the roads we might take. To draw off Wheeler and deceive the rebels again, I ordered Kilpatrick's cavalry to ride north, feint against Augusta and break the Augusta-Savannah Railroad, and then dash down to Millen. If possible, he was to seize the rebel prison there and liberate the captives. Kilpatrick, known as Little Kil, was reckless and unpopular. "I know he's a hell of a damned fool," I said, "but I want just that sort of man to command my cavalry on this march."

Still traveling with Slocum's wing, I rode with my staff east by southeast toward Sandersville. The country was swampy, and the moss-hung forests were full of croaking, screeching creatures and slithering snakes. At one homestead a sharp-tongued young hussy bawled us out for taking her stock. "You got no right to punish helpless women who've never done anything," she said. We asked where her young men friends had gone. "In the army," she said. Had she used her influence to keep them at home? "No. If they hadn't gone to war, the women here would've called them cowards."

"That's why you're getting punished," I said. "You've done all you could to help the war, and have not done what you could to prevent it."

Our scouts reported that the enemy had burnt the bridge in the swamplands over Buffalo Creek. The Negroes said it was done by a party from Sandersville, and it pissed me off that we had to waste time repairing it.

"In war," I said, "everything is right which prevents anything. If bridges are burned, I've got a right to burn all the houses near it. Goddamn it, I mean to do it, too."

Major Hitchcock protested. "Indiscriminate punishment isn't right. There ought to be proof connecting a man to the burning of a bridge before destroying his house."

"Well, let him look to his own people," I said. "If they find that burning bridges destroys their neighbors' houses, they'll stop it."

"I suppose you're right," Hitchcock said. "Like you say, war is war, a horrible necessity at best, and when forced on us, as this war is, we must make it so terrible that when peace comes it will *last*."

After a four-hour delay to repair the bridge, we were on the march again. That evening we halted at a double-log house with a cotton screw-press and huge stacks of fodder in the yard. Soldiers swarmed across the yard, overturning a beehive. Impervious to the attacking bees, they took out the honeycomb and carted all the fodder to the wagons. I ordered the cotton screw-press burned, and it was done.

Inside the cabin there wasn't much left—soldiers had evidently been here earlier. In one room we found an old lady and a young woman with several little kids. Both women were in great distress, weeping and carrying on, Jesus, it was disturbing. The old woman cried out bitterly, "I hope the Lord will reward us all by our *deeds*. It's very hard for a poor old woman like me to have *everything* she has taken from her, *everything*."

After we rode on, the old lady troubled me so much that I had coffee and other supplies taken back to her.

As we approached Sandersville, the rendezvous point for the two wings, our scouts reported that Wheeler's cavalry had occupied the town, prepared to fight a rear-guard action, and that a lynch mob had hanged some of Wheeler's Union prisoners. When word of that spread down the line, the entire wing was spoiling for a fight. Slocum's lead brigade deployed and went forward in line of battle. Ahead of 'em, our skirmishers charged Wheeler's cavalry at double quick and, cheering wildly, chased 'em out of town.

When we entered Sandersville, we learned that the rebels had fired at our skirmishers from street corners, from behind houses, and from the second-story parapet of the courthouse. I dismounted and sat on the steps of a large brick house. I was mad as hell about the lynching of the Federal prisoners and the firing on my men from the Goddamn courthouse. When the lady of the house came out and demanded Federal protection, I glared at her. "You'll be protected," I said, "but I mean to burn the town as punishment for the people who burned the bridge and hanged our soldiers."

A Methodist minister came up and begged me to spare the women and children. "The men who lynched your soldiers were not Georgians, much less inhabitants of Sandersville."

"I don't make war on women and children," I said, and turned to several women who had gathered around. "Your houses won't be burned. But the courthouse will, because it was used as a fort to fire on my men."

We stayed long enough to see the courthouse go up in flames. Then we rode down to Tannille Station and found it, too, a smoking ruins. An old nigger described how our men had burnt it. "Dem Yankees, some of 'em come down here and first burn the depot. Den some more come and dey burn de railroad, then some more come and dey burn up de well. Dem Yankees is de most *destructionist* people ever I see."

My staff and I now switched over and rode with Howard's right wing, which had been tearing up the Georgia Central and continued to do it as we moved south toward Savannah. The Georgia Central, which led from Macon to Savannah, was Richmond's vital railroad connection with the fertile regions of Georgia, Alabama, and Mississippi. Its destruction was an irreversible blow to Davis and Lee—"to say nothing," added Major Hitchcock, "of the moral effect at home and abroad of such a march as this through the heart of the South's Empire State."

As we rode along sandy roads through the pine woods, we often laughed about Jeff Davis's idea that this army would be starved out. Hell, no army on earth had ever had so much to eat. General Frank Blair, commander of the Seventeenth Corps, was riding with us, and he mentioned that he'd read some "absurdly desperate stuff" in a Georgia paper of the twentieth. "Paper claimed that Hood had completely succeeded in 'cutting Sherman's communications,'" Blair said, which made us laugh like hell. "Said that Sherman was forced to his present 'desperate retreat through Georgia to the seacoast' with an army of not over twenty-five thousand men. Ever hear such Goddamned lunacy?"

As we approached the Ogeechee River, we learned that General Hardee had assumed command of the defense of Savannah with a small force of infantry and some irregulars. He meant to make a stand on the Ogeechee line behind fortifications at the railroad bridge. I had no intention of attacking him there and sent the Fourteenth Corps to Louisville to turn his flank, which it did, forcing him to retreat. We crossed the Ogeechee River on a pontoon bridge and continued to wreck the Georgia Central, leaving the trees decorated with Sherman's neckties.

At night, I slept little and prowled the camp restlessly, wearing slippers, red flannel drawers, a woolen shirt, and an old dressing gown. I poked at the embers of the fire and talked with whoever was still awake about the march, the war, the weather, the magnificent live oaks and magnolias in the area, and my late hours. I always woke up at three or four in the morning and liked to get up and be about because it was the best time to hear any movement in the distance. I made up the lost sleep by taking naps in the daytime.

On our way to Millen, we finally heard from Kilpatrick: his cavalry had routed the few militia and irregulars in front of the army and had fought Wheeler's cavalry near Augusta, but Wheeler made such a ferocious battle of it that Little Kil and his horsemen found themselves in a desperate struggle—had to fight a delaying action, falling back from one road barricade to another, fighting enemy horsemen hand to hand with clanging sabers and cracking pistols. Kil was finally rescued when Slocum hurried a full infantry division to his support.

On December third, I rode into Millen with Blair's corps. This was a vital railroad junction, with lines converging from Savannah, Augusta, and Macon and Atlanta. There was a wretched prison pen at Millen whose captives we'd hoped to liberate, but the rebels had removed 'em to some other hellhole. The Millen prison was a crude, foul-smelling stockade without shelter or a well or a spring inside the enclosure. We counted 750 graves and one bloated body still lying on the ground, unburied. Said one of my officers: "Gives convincing proof, doesn't it, that the criminal suffering of our men at Andersonville was not exaggerated."

Made me and everybody who saw it mad as hell. I told Kilpatrick: "Make the most complete and perfect possible break of the railroads about Millen. Let it be more devilish than can be dreamed of." His men ripped up the track in all directions and put the torch to the railroad depot, storehouses, and a hotel, which sent dense columns of black smoke and flames boiling into the sky. When we left for Savannah, Millen had ceased to exist as a railroad center.

We learned at Millen that Bragg was in Augusta and that Richmond, thinking that was our destination, had sent Wade Hampton there to organize a large cavalry force to stop us. Ha! Did we have the bastards fooled! We'd severed the rail line connecting Augusta to Millen and Savannah—no way they could bring their forces down by train. Hardee was between us and Savannah, with a force of about fifteen thousand men, but he didn't know where we were heading either, and in any case his force was too small to cover the roads.

65. DAVIS

We were desperately trying to concentrate troops to stop Sherman in his relentless march of destruction through Georgia. I sent Bragg to Augusta with orders to assemble and employ all available forces against Sherman, and I telegraphed Hardee that when Sherman's purpose was known, Hardee was to make every effort to obstruct his route. But when Sherman approached, Hardee fell back to Savannah, leaving us all in despair.

Frantic appeals for help poured into Richmond from every corner of Georgia, which caused me the most acute anxiety I had ever felt. A trail of vandalism unmatched in modern history marked Sherman's course through Georgia, where he encountered only helpless women and children. Not a single house was spared, not even a church, from Atlanta southward. The arson of the houses of noncombatants and the robbery of their property, extending even to trinkets worn by women, made the devastation as relentless as savage instincts could dictate. Even worse was their assaults on our women. A newspaper reported that the Yankee soldiers ravished white women in Milledgeville, driving one victim insane, and then held a miscegenation ball with nigger women. The raping and looting and burning frightened the poor white women of Georgia so badly that they fled into the woods and fields, weeping and crying out to God to help them.

The responsibility for such atrocities extended to the Administration in Washington, which, in order to effect our subjugation, ordered the devastation of our fields and the destruction of our crops and railroads, which reduced our soldiers, our people, and our prisoners to the most frightful condition for food. Our medicines for the sick were exhausted, and contrary to the usages of civilized warfare, were made contraband of war by our enemy. The responsibility for these distressing events rested on Abraham Lincoln, who repeatedly turned to the northern people and, charging us with atrocious cruelties to their sons, who were our prisoners, appealed to them to fill up his armies and take vengeance on us by our abject subjugation or entire extermination.

It all made me sick, so sick that rumors flew through Richmond that I was dying, was perhaps already dead. It was all I could do to drag myself to my desk and run my one good eye over the depressing dispatches from Georgia and Tennessee. I could not believe Hood's misfortune in Tennessee. At Franklin, he found an entire enemy corps drawn up behind fortifications and sent his army forward in a futile frontal attack, across two miles of open fields in what amounted to a reversal of Fredericksburg. Hood suffered seven thousand casualties, lost twelve generals and nearly sixty regimental commanders, which left him with only twenty-five thousand men. Would the chain of woes never cease? I cursed myself for ever letting Hood move into Tennessee. He should have gone after Sherman, as I had originally instructed him to do. Instead, he drove his battered, spiritless little army in the opposite direction, toward Nashville, where a huge Federal force and utter disaster awaited him.

66. LINCOLN

Sherman's brother called at the Executive Mansion and asked if I knew where the general was heading. "Nope," I said. "I know the hole he went in at, but I can't tell you what hole he'll come out of." Sherman was so much on my mind that at a public reception I shook hands absently and stared into space. "Sorry," I told an old acquaintance I hadn't recognized. "I was thinking of a man down South." I praised Sherman and his march in my message to Congress in early December. "The most remarkable feature in the military operations of the year," I said, "is General Sherman's attempted march of three hundred miles directly through the insurgent region. It tends to show a great increase of our relative strength that our general in chief should feel able to confront and hold in check every active force of the enemy, and yet to detach a well-appointed large army to move on such an expedition."

I was holding a conference when Colonel A. H. Markland, of the army postal service, stopped by on his way south with mail for Sherman. I walked across the room and shook Markland's hand. "Colonel, I heard from General Grant that you were going to find Sherman. When you see him, take his hand and tell him, for me, God bless him and God bless his army. That's as much as I can say, and more than I can write." As Markland started to leave, I called to him. "Now remember what I said. God bless Sherman and all his army."

67. SHERMAN

We were just nine miles from Savannah when I came upon General Blair and a group of men standing around a handsome young officer whose leg had been blown to pieces by a torpedo planted in the road. Tupper was his name—he was the adjutant of the First Alabama Union Cavalry. He was waiting for a surgeon to amputate his leg. Another torpedo had exploded and wounded several others less seriously.

"I was riding along with the rest of my staff," Tupper said, "when my horse stepped on the torpedo. The explosion killed my horse and did a pretty good job on my leg." I looked at his leg, which was badly torn and mutilated; muscles were ripped, the bloody end of a bone stuck out, the knee was shattered. I gritted my teeth in anger. The rebels had the Goddamn nerve to call *us* barbarians. The fucking cowards had planted eight-inch shells in the road, each loaded with about five pounds of powder with friction matches to explode them when they were stepped on. This wasn't war, I stormed, it was Goddamned *murder*!

Blair had brought a group of rebel prisoners up from the rear, armed 'em with spades and picks, and ordered 'em to clear the land mines from the road.

They appealed to me for mercy. "You can't send us out there to get blowed up—in the name of humanity, General."

"Your people put 'em there to assassinate our men." I pointed to Tupper's leg. "Is that humanity?"

"It wasn't us, General. We don't know where the things are buried."

"I don't give a damn if you're blown up. I'll not have my own men killed like this."

The rebels went ahead, and I could hardly help laughing as they tiptoed gingerly along the road, fearful that sunken torpedoes might explode at each step. With great care, without an accident, they uncovered seven additional torpedoes.

The two wings of the army were united now, and next day, December tenth, moving four corps abreast, we reached the rebel fortifications protecting Savannah. I wanted to reconnoiter the rebel lines in person and with my staff rode down the road into a dense forest of oak, pine, and cypress. We dismounted and walked over to the railroad track, which led straight into the city. About eight hundred yards away was a rebel parapet and a battery of guns. The cannoneers at one gun were preparing to fire, and I told my aides to scatter. I saw the white puff of smoke, heard the boom, and caught sight of the ball as it rose in flight and fell straight toward me. *Those bastards are trying to kill me*, I thought, and stepped aside. The ball, a thirty-two-pound shot, struck the ground near me and ricocheted into a Negro who was crossing the track at that instant. The ball took his head clean off, splattering the ground with brains and blood. His headless body quivered violently as blood spewed out of his severed neck. A soldier spread an overcoat over the body and we all got the hell away from that railroad.

The Savannah defenses were too strong to try a frontal attack, so I resolved to put Hardee under siege and starve him out. My corps commanders proceeded to invest the city from the Savannah River north of it to the Ogeechee south of it. With that, the march through Georgia was over. Behind us lay a swath of unredeemable destruction sixty miles wide and a hundred and sixty miles long. The railroads in all directions were so completely wrecked that they could not be used again. We burned all the cotton, took all the provisions and livestock, burned every building of military value and a great many that weren't, and left the entire area a smoldering, fire-scarred wasteland. In my report to Washington, I estimated the damage at $100 million and pointed out that we'd consumed stores and provisions essential to Lee's and Hood's armies. To some in the North, I said, the march might seem a hard species of warfare, but it brought the harsh realities of war home to the southern people. It demonstrated the complete *inability* of their armies and leaders to protect them, and it effectively knocked the state out of the war. I thought Georgians would not forget the grief and terror of that march for as long as they lived.

Our immediate goal was to establish a coastal base and open communications with the Federal fleet waiting for us offshore. The shortest route to the ocean was along the Ogeechee River south of Savannah, but Fort McAllister, which guarded the river near its mouth, would have to be taken first. I ordered General William B. Hazen to take his Second Division of the Fifteenth Corps—my old division, veterans of Shiloh and Vicksburg—and carry the fort by storm. It was strong in heavy artillery on the seaward side, I told Hazen, but was weak in the rear, on the landward side. He was to attack it there.

Howard, myself, and several staff officers mounted the roof of a rice mill to watch the assault. While Hazen was marching into position, someone pointed to a small column of smoke and an object gliding along the horizon, which grew little by little until we recognized it as the smokestack of a steamer coming up the river. When I saw Old Glory flying on its mast, I said, "My God, Howard, it's one of our gunboats!" A navy signal man waved a question from the deck: "Who are you?" Our flag man answered: "General Sherman. Who are you?" The answer: "Admiral Dahlgren. Is the fort taken?"

I told my man to reply: "No, but it will be in a few minutes."

Through our glasses, we saw Hazen's troops come out of the dark ring of woods encircling the fort and move toward it at a brisk pace with all colors flying.

"There they go, Howard," I said. "Not a waver. Grand, grand."

The fort's big guns sprang alive, belching forth dense clouds of smoke, which soon obscured our assaulting lines. One flag went down, but rose again. Through rifts in the sulfurous smoke, we saw our lines again, advancing toward a ravine in front of the fort. "They're up," somebody cried. "They're going in!" They hurled logs across the ravine and moved up the slope toward the parapets. Explosions sounded; bodies and body parts flew into the air. "Torpedoes!" I cried. "God*damn* it!" Then the guns stopped. "They're on the parapets," I said. "They've taken it, Howard. I've got Savannah." I danced a jig on the roof and said: "Hardtack tonight, boys! Hardtack tonight!" Then I sent a message back to Slocum. "Take a good big drink, a long breath, and then yell like the devil. The fort is ours. We've got a coastal base. The cracker line is open."

Next day I visited Dahlgren on his flagship. I was in a fine mood and told the naval officers about the destruction my army had visited on Georgia. "I could look forty miles in each direction and see smoke rolling up like one great bonfire," I said. "The march demonstrates a great truth: that armies even of vast magnitude do not have to be tied down to a base. I can't say enough good things about my men, they are in splendid order and equal to anything. With the fall of Fort McAllister, I regard Savannah as already ours." I went to the officers room and scribbled off hasty messages to Grant, Stanton, and Halleck, then returned to the naval officers. "I'm going to march to Richmond next," I said. "I expect to turn north by the end of the month, and when I go through South Carolina, where treason began, it will be one of the most horrible things in the history of the world. The devil himself won't be able to restrain my men in that state."

I returned to our lines before Savannah and found Colonel Markland at my headquarters with mail from the North. "I've brought you a message from the president," he said. "He asked me to shake your hand and say, 'God bless you and the army.'"

"Thank the president for me," I said. "Tell him my army is fine."

There was a dispatch from Grant. "I have concluded," he said, "that the most important operation toward closing out the rebellion will be to close out Lee and his army. My idea now is that you establish a base on the seacoast, leave in it all your artillery and cavalry, and enough infantry to protect them, and with the balance of your command come here by water with all dispatch."

That order frustrated the shit out of me. I turned to one of my aides. "Come here, Dayton!" I went into my headquarters, slammed the door, and swore. "I won't do it, Goddamn it! I won't do anything of the kind." I calmed down, though, when I realized that it would take a hundred steamers to transport my army to Virginia and that it would take weeks to get 'em all here. I had plenty of time to plead my case to Grant and Washington. I told Grant that if given time I would have possession of Savannah and implored him to let me turn north after that and punish South Carolina as she deserved. I wrote Halleck that every step I took from this point northward was as much an attack on Lee as if I were operating within the sound of his artillery. Halleck agreed, and Grant too came around, telling me I could operate from Savannah as I saw fit.

In his earlier dispatch to me, Grant had complained bitterly about Thomas. "Hood has him close in Nashville," Grant said. "I have said all I can to force him to attack without giving a positive order. Today I could stand it no longer and gave the order without any reserve." Slowtrot Thomas was at it again, dallying in Nashville while a tattered little rebel army held him hostage. It was disgusting in the extreme. I learned later that Grant was so upset with Thomas that he considered going to Nashville and relieving him in person. But on December fifteenth, Thomas finally attacked Hood with sledgehammer blows, all but annihilating his army as a fighting force, with Wilson's cavalry chasing the remnants of it clear back into Mississippi. I never liked Thomas personally, thought him too Goddamn docile and slow as a cow, but I had to concede him a magnificent victory at Nashville. I even sent him my congratulations: "I do not believe your own wife is more happy at the result than I am."

On December seventeenth I demanded that Hardee surrender Savannah, but he refused. Briefly I considered an assault, but opted instead for a complete investment of the city. We had it closed off on the north, west, and south, but there remained open, to the east, the Union Causeway, an old plank road leading into South Carolina. I knew Hardee would put a pontoon bridge across the Savannah River so that he could escape on that road, so I took a steamer up to our military base on Hilton Head and arranged for transports to carry a body of troops from our right flank around to the east side of the

Savannah River, to cut off Hardee's escape route. On my way back, a quartermaster tug pulled alongside and reported that Hardee and his little garrison had already made good their escape and that my army was in Savannah. I was damned disappointed that we hadn't bagged Hardee, but we had the big prize, the city of Savannah.

Next day, December twenty-second, I sent a message to the president. "I beg to present you as a Christmas gift the city of Savannah, with one hundred and fifty heavy guns and plenty of ammunition, also about twenty-five thousand bales of cotton."

68. LINCOLN

"Many, many thanks for your Christmas gift," I wrote Sherman. "When you were about leaving Atlanta for the Atlantic coast, I was *anxious*, if not fearful; but feeling that you were the better judge, and remembering that 'nothing risked, nothing gained,' I did not interfere. Now, the undertaking being a success, the honor is all yours, for I believe none of us went further than to acquiesce. And, taking the work of Gen. Thomas into the count, it is indeed a great success. Not only does it afford the obvious and immediate military advantages; but, in showing to the world that your army could be divided, putting the stronger part to an important new service, and yet leaving enough to vanquish the old opposition force—Hood's army—it brings those who sat in darkness, to see a great light. But what next? I suppose it will be safer if I leave Gen. Grant and yourself to decide."

It was indeed. No need for me to interfere with those two in charge. In any case I had my hands full that winter, trying to get Congress to seat the elected representatives from Louisiana and Arkansas, which I'd reconstructed by my 10 percent plan as set forth in my Proclamation of Amnesty and Reconstruction in late 'sixty-three. When Congress convened in early December, Sumner was the chief opponent of my reconstruction program, particularly in Louisiana. I called him to the Executive Mansion and tried to make him see the light about Louisiana.

"The state's hostile rebel majority would love to see the new government fail," I told him. "That's how you measure how worthwhile it is—by the color of its opposition. And Louisiana's new free-state constitution is excellent, better for the poor black man than what we have in Illinois. Thanks to the army's protection, Louisiana has a foundation to build on for the future. We'll sooner have the fowl by hatching the egg than by smashing it."

"Mr. President," he said in his Boston accent, "the eggs of crocodiles can produce only crocodiles. I fail to see how eggs laid by military power can be hatched into an American state. And in any case, reconstruction is not your responsibility. It's Congress's and Congress's alone. But my chief objection to your so-called reconstructed governments is their failure to enfranchise the blacks. They are the only true Unionists in the South. Their votes are as necessary as their muskets. I think you realize the shortcomings of what you've done in Louisiana and Arkansas. Didn't you allude to that in your message the other day, warning that more rigorous measures are likely to come?"

I had indeed. It was a signal that I was willing to compromise with congressional Radicals over reconstruction. The bitter rift between us, caused by my pocket veto of the Wade-Davis bill, had pretty much disappeared when the party won big in the state and national elections. Old Taney had died recently, and my appointment of Chase, a Radical, as chief justice of the Supreme Court also helped bring us together. When I told the Radicals in the House I was willing to meet 'em halfway, we worked out a deal: they would accept my reconstruction governments in Louisiana and Arkansas, and I would sign legislation that reconstructed the other rebel states along the lines of the Wade-Davis bill, which had a tougher oath and voter qualifications than my 10 percent plan.

The sticking point was black suffrage. The Democrats and many Republicans, like most of the country, opposed any form of suffrage for Negroes. The Radicals, on the other hand, wanted to enfranchise all male citizens "without distinction of color." I favored the ballot for our black soldiers and literate folk like the free Negroes of New Orleans, but doubted the propriety of universal suffrage for the freedman in his unprepared state. I didn't oppose the justice of universal Negro suffrage; but I did think it was of doubtful political policy and worried it would boomerang on the Republicans and the freedman himself. In any case, my endorsement of limited black suffrage brought me blistering criticism from the Democrats and conservative Republicans that I'd surrendered to the "nigger vote." Turned out, neither position could muster a majority vote, and the result was no reconstruction bill at all.

In the Senate, meanwhile, Sumner, Wade, and other Radicals moved to overturn my reconstruction efforts in Louisiana and Arkansas, for fear that they would become models for restoring the other rebel states. They damned my "seven months abortion" in Louisiana and fought it with every parliamentary trick they knew. In the end, Congress voted not to seat the representatives from Louisiana and Arkansas, which left the entire question of reconstruction in limbo. The Democratic *New York Herald* gloated that Senator Sumner had "kicked the pet scheme of the President down the marble steps of the Senate chamber."

Rumors flew that the battle over reconstruction had destroyed my personal friendship with Sumner. It wasn't true, not at all. He still accompanied me on my afternoon carriage rides and still advised me on foreign affairs. He enjoyed calling on Mary—they were also good friends—and liked to drop by my office just to talk. When we were together, Mary said, we laughed like a couple of schoolboys.

One issue Sumner and I saw eye to eye on was the Thirteenth Amendment. If there was an issue closest to my heart, that was it. In my congressional message that December, I implored the House to approve the amendment as the Senate had done. Yes, I said, this was the same House that had earlier rejected the amendment. But since then an election had shown that the next Congress would pass the measure if this one did not. It was only a question of *time*, then, as to when it would go to the states for ratification. And so, at all events, could we not agree that the sooner the better?

On that note, I used every political trick I knew to get the amendment approved. I plotted with House Radicals how to pressure conservative Republicans and dissident Democrats who opposed the measure. Debates began on January sixth and James Ashley, the measure's chief sponsor, quoted me: *"If slavery is not wrong, nothing is wrong."* When it appeared that the amendment would fail, I called Rollins of Missouri to the White House and told him: "You and I were old Whigs, both of us followers of Henry Clay. This amendment is my chief hope and reliance to bring the war to a speedy close. I need your support, Rollins, and I want you to work on the rest of the Missouri delegation. If the congressmen from the border states unite, enough of 'em to pass the amendment, the fellows down south couldn't expect much help from that quarter and would be willing to stop fighting."

I also singled out sinners on the Democratic side who were on praying ground, and told 'em they had a better chance for the Federal jobs they wanted if they voted for the amendment. Next day two of the sinners announced their conversion. With the outcome still very doubtful, I participated with congressional Republicans in certain secret negotiations to win over wavering opponents. Let's just say the negotiations involved the patronage, a New Jersey railroad, and the release of rebel prisoners who were related to congressional Democrats. That's all I'll say about it.

The amendment came up for a vote on January thirty-first, with spectators filling the galleries and the corridors of the Capitol. Every Republican member cast an "aye" for the measure, and when it passed by just three votes, the Republicans cheered, embraced one another, and danced in the aisles. "I feel like I've been born into a new life," Congressman George Julian beamed. "The world *does* move."

I signed the amendment bill the same day it passed the House. For me, it was a great moral victory, and I felt deeply gratified. I pointed out that Maryland and Missouri had already abolished slavery by state action, and so had my reconstructed governments in Louisiana and Arkansas. Once the Thirteenth Amendment was ratified by three-fourths of the states, slavery would be abolished everywhere in the land and our venerable Constitution would be transformed into a charter of freedom under which no one could ever again be a slave.

I pointed across the Potomac. "If the people across the river had behaved themselves, I couldn't have done what I've done."

69. DOUGLASS

William Lloyd Garrison credited Mr. Lincoln more than any other man for getting the Thirteenth Amendment passed, and black people cheered him and the amendment in boisterous mass meetings, crying "Glory, glory, Jehovah has triumphed!" There was no denying the importance of this great amendment for a people just liberated from the pain of the whip. But it did not go far enough. It did not provide for the one idea I had presented to the American people for the last three years of civil war, and that idea was clothed in the old abolition phraseology. It was the "immediate, unconditional, and universal" enfranchisement of the black man, in every state in the Union, so that he could vote freely in state and Federal elections for candidates of his choice.

"Without this," I argued on the platform, "the black man's liberty is a mockery. Without this, you might as well retain the old name of slavery for his condition; for in fact, if he is not the slave of the individual master, he is the slave of society, and holds his liberty as a privilege, not as a right. He is at the mercy of the mob, and has no means of protecting himself."

Freedom was not only the right to vote, I said. It was also the right to choose one's own employment. "When any individual or combination of individuals undertakes to decide for any man when he shall work, at what he shall work, and for what he shall work, he or they practically reduce him to slavery. He is a slave. Yet that is what General Banks has done in Louisiana, with the approval of the president: Banks has determined for the so-called freedman, when, and where, and at what, and for how much he shall work, when he shall be punished and by whom punished. This defeats the beneficent intention of the government in regard to the freedom of our people."

When I looked over the country, I saw Educational Societies, Sanitary Commissions, Freedmen's Associations, and the like. They were all very good, but as far as we were concerned they manifested more benevolence than justice. What I asked for the Negro was not benevolence, not pity, not sympathy, but simple justice. The American people had always been anxious to know what they should do with us. General Banks, in Louisiana, was distressed as to what he should do with the Negro. Everybody had asked the question, and they learned to ask it early of the abolitionists, "What shall we do with the Negro?" I had but one answer from the beginning. "Do *nothing* with us! Your doing with us has already played mischief with us. Do nothing with us! If the apples will not remain on the tree of their own strength, if they are worm-eaten at the core, if they are early ripe and disposed to fall, let them fall! I am not for tying or fastening them on the tree in any way, except by nature's plan, and if they will not stay there, let them fall. If the Negro cannot stand on his own legs, let him also fall. All I ask is, give him a chance to stand on his own legs! Let him alone! If you see him on his way to school, let him alone, don't disturb him! If you see him going to the dinner table at a hotel, don't disturb him! If you see him going to the ballot box, let him alone, don't disturb him! If you see him going into a

workshop, if you see him working his own field, just let him alone—
your interference is doing him a positive injury. General Banks's program to 'prepare' the former slave for freedom is of a piece with this
attempt to prop up the Negro. Let him fall if he cannot stand alone!
Let him live or die by the principle of self-help. If you will only untie
his hands, and give him a chance, I think he will live. He will work
as readily for himself as the white man. A great many delusions have
been swept away by this war. One was that the Negro would not
work; he has proved his ability to work. Another was that the Negro
would not fight; that he possessed only the most sheepish attributes,
was a perfect lamb; disposed to take off his coat whenever required,
fold his hands, and be whipped by anybody who wanted to whip
him. But the war has proved that there is a great deal of human
nature in the Negro, and that he 'will fight,' in the words of abolitionist Josiah Quincy, 'when there is a reasonable probability of his
whipping anybody.'"

As we approached the war's fifth year, tens of thousands of
black men were fighting in Mr. Lincoln's armies and many of them
were dying. They were fighting and dying for the right of the black
man to enjoy *full citizenship*, to *vote*, to *work* for an employer of his
own choosing, to *improve* himself, and to be *left alone*.

70. SHERMAN

I got a long letter from Halleck, warning me that a certain class of
men with great influence over the president were disturbed about my
treatment of the black race. "They say that you have manifested an
almost criminal dislike to the negro," Halleck wrote, "and that you
are not willing to carry out the wishes of the government in regard
to him, but repulse him with contempt! They say you might have
brought with you to Savannah more than fifty thousand, thus stripping Georgia of that number of laborers and opening a road by
which as many more could have escaped from their masters; but that
instead of this, you drove them from your ranks, prevented their following you by cutting the bridges in your rear, and thus caused the
massacre of large numbers by Wheeler's cavalry." He hinted that I
ought to do more for the niggers, by opening avenues of escape that
would bring 'em to Savannah, where they could subsist off the rice

fields around the city and find occupation in the cotton and rice plantations on the coast.

"Jesus Christ," I said and slammed the letter down. I was sitting in the office of my headquarters, an opulent mansion with a cast-iron porch and stained-glass windows. Why in God's name, I asked, couldn't sensible men leave the nigger alone? Just because I refused to load my army down with hundreds of thousands of poor Sambos, or recruit 'em as soldiers, I was supposed to be hostile to the black race? That was cock-and-bull! And that stuff about cutting the bridges and leaving the blacks to be massacred, that was *humbug*. I'll tell you what happened. It was at Ebenezer Creek. General Jeff C. Davis, one of my division commanders, put a pontoon bridge across the creek and withdrew it when his men were across. The darkies on the other side panicked and many of 'em jumped in the creek and drowned. Davis didn't pull the bridge up so that Wheeler could massacre the blacks. He took it up because he wanted his bridge for the next creek. He and Slocum told me they didn't believe Wheeler killed even one of the refugees.

I wrote Halleck all this, pointing out that I was the best kind of friend to Sambo. "Darkies of Savannah gather around me in crowds, and I can't find out whether I am Moses or Aron, or which of the prophets; but surely I am rated as one of the congregation, and it is hard to tell in what sense I am most appreciated by Sambo—in saving him from his master or the new master that threatens him with a new species of slavery. I mean state recruiting agents trying to enlist him in the army. I wouldn't let those agents in my camps in the Atlanta campaign. Of course sensible men understand such humbug. The South deserves all she has got for her injustice to the Negro, but that is no reason why we should go to the other extreme. Still, I thank you for your kind hint. I do and will do the best I can for Negroes."

Several days after I got Halleck's letter, Secretary of War Stanton arrived in Savannah on a revenue cutter. Wheezing from an attack of asthma, Stanton said he'd come down here to recuperate and escape the hell of wartime Washington. But the real reason, I soon learned, was the Goddamned nigger question. Jesus, when would they leave me alone about that?

"Tell me about Jeff C. Davis," Stanton said. "He's known as a proslavery man who hates blacks."

"I assure you, he's an excellent soldier," I said. "I don't believe he has any hostility to the Negro."

Stanton produced a newspaper article about the "massacre" on

Ebenezer Creek caused by Davis's pulling the bridge up. I called Davis to headquarters and asked him to answer the charges.

"I'm innocent," he said. "My men used pontoon bridges all the time, to get across the creeks as fast as possible and continue to march. We couldn't be encumbered with huge numbers of refugees."

I don't know what Stanton thought of this: he didn't say a word, just stared irritably at Davis through those tiny round spectacles of his. After Davis left, Stanton told me to set up a meeting with Savannah's Negro leaders. I rounded up a group of twenty preachers and lay leaders. Their spokesman was a sixty-seven-year-old Baptist preacher named Garrison Frazier. We met them one night in an upstairs room of my headquarters mansion. Stanton sat at a desk writing notes while I stood by the fireplace.

Stanton asked Frazier a pointed question. "State what you understand by slavery, and the freedom that was to be given by the president's proclamation."

"Slavery," he said, "is receiving by irresistible power the work of another man, and not by his consent. The freedom promised by the proclamation, as I understand it, is taking us from under the yoke of bondage and placing us where we can reap the fruits of our own labor, and take care of ourselves, and assist the government in maintaining our freedom."

Stanton looked at him in amazement. He put his pen down and touched his glasses, as if he could not quite comprehend the preacher's intelligence. I was pretty astonished myself.

"How can you support yourselves?" Stanton asked.

"The best way we can take care of ourselves is to have land and till it by our own labor. We want to be placed on land until we are able to buy it. We also need military protection and the right to govern ourselves."

When Stanton was finished, he invited me to leave the room. I walked out fuming. I knew he was going to ask that bunch what they thought of me, so he could report it to Lincoln and the powers in Washington, and I wanted it said to my face. It was Goddamned strange that the *great* War secretary would catechize *Negroes* concerning the character of a general who'd commanded a hundred thousand men in battle, captured cities, conducted sixty-five thousand men across four hundred miles of territory, and had just brought tens of thousands of black refugees to a place of security in Savannah.

After the blacks left, Stanton told me not to worry. "Frazier praised you, said the black people of Savannah felt inexpressible gratitude toward you." Stanton read from his notes what Frazier had said: "Some of us called upon General Sherman immediately upon his arrival, and he was courteous. We have confidence in him, and think what concerns us could not be in better hands."

In response to Frazier and his group, I issued Special Field Orders No. 15, on January sixteenth of 'sixty-five. The document went through several drafts, which Stanton edited. The orders set aside four hundred thousand acres of land on the Georgia and South Carolina sea islands, and thirty miles inland in South Carolina and parts of Georgia and Florida, as an exclusive settlement for the coloreds. No whites could go there. The land, of course, had once belonged to slaveowners. The head of each refugee family would get forty acres, clothes, seed, and farm equipment, and a possessory title in writing. The blacks would have sole management of their own affairs subject only to Congress.

Stanton and I appointed General Rufus Saxton, commander of Union occupation forces on the islands, to supervise the operation, and he eventually settled forty thousand niggers there. I hated the son-of-a-bitch—he was a Goddamned Radical Republican. But I liked the appointment—the refugee problem was no longer my problem. It was his.

Stanton, as one of my officers said, was "boorish and bearish," and I was Goddamned glad when he finally left. I wrote Ellen that Stanton's visit cured him of this Negro nonsense. "General Halleck and others have written me to modify my opinions. I was unwilling to weaken my forces by filling it with Negro troops, which many took for hostility to blacks. But you know I cannot change—if I attempted the part of a hypocrite it would break out at each sentence." I said I'd found a way to avoid enlisting blacks as soldiers. Give 'em land under my special field orders and turn 'em over to Saxton. That would keep 'em out of my army. "I want soldiers made of the best bone and muscle in the land," I told Ellen, "and won't attempt military feats with doubtful materials. I have said that slavery is dead and the Negro is free, and want him treated as free, and not hunted and badgered to make a soldier of, when his family is left back on the plantations. *I am right and won't change.*"

Still, I knew I was being watched. Any wrong move on the nigger question would tumble my fame down into infamy. So I avoided the question and flung myself into preparations for the invasion of South Carolina.

71. BOOTH

A few days before Christmas I took the stage down to Bryantown, spent the night with Dr. Queen, and the next day met Dr. Mudd in a tavern, where we shared a bottle of brandy. Mudd introduced me to Thomas Harbin, a Confederate agent stationed in King George County in northern Virginia, and we went to an upstairs room for a private conversation. He told me he went by an alias, "Wilson," and reported to Jefferson Davis. I told him about our plan to abduct Lincoln.

"He goes on a carriage ride at four every afternoon," I said. "We'll seize his carriage and subdue him. Two or three of us will drive it to the Navy Yard bridge, tell the guard, 'This is the president,' and then race south through lower Maryland. About halfway down we'll get fresh horses. That night we'll put Lincoln on the boat to Port Tobacco and then take him to rebel lines. I'm down here to get help from the right people. We could use your help, if you'll join us."

"Count on it," he said. "I'll meet you on the road and help you get him into Virginia."

I told him I would contact him when we were prepared to move, and we parted. I spent that night with Dr. Mudd, and the next day he introduced me to the neighbor who had horses for sale, and I bought a one-eyed, dark bay from him, rather an old bay but a good mover. By now, I thought I could trust Mudd, his sentiments being so close to my own, and I told him I was looking for trustworthy recruits for a secret plan that would enable the Confederacy to win the war. He said he knew a man, an old friend named John Surratt, who was a Confederate spy and "runner." He carried secret dispatches from Washington to Richmond hidden under the floorboards of his buggy. He lived at his mother's boarding house in Washington, Mudd said, and offered to introduce us.

I rode my horse back to Washington and put it in a stable. Next day Mudd met me at the National Hotel, and we walked off toward the Surratt boarding house. We hadn't gone far when Mudd spotted Surratt on Pennsylvania Avenue, walking with a heavy-set man wearing a short blue cloak with a cape.

Mudd called out: "Surratt! Surratt!"

"Dr. Mudd!" Surratt said and walked over. "I'm glad to see you. Let me introduce you to my friend, Mr. Weichmann, who works in the War Department."

"Gentlemen," Mudd said, "this is my friend, Mr. Boone."

I shook Surratt's hand and looked him over. He has a strong resemblance to Jefferson Davis, I thought: tall, slender, and erect, with piercing gray eyes and a small goatee on his chin. Didn't think he was older than twenty. I invited the three men up to my room, pulled the call bell for the waiter, and ordered cigars and milk punches all around. We talked and drank for a while. Then I asked Mudd and Surratt to step out into the hallway, closed the door, and told Surratt who I really was and said I would like to see him again, when he was alone.

He called at my room a day or so later, and I told him in a subdued voice, almost a whisper, why I had invited him here. "The northern prisons are full of thousands of our men the United States government refuses to exchange. You know how bad the war is going for us. We need those men desperately. I have a plan that will bring about their exchange." I went to the door and looked up and down the hallway. "We've got to be careful," I said. "Walls have ears." I pulled my chair closer to Surratt. "The plan is to kidnap Lincoln and carry him to Richmond, so the Confederate government can—"

"Kidnap Lincoln!" he said. "Isn't that a rather foolish idea? You can't just grab Lincoln in Washington, in the middle of thousands of Union soldiers."

"There are several points around Washington where he can be seized. The Soldiers' Home in the country would be the best place. It's away from those thousands of soldiers."

"Even if you do manage to kidnap him, you'd have to drive over a hundred miles to the Potomac without getting caught. If you get across the river, provided you don't run into Yankee gunboats, you'd have to drive through northern Virginia to the Rappahannock, and the area is swarming with Yankees. I know, I've just come from there. I know northern Virginia and southern Maryland by heart, and I don't think it can be done."

"That's why we need your support, because you know the area well. Three other men are with me. One is a Confederate agent who reports to President Davis. We all think the plan can work. Once Lincoln is in Richmond, the Confederate government will offer to exchange him for all our prisoners in the North."

Surratt kept shaking his head. "The President of the United States can't be spirited away like an ordinary citizen. It's too dangerous."

"I'm willing to take any risk. I've brooded so long over Lincoln's wrongs against the South that it's affected my mind. Can't think of anything else. Lincoln's a despicable, low-born tyrant—he needs to be punished and publicly humiliated. Kidnapping will humiliate him plenty. If we succeed, it will save the Confederacy. It will make us famous, we'll be heroes to all the South, our names will go into history. I would die for that."

Surratt said he wanted to think about it. In a day or two he came back and said he was with us.

"You won't regret it," I said. "If anyone asks, tell them we're in oil speculation together." I used the same cover with Arnold and O'Laughlin.

With rising expectation, I took the train to New York City to spend Christmas with my mother. She said she was having fearful dreams about me and with tears in her eyes begged me to stay home. I told her I *couldn't* stay, I had important *work* to do, God had given me a *special destiny*, I had to go back to Washington.

Before I left New York, I bought two seven-shot Spencer rifles, three revolvers, several boxes of ammunition, and three knives, which we would need in case we were pursued, and a pair of handcuffs to use on Lincoln. I put everything in a trunk and took it to Baltimore by train and left it with Arnold to store. I gave him and O'Laughlin money to buy a horse and buggy and told them to bring the cache of weapons to Washington in two weeks.

I returned to Washington and went to see Surratt at his mother's boarding house. It was now after the New Year, but the Surratts still had a Christmas tree by the window. Louis Weichmann, the War Department clerk, boarded here and was sitting in the parlor with three women. Surratt introduced them as his mother, Mary, his sister, Anna, and another boarder, a seventeen-year-old girl named Honora. The two girls kept stealing looks at me and whispering to themselves, and why not? I was well dressed in polished black boots, woolen pants, a bright red vest, a fur coat, and an expensive black felt hat. I was also strikingly handsome, with a thick black mustache, thick black curly hair, and dark eyes that made the hearts of many a lady flutter. The maids in the National Hotel fought over who would make my bed, and Washington belles swooned when I walked by with the spring of a cat.

"John," I said, "can you go upstairs and spare a word with me?"

When we were alone, I asked Surratt about Weichmann. "Is he suspicious? He seems the type. Busy eyes. Takes in everything. "

"He doesn't suspect a thing. I told everyone you and I are involved in the oil business, like you told me."

"Good. Listen, I've got the weapons. I think we can move in two weeks."

But a spell of severe winter weather set in, with snow and brutal cold. The weather, I discovered, restricted Lincoln's carriage rides; he no longer went to the country. That meant we had to postpone the abduction till warm weather came, or devise a new plan. I talked several times with Surratt and came up with another abduction scheme I thought would work brilliantly. In mid-January, Arnold and O'Laughlin brought the weapons to Washington, as planned, and I met them in a tavern for drinks.

"Listen closely," I said. "I've changed the script for abducting Caesar. We're going to seize him at Ford's Theater, not the Soldiers' Home. He doesn't go there in the winter. But he attends the theater regularly. I get my mail at Ford's, I've acted there many times and know every foot of it. Here's the plan. We'll leave the buggy in the alley behind the theater. One man will turn off the gaslights inside. In the darkness and confusion, the rest of us will seize Lincoln in his box, handcuff him, carry him offstage by the back entrance, and escape in the buggy through lower Maryland."

Arnold didn't like the plan. "Too dangerous," he said. "It could lead to the sacrifice of us all."

"Nonsense!" I said. "We've got to be brave. We're like soldiers going forth to battle. How can we fail? *God* is with us. *Justice* is with us. We'll watch the morning papers. They announce Lincoln's theater plans. When he goes to Ford's, we'll spring the trap and reverse the course of the war."

THE WINDS OF 'SIXTY-FIVE

When Johnny comes marching home again,
     Hurrah! Hurrah!
We'll give him a hearty welcome then,
Hurrah! Hurrah!
The men will cheer, the boys will shout,
The ladies they will all turn out.
     And we'll feel gay,
When Johnny comes marching home.

Furl that Banner, for 'tis weary;
Round its staff 'tis drooping dreary;
Furl it, fold it—it is best;
For there's not a man to wave it,
And there's not a sword to save it,
And there's not one left to lave it
In the blood which heroes gave it;
And its foes now scorn and brave it;
Furl it, hide it—let it rest!
For its people's hopes have fled.

1 . SHERMAN

By late January we were ready to invade South Carolina. Opposing us were scattered and inconsiderable forces that could hardly delay us an hour. We had cut ourselves off from our base, Savannah, and would once again live off the country. I meant to show South Carolina the scourge of war in its worst form, to visit utter destruction against that hellhole of secession. I knew we wouldn't be able to restrain our men as we'd done in Georgia. Hell, the devil himself couldn't restrain 'em in the state where treason had begun. I had no intention of holding 'em back lest it impair the vigor and energy of the army.

My only question was Lee. Would he sit on his ass in Petersburg and permit us, almost unopposed, to march through South and North Carolina, cutting off and consuming the very supplies he depended on to feed his army in Virginia? Or would he make an effort to escape Grant and try to catch us inland somewhere between Columbia and Raleigh? I knew full well that the broken fragment of Hood's army, about twenty-five thousand men, was being hurried across Georgia, by way of Augusta, to make a junction with the forces in my front under Hardee, Wheeler, and Hampton, which would give them a total of about forty thousand men. Against them I fielded an army of just over sixty thousand men, with 2,500 mule-drawn wagons and 600 two-horse ambulances. We had an edge not just in numbers: the soldiers and people of the South had an undue fear of our western men and made up such exaggerated stories of our prowess in Georgia that their own inventions scared them shitless.

Howard's right wing was poised at Pocotaligo, on the Charleston & Savannah Railroad, about twenty miles inland from Beaufort. Slocum's left wing was moving through the swamps on the south side of the Savannah River, but that whole country was under water from constant storms and rains, and it delayed Slocum's advance. On February first, with my staff and I riding with them, Howard's column headed up the muddy road along the Salkehatchie, through a tangled jungle of creeks and swamps which were full of squawking birds. Just ahead of our lead troops, rebel cavalry tried to obstruct our advance by cutting down trees. You could hear the thump of their axes against wet logs and trees. But we moved so fast that they never could complete their obstructions, and we got past 'em easily.

Word reached us that Slocum had crossed the Savannah and was now marching north with Kilpatrick's cavalry in the lead. Meanwhile Howard's wing came to the bridges over the Salkehatchie, crossed the river there, and headed into the densely wooded Salk swamps, which were about a mile and a half wide and fed by many streams. The rebels boasted that the Salk swamps were impenetrable, and they Goddamned sure looked that way. But our lead soldiers, by wading in brown-colored water up to their shoulders, built corduroy roads that allowed the army to get through the swamps, over the water and mud and treacherous quicksand. It was no holiday march like our journey through Georgia. We had to construct many miles of roads, day after day, across fifteen separate streams, dragging artillery and 2,500 loaded army wagons as we moved.

Our miracle march through the swamps stunned and demoralized Hardee's little force in our front. I heard he said: "I wouldn't have believed it if I hadn't seen it happen." Joe Johnston said later: "When I learned that Sherman's army was marching through the Salk swamps, making its own corduroy roads at the rate of a dozen miles a day and more, and bringing its artillery and wagons with it, I made up my mind that there had been no such army in existence since the days of Julius Caesar."

When we reached higher country, the roads improved, and we marched rapidly toward the South Carolina Railroad at Midville. The army advanced in a Y formation, with the two wings pointing in different directions to confuse the enemy and keep 'em divided. As we moved, my boys burnt and destroyed everything within our reach, leaving the lower part of the state a smoking ruin.

We reached the South Carolina Railroad in the middle of a rainstorm. The destruction of this road, which would sever all enemy communications between Charleston and Augusta, was the first great objective of the march. Details of men tore up the rails, burned and twisted 'em on bonfires, and left 'em twisted around trees as a reminder, to the rebel population, of the folly of starting this war. After wrecking the railroad for fifty miles, I ordered both wings to march on Columbia, our next big objective. To continue deceiving the rebels, I sent Kil's cavalry on a raid against Aiken, in the direction of Augusta.

We crossed the South Edisto and captured Orangeburg, which cut communications between Columbia and Charleston. The first of our soldiers in town torched several houses. As other troops came up, they demolished the railroad depot, burnt cotton bales, and wrecked two miles of the railroad south of the city. They found an orphan asylum with three hundred emaciated kids eating molasses and cornmeal mush for breakfast. When I rode up, several of my men were wiping tears from their eyes. I ordered decent rations to be left for the poor kids.

So far, we had the rebels completely fooled. Hardee, now at Charleston, assumed we would attack there. Rebel troops in Augusta believed that city was our objective. As a consequence they abandoned Columbia to the care of Hampton's cavalry, who were confused by the rumors that poured in on them.

Both wings of my army were now converging on Columbia. As they tramped along, the boys sang "John Brown's body lies a moldering in the grave, but his soul is marching on!"

2 . CHESNUT

James and I were in Columbia when Sherman invaded South Carolina. The news filled me with abject terror. I spent the days wrapped up on the sofa, too dismal even to moan. Nobody knew whether his target was Charleston, Augusta, or Columbia. One day we heard the Yankees were at Orangeburg. The next day they were reported to be marching on Columbia, and people were fleeing the city. Our friends, the Martins, had already gone to Lincolnton, North Carolina. Where should we go? James wanted me to return to Camden, and so did Molly, our servant; she wept and wailed and begged me to go home, saying that our black people would protect me. So I agreed to go—but then a Miss Patterson called. She was a refugee from a section of Tennessee overrun by the Yankee invaders, and she described graphically all the horrors to be endured by those subjected to fire and sword and rapine and plunder. She said that our slaves would fare even worse if the Yankees found me at Mulberry. James and I agreed: no matter how loyal our slaves might be, they could not protect me from an army bent upon sweeping us from the face of the earth. Frightened beyond description, I resolved to follow the Martins to Lincolnton.

I said farewell to no one and hurried to the depot with James. He tried to put his head through the car window to tell me good-bye, but a rude woman prevented him from doing it. After a horrible ride, twelve hours on the road with many delays, I reached John-ston's hotel in Lincolnton, broken-hearted and in exile. Such a place! No carpet—a horrid feather bed—soiled sheets—a pine table—for this I paid thirty dollars a day!

I met a Miss McLean, who had a comfortable house, and I per-suaded her to take me in. A clean, spacious room at last! She was a kind, beautiful, well-educated young woman, but alas she didn't brush her teeth, the first evidence of civilization, and lived in the midst of dirt in ways that would shame even the poorest overseer's wife. Still she was a flower, a pure white lily.

Next day I went for a walk and met General Joseph E. Johnston, a spry little man with keen black eyes and a Vandyke beard almost completely white. He was angry and rude. The president had ordered him to assume command of all our troops outside Virginia, and the general was not at all happy about it. Neither was I. I feared the great retreater would pull another Vicksburg and run from the invaders.

I had been in Lincolnton just three days when we learned that Columbia had fallen. A letter from James, who had escaped to Char-lotte, confirmed it; he had almost been taken prisoner! I did not care ever to see another paper, all the shame—disgrace—misery. How I wept that day! My poor heart was weary—and then how it poured—rain, rain, rain. I wanted so to get away, far, far away from Sherman's evil horde. I was so utterly heartbroken. "Oh my heav-enly Father," I prayed, "look down and pity us."

3 . SHERMAN

When my staff and I reached the Congaree River, opposite Columbia, Slocum was there with his lead troops. I rode down to the riverbank and saw that the Johnnies had burned the large bridge across the river. Across the Congaree lay Columbia in plain view. I could see the unfinished statehouse, a handsome granite structure, and the ruins of the railroad depot, which were still smoldering. That had to be the work of Hampton's cavalry. Clearly they were about to abandon the city. I could see a few citizens and soldiers running across the streets, and a number of niggers carrying off bags of grain or meal, which were piled up near the burned depot.

Captain DeGress of our artillery had a section of twenty-pound Parrott guns unlimbered, and I told him to aim a few shells near the depot to scare the niggers away. "They're stealing bags of cornmeal I want for our men," I said.

Because of the wide swamp bordering the Congaree, I decided not to enter Columbia from the west, and I told Slocum, once his main body was up, to march fifteen miles to the north, cross the Broad River above the town, and encamp. Howard's Fifteenth Corps had already reached the Broad River, which flowed south into the Congaree, and I directed that corps to cross the Broad and enter the city from the north. I ordered Howard to destroy the public buildings, railroad property, manufacturing and machine shops, but to spare libraries, asylums, and private dwellings.

I'd already issued the order when I learned that hidden rebel gunners had bombarded our camps the night before.

"The murderous bastards," I fumed. "Nothing but a bunch of Goddamned guerrillas. I ought to put the whole damn city to the torch." But when my temper cooled, I let my order to Howard stand.

Next morning I rode to the front of Howard's column, which was lined up to cross the river once his engineers completed a pontoon bridge. Stone's brigade had already floated across the river on pontoons and was deployed on the opposite shore. Through my field glasses, I saw four civilians ride up in a carriage sporting a white flag, and say something to Stone. A courier brought me a letter from the four men: it surrendered the city and begged me to treat the civilians by the rules of civilized warfare.

Once the bridge was done, Howard and I with our staffs led the Fifteenth Corps across the river, over a hill, and down a long road that led into Columbia between fields of corn and cotton. Behind us, the soldiers were singing:

> Hail Columbia, happy land,
> If I don't burn you, I'll be damned.

We passed an immense warehouse full of plug tobacco, and some niggers threw plugs to us as we rode by. Some of our men were already in the city. One fellow was wearing a long dressing gown and plug hat. As I approached, he stepped unsteadily off the side-walk and lifted his hat to me. He was so drunk he could barely stand up. "I have the honor (hic), General, to present (hic) you with (hic) the freedom of the (hic) city." I turned my head around to my staff and grinned. Then someone took charge of the soldier and hauled him off to the guardhouse.

As we moved on, we came to piles of cotton burning in the cen-ter of the wide streets. The niggers told us that Hampton's cavalry had cut the bales open and set them on fire as they left the city. A high and boisterous wind prevailed from the north, and flakes of cotton flew about in the air and lodged in the limbs of trees. Reminded me of a northern snowstorm. Near the market square we found Stone's brigade halted, with arms stacked. A large detail of his men and some civilians were trying to put the fires out with an old fire engine. Other troops avoided the burning cotton by marching on the sidewalks—they were on their way to camp outside of town.

One soldier reported an alarming development. "Some of our boys got some whiskey as we came through the city," he said. "The Negroes are running around with pails of the stuff." Major Hitch-cock saw it, too. "The citizens themselves," he said, "brought out large quantities of liquor and distributed it freely among our men, even to the guards General Howard posted all over the city."

We found a large crowd of whites and niggers at market square, where anxious female faces, white faces, stared at us from upper windows. About then I noticed several men trying to get through the crowd to see me. I told the crowd to make room for them. When they reached me, they said they were officers of our army who'd been prisoners of war. They had escaped from prison and were over-joyed to find themselves safe with us. Nichols of my staff told me afterward: "General, not even in the moment of victory have I seen your face beam with such exultation."

I did not know then what Major Hitchcock would tell me later: the prisoners told my soldiers about the cruel treatment they had received—exposed to the weather, they had to burrow under-ground—and all were burning for revenge. Nor did I know that a New England schoolteacher, back in 'sixty-one, had been tarred and feathered and run out of town for having abolitionist sentiments. That story passed through the ranks, and further embittered the troops. By nightfall drunken soldiers of the Fifteenth Corps were ready to retaliate against the town that called itself the "cradle of secession."

That night I took quarters, arranged by a respectable old physician, in a very good modern dwelling near the statehouse. After dark I noticed a bright light shining on the walls. I asked Major Nichols to find out what it was. He reported that a house was on fire near the market square. The high wind was still blowing, and I sent Nichols to see if the provost guards were doing their duty. He returned and said that an entire block of buildings was on fire near where the rebels had torched the cotton. General Woods was on the ground with plenty of men, all trying to put the fire out, but the gale-force wind was spreading the flames beyond control.

I hurried downtown with Colonel Dayton and advised several ladies in one house to move to my headquarters—I even had our wagons carry their effects there. Moving on, we could see flames leaping high into the air, casting the entire heavens in a lurid light. The fire roared and bellowed like an obscene monster. From the roofs of blazing buildings, pieces of board and burning shingles flew in the wind for several blocks and started new fires. We saw a mob of drunken soldiers, escaped prisoners, escaped convicts from the penitentiary, and niggers running from house to house, carrying off booty and spreading the fire with cans of turpentine and cotton torches soaked in combustible material. One soldier told a man whose store had burned down: "Did you think of this when you hurrahed for secession? How do you like it, hey?"

Homeless women and children, many in their nightclothes, milled about in shock, unable to believe that their houses had burned down. A few carried little valuables they had managed to grab as they fled outside. Our soldiers took 'em to a safe place—had to carry some of the women and children—and gave 'em rations. No doubt other civilians lay buried in the ashes of their houses.

I joined Howard and other officers on main street and we all shouted orders to stop the incendiaries and extinguish the flames. Provost guards set about arresting drunken soldiers; I myself ordered the arrest of one liquored-up private. When he resisted, Colonel Dayton shot him. Finally, I brought up Hazen's division to clear the streets and restore order.

About four in the morning the wind moderated, and gradually we got the fire under control. The sun rose that morning over a ruined city. From the center of town as far as the eye could reach, nothing could be seen but heaps of ashes, smoldering debris, shattered brick walls, and blackened chimneys.

The homeless were gathered in groups in the suburbs and in

open parks. A committee of irate women came to my headquarters and demanded: "Why did you burn our town, or allow your army to burn it?"

"I didn't burn your town, nor did my army. Your brothers, sons, husbands, and fathers set fire to every city, town, and village in the South when they fired on Fort Sumter. The fire they kindled there has been burning ever since, and it reached your houses last night."

You want to know who was to blame for the Goddamned fire? It was Wade Hampton. In my official report of the campaign, I charged him with burning his own city of Columbia, not with malicious intent but from folly and want of sense in ordering the bales of cotton set on fire. If I had made up my mind to burn Columbia, I would have done it with no more feeling than I would a common prairie village. But I didn't do it. God Almighty started wind sufficient to carry the burning cotton wherever He wished it. Our officers and men on duty worked hard to extinguish the flames; but I conceded that other soldiers not on duty, including the men who'd long been imprisoned there, helped spread the fire after it began, and indulged in unconcealed joy to see the ruin of the capital of South Carolina. Though I never ordered it or wished it, I've never shed a tear over the conflagration, because I believed it hastened what we all fought for: the end of the war.

I wasn't finished with Columbia. By my orders, groups of soldiers destroyed the Confederate printing office, the arsenal, gasworks, foundries, and a good stretch of the railroad. Then my troops set out for North Carolina. As the rear column swept through the streets, people booed and hissed, and shrieking harridans tried to hit the soldiers with their fists.

Slocum marched westward, wrecking the railroad that led to Abbeville, and then turned north toward Winnsboro. Blair, leading Howard's wing, moved along the railroad farther to the east, toward Charlotte, North Carolina, ripping the rails up for some forty miles. Following the army was a horde of refugees, hundreds of niggers, and maybe four hundred whites, most of 'em Unionist sympathizers and escaped prisoners. The slaves of South Carolina communicated the direction of our march by word of mouth over great distances. Every day you could see 'em coming to us down roads and across fields, carrying all their earthly belongings and things they had pilfered in old stages, carts, family carriages, and lumber wagons. They joined the crowd in the rear of the army, and sometimes their numbers almost equaled the number of troops they followed.

Slocum told a very funny story about one nigger family. "The head of the family was mounted on a mule," he said, "and safely stowed away behind him in pockets or bags attached to the blanket which covered the mule were two little pickaninnies, one on each side. Behind him was another mule, covered by old tent-flies or strong canvas, and ten or fifteen pockets were attached to each side, so that nothing of the mule was visible except the head, the tail, and feet, all else being covered by the black woolly heads and bright eyes of the little darkies."

When Slocum bore down on Winnsboro, the townspeople screamed, "Yankees are coming! Yankees are coming!" and fled hysterically in the opposite direction. Slocum's boys then plundered and torched the town, burning down thirty homes, the Episcopal church, and all the public buildings. I tried to stop the Goddamned looting—had the trains searched and found five tons of purloined clothes, silverware, tobacco, and other goods. Ordered the men to burn it all. Before we left, one of my officers married a pretty mulatto girl, with a Roman Catholic priest performing the ceremonies. I don't approve of race mixing myself, but I didn't interfere—it was the officer's business if he wanted to marry a half nigger.

Howard's right wing now turned eastward and took off for Cheraw in the northeast corner of the state. We learned that Hardee was in Cheraw, which meant that he'd evacuated Charleston. We soon heard that Federal troops from the sea islands had occupied the city. As Hitchcock said, "the capture of Charleston had only a *moral*, not a military value to us."

Slocum meanwhile destroyed the railroad to Chester, far to the west of Howard, and then turned east to the Catawba River. By my orders, Kilpatrick's cavalry crossed the river and feinted north, to make the rebels believe we were heading for Charlotte, North Carolina. I'd heard that Beauregard had directed all his forces there, including one corps of Hood's old army.

But I had no intention of going to Charlotte. I was heading for Fayetteville and Goldsboro far to the east. As Slocum approached the Catawba, Howard, farther to the east, had got his right wing across the Wateree River and was already marching rapidly toward Cheraw and Fayetteville. Slocum got part of his command across the Catawba in a driving rainstorm, but the swollen river swept the pontoon bridge away, leaving the Fourteenth Corps stranded on the western shore. I was riding with Slocum, and the delay in getting the Fourteenth Corps across the river irritated me beyond endurance. I was ready to spike their Goddamned artillery, destroy their wagons, and shoot their fucking mules to get the left wing moving again.

To make matters worse, Slocum reported that Hampton's rebel cavalry was executing his foragers. Found twenty-one of 'em murdered in a ravine. Kilpatrick reported that some of his horsemen had also been executed. I wrote Wade Hampton that foraging was a right of war as old as history and that I would retaliate in kind. "I have ordered a number of prisoners in our hands to be disposed of in like manner," I said. "I hold about one thousand prisoners and can stand it as long as you."

Hampton answered that he would hang two Federals for every one of his men I killed, and that he'd ordered his troops to execute any Federal prisoner who'd burned a house. "This order shall remain in force so long as you disgrace the profession of arms by allowing your men to destroy private dwellings."

The insolent son-of-a-bitch. I didn't bother to reply. But when we found another forager murdered by the wayside, I ordered our prisoners to draw lots. An old man who drew the black mark was shot by a firing squad. After that we found no more murdered foragers.

Meanwhile, as Slocum waited for rains to stop, I sent a detachment of troops to wreck Camden. They liberated fourteen Union prisoners and burned two thousand bales of cotton, a big flour mill filled with wheat and corn, the Masonic hall and other buildings, and plundered the town in every direction.

After four days it finally stopped raining. Slocum's engineers threw a pontoon bridge across the Catawba, and the Fourteenth Corps got across at last. We then marched rapidly to Cheraw, where Howard was waiting for us; Hardee had long since left that place.

General Blair, one of my corps commanders, sent to my bivouac a case of the finest Madeira wine I'd ever tasted. He'd confiscated it from the private store of one of Charleston's old aristocratic families, who'd sent it to Cheraw for safety. Ha! My staff and I drank a toast: "To our great army and our successful march through the heart of South Carolina, the first and most bitter and obstinate of all the rebel states, without a single check, defeat, or disaster."

North Carolina was next. Waiting for us there was Joe Johnston, with a patchwork army that was no match for my tall, red-bearded, hard-bitten westerners.

4. CHESNUT

Lincolnton crawled with rumors about Sherman's atrocities. They said he had burned Lancaster as he had burned Columbia, the ghoul, the hyena. Another letter came from James, who was in Charlotte: "The restoration of Joe Johnston, it is hoped, will redound to the advantage of our cause and the reestablishment of our fortunes. I am informed that a detachment of Yankees went to Camden with a view to destroying all the houses, mills, and provisions about the place. No particulars have reached me about Mulberry."

It was not until later that we learned that a Yankee column had gone out to the Chesnut plantation, where James's sister was looking after their ninety-three-year-old father.

"I suppose you've come to rob us," she told the officer in charge. "Please do so and go. Your presence agitates my blind old father."

The commander retorted, "What do you take me for, a thief?" And he stormed out. His men smashed up one entire side of the house and took all the horses.

In Lincolnton famine stalked the houses and the streets. I could find no one who would exchange food for Confederate money. In despair I read Shakespeare and quoted Job. A week or so later James came for a brief visit. Wearing his uniform and heavy cavalry boots, he stood gazing out my window and related in a low and steady monotone what he had seen when our soldiers fled from Columbia: "So much straggling, so many camp followers, no discipline among the troops." Before he left, he gave me his last cent.

It was a sad parting.

5. DAVIS

The croaking malcontents blamed me for the disasters in Georgia and South Carolina. They magnified every reverse and prophesied ruin, which produced public depression and sowed the seeds of disintegration. The *Richmond Examiner* demanded my removal, and certain congressmen and clerks in the War Department openly declared for Lee as dictator. The head of the War Bureau reported that "the last meat ration has been issued to Lee's army and not a pound of it remains in Richmond. The truth is we are prostrated in all our energies and resources."

"Where is this to end?" asked Josiah Gorgas, our chief ordnance officer. "No money in the Treasury, no food to feed General Lee's army, no troops to oppose Sherman. Is the cause really hopeless? Is it to be lost and abandoned in this way? My wife and I talk of going to Mexico to live out the rest of our days."

The West, I conceded, was irretrievably lost. To compound our misery, Yankee naval and army forces, in mid-January, had captured Fort Fisher, which protected Wilmington, and closed off our last blockade-running port. How the croakers fumed about that disaster! The fall of Fort Fisher and the march of Sherman's Goths through South Carolina had a devastating effect on Lee's army. He reported that hundreds of his men were deserting every day and taking their firearms with them. Many of them left, he said, because their friends and families at home wrote them that the cause was hopeless and begged them to return home and save them from roving gangs of deserters. "Unless the epidemic of desertions can be stopped," Lee said, "it will bring us calamity."

The clamor of the defeatists sounded all around me, but I refused to concede that we were losing the war, even with the Confederacy shrunk to the lower half of Virginia and part of North Carolina as far as my ability to govern was concerned. I remained implacably committed to our independence, and I paid for it with my health. I overheard the daughter of one of my old friends say that I looked bad—"old, gray, and wrinkled," was how she put it. "I never saw a more troubled countenance," she added.

In an attempt to save our Confederate nation, I resorted to desperate measures that winter. I dispatched my friend and fellow planter Duncan F. Kenner on a secret mission to Europe. It was his belief that the Confederacy could not win its independence if it held on to slavery because the entire civilized world opposed it. I agreed. I no longer cared about slavery anyway—I was fighting first and foremost to make a *nation*, and that required flexibility. Therefore, I authorized Kenner to offer, through our envoys, a proposition to the governments of England and France. The Confederate states would abolish slavery if England and France would recognize us as an independent nation. Napoleon the Third let it be known that he would follow England's lead. But when Kenner and Mason sounded out Prime Minister Palmerston indirectly, he gave them an emphatic no.

Great Britain, he said by an indirect communication, would not under any circumstances recognize the Confederacy—his government believed our cause was lost

Perhaps my proposal was "rash" and "reckless," as the croakers said when news of the secret mission leaked out. I knew that my proposal could not be implemented by an executive decree or a congressional act. The Confederate government could make no agreement nor arrangement with any nation that would interfere with state institutions, and it would have been necessary to submit the proposal of emancipation to the states for their separate action. The states probably would not have abolished slavery; the state righters would have surrendered before allowing that to happen. I hoped that England and France would recognize the Confederacy on the basis of my offer alone. In any event, the Kenner mission failed.

The second desperate step was to enroll slaves as soldiers. The idea had been hotly debated for months. Back in the fall, several newspapers, including the *Richmond Examiner*, had demanded that we enlist black troops. "We believe," said the *Examiner*, "that the negroes, identified with us by interest, and fighting for their freedom here, would be faithful and reliable soldiers." General Lee contended that the only hope of replacing our losses from attrition and desertion lay in conscripting the slaves, using them as "sappers and miners" and as cooks, teamsters, and artillery drivers. When I proposed that the Confederacy purchase forty thousand slaves to be used in noncombat military services, it provoked a storm of protest from the planters and their representatives in Congress, and my proposal had not been acted upon.

Now, early in 1865, with the military situation growing worse every day, General Lee endorsed the general idea of employing slaves as soldiers, and Secretary of War Benjamin and I agreed. When I recommended that the slaves should be admitted into the service and freed after their service was over, it provoked an even louder roar of protest from the planter class and caused universal gloom in Richmond. General Howell Cobb of Georgia summed up the opposition in a letter to Secretary of War Seddon. "I think that the proposition to make soldiers of our slaves is the most pernicious idea that has been suggested since the war began. It is to me a source of deep mortification and regret to see the name of that good and great man and soldier, General R. E. Lee, given as authority for such a policy. You cannot make soldiers of slaves, nor slaves of soldiers. The moment you resort to negro soldiers your white soldiers will be lost to you.

The day you make soldiers of the negroes is the beginning of the end of our revolution. If slaves will make good soldiers our whole theory of slavery is wrong."

Benjamin and I disagreed. At a mass meeting in Richmond, Benjamin spoke for the Administration in calling for a slave soldier bill. "Let us say to every negro who wishes to go into the ranks on condition of being made free—'Go and fight. You are free.' There is nothing wrong with trying this experiment. I'm willing to try it with my own slaves." Someone cried, "Put in the niggers," and there were cheers from the crowd. In mid-February Congressman Ethelbert Barksdale, one of my most loyal supporters, introduced an Administration bill to arm 200,000 slaves. He also read an open letter from Lee defending the measure. "It is not only expedient but necessary," Lee wrote. "The enemy will use them against us if he can get possession of them. I cannot see the wisdom of the policy of holding them to await his arrival, when we may, by timely action and judicious management, use them to arrest his progress." Lee added that the slaves, in his opinion, would make "efficient soldiers."

The measure plunged Congress into the most raucous debates of the war. With great skill, Barksdale got the bill approved in the House, but R. M. T. Hunter led a strident opposition to it in the Senate. "Pass this abolition bill," he cried, "and it means the end of white superiority in our society." That argument ended debate on the bill in the Senate.

Meanwhile, in a vote of no confidence in me, Congress demanded that Lee be made supreme commander, even though Lee made it clear he did not want the position. On January twenty-third, Congress enacted a bill creating "the General in Chief of the Armies of the Confederacy" and pressured me to appoint Lee. I signed the bill without hesitation and named Lee general in chief. From that patriotic gentleman and friend came a soothing letter: "If I can relieve you from a portion of the constant labor and anxiety which now presses upon you, and maintain a harmonious action between the great armies, I shall be more than compensated for the addition to my present burdens."

During that same January, Frank Blair, Sr., called on me for an interview. "I'm a man of southern blood," he said, "and I'm anxious to see the war between the states terminated. I come here with a pass from President Lincoln to see if I can persuade you to enter into negotiations to stop the war. I have no credentials—no authority from Lincoln—and my views are to be regarded as merely my own."

Our conference ended with no other result than an agreement that Blair would learn whether Lincoln would send or receive commissioners to negotiate for a peaceful solution to the questions at issue. "Report to him my readiness to enter upon negotiations," I said, and I wrote a letter to that effect, which he would give to Lincoln. It said: "Notwithstanding the rejection of our former offers, I would, if you could promise that a commissioner, minister, or other agent would be received, appoint one immediately, and renew the effort to enter into conference with a view to secure peace *to the two countries*."

Blair returned with Lincoln's reply: "You may say to him that I have constantly been, am now, and shall continue to be ready to receive any agent whom he or any other influential person now resisting the national authority may informally send to me with the view of securing peace *to the people of our common country*."

That final line revealed Lincoln's hand: he would not recognize our independence. The cruel and arbitrary conditions he had laid down for peace last year were still on the table. Nevertheless I decided on a conference with Lincoln, to show Vice President Stephens, Senator R. M. T. Hunter, and my other bitter critics the utter futility of peace negotiations with the Yankees. I appointed Stephens, Hunter, and Assistant War Secretary John A. Campbell to meet informally with Lincoln in Washington.

"Stress to him that there are *two countries* instead of one common country," I said. "We can't be too particular on that point."

The three men proceeded to Grant's lines and took his boat to Hampton Roads, but they were not allowed to proceed farther. Lincoln and Seward came down from Washington, and the informal meeting took place on February third, on a Yankee steamer anchored off Hampton Roads. Then the three commissioners returned to Richmond and called on me at the Executive Mansion, handing me a written report. Mr. Campbell, glancing at his memoranda, told me informally all that had passed.

"Lincoln," he said, "refused to make any treaty or agreement with the Confederacy that looked to an ultimate settlement of the war, because that would recognize its existence as a separate power, which under no circumstance would be done. Nor would he make any such terms with the states separately. In the ensuing discussion, Lincoln laid down three conditions. 'First, no truce or armistice would be granted or allowed without satisfactory assurance in advance of a complete restoration of the authority of the United States over all places within the states of the Confederacy. Second, he would not recede on the slavery question. Third, no cessation of hostilities would be accepted short of an end of the war and the disbanding of all forces hostile to the government.'

"Mr. Hunter proposed an armistice and a convention of the states, but Lincoln and Seward rejected that, on the grounds that it would be tantamount to recognition. Hunter pointed out that there had been frequent conventions between Charles I and the English Parliament. 'And Charles lost his head,' Lincoln said. When the subject of punishment for rebellion came up, Lincoln said, 'You must accept all the consequences of the application of the law, but I would be disposed to a liberal use of the power confided to me for the remission of pains and penalties.' To that Campbell said: 'I have never regarded my neck as being in danger.' Lincoln replied angrily: 'There are a great many oak trees where I live, whose limbs afford convenient points from which you might be dangled.'

"We asked Lincoln what he meant by not receding on the slavery question. He remained committed, he said, to the terms in his message of last December. In it, he'd said: 'I repeat the declaration made a year ago, that while I remain in my present position I shall not attempt to retract or modify the emancipation proclamation, nor shall I return to slavery any person who is free by the terms of the proclamation, or by any act of Congress.' We asked if those measures would continue to operate after the war ended. That would depend on the courts, Lincoln said. Seward pointed out that the House had recently approved the Thirteenth Amendment, which outlawed slavery throughout the United States. When ratified by the states, the amendment would dispose of all legal questions about slavery.

"In conclusion, Mr. Hunter summed up what seemed to be the result of the conference: that there could be no peace treaty between the Confederacy and the United States, that Lincoln left nothing to us but unconditional submission."

Hunter turned to me and said: "We are to be held criminally responsible for a war we did not begin. We are to atone for all the blood that has been shed; confess that we have kept up a wicked war, and submit to all the laws as they are. If we go back to the bonds of the Union, we go back without representation in Congress, as Lincoln intimated; three million slaves will be loose in our midst. *We* will be slaves, and our slaves will be freedmen. Such were the terms of submission and reunion; it was subjugation in either form."

So spoke his Majesty, Abraham the First. "This demonstrates to the world," I said bitterly, "the *folly* and *danger* in trying to negotiate with that blackguard. Gentlemen, I would like you to add 'humiliating surrender' and 'degrading submission' to your report."

When they declined to do it, on the grounds that the report as written would speak for itself, I added the phrases myself and released the report to the public.

A few weeks later the slave soldier bill went down to defeat in the Senate. Thanks to Lee's influence, however, the Virginia legislature enacted a measure authorizing the Confederacy to press one-fourth of Virginia's male slaves into the army. There was no mention of emancipating them. Not even Lee could persuade the legislature to do that. The legislature also directed Virginia's congressmen to vote for a Confederate law that would arm the slaves. With the support of the Virginia senators, the Confederate Senate voted again on Barksdale's slave soldier bill and approved it by a margin of one vote.

Meanwhile General Lee came up to Richmond to confer with me. Though his hair and beard were totally white, he looked in vigorous health. His voice, however, was somber. "May I speak frankly, Your Excellency?"

"By all means," I said.

"When Sherman invades North Carolina, I've ordered General Johnston, if he thinks it practicable, to attack him before he can connect with Federal troops advancing inland from Wilmington. Sherman must be stopped before he reaches the Roanoke River, our last strong defensive line south of the Appomattox." He paused. "The best way to stop him is for me to unite with Johnston and attack Sherman with our combined armies. But I must warn Your Excellency that a joint operation against Sherman would require me to abandon Petersburg and Richmond. In any case, I fear that the evacuation of the two cities is but a matter of time."

"Would it not be better to withdraw at once?" I asked.

"My artillery and draught animals are too weak to pull anything on the muddy roads. We must wait till the weather warms and the roads are firmer. But we must move before Grant launches a spring campaign. When we do retreat, it must be toward the country we're drawing supplies from. I propose that we retire to Danville, on the North Carolina border, collect supplies and effect a junction with General Johnston's forces. Our combined armies can then defeat Sherman before Grant can come to his relief. Then the more southern states, encouraged by our success, might send us large reinforcements. Grant meanwhile, on his way to help Sherman, will find himself far from his base of supplies, in the midst of a hostile population. Maybe then we can destroy him and free Virginia of all invaders."

Lee returned to Petersburg, and General Johnston officially took command of all troops in North Carolina and south of Petersburg. But when Sherman invaded North Carolina, Johnston retreated without even trying to fight. I cursed his infernal proclivity to retreat and feared he would surrender the region in North Carolina from which we were drawing supplies. I urged General Lee to give Johnston specific instructions to avert so great a calamity. Lee replied that Johnston's forces were so badly depleted that it was better to avoid a general engagement and instead try to strike Sherman in detail, when his army was divided. "This is General Johnston's plan," Lee said, "in which I hope he may succeed, and he may then recover all the ground he may be obliged to relinquish in accomplishing it. The greatest calamity that can befall us is the destruction of our armies."

We had other ways of saving our armies and avenging the violence that Lincoln had visited on our people and our land. We had changed the key phrase in our cipher from "Complete Victory" to "Come Retribution," which meant that clandestine operations by our agents in Washington were to play a major role in Lee's and Johnston's military operations.

6. BOOTH

During the winter, Surratt slipped down the corridor into Richmond and returned with exciting news. He had seen Secretary Benjamin and they had discussed my plan to kidnap Lincoln. Benjamin assured him that rebel signal corps camps in the lower Potomac were ready to assist us when we struck. From what we could learn from other agents, an abduction scheme was part of Richmond's military strategy, which called for Lee and Johnston to attack Sherman before Grant began a spring campaign at Petersburg. If we could capture Lincoln and force negotiations, General Lee and General Johnston might not have to attack Sherman. The word from Richmond was that Lincoln must be abducted *by late March*, before Lee launched his campaign. Once it was under way, the kidnapping plan would have to be abandoned.

I was certain our operation would be the most *daring* and *victorious* deed of the entire war. To carry it off, we'd enlisted several new recruits who were mesmerized by my rages against Caesar, whose latest crime was the failed peace conference at which he had demanded unconditional submission. The first of our new conspirators was George Atzerodt, alias Andrew Atwood, a German-born blacksmith and wagon master from Port Tobacco. He was twenty-nine years of age, spoke broken English, and was short and thickset with a pinched face and narrow slits for eyes. "Rough-looking" was how Surratt's mother described him. He had ferried rebel secret service agents back and forth across the Potomac, and was exactly the man we needed to get a boat for us and ferry Lincoln across the river at Port Tobacco. When Surratt promised him a great prize and said his knowledge of the Potomac was invaluable to our operation, he threw in with us, moved to Washington, and stayed a night at Mrs. Surratt's boarding house before taking a room at the Pennsylvania House. Anna and Honora couldn't pronounce his last name, so he told them to call him "Port Tobacco"—others did—and that is what they called him, "Mr. Port Tobacco." I told them he was in the oil business with John and me.

The second recruit was Lewis Paine of Florida, a fellow Lincoln hater and a one-time rebel soldier currently staying at the Branson boarding house in Baltimore. Surratt went to Baltimore and enlisted him in our plot, saying we needed a man of his strength and experience. He's tall, over six feet, and strong as an ox, with coarse black hair and a wild look in his eyes. He told Surratt he'd fought in the major battles of Virginia, from Seven Pines to Chancellorsville, and was wounded and captured at Gettysburg. He escaped from the hospital, fled to Virginia, and joined Mosby's rangers as a part-time partisan. When his term with Mosby was up, he made his way to Alexandria, took the oath of allegiance to the United States, and went north to Baltimore and the Branson boarding house, a center for rebel secret service operations. Prominent gentlemen of Baltimore, who were secret friends of the Confederacy, supplied him with funds, so that he could journey back and forth from Baltimore to Richmond.

The last recruit was Davy Herold, whose widowed mother and six sisters lived in Washington, on Eighth Street near the Navy Yard. He'd once worked as a druggist's clerk in a pharmacy near the White House. My eyes shone when Surratt said that Caesar had bought his medicines from that very pharmacy. When I spoke with

Herold, he said he had a passion for partridge shooting and took off every fall for two or three months to hunt the birds. He's about twenty-two, and though slight and slow of foot is no halfwit—he'd attended Georgetown College. He looked up to me in awe when I declaimed what heroes we would become when Caesar was in chains in Richmond.

The abduction team was now complete: me, agent Harbin, Surratt, Arnold, O'Laughlin, Atzerodt, Paine, and Herold. When we got Lincoln across the Potomac, we would turn him over to Benjamin B. Arnold, a rebel courier stationed at a signal camp in King George County, and Arnold would take him to Richmond.

It was now March first, three days before Lincoln's Second Inauguration. I had hoped to strike before that event, but it was impossible to get all my men together and the fine points of our plan worked out in time. O'Laughlin and Arnold, in fact, had gone back to Baltimore but promised to return the moment I sent for them. To keep morale high, I went to each of the other recruits and reminded him of Lincoln's ungodly atrocities, the niggers freed, entire towns burnt, countless homesteads devastated, women raped, children left without homes, untold thousands of our brothers killed and buried in cold graves on a thousand hillsides.

We heard rumors from our friends that rebel agents were going to assassinate Lincoln on March fourth. *Robert Martin*, I said to myself, *the fellow I met in Canada last year. He'd said there would be an assassination attempt during Lincoln's inauguration!*

"We have to be in the crowd that day," I told my men, "to help our friends any way we can." At my signal, Paine came down from Baltimore, wearing a slouchy felt hat and a ragged black overcoat. Lincoln, I said, would speak from a platform on the east front of the Capitol. I would be among the dignitaries in back of Lincoln, as the guest of Miss Lucy Hale, who would provide me with a ticket. Paine, Surratt, Atzerodt, and Herold would stand below Lincoln, facing the crowd. I too would be facing the crowd, all of us ready to assist any assassination attempt from that direction.

March fourth was not quite the Ides of March, but the day of Caesar's coronation as emperor was the perfect day for him to fall.

7 · LINCOLN

I heard my old friend Joshua Speed was in town, and I sent for him and told the guard to admit him as soon as he arrived. I had roomed with Speed in Springfield back in 'forty-two. We were best friends then and had shared our political opinions and our feelings and fears about the fairer sex. Hadn't seen Speed since he and his wife joined Mary and me for Thanksgiving dinner back in 'sixty-one.

It was about ten days before the Second Inaugural, and my office was full of visitors, with several senators and congressmen still waiting in the corridor. When Speed entered, I rushed over and took his hand with both of mine. "Good to see you, Speed. I still have some audiences to give. Why don't you take the papers and amuse yourself? When I'm done, we can visit."

One by one my visitors came and left until only two women remained in the room, sitting near the fireplace.

I was tired and irritable and it sounded in my voice. "What can I do for you?"

They both spoke at once. They wanted me to release two draft dodgers from western Pennsylvania who were in prison. From what I could make out the older lady was the mother of one of the men and the younger woman was married to the other.

"Stop," I said. "Don't say any more. Give me your petition."

"Mr. Lincoln," the older lady said, "we don't have a petition. We couldn't write one and had no money to pay for writing one. We thought it best to come and see you."

"I see." I rang the bell and told a messenger to have General Dana bring me the names of all the draft dodgers in prison from western Pennsylvania. Dana soon came with the list. "Any differences in the charges or degrees of guilt?" I asked. He said none that he knew of. I looked at the two ladies and felt a rush of sympathy for them and their men folk. "Well, these fellows have suffered long enough. I've thought so for some time. I think I'll just turn the whole flock loose. General Dana, draw up the order." He did so and I signed it.

"You can go now," I told the ladies. The younger one came to me and started to kneel. "Get up," I said. "Don't kneel to me, but thank God and go." The older lady approached me with tears in her eyes. "Thank you, Mr. Lincoln, and good-bye." I took her hand with both of mine and showed her out the door.

"Lincoln," Speed said, "from what I know about your nervous sensibility, it's a wonder such scenes don't kill you."

"I tell you what, Speed. It's the only thing today that's given me pleasure and made me forget how bad I feel. I'm not well. Feet and hands cold. Told Browning I've got a class A case of the hypo. Probably ought to be in bed. But you know, that old lady, she was no counterfeit. Her honesty showed in the features of her face. At least I made two people happy today. I don't know when I'm going to die—probably before I get out of this damn job—but when I do, I want it said that I always plucked a thistle and planted a flower when I thought a flower would grow."

One thing that weighed on me were the endless rumors that I was going to be killed or kidnapped on Inauguration Day. Somebody reported a possible abduction plot to an officer in the War Department, and the officer passed the report on to Stanton. A fanatic on the subject of my safety, Stanton assigned extra guards to protect me. "I'm not a damned emperor!" I protested. "I don't need a royal bodyguard." When I told the guards to go away and leave me alone, they said Stanton would have 'em shot if they did. I knew he'd do it, too, so they stayed. Stanton also deployed a large force of detectives throughout Washington, to keep an eye on the hundreds of rebel deserters and northern riffraff roaming about the city. On Stanton's orders, soldiers patrolled the streets and secured the roads and bridges leading into the capital.

As Inauguration Day approached, I worked late into the night, putting the finishing touches on my Inaugural Address. Sitting at my desk with my legs crossed, I stared at my inchoate script and thought about the meaning of this great war. *I admit it, I haven't controlled events, they've controlled me. No, God's controlled me, and toward what end? Certainly emancipation, the central act of my Administration and the great event of the nineteenth century. But the horrendous casualties and untold destruction, what does God mean by that? Why did the contest begin as a ninety-day frolic for both sides and swell into a vast hurricane of violence that's left hardly a single family, black or white, northern or southern, unscathed? I dreamed of the right to rise, and my dream came true: I rose to the top. But where is the glory? Ashes and blood, whole cities wrecked, railroads—the sign of our technological genius—torn up and wrapped around tree trunks, whole farms and plantations burned. Americans slaughtering Americans, fathers slaying sons, brothers killing brothers. What does it all mean? And the graves—God knows how many there will be before this thing ends. Half a million? a million? God knows how many survivors will live out their remaining years with mutilated and amputated bodies, and memories so horrifying they'll wake up screaming in the night. I've lived with aching heart through it all and envy the dead their rest on the battlefields.*

I remembered old John Brown's last words before they hanged him for trying to free the slaves. *The crimes of this guilty land cannot be purged away except by blood.* He was right. A staggering insight. The whole land, North and South, guilty of complicity in the crime of slavery. God's punishment, this terrible war, His wrath roaring in the thunder of the guns, His tears falling as rain on the human wreckage of blood-soaked battlefields.

I dipped my pen in the inkwell and started writing again.

8. Douglass

I was present at the Second Inauguration of Mr. Lincoln, admiring the great parade—the blaring bands, the marching soldiers, the flag-waving spectators. But I felt there was murder in the air, and I kept close to the president's carriage on the way to the Capitol, for I feared I might see him fall that day.

On that day, the Confederacy was crumbling, and there was a *feeling* in the atmosphere in Washington. I didn't know exactly what it was, but I feared the president might be shot on his way to the Capitol. I hadn't heard of any plot; it was just a presentiment that troubled me deeply.

Ahead, the new dome of the Capitol moved against heavy rain clouds. Crowning the new dome was a statue with spectacular white wings and a sword and shield. A huge crowd had already gathered before the platform in front of the east portico. I made my way to the front of the crowd and stood by my friend Mrs. Thomas Dorsey as clouds scudded across the sky, rolling and turning in the wind. I noticed that thousands of other Negroes were also present, which was another sign of the revolutionary changes the war had brought about. Until now, Negroes had always been excluded from the inaugural ceremonies.

Presently Lincoln and the Supreme Court justices emerged from the door of the rotunda and made their way along a passageway leading to the platform. A line of police guarded the passageway, and there was a ruckus of some sort: I caught a glimpse of a policeman struggling with a wildly excited man. Finally the officer pushed him back into the crowd.

Lincoln took his seat on the platform, looked over the throng of spectators, and saw me. He touched Andrew Johnson and pointed me out to him. When Johnson looked at me, his expression was one of contempt and aversion, which gave me a glimpse into his heart and soul. "Whatever Andrew Johnson may be," I told Mrs. Dorsey, "he's no friend of our race." Seeing that I was observing him, he tried to look more friendly, but what he really looked was drunk. I hoped to God that nothing would happen to Lincoln this day. I couldn't bear the thought of the profane and drunken Johnson as our president.

Lincoln rose now and stepped to a podium at the front of the platform. At that very moment, the sun broke through the clouds, flooding the entire gathering with brilliant sunlight. It took my breath away. Then the clouds closed in again as Chief Justice Chase administered the oath, and Lincoln kissed the Bible. Then he donned his spectacles, took out his speech, and proceeded to read. I looked beyond him, at a man standing behind the railing of the right buttress. He had a mustache and wore a stovepipe hat and looked like the actor Booth. I had heard he was a Confederate sympathizer. Below the platform, just beneath Lincoln, not far from where I stood, several seedy-looking characters were staring at the crowd, or maybe at the soldiers stationed in the windows and on the roofs of nearby buildings.

I turned my attention back to Lincoln, who was talking about what had caused the war to break out four years ago. "One-eighth of the whole population were colored slaves," he said in his high-pitched voice, "located in the Southern states. All knew that this interest was, somehow, the cause of the war. To strengthen, perpetuate, and extend this interest was the object for which the insurgents would rend the Union, even by war; while the government claimed no right to do more than to restrict the territorial enlargement of it. Neither party expected for the war, the magnitude, or the duration, which it has already attained. Neither anticipated that the *cause* of the conflict might cease with, or even before, the conflict itself should cease. Each looked for an easier triumph, and a result less fundamental and astounding. Both read the same Bible, and pray to the same God; and each invokes His aid against the other. It may seem strange that any men should dare to ask a just God's assistance in wringing their bread from the sweat of other men's faces; but let us judge not that we be not judged. The prayers of both could not be answered; that of neither has been answered fully. The Almighty has His own purposes. 'Woe unto the world because of offences! for it must needs be that offences come; but woe to that man by whom the offence cometh!' If we shall suppose that American slavery is one of those offences which, in the providence of God, must needs come, but which, having continued through His appointed time, He now wills to remove, and that He gives to both North and South, this terrible war, as the woe due to those by whom the offence came, shall we discern therein any departure from those divine attributes which the believers in a living God always ascribe to Him? Fondly do we hope—fervently do we pray—that this mighty scourge of war may speedily pass away. Yet, if God wills that it continue, until all the wealth piled by the bondsman's two hundred and fifty years of unrequited toil shall be sunk, and until every drop of blood drawn with the lash, shall be paid by another drawn with the sword, as was said three thousand years ago, so still it must be said 'the judgments of the Lord are true and righteous altogether.'"

I had a lump in my throat: in one striking sentence Lincoln had answered all objections to his prolonging the war. He had declared it God's punishment on a guilty land, North and South alike, for the offense of slavery. How close he was to John Brown's vision! How close he was to the colored man who had heard in the roaring of the guns at Bull Run, Shiloh, and Antietam God's angry voice announcing that Judgment Day was at hand!

"With malice toward none," Lincoln said, "with charity for all; with firmness in the right, as God gives us to see the right, let us strive on to finish the work we are in; to bind up the nation's wounds; to care for him who shall have borne the battle, and for his widow, and his orphan—to do all which may achieve and cherish a just and a lasting peace among ourselves and with all nations."

It was a magnificent address—more like an inspired sermon than a state paper. I marveled at how Lincoln could say so much in a space so narrow. Yet when Lincoln bowed and I clapped my hands in gladness and thanksgiving, I saw in the faces of many whites about me expressions of widely different emotion.

That evening President Lincoln held the usual inaugural reception in the White House. In the past, colored people had been barred from such occasions. But now that freedom had become the law of the Republic, and colored men were mingling their blood with the blood of white men to save the country, a colored man ought to be able to offer his congratulations to the president like any other citizen, and I resolved to attend the reception. Someone had to lead the way. If the colored man was to have his rights, he had to take them.

At the White House, I joined a grand procession of citizens. I had long viewed myself as a man, but now in this multitude of the *elite* of the land, I felt myself a *man* among *men*. When I reached the front door of the White House, however, two policemen took me rudely by the arm and ordered me to stand back.

"No niggers are allowed inside," one said. "That's our orders."

"There must be some mistake," I said. "The president would never give such an order. If he knew I was at the door, he would have me admitted."

Since I was blocking the doorway and was obviously not going away, they changed their minds and conducted me inside. I soon found myself walking on some planks out of a window, which had been arranged as a temporary exit for visitors.

"You've deceived me," I cried to the policemen. "I'm not leaving till I see President Lincoln."

At that moment a gentleman who was passing recognized me. I asked him: "Would you be kind enough to tell Mr. Lincoln that Frederick Douglass is detained by officers at the door?"

When told about my predicament, the president had me shown at once into the East Room. "Here comes my friend Douglass," he said as I entered the room. He grasped my hand and said, "I'm glad to see you. I saw you in the crowd today, listening to my Inaugural Address. There is no man's opinion I value more than yours. I want to know what you thought of it."

"Mr. Lincoln," I said, "it was a sacred effort."

"I'm glad you liked it!" he said, and I passed on, feeling that anyone, however distinguished, would be honored by such remarks, from such a man. I was proud, too, because it was the first inaugural reception in the history of the Republic in which a president had received a free colored man and solicited his opinion.

I was profoundly relieved that nothing evil had befallen Mr. Lincoln that day. But as I walked through Washington's streets that night, I still felt it—the sensation of murder in the air.

9. BOOTH

I was disappointed that rebel agents didn't assassinate Lincoln on Inauguration Day. From where I stood at the Capitol, I had an *excellent* chance to kill him myself. But at this time that was not my game. Anxious to implement the abduction scheme before the late March deadline, I called Arnold and O'Laughlin down from Baltimore. Paine had gone back there after the Inauguration, and I summoned him to Washington as well. He took a room at the Surratt House, where he pretended to be a Baptist preacher and wore a new gray suit and a black tie. Surratt didn't think he fooled the girls— one said he was "queer-looking" and wouldn't convert many souls.

I liked Paine: he was a powerful man with a mean look in his eyes. He called me Captain and nodded furiously during my fiery soliloquies about Lincoln and the glory awaiting us. I knew he was one conspirator who would do whatever I asked.

On March fifteenth, I held a secret conference with my recruits in a back room of Gautier's saloon and restaurant on Pennsylvania Avenue. Only the two Confederate agents were absent. It was the first time we'd all met as a group: Arnold and O'Laughlin, Surratt and Paine, Atzerodt and Herold. I ordered champagne all around and told the bartender to keep the drinks coming.

"Gentlemen," I said, "we strike the next time Caesar attends Ford's Theater. Everything is in readiness. Paine, you'll seize Lincoln in the president's box. Harold and O'Laughlin will turn off the gaslights. Arnold, you'll leap on the stage and help Paine and me lower Lincoln from the box. We'll take him out the back door where the buggy and horses will be waiting in the alley. Surratt and Port Tobacco, you'll already be on the other side of the Navy Yard Bridge and will join us when we get there. Harbin will meet us on the road through southern Maryland. I've already bought boats to get us across the Potomac. Atzerodt and Surratt will be our pilots. Once in Virginia, we'll turn Caesar over to Benjamin Arnold, who'll take us all to Richmond."

Nobody said anything at first. Then Arnold objected again. "You'll never get him out of the box," he said. "And even if you do, you'll never get him across the bridge. The sentinel will stop us."

"We'll shoot the sentinel," I said.

"The gunshot would sound the alarm. Police and soldiers would be after us in no time."

"I agree with Sam," O'Laughlin said. "It's too dangerous."

"Besides, John, this whole abduction idea is obsolete," Arnold said. "Didn't you see it in the papers? They've started exchanging prisoners again. Your objective has already been accomplished. I want to help the Confederacy, but I want an operation that promises success and gives me a shadow of a chance for my life."

"You find fault with everything I propose," I said angrily.

"John, you can be the leader of our party, but not my executioner."

I glared at him. "Do you know you're liable to be shot?"

"Are you threatening me? Two can play that game."

By then I was so furious I could not speak. He sensed that I was close to strangling him, friend or not. "Okay," he said. "Okay. I'm still with you. But if the thing isn't accomplished within a week, I'll have nothing more to do with it."

Surratt spoke up. "The government may have wind of our movement. They've started building a stockade and gates at the Navy Yard Bridge. The gates open only to the south, as though they expect danger from within, not from without. Maybe it's wise to abort the plot."

"Abort the plot!" I rose and smashed my fist on the table. "We can't do that. By God, if worse comes to worst, *I'll* know what to do."

"What do you mean by that?" O'Laughlin said. "If you mean anything more than the capture of Lincoln, I'm out." Arnold and Surratt agreed. All three stood and put on their hats.

"Gentlemen," I said, "sit down, sit down. I've drunk too much champagne. I think we all have. I assure you, I mean nothing more than the abduction of Lincoln. Even if they are exchanging prisoners, holding him hostage will speed up the process. Richmond could even demand independence as the price for letting the tyrant go." We talked for another hour or so until we had our differences resolved. They were all still with me. The meeting broke up at dawn.

On March seventeenth, I learned that Lincoln planned to attend a benefit play at Campbell Hospital at two o'clock that very afternoon. I knew that hospital: it was located on the outskirts of Washington, on the road to the Soldiers' Home. *Forget Ford's Theater!* I said. *We'll seize Caesar today.* I summoned my men and told them the change of plans. I gave Herold my black box, which contained two carbines, ammunition, a monkey wrench, and a coil of rope to trip up any pursuing cavalry, and told him to take the box to Sur-rattsville, the Surratt family's farm and village inn in lower Mary-land. I told the others we would intercept Lincoln as he rode to the hospital. "Surratt, since you're the best driver, you'll drive Lincoln's carriage and we'll ride horseback. We'll race to Surrattsville, pick up Herold and the box of equipment, and head for the Potomac and Port Tobacco as fast as we can go. This will work, gentlemen. By tomorrow night, Lincoln will be in Richmond."

Herold set out for Surrattsville in my horse-drawn buggy, and the rest of us split up to get our horses and firearms. I went to the National Hotel and met Surratt at the boarding house, and we took off at a gallop. He was armed with a revolver and wore spurs on his boots, with his trousers tucked into their tops. When we reached the restaurant, the others were already there. To avoid suspicion, Arnold and O'Laughlin sat in one part of the room, Atzerodt and Paine in another

"Any sign of the Old Man?" I asked Arnold.

He shook his head. "Me and Michael rode down near the hospi-tal and didn't see him or any guards."

To find out what I could, I rode to the hospital and saw an actor I knew standing outside. I inquired about Lincoln, and the actor said he wasn't coming. He'd changed his plans and was speaking to an Indiana regiment instead. I was furious! Cursing our bad luck, I spun my horse around and galloped back to the restaurant and told the others what had happened, and we stormed out and rode back into the city by separate routes.

We'd agreed to rendezvous at Surratt's house. When I got there, Surratt's and Paine's horses were tied up outside. I found them in an upstairs room, still armed and still excited. I was carrying my riding whip and walked furiously around the room, slashing the air with the whip. Surratt was almost hysterical—he kept threatening to shoot anyone who came into the room. Then I noticed Weichmann sitting there. *Damn!* I thought. *What the devil is he doing here?* "I didn't see you," I said. I motioned to Surratt and Paine, and we went to a small back attic where Paine stayed.

"All my hopes are ruined," Surratt said bitterly.

"Don't despair," I said. "We'll have other opportunities." I struck the air with my whip.

Arnold and O'Laughlin never showed at the Surratt House. When I saw them next, they said they were through with the con-spiracy and in a few days went back to Baltimore. Those turncoats! I was so angry at them my hands shook violently. To settle my nerve, I drank a great deal of brandy. Well, I told myself, I still have Paine, Atzerodt, Herold, Surratt, and the two rebel agents—more than enough to handle Lincoln. We'll get him the next time he goes to Ford's Theater. I took another shot of brandy.

The day after the failed abduction attempt, on my instructions, Surratt and Atzerodt rode down to Surrattsville, told Herold what had happened, and emptied the contents of my black box on a sofa in the house. Surratt showed the things to John Lloyd, who was renting the farm and inn from Surratt's mother, and persuaded him to hide the carbines and ammunition. The coil of rope and monkey wrench could stay in the box; nobody would be suspicious of them. Surratt even showed Lloyd where to conceal the weapons and ammunition: between the joists of an unfinished little room above the storeroom at the back of the house.

A few days later I left for New York City on oil business. But first, I paid a brief call on my mother, who complained about how lonely and miserable she was. "I never doubted your love and devotion to me," she said, "I always gave you praise for being the fondest of all my boys, but since you leave me to grief, I've begun to doubt it. I'm no *Roman mother*. I love my dear ones before country and anything else. Heaven guard you is my constant prayer." I remarked that I was a Roman son, kissed her, and left to discuss the oil business with a gentleman who had connections with the rebel secret service. Then I returned to Washington, ready to spring our trap on Caesar again, only to find out that he and his family had gone to City Point to visit Grant.

"Curses!" I cried. "The fates have foiled us again."

10. LINCOLN

When Grant invited me to visit City Point, I accepted, gladly, because I wanted to be there when the final victory came. And that would be soon, if Sherman could unite with Grant at Petersburg. Sherman had already slashed into North Carolina, destroyed the Confederate stronghold of Fayetteville, and set out for Goldsboro. On the way, his army was divided into two wings, and Johnston's rebel force attacked Sherman's left wing at Bentonville, hoping to whip him in detail. But Sherman rushed reinforcements to his beleaguered flank, united his army, and drove the rebels off toward Raleigh. Which showed that redheaded Bill Sherman could fight with the best of 'em in a crisis. The day I left for City Point, March twenty-third, Sherman reached Goldsboro and linked up with Alfred Terry's force marching inland from Wilmington. Schofield's Army of the Ohio soon joined them from Tennessee, giving Sherman a powerful force of ninety thousand men. Sherman had wired Stanton in triumph: "There is now no place in the Confederacy safe against the Army of the West."

We traveled down to City Point on the *River Queen*, an unarmed side-wheel steamer. The *Bat*, a captured blockade runner converted into a gunboat, went along as an escort. With me were Mary and Tad and a couple of guards, Captain Charles Penrose, a tall, fair-skinned man, and William H. Crook of the Washington Metropolitan Police, who'd been detailed as my bodyguard. Captain John Barnes of the navy went along to keep the *River Queen* in convoy. We ran into a fierce gale on the Chesapeake, and the boat rolled and tossed so badly in the waves that it upset my stomach. But I felt better when we docked at City Point the next evening. Crook couldn't get over all the different colored lights on the scores of boats in the harbor, and the lights of the military base along the high bluffs of the shore, which looked like a fair-size city.

Grant came on board with his staff and his wife, Julia, and we shook hands all around. I told Mary: "I'm going to leave you two ladies together while the general and I go to my room where we can have a little talk without being interrupted."

We sat down in my room, and Grant lit a cigar. "Mr. President," he said, "the end of the war is close at hand, nearer than I expected. When Sheridan reaches us with his cavalry in a few days, we'll be ready to complete the investment of Petersburg and force Lee to surrender or retreat."

"General," I said. "I can *sense* the end, and it touches the tired spot."

The general and his party left, and the next morning I rose early and went on deck to stretch my legs. What a scene! Ships of every description crowded the harbor: transports, monitors, gunboats, passenger boats, and fishing boats. Vessels lined the quartermaster's docks, where colored workmen were unloading munitions and stores. Huge storehouses covered the docks, and wagon trains passed one another on their way to and from the front. Before dawn, I'd heard terrific firing in that direction, but I didn't know what it meant until my son Robert, an officer on Grant's staff, came on board the *River Queen*. He told me that the rebels had broken through our lines and captured Fort Stedman. Our troops counterattacked, though, and recaptured Fort Stedman and the part of our lines that had been lost.

Robert also handed me a telegram from Stanton: "Nothing new has transpired here. Your tormentors have taken wings and departed. I would be glad to receive a telegram from you dated at Richmond before you return. Compliments to Mrs. Lincoln." I wired him back: "Robert just now tells me there was a little rumpus up the line this morning, ending about where it began."

After breakfast, I went up to Grant's headquarters on top of the bluff. He occupied a log cabin, with one room for his sleeping quarters and a larger one for conferences. The tents of his aides were grouped around it. I asked Grant if I could see the Fort Stedman battlefield. At first he thought it was too dangerous, but came around when he saw how much I wanted to go.

We rode a jolting military train up to the front and stopped on part of the battlefield near Fort Stedman. The ground was still covered with the dead and wounded of both sides. We got off the train and rode horseback to Meade's headquarters. I was on Grant's little black pony, Jeff Davis, with my feet practically dragging along the ground.

"Well," I said, "he may be Jeff Davis and a little too small for me, but he *is* a good horse."

When we reached Meade's headquarters, 1,600 prisoners stood on the parade ground. I thought they were skinny, wretched-looking fellows, with tangled beards and matted hair. I wondered what they were thinking now that the war was over for them. "They sure look sad and unhappy," I said to nobody in particular.

General Meade, who's the most irritable man I've ever met, a perpetual grouch, took us up to the front. We could see the long curved line of the enemy's entrenchments stretching around Petersburg and facing the longer curved line of our works. We got to the front just in time to see units of the Sixth Corps attack the enemy picket lines. Our guns blasted 'em with round shot and shells, but the shells exploded in the air, doing little damage. I took a map from my pocket, where I'd marked the location of our troops and the enemy, and spread it across my knees so I could get a clearer picture of the battle lines.

When we returned to the train, a number of wounded men, bandaged, bloodied, and forlorn, lay around the depot, waiting to be evacuated back to City Point. The sight of those poor fellows saddened me. Probably showed on my face, because Crook was staring at me as if to ask if I was okay. "I've seen enough of the horrors of war," I said. "I hope this is the beginning of the end and there won't be any more bloodshed or ruined homes." Didn't say much else on the ride back. Kept my face at the window, staring at the scenes of other battles as the train rocked along.

Back at City Point that night, I joined Grant and his staff around a crackling fire. The general wore an old cavalry coat and a scruffy black hat, smoked a cigar and whittled on a stick. You would never have known this plainly dressed, quiet little man was the general in chief of all our armies. I brushed smoke away from my face and spoke of the awful difficulties we'd faced since the war began: the mounting casualties in the field, the foreign troubles, and the vexing financial problems. We'd pretty much solved the problem of paying for the war, thanks mainly to the sale of war bonds, which brought in two-thirds of our revenues. We'd also resorted to extensive taxation and to issuing greenbacks—paper money backed up by specie—which were made legal tender. Congress created a National Banking system to issue the greenbacks and sell government bonds—it was the first national financial system we'd had since Andy Jackson destroyed the Second United States Bank. Had to hand it to Congress and to Treasury Secretary Chase, I said, for solving our financial troubles, which left me free to concentrate on the war.

Next morning, General Sheridan's forces reached Deep Bottom on the James, and Sheridan came across to City Point to discuss the upcoming campaign against the enemy right and the South Side Railroad. On the way from Winchester, he'd utterly destroyed the Virginia Central Railroad and the James River Canal and liberated more than two thousand slaves. Now the enemy's only remaining supply routes were the Southside Railroad out of Petersburg and the Danville Railroad out of Richmond. I went up to Grant's headquarters and shook hands with Sheridan, who had a red, weather-beaten face and stood chest high to me.

"General," I said, "when this peculiar war began I thought a cavalryman should be at least six feet four high, but I've changed my mind. Five feet four will do in a pinch."

I went inside the telegraph operator's tent and found several of Grant's staff sitting there. I took a telegram from my pocket and smiled. "It's from Stanton," I said. "He's a good, loyal friend, but he's famous for his gruff ways. Now he's getting facetious. Listen to this." I read the dispatch: "Your telegram and General Parke's report of the 'scrimmage' this morning are received. The rebel rooster looks a little the worse as he could not hold the fence. We have nothing new here. I hope you will remember Gen. Harrison's advice to his men at Tippecanoe, that they can 'see as well a little farther off.'" I chuckled at the protective instincts of my gruff old Mars.

I noticed three kittens meowing and crawling around inside the tent. "What happened to their mother?" I asked Grant's assistant adjutant, Lieutenant Colonel Bowers.

"The mother is dead," he said.

"I'm sorry, my little friends," I said and lifted them into my lap. "Don't cry. You'll be taken care of." I turned to Bowers. "Colonel, I hope you'll see that these little waifs get plenty of milk and are treated kindly." He promised to see to it. I wiped their eyes with my handkerchief and smoothed their coats, which set them to purring.

Next day Mary and I and General and Mrs. Grant set off by boat to review the Army of the James, now commanded by General Edward Ord, a capable soldier with thick eyebrows and a bushy mustache. General Butler, the last of the political generals, was gone. He'd bungled the first expedition against Fort Fisher, and Grant had relieved him of command and ordered him home to Lowell. I happen to like Butler, he was a good military administrator, but Grant was undoubtedly right in sacking him. Grant had then dispatched a second expedition under General Terry, which succeeded in capturing the fort.

As we steamed up the James, Mary kept fiddling with my tie and ruffled white shirt. I reckon I didn't look too presidential in my long-tailed black frock coat, which I wore unbuttoned, and strapless black trousers, which kept working their way up to reveal my skinny legs. I worried about Mary: she'd felt a headache coming on this morning and the pain showed in her eyes. By and by we past Admiral Porter's warships, which were lined up in the river in double file. I tipped my stovepipe hat at the sailors, who stood on deck and saluted me as we steamed past.

When the boat docked at Aiken's Landing, Grant, Ord, and I and several other officers rode off to the parade ground on horseback. Mary and Mrs. Grant came along in an ambulance with Porter and Badeau of Grant's staff. I noticed that Ord's wife, a handsome woman who could ride a horse with great skill, was with our group. I was having a heck of a time, laughing and joking with the two generals as we rode through the woods. We soon reached a wide field where the troops were drawn up for review—an officer said they'd been there for several hours. When the ambulance with Mary and Julia didn't show up, we thought maybe they had taken the wrong road. So the men wouldn't have to wait any longer, we proceeded with the review. As we passed in front of the soldiers, who stood at parade rest while a band played, I realized that Mrs. Ord was riding with me, with Grant and Ord just ahead of us. We were about halfway through the review when the ambulance arrived with Mary and Mrs. Grant. Uh-oh, I thought. Mary's going to have a fit when she sees me with Mrs. Ord.

That wasn't the half of it. When we rode over to the ambulance, Mary gave Mary Ord a terrible tongue-lashing. "What do you mean by riding next to my husband!" she shrieked. "It's vile and insulting! The soldiers will think *you're* his wife! Don't you have any manners? Your wretched behavior makes me sick." On and on she went until poor Mary Ord broke into tears. I was too embarrassed to speak. We all were—Grant, General Ord, the other officers.

When we got back to City Point after dark, I invited a band to come down to the boat and entertain us—I thought it might ease the tension. It didn't. In front of the officers and several guests, Mary demanded that Grant relieve General Ord of command of the Army of the James. Grant defended him with as much tact as he could. But I was mortified. I tried to calm Mary—now, now, Mother, I said—but she turned on me, too. Called me an "ass" for siding with Ord and accused me of all sorts of ugly things regarding Mrs. Ord. I just walked away and went back to my room. I tried to have pity on my poor wife. She'd become increasingly jealous of other women, especially the young ones: didn't want me to talk with 'em or even be near 'em. It was the terrible pressures of the war and the loss of our darling Willie that strained Mary's nerves so badly. I understood that. But I was still mortified, hurt, and angry at her tirade in front of all those people.

For several days after that, Mary remained "indisposed" in her cabin on the *River Queen*. Then she left Tad with me and returned to Washington on the U.S.S. *Monohassett*. She did send me a telegram saying she missed me "very, very much," which was her way of apologizing. But I couldn't help it, I still felt hurt and mortified.

One day late in March, I was sitting in the after cabin on the *River Queen* when Grant and Admiral Porter brought me a visitor. It was Bill Sherman. He'd left his army at Goldsboro and arrived at City Point on a captured steamer named the *Russia*. He wore an old slouch hat and a frayed and faded uniform and was as restless as ever. He paced and puffed on a cigar and spoke nonstop about his 525-mile campaign of destruction through Georgia and the Carolinas. I listened, fascinated, and asked him questions about how he'd lived off the country. But I told him I was anxious about his absence from his army and feared Joe Johnston might do it harm. He assured me that General Schofield was fully capable of commanding in his absence.

Next day the three men returned to my cabin for a war conference. We huddled over my large military maps on the table, with blue and red pins marking the positions of the rival forces about Petersburg and in North Carolina. The lines of the Army of the Potomoc now stretched beyond Thatcher's Run, and the army was poised to make its final move.

"Meade's army," Grant said, "will attack the enemy's right flank, for the double purpose of forcing Lee out of his position at Petersburg and ensuring the success of General Sheridan's cavalry. Sheridan has already crossed the James south of City Point and will move around Lee's right and strike the South Side and Danville railroads so as to cut off Lee's last supply lines and sever his communications with Johnston in North Carolina. My only worry is, Lee might evacuate Petersburg before Sheridan can cut the roads, and try to reach Johnston. If that happens, I assure you, Mr. President, the Army of the Potomac will pursue vigorously."

"If Lee lights out for North Carolina," Sherman said, "I'll hold him and Johnston off till Grant comes with the Army of the Potomac. Then we'll trap Lee between our two thumbs."

"Is it possible to avoid another battle?" I asked.

"Beyond our control," Grant said. "Sherman or me will probably have to fight one more bloody battle, but that *will be* the last."

"And after that battle," I said, "this will be one country."

Sherman left for North Carolina that afternoon, and the next day, March twenty-ninth I believe it was, Grant was ready to move his headquarters to the front. He kissed his wife repeatedly as they stood at the door of his log cabin. Then I walked with him down to the railroad station and shook hands with him and his staff.

"Good-bye, gentlemen," I said. "God bless you all. Remember, your success is my success."

"I think we can send you some good news in a day or two," Grant said.

I went back to the *River Queen* and paced the deck, waiting for news from Grant. That night, a terrific cannonade sounded near Petersburg. It was a dark and rainy night, and I could see the flashes of the guns on the clouds. Sounded to me like a great battle was under way, but the older hands hardly seemed to notice. Next day a wire came from Grant describing last night's action, which hadn't accomplished much. I telegraphed Stanton that I felt I ought to be at home and yet I hated to leave without seeing the end of Grant's present movement. Next day, the last day of March, Stanton wired me back that all was well in Washington and that I should stay to see the campaign out. "A pause by the army now would do harm," he said. "If you are on the ground there will be no pause."

A telegram from Grant that day reported a great deal of hard fighting southwest of Petersburg. "Our troops after being driven back on to Boydton Plank Road turned and drove the enemy back and took the White Oak Road. This gives us the ground occupied by the enemy this morning. I will send you a rebel flag captured by our troops."

The correspondent Cadwallader brought me several rebel battle flags from Grant's field headquarters "Here is something material," I said, "something I can see, feel, and understand. This means victory. This *is* victory."

11. GRANT

We were camped in a cornfield near Gravelly Run in the midst of a torrential downpour. The rain and mud and quicksand in this section exceeded anything I'd ever seen and greatly hampered the movement of the army. Roads had to be corduroyed in front of the teams and artillery before they could advance. By now Sheridan was at Dinwiddie Courthouse on the Boydton Plank Road some fifteen to eighteen miles southwest of Petersburg. That night he rode up to my headquarters in the rain and told me he could drive the entire rebel cavalry force with ease.

"If I had an infantry corps," he said, "I could strike Lee's right and either crush it or force him to reinforce it by weakening his entrenched lines. Then our troops in front of them could break through and march into Petersburg."

"How can you supply your troops with forage in this weather?" an aide asked.

"Forage! I'll get up all the forage I want. I'll haul it out, if I have to set every man in the command to corduroying roads, and corduroy every mile of them from the railroad to Dinwiddie. I tell you," he said, pacing up and down, "I'm ready to strike out tomorrow and go to smashing things."

He returned to Dinwiddie and reported next the day that a large body of rebel infantry and cavalry under George Pickett was entrenched at Five Forks, a strategically important junction just south of the South Side Railroad, at the extreme right of the enemy line. Sheridan said if I'd give him an infantry corps, he would attack Five Forks next morning and cut off the entire rebel force there. On my instructions, Meade sent him Warren's corps and a small division of cavalry.

Next day, April first, I sent Colonel Porter to stay with Sheridan and send back reports by courier every half hour. The reports were fragmentary: Sheridan's cavalry, fighting dismounted, had assaulted the front of the enemy line while Warren moved against his left. At the height of the battle, Sheridan asked permission to sack Warren for moving too slowly and disobeying orders, and I told him by courier to go ahead.

That night, I was sitting around a campfire with most of my staff when Colonel Porter galloped up with news from Sheridan. "A tremendous victory!" he shouted. "Sheridan's crushed Pickett's force and seized Five Forks. Lee's right is destroyed. We've almost completed the encirclement of Petersburg and we're close to the South Side Railroad, Lee's last route of escape by rail from St. Petersburg. This means the beginning of the end, the reaching of the last ditch. It points to peace and home!"

I wired Lincoln the news, said I'd ordered everything else to advance and prevent a concentration of the enemy against Sheridan. At a quarter to five the next morning, Sunday, April second, two hundred guns opened a furious cannonade on the enemy trenches followed by infantry assaults all along the line. At the same time Sheridan with his cavalry and infantry came sweeping down from the west. Parke's Ninth Corps dashed through the enemy lines at Fort Mahone, and Wright's Sixth Corps broke through the enemy defenses and seized the South Side Railroad. With my aides I rode to a farmhouse on top of a knoll where I could see the fighting through my glasses. I sat down under a tree and wrote out orders, which couriers took away at a gallop. Suddenly bullets struck the leaves and the ground nearby. "Rebel sharpshooters," somebody cried. "General Grant, you've got to move back to safety." But I ignored the bullets and kept on writing orders. Finally, I got up, looked around, and walked around to the other side of the farmhouse. "Well," I said, "they do seem to have the range on us."

By noon, we'd seized most of the enemy's outer defenses save Forts Gregg and Whitworth. On my orders, three infantry brigades stormed and captured Gregg in fierce hand-to-hand combat. The rebels then abandoned Whitworth and fell back to Petersburg's inner fortifications. We'd now cut all the railroads out of Petersburg and had the city encircled from the Appomattox above it to the Appomattox south of it. With the fall of Petersburg imminent, I wired the president to join me at the front.

12. DAVIS

I was attending Sunday services at Saint Paul's Episcopal Church when a soldier came down the aisle with a telegram from General Lee. "I think it is absolutely necessary that we should abandon our position tonight. I have given all the necessary orders on the subject to the troops. I have directed General Stevens to send an officer to Your Excellency to explain the routes to you by which the troops will be moved to Amelia Court House and furnish you with a guide and any assistance that you may require for yourself." I folded the telegram and walked out of the church and down to the War Office, where I wired General Lee that we would evacuate Richmond. He replied that he would abandon Petersburg that night by way of the Appomattox River. "The enemy is so strong that they will cross above us and close us in between the James and the Appomattox, if we remain."

I went to my office and gave directions for the evacuation of Richmond. So the event I had dreaded had come at last. The slave soldier act had come too late to save Petersburg and the capital. Only two Negro companies had been formed, against bitter opposition from the planters, who warned us that there was no way of knowing in which direction the niggers would shoot if they were sent to the front with guns. The Saturday before I received Lee's telegram, an explosive expert—I won't reveal his name—left Richmond on a secret mission to remove the tyrant in Washington and his evil Cabinet. If successful, the mission would create great confusion in Washington and in Grant's army of mercenaries and niggers, which would aid us in our retreat into the interior of our country.

Having collected my personal papers and packed our treasury— $500,000 in gold and silver—in bags, I strode home through the streets, which were filled with women in black weeping over our terrible misfortunes. At the Executive Mansion, I packed what I could take and gave friends the rest. To one I entrusted an oil painting and a marble bust of myself. "I'll put them where they'll never be found by a damned Yankee," he said. I changed into fresh trousers, put on my gray Confederate waistcoat, a frock coat, and donned my full-brimmed planter's hat, and waited for word that the evacuation train was ready to carry me and the Cabinet to Danville. I had already sent Varina and the children and her sister Maggie Howell to Charlotte by train. Their protector, Burton Harrison, had gone with them. I shall never forget our leave-taking at the Richmond depot. Little Jeff begged to stay with me, and Maggie clung to my arm. When Varina and the children got on the train, I feared I was looking on them for the last time.

Just after eight o'clock that night, word came that the train was ready. I mounted my horse, Kentucky, and rode through the streets, which were lit by gas lanterns. There were signs of panic everywhere, hungry people breaking into the government commissary and men rolling barrels ahead of them. A long line of refugees was on the way out of town, thin women staggering under the weight of their belongings and leading thin children by the hand. Soldiers and officers were hurrying off with their trunks, and here and there a few squads of reserves and local troops were trying without success to maintain order. On Main Street a few provost guards were emptying barrels of whiskey into the gutters. I saw mobs of civilians looting stores and shops, jumping and shouting in demonic revelry. Women whose arms were filled with plunder and whose hair hung over their ears, were running off through the night. The sight of our people pillaging their own city made my face burn.

When I reached the station on the James, the Cabinet secretaries were already on board the train except for Breckinridge, now my secretary of war, who planned to remain in the city to supervise the last stage of the evacuation. Then he would follow Lee and report to me at Danville. I sat in the same car with my Cabinet, but there were more delays: the treasure train ahead of us had to clear the track and bridge across the river. Finally, around eleven that night, our train pulled out with a shriek of its whistle, crossed the bridge over the James, and roared west for Danville, 140 miles distant. Behind us, fires and giant columns of smoke boiled up from Richmond. That was the work of the cavalry rearguard, which set fire to everything of military or industrial value, including tobacco warehouses, munitions, and the armory. A strong south wind fanned the flames into an inferno which swept over the city to the waterfront and consumed the giant flour mills there. Through the train windows, we could see the horizon glowing from the blazing dumps and burning mills.

When we reached Danville the next morning, we obtained rooms and the different administrative departments resumed their routine labors. I issued a proclamation to the people of the Confederate States of America:

Animated by that confidence in your spirit and fortitude, which never yet has failed me, I announce to you, fellow countrymen, that it is my purpose to maintain your cause with my whole heart and soul; that I will never consent to abandon to the enemy one foot of the soil of any one of the States of the Confederacy. If by stress of numbers, we should ever be compelled to a temporary withdrawal from Virginia, or from any other border state, again and again will we return, until the baffled and exhausted enemy shall abandon in despair his endless and impossible task of making slaves of

*a people resolved to be free. Let us not despond, my country-
men, but, relying on the never failing mercies and protecting
care of our God, let us meet the foe with fresh defiance, with
unconquered and unconquerable hearts.*

13. LINCOLN

Tad and I and Admiral Porter took a one-car train from City Point
to Hancock Station, and from there rode horseback over the captured rebel fortifications toward Petersburg. The dead and the dying
still lay in and around the trenches, rifle pits, forts, and sunken roads
of the rebel lines. One poor fellow had a bullet hole in his forehead.
Another had both arms shot away: his wide accusing eyes stared
right at us. I tell you, it unnerved me.

After a bit we reached the city, where Old Glory now flew over
the battered courthouse. The streets were full of debris and drifting
smoke. Many buildings, blasted by shells, were still burning as we
rode by. The rebels had set fire to the tobacco warehouses, and bundles of tobacco lay about in yards and streets, which Negro boys
were hauling off to sell to our soldiers. Save for the Negroes, who
thronged the streets, singing and yelling, the city was all but
deserted. The few whites we saw looked like they were half-starved.

We came to Market Square and saw Grant standing on the steps
of a house. I dismounted, strode through the gate with a big grin on
my face, and shook his hand. "You know, General, I had a sneaking
idea all along you intended to take Petersburg before Sherman came
up."

"One time I thought Sherman ought to come up and support
us," Grant said. "Changed my mind. Thought it would be better to
let Lee's old antagonists give his army the final blow, and finish the
job."

"My anxiety's been so great," I said, "I didn't care where the
help came from, so that the work was perfectly done."

Grant waited in Petersburg for an hour and a half, hoping to get
word that Richmond had fallen. When no word came, he said he'd
best be gettin' on—had to catch up with the army, which was pursuing Lee. We said good-bye, and I watched Grant and his staff ride

off until the buildings cut them off from view. Yes, that little fellow was my kind of general.

We returned to City Point and found a telegram from General Godfrey Weitzel, commander of a corps in the Army of the James. "Richmond fell to us at 8:15 this morning," the telegram said. I learned later that black troops in his command were the first of our soldiers to enter the city, which was altogether fitting. I wired Stanton that Richmond was ours at last. He telegraphed back: "I congratulate you and the nation on the glorious news in your telegram just received. Allow me respectfully to ask you to consider whether you ought to expose the nation to the consequence of any disaster to yourself in the pursuit of a treacherous and dangerous enemy like the rebel army. Commanding generals are in the line of their duty in running such risks. But not the political head of the nation."

"Thanks for your caution," I wired him. "But I have already been to Petersburg and think I will go to Richmond tomorrow. I will take care of myself."

Next morning, as we prepared to steam up the James, I told Admiral Porter: "Thank God I've lived to see this. It seems to me I've been dreaming a horrible dream for four years, and now the nightmare's gone. I can hardly wait to see Richmond."

"If there's anything left of it," he said. "Did you see the red glare last night? Richmond's still burning and there's a black smoke over the city. It'll be a dangerous trip. The river's full of torpedoes; we'll have to remove them first."

I didn't care. I was even more excited than Tad when we steamed up the James, past Deep Bottom and Chaffin's Bluff. Ahead of us Union boats were busy sweeping the channel of torpedoes. At Drewry's Bluff we ran into a line of obstructions the steamers couldn't get around, so we continued upriver on a barge rowed by twelve sailors. On both sides of the barge, broken ordnance, wrecked boats, and dead horses floated by. We passed so close to torpedoes we could've reached out and touched them. As we rounded a curve, the church steeples of Richmond came into view. The city was still in flames all right, and a dense mass of smoke hung over the city.

When we reached a landing near Libby Prison, an ominous-looking brick building, I stepped ashore with Tad in hand. Crook, Porter, and the twelve sailors armed with carbines walked with us. Behind a small house black workers were digging with shovels. One recognized me, shouted to the others, and they ran over and cried

and cheered, and one even knelt at my feet. "Don't kneel to me," I
said, "this is not right. Kneel only to God and thank Him for your
freedom. I've only been His instrument. But I'll tell you this: as long
as I live I'll let nobody enslave you again."

As we made our way toward capitol hill, hundreds of more
Negroes flocked around us, cried my name, and struggled to touch
me. I tell you, I was so embarrassed my face was red. One woman
clapped and shouted "Glory! glory! glory!" over and over. "My
poor friends," I said, "you're free. Liberty is your birthright. God
gave it to you as He gave it to others, and it's a sin you've been
deprived of it all your lives. Now, please let me pass on; I have little
time to spare."

It was a hot day and I fanned my face with my hat as we made
our way through the dust and smoke. I noticed white people staring
at us from behind the windows of their homes. "Something oppressive in those silent faces," Crook said. "I would welcome *something*,
a yell of defiance." On other windows the green venetian blinds
were shut, but occasionally I saw fingers parting them and eyes peering out. Suddenly Crook stepped in front of me and pointed at an
open second-story window of a house on our left. For a moment, a
man in gray seemed to be pointing something that looked like a gun,
but then he disappeared.

As we neared Richmond center, a great crowd of blacks and a
few whites made it impossible for us to go on. Porter and the sailors
formed a protective circle around Tad and me, just in case. Suddenly
a white man dashed toward me from the sidewalk, and Porter drew
his sword, ready to run him through. But the fellow stopped,
removed his hat, and cried, "Abraham Lincoln, God bless you!
You're the poor man's friend." He tried to force his way through the
circle of sailors—I think he wanted to shake my hand. But Porter
yelled *no* and shoved him back. Didn't daunt his enthusiasm. He
went away tossing his hat into the air.

Couple of minutes later, Porter was trying to clear a path for us
when a beautiful girl stepped forward with a bouquet of flowers. She
smiled so sweetly that Porter ordered the guards to let her through,
and she handed the flowers to me. The card on it said: "From Eva to
the Liberator of the slaves."

Eva and the hat-tossing fellow were aberrations in this rebel city,
where most whites remained behind locked doors and closed windows. When Porter called the cavalry to clear the streets and we
were able to move forward again, I saw a young white woman

standing on a kind of bridge connecting the Spotswood House with another hotel across the street. She wore a Union flag draped over her shoulders. Couldn't tell whether this was an act of defiance or her way of rejoining the Union.

I was walking in my flat-footed gait, at the head of my party and the immense crowd following us, when I met an aide of General Weitzel, who commanded the city. "How far is it to the rebel White House?" I asked the aide. "I'd like to see it." He took us to a gray stucco mansion on a hilltop near the railroad to Danville. General Weitzel had installed his headquarters there, and the Union flag was flying over it. Weitzel's aide took us inside and into a reception room Jefferson Davis had used as his office. I walked over to a big leather-covered armchair near a desk. "This must have been Davis's chair," I said, and sat down in it. "I wonder if I could get a drink of water?" I lay back and stretched my legs.

By and by Weitzel arrived and offered to take us on a carriage ride through the city. We set out with me, Weitzel, Tad, and Porter in the buggy and Crook riding horseback at my side. The devastation we saw was unreal: skeletons of burned-out homes, buildings still on fire, streets piled with rubble. I pointed the ruins out to little Tad, who sat silent and wide-eyed by my side. At one point Weitzel asked me how he should handle the conquered people. "I'm not ready to answer that yet," I said, "but if I were in your place I'd let 'em up easy, let 'em up easy."

A Negro woman we passed apparently thought I was the second coming and could perform miracles like healing the sick. She held her child aloft, crying, "Honey, look at Mr. Lincoln and you'll get well." I tipped my hat and smiled at 'em. When we reached capitol hill, an old black man in rags, with crisp white hair protruding through a hole in his straw hat, recognized me when we rolled to a stop. He lifted his hat, knelt on the ground, and reached up for my hand. "May the good Lord bless and keep you safe, President Lincoln," he said.

We went inside the rebel capitol and found both chambers wrecked: furniture broken, tables and desks overturned, chairs hacked to bits. The floors were littered with bales of worthless Confederate paper money and bundles of public documents. "Looks like the legislators took off in a hurry," Admiral Porter said. Outside, as we climbed into the carriage, we saw thousand-dollar Confederate bonds, letters, and official papers scattered about the lawn and in the streets.

It was getting late, so Weitzel took us back to the landing on the river where we'd left the barge. Porter's flagship, *Malvern*, was waiting for us there; somehow it had got around the obstructions at Drewry's Bluff. We spent the night on the *Malvern* while it was docked at the landing—I bunked in the stateroom and Crook slept with Tad in another cabin. My sailor escort stood guard outside my door, but as usual I couldn't sleep. At one point I got up and made my way to Tad's cabin, dressed only in my long white nightgown. I opened the door and walked quietly to the bed. "Who's there!" a voice rang out. It was Crook. "It's just me," I said. "Checking to see if Tad's all right."

Next morning, General Edward H. Ripley of the Army of the James came to see me with an urgent look on his face. "Mr. President," he said, "a rebel soldier is outside with alarming information. He claims to be in Rain's Torpedo Bureau, which he says is a secret service organization specializing in explosives. He's signed a sworn statement that the Torpedo Bureau sent a group of men on a top secret mission against the head of the Yankee government. He doesn't know any names or the details of the plan, but he thinks the war's over and further bloodshed is useless, and he wants to warn you that you're in danger, grave danger. Please let me bring him in to talk to you."

I heard all this with my elbows on the table of my cabin, holding my head in my hands. "I'm sick of hearing about plots to kill me," I said. "This sounds more far-fetched than any of the others. The Confederacy is whipped; why would a bureau of the government want to blow me up? I can't believe it. Tell the rebel soldier or whatever he is to go away." Ripley kept begging me to see the man, but I told him no, emphatically, and he finally left.

Shortly after that, John A. Campbell, Davis's assistant secretary of war, and a Richmond attorney named Myers came to talk to me about restoring Virginia to the Union. Campbell was one of the rebel commissioners I'd talked to at the Hampton Roads conference. "All we ask," he said, "is an amnesty and a military convention—you understand, to cover appearances. We admit that slavery is dead. I'm sure if you offer us amnesty the rebel armies will dissolve and all the rebel states will return to the Union."

"My terms for peace haven't changed," I said. "The rebel armies must lay down their arms and disperse. Your people must recognize emancipation and the supremacy of the Union. These are indispensable. If your armies and your people persist in fighting, confiscated rebel property will be sold to bear the additional cost. But I will remit confiscated property to any state that promptly and in good faith withdraws its troops and support from the rebellion." I wrote this down as an informal paper and handed it to Campbell. "What I want," I said, "is for the Virginia legislature, the very legislature that's been sitting up yonder"—I pointed in the direction of the wrecked capitol—"to come together and vote to restore Virginia to the Union and recall her soldiers from the Confederate army."

"I believe that can be arranged," Campbell said, "if you'll authorize it."

"As for amnesty," I said, "there'll be no blanket pardon. But I do have the power to save any individual sinner from hanging. One man I won't pardon is Jefferson Davis. Once we get him—and we *will* get him—he has to stand trial for his crimes against the government."

Later that day we returned to City Point, and the next day I sent a private letter to Weitzel authorizing the Virginia legislature to meet in order to withdraw Virginia troops from the rebel army and end all other support for the rebellion. I wrote Grant what I'd done and added that I didn't think anything would come of it. "From your recent dispatches," I said, "it seems that you are pretty effectually withdrawing the Virginia troops from opposition to the government."

That same day Mary returned to City Point with "a choice little party," as she put it, that included Sumner and Lizzie Keckley, Mary's Negro seamstress. Mary said she was "disappointed" that I'd gone to Richmond without her. I didn't say anything—there was still a good deal of hurt between us.

Next morning I went up to Colonel Bowers's telegraph tent to check on dispatches from the front. One from Sheridan reported that the retreating rebels had made a stand on Burke's Station Road, and he'd attacked and routed 'em.

"If the thing is pressed," he said, "I think Lee will surrender."

I wired Grant: "Let the *thing* be pressed."

14. LEE

When my army abandoned Petersburg, Bermuda Hundred, and Richmond, we numbered only twenty-eight thousand men. I rode with the main force from Petersburg, which escaped across the Appomattox and then recrossed to the south side of it. Our first objective was Amelia Court House, where we expected rations to be awaiting us from Danville, which was our main objective. When we reached Amelia Court House, however, there were no rations, none at all, and we had to waste a day collecting what little we could from the countryside. Then we set out for Jetersville, the next station on the Danville Railroad, only to discover that the Yankees were there in force, blocking our way to Danville. They were Sheridan's cavalry, we learned, plus two entire infantry corps. The rest of the Army of the Potomac and the Army of the James were coming up fast in our rear. The vigor of Grant's pursuit depressed me, and I felt badly for my brave men—none had fought better than those who were still with me.

We weren't strong enough to break through Sheridan's forces ahead of us, and yet we had to have rations or face starvation. That night I turned the army northwest and set out for Farmville on the South Side Railroad, hoping by a rapid night march to get around Sheridan's flank and ahead of the pursuing Yankees. From Farmville we could order rations to be brought down the railroad from our supply depot at Lynchburg. Then we could turn south, march to Danville, and then effect a junction with Johnston in North Carolina.

Longstreet's corps with Field's division was in the lead, followed by the two skeletal corps of Richard Anderson and Dick Ewell and the bulk of our wagons. General Gordon's command brought up the rear, with orders to keep the wagons and stragglers ahead of them. The forced night march was a terrible hardship on the army: hundreds of starving men fell out of the ranks, others discarded their guns to lighten their load, and horses collapsed from hunger.

We reached Rice's Station on the morning of April sixth and set out for Farmville, located on the railroad and the Appomattox, with Longstreet still in the lead. The army was strung out badly now and lurched forward with little coordination through the valley of Sayler's Creek, which emptied into the Appomattox. Anderson's and Ewell's commands, which formed the middle of our column, became separated from the front and rear. I rode back to investigate and found Gordon's corps fighting an undetermined number of Yankees on the other side of Sayler's Creek where it emptied into the Appomattox. Gordon's troops were our rear guard! Where were Anderson and Ewell? I turned back toward the front of our column and rode to where Anderson and Ewell ought to be marching. Not a sign of them anywhere. I became desperately alarmed when I caught up with Longstreet's rear division under William Mahone. "Where is Anderson?" I said. "Where is Ewell? It's strange I haven't heard from them." I rode back to Sayler's Creek with Mahone's division, only to see, across the valley, the remnants of our middle divisions fleeing in great disorder. The Yankees, we learned, had attacked Anderson and Ewell from three directions in overwhelming numbers. Their two corps had been obliterated, and Ewell and my oldest son had been captured.

"My God!" I cried. "We've lost a third of the army!"

All that remained of the once-proud Army of Northern Virginia were Longstreet's forces, Gordon's, and the cavalry, about ten thousand men. We marched all that night on rain-drenched roads, men, horses, artillery, ambulances, and cavalry wallowing forward in deep mud and darkness. At sunup of the seventh we passed through Farmville and crossed to the north side of the Appomattox, and I ordered the rear column to burn the bridges behind us. They destroyed the railroad bridge, but not the wagon road bridge, and two entire corps of Yankee infantry got across to the north side of the river with us. I didn't know where Grant's cavalry was, but the rest of his well-fed infantry corps were coming up fast south of the river.

My staff and I halted briefly at a house, and I had just washed my face and was drying off when Brigadier General Henry A. Wise came up. "General Lee," he said, "my brave men are more dead than alive. For more than a week, they've been fighting day and night, without food, and, by God, sir, they won't move another step until *somebody* gives them something to eat."

"General," I said, "I assure you we'll get rations from Lynchburg. I must ask you now what you think of the situation."

"Situation? There is no situation. Nothing remains, General Lee, but to put your poor men on your poor mules and send them home in time for spring plowing. This army is hopelessly whipped, and is fast becoming demoralized. These men have endured more than I believed flesh and blood could stand, and I say to you, emphatically, sir, that to prolong the struggle is murder, and the blood of every man killed from this time forth is on your head, sir."

My neck turned red with anger. "Don't talk so wildly! My burdens are heavy enough! What would the country think of me, if I did what you suggest?"

"Country!" Wise exclaimed. "There is no country. There has

been no country, General, for a year or more. *You* are the country to these men."

I stood at an open window, staring at a column of those men plodding up the road and adjacent field. I couldn't respond to Wise's outburst.

That night, in camp near Cumberland Church, I received a letter from General Grant pointing out the hopelessness of further resistance and urging me to surrender. I showed the letter to Old Pete, and he shook his head. "Not yet," he said. I agreed—but I did send a reply asking what terms Grant would offer on condition of surrender.

Next morning, the eighth, the army set out for Appomattox Court House and Appomattox Station two or three miles beyond, where I hoped to draw supplies from Lynchburg. Gordon was now in the lead and Longstreet in the rear. Before noon, I halted for a rest, and General William Pendleton came up. He said a group of his officers asked him to advise me that further bloodshed was useless and that I ought to start negotiations for surrender.

"I trust it has not come to that," I snapped. "We've got too many brave men to think of laying down our arms."

By great effort, the head of the army reached Appomattox Court House that evening, and the troops halted for a rest. We had just made camp when our scouts reported enemy troops across my front, at Appomattox Station on the railroad. "They've cut us off from Lynchburg," I said and shook my head. I summoned Longstreet, Gordon, and Fitz Lee for an emergency war council. The enemy is in force in front of us and behind us, I said. Should we surrender? No, they said in unison. We all agreed we should try to cut our way out by attacking the enemy in our front. Gordon's infantry and Fitz Lee's cavalry would make the attack. Old Pete would close up and be prepared to hold off any Federal thrusts from the rear.

The roar of our guns opened the battle at dawn on the ninth. I rode to the front to watch the attack, but could see nothing because a thick fog hung over the landscape, and I sent Venable to find out what was happening. At the same time, the roar of artillery and rattle of musketry sounded to our rear. Longstreet sent word that he was fighting desperately against two entire Federal corps. I prayed to merciful Providence that Gordon could open a way of escape on our front.

Suddenly Venable came galloping out of the mist and whirled his mount to a stop. "General Lee, sir. Gordon moved through Appomattox Court House, found the Federals behind fieldworks, and launched an attack. Then the cavalry saw a heavy force of Federal infantry hidden in the woods in back of Gordon's right. They attacked our cavalry and then headed for Appomattox Court House to cut Gordon off from Longstreet. At the same time, enemy cavalry struck Gordon's left. They're pressing him on three sides. He said, 'Tell General Lee I've fought my corps to a frazzle, and I fear I can do nothing unless I'm heavily supported by Longstreet's corps.'"

"That's impossible," I said. "Longstreet is heavily engaged in our rear." That meant we were whipped. It was over. "There is nothing left for me to do but to go and see General Grant," I said, "and I would rather die a thousand deaths." I donned a new uniform with sash and sword and boots with gold spurs in which to meet Grant. To an aide I dictated a letter to Grant requesting an interview, at such time and place as he might designate, to discuss the surrender of my army.

15. GRANT

With our forces pressing Lee's army from the front and rear, I set out for Sheridan's front with my staff, riding along the south side of the Appomattox. I'd had a terrible headache since yesterday. Hurt so bad I felt sick. We hadn't gone far when Lieutenant Charles E. Pease of Meade's staff overtook us with a dispatch from Lee. I tore it open and read it. "He's asking for an interview for the purpose of surrendering his army," I said. The instant I saw the contents of that dispatch I was cured of the headache.

Pease also handed me a note from Meade. Said he'd read the dispatch from Lee and had granted him a truce. I dismounted and sat down on the grass by the side of the road and wrote a reply to Lee asking him to tell me where the interview would take place. I gave the note to Colonel Babcock, and he rode off to find Lee. Then I rode at once to Sheridan's front, where his troops were drawn up in line of battle facing the Confederate army nearby. Sheridan's men were very much excited and said that the offer to surrender was a damned rebel trick so they could get away. But I had no doubts about Lee's good faith, and with my staff I rode on to Appomattox Court House, which consisted of a half dozen houses and a single street. Saw a group of our officers standing at the edge of the village. Recognized Sheridan and Ord.

"How are you, Sheridan?" I asked.

"First rate, thank you. How are you?"

"Never felt better. Is Lee over there," I asked, pointing up the street.

"Yes, he's in that brick house, waiting to surrender to you."

I rode on with Sheridan, Ord, and several other officers and saw Babcock's orderly sitting in the street in front of the brick house.

"Colonel Babcock posted me here," he said. "Told me to tell you he and General Lee are inside."

"Who's house is it?" I asked.

"Fella by the name of McLean."

When I left camp that morning, I was in rough garb. Had no sword or spurs, wore a stiff-brimmed black hat and a mud-spattered private's uniform, with the shoulder straps of my rank on the coat to indicate who I was. I went inside to the parlor and saw General Lee sitting by a small oval table near the front window. His hair and beard were almost completely white, and he wore a beautiful new uniform—a gray coat buttoned to his throat, polished top boots, large spurs, and a fine long sword whose hilt was studded with jewels. His gray felt hat and a pair of buckskin gauntlets lay on the table. Didn't know what his feelings were—he was a man of much dignity, with an impassive face. My own feelings were sad and depressed. I felt like anything but rejoicing at the downfall of a foe who'd fought so long and valiantly, and who'd suffered so much for a cause, though that cause was one of the worst a people had ever fought for.

I sat down by a marble-topped table in the center of the room and spoke to Lee, who remained at the small table. "I met you once before, while we were serving in Mexico. I've always remembered your appearance. I think I would recognize you anywhere."

"I remember meeting you," he said. "I've often thought of it and tried to remember how you looked, but I've never been able to do so."

We talked a little more about Mexico, and then he said: "I asked to see you to find out on what terms you would receive the surrender of my army."

"The officers and men who surrender will be paroled and disqualified from taking up arms again. All arms, ammunition, and supplies are to be delivered up as captured property."

Lee nodded. "Those are about the conditions I expected would be proposed. May I ask you to write them down so they can be formally acted on?"

"Very well," I said, and asked for my order book. I wrote down the terms rapidly, pausing only after I'd written, "The arms, artillery, and public property to be parked, and stacked, and turned over to the officers appointed by me to receive them." I glanced at Lee's sword and thought it would cause undue embarrassment and humiliation to relieve officers of their side arms. So I wrote that the terms of surrender would not embrace the officers' sidearms, private horses, and baggage. Then I handed the order to Lee.

He took a pair of steel-rimmed spectacles out of his pocket, slowly wiped them clean with a handkerchief, placed them on his nose, crossed his legs, and read the order carefully. When he finished, he said, in reference to the officers' sidearms: "This will have a very happy effect on my army."

"I'll have a copy made in ink unless you have any suggestions."

"There is one thing," he said. "Unlike your army, the cavalrymen and artillerymen in our army own their own horses. I wonder if these men will be permitted to retain their horses."

"I didn't know your private soldiers owned their animals," I said. "I take it most of the men in your ranks are small farmers. Since the country has been stripped bare by our two armies, it's doubtful they can put in a crop to carry them and their families through next winter without their horses. I won't change the terms as written, but I will instruct my paroling officers to let the men take their horses or mules home with them to work their little farms."

Lee nodded his thanks. Then he had an aide draw up a formal acceptance of my terms of surrender, which he signed.

"One more thing," he said. "I have a thousand or so of your men as prisoners. I'll be glad to send them to your lines as soon as it can be arranged, because I have no provisions for them. In fact, I have nothing for my own men. They've been living the last few days on parched corn, and we are badly in need of rations and forage."

"Don't have any forage for your animals," I said, "but I'll have your army supplied with rations at once. How many men do you have?"

"I can't say."

"Suppose I send over twenty-five thousand rations. Do you think that will be sufficient?"

"I think it will be ample. And a great relief, I assure you."

It was just before four in the afternoon. Lee and I rose and shook hands. He bowed to the other officers in the room, put on his hat and gauntlets, and went outside and signaled his orderly to bring his horse. He stood on the bottom step of the porch, striking his hands together as he stared at a hill beyond the valley where his army lay. As he mounted his horse, I stepped off the porch and raised my hat in salute. He raised his hat in return, then rode away, across the valley, and up the hill where his army was waiting for him.

16. LEE

When my old soldiers saw me riding up the road, they broke into cheers. "General," one cried, "are we surrendered?" When they crowded around me, tears filled my eyes. "Men," I said, "we've fought the war together, and I've done the best I could for you. You will all be paroled and must go to your homes until exchanged for captured Yankee soldiers." Many of them wept openly, others cursed and said they wanted to die. One man cried, "General, we'll fight 'em yet. Just say the word and we'll go in and fight 'em yet!" I shook my head. "There will be no more of that." I tried to say something more to them, but couldn't. I wiped the tears from my eyes, said good-bye, and rode on with my staff.

We halted at an orchard to await the rations from Grant's army. Only now did the full realization of our surrender hit me. All the terrible sacrifices, the deaths of so many brave and gallant men—all was in vain, *in vain*. I paced back and forth in the orchard, slapping my hands together in anger. My staff knew I was in a savage mood and stayed back. After a while, some Yankee officers came and said they wanted to see me. I turned and glared at them until they retreated down the road.

When the rations began arriving, I rode back to headquarters with my staff. Many of my old soldiers followed us, cheering and weeping and crying out, "We love you, General Lee!" I loved them too, and the pain in my heart was so great I thought I could not bear it. One private who wore nothing but rags reached for my hand. "General," he said, "I've had the honor of serving in this army since you took command. If I thought I was to blame for what's happened today, I couldn't look you in the face. But I've always tried to do my duty. I hope to have the honor of serving under you again. Good-bye, General. God bless you."

I turned my head away so he wouldn't see the look on my face.

Next day I issued a general order, which became known as "Lee's Farewell Address," to the Army of Northern Virginia.

> *After four years of arduous service, marked by unsur-passed courage and fortitude, the Army of Northern Virginia has been compelled to yield to overwhelming numbers and resources.*
>
> *I need not tell the brave survivors of so many hard fought battles, who have remained steadfast to the last, that I have consented to the result from no distrust of them.*
>
> *But feeling that valor and devotion could accomplish nothing that would compensate for the loss that must have attended the continuance of the contest, I determined to avoid the useless sacrifice of those whose past services have endeared them to their countrymen.*
>
> *By the terms of the agreement officers and men can return to their homes and remain until exchanged. You will take with you the satisfaction that proceeds from the conscious-ness of duty faithfully performed, and I earnestly pray that a Merciful God will extend to you His blessing and protection.*
>
> *With an increasing admiration of your constancy and devotion to your country, and a grateful remembrance of your kind and generous considerations for myself, I bid you all an affectionate farewell.*

As word of the surrender spread, thousands of stragglers came in to give themselves up, so that by the time of the official surrender, April twelfth, the army totaled 26,018 officers and men. That day they marched together for the last time and stacked their arms before their conquerors. I did not attend the ceremony, but I did stay on at my headquarters, letting my old soldiers know that they would not go through this humiliating ordeal without me.

I sent a dispatch to President Davis, saying it was with pain that I announced to His Excellency the surrender of the Army of North-ern Virginia. I left Appomattox later that day with my aides, Taylor and Marshall, and my ambulance and headquarters wagon with their drivers. We rode through Buckingham Court House and found

Old Pete camped two miles outside of town. My old warhorse looked exceedingly tired, with dark circles under his eyes.

"I've thought the cause was hopeless for months," he said bitterly. "Next time I fight, I'll make certain it's necessary."

We parted the next day, and I sat my horse, watching Old Pete as he rode off and finally disappeared from view. I felt a pain in my heart and an emptiness that would never go away. For three long years, we had fought hard together, had won great victories and suffered painful defeats together. It was difficult to believe our efforts had come to such a bitter parting.

On the ride to my brother's farm in Powhatan County, I kept telling myself I had done the right thing in surrendering the army and not turning the men loose to continue the war through guerrilla operations. Before I went to see Grant, Colonel Alexander had proposed that the men should take to the woods and fight as partisans. "Two-thirds of us would get away," Alexander said. "We would scatter like rabbits and partridges in the woods, and they couldn't scatter to catch us."

"We have to consider how that would affect the country as a whole," I told him. "Already it's demoralized by four years of war. If I took your advice, the men would be without rations and under no control of officers. They would become mere bands of marauders, and the enemy's cavalry would pursue them. A partisan war like that would cause great suffering and the devastation of the country. We would bring on a state of affairs it would take the country years to recover from. You young fellows might go to bushwhacking, but the only dignified course for me is to go to General Grant and surrender myself and take the consequences of my acts."

I still think I made the right choice. But my bitter feelings about what had befallen us would not go away. I was sorry, extremely sorry, I had ever become a soldier. It was the worst mistake of my life.

We stayed the night with my brother and next morning my son Rooney and my nephew John joined us for the ride into Richmond. On April fifteenth we passed through Manchester on the south side of the James. The sky was overcast and the day was dark as we crossed the river on a pontoon bridge laid down by the Yankees. Ahead of us, the entire waterfront of Richmond was burned out— flour mills, the arsenal, factories, tobacco warehouses, homes, stores, all. East of the Tredgar Iron Works and the blackened walls of plants that had once produced shells and small arms, the fire had leveled Richmond for almost a mile.

It was raining when we entered the ruins of the city—we could see the top of the statehouse, moving against the clouds. A Yankee flag was flying over the capitol, and the sight disturbed me so much that I raised my hand to shield it from my sight. At last, we reined up at the little red brick house on East Franklin Street where my family was staying. I dismounted and went inside to see my dear Mim. She was in her wheel-chair, her face contorted in pain, and I bent down and kissed her. Then I unbuckled my sword, never to wear it again.

17. DAVIS

When we heard that Lee had surrendered, we abandoned Danville and hastened to Greensboro, North Carolina, by train. A few days later, Rob Lee arrived with his father's letter to me officially announcing his surrender to Grant. I turned away and wept silently. Still, I did not think the cause was lost. I had already summoned Generals Johnston and Beauregard to Greensboro. Now, with three members of the Cabinet, we held a war council in the house in which I was staying.

"Our late disasters are terrible," I said, "but I do not think we should regard them as fatal. I think we can whip the enemy yet, if our people will turn out." I asked General Johnston what he thought.

"Sir, my view is that the people are tired of war and will not fight any longer. Our country is overrun, our military resources are gone, my men are deserting in large numbers every day—my little army is melting away like snow before the sun. Since Lee's defeat, they believe the war is lost. I think we ought to ask Sherman for terms."

I turned to General Beauregard. "And you, sir?"

"I agree with General Johnston."

"Gentlemen," I said, "I did not call you here to ask your opinions about negotiating with Lincoln, but to find out what is feasible to do with your army."

"Sir," Johnston said in a tone that bordered on disrespect. "I'm convinced that Sherman will offer terms that will be to our advantage."

"You can ask him for terms, but I am not sanguine about the ultimate results. Mind you, sir, I will do nothing that will obligate me to the enemy government. I expect you to stand at Charlotte and if forced to do so, to retreat to the southwest. If we have to, we will go to Texas and continue the war from there. I will not leave Confederate soil as long as there are men in uniform willing to fight for the cause."

After the meeting, I wrote Varina by courier: "Dear Winnie, I will come to you if I can—Everything is dark—you should prepare for the worst by dividing your baggage so as to move in wagons. If you can go to Abbeyville it seems best to do so. I have lingered on the road and labored to little purpose. My love to the children and Maggie—God bless, guide, and preserve you. Your affectionate Banny."

With a small band of Tennessee cavalry as my escort, I hastened to Charlotte, to await news from Johnston. On the way there, I received a letter from a battalion of Virginia troops serving with Johnston; they wanted permission to go home to protect their families. I answered with an emphatic no. "Our necessities exclude the idea of disbanding any portion of the force which remains to us and constitutes our best hope of recovering from our reverses and disasters."

Still, I could not be blind to the signs: panic had seized the country, and I began to despair. I wrote Winnie that the dispersion of Lee's army and the surrender of the remnant which remained with him destroyed the hopes I had entertained when she and I had parted. Had that army held together, I said, I was confident we would have successfully executed the plan of operations I had worked out and would now be on the high road to independence. Even after that disaster, if the men who straggled, say thirty or forty thousand in number, had come back with their arms and with a disposition to fight, we might have repaired the damage; but all was sadly the reverse of that.

"The issue is one which it is very painful for me to meet," I wrote. "On one hand is the long night of oppression which will follow the return of our people to the 'Union.' On the other, the suffering of the women and children and carnage among the few brave patriots who would still oppose the invader, and who, unless the people would rise en masse to sustain them, would struggle but to die in vain. I have prayed to our Heavenly Father to give me wisdom and fortitude equal to the demands of the position in which Providence has placed me. I have sacrificed so much for the cause of the Confederacy that I can measure my ability to make any further sacrifice required.

"How you and the children are to be saved from degradation is much on my mind. Your best opportunity would be to go to Mobile and sail to a foreign port, or try to reach Texas. As for myself, I intend to force my way across the Mississippi, and if nothing can be done there, then I can go to Mexico, and have the world from which to choose a location.

"Dear wife, this is not the fate to which I invited you when the future was rose colored to us both; but I know you will bear it even better than myself. Farewell, my dear, there may be better things in store for us than are now in view, but my love is all I have to offer, and that has the value of a thing long possessed, and sure not to be lost."

18. LINCOLN

Before leaving City Point, I toured Depot Hospital on the Appomattox with Mary. I was struck by the citylike appearance of the hospital, which consisted of scores of white tents separated by dirt streets. We spent five hours there, visiting every ward in the hospital. The men who were able stood in line and shook my hand. I went to the bedsides of those who couldn't stand and spoke to them. One poor fellow had lost a leg at Fort Stedman and had a fever. I put my hand on his forehead, then bent over and kissed his cheek. When the surgeons pulled the sheet back to show me his bloody, unhealed stump, I got tears in my eyes and whispered to him that he had to live.

I met many of the nurses and surgeons, too. One of the nurses was a pretty Quaker girl with rosy cheeks. She couldn't have been much more than twenty-one, yet she smiled brightly and was clearly proud of her hospital work. Thank God for the women of the North who came to the battlefield to patch up our mutilated soldiers. I assured her and the others that this cruel war would soon be over.

The surgeons were afraid I would tire out and urged me to rest. "No," I said, "I aim to see as many of the boys as possible. I'll never see 'em again, and I want 'em to know how much I appreciate what they've done for the country." In all, I reckon I shook hands with seven thousand patients that day.

A surgeon said my arm must be lame. "Doesn't it ache?" he asked.

"Nope," I said. "My muscles are pretty strong." I stepped outside and spotted a heavy ax lying by a wood pile. I picked it up and split a few logs, and then said: "I wonder if I can lift this thing by the end of the handle." I held the ax out horizontally at arm's length—the thing didn't quiver as I held it there. "When I used to split rails back home, that was thirty years ago, I could lift two axes that way." Couple of strong-looking fellows tried to lift the ax as I had, but couldn't do it.

We left for Washington on the night of April eighth on board the *River Queen.* Seward had been hurt in a carriage accident, and I was anxious to get back to Washington and see how he was doing. We anchored for the night at Fort Monroe, and the next morning, Palm Sunday, we set out for Washington. On the way, I entertained the group by reading the scene from *Macbeth* where Duncan is assassinated.

> *Duncan is in his grave,*
> *After life's fitful fever he sleeps well;*
> *Treason has done his worst; nor steel, nor poison,*
> *Malice domestic, foreign levy, nothing*
> *Can touch him further.*

We reached Washington that evening and found the presidential carriage waiting for us at the wharf. We climbed in—Tad, Crook, Mary, and me—and headed for the White House. We were amazed to see bonfires blazing in all directions, firecrackers going off, people dancing and shouting in the streets. I asked a bystander what had happened. "Haven't you heard?" he said. "Lee has surrendered!" When we reached the White House, Stanton handed me a telegram that confirmed the news.

"Any word from Sherman?" I asked.

"Nothing," Stanton said.

I went to see Seward in his red brick house on Lafayette Square. Found him lying in bed upstairs, with his jaw fractured and his right arm broken. His head and neck were in a steel frame and covered with bandages.

"You're back from Richmond," he whispered.

"Yes," I said. "I trust you've heard the good news?"

"Lee's surrender? Oh yes. But don't proclaim a day of thanksgiving just yet. We still haven't heard that Johnston has given up."

I told him about my trip to City Point and my visit to the ruins of Richmond. Pausing from time to time to get his breath, he told me how Stanton had come to see him repeatedly and how he'd said: "God bless you, Stanton. You've made me cry for the first time in my life."

The next day, by Stanton's orders, five hundred guns shattered the dawn stillness, celebrating the official news of Lee's surrender. Welles, secretary of the navy, reported that the country was delirious with joy. "Guns are firing, bells ringing, flags flying, men laughing, children cheering, all, all are jubilant."

I had breakfast with young Brooks while "hurrahing legions," as he described 'em, marched by outside. Later in the day a band and a cheering crowd gathered on the White House grounds. Tad went to a window and waved a captured rebel flag, and the crowd roared with delight. Tad turned and said, "They want you to speak, Papaday." I promised 'em a formal speech on the night of the eleventh and then asked the band to play "Dixie." "I've always thought 'Dixie' the most beautiful of our songs," I told the crowd. "The rebels took it as theirs, but we've captured it back"—there were happy shouts from below—"and it's our lawful prize." The band struck up "Dixie," with its cornet trills, and then launched into a rousing rendition of "Yankee Doodle."

While Washington celebrated that April tenth, I sat at my desk and worked on the speech I'd promised. It wasn't going to be an ode to patriotism and victory. Nope, I aimed to talk about the problems of reconstruction and how I hoped to solve them. But I tell you this, it was like trying to blaze a way through the swamp. When the Cabinet met that day, I said I was glad and relieved that the war was over, but I didn't have time to rejoice because our postwar burdens were among the worst we'd ever faced. We had to restore and rebuild the conquered states of the so-called Confederacy, had to keep the loyalty of the white Unionist minority there, and had to protect the freedom of the former slaves. The new Freedmen's Bureau, which we'd created in March, would provide the Negroes with food, schools, and transportation, would help 'em find jobs at fair wages, and would settle 'em on confiscated or abandoned lands. But hatred and fear of the Negro ran deep all across the South, and the bureau was certain to meet bitter resistance from the former rebels.

Another problem of course was Negro suffrage. Most northern states didn't let Negroes vote, and most Republicans, including some Radicals, shrank from enfranchising the former slaves, for fear it would alienate their white constituencies. On the other hand, I was impressed with Sumner's argument that the Negroes were the best Unionists we had in Dixie and that they deserved the elective franchise. Chief Justice Chase told me bluntly it was criminal to deny southern Negroes the suffrage because it left 'em under the political control of their former masters, and that argument struck me as very persuasive. Beyond their freedom, what else should the former slaves have? Civil rights, all legal rights, the right to work freely and for decent wages, and the right to rise—to go as far as their talent and toil will take them. That much we had to guarantee them. On that note, I was glad the new Louisiana constitution had not adopted an apprentice system for the freed people. Douglass was right: they deserved the right to choose their own employers, to "stand on their own legs," as he put it.

Stanton came in later that day, complaining that he was sick and exhausted. "I promised myself I would resign when Richmond fell and Lee surrendered," he said. "I'm here to offer my resignation."

I looked at him, his burly figure, long beard, and tired eyes, and thought how irreplaceable he'd been as my secretary of war. I walked over to him and put my hands on his shoulders. "Stanton, you've been a good friend and a faithful public officer, and it's not for you to say when you're no longer needed here. With the problems we face in the South, I'll need you more than ever."

He was silent for a few minutes. Then he said: "I guess I can stay on a little longer, Mr. President."

On the evening of April eleventh, hundreds of people showed up on the White House lawn as I prepared to speak to them from an upstairs window. It was drizzling and misty out, but you could still see the new illuminated dome of the Capitol and the lights along Pennsylvania Avenue. In the distance, beyond the Potomac, Arlington House—Lee's old house—was ablaze with colored candles and exploding rockets, as hundreds of former slaves sang "The Year of Jubilee."

With young Brooks holding a candle from behind a curtain, I stepped to the window and unrolled my speech. Little Tad sat beside me, ready to grab the pages as I dropped them on the floor. The lights of the White House illuminated the vast sea of upturned faces stretched out below, and I bowed when they broke into a resounding hurrah.

"We meet this evening, not in sorrow, but in gladness of heart," I began. "The evacuation of Petersburg and Richmond and the surrender of the principal insurgent army, give hope of a righteous and speedy peace whose joyous expression can not be restrained." But our recent successes, I said, forced our attention to the re-inauguration of the national authority—reconstruction. "It is fraught with great difficulty," I said. "Unlike the case of a war between independent nations, there is no authorized organ for us to treat with. No one man has the authority to give up the rebellion for any other man. We simply must begin with, and mold from, disorganized and discordant elements. Nor is it a small additional embarrassment that we, the loyal people, differ among ourselves as to the mode, manner, and means of reconstruction." We all agreed, however, that the insurgent states were out of their proper practical relation with the Union; and that the sole object of the government, civil and military, was to get those states back into that proper practical relation.

I pointed out that I had been much censored for setting up and sustaining the new state government in Louisiana, even though the plan I used to do it—the 10 percent plan—had been approved by every member of the Cabinet and had received many commendations from members of Congress. I admitted that the amount of constituency on which the new Louisiana government rested would be more satisfactory to all if it contained fifty, thirty, or even twenty thousand, instead of only about twelve thousand, as it did.

Then I brought up the matter of Negro suffrage in Louisiana. "It is also unsatisfactory to some that the elective franchise is not given to the colored man," I said. "I would myself prefer that it were now conferred on the very intelligent, and on those who serve our cause as soldiers. Still the question is not whether the Louisiana government, as it stands, is quite all that is desirable. The question is 'Will it be wiser to take it as it is, and help to improve it; or to reject, and disperse it?' 'Can Louisiana be brought into proper practical relation with the Union *sooner* by *sustaining* or by *discarding* her new state government?'

"Some twelve thousand voters in the heretofore slave state of Louisiana have sworn allegiance to the Union, held elections, organized a state government, and adopted a free-state constitution, which gives the benefit of public schools equally to black and white and empowers the legislature to confer the elective franchise upon the colored man. Their legislature has already voted to ratify the constitutional amendment recently passed by Congress, abolishing slavery throughout the nation. These twelve thousand white men are thus fully committed to the Union, and to perpetual freedom in the state—committed to the very things and nearly all the things the nation wants—and they ask the nation's recognition and its assistance to make good their committal. If we *reject* and *spurn* them, we tell the white men they are worthless and we tell the colored men, 'The cup of liberty, which your old masters hold to your lips, we dash from you and leave you to the chances of gathering the spilled and scattered contents in some vague and undefined when, where, and how.' If this course, discouraging and paralyzing both white and black, has any tendency to bring Louisiana into proper practical relation with the Union, I have been unable to perceive it.

"If, on the contrary, we recognize and sustain the new government of Louisiana, we encourage the hearts and nerve the arms of the twelve thousand to adhere to their work, and argue for it, and fight for it, and feed it, and grow it, and ripen it to a complete success. The colored man too, in seeing all united for him, is inspired with vigilance, and energy, and daring, to the same end."

I granted that the colored man deserved the elective franchise. But would he not attain it sooner by saving the already advanced steps toward it, than by running backward over them? I also pointed out that if we rejected Louisiana, we also rejected one vote in favor of the proposed Thirteenth Amendment.

"What has been said of Louisiana," I went on, "will apply generally to other states. And yet so great peculiarities pertain to each state; and such important and sudden changes occur in the same state; and withal, so new and unprecedented is the whole case, that no exclusive and inflexible plan can safely be prescribed as to details and colatterals. Such exclusive and inflexible a plan would surely become a new entanglement."

Still, the vexing problems of reconstruction, of how to control the rebellious white majority and protect southern Unionists whether white or colored, were far from being solved. Therefore I concluded with a warning: "In the present '*situation*' as the phrase goes, it may be my duty to make some new announcement to the people of the South. I am considering, and shall not fail to act, when satisfied that action will be proper."

It was an unpopular speech. What my listeners wanted was not a technical treatise about reconstruction, but a rousing oration about our victorious arms. While I read the speech, dropping the pages to

Tad, many people got bored and wandered off in the mist. Others frowned when I said the colored man deserved the right to vote, and the look on their faces made me anxious.

19. BOOTH

I heard the speech Caesar gave from the White House window. When he finished, I turned to Herold and Paine. "That means nigger citizenship. Now, by God, I'll put him through. That's the last speech he'll ever make." I spun around and stomped off. The fall of Richmond and Lee's surrender had put me in the blackest mood of my life. I hated all the celebrations, the singing and hurrahing in the streets for Caesar's victorious armies. That diabolical tyrant had *destroyed* my country, had *burned* Richmond, *burned* Columbia, *burned* Charleston, had *laid waste* to the most perfect society ever made. I could never see Richmond again—I couldn't bear the sight of nigger troops patrolling the ruins of that once beautiful city—and the thought *tormented* me. At the saloon and billiard parlor on E Street, I tried to drown my sorrow in bottle after bottle of brandy, but the brandy only fueled my hatred for Caesar, and I cursed him till tears burned my eyes.

For six months we had worked to capture him, but now our great cause was all but lost and abduction was useless. No, something decisive and great had to be done. Death to Caesar! That was my vow. I'd heard that Confederate agents had a secret plan to blow Lincoln up in the White House, and I told Atzerodt we had to kill him before they did. Vengeance would be ours! Then we learned that the team of agents had been captured, which left the field clear for us. Surratt had gone to Canada after Richmond fell, so we were now down to four—Atzerodt, Herold, Paine, and myself. We would need the help of Mrs. Surratt, who had closed her home and wept at the news of Lee's surrender. I called at her boarding house and persuaded her to ride out to Surrattsville and tell Lloyd to have the concealed weapons ready for us. Before I left, Weichmann, Mrs. Surratt's boarder, asked me why I wasn't acting. "I'm done with that," I said, glaring at him. "The only play I care to act in is *Venice Preserved*." He looked blankly at me, so the import of my remark didn't register. The play involves a group of conspirators who plan to preserve Venice by assassinating all the tyrannical senators.

On the day of Lincoln's speech, Mrs. Surratt ran her errand to Surrattsville. The next day, in my room at the National Hotel, I drew up a list of targets: Lincoln, Johnson, and Seward, all would die for their crimes against my country. On the thirteenth, Atzerodt, on my orders, went to the Kirkwood House where Johnson was staying, and took a room for the next day. His room was directly above Johnson's. Paine and I went to Seward's house on Lafayette Square to find out how we could get inside to kill him. I knew Seward was confined to his bed—I'd read about his accident in the paper. I spoke to a lovely chambermaid at Seward's residence and charmed her so much she blushed. I had a good mind to give her my diamond pin. If necessary, I felt sure we could gain entrance into Seward's house through her.

That same day General Grant arrived in Washington and took rooms at Willard's Hotel. I put that drunken swine on my list for the heinous slaughter of so many thousands of my countrymen. On the way back to my hotel, I met a friend. "Ed," I said, "I've got the biggest thing on my hands that has ever turned up."

20. LINCOLN

My speech didn't win many converts from Sumner's camp. The senator himself let me know that he remained "categorically" opposed to my efforts in Louisiana. As it turned out, the hottest controversy was not over my speech but over my letter authorizing the Virginia legislature to meet. "Alas! Alas!" Sumner cried when he heard about it. Stanton and James Speed, my new attorney general, rushed in to protest, pointing out that this was tantamount to recognizing the legislature as a legal body. All I meant to do, I told 'em, was to have the legislature undo its own work, disband Virginia's troops, and have 'em come together and turn themselves and their neighbors into good Union men. But since the Cabinet opposed the move, I admitted I had perhaps made a mistake. I wrote General Weitzel in Richmond not to let the legislature convene.

Last night I had the dream again—the one where I'm on a phantom ship moving swiftly toward a dark and indefinite shore. That dream had always come to me on the eve of important tidings from the front. When I woke this morning, I was in a good mood.

It's Good Friday, and I think the dream surely portends momentous news for today—probably that Johnston has surrendered in North Carolina. I'm sure the other pockets of resistance in Louisiana and Texas will end shortly after, bringing the war officially to a close.

I walked to my shop and lit the fireplace to take off the morning chill. Then I went to a window and looked outside. It was a beautiful spring day—the dogwoods and Judas trees were blooming. In a few days young couples would be riding to the Great Falls for picnics and romance. Like me and Mary in the old days.

At eight I had a light breakfast with Mary and Tad in the dining room. Robert had come back to Washington with General Grant and joined us for breakfast. He told us, in his quiet way, that he'd stood on the porch when Lee surrendered to Grant at Appomattox. It was comforting to Mary and me to have our little family together again. She and I were in better spirits now, mainly because I'd tried to put her jealous fit at City Point behind me. A couple of days ago I'd written her a playful and tender note about going on a carriage ride together, and she'd smiled and hugged close to me as we rode about the city with the cavalry escort. At breakfast this morning, I told her we would ride again in the afternoon, by ourselves. Tonight we're going to Ford's Theater to see the British farce *Our American Cousin*, starring Laura Keene. I hope it'll make me laugh—I need to get my mind off reconstruction. We invited the Grants to go with us and today's papers announced our plans.

After breakfast, I shaved, combed my hair and whiskers, put on a freshly brushed black suit, and went over to the telegraph office in the War Department. Stanton was in a huff about my going to the theater, said he was worried that some crazy rebel sympathizer might take a shot at me, and begged me to stay at home.

"No way," I said. "I need a laugh over the country cousin."

"Well," he said, "at least take along a responsible guard."

"Stanton," I said, "do you know that Major Eckert can break an iron poker over his arm?"

"No. Why do you ask a question like that?"

"Well, Stanton, I've seen Eckert break five pokers, one after the other, over his arm, and I'm thinking he would be the kind of man to go with me this evening. Can I take him?"

"He's got important work to do this evening. He can't be spared."

I knew Stanton was saying this to discourage me from going out tonight. "I'll ask the major myself," I said. "He can do his work tomorrow."

I went into the cipher room and told Eckert what Stanton had said. Eckert's a muscular, clean-shaven fellow with a receding hairline and a prominent nose. "Come now, Major," I said. "Go to the theater with us. Mrs. Lincoln also wants you to go." He thanked me for the invitation, but toed the Stanton line and said he absolutely had to do his work tonight. "Very well," I said, "I'll take somebody else along, because Stanton insists on having somebody to protect me. But I would much rather have you, since you can break a poker over your arm." Don't think he realized I was joking. I *know* Stanton didn't realize it.

At eleven this morning I met with Grant and my Cabinet secretaries in the Cabinet room. I was as cheerful as I've ever been. Grant, chewing on a cigar, looked a little tired. I shook his hand warmly and asked if he'd heard from Sherman. He said he expected news any hour now. I said favorable news must be on the way and told him and the Cabinet about my dream, which I'd had before great victories like Gettysburg and Vicksburg.

We turned to reconstruction. I confessed that I'd been too fast in my desire for an early reconstruction. I'd asked Stanton to draft a tentative plan, and he read it to us. It called for an army of occupation for the conquered South and for Virginia and North Carolina to be combined into a single military district, which would be run by the army and the War Department under military law.

"Consider the plan carefully," I said. "Reconstruction is the great question before us, and we must act soon. I'm glad Congress isn't in session now to impede our work."

There was considerable discussion on Stanton's report. We all agreed on the need for a temporary military government for the conquered South, and we thought an army of occupation might well be necessary to protect the freedmen and safeguard the reconstruction process. This was pretty much what I'd had in mind in the closing line of my speech the other night: "It may be my duty to make some new announcement to the people of the South. I am considering, and shall not fail to act, when satisfied that action will be proper."

What I didn't like about Stanton's plan was the combination of Virginia and North Carolina into a single department. Welles argued that the two states should be dealt with separately, and I agreed. I instructed Stanton to rewrite his plan so as to apply military reconstruction separately to the two states. We would discuss the revised proposals at the next meeting.

On other reconstruction matters, we deferred the question of Negro enfranchisement for later discussion. But I did ask Stanton to draw up a program to try in North Carolina. The Cabinet then asked about punishing the rebels. Would there be persecutions?

"No," I said, "no bloody work, no war trials or hangings. But I'd like to frighten the rebel leaders out of the country, open the gates, let down the bars, and scare 'em off." As I said that, I waved my hands as if I was shooing chickens.

After the meeting, Grant stayed behind to talk with me in private. "We appreciate your invitation to attend the theater," he said, "but I'm sorry we have to decline. Mrs. Grant and I have made arrangements to go to Burlington, New Jersey, to see our children, who're in school there. It would be a great disappointment to Julia to delay our trip."

"The people would love to see you, General," I said. "You ought to stay and see the play on that account."

He looked unhappy, and I can't say I blamed him: he's a private man with little stomach for public demonstrations. As we talked, a message came from Mrs. Grant. "She says she's anxious to start for Burlington on the four o'clock train," Grant said. "I'm very sorry—"

"That's all right," I said. "No need to say more. I understand."

Early this afternoon I had lunch with Mary and we talked about who would replace the Grants as our guests tonight. We'd sent invitations to the Stantons, too, but of course Stanton turned us down since he disapproved of my going out at all. I told Mary I had half a mind not to go, but she thought it best to stick to our plans, since they'd been announced in the papers. Later we sent an invitation to Major Henry Rathbone and Clara Harris, his fiancée and the daughter of Senator Ira Harris of New York, and they accepted. They're a handsome young couple—I'm glad they'll be going with us.

At five I fetched Mary for our carriage ride. We drove out the White House gates and headed for the Navy Yard with our cavalry escort jingling noisily on both sides of us. It was raw and gusty out, and we sat close together as the carriage rolled along the streets. I noticed lilacs blooming in the dooryards and smelled their scent in the wind. I felt as happy and playful as a young boy, and it showed.

"You seem so gay, Father. So very cheerful."

"And well I might," I said. "I consider this day the war has come to a close." I smiled tenderly at her. "We must both be more cheerful in the future," I said. "Between the war and the loss of our darling Willie, we've been very miserable."

We talked about the years ahead, after my second term is over. "We'll travel to Europe with the boys," I said, "and maybe visit Jerusalem. I've always wanted to see it. Then we'll go out west, to California, where the soldiers are going to be digging up gold to pay the national debt. Then I'd like to return to the law, Mary. Open an office in Springfield or Chicago." I sighed. "What a great relief it'll be to get back to my practice, my old friends, the circuit, the jokes and laughter around a hotel fireplace with other lawyers." Then I fell silent and my mind wandered back over the war and the terrible storms we'd passed through since it all began.

21. BOOTH

When I dropped by Ford's Theater on Good Friday morning, I learned about Caesar's plans for the evening. I sported a cane and was dandily dressed in riding boots with spurs, dark pants, a black cloak, a black felt hat, and white kid gloves. Harry Ford, co-owner of the theater, was standing in front with several other men. "Here comes the handsomest man in the United States," Ford said when he saw me. I knew him and his brother well.

"What's on tonight?" I asked.

"*Our American Cousin,*" he said, "and we're going to have a big night. The president and General Grant are going to occupy the president's box, and General Lee is going to have the adjoining one." I found nothing funny about that last remark—he said it to annoy me because of my love for the Confederacy.

I walked off. The news about Lincoln and Grant was what I'd been waiting for. *Tonight* we would strike, *tonight* we would avenge the destruction of my country. In a moment, I spotted John Coyle, editor of the *National Intelligencer,* with another man. I told Coyle I wanted to talk to him in private, and we slipped inside a restaurant.

"You've heard the talk," I said. "Suppose Lincoln is killed."

"Johnson would succeed him," Coyle said.

"But if he's also killed?"

"Then Seward would be president."

"But suppose he's killed, then what?"

"Then anarchy, I suppose, until they choose another president by whatever the Constitution provides." Coyle laughed. "But what nonsense. They don't make Brutuses nowadays."

"No. No, they don't," I said.

Around noon I saw Grant's wife and boy eating lunch with another woman and a girl in the dining room of Willard's. I went inside, ordered some soup, and tried to hear what Grant's wife was saying. Just woman's talk, as much as I could make out, so I left and returned to Ford's Theater. I was well known there and no one paid me any attention when I went inside. By the time I left, a peephole had been bored in the door to the president's box and the door at the end of the hallway leading to the first balcony had also been fixed—plaster had been chipped from the frame so that a bar could be inserted to lock the door from the inside.

When I learned that Mrs. Surratt planned a trip to Surrattsville that afternoon, I went to her house and gave her a package containing my splendid French field glasses; I asked her to leave them at Surrattsville. She agreed to do it and said that Weichmann would drive her there. It was around four, I think, when I returned to the National Hotel and wrote a letter addressed to the editors of the *National Intelligencer*.

> *For a long time I have devoted my energies, my time and money to the accomplishment of a certain end. I have been disappointed. The moment has now arrived when I must change my plans. Many will blame me for what I am about to do; but posterity, I am sure, will justify me.*
> *Men who love their country better than gold or life.*
> JOHN W. BOOTH, PAINE, HEROLD, ATZERODT

A few minutes later, I rode my bay mare out of Pumphreys Livery Stable and headed for Pennsylvania Avenue. My horse was a bad little bitch, and I was fond of her. I reined up at the curb to talk to Johnny Matthews, a friend and fellow actor who was playing in *Our American Cousin*. A column of rebel prisoners had just gone by, and Matthews asked me if I'd seen them. "Yes, I did." I lifted my hand to my forehead. "Great God, Johnny, I no longer have a country!"

"Jesus, you're nervous," he said. "What's the matter?"

"It's nothing," I said. "Johnny, I have a favor to ask of you." I handed him my letter to Coyle. "I may leave town tonight. I want this published in the *National Intelligencer*. Please see to it for me."

He took the letter and then turned. "There goes General Grant," he said. "I thought he was going to the theater this evening with the president."

"Where?" I said, and he pointed to a carriage that had just passed. I spurred my horse and galloped after it.

22. GRANT

Mrs. Rucker, wife of the chief quartermaster, took us to the train depot in her carriage. Jesse and the women sat in the back while I rode in front with the driver. I felt bad about turning down Lincoln's invitation to attend the theater with him and Mrs. Lincoln, but Julia couldn't stand being around her for a minute. Julia was still going on about a strange man who'd sat across from her and Jess and Rawlins's wife and little girl while they were eating at Willard's dining room. "He stared at us the whole time," Julia said, "and seemed to be listening to our conversation. He had dark hair and a dark mustache and a face as pale as ivory. He was really wild-looking, Ulys. He played with his soup spoon, sometimes filling it and holding it half-lifted to his mouth, but never tasting it. He did this many times. I thought he was crazy. I called Mrs. Rawlins's attention to the man, and she glanced at him. 'I believe there is something peculiar about him,' she told me. We were so frightened we got up and left."

"He was probably just curious," I said.

"He had the wildest look in his eyes—it gave me goose bumps. Wouldn't surprise me if he was one of Mosby's guerrillas. I'm afraid there'll be an outbreak tonight. I just feel it, and I'm glad we're going away."

We hadn't gone far on Pennsylvania Avenue when a man galloped past us on a dark horse, peering inside as he swept by. He had a black mustache and wore a soft black felt hat. He rode about twenty yards ahead, then wheeled about and rode back and peered into the carriage again.

"That's the wild-looking man who stared at us in the dining room," Julia said. "I don't like his looks, Ulysses."

"Not very friendly," I said and glanced back at him.

23. BOOTH

There were trunks and other baggage in Grant's carriage and it was heading for the Baltimore & Ohio railroad station. Curses! They were leaving town! Well, I had other ways of killing Grant—I would send a wire to the right people in Baltimore. To steady my nerve, I rode to Grillo's place next to Ford's Theater and joined Ed Spangler, a stagehand at Ford's, and several other men for drinks. Then I went back to my room at the National Hotel and armed myself with a razor-sharp dagger and a .44 caliber rifled Deringer pistol. I took a last look around. On the bureau was a broken comb, a clothes brush, embroidered slippers, and a half pound of Killikinich tobacco in brown paper. Several sheets of notepaper and hotel envelopes lay on the nearby table. I knelt down and locked my trunk, which contained my correspondence and the gimlet used to carve the hole in the door to the presidential box. Then I went downstairs and handed my key to the clerk.

"Are you going to Ford's Theater tonight?" I asked.

"No," he said.

"You ought to go. There's going to be some splendid acting there tonight."

At eight I met Atzerodt, Paine, and Herold in Paine's room at the Herndon House on Ninth Street. Atzerodt's little green eyes had a dull look in them—he'd been drinking heavily.

"Men," I said, "we strike tonight, and it will be the greatest thing in the world. I will kill Lincoln at Ford's Theater and the South will be avenged! Paine, you'll go up to Seward's house and kill him. Herold will go with you and hold your horses. What weapons do you have?"

"Pistol and a knife," Paine said.

"Good. Here's a package—tell them you're from the druggist with medicine for Seward. Herold came up with the idea." Herold grinned proudly. I turned to Atzerodt. "You get some coffee and sober up. Your job is to kill Johnson at the Kirkwood House. Herold will help you after Paine's done his work. Check your watches: we'll all try to strike at about the same time, around ten or a little after. General Grant left town today for Baltimore. I've sent word to our friends in Baltimore to kill him on the train."

"Can't do it," Atzerodt said drunkenly. "Can't murder nobody."

"You damn fool!" I cried. "You're going to hang anyhow. It's death to any man who backs out now. Do you understand? Do you *understand*!" He mumbled yes.

"All right, then. We'll rendezvous at the Navy Yard Bridge, ride to Surrattsville around Piscataway, and make our way to the Potomac. We can depend on friends to provide us with food and water along the way. Once we're across the river, we'll be with our countrymen. Maybe we can eventually make it to Canada. I have friends there."

I left them and stopped at a saloon for a few shots of whiskey. I knew every line and scene of *Our American Cousin* and looked at my watch to check the progress of the play. I planned to shoot Lincoln during the second scene of the third act, when only one actor, Harry Hawk, would be onstage.

I left the saloon and led my horse down the alley in back of Ford's Theater. It was a little before ten o'clock. I opened the back door, called Spangler out, and told him to hold my horse for ten or fifteen minutes. Then I entered the back door, crossed under the stage, made my way through the little side passage, and stepped out onto Tenth Street. Caesar's carriage was parked in front of the theater, which was brilliantly lit. It had been cloudy and foggy earlier in the evening, but the sky had cleared and the moon was just beginning to rise. I went into Grillo's place next to Ford's and ordered a whiskey with a water chaser. I downed the whiskey and put money on the counter, then strode back outside and entered the theater. When the doorkeeper reached for a ticket, I seized his hand by two fingers and said, "I don't need a ticket, Buck. What time do you have?" He directed me to the clock in the lobby. It was ten past ten. The play was now in the second scene of the third act.

Humming a tune, I climbed the stairway to the second balcony. I paused to admire the play and then crossed the dress circle, making my way along the wall toward the narrow hallway leading to the president's box. A man was sitting in a chair which blocked the aisle. At first he refused to move when I indicated I wanted by. Then he let me pass. The house was crowded with well-known civilians and many ladies in rich costumes and army officers in their uniforms, sitting under clusters of gaslights. I took a long look around the dress circle and then at the orchestra and the president's box, which overlooked the stage and was draped with flags. Then I pushed the door open and slipped into the hallway to the president's box. There was no guard. I could not believe my good fortune! I closed the door and barred it from the inside, then made my way to the door to Caesar's box and peered through the peephole. In the narrow beam of light, I could see the back of Caesar's head. He was sitting in a rocking chair, holding the hand of his wife, who set next to him. A young officer and a young woman sat on a sofa to their right, staring raptly at the stage below them, where Hawk was standing alone. "Don't know the manner of good society, eh?" Hawk called out. "Wal, I guess I know enough to turn you inside out, old gal—you sockdologizing old mantrap."

At that instant I entered the box, aimed my derringer point blank at the back of Lincoln's head, and pulled the trigger. The shot rang out and smoke from the pistol drifted in front of me. Blood and brain matter spewed from Lincoln's head as he fell forward into his wife's lap. I dropped the gun and cried "Freedom!" The army officer jumped up, and I lunged at him with the dagger—I intended to stab him in the heart—but he parried the blow with his arm. I jumped on the front of the box and leaped, but my spur caught in a flag and I fell to the stage, breaking my left leg. Cries of surprise swept over the house. Above me, the officer screamed: "Stop that man!" The girl with him yelled: "Won't somebody stop that man? The president is shot!"

I got to my feet and, facing the audience with a clinched fist, shouted "*Sic semper tyrannus*," thus be it ever to tyrants, the motto of the state of Virginia. I turned to see Hawk staring wildly at me. I brandished the dagger at him, and he turned and fled. Then I limped backstage and knocked the orchestra leader aside, stabbing him twice with my knife. I escaped out the back door and found Peanuts—Joe Burroughs—holding my horse. He said, "Spangler asked me—" But I shoved him out of the way and got one foot in the stirrup when the horse spun around in a circle. Somebody tried to grab the reins as I brought my broken leg over the saddle, but I crouched over the pummel and spurred the horse in the flanks and we flew up the alley, away from outstretched hands.

I raced to the Navy Yard Bridge, where a guard stopped me, demanding to know my name and where I was going. "Name's Booth," I said. "Live in Charles. I'm going home."

"Why are you out so late? Don't you know there's a curfew after nine?"

"Had business in the city," I said. "Thought I could ride home by the moon."

The guard stared at me briefly, then let me pass. I galloped away on the moonlit road, heading through lower Maryland. Halfway up Good Hope Hill I met a man in a wagon and asked if he'd passed any other horsemen. He said no. I took off again, with the broken bone of my leg tearing at my flesh—the pain was unbearable. About seven or eight miles from Washington, I heard a rider in back of me coming up fast. I turned around. It was Herold.

"I killed Caesar," I said. "Walked into his box and shot him with my derringer behind his left ear. Head exploded. Spattered blood and brains all over his wife. A soldier in the box tried to stop me but I stabbed him and leaped from the box. My spur caught in a flag and I broke my leg in the fall. What happened at Seward's? Did Paine kill him?"

"I think so," Herold said. "We went to his house and I held Paine's horse while he went inside with the fake package of medicine. A few minutes went by, then people inside the house started yelling and screaming. I figured Paine had done his work, so I tied his horse up and went to find Atzerodt, like you told me. He wasn't at the Kirkwood House. Couldn't find him anywhere, so I took off."

"Damn that Atzerodt," I said bitterly. "We'd better get going. They'll be after us soon."

We reached Surrattsville at midnight, and Herold woke up Lloyd while I stayed on my horse. Herold went inside the house and a few minutes later came out with the two carbines, my field glasses, the box of shells, the coil of rope, and a bottle of whiskey. I took a long drink from the bottle but told Herold I couldn't carry my carbine—my leg hurt so much it was all I could do to hold myself in the saddle. Lloyd staggered up, obviously drunk. "Want to hear some news?" I asked him. He mumbled, "What?" "I've murdered the president." Herold added: "And I've fixed Seward." Lloyd just looked at us, the drunken scum.

We set off for Dr. Mudd's house at Bryantown, twenty-five miles from Washington. Got there about four in the morning. Herold dismounted and knocked on Mudd's door while I clung to my saddle. In a few minutes, Mudd came out and helped me inside to a sofa in the parlor. I lay there, groaning in pain. He got a lantern and took me to a bed upstairs, where he cut the boot off, because my leg was so swollen. He examined the leg and said the front bone was broken about two inches above the instep. He gave me some whiskey and then set the leg, applied a splint fashioned out of some old boards, and left me to sleep for an hour or so.

When I woke, I sent Herold downstairs to borrow Mudd's razor, and I used it to shave off my mustache. Then Herold helped me downstairs, and Mudd made a pair of crude crutches out of some plank boards. In the early afternoon, Herold and Mudd rode over to his father's place to get a carriage for me. But Mudd reported back that all of his father's carriages were broken down save one, and he couldn't spare it. I asked Mudd the way to Allen's Fresh and the Potomac, and he described the main road.

"Isn't there a shorter way?" I asked.

"Yes," he said, "a road across yonder swamp."

I thanked Mudd for his help, and Herold and I rode into the swamp. It was a black, drizzly, foggy evening and we got lost and wandered around in the swampy thickets till we came across a farmhouse. Herold knocked on the door and a nigger answered and said he lived there. We gave him two dollars to take us to William Bertle's farm, east of St. Mary's Catholic Church, which had been a haven for Confederate agents. The nigger said he'd heard rumors of Federal cavalry in the area.

"Don't you tell anybody about us," Herold said. "If you do, you won't live long."

I changed my mind about going to Bertle's farm and told the nigger to take us to Samuel Cox's place near the Potomac. Like his neighbors, Cox had been a Confederate sympathizer and was sure to help us get across the river. When we reached his place, the nigger left us, and Herold went to get Cox.

"I'm John Wilkes Booth," I told him. "I killed President Lincoln." He didn't say anything. "You're a friend of the Confederacy—will you help us get across the Potomac?"

"Yes, of course," he said. "You can hide in the woods till I can arrange the crossing." His overseer took us to a hiding place deep in the woods, where I lay on blankets on the ground. My leg was killing me. I think it was Sunday when Cox's foster brother, Tom Jones, brought us food and the latest newspapers. During the war, he said, he'd been a Confederate signal officer and a mail agent for rebels in the area.

"The government's offering a reward of a hundred and seventy-five thousand dollars for you," he said. "They've mounted a massive manhunt. The area's swarming with Federal cavalry and detectives. When it's safe, I'll take you to the Potomac and arrange for a boat to ferry you to Virginia."

When he left, I leafed through a copy of the *National Intelligencer*, looking for my letter. It wasn't there! I cursed Matthews and Coyle, the damned traitors. I was shocked at the papers; they decried the murder of Lincoln as a foul and horrendous act and called me a cowardly fiend and a common cutthroat.

I took out my memorandum book and wrote a reply. "I struck boldly and not as the papers say. I walked with a firm step through a thousand of his friends; was stopped, but pushed on. A colonel was at his side. I shouted *Sic semper* before I fired. In jumping broke my leg. I passed all his pickets. Rode sixty miles that night, with the bone of my leg tearing the flesh at every jump.

"I can never repent it, though we hated to kill. Our country owed all our troubles to him, and God simply made me the instrument of his punishment. This forced Union is not what I have loved. I care not what becomes of me. I have no desire to out-live my country." Tears welled in my eyes. No, I had no desire to out-live the Confederacy.

Jones came back a few days later and said the cavalry had thinned out, it was time to make a dash for the river. We left under cover of darkness and made our way to a rowboat Jones had hidden in a little creek that emptied into the Potomac. He and Herold helped me into the boat, and Jones showed me how to use a compass to reach Machodoc Creek, downriver on the Virginia side.

"When you land," he said, "go see Elizabeth Quesenberry. She'll lead you to Thomas Harbin and Joseph Barden."

Herold took the oars and rowed us out into the Potomac, which at this point was two miles wide. But we caught the high tide at midnight and the tide and the strong wind swept us far beyond our destination, close to a Federal gunboat. Herold rowed furiously upstream until we struck the Maryland shore again. We made a fire and I wrote another entry in my memorandum book: "After being hunted like a dog through swamps, woods, and last night being chased by gunboats till I was forced to return wet, cold, and starving, with every man's hand against me, I am here in despair. And why? For doing what Brutus was honored for—what made Tell a hero. And yet I, for striking down a greater tyrant than they ever knew, am looked upon as a common cutthroat. My action was purer than either of theirs. One hoped to be great. The other had not only his country's, but his own wrongs to avenge. I hoped for no gain. I knew no private wrong. I struck for my country and that alone. God cannot pardon me if I have done wrong. Yet I cannot see my wrong. The little, the very little, I left behind to clear my name, the government will not allow to be printed. So ends all. For my country I have given up all that makes life sweet and holy, brought misery upon my family, and am sure there is no pardon in

Heaven for me, since man condemns me so. I have only heard of what has been done, (except what I did myself), and it fills me with horror. God, try and forgive me, and bless my mother. Tonight I will once more try the river with the intent to cross. Though I have a greater desire and almost a mind to return to Washington, and in a measure clear my name—which I feel I can do. I do not repent the blow I struck. I may before my God, but not to man. I think I have done well. Though I am abandoned, with the curse of Cain upon me, when, if the world knew my heart, that one blow would have made me great. I have too great a soul to die like a criminal. O, may He, may He spare me that, and let me die bravely."

24. GRANT

We rode north in a private car attached to the train. It belonged to the president of the Baltimore & Ohio Railroad, who'd kindly let us use it. As the train roared through Maryland, trailing pluffs of black smoke, I tried to shake off the unsettled feeling I'd gotten when the wild-looking horseman peered into our carriage. That night, before we reached Baltimore, a noise sounded at the door of the car's front platform. Sounded like somebody was trying to open the door, but the door was locked. Good thing. Few more sounds at the door, and then nothing except the drone of the train.

We passed through Baltimore and reached Philadelphia about midnight. We took a carriage through the city and stopped at a large restaurant so I could get some oysters—hadn't eaten since nine that morning. Before the oysters came, a servant handed me a telegram, but before I could open it a second telegram came and a third. I read them and groaned.

"Is anything the matter?" Julia asked.

"Something terrible has happened. Don't get excited now. The president has been assassinated at Ford's Theater, and I have to go back. I'll take you to Burlington first."

We took the ferry across the Delaware River and boarded the train for Burlington. Couldn't get my mind around what had happened.

"I was afraid something bad would happen," Julia said. "Didn't I tell you so? Who could've done such a thing?"

"I don't know."

"This will make Andrew Johnson president, won't it?"

"Yes," I said, "and I dread the change. He's not a twentieth the man Mr. Lincoln was."

I left Julia at Burlington and took a special train back to Washington. I went straight to the War Department, where I found Stanton hard at work, directing a relentless pursuit of the assassin. His eyes were bloodshot—he'd stayed up all night taking testimony from eyewitnesses, who positively identified the actor, John Wilkes Booth, as Lincoln's murderer. The president had died at seven-thirty that very morning, in a little room in a boarding house across from the theater. Stanton was inconsolable. At the mention of Mr. Lincoln's name, he broke down and sobbed bitterly.

At first I thought Seward had also been killed. Turned out to be false. A giant of a man had attacked him in his bedroom, cutting his face and neck badly with a knife. Then the man ran out of the house, screaming, "I'm mad! I'm mad!"

Stanton and I both believed the assassination plot had originated in Richmond, the last desperate act of the dying rebel government. So when I saw a dispatch from General Ord in Richmond, saying that Confederates Hunter and Campbell wanted permission to see Lincoln in Washington, I blew up. Telegraphed Ord to arrest both men, arrest the Richmond mayor, arrest all the members of the old Richmond council and all paroled officers and surgeons who hadn't taken the oath of allegiance, and throw the lot of 'em into Libby prison. Ord wired back that this would reopen the rebellion!

Talked to Stanton about it and canceled the order. A lot of evidence he'd uncovered still pointed to a rebel conspiracy. But if we'd held the ex-Confederate leaders responsible, it might've taken years, decades even, to reunite the sections and make our country whole again. When a letter came from Dick Ewell, one of Lee's corps commanders, saying that the southern people would never have sanctioned Lincoln's assassination, that they felt nothing but "unqualified abhorrence and indignation" over the deed, Stanton and I decided to accept that verdict and blame the assassination solely on Booth and his henchmen.

Had a huge manhunt under way—columns of cavalry and Federal detectives scouring the Washington area and southern Maryland. Captured two of Booth's henchmen, Atzerodt and Paine, only a few days after the assassination and confined 'em in chains in the holds of monitors anchored in the Potomac. Also arrested Ed Spangler, a stagehand at Ford's Theater; a Dr. Mudd, who set Booth's leg and helped him escape; and a Mrs. Surratt, who owned the boarding house where Booth and his gang had plotted the murder.

On April twenty-sixth, I think it was, Federal detectives and a detachment of cavalry cornered Booth himself in a tobacco barn near Port Royal, Virginia. A confederate named Herold surrendered, but Booth refused to come out of the barn and threatened to open fire with a carbine. When the commander of the Federal pursuit set the barn on fire, Booth appeared to want to fight his way out, so one of the pursuers, Boston Corbett, shot him with a revolver, claiming that Providence had ordered him to do it. They laid Booth on the grass, under a locust tree, just beyond the barn door. He muttered, "Tell my mother I died for my country"—which we interpreted to mean the Confederacy—and he died a little while later. Lieutenant Edward Doherty, commander of the cavalry detachment, sewed Booth's body up in a blanket and brought it back to Washington and we placed it in a monitor. Booth's dentist identified the body and so did Dr. May of Washington—he'd removed a carbuncle from Booth's neck several months earlier. Body was identified by several others who knew him and recognized the initials *JWB* tattooed on his wrist. Stanton was afraid rebel sympathizers might try to steal Booth's body, and make it "the instrument of rejoicing at the sacrifice of Mr. Lincoln." So Stanton had the body buried under the stone floor of the Old Penitentiary Building.

Since the war wasn't officially over, a military court tried the other conspirators and sentenced Paine, Atzerodt, Herold, and Mrs. Surratt to be hanged. The court voted life imprisonment at hard labor for Dr. Mudd and two of Booth's earlier confederates, Arnold and O'Laughlin, and six years at hard labor for Spangler. The four convicted men were sent to a penal island off the coast of Florida, where O'Laughlin died. President Johnson later pardoned the other three and had them released.

I've held off describing Lincoln's funeral because it hurts to talk about it. That day, Wednesday, April nineteenth, was the saddest day of my life. Funeral took place in the East Room, where Mr. Lincoln had greeted people in his receptions and public events. His coffin rested on a flower-covered catafalque, where a guard of honor had watched it day and night. His head lay on a white pillow, a faint smile was frozen on his lips, his face was pale and distorted. The room was festooned with black crepe.

Services began at eleven that morning, with some six hundred people crowded into the East Room. Nearly all official Washington was there—Johnson, members of the Cabinet, Senator Sumner and his congressional colleagues, Chief Justice Chase, the diplomatic corps, generals and naval officers, Lincoln's personal cavalry escort and bodyguards, and his personal secretaries. Robert Lincoln stood at the front of the coffin—he was the only member of the family who was present. Mrs. Lincoln stayed in her room, weeping hysterically. I wore a black mourning crepe on one arm and stood by myself at the head of the coffin, staring at a cross of lilies and thinking over and over again that this was the worst day of my life. I looked at Mr. Lincoln's sad face and thanked the Lord he'd spent most of his last days with me at City Point. Then I started to cry. He was incontestably the greatest man I have ever known.

Four ministers spoke and prayed, then twelve veteran reserve corps sergeants carried the coffin out to the funeral car. As bells tolled and minute guns fired salutes and bands played dirges for the dead, the funeral procession started up Pennsylvania Avenue. A detachment of black troops was in the lead, then came the funeral car followed by a riderless horse with Mr. Lincoln's boots turned backward in the stirrups, then columns of mourners, all moving to the steady muffled beat of drums. The lines swelled with wounded soldiers from the city's military hospitals: they'd gotten out of their beds and were marching with us now, some with arms in slings, others hobbling along on crutches, as they followed after their fallen chief. A procession of colored citizens walked in lines of forty from curb to curb, forty thousand of 'em in high silk hats and white gloves, holding hands as they moved.

When the procession reached the Capitol, the sergeants carried Lincoln into the rotunda, where he lay in state on another catafalque. All the next day, thousands of people filed past the coffin in two lines, paying the president their last respects. Two days later they took Lincoln to a nine-car funeral train draped with Union flags. Some friends of the president retrieved his son Willie from his grave in Georgetown, and put his coffin on the funeral car with his father's. The train crawled out with ringing bells, starting on a 1,600-mile journey back to Springfield, Illinois, where father and son would be buried together.

Meanwhile word came from Sherman that Joe Johnston was prepared to surrender and that they had agreed to terms. I'd sent Sherman my terms to General Lee, and assumed he would offer the same to Johnston. When I read Sherman's terms, I knew there was going to be trouble, because Sherman had strayed into political matters. His agreement with Johnston declared a general amnesty, guaranteed that the former rebels would retain their political rights and franchises and their rights of property, and declared that the president of the United States would recognize the governments of the formal rebel states.

Stanton and President Johnson denounced Sherman in very bitter terms. Some people went so far as to call him a traitor—a preposterous term to apply to a man who'd rendered so much outstanding service, even supposing he'd made a mistake in granting such terms to Johnston and his army.

At any rate, Stanton and President Johnson rejected the terms and sent me to North Carolina to tell Sherman so. When I reached his headquarters in Raleigh, I told him to inform Johnston that Washington had rejected the terms they had conditionally agreed on, and that he was to be offered the same terms I'd given General Lee. Sherman was outraged, cussed Stanton and Johnson in some of the bitterest language I've ever heard from him, and claimed that he'd acted according to Lincoln's wishes and in his spirit. I knew that wasn't right: Lincoln had made it clear to all of us what his terms and conditions were, which included the disfranchisement of the Confederacy's ruling class and its army and naval officers, not to mention his plan of creating new state governments out of the loyal Unionist minority in the South.

On April twenty-sixth, Sherman and Johnston met again, and Johnston surrendered his army according to the terms I'd given Lee. Eight days later Richard Taylor gave up his forces in Louisiana. On May tenth, a detachment of our cavalry captured Jefferson Davis near Irwinville, Georgia. He was trying to reach Texas to carry on the war from there. President Johnson then proclaimed that armed rebel resistance had ended, though the rebel commander in the Trans-Mississippi did not officially surrender till early June. Jeff Davis went to prison at Fort Monroe—they locked him up in an inner cell with seventy soldiers standing guard; they put his ankles in irons and kept a lamp constantly burning by his cot. He was indicted for treason but was never put on trial. President Johnson finally ordered him released, and he bitterly announced that he *had not repented* for what he'd done—said if he had the chance, he would do all over again what he'd done in 'sixty-one.

The cruel war was over. More than 600,000 soldiers on both sides had died, and nobody knows how many civilians and refugees, colored and white. Many folks have asked me how we won the war, and I always tell 'em it was simple: we whipped 'em in the West, captured the Mississippi and cleared 'em out of Mississippi and Tennessee, which made Sherman's invasion of Georgia and the Carolinas possible. From the summer of 'sixty-four on, I'd pinned Lee down at Petersburg while Sheridan and Sherman destroyed his railroads and sources of supplies and starved him out. Ought to mention that a Federal cavalry force under General James Wilson, near the end of the war, cut a swath of devastation clear across Alabama and into western Georgia; it was the most destructive cavalry raid of the war and contributed to our triumph of arms.

Now that the war was over, I faced a Herculean task as general in chief of the greatest army in the world, which included an occupying army in the states of the dead Confederacy. What a spectacle it was to see our country able to put down a great rebellion and come out whole again. I wrote Julia that our nation, united, would have a strength which would enable it to dictate to all others, making them conform to justice and right.

25. CHESNUT

At war's end I was at Chester, South Carolina, with Mrs. Preston and her three daughters, and hundreds of other refugees. Sam Hood was there, too, still hoping to marry Buck Preston. But the Prestons refused to permit the wedding, and Hood left for Texas, holding his hat off his head until he was out of sight of my house.

"Why did he do that?" I asked.

"In honor of my being here," Buck said.

"Buck, my poor darling, they did you a cruel wrong when they didn't let you marry and share the fate of your poor wounded hero, the only true man I've seen in your train yet." But what could she do? The decision had been made.

The Wigfalls passed through on their way to Texas and the Rio Grande. "When the hanging starts," Wigfall said, "we'll be in Mexico."

Colonel Cad Jones came with a secret dispatch from my military husband. I opened it. "Lincoln—old Abe Lincoln—killed—murdered—Seward wounded!" I showed it to some ladies who were standing beside me.

"Who murdered him?" they asked.

"Who knows?"

Mary Darby thought the Yankees had murdered him themselves, since there were no Confederates in Washington.

"But if they see fit to accuse us of instigating it?" someone said. "See if they don't take vengeance on us, now that we're ruined and can't repel them any longer."

Mr. Heywood said: "The death of Lincoln—I call that a warning to tyrants. He won't be the last president put to death in the Yankee capital, though he is the first."

Yankee troops were everywhere, like the locusts that plagued Egypt. My husband had joined me, and we'd vowed to stay, no point in running. April twenty-third was our silver wedding anniversary, and the unhappiest day of my life. James, my cool captain, was extremely bitter: he'd been to Camden and Mulberry and reported that Yankee raiders had destroyed Mulberry.

One night we all sat talking in our parlor, and Mary Darby brought up Lincoln again. "One thing is respectable in those awful Yankees. If they did choose a baboon to reign over them, they stuck by him through weal and woe. They saw in his ugly hide the stuff to carry them through, and he saved them—if he couldn't save himself."

The men sat silent and the women talked. One said: "Now he'll be Saint Abe for all time, saint and martyr. It just makes you sick."

"When they print his life," another said, "I wonder if they'll put in all the dirty stories he delighted in."

"Faugh!" Mary Darby said. "Most of the anecdotes I heard were so off-color I've never been able to repeat them."

Someone else brought up Jeff Davis. "We chose a proud soldier to be our president, and what did we do? Hamstrung him instantly."

"Well," Mary Darby said, "the worst has come—and after so many left dead on the battlefields, so many dead in the hospitals and prisons."

"Or worse," I said, "left alive with hideous wounds and diseases."

"Some starved to death," another woman said. "And the brokenhearted women we've seen die."

"Yesterday those poor fellows were heroes," one woman added. "Today they're only rebels to be hung or shot, at the Yankees' pleasure."

"It's been a year since we left Richmond," I said, "a year since I stood by little Joe Davis's grave. Since then the Confederacy's double-quicked downhill. Nothing now but burned towns, deserted plantations, sacked villages."

James said: "You seem determined to look the worst in the face."

"Yes," I said, "poverty, no future, no hope."

James pointed at me. "Your sentence is pronounced—*Camden for life*."

In May we left for Camden and passed the ruins of Sherman's tracks through South Carolina. The land was desolate, nothing but tall blackened chimneys. The blooming of the gardens in the ruins gave a funereal effect. I wept and cursed Sherman, I hated him so. Except for one of the Preston slaves, we didn't see one living thing—man, woman, or animal. In crossing the Wateree at Chesnut's Ferry, we had not a cent to pay the ferry man, *silver* being required.

We reached Camden on the seventh and Mrs. Bartow rode out to Mulberry with me. The Yankee raiders had smashed up one entire side of the big house: every window broken, every bell torn down, every piece of furniture destroyed, every door knocked in. Old Colonel Chesnut was in a deplorable state—blind—feeble—fretful—miserable. He had suffered financial ruin: his cotton had all been destroyed, and he'd converted his stocks and bonds into worthless Confederate securities. Some of his debts had come from supporting more than five hundred slaves during the war. *Now they are free citizens of the U.S.A.*, I thought bitterly. All of them remained on the estate and agreed to work summer crops. They did not express the slightest pleasure at their sudden freedom, but I didn't fool myself: they would all leave after a while.

Without financial resources, we've tried to manage in the new state of things. We've brought in a little money by selling butter and eggs on shares. In my few leisure moments, I write in my journal, recording how sick at heart I feel, how ill and miserable. This on the fifteenth: "The uncertain state of the country, the certain ruin of all we hold dear. My nerves are unstrung, my brain on fire. No mails anywhere—so no letters written or received. No newspapers—no safety valves of any kind. So today I had a violent fit of hysterics. JC called, shut the door, and seized me—frightened to death—soothing me as if I was dying. I was ill enough and wish I *had* died."

There are nights here with the moonlight, cold and ghastly, and the whippoorwills and the screech owls alone disturbing the silence, when I tear my hair and cry aloud for all that is past and gone.

CODA

When lilacs last in the doorway bloom'd
And the great star early droop'd in the western sky in the night,
I mourn'd, and yet shall mourn with ever-returning spring.

Ever-returning spring, trinity sure to me you bring,
Lilac blooming perennial and drooping star in the west,
And thought of him I love.

WALT WHITMAN

That our national democratic experiment, principle, and machinery could triumphantly sustain the shock of civil war, and that the Constitution could weather it, like a ship in a storm, and come out of it as sound and whole as before, is by far the most signal proof yet of the stability of our experiment in democracy and our Constitution. That is, I think, how our great Captain would have expressed it, were he still with us.

How often since that dark and dripping Saturday my heart has entertained the dream, the wish, to give of Abraham Lincoln's death, its own special thought and memorial. Yet I find my notes incompetent and the tribute I dreamed of waits unprepared as ever.

I shall not easily forget the first time I ever saw Abraham Lincoln. It must have been about the eighteenth or nineteenth of February 1861. It was rather a plesant afternoon, in New York City, as he arrived there from the West, to remain a few hours and then pass on to Washington, to prepare for his inauguration. The broad spaces, sidewalks, and streets in the neighborhood of the Astor House were crowded with solid masses of people. Presently two or three shabby hack barouches drew up near the Astor House entrance. A tall figure stepped out of the center of these barouches, paused leisurely on the sidewalk, looked up at the granite walls and looming architecture of the grand old hotel—then, after a revealing stretch of arms and legs, turned round for over a minute to scan the appearance of the vast and silent crowds. There were no speeches—no compliments—no welcome—as far as I could hear. Much anxiety was concealed in that quiet. Cautious persons had feared some marked insult or indignity to the president-elect—for he possessed no personal popularity at all in New York City, and very little political. But it was evidently tacitly agreed that if the few political supporters of Mr. Lincoln would entirely abstain from any demonstration on their side, the immense majority, who were anything but supporters, would abstain on their side also.

From the top of an omnibus I had a capital view of it all, and especially of Mr. Lincoln, his look and gait—his perfect composure and coolness—his unusual and uncouth height, his dress of complete black, stovepipe hat pushed back on the head, dark brown complexion, seamed and wrinkled yet canny-looking face, black, bushy head of hair, disproportionately long neck, and his hands held behind as he stood observing the crowd of thirty to forty thousand people. I have no doubt, so frenzied were the ferments of the time, that many an assassin's knife and pistol lurked in hip or breast pocket there, ready, as soon as break and riot came.

But no break or riot came. The tall figure gave another relieving stretch or two of arms and legs; then with moderate pace ascended the portico-steps of the Astor House. As I sat on the top of my omnibus, and had a good view of him, the thought, dim and inchoate then, has since come out clear enough, that four sorts of genius, four mighty and primal hands, will be needed to the complete limning of this man's future portrait—the eyes and brains and finger touch of Plutarch and Eschylus and Michelangelo, assisted by Rabelais.

And now the rapid succession of momentous events—the national flag fired on at Sumter—the uprising of the North, in paroxysms of astonishment and rage—the chaos of divided councils—the call for troops—the first Bull Run—and the full flood of the secession war. Four years of lurid, bleeding, murky, murderous war. The secession war? Nay, let me call it the Union war. A great literature will yet arise out of the era of those four years, those scenes—era-compressing centuries of native passion, first-class pictures, tempests of life and death—an inexhaustible mine for the histories, drama, romance, and even philosophy of people to come.

During the course of the war, I saw Mr. Lincoln many times in Washington, riding in his carriage on his late-afternoon forays; I was sure he recognized me and tipped his hat, and I loved him personally and reflected much on the meaning of the war and his place in it. Truly the war's climactic moment was the murder of this powerful western star.

The day, April fourteenth, 1865, seems to have been a pleasant one throughout the whole land—the long storm, so dark, so fratricidal, full of blood and doubt and gloom, over and ended at last by the sunrise of such an absolute national victory and utter breakdown of secessionism at Appomattox. The day was propitious. Early herbage, early flowers, were out. In the dooryards, many lilacs were already in full bloom.

The popular afternoon paper of Washington, the little *Evening Star*, had spattered all over its third page, divided among the advertisements in a sensational manner, in a hundred different places, *The President and his Lady will be at the Theater this evening*. The president came that night and, with his wife, witnessed the play from the large state boxes on the second tier. The actual murder transpired with the quiet and simplicity of the commonest occurrence—the bursting of a bud or pod in the growth of vegetation. Through the general hum following a stage pause in the third act, came the muffled sound of a pistol shot, and from the president's box a sudden figure, Booth, his eyes like some mad animal's flashing with light and resolution, leaps and falls out of position, catching his boot heel in the copious drapery, the American flag, falls on one knee, gets up, makes a gesture to the audience, and walks off backstage.

A moment's hush—a scream—the cry of murder—Mrs. Lincoln leaning out of the box, with ashy cheeks and lips, with involuntary cry, pointing to the retreating figure, He has killed the president! And still a moment's strange, incredulous suspense—and then the deluge!—that mixture of horror, noise, uncertainty—the people burst through chairs and railings, and break them up—there is inextricable confusion and terror—women faint—feeble persons fall and are trampled on—many cries of agony are heard—the broad stage suddenly fills to suffocation with a dense and motley crowd, like some horrible carnival.

In the midst of all this, the soldiers of the president's guard, with others, suddenly drawn to the scene, burst in—some two hundred altogether—they storm the house, through all the tiers, inflamed with fury, literally charging the audience with fixed bayonets, muskets and pistols, shouting *Clear out! clear out! you sons-of-bitches!* And they cleared out, and the theater closed, never to open again.

And in the midst of that pandemonium, infuriated soldiers, the audience, the stage, and all its actors and actresses, its paint pots, spangles, and gaslights—the life blood from those veins, the best and sweetest of the land, drips slowly down, and death's ooze already begins its little bubbles on the lips. None will ever forget that moody, tearful night.

None will ever forget his coffin as it passed through the lanes and streets, with the pomp of the inloop'd flags with the cities draped in black, with the countless torches lit, the silent sea of faces and the unbared heads, the dirges through the night and the tolling tolling bells' perpetual clang. Ah, coffin that gently passed, I gave you my spring of lilac.

In Mr. Lincoln's death, a long and varied series of contradictory events arrives at last at its highest poetic, single, central, pictorial denouement. The whole involved, baffling, multiform whirl of the secession period comes to a head, and is gathered in one brief flash of lightning—one simple fierce deed. Its sharp culmination and solution illustrates those climax-moments on the stage of universal Time, where the historic Muse at one entrance, and the tragic Muse at the other, suddenly ring down the curtain, closing an immense act in the long drama of creative thought and giving it radiation, tableau, stranger than fiction. Fit radiation—fit close! How the imagination—how the student loves these things! America, too, is to have them. For not in all the great deaths—not Caesar in the Roman senate-house—not Napoleon passing away in the wild night storm at St. Helena—not Paleologus, falling, desperately fighting, piled over dozens deep with Grecian corpses—not calm old Socrates, drinking the hemlock—outvies the terminus of the secession war, in one man's life, here in our midst, in our own time—that seal of the emancipation of three million slaves—that parturition and delivery of our last really free Republic, born again, henceforth to commence its career of a genuine homogeneous Union.

Nor will ever future American patriots and Unionists over the whole land, North or South, find a better moral to their lesson. The final use of a heroic-eminent life—especially of a heroic-eminent death—is its indirect filtering into the nation and the race, its giving, age after age, color and fiber to the personalism of the youth and maturity of that age, and of mankind. Then there is a cement to the whole people, subtler, more underlying, than anything in written constitution, or courts, or armies—namely, the cement of a death identified thoroughly with that people, at its head, and for its sake. Strange, is it not, that battles, martyrs, agonies, blood, even assassination, should so condense—perhaps only really, lastingly condense—a nationality?

I repeat it—the grand deaths of the race—the dramatic deaths of every nationality—are its most important inheritance and value—in some respects beyond its literature and art, as the hero is beyond his finest portrait, and the battle itself beyond its choicest song or epic. Is not here indeed the point underlying all tragedy? the famous pieces of the Grecian masters—and all masters? Why, if the old Greeks had had this man, what trilogies of plays—what epics—would have been made out of him!

When, centuries hence, the leading historians and dramatists seek some personage, some special event, incisive enough to mark with deepest cut, and mnemonize, this turbulent nineteenth century of ours, perhaps the greatest century of the world, something to identify with the history of the United States—the absolute extirpation and erasure of slavery from the states—those historians will seek in vain for any point to serve more thoroughly their purpose, than Abraham Lincoln's death.

> O Captain! my Captain! our fearful trip is done,
> The ship has weather'd every rack, the prize we sought is won,
> The port is near, the bells I hear, the people all exulting,
> While fellow eyes the steady keel, the vessel grim and daring;
>   But O heart! heart! heart!
>   O the bleeding drops of red,
>   Where on the deck my Captain lies,
>   Fallen cold and dead.

REFERENCES

The following references indicate the sources on which each monologue is based. In quoting from them, I corrected spelling and capitalization for purposes of consistency and in some instances altered the wording for the sake of clarity. As I said in my prefatory remarks, I sometimes wove letters, speeches, interviews, and other recorded utterances into dialogue and scenes; these instances are pointed out in my references.

ABBREVIATIONS

(Listed alphabetically by author or title)

EPA FFC   Edward Porter Alexander, *Fighting for the Confederacy: The Personal Recollections of Edward Porter Alexander* (ed. Gary W. Gallagher, Chapel Hill: University of North Carolina Press, 1989)

EPA MM   Edward Porter Alexander, *Military Memoirs of a Confederate: A Critical Narrative* (reprint of 1907 ed., New York: De Capo Press, 1993)

AB MHG   Adam Badeau, *Military History of Ulysses S. Grant From April, 1861, to April, 1865* (3 vols., New York: Appleton and Co., 1881)

CBP LC   Clara Barton Papers, Library of Congress, Washington, D.C.

CBP SC   Clara Barton Papers, Smith College, Northampton, Mass.

JWBW   John Wilkes Booth, *"Right or Wrong, God Judge Me": The Writings of John Wilkes Booth* (ed. John Rhodehamel and Louise Taper, Urbana: University of Illinois Press, 1997)

NB WLT   Noah Brooks, *Washington, D.C., in Lincoln's Time* (ed. Herbert Mitgang, Chicago: Quandrangle Books, 1971)

OBD   Orville H. Browning, *Diary* (ed. Theodore Calvin Pease and James G. Randall, 2 vols., Springfield, Ill.: Illinois State Historical Library, 1925–33)

BBP   Benjamin F. Butler Papers, Library of Congress, Washington, D.C.

SC TYWG   Sylvanus Cadwallader, *Three Years with Grant* (ed. Benjamin P. Thomas, New York: Alfred A. Knopf, 1961)

FBC ILAL   Francis B. Carpenter, *The Inner Life of Abraham Lincoln: Six Months at the White House* (New York: Hurd and Houghton, 1868)

ZCP	Zachariah Chandler Papers, Library of Congress, Washington, D.C.
SC ILC	Samuel P. Chase, *Inside Lincoln's Cabinet: The Civil War Diaries of Salmon P. Chase* (ed. David Donald, New York: Longman's, Green and Co., 1954)
MCCW	Mary Boykin Chesnut, *Mary Chesnut's Civil War* (ed. C. Vann Woodward, New Haven: Yale University Press, 1981)
PMC	Mary Boykin Chesnut, *The Private Mary Chesnut: The Unpublished Civil War Diaries* (ed. C. Vann Woodward and Elisabeth Muhlenfeld, New York: Oxford University Press, 1984)
ABC UB	Asia Booth Clarke, *The Unlocked Book: A Memoir of John Wilkes Booth by His Sister* (New York: G.P. Putnam's Sons, 1938)
JD LPS	Jefferson Davis, *Constitutionalist: His Letters, Papers and Speeches* (ed. Dunbar Rowland, 10 vols., Jackson: Mississippi Department of Archives and History, 1923)
JDMP	Jefferson Davis, *The Messages and Papers of Jefferson Davis and the Confederacy* (ed. James D. Richardson, 2 vols., New York: Chelsea House, 1966)
JDP	Jefferson Davis, *Papers* (ed. Haskell M. Monroe and others, 9 vols., Baton Rouge: Louisiana University Press, 1971—)
JD PL	Jefferson Davis, *Private Letters, 1823–1889* (ed. Hudson Strode, New York: Harcourt, Brace & World, 1966)
JD R&F	Jefferson Davis, *The Rise and Fall of the Confederate Government* (reprint 1881 ed., 2 vols., New York: Da Capo Press, 1990)
VD JD	Varina Davis, *Jefferson Davis, Ex-President of the Confederate States of America: A Memoir* (reprint of 1890 ed., 2 vols., Baltimore: The Nautical & Aviation Publishing Co., 1990)
FD L&W	Philip S. Foner (ed.), *The Life and Writings of Frederick Douglass* (4 vols., New York: International Publishers, 1950)
FDP	Frederick Douglass, *Papers* (ed. John W. Blassingame, 5 vols., New Haven: Yale University Press, 1979—)
JGM	Julia Grant, *The Personal Memoirs of Julia Dent Grant* (ed. John Simon, New York: G. P. Putnam's Sons, 1975)
USGP	Ulysses S. Grant, *Papers* (ed. John Y. Simon, 18 vols., Carbondale, Illinois: Southern Illinois University Press, 1967—)
USG PM	Ulysses S. Grant, *Personal Memoirs* (2 vols., New York: Charles L. Webster & Co., 1885)
CHP SC	Cornelia Hancock Papers, Swarthmore College

CHP UM   Cornelia Hancock Papers, University of Michigan, Ann Arbor

JH D&L   John Hay, *Lincoln and the Civil War in the Diary and Letters of John Hay* (ed. Tyler Dennett, reprint 1939 ed., Westport, Connecticut: Negro Universities Press, 1972)

HMH MWS   Henry M. Hitchcock, *Marching with Sherman* (ed. M. A. DeWolfe Howe, New Haven, Conn.: Yale University Press, 1927)

ALAP   Investigation and Trial Papers Relating to the Assassination of Abraham Lincoln, U.S. National Archives and Records Administration, Washington, D.C.

B&L   Robert Underwood Johnson and Clarence Clough Buel (eds.), *Battles and Leaders of the Civil War* (4 vols., New York: Thomas Yoseloff, 1956)

JBJ WCD   J. B. Jones, *A Rebel War Clerk's Diary at the Confederate States Capital* (ed. Howard Swiggett, new and enlarged ed., 2 vols., New York: Old Hickory Bookshop, 1935)

REL L&L   J. William Jones, *Life and Letters of Robert E. Lee, Soldier and Man* (New York: the Neale Publishing Co., 1906)

RELD   Robert E. Lee, *Lee's Dispatches: Unpublished Letters of General Robert E. Lee, C.S.A., to Jefferson Davis and the War Department of the Confederate States of America, 1862–1865* (ed. Douglas Southall Freeman, N.Y.: G. P. Putnam's Sons, 1957)

RELP VHS   Rorbert E. Lee Papers, Virginia Historical Society, Richmond

RELC WL   Robert E. Lee Collection, Washington and Lee College, Lexington

REL WP   Robert E. Lee, *The Wartime Papers of Robert E. Lee* (ed. Clifford Dowdey and Louis H. Manarin, reprint 1961 ed., New York: Da Capo Press [n.d.])

ALCW   Abraham Lincoln, *Collected Works* (ed. Roy P. Basler and others, 9 vols., New Brunswick, N.J.: Rutgers University Press, 1953–55)

ALCWS   Abraham Lincoln, *Collected Works, Supplement, 1832–1865* (ed. Roy P. Basler, Westport, Conn.: Greenwood Press, 1974)

CWL   Abraham Lincoln, *Conversations with Lincoln* (ed. Charles M. Segal, New York: G. P. Putnam's Sons, 1961)

ALRW   Abraham Lincoln, *The Recollected Words of Abraham Lincoln* (ed. Don E. Fehrenbacher and Virginia Fehrenbacher, Stanford: Stanford University Press, 1996)

RTLC   Robert Todd Lincoln Collection of the Papers of Abraham Lincoln, Library of Congress, Washington, D.C.

TL WG&M   Theodore Lyman, *With Grant and Meade from the Wilderness to Appomattox* (reprint of 1922 ed., Lincoln: University of Nebraska Press, 1994)

AL DBD   Earl Schenck Miers (ed.), *Lincoln Day by Day: A Chronology, 1809–1865* (reprint 1960 ed., 3 vols., Dayton, Ohio: Mornside House, 1991)

MLP   Mary A. Livermore Papers, Boston Public Library

ML SML   Mary A. Livermore, *The Story of My Life* (Hartford: A. D. Worthington & Co., 1898)

ML MSW   Mary A. Livermore, *My Story of the War: A Woman's Narrative* (reprint 1887 ed., Williamstown, Massachusetts: Corner House Publishers, 1978)

JGNP   John G. Nicolay Papers, Library of Congress, Washington, D.C.

N&H ALH   John G. Nicolay and John Hay, *Abraham Lincoln: A History* (10 vols., New York: Century Co., 1890)

BP AL   Benn Pitman (comp.), *The Assassination of President Lincoln and the Trial of the Conspirators* (reprint of 1865 ed., Westport, Connecticut: Greenwood Press, 1974)

BPS CT   Ben Perley Poore, *The Conspiracy Trial for the Murder of the President* (3 vols., Boston: J. E. Tildon & Co., 1866)

HP CWG   Horace Porter, *Campaigning with Grant* (reprint 1897 ed., New York: Bonanza Books, 1961)

ATR RAL   Allen Thorndike Rice (ed.), *Reminiscences of Abraham Lincoln by Distinguished Men of His Time* (reprint 1888 ed., New York: Haskell House Publishers, 1971)

WTS HL   William Tecumseh Sherman, *Home Letters* (ed. M. A. DeWolfe, New York: Charles A. Scribner's Sons, 1909)

WTSM   William Tecumseh Sherman, *Memoirs* (Library of America ed., New York: Literary Classics of the United States, 1990)

WTSP   William Tecumseh Sherman Papers, Library of Congress, Washington, D.C.

SL   *The Sherman Letters: Correspondence Between General and Senator Sherman from 1837 to 1891* (ed., Rachel Thorndike Sherman, New York: Charles A. Scribner's Sons, 1894)

TJS   *Trial of John H. Surratt in the Criminal Court for the District of Columbia* (2 vols., Washington: French & Richardson, 1867)

LTP   Lyman Trumbull Papers, Library of Congress, Washington, D.C.

OR   U.S. War Department, *The War of the Rebellion: A Compila-*

tion of the Official Records of the Union and Confederate
Armies (70 vols. in 128, Washington, D.C.: Government
Printing Office, 1880–1901)

BFWP   Benjamin F. Wade Papers, Library of Congress, Washington,
D.C.

LMC   Patricia Allie Wall, "The Letters of Mary Boykin Chesnut"
(Master's thesis, University of South Carolina, 1977)

EWP LC   Elihu Washburne Papers, Library of Congress, Washington,
D.C.

EWP NLHC Elihu Washburne Papers, Norlands Living History Center,
Livermore, Maine

LJW AAL   Louis J. Weichmann, A True History of the Assassination of
Abraham Lincoln and of the Conspiracy of 1865 (ed. Floyd
E. Risvold, New York: Vintage Books, 1977)

GWD   Gideon Welles, Diary (ed. John T. Morse, Jr., 3 vols: Boston:
Houghton Mifflin Co., 1911)

THE WINDS OF 'SIXTY-ONE

1. **Lincoln.** Sumter: *ALCW*, 4:331–32, 425–28; *N&H, ALH*, 4:70–78;
Frederick W. Seward, *Reminiscences of a War-Time Statesman and
Diplomat, 1830–1915* (New York: G. P. Putnam's Sons, 1916), 151–52;
Union men of Virginia convention to AL, Mar. 10, 1861, RTLC; *GWD*,
1:39; David M. Potter, *Lincoln and His Party in the Secession Crisis*
(New Haven: Yale University Press, 1942), 373–74. Seward profile:
William Howard Russell, *My Diary North and South* (ed. Fletcher Pratt,
New York: Harper & Brothers, 1954), 19–20; Glyndon G. Van Deusen,
William Henry Seward (New York: Oxford University Press, 1967),
255–68, 274, 335, 339–41; *NB WLT*, 35–36. Old codgers in the War
Department: Russell, *Diary*, 209. Visit with Scott and Scott's regard for
Lee: Seward, *Reminiscences*, 167–68; *REL WTP*, 3. Seward's son does
not say that Lincoln was present when Seward and Scott discussed Lee,
but it's extremely unlikely that Lincoln would not have been there given
the vital importance of the discussion: the field command of the Union
army. Frank Blair, Sr., profile: William Ernest Smith, *The Francis Preston
Blair Family in Politics* (2 vols., New York: Macmillan Co., 1933), 1: 79,
187, 464; Elbert B. Smith, *Francis Preston Blair* (New York: Free Press,
1990), 4, 37. The evidence indicates that Lincoln called on Blair and
asked him to offer Lee field command of the army being raised. Blair did
make the offer, on the authority of the President.

2. Lee. Lee's first meeting with Scott: Margaret Sanborn, *Robert E. Lee* (2 vols., Philadelphia: J. B. Lippincott Co., 1966–67), 1:307–08. "Has it come so soon as this?" *B&L* 1:36. Lee's loyalty to Virginia took precedence over his loyalty to the Federal government: Sanborn, 1:306. Mr. Custis was like a father to Lee: Robert E. Lee, *"To Markie": The Letters of Robert E. Lee to Martha Custis Williams* (ed. Avery Craven, Cambridge: Harvard University Press, 1934), 41, 43; Paul C. Nagel, *The Lees of Virginia: Seven Generations of an American Family* (New York: Oxford University Press, 1990), 235; Sanborn 1:94. Mr. Custis's will: Sanborn, 1:270–71. Manager of Arlington: RELP VHS. Charge that Lee was cruel to slaves: *New York Tribune,* June 24, 1859; Sanborn, 1:282–83; Douglass Southall Freeman, *R. E. Lee: A Biography* (4 vols., New York, Charles Scribner's Sons, 1934–35), 1:391–92. See Lee's letter of July 8, 1858, RELP VHS. Mr. Custis's slaves an "unpleasant legacy": Nolan, 16; Emory M. Thomas, *Robert E. Lee: A Biography* (New York: W. W. Norton & Co., 1995), 178. Lee's affection for Arlington: Lee, *"To Markee,"* 43; Nagel 234–35. "The soft wild luxuriance of its woods" in Agnes Lee, *Growing Up in the 1850s: The Journal of Agnes Lee* (ed. Mary Custis Lee deButts, Chapel Hill: Robert E. Lee Memorial Association, by the University of North Carolina Press, 1984), 63; Children "intwined around my heart": Mary P. Coulling, *The Lee Girls* (Winston-Salem, North Carolina: John B. Blair, 1987), 10; Sanborn, 1:98. Lee's children tickled his toes: Captain Robert E. Lee, *Recollections and Letters of General Robert E. Lee* (Secaucus, N.J.: Blue and Gray Press [n.d.]), 9–10; Sanborn 1:199. Lee's nicknames for children and affection for daughters: Coulling 13, 23; Captain Lee, 14–15. Mary's difficulties in child birth: Coulling, 8; Sanborn, 1:107–08; Clifford Dowdey, *Lee* (New York: Bonanza Books, 1965), 62, 111, 127. "All other men are small in comparison": quoted in Mark Grimsley, "Robert E. Lee," *Civil War Times Illustrated* (November 1985), 15. Lee's attitudes on the slavery issue and the sectional crisis: Lee to Mary Lee, Dec. 27, 1856, in Sanborn, 1:255, in Freeman, 371–73, and in A. L. Long, *Memoirs of Robert E. Lee* (Secaucus, N.J.: Blue and Gray Press, 1983), 83–84; Alan T. Nolan, *Lee Considered: General Robert E. Lee and Civil War History* (Chapel Hill, University of North Carolina Press, 1991), 12–15, 23, 29, 48; Lee to Custis Lee siding with Buchanan, Dec. 14, 1860, in Rev. J. William Jones, *Life and Letters of Robert Edward Lee* (Harrisonburg, Virginia: Sprinkle Publications, 1986), 118–19; Lee to W. H. F. Lee, Jan. 23, 1861, in Long, 88–89, in Freeman, 1:420–422, and discussed in Thomas L. Connelly, *The Marble Man: Robert E. Lee and His Image in American Society* (New York: Alfred A. Knopf, 1977), 194–95; Lee to

Markie Williams, Jan. 22, 1861, Lee, *"To Markie,"* 58–59. See also Sanborn, 1:301–02, 306, and Thomas, 186, 188–90. Lee's meeting with
Blair: *REL WTP,* 4; Lee's conversation with William Allan, Feb. 15,
1868, RELC WL, and printed in Gary W. Gallagher (ed.), *Lee the Soldier*
(Lincoln: University of Nebraska Press, 1996), 10; Jones, 131; Sanborn,
1:310; Freeman, 1:436–37; Long, 92–93. Lee's meeting with Scott: Lee's
conversation with Allan, Feb. 15, 1868, RELC WL; Long, 93; Freeman,
437, 437n–438n; Sanborn 1:311. Lee's struggle with his conscience about
resigning: Freeman, 1:438–39. Lee in Leadbetter's Apothecary, Lee can't
raise his hand against his family and home: Sanborn, 1:312, 314. Lee's
resignation: *REL WTP,* 9, 10; Jones, 132; Freeman, 1:442. "I did only
what my duty demanded": Freeman, I, 447. Lee's appeal to Providence:
REL WTP, 12.

3. **Lincoln.** Lincoln's view of Lee as a traitor: *ALCW,* 6:265. Magruder:
N&H ALH, 4:142; *ALRW,* 431–32. Washington crawled with rumors:
Seward, *Reminiscences,* 157; *JH D&L,* 9; Nicolay to Theresa, Apr. 17,
1861, JGNP; Helen Nicolay, *Lincoln's Secretary: A Biography of John G.
Nicolay* (New York: Longman's Green & Co., 1949), 91.

4. **Mary Livermore.** Troops in Boston: *ML MSW,* 85, 91–92, 95–96. Garrison: ibid., 98–99; Mary Livermore to William Lloyd Garrison II, Apr. 8,
1886, Garrison Family Papers, Smith College. Tutor and cruelties on a Virginia plantation: *ML SML,* 139–188, 235, 355–56, 364. Something had
happened to the Sixth Massachusetts in Baltimore: *ML MSW,* 99–100.

5. **Lincoln.** Sixth Massachusetts mobbed in Baltimore: *JH D&L,* 3–4; *AL
DBD,* 3:36; *ALCW,* 4:340–41; AL to Ed Jones, *ALRW,* 269; Nicolay to
Theresa, Apr. 19, 1861, JGNP. Rumors and "vigilant watch": ibid.; *JH
D&L,* 5; Nicolay, *Lincoln's Secretary,* 91. Baltimore delegation inter-
cepted AL, "if I grant you this concession": *JH D&L,* 6; Nicolay memo-
randum, Apr. 19, 1861, JGNP; Nicolay, *Nicolay,* 93–94. AL's summons
to Hicks and Brown: *ALCW,* 4:341. Brown-Lincoln dispatches: Nicolay
memorandum, JGNP; Nicolay, 93–94; *JH D&L,* 6. Brown and second
Baltimore delegation: *ALCW,* 4:341–42; Nicolay memorandum, JGNP;
CWL, 112–13. The anxious wait for troops: *JH D&L,* 5–8; Nicolay to
Theresa, Apr. 26, 1861, JGNP; *N&H ALH,* 4: 149–53; J. G. Randall,
Lincoln the President (4 vols., New York: Dodd, Mead & Co., 1945–55),
1:364; *ATR RAL,* 377. Cabinet meeting: ibid.; *ALCW,* 5:240–43.
Cameron description: William Howard Russell, *My Diary North and
South* (ed. Fletcher Pratt, New York: Harper & Brothers, 1954), 27;
Robert V. Bruce, *Lincoln and the Tools of War* (Urbana: University of

Illinois Press, 1989), 28. Welles description: John Niven, *Gideon Welles: Lincoln's Secretary of the Navy* (New York: Oxford University Press, 1973), 318–19. Blair description: Russell, 27–28. Bates description: ibid., 28. Chase description: *SC ILC*, 1–7; Wade on Chase and the trinity in *JH D&L*, 53. "Why don't they come?" and "You are the only northern realities" in Nicolay, 95–96, and *JH D&L*, 11. Troops in Washington: *JH D&L*, 11; Margaret Leech, *Reveille in Washington, 1860–1865* (New York: Harper & Brothers, 1941), 66–69; Clara Barton to Elvira Stone, Apr. 29, May 14, 1861, CBP LC. AL's call for more troops: *ALCW*, 4:3554. Lincoln's Black Hawk war experience: ibid., 1:510. AL's plan of operations: *JH D&L*, 11; T. Harry Williams, *Lincoln and His Generals* (New York: Alfred A. Knopf, 1952), 16. Scott's plan: ibid., 16–18. AL's need to hold Kentucky and the other border slave states: *ALCW*, 4:532. Lincoln *had* to have Kentucky: Benjamin Quarles, *Abraham Lincoln and the Negro* (New York: Oxford University Press, 1962), 84. Lincoln's Kentucky policy: Randall, 1: 3–9; *CWL*, 115–16; *ALCW*, 4:368–69; David C. Mearns, *The Lincoln Papers* (reprint of 1948 ed., New York: Kraus Reprint Co., 1969), 619–20. Butler's occupation of Baltimore: "bag the whole nest" in *JH D&L*, 11–12; Hans L. Trefousse, *Ben Butler: The South Called Him BEAST!* (reprint of 1957 ed., New York: Octagonal Books, 1974), 65–76; Howard P. Nash, Jr., *Stormy Petrel: The Life and Times of General Benjamin F. Butler, 1815–1893* (Rutherford, N.J.: Fairleigh Dickinson University Press, 1969), 98–100; Randall, 1:366. Arrests of pro-secessionist Maryland legislators: Seward, *Reminiscenes*, 175–78; *ALCW*, 4:523, also 344, 5:24, 523; Mark E. Neely, Jr., *The Fate of Liberty: Abraham Lincoln and Civil Liberties* (New York: Oxford University Press, 1991), 15–18. "Necessity knows no law": J. G. Randall, *Constitutional Problems Under Lincoln* (revised ed., Urbana: University of Illinois Press, 1964, 26–27; Stephen B. Oates, *Abraham Lincoln: The Man Behind the Myths* (New York: Harper & Row, 1984), 120. Martial law and military arrests: *ALCW*, 4:430–31, 6:263; Neely, 3–65; Randall, *Constitutional Problems*, 118–85; Harold M. Hyman, *A More Perfect Union: The Impact of the Civil War and Reconstruction on the Constitution* (reprint 1973 ed., Boston: Houghton Mifflin Co. 1975), 65–155; Benjamin P. Thomas and Harold M. Hyman, *Stanton: The Life and Times of Lincoln's Secretary of War* (New York: Alfred A. Knopf, 1962), 157–58, 280–81, 375. Mobilization woes: *ALCW*, 4:369n, 370–76, 402ff; *JH D&L*, 18–19; Randall, *Lincoln the President*, 1:361, 372, 2:86. Medical difficulties and Dix: Stephen B. Oates, *A Woman of Valor: Clara Barton and the Civil War* (New York: The Free Press, 1994), 4, 9–10; Cameron's directive regarding Dix in *OR*, ser. 3, 1:107.

6. **Livermore**. Chicago mobilization: *ML MSW*, 101–10; *ML SML*, 458. Uprising of women: ibid., 109–35. Husband's support, Mary Livermore's activities: *ML SML*, 395, 457, 596–97; Lara Ruegamer, "'The Paradise of Exceptional Women': Chicago Women Reformers, 1863–1893" (Ph.D. dissertation, Indiana University, 1982), 84. Livermore and Jane Hoge: *ML MSW*, 160; Ruegamer, 9, 13, 85. Feeding the soldiers, the story of the young woman in uniform: *ML MSW*, 114. Scholars estimate that four hundred women joined the army masquerading as men. See Agatha Young, *The Women and the Crisis: Women of the North in the Civil War* (New York: McDowell, Obolensky, 1959), 43; Ann Douglas Wood, "The War within a War: Women Nurses in the Union Army," *Civil War History* (Sept. 1972), 202; and Richard Hall, *Patriots in Disguise: Women Warriors of the Civil War* (New York: Paragon House, 1993), 20–45. Mary's article in the *Covenant*: L. P. Brockett, *Women's Work in the Civil War: A Record of Heroism, Patriotism, and Courage* (Philadelphia: Zeigler, McCurdy and Co., 1967), 578–79. Formation of U.S. Sanitary Commission: William Q. Maxwell, *Lincoln's Fifth Wheel* (New York: Longman's, Green, & Co., 1956), 2–7, 298–99; George Washington Adams, *Doctors in Blue: The Medical History of the Union Army in the Civil War* (New York: Henry Schuman, 1952), 5–9. Livermore's and Hoge's association with Chicago Sanitary Commission: *ML MSW*, 136; Maxwell, 298, Dr. John S. Newberry, *The U.S. Sanitary Commission in the Valley of the Mississippi During the War of the Rebellion, 1861–1865* (Cleveland: Fairbanks, Benedict, & Co., 1871), 18–19; Mrs. Sarah Edwards Henshaw, *Our Branch and Its Tributaries: Being a History of the Work of the Northwestern Sanitary Commission and Its Auxiliaries During the War of the Rebellion* (Chicago: Alfred L. Sewell, 1868), 28–29, 38, 39, 42–45, 58. E. P. Teale quotation: ibid., 36–37.

7. **Lincoln**. AL and James W. Ripley: Bruce, *Lincoln and the Tools of War*, 23, 30–42, 53, 69, 81; William O. Stoddard, *Inside the White House in War Times* (New York: Charles L. Webster & Co., 1890), 42; William O. Stoddard, *Abraham Lincoln and Andrew Johnson* (New York: F. A. Stokes & Brother, 1888), 213, 223. Ellsworth's death: *ALCW*, 4:273n; *ALC*, 121–23; *N&H ALH*, 4: 310–14; *JH D&L*, 17. Description of Navy Yard: Russell, *My Diary*, 31–32; Bruce, 7. Ellsworth's burial: *AL DBD*, 3:43–44; Justin G. Turner and Linda Levitt Turner, *Mary Todd Lincoln: Her Life and Letters* (New York: Alfred A. Knopf, 1972), 92; Reinhold H. Luthin, *The Real Abraham Lincoln* (Englewood Cliffs, N.J.: Prentice-Hall, 1960), 286.

8. **Lee**. Loss of Arlington: Jones, *Life and Letters*, 156; *REL WTP*, 36, 48. REL's office: Alfred Hoyt Bill, *The Beleaguered City: Richmond,*

1861–1865 (reprint of 1946 ed., Westport, Conn.: Greenwood Press, 1980), 56. Brigadier General in CSA army: Freeman, *Lee,* 1:501. Sons in the army: ibid., 511. Lee urged Rob to stay in school: *REL WTP,* 15. Lee's guilts and fears of failure as a father: Lee letters quoted in Connelley, *Marble Man,* 178–79. Troubles with Rooney: Nagel, *Lees of Virginia,* 259, and Thomas, *Lee,* 169–70; description of Rooney in Freeman, 2:274, and Philip Van Doren Stern, *Robert E. Lee: The Man and the Soldier, A Pictorial Biography* (New York: Bonanza Books, 1963), 137. Lee dispersed troops and ordered commanders to resist invading Yankees: *REL WTP,* 41. Lee wanted to take the field: *REL WTP,* 54.

9. **Jefferson Davis.** JD's office building in Montgomery: Russell, *My Diary,* 93. JD's reactions to AL's "usurpations": *JD R&F* 2:137; *JDMP,* 63–82; *JDP,* 7:184–85. Davis's efforts at nation building: *VD JD,* 2:74; Paul D. Escott, *After Secession: Jefferson Davis and the Failure of Confederate Nationalism* (Baton Rouge: Louisiana State University Press, 1978), 56, 80. Assassination warnings: *VD JD,* 2:74–75. Train trip to Richmond: *VD JD,* 2:75; *JBJ WCD,* 1:44; *JD LPS,* 5:102; *JDP,* 7:183n; Wigfall description in Russell, *My Diary,* 62; Charlotte Wigfall quotation in Strode, *Davis,* 2:89. Lamar's response to JD's arrival: Strode, 2:90. JD's speech from hotel balcony (not an exact quotation): *JDP,* 7: 185. Richmond a sprawling military camp: *VD JD,* 2:86; Emory M. Thomas, *The Confederate Nation, 1861–1865* (New York: Harper & Row, 1979), 103. Executive offices in Treasury Building (formerly the Federal Custom House): *White House of the Confederacy* (Richmond: Cadmus Marketing [n.d.]), 17; Strode, 2:91–92. Lee's appearance: Freeman, 1:84–85, 450, 612. JD and Lee confer: Strode, 2:93; We may assume that Lee told JD what he said to others at this time ("the cruel enemy," "the evil designs of the North," "count on my voice," as quoted in Connelly, 201). JD's desire to recapture Arlington and take the offensive: *JDP,* 7:199, 203, 239. JD in command of rebel forces in northern Virginia: Douglas Southall Freeman, *Lee* (one volume abridgment by Richard Harwell, New York: Charles Scribner's Sons, 1961), 134. Johnston's retreat and biography: Strode, 2:97, 79; Steven E. Woodworth, *Jefferson Davis and His Generals: The Failure of Confederate Command in the West* (Lawrence: University Press of Kansas, 1990), 174, 176. Beauregard's forces and possible retreat: *JDP,* 7:234–35. JD's response: ibid., 238, 239. JD preferred field command: *JD R&F,* 1:230.

10. **Lincoln.** "On to Richmond": *CWL,* 125; Frank Moore (ed.), *The Rebellion Record: A Diary of American Events* (12 vols., New York: G. P. Putnam and D. Van Nostrand, 1861–69), 2:385. Lincoln's conference

with McDowell and Scott: *N&H ALH*, 4:360; E. D. Townsend, *Anecdotes of the Civil War in the United States* (New York: D. Appleton and Co., 1884), 57; Williams, *Lincoln and His Generals*, 21, Randall, *Lincoln the President*, 1:391. AL to Hay on central idea: *JH D&L*, 19–20; see also Nicolay memorandum, May 7, 1861, JGNP. AL's message: *ALCW*, 4:422–40. British monarchists ("the trial of Democracy," "riddance to a nightmare"): Ephraim D. Adams, *Great Britain and the American Civil War* (2 vols., New York: Longman's Green & Co., 1925), 2:284; Frank Lawrence Owsley, *King Cotton Diplomacy: Foreign Relations of the Confederate States of America* (2nd ed., Chicago: University of Chicago Press, 1959), 186. Lincoln's fears of returning class, caste, and despotism: *ALCW*, 3:375. Lincoln's hands-off policy regarding slavery derived from his and the party's prewar position, elucidated in full in Stephen B. Oates, *The Approaching Fury: Voices of the Storm, 1820–1861* (New York: HarperCollins, 1997), 156ff. Wade and Chandler profiles: Hans L. Trefousse, *The Radical Republicans: Lincoln's Vanguard for Racial Justice* (New York: Alfred A. Knopf, 1969), 7–9, 172–73; *NB WLT*, 34–35. Profile of Sumner: *NB WLT*, 33–34, *ATR RAL*, 223. I've cast into dialogue the senators' arguments for emancipation, which they presented to Lincoln and which are well documented in the following sources: Detroit *Post and Tribune, Zachary Chandler* (Detroit: *Post and Tribune*, 1880), 222, 253; George Washington Julian, *Political Recollections, 1840–1872* (Chicago: Jansen, McClurg, & Co., 1884), 153, 165–66, 223; Charles Sumner, *Selected Letters* (ed. Beverly Wilson Palmer, 2 vols., Boston: Northeastern University Press, 1990), 2: 65, 69, 72, 74–76, 78, 80, 82; David Donald, *Charles Sumner and the Rights of Man* (New York: Alfred A. Knopf, 1970), 17ff; Hans L. Trefousse, *Benjamin Franklin Wade, Radical Republican from Ohio* (New York: Twayne Publishers, 1963), 180–81; Trefousse, *Radical Republicans*, 30–32, 158–59, 172, 203–08; Stephen W. Sears, *The Civil War: The Best of American Heritage* (New York: American Heritage Press, 1991), 106, 112–113; *LRW*, 2; see also John Hope Franklin, *The Emancipation Proclamation* (Garden City, N.Y.: Doubleday & Co., 1965), 1–28. Lincoln's response ("always hated slavery," "too big a lick," "applecart" and "thunderbolt"): *ALCW*, 2:492; Donald, 60; *ALWR*, 295, 326; Carl Sandburg, *Abraham Lincoln, The War Years* (4 vols., New York: Harcourt, Brace & World, 1939), 1:356–57; Fawn M. Brodie, *Thaddeus Stevens, Scourge of the South* (New York: W. W. Norton, 1966), 155.

11. **Davis.** Response to AL's message, Yankee aggression, and First Confiscation Act: *JD LPS*, 5:114–18; *JD R&F*, 2: 1–5, 136–37, 159–60. Federal

advance against Manassas: *JDP*, 7:249, 251, 252n; *JD LPS*, 5:118–19; Strode, *Davis*, 2:111. Johnston's wire about his rank: *JDP*, 7:254. JD's message: *JD LPS*, 5:114–18. JD to battlefield: *JD R&F*, 1: 302–03; Strode, 2:114–16.

12. **William Tecumseh Sherman.** In Louisiana, views on the South, slavery, anarchy, secession, monarchism: WTS to John Sherman, Dec. 1, 9, 18, 29, 1860, Jan. 16 and Feb. 1, 1861, WTSP; *SL*, 78; *WTS HL*, 182, 190, 193, 195, 197, 200–01; Michael Fellman, *Citizen Sherman: A Life of William Tecumseh Sherman* (New York: Random House, 1995), 56–59, 74–75, 78, 87, 131; Lloyd Lewis, *Sherman, Fighting Prophet* (New York: Harcourt, Brace and Co., 1932), 126; John F. Marszalek, *Sherman: A Soldier's Passion for Order* (New York: The Free Press, 1993), 109. WTS to Louisiana professor: Lewis, 138, Marszalek, 137; Burke Davis, *Sherman's March* (New York: Random House, 1980), 15. WTS's resignation, warning to South: WTS to Gov. Moore, Jan. 18, 1861, WTSP; Marszalek, 137. WTS in command "rabble" troops: Fellman, 89; Lewis, 168. WTS's advance, pillaging soldiers: *WTSM*, 198; Lewis, 170; *WTS HL*, 209. WTS at Bull Run: based on WTS's long letter to his wife, Ellen, in *HL*, 205–09, 211–12; WTS's letter to John Sherman, July 19, 1861, WTSP; and *WTSM*, 199–205. The Lovejoy incident is reported in William F. G. Shanks, *Personal Recollection of Distinguished Generals* (New York: Harper & Brothers, 1866), 38–39.

13. **Lincoln.** At telegraph office during Bull Run: David Homer Bates, *Lincoln in the Telegraph Office* (New York: The Century Co., 1907), 38, 87–91; *AL DBD* 3:55; Nicolay to Theresa, July 21, 1861, JGNP, and quoted in Nicolay, *Lincoln's Secretary*, 108–10; Williams, *Lincoln and His Generals*, 22–23; Randall, *Lincoln the President,* 1:390. Lincoln in White House: Benjamin P. Thomas, *Abraham Lincoln: A Biography* (New York: Alfred A. Knopf, 1952), 272; *N&H, ALH*, 4:355; Russell, *My Diary,* 231 (for clouds swirling over moon). Wade and Chandler during battle, Chandler at White House: Trefousse, *Radical Republicans*, 173–75.

14. **Davis.** JD's arrival on battlefield: *JD, R&F*, 1: 303–06; Strode, *Davis*, 2:114–16. JD's account of his rallying troops to victory: *JDP*, 7:258n, 259–61n. JD conference with Johnston and Beauregard: *JDP* 7:394n; *JD R& F*, 1:307, 310, 313; Strode, 2:125–27, 131. Beauregard portrait: T. Harry Williams, *P. G. T. Beauregard, Napoleon in Gray* (Baton Rouge: Louisiana State University Press, 1954), 52–53; Hamilton Basso, *Beauregard, The Great Creole* (New York: Charles Scribner's Sons, 1933), 46–47, 116, 143. JD thanked Beauregard: *JDP*, 7:258. Johnston's remark

("more disorganized in victory"): Nicolay, *Lincoln's Secretary*, 111. JD's speech at Richmond depot: *JDP* 7:262. JD's love for administrative details and minutiae: William C. Davis, *Jefferson Davis, the Man and the Hour* (New York: HarperCollins, 1991), 389; *VD JD* 2:305 (JD's singing as he worked). JD wanted a strong central government, a national military system, and industrial self-sufficiency, but faced state-rights opposition: Escott, *After Secession*, 55–56, 59, 61, 79, 81; *JBJ WCD*, 1:198–99; *Charleston Mercury* (Sept. 11, 1861); *JD R&F*, 1:404–14. Offensive-defensive strategy and autonomous military departments: Thomas, *Confederate Nation*, 108; Woodworth, *Davis and His Generals*, 19; Davis, *Davis*, 373; *JD LPS*, 5:193, 131, 354–55, 462, 465–67. JD's command appointments: Davis, *Davis*, 374–76; Woodworth, 17–33. Polk profile: William M. Polk, *Leonidas Polk, Bishop and General* (2 vols., New York: Longman's, Green, 1915), 1:211, 2:213; Woodworth, 32. JD on Kentucky neutrality: Woodworth, 35–38; *JDP*, 7:310. Lee sent to West Virginia: *REL WTP*, 59–61, 69 (for Lee's sense of duty); Freeman, *Lee*, 1:541–42; *JD R&F*, 1:372, 374. Conditions at Manassas, JD and Johnston: *JD LPS*, 5:121, 123, 129, 135; Strode, 2:146–48, 152. Confederate White House: *JDP*, 7:204n–205n; *White House of the Confederacy*, 7, 17; *VD JD*, 2:198–200. Mary Chesnut description: Elisabeth Muhlenfeld, *Mary Boykin Chesnut: A Biography* (Baton Rouge: Louisiana State University Press, 1981), 53, 74. JD liked her to sit opposite him: *PMC*, 101, 108.

15. **Mary Boykin Chesnut.** JD liked her chat: *PMC*. Funerals and Dead March: *MCCW*, 107; *PMC*, 123; MC to "Sister Clay" [Virginia Caroline Tunstall Clay], c. Apr., 1866, LMC. Return of James Chesnut: *PMC*, 102. JD's and James Chesnut's speeches: ibid., 103. MC's ambitions for her husband: *MCCW*, xxxix; *PMC*, 112, 121. JD description: Russell, *My Diary*, 93–94. JD's opponents: *PMC*, 57; Eric H. Walers, *The Fire-Eaters* (Baton Rouge: Louisiana State University Press, 1992), 160 (Wigfall description). MC's sympathies for Davises: *PMC*, 122, *MCCW*, 136. Varina on carping against JD: ibid., 141. MC with Barnwell: *PMC*, 122–23. MC's ambitions (if only she were a man): *PMC*, 63, 72, 74, 130, 144, 145 ("I think these times"), 146; *MCCW*, 177. MC's hospital work and illness: *PMC*, 135–36, 138–39, 155, 162. MC's visits with Mrs. Davis and Mrs. Toombs: ibid., 140. JD's sickness: ibid., 150–51, 153; *JD LPS*, 5:135; Strode, *Davis*, 2:148, 151. Northern papers reported JD's death: *JDP*, 7:317n.

16. **Lincoln.** Reactions to Bull Run: Moore, *Rebellion Record*, 2:284–85; *ALC*, 125–26; *New York Herald*, July 25, 26, 1861; Randall, *Lincoln the President*, 1:389–92. AL and Scott: *CWL*, 126. Trumbull's criticism of AL: Horace White, *The Life of Lyman Trumbull* (Boston: Houghton

Mifflin Co., 1913), 171. AL's visit with Sherman: *WTSM*, 206–08; Lewis, *Sherman*, 180. Sherman description: Captain David P. Conyngham, *Sherman's March Through the South with Sketches and Incidents of the Campaign* (New York: Sheldon and Co., 1865), 50–51; *HP CWG*, 290; Marszalek, *Sherman*, 147. AL's plan of operations: *ALCW*, 4: 457–58. AL and Frémont: John Bigelow, *Memoir of the Life and Public Services of John Charles Frémont* (New York: Derby & Jackson, 1856), 461–62 (description of Frémont); Williams, *Lincoln and His Generals*, 33–35. AL and McClellan: *NB WLT*, 25; Williams, 24–31; Warren G. Hassler, Jr., *Commanders of the Army of the Potomac* (Baton Rouge: Louisiana University Press, 1962), 26–31. Lincoln's stories: *ALRW*, 27, 91–92; Albert B. Chandler, "As Lincoln Appeared in the War Department," *Independent* (Apr. 4, 1895), 448–49; *ALRW*, 256 ("tumbler of piss with a fart in it"). Quotation ("I tell you the truth"): John F. Farnsworth's testimony in Sandburg, *Abraham Lincoln: The War Years*, 3:305. AL's public opinion baths: Stephen B. Oates, *With Malice Toward None: A Life of Abraham Lincoln* (2nd ed., New York: HarperPerennial, 1994), 126–47. Soldiers' Home description: Julia Susan Wheelock, *The Boys in White: The Experience of a Hospital Agent in and around Washington* (New York: Lange & Hillman, 1870, 1870), 169–71. Mary and Washington society: Ruth Painter Randall, *Mary Lincoln: Biography of a Marriage* (Boston: Little, Brown, 1953), 196–97, 218–19, 312, 344, 346; Turners, *Mary Lincoln*, 77–79. Mary's headaches: ibid., 609. Hellcat: *JH D&L*, 41. AL and Shakespeare: *ALCW*, 6:392. AL and Holmes, *NB WLT*, 78–79. Douglas died from bad whiskey: Russell, *My Diary*, 183. Lincoln's depression, Browning's exhortation: Browning to AL, Aug. 19, 1861, RTLC; *OBD*, 1: 488–89; Nicolay, *Lincoln's Secretary*, 101 ("if to be the head of Hell"). Greeley quotation: Greeley to AL, July 29, 1861, RTLC. McClellan quotation: George B. McClellan, *McClellan's Own Story* (New York: Charles L. Webster, 1887), 229. Lincoln and ordnance: Bruce, *Lincoln and the Tools of War*, 49–56, 112 ("newfangled gimmracks"), 99–104, 107–11 (Berdan's sharpshooters), 117. Lincoln and Professor Lowe: ibid., 85–88; *ALCW*, 4:460; E. B. Long, *The Civil War Day-by Day: An Almanac, 1861–1865* (Garden City, N.Y.: Doubleday & Co., 1971), 86–87. Frémont's complaints: Williams, *Lincoln and His Generals*, 35; Blair's charges against Frémont: Frank Blair to Montgomery Blair, Sept. 1, Oct. 2, 1861, RTLC; Nicolay memorandum, Sept. 7, 1861, JGNP; Randall, *Lincoln the President*, 2:19. AL's reaction to Frémont's proclamation: *ALCW*, 4:531–32; Joshua Speed to AL, Sept. 1 and 3, 1861, RTLC; James Speed and Greene Adams to AL, Sept. 2, 1861, ibid.; Thomas, *Lincoln*, 275 ("over the mill dam"). Response of Radicals and abolitionists: Wendell Phillips Garrison and Francis Jackson Garrison, *William Lloyd Garrison, 1805–1879: The Story of His Life* (reprint of 118–89 ed, 4 vols., New York: Negro Universities Press, 1969), 4:32; *Douglass's Monthly* (Oct., 1861), in *FD L&W*, 3:165. AL's order to Frémont: *ALCW*, 4:506. Jessie Frémont's visit with AL: *ALCW*, 4:515; *LC*, 131–34; *N&H*, *ALH*, 415; *JH D&L* ("taxed me so violently"), 133. AL's order of Sept. 11, 1861, to Frémont, *ALCW*, 517–18; also 507. Reaction to AL's order: Donald, *Sumner and the Rights of Man*, 26; Wade to Chandler, Sept. 23 and Oct. 8, 1861, BFWP; *Douglass's Monthly* (Dec., 1861) in *FD L&W*, 3:177, also 161–62, 174; William Lloyd Garrison, *Letters* (ed. Walter M. Merrill and Louis Ruchames, 6 vols., Cambridge: Harvard University Press, 1971–81), 4:35, 40; Garrisons, 4:35; James M. McPherson, *The Struggle for Equality: Abolitionists and the Negro in the Civil War and Reconstruction* (Princeton: Princeton University Press, 1964), 74 (the "truce" was over). Dismal time: Nicolay, "Conversation with the President," Oct. 2, 1861, Nicolay, *Lincoln's Secretary*, 125–26.

17. Ulysses S. Grant. Paducah expedition: *USGM*, 1:264–67; *USGP*, 2: 189, 194, 196, 198; *AB MHG*, 1:11–12; Bruce Catton, *Grant Moves South* (Boston: Little, Brown, 1960), 49. USG to Julia: *USGP*, 2:214. USG in Cairo: ibid., 2:207, 238; Catton, 48, 44, 46; B. Franklin Cooling, *Forts Henry and Donelson: The Key to the Confederate Heartland* (Knoxville: University of Tennessee Press, 1987), 76. Rawlins: James Harrison Wilson, *The Life of John A. Rawlins* (New York: the Neal Publishing Co., 1916), 54, 58, 60–61; W. R. Rawley to E. B. Washburne, EWP LC; Catton, 67–69; *USGP*, 2:116, 182. Galena's public meeting: Wilson, 48; Albert D. Richardson, *A Personal History of Ulysses S. Grant* (Hartford: American Publishing Co., 1868), 179. USG and Julia Dent: Lloyd Lewis, *Captain Sam Grant* (Boston: Little, Brown, 1950), 111–12; Foster Coates, "The Courtship of General Grant," *Ladies' Home Journal* (Oct., 1890), 4. Rawlins's speech: Wilson, 48. USG's reaction: Richardson, 179, *USGP*, 2:3–4, 6–7. First battle in Missouri: *USGM*, 1:249–50. USG promoted: ibid., 1:254; *USGP*, 2:81, 82n; Catton, 17. USG under the tree: ibid., 26. Foote: *B&L*, 1:344, 359–60; John Mason Hoppin, *Life of Andrew Hull Foote* (New York: Harper & Brothers, 1874), 402–03. USG freed his slave: *USGP*, 1:347. USG's aggressiveness: *USGP*, 3:63, 64; Charles M. J. Cramer, *Ulysses S. Grant: Conversations and Unpublished Letters* (New York: Eaton & Mains, 1897), 93.

18. Davis. JD and Sidney Johnston: Woodworth, *Davis and His Generals*, 45–50; *JD R&F*, 1: 347–48; 2:54–56; Strode, *Davis*, 2:221. JD and Polk's seizure of Columbus: *JDP*, 7: 235, 327, 328, 328n; *JD R&F*,

1:333–42; Woodworth, 38–41, 45. Johnston's complaints: ibid., 52–55; JD R&F, 1:350; Strode, 2:153–55. Johnston's military actions in Tennessee: JDP, 7:342; Long, *Civil War Day by Day*, 119; Woodworth, 55–56.

19. **Sherman.** WTS in Louisville: *WTSM*, 213–14; WTS to Thomas Ewing, Sept. 30, 1861, and Apr. 4, 1862, Joseph H. Ewing, *Sherman at War* (Dayton, Ohio: Morningside House, 1992), 32, 48; Lewis, *Sherman*, 184. WTS and Anderson: *SL*, 127; *WTSM*, 210; Special Orders No. 41, Aug. 24, 1861, WTSP. WTS's western tour: *WTSM*, 211–14. War as a monster: WTS quoted in Marszalek, *Sherman*, 155. WTS at Muldraugh's Hill: *WTSM*, 213–15; Ewing, 33; WTS to John Sherman, Oct. 5, 1861, WTSP; Marszalek, 158–59; Lewis, 190 (WTS and the reporter). WTS as departmental commander: *WTSM*, 216–18; *SL*, 133; Lewis, 191 ("Answer"); Ewing, 36; *OR*, ser. 1, 4:335–36, 340–41, 350–51, 353–54; WTS to Thomas Ewing, Dec. 12, 1861, and to John Sherman, Dec. 17, 1861, WTSP. WTS's nervous characteristics: Shanks, *Personal Recollection*, 18–26, 54; Henry Villard, *Memoirs* (2 vols., Boston: Houghton, Mifflin, 1904), 1:209–20. WTS to Ellen, Oct. 6 and Nov. 1, 1861, in Fellman, *Sherman*, 96; see also Villard, 1:211. WTS's conference with Cameron and Thomas: *WTSM*, 219–20, 228–31; Shanks, 34; WTS to Lorenzo Thomas, Oct. 22, 1861, and to John Sherman, Oct. 26, Dec. 12, 1861, WTSP. WTS banished reporters: Ewing, 35; Villard, 1:209. Insanity charge: *WTSM*, 221, 223; *New York Tribune* (Oct. 30, 1861); Ewing, 40–41; *WTS HL*, 231; WTS to Thomas Ewing, Dec. 12, 1861, and to John Sherman, Dec. 17, 1861, and press clippings in WTSP. WTS relieved, Ellen's visit: *WTSM*, 232, Ellen to John Sherman, Nov. 10, 1861, WTSP; Fellman, 97–99. WTS's courtship: ibid., 29–45; *WTS HL*, 17–20; Marszalek, 49.

20. **Lincoln.** Baker's visit: *JH D&L*, 27 ("don't let them hurry me"); John Hay, "Edward Baker," *Harper* (Dec. 1861), 108; Randall, *Mary Lincoln*, 235. Mark E. Neely, Jr., *The Abraham Lincoln Encyclopedia* (New York: McGraw-Hill Book Co., 1982), 16, points out that Baker had "joked about becoming a 'venerable martyr' in June." We may assume that AL and Baker discussed McClellan and Baker's joking about his martyrdom. Baker's liking of champagne and cards: Neely, 16. AL and Baker's death: *ATR RAL*, 96, 172–73; Nicolay, *Lincoln's Secretary*, 10; *AL RW*, 54 ("smote like a whirlwind"). Lincoln's discussion with Wade, Chandler, and Trumbull: *JH D&L*, 31; Wade to Chandler, Oct. 8, 1861, and Wade to Mrs. Wade, Oct. 25, 1861, BFWP; Chandler to Mrs. Chandler, Oct. 27, 1861, ZCP; Trefousse, *Radical Republicans*, 179–80. We may assume

that the three Senators told Lincoln what they said about McClellan in their letters and other conversations. AL's visit with McClellan: *JH D&L,* 31.

21. **Grant.** USG's itching to advance against Belmont: *USGP,* 3: 64, 116; *USGM,* 1:270–80; Catton, *Grant Moves South,* 84. Confusing orders from St. Louis: *USGP,* 3:144n, 103n, 144n. Oglesby's operation: ibid., 108–09, 109, 114, 123. Belmont was Grant's objective: ibid., 3: 137, 141, 150n, 151n. The Belmont expedition: ibid., 3: 129, 133–34, 137–39, 141–42, 146n–47n, 155n–56n, 193n, 193–95, 197–98, 205; *USGM,* 270–80; *B&L,* 1:351–56; *AB MHG,* 1:15–20, Catton, 75–80, 84. Nathaniel Cheairs Hughes, Jr., *The Battle of Belmont: Grant Strikes South* (Chapel Hill: University of North Carolina Press, 1991), is the best scholarly account.

22. **Lincoln.** Washburne defended Grant: Wilson, *Rawlins,* 68–69, 71. Frémont relieved: *ALCW,* 4:513; Trefousse, *Radical Republicans,* 177. AL to Edward Everett about the capture of Mason and Slidell: *ALCW,* 5:26. Scott's retirement, McClellan's promotion: Bates, *Diary,* 196, 199; *ALCW,* 5:9–10. Lincoln-McClellan dialogue: *JH D&L,* 33. McClellan-Scott feud: Randall, *Lincoln the President,* 1:393–94; *CWL,* 135, 138; George B. McClellan, *The Civil War Papers of George B. McClellan* (ed. Stephen W. Sears, New York: Ticknor & Fields, 1989), 81; *McClellan's Own Story,* 86, 167, 169–70; Stephen W. Sears, *George B. McClellan, The Young Napoleon* (New York: Ticknor & Fields, 1988), 122–23, 125–26. McClellan's opinion of AL and Cabinet: McClellan, *Papers,* 85, 106, 135; Sears, 132. McClellan's avoidance of AL: ibid., 131; *McClellan's Own Story,* 170, 174–76; Randall, 2:72–73. McClellan's snubbing of AL, Seward, and Hay: *JH D&L,* 34–35; Nicolay, *Lincoln's Secretary,* 142. Hunter's complaint, AL's response: *ALCW,* 5:84–85, 85n. AL-McClellan strategy: Williams, *Lincoln and His Generals,* 32, 42–50; Kenneth P. Williams, *Lincoln Finds a General* (5 vols., New York: Macmillan, 1949–1959), 1:103–21. AL's blunt memorandum and McClellan's reply: *ACLW,* 5:34, 35n.

23. **Davis.** Victories, barbarous enemy, northern tyrant: *JD LPS,* 5:167–172; *JDP,* 7:412–19, 429. JD rejected an advance by J. E. Johnston and Beauregard: *JD LPS,* 5:163; Strode, *Davis,* 165–67; *JDP,* 7:352–53n. Lee's failed western Virginia campaign: *REL WP,* 60–79; Freman, *Lee,* 1:541–603; Fitzhugh Lee, *General Lee* (reprint 1894 ed., Wilmington, N.C.: Broadfoot Publishing Co., 1989, 112–27); *JD R&F,* 1:374–77. Lee sent to the coast: Freeman, 1: 607; Strode, 2:178.

24. Lee. Coastal command: *REL WP*, 82–92, 96, 98, 111–12, 118, 121–23; Freeman, *Lee*, 1:608–29.

25. Davis. The controversy over Johnston's rank: *JD LPS*, 5:132; *JDP*, 7:335n–36n, 340, 340n; *VD JD*, 2:144–53; Woodworth, *Davis and His Generals*, 176–77; Strode, *Davis*, 2:156–59; Craig L. Symonds, *Joseph E. Johnston: A Civil War Biography* (New York: W. W. Norton, 1992), 127–29. JD's difficulties with Beauregard: *JD LPS*, 5:156–57, 165; *JDP*, 7:383, 384–85, 392–94, 400–01; *JD R&F*, 1:315–21; Williams, *Beauregard*, 97–112. Judah Benjamin: description in Russell, *My Diary*, 96; Strode, 2:160–61. *Trent* affair: *JDP*, 7:417, 454; Strode, 2:185.

26. Lincoln. *Trent* affair: *OBD*, 1:516–19; Benjamin Lossing, *Pictoral History of the Civil War in the United States of America* (2nd vol., Hartford: T. Belknap, 1868), 156–57; *ALRW*, 307; *ALCW*, 5:62–64; *CWL*, 140–43; Nicolay to Theresa, Dec. 22, 1861, JGNP; Adams, *Britain and the American Civil War*, 1:231; Donald, *Sumner and the Rights of Man*, 36–41; *HP CWG*, 406–09; Sumner, *Selected Letters*, 2:87 ("There will be no war"), 91–94, 97 ("bring Lord Lyons here"); Randall, *Lincoln the President*, 2:45–49; Bates, *Diary*, 213–14; *SC ILC*, 53, 55; Frederic Bancroft, *Life of William H. Seward* (2 vols., New York: Harper & Brothers, 1900), 2:237–53.

27. Douglass. FD's reaction to the start of war: *FD L&W*, 3:89, 99; David W. Blight, *Frederick Douglass' Civil War: Keeping Faith in Jubilee* (Baton Rouge: Louisiana State University Press, 1989), 87, 106. Vincent Harding, *There Is a River: The Black Struggle for Freedom in America* (New York: Harcourt Brace Jovanovich, 1981), 221–23, lyrically describes how black folk saw the hand of God in the outbreak of hostilities. White abolitionists: McPherson, *Struggle for Equality*, 50–51 ("the hour has struck"); Garrison, *Letters*, 417 ("no time for criticism"). Blacks rushed to enlist: Boston *Daily Courier* (Apr. 24, 1861); *FD L&W*, 3:432; Quarles, *Negro in the Civil War*, 29. "White man's war": Cameron's announcement, *OR*, ser. 3, 1:133; *FD L&W*, 3:432. Slaves at Fort Pickens: *FD L&W*, 3:95. Lincoln Administration's vacillating policy on fugitive slaves: Quarles, 65–66; *OR*, ser. 2, 1:750–98. FD's efforts to convert AL to an abolition war: *FD L&W*, 3:16–17, 153. Mission of the war: ibid., 3:14, 94. Fight with both hands: ibid., 3:94, 153. The Negro is the key: ibid., 3:13, 94, 117. Useless to appease the border: ibid., 3:444. You are the statesman of the hour: ibid., 3:445. Long, desolating war: ibid., 3:172. Repent, break every yoke: ibid., 3:99. FD's reaction to Frémont's ouster: ibid., 3:161–62, 165, 174. White abolitionists' crusade: McPherson, 74, 75–77, 80–81, 93; *FDP*, 3:496n; Garrision, *Letters*, 4:35, 41n; *FD L&W*, 3:233; *FDP*, 3:488. Garrison himself regularly sent the *Liberator* to the White House. See Garrison, *Letters*, 5:254. Iron black hand: *FD L&W*, 3: 466, 483; FD, *Life and Times* (reprint of revised 1892 ed., New York: Collier Books, 1962), 336.

28. **Lincoln.** AL attended antislavery lectures at Smithsonian: McPherson, *Struggle for Equality*, 80–81; *ATR RAL*, 60. Greeley description in Hodding Carter, *The Angry Scar: The Story of Reconstruction* (Garden City, N.Y.: Doubleday, 1959), 169; William Harlan Hale, *Horace Greeley, Voice of the People* (New York: Harper & Brothers, 1950), 1–2, 4–5, 77–78, 295–96, 340. AL's gradual emancipation plan for Delaware: *ALCW*, 5:29–31; *OBD*, 1:512; *ALCW*, 5:48, 145. In December the Maryland General Assembly adopted resolutions opposing any attempt by the Federal government to intefere with slavery in the states (see the resolutions in RTLC). Redpath colonization scheme: McPherson, 77–89. AL's message to Congress: *ALCW*, 5:48–51. AL's objection to black soldiers, but not to black sailors and army laborers: Nivens, *Welles*, 395–96. Cameron's report: Alexander McClure, *Abraham Lincoln and Men of War-Times* (Philadelphia: Times Publishing Co., 1892), 393–96; *N&H ALH*, 5: 125, 127; Randall, *Lincoln the President*, 2:56–58; Thomas and Hyman, *Stanton*, 133–35; Bates, *Diary*, 203; Bradley, *Cameron*, 201–05. Sumner's speech on Baker: T. Harry Williams, *Lincoln and the Radicals* (Madison: University of Wisconsin Press, 1941), 61; AL and Sumner on emancipation: Sumner to Wendell Phillips, Dec. 8, 1861, Sumner, *Selected Letters*, 2:85; Sumner to John Andrew, Dec. 27, 1861, *AL RW*, 433, and Charles Sumner, *Works* (15 vols., Boston: Lee & Shepard, 1870–1883), 6:152. Edward Everett Hale memorandum, Apr. 26, 1862, in Hale, *Memories of a Hundred Years* (revised ed., 2 vols. in 1, New York: Macmillan Co., 1904), 2:189–97; Donald, *Sumner and the Rights of Man*, 48.

29. **Douglass.** Smith's reaction to AL's message: McPherson, *Struggle for Equality*, 94. Garrison's reaction: Garrison, *Letters*, 4:47; *Liberator* (Dec. 6, 1861). FD's reaction: *FD L&W*, 3:186–87.

30. **Davis.** Preston to JD, Dec. 28, 1861, *JDP*, 7:446.

THE WINDS OF 'SIXTY-TWO

1. **Lincoln.** Cameron and War Department corruption: Oates, *With Malice Toward None*, 276–78; *ALCW*, 5:96–97, 240–43. Stanton: Thomas and Hyman, *Stanton*, 354, 375–78, 390–93; Bryan, *Great American Myth*,

129–30 (Stanton had "a perpetually irritated look" and "Folks come up here"); George Templeton Strong, *Diary* (ed. Allan Nevins and Milton Halsey Thomas, 4 vols., New York: Macmillan Co., 1952), 4:266; *NB WLT*, 36–37; Allan Nevins, *The War for the Union* (4 vols., New York: Charles Scribner's Sons, 1959–71), 2:458–59; *ATR RAL*, 398. Lincoln's mind: Joshua Speed to William H. Herndon, Dec. 6, 1866, in *Herndon's Lincoln: The True Story of a Great Life* (3 vols., Springfield: Herndon's Lincoln Publishing Co. [n.d.]), 3:522. Wade on McClellan: *Congressional Globe*, 37th Cong., 2d Sess., 94; Trefousse, *Radical Republicans*, 184. Johnson description: Hans L. Trefousse, *Andrew Johnston: A Biography* (New York: W. W. Norton & Co., 1989), 21, 73; Eric McKitrick (ed.), *Andrew Johnson, A Profile* (New York: Hill & Wang, 1969), 85. Prostrate McClellan: Bates, *Diary*, 219; *ALCW*, 5:94. Wade's early January visit with AL about McClellan: Julian, *Political Recollections*, 201–03; *SC ILC*, 57–58; Trefousse, *Wade*, 159–60; Luthin, *The Real Abraham Lincoln*, 308. I've cast into dialogue the points discussed at this meeting. The quotations ("Anybody" and "Wade, anybody will do for you," are in Nicolay, *Lincoln's Secretary*, 149. Nicolay doesn't give a date for this Lincoln-Wade dialogue, but it fits with what was said at the early January meeting. Bates urged Lincoln to command: Bates, *Diary*, 218–20. Buell and Halleck: *ALCW* 5:87, 90, 91–92, 94–95. AL's visit with Meigs: Montgomery Meigs, "General Montgomery Meigs on the Conduct of the War," *American Historical Review* (Jan., 1921), 292–93, 302; Randall, *Lincoln the President*, 2:75. AL to Halleck and Buell: *ALCW*, 5:98–99. AL's meeting with McDowell, Franklin, and Cabinet: *ALCW*, 8:39, 40n; *CWL*, 150–53; Browning, *Diary*, 1:523. Conference of Jan. 13: *CWL*, 153–56; McClellan, *McClellan's Own Story*, 156–58; Randall, 2:76. McClellan before the Joint Committee: *Detroit Post and Tribune, Chandler*, 224–26; Trefousse, *Wade*, 162. Burnside's expedition: John G. Nicolay to Theresa, Jan. 26, 1862, JGNP. AL's General War Order No. 1: *ALCW*, 5:111–12; *JH D&L*, 36. McClellan's response, McClellan's own plan: Williams, *Lincoln and His Generals*, 63–64; McClellan, 228–29; *ALCW*, 5:118–19, 119n–20n, 124n–25n.

2. **Davis.** Loss of Roanoke Island, demands of governors: *JD LPS*, 5:193, 196, 204; Escott, *After Secession*, 62. JD and Sidney Johnston's staff officer: Stanley Horn, *Army of Tennessee* (Indianapolis: Bobbs-Merrill, 1941), 60; Charles P. Roland, *Albert Sidney Johnston: Soldier of Three Republics* (Austin: University of Texas Press, 1964), 277; Woodworth, *Davis and His Generals*, 55. Mill Springs, Beauregard: ibid., 68–69, 76–78.

3. **Grant.** Grant's proposal to Halleck: *USGP*, 4:94; *AB MHG*, 1:26; *USGM*, 1:287; Catton, *Grant Moves South*, 124; Cooling, *Forts Henry and Donelson*, 74. Foote to Halleck, USG to Halleck: *USGP*, 4:99n., 103. Halleck's approval: ibid., 132–33; Cooling, 89. USG's force: *USGP*, 4:122, 123; *AB MHG*, 1:24; *B&L*, 1:139–40, 361. USG's surveillance of Fort Henry, flotilla's arrival, USG to Julia: *USGP* 4:147, 150, 154n; *USGM*, 1:288–90; *AB MGH*, 1:28; Cooling, 283 (fort's ordnance); *USGP*, 4:153. USG and Foote on *Cincinnati*: *USGP* 4:150; Catton, 143 ("I'll have the fort"); Cooling, 101 (rained all night). Gunboats' attack: *B&L*, 1:367; *USGM*, 1:287–93; Catton, 143–44; Cooling, 103–06; *USGP*, 4:158n, 157 ("Fort Henry is ours"), 163 (to Julia). Impediments to taking Donelson: *USGP*, 4: 171–72, 175, 179, *USGM*, 1:287–93; Catton, 148, Cooling, 113. Grant's reconnoiter of Donelson: *USGP*, 4:180n, 201n; *AB MHG*, 1:50 ("Pillow will not fight"). USG's impatience: Cooling, 117; *USGP*, 4:183n. Investing Fort Donelson: *USGP*, 4:183n, 195, 200, 203, 207; *USGM*, 1:300–01; Cooling, 148–49. USG's visit with Foote: ibid., 153; *AB MGH*, 1:39–40; Catton, 155–56. USG watched from a point close to the river: Catton, 162. The gunboat attack: *USGP*, 4:213, 215n; *USGM*, 1:302; *AB MHG*, 1:42; Cooling, 155–60. USG's visit with Foote: *USGM*, 1:304–05; *AB MHG*, 1:42–43; Cooling, 170; Catton, 164. USG and the battle on the right of his line: *USGM*, 1:305–08; *AB MGH*, 1:45; Catton, 166–69; Cooling, 180–84. Smith description: *B&L*, 1:405. Smith's attack: *USGM*, 1:308–09; *AB MGH*, 1:45–46; Catton, 169–71; Cooling, 185–88. USG that night: Catton, 172–73. The surrender: ibid., 174–75; *USGM*, 1:310–12. Buckner description: Richardson, *Grant*, 233; Lewis, *Sam Grant*, 338. USG's visit with Buckner: *AB MHG*, 1:50–51; *USGM*, 1:312–15. USG to Halleck, USG's new command, USG to Julia: *USGP*, 4:225, 225n–226n, 271.

4. **Livermore.** "Donelson is taken!", civilian corps: Henshaw, *Our Branch and Its Tributaries*, 49, 52; *ML MSW*, 180. Hospital steamers: Henshaw, 51, 53; *ML MSW*, 120 ("better to heal a wound"), 180–81; Newberry, *Sanitary Commission*, 28, 484–85. Newberry's description of Donelson battlefield: Newberry, 30–31. Story of Mother Bickerdyke: Henshaw, 54. ML and Hoge at St. Louis hospital: *ML MSW*, 184–97. Cairo hospitals: ibid., 202–03.

5. **Lincoln.** Unconditional Surrender Grant's accomplishments: Catton, *Grant Moves South*, 181; *AB MHG*, 1:55; Cooling, *Forts Henry and Donelson*, 229 ("Columbus is ours"). Halleck had it in for USG: *USGP*, 4:197n, 196n, 321; *AB MHG*, 1:53; *USGM*, 1:328; Cooling, 119; Catton, 187–88. USG promoted: Nicolay, *Lincoln's Secretary*, 132–33;

USGP, 4:272n; *AB MHG*, 1:34. Mary's renovation of the White House: Oates, *With Malice Toward None*, 272–76; Randall, *Mary Lincoln*, 244–68; Turners, *Mary Lincoln*, 84–89, 96–100, 110–13, 120, 137. Willie's illness and death: Nicolay to Theresa, Feb. 2, 6, 11, 1861, JGNP; Nicolay, *Lincoln's Secretary*, 132–33; Elizabeth Keckley, *Behind the Scenes: Thirty Years a Slave and Four Years in the White House* (New York: Arno Press and the New York *Times*, 1968), 100–05 ("our cat has a long tail," "my poor boy"); Bates, *Diary*, 233, 235, 236; Nicolay memorandum in notebook for Feb.–Mar., 1862, JGNP ("Well, Nicolay"); *ALRW*, 345; Browning, *Diary*, 1:530–31. Willie's traits: Ruth Painter Randall, *Lincoln's Sons* (Boston: Little, Brown, 1955), 120, 127 ("the hope and stay of her old age"), Keckley, 98–99; Turners, 120. Mrs. Pomroy: Anna L. Boyden, *Echoes from Hospital and White House: A Record of Mrs. Rebecca R. Pomroy's Experiences in War-Times* (Boston: D. Lothrop and Co., 1884), 52–56. Willie's burial, Mary's suffering: Randall, *Lincoln's Sons*, 130–33; Randall, *Mary Lincoln*, 239, 285–302; Turners, 121ff; Keckley, 104–05, 120–21; Boyden, 58. AL shut himself up: *FBC ILAL*, 117. AL's doctrine of fatalism: Oates, 5; Richard N. Current, *The Lincoln Nobody Knows* (New York: McGraw-Hill Book Co., 1958), 71–75. Stanton's warning to Halleck: *OR*, ser. 1, 7:652; Catton, 188.

6. **Davis.** Floyd and Pillow relieved, Nashville lost: *JD R&F*, 2:31–32; *JD LPS*, 5:204. JD's inauguration: *JBJ WCD*, 1:111; Strode, *Davis*, 2:202; *JD LPS*, 5:199–202; *VD JD*, 2:180, 183. JD's enemies: Strode, 2:206; *JD R&F*, 2:30–34; *JDP*, 8:94 and 94n. JD to Brooks, Mar. 15, 1862, *JDP*, 8:101–02. Lee as JD's military adviser: *JDP*, 8:75; Strode, *Davis*, 2:211; Freeman, *Lee*, 2:4–5; *REL WP*, 124–27. Pea Ridge: Woodworth, *Davis and His Generals*, 115. Sidney Johnston's retreat, reinforced by Bragg: *JDP*, 8:94; *JD R&F*, 2:38; *JD LPS*, 5:215; Woodworth, 89.

7. **Lincoln.** USG relieved of his command: *USGP*, 4:319n. Halleck's complaints to McClellan: ibid., 4:320n, 331n; *USGM*, 1:327. McClellan supported Halleck's action: McClellan, *Civil War Papers*, 197.

8. **Grant.** Reaction to Halleck's telegram: *USGP*, 4:327, 313, 317, 318–19, 319n; Hamlin Garland, *Ulysses S. Grant: His Life and Character* (New York: Doubleday & McClure Co., 1898), 198; *USGM*, 1: 326–27; Catton, *Grant Moves South*, 208. Halleck's second bombshell (Mar. 7, 1862): *USGP*, 4:331n. Halleck didn't tell USG so, but it was Halleck who had complained to Washington (ibid., 4:320n). The anonymous complaint: ibid., 4:353n–54n. USG to Halleck, Mar. 7, 1862, Halleck to

USG, Mar. 8, 1862, USG to Halleck, Mar. 9, 1862, ibid., 4:331, 335n, 334. Catton, 202, points out that USG's dispatch of Mar. 9 "invited a showdown." Halleck reversed himself: *USGP*, 4:354–55. USG's reply, ibid., 4:358–59. Halleck's report to Washington exonerating USG: ibid., 4:416n; USG's reply, ibid., 4:415. USG to Julia: ibid., 4:413.

9. **Lincoln.** AL's interrogatories to Halleck: *USGP*, 4:416n. AL's warning to McClellan: McClellan, *McClellan's Own Story*, 195–97; *CWL*, 161–62. The Joint Committee believed that "Fighting, and *only* fighting," could win the war: Randall, *Lincoln the President*, 2:87. AL and Sumner on emancipation: Donald, *Sumner and the Rights of Man*, 50. AL on saving life and limb: *ALCW*, 7:281–82. AL read his message to Sumner: Hale, *Memories*, 2:193–96; Donald, 51–52. AL's message on state-guided emancipation: *ALCW*, 5:144–46. Greeley's response: *New York Tribune* (Mar. 7, 1862); Nicolay, *Lincoln's Secretary*, 134–35. Said Henry Ramond of the *New York Times*: "I regard the message as a master-piece of practical wisdom and sound policy" (*ALCW*, 5:153n). Wadsworth's response: Brodie, *Stevens*, 156. AL's appeal to the border-state delegation: *CWL*, 165–68; Nicolay Memorandum, Mar. 9, 1862, in Notebook for Feb.–Mar., 1862, JGNP; *ALRW*, 121–22. AL against return of fugitive slaves: *ALRW*, 123. Opposition to abolition of slavery in Washington, D.C.: *New York Herald*, Apr. 5, 1862; *NB, WLT*, 180–82. Sumner quotation: *FD L&W*, 3:21–22

10. **Douglass.** AL's message: *FDP*, 3:518–19. FD to Sumner: Apr. 7, 1862, Charles Sumner Papers, Harvard University; quoted in McPherson, *Struggle for Equality*, 98. Slavery abolished in Washington, D.C.: *FD L&W*, 3:22; Quarles, *The Negro in the Civil War*, 142; Benjamin Quarles, *Frederick Douglass* (New York: Atheneum, 1968), 196; Blight, *Douglass' Civil War*, 125.

11. **Davis.** *JD R&F*, 2: 145–50, 152.

12. **Lincoln.** AL and McClellan: McClellan, *Civil War Papers*, 195–97; *CWL*, 161–62; Oates, *With Malice Toward None*, 293–94, 461. *Monitor* v. *Virginia*: Bates, *Lincoln in the Telegraph Office*, 115–17; *N&H, ALH*, 5:226; *JH D&L*, 36–37; Nicolay notes quoted in Nicolay, *Lincoln's Secretary*, 135–36; *GWD*, 1:62–67; Browning, *Diary*, 1:532–33; Bruce, *Lincoln and the Tools of War*, 172–73. Manassas and the "Quaker guns": *JH D&L*, 37; Garrowski to Chandler, Mar. 12, 1862, ZCP; Francis Fessenden, *Life and Public Services of William Pitt Fessenden* (2 vols., Boston, 1907), 1:261 ("scorn of world"); *N&H ALH*, 5:177–78; Thomas and Hyman, *Stanton*, 182–83; McClellan, 202–03; Williams, *Lincoln and*

His Generals, 69–70; Trefousse, *Radical Republicans,* 191; Bates, *Diary,* 239–40. President's War Order No. 3: *ALCW,* 5:155–56. Peninsula plan: Williams, 72–84; *AL DBD,* 3:100–02; *ALCW,* 5:151n, 157, 182, 184; Thomas and Hyman, 187–88, 208–09; *OBD,* 1:537–39; Sumner, *Letters,* 2:112, Williams, *Lincoln Finds a General,* 1:152–86. AL called on McClellan at Alexandria: *AL DBD* 3:102. Description of expeditionary force: Leech, *Reveille in Washington,* 164–65; Sears, *McClellan,* 168. AL took McClellan's measure: *OBD,* 537–39. Stanton's discovery, McDowell's corps detained, argument over the size of McClellan's army: *ALCW,* 5:151n, 179, 182n, 184–85, McClellan, 228, 232–33. "Indefinite procrastination": *ALCW,* 5:203.

13. **Davis.** Johnston on McClellan: Johnston to Lee, Apr. 22, 1862, *OR,* ser. 1, 11 (pt. 3): 455–56, and quoted in Sears, *McClellan,* 180. Johnston on the peninsula: *JD R&F,* 2:67–69, 70–71. Sidney Johnston at Corinth: ibid., 2:38, 44; Woodworth, *Davis and His Generals,* 90; James Lee McDonough, *Shiloh—In Hell Before Night* (Knoxville: University of Tennessee Press, 1977), 9–11 ("vertebrae of the Confederacy"); *JDP,* 8:123, 128, 130–31.

14. **Grant.** Halleck's orders: *USGM,* 1:331; *AB MHG,* 1:71. Grant's army at Pittsburg and Crump's Landings: *WTSM,* 161; *USGM,* 1:332; Wiley Sword, *Shiloh: Bloody April* (Dayton, Ohio: Press of Morningside Bookshop, 1988), 13; McDonough, *Shiloh,* 25, 45–52, 96; Catton, *Grant Moves South,* 218. USG's regard for Sherman: John Russell Young, *Around the World with General Grant* (2 vols., New York: American News Co., 1879), 2:293 ("not a false line in Sherman's character"). Sickness in the army: Sword, 37; Lewis, *Sherman,* 217 ("Tennessee quickstep"); *USGP,* 4:443. USG's injury: ibid., 5:103; *USGM,* 1:334–35; *AB MHG,* 1:72. USG's visit with Sherman, Apr. 5: *USGP,* 5:9, 13–14; *WTSM,* 254–55; *USGM,* 1:333–34, 338–39; *AB MHG,* 1:71–74, 77; McDonough, 57; Catton, 219; Sword, 133. Sherman's view of his troops: Sword, 122. Sherman description: *AB MHG,* 2:19 ("as if his superabundant energy"). USG and the sound of battle, dialogue, morning of 6th: Richardson, *Personal History of Grant,* 244–45; Garland, *Grant,* 202–03; *USGM,* 1:336; *USGP,* 5:17, Catton, 223–24, 228. Crump's Landing: Richardson, 245; Garland, 203; *USGM,* 1:336.

15. **Sherman.** Attacked on first day of Shiloh: WTS to Ellen, Apr. 11, 1862, *WTS HL,* 220–23; WTS to Thomas Ewing, May 3, 1862, Ewing, *Sherman at War,* 53–54; WTS to John Sherman, Apr. 22, 1862, WTSP; *WTSM,* 256–60; Sherman's report in *OR,* ser. 1, 10 (pt. 1): 248–54;

Marszalek, *Sherman*, 177, 186–87; Lewis, *Sherman*, 204; Fellman, *Citizen Sherman*, 107 (*"I have given you pain"*); Halleck to WTS, Dec. 14, 18, 1861, WTSP. WTS in his element, in control: *WTSM*, 257; Fellman, 117–18. USG's arrival: *WTSM*, 266.

16. **Grant.** USG and Sherman: Lewis, *Sherman*, 222–23; Sword, *Shiloh*, 188, 209, 211, 220, 324; *WTSM*, 266; *USGP*, 5:34; J. T. Headley, *The Life of Ulysses S. Grant* (New York: E. B. Treat & Co., 1868), 103 ("gallant stand"). WSG's dispositions: *AB MHG*, 1:76; McDonough, *Shiloh*, 90, 124, 161; Catton, *Grant Moves South*, 227; *USGM*, 1:336–40; *B&L*, 1:607. USG found McClernand: McDonough, 125. USG on the Union left: ibid., 105–06, 125; *OR*, ser. 1, 10 (pt. 1): 279 (hold "at all hazards"). USG under enemy artillery fire: *USGM*, 1:353–54. USG said this took place on Monday, Apr. 7; Sword, 350, and McDonough, 183, say it occurred on Sunday. Praise for Sherman: Fellman, *Citizen Sherman*, 115–16; *USGM*, 1:339. Rowley sent to find Wallace: *OR*, ser. 1, 10 (pt. 1): 181; McDonough, 128. Stragglers: *USGM*, 1:343–44; *AB MHG*, 1:82; *B&L*, 1:494; Catton, *Grant Moves South*, 235. USG and Buell: Sword, 351; *USGM*, 1:344; *B&L*, 1:493–94; *AB MHG*, 1:82 ("What preparations" and "haven't despaired"); also quoted in Wilson, *Rawlins*, 88. USG on every part of the field: *AB MHG*, 1:80; *USGM*, 1:343. Peach orchard, men tore paper cartridges, the carnage: Lewis, 224. Lew Wallace: *B&L*, 1:609; *USGM*, 1:336–37. Rebel bombardment, collapse of Union left: Sword, 293, 298, 306; McDonough, 162, 164; Horace Cecil Fisher, *A Staff Officer's Story* (Boston: Thomas Todd Co., 1960), 14; *USGP*, 5:32–33. New defensive line: D. Leib Ambrose, *History of the Seventh Regiment Illinois Volunteer Infantry* (Springfield: Illinois Journal Co., 1868), 51; *USGM*, 1:345; Catton, 240 ("think we'll stop 'em here"); McDonough, 171. USG's pleading with stragglers: ibid., 170–71; John A. Cockerill, "A Boy at Shiloh," in George Morley Vickers (ed.), *Under Both Flags, A Panorama of the Great Civil War: Tales of the Civil War as Told by the Veterans* (Chicago: W. S. Reeve Publishing Co., 1896), 369. Arrival of Nelson's division: Sword, 359; McDonough, 178–79; Fisher, 13; Lewis, 228. Final rebel attack: T. W. Connelly, *History of the Seventieth Ohio Regiment From Its Organization to Its Mustering Out* (reprint 1902 ed., Adams County Historical Society, 1978), 51–52 ("Army of Tennessee, stand firm!"); *USGP*, 5:33; Fisher, 14; McDonough, 173, 175; Sword, 369; *AB MHG*, 1:85; *WTSM*, 266. Gunboat salvos, fierce storm: Cockerill, 370; *USGM*, 1:368; *AB MHG*, 1:87; Sword, 374; McDonough, 184. WTS and USG ("Well, Grant," and "Lick 'em tomorrow"): Catton, 242; McDonough, 183; Douglas Putnam, Jr., "Reminis-

cences of the Battle of Shiloh," *Sketches of War History, 1861–1865* (vol. 3 of Military Order of the Loyal Legion of the United States, Ohio Commandery), 205, reports that Grant had a similar conversation with McPherson. Second day: *WTSM*, 259–60; *USGM*, 1:350–51 ("Charge!"); Lewis, 231; *AB MHG*, 1:89–91. USG examined battlefield: *USGM*, 1:336; *USGP*, 5:34; Cockerill, 372; Sword, 428–29; McDonough, 215. Forces engaged, casualties: Sword, 430; *USGM*, 1:367. USG's praise for WTS: *USGP*, 5:34, 111.

17. **Sherman.** Description of battlefield: Marszalek, *Sherman*, 181–82; WTS to Ellen, Apr. 16, 1862, WTSP. Log house hospital, transports: Lucien B. Crooker and others, *The Story of the Fifty-Fifth Regiment Illinois Volunteer Infantry in the Civil War, 1861–1865* ([no place]: by a committee of the Regiment, 1887), 116; Sword, 430; Annie Wittenmyer, *Under the Guns: A Woman's Reminiscences of the Civil War* (Boston E. B. Stillings & Co., 1895), 30; *WTSM*, 267. WTS on the terrible nature of the war: *WTS HL*, 222–23. WTS reborn: Fellman, *Citizen Sherman*, 118, 122; *WTSM*, 276. Halleck's and Grant's praise: *USGP*, 5:34; Fellman, 115–16; Lewis, *Sherman*, 232–33. Newspaper attacks: *WTSM*, 265, 267; Headley, *Grant*, 117; *USGP*, 5:79n. Insanity charge reasserted: Louis Morris Star, *Reporting the Civil War* (New York: Collier, 1962), 143. USG accused of drunkness: Catton, 259; William R. Rowley of USG's staff denied the charge and defended USG in letter to E. Hempstead, Apr. 19, 1862, EWP LC. WTS's loathing for journalists: Fellman, 125, 126, 134; WTS to John Sherman, May 12, 1862, WTSP; Ewing, 56; WTS to Lieutenant Governor Stanton, July 12, 1862, WTSP. The press caused the war: *WTS HL*, 227, 295–96; WTS to S. Homm, July 7, 1862, WTSP. WTS to John Sherman, Apr. 22, May 7, 12, 1862, WTSP. WTS to USG, Aug. 18, 1862, *OR*, ser. 1, 17 (pt. 2): 178–79. Ellen said that Sherman "opened a regular warfare upon the correspondents, whom he detests" (Fellman, 127). Army reorganization: *USGM*, 1:371–72; *WTSM*, 271; *AB MHG*, 1:100, 101n. WTS's esteem for Halleck: WTS to Thomas Ewing, May 3, 1862, Ewing, *Sherman at War*, 54; *WTSM*, 274. Hardest fighting lay ahead: *SL*, 169.

18. **Davis.** Beauregard's telegram to JD: *JDP*, 8:131. JD's reaction to Sidney Johnston's death: *JDP*, 8:132; *JD R&F*, 2:54; *VD JD*, 2:229–32. JD's message: *JDMP*, 1:155. JD blamed Beauregard for the defeat: *JDP*, 8:139; *JD R&F*, 2:47–48, 50, 53, 55; *VD JD*, 2:241. JD on Johnston's fall: *JD R&F*, 2:55. JD sent reinforcements, wrote governors: Woodworth, *Davis and His Generals*, 103; *JD LPS*, 5:230, 231; *OR*, 10 (pt. 2), 407; Woodworth, 104. Critical want of manpower, conscription: Strode, *Davis,*

2:237; Escott, *After Secession*, 64, 118; *JDP*, 8:572. Brown's protest: *JDP*, 8:151, 167. JD's replies: ibid., 262, 284, 476–77; *JD LPS*, 5:297. Fall of New Orleans: *VD JD*, 2:248, 250; *JD R&F*, 2:188–89, 193; *JD LPS*, 5:236; Clement Eaton, *Jefferson Davis* (New York: Free Press, 1977), 152; Long, *Civil War Day by Day*, 202–03, 205. Butler's atrocities: *JD R&F*, 2:195, 241–44. Lee's proposed valley campaign: *REL WP*, 127, 156–57, 163; Freeman, *Lee*, 2:32–40, 50. Johnston's retreat: *JDP*, 8:158, 175, *JD R&F*, 2:74–78. Mary Lee's ordeal: Clifford Dowdy, *Lee* (New York: Bonanza Books, 1965), 205; Freeman, 2:252. JD and Varina on family's safety, family's departure: *JDP*, 8:168, 172, 173; *VD JD*, 2:268–69. JD and REL's visit with Johnston: *JBJ WCD*, 1:125; *JD R&F*, 2:84. Drewry's Bluff fight: *JDP*, 8:178–79, 180; *JBJ WCD*, 1:125–26. Johnston across the Chickahominy, JD's warning to and visit with: *JD R&F*, 2:85–86, 99; *JDP*, 8:184–85. McClellan at Richmond's gates, Johnston must stand and fight: Strode, 2:150; *JD LPS*, 245.

19. **Lincoln**. Peninsula operations, McDowell's plan: *ALCW*, 5:219–20, 226–27; McClellan, *Civil War Papers*, 270–72; Williams, *Lincoln and His Generals*, 94–96. AL to Aquia Creek: *AL DBD*, 3:114; Williams, 96. AL and Jackson's valley campaign: *AL DBD*, 115–16; *ALCW*, 5:232–33, 235–36, 236n, 236–37; McClellan, *McClellan's Own Story*, 346, 396–97; AL to Frémont, McDowell, and Banks, *ALCW*, 5:243–71; Williams, 100–03. AL and McClellan: McClellan, *Civil War Papers*, 279; *ALCW*, 5:245. Halleck wanted reinforcements, size of his army: ibid., 5:231; McDonough, *Shiloh*, 220. Lincoln couldn't spare Grant: McClure, *Lincoln and Men of War-Times*, 193.

20. **Grant**. "Pick and shovel campaign": Frank A. Burr, *Life and Deeds of General U. S. Grant* (Philadelphia: National Publishing Co., 1885), 283; *USGM*, 1:372–74, 376–77; USG to Julia, Apr. 30, 1862, *USGP*, 5:102. Last great battle: *USGP*, 5:118, 124. USG's protest to Halleck, Halleck's reply: ibid., 5:114, 115n. Corinth besieged, USG's proposed attack: *AB MHG*, 101–02; Catton, *Grant Moves South*, 271. Corinth evacuated: *AB MHG*, 1:102–03; *USGM*, 1:379–80; *USGP*, 5:134, 137, Villard, *Memoirs*, 1:275–76; *SL*, 155. USG's leave of absence: *USGP*, 5:136–37, 140.

21. **Sherman**. WTS begged USG not to leave: scene and dialogue from *WTSM*, 276; *USGP*, 5:141; scene confirmed in ibid. and *HL*, 228. USG wrote Washburne that Halleck asked him to stay "a little longer" (*USGP*, 5:145). WTS to USG, June 6, 1862, ibid., 5:141.

22. **Davis**. Beauregard's retreat: Woodworth, *Davis and His Generals*, 105 ("last extremity"); *JDP*, 8:224 ("brilliant and successful"); JD to Varina,

June 13, 1862, ibid., 8:243–44. Change of command: *JD R&F*, 2:60–61; *JDP*, 8:256, 269. Lee's conference with Johnston, offensive-defensive program: *JD, R&F*, 2:99–100; *JDP*, 8:200. JD to the front, demanded that Johnston fight: *JD, R&F*, 100–01; Woodworth, 178. Musketry sounded like hail: Alfred Bill, *Beleaguered City,* 134. Destruction of JD's plantation: *JDP*, 8:203–04; *VD JD*, 2:267. As it turned out, the reports were exaggerated: the two plantations were not destroyed at this time. Later, on June 24, a Federal raiding party did burn them both (*JDP* 8:204n). JD and Battle of Seven Pines: *JDP*, 8:208, 209; *JD R&F*, 101–02, 105, 108; Freeman, *Lee*, 2:67–74.

23. **Lincoln.** McClellan's telegrams of June 1, 2, and 4: McClellan, *Civil War Papers*, 285, 286, 288–89. AL's worry, McClellan's response: *ALCW*, 5:257, 258n. McClellan on Lee: McClellan to AL, Apr. 20, 1862, RTLC, and quoted in Sears, *McClellan*, 180. McClellan's excuses for inaction: McClellan, *Civil War Papers*, 291; Williams, *Lincoln and His Generals*, 106–07; McClellan, *McClellan's Own Story*, 392–93. AL's complaints about McClellan: Thomas, *Lincoln*, 325 ("Heaven sent rain only on the just"); *OBD*, 1:552. AL's visit with Scott: New York *Herald* (June 26, 1862); Williams, 113. McClellan's telegram ("Several contrabands"), AL's reply: McClellan, *Civil War Papers,* 309–10; *ALCW*, 5:286; P. M. Zall, *Abe Lincoln Laughing: Humorous Anecdotes from Original Sources by and about Abraham Lincoln* (Berkeley: University of California Press, 1982), 29 ("shoveling flees"). Pope and the Army of Virginia: *ALCW*, 5:287; Williams, 119–23; Oates, *With Malice Toward None*, 303–04. McCellan's telegram of June 26: McClellan, *Civil War Papers*, 316.

24. **Lee.** Long odds: Freeman, *Lee*, 2:117; *REL WP*, 211. Stuart's ride, enemy's right flank in the air: ibid., 197–98; Emory Thomas, *Bold Dragoon: The Life of J. E. B. Stuart* (New York: Harper & Row, 1986), 113–26, 129. REL's plan of attack to JD: *JD, R&F*, 2:109–10; *REL WP*, 198–200, 212; Freeman, 2:110–12. REL's audacity and willingness to take risks: Connelly, *Marble Man,* 205–06. REL's sense of McClellan's caution: Stephen W. Sears, *Landscape Turned Red: The Battle of Antietam* (reprint of 1983 ed., New York: Popular Library, 1985), 59. Mechanicsville, June 26: *REL WP*, 201, 212–13; Freeman, 2:131–35; *JD R&F*, 2:113–14.

25. **Lincoln.** McClellan's "complete" victory, June 26, attacked again next day: McClellan, *Civil War Papers,* 317, 319. Washington was "almost wild with rumors": Nicolay to Theresa, June 29, 1862, JHNP; AL lay on

Stanton's sofa, Pope enjoined him not to let McClellan retreat: Williams, *Lincoln and His Generals*, 123–24.

26. **Lee.** Yankee retreat to Powhite Creek: *REL WP*, 214. Jackson description: Henry Kyd Douglas, *I Rode with Stonewall* (Chapel Hill: University of North Carolina Press, 1940), 162, 234; James I. Robertson, Jr., *Stonewall Jackson: The Man, the Soldier, the Legend* (New York: Macmillan, 1997), xi, 273, 301, 409–10, 470–71, 476, 480; Freeman, *Lee*, 1:307, 308, 2:122, 200; John Bowers, *Stonewall Jackson, Portrait of a Soldier* (reprint 1989 ed., New York: Avon Books 1990), 176, 203, 220–21, 246, 441–42. Robertson, Jackson's best biographer, demolishes the myth that old Stonewall had a peculiar habit of sucking lemons. The general, Robertson says, liked all manner of fruit, including lemons, but peaches were his favorite (Robertson, xi). REL's conference with Jackson: Freeman, 2:138–41; Robertson, 476. REL description: *REL WP*, 197. Battle of Gaines' Mill: ibid., 214–17; Freeman, 2: 147–152, 153–54 (Stonewall on a homely horse and sucking a lemon, horseback conference with Lee), 155; Robertson, 476–83; James M. McPherson, *Battle Cry of Freedom: The Civil War Era* (New York: Oxford University Press, 1988), 468 (Magruder's theatrics); *REL WP*, 202 ("profoundly grateful to Almighty God").

27. **Lincoln.** McClellan's June 28 telegram, AL's reply: McClellan, *Civil War Papers*, 322–23; *ALCW*, 5:289. Reinforcements: ibid., 4:295, 305–06. AL's open letter to council of governors, call for 300,000 volunteers: ibid., 291–97. AL to McClellan ("we still have strength"): ibid., 298.

28. **Lee.** June 28 and Battle of Savage Station next day: *REL WP*, 216–18; Freeman, *Lee*, 2:159–78; *EPA FFC*, 105; McPherson, *Battle Cry of Freedom*, 468. Lee's pursuit on June 30, REL and JD, Hill's order: *REL L&L*, 181–82; Freeman, 2:181–82; *REL WP*, 218; *EPA FFC*, 107. Battle of Glendale: *REL WP*, 218–19; Freeman, 2:196–99; Robertston, *Jackson*, 495–99; *EPA FFC*, 109–10. REL's bitterness: Freeman, 2:202, also 199. Battle of Malvern Hill: *EPA FFC*, 112, and McPherson, *Battle Cry of Freedom*, 469 (Lee's sense of panic in enemy army); REL WP, 219–20; Freeman, 2:215–19; *B&L*, 2:394 ("It was not war"), 409–21; Jeffry D. Wert, *General James Longstreet, The Confederacy's Most Controversial Soldier: A Biography* (New York: Simon & Schuster, 1993), 145–49; *EPA FFC*, 113; Stephen W. Sears, *To the Gates of Richmond: The Peninsula Campaign* (New York: Ticknor & Fields, 1992), 309–38. Thomas, *Lee*, 243, called Malvern Hill "a mismanaged macabre farce." July 2:

REL WP, 221; Freeman, 2:20–23, and Wert, 149–50 (Lee and Longstreet, description of battlefield). JD's arrival: Freeman, 2:224; *REL WP*, 221. REL's conclusions about Seven Days campaign: ibid., 208, 210, 221, 229–30; Fitzhugh Lee, *Lee*, 171. Rebel casualties: Thomas L. Livermore, *Numbers and Losses in the Civil War in America, 1861–1865* (reprint of original ed., Dayton, Ohio: Morningside, 1986), 86.

29. Davis. JD's letter of thanks: *JDP*, 8:275–76. JD's optimism, letter to Varina: Strode, *Davis*, 2:419; *JD LPS*, 5:291, and *VD JD*, 2:323. JD pined for the day: *JDP*, 8:294. Lee the hero: Sears, *Landscape Turned Red*, 60; Freeman, *Lee*, 2:245, 277. JD's criticism of McClellan: *JD LPS*, 5:291, and *VD JD*, 2:322.

30. Lincoln. McClellan's telegrams to Washington: McClellan, *Civil War Papers*, 329 ("I have not yielded"), 338 ("When the circumstances," "our honor," "bands playing"), 333 (100,000 reinforcements). AL's response: *ALCW*, 5:301, 303, 305, 307. AL inconsolable, press criticism, public outcry, Republicans wanted McClellan's head: *AL RW*, 137; *New York Herald* (July 8 and 9, 1862); Nicolay to Theresa, July 13, 1862, JGNP; Oates, *With Malice Toward None*, 306; Thomas, *Lincoln*, 327. Arrival of wounded: Nicolay, *Lincoln's Secretary*, 148; Leech, *Reveille in Washington*, 232. Harrison Landing conference: *AL DBD*, 3:126–27; Williams, *Lincoln and His Generals*, 131–33; *ALCW*, 309–12. McClellan's letter: McClellan, *Civil War Papers*, 336–38 (mine is an edited version of the letter). Stanton's advocacy of abolition and Negro troops: Thomas and Hyman, *Stanton*, 229–34. Pressures on Lincoln to strike at slavery: Gideon Welles, "The History of Emancipation," *Galaxy* (Dec. 1872), 842; *CWL*, 175; McPherson, *Struggle for Equality*, 107–12. New confiscation bill: Brodie, *Stevens*, 156–57; Donald, *Sumner and the Rights of Man*, 65–67; V. Jacque Voegeli, *Free but Not Equal: The Midwest and the Negro during the Civil War* (Chicago: University of Chicago Press, 1967), 24–25. Sumner's argument with AL: Donald, 60; Charles Sumner, *Complete Works* (20 vols., New York: Negro Universities Press, 1969), 9:182–86; Sumner, *Letters*, 2:121; *AL RW*, 434; *CWL*, 269. End of the rope, last card or lose the game: *FBC ILAL*, 20–21, 83–84. AL's appeal to border representatives: *ALCW*, 5:317–19, 319n. AL must strike at slavery: Welles, "The History of Emancipation," *Galaxy*, 842. Carriage ride with Seward and Welles: ibid., 842–43; *CWL*, 175–77; *GWD*, 1:70–71. Browning and Second Confiscation Act: *OBD*, 1:558. AL and the Act: *ALCW*, 5:328–31, 328n–329n; *N&H, ALH*, 10:101; Stanton to Benjamin F. Butler, July 3, 1862, Butler, *Private and Official Correspondence of Gen. Benjamin F. Butler during the Period of the Civil War*

(5 vols., Norwood, Mass.: Plimpton Press, 1917), 2:41, also quoted in
ALRW, 416. Radicals' response to Lincoln threatened veto: Julian, *Political Recollections*, 219–20; Trefousse, *Radical Republicans*, 221–22.
Julian's conference with AL: Julian, 219, 246; Patrick Riddleberger,
*George Washington Julian, Radical Republican: A Study in 19th Century
Politics and Reform* (Indianapolis: Indiana Historical Bureau, 1966), 172.
Preliminary emancipation proclamation and Cabinet: *ALCW*, 5:336–37,
337n; *FBC ILAL*, 21–22, 89–90; *SC ILC*, 98–99; *N&H, ALH*, 6:127;
Glyndon G. Van Deusen, *William Henry Seward* (New York: Oxford
University Press, 1967), 331; Thomas and Hyman, *Stanton*, 238–39;
Niven, *Welles*, 419–20. Halleck to USG: *OR*, ser. 1, 17 (pt. 2): 150; Catton, *Grant Moves South*, 294. Pope: *OR*, 12 (pt. 3):473–74; Williams,
122–23. McClellan ordered to northern Virginia: *OR*, ser. 1, 12 (pt.
3):599.

31. **Davis.** The North's sweeping usurpations: *JD R&F*, 2:139–44. Pope's
despotic acts: *JDP*, 8:311; *JD R&F*, 2:262–63; *JD LPS*, 5:306–07;
Thomas, *Lee*, 249. Prisoner exchange, JD's retaliation: *JD R&F*, 2:495–96,
JDP, 8:311. JD to Lee, Halleck's response: ibid., 8:310–11, 312. Lee
wanted to suppress Pope: *REL WP*, 239–40; James Longstreet, *From
Manassas to Appomattox: Memoirs of the Civil War in America* (reprint
of original ed., New York: Smithmark, 1992), 155. Jackson's and then
Lee's moves against Pope: *REL WP*, 271–76; Freeman, *Lee*, 2:261–73.

32. **Lee.** REL mortified at McClellan's escape, wanted to suppress Pope:
REL WP, 257, 258–59, 239, 240. Army reorganization and Longstreet:
Freeman, *Lee*, 2:246–50; Gary W. Gallagher, "Scapegoat in Victory:
James Longstreet and the Battle of Second Manassas," *Civil War History*
(Dec., 1988), 302. REL's plan of battle: *REL WP*, 276; Freeman,
2:279–81. Stuart's raid against Catlett's Station: Thomas, *Bold Dragoon*,
144–51; *REL WP*, 227, 262–64, 277; Freeman, 2:296–300. Stuart
description: Thomas, 18, 69, 128–29, 170, 233–34. REL's plan to
maneuver Pope away from McClellan: *REL WP*, 267, Freeman,
2:297–303. Jackson's famous march in Pope's rear: Sears, *Landscape
Turned Red*, 68 ("close up, men"); Robertson, *Jackson*, 547–53; *REL
WP*, 227, 279; *RELD*, 54. Reinforcements from JD: *JDP*, 8:358; Freeman, 2:310. Longstreet's march to join Jackson: *REL WP*, 267, 278–81;
Freeman, 2:312–19; Wert, *Longstreet*, 162–65. Lee deferred to Longstreet:
Gallagher, 303–06; Wert, 168–70. Second Manassas (Aug. 30): *REL WP*,
281–85; Long, *Memoirs of Lee*, 198; Longstreet, *From Manassas to
Appomattox*, 185–92; Gallagher, 306; Freeman, 2:328–37; McPherson,
Battle Cry of Freedom, 531; Philip Van Doren Stern, *Robert E. Lee: The*

Man and the Soldier: A Pictorial Biography (New York: Bonanza Books, 1963), 157–58 (REL and son Rob). REL to JD: *REL WP*, 268.

33. **Lincoln.** Might as well stop fighting: *JH D&L*, 46. McClellan and Halleck, chaotic command system: *JH D&L*, 45; Williams, *Lincoln and His Generals*, 153–60; *ALCW*, 5:395–402. AL's changes, AL and McClellan: *JH D&L*, 46–47 (hurt the enemy, "use the tools we have," McClellan as organizer); *AL DBD*, 3:137; Williams, 159–61; Sears, *McClellan*, 259. Stormy Cabinet meeting: *ALCW*, 5:486n ("wrung by the bitterest anguish"); *GWD*, 1: 104–05, 124; *SC ILC*, 136; *OBD*, 1:589–90 (AL on McClellan's organizing ability). AL's "Meditation on Divine Will," Sept. 2, 1862: *ALCW*, 5:403–04.

34. **Davis.** JD extolled Lee's army, enemy cleared from northern Virginia: *JDP*, 8:372; *JD R&F*, 2:276. Situation in West: *JD LPS*, 5:313; Davis, *Davis*, 466; Woodworth, *Davis and His Generals*, 139. Offensive strategy: *JDP*, 8:293 ("My early declared purpose"), *JD LPS*, 5:313; Davis, *Davis*, 467; Woodworth, 339. Kentucky campaign: ibid., 139–46; *JD R&F*, 2:323–24. Lee's Maryland campaign, grand offensive: *REL WP*, 313; Davis, *Davis*, 469; *JD LPS*, 5:338–39.

35. **Lee.** Crossing the Potomac: *REL WP*, 295; James V. Murfin, *The Gleam of Bayonets: The Battle of Antietam and Robert E. Lee's Maryland Campaign, September of 1862* (Baton Rouge: Louisiana State University Press, 1965), 99. Description of the soldiers: Frederick resident quoted in Murfin, 108–09; *EPA FFC*, 139 ("magnificent morale"). REL in ambulance, injury: Fitzhugh Lee, *Lee*, 210; Long, *Memoirs of Lee*, 206; Freeman, *Lee*, 2:340. REL to JD: *REL WP*, 295. Army problems: ibid., 293–94; *OR*, ser. 1, 19 (pt. 2):144; Murfin, 93, 95. Jackson's injury, Longstreet's blister: ibid., 91 (Longstreet wore a carpet slipper); Wert, *Longstreet*, 182. Powell Hill's arrest: Robertson, *Jackson*, 585, 589–90; Murfin, 91–92. Need for food: *REL WP*, 293; REL's conversation with William Allan, Feb. 15, 1868, RELC WL; Long, 206. Victory at Richmond, Kentucky: *OR*, ser. 1, 19 (pt. 2): 596; Murfin, 100. REL at Frederick: *REL WP*, 297, 298; Freeman, 2:355–56; Murfin, 108–09. REL's campaign objectives: REL's conversation with Allan, RELC WL, and printed in Gary W. Gallagher (ed), *Lee the Soldier* (Lincoln: University of Nebraska Press, 1996), 7–8; *REL WP*, 301; Longstreet, *From Manassas to Appomattox*, 285; Sears, *Landscape*, 73, 90–91; Bruce Catton, "Crisis at Antietam," *American Heritage* (Aug. 1958), 55. REL's plan as told to Walker: *B&L*, 2:605–06; also *REL WP*, 304; REL's conversation with Allan, RELC WL, and printed in Gallagher, 8. REL's

proclamation and dispatch to Davis suggesting a peace proposal: *REL WP*, 299, 301.

36. **Lincoln.** Halleck's indecision: *JH D&L*, 176; *ALRW*, 44; Williams, *Lincoln and His Generals*, 176. McClellan in field command: Spears, *McClellan*, 263; McClellan, *Civil War Papers*, 435; Oates, *With Malice Toward None*, 317. McClellan's army on the march: Leech, *Reveille in Washington*, 198; *B&L*, 2:59; Sears, *Landscape Turned Red*, 112. AL's vow with God: *SC ILC*, 150; *GWD*, 1:143. AL's telegrams to McClellan: *AL DBD*, 3:139, 140; *ALCW*, 5:410, 412, 418.

37. **Lee.** REL's plan of attack against Yankee garrisons: *REL, WTP*, 304–05, 313–14; *OR*, 19 (pt. 1): 144–45, 19 (pt. 2):603–04; *B&L*, 2:663; REL's conversation with Allan, RELC WL, and printed in Gallagher, *Lee*, 8–9; Murfin, *Gleam of Bayonets*, 112; Sears, *Landscape Turned Red*, 100; Freeman, *Lee*, 2:363–64. REL at Boonsboro and Hagerstown: *REL, WP*, 306, 314–15; REL's conversation with Allan, RELC WL ("General, I wish we could stand still"); Freeman, 2:365–66 (a woman sang "The Star-Spangled Banner"). McClellan's rapid advance, decision to hold South Mountain, Longstreet's objections: ibid., 367–68, 369n; *REL, WP*, 315–16; REL's conversation with Allan, RELC WL; Sears, 138–39; *B&L*, 2:665–66. Battle of South Mountain: *REL WP*, 309–10, 315–16; REL's conversation with Allan, RELC WL; Freeman, 2:369–76; *B&L*, 2:559–81, 666; Sears, 166–67. D. H. Hill description: REL's conversation with Allan, RELC WL (D. H. Hill's "queer temperament"); Hal Bridges, *Lee's Maverick General: Daniel Harvey Hill* (reprint of 1961 ed., Lincoln: University of Nebraska Press, 1991), 2, 6; Douglas Southall Freeman, *Lee's Lieutenants: A Study in Command* (3 vols., New York: Charles Scribner's Sons, 1942–44), 1:xxxi. To Sharpsburg: *REL WP*, 316–18; REL's conversation with Allan, RELC WL (Lee would have attacked McClellan). Description of landscape: Catton, "Crisis at Antietam," *American Heritage*, 93; Freeman, 2:378 ("we will make our stand"), 378–81, 383–84. Word from Jackson: *REL WP*, 310, 318; Freeman, 2:379 ("That is good news"). REL's reconnoiter, assessment of McClellan: ibid., 378–80; Catton, "Crisis at Antietam," *American Heritage*, 93, 95, Sears, 180. Arrival of Jackson and Walker: Freeman, 2:382–83; *B&L*, 2:667; Sears, 182–83. REL's strength Sept. 16, disposition of troops, REL pondered the odds: *REL WP*, 318–19; Catton, "Crisis at Antietam," *American Heritage*, 93, 95; Sears, 192–93; *B&L*, 2:667; Murfin, 209 (rained that night). The battle on the rebel left: *REL WP*, 319–20; *B&L*, 2:668; Freeman, 2:387–92; Sears, 230–31, 237 ("Don't get excited"), 256. REL, Longstreet, Hill at command post hill: *B&L*,

2:671, Long, *Memoirs of Lee*, 221; Moxley G. Sorrel, *Recollections of a Confederate Staff Officer* (reprint of 1905 ed., New York: Bantam Books, 1992), 84. The battle at the rebel center: *REL WP*, 320–21; *B&L*, 2: 668–70 ("we're already badly whipped"); Murfin, 246, 257–61; Sears, 266, 279, 303–04; *EPA MM*, 262 ("The end of the Confederacy"); Freeman, 2:392–95. The battle on the rebel right: *REL WP*, 321–22; *B&L*, 2:661–62, 670–71; Sorrel, 84; Freeman, 2:395–403 (A. P. Hill's arrival, REL dialogue); Murfin, 269, 276, 281; Sears, 294–327. REL's conference with his generals: Freeman, 2:403 ("Where is Longstreet?"); *B&L*, 2:671–72 ("Here is my old warhorse"); Murfin, 291 (REL's dialogue with Longstreet, Jackson, and Hood, and "Gentlemen, we will not cross"); Sears, 327; McPherson, *Battle Cry of Freedom*, 544; *EPA FFC*, 153–54. Withdrawal: *REL WP*, 322–23; *B&L*, 2:672; Sears, 335–37; Murfin, 295; Freeman, 2:405–06; McPherson, 545.

38. **Lincoln.** McClellan's telegrams: McClellan, *Civil War Papers*, 467, 468, 470; *ALCW*, 5:425–26. Cabinet meeting, preliminary emancipation proclamation: *GWD*, 1:142–45; *SC ILC*, 149–52; Voegeli, *Free But Not Equal*, 52–53; *N&H ALH*, 6:162–63; McPherson, *Battle Cry of Freedom*, 558 (a war of subjugation, "The Old South is to be destroyed and replaced by new propositions and ideas"); *ALCW*, 5:433–37.

39. **Douglass.** *FD L&W*, 3:40, 273–77, 292–93, 295, 298.

40. **Davis.** *JD R&F*, 2:145; Beauregard to Miles in *OR*, ser. 2, 4:916, and *JBJ WCD*, 1:159 (raise the black flag); Richmond *Enquirer* (Oct. 1, 1862), and quoted in Herbert Mitgant (ed.), *Abraham Lincoln, A Press Portrait* (Chicago: Quadrangle Books, 1971), 315; Strode, *Davis*, 2:312–13; *JDP*, 8:422 (Lee's response to emancipation proclamation).

41. **Lincoln.** Democratic response: Franklin, *Emancipation Proclamation*, 81–82; Voegeli, *Free But Not Equal*, 54–57; McClellan, *Civil War Papers*, 471, 493; Williams, *Lincoln and His Generals*, 171–72. Colonization: Voegeli, 42, 97; *ALCW*, 5:371n; McPherson, *Struggle for Equality*, 95–96. Fall elections: Thomas, *Lincoln*, 344–45; Voegeli, 62–64; *CWL*, 214–15; *GWD*, 1:183; Sandburg, *Abraham Lincoln: The War Years*, 2:216; *ALCW*, 5:493–95, 503, 509–11. That the Republicans lost the off-year elections was AL's view and the view of many other Republicans. McPherson, *Battle Cry of Freedom*, 561–62, disputes that perception.

42. **Davis.** To Lee, *JDP*, 8:409. Van Dorn and Price: Strode, *Davis*, 2:314, 320–21; Woodworth, *Davis and His Generals*, 154–55, 169–73; John B. Jones, *A Rebel War Clerk's Diary* (one volume ed., ed. Earl Schenck

Miers, Baton Rouge: Louisiana State University Press, 1993), 93 ("Gibraltar of the Mississippi"). Failure in Kentucky: *JDP*, 8:417, 420, 448–49; *OR*, ser. 1, 16 (pt. 2): 845–46; Strode, 2:315–16; Woodworth, 147–48. JD's conference with Bragg, letter to Smith: *JDP*, 8:468–69, 471; Joseph H. Parks, *General Edmund Kirby Smith, C.S.A.* (Baton Rouge: Louisiana State University Press, 1954), 245. Bragg description: Grady McWhinny, *Braxton Bragg and Confederate Defeat* (New York: Columbia University Press, 1969), 28, 389; Walter Lord (ed.), *The Fremantle Diary* (reprint 1954 ed., New York: Capricorn Books, 1960), 115. The new Western Department: Davis, *Davis*, 475–76; *JDP*, 8:533; *JD R&F*, 2:338. Troubles with Randolph, Seddon description: ibid., 476–77; *JBJ WCD*, 1:312, 380; Davis, *Davis*, 480. Conscription, Brown's objections: *JDP*, 8:408; Shelby Foote, *The Civil War, A Narrative* (3 vols., New York: Random House, 1958–74), 1:779–80; Escott, *After Secession*, 71, 85, 87, 120; Richard N. Current (ed.), *Encyclopedia of the Confederacy* (4 vols., New York: Simon & Schuster, 1993), 3:397–98. Organized opposition: Davis, *Davis*, 441–47; *JDP*, 8:322; Escott, 70. Varina and entertainment: *VD JD*, 2:160–64; Davis, *Davis*, 448, 454.

43. **Lincoln.** AL to Schurz: *ALCW*, 5:509. Prodding McClellan: *ALRW*, 231; *ALCW*, 5:460–62. Buell and Rosecrans: *OR*, ser. 1, 16 (pt. 2):638, 639, 640–42; Williams, *Lincoln and His Generals*, 151–52, 181–87; *JH D&L*, 188. McClellan relieved, Burnside in command: *ALCW*, 5:462n, 474 ("Will you pardon me"), 475, 479, 485; *JH D&L*, 218–19; Nicolay to Hay, Oct. 26, 1862, and Nicolay to Theresa, Oct. 26, and Nov. 9, 1862, JGNP; *CWL*, 212; *ALRW*, 231; *OBD*, 1:619; Williams, 174–82, 194–97.

44. **Livermore.** Interview with AL: *ML MSW*, 233, 241–42, 555–62. In charge of Chicago Sanitary Commission: ibid., 136–37, 155–56, 165–69; *ML SML*, 472; Henshaw, *Our Branch*, 94,103–04, 206, 208, 229–30; Newberry, *U.S. Sanitary Commission*, 221, 228.

45. **Lincoln.** AL's message: *ALCW*, 5:520–21, 530–37; *OBD*, 1:591. Sumner called frequently on Lincoln that December to discuss emancipation and AL's proclamation. I've simulated what they surely said to one another, basing the dialogue on their recorded views and events at that time: Sumner, *Complete Works*, 9:193–236, 247; Sumner, *Selected Letters*, 2:133; Donald, *Sumner*, 79–85, 96–97; Boyden, *Echoes*, 122; *ALCW*, 5:420.

46. **Lee.** Concentration at Fredericksburg: *REL WP*, 326–27, 340, 342, 345 (letter to Davis), 351, 354 (letter to Mary), 357 (letter to Charlotte), 367;

Freeman, *Lee*, 2:433–34; Foote, *Civil War*, 2:23. Federal seizure of Freder#
icksburg: *REL WP*, 327, 357–58, 361, 369; *B&L*, 3:75; Clara Barton,
"Black Book," CBP SC; Clara Barton, Lecture [typescript], CBP LC; Free#
man, 2:443–50; Foote, 2:27; *EPA FFC*, 170–71. REL's army: *REL WP*,
369, 380; Freeman, 2:447, 451 ("I shall try"), 452; Thomas, *Lee*, 269
(REL had 306 guns). REL and officers at command post: Sorrel, *Recollec#
tions*, 111. Battle of Fredericksburg: *REL WP*, 361–62. 370–73; Longstreet,
From Manassas to Appomattox, 308–12; *EPA FFC*, 173, 176; *B&L*,
3:75–82; Freeman, 2:456–64; Foote, 2:35–39. Northern lights: Freeman,
2:466–67; Foote, 2:42 ("the heavens are hanging"), *REL WP*, 373. REL's
spirits, hopes for final victory: *REL WP*, 380; Freeman, 2:466–67; *B&L*,
3:82 ("General, I am losing faith"). Federal retreat, REL depressed: *REL
WP*, 364–65 ("They suffered heavily"), 373, 380; Freeman, 2:473.

47. **Lincoln.** AL's reaction to Fredericksburg: Francis B. Carpenter, *Six
Months at The White House with Lincoln* (ed. John Crosby Freeman,
Watkins Glen, New York: Century House, 1961), 73 ("If there's a
man"); Villard, *Memoirs*, 1:390–91. Popular outcry: Chandler to Trum#
bull, LTP ("unstable as water"); Donald, *Sumner*, 2:89 ("cowardly imbe#
cile"); *CWL*, 212–13 ("I am heartsick"); C. L. Stephenson to Eli Wash#
burne, Dec. 24, 1862, EWP LC; Bill, *Beleaguered City*, 154 ("God help
us"); *ALRW*, 202 ("Cavode, stop!"). AL's conversation with Trumbull:
USGP, 6:288n–289n. AL on Vicksburg: David Dixon Porter, *Incidents
and Anecdotes of the Civil War* (New York: D. Appleton and Co., 1885),
95–96; Edward Cole Bearss, *The Campaign for Vicksburg* (3 vols., Day#
ton, Ohio: Morningside, 1985–86), 3:1312. McClerndon's plan: *AB
MHG*, 1:128–30; *GWD*,1:386–87; Porter, 122–23; Bearss, 1:27–28; Cat#
ton, *Grant Moves South*, 325–27; *USGP*, 6:289n, 279n ("the depot of a
joint").

48. **Grant.** USG and Halleck: *USGP*, 6:288, 288n. USG and Sherman
worked out a plan: ibid., 6:390, 403 (Sherman would command the expe#
dition); 404, 408; Bearss, *Vicksburg*, 1:118; *USGM*, 1:431; *AB MHG*,
1:133–36, 119 ("The President may insist"). Sherman back to Memphis,
USG to Halleck: *USGP*, 7:6. Forrest's raid: ibid., 7:63–64, 69; Bearss,
1:300. Lincoln wanted McClernand to command: *USGP*, 7:62, 107;
USGM, 1:432. USG to McClernand, USG's communications cut: *USGP*,
7:68–69, 107; Catton, *Grant Moves South*, 337.

49. **Davis.** Appeals from Pettus and Phelan, battle in Virginia imminent:
JDP, 8:525, 539–40 ("Plant your own foot"); *JBJ WCD*, 1:199. JD to
Lee: *JD LPS*, 5:384. JD with Bragg's army: *JD LPS*, 5:294–95, 386;

Woodworth, *Davis and His Generals*, 183; Foote, *Civil War*, 2:9 ("robbing Peter to pay Paul," "fight if you can"). JD at Chattanooga: *JD LPS*, 5:295; Strode, *Davis*, 2:344; Foote, 2:9. Hostility and disaffection: *JD LPS*, 5:294–95, 386. JD at Vicksburg: *B&L*, 3:474; Foote, 2:10 ("immense, intrenched camp"), 11–12; *JDP*, 559 ("Banks is reported to be ascending"); 561–63 ("To prevent the enemy"); 585, 587n (Johnston's anger that JD hadn't ordered Holmes to send troops); Davis, *Davis*, 485; Woodworth, *Davis and His Generals*, 183–84; Symonds, *Johnston*, 193.

50. **Grant.** Reaction to Holly Springs raid: *USGM*, 1:432–34; *USGP*, 7:71n, 76; Bears, *Vicksburg*, 1:310–17, 327. Advance suspended, retreat to Holly Springs: *USGP*, 7:79, 81; *USGM*, 1:433; *AB MHG*, 1:139. USG to Oxford residents: *USGM*, 1:435–36; *SC TYWG*, 40. Army lived off the country: *USGP*, 7:94; *USGM*, 1:433, 435; *AB MHG*, 1:139–40. Changed plans: *USGP*, 7:83. 198, 204.

51. **Davis.** JD and Johnston with Pemberton's army: *B&L*, 3:474–75; *JDP*, 8: 560n; Michael B. Ballard, *Pemberton, A Biography* (Jackson: University Press of Mississippi), 127–28; Foote, *Civil War*, 16–17; Symonds, *Johnston*, 193–94. Pemberton description: Ballard, 3, 5, 11, 108 ("I have great confidence"), 122. JD in Jackson: *JDP*, 8:560; Russell, *My Diary*, 156–57 (description of Pettus and his office). JD's address: Foote, 2, 3–4, 13 (description of hall, Phelan and Pettus); *JDP*, 8:565–79. Back to Vicksburg: *JDP*, 8:587; Ballard, 128–29; *B&L*, 3:483 (Vicksburg's guns).

52. **Sherman.** WTS's force: Marszalek, *Sherman*, 205; Ewing, *Sherman at War*, 80. Proscription of journalists: General Orders No. 8, Dec. 18, 1862, WTSP. Failed attack on Walnut Hills: *WTSM*, 312–17; *SL*, 172–73; Marszalek, 205–07. Porter to WTS: "Extracts from Admiral Porter's Journal," WTSP. WTS and McClernand: Ewing, 82, 109 ("unscrupulous old politician"); Marszalek, 210 ("consumed by personal ambition"); Lewis, *Sherman*, 258, 260 ("he ranks me"), 261. McClernand description: WTS quoted in Lewis, 260.

53. **Davis.** Message from Bragg: Foote, *Civil War*, 2:18; *JDP*, 8: 590. Bragg's retreat, JD claimed victory: ibid., 2:19. JD's speech: *JD LPS*, 5:390–91, 394–95. JD traveled 2,750 miles: Strode, *Davis*, 2:358.

THE WINDS OF 'SIXTY-THREE

1. **Lincoln.** AL would stand by his pledge: Sumner to John Murray Forbes, Dec. 25, 1862, John Murray Forbes, *Letters and Recollections* (ed. Sarah Forbes Hughes, 2 vols., Boston: Houghton, Mifflin Co., 1899), 1:348–49;

ALCW, 435; Sumner, *Selected Letters*, 2:136; *OBD*, 1:606–07 ("there is no hope"). AL and colonization: AL's talk with Washington blacks in *ALCW*, 5:370–75; Haitian scheme in James M. McPherson, *The Negro's Civil War* (reprint 1965 ed., New York: Vintage Books, 1967), 96–97. AL made an oblique reference to blacks as a free-wage force in his recent message (*ALCW*, 5:535) and did so again in his final emancipation proclamation (ibid., 6:30). Black troops: *ALCW*, 6:149–50 ("available and unavailed of force"); Sumner, *Selected Letters*, 2:136; Forbes, 1:349, 353; *ALRW*, 435; Donald, *Sumner and the Rights of Man*, 97; Thomas and Hyman, *Stanton*, 256. AL's insomnia last night of 1862: Thomas, *Lincoln*, 364. Supreme irony of AL's life: undated clipping in Lincoln National Life Foundation, Fort Wayne, Indiana, as cited in Louis A. Warren, *Lincoln's Youth: Indiana Years* (New York: Appleton Century Crofts, 1959), 225. Final proclamation: *ALCW*, 6:28–30. AL's reasons for exemptions: ibid., 6:428–29. Reconstruction and King's cure: *ALCW*, 8:254; Oates, *Abraham Lincoln: The Man Behind the Myths*, 110, 139–40. Mary's condition and views on emancipation: Turners, *Mary Lincoln*, 144 ("furnace of affliction"), 141 ("cause of humanity"), 145–46 ("oppressed colored people"); Keckley, *Behind the Scenes*, 114. President's reception: Benjamin French, "At the President's Reception," Jan. 1, 1863, in Brown University Library, Providence, Rhode Island ("Oh, Mr. French"); *NB WLT*, 48–49. AL's signing of the emancipation proclamation: *N&H ALH*, 6:422; *CWL*, 235 ("I've been shaking hands," "soul is in it," "if my name ever gets into history," "He hesitated," "That will do"); Seward, *Reminiscences*, 227 ("doing the right thing"). Reactions: *JH DD&L, 50*; *ATR RAL*, 56 ("as much harm as good"); *CWL*, 278 (AL feared "the fire in the rear"); McPherson, *Negro's Civil War*, 50 ("time of times").

2. **Davis.** On emancipation proclamation: *JDMP*, 1:290–92; *JD R&F*, 2:160–62; *JDP*, 9:21; *VD JD*, 2:215–17. Other reactions: *Richmond Examiner* (Jan. 7, 1863); Strode, *Davis*, 2:362; Escott, *After Secession*, 188; Bill, *Beleaguered City*, 150 ("reign of hell" and "hoist the black flag"). JD's proclamation: *VD JD*, 2:251–58. JD's Address to the North: quoted in Quarles, *Negro in the Civil War*, 180.

3. **Douglass.** Impact of emancipation on Confederates: *FD L&W*, 3:315–16. FD on the proclamation: *FDP*, 3:549–52, 564. Wall of resistance: ibid., 3:566–67. Andrew and an elite black regiment: Louis F. Emilio, *A Brave Black Regiment: History of the Fifty-Fourth Regiment of Massachusetts Volunteer Infantry, 1863–1865* (3rd ed., Salem, New Hampshire: Ayer Company, 1990), 3. FD as recruiter: ibid., 11–12; *FD L&W*, 3:31–32, 319–20; *Liberator* (Mar. 13, 1863); William S. McFeely,

Frederick Douglass (New York: W. W. Norton & Co., 1991), 218 (FD's reluctance to fight as a common soldier), 224 (descriptions of Charles and Lewis Douglass). FD's arguments that blacks should enlist: *FD L&W*, 3:340–46; *Liberator* (Mar. 13, 1863). Regiment at Reading: Emilio, 20–21; Quarles, *Douglass,* 205–06; Henry Greenleaf Pearson, *The Life of John A. Andrew, Governor of Massachusetts, 1861–1865* (2 vols., Boston: Houghton Mifflin, 1904), 2:87–89 ("I know not"); also quoted in McPherson, *Struggle for Equality,* 206. Departure of Fifty-Fourth: *FD L&W*, 3:32, 346; *FDP*, 3:587; Quarles, 207–08; Emilio, 31–32.

4. **Lincoln.** Democratic response to emancipation proclamation, backlash in the army: Voegeli, *Free But Not Equal,* 76–90; *Chicago Times* (Jan. 3, 1863); *New York World* (Jan. 8, 1863); *New York Herald* (Jan. 20, 1863); Bell Irvin Wiley, *Life of Billy Yank: The Common Soldier of the Union* (reprint 1952 ed., Garden City, New York: Doubleday & Co., 1971), 40–43; Forrest G. Wood, *Black Scare: The Racist Response to Emancipation and Reconstruction* (Berkeley: University of California Press, 1968), 17–39. Republicans shocked: Edward L. Pierce, *Memoir and Letters of Charles Sumner* (4 vols., Boston: Houghton Mifflin, 1887–93), 4:114 ("These are dark hours"); *OBD*, 1:613 ("We all agree"), 616 (David Davis's objections); *CWL* ("slow walker"), 215; *CWL*, 278; *ALCW*, 6:48–49 ("broken eggs"). England: Charles Francis Adams, Jr., *Charles Francis Adams* (Boston, 1900), 299–300ff; Thomas, *Lincoln,* 360 ("It has rallied"); *ALCW*, 6:64. Utilizing black troops: *FD L&W*, 3:36; *ALCW*, 6:149–50 ("bare sight"). Refugee system: Voegeli, 95–112; Dudley Cornish, *The Sable Arm: Negro Troops in the Union Army, 1861–1865* (reprint 1956 ed., New York: W. W. Norton & Co., 1966), 112–31; Bell Irvin Wiley, *Southern Negroes, 1861–1865* (Baton Rouge: Louisiana State University Press, 1965), 199–250. Colonization fiasco in Haiti: Quarles, *Lincoln and the Negro,* 113–23, 191ff; McPherson, *Negro's Civil War,* 96–97; *ALCW*, 6:178–79; *N&H, ALH,* 6:359–67. Conscription, disaffected Democrats, arbitrary arrests: McPherson, *Battle Cry of Freedom,* 600–06; Thomas and Hyman, *Stanton,* 157–58, 245–81, 375; Hyman, *More Perfect Union,* 215–23; Voegeli, 76–78; *CWL* (AL feared "fire in the rear" more than military reversals); Neely, *Fate of Liberty,* 120–33. Vallandigham case: Frank L. Clements, *The Limits of Dissent: Clement L. Vallandigham and the Civil War* (Lexington: University of Kentucky Press, 1970), 102ff; Neely, 65–68; Bruce Catton, *Never Call Retreat* (Garden City, New York: Doubleday & Co., 1965), 102–04, 172–74. AL's defense: *ALCW*, 6: 260–69, 300–06.

5. **Grant.** McClernand-Grant contretemps: *OR*, ser. 1, 24 (pt. 3):19; Bearss, *Vicksburg*, 1:433–35; *USGP*, 7:264–65, 276n. USG and contrabands: ibid., 7:338–39, 8:49m 91–92, 93n–94n; Cramer, *Ulysses S. Grant: Conversations and Unpublished Letters*, 106. Lorenzo Thomas and refugee system: *USGP*, 8:355n–56n; Theodore F. Upson, *With Sherman to the Sea* (Bloomington: University of Indiana Press, 1958), 56; *OR*, ser. 1, 24: (pt. 3):220; Catton, *Grant Moves South*, 404. Sherman's objections to black soldiers, approval of draft: *WTS HL*, 193, 252, 243. USGP's army at Milliken's Bend: *USGM*, 1:446, 458–59; *AB MHG*, 1:161. Newspaper attacks: Earl Schenck Miers, *The Web of Victory: Grant at Vicksburg* (Baton Rouge: Lousiana State University Press, 1955), 106; Catton, 368.

6. **Sherman.** Knox description and dispatch: Bernard A. Weisberger, *Reporters for the Union* (Boston: Little, Brown and Co., 1953), 111; *New York Herald* (Jan. 18, 1863); Ewing, *Sherman at War*, 87–88, 90; *SL*, 188. WTS summoned Knox: ibid., 188, 197; Ewing, 88–89; Lewis, *Sherman*, 264. Knox's court-martial: Ewing, 91–92 ("no army"), 100–01; WTS to John Sherman, Feb. 7 and 18, Mar. 14, Apr. 3, 1863, WTSP; *SL*, 188. WTS threatened to quit the army: Fellman, *Citizen Sherman*, 129. Lincoln's intercession, Grant chewed Knox out, WTS's response: *ALCW*, 6:142–43; *USGP*, 8:30–31; Ewing, 102; Marszalek, *Sherman*, 216 ("if the press"); Weisberger, 114.

7. **Grant.** Long talks about Vicksburg: *USGM*, 1:443–45; *AB MHG*, 1:155, 160–62; Wilson, *Rawlins*, 108, 113–15; Bearss, *Vicksburg*, 1:341, 467 (Grant resolved to expore options); *WTS HL*, 238, 245–46. USG's winter projects: *USGM*, 1:446–55; *USGP*, 7:477–78; *AB MHG*, 1:163. Halleck to USG about Lincoln's impatience: *AB MHG*, 1:181. Scurvy description: Henshaw, *Our Branch and Its Tributaries*, 118.

8. **Livermore.** Anti-scorbutics for Grant's army: Henshaw, *Our Branch and Its Tributaries*, 102, 105, 118, 121–22, 124; Newberry, *U. S. Sanitary Commission*, 224. ML's trip down river: *ML MSW*, 283, 284–86. ML at Milliken's Bend: ibid., 281, 300–02, 307, 309–17, 321–26, 339–45, 354; Henshaw, 105–07; Newberry, 88–89.

9. **Lincoln.** Impatience with Grant: Madeleine Dahlgren, *Memoir of John A. Dahlgren* (New York: Boston: James R. Osgood & Co., 1892), 389; Luthin, *The Real Lincoln*, 370; *ALCW*, 6:326. Cincinnati editor charged USG with drunkenness: *SC TYWG*, 114. Dana mission: Charles A. Dana, *Recollections of the Civil War* (reprint of original ed., ed. Ida M. Tarbell, New York: Collier Books, 1963), 41–42, 47. AL and Benjamin Butler: *ALCW*, 6:76–77, 7:207, 207n; Butler, *Private and Official*

Correspondence, 3:13, *ATR RAL,* 143–46 ("Don't let Davis catch you," "That's a game"); Sumner, *Selected Letters,* 2:139. Mud March: Bruce Catton, *Glory Road* (Garden City, New York: Doubleday & Co., 1952), 103, 105; Foote, *Civil War,* 2:130 ("THIS WAY TO RICHMOND"). Army recriminations, Burnside relieved: *ACLW,* 6:52, 74n–75n, 77n, 78n; Williams, *Lincoln and the Radicals,* 265–66; Luthin, 367 ("incompetent," "played out imbecile"); *B&L,* 3:239–40; *OBD,* 1:619; Williams, *Lincoln and His Generals,* 210. AL's interview with Hooker: *AL DBD,* 3:165; *ALCW,* 6:78–79; Williams, *Lincoln and His Generals,* 232 ("If the enemy doesn't run"). Hooker description: ibid., 213–14; Walter H. Hebert, *Fighting Joe Hooker* (Indianapolis: Bobbs-Merrill Co., 1954), 23, 38; Helen Nicolay, *Lincoln's Secretary,* 166 ("stuck in the mud"); Nicolay to Theresa, May 17, 1863, JGNP. Description of Aquia Creek, devastated countryside, army camp: Seward, *Reminiscences,* 229–30; Oates, *A Woman of Valor,* 101–02. AL's visit with Hooker's army: *AL DBD,* 3:177–78; *NB WLT,* 51–60; *ALCW,* 6:164–65; *B&L,* 3:120 ("in your next battle").

10. **Lee.** Lincoln's visit, emancipation proclamation, need for more troops: *REL WP,* 388–90, 411("whole power of their country," "What has our Congress done"). Hill and Longstreet on detached duty: Foote, *Civil War,* 2:239–40, 252–61; *REL WP,* 376–77, 405–06. REL's strength, rations: Freeman, *Lee,* 2:483; *REL WP,* 378; Foote, 2:237. REL's conference with Davis: *REL WP,* 414, 417; Freeman, 2:481 ("the enemy will make every effort"), 498–503. Davis's poor health: *JBJ WCD,* 1:269; Davis, *Davis,* 494, 496.

11. **Davis.** Shortages, impressment: *JDP,* 9:vii, 341; Thomas, *Confederate Nation,* 196–201; *JD LPS,* 5:420, 6:120. Finances, inflation, taxes: Strode, *Davis,* 2: 379 (prices); Thomas, 198; *JD LPS,* 6:120 ("absolute necessity"). Richmond bread riot: *VD JD,* 2:373–76; *JBJ WCD,* 1:285–86; *JDP,* 9:146. JD's proclamation: *JD LPS,* 5:472–73. Complaints to JD: Escott, *After Secession,* 106–55. Runaway servants: *VD JD,* 2:218.

12. **Chesnut.** James's resignation, MC at Mulberry: Muhlenfeld, *Mary Chesnut,* 116; *PMC,* 49, 56, 58. James's commission, back to Richmond: Muhlenfeld, 117; *MCCW,* 431. Chesnut's quarters: ibid., 374, 429. Preston family, Preston girls: ibid., 275, 284–85. Social whirl: ibid., 430, 432, 433, 434, 438.

13. **Davis.** Kirby Smith: Parks, *Smith,* 251, 255–56; *JDP,* 9:45–46, 74–76, 130–31. JD's worries about Vicksburg, defense of Pemberton: *JD LPS,* 5:427, 433, 444, 447, 464–65. JD's illness: *JBJ WCD,* 1:291, 293–94; *JD LPS,* 5:490.

14. Lee. REL's illness: *REL WP*, 413, 419, 427–28 (REL's letter to Mary), 380 ("what a cruel thing is war"). Recovery: ibid., 431–32. REL's study of Hooker: ibid., 427, 433. REL's desire to take the offensive: ibid., 421, 430; Freeman, *Lee*, 2:503–04. REL's concerns about the West: *REL WP*, 434.

15. Davis. Pemberton's report, reinforcements to Bragg: Woodworth, *Davis and His Generals*, 202. JD's worsening health: *JD LPS*, 5:490; Strode, *Davis*, 2:385–94.

16. Grant. USG's diversion and plan: Ballard, *Pemberton*, 135–36 *USGM*, 1:574–75; *USGP*, 7:317, 486, 8:12; *AB MHG*, 1:186; USG quoted in Young, *Around the World with Grant*, 616; Bearss, *Vicksburg*, 2:129–76; *USGM*, 1:489; *AB MHG*, 1:188–89. Dana: Dana, *Recollections*, 9, 12, 49, 61; Wilson, *Rawlins*, 121. Sherman's objections: Dana, *Recollections*, 51, *WTSM*, 338–40; *AB MHG*, 1:183–84; *USGM*, 1:542n–543n. McClernand at New Carthage: *USGP*, 8:511; Bearss, 2:25, 53. USG's family at Milliken's Bend: *USGP*, 7:490–91, 8:30 (Grant's boils); *AB MHG*, 1:195 (Grant's boils); *JGM*, 111–12 ("The president has sent General Thomas," "I'm glad you arrived in time"). Grant watched as Porter's flotilla ran the batteries: ibid., 112; Dana, *Recollections*, 54–55; Fred Grant, "A Boy's Experience at Vicksburg: Personal Recollections of the War of the Rebellion," *Addresses Delivered Before the Commandery of the State of New York* (Military Order of the Loyal Legion of the United States, 3rd series, ed. A. Noel Blakeman, New York: G. P. Putnam's sons, 1907), 86; *USGM*, 1:463–64; *JGM*, 112; *AB MHG*, 1:190–92; Wittenmeyer, *Under the Guns*, 95; Catton, *Grant Moves South*, 414–15; Bearss, 2:67 (strength of rebel batteries). USG to New Carthage: *USGP*, 8:85; Grant, "Boy's Experience," 88; Catton, 515; *USGP*, 8:511; *USGM*, 1:465–68. McPherson description: *USGP*, 7:409, 467; Conyngham, *Sherman's March*, 53, 176; Richardson, *Personal History of Grant*, 323. More steamers and barges: *USGM*, 1:471; *AB MHG*, 1:196; Bearss, 2:79. USG's designs on Grand Gulf: *USGM*, 1:472–75. Porter and Grant's reconnoiter: *USGP*, 8:115n, 117, 130, 131n; Dana, *Recollections*, 56; *USGM*, 1:474–75; Bearss, 2:281–82.

17. Davis. *JD LPS*, 5:475–76, 479, 485; *JD R&F*, 2:335–36; *JDP*, 9:161; Ballard, *Pemberton*, 136–38, 155 (Vicksburg must be held, Lee and Vicksburg); Woodworth, *Davis and His Generals*, 204–05; Strode, *Davis*, 2:376; Davis, *Davis*, 501.

18. Grant. McClernand's slows: Dana, *Recollections*, 57–58; *USGP*, 8:122, 126–27, 132; Bearss, *Vicksburg*, 2:293–94; Catton, *Grant Moves South*,

428 ("keep it moving"). Naval attack against Grand Gulf: *USGP*, 8:135, 145, 512; Dana, 58; *USGM*, 1:475–76 (sight of dying men made USG sick); Grant, "Boy's Experience at Vicksburg," *Addresses Delivered Before the Commandery of the State of New York*, 88; Richardson, *Grant*, 302 ("It's no use, General"); *USGP*, 8:512; *AB MHG*, 1:200; Bearss, 2:310–12. Across the Mississippi: *USGP*, 8:512; Dana, 59–60; Grant, "Boy's Experience," 88–90; *AB MHG*, 1:200; Bearss, 2:318–46. USG's admiration for Porter: quoted in Young, *Around the World with Grant*, 305. Battle of Port Gibson: *USGP*, 8:138–47, 152, 155, 262, 512–13; *USGM*, 1:485–87; *AB MHG*, 1:205–14, 211, 226 (USG had only his toothbrush); Richardson, 306 ("Grant was everywhere on the front"), 308–09; Dana, 60–62; Grant, "Boy's Experience," 89–90; Bearss, 2:299–300. Grierson's raid: *USGP*, 8:139, 148; *AB MHG*, 1:189. Bearss, 2:211–36; Stephen Z. Starr, *The Union Cavalry in the Civil War* (3 vols., Baton Rouge: Louisiana State University Press, 1979–85), 3:190–94.

19. **Davis.** JD and Mississippi: *JBJ WCD*, 1:297; Strode, *Davis*, 2:391–94 (so ill he couldn't speak); *JD R&F*, 2:336–38; JD's advice to Pemberton in *OR*, ser. 1, 24 (pt. 3), 859; Ballard, *Pemberton*, 137–50. Enemy movement on the Rappahannock: *REL WP*, 434–36. JD and enemy cavalry raid: *JBJ WCD*, 1:307–08; Bill, *Beleaguered City*, 173; *MCW*, 477–78. Message from Lee: *REL WP*, 442.

20. **Lee.** REL and enemy movements, Apr. 28–30: *REL WP*, 442–46, 460–61; Foote, *Civil War*, 2:271 ("Mr. F. J. Hooker"); Freeman, *Lee*, 2:508–14 ("The enemy attack will come from above"). REL's decision to fight, divided army: *REL WP*, 461; Freeman, 2:515–17; Robertson, *Jackson*, 701–04. REL into the Wilderness, Hooker handed REL the initiative: *REL WP*, 461–62; REL's conversation with Allan, RELC WL, and printed in Gallagher, *Lee*, 9; Freeman, 2:516–18; Foote, 2:276–81, 314. REL's nighttime conference with Jackson, REL conceived of flank attack against the enemy right: REL's conversation with Allan, RELC WL; Freeman, 519–21 (dialogue between REL and Jackson); Long, *Memoirs of Lee*, 255; Robertson, 709–12; Thomas, *Bold Dragoon*, 211 (Stuart's new uniform). Jackson's departure and dialogue: G. F. R. Henderson, *Stonewall Jackson and the American Civil War* (reprint of 1898 ed., 2 vols., Secaucus, N.J.: Blue and Gray Press [n.d.]), 2:432; Robertson, 714. REL's admiration for Jackson: Henderson, 2:477 ("Such an executive officer"). REL during Jackson's attack: Freeman, 2:530–32; *REL WP*, 462–64. Captain R. E. Wilbourn's report: Freeman, 2:532–33; Long, 256 (Jackson's remark if he'd only had another hour of daylight); Foote, 2:303 (These people must be pressed"). Second day of battle: *REL WP*, 464–65;

EPA FFC, 209–10; Long, 259–60; Fitzhugh Lee, *Lee,* 252–54; Freeman, 2:538–42. Message from Jackson, REL's reaction: *REL WP,* 452–53; Freeman, 2:542–43; Long, 260. REL against Sedgwick: *REL WP,* 454, 466–67; *EPA FFC,* 213; Fitzhugh Lee, 255; Freeman, 2:543–51. Yankee retreat: ibid., 2:557 ("That is the way you young men"); *REL WP,* 457; Ernest B. Furgurson, *Chancellorsville, 1863: The Souls of the Brave* (New York: Alfred A. Knopf, 1992), 320–21. REL's casualties: Livermore, *Numbers and Losses,* 99; Freeman, 3:5; *REL WP,* 426. Jackson's death: Freeman, 2:560, 562 ("Give Jackson my affectionate regards," "Surely Jackson must recover"); *REL WP,* 426 ("It is a terrible loss"). REL to Seddon and Davis: ibid., 482, 483.

21. **Lincoln.** AL's anxiety about Hooker's army: *GWD,* 1:291; *NB WLT,* 60–61 ("My God, what will the country say?"); *ALCW,* 6:198–200; *AL DBD,* 3:182–83. AL's visit with the army: ibid., 183; Nicolay to Theresa, May 10, 1862, JGNP; *ALCW,* 6: 201; George Gordon Meade, *Life and Letters* (2 vols., New York: Charles Scribner's Sons, 1913), 1:372 (AL blamed no one); *ALRW,* 324; Williams, *Lincoln and His Generals,* 243–44. Hospital boats at Washington: Leech, *Reveille in Washington,* 232; Keckley, *Behind the Scenes,* 119 ("It is dark, dark everywhere"). Capital crawled with rumors: *NB WLT,* 61–62. AL's advice to Hooker: *ALCW,* 6:217; Meade, 1:385 ("he was not disposed to throw away a gun"); *ALRW,* 376. AL's confidence in Grant: *ALCW,* 6:230; *Chicago Tribune* (May 29, 1863); *ALRW,* 11; *ALCW,* 6:326.

22. **Grant.** Port Hudson operation canceled: *USGP,* 8:514; Bearss, *Vicksburg,* 2:435; *USGM,* 1:491–92; *AB MHG,* 1:218. USG's strength: *AB MHG,* 1:232. Despite what Grant claims in his *Memoirs* and what Catton and many other writers maintain, USG did not entirely cut himself off from his supply base when he moved inland. USG's mode of supplying his army is described in *USGP,* 8:178, 181, 183–84, 187–88; *AB MHG,* 1:228; Dana, *Recollections,* 72; Bearss, 2:480–81. USG's plan of operations against Pemberton: Bearss, 2:480; *USGP,* 8:514; Dana, 64; *AB MHG,* 1:219–20. Foraging: *USGM,* 1:493; *AB MHG,* 1:232–33, 238–39, 284, 292–93. USG to Banks and Halleck: *USGP,* 8:190, 196.

23. **Davis.** Pemberton's strategy against Grant: *OR,* ser. 1, 24 (pt. 3), 807–08, 850–51, 858–59; Ballard, *Pemberton,* 151. JD's efforts to help Pemberton: *JD R&F,* 2:336; Strode, *Davis,* 2:395 (Pemberton's "dispatches leave me in doubt"); *JD LPS,* 5:482 (suggestion that Pemberton cut Grant's supply line). JD's concerns about Johnston: Ballard, 141–43; *JD LPS,* 5:482, 488; *JDP,* 9:183; Strode, 2:401 (JD's illness); *JD R&F,*

2:339–40. JD ordered Johnston to Mississippi: ibid., 2:339–40, 345; Ballard, 153–54 (report of want of confidence in Pemberton). Report of fighting at Raymond: ibid., 152.

24. Grant. USG's decision to seize Jackson: *USGP*, 8:514; *AB MHG*, 1:216; *USGM*, 1:499–500; Bearss, *Vicksburg*, 2:513–14; *SC TYWG*, 70–72 ("Success to our campaign"). Advance against Jackson: *USGP*, 8:205, 207–08, 514–15; *USGM*, 1:505.

25. Davis. Johnston's arrival in Jackson: *JD R&F*, 2:339; *JD LPS*, 5:448, and *JDP*, 9:189 ("too late," "Anxiously wait"). JD's thoughts of sending part of Lee's army to Mississippi: *JBJ WCD*, 1:235; Strode, *Davis*, 2:402. JD's conference with Lee, Lee's plan to invade the North: I've simulated what JD, Lee, and Seddon said during their momentous meetings with the Cabinet, based on the information in ibid., 402–06; John H. Reagan, *Memoirs* (ed. Walter Flavius McCaleb, New York: Neale Publishing Co., 1906), 120–22, 150–53; *REL WP*, 476, 482–84; REL's conversation with Allan, RELC WL, and printed in Gallagher, *Lee*, 13; *JDP*, 9:201–03; Wert, *Longstreet*, 240, 244–46, and William Garrett Piston, *Lee's Tarnished Lieutenant: James Longstreet and His Place in Southern History* (Athens: University of Georgia Press, 1987), 44–45 (Longstreet's talks with Seddon, Longstreet agreed with Lee); *REL WP*, 482, 483–84, 476, 569–70; Freeman, *Lee*, 3:19–20; Foote, *Civil War*, 2:430–32; McPherson, *Battle Cry of Freedom*, 647; *REL WP*, 508–09, and *B&L*, 3:346 (Lee's political objectives); Thomas, *Lee*, 288. Johnston's retreat from Jackson: *OR*, ser. 1, 24 (pt. 3), 877–78, 882; Strode, 2:402. Pemberton after Grant's supply line: *JD R&F*, 2:340 ("The object is to cut the enemy's communications"); Symonds, *Johnston*, 208–09.

26. Grant. Occupation of Jackson: *USGP*, 8:215, 515; *USGM*, 1:505–06; *AB MHG*, 1:247–49; *WTSM*, 348 (Confederate Hotel); *SC TYWG*, 73–74; Richardson, *Personal History of Grant*, 315; Catton, *Grant Moves South*, 441–42. USG's directions to Sherman and McPherson: *USGP*, 8:515; *USGM*, 1:507; *AB MHG*, 1:252; *WTSM*, 347. USG's sleeping quarters, vandalism: *USGM*, 1:506; *SC TYWG*, 75. Jackson put to the torch: *USGP*, 8:515; *USGM*, 1:507, Dana, *Recollections*, 67; Bearss, *Vicksburg*, 2:550. Advancing west toward Edward's Depot: *USGP*, 8:224–26, 515–16; *USGM*, 1:510–12; Bearss, 2:579–80. Battle of Champion Hill: *USGP*, 8:516; Bearss, 2:592–640; *SC TYWG*, 77; *USGM*, 1:512–21; *AB MHG*, 1:260–67; Garland, *Grant*, 23 (USG under fire); Ballard, *Pemberton*, 160–64. Pursuit: *USGP*, 8:517; Thomas M. Stevenson, *History of the 78th Regiment Ohio Volunteers* (Zanesville,

Ohio: Hugh Dunne, 1865), 235 (abandoned supplies, train on fire). USG ahead of pursuit, bivouac: *AB MHG*, 1:272–73, *USGM*, 1:521. Significance of Champion Hill: *USGP*, 8:228, 231; *AB MHG*, 1:275; Bearss, 2:638. Advance to the Big Black River, rebel positions: *USGP*, 8:517; *USGM*, 1:523–24; *AB MHG*, 1:276; Dana, *Recollections*, 68; Bearss, 2:667. USG's conversation with Dwight: *USGP*, 8:221n; *USGM*, 1:524, 526; Bearss, 2:672, 682–86. Battle of the Big Black, Lawler's charge: Young, *Around the World with Grant*, 623; *USGM*, 1:523–26; *USGP*, 8:518; Catton, *Grant Moves South*, 446 (Lawler description, "When it comes to plain hard fighting," "Let's go for the cussed Rebels!"). Advance against Vicksburg: *USGP*, 8:518; *USGM*, 1:526–27; *WTSM*, 349. USG and Sherman at Walnut Hills: *USGM*, 1:528, 532–33; *WTSM*, 350–51; *AB MHG*, 1:281 ("Until this moment"), 284; Bearss, 3:752. May 19 assaults: *USGP*, 8:518; *USGM*, 1:529; *AB MHG*, 1:298–303; Stevenson, 238; Bearss, 3:763 (Thirteenth U.S. Infantry, "First at Vicksburg"), 772. Preparations: *USGM*, 1:529; *AB MHG*, 1:310; Stevenson, 238. May 22 assaults: *USGP*, 8:245–46, 518–19; *USGM*, 1:530–31; *AB MHG*, 1:309–22; *SC TYWG*, 90; Bearss, 3:815, 823, 835, 854–55. McClernand problem: *USGP*, 8:518–19; *SC TYWG*, 92; *AB MHG*, 1:325–26; Bearss, 3:836–37, 844–45. USG's anger at McClernand, McClernand relieved: Dana, *Recollections*, 71–72, 96; *OR*, ser. 1, 24 (pt. 1): 86–87; *USGP*, 8:385. Siege: ibid., 8:249, *USGM*, 1:532, 537, 540; *AB MHG*, 1:359 (strength of besieging army). Only a question of time: *USGP*, 8: 257, 261.

27. Lincoln. AL's anxiety about Vicksburg, but confidence in Grant: Oates, *With Malice Toward None*, 349; *ALCW*, 6:230; *USGP*, 8:343n. AL's difficulties with an inert Rosecrans: *OR*, ser. 1, 23 (pt. 2): 369, 371, 383, 23 (pt. 1): 8–10; Williams, *Lincoln and His Generals*, 247–51.

28. Davis. Vicksburg under siege: *JD R&F*, 2:346 ("the most important point"), 347; *VD JD*, 2:421; *JDP*, 9:264. JD's difficulties with Johnston: *JD LPS*, 5:489–90, 492, 496–97, 499–500, 502–03, 505, 513, 519–20, 522, 527–28, 531–35, 555–63; *JDP*, 9:218–20, 227, 252–53, 271; *VD JD*, 2: 422–23 ("I have not considered myself in command," "Your telegram grieves and alarms us," "Only my convictions"); Strode, *Davis*, 2:418–19; Symonds, *Johnston*, 209–14. Davis, *Davis*, 503, says that "Davis's unhappy and largely unwilling adherence to Johnston would be his greatest mistake of 1863." JD's difficulties with Lee: Edwin B. Coddington, *The Gettysburg Campaign: A Study in Command* (reprint of 1979 ed., New York: Charles Scribner's Sons, 1984), 21 ("the means which would make it quite safe"), 118; *REL WP*, 476; Freeman, *Lee*, 3:23.

29. Lee. REL's and JD's views on strategy: Coddington, *Gettysburg Campaign*, 21, 118; Wert, *Longstreet*, 24 (force Lincoln's hand, "play a little of that game"). Strength of REL's army: *REL WP*, 476–77; Coddington, 248; Freeman, *Lee*, 3:23. Reorganized army: *REL WP*, 488–89; *RELD*, 91–93; Thomas, *Bold Cavalier*, 215. Powell Hill description: Henry K. Douglas, *I Rode with Stonewall* (Chapel Hill: University of North Carolina Press, 1940), 147; *REL WP*, 488. Ewell description: Fremantle, *Diary*, 222; REL's conversation with Allan, RELC WL, and printed in Gallagher, *Lee*, 11; *REL WP*, 488, 490 (Jackson's "spirit is with us"); Fitzhugh Lee, *Lee*, 259; Freeman, *Lee*, 3:809. Invincible army: *REL WP*, 490; Walter Taylor, *Four Years with General Lee* (ed. James I. Robertson Jr., Bloomington: Indiana University Press, 1962), 101, observed that the Army of Northern Virginia had "an overweening confidence." Weapons: Coddington, 253. REL's plan of battle, talk with Long: Long, *Memoirs of Lee*, 268–69; Coddington, 9; *REL WP*, 500 ("I trust that a kind Providence"). No promise to Longstreet: REL's conversation with Allan, RELC WL, and printed in Gallagher, 15. REL's review of cavalry: Freeman, 3:30; *REL WP*, 507. Battle of Brandy Station: ibid., 570; Thomas, 221–27; Coddington, 56–58, 60–61, 65; Freeman, 3:31–32. Rooney: *REL WP*, 509, 511–12; Robert E. Lee, Jr., *Recollections*, 96–97. Campaign began: *REL WP*, 513, 517, 519, 570, 572; Coddington, 104.

30. Lincoln. Lee's advance north: *GWD*, 1:328; *AL DBD*, 3:190; *ALCW*, 6:273 ("If his head is at Martinsburg"), 274n; 277, 280–82; *GWD*, 1:332–33 (AL's joking about Orpheus Kerr). AL at telegraph office, confusion about Lee's objective: *AL DBD*, 3:190–92; Thomas, *Lincoln*, 382.

31. Lee. REL with Longstreet: Long, *Memoirs of Lee*, 271; Coddington, *Gettysburg Campaign*, 106; Fremantle, *Diary*, 176–78 (description of countryside). Stuart's plan, REL's directions: *REL WP*, 478, 526, 573–74; Coddington, 108; Freeman, *Lee*, 3:40–41, 43–48; Thomas, *Bold Dragoon*, 239–41. Longstreet across the Potomac: Fremantle, 187 (heavy rain); EPA FFC, 227; Harry W. Pfanz, *Gettysburg: The Second Day* (Chapel Hill: University of North Carolina Press, 1987), 9; Coddington, 114. Chambersburg: Wert, *Longstreet*, 253 (hostile women); Freeman, *Lee*, 3:54 (lock of hair); *EPA FFC*, 229 (prosperous Dutch farms). Foraging: Annette Tapert (ed.), *The Brothers' War: The Civil War Letters to Their Loved Ones, From the Blue and the Gray* (reprint of 1988 ed., New York: Vintage Books, 1989), 154; Coddington, 159–71; Fremantle, 224 ("Yes, Madam, it's very sad"). Lee's general orders on pillaging: *REL WP* 533–34; 508–09 (northern peace party). Ewell's and Early's commissary raids: Pfanz, 5, 8; Coddington, 159–71. REL's conversation with Trimble: Freeman, 3:58–59. No word from Stuart: ibid., 58; Long, *Memoirs of Lee*, 274.

32. **Lincoln.** Difficulties with Hooker, Hooker "took umbrage," sacked: *GWD*, 1: 340, 344, 347–50; *ALCW*, 6:281; Williams, *Lincoln and His Generals*, 258–59; *AL DBD*, 3:192–3. Reynolds offered command: Coddington, *Gettysburg Campaign*, 37. Meade description: Franklin Aretas Haskell, *Haskell of Gettysburg, His Life and Civil War Papers* (ed. Frank L. Byrne and Andrew T. Weaver, Madison: State Historical Society of Wisconsin, 1970), 132; Williams, 259–60, 329; Bruce Catton, *Mr. Lincoln's Army* (Garden City, N.J.: Doubleday & Co., 1951), 117 ("damned old goggle-eyed"). Instructions to Meade: *OR*, ser. 1, 27 (pt. 1):61, 62. Reports of rebel pillaging, seizure of free blacks: Coddington, 159–71.

33. **Lee.** Harrison's report, REL's concern: Coddington, *Gettysburg Campaign*, 180–81, 183, 185; Pfanz, *Gettysburg: Second Day*, 3–4; Freeman, *Lee*, 3:60–62; Long, *Memoirs of Lee*, 275. Advance toward Cashtown and Gettysburg: *REL WP*, 574–75; Coddington, 197 (REL sensed battle was imminent); Freeman, 3:62–65 ("General Meade will commit no blunder"). Camp at Greeenwood, news from Hill: *EPA FFC*, 230; *REL WP*, 575; Coddington, 263–64; Freeman, 3:65. **Gettysburg, July 1.** REL to Cashtown: REL upset about Stuart: ibid., 3:66; Long, 275; Fremantle, *Diary*, 202 ("pretty tidy bunch"); Coddington, 280–81; Longstreet, *From Manassas to Appomattox*, 357 ("I cannot think"); Pfanz, 22 ("nothing for three days"). REL to Gettysburg, battle west of town: *REL WP*, 575–76; Fremantle, 203–05; Freeman, 3:69–71; Coddington, 266–95, 309–10. REL on Seminary Ridge: *REL WP*, 576; *B&L*, 3:339; Freeman, 3:71–72. REL's conference with Ewell and Early: ibid., 77–80; Coddington, 364–65. REL back on Seminary Ridge, Ewell and Culp's Hill: *REL WP*, 576; *EPA FFC*, 234; Freeman, 3:80–83; Coddington, 365–67. REL's anxiety and diarrhea: Coddington, 361–62; Pfanz, 4. **Gettysburg, July 2.** REL's uniform, breakfast, scouts: Fremantle, 198; Freeman, 3:86; Pfanz, 4, 104, 106. REL to observation post on Seminary Ridge: ibid., 104–05; Freeman, 3:86. Some sources claim that REL's argument with Longstreet about fighting at Gettysburg took place on the late afternoon of July 1. Fremantle, in his diary, said it occurred in the early morning of July 2, and that seems to fit the logic of events. My account draws from Fremantle, 205–06; *B&L*, 3:339–40; Longstreet, 358–59; Longstreet to an uncle, July 24, 1863, *Southern Historical Society Papers* (1878), 5:54; *The Annals of the War Written by Leading Participants North and South* (reprint of original ed., Dayton, Ohio: Mornside Bookshop, 1988), 421; Taylor, *Four Years with Lee*, 77; Wert, *Longstreet*, 257–58. Hill and

Hood came up, whittling of sticks, scouting reports: Fremantle, 205–06; Pfanz, 106–07; Coddington, 374. REL's decision to attack by the round tops: *REL WP*, 577; *B&L*, 3:341; Pfanz, 106. Longstreet's objection, REL walked off: Freeman, 3:89; Pfanz, 112; Fremantle, 296n–97n. REL's orders to Ewell: *REL WP*, 577; Freeman, 3:91–92; Pfanz, 112. Longstreet still on Seminary Ridge, REL's anger: Wert, 268; *Annals of the War*, 311. Longstreet told Hood he "never liked to go into battle with one boot off" (Fremantle, 297n), but it seems highly likely he would tell REL the same thing. Alexander: *EPA FFC*, 235; Freeman, *Lee's Lieutenants*, 2:xliii. REL at overlook, what he could see, chafed at delay: Freeman, 3:95–97; Long, 281–82; Fremantle, 207–08. Cannonade: ibid., 207–08. Longstreet's attack: ibid., 208; *REL WP*, 577–78; *B&L*, 3:340–41; *Annals of the War*, 423–29; Coddington, 427–45; Freeman, 3:99–102; Pfanz, 390ff. REL's assessment, casualties: Coddington, 443 ("partial success," "concert of action"); Pfanz, 429, 431, Freeman, 3:103; Longstreet, 375 ("Tell father"). Stuart's arrival: Thomas, *Bold Dragoon*, 246 ("Well, General"), 247; *REL WP*, 480–81, 580–81; Freeman, 3:105. Moon-lit night, REL's orders to renew the attack: *EPA FFC*, 244; *REL WP*, 578–79; Coddington, 454–56, 466; Fremantle, 205 ("contempt" for the enemy). REL's diarrhea: Dowdey, *Lee*, 383–84. **Gettysburg, July 3.** REL's contretemps with Longstreet: *Annals of the War*, 429; Richard Rollins (ed.), *Pickett's Charge: Eye-Witness Accounts* (Redondo Beach, Cal.: Rank and File Publications, 1994), 12; Wert, 283; Freeman, 3:107; Coddington, 456–58. REL's decision to launch a frontal attack: Rollins, 55, 58; Coddington, 459–60, 463, 465; Long, 287–88; George R. Stewart, *Pickett's Charge: A Microhistory of the Final Attack at Gettysburg, July 3, 1863* (Boston: Houghton Mifflin, 1959), 7–22. Longstreet's objections, REL's retort: *B&L*, 3:342–43; Longstreet, 386–87; Rollins, 12; Wert, 283; Stewart, 83 (Napoleon III at Solferino). Assaulting force: Rollins, xxi-xxiii, 3–4; Coddington, 460–62, 520; Freeman, 3:114 (REL rode length of attacking force three times). Sources put the strength of the assaulting columns from 11,900 to about 14,000 men. Pickett description: Freeman, *Lee's Lieutenants*, 2:xi, 491; Foote, *Civil War*, 2:531–32. Strength and description of rebel guns: Coddington, 462 (159 guns); Rollins, 368–70; Stewart, 33–34. Description of bombardment: Rollins, 84–85, 89–90, 97, 99, 103, 162, 184, 248 ("loose grass, leaves, and twigs arose from six to eight inches above the ground"), 253–54, 349; Haskell, *Haskell of Gettysburg*, 152–53; Stewart, 125 (cannonade began at 1:07 p.m.), 127, 130–31, 137–38, 159, 260–61; Gary W. Gallagher (ed.), *Two Witnesses at Gettysburg: The Personal Accounts of Whitelaw Reid and A. J. L. Fremantle* (St. James, N.Y.: Brandywine Press, 1994), 65–66;

EPA FFC, 257–58. The charge: *REL WP*, 580; Stewart, 178–252; Rollins, xxiii–xxiv, 9–10, 14, 131–32, 147, 156, 165, 174; Gallagher, 70; Fremantle, 212; *B&L*, 3:346–47; *EPA FFC*, 262; G. W. Finley, "With Pickett at Cemetery Ridge," in Vickers (ed.), *Under Both Flags*, 306–09. REL during the charge: Coddington, 526; Freeman, 3:128; *EPA FFC*, 265. Aftermath: Fremantle, 214–16 ("all my fault," "a sad day for us," "Uncle Robert will get us"); *EPA FFC* ("all good men"); Stewart, 256–57, and Rollins, 335 (REL's exchange with Pickett); *B&L*, 3:346 ("It was my fault"). Stuart's failure: Coddington, 521–23; McPherson, *Battle Cry of Freedom*, 663. REL's decision to withdraw, casualties: *REL WP*, 581, 563. REL to Imboden, storm, Imboden's departure: *B&L*, 3:422, 425. REL to Mary and to Davis: *REL WP*, 542, 543–44, 547–48.

34. **Lincoln.** AL at telegraph office: *AL DBD*, 3:194; Bates, *Lincoln in the Telegraph Office*, 155–56; *ALCW*, 6:314. AL's anger at Meade: *ATR RAL*, 402 ("Is that all?"); *ALCW*, 6:318, 341; *JH D&L*, 67; *CWL*, 273. News of Vicksburg: *GWD*, 1:364; *ALCW*, 321; Nicolay, *Lincoln's Secretary*, 102. AL pressed Meade to pursue Lee: *ALCW*, 6:319. AL's rage at Meade's failure to destroy Lee's army: *GWD*, 1:368, 369–71, 374, 381; *NB WLT*, 80–82, 91–94; *JH D&L*, 67, 69; *ALCW*, 6:327–28, 328n, 341. AL's letter to Grant: ibid., 326. USG did get drunk once during the siege. See Dana's account in New York *Sun* (Jan. 28, 1887); Dana, *Recollections*, 9, 90–91; *USGP*, 8:322n, 325n; Wilson, *Rawlins*, 128–29. AL's remark on apocryphal story about Grant's brand of whiskey in Albert Chandler, "Lincoln and the Telegrapher" (ed. E. B. Long), *American Heritage* (Apr. 1961), 34. Medical conditions at Gettysburg: Adams, *Doctors in Blue*, 83–84; Majorie Barstow Greenbie, *Lincoln's Daughters of Mercy* (New York: G. P. Putnam's Sons, 1944), 169–70 ("Nurses, matrons").

35. **Cornelia Hancock.** CH's autobiography and letters housed in the University of Michigan Library were published in *After Gettysburg: Letters of Cornelia Hancock, 1863–1868* (ed. Henrietta Stratton Jaquette, New York: Thomas Y. Crowell Co., 1956). I've used the unedited original manuscripts, and my references are to them. CH would serve her country: CH's autobiography (typescript), 1–2, CHP UM. CH's departure for Philadelphia and excitement there: ibid., 2–3, 1 (CH's father). CH's encounter with Dix: ibid., 3–4; CH to cousin, July 7, 1863, CHP UM; Wittenmyer, *Under the Guns*, 120–21 (Dix description). Train to Gettysburg: Georgeanna Woolsey, "What We Did at Gettysburg," in Frank Moore, *Women of the War, Their Heroism and Self-Sacrifice* (Hartford: S. S. Scranton & Co., 1867), 132 (description of landscape, field where cavalry fought). Detritus of war in Gettysburg: CH autobiography, 4;

Woolsey, 139; Georgeanna Woolsey Bacon and Eliza Woolsey Howland, *Letters of a Family During the War for the Union, 1861–1865* (2 vols. [New Haven: Tuttle, Morehouse & Taylor, c.1899]), 2:533; Mrs. Edmund A. Souder, *Leaves from the Battlefield of Gettysburg: A Series of Letters from a Field Hospital* (Philadelphia: Caxton Press of C. Sherman Son & Co., 1864), 17, 22–23, 52–53. Church hospital (probably the Trinity German Reformed Church): CH autobiography, 4; Gregory A. Coco, *A Vast Sea of Misery: A Historical Guide to the Union and Confederate Field Hospitals at Gettysburg, July 1–November 20, 1863* (Gettysburg, Penn.: Thomas Publications, 1988), 13. CH to Second Corps hospital: CH autobiography, 5–7; Coco, 91–92 (location of hospital), 94; CH to cousin, July 7, 1863, CH UM; CH to dear sister, July 8, 1863, ibid. (casualties). CH's work at Second Corps hospital: CH to cousin and dear sister, ibid.; Coco, xvi ("my legs [were] swollen"); Greenbie, 172 ("I feel like a new person"); Anna Holstein, *Three Years in the Field Hospitals of the Army of the Potomac* (Philadelphia: J. B. Lippincott & Co., 1867), 10–11, 38–39; CH to dear Mother, July 21, 1863, CHP UM. Camp Letterman: Coco, 167. CH there: CH to dear sister, Aug. 16, 1863, to Dear Sallie [her niece], Aug. 18, 1863, to dear Mother, Aug. 23 and Sept., 1863, CHP UM.

36. **Lee.** Criticism of the army: Freeman, *Lee*, 3:146; REL WP, 560 (letter to Mary), 564–65. REL's contempt for criticism: REL's conversation with Allan, RELC WL, and printed in Gallagher, *Lee*, 15. Gettysburg was a success: *REL WP*, 565; Long, *Memoirs of Lee*, 296; Coddington, 573 (REL upset Union plans for a summer offensive); Gallagher, 22 ("a sucking dove"); Jones, *Personal Reminiscences of General Robert E. Lee*, 156 ("If I had had Stonewall Jackson with me," "establishment of our independence"); Freeman, 3:161, quotes a more cautious version of the remark about Jackson; but the quotation in Jones corresponds to REL's campaign objectives. REL rejected Pickett's report: *OR*, ser. 1, 27 (pt. 3), 1075; Freeman, 3:146. REL's prayers for his failings: *REL WP*, 560, 590. REL to Davis: ibid., 590.

37. **Davis.** JD's reply to Lee: *JD LPS*, 5:589–90; *JDP*, 9:337–38. JD's assessment of Gettysburg: *JD R&F*, 2:377–78. JD on Vicksburg loss: Josiah Gorgas, *The Journals of Josiah Gorgas, 1857–1878* (ed. Sarah Woolfolk Wiggins, Tuscaloosa: University of Alabama Press, 1995), 74 ("Yes, from a want of provisions inside"). JD on heinous Yankees: *JD LPS*, 5:549–50, *JDMP*, 1:329; Escott, *After Secession*, 191–92. Treatment of Union Negro troops: Cornish, *Sable Arm*, 161–62.

38. Douglass. FD's recruiting efforts: *FDP*, 3:590–98; *FD L&W*, 3:368. Blacks at Port Hudson: Cornish, *Sable Arm*, 142–44; Joseph T. Glatthaar, *Forged in Battle: The Civil War Alliance of Black Soldiers and White Officers* (New York: Free Press, 1990), 123–30; New York *Times* (June 11, 1863). Backs at Milliken's Bend: *USGP*, 8:327n–328n; Glatthaar, 130–35; Cornish, 144–45; Quarles, *Negro in the Civil War*, 220–24; *USGM*, 1:545; Dana, *Recollections*, 93 ("The bravery of the blacks"). Blacks at Battery Wagner: *FD L&W*, 4:220, 368 (black prisoners murdered); McPherson, *Negro's Civil War*, 190 ("perfect hail"); Emilio, *Brave Black Regiment*, 67–104; FD, *Life and Times*, 342 ("After that assault we heard no more"). Unequal pay and treatment: Cornish, 183–184, 187–88, Glatthaar, 65, 170; *FD L&W*, 3:372 ("meanness, ingratitude and cruelty of the government"). FD to Stearns: ibid., 3:367–69. AL's "Order of Retaliation": *ALCW*, 6:357; *FD L&W*, 3:369 ("What ought to have come"). Stearns urged FD to see Lincoln: Blight, *Douglass' Civil War*, 168. FD's interview with Lincoln: Washington *Post* (Feb. 13, 1888); *FD L&W*, 36–37, 606–08; FD's speech in *Liberator* (Jan. 29, 1864); Garrison's speech in ibid. (July 7, 1865); *ATR RAL*, 185–88; FD, *Life and Times*, 346–50, 541–42.

39. Lincoln. AL on Douglass: G. S. Borritt, *Lincoln and the Economics of the American Dream* (Memphis: Memphis State University Press, 1978), 174 ("There was a similarity"); *FD L&W*, 3:45 ("one of the most meritorious men"). Equal pay for black troops: Cornish, *Sable Arm*, 156 (Holt's letter to Stanton), 189. Grant and black soldiers: *ALCW*, 6:374; *USGP*, 9:196–97; Hurlbut to AL, Aug. 15, 1863, RTLC ("great river will bristle"). New York City draft riot: Nevins, *War for the Union*, 3:119–27; McPherson, *Negro's Civil War*, 69–75; Douglass, *Life and Times*, 356. AL refused to suspend the draft: *ALCW*, 6:369–70 ("butcher drives bullocks"), 381, 390–91. Obstructionist judges, AL's defense of draft, suspension of habeas corpus: ibid., 6:444–49, 451; *GWD*, 1:432–33. AL's public letter to Democrats: *ALCW*, 6:406–10; *GWD*, 1:470 ("good deal of emotion"). Hay praised Lincoln's letter in a letter of his own to Nicolay (*JH D&L*, 91). We may assume that Hay would tell AL the same thing. Sumner's praise: Donald, *Sumner and the Rights of Man*, 166; see also Sumner, *Selected Letters*, 2:190–91. Fall state elections: Thomas and Hyman, *Stanton*, 294–95; *GWD*, 1:469–70; Voegeli, *Free But Not Equal*, 118–32; Thomas, *Lincoln*, 398–99 ("Glory to God in the highest"); *ACLW*, 7:24 ("native depravity"). Livermore's request to AL: Oct. 11, 1863, RTLC. Arnold's intercession: *ML MSW*, 564; Isaac N. Arnold, *The Life of Abraham Lincoln* (4th ed., Lincoln: University of Nebraska Press, 1994), 267.

40. Livermore. Sanitary fair inception and gathering of articles: *ML MSW*, 411–16; Henshaw, *Our Branch and Its Tributaries*, 210–16; Ruegamer, "Paradise of Exceptional Women," 89; Greenbie, *Lincoln's Daughters of Mercy*, 187; William Quentin Maxwell, *Lincoln's Fifth Wheel: The Political History of the United States Sanitary Commission* (New York: Longman's, Green & Co., 1956, 224; ML to Lincoln, Oct. 11, 1863, RTLC. Difficulty with the builder of a temporary hall: *ML MSW*, 435–36. The fair: ibid., 417–56; *Chicago Tribune* (Oct. 28, 1863); Henshaw, 215–24, 315; ML to Lincoln, Nov. 26, 1863, RTLC ("During the progress"); Northwestern Sanitary Fair, Records, Chicago Historical Society. Fair mania: *ML MSW*, 455–56; Maxwell, 224, 226. ML and Hoge nationally famous: Henshaw, 94; Ruegamer, 90–91; ML MSW, 160. Women's expanded opportunities: Oates, *Woman of Valor*, 212, 376, 508; Mary Elizabeth Massey, *Bonnet Brigades* (New York: Alfred A. Knopf, 1966), 131–52. Women in the fields: *MSW*, 145–46.

41. Lincoln. On sanitary fairs: *ALCW*, 7:254. Troubles with Meade: ibid., 6:466–67, 518, 519n; *GWD*, 1:439–40 ("same old story"). AL's thanks to Burnside: *ALCW*, 6:439. Rosecrans: Williams, *Lincoln and His Generals*, 276.

42. Davis. Concern for Chattanooga, JD to Bragg: *JD LPS*, 6:23, 30, 36. JD's conference with Lee: I've simulated what the two told one another based on their views and actions as given in ibid., 36; Strode, *Davis*, 2:474; *REL WP*, 594, 596; Piston, *Lee's Tarnished General*, 66–68. Bragg's masterful plan: Woodworth, *Davis and His Generals*, 230, 233. Bragg's reports from Chickamauga: *JBJ WCD*, 2:49; *JDP*, 9:404–07.

43. Lincoln. Chickamauga: *GWD*, 1:439 ("awake and watchful"); *JH D&L*, 106; *CWL*, 280–81; *ACLW*, 6:469 ("Go to Rosecrans"), 474n–75n ("serious disaster," terrible defeat); 474 ("Please relieve my anxiety"), 475n ("brave and determined"); *OR*, ser. 1, 30 (pt. 1): 192–93 (Dana's report). Burnside's folly: *ALCW*, 6:480–81; Bates, *Lincoln in the Telegraph Office*, 202 ("Damn Jonesboro!"). Ride back from Soldiers' Home, War Department conference: *JH D&L*, 93. Hooker sent west: *ALCW*, 6:486; Long, *Civil War Day by Day*, 413–14; McPherson, *Battle Cry of Freedom*, 675 (twenty thousand men moved by train in eleven days). Rosecrans's failings: *OR*, ser. 1, 30 (pt. 1): 202 ("greatly lacking"); *JH D&L*, 106 ("stunned like a duck"). Command reorganization, Rosecrans relieved: *USGP*, 9:296–97, 297n–98n; Richardson, *Personal History of Grant*, 353 ("Lincoln supplanted one hero").

44. Davis. Poisonous bickering: *OR*, ser. 1, 30 (pt. 4), 705–06; Piston, *Lee's Tarnished Lieutenant*, 74; Woodworth, *Davis and His Generals*, 238–39; *JD LPS*, 6:55 ("The opposition to you"). Deserters and soldiers otherwise "evading duty": Ella Lonn, *Desertion During the Civil War* (reprint of 1928 ed., Gloucester, Mass.: Peter Smith, 1966), 29–30; Escott, *After Secession*, 126–27 JD's objectives on trip west: *JD LPS*, 6:57–58. JD at Missionary Ridge: ibid., 62, 70; Woodworth, 242–44; Strode, *Davis*, 2:481–82. JD at Bridgeport and Selma, Ala., instructions to Bragg, learns of Grant: ibid., 2:484–85, 490.

45. Grant. Situation in Chattanooga: Dana, *Recollections*, 124, 126; *USGM*, 2:17–24; *AB MHG*, 1:422–25; Bruce Catton, *Grant Takes Command* (Boston: Little, Brown & Co., 1969), 35; *USGP*, 9:302 ("Hold Chattanooga"), 302n. USG to Stevenson: Peter Cozzens, *The Shipwreck of Their Hopes: The Battles for Chattanooga* (Urbana: University of Illinois Press, 1994), 43; Catton, 35–36; Richardson, *Personal History of Grant*, 353. USG's injury: ibid., 348–49; *USGM*, 1:581–82; *USGP*, 9:222n, 238, 273. Horseback trip to Chattanooga: Dana, *Recollections*, 126, 129; *AB MHG*, 1:442; *USGM*, 2:28; Burr, *Life and Deeds of Grant*, 450; Headley, *Grant*, 242–43; Wilson, *Rawlins*, 165; *OR*, ser. 1, 31 (pt. 1): 69; Cozzens, 45 ("I have seen human misery"). USG and staff at Thomas's headquarters: *HP CWG*, 1, 5; Wilson, 165–66; James Harrison Wilson, *Under the Old Flag* (2 vols., New York: D. Appleton & Co., 1912), 1:273–75; Young, *Around the World with Grant*, 295 (USG's opinion of Thomas, old army joke); *USGM*, 2:28–29; Catton, 49. Baldy Smith description: from photographs and *USGP*, 10:475. Conditions in Chattanooga: *AB MHG*, 1:442–43; *SC TYWG*, 138. USG's reconnaissance: *AB MHG*, 1:442–43; *USGP*, 9:314; *USGM*, 2:34; Villard, *Memoirs*, 2: 180–82, 255–56. Opening the supply line: *USGP*, 9:556–58; Wilson, 169–70; Catton, 53–54, 56; *USGM*, 2:36–38; *AB MHG*, 1:442–45. USG's headquarters, USG to Julia: Garland, *Grant*, 244; Cozzens, 111; *USGP*, 9:334. Longstreet, Davis's visit: Dana, *Recollections*, 131; *AB MGH*, 1:461; *USGM*, 1:85–86. USG's plan to attack Bragg: Cozzens, 106–07; *USGM*, 2:96, Catton, 61; *USGP*, 9:371 ("The movement"). Thomas couldn't move: *AB MHG*, 1:463–64 ("unable to move," "a great disappointment"); *USGP*, 9:376, 559 ("I felt restless"). USG's order to Sherman: ibid., 9:380.

46. Sherman. Hated repairing railroads: Lewis, *Sherman*, 312; Marszalek, *Sherman*, 239–40. Willy: Ewing, *Sherman at War*, 118–22, 124; *WTSM*, 372–75; *USGP*, 9:274–75, *WTS HL*, 275–76, 278–79; WTS to John Sherman, Oct. 24, 1863, WTSP LC; Fellman, *Citizen Sherman*, 199, 201, 203. WTS with Grant: Catton, *Grant Takes Command*, 63 ("Take the chair of honor"). Reconnaissance: *WTSM*, 387 ("You're besieged"); *AB MHG*, 1:476. Grant's plan: *USGP*, 9:410–12, 560; Wilson, *Rawlins*, 171; Cozzens, *Shipwreck of Their Hopes*, 115, 145.

47. Lincoln. Preparing Gettysburg address: Frank L. Klement, "These Honored Dead: David Wills and the Soldiers' Cemetery at Gettysburg," *Lincoln Herald* (Fall, 1972), 123–31; *ALCW*, 7:17n; *NB WLT*, 252–53 ("short, short, short"); *ATR RAL*, 403 ("Well, I feel"); James Speed's statement in *Louisville Commercial* (Nov. 12, 1879). Departure: *ALCW*, 7:17–18; Turners, *Mary Lincoln*, 154–55; Randall, *Mary Lincoln*, 328–29; *AL DBD*, 3:220. At Wills's home: Klement, 129–30; Nicolay, *Lincoln's Secretary*, 175–77; *ALCW*, 7:16–17 ("In my position"); William E. Barton, *Lincoln at Gettysburg* (New York: Peter Smith, 1950), 60–65; Philip B. Kunhardt, Jr., *A New Birth of Freedom: Lincoln at Gettysburg* (Boston: Little, Brown & Co., 1983), 107–23, 185. Procession to Cemetery Hill: *JH D&L*, 121; Kunhardt, 155–64. Cemetery Hill, Everett's speech: Kunhardt, 181–211; Barton, 71–79. What AL actually said at Gettysburg: ibid., 81–83; Kunhardt, 214–20; *JH D&L*, 121; Klement, 130–31. Drafts of address, final version: *ALCW*, 7:16–23. Press criticisms: Kunhardt, 221. Everett's praise, AL's response: *ALCW*, 7:24, 25n. AL's illness: ibid., 25, 35; *JH D&L*, 128; Thomas, *Lincoln*, 403 ("now he had something he could give everybody").

48. Grant. Sherman's delay: *AB MHG*, 1:476; *USGP*, 9:421, 423, 426, 428–29. Deserter's report: ibid., 435, 560; *B&L*, 3:721; *USGM*, 2:54–64. Orchard Knobb: *B&L*, 3:721; Dana, *Recollections*, 137; *USGP*, 9:434; *AB MHG*, 1:489–90; Cozzens, *Shipwreck of Their Hopes*, 135. USG's plan: *USGM*, 2:95; USG claimed that he had 60,000 men, but Cozzens, 143, puts his force at 80,000 men. USG on parapet at Fort Wood, spectacle: *USGP*, 9:491, 495; Wilson, *Rawlins*, 171; *AB MHG*, 1:495. Battle of Lookout Mountain: *B&L*, 3:723; *USGP*, 9:441 ("Thomas's forces are confronting"), 442n (Meigs called it the "battle above the clouds"); *USGM*, 2:72–73; Dana, 139–40; *AB MHG*, 1:499–500; *SC TYWG*, 146; Wilson, *Under the Old Flag*, 1:293; Catton, *Grant Takes Command*, 69–74; Villard, *Memoirs*, 2:261. Sherman's claim about Tunnel Hill: Catton, 76–77; Cozzens, 200; *USGP*, 9:440, 443. Heavy fog, moonlight: *SC TYWG*, 144, Cozzens, 197. USG's plan for next day: *USGP*, 9:441–43, 443n; *USGM*, 2:75; *AB MHG*, 1:501. Brilliant sunrise, description of Missionary Ridge, Union flag atop Lookout Mountain: *SC TYWG*, 148–50; *AB MHG*, 1:503–04; *USGM*, 2:74; Dana, 140–41 (shell bursts and solid shot). Sherman's error, change of plans: Cozzens, 210, 217, 241; *USGP*, 9:446n, 561; *AB MHG*, 1:507; *USGM*, 2:78; Catton, 77.

Sherman's piecemeal attacks: Richardson, *Personal History of Grant*, 365; *SC TYWG*, 152 ("Driving our boys"); *USGP*, 9:562; *USGM*, 2:77; *AB MHG*, 1:504–05, Catton, 77–80; S. H. M. Byers, *With Fire and Sword* (New York: Neale Publishing Co., 1911), 106–07; Cozzens, 204–18, 224–35, 246–47; Wilson, *Rawlins*, 171. USG ordered Thomas to attack, Granger's delay: Wilson, *Rawlins*, 172–73; Wilson, *Flag*, 1:298; Garland, *Grant*, 249; Richardson, 365–66; *SC TYWG*, 153–54; *USGP*, 9:562–63; Cozzens, 246–48. Assaults against Missionary Ridge: *USGP*, 9:447n, 447–48, 563; Dana, 141–42; *B&L*, 3:725; *SC TYWG*, 149–50; Wilson, *Rawlins*, 173; *AB MHG*, 1:508; *B&L*, 3:725 ("Who ordered those men," "When those fellows get started"); E. Hannaford, *The Story of a Regiment: A History of the Campaigns, and Associations in the Field, of the Sixth Regiment Ohio Volunteer Infantry* (Cincinnati: published by the author, 1868), 508–09; Cozzens, 282, and Catton, 84 (USG bit on his cigar); Cozzens, 294 ("Chickamauga! Chickamauga!"); Richardson, 368 ("I'm going up there"). USG on top of Missionary Ridge: Dana, 14; Richardson, 369 ("Now we have a general!"), Wilson, *Flag*, 1:300 ("all we needed was a leader"); *USGP*, 9:446 ("I believe I'm not premature"), 451–52; *USGM*, 2:73 ("Remember Burnside"). Pursuit: *USGP*, 9:456, 496, 458, 563–64; Cozzens, 368–69, 384; *AB MHG*, 1:517–18, 524; Dana, 143. Wilson's criticism of Sherman, USG's defense: Wilson, *Rawlins*, 177; *USGP*, 9:561–62. Sherman to Burnside's relief: *USGP*, 9:473, 565; *USGM*, 2:92–94; AB MHG, 1:543; Cozzens, 354, 387.

49. Lee. Longstreet wanted REL in the West: Sorrel, *Recollections*, 259. REL's maneuvers against Meade: *REL WP*, 513–14, 534, 584, 587–88, 609, 612–14, 620–22, 632. Appalled at wanton destruction: ibid., 636, 513, 584, 588. Desertions, REL's rheumatic pains: ibid., 587, 591, 595, 623–24. REL missed Longstreet: *B&L*, 3:349 ("If I only had taken your counsel"). REL's interview with Captain Blackford: W. W. Blackford, *War Years with Jeb Stuart* (New York: Charles Scribner's Sons, 1946), 245–46. Meade's escape: *B&L*, 4:240 ("I'm too old").

50. Lincoln. Thanks to Grant and his army: *ALCW*, 7:53. Early reconstruction efforts in Tennessee: ibid., 6:440, 440n–441n, 469. In Louisiana: ibid., 5:504–05, 6:365, 7:66–67, 102; Trefousse, *Radical Republicans*, 280–82; Herman Belz, *Reconstructing the Union* (Ithaca, N.Y.: Cornell University Press, 1969), 145. Sumner's objections: Donald, *Sumner and the Rights of Man*, 117–22; Sumner, *Selected Letters*, 2:105–06 (state-suicide theory). Blair-Sumner split: Donald, 137–41; Smith, *Francis Preston Blair Family in Politics*, 2:244–24; *JH D&L*, 112–13. Washburne's visit, AL's support of Grant, AL read his message and proclamation:

Washburne to his wife, Dec. 6, 1863, EWP NLHC; *USGP*, 9:503n, 523, 523n. AL's message and Proclamation of Amnesty and Reconstruction, *ALCW*, 7:48–56. Reactions: *JH D&L*, 131–35; *NB WLT*, 150–51; Sumner, *Selected Letters*, 216–17; Edward Magdol, *Owen Lovejoy: Abolitionist in Congress* (New Brunswick: Rutgers University Press, 1967), 379. Louisiana reconstruction: *ALCW*, 7:66–67, 89–91, 95, 123–25, 161–62, 217–18, 243 ("I barely suggest"), 269–70, 8:30–31, 106–07, 402, 8:402–04 (defense of Louisiana government); Peyton McCrary, *Abraham Lincoln and Reconstruction: The Louisiana Experiment* (Princeton: Princeton University Press, 1978), 186–270; Jefferson Davis Bragg, *Louisiana in the Confederacy* (Baton Rouge: Louisiana State University Press, 1941), 212–13, 290–91; John D. Winters, *Civil War in Louisiana* (Baton Rouge: Louisiana State University Press, 1963), 394–95. Congressional opposition: Donald, 179–80; Nevins, *War for the Union*, 3:417–44. See also the controversial Wadsworth letter in *ALCW*, 7:101–03; and discussion in Trefousse, 286.

51. Douglass. Banks's regime: McPherson, *Struggle for Equality*, 289–90; *FD L&W*, 3:429n. FD's anger at Banks's system and AL, need for black suffrage and full citizenship: ibid., 3:42, 394, 404, 406, 420, 4:158, 164; *FDP*, 3:604–05.

52. Davis. Lincoln's plan of reconstruction: *JD R&F*, 2:240, 249–53, 259; *JD LPS*, 6:145–46; *VD JD*, 2:455–56. Bragg's disaster, Bragg relieved: Woodworth, *Davis and His Generals*, 253; Strode, *Davis*, 2:496–97. Lee declined western command: *JD LPS*, 6:93; *REL WP*, 642. JD's message: *JD LPS*, 6:93–128. Bitter attacks against JD: Davis, *Davis*, 529–30; Strode, 2:506. Conference with Lee, Johnston restored to command in the West: *REL WP*, 642–43; Strode, 2:503; *JD LPS*, 6:132, 135–37; *OR*, ser. 1, 32 (pt. 2), 510–11, 559–60; Woodworth, 257–59 ("difficulties appear to be in the way").

53. Chesnut. Wigfalls: *MCCW*, 498–99. Tea at rebel White House, MC on Davis: ibid., 504, 509, 549, 551; Woodworth, *Davis and His Generals*, 280 (Davis's dyspepsia, Varina's lunch trays). Lees: *MCCW*, 450, 504, 516, 569, 573. Sam Hood description, summer 1863 love affair with Sally "Buck" Preston: Richard M. McMurry, *John Bell Hood and the War for Southern Independence* (reprint of 1982 ed., Lincoln: University of Nebraska Press, 1992), 33, 69, 83; *MCCW*, 430, 509, 574 (description of Buck Preston); Mullenfeld, *Mary Chesnut*, 119. Hood's visit with MC: *MCCW*, 502. Dinner party, Preston's flirtations: ibid., 505. Hood's precarious romance with Buck Preston: ibid., 509–10, 515–16, 551–52,

559–60, 561–65, 576, 592, 616, 708; McMurry, 83–92. MC on the winter reprieve: *MCCW*, 519, 523, 607.

THE WINDS OF 'SIXTY-FOUR

1. **Sherman.** Genesis and objectives of Meridian raid: *WTSM*, 416–19; WTS to McPherson, Jan. 17, and WTS to John Sherman, Jan. 19, 1863, WTSP; *OR*, ser. 1, 17 (pt. 2), 260–61 ("We cannot change the hearts of these people"); *SL*, 230–32 (slaveholding class); Marszalek, *Sherman*, 235, 249, 252. The raid: *USGM*, 419–23; Marszalek, 252–54; Lewis, *Sherman*, 333–34; *WTS HL*, 287–88.

2. **Davis.** Manpower woes: *JBJ WCD*, 2:175. Cleburn proposal, slave impressments: Robert F. Durden, *The Gray and the Black: The Confederate Debate on Emancipation* (Baton Rouge: Louisiana State University Press, 1972), 51–66. JD to Vance: *JD LPS*, 6:141–42, 144–46. JD's suspension of writ, protests from Georgia: ibid., 6:168; Louise Biles Hill, *Joseph E. Brown and the Confederacy* (Chapel Hill: University of North Carolina Press, 1939), 206–13; Thomas E. Schott, *Alexander H. Stephens of Georgia,: A Biography* (Baton Rouge: Louisiana State University Press, 1988), 392–409; Strode, *Davis*, 3:9, 18–19; Escott, *After Secession*, 204–05. Bragg: Davis, *Davis*, 542–43. Yankee cavalry raid, Dahlgren's captured documents: *MCCW*, 578 ("It is not the army"); *JBJ WCD*, 2:162–69; *JD R&F*, 2:425; *VD JD*, 2:467–70; Starr, *Federal Cavalry*, 2:57–65; *Richmond Sentinel* (Mar. 5, 1864); *Richmond Dispatch* (Mar. 5, 1864); David E. Long, "Lincoln the Assassin?" *The Lincoln Newsletter* (summer 1994), 1, 4–5; *B&L*, 4:95–96. Lee's reaction, protest to Meade: *REL WP*, 678; *B&L*, 4:96; Freeman, *Lee*, 3:219n. JD's and the Confederacy's modes of retaliation: my account draws heavily from William A. Tidwell, with James O. Hall, and David Winfred Gaddy, *Come Retribution: The Confederate Secret Service and the Assassination of Lincoln* (Jackson: University Press of Mississippi, 1988), 189–207, 236–38, 246–51; also *JD LPS*, 6:237–38; William Hanchett, *The Lincoln Murder Conspiracies* (Urbana: University of Illinois Press, 1983), 15–16, 29, 33–34; *The Assassination and History of the Conspiracy* (reprint of J. R. Hawley & Co., ed., 1865, New York: Hobbs, Dorman & Co., 1965), 38–41. Other forms of retaliation that passed before JD's eye were proposals to abduct and even assassinate Lincoln. See *BP AL*, 52, 375; Tidwell, 233, 235–36, 247–48, 251; Hanchett, 29, 30, 32.

3. **John Wilkes Booth.** On Lincoln's vile deeds: JWB's memorandum, Apr. 13, 14, 1865, in *TJS*, 1:310; JWB's letter, "To Whom It May Concern,"

in Philadelphia *Enquirer* (Apr. 19, 1865), and republished in Stanley Kimmel, *The Mad Booths of Maryland* (2nd revised and enlarged ed., New York: Dover Publications, 1969), 396–98, in George S. Bryan, *The Great American Myth* (New York: Carrick & Evans, 1940), 240–43, and in *JWBW*, 124–27; *ABC UB*, 114–15. See also JWB's December 1860, speech on Lincoln's election and secession in *JWBW*, 55–64. JWB played before Lincoln, preferred that a Negro had applauded him: Kimmel, 393–94. JWB at St. Timothy's Hall: *ABC UB*, 58–59, 156–57; Bryan, 81; Kimmel, 153. Gypsy's hand-reading: *ABC UB*, 57. JWB's quarrels with Edwin: *ABC UB*, 114; Bryan, 141; Kimmel, 176. JWB's threat to James Clarke: *New York Herald* (June 27, 1909), magazine section; Bryan, 141–42. JWB's conversation with Asia, JWB a rebel agent: *ABD UB*, 115–17; Hanchett, 42; *BP AL*, vi.

4. **Lincoln.** Murder conspiracy: *FBC ILAL*, 63; *New York Tribune* (Mar. 19, 1864). AL's dislike of military guards: *FBC ILAL*, 64–67; Bryan, *Great American Myth*, 57–65. Arnold and Thirteenth Amendment: Arnold, *Life of Lincoln*, 352, 354, 356. AL and reelection: Brooks's letter in Sacramento *Union* (Oct. 31, 1863); Bryan, 127 ("eating my life out"); Wendell Phillips Garrison and Francis Jackson Garrison, *William Lloyd Garrison, 1805–1879: The Story of His Life* (reprint of 1885–89 ed., 4 vols., New York: Negro Universities Press, 1969), 4:97–98 ("he is the best possible"). Republican opposition to AL: *SC ILC*, 24–27; Richardson, *Personal History of Grant*, 407, 434. Chase boom: *ALRW*, 2; *SC ILC*, 5, 24–27, 32, 176, 183–84; Bates, *Diary*, 310. Pomeroy circular: New York *Herald* (Feb. 22 and 24, 1864); *ALCW*, 7:200n–01n; Nicolay to Theresa, Feb. 28, 1864; JGNP; Randall and Richard N. Current, *Lincoln the President*, 4:85–110; *SC ILC*, 210–11; *CWL*, 310–11; Frederick J. Blue, *Salmon P. Chase: A Life in Politics* (Kent, Ohio: Kent State University Press, 1987), 222–26. AL's worries about Grant's presidential aspirations, Jones visit: *USGP*, 9:543n. Grant's promotion to lieutenant general: *USGP*, 9:523.

5. **Grant.** USG's worries about his promotion: ibid., 9:543n; Rawlins to Washburne, Jan. 20, 1864, EWP LC. USG to Sherman, Sherman's response: *USGP*, 10:187, 187n. USG's arrival in Washington: *NB WLT*, 133–34; *HP CWG*, 22; Catton, *Grant Takes Command*, 124–25. USG at White House: Nicolay memorandum, Mar. 8, 1864, JGNP; *USGM*, 2:122–23; *HP CWG*, 20–21; *NB WLT*, 135; *AL DBD*, 3:245. Train ride to Meade's headquarters, description of countryside: *AB MHG*, 2:40; Oates, *Woman of Valor*, 59; Catton, 131. USG knew only two tunes: *HP CWG*, 83. Meade description: Dana, *Recollections*, 171; *TL WG&M*, 6;

AB MHG, 2:369; Morris Schaff, *The Battle of the Wilderness* (Boston: Houghton Mifflin Co., 1910), 40–41. USG's interview with Meade: dialogue based on descriptions of the interview in *USGM*, 2:116–17; *AB MHG*, 2:11–12, 15–17; Andrew A. Humphreys, *The Virginia Campaign of '64 and '65: The Army of the Potomac and the Army of the James* (New York: Charles Scribner's Sons, 1883), 5; *HP CWG*, 29. USG back in Washington: ibid., 22; *FC ILAL*, 56–57. USG's meeting with Sherman: *AB MHG* 2:23. USG and Sherman on train to Cincinnati: *JGM*, 128–29; *USGM*, 2:120; *USGP*, 9:500–01, 501n–02n, 10:200–01; 273–74; *AB MHG*, 2:40; David Long, *The Jewel of Liberty: Abraham Lincoln's Reelection and the End of Slavery* (Mechanicsburg, Penn.: Stackpole Books, 1994), 197 (USG had topographical maps).

6. **Lincoln**. AL's meeting with Grant: dialogue based on descriptions of the meeting in *USGM*, 2:122–23; *AB MHG*, 2:13–14; *HP CWG*, 26–27; Williams, *Lincoln and His Generals*, 304–06; *JH D&L*, 178–79 ("those not skinning"); Brooks Simpson, *"Let Us Have Peace": Ulysses S. Grant and the Politics of War and Reconstruction* (Chapel Hill: University of North Carolina Press, 1991), 54–57; Stoddard, *Inside the White House*, 220–22; *ALRW*, 426–27. Williams says that, despite Grant's claim, AL did not give him "a free hand" in conducting military operations; AL did not want to know the details of those operations, Williams points out, but he did want to know about Grant's strategic plans.

7. **Grant**. USG at Brandy Station, army reorganization: *HP CWG*, 24; Schaff, *Battle of the Wilderness*, 52; Humphreys, *Virginia Campaign of '64 and '65*, 3; *USGM*, 2:128. USG's reconnaissance, description of countryside: Schaff, 52, 57, *AB MHG*, 2:40; Gordon C. Rhea, *The Battle of the Wilderness, May 5–6, 1864* (Baton Rouge: Louisiana State University Press, 1994), 30. Opinions of Lee: *TL WG&M*, 87; *USGM*, 2:292; Dana, *Recollections*, 192. After the war, USG said of Lee: "The illusion that nothing but heavy odds beat him will not stand the ultimate light of history" (Young, *Around the World with Grant*, 459). Hancock description: *TL WG&M*, 82, 107; Schaff, 42. Warren description: Rhea, 39, 95. Sedgwick description: Schaff, 43. Sheridan's arrival, description: *USGM*, 2:133; *AB MHG*, 2:42; *TL WG&M*, 82; Young, 297; Schaff, 43; *HP CWG*, 24; Roy Morris, Jr., *Sheridan: The Life and Wars of General Phil Sheridan* (New York: Crown Publishers, 1992), 1 (head shaped like a bullet, Lincoln's description of Sheridan). Details of USG's grand plan: *USGP*, 10: 236–37, 242, 245–47, 251–52, 257, 273–75, 327; 14:165, 171; *AB MHG*, 2:46; *USGM*, 2:131–32. USG's plan to turn Lee's flank: *USGP*. 10:274–75, 309, 371; Humphreys, 6, 12–13; *HP CWG*, 37; Rhea,

32, 49–58. Fort Pillow massacre, suspension of prisoner exchange: *USGP*, 10:284–85, 285n; McPherson, *Battle Cry of Freedom*, 792, 794; Simpson, 58–59. Banks's disaster: *USGP*, 10:340, 341n, 342, 374; Williams, *Lincoln and His Generals*, 310. USG's birthday: *USGP*, 10:363. USG's dates to commence operations: ibid., 10:364, 371; *USGM*, 2:140. USG and Lincoln exchange dispatches: *ALCW*, 7:324; *USGP*, 10:380.

8. **Chesnut.** Death of Mrs. Chesnut, James's promotion, Varina to MC: *MCCW*, 594. Joe Davis's death and funeral: ibid., 601–02, 609; *VD JD*, 2:496–97. Mulberry in spring: *MCCW*, 606. Dreadful work of killing would commence again: ibid., 609, 625.

9. **Lee.** REL on Clark's Mountain, May 2: *B&L*, 4:118. REL's preference for offensive, Longstreet's return, REL's dislike of defensive: *REL WP*, 698–700, 703; Wert, *Longstreet*, 372; Clifford Dowdey, *Lee's Last Campaign: The Story of Lee and His Men Against Grant—1864* (reprint of 1960 ed., Lincoln: University of Nebraska Press, 1993), 4–5; Jones, *Personal Reminiscences*, 40 ("We must destroy Grant's army," "a question of time"); see also *REL WP*, 759–60. REL's officers dismissed Grant: *B&L*, 4:142. Longstreet on Grant: *HP CWG*, 46–47. REL's intention to inflict crippling casualties on Grant's forces and strengthen the northern Peace party: the dialogue is based on descriptions of REL's views in *RELD*, 160n, 161, 185; Herman Hattaway and Archer Jones, *How the North Won: A Military History of the Civil War* (Urbana: University of Illinois Press, 1983), 532. JD and Longstreet shared Lee's views: Davis, *Davis*, 564, 696; Wert, *Longstreet*, 372; *OR*, ser. 1, 32 (pt. 3), 588. REL predicted Grant's advance: Rhea, *Battle of the Wilderness*, 25–26; Dowdey, 32, 53; *B&L*, 4:118 ("Grant will cross the river at Ely's"), 122; Gene Smith, *Lee and Grant: A Dual Biography* (New York: McGraw-Hill Book Co., 1984), 187 ("Gentlemen, we've got to whip him").

10. **Grant.** USG's apprehension: *B&L*, 4:145. Humphreys' description: Schaff, *Battle of the Wilderness*, 43–44. Humphreys's plan: Rhea, *Battle of the Wilderness*, 55. USG to Germanna Ford: Schaff, 83, 86, 298 (undertaker story); *SC TYWG*, 174–75 (description of countryside and marching troops); *HP CWG*, 41–43 (USG's uniform, headquarters in farmhouse, "Well, so far"). Dispositions of corps on May 4: *B&L*, 4:145; Humphreys, *Virginia Campaign*, 18–19; Rhea, 74–75; Schaff, 96. Rebels on the move: *EP CWG*, 44; *USGP*, 10:397. Supper with staff, Meade's visit: *HP CWG*, 45–46; *AB MHG*, 2:100.

11. **Lee.** REL's plan, army strength: Rhea, *Battle of the Wilderness*, 80–81; *REL WP*, 719; Freeman, *Lee*, 3:269–70; Dowdey, *Lee's Last Campaign*,

71. Army's advance, May 4: *REL WP*, 719–22; Rhea, 87–88; Freeman, 3:274–75. REL's plan, May 5: Rhea, 90, 120; *B&L*, 4:240–41; Long, *Memoirs of Lee*, 326–27; Dowdey, 83; William L. Royall, *Some Reminiscences* (New York: The Neale Publishing Co., 1909), 28 ("Marse Bob is going for them").

12. **Grant.** Army in motion, messages from Meade, USG to the front: *HP CWG*, 47–48; Humphreys, *Virginia Campaign*, 21; *B&L*, 4:154; Rhea, *Battle of the Wilderness*, 97, 129–30; *USGP*, 10:397–98, 399n ("The enemy have appeared"); 10:399 ("If any opportunity"), 399n; Rhea, 109, 131. USG with Meade near Wilderness Tavern: Rhea, 131; *HP CWG*, 48–49; Schaff, 135; Edward Steere, *The Wilderness Campaign* (Harrisburg, Penn.: The Stackpole Company, 1987), 119–22. Battle instructions: Humphreys, 25; *TL WG&M*, 88; *HP CWG*, 49–50; Rhea, 133. Headquarters on piney knoll, reluctant Warren: *HP CWG*, 49–50; Humphreys, 25; *AB MHG*, 2:105; Schaff, 142; Catton, *Grant Takes Command*, 187–88 ("army seems reluctant").

13. **Lee.** REL with Hill, messengers from Ewell: Rhea, *Battle of the Wilderness*, 124, 126; Freeman, *Lee*, 3:277–78; *OR*, ser. 1, 36 (pt. 1), 1028, 1070. REL at Widow Tapp's farm: Dowdey, *Lee's Last Campaign*, 104–08; Freeman, 3:278; Rhea, 129.

14. **Grant.** USG at Warren's front: *HP CWG*, 51; *AB MHG*, 2:108; Schaff, *Battle of the Wilderness*, 166 (Indiana soldier's description of the fire); Rhea, *Battle of the Wilderness*, 191 ("The commanding general").

15. **Lee.** Federal attacks against Heth, REL at Tapp farm: Rhea, *Battle of the Wilderness*, 196, 204, 207, 240; Dowdey, *Lee's Last Campaign*, 117–18, 123–25; Freeman, *Lee*, 3:278–80; Andrew E. Ford, *The Story of the Fifteenth Regiment Massachusetts Volunteers in the Civil War, 1861–1865* (Clinton: Press of W. J. Coulter, 1898), 323–24 (description of combat); E. M. Haynes, *A History of the Tenth Reg., VT. Vols.* (Rutland, Ver.: The Tuttle Co., 1894), 106–07 (description of combat, torn whirling body of one man). REL revised battle plan: Longstreet, *From Manassas to Appomattox*, 556–57; Rhea, 272–74. Ewell's report, REL's orders to him and to Longstreet: *OR*, ser. 1, 51 (pt. 2, supplement): 887–90, 902–03; Rhea, 275–76, 278; *REL WP*, 722; Dowdey, 99–100.

16. **Grant.** Fires, both armies entrenched: Catton, *Grant Takes Command*, 193. USG's anxieties about wounded: *HP CWG*, 53. USG's frustrations with Army of the Potomac: Rhea, 222, Catton, 189. USG's orders for an attack on May 6: Humphreys, *Virginia Campaign*, 37; *HP CWG*, 54;

USGP, 10:400; *USGM*, 2:195; *TL WG&M*, 93; Rhea, 266–67; Schaff, *Battle of the Wilderness*, 223–24. USG up at 4 A.M., breakfast: *HP CWG*, 56. Sedwick attacked, sound of Hancock's attack: Rhea, 321.

17. **Lee.** Attack against Hill: Rhea, *Battle of the Wilderness*, 289 ("one of the worst stampedes"), 290–93. REL to McGowan: *EPA FFC*, 357. REL's army on the brink of disaster: *B&L*, 4:241; Dowdey, *Lee's Last Campaign*, 145–49; Rhea, 294–95. Arrival of Texas brigade and Longstreet: J. B. Polley, *Hood's Texas Brigade: Its Marches, Its Battles, Its Achievements* (New York: Neal Publishing Co., 1910), 231, 239; Long, *Memoirs of Lee*, 330–31; *B&L*, 4:124–25; also in Freeman, 3:287–90; Rhea, 301, 303. Longstreet's attack, Sorrel's flank attack: ibid., 301, 304, 310, 315–16, 353–66, 446; Long, 331, 333; Longstreet, *From Manassas to Appomattox*, 561; Dowdey, 160–63. Longstreet shot, REL met his ambulance: Freeman, 3:294; Longstreet, 563–64; Francis W. Dawson, *Reminiscences of Confederate Service, 1861–1865* (ed. Bell I. Wiley, Baton Rouge: Louisiana State University Press, 1980), 116; Rhea, 373; Dowdey, 165–66. REL and Field took charge, attack of Longstreet's men, Gordon's dusk attack: Rhea, 390–96, 403, 412–18, 444; Dowdey, 170–71; *EPA FFC*, 363; John B. Gordon, *Reminiscences of the Civil War* (reprint of 1903 ed., Lincoln: University of Nebraska Press, 1993), 258. REL assumed the defensive: Taylor, *Four Years with General Lee*, 129; Rhea, 441, 443; Freeman, 3:329; Dowdey, 174–75, 182.

18. **Grant.** USG's frustrating battle: Schaff, *Battle of the Wilderness*, 226, 247–48; Rhea, 431–32, 434, 439. USG's headquarters almost overrun: *HP CWG*, 59 ("General, wouldn't it be prudent," "It would be better," "General Grant, this is a crisis," "I'm tired of hearing"); Schaff, 237; *AB MHG*, 2:119. USG and enemy's sundown attack: *HP CWG*, 68–71; *USGP*, 10:404n; *TL WG&L*, 98; Rhea, 417. USG couldn't sleep: *HP CWG*, 72–73; Humphreys, *Virginia Campaign*, 54. USG in an army chair by the fire: *SC TYWG*, 181–82; Schaff, 326. USG's thinking on the drawn battle: Catton, *Grant Takes Command*, 201, 204 (Wilderness was worse than Shiloh); Rhea, 434, 439 (USG's resolution about leading the Army of the Potomac).

19. **Lincoln.** AL's joke and anxieties about Grant: *HP CWG*, 98; *FBC ILAL*, 31. USG's dispatch: *USGP*, 10:400–01. AL's pacing in White House: *FBC, ILAL*, 31; *AL DBD*, 3:257. Dana mission: Dana, *Recollections*, 170–71 ("we've been pretty much in the dark"); Schaff, *Battle of the Wilderness*, 326.

20. Grant. Fog and smoke, Ferrero's black division: *HP CWG*, 329–30; *TL WG&M*, 102. USG's flank movement to Spotsylvania Court House: *USGP*, 10:408–09; *HP CWG*, 74, 76; *AB MHG*, 2:17; Humphreys, *Virginia Campaign*, 52. Hospital train to Fredericksburg: Schaff, *Wilderness Campaign*, 339–40. Men cheered when USG didn't retreat: *USGM*, 2:210; *AB MHG*, 2:1134; Catton, *Grant Takes Command*, 208–09. USG at Piney Branch Church, Dana's arrival: *AB MHG*, 2:142; *HP CWG*, 83; Dana, *Recollections*, 172; *TL WG&M*, 104 ("an ill omen").

21. Lee. REL anticipated Grant's move to Spotsylvania, ordered Anderson there: Rev. John K. White, "General Lee—Through the Eyes of a Staff Officer," in Vickers (ed.), *Under Both Flags*, 405; Freeman, *Lee*, 3:298–303; William D. Matter, *If It Takes All Summer: The Battle of Spotsylvania* (Chapel Hill: University of North Carolina Press, 1988), 15, 33, 52; Dowdey, *Lee's Last Campaign*, 183. REL and rest of army moved to Spotsylvania, beat Grant there: *REL WP*, 723–27; Long, *Memoirs of Lee*, 335–36; Freeman, 3:304–07; Matter, 57–59, 87–95; Dowdey, 185–93. Lee's intricate field works: *B&L*, 4:174; Dowdey, 195–97; Matter, 103–10, 129–30. Lee's defensive-offensive plans: Long, 349.

22. Grant. USG's frustrations with Warren and Sedgwick: Humphreys, *Virginia Campaign*, 65; *AB MHG*, 2:144–45; *HP CWG*, 87. USG and Meade inspected lines: *AB MHG*, 2:146–47, and Matter, *If It Takes All Summer*, 105 (description of countryside and rival fieldworks); *HP CWG*, 88–89. Sedgwick's death: ibid., 89–90; *TL WG&M*, 107–08. Wright description: from photographs and from Catton, *A Stillness at Appomattox* (Garden City, N.Y.: Doubleday & Co., 1954), 116. Sheridan's raid: *USGM*, 2:153; *B&L*, 4:189; Morris, *Sheridan*, 164–65. Dispatches from Washington: *HP CWG*, 91; Catton, *Grant Takes Command*, 20. USG to Halleck: *USGP*, 10:418–19. Grant's maturing plans: Humphreys, 83 ("vulnerable to a systematic"); *HP CWG*, 94; *USGP*, 10:419–20 ("Reconnoiter the enemy's position"); Matter, 161–62; *HP CWG*, 96–97 ("Ulysses don't scare"). Mott's botched attack, Upton's attack: Matter, 161–62; Humphreys, 85–87, *HP CWG*, 96; Catton, *Grant Takes Command*, 220–21; *USGM*, 2:224; Charles E. Davis, *Three Years in the Army: The Story of the Thirteenth Massachusetts Volunteers* (Boston: Estes and Lauriat, 1894), 338 (horse shot near USG, USG kept his eye on the battle); Matter, 167 (Upton's attack produced useful information); *USGP*, 10:427. USG to Halleck and to Julia: *USGP*, 10:422–23; *HP CWG*, 98; Catton, *Grant Takes Command*, 233. USG's plan of attack for May 12: *USGP*, 10:424–25, 427; *HP CWG*, 100. USG up before dawn, May 12, inclement weather: *HP CWG*, 102. New headquarters location, battle began: *AB MHG*, 2:174; *HP CWG*, 102; Humphreys, 92.

23. **Lee.** REL to the front, inclement weather: *B&L*, 4:242; *EPA FFC*, 376; Matter, *If It Takes All Summer*, 189. REL encountered routed rebels: Freeman, *Lee*, 3:317 ("Hold on!"); *B&L*, 4:243; Dowdey, *Lee's Last Campaign*, 201–05. REL tried to accompany Gordon into battle: Long, *Memoirs of Lee*, 338; Freeman, 3:319; Dowdey, 205–07; Matter, 199–202. Rodes's dilemma, Venable and reinforcements: ibid., 205–11; Freeman, 3:319. REL with Nat Harris, enemy driven from salient: Dowdey, 209–10, 213; Freeman, 3:320–24; Matter, 211–12, 244–45. Close quarter combat at Bloody Angle: Humphreys, *Virginia Campaign*, 99–100; Matter, 373 (tree twenty inches in diameter cut down); Andrew E. Ford, *The Story of the Fifteenth Regiment Massachusetts Volunteer Infantry in the Civil War* (Clinton: Press of W. J. Coulter, 1898), 328; History Committee, *History of the Nineteenth Regiment Massachusetts Volunteer Infantry, 1861–1865* (Salem, Mass.: Salem Press, 1906), 309–11; *B&L*, 4:172; *HP CWG*, 110. Stuart's death: *REL WP*, 731 ("A more zealous, ardent, brave"); Gordon, *Reminiscences*, 273 ("I can scarcely think of him"). Evacuation of Mule Shoe: ibid., 3:326; Matter, 259–60, 267 (casualties); Dowdey, 223; *EPA FFC*, 378 (duration of battle). Rebel officer on Grant: Tapert, *Brothers' War*, 198.

24. **Grant.** USG's praise for Hancock's and Wright's generalship: *HP CWG*, 102–03; *B&L*, 4:170; *AB MHG*, 2:175; Matter, *If It Takes All Summer*, 209, 215; *TL WG&M*, 112 ("a sterling soldier"). Burnside's ineptitude: *HP CWG*, 104–05; *AB MHG*, 2:175; Matter, 226. Warren's ineptitude: *AB MHG*, 2:177, 183; Matter, 229–33. USG on battleline, Porter's report of the fighting at Bloody Angle: *HP CWG*, 110–11, 122; also *B&L*, 4:172, 174; Dana, *Recollections*, 177–78. We may assume that Porter described to Grant what he saw at the Bloody Angle; therefore I cast into dialogue the stylized written expression found in Porter's book. USG to Julia: *USGP*, 10:443–44. Trains of wounded to Fredericksburg: Oates, *Woman of Valor*, 229, 233.

25. **Hancock.** CH to Fredericksburg: CH, Autobiography (typescript), CHP UM; CH to her sister, May 12, 1864, ibid.; L. P. Brockett, *Women's Work in the Civil War: A Record of Heroism, Patriotism, and Courage* (Philadelphia: Zeigler, McCurdy and Co., 1867), 285. CH first and only woman there: Dr. Henry T. Child to Ellen Child, May 12, 1864, and CH to her mother, ca. May, 1864, CHP UM; letter from "V" [Dr. Vanderpool] in New York *Tribune* (May 31, 1864); John Vassar of Christian

Commission cited in Brockett, 285. CH's stylish clothes: CH to her sister, Mar. 30–Apr. 2, 1864, CHP UM. Description of wounded in Fredericksburg and at Belle Plain: CH to her sister, May 12, 1864, ibid.; CH to her mother, "about May, 1864," ibid.; Joseph K. Barnes et al., *The Medical and Surgical History of the War of the Rebellion (1861–65)* (2 vols. in 6, Washington, D.C.: Government Printing Office, 1875–83), 1 (pt. 1):155; undated fragment in Clara Barton, Journals and Diaries, CBP LC; Clara Barton, "Black Book," CBP SC; Rev. Lemuel Moss, *Annals of the United States Christian Commission* (Philadelphia: J. B. Lippincott, 1868), 432; Oates, *Woman of Valor*, 229–31. Conditions in Fredericksburg: Moss, 432; CH to her sister, May 12, 1865, CHP UM; John Anderson, *History of the Fifty-seventh Regiment of Massachusetts Volunteers in the War of the Rebellion* (Boston: E. B. Stillings & Co., 1896), 58; Clara Barton quoted in Frances Gage's letter of May 29, 1864, newspaper clipping, CBP LC; Ned Barton to his mother, May 17 and 19, 1864, Edward Mills Barton Letters and Diary, American Antiquarian Society, Worcester, Mass.; Sanitary Commission worker's letter of May 12, 1864, from Fredericksburg, newspaper clipping, New England Women's Auxiliary Association Papers, Massachusetts Historical Society, Boston; *Daily Advertiser*, June 3, 1864, clipping, ibid.; Oates, 231–33. CH at Second Corps hospital with Dr. Detmold and Dr. Vanderpool: CH to her sister, May 12, 1864, CHP UM; CH to her mother, "about May, 1864," ibid. New hospital in Methodist Church: CH to her sister, May 12, 1864, to her mother, "about May, 1864," ibid; letter from "V" in *New York Tribune* (May 31, 1864); Capt. H. A. Mattison to CH, May 25, 1865, CHP SC. Description of amputations: Oates, 61–62. Dr. Miller's message from Dr. Dudley, CH-Dudley friendship: CH to her mother, "about May, 1864," CHP UM; CH to her mother, Feb. 13, 1864, to her sister, Feb. 24, 1864, to Dear Sarah, Mar. 2, 1864, and to her sister, Mar. 5, 1864, ibid. Georgianna Woolsey's description of Belle Plain: Georgiana Woolsey Bacon and Eliza Woolsey Howland, *Letters of a Family During the War for the Union*, 2:587, 589. Terrible shortages, Sanitary Commission train: ibid., 2:589–90; CH to her sister, May 14, 1864, CHP UM. CH in dark stone house: ibid.; CH to her sister, May 20, 1864, and to her mother, May 21, 1864, ibid. CH's certainty she was in the right place: CH to her sister, May 14, 1864, ibid.

26. Davis. Petersburg reinforced: *JD R&F*, 2:549, *JBJ WCD*, 2:202–04; Strode, *Davis*, 3:36–37; *JD LPS*, 6:251. Difficulties in reinforcing Lee: *REL WP*, 728, 729; Long, *Civil War Day by Day*, 501; *JD LPS*, 6:249, 251, 253 ("The country could not bear the loss"). Butler repulsed at

Drewry's Bluff, JD there: *JBJ WCD*, 2:211–12, 216; *JD R&F*, 2:430–32; *VD JD*, 2:511; Long, 503; William Glenn Robertson, *Back Door to Richmond: The Bermuda Hundred Campaign, April-June 1864* (Baton Rouge: Louisiana State University Press, 1987), 53–242. Beauregard's outrageous proposal, Lee's response: *JD R&F*, 2:432; *JD LPS*, 6:257. JD's bitter disappointment with Johnston's retreat: *JD R&F*, 2:468; Woodworth, *Davis and His Generals*, 275, 277.

27. Sherman. Strength of WTS's forces, logistics: *WTSM*, 466, 470–88; *WTS HL*, 306; Marszalek, *Sherman*, 261 (1,300 tons of stores per day). Resaca: *WTSM*, 500, 503; Marszalek, 265 ("Take it easy today"). WTS flanked Johnston and forced him to retreat to Kingston, WTS's objectives: *WTSM*, 503–05; *WTS HL*, 290–91; WTS to John Sherman, May 26, 1864, WTSP. WTS's proscription of journalists: Ewing, *Sherman at War*, 131–32; WTS to John Sherman, June 9, 1864, WTSP. Cassville: *WTSM*, 505–07. WTS slept little: Lewis, *Sherman*, 358; *B&L*, 4:301 ("A pretty way we're commanded"); Fellman, *Citizen Sherman*, 193. Johnston abandoned Cassville: *WTSM*, 506, 508, 511. WTS knew the country: ibid., 512. WTS to Ellen: *WTS HL*, 293–94.

28. Davis. Alarm over Johnston's retreat to Allatoona, recriminations in his army, refugees: *JD R&F*, 2:469–71; Samuel Carter, III, *The Siege of Atlanta* (New York: St. Martin's Press, 1973), 130; Albert Castel, *Decision in the West: The Atlanta Campaign of 1864* (Lawrence: University Press of Kansas, 1992), 209–211; McPherson, *Battle Cry of Freedom*, 747; Gorgas, *Journals*, 111 ("Johnston has fulfilled"); Strode, *Davis*, 3:45; Symonds, *Johnston*, 291–95. Johnston must be removed, JD left him in command: Strode, 3:46–48; Symonds, 295–96; Woodward, *Davis and His Generals*, 277.

29. Sherman. WTS to Dallas: *WTSM*, 512; *B&L*, 4:306 (description of country); Marszalek, *Sherman*, 267 ("soldiers so bespattered with mud"). Battle of New Hope Church: *WTSM*, 513–15, 519; Conyngham, *Sherman's March*, 107 (episode with frightened soldier); Marszalek, 268. WTS's remarks to his officers: we may assume that he told them pretty much what he wrote Ellen and his brother John (*WTS HL*, 294–97; WTS to John Sherman, June 9, 1864, WTSP, and published in *SL*, 236).

30. Grant. USG on Sherman: *USGP*, 10:455, 461. Sigel's disaster: *AB MHG*, 2:199–200, 202; *USGP*, 10:460n ("do nothing but run"); *HP CWG*, 124. Butler's fiasco, Baldy Smith ordered to join Potomac Army: *USGP*, 15: 171–72; *B&L*, 4:147; *USGM*, 2:150–52; *AB MHG*, 2:257; *HP CWG*, 147. USG to his staff: ibid., 124–25 ("Lee will undoubtedly"),

131, 147; *USGP*, 10:464; *AB MHG*, 2:201. USG to North Anna: *HP CWG*, 132–43; *TL WG&M*, 118–27. Sheridan's arrival, details of his raid: *HP CWG*, 143; *B&L*, 4:188–89; *TL WG&M*, 125; Catton, *Grant Takes Command*, 244–46. Cipher dispatch from Sherman, Meade's anger: *TL WG&M*, 126. Lee's trap: ibid., 127, 127n; Freeman, *Lee*, 3:356; Dowdey, *Lee's Last Campaign*, 260–65; *HP CWG*, 145. USG withdrew, another flanking maneuver, new base: *USGM*, 2:253; *USGP*, 10:490–91 ("Lee's army is really whipped").

31. **Lee.** REL's illness, frustration: Dowdey, *Lee's Last Campaign*, 256, 260; Freeman, *Lee*, 3:359, and *B&L*, 4:244 ("We must strike them a blow"). REL to Hill: *REL WP*, 759–60. Starving army: *B&L*, 4:231. REL's need for reinforcements: *REL WP*, 756, 757; Dowdey, 277–78; Freeman, 3:368–69 ("If General Grant advances"). Cavalry to Old Cold Harbor, calamity in the making: ibid., 3:369–72; *REL WP*, 740, 758–59; Dowdey, 278–83. REL's illness worsened: *B&L*, 4:244 ("the head and front"); Taylor, *Four Years with Lee*, 134. REL tried to think like Grant: Freeman, 3:374; *REL WP*, 762; Dowdey, 284–86. Race for Old Cold Harbor: Freeman, 3:375–77. Anderson's failure, REL to Old Cold Harbor, chafed at being thrown on defensive: ibid., 377–87; Dowdey, 286–94, 296; *REL WP*, 761.

32. **Grant.** Rebels preparing for another desperate fight, Hancock ordered to attack, unable to do so: *USGP*, 11:5; *HP CWG*, 166–67; *TL WG&M*, 138 ("Sharp as steel traps"), 140, 141n ("We ought to be able to eat them up"). USG's headquarters to near Bethesda Church, USG's reconnaissance of rebel lines: *HP CWG*, 172–74; Daniel George Macnamara, *The History of the Ninth Regiment Massachusetts Volunteer Infantry* (Boston: E. P. Stillings & Co., 1899), 404 (description of lines and terrain); *AB MHG*, 2:290 (had to attack to ascertain weakness in enemy lines). USG's option, ordered an attack all along the line: *HP CWG*, 172–74; *USGP*, 11:8; *B&L*, 4:225. Severe rainstorm: James L. Bowen, *History of the Thirty-Seventh Regiment Mass. Volunteers in the Civil War of 1861–1865* (Holyoke, Mass.: Clark W. Bryan & Co., 1884), 332. Battle of Cold Harbor: Dowdey, *Lee's Last Campaign* (roar of guns rattled Richmond windows); *HP CWG*, 177; *AB MHG*, 2:291 (morning mist); *USGP*, 11:14; Bowen, 333; Capt. A. W. Bartlett, *History of the Twelfth Regiment New Hampshire Volunteers in the War of the Rebellion* (Concord, N.H.: Ira C. Evans, 1897), 203–04; *B&L*, 4:226–28; Alfred S. Poe, *The Tenth Regiment Massachusetts Volunteer Infantry 1861–1865* (Springfield, Mass.: Tenth Regiment Veteran Association, 1909), 286 ("The immobile lines"). USG suspended the battle: *USGM*,

2:272; *AB MHG*, 2:297; *HP MHG*, 177. USG regretted the assaults: ibid., 179; *USGM*, 2:276.

33. **Hancock.** Hospital corps to White House Landing: CH to her sister, May 31–June 3, 1864, CHP UM; Julia Susan Wheelock, *The Boys in White: The Experience of a Hospital Agent in and around Washington* (New York: Lange & Hillman, 1870), 221 (description of river). White House Landing description: ibid., 230; Anna Morris Holstein, *Three Years in Field Hospitals of the Army of the Potomac* (Philadelpia: J. B. Lippincott & Co., 1867), 73; Sophronia E. Bucklin, *In Hospital and Camp: A Woman's Record of Thrilling Incidents among the Wounded in the Late War* (Philadelphia: John E. Potter and Co., 1869), 247. Arrival of wounded, terrible suffering: William Howell Reed, *Hospital Life in the Army of the Potomac* (Boston: William V. Spencer, 1866), 59 (eight thousand wounded arrived before the hospital was set up); CH to her sister, May 31–June 3, 1864, and to Joanna Dickeson, July 18, CHP UM; Wheelock, 225; Bucklin, 249; Holstein, 66. Bucklin's description (not an exact quotation): Bucklin, 253, 255, 258, 261, 268. Men cried for food: ibid., 258. CH and Barlow to First Division, Second Corps, hospital at front: CH to her mother, June 7, 1864, CHP UM; Eileen F. Conklin, *Women at Gettysburg 1863* (Gettysburg: Thomas Publications, 1993), 21–22 (Barlow biography). CH and Dr. Dudley, CH stayed a week: CH to her mother, June 7, 1864, to her sister, June 9, 1864, to Joanna Dickeson, July 18, 1864, CHP UM. White House Landing hospital moved to the James: ibid.; CH to her mother, June 15, 1863, CHP UM.

34. **Grant.** USG's plan to cut off Lee's supply lines and seize Petersburg: *B&L*, 4:148, 150–51; *USGP*, 10: 487, 88, 11:19–21; *HP CWG*, 183; Catton, *Grant Takes Command*, 277. Sheridan's departure, Lee's cavalry pursuit: *B&L*, 4:148; *USGP*, 11:21, 23, 24; *HP CWG*, 190; Catton, 280–81.

35. **Lee.** REL sent Hampton and Fitz Lee after Sherman: *REL WP*, 771, 773; Freeman, *Lee*, 3:393, 397. REL sent Early to the valley: ibid., 3:401, 406; *REL WP*, 777–78.

36. **Grant.** To Wilcox Landing on the James: *HP CWG*, 189–96. USG conferred with Butler on Bermuda Hundred: ibid., 197–98; *B&L*, 4:151; *USGP*, 11:45 ("Our forces commenced"). Hancock and Smith on the way to Petersburg: *HP CWG*, 198–99. USG on the bluff above the river: ibid., 199–200; *ALCW*, 7:393 ("Have just recd. your dispatch"). USG back to City Point: *USGP*, 11:47 ("Have just arrived"), 47n ("Genl Butler at Lookout").

37. **Lee.** Grant on the move, Sheridan "handsomely whipped": *REL WP*, 776–77; Freeman, *Lee*, 3:405. REL to Richmond: *REL WP*, 778. Grant indeed at James River: ibid., 780; *RELD*, 228n. REL on June 15: *REL WP*, 781.

38. **Grant.** USG on June 15: *USGP*, 11:47, 47n, 49, 49n, 50n ("I have been watching," "A train of eleven cars"), 52n ("Hancock seems to be driving them"), 53 ("The enemy are now seen"). USG learned what had happened at Petersburg: *B&L*, 4:151; *USGM*, 2:294–95; *HP CWG*, 202–03; *AB MHG*, 2:361; Catton, *Grant Takes Command*, 285–89. Dispatches from Butler, morning of June 16: *USGP*, 11:57n; 61, 56 (USG orderded Meade to hurry Warren). USG to Petersburg front: *HP CWG*, 206; *B&L*, 4:151; *TL WG&M*, 162–65; Dana, *Recollections*, 196 ("Negro troops fought magnificently"); *USGP*, 11:56. USG met Meade: *HP CWG*, 206; *B&L*, 4:151; *TL WG&L*, 163–64, 164n. Meade's attack: ibid. (smoke rose across the sun). Butler to USG, USG to Meade: *USGP*, 11:59n.

39. **Lee.** REL baffled as to Grant's whereabouts: *REL WP*, 784–86; Thomas, *Lee*, 337–38. REL recaptured rebel lines on Bermuda Hundred: ibid., 787–90; *B&L*, 4:245. REL on morning of June 17: *REL WP*, 787, 788.

40. **Grant.** Report of Meade's June 16 attack: *USGP*, 11:63; *B&L*, 4:151. Assaults of June 17: *HP CWG*, 207; *TL WG&M*, 167; *USGP*, 11:63n ("so soon as Lee's army"); Catton, *Grant Takes Command*, 292–93.

41. **Lee.** Beauregard's frantic messages, REL moved army to Petersburg: *REL WP*, 787–89, 791–92, 794; *B&L*, 4:245 ("*coup de main*").

42. **Grant.** June 18 assaults: *USGP*, 11:78n, 79n–80n (Meade's report). USG "greatly chagrined" at Potomac Army's lackluster performance: *AB MHG*, 2:372–73; George A. Bruce, *The Twentieth Regiment of Massachusetts Volunteer Infantry, 1861–1865* (Boston: Houghton, Mifflin & Co., 1906), 406 (report of corps, division, and brigade commanders); *TL WG&M*, 165. McPherson, *Battle Cry of Freedom*, 741, writes that "The Cold Harbor syndrome inhibited Union soldiers from pressing home their assaults." Casualties: Catton, *Grant Takes Command*, 303, puts the figure at sixty-four thousand; Livermore, *Numbers and Losses*, estimates total Federal losses at 51,896. Lee pinned down, loss of mobility: McPherson, 741. USG settled for a siege: *USGP*, 11:111; *HP CWG*, 210; Catton, 296–97, 301–02. Sheridan's return, campaign: ibid., 297–300; Starr, *Union Cavalry*, 2:127–47. USG's optimism, letter to a friend: *USGP*, 11:176.

43. **Sherman.** WTS's destruction in northwest Georgia: *SL*, 236; Upson, *With Sherman to the Sea,* 119; *ALCW*, 7:330n–31n; Fenwick Y. Hedley, *Marching Through Georgia: Pen-Pictures of Every-Day Life* (Chicago: M. A. Donohue & Co., 1884), 138; Ewing, *Sherman at War*, 130; Marszalek, *Sherman*, 273, and Lewis, *Sherman*, 421 ("They call me a barbarian, vandal, a monster"); *WTS HL*, 298 ("To realize what war is"). At Kennesaw Mountain: ibid., 296–97; *WTSM*, 520; Upton, 115. WTS to his advanced line, Bishop Polk killed: *WTSM*, 520, 523–24; Lewis, 374 ("saucy they are," "Shust teeckle them"). Johnston constricted his lines, rains: *WTSM*, 525–27. WTS resolved to attack: ibid., 530 (Kennesaw was "the key"), 531; *OR*, ser. 1, 38 (pt 1):68–69, (pt. 4): 492, (pt. 5):150–51; *WTS HL*, 298, 301; Hedley, 127; Lewis, 375–76, 378. Battle of Kennesaw Mountain: *USGM*, 531–32; Upson, 116; Lewis, 378 ("The assault I made was no mistake"); *WTS HL*, 299–300. Johnston's retreat to the Chattahoochee, WTS's pursuit: *WTSM*, 532–33, 535–40; Ewing, 130 (WTS's summary of the campaign). WTS forced Johnston to retreat to Atlanta: *WTSM*, 541–42. WTS learned that Hood had replaced Johnston: ibid., 543–44; *WTS HL*, 304. Battle of Peach Tree Creek, investment of Atlanta: *WTSM*, 544–49; Castel, *Decision in the West*, 365–83; *B&L*, 4:319 (half-circle investment). Death of McPherson, Battle of Atlanta: *WTSM*, 548–51, 555–57; *B&L*, 4:327–28; *WTS HL*, 302; Lewis, 385, 387; Hedley, 160–61; *OR*, ser. 1, 38 (pt. 5):241 (McPherson fell "booted and spurred," "History tells us"). Howard in command of the Army of Tennessee, Slocum in command of the Twentieth Corps: *WTSM*, 559–60. Slocum description: *In Memoriam: Henry Warner Slocum, 1826–1894* (Albany: J. B. Lyon Co., 1904), 53, 70, 72, 88. Warning from Grant: *WTSM*, 559–60. WTS to Ellen: *WTS HL*, 301–02.

44. **Lee.** REL wrote his wife that he called on Davis in early August "on matters of business" (*REL WP*, 829). There is no record of what that business was, but it undoubtedly included the critical situation in Atlanta. I've simulated what Davis surely told REL on the basis of descriptions of his views in *JD R&F*, 2:471, 474–75; *JD LPS*, 6:291–92; Strode, *Davis*, 3:73; Davis, *Davis*, 562 (It was "a sad alternative"); *VD JD*, 2:494 (JD wanted to take command in the West and help Lee win "one great decisive battle"). REL's pessimism about Petersburg siege: *REL WP*, 744; *EPA MM*, 557–58 ("However bold we might be"). Description of rival works, REL's headquarters: Oates, *Woman of Valor*, 254, 266; *REL WP*, 812. Early's raid: *REL WP*, 807, 811, 819–20, 822–24; Frank Vandiver, *Their Tattered Flags* (New York: Harper's Magazine Press Book, 1970),

289 (Early carried off his mission "with verve almost worthy of Stonewall").

45. **Lincoln.** Early's raid: Seward, *Reminiscences*, 244–48; GWD, 2:72–73; Long, *Civil War Day by Day*, 537; NB WLT, 160, 208–09; ALCW, 7: 437, 438; USGP, 11:198, 203–04. AL at Fort Stevens: Seward, 248–49; AL DBD, 3:271–72; GWD, 2:75; JH D&L, 208–09; FBC ILAL, 301–02; John H. Cramer, *Lincoln Under Enemy Fire* (Baton Rouge: Louisiana State University Press, 1948), 13–105 ("Get down, you fool!"); Sandburg, *Abraham Lincoln: The War Years*, 3:140, 142. AL on Grant's bulldog tenacity: JH D&L, 180; FBC ILAL, 283. AL called up 500,000 volunteers: ALCW, 7:448–49; FBC ILAL, 282 ("If I go down"). AL's renomination: ALCW, 7:376–77, 380–82; FBC ILAL, 168; JH D&L, 183, 185–86; NB WLT, 142; Arnold, *Life of Lincoln*, 358. Garrison's visit: William Lloyd Garrison, *Letters* (ed. Walter M. Merrill and Louis Ruchames, 6 vols., Cambridge: Harvard University Press, 1971–81), 5:211–12; Garrison, *Life*, 4:117; FBC ILAL, 167. Stowe's visit: Milton Rugoff, *The Beechers: An American Family in the Nineteenth Century* (New York: Harper & Row, 1981), 356 ("So this is the little lady"); ATR RAL, 251 (AL didn't think he would live long after the war). Chase's resignation: SC ILC, 30–31, 37–44, 223–235, 255; ALCW, 7:419; NB WLT, 120–22. Fessenden's appointment: ibid., 121–22; JH D&L, 201–03. Fessenden description: Charles A. Jellison, *Fessenden of Maine: Civil War Senator* (Syracuse, N.Y.: Syracuse University Press, 1962), 51, 93, 112–13, 177–78. AL versus Winter Davis, Wade-Davis bill: NB WLC, 28–29 (description of Davis), 150–52; the bill and the Wade-Davis Manifesto: Henry Steele Commager, *Documents of American History* (7th ed., New York: Appleton-Century-Crofts, 1963), 436–39; Trefoussee, *Radical Republicans*, 286–87. AL's objections and pocket veto: JH D&L, 204–05; NB WLT, 153–54; Trefousse, 288, 292–93 (Davis's reaction); Donald, 184 (Sumner "inconsolable"). AL's proclamation: ALCW, 7:433–34. Stevens's and Sumner's reactions to pocket veto: Brodie, *Stevens*, 208; Donald, 185–86. AL's story about the wrigglers: FBC ILAL, 145; NB WLT, 156 ("To be hurt"). Greeley's peace feeler: ALCW 7:435, 435n, 451n. AL's "To Whom It May Concern" in ibid., 7:451.

46. **Davis.** Reaction to Lincoln's peace terms: Hanchett, *Lincoln Murder Conspiracies*, 16–17; JD R&F, 2:517 (hope in northern Peace party). JD's interview with the two northerners (Colonel James F. Jacques of the Seventy-Eighth Illinois Infantry and James R. Gilmore of Massachusetts): ibid., 2:515–16; Durden, *Gray and Black*, 69–71; Strode, *Davis*, 3:76–81.

47. **Lincoln.** Dix's report of rebel assassination plot, AL's reaction: New York *Times* (Dec. 30, 1880); Tidwell, *Come Retribution*, 332, identifies Sanders as the commissioner who told the story to Stevens. AL shot at: Ward Hill Lamon, *Recollections of Abraham Lincoln, 1847–1865* (ed. Dorothy Lamon Teillard, reprint of expanded second ed., 1911, Lincoln: University of Nebraska Press, 1994), 267–69; Tidwell, 237. Lamon claimed that the incident took place in August 1862, but that is not so. It occurred in August 1864. See *ALRW*, 286.

48. **Booth.** Rebel partisan's abduction plan: Hanchett, *Lincoln Murder Conspiracies*, 30; Tidwell, *Come Retribution*, 235–36. JWB's response to Lincoln's "To Whom It May Concern" appeared in the Philadelphia *Enquirer* (Apr. 19, 1865); it is also in Bryan, *Great American Myth*, 240–43, in Kimmel, *The Mad Booths of Maryland*, 396–98, and in *JWBW*, 124–27. JWB's meeting with rebel agents in Boston: Tidwell, 262–63; *JWBW*, 119. JWB's visit with Asia: *ABC UB*, 123–25. JWB summoned Arnold and O'Laughlin: Arnold statement, Apr. 18, 1865, ALAP.

49. **Grant.** The mine scheme: USG and Meade's discussions of it based on *HP CWG*, 258–59; William Marvel, *Burnside* (Chapel Hill: University of North Carolina Press, 1991), 390–97; Duane Schultz, *Glory Enough for All: The Battle of the Crater* (New York: St. Martin's Press, 1993), 124–32, 163–70, 212–17, 243–45, 255–58, 261–67, 279–81, 284–85. I owe a great debt to Schultz's brilliant novel, which helped me understand the genesis and digging of the mine as well as the hatred between Burnside and Meade and the maladroit command decisions by them and Grant that doomed the project. Battle of the Crater: *USGP*, 11:345–46, 12:111; *B&L*, 4:551–62; *HP CWG*, 261–69; *TL WG&M*, 196–204; Warren Wilkinson, *Mother, May You Never See the Sights I Have Seen: The Fifty-Seventh Massachusetts Veteran Volunteers in the Army of the Potomac, 1864–1865* (New York: Harper & Row, 1990), 235–64; Noah Andrew Trudeau, *The Last Citadel: Petersburg, Virginia, June 1864–April 1865* (Boston: Little, Brown and Co., 1991), 103–127; Catton, *Stillness at Appomattox*, 251–52. The best description of the battle and the court of inquiry that followed is in Schultz, 290–348. Dust and fire engines at Depot Hospital: Wheelock, *Boys in White*, 242; Holstein, *Three Years*, 77, 80; Moss, *Christian Commission*, 323, 324; Donald C. Pfanz, "The Depot Field Hospital at City Point" (unpublished, 1988, copy at Petersburg National Battlefield), 48.

50. **Hancock.** Terrible conditions at Depot Hospital: CH to her sister, July 1, 1864, CHP UM. Hospital description: ibid.; Pfanz, "Depot Field Hos-

pital," 7ff; Wheelock, *Boys in White*, 238, 240; Adelaide Smith, *Reminiscences of an Army Nurse During the Civil War* (New York: Greaves Publishing Co., 1911), 96–99. Helen Gilson: Reed, *Hospital Life*, 81, 86, 140, 154–55; Maxwell, *Lincoln's Fifth Wheel*, 258; CH to her sister, July 14, 1864, CHP UM. CH's diet kitchen: CH to her mother, June 29, 1864, to her niece, July 7, 1864, and to her sister, July 14 and 23, 1864, ibid. CH's stylish dress: Pfanz, 20; CH to her mother, June 27, 1864, CHP UM ("I have the confidence"). CH and Capt. Dod: CH to her sister, Aug. 17 and 27, 1864, to her mother, Aug. 27, 1864, ibid.; Capt. Dod to his Mother, Aug. 17, 1864, ibid. ("She is well known"). Canonading, one poor fellow: Wheelock, 238–39; Bucklin, *In Hospital and Camp*, 312. CH sick, Barlow's death: CH to her sister, early July 1864, and to her mother, July 4, 1864, CHP UM; Conklin, *Women at Gettysburg*, 22; Reed, 60. CH and Dr. Dudley: CH to her sister, early July, "about" Aug., Aug. 17, Sept. 2, and Oct. 17, 1864, and to her mother, July 20, Aug. 15 and 27, 1864, CHP UM; Trudeau, *Last Citadel*, 289 ("troglodytes"). City Point and Grant's headquarters: informational brochure provided by park ranger, Appomattox Manor, City Point; Wilkinson, *Mother, May You Never See the Sights I Have Seen*, 209–10; Trudeau, 132.

51. **Grant.** USG's meeting with Lincoln at Fort Monroe: *AL DBD*, 3:276; Catton, *Grant Takes Command*, 336–42; *GWD*, 2:90. USG put Sheridan in command of upper Potomac: *USGP*, 11:368; *ALCW*, 7:476 ("This, I think"); Catton, 344. USG to Washington and Monacacy River: *HP CWG*, 271–72; *USGP*, 11:377n. USG's instructions to Sheridan: *USGP*, 11:242–43, 378, 12:97.

52. **Lincoln.** AL agreed with Grant: *ALCW*, 7:476. *Illinois State Register*'s derision of AL: Bryan, *Great American Myth*, 391. AL couldn't be reelected: Weed to Seward, Aug. 22, 1864, RTLC; Nicolay to Theresa, Aug. 21 and 28, 1864, JGNP; *SC ILC*, 236–38; Randall and Current, *Lincoln the President*, 4:198–232; Butler, *Private and Official Correspondence*, 5:35 ("I'm going to be beaten"); FBC ILAL, 306 ("weal or woe"). AL's conversation with Mills and Randall: ibid., 306–08. AL's memorandum on his probable failure: *ALCW*, 7:515; *JH D&L*, 238 ("General, the election"). AL's concerns about Douglass: *FD L&W*, 4:44–45 ("the condition he had risen from"). Rev. John Eaton was the mutual friend who arranged AL's second interview with Douglass. AL wavered: ibid., 422–24; *ALCW*, 7:517–18. AL's interview with Douglass: *FD L&W*, 3:45–46, 422–24; Douglass, *Life and Times*, 358–59. AL's awakened resolution: *N&H ALH*, 9:221. Democratic platform, McClellan's repudiation of it and peace terms: Sears, *McClellan*, 371–76; McClellan, *Civil*

War Papers, 590–92; McPherson, *Battle Cry of Freedom*, 772; Long, *Jewel of Liberty*, 243–44. AL insisted that the election take place, refused to rescind emancipation: *ALCW*, 8:1–2, 41, 52, 75, 101. AL's remarks to 148th Ohio and 166th Ohio: ibid., 7:528, 512. Cincinnati call: Randall and Current, 4:224–25; *New York World* as quoted in *New York Herald* (Aug. 2, 1864). Campaign: *GWD*, 2:136; Voegeli, *Free But Not Equal*, 151–52; Randall and Current, 4:237–49; Wood, *Black Scare*, 53–79; La Crosse (Wis.) *Democrat* (Aug. 29, 1864) as quoted in Bryan, 391.

53. **Booth.** Reunion with Arnold and O'Laughlin: Arnold statement, Apr. 18, 1865, ALAP. Arnold description: Samuel Bland Arnold, *Defence and Prison Experience of a Lincoln Conspirator* (ed. Charles F. Heartman, Hattiesburg, Miss.: The Book Farm, 1943), 34–36. O'Laughlin description: Tidwell, *Come Retribution*, 263; BP AL, 222, 232–33. JB's abduction plan: dialogue based on descriptions of plan and conversation in Arnold's statement, Apr. 18, 1865, and Arnold's affidavit, Dec. 3, 1867, ALAP; Arnold, *Defence*, 18–19, 30–31, 38–39.

54. **Lincoln.** AL's reaction to fall of Atlanta based on *ALCW*, 7:532–34; *WTSM*, 582–83. AL's old friend Leonard Swett wrote his wife from the White House: "God gave us the victory at Altanta, which made the ship right itself, as a ship in a storm does after a great wave has nearly capsized it." See Ida Tarbell, *The Life of Abraham Lincoln* (2 vols., New York: Doubleday & McClure Co., 1900), 2:203.

55. **Davis.** Hood abandoned Atlanta: *JBJ WCD*, 2:276–77; *JD R&F*, 2:476. JD on Sherman's expulsion order: ibid., 2:478. Hood's protest: *WTSM*, 598.

56. **Sherman.** WTS's reply to Hood: *WTSM*, 602. WTS to Atlanta's mayor and two city councilmen: ibid., 601; *WTS HL*, 311 ("the people of the South made a big howl").

57. **Davis.** Absenteeism in army: Lonn, *Desertion During the Civil War*, 30; Escott, *After Secession*, 127; *REL WP*, 847–49. Conscription intensified, JD to Brown: *JBJ WCD*, 2:308; Robert Garlick Hill Kean, *Inside the Confederate Government: The Diary of Robert Garlick Hill Kean* (ed. Edward Younger, Baton Rouge: Louisiana State University Press, 1957), 174; *JD LPS*, 6:336–38; *JD R&F*, 2:479, 565. Rumors that Sherman had offered to treat with Brown and Stevens: *JBJ WCD*, 2:287. JD's goals on trip west: *JD R&F*, 2:479. Plan of operations for Hood: Davis, *Davis*, 565, says that JD proposed the plan. JD's dialogue based on descriptions of the plan in ibid.; *JD R&F*, 2:480–81; Strode, *Davis*, 3, 607. Johnston

to coordinate Hood and Taylor: Woodworth, *Davis and His Generals*, 292; Foote, *Civil War*, 3:607. Brown's distempered letter: *JBJ WCD*, 2:292. JD's speeches at Macon and elsewhere: *JD LPS*, 6:341–42, 346–47, 349, 352–60. JD and Beauregard in Augusta: *JD R&F*, 2:480–81; Davis, *Davis*, 566–67 ("Wherever you are present"). JD's reunion with Chesnuts: *MCCW*, 651–52; Strode, 3:101 (sixty-year-old Madeira); Muhlenfeld, *Chesnut*, 122 ("the best ham—the best Madeira"). JD back in Richmond: *JBJ WCD*, 2:300.

58. **Sherman.** Chasing Hood, Allatoona: *WTS HL*, 312; *SL*, 242–43; *WTSM*, 622–26; Hedley, *Marching Through Georgia*, 216–22; Marszalek, *Sherman*, 291–92; Lewis, *Sherman*, 426–28 ("Corse, they came damn near"). WTS's proposals to march to the sea, Grant's responses: *USGM*, 627–34; *HP CWG*, 317; *USGP*, 12:272–73, 290n, 289–90, 303n, 302–03, 371n, 370–72, 373, 373n–75n; *OR*, ser. 1, 39 (pt. 3): 364–65, 412, (pt. 2):378, (pt. 3):202–03, 222, 239, 358, 576–77, 594–95; *WTS HL*, 313–14; *HMH MWS*, 34 ("It's a big game"). Grant wavered, WTS's response: USG to WTS, Nov. 1 and 2, 1864, WTSP and *USGP*, 370–73; *WTSM*, 639–40, 643 ("I believe you will be"); *OR*, ser. 1, 39 (pt. 3):240.

59. **Lincoln.** Victories in the Valley, operations on Grant's front: *USGP*, 12:177, 191, 229n, 228–29 ("I am taking steps"), 231, 242, 251–52. Chandler's deal, Blair ousted: Winfred A. Harbison, "Zacharia Chandler's Part in the Re-election of Abraham Lincoln," *Mississippi Valley Historical Review* (Sept., 1935), 267–76; Long, *Jewel of Liberty*, 240 ("I may accomplish nothing"); Trefousse, *Radical Republicans*, 295–96; *ALCW*, 8:18; *JH D&L*, 219–20; *GWD*, 2:156–59; *CWL*, 352. Republicans closed ranks behind AL: Thomas, *Lincoln*, 447 ("fight like a savage"); *New York Tribune* (Sept. 6, 1864) endorsed Lincoln. Douglass's and abolitionists' support: *FD L&W*, 3:404 ("heaviest calamity"), 424; McPherson, *Struggle for Equality*, 283–84. AL and fall state elections: *ALCW*, 8:46, 47, 58, 332 ("The progress of our arms, upon which all else chiefly depends"); *USGP*, 12:16–17 (Grant wrote Washburne he supported AL); 213–14; *JH D&L*, 226–30. Of the two presidential candidates, Sherman the monarchist said: "I almost despair of popular government, but if we must be so inflicted I suppose Lincoln is the best choice" (WTS to John Sherman, Oct. 11, 1864, WTSP). AL also said of Sheridan: "This Sheridan is a little Irishman, but he is a big fighter" (*ALRW*, 507).

60. **Davis.** JD's anger at Federal strategy to starve rebels into submission: *JD R&F*, 2:483, 513–15. Hood's change of plans: ibid., 2:481–82; Foote,

Civil War, 3:616–17; Woodworth, *Davis and His Generals*, 294–96; McMuray, *Hood*, 161–632; John Bell Hood, *Advance and Retreat: Personal Experiences in the United States and Confederate States Armies* (New Orleans: published for the Hood Orphan Memorial Fund, 1880), 273 ("it would be the best thing"). JD's objections, reluctant approval: *JD R&F*, 2:482–83; *JD LPS*, 6:398–99; Strode, *Davis*, 3:107, 109, 122. That JD approved of Hood's chimerical plan of operations "shows just how distracted and exhausted he was by now" (Davis, *Davis*, 576). JD had thought he could negotiate with McClellan, hopes dashed: Strode, 3:87; Escott, *After Secession*, 217; *JD LPS*, 6:347 ("Victory in the field").

61. Booth. Closed out oil investments: Tidwell, *Come Retribution*, 265. In Canada: ibid., 24–25, 328–34; *LJW AAL*, 46–47; *BP AL*, 39, 42, 45–46; Arnold's statement, Dec. 3, 1867, ALAP; Arnold, *Defence*, 19–20. JWG moved into Washington's National Hotel on Nov. 9, the day after the election (Bryan, *Great American Myth*, 102).

62. Lincoln. AL's conversation with Brooks: *NB WLT*, 195–97. AL at War Office: *JD D&L*, 233–36; *NB WLT*, 196–98; Dana, *Recollections*, 227–28; Keckley, *Behind the Scenes*, 157 ("Poor Mr. Lincoln"). AL's story about the looking glass: *NB WLT*, 198–200; *FBC ILAL*, 164–65; Lamon, *Recollections of Lincoln*, 112–13. See Don Fehrenbacher's analysis of this incident in John L. Thomas (ed.), *Abraham Lincoln and the American Political Tradition* (Amherst: University of Massachusetts Press, 1986), 33–35. Election returns: Long, *Jewel of Liberty*, 233; *USGP*, 395–96. AL on the victory: *ALCW*, 8:101 ("he who is most devoted to the Union"), 149 ("the voice of the people"), 100–02 ("It has long been"). Long's *Jewel of Liberty* is superior to all previous treatments of the election of 1864, which Long believes was the most crucial in American political history.

63. Booth. JWB's dialogue based on descriptions in *LJW AAL*, 444; Arnold's and Herold's statements in ALAP; Atzerodt's "confession" in Baltimore *American* (Jan. 18, 1869). JWB in National Hotel: Bryan, *Great American Myth*, 102, 105–06. Conrad mission: Tidwell, *Come Retribution*, 20–21, 264, 273–74, 281–88, 291–95, 334; Hanchett, *Lincoln Murder Conspiracies*, 30–31. JWB's trip into Lower Maryland, met Dr. Queen and Dr. Mudd: *LJW AAL*, 46–47, 61–62; Bunker's testimony, *TJS*, 1:329–31; Tidwell, 331–36; *BP AL*, 178, 320; Mudd's sworn statement, Apr. 21, 1865, ALAP. JWB's bank deposit, played in *Julius Caesar* in New York: Tidwell, 335; *BP AL*, 44; Asia Booth Clark, *The Elder and the Younger Booth* (Boston: James R. Osgood & Co., 1882), 159. Rebel sabotage in New York: Bryan, 102; Tidwell, 336, Hanchett, 19–20. JD's talk with Samuel Chester: *BP AL*, 44. JWB's visit with sister Asia: *ABC UB*, 119–22, 125–27; *LJW AAL*, 49–52; *Lincoln Log* (May/June 1977), 2; Hanchett, 46–47. Burning of Atlanta: the papers did report that event; we may assume that Booth read the accounts and reacted accordingly.

64. Sherman. Army organization and strength: *WTSM*, 649; Hedley, *Marching Through Georgia*, 259 ("little devils"); Marszalek, *Sherman*, 297. Foraging: ibid., 298; *WTSM*, 652; *WTS HL*, 321; *HMH, MWS*, 58; Upson, *With Sherman*, 134. No refugees: Lewis, *Sherman*, 439. WTS's conversation with Howard: *B&L*, 4:663–64; Burke Davis, *Sherman's March* (New York: Random House, 1980), 27. Destruction of Atlanta: *USGM*, 634; Davis, 5–6; *HMH MWS*, 56; Upson, 56. WTS watched the flames from hilltop mansion: *HMH MWS*, 57–58; Davis, 3–4 ("I've been fighting Atlanta"). First day's march, railroad destruction: *WTSM*, 655–56; *HMH MWS*, 64; General Jacob D. Cox, *Sherman's March to the Sea* (reprint of 1882 ed., New York: Da Capo Press, 1994), 36; Davis, 31. Camp at Lithonia, foraging procedure: *USGM*, 656, 659; Davis, 29; Cox, 39. Covington: *USGM*, 657. Plundering: *HMH MHS*, 77 ("I'll have to harden my heart"); *WTSM*, 659; Conyngham, *Sherman's March*, 268–77. WTS blamed Davis for the plundering: *HMH MWS*, 77; Davis, 37, 79. WTS's waging war against a hostile people: *WTSM*, 705 ("hostile people"), 729; Byers, *With Fire and Sword*, 177 ("war is hell"); *HMH MWS*, 35–36; Marszalek, 305 (no major battles, minimal loss of human life). Griswoldville: Cox, 30; Upson, 136–37; Marszalek, 304. At Judge Harris's plantation, WTS's discussions with blacks: *HMH MWS*, 69–72; *USGM*, 657–58; Davis, 32. Black refugees followed the army: Ewing, *Sherman at War*, 151; Lewis, *Sherman*, 439 (up to twenty-five thousand "at one time or another"), 440; Hedley, 311–12; Conyngham, 277; Cox, 37; *B&L*, 4:664; Upson, 136; Davis, 45–46. Gypsy camps: Cox, 37; Davis, 46, Lewis, 440. At Madison: Davis, 48; Cox, 27; *WTS HL*, 241–42 ("There goes the old man"). At Howell Cobb's plantation: *HMH MWS*, 84–85; *USGM*, 662; Davis, 60–61 ("Our white folks"). At Milledgeville: *USGM*, 663–34; *HMH MWS* ("First act of the drama"); Davis, 58 (description of the town). Mock session of legislature: *USGM*, 666; Conyngham, 254–58; Lewis, 446; Davis, 64. Andersonville escapees: Davis, 66; Lewis, 448. Davis and Beauregard's pleas for a guerrilla war: *USGM*, 665; Cox, 29; Davis, 50; Lewis, 441, 449–50 ("a devastation more or less relentless"). Kilpatrick's raid: Cox, 31–32, 69–70; Davis, 70 ("I know he's a hell of a damned fool"). Heading for Sandersville: Davis,

69; *HMH MWS*, 88–90, 92 (sharp-tongued young woman, "You've done all you could"). Rebels burned Buffalo Creek Bridge, WTS's retaliation, exchange with Hitchcock: *HMH MWS*, 92–93. WTS and elderly woman's homestead: ibid., 94, 97. Skirmish at Sandersville: ibid., 95, 105; Davis, 72–73, 75, WTS in town, courthouse burnt: *HMH MWS*, 96–97; Davis, 77. To Tennille Station: *HMH MWS*, 100, 119 ("Dem Yankees is de most"). Destruction of the Georgia Central: ibid., 135 ("to say nothing of the moral effect"). WTS laughed at Jeff Davis: ibid., 108. Flanking maneuver, army across the Ogeechee: ibid., 107, 112, 119. WTS's insomnia, nocturnal prowling: ibid., 113. Word from Kilpatrick: ibid., 123; Cox, 33; Davis, 70–71. At Millen: *WTSM*, 669; Cox, 34; *HMH MWS*, 130. Rebel prison: ibid., 150; Lewis, 460 ("convincing proof," "Make the most complete"). Destruction of Millen: *HMH MWS*, 133, 135. Had the rebels fooled: *WTSM*, 669; *HMH MWS*, 135, 149.

65. Davis. JD's concentration of troops: *JD LPS*, 6:410, 412. Frantic appeals for help, JD on Sherman's trail of destruction and Lincoln Administration's complicity: Strode, *Davis*, 3:115, 116; *JD R&F*, 2:483, 512. JD sick again, rumors of his death: *JBJ WCD*, 2:344. Battle of Franklin: *B&L*, 4:432–36, 444–51; Woodworth, *Davis and His Generals*, 298–301.

66. Lincoln. AL on Sherman: McClure, *Lincoln and Men of War-Times*, 238 ("I know the hole"); see also *ALCW*, 8:154, for a similar expression; *FBC ILAL*, 459 ("thinking of a man down South"); *ALCW*, 8:148 (AL's praise for Sherman). AL to A. H. Markland: Davis, *Sherman's March*, 90.

67. Sherman. Topedo incident: *HMH MWS*, 164; *WTSM*, 670. At the parapets of Savannah, WTS's reconnaissance: *HMH MWS*, 168–71; *WTSM*, 670–71; *WTS HL,* 317; Hedley, *Marching Through Georgia*, 322–24. Savannah invested, swath of destruction: *HMH MWS*, 166; *OR*, ser. 1, 44:13–14; *WTS HL*, 318; *HMH MWS*, 167–68; Cox, *Sherman's March*, 36; *WTSM*, 677. WTS and capture of Fort McAllister: *WTS HL*, 316–17; *WTSM*, 675; Cox, 53–54; *HMH MWS*, 179–80, 195; Davis, *Sherman's March*, 105; Lewis, *Sherman*, 463–64. WTS with Dahlgren: Davis, 106–07; *WTSM*, 676–77; Lewis, 465. Markland's message from Lincoln: ibid.; Davis, 107–08. Dispatch from Grant: *WTSM*, 682; Lewis, 467–68, and Davis, 108–09 (WTS enraged, "Won't do it, Goddamn it!"); *WTSM*, 682–83. Grant changed his mind: *WTSM*, 686; Cox, 58; Halleck to WTS, Dec. 16, 1864, WTSP. Grant's troubles with Thomas: *WTSM*, 682 ("Hood has Thomas close in Nashville"), 690–92; Halleck to WTS,

Dec. 15, 1864, WTSP (report of Thomas's victory); Feldman, *Citizen Sherman*, 190 (WTS's praise for Thomas). WTS and fall of Savannah: *WTSM*, 687, 692–95; *HMH MWS*, 198; Cox 59–60; Davis, 109–11, 114; Lewis, 469. WTS's Christmas gift to Lincoln: *WTSM*, 711.

68. **Lincoln.** AL's thanks to Sherman: *ALCW*, 8:121–22. AL summoned Sumner to the White House for a talk about Louisiana and Arkansas: my dialogue is based on descriptions of their views in ibid., 106–08, 404; Sumner, *Collected Works*, 10:44; Sumner, *Selected Letters*, 2:105–07, 196–97, 204, 256, 270–74. AL's Message: *ALCW*, 8:152. AL's compromise plan with Sumner and Radicals, which fell apart: Sumner, *Selected Letters*, 258; McPherson, *Battle Cry of Freedom*, 843–44; LaWanda Cox, *Lincoln and Black Freedom: A Study in Presidential Leadership* (Columbia: University of South Carolina Press, 1981), 119–21; Belz, *Reconstruction of the Union*, 244–76; Donald, *Sumner and the Rights of Man*, 196–207; McCrary, *Lincoln and Reconstruction*, 287–92. AL-Sumner friendship: Turners, *Mary Lincoln*, 185 ("two schoolboys"). AL's promotion of Thirteenth Amendment: *ALCW*, 8:149; Trefousse, *Radical Republicans*, 299, and *ALCW*, 7:281 ("If slavery is not wrong"); Arnold, *Life of Lincoln*, 358–59, and *ALRW*, 384. AL's talk with Rollins: Albert G. Riddle, *Recollections of War Time: Reminiscences of Men and Events in Washington, 1860–1865* (New York: G. P. Putnam's Sons, 1895), 323–24 (AL's use of the patronage); Brodie, *Stevens*, 204; Julian, *Political Recollections*, 251 ("I feel like I've been born"); *FBC ILAL*, 202 ("If the people over the river").

69. **Douglass.** Garrison credited Lincoln: *Liberator* (Feb. 10, 1865). Limitations of Thirteenth Amendment: Harding, *There Is a River*, 270. FD's speech about immediate and universal enfranchisement and self-help: *FD L&W*, 4:158–60, 164.

70. **Sherman.** Halleck's warning to WTS, Dec. 30, 1864, WTSP. WTS's headquarters: *HMH MWS*, 202, 207; *WTS HL*, 319. WTS's reaction to Halleck's letter: Davis, *Sherman's March*, 132 ("Because I had not loaded"); WTS to Halleck, Jan. 12, 1864, *OR*, ser. 1, 47 (pt. 2):36–37 ("But the nigger! Why, in God's name, can't sensible men leave him alone?" "humbug," "cock-and-bull," "darkies gather around me in crowds"); Fellman, *Citizen Sherman*, 163–64; Lewis, *Sherman*, 478. Stanton's arrival, questioned WTS about Jeff C. Davis: Lewis, 479; Davis, 133, 136. Meeting with black leaders: *WTSM*, 726–27; minutes of the meeting in *OR*, ser. 1, 47 (pt. 2): 37–41; Thomas and Hyman, *Stanton,*

344. Special Field Orders No. 15: *OR*, ser. 1, 47 (pt. 2): 60–62; Marszalek, *Sherman*, 314 (several drafts which Stanton edited); Fellman, 166–68 (WTS "despised" Saxton). Stanton was "boorish": Thomas and Hyman, 345. WTS to Helen: *WTS HL*, 327–28. WTS knew he was being watched: Davis, 139.

71. **Booth.** JWB's talk with Harbin: *LJW AAL*, 46–48; Tidwell, *Come Retribution*, 337, 342; Atzerodt's "confession" in Baltimore *American* (Jan. 19, 1869). JWB bought a horse: *BP AL*, 71, 169, 320; Mudd's sworn statement, Apr. 21, 1865, ALAP. John Surratt a rebel spy: Bryan, *Great American Myth*, 118; *BP AL*, vii; *TJS*, 1:118. Mudd and JWB met Surratt in Washington: *BP AL*, 114, 117, 191, 421; *LJW AAL*, 32–34; Tidwell, 338. Surratt description: *BP AL*, 116; *LJW AAL*, 14, 30, 443; Bryan, 118; *Trial of John Surratt*, 2:994. JWB's meeting with Surratt in JWB's hotel room: Surratt's Rockville lecture in *LJW AAL*, 430–31; Hiss interview in ibid., 444; *BP AL*, 120 ("oil speculation" cover). JWB in New York with mother, her fearful dreams: Tidwell, 338; Arnold's statement, Dec. 3, 1867, ALAP; Arnold, *Defence*, 21. JWB told Arnold that his mother wrote him about her fearful dreams; we may assume she talked with JWB about them during his Christmas visit. Sources and authorities do not agree exactly when JWB acquired his arsenal of weapons. Hanchett, *Lincoln Murder Conspiracies*, 44–45, thinks he bought them in New York in early November 1864; Tidwell, 338, believes that the date was later in November. I think Booth purchased the weapons during his late December trip to New York City, after he'd recruited Surratt and Mudd to help him. On his way back to Washington, he left the weapons with Arnold and O'Laughlin in Baltimore. As Tidwell, 336–37, points out, it's entirely possible that rebel agents helped JWB purchase the Spencer carbines. JWB's visit to Surratt Boarding House: this is a composite scene based on several visits as described in *BP AL*, 114, 120, 131, 133, 139; Mary Surratt's statement, Apr. 17 and 28, 1865, ALAP; *LJW AAL*, 104; L. C. Baker, *History of the United States Secret Service* (Philadelphia: published by L. C. Baker, 1867), 563 (Anna and Honora swooned when JWB called). JWB description, cast a spell over women: Ralph Borreson, *When Lincoln Died* (New York: Appleton-Century, 1965), 21, 138; Carl Sandburg, *Abraham Lincoln: The War Years*, 4:301, 314–15. JWB's revised abduction plan, winter postponement: dialogue based on descriptions in Arnold's statements, Apr. 18, 1865, and Dec. 3, 1867, ALAP; Arnold, *Defence*, 20–21, 41–42; Bryan, 117–18.

The Winds of 'Sixty-Five

1. **Sherman.** WTS would show South Carolina the scourge of war: *WTSM*, 752 (WTS's contempt for opposing force); Lewis, *Sherman*, 486, 488; Davis, *Sherman's March*, and John G. Barrett, *Sherman's March Through the Carolinas* (Chapel Hill: University of North Carolina Press, 1956), 38–39 ("the Devil himself"). Lee was the big question, strength of opposing forces: *WTSM*, 750, 752; Barrett, 49; Lewis, 488 ("undue fear of our western men"). WTS moved out with Howard: *HMH MWS*, 236–37, 247, 251; Davis, 142; *WTSM*, 753–54. Through the Salk swamps: *HMH MWS*, 254–55, 259, 263–64, 266; Cox, *Sherman's March*, 171; *WTSM*, 754; Hedley, *Marching Through Georgia*, 356–57; Davis, 147 ("I wouldn't have believed it"); Lewis, 490, and Cox, 168n ("When I learned that Sherman's army"). Army moved in a Y formation: Barrett, 41, 52 ("lower part of the state lay in smoldering ruins"). Destruction of South Carolina Railroad: *WTSM*, 754–55; *HMH MWS*, 259, 261; Cox, 172; *B&L*, 4:685. March to Orangeburg, Kilpatrick's cavalry raid: Davis, 150; Barrett, 56–58. Destruction at Orangeburg: *WTSM*, 755; Conyngham, *Sherman's March*, 323–24; Davis, 148; Barrett, 59. To Columbia: *WTSM*, 757; Upson, *With Sherman to the Sea*, 150 (the boys sang "John Brown's body").

2. **Chesnut.** MC's fears of Sherman: *MCCW*, 702, 715–16. MC at Lincolnton: *PMC*, 228–31, 234–36.

3. **Sherman.** WTS at the Congaree: *WTSM*, 758–59. WTS's orders to Howard: ibid., 758; General Field Order No. 26, Feb. 16, 1865, WTSP. Hidden rebel gunners: Davis, *Sherman's March*, 152; Fellman, *Citizen Sherman*, 230; Lewis, *Sherman*, 501. Mayor's letter of surrender: *WTSM*, 759–60; Davis, 160. WTS and Fifteenth Corps entered Columbia: *WTSM*, 760; Barrett, *Sherman's March*, 75 ("Hail Columbia, / happy land"). Tobacco warehouse, drunken soldier: Upson, *With Sherman to the Sea*, 152; Hedley, *Marching Through Georgia*, 380. Burning cotton: *WTSM*, 761; Cox, *Sherman's March*, 173; Upson, 152 ("Some of our boys"); *HMH MWS*, 269 ("The citizens themselves"). WTS at Market Square, escaped prisoners: *WTSM*, 761; Davis, 162 ("not even in the moment"); *HMH MWS*, 269. WTS's quarters: *WTSM*, 761. WTS during the night of the fire: ibid., 766–67; *HMH MWS*, 269; Cox, 174–75; Upson, 152–54; Conyngham, *Sherman's March*, 330–36; Hedley, 386; Davis, 168 ("Did you think of this"); Barrett, 88; *WTSM*, 767 (sun rose "over a ruined city"); Hedley, 395 ("Why did you burn our town," "I did not burn your town"). WTS blamed Hampton: *WTSM*, 767; *OR*, ser. 1,

47 (pt. 1):21–22; Lewis, 506–08; Sherman's testimony in *A. Barclay* v. *U.S.*, Mar. 26, 1872, WTSP; Barrett, 90–91. Says Barrett, 77: "there is conclusive evidence . . . that at least some cotton was fired before Sherman entered Columbia." Further destruction in Columbia: Lewis, 508; Barrett, 93 (booing civilians). Refugees: Lewis, 508; Slocum's account in *B&L*, 4:688–90. Slocum at Winnsboro: Barrett, 96 ("Yankees are coming!"), 97; Davis, 189–91 (marriage of officer and "a pretty mulatto girl"). Fall of Charleston: Barrett, 106; Cox, 178; *HMH MWS*, 265 ("the capture of Charleston"). Slocum turned east, Kilpatrick's cavalry feinted north, WTS was heading for Fayetteville and Goldsboro: *WTSM*, 768, 771. Slocum's delay at Catawba, WTS's irritation: ibid., 771; *B&L*, 4:686; Barrett, 99; New York *Herald* (Mar. 15, 1865) (Sherman "was ready to destroy the wagons, spike the cannons, shoot the mules"). Murdered foragers: Davis, 188. WTS to Hampton, Hampton's reply: *OR*, ser. 1, 47 (pt. 2):546–47, 596–97; Barrett, 104–05; Marszalek, 326; Davis, 204–05 (no more murdered foragers). Camden wrecked: Barrett, 101–03. WTS at Cheraw: Barrett, 100; *WTSM*, 773–74 (Blair's gift of Madeira wine); *HMH MWS*, 265 (successful march through "the first and most bitter and obstinate" rebel state).

4. **Chesnut.** Sherman the ghoul: *MCCW*, 740–41; ibid., 738–39 ("The restoration of Joe Johnston"). Federals at Mulberry: Davis, *Sherman's March*, 197. Famine stalked Lincolnton: *MCCW*, 761, 733. James's brief visit: ibid., 745, 747 ("It was a sad parting").

5. **Davis.** Croaking malcontents, demands for JD's removal: *JD PL*, 140; *JBJ WCD*, 2:364–65; Strode, *Davis*, 3:126; Gorgas, *Journals*, 147–48; McPherson, *Battle Cry of Freedom*, 816 ("Wife and I sit talking"). Desertions in Lee's army: *REL WP*, 910; Lonn, *Desertions during the Civil War*, 28–30. JD implacably committed to CSA independence, daughter of old friend on his appearance: Escott, *After Secession*, 215, 224 ("old, gray, and wrinkled"). Kerner mission: Durden, *Gray and Black*, 147–49; Thomas, *Confederate Nation*, 294; *JD LPS*, 6:518–19 ("The Confederate government can make no agreement"). As Davis, *Davis*, 598, observes: JD's "ardent Confederate nationalism" had become more important to him than saving slavery. Slave soldier debate: Durden, 75 ("We believe that the negroes"), 135–37, and Freeman, *Lee*, 3:499, 517–18 (Lee's approval). JD's proposal to buy forty thousand slaves: *JD LPS*, 6:384–98. Howell Cobb's objection to slave soldiers: Durden, 184. JD and Benjamin defend slave soldiers: ibid., 193–95 ("Let us say to every negro," "put in the niggers"). Barksdale introduced slave soldier bill, Lee's support: ibid., 202–03, 206. Lee as general in chief: *JD LPS*, 6:453–54; *JDMP*, 1:570;

REL WP, 884, 892 ("If I can relieve you"). Blair interview, JD's letter, Lincoln's reply: *JD R&F*, 2:517–21. JD decided on conference: ibid., 2:521; Strode, 3:137; Davis, *Davis*, 591 ("there are *two* countries"). Report of commissioners on Hampton Roads conference: *JD R&F*, 2:522–23; Kean, *Inside the Confederate Government*, 194–97, 201–02; *ALCW*, 8:279 (Lincoln's three conditions); *JDMP*, 1:306; *JD LPS*, 6:465–78; *JBJ WCD*, 2:411 ("His Majesty Abraham the First"). Passage of slave soldier bill: Durden, 245–50; Long, *Civil War Day by Day*, 649; Keane, 204; Strode, 3:153 Lee's conference with JD: this is a composite of several meetings based on descriptions of those meetings and of JD's and Lee's views in Freeman, *Lee*, 4:5, 9–10; Strode, 3:156; *REL WP*, 909–10; *JD R&F*, 2:550–51; Tidwell, *Come Retribution*, 363. JD on Johnston's retreat, Lee's reponse: *JD LPS*, 6:512; *REL WP*, 914–15. "Come Retribution": Tidwell, 346–47.

6. **Booth.** Surratt's trip to Richmond: Tidwell, *Come Retribution*, 340–41, 363–64, 382. Atzerodt description: Atzerodt statement, Apr. 25, 1865, Mary Surratt statement, Apr. 28, 1865, ALAP; *LJW AAL*, 75–76; *BP AL*, 115–18, 133. Lewis Paine description: *Trial of John Surratt*, 1:373; *LJW AAL*, 84; Betty J. Ownsbey, *Alias "Paine": Lewis Thornton Powell, the Mystery Man of the Lincoln Conspiracy* (Jefferson, N.C.: McFarland & Co., 1993), 10–44; Dr. A. D. Gillette, "Last Days of Payne," *New York World* (Apr. 3, 1892). Paine's real name was Louis Thornton Powell; he assumed the alias Paine or Payne when he took the oath of allegiance at Alexandria in January 1865 (Ownsbey, 33). JWB referred to him as Paine. Davy Herold description: *LJW AAL*, 22, 43; Herold's statement, Apr. 27, 1865, ALAP; *BP AL*, vii-viii, 274; *TJS*, 1:510, 517; Bryan, *Great American Myth*, 138–39; Tidwell, 341; Ownsbey, 74. Benjamin Arnold's involvement: Tidwell, 410. Rumors that Lincoln would be assassinated: Tidwell, 336; *BP AL*, 420. Paine's dress: *LJW AAL*, 84. JWB's ticket and Miss Hale: ibid., 89. Booth and four of his cohorts were in the inaugural crowd; his men did face the audience, as if to help in any abduction or assassination attempt, which is why I think they were there. See the photographs in Dorothy Meserve Kunhardt and Philip B. Kunhardt, Jr., *Twenty Days* (New York: Harper & Row, 1965), 30, 33, 34–35. Louis Weichmann, however, apparently thought they planned to abduct Lincoln during his inauguration (see Bryan, 120–21). I could find no other evidence to corroborate that claim; and the absence of Arnold and O'Laughlin seems to belie it.

7. **Lincoln.** Interview with Speed: William H. Herndon and Jesse William Weik, *Herndon's Lincoln: The True Story of A Great Life* (3 vols.,

Springfield, Ill.: The Herndon's Lincoln Publishng Co., [n.d.]), 3:525–27. Stanton's concerns for AL's safety, military guards, tip on abduction plot: Oates, *Abraham Lincoln: The Man Behind the Myths*, 174–75; *BP AL*, 119–20; Bryan, *Great American Myth*, 63–72, 120–21, 127, 136–37; *LJW AAL*, 102–09; *BP AL*, 120; Thomas Reed Turner, *Beware the People Weeping: Public Opinion and the Assassination of Abraham Lincoln* (Baton Rouge: Louisiana State University Press, 1982), 65–73; Thomas and Hyman, *Stanton*, 349, 393–94. I've simulated AL's thoughts about "this great war" as he wrote his Second Inaugural Address: many of those thoughts are in the address itself; the others are recorded in *ALCW*, 7:282–83 ("I claim not to have controlled events"); *FBC ILAL* (emancipation as "the central act of my Administration"); L. Pierce Clark, *Lincoln, A Psycho-Biography* (New York: Charles Scribner's Sons, 1933), frontal quotation ("I had my ambitions" but "where is the glory? Ashes and blood," "I envy the dead"); AL's remarks on being cast into "a great civil war," clipping, Lincoln National Life Foundation, Fort Wayne, Ind., as cited in Warren, *Lincoln's Youth*, 225. AL on John Brown: AL's Inaugural Address, in fact, echoed Brown's last message to his country: "I John Brown am now quite *certain* that the crimes of this *guilty, land*: will never be purged *away*; but with Blood."

8. **Douglass.** FD at Lincoln's inauguration: FD, *Life and Times*, 362–64; FD in *ATR RAL*, 190–91. Ruckus of some sort, wildly excited man: Bryan, *Great American Myth*, 121–22; *LJW AAL*, 90–93. FD said that from where he stood he could "hear and see all that took place" (*Life and Times*, 363). He could not have failed to notice Booth, who stood above and behind Lincoln, and Booth's four seedy-looking henchmen, who stood just below Lincoln, facing the crowd. AL's address: *ALCW*, 8:332–33. FD at White House reception: FD, *Life and Times*, 365–66; FD in *ATR RAL*, 191–93.

9. **Booth.** JWB's "excellent chance" to kill Lincoln: *BP AL*, 45. Paine at Surratt Boarding House: *LJW AAL*, 97; *BP AL*, 115, 118 ("queer-looking"), 132; Hanchett, *Lincoln Murder Conspiracies*, 52 (Paine worshipped JWB, called him "Captain"). Secret conference at Gautier's saloon and restaurant: Arnold's statements, Apr. 18, 1865, and Dec. 3, 1867, ALAP; Arnold, *Defence*, 21–23, 45–47; Atzerodt's "confession" in Baltimore *American* (Jan. 18, 1869); *LJW AAL*, 116; Surratt's Rockville lecture in ibid., 431–32; Bryan, 139. Abortive abduction attempt at Campbell Hospital: *LJW AAL*, 115–17; Surratt's Rockville Lecture in ibid., 432; *TJS*, 1:511–12; Arnold's statement, Dec. 3, 1867, ALAP; Arnold, *Defence*, 23–24, 31, 48; Atzerodt's "confession" in Baltimore

American (Jan. 18, 1869); *BP AL*, 118; Ownsbey, *Alias "Paine,"* 61 (JWB asked about "the old man"); *AL DBD*, 3:32. Rendezvous at Surratt Boarding House: *BP AL*, 118, 120; *LJW AAL*, 101–02. Arnold and O'Laughlin back to Baltimore: Arnold, *Defence*, 48; Arnold's statement, Dec. 3, 1867, ALAP; *BP AL*, 232, 236. Surratt and Atzerodt hid JWB's tools and weapons at Surrattsville: *BP AL*, 293; *TJS*, 1:278. JWB's visit with his mother: her sad sentiments are in a letter she wrote JWB after the visit, but it's clear from the letter that she expressed something like that during the visit. See Bryan, 141. While in New York, JWB spoke with Roderick D. Watson of Maryland, who was involved with the rebel underground (Tidwell, *Come Retribution*, 415). JWB was back in Washington on Mar. 25 (Bryan, 119, 139); Lincoln had left for City Point two days before.

10. **Lincoln.** Sherman at Goldsboro: Davis, *Sherman's March*, 241 (Schofield joined him, combined army of ninety thousand); *WTSM*, 778 ("no place in the Confederacy is safe"). AL's trip to City Point: John S. Barnes, "With Lincoln from Washington to Richmond," *Appleton's Magazine* (May and June 1907), 517–20; *ALCW*, 8:373; William H. Crook, "Lincoln As I Knew Him," *Harper's Monthly Magazine* (June 1907), 46. The Grants and staff greeted AL: *JGM*, 142 ("I'm going to leave you two ladies"). AL's conference with Grant: dialogue based on description of meeting in Crook, 46. The scene before AL: Crook, 47; Barnes, 524. Robert Todd Lincoln brought AL news of Fort Stedman battle, plus telegram from Stanton, AL's reply: ibid., 521; *ALCW*, 8:373n–74n, 373. AL at Grant's headquarters: Barnes, 521, 742 (description of headquarters). AL at Meade's headquarters: Crook, 347 ("he may be Jeff Davis"); *ALCW*, 8:374 (1,600 prisoners); *TL WG&M*, 324 (prisoners' appearance); Barnes, 521 ("sad and unhappy"). AL at the front: Donald C. Pfanz, *The Petersburg Campaign: Abraham Lincoln at City Point, March 20–April 9, 1865* (Lynchburg, Va: H. E. Howard, Inc., 1989), 10; Barnes, 521; Crook, 47; *HP CWG*, 406, and Admiral David Dixon Porter, *Incidents and Anecdotes of the Civil War* (New York: D. Appleton and Co., 1885), 282 (AL studied his map or "chart"). AL back at depot: Pfanz, 10; Barnes, 521–22 ("he had seen enough of the horrors of war"). AL, Grant, and staff around campfire: *HP CWG*, 406–07. Sheridan's arrival, campaign of destruction: *USGP*, 14:181, 202; Crook, 42 (Sheridan description); Sandburg, *Abraham Lincoln: The War Years*, 4:147 ("when this peculiar war began"). AL at telegraph operator's, Stanton's dispatch: *HP CWG*, 409–10; *ALCW*, 8:374n. The kittens: *HP CWG*, 410; Porter, 286–87. Review of Army of James, Mary Lincoln's jealous fit: Barnes,

522–24; *HP CWG*, 413–16; *JGM*, 146; Randall, *Mary Lincoln*, 372–74; Turners, *Mary Lincoln*, 206–08, 211; Pfanz, 15–19, 38. Sherman at City Point: *HP CWG*, 417–19, 423; *WTSM*, 810–13; Barnes, 743–44; Charles Carlton Coffin's account in *ATR RAL*, 177. Grant's departure for the front: *HP CWG*, 425–26. AL back on *River Queen*: *ALCW*, 8:377 (flashes of the guns); 378n–79n ("A pause by the army," "I will send you a rebel flag"); *SC TYWG*, 307 ("Here is something material").

11. **Grant.** Rain and bad roads: *ALCW*, 8:380n. Sheridan with USG: *HP CWG*, 428, 430 (ready to go "smashing things"). Reinforcements to Sheridan: ibid., 430–31, 434, 440–41 (Warren relieved). Porter brought USG news of Five Forks: ibid., 442–43, 443n; *ALCW*, 8:382n; *USGP*, 15:202. Federal assaults, Apr. 2: *USGP*, 14:314, 319n, 325, 15:202–03; *HP CWG*, 446–47 (USG under fire), 448, and *USGP*, 14:327n (USG invited Lincoln to the front).

12. **Davis.** St. Paul's, telegrams from Lee: *REL WP*, 925–26, 928. Two companies of black troops, bitter opposition: *JD LPS*, 6:526; Quarles, *Negro in the Civil War*, 280–81; *JBJ WCD*, 2:282; Durden, *Gray and Black*, 172–73; Escott, *After Secession*, 253–55. Explosive expert's mission: Tidwell, *Come Retribution*, 27–28, identifies the expert as Thomas F. Harney. Richmond dispatched him to Mosby with a secret team. Their goal, Tidwell believes, was to sneak into Washingon and blow up the White House while Lincoln and the Cabinet were meeting there. Atzerodt claimed that Booth and his men had talked about doing the same thing. Tidwell speculates that Richmond had ordered Booth to cooperate with Harney. On April 10, however, Federal cavalry captured Harney and his men. JD at Executive Mansion: Foote, *Civil War*, 3:886–87. Family sent to Charlotte, leave-taking: *VD JD*, 2:575–77. JD to train station: Foote, 3:887. Departure: *JD LPS*, 5:532–33; Strode, *Davis*, 3:165–69; Foote, 3:889; Davis, *Davis*, 606–07; Bill, *Beleaguered City*, 272–73. JD at Danville, proclamation: *JD R&F*, 2:573–74; *JD LPS*, 6:529–31.

13. **Lincoln.** AL and Tad to Petersburg, description of rebel works: *ALCW*, 8:384; Crook, "Lincoln As I Knew Him," *Harper's Monthly Magazine*, 519, 529; Barnes, "With Lincoln from Washington to Richmond," *Appleton's Magazine*, 744; Reed, *Hospital Life*, 160; Pfanz, *Petersburg Campaign*, 54. AL's ride through Petersburg: *ATR RAL*, 178; Crook, 519; Barnes, 744–45; Porter, *Incidents*, 291; Reed, 161; Adolphe de Pineton, Marquis de Chambrun, *Impressions of Lincoln and the Civil War* (New York: Random House, 1952), 78. AL met Grant: Crook, 519; *HP CWG*, 451 ("You know, General," "I thought at one time," "My anxiety

has been so great"). Grant's departure: ibid., 452. AL back at City Point: *USGP*, 14:340–41 ("Richmond fell"); *ALCW*, 8:384n–85n ("I congratulate you"), 385 ("Thanks for the caution"). AL and Tad to Richmond: Porter, 294 ("Thank God I have lived," "If there is anything left"), 295; Crook, 520–21; Barnes, 746–47; Marquis de Chambrun, 74–75; Pfanz, 60. The landing: Porter, 295 ("Don't kneel to me"). The walk to Capitol Hill: *ATR RAL*, 181 ("Glory! Glory!" "My poor friends"); Porter, 298, 299 (warm day, AL fanned his face); Barnes, 748; Marquis de Chambrun, 75; Crook, 521 ("Something oppressive"). White man dashed up, beautiful girl with flowers: Porter, 300–01. Girl wearing U.S. flag: Crook, 521. AL to rebel White House: Barnes, 748; *B&L*, 4:728 (AL sat in Davis's chair); Barnes, 749 ("I wonder if I could get"). AL's carriage ride: Crook, 522; *B&L*, 4:728 ("If I were in your place"); Pfanz, 66 (AL the miracle healer); *ATR RAL*, 182 ("May the good Lord"). At the state capitol: Pfanz, 66; Barnes, 749, Crook, 522; Porter, 302; *JGM*, 150. AL and Tad on *Malvern*: Crook, 522; Porter, 304. Ripley's alarming report: Sandburg, *Abraham Lincoln: The War Years*, 4:242; Pfanz, 69. There was, of course, just such a mission as Ripley described; it was led by rebel explosives expert Thomas Harney. See Tidwell, *Come Retribution*, 27–28. AL's meeting with Campbell and Myers: *ALCW*, 8:386–88; Pfanz, 71 ("sitting up yonder," Davis must stand trial). AL back at City Point: *ALCW*, 8:389 (letter to Weitzel); Turners, *Mary Lincoln*, 212 ("choice little party"), 220; Pfanz, 77–78. AL at Bower's telegraph tent: *ALCW*, 8:389, 392.

14. **Lee.** To Amelia Court House: Freeman, *Lee*, 4:58, 60–61 ("no men ever fought better"), 67–68; *REL WP*, 900–01, 935–36, 938. Sheridan blocked the way: *EPA FFC*, 521, and *EPA MM*, 594; *REL WP*, 901; Freeman, 4:73–75. To Farmville: *REL WP*, 901, 936. Battle of Sayler's Creek: *EPA FFC*, 521; *REL WP*, 901, 931, 936–37; Freeman, 4:84 ("Where is Anderson?" "My God"), 88; Long, *Civil War Day by Day,* 668 (REL had lost a third of his army). Night march, through Farmville to north side of the Appomattox: *EPA FFC*, 524–25; *EPA MM*, 597; *REL WP*, 936; *USGM*, 2:476. REL's discussion with Wise: dialogue in *EPA MM*, 598–99. Cumberland Church, first letter from Grant: *USGP*, 14:361; *REL WP*, 901; *B&L*, 4:730; Freeman, 4:104 ("Not yet"); *REL WP*, 931–32 (REL's reply to Grant). Toward Appomattox Station, REL's discussion with Pendleton: *EPA FFC*, 528; *EPA MM*, 600–01; Freeman, 4:109–10. At Appomattox Court House, emergency war council: *REL WP*, 902, 937; Gordon, *Reminiscences*, 436; Freeman, 4:114. The last battle, Apr. 9: *REL WP*, 902, 937; Gordon, 436–38; *EPA MM*, 603

("Tell General Lee"); Freeman, 4:120–21. REL's despair ("There is noth-ing left for me"): *EPA MM*, 603; Gordon, 438.

15. **Grant.** USG's headache: *HP CWG*, 462; *USGM*, 483. Pease brought Lee's request for an interview and Meade's note: *REL WP*, 932; *HP CWG*, 466–67; *B&L*, 4:733; *USGM*, 2:485 (USG cured of headache); *USGP*, 14:372–73 (USG to Lee asking where they should meet); *B&L*, 4:734–35 (Babcock's mission). USG to Sheridan's front, then to Appo-mattox Court House: *USGM*, 2:486, 488; *HP CWG*, 469–70 ("How are you, Sheridan?" "First-rate," Babcock in the street). USG's dress: *USGM*, 2:489. USG and Lee in McLean House: ibid., 2:489–95; *B&L*, 4:737–423; *USGP*, 14:373–76 (USG's terms); *REL WP*, 933–35, 937–38.

16. **Lee.** REL rejoined his army: *EPA FFC*, 539; Freeman, *Lee*, 4:145–47 ("General, are we surrendered?" "Men, we have fought," REL's anger in peach orchard, "we love you, General Lee!" "General, I have the honor"); Thomas, *Lee*, 366. REL's farewell, stragglers arrived by the thousands, REL to Davis: *REL WP*, 934–35, 935–39. REL through Buckingham Court House, talk with Longstreet: Freeman, 4:159 ("Next time I fight"). Alexander proposed a guerrilla war, REL rejected it: *EPA MM*, 604–05; *EPA FFC*, 532–33; *REL WP*, 939. REL to Richmond: Freeman, 4:161–63; *REL WP*, 903; Thomas, 368–69 (it was raining). REL unbuckled his sword: Freeman, 4:164.

17. **Davis.** JD's conference with Johnston, Beauregard, and Cabinet mem-bers in Greensboro: *JD R&F*, 2:576–79; Strode, *Davis*, 3:187–89; Foote, *Civil War*, 3:968–69; Symonds, *Johnston*, 353–55. JD in flight: *JD LPS*, 6:545 ("I will come to you"), 549 ("Our necessities exclude"). JD's long letter to Vinnie: ibid., 6:559–62.

18. **Lincoln.** AL's tour of Depot Hospital: *ALRW*, 396; Pfanz, *Petersburg Campaign*, 84–85 (the patient's bloody, unhealed stump); Marquis de Chambrun, *Impressions*, 79; *FBC ILAL*, 287–89 (surgeon's worry that Lincoln's arm would ache). AL's ax trick: ibid., 289; *ALRW*, 279. It was in 1864 that AL said: "When I used to split rails, I could lift two axes that way." We may assume he said the same thing at Depot Hospital. The pretty Quaker girl was Cornelia Hancock, who in a letter to her sis-ter, Apr. 11, 1865, *CHP UM*, described AL's visit to the hospital, saying that he shook hands with those patients who could stand and went to the beds of those who could not, and that he assured them all that "the war would be over in six weeks." AL's trip back to Washington, AL read Duncan's assassination scene in *Macbeth*: Adolphe de Pineton, Marquis de Chambrun, "Personal Recollections of Mr. Lincoln," *Scribner's Maga-*

zine (Jan., 1893), 35; Marquis de Chambrun, *Impressions*, 83; Pfanz, 90. AL and family to White House: Crook, "Lincoln As I Knew Him," *Harper's Monthly Magazine*, 523 ("Lee has surrendered!"); Thomas and Hyman, *Stanton*, 353; *USGM*, 2:495; Bryan, *Great American Myth*, 134. AL's visit with Seward: Seward, *Reminiscences*, 253 ("You are back from Richmond"); *FBC ILAL*, 290; Van Deusen, *Seward*, 412 ("God bless you, Stanton"). The country was delirious: *GWD* 2:278; Marquis de Chambrun, *Impressions*, 90. Cheering crowd at White House, "Dixie": *NB WLT*, 224–25; Crook, 524; *ALCW*, 8:393. AL worked on reconstruction: *ALRW* ("trying to blaze a way through the swamp"). Negro suffrage: *ALCW*, 8:393n (Chase said it was criminal). Attorney General Speed, also an advocate of Negro enfranchisement, told Chase that Lincoln "never seemed so near our views" (*SC ILC*, 268). What AL and Republicans had to guarantee former slaves: Harold Hyman, *A More Perfect Union: The Impact of the Civil War and Reconstruction on the Constitution* (reprint of 1973 ed., Boston: Houghton Mifflin Co., 1975), 281; Harold M. Hyman, *Lincoln's Reconstruction: Neither Failure of Vision Nor Vision of Failure* (Third Annual R. Gerald McMurtry Lecture, Fort Wayne, Ind., 1980), 21; Oates, *Abraham Lincoln: The Man Behind the Myths*, 144–46. Stanton tried to resign: *FBC ILAL*, 265 ("you've been a good friend"); *ALRW*, 417. Illuminations and celebrations on evening of Apr. 11: Wheelock, *Boys in White*, 251–52; *NB WLT*, 225. AL's last speech: ibid., 227; Crook, 524; *ALCW*, 8:399–405.

19. **Booth.** JWB's reaction to Lincoln's speech: *LJW AAL*, 490; Bryan, *Great American Myth*, 144; Hanchett, *Lincoln Murder Conspiracies*, 37. JWB drank heavily after Lee's surrender: ibid., 51–52; Bryan, 142. Decision to assassinate: Booth's memorandum book, Apr. 13, 14, 1865, *TJS*, 1:310. JD enlisted Mary Surratt's aid: *BP AL* (Mrs. Surratt wept); Tidwell, *Come Retribution*, 421; *LJW AAL*, 131 (Booth was done acting; the only play he would act in was *Venice Preserved*); Thomas Otway, *Venice Preserved* (ed. Malcolm Kelsall; Lincoln: University of Nebraska Press, 1969). Mary Surratt's errand: *BP AL*, 113, 116–19, 121; *LJW AAL*, 133; *TJS*, 1:28, 295, 299. JWB drew up list of targets: Tidwell, 421–22; Atzerodt's statement, Apr. 25, 1865, ALAP; *BP AL*, 145; Tidwell, 423, and Atzerodt's "confession" in Baltimore *American* (Jan. 18, 1869) (JWB and Paine to Seward's house). JWB to friend ("Ed, I've got"): Tidwell, 422.

20. **Lincoln.** Controversy over the Virginia legislature: Donald, *Sumner and the Rights of Man*, 215 ("Alas! Alas!"); *GWD*, 2:279–80 (AL admitted he had perhaps made a mistake); *ALCW*, 8:406–07 (AL canceled meeting

of legislature). AL's dream: *FBC ILAL*, 292; Bryan, *Great American Myth*, 145 ("Judas trees and dogwoods were in bloom"). Breakfast on Good Friday: Randall, *Lincoln's Sons*, 208; Keckley, *Behind the Scenes*, 138; Turners, *Mary Lincoln*, 257 ("playful note"); Bryan, 150. AL well groomed: Hugh McCulloch, *Men and Measures of Half a Century* (New York: Charles Scribner's Sons, 1889), 222. AL at telegraph office: Bates, *Lincoln in the Telegraphic Office*, 366–68. Cabinet meeting: McCulloch, 222 (president was cheerful); *CWL*, 396; Thomas and Hyman, *Stanton*, 357–58; *GWD*, 2:280–83; Seward, *Reminiscences*, 254–57; *SC ILC* ("perhaps been too fast"); Welles, "Lincoln and Johnson," *The Galaxy* (Apr. 1872), 525–27; Thomas, *Lincoln*, 517 ("Frighten them out of the country"). Grant declined theater invitation: *HP CWG*, 498; *USGM*, 2:508; *JGM*, 155. Stantons declined theater invitation: Bryan, 161. AL wavered about attending the theater: *NB WLT*, 229. Carriage ride with Mary: *FBC ILAL*, 293, and Turners, 218 ("And well I might," "Between the war and the loss of our darling Willie"); Arnold, *Life of Lincoln*, 429–30.

21. **Booth.** JWB at Ford's Theater in the morning: *LJW AAL*, 136 ("Here comes," "What's on," "*Our American Cousin*"). JWB's conversation with Coyle: ibid., 138. JWB eyed Julia Grant: *JGM*, 155–56; *HP CWG*, 498. For a discussion of JWB's preparations in the hallway and president's box in Ford's Theater, see Oates, *Abraham Lincoln: The Man Behind the Myths*, 159, 211–12. JWB's package to Mary Surratt: *BP AL*, ix, 113, 118; *LJW AAL*, 165–66, 170; *TJS*, 1:288; Tidwell, *Come Retribution*, 423. JWB's letter addressed to the editors of the *National Intelligencer*: *National Intelligencer* (July 18, 1867), and *JWBW*, 147–53. JWB's conversation with Matthews: ibid.; *TJS*, 2:821; *LJW AAL*, 140.

22. **Grant.** *JGM*, 155–56; *HP CWG*, 498–99; *LJW AAL*, 140–41; *ABC UB*, 168–70.

23. **Booth.** The right people in Baltimore: as the Grants rode the train to Baltimore that evening, somebody appeared on the front platform of the Grants' car and tried to open the door, only to find it locked (*HP CWG*, 500; *JGM*, 156–57, 167n; Young, *Around the World with Grant*, 2:356). If this was an attempted assassination, and it probably was, JWB had indeed contacted his friends in Baltimore. JWB at Grillo's place: *BP AL*, 73, 80; *TJS*, 1:176. JWB back to National Hotel: *New York Tribune*, Apr. 17, 1865 (description of articles in his room). JWB's Deringer: *LJW AAL* ("Are you going to Ford's"); Philip B. Kunhardt, Jr., Philip B. Kunhardt III, Peter W. Kunhardt, *Lincoln: An Illustrated Biography* (New

York: Alfred A. Knopf, 1992), 355. JWB's meeting with conspirators: *BP AL*, xii, 307, 314; Atzerodt's statement, Apr. 25, 1865, ALAP; Atzerodt's "confession" in *Baltimore American* (Jan. 19, 1869); Tidwell, *Come Retribution*, 437, 442; Ownsbey, *Alias "Paine,"* 74. JWB to Ford's that night: Spangler's examination, Apr. 15, 1865, ALAP; *BP AL*, 74–75, 105. JWB crossed under Ford's, in Grillo's: ibid., 72, 106. The moon: *LJW AAL*, 476n; *TJS*, 1:577, 578. JWB and doorkeeper: *BP AL*, 73; Bryan, *Great American Myth* (seized doorkeeper's hand by two fingers, JWB didn't need a ticket, hummed a tune). A man let JWB pass, JWB surveyed the house, entered narrow passageway, barred door: *BP AL*, 76, 78; *TJS*, 1:129; *LJW AAL.* 151. The shooting, JWB's escape: *BP AL*, 39, 74–76, 78–80; *TJS*, 1:130, 2:985; Herold's statement, Apr. 27, 1865, ALAP; *LJW AAL*, 152–54; Clara Harris's affidavit, Apr. 17, 1865, Baker, *Secret Service*, 473; Borreson, *When Lincoln Died*, 26. JWB at Navy Yard Bridge: *BP AL*, 84. JWB's flight to Mudd's house: ibid., 85–87, 124–25; Herold's statement, Apr. 27, 1865, ALAP; *TJS*, 1:282–86, 295–96. JWB at Mudd's: *BP AL*, xiii-xiv, 87–89, 168–70, 176 (the weather), 421; Mudd's sworn statements, Apr. 21 and Apr. 27, 1865, ALAP; Tidwell, 445–46. JWB and the Negro guide: ibid., 446; *BP AL*, xiv; *LJW AAL*, 192. Cox hid JWB and Herold, Jones brought papers and food, JWB's entry in his memorandum book: Tidwell, 449–50; *LJW AAL*, 193–95, 197; Herold's statement, Apr. 27, 1865, ALAP; *TJS*, 1:310.

24. **Grant.** USG learned of the assassination: *HP CWG*, 500; Young, *Around the World with Grant*, 2:354; *JGM*, 156; *USGM* 2:509; Catton, *Grant Takes Command*, 475–76. Stanton: *HP CWG*, 501. Seward: *BP AL*, 156 ("I'm mad! I'm mad!"). USG to Ord: Catton, *Grant Takes Command*, 478. USG and Stanton decided not to blame the dying Confederacy for Lincoln's death, but attributed it to a "mad" Booth: Barbara Hughett, "William Hanchett on 'Lincoln's Assassination After 130 Years,'" *Civil War Round Table* (Chicago: Apr. 1995), 1. Capture of Booth: Herold's statement, Apr. 27, 1865, ALAP; *BP AL,* xvii–xviii, 91–95; *TJS*, 1:304, 307–08; Tidwell, 474–76; *ABC UB*, 140. Identification of Booth's body: *BP AL*, xviii, 95. AL's funeral: Arnold, *Life of Lincoln*, 436; Young, 2:354–57; *NB WLT*, 234; Kunhardts, *Twenty Days*, 121–22; *NB WLT*, 234; Catton, 479–80. Johnston's surrender to Sherman: *USGM*, 2:513–17; *WTSM*, 837–56. Davis in prison: Strode, *Davis*, 3:230–52; Foote, *Civil War*, 3:1035–49. JD's address to Mississippi legislature, 1884: Hodding Carter, *The Angry Scar*, 75; *VD JD*, 2:816–17. Wilson's raid: James Pickett Jones, *Yankee Blitzkrieg: Wilson's Raid Through Alabama and Georgia* (Athens: University of Georgia Press,

1976). UAG's Herculean task: USG, *Memoirs of U. S. Grant and Selected Letters, 1839–1865* (New York: Library of America, 1990), 1088.

25. **Chesnut.** At Chester, Sam Hood, Wigfalls: *MCCW*, 771, 776–77, 782–83, 791; *PMC*, 243. Lincoln's assassination, MC unhappy, Mary Darby on Lincoln: *MCCW*, 790–92, 793–94, 796. At Camden: *MCCW*, xli, 800–03; *PMC*, 237, 243–47, 254; Muhlenfeld, *Mary Chesnut*, 128; LMC, 73.

CODA

Walt Whitman. Whitman, *Collected Writings* (ed. Floyd Stovall 431 ("That our national democratic experiment"); Walt Whitman, "Death of Abraham Lincoln," *Complete Prose Works* (7 vols., New York: Knickerbocker Press, 1902), 2:239–56; *ATR RAL,* 469–75; Charles I. Stovall, (2 vols., New York: New York University Press, 1964), Glicksberg (ed.), *Walt Whitman and the Civil War* (reprint of 1933 ed., New York: A. S. Barnes and Co. [no date]), 138n–139n, 173–76; Floyd Stovall (ed.), *Walt Whitman: Representative Selections* (New York: American Book Co., 1934), 232–33.

ACKNOWLEDGMENTS

I am most grateful to the editors of the published papers, collected works, writings, diaries, and reminiscences of my speakers, which are listed in my references. Without these massive and meticulously assembled works, my book could not have been written. I am especially indebted to John Y. Simon, editor of the *Papers of Ulysses S. Grant,* a monumental work of scholarship that made my depiction of Grant immeasurably easier.

I owe a debt, too, to the many biographers of my speakers and to numerous other specialists for breaking the ground ahead of me and showing me where to go. My debt to these distinguished scholars is indicated in my references. To the staff of the library of the University of Massachusetts, Amherst, I offer my sincere appreciation for the professional services they rendered. My thanks, too, to the officers and staffs of all the repositories listed at the beginning of my references for their professional help and courtesies. The publications of the John Surratt Society, especially the compilation of source materials on the Lincoln assassination, proved to be invaluable, and I am especially grateful to that organization.

Special thanks go to my talented research assistants, Melba Jensen, Anne-Marie Taylor, Karl Anderson, Don Valentine, Shelly Weinstein, James Leach, Glendyne Wergland, and Beth Weston, who performed myriad duties with alacrity and skill. I am most grateful to my colleagues in the Department of History at the University of Massachusetts, Amherst, especially Robert Jones, Bruce Laurie, Roland Sarti, and Mary Wilson, who provided me with research assistants and in countless other ways helped make *The Approaching Fury* and *The Whirlwind of War* a reality. Professor Emeritus Robert E. Taylor and Olga Taylor also gave me invaluable support. Linda Davis, my friend and fellow biographer, understood perfectly what I was attempting to do, and I thank her for her encouragement. Members of the Amherst Creative Biography Group—Sandra Katz, William Kimbrel, Elizabeth Lloyd-Kimbrel, Ann Meeropol, Helen Sheehy, and Harriet Sigerman, accomplished biographers all—heard segments of the book during our monthly meetings and proffered trenchant advice on structure, content, and technique. Professor

Michael Meeropol of Western New England College also made help-ful suggestions, for which I am most thankful.

I owe a great debt to Harold Holzer, Frank J. Williams, Paul Simon, John Y. Simon, William C. Davis, Ralph G. Newman, Richard N. Current, Hans L. Trefousse, Robert V. Remini, David Herbert Donald, James M. McPherson, Gary W. Gallagher, William S. McFeely, Emory M. Thomas, Gabor S. Boritt, Herman Belz, Eric Foner, John Hope Franklin, Robert W. Johannsen, Kenneth M. Stampp, and Thomas R. Turner, for their professional support when I most needed it, and for their magnificent studies of the antebellum and Civil War era, without which my own books could never have been written. My agent, Gerard McCauley, and my new editor at HarperCollins, Paul McCarthy, gave unstinting encouragement throughout my long labor of creation. Paul turned out to be a spe-cial gift: his intuitive understanding of what I was attempting to do in *The Whirlwind of War* and his brilliant and creative editing of the manuscript made it a far better book than it otherwise would have been. I am deeply grateful to my copy editor, Shelly Perron, for her careful and professional preparation of the manuscript.

I owe a special acknowledgment to Davis Grubb, whose novel, *The Voices of Glory,* served as a model of how to tell a story through various first-person narrators. Michael Shaara's *The Killer Angels*, the best novel ever written about the Civil War, continued to be an inspiration for how to tell a story from shifting perspectives and how to describe Civil War combat. I learned a great deal from Cynthia Bass's novel, *Sherman's March*, which tells the story in the voices and from the viewpoints of Sherman and two fictional charac-ters—a Union army captain and a Georgia farm wife and refugee. I am also much indebted to the late Bruce Catton, whose splendid tril-ogy on the Army of the Potomac inspired me to become a Civil War historian.

My warmest thanks to Bob Maher and Catherine Boyers of the Civil War Education Association for inviting me to read a chapter of my *Voices* at the Association's Civil War symposium, held in West Palm Beach, Florida, in February, 1997. My fellow Civil War histo-rians who served as faculty at the symposium—Frank J. Williams, Harold Holzer, Lesley J. Gordon, Craig L. Symonds, John F. Marszalek, John T. Hubell, Jeffry D. Wert, and Richard M. McMurry—offered cogent comments about my *Voices*, especially in the sunlit afternoons at the hotel's outdoor bar, and I thank them for their encouragement and camaraderie.

I am also indebted to the Lincoln Forum, the foremost Lincoln organization in the world, for inviting me to read a segment of *The Whirlwind of War* at the Forum's Second Annual Symposium, held at Gettysburg in November, 1997. This grand event attracted Lincoln scholars and enthusiasts from all over the country, and I was honored to have played a part. I want to thank my fellow faculty members at the symposium—Gabor S. Boritt, Richard N. Current, Avram Fechter, Gary W. Gallagher, Harold Holzer, Gary Kross, Edna Greene Medford, Lloyd Ostendorf, John Y. Simon, and Frank J. Williams—for their constructive comments and support. Brian Lamb, founder and creative genius of C-Span, which taped the symposium, again showed his appreciation for Lincoln and the Civil War, and we are all deeply in his debt. Finally I owe a special thanks to David E. Long, whose path-breaking book, *The Jewel of Liberty: Abraham Lincoln's Re-election and the End of Slavery*, gave me a deeper understanding of the momentous presidential canvass of 1864, which Long rightly calls "the most important electoral event in American history."

INDEX